are saturated with Scripture, references to the Latin classics, the early Church Fathers, his theological predecessors, English poets and playwrights, and those "natural philosophers" exploring the wonders of God in creation. Research for this project was necessarily intensive. From the finest libraries of Europe and America, resources were scrutinized in order to trace the literary sources behind Wesley's thoughts. Each volume is rich with footnotes that include the identification of quotations, the elucidation of references, the tracing of key themes, and vital background information on each sermon.

Representing the culmination of twenty years of exhaustive research, it is the purpose of these conclusive volumes to keep alive the growing interest in Wesleyan studies for the entire Christian church. Generations will look to them for scholarship, insight, and inspiration.

Gifted scholar and world renowned leader in Wesleyan studies, Dr. ALBERT C. OUTLER is Professor Emeritus of Theology at Perkins School of Theology, Southern Methodist University, Dallas, Texas.

THE BICENTENNIAL EDITION
OF THE
WORKS OF JOHN WESLEY

Editor-in-Chief FRANK BAKER

*The Directors of the Bicentennial Edition of
the Works of John Wesley
gratefully acknowledge the financial support
in the preparation of this volume of
Mary Luccock Livermore of Lubbock, Texas
as a memorial to Halford E. Luccock*

JOHN WESLEY

(FROM THE BUST IN THE NATIONAL PORTRAIT GALLERY, LONDON)

THE WORKS OF
JOHN WESLEY

VOLUME 1

SERMONS
I
1–33

EDITED BY

ALBERT C. OUTLER

ABINGDON PRESS

NASHVILLE

1984

87-565

The Works of John Wesley, Volume 1
SERMONS, I, 1–33

Copyright © 1984 by Abingdon Press
Second Printing 1984
All rights reserved.

Library of Congress Cataloging in Publication Data

Wesley, John, 1703-1791.
  The works of John Wesley.
  Includes indexes.
  Contents: v. 1. Sermons I, 1-33 / edited by Albert C.
Outler.
  1. Methodist Church—Collected works. 2. Theology—
Collected works—18th century. I. Outler, Albert Cook,
1908-   . II. Title.
BX8217.W5 1984   252'.07   83-22434

ISBN 0-687-46210-X

THE MONOGRAM USED ON THE CASE AND HALF-TITLE IS
ADAPTED BY RICHARD P. HEITZENRATER FROM ONE OF
JOHN WESLEY'S PERSONAL SEALS

MANUFACTURED BY THE PARTHENON PRESS AT
NASHVILLE, TENNESSEE, UNITED STATES OF AMERICA

THE BICENTENNIAL EDITION OF
THE WORKS OF JOHN WESLEY

This edition of the works of John Wesley reflects the quickened interest in the heritage of Christian thought that has characterized both ecumenical insurgency and dominant theological perspectives during the last half-century. A fully critical presentation of Wesley's writings had long been a desideratum in order to furnish documentary sources illustrating his contribution to both catholic and evangelical Christianity.

Several scholars, notably Professor Albert C. Outler, Professor Franz Hildebrandt, Dean Merrimon Cuninggim, and Dean Robert E. Cushman, discussed the possibility of such an edition. Under the leadership of Dean Cushman, a Board of Directors was formed in 1960 comprising the deans of four sponsoring theological schools of Methodist-related universities in the United States: Drew, Duke, Emory, and Southern Methodist. They appointed an Editorial Committee to formulate plans, and enlisted an international and interdenominational team of scholars for the Wesley Works Editorial Project.

The works were divided into units of cognate material, with a separate editor (or joint editors) responsible for each unit. Dr. Frank Baker was appointed textual editor for the whole project, with responsibility for supplying each unit editor with a collated critical text for his consideration and use. The text seeks to represent Wesley's thought in its fullest and most deliberate expression, in so far as this can be determined from the available evidence. Substantive variant readings in any British edition published during Wesley's lifetime are shown in appendices to the units, preceded by a summary of the problems faced and the solutions reached in the complex task of securing and presenting Wesley's text. The aim throughout is to enable Wesley to be read with maximum ease and understanding, and with minimal intrusion by the editors.

It was decided that the edition should include all Wesley's original or mainly original prose works, together with one volume devoted to his *Collection of Hymns for the use of the People called*

Methodists, and another to his extensive work as editor and publisher of extracts from the writings of others. An essential feature of the project is a Bibliography outlining the historical settings of over 450 items published by Wesley and his brother Charles, sometimes jointly, sometimes separately. The Bibliography also offers full analytical data for identifying each of the two thousand editions of these 450 items that were published during the lifetime of John Wesley, and notes the location of copies. An Index is supplied for each unit, and a General Index for the whole edition.

The Delegates of the Oxford University Press agreed to undertake publication, but announced in June 1982 that because of severe economic problems they would regretfully be compelled to withdraw from the enterprise with the completion in 1983 of Volume 7, the *Collection of Hymns*. The Abingdon Press offered its services, beginning with the publication of the first volume of the *Sermons* in 1984, the bicentennial year of the formation of American Methodism as an autonomous church. The new title now assumed, however, refers in general to the bicentennial of Wesley's total activities as author, editor, and publisher, from 1733 to 1791, especially as summarized in the first edition of his collected works in thirty-two volumes, 1771–1774.

Dean Robert E. Cushman of Duke University undertook general administration and promotion of the project until 1971, when he was succeeded by Dean Joseph D. Quillian, Jr., of Southern Methodist University, these two universities having furnished the major support and guidance for the enterprise. During the decade 1961–70 literary planning was undertaken by the Editorial Committee, chaired by Dean Quillian. International conferences were convened in 1966 and 1970, bringing together all available unit editors with the committee, who thus completed their task of achieving a common mind upon editorial principles and procedure. Throughout this decade Dr. Eric W. Baker of London, England, serving as a General Editor along with Dean William R. Cannon and Dean Cushman, assisted the Directors in British negotiations, as well as at the conferences. In 1969 the Directors appointed Dr. Frank Baker, early attached to the project as bibliographer, and later as textual editor, their Editor-in-Chief also. In 1971 they appointed a new Editorial Board to assist him in coordinating the preparation of the various units for publication. Upon Dean Quillian's retirement in 1981 he was succeeded as President of the project by Dean James E. Kirby, Jr., also of Southern Methodist University.

Other sponsoring bodies were successively added to the original four: The United Methodist Board of Higher Education and Ministry, The Commission on Archives and History of The United Methodist Church, and Boston University School of Theology. For the continuing support of the sponsoring institutions the Directors express their profound thanks. They gratefully acknowledge also the encouragement and financial support that have come from the Historical Societies and Commissions on Archives and History of many Annual Conferences, as well as the donations of The World Methodist Council, The British Methodist Church, private individuals, and foundations.

On June 9, 1976, The Wesley Works Editorial Project was incorporated in the State of North Carolina, U.S.A., as a nonprofit corporation. In 1977 by-laws were approved governing the appointment and duties of the Directors, their Officers, and their Executive Committee.

THE BOARD OF DIRECTORS

The Board of Directors

President: James A. Kirby, Dean of Perkins School of Theology, Southern Methodist University, Dallas, Texas

Vice-President: Robert E. Cushman, The Divinity School, Duke University, Durham, North Carolina

Secretary: Gerald O. McCulloh, Nashville, Tennessee

Treasurer: Thomas A. Langford, The Divinity School, Duke University, Durham, North Carolina

Editor-in-Chief: Frank Baker, The Divinity School, Duke University, Durham, North Carolina

Associate Editor-in-Chief: Richard P. Heitzenrater, Perkins School of Theology, Southern Methodist University, Dallas, Texas

Dennis M. Campbell, Dean of The Divinity School, Duke University, Durham, North Carolina

William R. Cannon, Bishop of The United Methodist Church, Raleigh, North Carolina

Rupert E. Davies, Bristol, England

Joe Hale, General Secretary of The World Methodist Council, Lake Junaluska, North Carolina

Dwight E. Loder, Bishop of The United Methodist Church, Columbus, Ohio

Richard Nesmith, Dean of Boston University School of Theology, Boston, Massachusetts

Thomas W. Ogletree, Dean of The Theological School of Drew University, Madison, New Jersey

Donald H. Treese, Associate General Secretary of the Division of the Ordained Ministry, The United Methodist Board of Higher Education and Ministry, Nashville, Tennessee

Jim L. Waits, Dean of Candler School of Theology, Emory University, Atlanta, Georgia

Charles Yrigoyen, Jr., Executive Secretary of The Commission on Archives and History of The United Methodist Church, Drew University, Madison, New Jersey

The Editorial Board

The Editor-in-Chief (*chairman*); the President and the Associate Editor-in-Chief (*ex officio*); William R. Cannon, Robert E. Cushman, Rupert E. Davies, and Gerald O. McCulloh, Directors; together with John Lawson, Exeter, Devon, England.

PREFACE

THE chief aim and warrant for this edition of the extant sermons of John Wesley is to present them in reliable and readable texts, in a sequence that reflects Wesley's own sense of their proper order, with editorial comments focused on contexts and sources. In this undertaking, I have had the generous collaboration of Professor Frank Baker of Duke University, who stands without a peer in his mastery of the details of Wesley's texts and bibliography. Early on, he provided a model copy-text so meticulous that my own collations of it were almost redundant. His expert analysis of the methodological problems involved appears as Appendix A in Volume 4.

After extensive experiments with alternatives we came to agree in preferring the freshness of Wesley's first editions. They come closer to reflecting what we know of his actual preaching style than some of the later revisions (many of which were managed by editorial assistants and printers and not always carefully reviewed by Wesley). Revisions that reflect substantive changes are, of course, footnoted, and important variants are listed by Professor Baker in his Appendix already noted. To help readability, we have undertaken to 'modernize' the orthography of the texts. This, we feel, is consonant with Wesley's own openness to the important shifts in orthographical styles occurring in his century. There was nothing consciously quaint about him; thus, mere facsimile texts would not re-present him realistically. He was, however, an eighteenth-century Englishman, and we have taken care to preserve those features of his syntax that were, in fact 'good English' usage in his time.

The search for an ideal order for the entire sermon corpus proved frustrating and finally fruitless. The most obvious scheme, at first glance at least, would have been a straightforward chronological sequence, either in the order of composition or of first publication. The clear advantage here would have been the exhibition of Wesley's thought in its successive stages of development. Read in this light, the sermons shatter most of the conventional views of the 'constancy' of his theological course 'after his conversion on 24th May, 1738' (Schmidt). This problem of development in Wesley is thus far woefully underdeveloped, and for those who may be interested, we have provided a chronological listing of all the sermons (pp. 707-13 below).

Three counter-considerations finally tilted the scale against this first impulse. To begin with, the question of *exact* sequence is not yet fully solved, especially within the blocs of sermons included in the first collection of *Sermons on Several Occasions*, 1746–60. A second hesitation was rather different: it is simply the fact that Wesley's earliest sermons are the least impressive of the lot, and there was no way of ensuring any general reader's perseverance until the question of 'stages' could rightly be weighed and balanced out. The really decisive point, however, was the basic principle that an author has a right to be read, in the first instance, in his own preferred order. On this point, the case is clear: Wesley regarded his three sermon collections (1746–60, 1771, 1787–88) as the core of his doctrinal teaching; the other sermons were reckoned as supplementary. Even here, however, the principle is not without complications; those three collections differ sufficiently in their orderings to require still further analysis (as in the Introduction and introductory comments below).

In Volume 4 several special aids are provided for the more curious. The first of these is Professor Baker's essay on textual analysis. The second is a report of some sermons ascribed to Wesley on inconclusive grounds, but deserving of notice. Appendix C summarizes a group of sermons that Wesley valued sufficiently to copy out from other authors and then to preserve in his personal papers for more than half a century. Included here is a sermon by John Gambold, in Gambold's handwriting, which Wesley must have cherished. Thomas Jackson found its pneumatology so nearly consonant with Wesley's that he chose to publish it in 1825 and 1829—thus provoking several ingenious explanations as to how a university sermon dated 'On Whitsunday, 1736' could have been preached in St. Mary's, Oxford, by a man who was then in Georgia. Appendix D reproduces samples from Wesley's sermon registers still extant in Wesley's hand, which record his preaching during the years 1747–61, 1787–88. A more nearly complete 'register' of Wesley's preaching—dates, places, and texts—is in preparation by my former research assistant, Wanda Willard Smith. It is hoped that this will appear in due course as a monograph in its own right; much of its basic research has already been incorporated in this edition. The Indexes for the four volumes are contributed by John A. Vickers.

It is obvious, however, that this edition has a second concern, almost as urgent as the first: *viz.*, a methodological redefinition of 'Wesley Studies', with special emphasis on Wesley's sources and his special way of using them. Traditionally, Wesley has been viewed (by Methodists and non-Methodists alike) rather more in the light of the consequences of his career (i.e., as founder and patriarch of the Methodists) than in the light of his involvements in the crowded forum of eighteenth-century theological debate. What have been missed thereby are his deep roots in the Christian tradition, and his refocusing of this tradition in an age of radical transitions. Prolonged immersion in his texts, however, has nourished the conviction that he becomes more and more intelligible (and interesting) as his ideas and rhetoric are weighed against the vast mosaic of his sources—a background so artfully concealed that almost every Wesley text is something like a palimpsest. Seen in such a perspective these sermons may be taken as prisms that gather rays from a wide range of sources, and that refract them in ways that would serve the needs of a popular revival ('plain truth for plain people'). The result is a deliberate programme of simplification (easily stretched to over-simplifications). But this has obscured our awareness of the breadth, depth, and originality of Wesley's recombinations of his complex heritage.

It is, therefore, an avowed hope of this edition to serve the cause of 'relocating' Wesley's place in the history of Christian preaching and theology. This would mean to see him more clearly (as he saw himself) as an Anglican folk-theologian whose theological competence and creativity were dedicated to popular evangelism, Christian nurture, and reform, so that his theology could be evaluated more directly by his own stated (Anglican) norms: 'Scripture, reason, and Christian antiquity'. This 'new image' of Wesley need not replace the old, but it is needed to redress an imbalance. The credibility of any such perspective, however, depends upon an adequate display of Wesley's sources, and a demonstration of his way with the diverse traditions that converged in him.

The first level of such a venture is, of course, with Wesley's biblical quotations, echoes, and allusions. He left these uncited, as a rule, since he assumed in his readers a high degree of shared familiarity with Holy Scripture. But it would be interesting to know how many of them appreciated his remarkable interweavings of biblical language with his own, and this so smoothly that the seams rarely show. For our purposes, however, it is important for modern readers to be able to visualize this phenomenon and thus to have ample data for probing the still unplumbed questions of Wesley's hermeneutics and his working notions about biblical inspiration and authority. The question of Wesley's rhetoric and its correlation with the substance of his thought is important and still open. Thus it seemed justified to footnote the full repertory of his biblical citations. This part of the work was, however, mostly a matter of diligence, together with some familiarity with Wesley's preferred translations; this included his marked preference for the Book of Common Prayer Psalter.

What proved our chief challenge, and final despair, was the unexpected range and prolixity of his non-biblical sources, from Hesiod to Prior and Fontenelle. He quoted mostly from memory, altering his originals without hesitation. There are, of course, his own occasional footnotes, and we have designated these by superior indicators 'a', 'b', 'c', etc. Our search for sources led in all directions: they required the compilation of a bibliography of Wesley's recorded readings (and many other titles besides). What is offered here is more of a brave beginning than a finished job: we are hoping to enlist our readers to amend and improve on these footnotes as they now stand. Our problem was the overabundance of both needles and haystacks—and all those promising-looking haystacks that turned out to have no needles after all. This is the point to the plaintive siglum π;, which we use with quotations that we had finally to leave unlocated. It came, of course, from $\pi\acute{o}\vartheta\varepsilon\nu$; (whence?) or $\pi o\hat{v}$; (where?)—and is a cry for help from anyone who can fill in our blanks. The footnotes, therefore, are not merely plums for pedants. They are integral parts of our project of exhibiting Wesley's sources, his use of them, and their relevance for contemporary interpretation.

It was inevitable, perhaps, that our reach would exceed our grasp by so much more than we had expected. We realize that many questions are left unanswered here, still more half-answered. But this beginning may be enlarged upon, and nothing would please us more than for this to happen. Those who find the footnotes superfluous need only to treat them as—*footnotes.*

Surely, however, there will be some who will recognize in this approach to Wesley studies at least a few fresh horizons of inquiry.

Of all the genres in the Wesley corpus the sermons focus and expound his understanding of Christian existence most clearly. Wesley saw theology chiefly as practical; the idea of a speculative *summa* seems never to have crossed his mind. But his sermons—together with the hymns of his brother Charles—were practical tools for teaching and spiritual formation. Together, they constitute 'a small body of divinity' more accessible than any systematic treatise could have been. To know the sermons is by no means to know the whole of Wesley. But not to know them (or to know only the so-called Wesleyan standards, *Sermons on Several Occasions*, 1–44) is to have missed an important resource both for historical and contemporary theology.

This project has been stretched out over the course of twenty years and has involved a host of helpers along the way. First of all, there were successive generations of students who kept asking honest questions about the relevance of it all. Then there were academic colleagues and fellow churchmen, whose initial doubts about any such an investment of time and energy turned into positive interest and support. There were a host of specialists in cognate fields who dealt patiently with importunate queries about this quotation or that allusion; even when they could not help, it was always a comfort to learn that something that we had missed was not already a commonplace to others.

Thus the debts of gratitude went on piling up: to men such as Dr. Frank Cumbers and Dr. John Bowmer, who opened up The Methodist Archives (while they were still in London); to men like John Walsh of Oxford and Reginald Ward of Durham, who greatly stretched the horizons of my knowledge of British church history. I remember thankfully the efficient staff of The British Library and Dr. Williams's Library in London, and in other libraries as well: at Oxford, Union Theological Seminary (New York), Drew, Duke, Wesley College (Bristol). Closer to home I had the loyal cooperation of colleagues in the Bridwell, Fondren, and Underwood libraries here at Southern Methodist University.

The full roster of my allies in this venture is too long to tally. But not to mention the following would stifle my feelings of genuine appreciation: Wm. S. Babcock, Hugh Barbour, Henry Chadwick, Edward Corbin, Rupert Davies, Martha England,

Roland M. Frye, Fr. Placid Gilbert, V. H. H. Green, Arthur Liston, Charles Love, Pamela Naylor, Frank Northam, John Newton, Peter Opie, Jaroslav Pelikan, Klaus Penzel, Colin Roberts, Charles Rogers, Massey Shepherd, Jr., George A. Snyder, Page Thomas, Robert Tuttle, Jr.

Besides these, there are six people whose shares in the project would rank them almost as co-editors, save only on the point of responsibility. Professor Baker, as Editor-in-Chief, has been colleague and critic from beginning to end, and shares with the Unit Editor the responsibility for the flaws that still remain. Professor Richard P. Heitzenrater has generously shared his special expertise in the Oxford phase of Wesley's career. Professor Patrick Henry of Swarthmore (himself also an alumnus of Christ Church) read the penultimate manuscript with an eagle eye and supplied many shrewd and helpful comments. Mrs. John Warnick, while Curator of the Methodist Historical Collection in Bridwell Library, was indefatigable in her searchings for Wesley's classical tags and poetic snatches. There was my former research assistant, Wanda Willard Smith, without whose diligence, competence, and zeal, the project would simply never have been finished. And finally there has been my wife, whose active help and patience gave the task a meaning that it could not have had otherwise. Happy the man with so interesting a cause, with so many good comrades in it, who lives to see it through!

Albert C. Outler

Dallas, Texas
February 24, 1981
The Feast Day of St. Matthias

CONTENTS

Contents

ILLUSTRATIONS

SIGNS, SPECIAL USAGES, ABBREVIATIONS

[ ]	Indicate editorial insertions or substitutions in the original text, or (with a query) doubtful readings.
. . .	Indicate a passage omitted by the writer from the original and so noted by Wesley, usually by a dash.
[. . .]	Indicate a passage omitted from the original text to which the present editor is drawing attention. (N.B. The distinguishing editorial brackets are not used in the introductions and footnotes.)
[[ ]]	Entries within double brackets are supplied by the editor from shorthand or cipher, from an abstract or similar document in the third person, or reconstructed from secondary evidence.
a,b,c,	Small superscript letters indicate footnotes supplied by Wesley.
1,2,3,	Small superscript figures indicate footnotes supplied by the editor.
Cf.	'Cf' before a scriptural or other citation indicates that Wesley was quoting with more than minimal inexactness, yet nevertheless displaying the passage as a quotation.
See	'See' before a citation indicates an undoubted allusion, or a quotation which was not displayed as such by Wesley, and which is more than minimally inexact.
π;	π; indicates a quotation which has not yet been traced to its source.

Wesley's publications. Where a work by Wesley was first published separately its title is italicized—except in the Contents, opening titles, and Appendices A and B—even where (as occasionally in the *Sermons*), the eventual title thus italicized is not that under which it was first published; where it first appeared within a different work, such as a collected volume, the title is given within quotation marks. References such as '*Bibliog,* No.3' are to the forthcoming Bibliography in this edition (Vols. 33–34), which has a different numbering system from Richard Green's *Wesley Bibliography,* although cross-references to Green's numbers are given in the new Bibliography.

Abbreviations. The following are used in addition to many common and obvious ones such as B[oo]k, ch[apter], c[irca], col[umn], com[ment], cont[inued], ed[itio]n, espec[ially], intro[duction, ductory], l[ine], MS[S], n[ote], orig[inal], p[age], para[graph] or ¶, P[ar]t, Sect[ion] or §, st[anza], ver[se/s], Vol[ume].

AM	Wesley, John, *Arminian Magazine* (1778–97), cont. as *Methodist Magazine* (1798–1821) and *Wesleyan Methodist Magazine* (1882–1913).
AV	Authorized Version of the Bible, 1611 ('King James Version').

BCP   *The Book of Common Prayer as Revised and Settled at the Savoy Conference, Anno 1662*, London, William Pickering, 1844 (which adds marginal numbering for the successive liturgical units).

BL   The British Library, London (formerly British Museum).

Boston   Boston, Thomas, *Human Nature in its Fourfold State*, Edinburgh, 1720.

Bibliog   Bibliography of the publications of John and Charles Wesley, in preparation by Frank Baker to form Vols. 33–34 of this edn.

Christian Lib. Wesley, John, ed., *Christian Library*, 50 vols., Bristol, 1749–55.

Curnock   Curnock, Nehemiah (ed.), *The Journal of the Rev. John Wesley, A. M., . . . enlarged from Original Manuscripts*, 8 vols., London, 1909–16.

CWJ   Wesley, Charles, *Journal*, ed. Thomas Jackson, 2 vols., London, 1849.

DNB   *The Dictionary of National Biography*, ed. Sir Leslie Stephen and Sir Sidney Lee, 22 vols., Oxford, Oxford University Press, 1921–23.

General Rules Wesley, John, *The Nature, Design, and General Rules of the United Societies . . .*, Newcastle, Gooding, 1743 (*Bibliog*, No. 73).

Homilies   *Certain Sermons or Homilies appointed to be read in Churches in the Time of the late Queen Elizabeth* (1623), Oxford, University Press, 1840.

Jackson   Jackson, Thomas (ed.), *The Works of the Rev. John Wesley*, 3rd edn., 14 vols., London, Mason, 1829–31.

JWJ   Wesley, John, *Journal*, in preparation by W. Reginald Ward to form Vols. 18–24 of this edn.; cf. Curnock.

Kempis   *De Imitatione Christi*, published by John Wesley as *The Christian's Pattern*, London, Rivington, 1735 (*Bibliog*, No. 4).

LACT   Library of Anglo-Catholic Theology (Oxford, 1841–63).

Law,   Law, William, *A Serious Call to a Devout and Holy Life* (1729),
  Serious Call as reprinted in his *Works*, 9 vols., London, 1762, Vol. IV.

LCC   Library of Christian Classics (Philadelphia, 1953—).

LPT   Library of Protestant Thought (Oxford, 1964—).

Loeb   The Loeb Classical Library, London, Heinemann; Cambridge, Massachusetts, Harvard University Press.

MA   Methodist Archives, The John Rylands University Library of Manchester.

MM   *Methodist Magazine* (London, 1798–1821).

Migne, *PG, PL* Migne, J. P. (ed.) *Patrologiae Cursus Completus, Series Graeca* (Paris 1857–66), and *Series Latina* (Paris, 1878–90).

Moore   Moore, Henry, *Life of the Rev. John Wesley*, 2 vols., London, Kershaw, 1824–25.

NEB	New English Bible.
Notes	Wesley, John, *Explanatory Notes upon the New Testament*, London, Bowyer, 1755 (*Bibliog*, No. 209).
NPNF, I, II	*Nicene and Post-Nicene Fathers of the Christian Church*, First Series (New York, 1886–90), and Second Series (New York, 1890–1900).
OED	*The Oxford English Dictionary upon Historical Principles*, Oxford, Clarendon Press, 1933.
Poet. Wks.	Wesley, John and Charles, *The Poetical Works*, ed. G. Osborn, 13 vols., London, Wesleyan-Methodist Conference Office, 1868–72.
Seymour	[Seymour, A. C. H.], *The Life and Times of Selina, Countess of Huntingdon*, 2 vols., London, Painter, 1840.
SOSO	Wesley, John, *Sermons on Several Occasions*, 1746–60, 1771, 1787–88.
Southey	Southey, Robert, *The Life of Wesley*, ed. C. C. Southey (including *in full*, as does that of 1846, 'Remarks on the Life and Character of John Wesley', by Alexander Knox), 2 vols., London, Longman, etc., 1864
Sugden	Sugden, E. H., ed., *Wesley's Standard Sermons*, 2 vols., London, Epworth Press, 1921.
Telford	Telford, John, ed., *The Letters of the Rev. John Wesley*, 8 vols., London, Epworth Press, 1931.
TR	*Textus Receptus* (the 'Received Text', which underlies the AV).
Tyerman (*JW*)	Tyerman, Luke, *The Life and Times of the Rev. John Wesley*, 3 vols., London, Hodder and Stoughton, 1870–71.
[Wesley,] *Works*	Wesley, John, *The Works of the Rev. John Wesley*, 32 vols. Bristol, Pine, 1771–74 (*Bibliog*, No.334).
WHS	*The Proceedings of the Wesley Historical Society* (Burnley and Chester, 1898—).
WMM	*Wesleyan Methodist Magazine* (1822–1913).

INTRODUCTION

I. A CAREER IN RETROSPECT

It was John Wesley's settled habit to spend his winter seasons in and around London; these seasons were interludes between his annual preaching tours throughout Great Britain during the rest of the year.[1] Sunday, December 15, 1772, found him in the Kentish village of Shoreham visiting an old, cherished friend, the Revd. Vincent Perronet, vicar of the parish church. Such a welcome respite seems to have prompted a brief moment of wistfulness. At the time, he had been leading the Methodist Revival Movement for more than a full generation; it was still flourishing despite an unending round of problems. During this peaceful day in Shoreham, he dashed off a revealing note to his brother Charles, once so active in the Revival but now happily married and comfortably ensconced in his London home on Marylebone Road. Charles was the only person in the world to whom John was prepared to open his heart freely. The letter begins with three paragraphs about current affairs and then turns, without clear connection, to a long-vanished past:

> I often cry out, *Vitae me redde priori!*[2] Let me be again an Oxford Methodist! I am often in doubt whether it would not be best for me to resume all my Oxford rules, great and small. I did then walk closely with God, and redeem the time. But what have I been doing these thirty years?

John could count on Charles to understand such a sudden uprush of nostalgia. Actually, Charles had been his brother's closest comrade during 'these thirty years'—and his most effective ally. He knew, as the others could not, how deeply John still cherished their 'former life' at Oxford, how truly a part of him still longed for a 'sweet retirement' in 'the groves of Academe'.[3]

---

[1] See his letter to Mrs. Savage, Sept. 19, 1771: 'My course has been for several years as fixed as that of the sun.' See also his letter to Samuel Sparrow, July 2, 1772: '. . . In the summer months I am almost continually in motion'.

[2] 'Give me back my former life'; Horace, *Epistles*, I. vii. 95. See also Wesley's earlier *Notes* on Eph. 5:16 and notice the contrast here between personal self-exposure and 'business as usual'.

[3] 'Having now obtained what I had long desired, a company of friends that were as my own soul, I set up my rest, being fully determined to live and die in this sweet retirement.' ('A Short History of the People Called Methodists', §4; cf. *Bibliog*, No. 420.i, and Vol. 9 of

Charles had his own lively memories of the rigours and joys of life in the Holy Club from 1729 to 1735; he could recall how popular a university preacher his brother had been from 1730 to 1735, despite much snide merriment about the enthusiasm of the 'Methodists', 'Bible Moths', 'Supererogation men', etc.[4] But he also remembered, more realistically than John, how barren of happiness and holiness those years had been, how ill-fated their Georgia mission, how unpromising their prospects in England after their return. He could have reminded John of how exciting it had been, after 1738, when their new-found experience of faith and their latent talents for communicating saving faith to 'plain people' had added a new impetus to the revival movements already stirring in many parts of Britain. Thus, he would have understood how to interpret John's passing spasm of nostalgia; he knew that only a part of John could have ever been content again with that *vita priori* in Oxford.

Moreover, despite a deepening dismay about his brother's irregular 'churchmanship', Charles had a clearer view than anyone else of the positive achievements of the three decades since 1738.[5] He had himself become the poet laureate of the Methodist people and a rousing preacher in his own right.[6] His main ecclesial concern had been to keep the Methodists safely within the Church of England as a 'religious society'. As the threat of 'separation' had loomed larger, however, he had fled the Conference of 1755, protesting what he foresaw in an anguished

this edn. Cf. the reference to *inter sylvas academicas* in Wesley's letter to 'John Smith', June 25, 1746, and in 'Some Remarks on Article X of Mr. Maty's New Review for December, 1784', §6, in the *Arminian Magazine* (henceforth *AM*), 1785, 152 (Vol. 9 of this edn.). See also a similar quotation from Horace in *A Farther Appeal*, Pt. III, III. 18 (11: 303 of this edn.). For a reference to 'beloved obscurity', cf. Sermon 112, *On Laying the Foundation of the New Chapel*, I.5 and n.)

[4] At the invitation of Bishop Potter, Wesley had preached an ordination sermon in Christ Church Cathedral, Sept. 19, 1730, just two years after his own ordination as priest. Thereafter, until he left for Georgia, his invitations to preach before the university far exceeded the normal rotation; see below, pp. 109-10.

[5] None of Charles's diaries, journal, or letters was published in his lifetime. A biography based on his surviving papers, preserved by his daughter, Sarah, was written by Thomas Jackson in 1841. Jackson then edited and published *The Journal of the Rev. Charles Wesley, M. A. . . . [with] Selections from his Correspondence and Poetry*, 2 vols., 1849 (henceforth 'CWJ'). A collection of *Sermons by the Late Rev. Charles Wesley, A. M.* was published in 1816.

[6] Cf. John Wesley's letter to Charles, June 27, 1766: 'In connexion I beat you; but in strong, pointed sentences you beat me.' John Whitehead said Charles's sermons were more 'awakening and useful' than John's; cf. his *Life of the Rev. John Wesley*, 2 vols. (1793, 1796), I. 292. Henry Moore's assessment was that 'John's preaching was all principles;

poetical *Epistle* to his brother.[7] In 1756 he had settled in London and, thereafter, had loosened his connection with the Conference. His own retrospective would, therefore, have been different from John's, and yet he would have realized his brother's unstated appeal that his unique ministry, 'these thirty years', had not been in vain.

There was, of course, a voluminous public record of that ministry (1738–72). Wesley's own version of those years had appeared in the successive *Extracts from the Journal of the Rev. John Wesley*,[8] in *A Short History of Methodism* (1765), and in a series of *Appeals to Men of Reason and Religion* (1743–45).[9] Besides, there had been a steady stream of critics of Methodism, from Josiah Tucker's 'Three Queries' in the *Weekly Miscellany* (1739), and *A Brief History of the Principles of Methodism* (1742), down to the furious controversy with the Calvinists that was still roiling.[10] No other religious leader in his century had provoked so varied an array of opponents, from clerics (and a few laymen), to the Bishops of Exeter and Gloucester.[11] On that Sunday at Shoreham, Perronet was entertaining the most widely exposed private person in England.[12]

His career as a truly effective evangelist ran back to 1739 when,

Charles's was all aphorisms'; cf. E. H. Sugden, ed., *Wesley's Standard Sermons* (London, Epworth Press, 1921—henceforth 'Sugden'), I. 69.

[7] *An Epistle to the Reverend Mr. John Wesley. By Charles Wesley, Presbyter of the Church of England*, 1755 (*Bibliog*, No. 210).

[8] Pts. 1–11 had been published by 1772, seven were to follow (abbreviated to 'JWJ' in this edn.).

[9] Vols. 9 and 11 of this edn.

[10] Cf. the Calvinist onslaught in *The Gospel Magazine* and the polemical attacks of Augustus Toplady (*A Caveat against Unsound Doctrines*, 1770; *A Letter to the Rev. Mr. John Wesley relative to his pretended Abridgment of Zanchius on Predestination*, 1770; *More Work for Mr. John Wesley*, 1772) and Richard Hill (*Pietas Oxoniensis* [anon.], 1768; *A Conversation between Richard Hill, Esq., The Rev. Mr. Madan, and Father Walsh, the Superior of a Convent of English Benedictine Monks at Paris . . . Relative to Some Doctrinal Minutes advanced by the Rev. Mr. John Wesley and Others at a Conference held in London, Aug. 7, 1770* [also anon.], 1772; *A Review of all the Doctrines Taught by the Rev. Mr. John Wesley*, 1772). The controversy continued fiercely, as in *Logica Wesleiensis: Or the Farrago Double-Distilled* (1773).

[11] Cf. George Lavington, *The Enthusiasm of Methodists and Papists Compared . . .*, Pts. I and II, published anonymously in 1749; Pt. III in 1751. See also the spirited replies of Whitefield, Vincent Perronet, and John Wesley. Cf. also William Warburton, *The Doctrine of Grace: Or, the Office and Operations of the Holy Spirit Vindicated from the Insults of Infidelity and the Abuses of Fanaticism* [i.e., Methodism] . . . , 2 vols., 1763. For the whole panoply of anti-Methodist polemic, see Richard Green, *Anti-Methodist Publications Issued During the Eighteenth Century* (1902).

[12] Cf. Joseph G. Wright, 'Notes on Some Portraits of John Wesley', in WHS, III. 185-92.

with grave misgivings, he had joined George Whitefield (former colleague in the Holy Club and fellow missionary to America) in a preaching mission to the poor on the outskirts of Bristol.[13] This reluctant venture had followed a succession of climactic experiences strung out over the entire year of 1738. Even before that, Wesley had pressed his quest for a personal assurance of God's pardoning grace in reaction to challenges from the Moravians and Salzburgers in Georgia. Following his return to England there had been an intense two-month span of soul searching that had reached a climax in the famous experience in 'a society in Aldersgate Street' on the evening of May 24th.[14] This, in turn, had prompted a pilgrimage to the Moravian heartland (Marienborn and Herrnhut) that had enabled him to make a probing study of Moravian life and doctrine—and of the personality cult that had grown up around their leader, Count Ludwig von Zinzendorf.[15] Then, in the following October, he had been shaken, yet again, by his discovery of Jonathan Edwards's *Faithful Narrative of a Surprising Work of God in New England* (1736).[16] The cumulative effect of this series of experiences was to drive him back to his own Anglican heritage, specifically to the Edwardian *Homilies* of 1547. There he had found a resolution to his doctrinal perplexities to match his new-found sense of assurance. This had prompted him to extract from Homilies I–IV an abridgement, which he then published and used as a theological charter throughout his whole career.[17] The end product of this series of conversions was a radical shift in his self-understanding of 'the order of salvation'—away from holy

[13] See JWJ, Mar. 10–Apr. 8, 1739.

[14] Cf. the carefully composed account of this in the *Journal* entry for that date; note the review of his spiritual pilgrimage from childhood to the very moment ('about a quarter before nine') when, as he says, 'I felt my heart strangely warmed . . .; and an assurance was given me that [Christ] had taken away *my* sins, even *mine*, and saved *me* from the law of sin and death.' The parallel here with St. Augustine's famous account of his conversion in the Milanese garden is clearly not unconscious; cf. *Confessions*, VIII. vii-xii (§§16-30).

[15] Cf. Edward Langton, *History of the Moravian Church* (New York, Macmillan, 1956); J. E. Hutton, *A History of the Moravian Church* (2nd edn., 1909); W. G. Addison, *The Renewed Church of the United Brethren, 1722–1930* (London, SPCK, 1932); Daniel Benham, *Memoirs of James Hutton* (1856). See also, Wesley's letter of Aug. 8, 1740, 'To the Church of God at Herrnhut in Upper Lusatia'.

[16] See below, p. 39.

[17] Cf. JWJ, Nov. 12, 1738: 'In the following week, I began more narrowly to inquire what the doctrine of the Church of England is concerning the much-controverted point of justification by faith; and the sum of what I found in the Homilies I extracted and printed for the use of others'—*The Doctrine of Salvation, Faith, and Good Works* (1738); it went through thirteen edns. in Wesley's lifetime (see *Bibliog*, No. 11, and Vol. 12 of this edn.).

living as a precondition to saving faith, to faith itself as the threshold of any valid experience of true holiness.

When he began his field preaching in 1739, Wesley had known next to nothing of the scattered revival movements elsewhere in England.[18] He was, however, aware of Whitefield's exciting work in and around Bristol, and he must have known of the tradition of the Quaker and Baptist field preachers who had ministered in these outlying districts during the turmoils of the Restoration.[19] What no one had counted on was that the upshot of his field preaching would be the discovery of his true vocation as an evangelist and the launching of a revival movement destined to eclipse the others both in its scope and staying power. Wesley's 'Methodism' quickly took on a character of its own—a 'connexion' of religious societies within the Church of England, with 'class-meetings' for prayer, study, and mutual help, together with active philanthropic programmes for the needy.[20] For 'these thirty years', then, Wesley had directed and governed this movement, and would continue to do so till his death in 1791. And yet, despite his gifts as leader and organizer, it was his impression that he had never *planned* the Methodist Revival. He had instead been gathered up into it and swept along by what seemed to him the clear leadings of divine providence.[21] It was Wesley's way to *re*-act to opportunities and openings as they came along rather than to preform the future by his own design. From childhood, he had had a sense of being set apart for a special destiny, 'a brand plucked out of the burning';[22] he had also come

---

[18] Cf. J. D. Walsh, 'Origins of the Evangelical Revival', in G. V. Bennet and J. D. Walsh, eds., *Essays in Modern English Church History* (London, Adam & Charles Black, 1966), pp. 132-62.

[19] Cf. the commemorative plaques on Hanham Mount near Bristol: 'Dedicated to the Field Preachers, 1658–1739'; [they] 'often forded the flooded Avon and risked imprisonment and death for their faith'; 'Out of the Wood came Light.' What is not so easy to explain is the absence of any reference to Whitefield, Wesley, or their ministries, on any of the plaques.

[20] Note the similarities and differences between this new United Society and the older ones described by Josiah Woodward in *An Account of the Rise and Progress of the Religious Societies in the City of London* (1698). See also John S. Simon, *John Wesley and the Religious Societies* (London, Epworth Press, 1923).

[21] See his letter to James Hutton, June 7, 1739: 'I enforced (as not my choice, but the providence of God, directed me) those words of Isaiah. . . .'; a letter to Charles, Sept. 28, 1769: 'All our lives and all God's dealings with us have been extraordinary from the beginning. . . .'; his annual *Minutes* for 1765 (*Q.* [26]): 'God . . . thrust us out, utterly against our will, to raise an holy people;' see also No. 107, 'On God's Vineyard', II. 3.

[22] This was associated with his experience of a dramatic rescue from a fire that

to lend special meanings to the metaphors of 'fire', 'flame', and 'light'.[23]

Any proper answer, then, to his rhetorical question about 'these thirty years' would have amounted to a survey of the middle third of his career. Among many other things, it would have included the story of his organization of the United Methodist Societies and his employment of laymen as 'Assistants'; this would have explained the origins and unique functions of the 'Annual Conference' of his clerical and lay brethren (with himself as host and president). It had also included an extensive programme of editing and publishing that was still going forward.[24] In 1772 he was deeply engaged with the only edition of his *Works* that he himself would collect and order: thirty-two volumes headed by fifty-three sermons in Volumes I–IV.[25] Throughout, he had been engaged in a relentless succession of controversies in which he had undertaken to clarify, develop, and defend his theological ideas. It was, therefore, natural enough that, with all these cumulative pressures, he would have been prompted wistfully to recall that quieter, more ordered 'former life' at Oxford.

We know less about John Wesley, as person and preacher, from those earlier days than from his later years of fame and notoriety. There are remembrances of him from his Oxford days: of his charming manners and sprightly conversation.[26] But a rather different impression comes from the reports of William Stephens, secretary to the Trustees for the Georgia Colony, who

destroyed the Epworth Rectory in 1709. For the story of that rescue in Susanna Wesley's words, see her letter of Aug. 24, 1709, to the Revd. Mr. Hoole, in Henry Moore, *The Life of the Rev. John Wesley* (London, John Kershaw, 1824, 1825—henceforth 'Moore'), I. 112–14; for Wesley's remembrance of it as told to Moore, cf. *ibid.*, pp. 114-15; see also his MS. Journal for Mar. 7, 1737, and JWJ, Feb. 7, 1750.

[23] Cf. James Downey, *Eighteenth Century Pulpit* (Oxford, Clarendon Press, 1969), p. 221.

[24] Cf. T. W. Herbert, *John Wesley as Editor and Author* (Princeton, Princeton University Press, 1940); see also Vol. 16 of this edn. and *Bibliog*, Vols. 33-34. Wesley's theological biases and editorial methods may be studied at firsthand in his *Christian Library* (henceforth *Christian Lib.*) and the *AM*.

[25] By 1772 sixteen vols. had been published; Vols. 17–25 appeared in 1773, 26–32 in 1774.

[26] See Samuel Badcock's description of Wesley as a 'very sensible and acute collegian, baffling every man by the subtleties of logic, and laughing at them for being so easily routed; a young fellow of the finest classical taste, of the most liberal and manly sentiments', whose pen could produce surprisingly 'gay and sprightly' verse (*Westminster Magazine*, Apr. 1774, p. 180). See also V. H. H. Green, *The Young Mr. Wesley: A Study of John Wesley at Oxford* (London, Edward Arnold, 1961), chs. IV, VI, X-XI.

visited him in Savannah just as his troubled ministry there was nearing its inglorious end.[27] The Earl of Egmont, a Trustee for the Georgia Colony, remembered Wesley as 'an odd mixture of a man'; he and many of the other trustees were clearly dissatisfied with his work as chaplain.[28]

With increasing fame, however, there had come more notice from competent observers, but notoriety, too, not to mention the swelling flood of portraits, busts, medallions, and relics (in a burgeoning hero-cult).[29] Howel Harris wrote approvingly of a sermon of Wesley's that he had heard in May, 1743.[30] From many sources there are two of uncommon interest and trustworthiness. Just three years before John's letter to Charles, a visiting Swedish professor, Johan Henrik Liden, of Uppsala, had met the elder Wesley in London (on Sunday, Oct. 15, 1769). His report to his friends back home is revealing:

Today I learned for the first time to know Mr. John Wesley, so well known here in England, and called the spiritual father of the so-called 'Methodists'. He arrived home yesterday from his summer journey to Ireland, where he has visited his people. He preached today at the forenoon service in the Methodist Chapel in Spitalfields for an audience of more than 4,000 people. His text was Luke 1:68. The sermon was short but eminently evangelical. He has no great oratorical gifts, no outward appearance, but he speaks clear and pleasant. After the Holy Communion (which in all English churches is held with closed doors at the end of the preaching service, when none but the communicants usually are present, and which here was celebrated very orderly and pathetic), I went forward to shake hands with Mr. Wesley . . . and was received by him in his usual amiable and friendly way. He is a small, thin old man, with his own long and straight hair, and looks as the worst country curate in Sweden, but has learning

[27] See *Journal of the Proceedings in Georgia*, Vol. I, pp. 10, 11-12, 14-15, 19-20, 30-31, 36-37, 40-41, 45-46, 53, 65, 234-35; this last entry notes Stephen's dismay at discovering the parish register 'filled with the names of communicants at the Sacraments . . . instead of an account of births and burials'.

[28] *Diary of Viscount Percival, Afterwards First Earl of Egmont*, R. A. Roberts, ed., 3 vols. (1920-23), II. 481 (Apr. 26, 1738).

[29] E.g., his silver buckles were passed on from family to family till finally they were bequeathed to the museum in Wesley's House on City Road, London; see T. Francis Glasson in WHS, XXXIII.177-78. There was even a vogue for 'Wesley tablecloths', etc.; cf. WHS, XXXVII.31-33. No other Englishman of his time had had as many likenesses struck off—but with such wide differences between them that it is impossible to decide on one above the others as the most accurate.

[30] See his letter of May 12th to George Whitefield: 'Last Sunday I heard Bro. John Wesley preach upon the seventh of the Romans. He was very sweet and loving, and seemed to have his heart honestly bent on drawing the poor souls to Christ' (Nehemiah Curnock, ed., *The Journal of the Rev. John Wesley*, 8 vols., London, Epworth Press, 1909-16—henceforth 'Curnock'—III. 77n.).

as a bishop and a zeal for the glory of God which is quite extraordinary. His talk is very agreeable. . . . He is the personification of piety, and he seems to me as a living representation of the loving Apostle John. The old man Wesley is already 66 years, but very lively and exceedingly industrious. I also spoke with his younger brother, Mr. Charles Wesley, also a Methodist minister and a pious man, but neither in learning or activity can he be compared with the older brother.[31]

A later account comes from the well-known evangelical historian, Thomas Haweis, who had collected all eyewitness evidence available to him:

John Wesley was of the inferior size [five feet, three inches], his visage marked with intelligence, singularly neat and plain in his dress, a little cast in his eye observable upon particular occasions, upright, graceful, and remarkably active. His understanding, naturally excellent and acute, was highly stored with the attainments of literature, and he possessed a fund of anecdote and history that rendered his company as entertaining as instructive. His mode of address in public was chaste and solemn, though not illumined with those coruscations of eloquence which marked, if I may use that expression, the discourses of his rival, George Whitefield. But there was a divine simplicity, a zeal, a venerableness in his manner which commanded attention and never forsook him in his latest years. When at fourscore he retained all the freshness of vigorous old age, his health was remarkably preserved amidst a scene of labour and perpetual exertions of mind and body to which few would have been equal. Never man possessed greater personal influence over the people connected with him, nor was it an easy task to direct so vast a machine [the Methodist Societies] when amidst so many hundred wheels in motion some moved eccentrically and hardly yielded to the impulse of the mainspring. I need not speak of the exemplariness of his life. Too many eyes were upon him to admit of his halting, nor could his weight have been maintained a moment longer than the fullest conviction impressed his people that he was eminently favoured as a saint of God and as distinguished for his holy walk as for his vast abilities, indefatigible and singular usefulness.[32]

Thus, at the time he was giving voice to his passing nostalgia, John Wesley had already set a notable mark on English Christianity, had brought new form and power to popular religion, had altered and enriched the theological climate of his time. This harvest of a unique career had come, more than he or

---

[31] WHS, XVII.2.

[32] See Thomas Haweis, *An Impartial and Succinct History of the Rise and Declension and Revival of the Church of Christ* (1807), II. 435-36. For a thoughtful disciple's considered (and generally reliable) retrospect on Wesley as person and preacher, see Whitehead, II. 466-68. There is a useful collection of other eyewitness accounts in R. Denny Urlin, *A Churchman's Life of Wesley* (1880), Appendix XIII, 'Portraiture and Character', pp. 344-46.

the others realized, from a radical role-reversal from his original identity as academic don and regular cleric to a virtual identification with the English underclass. They, in turn, had accepted him as one of their own and yet also as their spiritual director, theological mentor, and pastoral counselor. His unconventional ministry had given them not only a new hope of grace and salvation *in this life* but also a new sense of human dignity, also *in this life*. Judged by almost any norm, it had been a unique career, and in 1772 it still had two remarkable decades left.[33]

He had been born in an out-of-the-way Lincolnshire village in an England still shaken by the shocks of civil war and dynastic violence. He had grown up amidst the dying throes of the feudal system in the English Church and civil state, nowhere more vividly described than in Gilbert Burnet's classic autobiography, which Wesley had read in Oxford.[34] His career had been cast in a century of bewildering transitions in English society: political and cultural changes that gave the label 'Georgian' to an epoch, social and economic changes that prepared the way for the cruelly unequal prosperity of the late eighteenth century. He had done more than survive these transitions passively; he had himself been one of the forces of significant change. His firsthand acquaintance with the English masses, and with Britain generally, was unmatched—certainly by any churchman.

Wesley's backward glance, then, was obviously less concerned with onward events of his career than with their meaning and lasting value. It was a rare lapse of self-confidence in the midst of conflict in which he usually moved serenely. He realized that many of his Anglican critics saw nothing but confusion in his theological endeavours to synthesize the two rival traditions of evangelical faith and 'holy living'. The Calvinists had denounced him, not only as 'Arminian', but also as a 'Papist', a 'Presbyterian Papist', 'a puny tadpole in divinity'.[35] His steadfast reply to all this

---

[33] Cf. W. E. H. Lecky's fulsome account of Wesley and Methodism in *A History of England in the Eighteenth Century* (1892), III. 37-153. See also Charles Grant Robertson, *England Under the Hanoverians* (London, Methuen and Co., 1911); and Basil Williams, *The Whig Supremacy, 1714–1760* (Oxford, Clarendon Press, 1939).

[34] *History of His Own Time* [1643–1715], 2 vols. (1724, 1734); Wesley had read Vol. I in 1725.

[35] His ablest Anglican critics were Josiah Tucker (see above, nn.10, 11) and 'John Smith', for whose correspondence with Wesley see Vol. 26 of this edn. See also Thomas Church, *Remarks on the Rev. Mr. John Wesley's Last Journal* (1745).

For the charges of 'papism', see JWJ, Oct. 30, 1743; Aug. 27, 1739; Apr. 11, 1740; and

was an unwavering profession of loyalty to the Church of England as defined by her Homilies, the Articles of Religion, and the Book of Common Prayer. Very late in life, with his movement headed toward eventual separation, he would go on repeating his old profession: 'I declare once more that I live and die a member of the Church of England, and that none who regard my judgment or advice will ever separate from it.'[36] He never saw himself as a rebel, even though the blithe irregularities in his churchmanship left the impression that, although he was certainly *in* the Church of England as defined by her tradition, he was never altogether *of* it, as defined by her eighteenth century self-understanding.[37]

The evidence about his personal disposition and temperament is curiously inconsistent. Aaron Seymour speaks of him as 'cheerful'; Richard Viney, who knew him better, commented on his 'choleric complexion'. His sister Emily complained that he had reined his feelings so tightly that he regarded 'natural affections as a great weakness if not a sin'.[38] Even so, he shed

Sept. 24, 1742. Some of his opponents were even more colourful in their epithets. Cf. Augustus Toplady, 'An Old Fox Tarr'd and Feather'd', *Works* (1837), p. 762. In a pamphlet of no more than forty pages Rowland Hill calls Wesley 'a designing wolf', 'a dealer in stolen words', 'as unprincipled as a rook and as silly as a jackdaw', 'a grey-headed enemy of all righteousness', 'a wretch' guilty of 'wilful, gross and abominable untruth', 'a venal profligate', 'a wicked slanderer', 'an apostate miscreant', 'libeller', 'crafty slanderer', 'an unfeeling reviler', 'a liar of the most gigantic magnitude', 'a Solomon in a cassock', 'a disappointed *Orlando Furioso*', 'Pope John', 'this living lump of inconsistencies', etc., etc.; see *Imposture Detected and the Dead Vindicated: in a Letter to a Friend* (London, 1777).

[36] See 'Farther Thoughts on Separation from the Church', §7, in *AM*, 1790, 216 (Vol. 9 of this edn.); cf. his letter to *The Dublin Chronicle*, June 2, 1789 ('In my youth I was not only a member of the Church of England but a bigot to it.'); his letter to Henry Moore, May 6, 1788 ('I am a Church of England man; . . . in the Church I will live and die, unless I am thrust out.'); to Joseph Taylor, Jan. 16, 1783, and to John Mason, Mar. 22, 1772. See also Sermon 121, 'Prophets and Priests', §18.

The term 'Anglican' was not in common use in Wesley's time (cf. *OED*), but the basic equation of the terms 'national', 'establishment', 'Church of England men', and 'Anglican' had already been made by Joseph Glanvill, *A Seasonable Defence of Preaching* (1678), pp. 74-75. Later, the Tractarians would co-opt the phrase and associate it with the medieval notions of an *ecclesia anglicana* as a regional catholic church. For the propriety of the label 'Anglican' in Wesley's case, cf. Frank Baker, *John Wesley and the Church of England* (Nashville and New York, Abingdon, 1970), p. 6.

[37] For a comprehensive analysis of this complex relationship, see Frank Baker, *ibid.*, *passim*, but espec. chs. 14-17, 'Epilogue', and Appendix (pp. 326-40).

[38] See his letter to 'Mrs. Harper', June 30, 1743, and note Wesley's surprised denial of such a charge. See also A. C. H. Seymour, *Life and Times of Selina, Countess of Huntingdon* (London, W. E. Painter, 2 vols., 1840—henceforth 'Seymour') I. 58, and 'Richard Viney's Diary', May 29, 1744, in WHS, XIV.198. For other comments on the question of 'inordinate affection', cf. Nos. 14, *The Repentance of Believers*, I. 5; and 84, *The Important Question*, III. 10; and his letters to Ann Bolton, Nov. 28, 1772, to Sarah Mallet, Oct. 6, 1787 and Mar. 11, 1788, and to Adam Clarke, Jan. 3, 1791.

resentments easily and was honestly averse to controversy unless
sorely provoked. By the same token, though, he reacted to
criticism with the instincts of a born debater, with a habit of
logic-chopping and a notable gift for sarcasm.[39] And yet, one of
his wisest and most discerning friends, Alexander Knox (himself
a mentor to Pusey, Keble, and Newman), said of him: 'He was, in
truth, the most perfect specimen of *moral happiness* which I ever
saw.' Yet Knox spoke also of the 'sudden revolutions of [Wesley's]
mind', 'his proneness to attribute to the Spirit of God what might
more reasonably be resolved into natural emotions.'[40] This throws
a flood of light on the twists and turns of his personal life: e.g., the
Sophy Hopkey affair in Georgia, the tragic breach with George
Whitefield, his resort to pious sortilege in making important
decisions, his aborted courtship of Grace Murray, his unhappy
marriage—and so on and on.[41]

He was a truly humble man, at home with great and small; he
loved and was loved by little children everywhere.[42] But he also
commanded respect, even from the mobs, and was immensely

[39] See his unprovoked attack on his former mentor, William Law; cf. A. Keith Walker,
William Law: His Life and Thought (London, SPCK, 1973), espec. pp. 127-39. Cf. his
anti-Calvinist polemic in *Predestination Calmly Considered* (1752), *passim*, and his even
larger debate with John Taylor of Norwich in *The Doctrine of Original Sin: According to
Scripture, Reason, and Experience* (1757), (*Bibliog*, Nos. 194, 222) both in Vol. 12 of this edn.

[40] See Knox's 'Remarks on the Life and Character of John Wesley', in Robert Southey,
Life of Wesley, New edn., ed. C. C. Southey, with Knox's 'Remarks', (London, Longman,
et al., 1864—henceforth 'Southey'), II. 344, 339. In defending Wesley from the charge of
vanity, however, Knox wrote: 'Great minds are not vain: and [Wesley's] was a great mind,
if any mind can be made great by distinterested benevolence, spotless purity, and simple
devotedness.' (*Thirty Years' Correspondence between John Jebb and Alexander Knox*, 2nd edn.,
London, Duncan, 1836, II. 460).

[41] Cf. Wesley's MS account of his relations with Sophy Hopkey, Mar. 1736 to Mar. 12,
1737, in the Methodist Archives, John Rylands University Library of Manchester—henceforth 'MA.' For the breach with Whitefield see Southey, ch. xi, Luke
Tyerman, *Life and Times of John Wesley* (New York, Harper and Brothers,
1872—henceforth 'Tyerman (*JW*) '), I. 311-25, and for Whitefield's side *George
Whitefield's Journals*, Iain Murray, ed. (London, Banner of Truth Trust, 1960), Appendix
III, pp. 563-88. For a MS account of the Grace Murray affair, see British Library
(henceforth 'BL') Add. MS No. 7119; cf. J. A. Leger, *John Wesley's Last Love* (London,
J. M. Dent and Sons, Ltd., 1910). For samplings of his use of lots, see JWJ, Mar. 4, 1737
(cf. diary), Mar. 28, 1739, and also his open letter to Thomas Church, June 17, 1746 (IV.
3-4), in Vol. 9 of this edn.

[42] Charles Atmore recalls a sermon to children at Bolton, 'literally composed and
delivered in words of not more than two syllables' (Curnock, VIII. 63n.); see also Tyerman
(*JW*), III. 472; and Banning's account in his *Memoir*, (WHS, IV.119-20). Matthias Joyce,
one of Wesley's preachers, recalled the first time he heard Wesley preach (in 1773) and
added: 'What endeared him still more to me was seeing him stoop to kiss a little child that
stood on the stairs.' (John Telford, ed., *Wesley's Veterans*, VII. 191).

popular with many of Britain's 'plain people'. He was a High Church Tory who made it a point to wear his clerical vestments whenever he preached, even in the fields.[43] He also understood himself as an Anglican theologian with a special mission to teach the masses, well content for his teachings to be judged by the immemorial Anglican canons of 'Scripture, reason, and Christian antiquity'.[44] Into the bargain, however, he was also a decisive influence in the reformation of manners that had already been noticed before the century was out.[45]

Wesley's character, then, was complex and paradoxical in many ways. And yet there were two wholly consistent concerns running throughout his ministry after 1739 and clearly mirrored in his sermons. One of these was his special sense of calling to an 'extraordinary ministry' to the masses beyond the reach of the 'ordinary ministries' of a state church so hobbled by the suspensions of her Convocation that she could not respond to new needs created by out-dated parish boundaries, conflicting jurisdictions, and tragic human dislocations.[46] Even before his own Revival had been launched, Wesley had claimed, 'I look upon *all the world* as *my parish*; thus far I mean, that in whatever part of it I am I judge it meet, right, and my bounden duty, to declare unto all that are willing to hear the glad tidings of salvation. This is the work which I know God has called me to.

[43] See JWJ, Sept. 9, 1743 (during a visit to the wild country of St. Hilary Downs in Cornwall): 'The Downs I found, but no congregation, neither man, woman, nor child. But by that [time] I had put on my gown and cassock about an hundred gathered themselves together.' Frederick Gill, *In the Steps of John Wesley*, pp. 149-50, gives an account of an old man at Hull who remembered Wesley as 'a bonny little man, with such a canny nice face', wearing 'knee breeches, black stockings, and buckles on his shoes, with his bonny white hair hanging on his black gown, and a clean white thing like two sark necks, hanging down on his breast'.

[44] See 'To the Reader', § 4, in *Works* (1771), Vol. I.

[45] See Bernard Semmel, *The Methodist Revolution* (New York, Basic Books, 1973), chs. 1-4; see also Dorothy George, *London Life in the Eighteenth Century* (London, George Routledge and Sons, 1930), pp. 16-17: 'By the end of the [eighteenth] century we are in a different world. . . . We see a revolution comparable with conversion.' Cf. Christopher Hill, *Reformation to Industrial Revolution*, Vol. 2 in *The Pelican Economic History of Britain* (Harmondsworth, England, Penguin Books, 1971), p. 276; note Hill's complaint that the Methodists 'liberated people without democratizing society'; see also John D. Gay, *The Geography of Religion in England* (London, Duckworth, 1971), p. 146.

[46] The Whigs had prorogued both Convocations of Canterbury and York in 1717; they were reconvened briefly in 1741, and then silenced until 1852 (for Canterbury; 1861 for York). This had the effect of freezing the church's administration in its *status quo* during a crucial period of rapid social change.

And sure I am that his blessing attends it.'[47] Thus, he felt free not only to preach wherever he found an auditory, but he was equally concerned to organize his converts into religious societies and to enlist them in the ongoing tasks of Christian nurture in mutually sustaining small groups.[48]

The other clue to Wesley's inner consistency, despite all his 'sudden revolutions', may be seen in his intensely practical concern with the order of salvation in the Christian life. The controlling theological inquiry throughout his life was into the meaning of becoming and being a Christian in all the aspects of Christian existence. Here one may find the genuine integration of what seemed to some of his critics as nothing better than 'a medley of . . . Calvinism, Arminianism, Montanism, Quakerism, Quietism, all thrown together'.[49] This preoccupation with the *ordo salutis* and his cumulative insights into its wholeness may be recognized in all the developments in his preaching and in his personal pilgrimage as well.[50]

By 1772, therefore, there was no way back to that 'former life' of Wesley; there never had been, really. He had had a slow start, and one or two false starts. But, finally, he had found his unique calling, and his sermons (early, middle, and late) are mirrors to that.

II. THE PREACHER AND HIS PREACHING

For Wesley it was preaching that defined his vocation preeminently.[1] This was the principal means of gathering converts into Christian fellowship and of nurturing them in it. 'In

---

[47] See letter of Mar. 28 (?), 1739; long tradition has this letter dated as Mar. 20 and as written to James Hervey, but incorrectly. It was addressed to some clergyman (possibly John Clayton) who had already raised the issue of Wesley's right to invade other men's parishes without invitation (see *Letters*, Vol. 25 in this edn., pp. 614, 616). See also the carefully edited account of Wesley's conversation with Bishop Butler of Bristol, Aug. 16, 1739, in WHS, XLII. 93-100.

[48] Cf. Thomas Oden, *The Intensive Group Experience: The New Pietism* (Philadelphia, The Westminster Press, 1972), pp. 56-88.

[49] See *The Principles of a Methodist*, § 30 (*Bibliog*, No. 67, and Vol. 9 of this edn.), in response to Josiah Tucker's *Brief History*, p. 39.

[50] On this point, a careful comparison and contrast between Wesley and Søren Kierkegaard might be very fruitful; cf. Kierkegaard's stress on 'becoming a Christian', generally, and espec. in *Training in Christianity*, Walter Lowrie, tr. (London, Oxford University Press, 1941).

[1] See JWJ, July 28, 1757: 'About noon I preached at Woodseats, in the evening at Sheffield. I do indeed *live* by preaching!'

the first church', as he believed, 'the primary business of apostles, evangelists, and bishops was to preach the Word of God';[2] he had taken this as his own chief business. Even before he left England for Georgia, he could say, unpompously, to John Burton, 'My tongue is a devoted thing.'[3] His first venture into field preaching had wrenched all his habits and preferences out of shape,[4] but the startling response had overcome his reluctance. His experiences in Kingswood and Moorfields had convinced him that this 'extraordinary' ministry, beyond the confines of parish and campus, had become his special ministry.

He had already learned to preach extempore in Oxford.[5] After 1739 he was even more earnestly convinced that preaching, to be effective, must be an interpersonal encounter between the preacher and his hearers. Hence, he believed that oral preaching was the norm. Written sermons could only be regarded as either preparatory for more effective oral utterance or else distillates of it: the written word as substitute for personal presence. However, he saw an important difference between the principal aims of an oral and a written sermon: the former is chiefly for *proclamation* and invitation; the latter is chiefly for *nurture* and reflection. Many of Wesley's favourite texts for oral preaching do not appear at all in the corpus of his written sermons and vice versa. This fact, plus the enormous range of his oral sermon texts, disposes of the suggestion that Wesley had a limited repertory of memorized discourses which he merely repeated to different auditories. As far as we can tell, the doctrinal substance of the two genres was identical; and when Wesley finally resorted to a *written* corpus as an extension of his wider ministry, it was designated for his own people as well as for any others who also might be interested.

[2] *Notes*, Acts 6:2.

[3] Letter, Oct. 10, 1735.

[4] JWJ, Apr. 2, 1739; his first experiment of preaching in the open air had been on the deck of the ship *Simmonds*, Oct. 19, 1735, but that had clearly been exceptional.

[5] The Puritan traditions of extempore prayer and preaching go back at least to their early leaders like William Fulke (1538–89); cf. his *Brief and Plain Declaration Concerning the Desires of all Those Faithful Ministers that Have and Do Seek for the Discipline and Reformation of the Church of England* (1584), in Leonard J. Trinterud, ed., *Elizabethan Puritanism*, A Library of Protestant Thought (New York, Oxford University Press, 1971), pp. 267-69. The first record of Wesley's extempore preaching is in his diary, Nov. 10, 1734: 'Began preaching extempore on the Beatitudes'—in the Castle at Oxford. Much later (JWJ, Jan. 28, 1776), he would (incorrectly) remember that his first such experiment was in the year 1735, in All Hallows Church, Lombard Street, London: 'This was the first time that, having no notes about me, I preached extempore.'

His compulsion to preach wherever opportunity offered had driven him into the fields.[6] His self-justification here was twofold. The first was his 'right to preach anywhere' (*ius predicandi ubique*) that he understood as having been implied in his Oxford ordination.[7] 'Being ordained as Fellow of a College [he had claimed in 1739], I was not limited to any particular cure, but have an indeterminate commission, to preach the Word of God in any part of the Church of England.'[8] Later, he would be even more specific: 'I . . . was ordained as a member of that "College of Divines" [i.e., Lincoln] (so our statutes express it) "founded to overturn all heresies, and defend the Catholic faith".' [9] Wesley's second justification rested on the distinction, already mentioned, between the settled parish ministry (*ministerium ordinarium*) and the validity, *in exceptional circumstances*, of an irregular and informal ministry (*ministerium extraordinarium*). This, as we shall see, was a tradition that ran back into the Middle Ages and still seemed warranted in the special circumstances of the eighteenth century. These two different types of ministry, in Wesley's view, need not be rivals; they ought to be partners. As an itinerant, he rarely preached during 'church hours'; there were other times when people might conveniently be gathered. But this also meant that he was always preaching to people on the move; wherefore, it was important that every sermon should proclaim the essential

---

[6] Beginning in 1738, Wesley began to be barred from many regular pulpits (e.g., St. Lawrence Jewry; St. Katherine Cree; St. John's, Wapping; St. Benet, Paul's Wharf; St. Antholin), as he explained to Samuel Walker (Sept. 19, 1757), for preaching 'repentance and remission of sins and [for] insist[ing] that we are justified by faith. . . . (I say for *this*: as yet there was no field preaching). And this exclusion occasioned our preaching elsewhere, with the other irregularities that followed.' Later, he would become 'an honourable man', welcomed into many pulpits, so that he would write, 'I have more invitations to preach in churches than I can accept of' (JWJ, Jan. 19, 1783). In a single four-year span (1780–84) he was invited into more than fifty regular pulpits and barred from only one thereafter. For a list of churches where Wesley preached again after having been shut out of these pulpits in 1738–39, see A. Skevington Wood, *The Burning Heart*, p. 201.

[7] Hastings Rashdall, *The Universities of Europe in the Middle Ages*, Frederick Maurice Powicke and Alfred Brotherston Emden, eds. (Oxford, Clarendon Press, 1936), III. 136, notes that the Chancellor of Oxford had by tradition the right to 'license preachers to preach in every diocese in England'.

[8] See p. 13, n. 47 above, Wesley's interview with Bishop Butler.

[9] *Farther Appeal*, Pt. I, VI. 9 (11: 183 in this edn.). The heresies first here in view were those of Wycliffe and the Lollards. Cf. Wesley's *Principles of a Methodist Farther Explain'd* (1746), III. 5, Vol. 9 of this edn. See also F. Makower, *The Constitutional History and Constitution of the Church of England* (1895), 491, on Canon 33 of 'The Canons of 1604'. Wesley also seems to have believed that he had the personal support of King George himself in his irregularities; see JWJ, Sept. 3, 1750.

gospel as if for that one time only.[10] This constant itinerancy (both for himself and for his assistants) was of the essence of Wesley's idea of the 'extraordinary ministry'; he never intended to lead a schismatic movement. In 1756 he wrote to Samuel Walker of Truro, 'Were I myself to preach one whole year in one place, I should preach both myself and most of my congregation asleep.'[11] 'The preachers *must* change regularly;' said he to Mrs. Bennis, 'it would never do to let one man sit down for six months with a small society.'[12]

Wesley was by no means the most exciting or eloquent preacher of his time. J. L. von Mosheim, 'the father of modern church history', had not even heard of him in 1755.[13] In Aaron Seymour's dramatic account of the Evangelical Revival Wesley appears as a marginal figure.[14] And yet his influence was cumulative and longer lasting than that of any of the other evangelists of the century. *His* explanation for this, and it is crucial, was that the system of pastoral care and Christian nurture provided for the converts in the 'Methodist connexion' forged them into a mutually sustaining community.[15] He compared the efforts of some of his fellow evangelists among the clergy to 'ropes of sand'.[16] More than anything else, it was Wesley's *message* that

[10] See 'Disciplinary' *Minutes*, June 28, 1744: '*Q.* 13. What is the best general method in preaching? *A.* (1). To invite. (2). To convince. (3). To offer Christ. Lastly, To build up, and to do this (in some measure) in every sermon.' See also the MS Minutes for May 23, 1753: 'The most effectual way of preaching Christ is to preach him in all his offices, and to declare his law as well as gospel to believers and unbelievers,' and Wesley's open letter, 'Of Preaching Christ', Dec. 20, 1751.
Samplings of Wesley's habit of summarizing the essence of his gospel message in encapsulated form may be seen in Sermons 7, 'The Way to the Kingdom', I. 7-8; 24, 'Sermon on the Mount, IV', III. 1-3; 122, 'The Causes of the Inefficacy of Christianity', §6; and 39, 'Catholic Spirit', §§12-18, etc. Similar summations are scattered through the *Notes* and letters.

[11] Letter, Sept. 3, 1756, to Samuel Walker.

[12] Letter of July 27, 1770; see also his letter to Joseph Benson, Dec. 11, 1772.

[13] Cf. J. S. Reid, *Mosheim's Institutes of Ecclesiastical History* (1st edn. in Lat., 1747), 1849, p. 873, for a brief notice of Whitefield.

[14] Cf. his *Countess of Huntingdon*, I, chs. xii, xiv-xv; II, ch. xxxix. W. Fraser Mitchell, *English Pulpit Oratory* (New York, Macmillan, 1932), p. 312, ignores Wesley in his list of 'the greatest English preachers'. He was ignored by Erasmus Middleton's survey in his *Evangelical Biography* (1812), and also by John C. Ryle's *Five Christian Leaders of the Eighteenth Century* (London, Banner of Truth Trust, 1960); Ryle gives John Berridge of Everton a chapter instead.

[15] Cf. his letter to the 'Travelling Preachers', Aug. 4, 1769, appended to the Annual *Minutes* that year; *A Plain Account of the People called Methodists*, II. 7-10, VI. 1-6 (*Bibliog*, No. 156, Vol. 9 of this edn.); and 'Thoughts upon Methodism' (Aug. 4, 1786, in *AM*, 1787).

[16] *Ibid.*, Aug. 4, 1769; cf. Sermon 113, *The Late Work of God in North America*, I. 9 and n.

struck home: people not excited by his eloquence were moved by his vision of the Christian life and his gospel of universal redemption. This opened the door of hope for men and women who had been crowded off onto the margins of society.[17] Moreover, it was hope in this world as well as in the world to come. Victims of the social and economic dislocations of Hanoverian England had been huddled together on the outskirts of the great cities and around the pitheads of new mines in Cornwall and the North.[18] Wesley had found his new underclass where they were and had gathered them into new social groups in which each person found acceptance and a new sense of dignity. Whitefield and most of the other evangelists found their constituencies largely among the rising middle class and lesser nobility.[19] Thus, if the Church of England was unable to adapt to the new circumstances,[20] Wesley's itinerant system could and did. There is no record of a Methodist society within the bounds of the great cities or their affluent suburbs. But they struck quick root in Moorfields, Spitalfields, Southwark, and similar pockets of poverty around Bristol, Newcastle, and elsewhere.[21] 'I love the poor', said Wesley to Dorothy Furly; 'in many of them I find pure, genuine grace, unmixed with paint, folly, and affectation.'[22] For all the resentment he aroused within the established churches (Anglican and Nonconformist), the common people heard him gladly and took him to their hearts.

[17] Cf. Christopher Hill, *Society and Puritanism in Pre-Revolutionary England* (London, Secker and Warburg, 1964), pp. 456-57; the 'poor' were excluded from the political process and from most of the protections even of the common law; see also, *ibid.*, p. 241, for a comment on the affinities between the Puritans and the rising bourgeoisie.

[18] Cf. George Rudé, 'The Other London' in *Hanoverian London, 1714–1808* (London, Secker and Warburg, 1971), pp. 82-99.

[19] It is true, of course, that Whitefield attracted huge masses to his outdoor services, and he had built a Tabernacle in Moorfields within sight of the Foundery. Even so, his support came largely from the constituency of the Tottenham Court Road Tabernacle and from Lady Huntingdon's Connexion.

[20] Cf. Jonathan Swift's hyperbolic claim that 'five-sixths of the people in England are absolutely hindered from hearing divine service', in *The Prose Works*, ed. Temple Scott (1897), I. 45. Even so, his point that the churches could not reach beyond their bounds of coterie and custom is valid enough.

[21] Cf. Gay, *Geography*, p. 146.

[22] Letter of Sept. 25, 1757; cf. his letter of Sept. 29, 1764, to Ann Foard: 'I *bear* the rich and love the poor; therefore I spend *almost all* my time with them.' See also his comment in a letter to one of his more sophisticated friends, Brian Bury Collins, Jan. 14, 1780: 'You have seen very little of the choicest part of the London society. I mean the poor. Go with me into their cellars and garrets, and then you will taste their [gracious] spirits.'

Outcasts of men, to you I call,
    Harlots and publicans, and thieves!
He spreads his arms t'embrace you all;
    Sinners alone his grace receives:
No need of him the righteous have,
He came the lost to seek and save.[23]

The Tradition of Popular Preaching in England

In Wesley's break with eighteenth century taboos against field preaching, extempore prayer, and lay leadership (including his own), he was appealing to larger precedents than those currently being set by men like Howel Harris and George Whitefield. Actually, he was reclaiming a longer, richer tradition that reached back into medieval times and the English Reformation. We have, from G. R. Owst, the fascinating story of the 'lewd' (i.e., popular) preachers and the wandering friars, pardoners, and almoners of the fourteenth and fifteenth centuries.[24] Those men had addressed themselves, as they said, *ad populum* (to the multitude); their messages had ranged from vigorous protests against immorality and injustice to pleas for true compassion and help for the disconsolate poor who had little to hope for from their settled pastors. They, too, had been itinerants, and had 'preached abroad' at the numerous 'preaching crosses' scattered across the land—and not seldom in churchyards and cemeteries.[25] They, too, had been criticized by the generality of bishops and clergy; but they had also found occasional encouragement, as, for example, by so eminent a churchman and scholar as Robert Grosseteste in Wesley's native Lincolnshire.[26] Many of these men were refreshingly free spirits, seeking to redress the imbalance they saw in their times between the Eucharist and the sermon in Christian worship. Overall, they were also partisans of a Christian

[23] 'Where shall my wondering soul begin?' st. 5 in *Hymns and Sacred Poems*, 1739, pp. 101-3, No. 29 in Wesley's *Collection of Hymns* (1780, *Bibliog*, No. 408, Vol. 7 of this edn.).
[24] In his *Preaching in Medieval England* (Cambridge, Cambridge University Press, 1926). Cf. also, E. C. Dargan, *A History of Preaching* (Grand Rapids, Baker Book House, 1954), I. 336-42; and R. C. Petry, *No Uncertain Sound* (Philadelphia, The Westminster Press, 1948), 251-60.
[25] For Wesley's re-enactment of this old populist tradition (*ad populum*), see his Preface, below, p. 103; for the story about preaching from his father's tombstone in the Epworth churchyard, see JWJ, June 6-7, 1742.
[26] Bishop of Lincoln (1235–53), great preacher, reformer, and staunch friend of the Franciscan friars. Matthew Paris's description of him stresses the range of his roles: 'confuter of the pope and the king, . . . preacher to the people (*ad populum*)'; see Henry R. Luard, in *DNB*, 'Grosseteste'.

puritanism, champions of 'the righteous poore [as] Goddes knyghtes (*patientes pauperes, fideles simplices*)'. They insisted on a radical equality of all persons before God. They denounced pride and avarice as the most pervasive of all the deadly sins, even as they laid great stress on thrift, industry, sobriety, and generosity, as essential Christian virtues.[27] Finally, just as they taught a Christian unworldliness in life, they also taught the Christian 'craft of dying well'.[28] That Wesley stood in their line is clear, and this is important in any interpretation of his self-chosen role as a folk-theologian.

It was inevitable that such a populist tradition would be in disfavour with the establishment at large; after the Lollard ferment, it had been harshly suppressed. At the Reformation, it was partially revived by men like Hugh Latimer and Bernard Gilpin.[29] The same populist tradition, although with a very

---

[27] Cf. G. R. Owst, *Literature and Pulpit in Medieval England* (Oxford, Basil Blackwell, 1961), pp. 569, 556, 566-68. William Langland's *Piers Plowman's Vision* (1362 ±) may be taken as a kind of distillate of this tradition; cf. *The Cambridge History of English Literature* (New York, Macmillan, 1933), II. 1-48. Its mysticism and moralism are echoed in Richard Rolle's Northumbrian *Pricke of Conscience* (1430 ±), first published in 1863; cf. *The Fire of Love* (1435) and *The Mending of Life* (*Cambridge History*, II. 49-54). See also its Kentish predecessor, Dan Michel's tr. of Frère Lorens's *La Somme des vices et vertues* (compiled in 1279), under the title of *The Ayenbite of Inwyt* (1340); cf. *Cambridge History*, I. 395-96. Chaucer is obviously aware of this tradition, although critical of it, too, as in 'The Wife of Bath, Prologue', and the 'tales' of friar, parson, and pardoner; cf. Owst, *Literature and Pulpit*, pp. 207-29, 385-97, *et passim*. See the concluding 'tale' ('The Parson's Tale') which turns out to be a *sermon* and, in the end, a kind of 'retraction' of Chaucer's literary enterprise softened by a reaffirmation of the abiding worth of his tr. of Boethius, *De consolatione*. It is worth noting that in the sermon the text (Jer. 6:16 in the Vulgate) is ignored, the discourse is actually about 'Penitence', 'Confession', and 'Satisfaction'. Thus, it amounts to yet another elaboration of the seven deadly sins, with divisions and subdivisions for each heading, and this makes for a striking parallel with *The Ayenbite of Inwyt* and *The Pricke of Conscience*. Clearly, this was a moral and religious tradition that had sunk so deeply into the English conscience that Wesley could take it for granted—as indeed he did. For exhortations to generosity, cf. Owst, *Literature and Pulpit*, pp. 554-56, with Wesley's 'third rule' for 'The Use of Money'—'Give all you can' (see Sermon 50).

[28] See Nancy Lee Beaty, *The Craft of Dying: A Study in the Literary Tradition of the Ars Moriendi in England* (New Haven, Yale University Press, 1970), ch. 1, and espec. ch. 5 (on Jeremy Taylor). The tradition had come to Wesley most directly from Jeremy Taylor's classic, *The Rule and Exercises of Holy Dying* (1651), *Works* (1844), 1. 516-604.

[29] Latimer was a priest of the diocese of Lincoln and licensed in the time of Edward VI to preach 'anywhere in the Kingdom'. He was a vigorous reformer and an obvious target when Mary Tudor came to the throne; he and Nicholas Ridley were martyred together in Oxford in 1555.

Bernard Gilpin (1517–83) was a popular itinerant and reformer in Elizabeth Tudor's reign (famed as 'the Apostle of the North'). Wesley included an extract of *The Life and Death of Bernard Gilpin* (from Samuel Clarke's *Lives of Eminent and Sundry Persons*, 1683) in the *Christian Lib*, XXVI. 99-138, and also again in *AM*, 1778, 315-25, 363-74, 407-17.

different message, had been continued by the early Protestant tractarians, as in, for example, John Frith's widely popular translation of Hamilton's *Places*.[30] During their brief ascendancy in the mid-seventeenth century, the Puritans renewed the tradition yet again by moving their pulpits from the churches to lecture halls and the Parliament.[31] During the Civil War and even after the Restoration, the tradition of 'running lectures' and 'house-creeping ministers' was continued.[32] Meanwhile, the radicals (Quakers, Baptists, Levellers, Ranters, etc.) had also revived the tradition of field preaching without license, to the grave consternation of souls as gentle as that of Richard Baxter.[33] When Whitefield and Wesley took to the fields and to 'itinerating', they were, therefore, renewing an old tradition and giving it new life and power.[34] Even the form of the typical Methodist chapel service reflected a sense of this heritage:

From the beginning the men and women sat apart, as they always did in the primitive church. And none were suffered to call any place their own, but the first comers sat down first. They had no pews, and all the benches for rich and poor were of the same construction. Mr. Wesley began the service with a short prayer; then sung a hymn and preached (usually about half an hour), then sang a few verses of another hymn, and concluded with prayer. His constant doctrine was salvation by faith, preceded by repentance, and followed by holiness.[35]

'Plain Truth for Plain People'

In his Preface to his very first collection of *Sermons on Several Occasions* (1746) Wesley goes out of his way to stress his

[30] I.e., 'Loci'; Patrick Hamilton (1504?–1528) was Abbot of Dearn, and his *Places: A Treatise on the Law and the Gospel* was translated by John Frith in 1529 (?). See also, William A. Clebsch, *England's Earliest Protestants, 1520-1535* (New Haven, Yale University Press, 1964), pp. 81-85.

[31] John F. Wilson, *Pulpit in Parliament: Puritanism During the English Civil Wars, 1640–1648* (Princeton, Princeton University Press, 1969).

[32] Cf. Christopher Hill, *Society and Puritanism*, pp. 80-81; and his *Reformation to Industrial Revolution*, p. 131.

[33] Cf. John R. H. Moorman, *A History of the Church of England* (London, Adam and Charles Black, 1963), ch. xv, 243-48; see also C. E. Whiting, *Studies in English Puritanism* (London, SPCK, 1931), ch. vi; Hugh Barbour, *The Quakers in Puritan England* (New Haven and London, Yale University Press, 1964), chs. 2–3; and *Reliquiae Baxterianae* (1696), Pt. I, pp. 74-78; note that Baxter's list runs: 'The Vanists—disciples of Sir Henry Vane—The Seekers, The Ranters, The Quakers, and The Behmenists'.

[34] Cf. Horton Davies, *Worship and Theology in England* (Princeton, Princeton University Press, 1961), III. 202-5.

[35] Cf. 'Thoughts Upon Methodism', §4, *AM*, 1787, 101 (Vol. 9 of this edn.); see also Wesley's letter to Mary Bishop, Nov. 27, 1770.

commitment to a 'plain style' in preaching.[36] Here again, we have something more than a personal crotchet: it is an echo of a longstanding rivalry between a variety of rhetorical traditions in English preaching that Wesley understood very well and on which he had taken a partisan stand. He knew the tradition of classical learning that had shaped English prose.[37] He understood how eloquence in Greek and Latin depends upon rhythms, sonorities, and images, on neologisms and 'conceits'; he also knew how this had evolved into an 'ornate style' in English preaching, strikingly similar to baroque art and music. The great ones in this latter tradition were Lancelot Andrewes (1555–1626), John Donne (1573–1631), Thomas Playfere (1561?–1609), and Jeremy Taylor (1613 1667). The sermons of Andrewes (Bishop of Ely, Chichester, and, finally, Winchester) are not only richly ornamented; they are intertwinings of intricate prose and poetry, prayer and piety. Donne (Lincoln's Inn and St. Paul's) had delivered and then written out some of the most eloquent sermons in the English language, with rhetorical coruscations as exalted as they are sustained (as in 'Death's Duell', 'The Bells', 'The Church Catholic', etc.). Playfere (a Cambridge professor of divinity) had carried the tradition to excess, a dazzling display of images and conceits where the style often outshines the substance. Jeremy Taylor (Bishop of Down and Connor in Ireland) has more to say than Playfere, but in rhetoric not much less involuted. Over against this there had arisen a plainer, more direct style in the great Edwardian preachers (Thomas Cranmer, John Jewel, Nicholas Ridley)— men who strove for clarity even as they strove to shape their sermons as works of literary art.[38]

It was the Puritans, however, who had elevated the sermon to

---

[36] See below, p. 104: 'I design plain truth for plain people' (§3).

[37] As in Richard Hooker's *Laws of Ecclesiastical Polity* (1594–97), the first great theological treatise by a man who thought in Latin and wrote in English.

[38] Cf. Jewel, *Oratio contra Rhetoricam* (1548), where he decries ornate rhetoric and implies that it was common practice for preachers 'to thrash about with the body, . . . stamp one's feet and to indulge in wild gestures'; see Wilbur Howell, *Eighteenth Century British Logic and Rhetoric* (Princeton, Princeton University Press, 1971), pp. 123 ff. The revival of preaching in the Edwardian prayerbooks and homilies and the eloquence of the prayerbooks themselves, raised the standards of pulpit rhetoric but also contributed to the custom of written sermons to be read to a congregation; the sectaries and the Puritans derided this 'preaching by the book'.

its place as 'the chief regular means of grace';[39] hence their preference for a centred pulpit with its great sounding board and a red velvet cushion for the great pulpit Bible. So also they could speak of preaching as an act of prophecy, as in William Perkins's influential *Art of Prophesying* (1613). *The Order of Prophecy at Norwich* . . . (1575) was a brief directive to the preachers who would be occupying the pulpit of 'Christ's in Norwich' during the absence of a called and settled pastor. The section of 'prophesying' in *The Directory for the Publique Worship of God* issued by the Westminster Assembly in 1646 reflects this same conception.[40]

The essence of preaching in this tradition was *biblical exposition.* The prophet-preacher's prime task was to find and expound a word from God to his hearers. This freed him from a lectionary but heightened the demand that he choose his texts with the utmost care and then develop them so that no clause or phrase or even word was disregarded. This was implied, as they thought, in the task of 'rightly dividing the word of truth'. This, in its turn, produced some intricate homiletical forms which, in lesser hands, tended toward the ponderous and pedantic 'crumbling of texts' and to elaborations of heads and subheads. Great names in this tradition, after Perkins, were John Owen, Richard Baxter, Stephen Charnock, Isaac Ambrose, Samuel Annesley (Wesley's maternal grandfather), and Isaac Watts (Wesley's older contemporary and something of a rival).

Almost apart from the Anglican-Puritan tensions, the sectaries (Baptists, Quakers, Levellers, etc.) had developed their own tradition of preaching—this one populist and anti-intellectualist. Rejecting 'steeple-houses' and a tax-supported clergy, they took to the fields and meeting-houses, updating, in their way, the older traditions of populist preaching. Their interest in charismatic

---

[39] Cf. Davies, *Worship and Theology in England,* III. 31; see also Christopher Hill, *Puritanism and Revolution* (London, Panther Books, 1969), pp. 261-62.

[40] Perkins's full title is, *The Art of Prophesying; Or, a Treatise Concerning the Sacred and Only True Manner and Method of Preaching,* and the essay appears in Perkins's *Works* (1612–13), II. 646-73; see espec. chs. i, ii ('The only two duties of the prophet are . . . the preaching of the Word, and praying unto God in the name of the people'), and ch. iii ('Of the Word of God'). See also William Fulke, *A Brief and Plain Declaration* . . . , in Leonard Trinterud, ed., *Elizabethan Puritanism,* pp. 256-65 (and Trinterud's comments on the early 'prophesyings' on pp. 191 ff.); cf. these with the directions on preaching in *The Directory for the Publique Worship of God Throughout the Three Kingdoms of England, Scotland, and Ireland* (1646), pp. 13-18. Much of this lies back of Wesley's description of 'the prophetic ministry' in Sermon 121, 'Prophets and Priests'.

experiences and their enthusiasm provoked nicknames: Quakers, Ranters, Jumpers. Wesley and the Methodists would, in their turn, face the same sort of ridicule for slightly different reasons.

An alternative to these polarizations had emerged in the seventeenth century, which valued simplicity and clarity above all other homiletical virtues. One may see it in Joseph Mede at Cambridge (who ought to be better known for his doctrine of justification than for his millenarian speculations). Its classic expression had been provided by John Wilkins (Bishop of Chester, natural scientist and author of a 'new theory of language') in his *Ecclesiastes: Or, A Discourse Concerning the Gift of Preaching As It Falls Under the Rules of Art* (1679). It was further adapted by Offspring Blackall (Bishop of Exeter) whose *Eighty-Seven Practical Discourses Upon Our Saviour's Sermon on the Mount* (1717–18)[41] served Wesley as a model; and it was reinforced by the essays of James Arderne, *Directions Concerning the Matter and Stile of Sermons* (1671), and Joseph Glanvill, *Essay Concerning Preaching* (1678).

John Wesley knew enough of this background to make his own choice of rhetorical style deliberate. He records reading *The Whole Sermons of that Eloquent Divine of Famous Memory, Thomas Playfere* (1623); if he read them all, he must have been wearied by their 'conceits', which are carried to the edge of caricature. He had also read that charming account in Thomas Fuller of a rhetorical flight in St. Mary's (Oxford) by a 'Mr. Tavernour' in 1558.[42] His reading had included other practitioners of the ornate style of preaching: Richard Sherry, Henry Peacham, Henry Smith, William Chappell—a Puritan—and John Scott.[43] That he knew the Puritans is amply demonstrated in his *Christian Library*[44]

---

[41] These occupied the major part of his *Works*, in two folio vols. (1723), Vol. 1, pp. 1-561, and Vol. II, pp. 609-939.

[42] Cf. *The Church History of Britain* (1656), Bk. IX, 65: 'Surely preaching now is very low if it be true what I read [in the Preface to Sir John Cheke's *The True Subject to the Rebell* (1st edn., 1549; rev. edn., 1641)], that Mr. Tavernour, of Water-Eaton in Oxfordshire ... gave the scholars a sermon in St. Maries ... beginning with these words: "Arriving at the mount of St. Maries in the stony stage where I now stand [i.e., the high pulpit], I have brought you some fine biskets baked in the oven of charity and carefully conserved for the chickens of the church, the sparrows of the Spirit, and the sweet swallows of salvation." '

[43] Cf. Sherry's Erasmian paraphrase in *A Treatise of Schemes and Tropes* (1555); Peacham, *The Garden of Eloquence* (1577); Henry Smith, *Sermons* (1652); Chappell, *The Preacher: or the Art and Method of Preaching* (1656); John Scott, *Sermons Upon Several Occasions* (1704).

[44] Cf. Robert C. Monk, *John Wesley: His Puritan Heritage* (New York, Abingdon, 1966).

and in his Preface to *SOSO*, V–VIII (1788).[45] But he also deplored their zeal for 'text crumbling'; he understood Robert South's fierce scorn of those so-called 'scribes', whose 'sermons are garnished with quibbles, shreds of Latin and Greek, luxuriant allegories, rhyming cadences . . . '.[46]

Wesley's championship of plain-style preaching had been influenced by his early admiration for his father's plain-style sermons and his discovery in Oxford of the sermons of Benjamin Calamy, William Tilly, and John Tillotson.[47] At Oxford he had read Quintilian's *Institutes*, probably in the great new Burmann edition of 1720. He also read Bartholomew Keckerman's *Rhetoricae Ecclesiasticae* in one of its editions after 1606. But when he decided to furnish his own preachers with a suitable brief manual, he chose an anonymous essay on *The Art of Speaking*,[48] possibly remembered from Oxford; he abridged it under the title, *Directions Concerning Pronunciation and Gesture.*[49] He strove mightily to improve his preachers' pulpit style and general manners,[50] and he deplored excess of any sort. Late in life he

[45] Cf. his references (§5) to 'Dr. [William] Bates, or Mr. John Howe, . . . or Mr. [Jeremiah] Seed'.

[46] Cf. 'The Scribe Instructed', in South's *Sermons Preached Upon Several Occasions* (1st edn., 1737; Philadelphia, Sorin and Ball, 1844), II. 81-85.

[47] Calamy (1642–1686) had been vicar of London's St. Lawrence Jewry; cf. his *Sermons Preached Upon Several Occasions* (1687). Tilly was a Fellow of Corpus Christi College, Oxford; M.A. (1697), B.D. (1707), D.D. (1711); cf. his *Sixteen Sermons . . . Preached Before the University of Oxford Upon Several Occasions* (1712). Tillotson was England's most popular preacher in the generation just before Wesley's; cf. his *Sermons on Several Occasions* in *Works* (1722). It is interesting that all of these men had the habit of using phrases with paired adjectives (e.g., 'honest and upright'). In abridging their texts Wesley would, almost invariably, strike off one adjective or the other in these pairings.

[48] *The Art of Speaking in Publick: Or an Essay on the Action of an Orator as to His Pronunciation and Gesture* (1727).

[49] Bristol, Farley, 1749, see *Bibliog*, No. 161, and Vol. 15 of this edn.

[50] See the *Minutes* for June 18, 1747, an answer to *Q*. 11 about 'smaller advices concerning preaching':

'(4). Choose the plainest texts you can.

(5). Take care not to ramble from your text, but to keep close to it, and make out what you undertake.

(6). Always suit your subject to your audience.

(7). Beware of allegorizing or spiritualizing too much.'

'Disciplinary' *Minutes*, 1749 (see Vol. 10 of this edn.). In Wesley's last revision of the Large *Minutes* (1789) there are twenty-one subheads in answer to this question. Note, however, John Hampson's opinion that Wesley's own sermons were not wholly 'superior in elegance' to some of those of his preachers (*Memoirs of the late Rev. John Wesley* (1791), III.137).

would lash out against the superficiality of so-called gospel sermons.[51]

Wesley saw this matter of style as a moral issue; indeed, as a point of national pride. He says as much in the Preface to *SOSO*, V–VIII (1788): 'I *could* even now write as floridly . . . as even the admired Dr. [Hugh] B[lair]. But I dare not. . . . I dare no more write in a "fine style" than wear a fine coat. . . . I cannot relish French oratory—I despise it from my heart. . . . I am still for plain, sound English.'[52]

There is, therefore, only an apparent irony in Wesley's first Preface (1746), when he ornaments the advertisement of his plain style with two 'shreds of Latin': 'I now write, as I generally speak, *ad populum*, to the bulk of mankind'; and 'Let me be *homo unius libri*' (a man of one book).[53] On first glance, such tags seem out of place. But one would recall how the first phrase, *ad populum*, was not only an echo from an older usage, but also a technical term made recently familiar by yet another great Bishop of Lincoln, Robert Sanderson. In his *Thirty-six Sermons* (1689) Sanderson had distinguished four categories of sermons: (1) *ad aulam* (addresses to a learned audience); (2) *ad magistratum* (sermons on civil occasions to the court or to an assize); (3) *ad clerum* (sermons to clergy); and (4) *ad populum* (sermons to plain people).[54] One should also remember that Wesley *and* his readers would think of such 'shreds' as tokens of a preacher's academic credentials;[55] this is why they were also almost always translated lest a reader be embarrassed or miss the point. Thus, Wesley's tags were not really lapses from his overall claim to plainness. It is a fair guess

[51] Cf. Sermon 123, 'On Knowing Christ After the Flesh', §11; see also his letter to Mary Bishop, Oct. 18, 1778: 'I myself find more life in the Church prayers than in the formal extemporary prayers of Dissenters. Nay, and I find more profit in sermons on either good tempers or good works than in what are vulgarly called "gospel sermons". That term is now become a mere *cant* word. I wish none of our society would use it. It has no determinate meaning. Let but a pert, self-sufficient animal, that has neither sense nor grace, bawl out something about Christ, or his blood, or justification by faith, and his hearers cry out, "What a fine gospel sermon!" Surely the Methodists have not so learnt Christ. We know no gospel without salvation from sin.' See also No. 99, *The Reward of Righteousness*, I. 3, and Wesley's letter to John Broadbent, Feb. 23, 1785: 'Take care you do not *scream* again, unless you would murder yourself outright.'

[52] See Vol. 2, between Sermons 53 and 54.

[53] See below, Preface, §§2, 5, pp. 104–6.

[54] The names of Wesley's father and older brother appear in the 'List of Subscribers' in the front of Sanderson's handsome folio. Thus a copy would have been in the Epworth rectory library, though it probably did not survive the fire of 1709.

[55] Cf. Peter Gay, *The Enlightenment*, Vol. I, in *The Rise of Modern Paganism* (New York, Alfred Knopf, 1966), p. 119.

that such scraps of learning were a sort of reassurance to the Methodists of the superior culture of their leader.

In that same first Preface, Wesley had gone out of his way to stress his intention, in these sermons, 'to forget all that ever I have read in my life'. The only credible meaning for such a disavowal is that he was willing to forego any outward show of learning that might distract his readers. It is obvious that he retained the substance of his reading; his voracious appetite for books of all sorts was never satiated. He read widely all his life, choosing his mentors with care from among the great, near-great, and yet also quite obscure authors whom he 'discovered'. Moreover, he retained a rich concealed deposit of all this for use throughout his life. Thus, as mentor to the Methodists, he digested this material and simplified it to the end that his 'plain people' could hear its 'plain truth' in a rhetoric suited to their needs.

He wore his learning so lightly that many have been deceived thereby. His quotations and allusions are careless (although rarely misleading); his abridgements are invariably biased, and yet often very deft. His *Christian Library* is an anthology culled from a huge bibliography, reduced by a ratio of roughly one page to fifty. The bulk of his 'sources' were Puritans (in one or another sense of that indefinable term), but 'predestination' had been carefully screened out of their treatises, to adapt them to what Wesley judged was their edifying core of common Christian piety.[56] His *Extract of Mr. Richard Baxter's Aphorisms of Justification* (1745) is an instructive example of Wesley's way with sources. Baxter had published the *Aphorisms* in 1649, but had quickly thereafter disavowed them as a misleading statement of his actual views. Thus there were no further editions of the *Aphorisms* after 1649; in their place Baxter had composed a *Confession of Faith* (1655), with the same doctrine of divine initiative and human response more carefully nuanced. Wesley discovered a copy of

---

[56] In 1772 Sir Richard Hill denounced Wesley in *A Review of All the Doctrines Taught by the Rev. Mr. John Wesley*; he was particularly incensed by Wesley's editorial biases, and asked, 'Why must poor John Bunyan be disembowelled to make him look like Mr. Wesley?' Wesley's bland reply in *Some Remarks on Mr. Hill's Review* (*Bibliog*, No. 341, Vol. 13 of this edn.), 12. (34), is that Bunyan's Calvinism had been omitted 'to make him like the authors going before him. . . . However, those that are fond of his bowels may put them in again and swallow them as they would the train of a woodcock.' Earlier (12. (1)) he had explained that he had not proofread *A Christian Lib.*, and blamed 'the correctors of the press', 'through whose inattention an hundred passages were left in which I had scratched out'. (For the *Christian Lib.* see *Bibliog*, No. 165, and Vol. 16 of this edn.)

the original *Aphorisms* in 1745, a rare book then, and rarer since. Preferring the *Aphorisms* over the *Confession*, Wesley 'extracted' them for the use of his preachers and people, blithely ignoring Baxter's disavowals.[57] In his *Extract* Wesley discarded all of Baxter's copious technical references, along with the careful distinction between God's 'decretive' and 'elective' will; Baxter's eighty 'theses' were reduced to Wesley's forty-five 'propositions'.

Two further examples of Wesley's habit of editing obscure texts according to his special purposes may be worth noting here; both appear in the *Arminian Magazine*. The first is a highly condensed extract from an important book by an obscure author, one John Plaifere: *Appello Evangelium* (1651). Plaifere is missing from the *Dictionary of National Biography*, and there are only six copies of his only book listed in the *National Union Catalog, Pre-1956 Imprints*. It is merely typical that Wesley took an elaborate text of four hundred and thirty-five octavo pages and reduced it to less than seventy; what is significant is that, in the process, the longest passage that remains almost intact is a brief discussion of justification from the so-called 'King's Book' of 1543 (*A Necessary Doctrine and Erudition for Any Christian Man*), a passage contributed by Stephen Gardiner.[58] Wesley may or may not have known Plaifere's source for this quotation. What matters is that he found the passage worth retaining.

Still another sampling from Wesley's extraordinary repertoire (and a good example of how he put his learning to unobtrusive use) is an English translation of Sebastian Castellio's dialogues on predestination, election, freewill, and faith.[59] Wesley had found them bound together with Castellio's elegant Ciceronian translation of à Kempis's *De Imitatione Christi* from its rude Latin original (*in latinum è latino*); this he wanted for his students at

[57] *Bibliog,* No. 99. None of his readers would have known anything about this history of the *Aphorisms;* Wesley knew it from Baxter's own comments in *Reliquiae Baxterianae,* Pt. I, pp. 107-8, 111. He also knew and 'extracted' Baxter's *Call to the Unconverted* (1658) in 1782. There is no recorded evidence of his having read Baxter's *Confession of Faith,* but more than once he recommended Baxter, e.g., his letters to Richard Locke, Sept. 14, 1770, and to Thomas Davenport, Dec. 23, 1782.

[58] Catholic bishop of London until exiled by Edward VI; he was recalled by Mary Tudor as Bishop of Winchester; there he married the beleaguered queen to Prince Philip of Spain in 1554; cf. Carolly Erickson, *Bloody Mary* (Garden City, N.Y., Doubleday and Co., 1978), Pt. V, pp. 373ff.

[59] *Dialogi IIII. De praedestinatione, De electione, De libero arbitrio, De fide* ('of Predestination, Election, Free Will, Faith') (Gouda, 1578). This 1st edn. had been interdicted by Queen Elizabeth's advisers; the dialogues were never published in England.

Kingswood School. But he also decided that Castellio's dialogues would be edifying for his people, and so he prepared an English translation for publication in the volumes of the *Arminian Magazine* for 1781 and 1782. It is a very good translation, too, and the only one in English that these dialogues have ever had; it still remains ignored by Castellio scholars.[60] Wesley's prefatory note is quietly understated:

> Numberless treatises have been written in this and the last age on the subject of predestination; but I have not seen any that is written with more good sense and good humour than Castellio's *Dialogues*, wrote above two hundred years ago. Yet I know not that they have ever appeared in our tongue. I believe therefore the putting them into an English dress will give pleasure to every impartial reader.[61]

Wesley's stake in this sort of learning and his 'concealment' of it came from his passion for a message that would gather into itself the riches of both Christian and classical traditions and that still could be shared with his 'plain people'. This is what lies behind and beneath the surface rhetoric of the sermons, including his claim to be *homo unius libri*. It is this veiled background which, nevertheless, gives the sermons themselves an extra dimension of depth and originality rarely found in typical popularizers.[62] By and large, such men work within cultural limitations and with even less care for the Christian tradition as a whole. Their strength has usually come from their fluency with Scripture and their confident self-reliance on personal experience and charisma. The great exceptions are quite different: geniuses who are great theologians and popular preachers both in

---

[60] There is no reference to Wesley's translation in any of the Castellio literature that I have seen; cf. Ferdinand Buisson, *Sébastien Castellion: sa Vie et son Oeuvre, 1515–1563*, 1964, *Appendice, Pièces Inédites*, cxviii, II. 498-99.

[61] *AM*, 1781, vi.

[62] Cf. William Perkins, *The Art of Prophesying*, in *Works*, II, ch. x: 'In the promulgation [of a sermon] two things are required: the hiding of human wisdom and the demonstration or showing of the Spirit. . . . Human wisdom must be concealed whether it be in the matter of the sermon or in the setting forth of the words, because the testimony of the Word is the testimony of God, and the profession of the knowledge of Christ and not of human skill: and again because the hearers ought not to ascribe their faith to the gifts of men but to the power of God's Word. . . . If any man thinketh that by this means barbarism should be brought into pulpits, he must understand that the minister may, yea and must privately, use at his liberty the arts, philosophy, and a variety of reading whilst he is inframing his sermon, but he ought in public to conceal all these from the people and not to make the least ostentation.' See also p. 37, n. 35 below.

one. Luther comes to mind,[63] or St. Chrysostom,[64] or even St. Augustine *in his sermons*.[65] No claim could ever be made that Wesley's talents ranked him in such a company. And yet, the analogy of effective preachers preaching out of a rich overflow is not amiss, and it is only fair to see Wesley apart from the generality of popularizers. These sermons in their contexts may, therefore, help to exhibit Wesley as the special sort of theologian that he was; and such an exhibition might further suggest that his theology deserves more serious consideration than it has yet had from historians of Christian thought in general.

III. THE SERMON CORPUS

The Early Sermons

CONVENTIONAL wisdom among Wesley biographers is to the effect that, during his Oxford years, he was something of a recluse and an 'enthusiast'.[1] They have ignored the fact that the young Mr. Wesley was actually a more popular preacher than most of his colleagues; his record of preaching in and around Oxford, in Christ Church Cathedral and St. Mary's, in the decade between his ordination as deacon (Sept. 19, 1725) and his departure for Georgia (Oct. 21, 1735) suggests a man of parts and of general acceptance as well. In that one decade he wrote some sixty-eight sermons of his own, and he preached many of them more than once.[2] He also 'collected' a full notebook of sermons from other

---

[63] See *The Liberty of a Christian Man*, §1; see also his *Catechisms* addressed to children, still grist for professional theologians.

[64] See W. R. W. Stephens, *Saint Chrysostom; . . . A Sketch of the Church and Empire in the Fourth Century* (2nd edn., 1880), pp. 422, 426 ff. See also Stephens's editing of Chrysostom's treatises and homilies in *NPNF, II*, Vol. IX (1889).

[65] As in Sister Sarah Muldowney, R.S.M., *St. Augustine: Sermons on the Liturgical Seasons*, in *Fathers of the Church* (1959), and in Quincy Howe, Jr., *Selected Sermons of St. Augustine* (New York, Holt, Rinehart and Winston, 1966); see espec. Howe's 'Introduction'.

[1] Cf. Richard Watson, *Life*, ch. ii; Tyerman (*JW*), I. 66-71; even Southey, *Wesley*, ch. 2. Wesley had given credence to this image in his JWJ retrospective for May 24, 1738 (§§4-7): 'Removing soon after to another college, I executed a resolution which I was before convinced was of the utmost importance, shaking off at once all my trifling acquaintance. . . . I abridged myself of all superfluities. . . . I soon became "a byword" for so doing.'

[2] Most of what we know of these early sermons and their sequence comes from the pioneering work of Richard P. Heitzenrater and his decipherings of Wesley's Oxford

authors and preached these to various audiences, too (e.g., in the Oxford prisons).[3] These sermons are important, therefore, as reflections of Wesley's early views and as portents of his later developments. But for the most part they are unimpressive as sermons, and so have been all too easily ignored by most students of Wesley's thought.

The reasons for this are obvious: they simply do not fit the conventional Methodist stereotypes or the stereotypes of others about Wesley. Wesley's tacit acknowledgement of their mediocrity is suggested by the fact that he included only one of them (lightly revised) in his later collection of *Sermons on Several Occasions*, Volumes I–IV.[4] Nor does he tell us how far some of them may have served him as 'first drafts' for later sermons on the same texts in the *Arminian Magazine* and *SOSO*, V–VIII. Eighteen of these manuscript sermons have survived, and also two fragments. Of these, Joseph Benson published four,[5] along with three others mistakenly attributed to Wesley.[6] Thomas Jackson followed Benson's order generally but added another manuscript sermon, on Isa. 1:21, which he entitled, 'True

---

Diaries; see his 'John Wesley's Early Sermons', in WHS, XXXVII. 110-28, and also his unpublished dissertation, 'John Wesley and the Oxford Methodists, 1725–35' (Durham, North Carolina, Duke University, 1972), in University Microfilms, Ann Arbor, Michigan. Heitzenrater's decipherment and transcription of Wesley's Oxford Diaries will be published in Vol. 32 of this edn., of the 1735–41 Diaries in Vols. 18–19—the first two volumes of the *Journal*; his work supersedes Curnock's and Green's, and provides us, for the first time, with adequate data for a detailed study of Wesley's day-to-day life and work. My narrative here is greatly indebted to Heitzenrater's findings.

[3] See Vol. XIX in the Colman Collection, MA, The John Rylands University Library of Manchester.

[4] Henceforth, '*SOSO*', I–IV. See below, No. 17, 'The Circumcision of the Heart'; No. 48, 'Self-denial' is from the same text as one of the Oxford sermons.

[5] (1) A funeral sermon of Jan. 11, 1727, but not at Epworth, *pace* Benson (on 2 Sam. 12: 33; see No. 136); (2) an Epworth sermon, 'On Corrupting the Word of God', of Oct. 6, 1727, on 2 Cor. 2:17 (see No. 137); (3) his inaugural sermon in Savannah, Feb. 20, 1736, 'On Love', on 1 Cor. 13:3 (see No. 149); and (4) another Epworth sermon of Sept. 3, 1732, from Amos 3:6 (see No. 143); this latter is in John's hand and is based on an incident recorded in his diary, but it reads more like it might have been preached by his father and copied out by John.

[6] (1) 'On the Resurrection of the Dead' (1 Cor. 15:35), from Benjamin Calamy, *Sermons*, xi (published by Wesley in the *Christian Lib.*, XXXIX. 246-73; see Vol. 4 of this edn., Appendix B); (2) 'On Grieving the Holy Spirit' (Eph. 4:30), from William Tilly, *Sermons*, xi (published in *MM*, 1798, as 'an original sermon of Mr. Wesley's', pp. 607-13; see Vol. 4, Appendix B); and (3) a university sermon of June 13, 1736, 'On the Holy Spirit' (2 Cor. 3:17) by John Gambold, and in John Gambold's handwriting (see Vol. 4, Appendix B).

Christianity Defended'.[7] He also felt bound to warn his readers that

these discourses, it will be observed, were written before Mr. Wesley obtained correct views of the way of salvation; and as they were not published either with his knowledge or appointment, he should not be made responsible for the sentiments which they contain.[8]

Jackson also added Wesley's first published sermon, on Job 3:17, to which he assigned a title, 'The Trouble and Rest of Good Men'.[9]

A legend soon sprang up based on a misleading *Journal* entry from October 16, 1771, that Wesley's first venture into a pulpit had been in the parish church of South Leigh on Sunday, September 26, 1725, with his text from Matt. 6:33.[10] In 1903 a crude transcript of this sermon was published in pamphlet form (in London) entitled, 'Wesley's First Sermon'. Professor Heitzenrater, however, has identified 'a listing of John Wesley's early sermons numbered *in the order that he wrote them*' on the verso, 'opposite a page [of the first Oxford diary] dated 24th September 1726'.[11] From this list and its enumerations it would appear that Wesley's very first sermon had been preached most probably in the church at Fleet Marston (from Job 3:17) and probably on October 3, 1725; which is to say, a bare fortnight after his diaconal ordination.[12] There are entries on this manuscript that indicate a repetition of the same sermon more than ten times during the next sixteen months in other small churches in the vicinity, including South Leigh (Feb. 12, 1727).[13] The sermon on Matt. 6:33 was his second sermon; it was written in November of 1725 and preached at several places noted on the manuscript: 'Buckland, Stanton, Wroot, Broadway, Binsey', etc. The next holograph in this sequence is a funeral sermon for a

---

[7] This was Wesley's own composition, in two versions (Lat. and Eng.); see Sermons 150 and 151 ('Hypocrisy in Oxford'), and the intro. com. on their respective circumstances.

[8] Jackson's prefatory note to his 'Fifth Series' of sermons in *Works*, VII. 451.

[9] Wesley had preached this in St. Mary's on Sept. 21, 1735, and Charles Rivington had published it in November. See Thomas Jackson's disparaging estimate of it in his edn. (*Works*, VII. 365).

[10] Cf. Curnock's imagined reconstruction of this event in his edn. of the JWJ, I. 60.

[11] 'John Wesley's Early Sermons', p. 111.

[12] The holograph of this sermon is in the Morley Collection of Wesleyana in Wesley College, Bristol (No. 133), along with 'On Dissimulation' (No. 138A) and the Latin text of 'Hypocrisy in Oxford' (No. 151).

[13] It was in *this* sense that he preached 'his first sermon at South Leigh'.

close friend, Robin Griffiths, preached in the parish church of Broadway on January 15, 1727. It is Wesley's first sermon with an idea somewhat out of the ordinary: *viz.*, that bodily death amounts to a conquest of sin which has its seat in the flesh; hence, Christians need not mourn unduly for their loved ones who have died in the faith.[14] The fourth surviving sermon from this sequence (No. 137, 'On Corrupting the Word of God') was written while Wesley was assisting his father in Epworth and Wroot in 1728–29; one thinks it may have been an oblique tribute to his father's stubborn integrity and faithfulness in interpreting the Bible to his obdurate parishioners. It is interesting that Wesley preserved this manuscript in his papers for more than sixty years; a slightly revised version of it was published posthumously in *The Methodist Magazine* in 1798. Yet another manuscript surviving from those Epworth days is dated January 17, 1728;[15] this is not the same sermon that appeared much later in the *Arminian Magazine* (1785), and in *SOSO*, VII (1788), even though their Scripture texts are identical.[16] We know of a sermon on Gen. 3:19 that was written in Epworth in 1728; a sermon on the same text was later published in the *Arminian Magazine* (1782), and in *SOSO*, V (1788). Still another sermon (on Matt. 26:26) was written in 1728; it may have been a prototext for No. 84, *The Important Question*, which was first published in 1775 and then included in *SOSO*, VII (1788). This may also have been the case with his first sermon on Luke 9:23 and his later Sermon 48, 'Self-denial'. We know of an undated sermon on Ps. 8:4 that may still have been in Wesley's papers when he wrote the sermon that appeared in the *Arminian Magazine* in 1788 and was later reprinted in the posthumous *SOSO*, IX (1800). Another Epworth sermon of late 1728 or early 1729 was based on Rom. 11:33; No. 68, 'The Wisdom of God's Counsels', published in the *Arminian Magazine* in 1784 and in *SOSO*, VI (1788), has the same text. Similar duplication of texts, from the Epworth period to the time of the later Wesley, may be seen in the case of a sermon on Eph.

---

[14] An echo of a doctrine that runs back at least to the *Apology of the Augsburg Confession* (1531), Art. XII, 151-61—as, e.g., 'Death itself serves this same [positive] purpose: to destroy this sinful flesh so that we may rise completely renewed' (l. 153); cf. T. G. Tappert, ed., *The Book of Concord* (1959), pp. 206-8. See also Heinrich Schmid, *Doctrinal Theology of the Evangelical Lutheran Church* (1899), pp. 263, 624.

[15] See No. 138A, 'On Dissimulation'.

[16] See No. 90, 'An Israelite Indeed'.

5:16 (see No. 93, 'On Redeeming the Time'), and a sermon recorded in Wesley's diary list prior to August, 1729; also a sermon on Luke 12:7.[17]

One reason for this conjecture that Wesley's early sermons may have been prototexts for his later ones is simply that they have not survived; all the manuscripts of the sermons that Wesley published seem to have been discarded by his printers. Thus the holographs in his papers at his death must have been pieces that he had cherished, and, presumably, had put to some use or other instead of handing them over to a printer.

At any rate, he returned to Oxford in late November of 1729 at the behest of his rector, John Morley, to resume his duties there. He continued to write sermons and preach them in nearby churches, and also, presently, in the prisons. What would seem to have been his first 'university sermon' was produced in late October, and preached in St. Mary's on November 15, 1730. Its text is Gen. 1:27, and it is easily Wesley's most interesting and original effort up to that date. His earlier sermons do not prepare his readers for the new flights of speculation here about Adam's perfections ('the image of God') or the tragic consequences of Adam's fall (including bodily weaknesses, one of which sounds very much like atherosclerosis). After fifty mediocre sermons, here is finally one with a touch of genius;[18] Wesley preached it at least four times more (in London, at Stanton, again in London, and in St. Miles', in Oxford). In September, 1731, Wesley wrote a sermon on Mark 9:48 which has not survived; a sermon on the same text appeared in the *Arminian Magazine* in 1782, but it would have had to have been written after 1759, since one of its most striking illustrations has to do with an asbestos handkerchief that Wesley had seen in the 'new' British Museum, not opened to the public till 1759.

The most outstanding of these early sermons—destined to stand as a landmark in Wesley's entire theological development thereafter—was his second 'university sermon', preached in St. Mary's, January 1, 1733.[19] His diaries record the fact that he spent

---

[17] The sermon on this text is dated in the fortnight of Aug. 7-22, 1729, when Wesley was back in Oxford for a visit; the published sermon on Luke 12:17, 'On Divine Providence' (No. 67), appeared first in the *AM*, 1786.

[18] See No. 141, 'The Image of God'; its publication in this edn. may be one of its more important contributions.

[19] See below, No. 17, 'The Circumcision of the Heart'.

the better part of a month preparing his manuscript; what they do not explain is its marked advance beyond any of Wesley's previous statements of his vision of the holy life. In it, all that he had learned from Taylor, à Kempis, William Law, and the traditions of Christian will-mysticism behind them comes to focus. It provides the earliest summing up of what would thereafter be the essence of his doctrine of grace. That he realized later how nearly successful he had been is suggested by his careful placement of it in a slightly revised version at the head of his second volume of *SOSO* (1748), which is also to say, as the first in the series of his sermons on holy living as the fruit of justifying faith. As an old man, he would confirm this earlier judgment: 'I know not that I can [even now] write a better [sermon] on "The Circumcision of the Heart" than I did five-and-forty years ago.'[20]

One of Professor Heitzenrater's more unexpected discoveries is that nine of John Wesley's early sermons have survived through the undesigned good offices of his brother Charles.[21] The evidence for this comes from the volume of thirteen sermons in Charles's handwriting in the Methodist Archives; eleven of these, heavily edited, were published posthumously in *Sermons by the Late Rev. Charles Wesley, A.M.* (1816). From the shorthand notes on the manuscripts, and from other references, Heitzenrater has concluded that Charles, newly ordained just before the Georgia mission, had borrowed and transcribed some of John's manuscript sermons, 'at various times during Charles' excursion to America in 1735-36'. One of these (on Ps. 91:11) would date back as early as September, 1726.[22] Another ('On the Sabbath') had been written in July of 1730 and preached twelve times between July 19, 1730 and September 9, 1733. The sermon of his brother's that Charles seems to have liked best (as far as we can tell from his own *Journal*) was the one on Luke 10:42.[23]

Besides these sermons that have survived either in John's handwriting or in Charles's transcriptions, there are eight other manuscripts also in John's hand that he had 'collected' and used in his preaching as occasions seemed to warrant.[24] The

[20] JWJ, Sept. 1, 1778.

[21] Heitzenrater, *op. cit.*, pp. 112-13; see also his chart on pp. 116-27.

[22] And this would mean that No. 135, 'On Guardian Angels', would be one of the earliest in the entire sermon corpus.

[23] See No. 146, 'The One Thing Needful', which had, in its turn, been based on Jeremy Taylor's *Unum Necessarium: Or, the Doctrine and Practice of Repentance* (1655).

[24] See Vol. 4, Appendix A.

significance for us of such borrowings is their indication of Wesley's instinctive dependence upon typical Anglican authors for his doctrine of holy living.[25] They also remind us that at this stage of his career Wesley felt no special need to establish himself as an original preacher in his own right: this practice of adapting and using material from others was a commonplace in his time.

These early sermons have been neglected by Wesley's disciples chiefly on the grounds of their doctrine; others have found them scarcely worth the trouble of serious analysis; others have never even noticed them at all.[26] And there is no denying that even in an age of perfunctory preaching they are generally unmemorable. This fact sheds some light on another one: that, for all of Wesley's zeal in that first decade, his early preaching was largely ineffectual.[27]

And yet they contain many a seed of Wesley's later, mature ideas. His conception of the essence of 'holiness' as love of God and neighbour is there, along with his view of sanctification as more of a process than a state. There is also his platonizing theory of religious knowledge as more intuitive than discursive, along with his distinctive sense of the personal, prevenient action of the Holy Spirit in all authentic spirituality. These sermons reflect a version of the ascetical-mystical tradition in English Christianity, and its succession from the medieval mystics (and moralists) down to his father's friend, John Norris, and to his own mother. Here is the source of a conviction that never left him: that holiness and true happiness are correlates, and this by God's specific design.[28] Behind his identified sources (Taylor, à Kempis, Law) there loomed a great cloud of witnesses whose

[25] There is a special case with respect to No. 101, 'The Duty of Constant Communion'. As it stands, it is enough of Wesley's own work to be printed with his *SOSO*; its substance, however, is greatly indebted to an earlier essay of Robert Nelson on *The Great Duty of Frequenting the Christian Sacrifice* (1707); cf. intro. com. for Wesley's adaptations of this.

[26] As, e.g., Martin Schmidt.

[27] Cf. *The Principles of a Methodist Farther Explained*, VI. 1: 'From the year 1725 to 1729 I preached much, but saw no fruit of my labour; . . . from 1734 to 1738, speaking more of faith in Christ, I saw more fruit of my preaching . . . than ever I had done before; . . . from 1738 to this time, speaking continually of Jesus Christ, . . . the "Word of God ran" as fire among the stubble.'

[28] See No. 5, 'Justification by Faith', I. 4 and n.; in no less than thirty of his sermons Wesley rings the changes on the theme: *only the holy can ever be truly happy*. Cf. Franklin L. Baumer's comment that 'happiness was the universal obsession of the age', in *Modern European Thought; Continuity and Change in Ideas, 1600-1950* (New York, Macmillan, 1977), p. 142; see also Paul Hazard, *La Pensée Européenne au XVIII Siècle* (Paris, 1946), Vol. I, ch. ii; and Robert Mauzi, *L'Idée du bonheur* . . . (Paris, 1960).

names we have to glean elsewhere (Henry Scougal, Lorenzo Scupoli [Juan de Castañiza], John Cardinal Bona, Gaston de Renty, Gregory Lopez, and many another).[29] And behind this Latin tradition lay the balancing, deepening influence of Greek Catholic spirituality (with its distinctive pneumatology that Wesley embraced wholeheartedly), with roots that run from Ignatius of Antioch through Irenaeus and Clement of Alexandria, to Macarius, Gregory of Nyssa, Ephrem Syrus, and the great Eastern liturgies.[30]

On its other side this same Anglican tradition reflected in these early sermons includes a radical emphasis on human freedom and responsibility. Men, it seems to say, *can* live blamelessly if they so choose and, therefore, ought to—although for all venial lapses the church has an ample store of 'the means of grace' on which the repentant faithful may rely for 'pardon and amendment of life'. Calvinists lumped all such views under their epithet, 'Arminian', and included Wesley, too. But the young Wesley had never read Arminius, as far as we know;[31] he had inherited this part of his tradition from men like William Laud, Charles Hickman, John Hinton, Browne Willis, and still more recently, George Bull, Peter Heylyn, Benjamin Hoadly, and John Tillotson.[32] There is no sign that he

---

[29] Cf. Jean Orcibal, 'Les Spirituels Francais et Espagnols chez John Wesley et ses contemporains', in *Revue d'Histoire des Religions*, CXXXIX (1951), pp. 50-109, and 'The Theological Originality of John Wesley and Continental Spirituality', in Rupert Davies and Gordon Rupp, eds., *A History of the Methodist Church in Great Britain* (London, Epworth Press, 1965), Vol. I, pp. 83-111; also Robert G. Tuttle, Jr., *John Wesley: His Life and Theology* (Grand Rapids, Mich., Zondervan, 1978), pp. 217-27.

[30] Cf. Albert C. Outler, *John Wesley*, in A Library of Protestant Thought (New York, Oxford University Press, 1964), pp. 9, 12-13, 31, 119. For Wesley's chief early source in the ancient liturgies, cf. William Beveridge's massive Συνόδικον, *Sive Pandectae Canonum SS. Apostolorum, et Conciliorum ab Ecclesia Graeca Receptorum* (1672), 2 vols.

[31] Frank Baker doubts if he ever read much of Arminius's own writings; see WHS, XXII. 118-19. The fact that he was labelled 'Arminian' is no proof of his direct dependence upon Arminius himself.

[32] William Laud, Archbishop of Canterbury, 1633–45; cf. Edward C. E. Bourne, *The Anglicanism of William Laud* (London, SPCK, 1947). Charles Hickman, Bishop of Derry, 1703–13; cf. *The Christian Faith Explain'd and Vindicated . . .* (1713), and *Twelve Sermons Preached at St. James's, Westminster* (1713). John Hinton, Prebendary of Sarum; cf. *A Sermon . . . on the Day of Thanksgiving for His Majesty's late Victory over the* [Monmouth] *Rebels* (1685). Browne Willis (1682–1760) was the anonymous author of a new treatise on *The Whole Duty of Man, Abridged for the Benefit of the Poorer Sort* (1717). Wesley refers to this in his Preface to his abridgement of [Richard Allestree?], *The Whole Duty of Man* (1657) in the *Christian Lib.*, XXI (1753): '. . . the ensuing tract [i.e., of 1657] far better deserves its title than that miserable thing which has lately usurped the name' [i.e., Willis's version]. Seth Ward (1617–89), successively Bishop of Exeter and Salisbury; cf. *Seven Sermons*

was ever tempted to the deistic tendencies of this tradition.[33]

Likewise, there is no discernible evidence in these early sermons of any acquaintance with 'England's earliest Protestants'—Robert Barnes, Patrick Hamilton, Simon Fish, and others.[34] Nor can it be proved, *from the sermons*, that he knew the great Puritans (William Perkins, William Ames, John Bunyan), or even the Lambeth Articles of 1595.[35] This makes it all the more interesting that as early as 1739 he could write and publish a sermon against George Whitefield's Calvinism that reflects a competent knowledge of the Puritan cause and, in the same year, publish an 'extract' of *Two Treatises* . . . of Robert Barnes, the Austin friar turned Lutheran, who had been burned by Henry VIII.[36] And since he could scarcely have discovered Barnes and Perkins and the others in the months after Aldersgate, this suggests that his theological orientation at Oxford had been very much more complete than he would afterward report.

In any case, there is a drastic contrast between these early sermons and the later ones, in substance, verve, and spirit. And this poses one of the most interesting problems in Wesley studies: the metamorphosis of an ineffectual zealot into an effectual evangelist, the sudden growth of a purveyor of commonplaces

---

(1673). For Hoadly and Tillotson, cf. Irène Simon, 'Anglican Rationalism in the Seventeenth Century', ch. ii in *Three Restoration Divines* (Paris, 1967); see also H. R. McAdoo, *The Structure of Caroline Moral Theology (London and New York, Longmans, Green, 1949)*, and E. C. Mossner, *Bishop Butler and the Age of Reason* (New York, Macmillan, 1936), espec. ch. i.

[33] The deists he knew best were Matthew Tindal (cf. his *Rights of the Christian Church asserted against the Romish and all other Priests who claim an Independent Power Over It*, 1706, and *Christianity as Old as the Creation*, 1730); Anthony Collins (see his *Essay Concerning the Use of Reason*, 1707, and *A Discourse of Freethinking*, 1713); and Anthony Ashley Cooper, Third Earl of Shaftesbury (*Characteristicks of Men, Manners, Opinions, Times*, 1711). His best known rationalists, by far, were John Locke (*The Reasonableness of Christianity*, 1695) and Samuel Clarke (*The Evidences of Natural and Revealed Religion*, 1706).

[34] So convincingly 'recovered' by Clebsch, *op. cit.*, p. 20 above.

[35] William Perkins (1558–1602); cf. his *Armilla Aurea* (1590, 1592); Eng. tr., *A Golden Chaine; Or the Description of Theology, Containing the Causes of Salvation and Damnation, According to God's Word* (1591—including a 2nd edn., much enlarged, 1597, and a 3rd edn., 1600). William Ames (1576–1633), a student of Perkins at Cambridge; cf. his *Medulla S. S. Theologiae* (1629); Eng. version, *The Marrow of Sacred Divinity* (1638). Cf. Bunyan's *The Doctrine of Law and Grace Unfolded* (1659), *A Defence of the Doctrine of Justification by Faith in Christ* (1672), and *Reprobation Asserted* (1674?).

[36] Cf. Barnes, *Two Treatises. The First, On Justification by Faith Only. . . . The Second, On the Sinfulness of Man's Natural Will* (Bibliog, No. 16). The original is from *The Workes of Doctour Barnes* [together with 'The Whole Workes' of W. Tyndale, John Frith, etc.], 1573. Wesley's extract is from Pt. 4 of Barnes's text, entitled, 'Faith onely justifieth before God' (pp. 226-27); Barnes's second treatise is entitled, 'Freewill of Man, after the fall of Adam, of his natural strength, can he nothyng but sinne afore God' (pp. 267-68).

into a folk-theologian whose influence would be perduring. It goes without saying, however, that all simplistic explanations of this metamorphosis are just that.

Sermons on Several Occasions, Volumes I–IV

During the summer of 1746 Wesley interrupted his itinerant schedule for several weeks in order to prepare a slight volume of sermons for publication—the first of three designed to exhibit 'the substance of what I have been preaching for between eight and nine years last past'. It was his hope that 'every serious man who peruses these [might] see, in the clearest manner, what these doctrines are which I embrace and teach as the essentials of true religion'.[37]

That phrase, 'for between eight and nine years last past', points to a self-conscious and radical shift in Wesley's understanding of the priorities in the order of salvation; it also reflects a radical new turn that his career had taken since 1738. Its vagueness ('between eight and nine years') implies that his evangelical conversion was not to be tied to any one single event, but rather to a series of them that had run throughout that year, beginning with his deep depression in the wake of his Georgia fiasco.[38] The essence of the shift had been a reversal of his earlier view that holy living is in order to justifying faith into an evangelical conviction that justifying faith is in order to holy living. This change had not come easily. He had been challenged to it by the Moravians and Salzburgers in Georgia.[39] The turmoil had then been intensified in a protracted dialogue between Wesley and Peter Böhler, a Moravian missionary who happened to be in England in transit to America. Wesley had met Böhler on February 7, 1738, and the two were nearly constant companions till the latter's departure on May 8.[40] The dialogue had borne its fruits in Wesley's climactic

---

[37] See below, Preface, § 1.

[38] Reported in two vivid memoranda, the first in JWJ, Jan. 8-9, 1738; and a 'Second Paper' of Jan. 25, given partly in Moore I. 342-44, and more fully in Journal I of this edn. (Vol. 18). Together, these constitute one of Wesley's more important theological self-revelations.

[39] One of Martin Schmidt's more important contributions in this area was his demonstration of the special influence of the Salzburgers along with the Moravians in preparing Wesley for his 'new' gospel. Cf. his essay, 'Wesley's Place in Church History', in Kenneth E. Rowe, ed., *The Place of Wesley in the Christian Tradition* (Metuchen, N. J., Scarecrow Press, 1976), pp. 67-93.

[40] See also Böhler's 'last word' in the debate, in his letter to Wesley from the dockside in Southampton; Wesley printed it in JWJ, May 10.

experience of *personal assurance* in an Anglican-Moravian society in Aldersgate Street in the evening of May 24 when, during the reading of 'Luther's preface to the *Epistle to the Romans*', he had suddenly 'felt [his] heart strangely warmed.'[41] He had then promptly declared his new-found faith in faith at St. George's, Bloomsbury, on the following Sunday, at Stanton Harcourt a fortnight later (June 11), and in a sermon to the university on that same afternoon.[42]

Wesley spent the following summer in Germany with the Moravians at Herrnhut and Marienborn, where his confidence in the doctrine of faith alone had been strengthened and his personal attachment to the Moravians weakened. Still another crisis followed in October with his discovery of Jonathan Edwards's newly published *Faithful Narrative*, with its details about an actual revival being stirred by a pietism very like his own, even though he himself was still 'beating the air'.[43] What is most significant here is that these cumulative challenges drove him back, as if by instinct, to his own Anglican roots. There, in the *Homilies*, he had finally found the theological font of his own heritage; this doctrine of justification remained as a fixed benchmark for the rest of his theological development.[44]

He had now settled his soteriology in what would be its stable order thenceforth; he had experienced for himself the assurance of grace;[45] and yet his preaching was still comparatively fruitless. This had changed abruptly in April of 1739 when, with grim distaste, he had ventured into the fields near Bristol and had found an unexpectedly positive response. This, in effect, had confirmed his own faith, and had launched his new career as an

---

[41] But note the striking parallels between the account of the Aldersgate heartwarming and an earlier experience in connection with William Law's *Practical Treatise Upon Christian Perfection* (1726) and *A Serious Call to a Devout and Holy Life* (1729): 'The light flowed in so mightily upon my soul that everything appeared in a new view. I cried to God for help . . . and I was persuaded that I *should be* accepted of him and that I was *even then* in a state of salvation.' (JWJ, May 24, 1738, §§ 5, 14). See also *A Plain Account of Christian Perfection (Bibliog*, No. 297, Vol. 12 of this edn.), §§ 4-5.

[42] He had already been scheduled for this engagement in St. Mary's; the university officials had had no way of knowing how different this new sermon would be from his last one there. Cf. JWJ, May 28, June 11, which contains no notice of his sermon in St. Mary's.

[43] JWJ, Oct. 9: 'I read the truly surprising narrative of the conversions lately wrought in and about the town of Northampton, in New England. Surely "this is the Lord's doing, and it is marvellous in our eyes"!'

[44] See above, p. 4.

[45] This assurance, however, was not constant, as we can see from JWJ, Jan. 4, 1739: 'That I am not a Christian at this day I as assuredly know as that Jesus is the Christ.'

evangelist—the spiritual director of a revival movement that was to take on a life of its own, sweeping Wesley along with its progress as its not always comprehending leader.[46] He had been forced by circumstances to rely on lay assistants as colleagues in this new 'extraordinary' ministry; doctrinal pluralism had followed from this as a matter of course. Wesley's reaction was to institute an annual gathering of the preachers, by his personal invitation, into a 'Conference' in which questions of doctrine and discipline were canvassed and worked through. Increasingly, however, the need for more and more doctrinal guidance became evident, and again Wesley responded, not with a creed or a confession, or even a doctrinal treatise, but with something analogous to a set of Methodist 'Homilies'—not in this case 'appointed to be read in the churches' (as Cranmer's had been) but rather to be studied and discussed by the Methodists and their critics. This decision that a cluster of *sermons* might serve as doctrinal standards for a popular religious movement is a significant revelation of Wesley's self-understanding of his role as spiritual director of 'the people called Methodists'. Sermons, as a genre, do not lend themselves to legalistic interpretation; these sermons in particular were the distillates of eight years of popular preaching and of a vigorous popular reaction. Wesley explains his motives in a crucial Preface which reads as if addressed as much to his non-Methodist critics as to his own disciples.

For his general title he resorted to an irony that would not have been lost on any well-read Anglican: *Sermons on Several Occasions*. This was, as they knew, a wholly conventional entitlement for sermons preached by ecclesiastical dignitaries in palaces and cathedrals.[47] Wesley's occasions had been far humbler; he was suggesting that they were not a whit less important. It is equally clear that his original design for this sermon series was open-ended. His first project was for a three-volume set of

[46] Cf. his description of his feelings of being 'swept along' by events (φερόμενος), letter of June 27, 1766 to his brother.

[47] Cf., e.g., Anthony Tuckney, *Forty Sermons on Several Occasions* (1676); William Bates, *Sermons Preached on Several Occasions* (1693); John Sharp, *Sermons Preached on Several Occasions* (1700); John Scott, *Sermons Upon Several Occasions* (1704); William Tilly, *Sixteen Sermons . . . Preach'd Before the University of Oxford . . . Upon Several Occasions* (1712); John Tillotson, *Sermons on Several Occasions* (1671); George Smalridge, *Sixty Sermons Preached on Several Occasions* (1724); William Reeves, *Fourteen Sermons Preached on Several Occasions* (1729); John Rogers, *Nineteen Sermons on Several Occasions* (1735)—we have identified at least twenty such collections thus entitled.

thirty-six sermons—1746, 1748, 1750. But as the revival burgeoned, so also there were new occasions for still more published sermons. Thus, in 1760, Wesley produced a fourth volume with the same title, but at first unnumbered; it is a curious medley of seven occasional sermons plus six paranetic tracts.[48] This brought the number of *SOSO* to forty-three—still with no suggestion that they were legal documents; otherwise, the inclusion of those tracts would make no good sense. Later (the details are hazy), a forty-fourth sermon (No. 41, *Wandering Thoughts*) turned up in the second edition of Volume III, published about 1762.[49] Meanwhile (1755), Wesley had provided his people with a specially designed exegetical tool for their biblical studies: his own revision of the AV New Testament with brief *Explanatory Notes*. These notes were partly original but also partially borrowed from other commentaries that he had found useful.[50] Thus, when problems of doctrinal variance among the Methodist preachers became acute enough, Wesley already had a practical solution. In the first trust deed of the Newcastle Orphan House (1746) he had specified in clearly nonforensic language that preaching in that chapel must be 'in the same manner, as near as may be, as God's Holy Word is now preached and expounded there' (i.e., by the Wesleys). By 1762 the situation called for

[48] (1) 'Advice to the People Called Methodists, with Regard to Dress'; Wesley later (1786) published a sermon on this topic (see No. 88); (2) 'The Duties of Husbands and Wives', extracted from William Whateley, *A Bride-Bush; Or, a Direction for Married Persons* (1619); (3) and (4), 'Directions to Children' and 'Directions to Servants', were probably paraphrased by Wesley from William Gouge (cf. *Works . . . in two volumes: the first, Domestical duties,* 1627); (5) 'Thoughts on Christian Perfection', the Preface of which is dated, Bristol, Oct. 16, 1759, and later (1766) incorporated in *A Plain Account of Christian Perfection*; (6) 'Christian Instructions, Extracted from a Late French Author'.

[49] It was inserted, without explanation, between the sermon, *Christian Perfection* and the one 'Satan's Devices'. One may guess that it had been written in 1761 (or early 1762), that it had been printed as a separate pamphlet by Felix Farley in 1762, and had then been quietly added to the new edn. of *SOSO*. Its obvious function is to serve as a qualifying comment on the rather ambitious claims that had been registered in the sermon on *Christian Perfection*. Here again, we are reminded of the open-ended character of the *Sermons* project.

[50] E.g., Matthew Henry, *An Exposition of All the Books of the Old and New Testament* (1725); Matthew Poole, *Annotations Upon the Holy Bible* (1696); John Guyse, *A Practical Exposition of the Four Evangelists, in the Form of a Paraphrase, with Occasional Notes,* 3 vols. (1739–42); John Heylyn, *Theological Lectures, With an Interpretation of the Four Gospels,* 2 vols. (1749, 1751); Philip Doddridge, *Family Expositor; Or a Paraphrase and Version of the New Testament, with notes* (1739); and J. A. Bengel, *Gnomon Novi Testamenti* (1742). For the *Explanatory Notes upon the New Testament*—henceforth *Notes*—see *Bibliog,* No. 209, and Vols. 5–6 of this edn.

something more precise, and in 1763 Wesley supplied it: a 'Model Deed' that set forth a sort of negative norm for Methodist orthodoxy, though still open-ended in principle. The trustees of the Methodist chapels were enjoined to welcome preachers appointed by Mr. Wesley, provided that they 'preach no other doctrine than is contained in Mr. Wesley's *Notes Upon the New Testament* and the four volumes of Sermons'.[51]

In the autumn of 1753 Wesley had been ill enough to feel prompted to compose his own epitaph.[52] In October of 1759 he spoke of 'the fourth volume of discourses' as 'probably the last which I shall publish'.[53] Actually, the growth rate of the Methodist societies and chapels quickened markedly after 1760,[54] and Wesley's health and vigour returned. Inevitably, then, he continued to write and publish new sermons, seeking always to refine and reinforce his basic doctrines. Nine of these new sermons appeared between 1758 (No. 15, *The Great Assize*) and 1770 (No. 53, *On the Death of George Whitefield*). Two of them are landmark sermons, crucial for any analysis of Wesley's maturing theology: *viz.*, No. 43, *The Scripture Way of Salvation* (1765)—a clear advance beyond No. 5, 'Justification by Faith'—and No. 20, *The Lord Our Righteousness* (1765), Wesley's clearest statement of the essential differences between his own soteriology and that of the English Calvinists.[55]

In 1770 he set out to finish a long-considered major project: the collection and ordering of those writings and publications of his which he now regarded as most fully representative: *The*

[51] This comment first appeared in the Large *Minutes* of 1763, and was maintained verbatim in all succeeding versions. Taken literally, it could have been construed as giving the six paranetic tracts in Vol. IV an authoritative status of some sort; Wesley obviously never intended this—further proof that not even his Model Deed had to be construed constrictively.

[52] 'To prevent vile panegyric'; see JWJ, Nov. 26 (but cf. also the longer period between early October 1753 and mid-April 1754).

[53] JWJ, Oct. 1.

[54] There were 31 chapels 'in connexion with Mr. Wesley' in 1760, 126 in 1771; cf. William Myles, *A Chronological History of the People Called Methodists* (4th edn., 1813), pp. 427-45.

[55] Seven of the nine sermons produced from 1758 to 1770 reflect the theological transition from the 'middle Wesley' (1738–65) to the 'late Wesley' (1765–91): Nos. 15, *The Great Assize* (1758); 13, *On Sin in Believers* (1763); 43, *The Scripture Way of Salvation* (1765); 20, *The Lord Our Righteousness* (1765); 11, *The Witness of the Spirit*, II (1767); 14, *The Repentance of Believers* (1767); 51, *The Good Steward* (1768). The other two were occasional in the more literal sense: Nos. 52, *The Reformation of Manners* (1763), and 53, *On the Death of George Whitefield* (1770).

Works of the Rev. John Wesley, M. A., Late Fellow of Lincoln College, Oxford.[56] His estimate of *SOSO* by this time is suggested by the fact that he placed them at the head of his edition (Vols. I–IV), with the nine new sermons inserted here and there (together with the tracts from the original Vol. IV).[57] In his Preface he speaks of this new and personally authorized edition as reflecting his 'last and maturest thoughts, agreeable, I hope, to Scripture, reason, and Christian antiquity'. The inference is plain: at the heyday of his career (age 68) Wesley's own preferred order for the four volumes of *Sermons* was as we are presenting them here.

Despite unending controversy, and in some degree because of it, the Methodist Revival continued to flourish. In 1778 Wesley felt goaded enough to counterattack with a magazine frankly aimed at his Calvinist critics.[58] The first three volumes of this mélange had no sermons of Wesley's. In 1781, however, he began to include a numbered series of 'Original Sermons by the Rev. John Wesley, M. A.'; they appeared in instalments (half a sermon per issue, or six in each annual volume). Six years later a rumour reached him that a clergyman 'in the West of England . . . designed to print, in two or three volumes, the sermons which had been published in the ten volumes of the *Arminian Magazine*'. To forestall this he undertook yet another edition of *SOSO*, explaining that if there were any call for such a thing he was 'the properest person to do it'.[59] Thus, in 1788 his new (and last) collection of sermons appeared, a hundred sermons in eight volumes. In Volumes I–IV, however, Wesley reverted to his earlier ordering, as before 1771, with eight of the nine additional sermons in the *Works* omitted, apparently discarded.[60] The decisive consideration here may have been the fact that to a certain degree since 1763, and especially after the legal establishment of 'The Conference' in 1784, 'the first four volumes of sermons' had

[56] *Works* (Bristol, Pine, 32 vols., 1771–74); see *Bibliog*, No. 334.
[57] Except that in the new Vol. IV the tract on 'Christian Instructions' was replaced by 'An Extract from [the first five chs. of] Mr. Law's Treatise on *Christian Perfection*'.
[58] *The Arminian Magazine: Consisting of Extracts and Original Treatises on Universal Redemption.* Vol. I, For the Year 1778: 'Our design is to publish some of the most remarkable tracts on the universal love of God, and his willingness to *save all men* from *all sin*, which have been wrote in this and the last century. Some of these are now grown very scarce; some have not appeared in English before. To these will be added original pieces, wrote either directly upon this subject or on those which are equally opposed to the patrons of "particular redemption".' (§ 4—see *Bibliog*, Nos. 371-84, Vol. 16 of this edn.).
[59] *SOSO*, V (1788), Preface, § 1.
[60] The sole exception was *The Lord Our Righteousness*, retained in Vol. III.

acquired a legal role in what was virtually a new denomination.[61] In terms of any overview of Wesley's theology, the omission of these eight sermons would represent a serious loss.

In the Preface to *SOSO*, I (1746), Wesley had explained: 'By the advice and at the request of some of my friends, I have prefixed to the other sermons contained in this volume three sermons of my own and one of my brother's, preached before the university of Oxford.'[62] These four sermons and their particular placement served two related purposes: first, they were manifestoes of the 'new' doctrine of 'faith alone'; second, they were signals of the pair's rejection of 'the groves of Academe' in favour of their new ministries to the English underclass.[63]

Wesley was not exaggerating when he claimed that these sermons (thirty-six, or forty-three, or forty-four) contained the gist of his understanding of 'the essentials of religion'.[64] The twelve sermons in Volume I (1746) are variations on the theme of his distinctive soteriology: salvation by unmerited grace, justification by faith as pardon and reconciliation, personal assurance of God's mercy confirmed by an 'inner witness of the Holy Spirit'. In the augmented edition of 1771 (the order followed here) one of the four added sermons is a revised formulation of the doctrine of *The Witness of the Spirit*; the second

---

[61] Technically, the Methodists were still a religious society within the Church of England; actually, they were already on their way to eventual separation and their division into a congeries of separate denominations; cf. Frank Baker, *John Wesley and the Church of England*, pp. 283-303; see also John S. Simon, *John Wesley, the Last Phase* (London, Epworth Press, 1934), pp. 19-22. Cf. also 'The Deed of Declaration' of 1784 (Vol. 10 of this edn.) and Curnock, VIII. 335-41. For a lively account of the protracted debate over the number of Wesley's 'standard sermons' and for its legal solution for the Methodists, cf. John S. Simon, 'The First Four Volumes of Wesley's Sermons', in WHS, IX. 36-45; see also E. H. Sugden, 'The Conference and the Fifty-three Sermons', in *The Standard Sermons of John Wesley*, II. 331-40.

[62] Preface, § 7.

[63] Cf. JWJ, Aug. 24, 1744 ('St. Bartholomew's Day'): 'I preached, I suppose, the last time at St. Mary's. Be it so. I am now clear of the blood of these men. I have fully delivered my own soul' (cf. Ezek. 3: 9). This last phrase is used by Wesley invariably as an expression of frustration and rejection. Cf. JWJ, June 9, 1779, and Apr. 2, 1787; see his letter to the Mayor of Newcastle upon Tyne, July 12, 1743, to William Law, Jan. 6, 1756, and to Mary Bishop, May 27, 1771; and cf. Sermon 88, 'On Dress', § 22. It is true that Wesley did not resign his Lincoln fellowship or its stipend until forced to do so by his marriage in 1751. But after 1744 all his effective ties with Oxford were severed, and more on his own initiative than that of the university.

[64] Preface, § 1. When Wesley first spoke of his sermons thus, he had only three vols.—and thirty-six sermons—in prospect (cf. the title-page of *SOSO*, I (1746)). The first edn. of 'four volumes' (1760) contained forty-three sermons. By 1763, the phrase denoted forty-four. The project remained open-ended in his own mind.

and third are rejections of all doctrines of guiltless 'perfection' (Nos. 13, *On Sin in Believers* and 14, *The Repentance of Believers*); the fourth is Wesley's sole *concio ad magistratum* (No. 15, *The Great Assize*). Volume II is concerned with the right 'order of salvation', from 'The Circumcision of the Heart' (No. 17) to the outworkings of faith in holy living (including No. 50, 'The Use of Money'). This is why, in the edition of 1771, Wesley could insert *The Lord Our Righteousness* (No. 20) between a sermon on the restoration of the power not to commit wilful sin (No. 19, 'The Great Privilege of those that are Born of God') and the true centrepiece of the whole collection (*viz.*, his thirteen-sermon series 'Upon Our Lord's Sermon on the Mount'), followed by a three-sermon series on the positive correlations of Law and Gospel.[65] The central thesis throughout this series is that the Law had served a proto-Christological function and, therefore, that the 'law' of 'love' continues to define the essence and end of Christian existence. Volume III is a sort of ellipse with its twin foci Wesley's understanding of the graciousness of grace (No. 39, 'Catholic Spirit') and the fullness of grace (No. 40, *Christian Perfection*). The resultant view of Christian living is brought into a balanced conspectus in the added sermon on *The Scripture Way of Salvation* (No. 43); the other sermons deal with one or another facet of this larger view. In the edition of 1771 there are three new and literally occasional sermons: *The Good Steward, The Reformation of Manners*, and Wesley's memorial sermon for George Whitefield (Nos. 51-53).

Even a casual analysis of these 'first four volumes of sermons' reveals that questions of chronology and provenance are incidental. Their order is shaped by the inner logic of Wesley's special view of the mystery of salvation. It is in this sense that they may rightly be regarded as a normative statement of the foundations of Wesleyan soteriology, even if not as his complete account of Christian existence.[66]

[65] Nos. 34-36, 'The Original, Nature, Properties, and Use of the Law': 'The Law Established through Faith, I'; and 'The Law Established through Faith, II'.

[66] Henry Moore, one of Wesley's closest friends, summarized them thus: '[Wesley's] first four volumes contain the substance of what he usually declared in the pulpit. He designed by them to give a view of what St. Paul calls . . . "the analogy of faith", *viz.*, the strong connection and harmony between those grand fundamental doctrines, original sin, justification by faith in the divine atonement of the Son of God, the new birth, inward and outward holiness.' (Moore, II. 405.) See also J. A. Beet's compact summary of the theological problem of the so-called Wesleyan 'standards' in 'The First Four Volumes of Wesley's Sermons', WHS, IX. 86-89.

Sermons on Several Occasions, Volumes V–VIII (1788)

As he approached his own 'three-score years and ten', Wesley took heart from the fact that the Revival had outlasted a generation.[67] As we have seen in the case of the Methodist chapels,[68] the Methodist movement grew more rapidly in its second generation than in its first, and its general impact on English society became more and more noticeable.[69] What has been less carefully noted is that Wesley, in the last two decades of his life, was even more productive than before both of written sermons and of edited materials for his people. This was the period of his collected *Works* (1771–74), of the *Arminian Magazine* (1778–91), and of the pamphlet war with Calvinists.[70] But more, it was a time of still further theological maturation, especially in the development of his views of Christian praxis. It is as if, after laying the firm foundations of his soteriology, Wesley had set himself to work out its practical consequences—without weakening any of those foundations. And yet it is just this rich vein of Wesley's *thought* that has suffered the most neglect in Wesley studies generally, even though such ancillary questions as his churchmanship (the Deed of Declaration and his ordinations)

[67] Cf. No. 63, 'The General Spread of the Gospel', § 16 (and n.), where Wesley quotes Luther as having said a revival 'never lasts above a generation, that is, thirty years (whereas the present revival has already continued above fifty)'; see also Nos. 94, 'On Family Religion', § 3; and 122, 'Causes of the Inefficacy of Christianity', § 17.

[68] See above, p. 42, n. 54.

[69] E.g., the *Minutes* of 1767 records a total of 25,911 members in all the Societies in England, Ireland, Scotland, and Wales (not really a mass movement even when it is remembered that this is a carefully winnowed membership list). In 1791 this same statistic had nearly trebled for the British Isles (to 72,476), together with 6,525 members in the missionary societies in 'The British Dominions' of America. To these were added the 57,621 reported members in 'The United States', giving a grand total of 136,622. For a comment on the social visibility and impact of the Methodists in this last third of Wesley's life cf. Semmel, *Methodist Revolution*, chs. i, iv. See also Stuart Andrews, *Methodism and Society* (London, Longmans, 1970), chs. 1 and 2.

[70] In this he was vigorously assisted by John William Fletcher, Walter Sellon, Thomas Olivers, and others. Fletcher (1729–85) was the Swiss-born and educated vicar of Madeley in Shropshire, and erstwhile president of the Countess of Huntingdon's college at Trevecca, Wales. He became embroiled in the controversy after 1770 and published a series of five *Checks to Antinomianism* in 1774 and 1775, and *The Doctrines of Grace and Justice Equally Essential to the Pure Gospel* in 1777. Walter Sellon, another Anglican priest, published a number of pamphlets for John Goodwin and against Augustus Toplady and Elisha Cole in the period of 1774 and thereafter; they are most easily consulted in his *Works* (London, 2 vols., 1814–15). Thomas Olivers (1725–99) entered the lists against Toplady and the brothers Hill; see his *Full Defence of the Rev. John Wesley . . .* (1776), *A Defence of Methodism . . .* (1785), and *A Full Refutation . . . of Unconditional Perseverance* (1790).

have been pored over endlessly. The sermons from these last two decades are, therefore, of great importance for any rounded view of his vision of the Christian life. This is why his second collection of *SOSO* (in a second set of four volumes) is so much more than an addendum to Volumes I–IV. They reveal new, and some fresh, facets of Wesley's mind and heart, and lend further complications to any explanation of his role as folk-theologian.

As we have seen, the decision to collect and publish these last four volumes came late (1787). It was taken under pressure, and the project itself was carried out in evident haste. But he had conserved a rich store of sermon manuscripts that he had been writing as 'original sermons' since 1775 and publishing in the *Arminian Magazine* since 1781. Incidentally, the ordering of the sermons as published in the *Arminian Magazine* differs from the order of their composition. The sequence of *SOSO*, V–VIII, differs still further. There is an ambiguous comment on this in his Preface. There he says, quite straightforwardly (§ 3): 'To make these plain discourses more useful, I purpose now to range [this series of fifty-six sermons] in proper order; placing those first which are intended to throw light on some important Christian doctrines, and afterwards those which more directly relate to some branch of Christian practice. And I shall endeavour to place them all in such an order that one may illustrate and confirm the other.' Actually, however, he begins Volume V with two of the most speculative sermons he ever wrote (Nos. 54, 'On Eternity', dated June 28, 1786, and 55, *On the Trinity*, dated May 7, 1775). The sequence thereafter seems somewhat more random than cumulative. He claims the right to alter his own texts at will, 'either to retrench what is redundant, to supply what is wanting, or to make any farther alterations which shall appear needful' (§ 2). Actually, the variations between the texts as they had appeared in the *Arminian Magazine* and again in *SOSO*, V–VIII, are negligible on points of substance. Also in this second Preface (to V), he reviews his praise of 'plain style' and his disparagement of 'French oratory'. And yet it will quickly be noticed that these late sermons are more copiously 'ornamented' (with classical tags, poetry, obscure quotations, and learned references) than any of the earlier sermons. Moreover, there is no explanation whatever of his omission of the extra sermons in *Works* (1771) I–IV, or of his salvaging of *The Lord Our Righteousness* from that group.

What is most striking about these late sermons is their range, as well as their reflection of Wesley's intense concern for all the practical aspects of 'contemporary Christian living'. Obviously, they are the work of an aging man, preoccupied with the pressures of the Revival. Their quality is uneven and only a few (Nos. 62, 'The End of Christ's Coming'; 73, 'Of Hell'; 85, 'On Working Out Our Own Salvation'; 115, 'Dives and Lazarus'; and 127, 'On the Wedding Garment') represent significant reformulations of older ideas. And yet there is nothing senescent in their spirit and nothing outdated in their sensitivity to current issues. They are the results of the aging Wesley's efforts to integrate the evangelical soteriology already established in *SOSO*, I–IV, with the sort of theology of culture he could see that his 'plain people' needed. There are sermons here to fortify and edify believers in the face of new challenges to historic Christian doctrine from Enlightenment scepticism and secularism. There is ammunition here for the Methodists in their protracted debates with the Calvinists, on one flank, and Anglican traditionalists, on the other. Their primary audience is the growing company of mature Christians long since converted, but newly confounded with new perplexities, in urgent need of wise pastoral counsel about their actual tasks in a changing world. Most specifically, as Wesley saw with increasing alarm, the earlier Methodist zeal for stewardship was lagging among those whose thrift, industry, and sobriety had rewarded them with unaccustomed affluence. These late sermons are mirrors to an age in which the ideas of Adam Smith's *Wealth of Nations* (published in 1776) were gaining the status of economic dogma; in their stress on surplus accumulation these 'new' ideas directly contradicted Wesley's 'third rule' for 'the use of money'—*viz.*, 'Give all you can.' It is no accident, therefore, that he would denounce surplus accumulation more frequently—and more stridently.

At the heart of all these practical counsels about the Christian family, 'attending the church services', 'the imperfections of human knowledge', etc., lay a rich and complex doctrine of *free grace* and its implications for a Christian's everyday problems of loving God above all else and of loving one's neighbour (defined as 'every child of man'). They suggest that Wesley may have had in mind something of an analogy between these late sermons and one or more of the classical manuals of Christian praxis that he knew had served earlier generations of English Christians so well—Richard Baxter's *Poor Man's Family Book* (1674), Jeremy

Taylor's *Ductor Dubitantium* (1660), or *The Whole Duty of Man* (1657), probably by Richard Allestree. Indeed, Wesley had published an extensive 'extract' of *The Whole Duty of Man* in his *Christian Library*, XXI. 3-194, with a significant foreword 'To the Reader':

> Whoever reads the following treatise should consider the time wherein it was wrote [*viz.*, the Cromwellian Commonwealth]. Never was there more talk of faith in Christ, of justification by faith, and of the fruits of the Spirit. And scarce ever was there less practice of plain, moral duties, of justice, mercy, and truth. At such a time it was peculiarly needful to inculcate what was so generally neglected. . . .
>
> I do not apprehend that any one page herein contradicts that fundamental principle, 'By grace ye are saved through faith', being justified freely 'through the redemption which is in Jesus'. Nor am I afraid that any who have read the preceding volumes should be induced by any part of this to build again the things which they had thrown down, to seek salvation by their own righteousness. But I trust, many who have already experienced the free grace of God in Christ Jesus may hereby be more fully instructed to walk in him, and more throughly furnished for every good word and work.

Something like this may be said of the whole of *SOSO*, V–VIII; it enlarges the notion of pastoral theology in a fresh and edifying way.

The Other Sermons

Meanwhile, between 1739 and 1788 Wesley published five sermons which he never included in any of his collections. They are not negligible items in the corpus, but, for various reasons, they did not fit the 'logic' of any of Wesley's orderings. The first of these was his intemperate attack on George Whitefield's doctrine of 'the decrees' in 1739 (No. 110, *Free Grace*). This had caused a breach between the two that never thereafter was fully healed despite a wary sort of reconciliation and a tenuous relationship that Wesley managed with Whitefield's patroness, the Countess of Huntingdon, until 1770. Moreover, Wesley was invited, by Whitefield's prior designation, to preach his 'official' memorial sermon in the two London 'Tabernacles' on November 18, 1770. Wesley must have realized, therefore, that republishing *Free Grace* in *SOSO* would serve no good purpose. It was Joseph Benson who decided that it should be included in his edition of Wesley's *Works* (1809–13), Vol. VIII, No. 55 (but without the long poem that Charles had written to match the sermon's prose).

Thomas Jackson simply followed Benson's lead both in his separate edition of the *Sermons* in 1825 (Vol. I, No. 54) and in the collected *Works* of 1829–31 (Vol. VII, No. CXXVIII).

No other such maverick sermon appeared till 1775, when Wesley published a charity sermon preached by invitation in St. Matthew's, Bethnal Green, on November 12, 'for the benefit of the widows and orphans of the soldiers who lately fell near Boston, in New England'. The reference here was to the opening skirmishes of the American Revolution (April 19 and June 17, 1775). In this sermon, on 2 Sam. 24:17, besides his incidental criticisms of the rebellious Americans, Wesley expounds a long-standing Christian platitude: a nation's miseries are usually the fruits of that nation's sins.[71] There was, however, no obvious place for it in *SOSO*, V–VIII, and Benson may have overlooked it. Thomas Jackson decided that it should not be lost, and included it in both of his editions (No. 58 in that of 1825; No. CXXX in *Works* of 1829–31, Vol. VII) and supplied the title still retained here, *National Sins and Miseries*.

Much earlier—indeed, shortly after *Free Grace*—Wesley had written two sermons that fall outside our category of published sermons but may be mentioned here. They were bold denunciations of hypocrisy in Oxford (or maybe the same sermon in a Latin and an English version). They may have been connected with the exercises for the B.D. degree he was expected to take as a Fellow of Lincoln. Very prudently, he published neither (and was never awarded the B.D. degree, either), but nevertheless he preserved them in his papers. What little we know about their history is sketched out above,[72] but what needs to be noted here is that they belong to that strange love-hate relationship that Wesley had with Oxford, and that they are also the most convincing demonstration we have of his facility and actual eloquence in Neo-Ciceronian Latin. Benson may not even have known of them; the English version appeared in Jackson's 'Fifth Series' (*Works*, VII, No. CXXXIV) with its triumphalist title, 'True Christianity Defended'.[73] The Latin version is being published here for the first time.

[71] For a review of how the Puritans had rung the changes on this same theme, cf. John Wilson, *Pulpit in Parliament*.

[72] See p. 31.

[73] Cf. his edn. of the *Works* (1829–31), VII. 451, where Jackson sees only a martyr's heroic courage: 'To deliver such a sermon before that learned body [more probably in The

In 1777 Wesley wrote and published a truly 'occasional' sermon which he omitted from *SOSO*, V–VIII. Its occasion was the laying of the foundation for his new Chapel in the City Road, April 21.[74] This was an interesting move away from the old Foundery on 'Windmill Hill' (which had served as his London centre since 1739) to a much more impressive headquarters closer to Whitefield's fine brick Tabernacle[75] and directly across City Road from the Nonconformist cemetery of Bunhill Fields.[76] It was natural enough that, given such a new beginning with its inescapable sectarian overtones, Wesley would be prompted to a somewhat complacent review of his particular movement and to a mildly triumphalist reflection upon its prospects. The sermon was published shortly thereafter, and as promptly denounced by the Revd. Rowland Hill, Minister of Surrey Chapel, Blackfriars Road.[77]

In the year following Wesley wrote and published a sermon on Ezek. 1:16 which he himself entitled, *Some Account of the Late Work of God in North America*. Tyerman judged it 'almost a misnomer to designate this a sermon';[78] it is, however, an exposition of one of Wesley's favourite themes: 'the adorable providence of God' in the midst of tragic circumstance. In it he deplores the American rebellion and then turns seer to prophesy a British victory which would 'make way for the happy return of [the Americans to their erstwhile] humility, temperance, industry, and chastity'. The sermon was popular enough to run through four printings in 1778, but history quickly outran the prophecy; it was not published again until the Jackson edition of 1825 and, again, slightly revised, in 1829.

The one other sermon that Wesley wrote and published in this period, but then omitted from his collection, was the memorial eulogy for his old friend and ally, John William Fletcher.

Divinity School than in St. Mary's if, indeed, it were ever "delivered"] required no small degree of pious resolution; it is a striking display of that spirit of sacrifice by which Mr. Wesley was actuated.'

[74] Cf. JWJ, Apr. 21, 1777, and Curnock's note. For a detailed account of this event and its history, see George J. Stevenson, *City Road Chapel* (1873).

[75] Cf. Seymour, I. 198-202, for the history of the modest beginning of the 'Tabernacle' in 1741 (a large 'shed') to its more spacious rebuilding in 1752–53.

[76] The Meeting-House and burying ground of the London Society of Friends (grave of George Fox) is only some fifty yards farther west of Bunhill Fields.

[77] In his *Imposture Detected* (1777); see above, p. 10, n. 35. See Vol. 9 of this edn. for Wesley's *Answer*.

[78] *Wesley*, III. 280.

Fletcher, 'Wesley's designated successor,'[79] had died in Madeley on August 14, 1785, while Wesley was on his itinerant rounds in Wiltshire and the West of England. He had returned to London on November 4 and on the sixth had delivered the eulogy in his bright new chapel. As may be seen, its emphasis was biographical; Wesley had based it on materials furnished him by Fletcher's wife, the former Mary Bosanquet.[80] Wesley had it published within the year, and it was widely reprinted thereafter.[81] However, it was not included in *SOSO*, V–VIII; it appeared again in Benson, and in Jackson's 'Fourth Series', No. CXXXIII.

Even after the publication of *SOSO*, V–VIII, Wesley continued to write and publish sermons. These appeared in the *Arminian Magazine* from May–June, 1789, through July–August, 1792, in a somewhat random order as far as any substantive logic may be discerned, but still in the numbered series as before. In 1800 George Story collected seventeen of these 'new' sermons in a posthumous ninth volume of *SOSO* in the same order as in the *Arminian Magazine*, *except* for Wesley's sermon on Heb. 5:4, in which he had defended his longtime practice of forbidding his lay preachers to administer the sacraments.[82] By 1800 the Methodists were in no mood to be edified by an argument of this sort; Story, therefore, simply dropped it out, leaving Thomas Jackson to 'restore' it in his edition of the *Works* (1829–31, Vol. VII, No. CXV), with, however, an explicit disavowal of its main thesis.

These very late sermons display the same intent and something of the quality of their predecessors. The most remarkable of them is No. 127, 'On the Wedding Garment', in which Wesley openly rejects the Puritan interpretation of 'the wedding garment' as 'the spotless robe of Christ's righteousness', imputed to us vicariously as our own, but rather as that 'holiness' itself, 'without which no man shall see the Lord.' Here, finally, the venerable evangelist comes back round to the same motif he had expounded so long

---

[79] Cf. Luke Tyerman's biography with this title (1882).

[80] Cf. her *Letter to the Rev. Mr. Wesley on the Death of the Rev. Mr. Fletcher, Vicar of Madeley*, dated Aug. 18, 1785, and printed by J. Edmunds of Madeley; see also her other letter to her husband's brother which was published in 1786: *A Letter to Mons. H. L. de la Flechere . . . on the death of his brother, the Reverend John William de la Flechere, twenty-five years vicar of Madeley, Shropshire.*

[81] Cf. *Bibliog*, No. 441.

[82] See No. 121, 'Prophets and Priests' (and intro. com.). It was promptly dubbed 'the Korah sermon' and openly criticized by Henry Moore and others; cf. Moore, II. 338-40.

ago in 'The Circumcision of the Heart'.[83] It is the end-point of a convoluted 'progress'—from faith in faith to faith in grace.

Three sermons that could not be included in the Wesley corpus on the same terms as the others still deserve our passing notice here. The first is one on 'The Cause and Cure of Earthquakes', a topic of general interest to all eighteenth-century defenders of God's good providence in nature.[84] Jackson published it as John's: 'no doubt can be entertained about its being the production of Mr. Wesley's pen.'[85] The 'Mr. Wesley' in question, however, turns out to have been Charles, who could, on such a question, have spoken for both brothers.[86]

A second sermon that has traditionally been attributed to Wesley with insufficient evidence is a stenographic transcription of what is said to have been Wesley's sermon on the occasion of the opening 'of the new house at Wakefield', April 28, 1774.[87] The transcript was made in shorthand 'at the time of delivery' and then promptly published 'at the request of many hearers'.[88] If we could be certain of this text (if, e.g., we had Wesley's corroboration of it or his inclusion of it in any collection), we would have to reckon with its indication that at least some of Wesley's oral sermons were remarkably similar to his written texts in both rhetoric and substance—except that this one is duller than most. As the data stand now, however, this text had better be classified as dubious, which is not to say 'spurious'.

Another instance of an interesting text that remains uncertain is a manuscript sermon on Heb. 4:9 that was published by Albert F. Hall in *The London Quarterly and Holborn Review*, April 1940 (Vol. CLXV, pp. 139–46). Earlier efforts to locate the manuscript for collation proved unavailing; it was not included in the papers and books bequeathed by Mr. Hall to Lincoln College in 1972. It has, however, finally surfaced, and is now in the collection of Dr.

---

[83] See Sermon, No. 17.

[84] It was an example of an extensive sermonic literature occasioned by the London earthquakes of Feb. 8 and Mar. 8, 1750; cf., e.g., William Whiston, *Memoirs, . . . to which are added his lectures on the late remarkable meteors and earthquakes* . . .(2nd edn., 1753), Pt. III, pp. 216-20. Cf. JWJ for the above dates; also Moore, II. 158-59, whose vivid description of London's panic reaction to these quakes includes an account of Whitefield's preaching at midnight to crowds who had flocked together in Hyde Park.

[85] Cf. Editor's Preface to *Wesley's Sermons* (1825).

[86] Cf. CWJ, Mar. 9, 1750; see also his *Hymns Occasioned by the Earthquake* (1750).

[87] Cf. JWJ: 'So I preached in the main street [of Wakefield]. . .'.

[88] See Vol. 4, Appendix B, and cf. *Bibliog*, No. 623.

Frederick E. Maser of Philadelphia. The text is undoubtedly in John Wesley's hand, but in substance it turns out to be a sort of homiletical outline of Richard Baxter's *Saints' Everlasting Rest.* In form it is original, and might well have been published here in full. In substance, however, it ranks with other 'extracts' by Wesley from his favorite authors.[89] Its chief significance is as a further testimony to Baxter's influence on Wesley's thought.

A Conspectus

From any such survey of the development of Wesley's sermon corpus, at least five general conclusions emerge that lend support to the 'logic' of the order adopted in this present edition. The first is that Wesley himself understood *SOSO*, I–VIII, as definitive of his role as preacher, teacher, evangelist, and pastor. In two successive personal wills (in 1768 and again in 1789), he bequeathed a set of these sermons (first, in their four-volume format, the second, 'the eight volumes') 'to each travelling preacher who should remain in the connexion six months after [his] decease'.[90] Moreover, the Model Deed of 1763 continued in force in all the Methodist Chapels 'in connexion with Mr. Wesley'. A second reasonably clear conclusion is that Wesley's understanding of *SOSO*'s primary function was not as a legal instrument with a fixed, exclusive number of sermons intended for literal construction by title or canon lawyers. The title had an open-ended connotation; Wesley meant to allow for enlargement and development in his own unfolding thought and that of others. George Story was not presumptuous in his entitlement of the posthumous Volume IX as *SOSO*. By the same token, the miscellaneous sermons, both early and late, have an interest in their own right in any critical or comprehensive review of Wesley's thought. They expose his understanding of the 'order of salvation' (always his central concern) in other facets and dimensions that have yet to be probed and fully integrated into a fully-orbed study of his life and work. A fourth generalization may only reflect a personal impression that has grown firmer in the course of this particular project: *viz.*, that the *later* Wesley who emerges here is the neglected Wesley and that there is a sorely

[89] See Vol. 4, Appendix.
[90] Cf. Tyerman *(JW)* III. 15, 616-17; also Hampson, *Memoirs*, III. 231-35.

needed redress of this imbalance if the agenda of Wesley studies is ever to regain its due proportions. And, finally, the manuscript sermons here newly edited and published may add more than mere quantity to our resources for a critical reconstruction of the Wesleyan theology. Most of them are mediocre and one of them, 'Hypocrisy in Oxford', like the published *Free Grace*, reflects an *un*catholic spirit. But the best of them ('The Image of God', 'The Wisdom of Winning Souls', 'The One Thing Needful', etc.) open up new facets of Wesley's early thought and later more than a few uncritical stereotypes.

It is admittedly awkward that each new edition of Wesley's sermons requires a new and different enumeration from any of its predecessors. This can scarcely be avoided. Not since *Wandering Thoughts* turned up unannounced in 1763, in the second edition of *SOSO*, III, has the problem of order and enumeration ever been as simple as an editor or reader might have preferred.

IV. THEOLOGICAL METHOD AND THE PROBLEMS OF DEVELOPMENT

It was Wesley's way to speak as directly as he could to his actual audiences; this is plain in his letters, polemical rejoinders, and essays, but most of all in his sermons.[1] This would follow from his conviction that preaching is the chief business of the evangelist, and it explains his choice of the sermon as the chief genre for his theological expositions. He understood the difference between the dialectical character of sermons and the didactic character of systematic treatises. Quite consciously, and from the beginning, he preferred the former. He knew as much as most of his contemporaries about the history of the creeds and confessions, but he seems never to have felt any compulsion to compose yet another creed or confession. It is noteworthy that in his sermons and letters he would, here and there, strike off apt summaries of the essence of Christian truth. But these are clearly distillates for edification rather than doctrinal formularies demanding a yes or no response. This general view of his role as preacher fitted well with his eclectic impulses as a theologian: he was a born borrower

---

[1] Not even his *Notes* on the New Testament are an exception to this rule (espec. when compared to other commentaries) nor his one long treatise (*The Doctrine of Original Sin*), which is less a conventional essay than a protracted debate with a single disputant. All his other extracts reflect this same impulse toward personal address: he is always the preacher-teacher trying to edify a targeted clientele.

who nevertheless put his own mark on every borrowing. There is, therefore, a crucial methodological question as to whether in the sprawling array of his writings and editings there are consistent interests that amount to a coherent self-understanding. One of the aims of this edition is to make it possible to sift such a question in a larger context.

It is important to begin with the recognition that Wesley's baseline tradition was Erasmian, as this particular perspective had been shaped through the course of the English Reformation (Bucer, Cranmer, Hooker) and the ensuing struggles between the Puritans and the Anglicans (Mede, Pearson, Beveridge). When hard-pressed by the Lutheran and Calvinist challenges (from the Moravians and from Edwards), Wesley fell back instinctively on Erasmians like Cranmer and Harpsfield.[2] This tradition involved a sincere commitment to the ideals of Christian humanism (non-dogmatic in mood and style), open to an alliance between reverent faith and reverent learning, concerned above all else with a gracious Christian lifestyle. By Wesley's time, however, it had evolved into a gospel of moral rectitude, but still with its three professed guidelines: Scripture, reason, and Christian antiquity.[3] To this Wesley had added a strong element of mystical piety.[4] It was this that sustained his lifelong interest in the patristic ideal of divine-human 'participation'—expressed in every Eucharist in the Prayer of Humble Access: '. . . that we may evermore dwell in him, and he in us'.[5] Wesley brought to this

---

[2] But note his quite self-conscious balancing act of matching his extract from the Anglican *Homilies* with a similar extract from Barnes's *Two Treatises on Justification*; see above, p. 37, n. 36, and cf. *Bibliog*, Nos. 11 and 16.

[3] Cf. Irène Simon, *Three Restoration Divines*, chs. 1–2; see also P. E. More and F. L. Cross, eds., *Anglicanism* (Milwaukee, Wisconsin, Morehouse Publishing Co., 1935), ch. 5(2), pp. 132–41. See also Francis Paget, *An Introduction to the Fifth Book of Hooker's Ecclesiastical Polity* (1907), p. 284.

[4] Cf. his review of his theological history to the end of 1737 in his memorandum of Jan. 25, 1738 (cf. Moore, I. 342-44). Note in this self-criticism of his overstress on tradition, his negative judgments on the Lutherans and Calvinists, and his discovery of the dangers of the mysticism which had nonetheless influenced him deeply and would continue to do so.

[5] Cf. BCP, Communion (359). The reference copy used is *The Book of Common Prayer as Revised and Settled at the Savoy Conference, Anno 1662* (London, William Pickering, 1844, folio), from which we frequently use the added marginal numbers assigned to the successive liturgical units of the text (excluding the Act of Uniformity, etc., the Psalter, and the rubrics).

Wesley's first discovery on the day of his Aldersgate experience was the promise in 2 Pet. 1: 4, 'that ye should be partakers of the divine nature' (JWJ, May 24, 1738, § 13). Cf. also the review of the 'participation' theme in the patristic churches in David Bálàs,

complex heritage two new elements: the first, a distinctive stress on the primacy of Scripture (not merely as 'standing revelation'[6] but as a 'speaking book'); and, second, as insistence upon the personal assurance of God's justifying, pardoning grace (which is what he always meant by such terms as 'experience', 'experimental', 'heart religion'). The constant goal of Christian living, in his view, is sanctification ('Christian perfection' or 'perfect love'); its organizing principle is always the *order of salvation*; the divine agency in it all is the Holy Spirit. Thus it was that Wesley understood prevenience as the distinctive work of the Holy Spirit and as the primal force in all authentic spirituality. This perspective was expounded in unsystematic forms, and yet it was inwardly coherent and relatively consistent in its development. And it is this basic viewpoint that is to be looked for in all the sermons: early, middle, and late.

Wesley's point of departure was always Holy Scripture, understood according to the 'analogy of faith' (i.e., its general sense),[7] and as 'the standing revelation' in the Christian church throughout her long history. He had grown up with Scripture as a second language; even in his early sermons one sees the beginnings of his lifelong habit of interweaving Scripture with his own speech in a graceful texture. Later, he will recall that it was not until 1729 that he began to be *homo unius libri*,[8] but this could only mean a rearrangement of priorities, not a novelty. There was never a thought that he should restrict his reading to the biblical text alone. It was, instead, a matter of hermeneutical principle that Scripture would be his court of first and last resort in faith and morals. This was the entire Scripture, too, and not just a biblical anthology; his view of the canon (not excluding the Apocrypha) was of a whole and integral revelation, inspired by the same Holy Spirit who continues to guide all serious readers into

---

Metousia Theou: Man's Participation in God's Perfections According to St. Gregory of Nyssa (Rome, Herder, 1966).

[6] Cf. Offspring Blackall, 'The Sufficiency of a Standing Revelation', Discourses LXXXVIII–XCV, *Works*, II. 941-1052—his Boyle Lectures for 1700.

[7] For Wesley's references to the 'analogy of faith', cf. No. 5, 'Justification by Faith', § 2 and n.

[8] In the Preface, § 5, to *SOSO*, I (1746), it is implied that his commitment to *sola Scriptura* came with the conversion of 1738. However, in a letter to William Dodd, Feb. 5, 1756, he speaks of his resolve 'to make the Scriptures my study about seven-and-twenty years ago' (i.e., 1729). This same dating is repeated in *A Plain Account of Christian Perfection* (1765), §§ 5, 10.

its unfathomable truth, parts and whole together. And it was from this basic doctrine of biblical inspiration that his main principles of interpretation were derived—all five of them. The first was that believers should accustom themselves to the biblical language and thus to the 'general sense' of Scripture as a whole. This general sense is omnipresent throughout the canon even if not equally so in every text; there is a 'message' in every part of Holy Writ, and it is always the same, in essence. This leads to a second rule, adapted from the ancient Fathers and from the Reformers as well: that the Scriptures are to be read as a whole, with the expectation that the clearer texts may be relied upon to illuminate the obscurer ones. There is no authority above Scripture from which a more definitive interpretation of revelation may be sought. Wesley was not indifferent to historical and literary questions in exegesis; he was living in the early days of the new biblical criticism, and he had a lively interest in the commentators (old and new).[9] But his constant focus was the text itself; his constant concern was with its direct address to the reader. Moreover, despite the fact that he had his favourite texts and passages in both Old and New Testaments, he had no 'canon within the canon'. This holistic sense of biblical inspiration suggested his third hermeneutical principle: that one's exegesis is to be guided, always in the first instance, by the literal sense, unless that appears to lead to consequencs that are either irrational or unworthy of God's moral character as 'pure, unbounded love'.[10] Then, and only with caution, the exegete may seek for an edifying allegory or anagogy, but only within the terms of the analogy of faith. A fourth hermeneutical rule follows from his doctrine of grace and free will: that all moral commands in Scripture are also 'covered promises', since God never commands the impossible and his grace is always efficacious in every faithful will.[11] His last rule is actually a variation on the Anglican sense of the old Vincentian canon that the historical experience of the church, though fallible, is the better judge overall of Scripture's meanings than later interpreters are likely to

[9] For Wesley's indebtedness to Matthew Henry, Matthew Poole, John Heylyn, Philip Doddridge, *et al*, cf. above, p. 41, n. 50.

[10] Cf. No. 21, 'Sermon on the Mount, I', § 6 and n.

[11] Cf. No. 25, 'Sermon on the Mount, V', II. 2 and n.

be, especially on their own.[12] Thus, radical novelty is to be eschewed on principle.[13]

One of the bonuses of an Oxford education for most of its alumni was a living sense of the continuity of the past into the future. Wesley had had the additional advantage of an acquaintance with John Clayton, the ardent patrologist of the Holy Club.[14] This discovery of 'the Fathers of the Church' reinforced Wesley's natural tendency to set most of his problems in their historical perspectives; one cannot point to another popular theologian with as lively a sense of the normative role of Christian antiquity for contemporary theology. The sermons do not display their larger historical background, but it is almost always there; for the purposes of any critical analysis this background will almost always reward a careful probing.

This general approach to biblical hermeneutics presupposed (or required) a matching theory of religious knowledge if the interpreter was to avoid the open trap of literalism, on the one side, or traditionalism on the other. Here Wesley found himself in an interesting dilemma. He was an avowed empiricist[15] in an age of empiricism;[16] yet he was also an unembarrassed intuitionist who openly claimed his heritage of Christian Platonism.This had come to him more generally from the Fathers, William of St. Thierry, the Victorines, St. Bonaventura, and the Cambridge Platonists. More directly, however, he had been instructed by his father's friend, John Norris, and also by Richard Lucas. Norris was the chief English disciple of the French Cartesian, Nicholas Malebranche, and Wesley was more heavily influenced by Malebranche's 'occasionalism' than was any other eighteenth-century British theologian.[17]

---

[12] Cf. No. 13, *On Sin in Believers*, III. 9 and n.; see also the memorandum for Jan. 25, 1738 [see p. 38, n. 38, above]. The reference there is to *The Commonitory of Vincent of Lerins* (A.D. 435), ch. ii, § 6.

[13] Cf. No. 25, 'Sermon on the Mount, V', § 1 and n.; and see also No. 17, 'The Circumcision of the Heart', § 1.

[14] Cf. V. H. H. Green, *The Young Mr. Wesley*, pp. 173-74.

[15] He repeats, almost casually, the Thomist formula that 'there is nothing in the mind not previously in the senses'; cf. No. 117, 'On the Discoveries of Faith', § 1 and n.

[16] Cf. Isaiah Berlin, ed., *The Age of Enlightenment: The 18th Century Philosophers* (New York, Mentor Books, 1956); see also Frederick Coplestone, *A History of Philosophy* (London, Burns Oates and Washbourne, 1959), Vol. V, chs. iv-xvii; and Etienne Gilson and Thomas Langan, *Modern Philosophy, Descartes to Kant* (New York, Random House, 1963), Pt. 5.

[17] That Malebranche had been read in the Holy Club we know from John Clayton's

He was reasonably well-versed in the history of 'natural philosophy'; he was very much aware of the knowledge explosion of his times; he shared the rationalist temper of his age; he was a trained logician. But he never supposed that theology was an empirical science, and he was careful to mark off the proper limits of reason.[18] He could, therefore, discuss the empirical 'orders of creation' in terms of a strictly empirical knowledge of tangible reality, and still insist that our knowledge of God and 'the things of God' must be intuitive, since reality at this level does not fall within the scope of empirical knowledge.

For even Locke himself had recognized a special domain for 'truths above reason'.[19] And thus, like many another dualist before him, Wesley drew what he thought was a clear line between our knowledge of things and our knowledge of spiritual reality; he found a persuasive analogy between our empirical sensorium and what he could think and speak of as our 'spiritual senses'. He understood how Descartes had conceived of our awareness of immaterial reality as truly primitive (*simplici mentis intuitu*); he knew Malebranche's variations on this theme. With a supporting tradition, therefore, he regarded the case for intuitionism as a wholly respectable option which he had consciously chosen and maintained consistently. Within this tradition, he had developed the integrating principles of his eclectic method: *viz.*, that theology is the interpretation of spiritual and moral insights sparked by the prevenient action of the Holy Spirit, deposited in Holy Scripture, interpreted by the

letter of Aug. 1, 1732 (see this edn., Vol. 25, pp. 331-34).Wesley recommended *The Search After Truth* in a letter to Samuel Furly, Feb. 18, 1756, and included it in the curriculum for Kingswood School; see another recommendation of it to Mary Bishop, Aug. 18, 1774. For competent reviews of Malebranche's epistemology, cf. Morris Ginsberg, *Dialogues on Metaphysics and on Religion by Nicholas Malebranche* (London, Allen and Unwin, 1923), pp. 21-42; and also Gilson and Langan, *Modern Philosophy*, ch. vii. A critical analysis of the similarities and differences between Malebranche, Norris, and Wesley would be a very useful exercise. For Lucas's influence upon Wesley see Alexander Knox, 'Remarks . . .' in Southey, II. 327-30.

[18] Cf. No. 70, 'The Case of Reason Impartially Considered'; also Nos. 10, 'The Witness of the Spirit, I', I.12 and n., and 69, 'The Imperfection of Human Knowledge'.

[19] *An Essay Concerning Human Understanding* (1690), Bk. IV, ch. 17, § 23. Locke distinguishes between assertions 'above, contrary, and according to reason': '(1) According to reason are such propositions whose truth we can discover by examining and tracing those ideas we have from sensation and reflection, and by natural deduction find to be true or probable; (2) *Above reason* are such propositions whose truth or probability we cannot by reason derive from these principles . . .'. For an example of an analytic discussion of (2), cf. *The Reasonableness of Christianity* (1695).

Christian tradition, reviewed by reason, and appropriated by personal experience.

From the same heritage came his understanding of an ascetical ethics, rooted in traditions of monasticism, finding its expression in a *contemptus mundi* that raises the human spirit above all inordinate attachments to 'this world'. After 1727 Wesley would come to understand this otherworldly view in richer detail—from à Kempis, Law, De Renty, Gregory Lopez, and many another; but he had already seen it much earlier, and at first hand, in the Puritan consciences of his parents and forebears. This rejection of 'the world' was less a loathing of God's good creation than a declaration of independence from bondages of worldliness and self-indulgence.[20]

This *asceticism-within-the-world* lay behind Wesley's moralism, and matched exactly his commitment to the great tradition of *ars moriendi*, 'the art of holy dying'.[21] This had been best described in English by Jeremy Taylor; a secularized version of it may be seen in Samuel Richardson's *Clarissa*.[22] It had then been sentimentalized and popularized by Edward Young's *Night Thoughts* (1742), Thomas Parnell's 'The Hermit' (1721), and James Hervey's *Meditations Among the Tombs* (1745–46). Wesley, for his part, scorned the sentimentality in these romanticized versions of otherworldliness. The Christian ideal in life and death, as he saw it, was equanimity and courage in the face of whatever providence might bring. And always the warrant for any such confidence was the God-given miracle of justifying faith and its assurance of grace. His notion, then, of holy living was a life emptied of spiritual pride but filled with the serenities of holiness—understood always as the Christian's love of God and neighbour.

Any such pluralistic method in theology was bound to generate tensions in Wesley's own mind and in those of his eager critics. It was neither neat nor clean-cut: the effort to gather and hold together so many disparate traditions was bound to strain the

[20] He came to label this 'dissipation', defined as 'the uncentring of the soul from God'; see No. 79, 'On Dissipation'.

[21] Cf. Beaty, *The Craft of Dying* (p. 19, n. 28, above).

[22] Cf. Clarissa's dying words: 'God Almighty would not let me depend for comfort [i.e., strength] upon any but himself . . .', in *Clarissa, Or, the History of a Young Lady . . .* (1747–48), Bk. XII, 92. One can take this novel as an important mirror to the eighteenth-century mind.

bonds of consistency—and all the more since Wesley was more interested in speaking to the needs of any given moment than in formulating a generalized view that might cover a multitude of conceivable instances.

From the earliest days of the Revival it appeared to half-friendly critics, like Josiah Tucker and 'John Smith', that Wesley's attempts to integrate an evangelical soteriology (*sola fide*) with a catholic doctrine of grace had involved him in serious inconsistencies.[23] Later, Sir Richard Hill would repeat Tucker's complaint that Wesley's theology was 'a medley of Calvinism, Arminianism, Montanism, Quakerism, Quietism—all thrown together . . .'.[24] The Moravians and, afterwards, their solifidian allies (men like James Relly and William Cudworth) would add the further charge of 'Pelagianism'. The Calvinists claimed to have found 'the superior of a convent of English Benedictine monks at Paris' who had judged Wesley's *Minute* of 1770 as even more synergistic than 'popery'.[25] Both John Hampson and Augustus Toplady, from opposite sides, charged Wesley with absurdities in his attempted reconciliations of sovereign grace and human agency.[26] Bishops Lavington and Warburton had joined this chorus of critics of Wesley's confusions.[27] Alexander Knox stood almost alone in his judgment that Wesley's later sermons were more balanced than those from his middle period.[28]

For his part, however, Wesley stoutly maintained that his teachings *were* consistent, and this poses a problem for those who would interpret his thought and its own special dynamics. One might better begin, perhaps, with the fact that his critics were accustomed to a notion of consistency defined as literal identity in successive formulations (*semper eadem*). Wesley's idea of identity had much more to do with constancy of intention and perspective in successive circumstances. His critics could point to altered formulations and to the inner tensions in Wesley's writings— from 'early' to 'middle' to 'late'. His basic shift in 1738 had prompted drastic alterations in his understanding of the order of

[23] See above, p. 9, n. 35.

[24] *Logica Wesleiensis: Or the Farrago Double Distilled* (1773), p. 43.

[25] Cf. Sir Richard Hill, *A Conversation* . . . , above, p. 3, n. 10.

[26] Cf. Hampson's *Memoirs*, III, chs. vii-ix; see also Toplady's *Caveat* . . . (cf. above, p. 3, n. 10).

[27] See above, p. 3, n. 11.

[28] See Southey, II. 293-360, one of the most probing of all the theological appraisals of Wesley by any of his own contemporaries, and one of the most unjustly neglected.

Theological Method and the Problems of Development 63

salvation (from his early view of a progression from holy living to justifying faith to a direct reversal of that order). It was not very long, however, before he relaxed his original insistence on conscious assurance as an either/or sign of justification. During that same period he also shifted his ground on the point of 'the remains of sin' in believers (what the schoolmen and Luther had called the *fomes peccati*).[29]

There was no inconsistency, as he saw it, in tilting the balance of a theological argument now this way, now that, depending on whether he was facing the antinomians from their side or the moralists from theirs. What was consistent, certainly after 1738, was his unwearied effort to find a proper place in the new evangelical soteriology for his undiminished concern for holy living. His goal was an alternative to both of the older polarizations that had separated the notions of Christ's *imputed* righteousness in justification from an actual *imparted* righteousness. He was convinced that both aspects of righteousness belonged as concomitant fruits of grace in the one mystery of salvation—provided only that they were both understood as means to the still higher end of perfection in love.[30] Thus, he found himself adapting Thomas Boston's familiar scheme of the 'fourfold states' of the soul's progress in faith to a 'threefold' one ('natural', 'legal' and 'evangelical').[31] Note how he included Boston's category of 'eternal' so as to fit his own concept of 'evangelical': 'The natural man neither conquers [sin] nor fights [it]; the man under the law fights with sin but cannot conquer; the man under grace fights and conquers'.[32] In such terms he could speak of 'Christian perfection' as the *end* of the order of salvation, and yet could also speak of 'the repentance of believers'. He could, moreover, teach his people to 'go on to perfection' and to 'expect to be made perfect in love in this life' and still react strongly against all advocates of *guiltless* perfection.

[29] Luther had spoken of the believer as *simul justus et peccator* ('justified and yet still a sinner'). This paradox followed from his doctrine of invincible concupiscence, *viz.*, that the *fomes peccati* remains in the believer as long as he is in the flesh. For a further discussion of Wesley's difficulties with this problem, see below, Nos. 13 and 14, *On Sin in Believers*, and *The Repentance of Believers* (and their intro. com.).

[30] Cf. his analysis of the relation of faith to love as a means to an end, in No. 35, 'The Law Established through Faith, I', II. 1-6.

[31] Cf. St. Augustine, *Enchiridion*, XXXI, ¶¶ 118-19; see also Thomas Boston, *Human Nature in its Fourfold State*.

[32] Cf. No. 9, 'The Spirit of Bondage and of Adoption', III. 8.

All this, of course, was bound to strike all lovers of single-track traditions as the evidence of a muddled head. To Wesley, however, it was a way of talking about the Holy Spirit's freedom to work as he wills and as human wills respond. The root difference in these competing views of consistency and development in theological statements is in their radically different pneumatologies and, consequently, in their differing views of the nature and roles of theological discourse. The Calvinists denied flatly any validity to natural virtue; the deists (and not a few Anglicans) firmly asserted it.[33] Wesley had struggled with this problem for a long time; it had surfaced first in his 1730 sermon on 'The Image of God'.[34] He could see the partial truths on both sides; he rejected their fierce disjunctions. His own conclusion looked beyond any of the views of Butler or Hutcheson or the Calvinists:

> For, allowing that all the souls of men are dead in sin by *nature*, this excuses none, seeing there is no man that is in a state of mere nature. There is no man, unless he has quenched the Spirit, that is wholly void of the grace of God. No man living is entirely destitute of what is vulgarly called 'natural conscience'. But this is not natural: it is more properly termed 'preventing grace' [i.e., the grace of the Holy Spirit]. Every man has a greater or less measure of this, which waiteth not for the call of man.[35]

On another point, the Calvinists insisted on the radical depravity of all men, including the justified. Moralists like John Taylor of Norwich vigorously denied this.[36] Wesley's formal doctrine of original sin is stark, and yet he carefully nuances it with his rejection of invincible concupiscence and his emphasis on salvation as the restoration of the image of God (disabled but not destroyed by sin).[37] He could, therefore, deny the classical

[33] E.g., Francis Hutcheson, whom Wesley repeatedly criticized; cf. Hutcheson's *Inquiry into the Original of our Ideas of Beauty and Virtue* (1725) and his *Essay on the Nature and Conduct of the Passions and Affections with Illustrations Upon the Moral Sense* (1726), and see below, No. 12, 'The Witness of Our Own Spirit', § 5 and n. For an Anglican spokesman, cf. Joseph Butler's 'Dissertation Upon the Nature of Virtue', an appendix to *The Analogy of Religion* (1736), Bk. I, ch. 3; see also W. R. Matthews's edn. of Butler's *Fifteen Sermons Preached at the Rolls Chapel* (London, G. Bell and Sons, 1967), Sermons I-IV.
[34] See No. 141, 'The Image of God.'
[35] See No. 85, 'On Working Out Our Own Salvation', III. 4; this late sermon is Wesley's most nearly complete statement of his own third alternative to the Calvinist and moralist extremes.
[36] As in *The Scripture Doctrine of Original Sin: Proposed to Free and Candid Examination* (1740), the enlarged 3rd edn. of which brought forth Wesley's *Doctrine of Original Sin* (1757).
[37] See No. 44, *Original Sin.*

Protestant doctrine that all the good works of the unjustified are merely 'splendid sins'.[38] For if the Holy Spirit is God's personal agency of grace in the human heart, it is then possible in principle that the power of that grace might overcome the satanic power of sin and death, so that from being under bondage of not being able not to sin, a Christian might be endued, by grace, with the power not to sin wilfully—which is all Wesley ever really claimed for his doctrine of perfection.

From their side, however, the Lutherans and Calvinists were bound to read Wesley as teaching a doctrine of 'sinless perfection', and it is true that they could find enough occasional passages to stir their suspicions.[39] They could see inherent confusion in any effort to keep the distinction between voluntary and involuntary sins clear cut; they had long since swept away all Roman Catholic distinctions between mortal and venial sins. Thus, perfection as they could envisage it was eschatological, 'in the state of glory only'.[40] It was bound to seem to them that anything else ignored the full weight of sin and could serve only as a temptation to spiritual pride.

Wesley himself was always quick to correct any such interpretation of his doctrine of perfection by the antinomians (Maxfield, Bell, Cudworth). He was aware of the fatal dangers of self-righteousness, and gave voice to it in a lively little pamphlet, *Cautions and Directions, Given to the Greatest Professors* [of Perfection] *in the Methodist Societies* (1762). It is a sharp warning against pride, against 'that daughter of pride, *enthusiasm*', against 'antinomianism', and 'of *desiring* anything but God'.[41] He could speak as sensitively as any other Protestant of 'repentance in believers', since he understood that as we grow in grace, we grow in self-knowledge (*viz.*, true repentance); but he always stressed that repentance was also the work of the Holy Spirit and not a merely human act of remorse.

Between the 'early' and the 'mature' Wesley there is a great

[38] For Wesley's rejection of the idea of 'splendid sins', cf. No. 99, *The Reward of Righteousness*, I.4 and n.

[39] As in the 'standard sermon' No. 40, *Christian Perfection*, II. 4-24. It should also be noted that many of Wesley's followers also understood his doctrine as implying 'sinless perfection'; cf. John L. Peters, *Christian Perfection and American Methodism* (New York, Abingdon, 1956).

[40] Cf. *The Westminster Confession*, ix. 5: 'The will of man is made perfectly and immutably free to [do] the good alone, in the state of glory only (*non nisi in statu gloriae*);' see also xiii. 1.

[41] §§ II, IV. See Vol. 12 of this edn.

gulf fixed, by the transformations of 1738 and thereafter. The developments from the 'mature' Wesley to the 'late' are not so clearly marked. They are, however, considerable and important, and this is why the 'late Wesley' deserves so much more study than he has ever had. Even so, those developments that we can see did not constitute 'inconsistencies', *in his eyes*. Rather, as far as his intentions went, they express his unfolding understanding of the paradoxes of Christian insight. He scorned obscurantism in thought and rhetoric, but he took it for granted that the same truth spoken in love required different formulations in different circumstances. He was capable of short flights of speculation,[42] but he never supposed that the data of revelation could be conceptualized into a single system of coherent thought without ambiguous remainders. As long as he felt that a given formulation was in accordance with the general sense of Scripture and the winnowed wisdom of tradition, he believed that it was internally consistent with other formulations conceived in the same spirit. And this came from his conviction that it was the Holy Spirit who was leading all faithful Christians into all truth, even if not into identical formulations of it. Between 'The Circumcision of the Heart' and 'On the Wedding Garment' lie six lively decades of theological development. And yet, when they are read together, these two descriptions of the Christian life do not differ on any essential point. *That* is what Wesley meant by consistency.

V. WESLEY AND HIS SOURCES

IT is clear enough that Wesley never expected to be edited critically; it is even probable that he would have deplored such an exercise as pedantic.[1] His quotations are rarely exact and rarely identified; his allusions are casual and his borrowings acknowledged vaguely or not at all. His sermons were for his 'plain people', but he could also be casual with his citations before a

---

[42] As in his sermons 'On Eternity' and *On the Trinity* (Nos. 54, 55); note, however, his methodological distinction between the mysteries of revelation and all reductive rationalisms.

[1] His own view of the Christian's priorities is reflected in the exhortations he drew up for his 'Helpers': 'You have nothing to do but to save souls;' 'never be triflingly employed; . . . neither spend any more time at any place than is strictly necessary'. (Nos. 11 and 1 of his 'Twelve Rules of a Helper', in 'Large *Minutes*', Vol. 10 of this edn.) He also has a snide comment on William Derham's preoccupation with the classification of butterflies in County Essex when his first duty was the cure of souls in his parish in Upminster; see No. 78, 'Spiritual Idolatry', I. 14.

university audience.[2] His editors, by and large, have been content to reprint Wesley's texts as they stood in whatever edition they preferred.[3] The concern of this edition of the *Sermons* to reopen some of the critical questions posed by Wesley's texts *and* his use of sources may very well be tinged with a hubris of its own.

And yet it is a fact that Wesley was working against an immense background with a remarkable repertory. The core of his learning was basically sound and his use of sources is usually apt. The value of tracing them out lies in their contribution to a composite portrait of Wesley as a folk-theologian. It suggests a view of Wesley as a technically competent theologian with a remarkable power of creative simplification, a revivalist who took special pains to conceal his erudition in the interest of the edification of his particular audiences. If this meant oversimplification, he was well content.[4] The untoward outcome of all this, however, is that Wesley's success at concealment has actually encouraged both his disciples and his critics to ignore the intricate mosaic that lies behind his plain-style prose. The result has been a general underestimation of Wesley's actual stature as a theologian and, therefore, of his place in the transition from Protestant orthodoxy to 'modernity', and of his relevance in later ages. Yet another unfortunate side-effect of this has been the denominationalization of Wesley studies, with no more than a handful of exceptions.[5]

[2] E.g., in his sermons on 'Hypocrisy in Oxford' (Nos. 150-51) he misquotes the 'Statutes of the University' to men who either knew them from memory or could readily have checked the texts.

[3] A partial exception here was the Canadian scholar, Nathaniel Burwash, *Wesley's Doctrinal Standards . . . with Introductions, Analysis, and Notes* (1909); this follows Thomas Jackson's order for the first 'fifty-*two* standard sermons', but is addressed almost exclusively to the quasi-legal functions of the sermons in Methodist theology. A more fully annotated edn. was published in 1921 by an Australian Methodist, E. H. Sugden (see above, p. 3, n. 6) but, again, Sugden's interest was focused on the legal status of the 'mature Wesley's' sermons (the others are quietly ignored) and his annotations are largely for Methodist eyes only. Since Jackson's time, no new edn. of the sermon corpus has appeared.

[4] In his Preface (1746), § 4: 'My design is in some sense to forget all that ever I have read in my life. I mean to speak, in the general, as if I had never read one author, ancient or modern (always excepting the inspired). I am persuaded that . . . this may be a means of enabling me more clearly to express the sentiments of my heart, . . . without entangling myself with [the thoughts] of other men.'

Note the echoes here and elsewhere from William Perkins, *The Art of Prophesying*, ch. x: 'Human wisdom must be concealed, whether it be in the matter of the sermon or in the setting forth of the words. . . .'

[5] Southey's *Wesley* is still one of the few produced by an eminent literary figure, but he

This means, therefore, that the task of source-tracings in the Wesley corpus is still closer to its bare beginnings than one might wish, and it is both a formidable and frustrating business. The data are insufficient, the clues too meagre, the methods thus far developed too haphazard. Yet even such a beginning as is represented here may set out the thesis (requiring further study for its verification) that Wesley lived and worked in a plurality of cultural worlds with little self-consciousness about their pluralism and with next to no distraction from his chief business as the spiritual director of the Methodist Revival. In retrospect, however, this 'plurality of worlds' can be identified with some clarity. There was, of course, the biblical world, but there was the classical world as well, in which Wesley shared a citizenship along with all the other cultivated people of his age. Beyond these, however, he also felt at home in the world of historic Christianity, especially in the patristic age, but in its medieval extensions also. Interestingly enough, his knowledge of the continental Reformation and the so-called Counter Reformation did not reach far past the commonplaces of seventeenth and eighteenth-century church history. When we come to British Christianity, however, and its tangled history of controversy and polarization, his resources are truly remarkable: here is much grist for well-furnished experts.

But Wesley's 'worlds' were not all 'theological'. He had read enough English literature to use it freely and to form quite confident value-judgments about it that dissented from the fashions of his time and those of ours as well. Moreover, he was widely and well read in most aspects of the intellectual, cultural (and industrial and economic) transitions of his century, and was able to bring much of this to his task as tutor to the uninstructed folk in his societies.

was scarcely able to estimate Wesley's theological background, even if he had been interested in it. Alexander Knox understood it much better and appreciated it much more; see above, p. 62. In later times both Maximin Piette, *John Wesley in the Evolution of Protestantism* (New York, Sheed and Ward, 1937), and John Murray Todd, *John Wesley and the Catholic Church* (London, Hodder and Stoughton, 1958), have recognized the Catholic elements in Wesley's heritage. Martin Schmidt's massive theological biography is excellent as far as it goes, but it scarcely glances at the final third of Wesley's career: see *John Wesley: A Theological Biography* (Nashville, Abingdon Press, 1963, 1972, 1973 [two vols. in three]). A promising sample of what it would mean for Wesley to be studied in an ecumenical context may be seen in Kenneth Rowe, ed., *The Place of Wesley in the Christian Tradition*. By and large, however, the agenda in Wesley studies has been of, by, and for Methodists, and their implicit claims to a proprietary right has been too readily conceded to them by non-Methodists.

The attempted recovery of this complex array of sources is, therefore, much more than an exercise in historical curiosity. It displays Wesley in new dimensions; it makes it possible to read between his lines; it helps make sense of his eclectic aims and method; it illuminates his theological options at a level beyond his bare texts. The richer one's knowledge of this half-hidden mosaic, the more nearly full-orbed one's view of Wesley's mind and heart might be.

Holy Scripture

It would be redundant to say more about Wesley's self-understanding as a biblical theologian. A few added comments on his actual use of Scripture might, however, be in order. He knew it so nearly by heart that even his natural speech is biblical.[6] Unsurprisingly, judging by the texts from which he preached, the Gospel according to St. Matthew was his favourite book (1362 recorded usages); this, however, is followed by Hebrews (965), John (870), Luke (853), and 1 Cor. (779). His Old Testament favourite, again unsurprisingly, was Isaiah (668 citations), followed by the Psalms (624) and Jeremiah (208). His favourite New Testament preaching text was Mark 1:15 (190 usages), followed by 2 Cor. 8:9 (167), Eph. 2:8 (133), Gal. 6:14 (129), and Matt.16:26 (117). His favourite sermon text in the Old Testament was Isa. 55:7 (112 usages); this was followed by Jer. 8:22 (102), Isa. 55:6 (90),[7] Hos. 14:4 (87 times) and Ps. 147:3 (72 times). He could find the gospel even in the Wisdom literature, as in Eccles. 9:10 (55 times), and Prov. 3:17 (36 times). There are six books in the Old Testament from which he never preached:

---

[6] Many of his sentences are deft fusions of the biblical language and his own. For samplings of complete paragraphs that have more biblical texts in them than Wesley's own words and that still read quite smoothly, cf. Nos. 4, *Scriptural Christianity*, IV. 9; 22, 'Sermon on the Mount, II', III. 18; 44, *Original Sin*, § 4; and 107, 'On God's Vineyard', I.9.

From 1738 Wesley had Alexander Cruden's *Concordance*, which he speaks of as 'undoubtedly the best which hath yet been published in the English tongue'. In 1760 he published a very brief concordance (ten sheets) by John Fisher, one of his own preachers (see *Bibliog*, No. 516). In 1782 he published an abridgement of Cruden's 3rd edn. by another of his preachers, Thomas Taylor (*Bibliog*, No. 565). In addition to Cruden, he had access to some seventeen New Testament concordances, from John Marbeck (1550) to Matthew Pilkington (1749). The most popular of these was John Downame's (1630) which went through numerous edns. By middle life, however, he had become a walking concordance himself; cf., e.g., No. 75, 'On Schism', I. 9 and n.

[7] If the Isaianic texts in 55:6-7 are combined, the total comes to 202.

Ezra, Esther, Song of Solomon, Obadiah, Nahum, and Zephaniah. And while he seems never to have taken an apocryphal text for a sermon, his citations from the Apocrypha are frequent enough (e.g., from the Wisdom of Solomon) to suggest that his notion of the canon was more 'catholic' than 'protestant'.[8] In any case, it is clear that Wesley's sense of Scripture was organic and integrated.

His mastery of the κοινή Greek was thorough enough so that he read the New Testament in the Erasmian *textus receptus* for both devotion and study. He was, in fact, self-confident enough about his linguistic prowess that he could strike out on his own with independent translations and exegeses.[9] His knowledge of Hebrew seems to have been nominal,[10] but his interest in the medieval rabbinical commentators is more detailed than that of most of his contemporaries.[11] As for the Bible in English, his enthusiasm for the Authorized Version of 1611[12] (which he spoke of as 'our recent translation') was never better than lukewarm. But since it was so familiar and readily accessible, he used it more often than any other, and encouraged its use among his people. But he knew the other English translations also;[13] we are reminded of his rectory upbringing by the fact that when he quotes a Psalm, it is almost invariably from the Psalter of the Book of Common Prayer (which is also to say from the 'Great Bible' of Coverdale of 1539). In this edition we have attempted a visual display in the footnotes of Wesley's way with Scripture. This may deserve a special notice in the history of hermeneutics; at the very least it is a demonstration that Wesley's claim to being *homo unius libri* cannot be tested (or even fully understood) without close attention to the interactions of the rhetoric of Scripture and the rhetoric and substance of these sermons.

[8] Cf. No. 41, *Wandering Thoughts*, II.3 and n.

[9] E.g., his *Notes*, and No. 16, 'The Means of Grace', III. 17.

[10] Cf. Nos. 25, 'Sermon on the Mount, V', IV. 2; and 26 'Sermon on the Mount, VI', III. 7.

[11] Cf. No. 36, 'The Law Established through Faith, II', I. 3 and n.; see also No. 66, 'The Signs of the Times', I. 2, where Wesley seems to know more than Matthew Poole about the medieval rabbinical interpretations of Gen. 49:10 (cf. Poole, *Annotations, loc. cit.*).

[12] Cf. No. 82, 'On Temptation', I. 1; see also No. 103, 'What is Man?, Ps. 8: 3-4', II. 4: 'The new translation of the Psalms, that is bound up in our Bible, is perhaps more proper than the old, that which we have in the Common Prayer Book.'

[13] There was nothing in the eighteenth century to match Samuel Bagster's *The English Hexapla, Exhibiting the Six Important English Translations* (1841), and yet Wesley seems to have had a competent working acquaintance with those same translations.

The Classics

Wesley's biblical world was, however, no enclave. *Sola scriptura* was never a displacement of, or substitute for, classical learning; and this was natural enough in view of the fact that he had mastered the baseline curriculum of his Oxford education and had come to cherish the classical tradition as the font of Western civilization.[14] He was an accomplished Latinist before he turned to theology as a special study;[15] his grounding in classical Greek was at least adequate. Even as age wore on, he continued to quote the classics without checking the originals; indeed, his later sermons are more ornamented with such tags than the earlier ones.[16] There is a charming vignette of Wesley in his old age in the memoirs of Madame Sophie de la Roche, a cultivated German noblewoman visiting England in 1786. She recalls having Mr.

[14] Wesley's awareness of the bitter debates between the critics and advocates of the classical curriculum in the seventeenth century is crucial; it explains his concern to set the debate on a higher level; cf. Nos. 4, *Scriptural Christianity*, IV. 6 ('without love all learning is but splendid ignorance'); 87, 'The Danger of Riches', I. 15; 109, *The Trouble and Rest of Good Men*, II. 7; 146, 'The One Thing Needful', III. 1. But see also his *Address to the Clergy* (1756), I. 3-6, *et passim*; cf. his letters to Dr. Thomas Rutherforth, Mar. 28, 1768 (§§ II. 2, 10), and to Bishop Robert Lowth (London), Aug. 10, 1780. For the seventeenth-century debate, see the exchanges between William Dell (against classical curriculum), as in *The Trial of the Spirits . . . and The Right Reformation of Learning* (1653), and Sydrach Simpson (for it) as in his Cambridge Commencement sermon of the same year. See also Samuel How, *The Sufficiency of the Spirit's Teaching Without Humane Learning: Or, A Treatise Tending to Prove Humane Learning to be No Help to the Spiritual Understanding of the Word of God . . .* (1640). Christopher Hill has a lively and sympathetic summary of this controversy in *The World Turned Upside Down* (New York, Viking Press, 1971), pp. 241-46.

[15] This can be seen in the rhetorical sophistication of his Latin sermon, No. 151, 'Hypocrisy in Oxford'; see also his transcription of an informal debate with Count Ludwig von Zinzendorf in JWJ, Sept. 3, 1741. The style of the *sermon* is much more elevated than that of the *debate*. Henry Moore must have had it from John Wesley himself when he reported (II.103): 'In the year 1731 the two brothers began the practice of conversing together in Latin, whenever they were alone, chiefly with a view of acquiring a facility in expressing themselves in this language on all occasions with perspicuity, energy, and elegance. This practice they continued for nearly sixty years; and with such success that if their style did not equal, it certainly on some subjects approached nearer to the best model of conversation in the Augustan age than many of the learned have thought it possible to attain.' See also Wesley's correspondence with Dr. Jan de Koker (a physician at Rotterdam), in JWJ, June 14, 1738, and Nov. 10, 1749; cf. JWJ, Aug. 10, 1738 (while at Herrnhut): 'I had an opportunity of spending some hours with Christian David. . . . Most of his words I understood well; if at any time I did not, one of the brethren who went with me explained them in Latin.'

[16] One of the indications that he was not relying on anthologies and florilegia is the fact that his quotations are so generally inexact. If he had been using something like, say, Herbert's *Jacula Prudentum*, one would have expected more exact copying.

Wesley pointed out to her in the salon of the ship in which they both were sailing from Rotterdam to Harwich:

> Wesley sat and read Virgil, with spectacles, in an Elzevir edition. Heavens! I thought, if the Methodists' principles keep their sight as clear as that to the age of 83, then I wish I had been educated in their sect; for since their chief reads Virgil on the high seas, I too might have read my favourite works without damnation.[17]

His Methodist readers would scarcely have been impressed by more than the bare fact of Wesley's classical culture, but some of them would have been reassured by this evidence that his academic credentials were still in good standing. They were, however, more edified than they realized by this unadvertised alliance between sound learning and vital piety. In Wesley's own case this classical orientation was very much more than ostentation; it was an integral element in his theological perspective. He knew how deeply classical culture had shaped patristic Christianity.[18] He also knew how decisively, even in his own time, its *re*discovery was reshaping the emergent Enlightenment in Europe. The Graeco-Roman legacy was a living resource for his Christian understanding, representing, as it did to him, an impressive demonstration of the grandeur and misery of 'pagan' culture at its best and worst. Some of the implications of this soteriological outlook become apparent in his exegesis—as, for example, his comments on Acts 14:15-17 ('the living God . . . who left not himself without witness . . .') and on Rom. 1:18-32 and elsewhere when he speaks of his conviction that God's providence has room in it for the salvation of 'heathens'.[19]

---

[17] *Sophie in London, 1786*, Eng. tr. by Clare Williams (1933), p. 78.

[18] One can imagine how delighted he would have been with C. N. Cochrane's *Christianity and Classical Culture* (London, Oxford University Press, 1944); one can also guess at some of his critical reservations.

[19] It was, indeed, the chief presupposition of his agreement with the old monastic epigram, *Qui facientes quod in se est*, which the nominalists also espoused and which Luther had denounced so violently. Cf. Wesley's Oxford Diary, V, [vi]: 'Q. How steer between scrupulosity, as to particular instances of self-denial and self-indulgence? A. *Fac quod in te est, et Deus aderit bonae tuae voluntati.*' Cf. also Nos. 85, 'On Working Out Our Own Salvation', III. 6-7; 66, 'The Signs of the Times', II. 10; 63, 'The General Spread of the Gospel', § 9; 69, 'The Imperfection of Human Knowledge', § 1; and 75, 'On Schism', § 21.

See also, Heiko A. Oberman, *Harvest of Medieval Theology* (Cambridge, Mass., Harvard University Press, 1963), pp. 129-45; Albert C. Outler, 'Methodism's Theological

Besides, he understood that a classical education tends to breed up in men and women a love of graceful speech and style; he had had good reason to appreciate this in his own family.[20]

In the sermons (and elsewhere, too) Wesley's favourite classical source was Horace; there are twenty-seven quotations from him in the sermons alone, some repeated in different contexts. One senses that he read Virgil with more personal pleasure, but he quotes from him only twenty-one times. Ovid follows with ten, Cicero with nine, Juvenal with seven. Thirteen others are quoted at least once: Aristophanes, Hadrian, Homer, Lucan, Lucretius, Persius, Pindar, Sophocles, Suetonius, Symmachus, Terence, Velleius Paterculus.

This display was more than mere ornamentation; within these borrowings we can find the germs of some of Wesley's most distinctive general ideas (e.g., his participation theme, his mind-body dualism, and his ideas about psycho-physical parallelism). These are major sources for his notions about human nature, human volition, and the human passions. Out of this heritage had come his predilection for form over raw feelings, his concept of conscience as a universal moral sense. Plato had bolstered his convictions about the ontological primacy of good over evil. The whole of the Graeco-Roman tradition had stressed coherence as a criterion of rationality. Besides, these ancient authors were shrewd critics of human folly; thus Wesley found in them discerning witnesses to the flaws in contemporary proposals about 'natural' theology and ethics. It was in this sense that his long dialogue with the ancients was a genuine *preparatio evangelica*; one might even suppose that he might still commend it as such.

Heritage: A Study in Perspective', in *Methodism's Destiny in an Ecumenical Age*, Paul Minus, Jr., ed. (New York, Abingdon Press, 1969), pp. 52-60; and Michael Hurley, 'Salvation Today and Wesley Today', in Kenneth E. Rowe, ed., *The Place of Wesley in the Christian Tradition*, pp. 94-116.

[20] There was, however, an early outburst against classical learning in a letter to his brother Samuel (himself an instructor in classics at Westminster School), Oct. 15, 1735 (written aboard the *Simmonds* en route to Georgia): 'Elegance of style is not to be weighed against purity of heart; . . . Therefore whatever has any tendency to impair that purity is not to be tolerated. . . . But of this sort . . . are the most of the classics usually read in the great schools . . . . I beseech you, therefore, . . . that you banish all such poison from your school.' This was, of course, not a settled view; cf. the strong emphasis on classical studies in the curriculum of John's own school at Kingswood; cf. A. G. Ives, *Kingswood School in Wesley's Day and Since* (London, Epworth Press, 1970), espec. pp. 1-106, and Appendix III, for the 'advanced course' and books placed by Wesley in the library at Kingswood.

Christian Antiquity

Wesley had a powerful sense of constancy within the turbulent experience of the Christian community through the centuries; this explains in part his lifelong interest in church history. He took it for granted and proceeded to re-enter the Christian past in order to appropriate its best treasures for his own time, because, amidst all historical change, he saw an essential continuity that had perdured. This, for him, was the essence of 'tradition'. He understood it as having been most clearly focused in the early centuries ('Christian antiquity'). Moreover, he believed it had developed in a more stable fashion within the Greek Orthodoxy than in the Latin West. His interest in patrology was more of a curiosity; his time at Oxford had coincided with the waning of one of its great epochs of patristic learning.[21] For all his life, thereafter, Wesley lived with these Fathers as mentors and contemporaries. In his baggage for Georgia he had included William Beveridge's ponderous folios of patristic texts (all eighteen pounds of them in their two volumes) and had used them as authorization for some of those unwelcome liturgical experiments that he tried on his ungrateful parishioners in Savannah.[22] But he learned much more from Eastern spirituality than liturgy. He found there a distinctive pneumatology which became the shaping force in all his later ideas about mysticism ('will-mysticism' versus 'unitive mysticism'). Here is the font of Wesley's most distinctive ideas about prevenient grace and human freedom and, most crucially, of his peculiar doctrine of perfection as τελείωσις (perfecting perfection) rather than *perfectus* (perfected perfection).

Early on, he was challenged to describe the ideal Christian, and did so under the ironic title, *The Character of a Methodist*.[23] What

---

[21] This epoch was signalized by the great edn. of St. Cyprian's *Opera* by John Fell, Dean of Christ Church and afterwards Bishop of Oxford, and assisted by Henry Dodwell and John Pearson (1682; Eng. tr. by Nathaniel Marshall, Oxford, 1717), by William Beveridge's *Synodikon*, and by the pioneering work of Edward Pococke. It was true, as V. H. H. Green says in *The Young Mr. Wesley*, pp. 33, 37, that scholarly interests in Oxford were in a general decline in the 1720s and 1730s, but this great tradition had not died, and Wesley is a useful case in point.

[22] See JWJ, Sept. 13-20, 1736; see also Mar. 5, 1736, Aug. 1736 (Curnock, I. 386), for the 'List of Grievances presented by the Grand Jury for Savannah'. The first of these is that '. . . the said Revd. person . . . deviates from the principles and regulations of the Established Church. . . . *Prima*, by inverting the order and method of the Liturgy . . .'. Then follow eleven specific allegations of such deviations.

[23] 1742, *Bibliog*, No. 57, Vol. 9 of this edn.

he had done, with no sense of incongruity, was to turn to the Seventh Book of the *Stromateis* of Clement of Alexandria, take its description of the 'true Gnostic', and update it for the eighteenth century. His basic idea of the 'order of salvation'—as the process of the restoration of the image of God—is obviously an adaptation from St. Irenaeus's famous doctrine of ἀνακεφαλαίωσις (i.e., the recapitulatory work of Christ as the ground of all salvation). His central theme (divine-human participation) was learned in large part from Macarius, Gregory of Nyssa, and Ephrem Syrus.[24] His concept of Christian κοινονία was more Greek than Latin, and this explains his freedom to correct what he regarded as the excessive sacerdotalism within the Anglican ecclesiology that he had inherited. At the center of all these ideas was his understanding of the person and work of the Holy Spirit as God's personal presence in the believer's heart and will, and in the Spirit filled community and its sacraments. This enabled him to think of the Christian believer as indwelt and led by the Spirit within rather than being possessed by the Spirit as if by some irresistible force. He could, therefore, repudiate the charges of 'enthusiasm' brought against him, for he understood their mistaken assumptions as to what 'enthusiasm' really means.[25] Similarly, it was this Eastern Orthodoxy that helped save him from any temptation to the more conventional forms of 'unitive mysticism'.[26] Thus, just as he could refocus the will-mysticism of Scupoli, Scougal, and Bona, he also felt free to reinterpret the 'unitive mysticism' of such devout souls as Antoinette Bourignon, Madame Guyon, and De Renty.[27]

This distinctive view of the person and work of the Holy Spirit provides us with many a clue to aspects of Wesley's thought that are otherwise puzzling. Here, for example, is the source of his

[24] See Outler, *Wesley*, pp. 9-15.

[25] See No. 37, 'The Nature of Enthusiasm'.

[26] Which he knew in the teachings of Eckhardt and Tauler and others. Cf. also his criticism of Luther's *Commentary on Galatians* in JWJ, June 15, 1741: 'He [Luther] is deeply tinctured with *mysticism* throughout, and hence often fundamentally wrong. . . . How does he (almost in the words of Tauler) decry *reason* . . . , how blasphemously does he speak of *good works* . . . !'

[27] Cf. Jean Orcibal, 'The Theological Originality of John Wesley . . .', pp. 83-111 (see p. 36, n. 29 above). See also Robert Tuttle, *Wesley*, pp. 218-27, 330-45; but cf. Evelyn Underhill, *Mysticism* (London, Methuen and Co., 1911), Pt. III, ch. x. All of these have tended to deny the crucial distinction already made by W. R. Inge, *Christian Mysticism* (London, Methuen and Co., 1899), between the active and passive approaches to 'union'. Quite to the contrary, Wesley's own mysticism was self-consciously *dialectical*.

distinction between the irresistible sovereignty of God as *Creator* and the resistibility of the Spirit's prevenient action.[28] It is this pneumatology that lies at the heart of Wesley's visions of perfection; and it helps explain why his version of this doctrine was so readily misunderstood by persons long accustomed to the forensic orientations in Latin soteriology. In this older tradition, sanctification ('holiness', 'perfection in love') could be seen as the 'plerophory' (fullness) of faith. Thus also, the dominical command, 'Be ye perfect', could be seen as the covered promise that grace *can* triumph over sin. But the faith that generates holiness is itself a relationship that continues and grows in this life—in a dynamic process that is nuanced differently from any Latin concept of perfection as an achieved *state*. It was no accident, then, that Wesley regarded Montanus as having been misunderstood and maligned; he even thought that Pelagius had been slandered by St. Augustine.[29] His choice of Macarius's *Homilies* to stand in Volume I of the *Christian Library* (after the writings of Clement, Ignatius, and Polycarp) was symbolic; his references to St. Chrysostom, St. Cyprian, Tertullian, St. Athanasius suggest a long-standing familiarity. The result was that Wesley felt very much at home in 'Christian antiquity' and quite free to make full use of this resource in his own right.

From the Age of the Fathers to the English Reformation

Wesley's direct knowledge of church history from the fifth to the sixteenth centuries turns out to be no better than nominal. This may be explained partly by an Oxford curriculum which scarcely noticed the so-called Middle Ages; but there was also Wesley's conviction that the whole stretch of church history from what he regarded as the Constantinian 'Fall of the Church'[30] all

---

[28] A distinction already implicit in the canons of the Second Council of Orange (Arausiacum, 529); cf. Reinhold Seeberg, *Textbook of the History of Doctrines*, tr. by Charles E. Hay (Grand Rapids, Michigan, Baker Book House, 1954), I. 380-85. Wesley relies on it constantly; it is at the heart of the notion of prevenience, but see his comments on *Thoughts Concerning the Origin of Power* (1772), his *Thoughts Upon Necessity* (1774), and the opening paragraphs of *Predestination Calmly Considered* (1752).

[29] Cf. No. 68, 'The Wisdom of God's Counsels', § 7; see also 'The Real Character of Montanus' (*AM*, 1785, 35-36). For a showcase of Wesley's patristic knowledge, cf. his open *Letter to the Reverend Dr. Conyers Middleton*, 1749 (*Bibliog*, No. 160, Vol. 13 of this edn.), espec. §§ 3-12. For a critical analysis that tends to support Wesley's views on this point, see Robert Evans, *Pelagius: Inquiries and Reappraisals* (New York, Seabury Press, 1968), chs. 5–6.

[30] See No. 61, 'The Mystery of Iniquity', § 27 and n.

the way to the sixteenth-century reformations had been a retrograde epoch at best. We have noted his debt to the popular piety of medieval England[31] and his conviction that the Edwardian *Homilies* were normative for Anglican doctrine. We know also that he had read Thomas Fuller's vivid *Church History of Britain* (1656) along with Peter Heylyn's *Historia Quinquarticularis* (1659). Both had helped confirm him in his preference for the Anglican tradition over any other.[32]

He was stoutly anti-Papist, and never changed his childhood conviction that Roman Catholics were still committed, on principle, to intolerance and to the subversion of English liberties.[33] In 1756 he published, without acknowledgement, his own abridgement of Bishop John Williams's *A Roman Catechism, Together With a Reply Thereto*,[34] and he knew both *The Canons of the Council of Trent* and also the *Catechism* published in that council's name by Pope Pius V.[35] What he may have known but not fully

[31] See above, pp. 18-19.

[32] See No. 33, 'Sermon on the Mount, XIII', III. 1 ('so excellent a Church, reformed after the true Scripture model, blessed with the purest doctrine, the most primitive liturgy, the most apostolical form of government'); and his letter to Sir Harry Trelawney, Aug. 1780 ('Having had an opportunity of seeing several of the Churches abroad and having deeply considered the several sorts of Dissenters at home, I am fully convinced that our own Church, with all her blemishes, is nearer the scriptural plan than any other in Europe.') See also No. 13, *On Sin in Believers*, I. 3 and n., and below, pp. 87-88.

[33] Cf. No. 127, 'On the Wedding Garment', § 13 and n. Note Wesley's dictum in his letter to *The Public Advertiser*, Jan. 21, 1780: 'It is a Roman Catholic maxim, established not by private men but by a public Council, that "no faith is to be kept with heretics".... The members of that Church can give no reasonable security to any government of their allegiance or peaceable behaviour.' The Council in question was Constance (1414-18), where Jerome of Prague and Jan Hus had been burned for heresy despite safe-conducts issued them by the Emperor Sigismund. But this so-called maxim of Constance had been fixed upon it by its Protestant critics; there is no such statement (or inference) in the conciliar records themselves. Incidentally, this was the Council that deliberately refused to approve the doctrine of the moral right of 'tyrannicide' even by private citizens, as advocated by Johannes Parvus and Johan von Falkenberg. In view of the permission of reginacide in Pius V's excommunication of Elizabeth I (*Regnans in excelsis*, 1570), most English Protestants (and Wesley with them) were convinced that Roman Catholics were disloyal citizens, *ex professo*. This helps explain Wesley's passive complicity in the 'Gordon Riots' of 1778.

[34] *Bibliog*, No. 217.

[35] There were numerous edns. of the *Acta et Decreta* of the Council, from the first official edn. of the complete set (Rome, 1564) to Wesley's time; the Bodleian had both the Antwerp edn. (1694) and Cologne (1722), besides many earlier ones. The first Eng. tr. had been published in 1687. The *Catechism*, drafted under the guidance of Pius IV, was completed and published by his successor, Pius V; it was published even more widely and more often than the *Acta*. In addition, Wesley knew Paolo Sarpi's widely popular, but heavily tendentious, *History of the Council of Trent* (1619).

realized was that his own understanding of 'the *causes* of justification' tilted more toward the original proposals at Trent (Seripando, Contarini, Pole) than they did to those of the High Calvinists, especially on the crucial issue of justification's 'causes': *viz.*, whether Christ's atoning death was its formal or meritorious cause.[36] There is no record of Wesley's ever having read Bellarmine; we cannot tell how much better than common knowledge was his acquaintance with the famous *'De auxiliis'* controversy between the Dominicans and the Jesuits over grace and free will.[37] A direct comparison of Wesley's doctrine of justification with Bellarmine's *De Justificatione* (1601) is, therefore, all the more instructive, especially on the point of their shared view that justification effects both a relative and a real change in the believer.[38] Had he known it, he would have applauded the intention behind Philip Melanchthon's translation of the Augsburg Confession into Greek for the benefit of the Byzantines, where he chooses to translate *justificare* as ἁγιάζεσθαι rather than δικαιοῦσθαι (i.e., 'to make holy' rather than 'to make just').[39] In the same sermon in which Wesley finally came down firmly on the side of Christ's death as the meritorious, rather than formal, cause of our justification there is a sympathetic story about Bellarmine and his 'dying words'.[40] Bishop Lavington had been wrong in his invidious comparison of the Methodists and Papists;[41] what he had recognized, even if also

[36] The most credible account of the tragic process of the Tridentine debates has been provided by Hubert Jedin in three remarkable chs. in his *History of the Council of Trent* (London, Thomas Nelson and Sons, 1961), Vol. II (ch. v, 'The Opening of the Debate on Justification'; ch. vii, 'The September Draft [1546]'; and ch. viii, 'Completion of the Decree on Justification'). All that Wesley could have known of the official transactions of Trent, however, was the final result in the *Acta et Decreta*, which was rigidly anti-Lutheran. Jedin shows how close the 'progressives' at Trent had come to a doctrine of justification by grace—i.e., by faith, hope, and love alone—but *without* antecedent merit. Cf. Bellarmine, *De Controversiis . . .* (1601), IV. 934-36, *'Explicantur causae justificatione';* see also Wesley's 'A Disavowal of Persecuting Papists' (*AM*, 1782, 197-200, Vol. 13 of this edn.).

[37] Precipitated by Luis de Molina's *Concordia liberi arbitrii cum gratiae donis . . .* (Lisbon, 1588); in 1597 a '*Congregatio De Auxiliis'* was appointed by Clement VIII to adjudicate and settle the question. Their efforts continued, without success, till 1606. In 1609 the work was suspended by Paul V with a stipulation that no further discussions of 'efficacious grace' were to be published without express authorization by the Holy See.

[38] Cf. Bellarmine, *'De Justificatione'*, I. ii, in *De Controversiis*; see also No. 43, *The Scripture Way of Salvation*, I. 4 and n.

[39] Cf. Jaroslav Pelikan, *The Christian Tradition: A History of the Development of Christian Doctrine* (Chicago, University of Chicago Press, 1974), II. 281.

[40] No. 20, *The Lord Our Righteousness*, II. 4.

[41] *The Enthusiasm of Methodists and Papists Compared*; see above, p. 3, n. 11.

distortedly, was a limited affinity between Wesley's soteriology and that held by the more moderate of the Roman Catholic reformers.[42]

The Anglican and Puritan Traditions

Wesley's clearest competence in church history, however, begins with seventeenth century Britain; his most vivid sense of personal involvement focused on the tragic conflicts between the Puritans and the Anglicans. Unsurprisingly, then, this period —from 'the Elizabethan Settlement' (1552–60) to the death of Queen Anne (1714)—provided him with his richest storehouse of sources. We have already seen how he tried to hold this unstable heritage in equilibrium with his pairings of Cranmer and Barnes.[43] In the Preface to the *Christian Library* he pays smug tribute to his national tradition: 'There is not in the world a more complete body of practical divinity than is now extant in the English tongue, in the writings of the last and the present century' (§1). Even a brief survey of Wesley's selections in that *Library* suggests an extraordinary range of reading together with a consistent editorial bias.[44] Later, in the *Arminian Magazine*, his horizons open out even more widely, always with an eye for suitable instructions for his own people and ammunition for their continuing skirmishes with the Calvinists.[45]

Wesley had been reading Anglican and Puritan divinity in Oxford, and maybe before. He knew the Anglican titans: Richard Hooker, Henry Hammond, Joseph Mede, George Bull, John Pearson, William Beveridge, John Tillotson. But he had a special fondness for the lesser lights whom we shall notice presently. He knew the great Puritans equally well: William Ames, William

---

[42] One may wonder how Wesley would have adjudged such a restatement of Roman Catholic views of justification as that of Hans Küng, *Justification: The Doctrine of Karl Barth and a Catholic Reflection* (New York, Thomas Nelson, 1964), with its stress on *sola fide*; or, for that matter, how he would have appraised the 'secret histories' of Trent as now displayed in Jedin, *op. cit.*, and John Dolan, *History of the Reformation: A Conciliatory Assessment* (New York, Desclée, 1964). We know now, as Wesley could not have, that there were many reformers (Catholic and Protestant) who had already laid out the principles of grace and free will which he had then developed in ways not greatly different from his own.

[43] See above, p. 56, n. 2.

[44] See above, p. 26, n. 56.

[45] The editorial policy of the *AM* is accurately indicated by its first sub-title: *Consisting of Extracts and Original Treatises on Universal Redemption*. This would be altered in Vol. VIII (1785) to 'consisting *chiefly* of . . .'.

Perkins, John Davenant, Richard Baxter, John Goodwin, John Bunyan, Isaac Ambrose, Isaac Watts. Out of this jumble, and with his Eastern pneumatology as his key, Wesley had developed a soteriology which presents, as Professor John Deschner has rightly noticed, a 'new emphasis in Protestant theology up to his time'.[46] In this, therapeutic metaphors[47] tend to outweigh the forensic ones that had dominated Western traditions since Anselm. In this perspective it is the Holy Spirit who communicates all the graces of the Father and the Son, especially 'preventing grace': 'all the "drawings" of "the Father", the desires after God, which, if we yield to them, increase more and more; all that "light" wherewith the Son of God "enlighteneth every one that cometh into the world"....; all the *convictions* which his Spirit . . . works in every child of man'.[48] This is why he was so strongly convinced that the much vaunted disjunction between the *imputed* righteousness of Christ (the ground of our justification) and his *imparted* righteousness (the Spirit's work in regeneration) posed a false alternative. The order of salvation, as Wesley had come to see it, is an organic continuum: conscience, conviction of sin, repentance, reconciliation, regeneration, sanctification, glorification. All of these are progressive stages in the divine design to restore the image of God in human selves and society.

Wesley's theology was elliptical in its form. Its double foci were the doctrines of justification and sanctification in a special correlation—two aspects of a single gracious intention, but separated along a continuum of both time and experience. The problem in justification was how Christ's sufficient merits may be imputed to the penitent believer as the righteous ground for God's unmerited mercy (i.e., the formal cause of justification).[49] And it was on this point of formal cause that Wesley parted from

[46] Cf. *Wesley's Christology* (Dallas, Tex., Southern Methodist University Press, 1960), p. 185.

[47] Cf., e.g., his emphasis on salvation as 'healing', as in No. 13, *On Sin in Believers*, III. 8 and n.; see also No. 17, 'The Circumcision of the Heart', I. 5.

[48] Cf. No. 43, *The Scripture Way of Salvation*, I. 2.

[49] See below, No. 20, *The Lord Our Righteousness*, II. 9-12 and n. This issue of 'causality' was crucial for both Puritans and Wesley; cf. C. F. Allison, *The Rise of Moralism* (New York, Seabury Press, 1966). The sticking point was that all theories of 'formal causality' entailed the notion of irresistible grace; Wesley's rejection of this was already implied in both his pneumatology and his doctrine of grace. This was grounded in the tradition established by Caesarius of Arles and the Second Council of Orange (520) to the effect that grace is an *infusio et operatio* of the Holy Spirit and is, therefore, in a profound mystery,

the Calvinists. They had stressed the Father's elective will, the prime link in 'a golden chain' of logic which led them link by link to the famous 'Five Points' of High Calvinism.[50] Wesley tilted the balance the other way because of his sense of the importance of the Holy Spirit's prevenient initiative in all the 'moments' of the *ordo salutis*. He could thus make room for human participation in reaction to the Spirit's activity and for human resistance as well—yet always in a very different sense from any Pelagian, or even 'Semi-Pelagian', doctrine of human initiative.[51] The result of this was an interesting distinction between efficacious grace in all but not for all. This pneumatocentric soteriology had still further corollaries. One was the distinction between 'wilful' sins ('mortal' sins in the Catholic vocabulary) and 'sins of infirmity' or 'surprise' ('venial'). Another was the notion that assurance is never 'final' but may be forfeited by unrepented sins of any gravity, even venial ones.[52] A third corollary (Wesley's alternative to 'unconditional election') was a doctrine of covenant grace (echoing the famous covenant theology of Johannes Cocceius).[53] As a result, he could speak of 'the beautiful gradations of love' in faith's progress from its first assurance of God's pardoning grace all the way to its 'plerophory'.[54]

None of the elements in this special view of justification is

resistible; cf. Seeberg, *op. cit.*, I. 380-82. On this question Bellarmine and Wesley had, in effect, agreed that everything turns on prevenient grace as a specific activity of the Holy Spirit.

[50] Cf. William Perkins, *A Golden Chaine*. Match this with the nine Lambeth Articles (1595). Both of these statements antedate the Arminian controversy and the Synod of Dort. The 'Five Points' came to be listed in a familiar acronym, TULIP: *T*otal depravity, *U*nconditional election, *L*imited atonement, *I*rresistible grace, and the *P*erseverance of the saints.

[51] Cf. Seeberg, *op. cit.*, I. 375-85.

[52] For Wesley's most extended comment on this point, cf. *Predestination Calmly Considered*, §§ 78-79 (Vol. 12 in this edn.); but see also Sermon 1, *Salvation by Faith*, II. 4 and n.

[53] Namely, the biblical idea of God and man in dynamic interrelationship of divine action and human reaction, as in Cocceius's *Summa doctrinae de Foedere et Testamento Dei* (1648; enlarged edn., 1654). Cf. No. 6, 'The Righteousness of Faith', § 1 and n.

[54] Cf. No. 91, 'On Charity', II. 6: 'It is proper to observe here, first, what a beautiful gradation there is, each step rising above the other in the enumeration of those several things which some or other of those that are called Christians, and are usually accounted so, really believe will supply the absence of love. St. Paul begins at the lowest point, *talking well*, and advances step by step, every one rising higher than the preceding, till he comes to the highest of all. A step above eloquence is knowledge; faith is a step above this. Good works are a step above faith. And even above this, is suffering for righteousness' sake. Nothing is higher than this but Christian love—the love of our neighbour flowing from the love of God.' See also Wesley's letters to Arthur Keene, June 21, 1784, and to Thomas Olivers, Mar. 24, 1757.

original. But Wesley's assortment of sources for it is unprece-
dented—and so also is the way he compounded and simplified
their convergent agreements. It includes a cluster of men who
have long since dropped into undeserved oblivion: Hugh
Binning, William Allen, John Rawlet, William Reeves, Thomas
Grantham, John Plaifere, Samuel Harsnet, Valentine Nalson.[55]
With all these men Wesley shared an Anglican orthodoxy older
than Augsburg or Trent. But they, in turn, were scarcely more
than a supporting cast for his main sources: Joseph Mede;[56] John

[55] Binning was a brilliant Scottish theologian and preacher who had died young
(1627–53); his ideas on justification, in *The Common Principles of the Christian Religion.* . . .
(1659), *Several Sermons* . . . (1660), and *The Sinner's Sanctuary* . . . (1670), anticipate
Wesley's by a century. William Allen was a 'General Baptist' who published *The Glass of
Justification: Or the Work of Faith with Power* . . . in 1658; he 'conformed' in 1662 and
served as vicar of Bridgewater until his death in 1686. His phrase for 'the almost Christian'
was 'the *negative* Christian', and his distinction between the faith of *adherence* and the faith
of *confidence* is similar to Wesley's between 'adherence' and 'assurance'; so also are his
ideas of prevenience (p. 27) and of 'faith working by love' (pp. 31 ff.). Allen's soteriology
deserves a careful study in its own right. John Rawlet (1642–82) was a Cambridge trained
popular preacher in the north; his influence on Wesley came through his *Christian
Monitor, . . . An Earnest Exhortation to a Holy Dying* . . . (1689), which went through
twenty-five edns. before the end of the seventeenth century and was constantly reissued
throughout the eighteenth century. William Reeves (1667–1726) was another Cambridge
trained patrologist (vicar of Reading), who reinforced Wesley's sense of the normative
character of 'the undivided church'. Wesley had read his *Fourteen Sermons* in 1733 with
evident approval. Thomas Grantham (1634–92) was a self-educated 'General Baptist'
preacher in Lincolnshire whose habits of itinerancy and whose restorationist views in
Christianismus Primitivus (1678) turn up, duly adapted, in Wesley—as well as his notion of
justification by faith, *and love*. We have already noticed John Plaifere and the influence of
his *Appello Evangelium* on Wesley (see above, p. 27). Samuel Harsnet (1561–1631) was a
bellicose anti-Calvinist, a defender of Peter Baro against William Whitaker. The bulk of
his writings was unpublished in Wesley's lifetime; but he had read Harsnet's famous
anti-Puritan sermon preached at Paul's Cross in 1584. Valentine Nalson (1683–1723) was
a popular Yorkshire preacher; Wesley had recommended his *Twenty Sermons* (1724, 1737)
to his friends in their first 'Annual Conference' (MS Minutes, 1744, § 84—June 29,
Q. 14).

[56] Joseph Mede (1586–1638), Cambridge theologian whose main contribution to
Wesley's thought came from his 'Discourses', in *The Works of the Pious and Profoundly
Learned Joseph Mede*, published posthumously, 1677. In Discourse XXVI, pp. 113-15,
there is a passage on justification and sanctification that Wesley could have written, and
certainly subscribed to (e.g., p. 115: 'A saving and justifying faith is to believe [in Christ's
merits] so as to embrace and lay hold upon Christ for that end, to apply ourselves unto him
and rely upon him, that we may through him perform those works of obedience which God
hath promised to reward with eternal life'). Cf. Discourse XXXIV (p. 175) for a distinction
'between the Romanists and us' on *merit* and reward; see also Discourse XXXIX (pp.
213-15) on faith and good works. Mede's doctrine of repentance is developed in
Discourses XXXVIII and LXII; his distinction between 'the fundamentals of salvation'
and 'the fundamentals of ecclesiastical communion' (in a letter to Samuel Hartlib, Feb. 6,
1636) is one of Wesley's presuppositions in No. 39, 'Catholic Spirit'. See also Mede's
Clavis Apocalyptica (1627).

Pearson, whose exposition of the section on 'the Holy Ghost' in his *Exposition of the Creed* (1659) was one of Wesley's most important sources;[57] Richard Baxter;[58] John Goodwin;[59] and even Isaac Ambrose.[60] It would be an important study in itself to review 'the history of justification' in the thought of this galaxy and to show by critical comparison Wesley's indebtedness to them and to the tradition in which they all stand.

We have already noticed that the deeper roots of Wesley's doctrine of perfection run back into the early Fathers; they had been supplemented by the ideas of such mavericks of the Spirit as William of St. Thierry and Thomas à Kempis. But there had also been a similar tradition in Britain that Wesley knew and had appropriated. Beyond his childhood acquaintance with Scougal, Wesley had also discovered (in Georgia) the *Memoirs of . . . Thomas Halyburton* (1715),[61] and then later James Garden's *Comparative Theology* (1700), one of the few works in Scotland directly inspired by Antoinette Bourignon.[62] Moreover, there was

[57] See 4th edn., 1676, pp. 327-30, and Wesley's quotations from Pearson in *A Farther Appeal*, Pt. I, V. 22-23 (11:163-66 of this edn.). Cf. also Wesley's lavish praise of Pearson in his letter to Cradock Glascott, May 13, 1764.

[58] Baxter's influence in Wesley's thought was decisive, and deserves far more careful and detailed study than it has had thus far. On this point espec. cf. Baxter's remarkable retrospective of his own theological development and concerns placed at the end of Bk. I, Pt. I, of *Reliquae Baxterianae* (1696), pp. 124-38; see also its abridgement in the *Autobiography of Richard Baxter* (Everyman's Library, 1931), pp. 103-32.

[59] John Goodwin (1594?-1665), was a major Puritan source for Wesley's doctrine of justification, espec. his *Imputatio Fidei . . .* (1642). In 1765 Wesley extracted and published this as *A Treatise on Justification*, in connection with his controversies with James Hervey; this work he also included in his own collected *Works* (1771-74), Vols. XXII-III. Later (1780) he included an 'extract' of Goodwin's *Exposition of the Ninth Chapter of Romans* (1653) in *AM*, 1780, with the following prefatory 'advertisement': 'As many of my friends have long desired to see John Goodwin's *Exposition . . .* , and as the book is become so scarce that it is seldom to be found, I judge that [this extract] will be both acceptable and profitable to them.' Goodwin had been the Puritan vicar of St. Stephen's, in Coleman Street, London, a vigorous supporter of Parliament against the King and the Cavaliers and, later, a Nonconformist—still with a study in Coleman Street. He was, however, not a Calvinist in theology; indeed, he was denounced by the hyper-Calvinist, Thomas Edwards, as 'a monstrous sectary, a compound of Socinianism, Arminianism, antinomianism, independency, popery, yea and of scepticism, too'. It was Goodwin who was the real target of the pamphlet against 'the new Methodists' in *A War Among the Angels of the Church, Wherein is Shewed the Principles of the New Methodists in the Great Point of Justification* (1693).

[60] A Lancashire divine (1604-62/3) whose works were long held in esteem; it is worth noting that Wesley devoted three of the fifty vols. in the *Christian Lib.* to Ambrose's writings.

[61] Cf. Wesley's own *Abstract of the Life and Death of the Reverend Learned and Pious Mr. Tho. Halyburton* (1739), Bibliog, No. 12.

[62] Cf. the *DNB* entries on the brothers Garden—George and James. George, the

the decisive influence of Jeremy Taylor, whose works we have already noticed.[63] His personal acquaintance with William Law and their subsequent breach needs further detailed study; it began with undue veneration which then turned into uncharitable criticism as Law drifted more and more into the orbit of Jacob Boehme.[64] Wesley had also read the devotional works of Bishop Joseph Hall (1574–1656), and had learned from him how a Puritan soteriology and a Catholic spirit might be combined.[65] Even after the Revival was fully launched, he could claim encouragement from Bishop Edmund Gibson's explicit approval of his doctrine of perfection.[66] Wesley ignores the fact that a great canonist and church historian like Gibson would have known the background of this controversy about holiness at least as well as he did.

But none of these men had ever envisaged any such goal as that of a Christian's 'being perfected in love' *in this life*.[67] Where had this provocative notion come from? Even a partial answer is curious. In 1741 Wesley had discovered *An Essay Toward the Amendment of the Last English Translation of the Bible* (1659) by an obscure seventeenth century exegete named Robert Gell. It is a huge quarto, a disorganized series of comments on the problems of biblical translation and the need for a revised version of the Authorized Version; and yet for all its bulk it does not begin to

younger and more eminent, was officially deposed from the ministry on account of his 'Bourignonism'; cf. his *Apology for M. Antonia Bourignon* (1699). The elder brother, James, was also deposed (1696) for his mysticism, and for his refusal to renew his signature to the Westminster Confession. Wesley thought well enough of James Garden's *Comparative Theology: Or the True and Solid Grounds of a Pure and Peaceable Theology* (1700) to extract and include it in his *Christian Lib.* XXII. 243-87.

[63] See above, p. 19, n. 28.

[64] Cf. John B. Green, *John Wesley and William Law* (London, Epworth Press, 1945), and Eric W. Baker, *A Herald of the Evangelical Revival* (London, Epworth Press, 1945); see also A. K. Walker, *Law*.

[65] Cf. Josiah Pratt's edn. of *Select Works of Bishop Hall . . .* (1811), Vol. III, espec. *A Holy Rapture . . ., Susurrium Cum Deo: Or, Holy Self-Conferences of the Devout Soul*, and *The Invisible World Discovered to Spiritual Eyes*. But see also Vol. I, and Hall's own accounts of his exertions on behalf of the *Via Media, or Way of Peace*.

[66] See *A Plain Account of Christian Perfection*, § 12; see also the intro. com. to No. 40, *Christian Perfection*.

[67] See the questions that Wesley had from 1770 asked of his 'Helpers' before admitting them on trial into his 'Connexion': 'Every person proposed is then to be present, and each of them may be asked, "A.B., Have you faith in Christ? Are you going on to perfection? Do you expect to be perfected in love in this life? Are you groaning after it?" ' (Large *Minutes*, 1770, *Q.* 60, Vol. 10 of this edn.). See also, letters to Samuel Bardsley, Feb. 1, 1775, and to Miss March, June 9, 1775.

cover the whole of the canonical text. In an Appendix, however (pp. 785 ff.), Gell had added a series of his own sermons on perfection as pure intention. In Sermon 20, 'Some Saints Not Without Sin for a Season', there is a vague reference to a then-recent controversy now so far forgotten that its full history may be beyond historical reconstruction. It concerns 'the condemnation' of Thomas Drayton and William Parker for their treatise, *A Revindication of the Possibility of a Total Mortification of Sin in This Life; and of the Saints' Perfect Obedience to the Law of God to be the Orthodox Protestant Doctrine* (1658).[68]

This 'succession' of Drayton, Parker, Gell on the doctrine of perfection was clearly a minority tradition and something of an elitist one in its way. Its main stress was on the triumphs of grace and on the power of a wholehearted love of God and neighbour to displace all other loves and so to overcome the remains of sin. What Wesley did—and this may have been his chief offence— was to universalize such an idea and, so to say, 'vulgarize' it. In this way he enlarged its scope, but also its risks of over-simplification on the one hand, and self-righteousness on the other. He was confounded and frustrated by the easy abuses thus invited, but was never deterred. And he was vindicated in that this doctrine became one of the hallmarks of the Methodist ethos; he could affirm with their agreement that 'the doctrine of Christian perfection' was one that 'God [had] peculiarly entrusted to the Methodists',[69] and had called them out as a separate movement in order 'to spread scriptural holiness over the land'.[70] Given his background in Eastern spirituality and his distinctive view of the office and work of the Holy Spirit, Wesley could never really understand why his optimistic views of the triumphant power of grace should offend so many Christians and confuse so many more.

On many points of churchmanship and polity that seemed

[68] Their original *Vindication* has not survived; the *Revindication* is not listed in the catalogues of BL or of Dr. Williams's Library, nor even in Donald Wing's *Short Title Catalogue of Books Printed . . . 1641–1700*. The only copy that I have ever seen is in the McAlpin Collection, Union Theological Seminary, New York.

[69] See JWJ, Feb. 6, 1789.

[70] Large *Minutes*, 1789, *Q.* 3 (first added in 1763): 'What may we reasonably believe to be God's design in raising up the preachers called Methodists? *A.* Not to form any new sect, but to reform the nation, particularly the Church, and to spread spiritual holiness over the land.' See also Nos. 107, 'On God's Vineyard', II. 8; and 121, 'Prophets and Priests', § 21.

crucial to the Anglican establishment, Wesley was almost blithely irregular. One may see this in the smugness of his report of his defiance of Bishop Butler's attempt to interdict him from irregular preaching in the diocese of Bristol.[71] On this point, as on so many others, he had simply been borne along by the actual circumstances of the Revival. What is more, he was willing to rest his case for his 'irregularities' on appeals to dubious 'authorities'.[72] Thus, on this score of practical ecclesiology, Wesley was less Anglican than on any other; his self-justification here was strictly pragmatic. The Revival had not only outlasted all precedent and expectations;[73] it had actually served the Christian cause in England and, therefore, the Church of England. On yet another ecclesiological frontier, he was convinced, before his time, that the core of Christian belief was more widely and more deeply shared by otherwise bitterly divided Christians than such antagonists had ever realized or were prepared to admit. He could, therefore, plead for and manifest what he labelled 'a catholic spirit'. He could also envisage a possible reunion of shattered Christendom, though less by any sort of 'conformity' to a single 'true church' than by some scheme of 'comprehension' such as had been proposed, prematurely, in the ill-fated Savoy

[71] See above, pp. 12-13. For the text of a strikingly similar exchange between Wesley's grandfather (also named John) and an earlier Bishop of Bristol (Gilbert Ironside, the elder), see Edmund Calamy, *The Nonconformist's Memorial* ('Whitchurch' in the section on 'Dorsetshire' in Samuel Palmer's edn., 1802, Vol. II, pp. 164-75); cf. Adam Clarke, *Memoirs of the Wesley Family* (London, 1823), pp. 23-32. See also Glanville Davies, 'Evidence Against John Wesley (*c.* 1636–70)', in WHS, XL. 80-84.

[72] In a letter to James Clark, July 3, 1756, Wesley appeals to 'Dr. Stillingfleet's *Irenicon*' as authority for the essential quality of presbyterial and episcopal orders; he repeats this same appeal to the Earl of Dartmouth (Apr. 10, 1761), and finally to his brother Charles on June 8, 1780. Is it possible that Wesley did not know that Edward Stillingfleet (1635–99) had written his *Irenicum: Or, A Weapon-Salve for the Churches' Wounds* in 1659 while still a struggling tutor (age twenty-four) and in the peculiar circumstances of the tragic need for 'comprehension' in the forthcoming Restoration? Was he unaware that Stillingfleet had subsequently repudiated his earlier position and had argued, in the Danby case, for the special jurisdictions of the Anglican bishops? Wesley's other chief authority for his thesis about the parity of presbyterial and episcopal orders was Peter King, *An Enquiry into the Constitution, Discipline, Unity, and Worship of the Primitive Church* (published anonymously in 1691 when King was still a Nonconformist and twenty-two years old); cf. Wesley's references to Lord King's 'Account of the Primitive Church' in JWJ, Jan. 20, 1746, and in his open letter to 'Our Brethren in America', Sept. 10, 1784 (§ 2). It is hard to imagine Wesley's not knowing that King had subsequently become an Anglican, the Baron of Ockham, Lord Chancellor of England, and had repudiated the ecclesiological views of his youthful *Enquiry . . .* ; this was common knowledge in Oxford and elsewhere.

[73] See No. 63, 'The General Spread of the Gospel', § 13 and n.

Conference of 1661. And, despite his anti-Papist prejudices, he quietly rejected the 'conclusion' that Roman Catholics, as such, were beyond the Christian pale.[74] For all the bad blood the doctrine of predestination had stirred between the Calvinists and the Methodists, Wesley acknowledged it as an allowable 'opinion', if only it were not insisted upon as an essential dogma. He rejected Quaker and Baptist doctrines of 'the Spirit within' only in so far as it had hardened Christian folkways into divisive practices.[75] His open letter 'To a Roman Catholic' (1749) amounts to a basic agenda for a truly ecumenical dialogue.[76]

Wesley's critics charged that he was trying to have it both ways: justifying the perpetuation of separate traditions and yet also affirming the mutual recognition of a shared core and communion between them. And so he was; he believed that, beyond the polarizations that divided Christians into denominations, there continued a transcending *koinonia* into which they might all find their way back. Part of his theological mission was the discovery of such a *koinonia* that could stand equally and securely against sectarianism, on the one side, and secularism, on the other. This was the important premise behind his oft-quoted, oft-distorted, epigram that, on points not threatening essential truth, Methodists 'think and let think'.[77] His practical efforts on behalf of this idea of 'comprehension' failed. He was an 'ecumenist' born out of due time, long before that term had been coined or the idea itself had evolved into its modern connotations. Even so, he never faltered in his hopes for a recovered Christian unity—and so he continues as an underdeveloped resource for any ecumenical vision that can conceive of that unity restored on other terms than abjuration and return.

And yet, for all this, he never understood himself as anything

<hr/>

[74] Cf. No. 74, 'Of the Church', § 19, and his open letter of July 18, 1749.

[75] Cf. his comments on the Quakers in *A Farther Appeal*, Pt. II, III. 5-10, and in Pt. III, IV. 7 (11:254-60, 319 of this edn.); see also his letters of Feb. 10, 1748, June 25, 1746 (to 'John Smith'), and JWJ, July 6, 7, 12, 1739, Mar. 25, 1740, and Apr. 25, 1758. For the Baptists, cf. *A Farther Appeal*, Pt. II, III. 3-4 (11:252-54 of this edn.), and JWJ, Aug. 10, 1739, Jan. 13, 1746, Apr. 3, 1751, and July 24, 1757.

[76] Cf. Michael Hurley, ed., *John Wesley's Letter to a Roman Catholic* (Dublin, Geoffrey Chapman, 1968), espec. the intro.

[77] Cf. No. 7, 'The Way to the Kingdom', I. 6 and n. See also his letter to Mrs. Howton, Oct. 3, 1783: 'It is the glory of the people called Methodists that they condemn none for their opinions or modes of worship. They think and let think.' He had laid down the same principle, much earlier, in *The Character of a Methodist* (1742), § 1: 'As to all opinions which do not strike at the root of Christianity, we "think and let think".'

other than a staunch and loyal Anglican; he did not 'espouse any other principles . . . than those which are plainly contained in the Bible, as well as in the Homilies and Book of Common Prayer'.[78] We have already noticed his confidence that 'the Church of England is the most scriptural church in the world'.[79] The only points on which he quite deliberately deviated from the standing Anglican church order were: (1), open-air preaching (first begun aboard the *Simmonds* on Sunday, Oct. 19, 1735); (2), extempore prayers and preaching;[80] (3), the Methodist Societies as a connexion of persons acknowledging him as spiritual director; (4), the Conference as a conciliar alternative to any dependence upon episcopal authorization. For each of these irregularities he felt he had justifying precedents; besides, he had long since realized that there were no bishops able or even inclined to excommunicate him and his people.[81] Thus it was that he could see and interpret the breadth of the whole Christian tradition through Anglican spectacles but with wide-angled lenses. Even after his Deed of Declaration of 1784 and his ordinations for America, he continued to insist, sincerely, 'I live and die a member of the Church of England, and none who regard my judgment or advice will ever separate from it.'[82] He died in this vain hope.[83]

Contemporary Culture

Wesley's orientation toward the Christian past did not, however, divert his interest from his own world and his own time. The abandonment of his academic career and his identification with the masses did not assuage his voracious appetite for

[78] Letter to *Lloyd's Evening Post*, Dec. 1, 1760; see also JWJ, Sept. 13, 1739: 'A serious clergyman desired to know in what points we differed from the Church of England. I answered: "To the best of my knowledge, in none. The doctrines we preach are the doctrines of the Church of England; indeed, the fundamental doctrines of the Church, clearly laid down, both in her Prayers, Articles, and Homilies." ' See his final reiteration and his apology for his 'irregularities', JWJ, Apr. 12, 1789.

[79] See above, p. 77, n. 32.

[80] See above, p. 14.

[81] Cf. Charles J Abbey, *The English Church and Its Bishops*, 2 vols. (1887), I. 249-50, 353-55, 383-97; II. 92-93, 132-36, for the suggestion that episcopal disapproval of Wesley never amounted to a firm proposal to bring him under active ecclesiastical or civil discipline.

[82] 'Farther Thoughts on Separation from the Church', *AM*, 1790, 216. See also JWJ, Apr. 12 (Easter), 1789.

[83] Cf. Frank Baker, *John Wesley and the Church of England*, pp. 304-23; see also John

reading, even though much of that reading was in haste and on the run.[84] For the most part he sought out books that served his purposes as theological tutor to the Methodists, and yet it is equally clear that he was also driven by an unflagging intellectual curiosity that continued with him to the end.[85] He lived in an age of exploration; he read the reports of the great voyagers eagerly, with an interesting mixture of credulity and critical reserve.[86] He himself had long since lost his illusions about the myths of the 'noble savage' and the unspoiled 'children of nature', through his experiences with the native Americans in Georgia. He was, therefore, inclined to find in the various accounts of other native peoples (the Hottentots in South Africa and the Laplanders in arctic Europe)[87] still further confirmation of his belief that sin (in the sense of the wilful violation of acknowledged moral

Walsh, 'Methodism at the End of the Eighteenth Century', in Davies and Rupp, eds., *A History of the Methodist Church in Great Britain*, I. 277-315.

[84] There was this much warrant for Ronald Knox's otherwise snide remark that Wesley was 'not a good advertisement for reading on horseback'; see *Enthusiasm* (Oxford, Clarendon Press, 1950), p. 447.

[85] In the last seven years of his life there are thirty-five *Journal* listings of recorded readings amidst incessant travel, preaching, and the care of the Societies. They range widely, from a quite new translation of 'Voltaire's *Memoirs*' (JWJ, Aug. 26, 1784: *Memoirs of the life of Voltaire . . . written by himself* [1784]) to 'LeVayer's *Animadversions*' (JWJ, June 8, 1785: Francois de la Mothe LeVayer, *Notitia Historicorum Selectorum* . . . [1678]), to 'Perry's *Treatise upon the Gravel and Stone*, with a favourable comment on Perry's experimental use of 'lithontriptics' (cf. *OED*, JWJ, Nov. 3, 1785: *A Disquisition of the Stone and Gravel, with other Diseases of the Kidneys, Bladder, etc.* (1777), ... *With Strictures on the Gout* (added to 7th edn., 1785), to 'Dr. Withering's *Treatise on Foxglove*' (JWJ, Mar. 21, 1786: William Withering, 'the elder', *An Account of the Foxglove and some of its medical uses: with practical remarks on Dropsy* [Birmingham, 1785]).

Toward the end he let others read to him, but his range is still wide; see diary, Jan. 12, 1791, when Elizabeth Ritchie 'read Mexico', re-read Lewis Stuckley, *A Gospel Glass . . .* (already extracted in the *Christian Lib.*, XXXIII. 5-269) and also Archibald Campbell, *The Doctrine of a Middle State between Death and the Resurrection* (1721).

His last reading was the poignant biography of an African ex-slave; see diary, Feb. 23, 1791; 'read *Gustavus Vasa'—viz.*, Olandah Equiano, *The interesting narrative of the life of O. Equiano, or G. Vassa, the African . . . written by himself* (1789; 2nd edn., 1790). This may have influenced his famous 'last letter' to William Wilberforce in ardent support of the latter's anti-slavery struggles.

[86] See Thomas Salmon, *Modern History: Or the Present State of All Nations* (1744-46), 3 vols., Aubry de la Motraye, *Travels Through Europe, Asia, and Into Parts of Africa* (1732), 3 vols. See also JWJ, Feb. 17, 1787, where Wesley says of Du Halde's *Description of China and Chinese Tartary*, '[His] word I will not take for a straw; but there are many and just remarks in the treatise, to which few impartial men would have any objection, in whatever form they were proposed.' In 1785 he read William Coxe's 3-vol. account of his *Travels into Poland, Russia, Sweden, and Denmark*, published just the previous year.

[87] For Wesley's knowledge of the Hottentots and the Cape of Good Hope, see No. 28, 'Sermon on the Mount, VIII', § 9 and n.; and for the Laplanders, No. 38, 'A Caution against Bigotry', I. 4 and n.

standards) is more nearly the universal norm than mere innocence or ignorance. But he was also certain that the *chief* hindrance to 'the general spread of the gospel' was the blatantly inhumane behaviour of nominal and pseudo-Christians at home and abroad.[88] Thus, he could hold on to his doctrines of universal redemption in Christ, and of the Holy Spirit's universal presence and prevenient activity among all peoples, and still denounce various Christian betrayals of the gospel.[89]

Given his providentialist views of history, he found in Edward Brerewood's demographic calculations that no more than 'five parts in thirty' of the world's population 'are as much as nominally Christian'[90] a further proof of the relative failure of Christian missions.[91] And yet he also took heart from various reports of new missionary ventures and revivals in other parts of the world. He looked ahead to the future expansion of Christianity with rising expectations.[92] His favourite sources here were such books as Jonathan Edwards's *Faithful Narrative* and John Gillies's *Historical Collections Relating to Remarkable Periods of the Success of the Gospel* (1754). Moreover, he thought he saw how these visions of a Christianized world could be fitted into the secularized doctrines of human progress newly advertised by men like George Hakewill and Bernard Le Bovier de Fontenelle.[93] Here, again, one sees his unfaltering confidence that his optimism of grace could co-exist with emerging new ideas about the human condition and the human prospect.

Wesley was rationalist enough to realize that his theology had to be correlated with the scientific revolution of his time, and he was aware of some of the problems involved in this. He had grown up with the comfortable assurance that 'natural philosophy', when true, would always be in accord with the Christian vision of the wisdom of God in creation, which is to say, with the long

[88] See No. 63, 'The General Spread of the Gospel', § 22 and n.

[89] For Wesley's view on universal redemption, cf. Michael Hurley, 'Salvation Today and Wesley Today', pp. 101-12; see above, pp. 72-73.

[90] Cf. his *Enquiries Touching the Diversities of Languages and Religions Through the Chief Parts of the Earth* (1614); see No. 63, 'The General Spread of the Gospel', § 2 and n.

[91] For Wesley's other references to Brerewood, cf. No. 15, *The Great Assize*, II. 4 and n.

[92] Cf. No. 102, 'Of Former Times', intro. and n.

[93] Cf. George Hakewill, *Apologie or Declaration of the Power and Providence of God in the Government of the World* . . . (1627, 1630, 1635); and Bernard Le Bovier de Fontenelle, *Dialogues of the Dead* (1st edn., in French, 1683; Eng. tr. by John Hughes, 1708), and *Conversations on the Plurality of Worlds* (1st edn. in Fr., 1686; Eng. tr. by Mrs. Aphra Behn; four edns. from 1688 to 1760); see No. 102, 'Of Former Times', §§ 20-23, and n. on § 21.

tradition represented by such men as John Ray, William Derham, and the Boyle Lecturers.[94] He had read Bishop Thomas Sprat's *History of the Royal Society* (1667) and a rich bibliography of other samplings of 'the new science' besides.[95] But he was also aware of the waning of the older confidence that Christian theology could forever regard 'natural theology' as a 'handmaiden *(ancilla)* to theology' (herself *regina scientiarum*). 'The Age of Newton' had posed radical difficulties to all historical Christian world views and, most especially, to its doctrines of miracles and providence. Moreover, Wesley had more than an inkling of the drastic consequences for the *fides historica* in the scepticism of David Hume and the critical idealism of Immanuel Kant. In reaction, he sought out various critics of Newton and appealed to them, less in refutation of Newton's empirical findings than in support of his own views of the sovereignty of divine providence.[96] For a brief span he flirted with the bizarre anti-Newtonian hypotheses of John Hutchinson, to the effect that an entire and inspired cosmology had been encoded in the unpointed Hebrew of 'the first five books of Moses';[97] he quickly realized this as a false move and abandoned it.

[94] John Ray (1627–1705) was a theologian, natural scientist, and charter Fellow of the Royal Society; it was his *Wisdom of God Manifested in the Works of Creation* (1691; twelve edns. by 1759) that Wesley took as a model; cf. Charles Raven's biography, *John Ray, Naturalist, His Life nd Works* (Cambridge, Cambridge University Press, 1942), also *Organic Design, a Study of Scientific Thought from Ray to Paley* (London, Oxford University Press, 1954). William Derham (1657–1735), rector of Upminster (Essex) and a Fellow of the Royal Society; cf. his *Astro-Theology* (1715) and *Physico-Theology* (1716). The Boyle Lectures had been founded in 1692 by Robert Boyle with the general intent of confirming the then reigning religious consensus about the harmony between the new sciences and the old faith.

[95] For Wesley's interests in contemporary natural phenomena (earthquakes, volcanoes, electricity, astronomy), see Nos. 15, *The Great Assize*, and 55, *On the Trinity*, and nn. It may be mentioned here that he read everything on electricity he could lay hands on, and was espec. interested in the controversial accounts of geological origins—as between Thomas Burnet, *The Sacred Theory of the Earth* (2 vols.; 1684, 1689), and William Whiston, *A New Theory of the Earth* (1696). What was at stake here was a theological interpretation of the creation stories of Genesis (and of the Flood); that Wesley's interest in these questions never flagged is suggested by his reading of Oliver Goldsmith's 8-vol. *History of the Earth and Animated Nature* (1774), sometime before 1789; cf. No. 130, 'On Living without God', § 1.

[96] Cf. Wesley's *Survey* (1777), III. 328: 'It will be easily observed that I do not *deny* but only doubt of the present [Newtonian] system of astronomy.' Cf. Nos. 55, *On the Trinity*, § 10 and n.; and 77, 'Spiritual Worship', I. 6 and n.

[97] Cf. Hutchinson, *Moses' Principia* (1724); see Nos. 77, 'Spiritual Worship', I. 6 and n., and 69, 'The Imperfection of Human Knowledge', I. 5 and n.; see also Charles Singer, *A Short History of Scientific Ideas to 1900* (New York, Oxford University Press, 1959), ch. viii.

He was, however, no mere critic. He gathered together what he regarded as the best in contemporary science and produced his own *Survey of the Wisdom of God in Creation: Or, A Compendium of Natural Philosophy*, first in two volumes (1763), then in three (1770), and finally in five (1777).[98] Largely borrowed (from good sources), it is an impressive collection, well-organized and open to the problems of integrating religion and science. Moreover, in the sermons (especially the later ones) we are casually confronted with what turn out to be competent references to the new astronomy (planetary distances, comets and 'fixed stars', the speed of light, and 'the plurality of worlds'). Wesley was the first popular theologian to recognize the importance of the newly discovered phenomenon of electricity[99] (relating it to his own prescientific notions of 'ethereal fire'). Indeed, he became a pioneer in the therapeutic uses of mild electrical shock, installing 'electrification machines' in his paramedical clinics in London and Bristol.[100]

Just as he struggled with the challenges to faith from natural philosophy, so also he sought to defend his people from the secularization of morality, which he recognized in all theories of intrinsic human virtue in their beginnings, as he reckoned them, in Shaftesbury, the deists, and even in Joseph Butler.[101] We have noted how this polemic against 'intrinsic virtue' was matched by his violent alarm over the spread of the economic theories of laissez-faire that finally found a classic statement in Adam Smith's *Wealth of Nations* (1776). What offended Wesley here was

[98] See *Bibliog*, No. 259, and Vol. 17 of this edn. (for the 1763 edn.). Quotations in this vol. are from the 1784 reprint of the 1777 edn.

[99] See No. 15, *The Great Assize*, III. 4 and n.

[100] See JWJ, Nov. 9, 1756: 'Having procured an apparatus on purpose, I ordered several persons to be electrified who were ill of various disorders; some of whom found an immediate, some a gradual, cure. From this time I appointed, first some hours in every week, and afterward an hour in every day, wherein any that desired it might try the virtue of this surprising medicine. Two or three years after, our patients were so numerous that we were obliged to divide them; so part were electrified in Southwark, part at the Foundery, others near St. Paul's, and the rest near the Seven Dials.' Cf. *ibid.*, Nov. 16, 1747.

Few of Wesley's people could afford the services of physicians; he, therefore, sought to supply them with what he could, including a manual of *Primitive Physick: Or, an Easy and Natural Method of Curing Most Diseases* (1747, and twenty-two more edns. by 1791). It is no more than a sample of medical *curiosa* today; yet it does manage to enforce Wesley's point that health is *wholeness*—and 'natural'.

[101] See his long running battle with Francis Hutcheson after the latter's publication of *An Inquiry into the Original of Our Ideas of Beauty and Virtue* (1725) and his *Essay on the Nature and Conduct of the Passions* . . . (1726). Cf. above, p. 64, n. 33.

the thesis that surplus accumulation was, in fact, the very foundation of economic well-being. In flat contradiction, Wesley insisted that all surplus accumulation was mortal sin.[102] He was, of course, swimming against a massive current, and made scant headway. His people were prepared to follow his first two rules for 'the use of money': *viz.*, 'gain all you can honestly' and 'save all you can carefully'. But the third rule ('give all you can—namely, all you have over and above necessities and conveniences') was asking too much—then, or since.

Wesley's father before him had been something of a marginal figure in the literary world as contributor to *The Athenian Mercury*, *The Athenian Oracle*, and *The Athenian Gazette*.[103] On his own, he had produced a poetic *Life of Christ* (1693) and some very ambitious *Dissertations on the Book of Job* (1735).[104] Young John had grown up in the literary climate of *The Spectator*, *The Tatler*, and *The Guardian*; one suspects that he was always an essayist at heart. For all his notoriety as an 'enthusiast', he maintained a mutually admiring friendship with Dr. Samuel Johnson, the ruling 'Grand Cham' of eighteenth-century letters.[105] Thus, behind the conventional stereotype of the itinerant evangelist there was a man of letters whose literary lore and exacting tastes are discernible 'between his lines'. In the sermons there are echoes from English literature from Bede to Chaucer, to Dryden, to Pope, to Thomson. He found Milton more profound than Shakespeare, and, by the same criterion, he adjudged both Edward Young and Matthew Prior as major poets.[106] His appraisals of Alexander Pope were mixed, but he was familiar

---

[102] See No. 50, 'The Use of Money', espec. intro.; also Nos. 28, 'Sermon on the Mount, VIII'; 87, 'The Danger of Riches'; 108, 'On Riches'; and 131, 'The Danger of Increasing Riches'.

[103] In association with their eccentric editor, John Dunton, who was also the elder Wesley's brother-in-law.

[104] See *Bibliog*, No. 7. Cf. also his *History of the Old and New Testament Attempted in Verse*, 3 vols. (1704).

[105] This was shared by his brother Charles and also their sister, Martha Hall. See Moore, II. 253-55, for a summary of Johnson's comments on Wesley, and JWJ, Dec. 18, 1783, for a report of his last visit 'with that great man, Dr. Johnson, who is sinking into the grave by a gentle decay' (Johnson was then 74, Wesley 80). There are at least seven references to Wesley (all sympathetic) in James Boswell's *Life of Johnson* (3rd edn., 1799).

[106] In a letter of Oct. 26, 1745, he speaks of Shakespeare as 'our heathen poet'; but he knew him well (espec. *Hamlet*, *The Tempest*, and *Twelfth Night*). See No. 77, 'Spiritual Worship', III. 5, where Prior's *Solomon* is adjudged as 'one of the noblest poems in the English tongue'; in No. 92, 'On Zeal', III. 6, Edward Young is spoken of as 'our great poet'.

enough with his poetry to paraphrase it almost casually.[107] He
knew Dryden fairly well but used him sparingly. He admired
Dean Jonathan Swift's sermon 'On the Trinity', and shared
Swift's disdain for English arrogance in Ireland.[108] He could not
abide Laurence Sterne, Voltaire, or Lord Chesterfield.[109]

Wesley's 'plain people' knew well enough how sternly he
denounced the English theatre in general as 'a sink of all
profaneness and debauchery'.[110] What they can scarcely have
realized was the range of Wesley's interest in English drama from
the Restoration to his own day. There is a diary record for
November 18, 1729, of his attending in London a performance of
John Fletcher's *Scornful Lady*,[111] and there is ample evidence of
his having read a great deal of English melodrama. In the corpus
there are quotations from more than a score of plays.[112] In
addition, we have records of his readings of other dramatic works
by these same playwrights, not to mention various plays by at least
another dozen dramatists from which he never quoted.[113]

An odd instance of this paradox may be seen in Sermon 44,
Original Sin, II. 9; there a snatch of poetry that is very apt (but
uncited) turns out to be a quotation from a once famous

[107] Cf. Nos. 67, 'On Divine Providence', § 19; 60, 'The General Deliverance', III. 5;
and 78, 'Spiritual Idolatry', II. 2.

[108] Cf. his *Short Method of Converting All the Roman Catholics in the Kingdom of Ireland*
(1752, *Bibliog*, No. 196, Vol. 13 in this edn.).

[109] Cf. No. 100, 'On Pleasing All Men', I. 5, where Sterne is identified as 'a late witty
writer'; but in JWJ, Feb. 11, 1772, his comment on *A Sentimental Journey* (1768) is
peremptory: 'Sentimental! What is that? It is not English.... It is not sense.... For oddity,
uncouthness, and unlikeness to all the world beside, I suppose [Sterne] is without a rival.'
In a letter to Richard Locke, Sept. 14, 1770, Wesley speaks of Voltaire as 'that wretched
man'; see also Nos. 84, *The Important Question*, III. 11; and 120, 'The Unity of the Divine
Being', §§ 19-20. For Wesley's comments on Chesterfield, see Nos. 100, 'On Pleasing All
Men',§ 4 and n.; and 128, 'The Deceitfulness of the Human Heart', II. 7.

[110] Cf. Nos. 89, 'The More Excellent Way', V. 4 and n.; and 94, 'On Family Religion',
III. 14.

[111] See also, JWJ, Mar. 28, 1750, where Wesley records a meeting with 'the famous Mr.
Griffith, of Carnarvonshire—a clumsy, overgrown, hard-faced man, whose countenance I
could only compare to that (which I saw in Drury Lane thirty years ago) of one of the
ruffians in *Macbeth*'. Wesley was seventeen in 1720 and a student at the Charterhouse.

[112] E.g., Joseph Addison, *Cato*; John Dryden, *The Conquest of Granada;* John Hughes,
The Siege of Damascus; Nathaniel Lee, *Oedipus*; Thomas Otway, *The Orphan;* Nicholas
Rowe, *Tamerlane, The Ambitious Step-mother, The Fair Penitent;* Shakespeare, *Hamlet, The
Tempest, Twelfth Night;* Sophocles, *Ajax*; Terence, *The Eunuch, The Lady of Andros*, and *The
Self-Tormentor*.

[113] E.g., Lord Lansdowne, John Dennis, Richard Taverner, Thomas Southerne, Ben
Jonson, Charles Molloy, William Wycherley, George Etheridge, George Lillo, James
Miller, George Ruggle, William Mountfort, and David Mallet.

melodrama by a once famous dramatist, Thomas Otway. The source is *The Orphan*, published and staged in 1680, first read by Wesley in May of 1726, now quoted in 1759. *The Orphan* was still being performed in the eighteenth century, but would a quotation from it be readily recognizable by Wesley's readers? And whence would Wesley have retrieved it? Another interesting sample of this literary outreach—the longest quotation still, alas, unidentified—is a passage of eight lines in Sermon 67, 'On Divine Providence', § 19. Obviously, it was familiar enough to Wesley; it neatly ornaments his argument. One might think it would be equally obvious to at least some others; yet none of many probes has found its source. These illustrations of Wesley's casual recourse to his literary heritage make two important points: the heritage enriched his rhetoric, and yet he makes no show of it whatever. This was his way of heeding Ovid's counsel about the artistry of concealing one's art.[114]

The Revival's greatest literary influence, however, came from its hymnody. This is the common witness of all the reports we have from the Methodists and from others. The brothers Wesley set great store by the fact that their people *sang* the same doctrine in their hymns as they heard and read in their sermons. Accordingly, the most copious source of quotations in the written sermons, besides the Scripture itself, is from the succession of hymn collections provided for the Methodist people. Here, Charles's contribution to the Revival was unique;[115] far more of his hymns have been sung by more Christians (and not just Methodists alone) than any sermon of John's has ever been read. And yet, John's hymnody reached beyond his brother's poetry. In the quasi-official *Collection of Hymns for the Use of the People Called Methodists* of 1780 there are hymns by Isaac Watts, along with a small sheaf of excellent translations by John himself of great Lutheran hymns from the Reformation's first century.[116] As with so much else, Wesley had very definite notions as to the role of hymns and singing in the Methodist services; these were summed

---

[114] See letter to Samuel Furly, July 15, 1764.

[115] Cf. Frank Baker, *Representative Verse of Charles Wesley*; see also J. Ernest Rattenbury, *The Eucharistic Hymns of John and Charles Wesley* (London, Epworth Press, 1948).

[116] Of these, three from Paulus Gerhardt, two each from Gerhard Tersteegen and John Scheffler, and one each from Ernst Lange, Joachim Lange, J. A. Rothe, J. H. Schein, and J. J. Winckler still survive in *The Methodist Hymn Book* (1933). For the *Collection* see Vol. 7 of this edn.

up in his *Directions* for congregational singing, which appeared as an appendix to *Select Hymns: With Tunes Annext* in 1761.[117] Just as he scorned the ornate style in preaching, so also he denounced repetitiveness in hymns, anthems, and oratorios.[118] In the *Minutes* for 1768 (*Q.* 23 (6)) he deplores 'the repeating the same word so often (but especially while another repeats different words, the horrid abuse which runs through the modern church music); as it shocks all common sense, so it necessarily brings in dead formality, and has no more of religion in it than a Lancashire hornpipe'.[119] The relevance of all this for our purposes is that when Wesley sprinkled his sermons with hymn stanzas or couplets, as he did generously, he could count on hearers and readers who could respond to them from their own experiences.

VI. ON READING WESLEY'S SERMONS

WESLEY was not born a great preacher, nor did he come by his fame as a preacher by diligence alone. It was, in effect, thrust upon him by an unfolding succession of events in which he was always more reactor than actor. What is crucial, from the very beginning of the Revival, was that it was Wesley's message that counted for more than his manner, and this suggests a basic

---

[117] E.g., 'IV. Sing *lustily* and with good courage. . . . Be no more afraid of your voice now, nor more ashamed of its being heard, than when you sung the songs of Satan. . . . VI. Sing *in time*. Whatever time is sung, be sure to keep with it. Do not run before, nor stay behind it, but attend close to the leading voices, and move therewith as exactly as you can. And take care you sing not *too slow*. This drawling way naturally steals on all who are lazy, and it is high time to drive it out from among us, and sing all our tunes just as quick as we did at first.'
    Cf. also, *Minutes*, 1765: '*Q.* [28]: What can be done to make the people sing better? *A.* (1). Teach them to sing by note, and to sing our tunes first. (2). Take care they do not sing too slow. (3). Exhort all that can, in every congregation, to sing. (4). Set them right that sing wrong. Be patient therein.'

[118] See JWJ, Aug. 9, 1768: 'I . . . was greatly disgusted at the manner of singing [at Neath, where the choir] repeated the same words, contrary to all sense and reason, six or eight or ten times over . . . ;' cf. also Mar. 19, 1778: 'In the evening, I preached at Pebworth church; but I seemed out of my element. A long anthem was sung; but I suppose none beside the singers could understand one word of it. Is not that "praying in an unknown tongue"? I could no more bear it in any church of mine than Latin prayers.' See also Apr. 8, 1781: 'The service was at the usual hours. I came just in time to put a stop to a bad custom, which was creeping in here; a few men, who had fine voices, sang a psalm which no one knew, in a tune fit for an opera, wherein three, four, or five persons sung different words at the same time! What an insult upon common sense! What a burlesque upon public worship! No custom can excuse such a mixture of profaneness and absurdity.'

[119] See the full answer to *Q.* 39 ('How shall we guard against formality in public worship? Particularly in singing?') in the Large *Minutes*, 1780 (Vol. 10 of this edn.).

reference point in reading him. John Donne's sermons are aural feasts that delight the ear, stir the imagination, and move the heart; but they are most fully savoured when read aloud with a practiced actor's eye for word-play and nuance. Wesley's rhetoric is markedly different. There are only occasional flights of eloquence in them—all short. Wesley's message is Wesley's medium—it is a transaction with a reader responding to insights springing from shared traditions and a shared source in Holy Writ. The typical Wesley sermon begins with a brief proemium promptly followed by an expository 'contract' between the preacher and the reader ('I am to show . . .', etc.). The reader is thus entitled to judge between the preacher's intention and his performance.[1] And always, it is the 'application' on which the whole effort is focused; this makes most of the sermons intensely personal and practical.[2] Wesley was content that others might be more exciting if he could be more nourishing.

None of these sermons stands alone; none is norm for all the others. Wesley can quite readily be quoted against himself when this passage or that is taken out of context. His sermons are bound to be misread unless they are understood as experimental statements and restatements of his vision of the Christian life. On first scanning they may seem repetitious: one quickly comes to recognize favourite phrases, quotations—some of his illustrations are pressed into double duty. And yet, even such repetitions have their purpose: they represent Wesley's way of trying to expose old truths in new lights.

These sermons may be read in gulps, without the distraction of notes. Or, they may be savoured and probed, and this is more fruitful as one becomes more deeply immersed in their backgrounds. They can be read in different sequences or in

---

[1] That Wesley honoured this compact in the breach as well as in the observance may be seen, e.g., in No. 39, 'Catholic Spirit' (where the text is merely a pretext) or in the following folkloric anecdote from Scotland (where the standards of 'sermon-tasting' were higher than in England): 'In one of Wesley's visits to Dunbar, when preaching in the open air [and rambling], a young man in the crowd cried, "Stick to your text.". . . Wesley was so much confounded as if a thunderbolt had fallen at his feet, . . . struck dumb with astonishment, and had not a word to say. After a little, he went on with his discourse in a much less confident tone than formerly.' (quoted from the *Berwickshire News*, Oct. 26, 1883, in WHS, XVII. 146-47).

[2] Cf. Wesley's letter to Joseph Taylor, Feb. 14, 1787: 'A sermon should be all application.' See also Nos. 20, *The Lord Our Righteousness*, II. 20; and 5, 'Justification by Faith', IV. 9 and n.

topical clusters (as, e.g., the pivotal series on Law and Gospel in the thirteen sermons 'Upon Our Lord's Sermon on the Mount', Nos. 31-33, together with the three following, Nos. 34-36). There is no doubt that the sermons in *SOSO*, I–IV, stand as a bloc and that, together, they do define the evangelical substance of Wesley's message. But they do not display its entire breadth and range, and it is unfortunate that conventional preoccupations with them have encouraged a corresponding neglect of the corpus *as a whole*. Thus Wesley's stature as a theologian has been casually underestimated, by Methodists and non-Methodists alike; his oversimplifications have been taken too easily at face value, and not recognized as hints of a more resourceful mind than meets the eye. Reverence for him as cult-hero and patriarch in Methodism has not preserved Methodist theology from serious distortions in the course of its post-Wesleyan developments.[3] Methodists, therefore, have almost as much to gain from genuinely critical studies of Wesley (from his own sources and as a whole) as do his fellow Anglicans and other Christians of every persuasion. It is, however, equally misleading to handle Wesley's sermons chiefly as historical curios. He was no antiquarian himself, and he would scorn any proposal that his sermons should ever be turned into puzzlers for pedants. Their real test is in their continuing power of witness—the possibility that their essential message may be updated and reformulated, again and again, while generations succeed each other.

The heart of Wesley's gospel was always its lively sense of God's grace at work at every level of creation and history in persons and communities. He took the 'Protestant principle' for granted: that God alone is God, with no rivals in creation save those idols that make human pride the primal font of sin and self-delusion. But he also cherished the Greek Christian heritage as a needful balance and, most especially, in its understanding of the Holy Spirit as the mediator of all graces—sufficient grace in all, irresistible grace in none. His ecclesiology turned on the conviction that all the means of grace are the Spirit's gifts to the priesthood of all believers and, under the Spirit's guidance, to a

[3] Robert E. Chiles, *Theological Transition in American Methodism* (Nashville, Abingdon, 1965), provides a survey of the shallow roots of American Methodism in Wesleyan theology. See also Franz Hildebrandt, *From Luther to Wesley* (London, Lutterworth Press, 1951), for an example of how Wesley may be "Lutheranized'. But see Garth Lean, *John Wesley, Anglican* (London, Blandford, 1964), for a fresh perspective.

representative priesthood.[4] The 'catholic substance' of Wesley's theology is the theme of *participation*—the idea that all life is of grace and all grace is the mediation of Christ by the Holy Spirit. Wesley did not, of course, invent any of these ideas, but neither did he find them already compounded in the special syndrome that he struggled for and largely achieved.[5]

Moreover, if his theology was unsystematic by design, this was not because of his disdain for coherence. After all, he was a trained logician and much more of a rationalist than the pietists among his followers have ever recognized. And yet, from his knowledge of the history of Christian doctrine he was aware of the fate of theological systems; besides, he himself had been bred up in a tradition with fewer experiments in 'systematic theology', as such, than any other. He had, therefore, come to take it for granted that the ways to Christian wisdom cannot be mapped as neatly as one might wish. The Christian pilgrim's progress is more securely guided by controlling insights (themselves works of the Spirit) than by manuals or treatises or *summae*.

By the same token, if Wesley's theology is ecumenical in scope and spirit, this was not the product of a pliant disposition. He was a very strong-minded man, scarcely fazed by criticism. He rarely changed his mind under anything short of circumstances that he could recognize as providential. He could, and often did, provoke controversy; he never backed away from a debate; his store of oil for troubled waters was meagre. It is all the more remarkable, therefore, that such a man could see so clearly the positive values of valid pluralism in an age when dogmatism and indifferentism were posed as the only two live options. Actually, Wesley's ecumenical vision was less relevant in his own age than it may have since become. He was only dimly aware, even as his movement grew, that the *fides historica* had already begun to lose its grip upon the European mind.[6] He would have been uneasy with the salvaging efforts of Schleiermacher and Ritschl; he would have been horrified by the disintegrations of Strauss and

[4] Cf. 'Disciplinary' *Minutes*, Aug. 3, 1745 (*Qs.* 1-9), and the 'points of discipline', discussed in mid-morning of June 15, 1747 (*Qs.* 1-14).

[5] Cf. George, *London Life*, p. 269, for a comment on how relevant Wesley's peculiar doctrine of assurance would have been in its own special time.

[6] See Peter Gay, *The Enlightenment*, (p. 25, n. 55 above). Cf. Carl L. Becker, *The Heavenly City of the Eighteenth Century Philosophers* (New Haven, Yale University Press, 1959). For a Christian historian's celebration of the end of the history of dogma, see Adolf von Harnack, *Grundriss der Dogmengeschichte* (1889), and *Das Wesen Des Christentums* (1900).

Feuerbach. By the same token, though, he would have deplored all fundamentalist oppositions between the Christian tradition and 'contemporary culture'. One may honestly suppose, however, that he would have rejoiced at the surprises of the Spirit in the modern ecumenical movement, and in the new flood of Christian charity let loose in the world by Pope John XXIII and the Second Vatican Council.

The Christian tradition remains in every age to be rediscovered and transvaluated—an inexhaustible resource for new horizons of inquiry and venture.[7] This edition is therefore offered with its implied thesis that Wesley's sermons deserve a place in that tradition and deserve more careful appraisal by historians and theologians than they have had. By the same token, though, John Wesley merits a closer look by those 'plain people' he loved so dearly and who, as he was so well aware, 'are competent judges of those truths which are necessary to their present and future happiness'.[8]

[7] Cf. Albert C. Outler, *The Christian Tradition and the Unity We Seek* (New York, Oxford University Press, 1957).

[8] *SOSO*, Preface, § 2.

SERMONS

O N

Several Occasions:

I N

THREE VOLUMES.

B y

JOHN WESLEY, M. A.

Fellow of *Lincoln-College*, OXFORD.

VOL. I.

LONDON:

Printed by W. STRAHAN: And fold by
T. TRYE, near Gray's-Inn Gate, Holbourn;
and at the Foundery, near Upper Moorfields.
MDCCXLVI.

PREFACE

That Wesley regarded this Preface as definitive of the entire project of his published sermons would appear from the fact that it is reprinted, unrevised, in every edition in his lifetime from 1746 to 1787. It sets out to do many things at once and in very short compass: (1) to describe the enterprise and to explain Wesley's choice of the sermon form as the medium of his theology; (2) to defend his style and role as folk theologian, renouncing his academic identification; (3) to stress soteriology as the focus of his entire theology; (4) to leave the way open for dialogue and reconciliation since 'love, even with many wrong opinions [i.e., doctrinal formulations], is to be preferred before truth itself without love'. Clearly, the aim here is to set the mood for a mutual understanding between the evangelist and his readers, a reference point for their interpretations of his doctrines, rhetoric, and spirit.

The Preface

1. The following sermons contain the substance of what I have been preaching for between eight and nine years last past. During that time I have frequently spoken in public on every subject in the ensuing collection: and I am not conscious that there is any 5 one point of doctrine on which I am accustomed to speak in public which is not here—incidentally, if not professedly—laid before every Christian reader. Every serious man who peruses these will therefore see in the clearest manner what those doctrines are which I embrace and teach as the essentials of true 10 religion.

2. But I am throughly sensible these are not proposed in such a manner as some may expect. Nothing here appears in an elaborate, elegant, or oratorical dress. If it had been my desire or design to write thus, my leisure would not permit. But in truth I at 15 present designed nothing less, for I now write (as I generally speak) *ad populum*[1]—to the bulk of mankind—to those who neither relish nor understand the art of speaking, but who

---

[1] See above, Intro., p. 25. Cf. Horace Bushnell, *Concio ad Clerum* (1828), § 1, for a later but analogous usage of *ad populum*.

notwithstanding are competent judges of those truths which are necessary to present and future happiness. I mention this that curious readers may spare themselves the labour of seeking for what they will not find.

5 3. I design plain truth for plain people. Therefore of set purpose I abstain from all nice and philosophical speculations, from all perplexed and intricate reasonings, and as far as possible from even the show of learning, unless in sometimes citing the original Scriptures. I labour to avoid all words which are not easy
10 to be understood, all which are not used in common life; and in particular those kinds of technical terms that so frequently occur in bodies of divinity, those modes of speaking which men of reading are intimately acquainted with, but which to common people are an unknown tongue. Yet I am not assured that I do not
15 sometimes slide into them unawares: it is so extremely natural to imagine that a word which is familiar to ourselves is so to all the world.

4. Nay, my design is in some sense to forget all that ever I have read in my life.[2] I mean to speak, in the general, as if I had
20 never read one author, ancient or modern (always excepting the inspired). I am persuaded that, on the one hand, this may be a means of enabling me more clearly to express the sentiments of my heart, while I simply follow the chain of my own thoughts, without entangling myself with those of other
25 men; and that, on the other, I shall come with fewer weights upon my mind, with less of prejudice and prepossession, either to search for myself or to deliver to others the naked truths of the gospel.

5. To candid, reasonable men I am not afraid to lay open
30 what have been the inmost thoughts of my heart. I have thought, I am a creature of a day,[3] passing through life as an arrow through the air.[4] I am a spirit come from God and returning to

---

[2] Cf. John Norris, *Reflections* (1690), p. 156: 'I now intend to follow the advice of the heathen, Marcus Antoninus, as I remember, τὴν των βιβλιῶν δίψαν ῥίψαν (Rid thyself of the thirst after books . . .)'.

[3] Cf. Pindar, *Pythian Odes*, viii. 95. Cf. also Nos. 3, '*Awake, Thou That Sleepest*', II.5; 29, 'Sermon on the Mount, IX', §24; 54, 'On Eternity', §5; 124, 'Human Life a Dream', §1; and 146, 'The One Thing Needful', §3.

[4] Cf. Wisd. 5:9-13: 'All those things are passed away like a shadow, and as a post that passeth by; as a ship that passeth over the waves of the water, which when it is gone by, the

God;[5] just hovering over the great gulf,[6] till a few moments hence I am no more seen[7]—I drop into an unchangeable eternity! I want to know one thing, the way to heaven[8]—how to land safe on that happy shore. God himself has condescended to teach the way: for this very end he came from heaven. He hath written it down in a   5 book. O give me that book! At any price give me the Book of God! I have it. Here is knowledge enough for me. Let me be *homo unius libri.*[9] Here then I am, far from the busy ways of men.[10] I sit down

trace thereof cannot be found, neither the path of it in the floods; or as a bird that fleeth through the air, and no man can see any token of her passage, but only hear the noise of her wings, beating the light wind, parting the air through the vehemency of her going, and fleeth on shaking her wings, whereas afterward no token of her way can be found; or as when an arrow is shot at a mark, it parteth the air, which immediately cometh together again, so that a man cannot know where it went through. Even so we, as soon as we were born, began to draw to our end, and have showed no token of virtue, but are consumed in our own wickedness.'

Cf. Bede, *Ecclesiastical History*, II. xiii; see also Fuller's *Church History* (1656), p. 73, for the story of King Edwin's (*c.* 626) 'nameless courtier' counselling the reluctant king: 'Man's life, O King, is like unto a little sparrow, which, whilst your majesty is feasting by the fire in your parlour with your royal retinue, flies in at one window, and out at another. Indeed we see it that short time it remaineth in the house, and then it is well sheltered from wind and weather; but presently it passeth from cold to cold, and whence it came, and whither it goes, we are altogether ignorant. Thus we can give some account of our soul during its abode in the body, whilst housed and harboured therein; but where it was before, and how it fareth after, is to us altogether unknown. If, therefore, Paulinus in his preaching will certainly inform us herein, he deserveth, in my opinion, to be entertained.' The same metaphor reappears in Law's *Christian Perfection* (1726), ch. 1 (*Works*, III. 22).

[5] See Eccles. 12:7. Cf. also, Nos. 30, 'Sermon on the Mount, X', §7; and 150, 'Hypocrisy in Oxford' (Eng. text), II.1: 'an everlasting spirit who is going to God'. Cf. also Wesley's letter to Mary Cooke, Sept. 24, 1785: 'You are an immortal spirit come forth from God and speedily returning to him.'

[6] Luke 16:26.   [7] See Ps 39·13.

[8] Cf. No. 58, *On Predestination*, §16, where Wesley lists five steps from God's foreknowledge to God's final glory: '(1) God knows all believers; (2) wills that they should be saved from sin; (3) to that end, justifies them; (4) sanctifies; and (5) takes them to glory.'

[9] 'A man of one book'; see also Jeremy Taylor, *Life of Christ*, ii. 12, Wesley's most likely direct source. But in Tillotson's Sermon LXXV (*Works*, I. 565), a negative usage had been cited: 'It is a saying, I think of Thomas Aquinas, *Cave ab illo qui unicum legit librum* (beware a man who reads only one book).' The reference here to St. Thomas is unsubstantiated; a closer parallel to Tillotson's point is Roger Bacon's complaint against the dominance of the *Sentences* of Peter Lombard in the 'schools', where *Magister Sententiarum*—i.e., of Lombard's 'one book'—was a prestigious degree; cf. Bacon, *Opus minus*, in *Opera quaedam hactenus inedita* (1859), I. 328-29. See also M. D. Chenu, *Toward Understanding St. Thomas* (Chicago, Henry Regnery Company, 1964), 264-72. For Wesley, then, this phrase was a rhetorical flourish.

Cf. also No. 107, 'On God's Vineyard', I.1; Wesley's letter to John Newton, May 14, 1765; and *A Plain Account of Christian Perfection*, §10.

[10] See Milton, 'L'Allegro', l. 118: 'the busy hum of men'. Cf. No. 73, 'Of Hell', III.2, where Wesley quotes Milton exactly.

alone: only God is here. In his presence I open, I read his Book; for this end, to find the way to heaven. Is there a doubt concerning the meaning of what I read? Does anything appear dark or intricate? I lift up my heart to the Father of lights: 'Lord, is it not thy Word,
5 "If any man lack wisdom, let him ask of God"? Thou "givest liberally and upbraidest not".[11] Thou hast said, "If any be willing to do thy will, he shall know."[12] I am willing to do, let me know, thy will.' I then search after and consider parallel passages of Scripture, 'comparing spiritual things with spiritual'.[13] I meditate
10 thereon, with all the attention and earnestness of which my mind is capable. If any doubt still remains, I consult those who are experienced in the things of God, and then the writings whereby, being dead, they yet speak. And what I thus learn, that I teach.

6. I have accordingly set down in the following sermons what I
15 find in the Bible concerning the way to heaven, with a view to distinguish this way of God from all those which are the inventions of men. I have endeavoured to describe the true, the scriptural, experimental religion, so as to omit nothing which is a real part thereof, and to add nothing thereto which is not. And
20 herein it is more especially my desire, first, to guard those who are just setting their faces toward heaven (and who, having little acquaintance with the things of God, are the more liable to be turned out of the way)[14] from formality, from mere outside religion, which has almost driven heart-religion[15] out of the world; and
25 secondly, to warn those who know the religion of the heart, the faith which worketh by love,[16] lest at any time they make void the law through faith,[17] and so fall back into the snare of the devil.[18]

7. By the advice and at the request of some of my friends, I have prefixed to the other sermons contained in this volume three
30 sermons of my own and one of my brother's preached before the University of Oxford. My design required some discourses on those heads. And I preferred these before any others, as being a stronger answer than any which can be drawn up now to those who have frequently asserted that we have changed our doctrine
35 of late, and do not preach now what we did some years ago. Any man of understanding may now judge for himself, when he has compared the latter with the former sermons.

---

[11] Cf. Jas. 1:5. [12] Cf. John 7:17. [13] 1 Cor. 2:13.
[14] Job 31:7; Heb. 12:13. [15] Cf. No. 25, 'Sermon on the Mount, V', IV.13 and n.
[16] Gal. 5:6. [17] Rom. 3:31. [18] See 1 Tim. 3:7.

8. But some may say I have mistaken the way myself, although I take upon me to teach it to others. It is probable many will think this; and it is very possible that I have. But I trust, whereinsoever I have mistaken, my mind is open to conviction. I sincerely desire to be better informed. I say to God and man, 'What I know not, teach thou me.'

9. Are you persuaded you see more clearly than me? It is not unlikely that you may. Then treat me as you would desire to be treated yourself upon a change of circumstances. Point me out a better way than I have yet known. Show me it is so by plain proof of Scripture. And if I linger in the path I have been accustomed to tread, and am therefore unwilling to leave, labour with me a little, take me by the hand, and lead me as I am able to bear. But be not displeased if I entreat you not to beat me down in order to quicken my pace. I can go but feebly and slowly at best—then, I should not be able to go at all. May I not request of you, farther, not to give me hard names in order to bring me into the right way? Suppose I was ever so much in the wrong, I doubt this would not set me right. Rather it would make me run so much the farther from you—and so get more and more out of the way.

10. Nay, perhaps, if you are angry so shall I be too, and then there will be small hopes of finding the truth. If once anger arise, ἠΰτε κάπνος (as Homer somewhere expresses it),[19] this smoke will so dim the eyes of my soul that I shall be able to see nothing clearly. For God's sake, if it be possible to avoid it let us not provoke one another to wrath. Let us not kindle in each other this fire of hell, much less blow it up into a flame. If we could discern truth by that dreadful light, would it not be loss rather than gain? For how far is love, even with many wrong opinions, to be preferred before truth itself without love? We may die without the knowledge of many truths and yet be carried into Abraham's bosom.[20] But if we die without love, what will knowledge avail?[21] Just as much as it avails the devil and his angels!

The God of love forbid we should ever make the trial! May he prepare us for the knowledge of all truth, by filling our hearts with all his love, and with all joy and peace in believing.[22]

[19] 'Like a puff of smoke'; cf. *Iliad*, xviii.110.
[20] See Luke 16:22, and below, No. 115, 'Dives and Lazarus', *passim*.
[21] Cf. below, No. 4, *Scriptural Christianity*, IV.6: 'Without love, all learning is but splendid ignorance.'
[22] See Rom. 15:13; and No. 42, 'Satan's Devices', II.3, where the same text is also quoted without citation.

A

SERMON

O N

Salvation by Faith

By *JOHN WESLEY*, A. M.
Fellow of *Lincoln* College, OXFORD.

LONDON:

Printed for JAMES HUTTON, at the *Bible* and
Sun, next the *Rose-Tavern,* without *Temple-Bar.*
MDCCXXXVIII.

SALVATION BY FAITH
THE ALMOST CHRISTIAN
'AWAKE, THOU THAT SLEEPEST'
SCRIPTURAL CHRISTIANITY

AN INTRODUCTORY COMMENT

As we have seen, these first four sermons in this first volume of SOSO were 'prefixed' to the other eight on the advice of friends, and also as proof of the consistency of Wesley's new preaching, whether before the University of Oxford or to the masses in Moorfields. But they also serve another function, unavowed but crucial: they mark out the successive stages of Wesley's alienation from any further career as a reformer within the university, as he made the radical shift in his commitment to the Revival as his new vocation.

Along with other ordained Oxford M.A.s, the brothers Wesley were subject to occasional appointment as preachers in the rota of university services on Sundays and saints' days (most of them in the Church of St. Mary the Virgin, but others in St. Peter's in the East and certain college chapels).[1] Attendance upon these services was a stated obligation of 'all doctors, masters, graduates, and scholars', who were enjoined to 'be present at them from their beginning to their end . . .'; no one was 'permitted to wander abroad to another church, or churches, under pain of chastisement . . .', etc. (ch. 10). Even though these injunctions were often honoured in the breach, such occasions were still splendid sounding boards for eloquent preachers with earnest messages.

John Wesley's first 'university sermon' had been delivered in St. Mary's on November 15, 1730, 'On Gen. 1:27' (see No. 141, Vol. IV); a second on July 23, 1732 ('A Consecration Sermon', not extant); a third on January 1, 1733 ('The Circumcision of the Heart'; see No. 17 below). This last may be reckoned as a landmark in the development of Wesley's theology, and must also have made a favourable general impression, for in the next two and a half years he was invited to deliver

---

[1] Cf. *Oxford University Statutes*, tr. by G. R. M. Ward (1845), Vol. I, 'The Laudian Statutes' (1636), Title XVI, chs. 1–7.

six *more university sermons: March 26, 1733 (Easter); April 1, 1733 (Low Sunday); May 13, 1733 (Whitsunday); February 10, 1734; June 11, 1734 (St. Barnabas's); September 21, 1735 (St. Matthew's). This is out of all proportion to any typical rotation, and even if Wesley was serving as substitute for other appointed preachers, that would have required the approval of the Vice-Chancellor (cf.* Statutes, *XVI, ch. 6). The least that this can mean is that John Wesley was more widely appreciated at Oxford as a preacher than the popular stereotypes have suggested.*

This fact sheds some light on the arrangement by the university officials for Wesley to preach again in Oxford soon after his return from Georgia (probably in expectation of his resumption of his duties there); the new appointment was set for the Festival of St. Barnabas, June 11, 1738. By that time, of course, Wesley had undergone the radical change of heart and mind described in the Journal *for May 24, about which his Oxford colleagues would have known nothing.[2] Meanwhile, he had already tested his 'new gospel' ('salvation by faith alone') in several churches in and near London, and his presentation of it had almost invariably stirred up more offence than conversions.[3] In most of these instances, as he records with a trace of self-righteousness, he had been thenceforth barred from this pulpit and that. The Aldersgate experience had not produced a new doctrine, but a new resolution to make the most of his opportunities to expound the one to which he had already come.*

He was by now very well aware of the controversial character of his message, and he could not have expected a sympathetic hearing at Oxford. 'Salvation by Faith' was, however, the first public occasion after his 'Aldersgate' experience for a positive evangelical manifesto. It is worth noting that its Moravian substance is qualified by echoes from the Edwardian Homilies, *as in the claim that salvation involved a power not to commit sin* (posse non peccare). *There is also an obvious Anglican nuance in the definition of saving faith presented here.*

When his turn as university preacher came round again (July 25, 1741), the Revival was in full swing and Wesley had found in its

---

[2] Cf. Intro., above, p.4; see also Schmidt, *Wesley*, I. 141-95, for a careful analysis of the theological developments involved in this 'conversion'; JWJ, Feb. 7–May 28, sheds light on Wesley's mood as he revised his sermon for this crucial new occasion.

[3] See JWJ, Feb. 5 (Milbank, Westminster); Feb. 12 (St. Andrew's, Holborn); Feb. 26 (thrice in London, the first, in St. Lawrence Jewry, being the most blessed 'because it gave the most offence'); Mar. 6 (after being counselled by Böhler to 'preach faith *till* you have it; and then, *because* you have it, you *will* preach faith'); Mar. 17, 26, and 27; Apr. 2, 25, 26; May 7, 9, 14, and 21 (this last being also the day of Charles Wesley's experience of assurance).

leadership an alternative career. He had not only begun to shift his loyalties from Oxford to his own Societies; he had also become one of Oxford's harsher critics.[4] *John Gambold had already advised him that he would face a hostile audience, but Wesley was in no mood to mollify them.*[5] *Indeed, the whole* Journal *record for June and July reflects a mounting tension, as if Wesley was aware of the crisis. On June 28 he preached 'at Charles Square [London], to the largest congregation that, I believe, was ever seen there, on "Almost thou persuadest me to be a Christian" [cf. Acts 26:28]'. This was the sermon that, revised and with its new 'application' explicitly aimed at Oxford, he delivered on the festival day of St. James the Apostle, July 25.*

Its theme—the radical difference between nominal and real Christianity—was already a familiar one in Puritan preaching;[6] *it was, however, already conventional to ignore the text's plain reference to Agrippa's being almost persuaded to become a Christian rather than to his already being a nominal one. Wesley draws out the distinctions between the two stages of Christian experience ('almost' and 'altogether'). Part I paints a vivid picture of the high-minded hypocrite (the 'almost Christian') and concludes with Wesley's confession 'that this had been his own state in all his days at Oxford' (I.13). Part II delineates the 'altogether Christian' according to his new conceptions, and openly expresses doubt that there are many such in Oxford even now (II.7-9). There are no records of this sermon's reception on this occasion, but it would not have been lost on his Methodist readers that their leader had bearded the Anglican establishment in one of its citadels and had survived.*

In the following year Charles Wesley came up for an appointment as preacher in St. Mary's on April 4, 1742. His evangelical conversion had preceded his brother's, either on May 3, 1738 (when 'it pleased God to open his eyes so that he saw clearly what was the nature of [saving]

---

[4] This may be seen in the Latin and English versions of a sermon on Isa. 1:21 which he had first prepared in 1739, probably in connection with his exercises for the B.D. degree which, as Fellow of Lincoln College, he was expected to take in due course (see below, Nos. 150, 151).

[5] See JWJ, June 18, 1741: 'All here [Gambold had said of the Oxford community] are so prejudiced that they will mind nothing you say.' Wesley's reaction: 'I know that. However, I am to deliver my own soul, whether they will hear or whether they will forbear' (one of Wesley's standard formulae of alienation). A fortnight later even Wesley and Gambold had come to a parting of their ways (cf. JWJ, July 2). Earlier, he had finally got round to reading 'that celebrated book, Martin Luther's *Comment on the Epistle to the Galatians*'; his negative reaction to it was intemperate (see JWJ, June 15).

[6] Cf. below, No. 2, *The Almost Christian*, proem and n.

faith . . .'), or on May 19 (when he 'had found rest to his soul').[7] *In any case, Charles was more exuberant in temperament and rhetoric than his elder brother.*[8] *He had already preached a sermon on justification 'before the university [July 1739] with great boldness . . . '.*[9] *His bidding prayer*[10] *indicates that this preaching service had been held in Christ Church Cathedral rather than St. Mary's. On June 30, 1740, he reports having spent a week in Oxford 'preaching repentance' but also in discovering that 'learned Gallio cared for none of these things'.*[11] *Now, he was scheduled to preach in St. Mary's itself—for the first and last time.*

Charles's message, with a barrage of invidious questions for its climax, fell largely on deaf ears; this is reported by a visitor who was in the audience: Thomas Salmon, a popular historian.[12] *Charles Wesley's denial of Salmon's report appears in his* Journal *for April 15, 1750, and is emphatic;*[13] *he may have been right about the time, since the sermon as printed can be read aloud in thirty minutes. On the other hand, Charles's accusations must surely have aroused resentment in his auditory, and Salmon would have been a competent judge of that. In any case this sermon would have persuaded any Methodist reader of Charles's wholehearted identification with his brother's cause and theirs.* 'Awake, Thou That Sleepest' *is then a lively evangelical statement, a personal identification with the Revival and a valedictory to Oxford.*

By August 1744 the Revival was gaining momentum, the network ('connexion') of the Methodist Societies had extended over into Wales

---

[7] Cf. both CWJ and JWJ for these dates and experiences.

[8] See above, p. 2, n. 6: '. . . in connection I beat you; but in strong, pointed sentences you beat me.'

[9] CWJ, Sunday, July 1, 1739; this is followed (on Monday) by a note that the Vice-Chancellor and 'all were against [that] sermon as liable to be misunderstood'. Had this been Charles's reinforcing sequel to John's *Salvation by Faith?*

[10] In the unpublished MS of a sermon on Rom. 3:27-28.

[11] See Acts 18:17 for this analogy between a Roman proconsul's and Oxford's indifference.

[12] 'The times of the day the University go to this church are ten in the morning and two in the afternoon, on Sundays and holidays, the sermon usually lasting about half an hour. But when I happened to be at Oxford, in 1742, Mr. Wesley, the Methodist, of Christ Church, entertained his audience two hours, having insulted and abused all degrees from the highest to the lowest, was in a manner hissed out of the pulpit by the lads;' Thomas Salmon, *A Foreigner's Companion through the Universities of Cambridge and Oxford* (1748), p. 25, and quoted in CWJ, Apr. 15, 1750.

[13] 'And it would have been high time for them to do so, if the historian [Salmon] said true. But, unfortunately for him, I measured the time by my watch and it was within the hour; I abused neither high nor low, as my sermon in print will prove; neither was I hissed out of the pulpit or treated with the least incivility, either by young or old . . . .'

and had come under serious persecution by English mobs, the first 'conference' had just been held (June 25-29), and John Wesley had found his true mission in life. Even so, his turn as university preacher came up yet again for August 24 (another festival, this one for St. Bartholomew). This, of course, was an anniversary of the notorious Massacre of Paris (in 1572) and, again, of the Great Ejectment of the Nonconformists in England in 1662, in which both of Wesley's grandfathers had suffered. Benjamin Kennicott's explanation of Wesley's appointment was that 'as no clergyman [could] avoid his turn, so the university can refuse none; otherwise Mr. Wesley would not have preached.'[14] *Actually, though, that rule was flexible; there was ample precedent for substitutions. One must wonder, therefore, how the appointment came about. Was it a gesture of academic freedom? Did Wesley have a stronger base in Oxford than would appear from the record? There is no indication that he had claimed his turn as by right, but it would never have crossed his mind to avoid it. Thus, the stage was set for a confrontation—and another valedictory.*

Parts I–III of Scriptural Christianity *constitute a positive account of Wesley's conception of the 'order of salvation' (Part I), an interesting missiological perspective (Part II), and an early statement of Wesley's eschatological ideas (Part III)—the sum of these parts is evangelical and Anglican. The mood changes in Part IV where he comes to his 'plain and practical application'. Here the judgment is passed, with scant charity, that Oxford's hypocrisies are an intolerable offence to God and a general hindrance to the Christian mission. Kennicott's uncharitable suspicion was that this final salvo 'was what [Wesley] had been preparing for all along . . .':*

> *[In the conclusion] he fired his address with so much zeal and unbounded satire as quite spoiled what otherwise might have been turned to great advantage. . . . I liked some of his freedom: such as calling the generality of young townsmen 'a generation of triflers'. . . . But considering how many shining lights are here that are the glory of the Christian cause, his sacred censure was much too flaming and strong and his charity much too weak. . . . Having summed up the measure of our iniquities, he concluded with a lifted up eye in this most solemn form, 'It is time for* thee, Lord, *to lay to* thine hand*'—words full of such presumption and seeming imprecation that they gave an universal shock. . . . Had these things been omitted and his censures moderated, I think his discourse, as to style and delivery, would have been uncommonly pleasing to others as well as to myself. He is allowed to be a man of great parts, and that by the excellent Dean*

---

[14] At this time, Kennicott was an undergraduate at Wadham College, but he was destined to set Old Testament studies in England upon a new level with his great *Vetus Testamentum cum Variis Lectionibus* (Vol. 1, 1776; Vol. 2, 1780). His account of Wesley's sermon appeared in *WMM*, 1866, 47-48.

of Christ Church;[15] for the day he preached the dean generously said of him, 'John Wesley will always be thought a man of sound sense, though an enthusiast!' However, the Vice-Chancellor[16] sent for the sermon, and I hear that the heads of college intend to shew their resentment.

Another eyewitness report of the same event was recorded by William Blackstone, already a Fellow of All Souls and on his way to the fame he would earn as author of his Commentaries on the Laws of England *(1765–69). In a letter to a family friend (Aug. 28) the young Blackstone reports on Wesley's sermon, which seems to have become the talk of the town:*

> *We were last Friday [Aug. 24] entertained at St. Mary's by a curious sermon from Wesley the Methodist. Among other equally modest particulars, he informed us, lst, that there was not one Christian among all the Heads of Houses; 2ndly, that pride, gluttony, avarice, luxury, sensuality and drunkenness were general characteristics of all Fellows of Colleges, who were useless to a proverbial uselessness. Lastly, that the younger part of the University were a generation of triflers, all of them perjured and none of them of any religion at all. His notes were demanded by the Vice-Chancellor, but on mature deliberation it has been thought proper to punish him by a mortifying neglect. . . .[17]*

That 'mortifying neglect' began at once. Charles Wesley records that 'we [John Wesley, Charles Wesley, Messrs. Piers and Meriton] walked back in form, the little band of us four; for of the rest durst none join himself to us.'[18]

Methodists, then and later, could see no proper warrant for anyone to have taken offence at such a sermon; after all, Wesley had simply preached the gospel and applied it 'close and home'. Thomas Jackson's later comment on it is typical:

> Scriptural Christianity *contains a beautiful and forcible description of spiritual religion, with the manner by which it is acquired by individuals and then spreads from one to another until it shall cover the earth. The concluding application to the heads of colleges and halls, to the fellows and tutors and to the body of undergraduates, assumes their general and wide departure from the true Christian character, and [their] abandonment to formality, worldliness, levity, and sloth. It contains nothing sarcastic and irritating, nothing that was designed to give unnecessary pain or offence; but is marked throughout by seriousness, fidelity, and tender affection.[19]*

---

[15] John Conybeare, who succeeded Joseph Butler as Bishop of Bristol, and author of *Defence of Revealed Religion . . .*(1732), one of the eighteenth century's more famous replies to Tindal and other deists.

[16] Walter Hodges, Provost of Oriel.

[17] Cf. the facsimile of the letter in John Fletcher Hurst, *The History of Methodism*, II. 604-5.

[18] Cf. CWJ, Aug. 24, 1744.

[19] *The Life of the Rev. Charles Wesley* (1841), I. 403.

John Wesley himself was much more of a realist and also more aware of his own intention:

> *I preached, I suppose the last time, at St. Mary's. Be it so. I am now clear of the blood of these men. I have fully delivered my own soul.*
>
> *The Beadle came to me afterwards and told me the Vice-Chancellor had sent him for my notes. I sent them without delay, not without admiring the wise providence of God. Perhaps few men of note would have given a sermon of mine the reading if I had put it into their hands; but by this means it came to be read, probably more than once, by every man of eminence in the University.[20]*

That he never regretted the affair or its consequences would appear from a complacent recollection of it in 1781 in 'A Short History of the People called Methodists':

> *Friday, August 24, St. Bartholomew's Day, I preached for the last time before the University of Oxford. I am now clear of the blood of these men. I have fully delivered my own soul. And I am well pleased that it should be the very day on which, in the last century,[21] near two thousand burning and shining lights were put out at one stroke. Yet what a wide difference is there between their case and mine! They were turned out of house and home, and all that they had; whereas I am only hindered from preaching, without any other loss; and that in a kind of honourable manner; it being determined that when my next turn to preach came they would pay another person to preach for me. And so they did twice or thrice, even to the time that I resigned my fellowship.[22]*

What would have been most obvious to his Methodist readers was the heroic stature of their leader who had preached 'plain truth' to academic people to their face and at the cost of rejection by them. What clearer proof could there be of his fidelity to the gospel under all circumstances and of his total commitment in his ministry among them? It was no small matter for a tenured don to have forsaken his privileged status in a class-conscious English society in exchange for 'The Foundery', 'The New Room', and a career among the masses. They knew, all too well, how rudely the Methodists had been treated, to the point of savage persecution, condoned by magistrates and clergy alike in the years between 1739 and 1746; they could still foresee dangerous days ahead. Scriptural Christianity *as published was an evangelical proclamation; it was also an act of defiance.*

These 'prefixed' sermons, therefore, serve a particular function in SOSO *as a bloc: they proclaim the Wesleyan message in prophetic terms, and they signify Wesley's transference of his allegiance from the*

---

[20] JWJ, Aug. 24, 1744.

[21] *Viz.*, the Great Ejectment in 1662.

[22] §30. See Vol. 9 of this edn. and *Bibliog*, No. 420.

Academy to his new vocation as a preacher of 'plain truth for plain people'. Together they dispel any impression of inconsistency. His message in St. Mary's had been the same as it was now in Moorfields. Thus, these sermons could serve as a multifaceted introductory quartet to the larger endeavour of Sermons on Several Occasions.

* * * * * * * * * *

The edited text of Salvation by Faith *is based upon the first edition of 1738. For a stemma illustrating its publishing history through its thirty-one editions in Wesley's lifetime, together with substantive variant readings, see Vol. IV, Appendix. See also* Bibliog, No. 10.

The text for The Almost Christian *is based upon its first edition, 1741. For a stemma and table of variant readings through the twenty-eight extant editions during Wesley's lifetime, see Vol. IV, Appendix. See also* Bibliog, No. 50.

The first edition of 'Awake, Thou That Sleepest' *followed here, was published shortly after the sermon itself was preached in 1742. For a stemma and variant readings from the fifty-two extant editions in Charles Wesley's lifetime, see Vol. IV, Appendix. See also* Bibliog, No. 59.

Scriptural Christianity *was also published shortly after its delivery in 1744 and ran through at least fifteen editions in Wesley's lifetime. For a stemma of these editions and a list of variant readings, see Vol. IV, Appendix. See also* Bibliog, No. 92.

Salvation by Faith

A Sermon preached at St. Mary's, Oxford, before the University, on June 11, 1738[1]

Ephesians 2:8

By grace ye are saved through faith.[2]

1. All the blessings which God hath bestowed upon man are of his mere grace, bounty, or favour: his free, undeserved favour, favour altogether undeserved, man having no claim to the least of his mercies.[3] It was free grace that 'formed man of the dust of the ground, and breathed into him a living soul',[4] and stamped on that soul the image of God,[5] and 'put all things under

---

[1] The half-title in the first edition of *SOSO*, Vol. I (1746), and a footnote in *Works* I. 15, record the date as June 18, 1738—an obvious misremembrance, since Wesley was in Germany then; cf. JWJ.

[2] One of Wesley's favourite texts. In No. 16, 'The Means of Grace', II. 6, he speaks of its theme as 'that great foundation of the whole Christian building'; cf. John Telford, *The Life of the Rev. Charles Wesley* (London, Wesleyan Methodist Book Room, 1900), pp. 76, 79-80, and also John Hampson's comment (*Memoirs*, I. 199) that Wesley's definition of faith here, based upon the *Homilies*, remained constant thereafter.

[3] See Gen 32:10. [4] Cf. Gen. 2:7.

[5] This metaphor from Gen. 1:27 is the basic one in Wesley's anthropology; it first appears in the MS sermon on the Genesis text (see below, No. 141, 'The Image of God', dated 1730) and is often repeated throughout the corpus. Cf. Nos. 3, *'Awake, Thou That Sleepest'*, I.2; 5, 'Justification by Faith', I. 1-2; 6, 'The Righteousness of Faith', II.9; 12, 'The Witness of Our Own Spirit', §16; 14, *The Repentance of Believers*, III.2; 20, *The Lord Our Righteousness*, I.2; 22, 'Sermon on the Mount, II', II.6; 44, *Original Sin*, III.5; 45, 'The New Birth', I.1; 57, 'On the Fall of Man', II.6; 60, 'The General Deliverance', I.1, 2, III.11, 12; 62, 'The End of Christ's Coming', I.7; 85, 'On Working Out Our Own Salvation', II.1; 128, 'The Deceitfulness of the Human Heart', I.2; 129, 'Heavenly Treasure in Earthen Vessels', §2, I.1; 135, 'On Guardian Angels', II.2; 139, 'On the Sabbath', I.2; 146, 'The One Thing Needful', I.2, III.1; cf. also his letter to Richard Morgan, Jan. 15, 1734, and to William Dodd, Mar. 12, 1756. See also *Survey* (1784), IV. 54-55.

The phrase denotes for Wesley the human capacity for knowing and responding to God's prevenient, justifying, and sanctifying activities and, in this respect, is equivalent to his other phrase about our 'spiritual sensorium' (cf. No. 10, 'The Witness of the Spirit, I',

his feet'.[6] The same free grace continues to us, at this day, life, and breath, and all things.[7] For there is nothing we are, or have, or do, which can deserve the least thing at God's hand. 'All our works thou, O God, hast wrought in us.'[8] These therefore are so
5   many more instances of free mercy: and whatever righteousness may be found in man, this also is the gift of God.

     2. Wherewithal then shall a sinful man atone for any the least of his sins? With his own works? No. Were they ever so many or holy, they are not his own, but God's. But indeed they are all unholy
10   and sinful themselves, so that every one of them needs a fresh atonement. Only corrupt fruit grows on a corrupt tree.[9] And his heart is altogether corrupt and abominable, being 'come short of the glory of God',[10] the glorious righteousness at first impressed on his soul, after the image of his great Creator. Therefore having
15   nothing, neither righteousness nor works, to plead, his 'mouth is utterly stopped before God'.[11]

     3. If then sinful man find favour with God, it is 'grace upon grace' (χάριν ἀντὶ χάριτος).[12] If God vouchsafe still to pour fresh blessings upon us—yea, the greatest of all blessings,
20   salvation—what can we say to these things but 'Thanks be unto God for his unspeakable gift!'[13] And thus it is. Herein 'God commendeth his love toward us, in that, while we were yet sinners, Christ died'[14] to save us. 'By grace', then, 'are ye saved through faith.'[15] Grace is the source, faith the condition, of
25   salvation.

     Now, that we fall not short of the grace of God, it concerns us carefully to inquire:

        I. What faith it is through which we are saved.

       II. What is the salvation which is through faith.

30   III. How we may answer some objections.

I.12 and n.). The restoration of our corrupted and disabled 'image' to its pristine capacity is, indeed, the goal of Wesley's *ordo salutis*.

   [6] Ps. 8:6; a rare quotation of a psalm from the AV. See also 1 Cor. 15:27; Eph. 1:22.

   [7] Acts 17:25.

   [8] Cf. Isa. 26:12.

   [9] See Matt. 7:17, 18; 12:33.

   [10] Rom. 3:23.

   [11] Cf. Rom. 3:19.

   [12] John 1:16. Orig. Χάρις ἀντι Χάριτος, in the early editions; the Greek parenthesis was omitted from later separate editions (beginning in 1743), and from all the collected editions of the sermons.

   [13] 2 Cor. 9:15.

   [14] Rom. 5:8.   [15] Cf. Eph. 2:8.

I. What faith it is through which we are saved.

1. And, first, it is not barely the faith of a heathen. Now God requireth of a heathen to believe 'that God is, and that he is a rewarder of them that diligently seek him';[16] and that he is to be sought by 'glorifying him as God by giving him thanks for all things',[17] and by a careful practice of moral virtue, of justice, mercy, and truth, toward their fellow-creatures. A Greek or Roman, therefore, yea, a Scythian or Indian, was without excuse if he did not believe thus much: the being and attributes of God, a future state of reward and punishment, and the obligatory nature of moral virtue. For this is barely the faith of a heathen.[18]

2. Nor, secondly, is it the faith of a devil,[19] though this goes much farther than that of a heathen. For the devil believes, not only that there is a wise and powerful God, gracious to reward and just to punish, but also that Jesus is the Son of God, the Christ, the Saviour of the world. So we find him declaring in express terms: 'I know thee who thou art, the Holy One of God.'[a] Nor can we doubt but that unhappy spirit believes all those words which came out of the mouth of the Holy One; yea, and whatsoever else was written by those holy men of old, of two of whom he was compelled to give that glorious testimony, 'These men are the servants of the most high God, who show unto you the way of salvation.'[20] Thus much then the great enemy of God and man believes, and trembles in believing, that 'God was made manifest in the flesh;'[21] that he will 'tread all enemies under his feet';[22] and

---

[a] Luke 4:34.

[16] Cf. Heb. 11:6.

[17] Cf. Luke 2:20.

[18] For other uses of this phrase and for Wesley's denials of the efficacy of natural religion, see Nos. 2, *The Almost Christian;* 9, 'The Spirit of Bondage and of Adoption'; 54, 'On Eternity', §17; 69, 'The Imperfection of Human Knowledge', III.2; 74, 'Of the Church', §11; 106, 'On Faith, Heb. 11:6', I.3, II.2. See also his *Notes* on Acts 17:28, and *Survey* II. 276. For Susanna Wesley's comments on this topic, see John Newton, *Susanna Wesley and the Puritan Tradition in Methodism* (London, Epworth Press, 1968), p. 149. Cf. also South, Sermon XIX, on Rom. 1:20, 'Sinners Inexcusable from Natural Religion Only', §IV, in *Sermons,* I.313 ff.

[19] This phrase was familiar from the Homily 'Of Salvation', Pt. III, *Certain Sermons or Homilies Appointed to be Read in Churches...* (Oxford, Oxford University Press, 1840), p. 26 (hereafter cited as *Homilies*). For other instances of Wesley's insistence that orthodoxy may be no better than 'the faith of a devil', cf. Nos. 7, 'The Way to the Kingdom', I.6; and 150, 'Hypocrisy in Oxford', I.9; see also his letter to Richard Tompson, July 25, 1755.

[20] Cf. Acts 16:17.

[21] Cf. 1 Tim. 3:16.

[22] Cf. 1 Cor. 15:25.

that 'all Scripture was given by inspiration of God.'[23] Thus far goeth the faith of a devil.

3. Thirdly, the faith through which we are saved, in that sense of the word which will hereafter be explained, is not barely that
5 which the apostles themselves had while Christ was yet upon earth;[24] though they so believed on him as to 'leave all to follow him';[25] although they had then power to work miracles, 'to heal all manner of sickness, and all manner of disease';[26] yea, they had then 'power and authority over all devils':[27] and which is beyond
10 all this, were sent by their Master to 'preach the kingdom of God'.[28] Yet after their return from doing all these mighty works their Lord himself terms them, 'a faithless generation'.[29] He tells them 'they could not cast out a devil, because of their unbelief.'[30] And when long after, supposing they had some already, they said
15 unto him, 'Increase our faith,' he tells them plainly that of this faith they had none at all, no, not as a grain of mustard seed: 'The Lord said, If ye had faith as a grain of mustard seed, ye might say unto this sycamine tree, Be thou plucked up by the roots, and be thou planted in the sea; and it should obey you.'[31]
20 4. What faith is it then through which we are saved? It may be answered: first, in general, it is a faith in Christ—Christ, and God through Christ, are the proper object[32] of it. Herein therefore it is sufficiently, absolutely, distinguished from the faith either of ancient or modern heathens. And from the faith of a devil it is
25 fully distinguished by this—it is not barely a speculative, rational thing, a cold, lifeless assent, a train of ideas in the head; but also a disposition of the heart. For thus saith the Scripture, 'With the heart man believeth unto righteousness.' And, 'If thou shalt confess with thy mouth the Lord Jesus, and shalt believe with thy *heart*
30 that God hath raised him from the dead, thou shalt be saved.'[33]

---

[23] Cf. 2 Tim. 3:16.

[24] An allusion to the doctrines of Robert Sandeman and John Glas, that faith in the apostolic *kerygma* in itself was salvific. Cf. No. 43, *The Scripture Way of Salvation*, II.3.

[25] Cf. Mark 10:28, etc.   [26] Matt. 10:1.   [27] Luke 9:1.

[28] Luke 9:2; the text of 1746 ends here.   [29] Luke 9:41.

[30] Cf. Luke 9:40; Mark 6:6.   [31] Luke 17:5-6.

[32] In the text of 1771 (and several later edns., but not that of 1787) 'object' is altered to 'objects'. The 1771 edition is notorious for its careless printing and, in any case, it would have seemed natural to a printer to use a plural object after a plural verb. It is scarcely probable that Wesley would have meant 'objects' in this context since the theological connotation would have been di-theistic. 'Object', then, is more probably Wesley's own usage.

[33] Rom. 10:9, 10.

5. And herein does it differ from that faith which the apostles themselves had while our Lord was on earth, that it acknowledges the necessity and merit of his death, and the power of his resurrection. It acknowledges his death as the only sufficient means of redeeming man from death eternal, and his resurrection as the restoration of us all to life and immortality; inasmuch as he 'was delivered for our sins, and rose again for our justification'.[34] Christian faith is then not only an assent to the whole gospel of Christ, but also a full reliance on the blood of Christ, a trust in the merits of his life, death, and resurrection;[35] a recumbency upon him as our atonement and our life, as *given for us*, and *living in us*. It is a sure confidence which a man hath in God, that through the merits of Christ *his* sins are forgiven, and *he* reconciled to the favour of God; and in consequence hereof[36] a closing with him[37] and cleaving to him as our 'wisdom, righteousness, sanctification, and redemption'[38] or, in one word, our salvation.

II. What salvation it is which is through this faith is the second thing to be considered.

1. And, first, whatsoever else it imply, it is a present salvation. It is something attainable, yea, actually attained on earth, by those who are partakers of this faith. For thus saith the Apostle to the believers at Ephesus, and in them to the believers of all ages, not, 'Ye *shall be*' (though that also is true), but 'Ye *are* saved through faith.'[39]

2. Ye are saved (to comprise all in one word) from sin. This is

---

[34] Cf. Rom. 4:25.

[35] This is close to the definition of 'lively faith' in the Homily 'Of Faith', Pt. I (*Homilies*, p. 30). The crucial distinction, in both places, is between faith as 'assent' and faith as 'trust'. See also *An Earnest Appeal*, §59 (11: 68-69 of this edn.).

[36] The first edition here reads: 'It is a confidence in the goodness of God, through the Son of his love, living, dying, and interceding for us. It is an acceptance of him in all his offices, as our Prophet, our Priest, and our King.' No copy of the 2nd edition survives, but the 3rd (1740) turns back again to the language of the Homily 'Of Salvation', Pt. III (*Homilies*, pp. 26-27).

[37] 'Closing with Christ' was a favourite Puritan metaphor. Cf. Ralph Erskine, *Law-Death, Gospel-Life: Or, the Death of Legal Righteousness, the Life of Gospel-Holiness* (Edinburgh, 1724); also Matthew Mead, Ἐν ὀλίγῳ Χριστιανός, *the Almost Christian Discovered* (1661). Similar usages may be seen in William Allen, *The Glass of Justification* (1658), p. 26; Richard Alleine, *Vindiciae Pietatis* (1676), p. 176; William Guthrie, *The Christian's Great Interest* (1766), pp. 103, 118-19; Thomas Ridgeley, *A Body of Divinity* (1733), p. 551. See also George Whitefield's letter to Dr. Doddridge in Seymour, I. 202.

[38] 1 Cor. 1:30. The edition of 1771 omits the phrase following the scriptural quotation.

[39] Cf. Eph. 2:8.

the salvation which is through faith. This is that great salvation foretold by the angel before God brought his first-begotten into the world: 'Thou shalt call his name Jesus, for he shall save his people from their sins.'[40] And neither here nor in other parts of
5 Holy Writ is there any limitation or restriction. All his people, or as it is elsewhere expressed, all that believe in him, he will save from all their sins:[41] from original and actual, past and present sin, of the flesh and of the spirit. Through faith that is in him they are saved both from the guilt and from the power of it.

10   3. First, from the guilt of all past sin. For whereas 'all the world is guilty before God';[42] insomuch that should he 'be extreme to mark what is done amiss, there is none that could abide it';[43] and whereas 'by the law is only the knowledge of sin', but no deliverance from it, so that 'by fulfilling the deeds of the law no flesh
15 can be justified in his sight'; now 'the righteousness of God, which is by faith of Jesus Christ', 'is manifested unto all that believe'. Now they are 'justified freely by his grace through the redemption that is in Jesus Christ. Him God hath set forth to be a propitiation through faith in his blood, to declare his righteous-
20 ness for (or by) the remission of the sins that are past.'[44] Now hath Christ 'taken away the curse of the law, being made a curse for us'.[45] He hath 'blotted out the handwriting that was against us, taking it out of the way, nailing it to his cross'.[46] 'There is therefore no condemnation now to them which believe in Christ Jesus.'[47]

25   4. And being saved from guilt, they are saved from fear. Not indeed from a filial fear of offending, but from all servile fear, from that 'fear which hath torment',[48] from fear of punishment, from fear of the wrath of God, whom they now no longer regard as a severe master, but as an indulgent Father. 'They have not
30 received again the spirit of bondage, but the Spirit of adoption, whereby they cry, Abba, Father: the Spirit itself also bearing witness with their spirit, that they are the children of God.'[49] They are also saved from the fear, though not from the possibility, of falling away[50] from the grace of God, and coming short of the

---

[40] Matt. 1:21.   [41] See Acts 10:43, etc.   [42] Cf. Rom. 3:19.
[43] Ps. 130:3 (BCP).   [44] Cf. Rom. 3:20-25.   [45] Cf. Gal. 3:13.
[46] Cf. Col. 2:14.   [47] Cf. Rom. 8:1.   [48] Cf. 1 John 4:18.
[49] Cf. Rom. 8:15-16.

[50] Cf. 2 Thess. 2:3. In opposition to all notions of final perseverance Wesley stresses the risks of faith and the dangers of lapsing, even from peak experiences of faith. Cf. Nos. 21, 'Sermon on the Mount, I', II. 4; 24, 'Sermon on the Mount, IV', I.9; 61, 'The Mystery of

great and precious promises. They are 'sealed with the Holy Spirit of promise, which is the earnest of their inheritance'.[51] Thus have they 'peace with God through our Lord Jesus Christ. . . . They rejoice in hope of the glory of God. . . . And the love of God is shed abroad in their hearts through the Holy Ghost which is given unto them.'[52] And hereby they are 'persuaded' (though perhaps not all at all times, nor with the same fullness of persuasion) 'that neither death, nor life, nor things present, nor things to come, nor height, nor depth, nor any other creature, shall be able to separate them from the love of God, which is in Christ Jesus our Lord.'[53]

5. Again, through this faith they are saved from the power of sin as well as from the guilt of it.[54] So the Apostle declares, 'Ye know that he was manifested to take away our sins, and in him is no sin. Whosoever abideth in him sinneth not.'[b] Again, 'Little children, let no man deceive you. . . . He that committeth sin is of the devil.'[55] 'Whosoever believeth is born of God.'[56] And, 'Whosoever is born of God doth not commit sin; for his seed remaineth in him: and he cannot sin, because he is born of God.'[57] Once more, 'We know that whosoever is born of God sinneth not; but he that is begotten of God keepeth himself, and that wicked one toucheth him not.'[c]

[b] [1 John] chap. 3, ver. 5-6.
[c] Chap. 5, ver. 18.

Iniquity', §30; 76, 'On Perfection', proem; 86, *A Call to Backsliders*, 1. 2(3). For the earliest instances of its use see Nos. 133, 'Death and Deliverance' (Oct. 1, 1725), ¶16; and 149, 'On Love' (Feb. 20, 1737), §1.

See also *Predestination Calmly Considered*, §74; *Serious Thoughts Upon the Perseverance of the Saints* (*Bibliog*, No. 192, Vol. 12 of this edn.); JWJ, May 6, 1742; May 6, 1785; and Wesley's *Notes* on this text as well as on Heb. 6:6.

[51] Eph. 1:13. This sentence is omitted from the edition of 1771.
[52] Cf. Rom. 5:1, 2, 5.   [53] Cf. Rom. 8:38-39.
[54] In most separate editions the following passage is added: 'Indeed "the infection of nature doth remain: which hath in itself the nature of sin" [cf. Art. IX, 'Of Original or Birth Sin' in The Thirty-nine Articles of Religion; for minor variants, see Appendix, 'Wesley's Text', Vol. IV]. For it is "a coming short of the glory of God" [cf. Rom. 3:23]. And St. John accordingly declares, not only that "if a man say he hath not sinned he maketh God a liar" [cf. 1 John 1:10], but also, "If we say we have no sin" now remaining "we deceive ourselves" [1 John 1:8]. Many infirmities likewise do remain, whereby we are daily subject to what are called sins of infirmity. And doubtless they are in some sense sins, as being "transgressions of the perfect law" [cf. 1 John 3:4]. And with regard to these it may be said of us all our lives that "in many things we offend all" [Jas. 3:2]. But this notwithstanding, the same Apostle declares. . . .'
[55] 1 John 3:7-8.   [56] 1 John 5:1.   [57] 1 John 3:9.

6. He that is by faith born of God sinneth not,[58] (1), by any habitual sin, for all habitual sin is sin reigning; but sin cannot reign in any that believeth.[59] Nor, (2), by any wilful sin; for his will, while he abideth in the faith, is utterly set against all sin, and
5 abhorreth it as deadly poison. Nor, (3), by any sinful desire; for he continually desireth the holy and perfect will of God;[60] and any unholy desire[61] he by the grace of God stifleth in the birth. Nor, (4), doth he sin by infirmities, whether in act, word, or thought; for his infirmities have no concurrence of his will; and without
10 this they are not properly sins. Thus, 'He that is born of God doth not commit sin.'[62] And though he cannot say he *hath not sinned*, yet now *'he sinneth not'*.[63]

7. This then is the salvation which is through faith, even in the present world: a salvation from sin and the consequences of sin,
15 both often expressed in the word 'justification', which, taken in the largest sense, implies a deliverance from guilt and punishment, by the atonement of Christ actually applied to the soul of the sinner now believing on him, and a deliverance from the power of sin,[64] through Christ 'formed in his heart'.[65] So that
20 he who is thus justified or saved by faith is indeed 'born again'. He is 'born again of the Spirit'[66] unto a new 'life which is hid with Christ in God'.[67] And as a 'newborn babe he gladly receives the ἄδολον, the sincere milk of the word, and grows thereby';[68] 'going on in the might of the Lord his God',[69] 'from faith to
25 faith',[70] 'from grace to grace',[71] 'until at length he comes unto a

---

[58] I.e., 'sinneth not', deliberately or intentionally. It is a crucial point for Wesley to distinguish between 'sins properly so called' (intentional violations of known laws of God) and indeliberate 'sins' of various sorts. Cf. below, No. 13, *On Sin in Believers* (intro.).

[59] For other references to 'sin remaining but not reigning', cf. No. 13, *On Sin in Believers*, I.6 and n.

[60] Rom. 12:2.

[61] All editions except *Works* (1771) read, 'and any tendency to an unholy desire'.

[62] 1 John 3:9. The *Sermons* (1746) and the editions stemming from it omit here a passage present in most single editions: *'hath sin in him*, but'.

[63] Cf. 1 John 5:18.

[64] *Works* (1771) alters 'the whole body of sin' to 'the power of sin'.

[65] Cf. Gal. 4:19; the first and other early editions have 'Christ gradually "formed in the heart" '.

[66] Cf. John 3:3, 5, etc. See also Nos. 14, *The Repentance of Believers*, III.2 and n.; and 45, 'The New Birth'.

[67] Cf. Col. 3:3. All editions except the *Works* (1771) add here: 'He is a new creature: old things are passed away; all things in him are become new' (2 Cor. 5:17).

[68] Cf. 1 Pet. 2:2.

[69] Cf. Eph. 6:10.

[70] Rom. 1:17.

[71] Cf. John 1:16.

perfect man, unto the measure of the stature of the fullness of Christ'.[72]

III. The first usual objection to this is,

1. That to preach salvation or justification by faith only is to preach against holiness and good works. To which a short answer 5 might be given: it would be so if we spake, as some do, of a faith which was separate from these. But we speak of a faith which is not so, but necessarily productive of all good works and all holiness.[73]

2. But it may be of use to consider it more at large: especially 10 since it is no new objection, but as old as St. Paul's time, for even then it was asked, 'Do we not make void the law through faith?'[74] We answer, first, all who preach not faith do manifestly make void the law, either directly and grossly, by limitations and comments that eat out all the spirit of the text; or indirectly, by not pointing 15 out the only means whereby it is possible to perform it. Whereas, secondly, 'We establish the law', both by showing its full extent and spiritual meaning, and by calling all to that living way whereby 'the righteousness of the law may be fulfilled in them'.[75] These, while they trust in the blood of Christ alone, use all the 20 ordinances which he hath appointed, do all the 'good works which he had before prepared that they should walk therein',[76] and enjoy and manifest all holy and heavenly tempers, even the same 'mind that was in Christ Jesus'.[77]

3. But does not preaching this faith lead men into pride? We 25 answer, accidentally it may. Therefore ought every believer to be earnestly cautioned (in the words of the great Apostle): 'Because of unbelief the first branches were broken off, and thou standest by faith. Be not high-minded, but fear. If God spared not the natural branches, take heed lest he spare not thee. Behold 30 therefore the goodness and severity of God: on them which fell, severity; but toward thee, goodness, if thou continue in his

---

[72] Cf. Eph. 4:13.

[73] The first edition reads: 'But we speak of a faith which is necessarily inclusive of all good works and all holiness.' See Appendix 'Wesley's Text', Vol. IV, for full details of variants. Notice the emphatic correlation here between 'faith alone' and 'good works', and this within days after 'Aldersgate'.

[74] Cf. Rom. 3:31. See also the later sermons (Nos. 35, 36) on 'The Law Established through Faith', Discourses I and II, both on this text and, together, expounding the same conjunction of saving faith and good works as its fruitage.

[75] Cf. Rom.8:4.   [76] Cf. Eph. 2:10.   [77] Cf. Phil. 2:5.

goodness: otherwise thou also shalt be cut off.'[78] And while he
continues therein, he will remember those words of St. Paul,
foreseeing and answering this very objection: 'Where is boasting,
then? It is excluded. By what law? Of works? Nay; but by the law of
5 faith.'[d] If a man were justified by his works, he would have
whereof to glory. But there is no glorying for him 'that worketh
not, but believeth on him that justifieth the ungodly'.[e] To the
same effect are the words both preceding and following the text:
'God, who is rich in mercy, . . . even when we were dead in sins,
10 hath quickened us together with Christ (by grace ye are saved),
. . . that he might show the exceeding riches of his grace in his
kindness toward us through Christ Jesus. For by grace ye are
saved through faith: and that not of yourselves.'[f] Of yourselves
cometh neither your faith nor your salvation. 'It is the gift of
15 God,'[79] the free, undeserved gift—the faith through which ye are
saved, as well as the salvation which he of his own good pleasure,
his mere favour, annexes thereto. That ye believe is one instance
of his grace; that believing, ye are saved, another. 'Not of works,
lest any man should boast.'[80] For all our works, all our
20 righteousness, which were before our believing, merited nothing
of God but condemnation, so far were they from deserving faith,
which therefore, whenever given, is not 'of works'. Neither is
salvation of the works we do when we believe. For 'it is' then 'God
that worketh in us'.[81] And, therefore, that he giveth us a reward for
25 what he himself worketh only commendeth the riches of his
mercy, but leaveth us nothing whereof to glory.[82]

4. However, may not the speaking thus of the mercy of God, as
saving or justifying freely by faith only, encourage men in sin?
Indeed it may and will; many will 'continue in sin, that grace may
30 abound'.[83] But their blood is upon their own head. The goodness
of God ought to lead them to repentance,[84] and so it will those

---

[d] Rom. 3:27.
[e] Rom. 4:5.
[f] Eph. 2:4-5, 7-8.

---

[78] Cf. Rom. 11:20-22.   [79] Eph. 2:8.   [80] Eph. 2:9.
[81] Cf. 1 Cor. 12:6; Eph. 3:20; Phil. 2:13.
[82] Cf. No. 85, 'On Working Out Our Own Salvation', I.1-4, III.6-7, where the identical
point is made once again, much later (1785). For Wesley's other uses of the *in se est* theme,
cf. above, Intro., pp. 72-73.
[83] Rom. 6:1.   [84] See Rom. 2:4.

who are sincere of heart. When they know there is yet forgiveness
with him, they will cry aloud that he would blot out their sins also
through faith which is in Jesus. And if they earnestly cry and faint
not, if they seek him in all the means he hath appointed, if they
refuse to be comforted till he come, he 'will come, and will not 5
tarry'.[85] And he can do much work in a short time. Many are the
examples in the Acts of the Apostles of God's working this faith in
men's hearts as quick as lightning falling from heaven. So in the
same hour that Paul and Silas began to preach the gaoler *repented,*
believed, and *was baptized*[86]—as were three thousand by St. Peter 10
on the day of Pentecost, who all repented and believed at his first
preaching.[87] And, blessed be God, there are now many living
proofs that he is still thus 'mighty to save'.[88]

5. Yet to the same truth, placed in another view, a quite
contrary objection is made: 'If a man cannot be saved by all that he 15
can do, this will drive men to despair.' True, to despair of being
saved by their own works, their own merits or righteousness. And
so it ought; for none can trust in the merits of Christ till he has
utterly renounced his own. He that 'goeth about to establish his
own righteousness'[89] cannot receive the righteousness of God. 20
The righteousness which is of faith cannot be given him while he
trusteth in that which is of the law.

6. But this, it is said, is an uncomfortable doctrine. The devil
spoke like himself, that is, without either truth or shame, when he
dared to suggest to men that it is such. 'Tis the only comfortable 25
one, 'tis 'very full of comfort',[90] to all self-destroyed, self-condemned sinners. That 'whosoever believeth on him shall not be
ashamed';[91] that 'the same Lord over all is rich unto all that call
upon him'[92]—here is comfort, high as heaven, stronger than
death! What! Mercy for all? For Zaccheus, a public robber? For 30
Mary Magdalene, a common harlot? Methinks I hear one say,
'Then I, even I, may hope for mercy!' And so thou mayst, thou
afflicted one, whom none hath comforted! God will not cast out
thy prayer. Nay, perhaps he may say the next hour, 'Be of good
cheer, thy sins are forgiven thee;'[93] so forgiven that they shall 35

[85] Heb. 10:37.   [86] Cf. Acts 16:30-34.   [87] See Acts 2:37-41.
[88] Isa. 63:1.   [89] Cf. Rom. 10:3.
[90] Cf. 2 Cor. 7:4. Cf. Art. XI, 'that we are justified by faith only is a most wholesome
doctrine and very full of comfort', in Thirty-nine Articles of Religion. See also the Homily
'Of Faith', Pt. III, in *Homilies*, pp. 37-40.
[91] Rom. 9:33.   [92] Rom. 10:12.   [93] Matt. 9:2.

reign over thee no more; yea, and that 'the Holy Spirit shall bear witness with thy spirit that thou art a child of God.'[94] O glad tidings! Tidings of great joy, which are sent unto all people.[95] 'Ho, everyone that thirsteth, come ye to the waters; come ye and buy
5   without money, and without price.'[96] Whatsoever your sins be, 'though red, like crimson',[97] though 'more than the hairs of your head',[98] 'return ye unto the Lord, and he will have mercy upon you, and to our God, for he will abundantly pardon.'[99]

7. When no more objections occur, then we are simply told that
10 salvation by faith only ought not to be preached as the first doctrine, or at least not to be preached to all. But what saith the Holy Ghost? 'Other foundation can no man lay than that which is laid, even Jesus Christ.'[100] So, then, 'that whosoever believeth on him shall be saved'[101] is and must be the foundation of all our
15 preaching; that is, must be preached first. 'Well, but not to all.' To whom then are we not to preach it? Whom shall we except? The poor? Nay, they have a peculiar right to have the gospel preached unto them.[102] The unlearned? No. God hath revealed these things unto unlearned and ignorant men[103] from the beginning. The
20 young? By no means. 'Suffer these' in any wise 'to come unto Christ, and forbid them not.'[104] The sinners? Least of all. He 'came not to call the righteous, but sinners to repentance'.[105] Why then, if any, we are to except the rich, the learned, the reputable, the moral men. And 'tis true, they too often except themselves
25 from hearing; yet we must speak the words of our Lord. For thus the tenor of our commission runs: 'Go and preach the gospel to every creature.'[106] If any man wrest it or any part of it to his destruction, he must bear his own burden.[107] But still, 'as the Lord liveth, whatsoever the Lord saith unto us, that we will speak.'[108]

30 8. At this time more especially will we speak, that 'by grace ye are saved through faith:'[109] because never was the maintaining this doctrine more seasonable than it is at this day. Nothing but this can effectually prevent the increase of the Romish delusion among us. 'Tis endless to attack one by one all the errors of that

---

[94] Cf. Rom. 8:16.   [95] See Luke 2:10.   [96] Cf. Isa. 55:1.
[97] Cf. Isa. 1:18.   [98] Cf. Ps. 40:12.   [99] Cf. Isa. 55:7.
[100] Cf. 1 Cor. 3:11.   [101] Cf. John 3:16; Mark 16:16.
[102] See Matt. 11:5; Luke 7:22.   [103] Acts 4:13.
[104] Cf. Mark 10:14.   [105] Mark 2:17.   [106] Mark 16:15.
[107] See Gal. 6:5.   [108] Cf. 1 Kgs. 22:14.
[109] Cf. Eph. 2:8.

Church.[110] But salvation by faith strikes at the root, and all fall at once where this is established. It was this doctrine (which our Church justly calls 'the strong rock and foundation of the Christian religion'[111]) that first drove popery out of these kingdoms, and 'tis this alone can keep it out. Nothing but this can give a check to 5 that immorality which hath overspread the land as a flood. Can you empty the great deep drop by drop? Then you may reform us by dissuasives from particular vices. But let 'the righteousness which is of God by faith'[112] be brought in, and so shall its proud waves be stayed.[113] Nothing but this can stop the mouths of those 10 who 'glory in their shame',[114] 'and openly deny the Lord that bought them'.[115] They can talk as sublimely of the law as he that hath it written by God in his heart. To hear them speak on this head might incline one to think they were not far from the kingdom of God. But take them out of the law into the gospel; begin 15 with the righteousness of faith, with 'Christ, the end of the law to everyone that believeth',[116] and those who but now appeared almost if not altogether Christians[117] stand confessed the sons of perdition,[118] as far from life and salvation (God be merciful unto them!) as the depth of hell from the height of heaven. 20

9. For this reason the adversary so rages whenever 'salvation by faith' is declared to the world. For this reason did he stir up earth and hell to destroy those who first preached it. And for the same reason, knowing that faith alone could overturn the foundations of his kingdom, did he call forth all his forces, and employ all his 25 arts of lies and calumny, to affright that glorious champion of the Lord of Hosts, Martin Luther, from reviving it.[119] Nor can we wonder thereat. For as that man of God observes, 'How would it enrage a proud strong man armed to be stopped and set at nought by a little child, coming against him with a reed in his 30 hand!'[120]—especially when he knew that little child would surely overthrow him and tread him under foot. 'Even so, Lord Jesus!'[121] Thus hath thy strength been ever 'made perfect in weakness'![122]

---

[110] Orig., 'that apostate Church', revised in *Sermons* (1746) and *Works* (1771).
[111] Cf. 'Of Salvation', Pt. II, in *Homilies*, p. 22.   [112] Phil. 3:9.
[113] See Job 38:11.   [114] Cf. Phil. 3:19.   [115] Cf. 2 Pet. 2:1.   [116] Cf. Rom. 10:4.
[117] See No. 2, *The Almost Christian*.   [118] See John 17:12; 2 Thess. 2:3.
[119] 'that glorious champion of the Lord of Hosts . . .' was dropped from the text in *SOSO*, I (1746). For an earlier evaluation of Luther, cf. JWJ, June 15-16, 1741; see also No. 14, *The Repentance of Believers*, I.9 and n. for other references to Luther.
[120] Not yet located in Luther's own words. But cf. Samuel Clarke, *The Marrow of Ecclesiastical Historie* (1650), p. 97, which Wesley had read.
[121] Cf. Rev. 22:20.   [122] 2 Cor. 12:9.

Go forth then, thou little child that believest in him, and his 'right hand shall teach thee terrible things'![123] Though thou art helpless and weak as an infant of days, the strong man shall not be able to stand before thee. Thou shalt prevail over him, and subdue him, 5 and overthrow him, and trample him under thy feet. Thou shalt march on under the great Captain of thy salvation,[124] 'conquering and to conquer',[125] until all thine enemies are destroyed, and 'death is swallowed up in victory'.[126]

Now thanks be to God which giveth us the victory through our 10 Lord Jesus Christ,[127] to whom, with the Father and the Holy Ghost, be blessing and glory, and wisdom, and thanksgiving, and honour, and power, and might, for ever and ever.   Amen.[128]

---

[123] Ps. 45:4.
[124] See Heb. 2:10.
[125] Rev. 6:2.
[126] 1 Cor. 15:54.
[127] 1 Cor. 15:57.
[128] Rev.7:12. This use of a concluding ascription would seem conventional enough, especially in such a sermon, *ad aulam*. It is, however, quite rare for Wesley: only nine of his collected sermons carry such ascriptions: Nos. 1, *Salvation by Faith*; 9, 'The Spirit of Bondage and of Adoption'; 12, 'The Witness of Our Own Spirit'; 29, 'Sermon on the Mount, IX'; 56, 'God's Approbation of His Works'; 63, 'The General Spread of the Gospel'; 71, 'Of Good Angels' (a collect); 85, 'On Working Out Our Own Salvation' (where the benediction serves as an ascription); 107, 'On God's Vineyard' (where Wesley uses the Preface to the Sanctus as an ascription). Note that neither No. 2, *The Almost Christian*, nor No. 4, *Scriptural Christianity*, appears in this list. Nine of the early 'uncollected' sermons have formal ascriptions: Nos. 133, 'Death and Deliverance'; 134, 'Seek First the Kingdom'; 135, 'On Guardian Angels'; 136, 'On Mourning for the Dead'; 137, 'On Corrupting the Word of God'; 140, 'The Promise of Understanding'; 141, 'The Image of God'; 146, 'The One Thing Needful'; and 150, 'Hypocrisy in Oxford'.

The Almost Christian

A Sermon preached at St. Mary's, Oxford,

before the University,

on July 25, 1741

Acts 26:28

Almost thou persuadest me to be a Christian.

And many there are who go thus far: ever since the Christian religion was in the world there have been many in every age and nation who were 'almost persuaded to be Christians'. But seeing it avails nothing before God to go *only thus far,* it highly imports us 10 to consider,

First, what is implied in being *almost,*

Secondly, what in being *altogether* a Christian.[1]

I.(I).1. Now in the being 'almost a Christian' is implied, first, heathen honesty.[2] No one, I suppose, will make any question of 15 this, especially since by heathen honesty here I mean, not that which is recommended in the writings of their philosophers only,

---

[1] See 'Intro. Com.', p. 111 above; half-title from *SOSO*, I (1746). The distinction between 'almost' and 'altogether' Christians was by now a commonplace. Cf. *The Sermons of Mr. Henry Smith, Gathered into One Volume* (1657), pp. 420-23; William Sheppard, *Sincerity and Hypocrisy; or, the Sincere Christian and Hypocrite in their Lively Colours, Standing One by the Other* (1658); William Allen, 'Dedicatory Epistle', *The Glass of Justification*, p. 20, speaks of a 'negative Christian'; in 1661 Matthew Mead preached a series of seven sermons at St. Sepulchre's, Holborn, on *The Almost Christian Discovered;* John Cardinal Bona, *Precepts and Practical Rules for a Truly Christian Life* (1678), p. 2; John Norris has extended references to 'those who serve God by halves, . . . the almost Christians', in *Christian Prudence* (1710), pp. 16 20, and in *Practical Discourses,* IV (1728), 'Concerning Practical Atheism', pp. 100-24; James Knight, *Eight Sermons* (1721), p. 274, speaks of 'lukewarm spirits'; and William Bates, Sermon X, in *Sermons,* p. 383. Throughout the Wesley corpus one finds references to 'the almost Christian', 'half-Christians', 'the good sort of men', 'saints of the world' (cf. No. 4, *Scriptural Christianity,* II.5 and n.).

[2] Wesley here understands 'honesty', as his audience would have, in its classical Latin sense of honour (as in Plautus, Cicero, Quintilian) denoting that form of self-disciplined conduct approved of by Aristotle in his *Nicomachean Ethics* (I.5; III.8; IV.3), a shared source which Wesley knew very well.

but such as the common heathens expected of one another, and many of them actually practised. By the rules of this they were taught that they ought not to be unjust; not to take away their neighbour's goods, either by robbery or theft; not to oppress the
5 poor, neither to use extortion toward any; not to cheat or overreach either the poor or rich in whatsoever commerce they had with them; to defraud no man of his right, and if it were possible to owe no man anything.

2. Again, the common heathens allowed that some regard was
10 to be paid to truth as well as to justice. And accordingly they not only had him in abomination who was forsworn, who called God to witness to a lie, but him also who was known to be a slanderer of his neighbour, who falsely accused any man. And indeed little better did they esteem wilful liars of any sort, accounting them the
15 disgrace of humankind, and the pests of society.

3. Yet again, there was a sort of love and assistance which they expected one from another. They expected whatever assistance anyone could give another without prejudice to himself. And this they extended, not only to those little offices of humanity which
20 are performed without any expense or labour, but likewise to the feeding the hungry if they had food to spare, the clothing the naked with their own superfluous raiment, and in general the giving to any that needed such things as they needed not themselves. Thus far (in the lowest account of it) heathen honesty
25 went, the first thing implied in the being 'almost a Christian'.

(II).4. A second thing implied in the being 'almost a Christian' is the having a form of godliness,[3] of that godliness which is prescribed in the gospel of Christ—the having the *outside* of a real Christian. Accordingly the 'almost Christian' does nothing which
30 the gospel forbids. He taketh not the name of God in vain,[4] he blesseth and curseth not,[5] he sweareth not at all, but his communication is 'Yea, yea,' 'nay, nay.'[6] He profanes not the day of the Lord, nor suffers it to be profaned, even by the stranger that is within his gates.[7] He not only avoids all actual adultery,

---

[3] 2 Tim. 3:5. For references to Wesley's distinction between the 'form' and the 'power' of godliness, see the *General Rules* (in *The Nature, Design, and General Rules of the United Societies*, 1743, *Bibliog*, No. 73, Vol. 9 of this edn.), §2; Nos. 3, *'Awake, Thou That Sleepest'*, III.11; and 150, 'Hypocrisy in Oxford', II.2; *The Doctrine of Original Sin*, 1757, pp. 229-30; see also *Notes*, Matt. 13:28.
[4] See Exod. 20:7.   [5] See Rom. 12:14.
[6] Cf. Matt. 5:34, 37.   [7] See Exod. 20:10.

fornication, and uncleanness, but every word or look that either directly or indirectly tends thereto: nay, and all idle words, abstaining both from all detraction, backbiting, talebearing, evil-speaking, and from 'all foolish talking and jesting' (εὐτραπελία), a kind of virtue in the heathen moralist's account.[8] Briefly, from all conversation that is not 'good to the use of edifying', and that consequently 'grieves the Holy Spirit of God, whereby we are sealed to the day of redemption'.[9]

5. He abstains from 'wine wherein is excess',[10] from revellings and gluttony. He avoids, as much as in him lies, all strife and contention, continually endeavouring to live peaceably with all men.[11] And if he suffer wrong, he avengeth not himself, neither returns evil for evil. He is no railer, no brawler, no scoffer, either at the faults or infirmities of his neighbour. He does not willingly wrong, hurt, or grieve any man; but in all things acts and speaks by that plain rule, 'Whatsoever thou wouldst not he should do unto thee, that do not thou to another.'[12]

6. And in doing good he does not confine himself to cheap and easy offices of kindness, but labours and suffers for the profit of many, that by all means he may help some. In spite of toil or pain, 'whatsoever his hand findeth to do, he doth it with his might,'[13] whether it be for his friends or for his enemies, for the evil or for the good. For, being 'not slothful in' this or in any 'business',[14] 'as he hath opportunity he doth good', all manner of good, 'to all men',[15] and to their souls as well as their bodies. He reproves the wicked, instructs the ignorant, confirms the wavering, quickens the good, and comforts the afflicted. He labours to awaken those that sleep,[16] to lead those whom God hath already awakened to

---

[8] Wesley's translation of εὐτραπελία follows the AV of Eph. 5:4, where εὐτραπελία is disparaged. For the 'heathen moralist', however, cf. Aristotle, *Nicomachean Ethics*, II.7 (1108a), who had indeed reckoned it as a virtue: 'In the matter of "pleasantness" (παιδία) the mean is "wit" and the middle way is "wittiness" (εὐτραπελία); excess here is buffoonery . . . and its deficiency is boorishness.' Wesley could presume that his audience understood this discrepancy between the κοινή of the New Testament and the classical usage of 'the heathen moralist'. Cf. Irène Simon, *Three Restoration Divines*, I. 316.

[9] Cf. Eph. 4:29-30.   [10] Eph. 5:18.   [11] See Rom. 12:18.

[12] This particular form of the Golden Rule is ascribed in the Talmud (*Sabb.* xxxi.1) to Hillel: 'What is hateful to you, do not to your neighbour; that is the whole Torah, while the rest is the commentary thereof; go and learn it.' See also Tobit 4:15: 'And what thou hatest, do to no man.' Cf. Nos. 30, 'Sermon on the Mount, X', §§22, 24; and 150, 'Hypocrisy in Oxford', I.10. It is not clear how Wesley had come by this form of the 'Rule'.

[13] Cf. Eccles. 9:10.   [14] Rom. 12:11.

[15] Cf. Gal. 6:10. Note the similarity here with the second of Wesley's *General Rules*.

[16] See No. 3, '*Awake, Thou That Sleepest*'.

the fountain opened for sin and for uncleanness, that they may wash therein and be clean; and to stir up those who are saved through faith to adorn the gospel of Christ in all things.

7. He that hath the form of godliness uses also the means of
5 grace; yea, all of them, and at all opportunities. He constantly frequents the house of God; and that not as the manner of some is, who come into the presence of the Most High either loaded with gold and costly apparel, or in all the gaudy vanity of dress, and either by their unseasonable civilities to each other or the
10 impertinent gaiety of their behaviour disclaim all pretensions to the form as well as to the power of godliness. Would to God there were none, even among ourselves, who fall under the same condemnation: who come into his house, it may be, gazing about, or with all the signs of the most listless, careless indifference,
15 though sometimes they may *seem* to use a prayer to God for his blessing on what they are entering upon; who during that awful service are either asleep or reclined in the most convenient posture for it; or, as though they supposed God was asleep, talking with one another, or looking round, as utterly void of
20 employment.[17] Neither let these be accused of the form of godliness. No: he who has even this behaves with seriousness and attention in every part of that solemn service. More especially when he approaches the table of the Lord it is not with a light or careless behaviour, but with an air, gesture, and deportment
25 which speaks nothing else but 'God be merciful to me, a sinner!'[18]

8. To this if we add the constant use of family prayer by those who are masters of families, and the setting times apart for private addresses to God, with a daily seriousness of behaviour—he who uniformly practises this outward religion has the form of
30 godliness. There needs but one thing more in order to his being 'almost a Christian', and that is, sincerity.

(III).9. By sincerity I mean a real, inward principle of religion from whence these outward actions flow.[19] And indeed if we have

---

[17] An echo of frequent criticisms in the *Spectator* and other newspapers of indecorous behaviour in churches. E.g., in No. 460, Aug. 18, 1712, Richard Steele comments on 'the ceremonies, bows, curtsies, whisperings, smiles, winks, nods, with other familiar arts of salutation, which take up in our churches so much time that might be better employed'; he goes on to speak of gossips who could 'give a particular account how two or three hundred people were dressed' but no inkling of the sermon. Cf. also *The Tatler*, No. 140, May 2, 1710.

[18] Luke 18:13.

[19] 'Sincerity' was a shibboleth in eighteenth-century religion, especially among the

not this we have not heathen honesty; no, not so much of it as will answer the demand of a heathen, Epicurean poet. Even this poor wretch, in his sober intervals, is able to testify:

> *Oderunt peccare boni virtutis amore;*
> *Oderunt peccare mali formidine poenae.*[a]

So that if a man only abstains from doing evil in order to avoid punishment,

> *Non pasces in cruce corvos*[b]

saith the pagan—there, 'thou hast thy reward'.[20] But even he will not allow such a harmless man as this to be so much as a *good* 10

---

[a] Good men avoid sin from the love of virtue; wicked men avoid sin from the fear of punishment. [Cf. Horace, *Epistles*, I.xvi. 52-53:

> *Oderunt peccare boni virtutis amore;*
> *Tu nihil admittes in te formidine poenae.*

Here Wesley has garbled the second line for the sake of the contrast between *oderunt peccare boni* and *oderunt peccare mali*. The notion that Horace was an Epicurean was an eighteenth-century commonplace, and found support in Horace's jesting reference to himself as an Epicurean in *Epistles*, I.iv.16. There are frequent quotations from Horace in Wesley's sermons, usually prefaced by epithets as, e.g., 'the poor heathen' (Nos. 28, 'Sermon on the Mount, VIII', §18); 'your brother heathen' (56, 'God's Approbation of His Works', II.1); 'the old Roman' (78 'Spiritual Idolatry', I.4); 'the old heathen poet' (102, 'Of Former Times', §8); 'the heathen poet' (129, 'Heavenly Treasure in Earthen Vessels', II.1).]

[b] Thou shalt not be hanged [Horace, *Epistles*, I.xvi.48].

---

latitudinarians. C. F. Allison, *The Rise of Moralism*, p. 144, believes that Edward Fowler (1632–1714), Bishop of Gloucester, was the first to make sincerity a prerequisite to justification, in his *The Design of Christianity* (1671). Samuel Johnson, in the *Dictionary* (1755), defined sincerity as 'honesty of intention' and quotes John Rogers (1679–1729), *The Necessity of Divine Revelation and the Truth of the Christian Religion* (1727): 'Jesus Christ has purchased for us terms of reconciliation, who will accept of sincerity instead of perfection; but then this sincerity implies our honest endeavours to do our utmost.' Lecky, *A History of England in the Eighteenth Century*, I. 312-13, cites Benjamin Hoadly (1676–1761) as affirming that 'sincerity is the one necessary requirement for the Christian profession.' See also William Bates, *Whole Works* (1st edn., 1700; 1815), II. 63; and William Reeves, *Fourteen Sermons Preached on Several Occasions* (1729), p. 251.

The early Wesley had commented on the prime importance of sincerity in a letter to his mother, July 29, 1725, and to Ann Granville, Oct. 3, 1731; the late Wesley makes almost the same point in a letter to Arthur Keene, Dec. 25, 1787. In between, see the references in the *Minutes* of 1746 (May 13), and in the following sermons: Nos. 6, 'The Righteousness of Faith', III.5; 9, 'The Spirit of Bondage and of Adoption', IV. 1; 12, 'The Witness of Our Own Spirit', §11; 18, 'The Marks of the New Birth', II.2; 19, 'The Great Privilege of those that are Born of God', II.10; 30, 'Sermon on the Mount, X', §9; 137, 'On Corrupting the Word of God', proem.

[20] Horace, *Epistles*, I.xvi.47: '*habes pretium, loris non ureris*' ('You have your reward; you are not being flogged'). Cf. Matt. 6:2, 5, 16.

heathen. If then any man from the same motive (viz. to avoid punishment, to avoid the loss of his friends, or his gain, or his reputation) should not only abstain from doing evil but also do ever so much good—yea, and use all the means of grace—yet we
5 could not with any propriety say, this man is even 'almost a Christian'. If he has no better principle in his heart he is only a hypocrite altogether.

10. Sincerity therefore is necessarily implied in the being 'almost a Christian': a real design to serve God, a hearty desire to
10 do his will. It is necessarily implied that a man have a sincere view of pleasing God in all things: in all his conversation, in all his actions; in all he does or leaves undone. This design, if any man be 'almost a Christian', runs through the whole tenor of his life. This is the moving principle both in his doing good, his abstaining
15 from evil, and his using the ordinances of God.[21]

11. But here it will probably be inquired, Is it possible that any man living should go so far as this and nevertheless be *only* 'almost a Christian'? What more than this can be implied in the being 'a Christian altogether'? I answer, first, that it is possible to go thus
20 far, and yet be but 'almost a Christian', I learn not only from the oracles of God, but also from the sure testimony of experience.

12. Brethren, 'great is my boldness toward you in this behalf.'[22] And 'forgive me this wrong'[23] if I declare my own folly upon the housetop, for yours and the gospel's sake. Suffer me then to speak
25 freely of myself, even as of another man. I am content to be abased so ye may be exalted,[24] and to be yet more vile for the glory of my Lord.[25]

13. I did go thus far for many years, as many of this place can testify: using diligence to eschew all evil, and to have a conscience
30 void of offence;[26] redeeming the time,[27] buying up every opportunity of doing all good to all men;[28] constantly and carefully using all the public and all the private means of grace; endeavouring after a steady seriousness of behaviour at all times and in all places. And God is my record, before whom I stand,
35 doing all this in sincerity; having a real design to serve God, a hearty desire to do his will in all things, to please him who had

---

[21] Note that, on this basis, a person obeying Wesley's *General Rules* would be no better than an 'almost Christian'.
[22] Cf. 2 Cor. 7:4.   [23] 2 Cor. 12:13.   [24] See 2 Cor. 11:7.
[25] See 2 Sam. 6:21-22. See also JWJ, Apr. 2, 1739: 'I submitted to be more vile, and proclaimed in the highways the glad tidings of salvation . . . .'
[26] Acts 24:16.   [27] Col. 4:5.   [28] Gal. 6:10.

called me to 'fight the good fight', and to 'lay hold of eternal life'.[29] Yet my own conscience beareth me witness in the Holy Ghost that all this time I was but 'almost a Christian'.[30]

II. If it be inquired, 'What more than this is implied in the being "altogether a Christian"?' I answer: 5

(I).1. First, the love of God. For thus saith his Word: 'Thou shalt love the Lord thy God with all thy heart, and with all thy soul, and with all thy mind, and with all thy strength.'[31] Such a love of God is this as engrosses the whole heart, as takes up all the affections, as fills the entire capacity of the soul, and employs the 10 utmost extent of all its faculties. He that thus loves the Lord his God, his spirit continually 'rejoiceth in God his Saviour'.[32] 'His delight is in the Lord,'[33] *his* Lord and his all, to whom 'in everything he giveth thanks'.[34] All *his* 'desire is unto God, and to the remembrance of his name'.[35] His heart is ever crying out, 15 'Whom have I in heaven but thee? and there is none upon earth that I desire beside thee.'[36] Indeed, what can he desire beside God? Not the world, or the things of the world. For he is 'crucified to the world, and the world crucified to him'.[37] He is crucified to the desire of the flesh, the desire of the eye, and the 20 pride of life.[38] Yea, he is dead to pride of every kind: for love 'is not puffed up',[39] but he that dwelling in love 'dwelleth in God, and God in him', is less than nothing in his own eyes.

(II).2. The second thing implied in the being 'altogether a Christian' is the love of our neighbour. For thus said our Lord in 25 the following words: 'Thou shalt love thy neighbour as thyself.'[40] If any man ask, 'Who is my neighbour?'[41] we reply, 'Every man in

---

[29] 1 Tim. 6:12.
[30] Cf. No. 81, 'In What Sense we are to Leave the World', §23, where Wesley (in 1784) recalls that it had 'pleased God' to convert him from an 'almost' to an 'altogether Christian' in 1725. But see also JWJ, Jan. 4, 1739, and his letter to brother Charles, June 27, 1766, and cf. Benham, pp. 34-40. Note also that all editions of Wesley's *Plain Account of Christian Perfection* refer to 1725 as the beginning of his conscious quest for perfection. The fact is that Wesley wavered from time to time about what it means to confess oneself 'a Christian'.
[31] Mark 12:30.   [32] Cf. Luke 1:47.   [33] Cf. Ps. 1:2.
[34] Cf. 1 Thess. 5:18.   [35] Cf. Isa. 26:8.   [36] Ps. 73:25.
[37] Cf. Gal. 6:14.
[38] I.e., to all *sin* (see 1 John 2:16), since Wesley had long since agreed with Augustine that *autem tria genera vitiorum . . . OMNIA peccata concludunt* ('indeed, *all* sins may be included within these three classes of vice'); cf. *Enarratio in Psalmum*, VIII.13, in Migne, *PL*, Vol. 36, col. 115. He would reiterate this tirelessly; see No. 7, 'The Way to the Kingdom', II.2 and n.
[39] 1 Cor. 13:4.   [40] Matt. 22:39, etc.   [41] Luke 10:29.

the world; every child of his who is "the Father of the spirits of all flesh".[42] Nor may we in any wise except our enemies, or the enemies of God and their own souls. But every Christian loveth these also as himself; yea, 'as Christ loved us'.[43] He that would
5 more fully understand what manner of love this is may consider St. Paul's description of it. It is 'long-suffering and kind. It envieth not. It is not rash or hasty in judging. It is not puffed up,'[44] but maketh him that loves, the least, the servant of all. Love 'doth not behave itself unseemly',[45] but 'becometh all things to all
10 men'.[46] She 'seeketh not her own', but only the good of others, that they may be saved. Love 'is not provoked'.[47] It casteth out wrath, which he who hath is wanting in love. It 'thinketh no evil'. It 'rejoiceth not in iniquity, but rejoiceth in the truth'. It 'covereth all things, believeth all things, hopeth all things, endureth all
15 things'.[48]

(III).3. There is yet one thing more that may be separately considered, though it cannot actually be separate from the preceding, which is implied in the being 'altogether a Christian', and that is the ground of all, even faith. Very excellent things are
20 spoken of this throughout the oracles of God. 'Everyone', saith the beloved disciple, 'that believeth, is born of God.'[49] 'To as many as received him gave he power to become the sons of God, even to them that believe on his name.'[50] And, 'This is the victory that overcometh the world, even our faith.'[51] Yea, our Lord
25 himself declares, 'He that believeth in the Son hath everlasting life;'[52] and 'cometh not into condemnation, but is passed from death unto life'.[53]

4. But here let no man deceive his own soul. It is diligently to be noted, the 'faith which bringeth not forth repentance' and love,
30 and all good works, is not that 'right living faith' which is here spoken of, 'but a dead and devilish one. . . . For even the devils believe that Christ was born of a virgin, that he wrought all kind of miracles, declaring himself very God; that for our sakes he suffered a most painful death, to redeem us from death
35 everlasting; that he rose again the third day; that he ascended into

---

[42] Cf. Heb. 12:9; also No. 7, 'The Way to the Kingdom', I.8 and n.
[43] Cf. Eph. 5:2.   [44] Cf. 1 Cor. 13:4.   [45] 1 Cor. 13:5.
[46] Cf. 1 Cor. 9:22.   [47] Cf. 1 Cor. 13:5.   [48] Cf. 1 Cor. 13:5-7.
[49] Cf. 1 John 5:1.   [50] Cf. John 1:12.   [51] 1 John 5:4.
[52] John 3:36.   [53] John 5:24.

heaven and sitteth at the right hand of the Father, and at the end of the world shall come again to judge both the quick and the dead. These articles of our faith the devils believe, and so they believe all that is written in the Old and New Testament. And yet for all this faith, they be but devils. They remain still in their 5 damnable estate, lacking the very true Christian faith.'[c]

5. 'The right and true Christian faith is' (to go on in the words of our own Church) 'not only to believe that Holy Scripture and the articles of our faith are true, but also to have a sure trust and confidence to be saved from everlasting damnation by Christ'—it 10 is a 'sure trust and confidence' which a man hath in God 'that by the merits of Christ his sins *are* forgiven, and he reconciled to the favour of God'—'whereof doth follow a loving heart to obey his commandments.'[54]

6. Now whosoever has this faith which 'purifies the heart',[55] by 15 the power of God who dwelleth therein, from pride, anger, desire, 'from all unrighteousness',[56] 'from all filthiness of flesh and spirit';[57] which fills it with love stronger than death both to God and to all mankind—love that doth the works of God, glorying to spend and to be spent for all men, and that endureth 20 with joy, not only the reproach of Christ, the being mocked, despised, and hated of all men, but whatsoever the wisdom of God permits the malice of men or devils to inflict; whosoever has this faith, thus 'working by love',[58] is not *almost* only, but *altogether* a Christian. 25

---

[c] Homily on the Salvation of Man [Pt. III, in a slight revision of Wesley's own earlier extract therefrom in *The Doctrine of Salvation, Faith, and Good Works*, §13, for which see Vol. 12 of this edn.]

---

[54] Cf. Wesley, *The Doctrine of Salvation, Faith, and Good Works*, §14; cf. also the Homily on the Salvation of Man, Pt. III.

[55] Cf. Acts 15:9; Jas. 4:8.

[56] 1 John 1:9.

[57] Cf. 2 Cor. 7:1.

[58] Cf. Gal. 5:6, Wesley's favourite text for his teachings on faith and good works (*fides caritatem formata*), the linch-pin by which he joined his double doctrine of 'faith alone' and 'holy living'. Cf. Nos. 8, 'The First-fruits of the Spirit', III.3; 10, 'The Witness of the Spirit, I', I.8; 19, 'The Great Privilege of those that are Born of God', III.1; 25, 'Sermon on the Mount, V', III.9; 35, 'The Law Established through Faith, I', II.3; 39, 'Catholic Spirit', I.14; 47, 'Heaviness through Manifold Temptations', II.3, IV.5; 62, 'The End of Christ's Coming', III.6; 65, 'The Duty of Reproving our Neighbour', III.14; 66, 'The Signs of the Times', II.8; 79, 'On Dissipation', §16; 90, 'An Israelite Indeed', II.4, II.11; 91, 'On Charity', III.11; 106, 'On Faith, Heb. 11:6', II.3; 107, 'On God's Vineyard', II.8; 109, '*The Trouble and Rest of Good Men*', I.3; 114, *On the Death of John Fletcher*, I.3; 146, 'The One Thing Needful', III.3. Wesley records having preached from this text fifteen

7. But who are the living witnesses of these things? I beseech you, brethren, as in the presence of that God before whom 'hell and destruction are without a covering: how much more the hearts of the children of men!'[59]—that each of you would ask his
5 own heart, 'Am I of that number? Do I so far practise justice, mercy, and truth, as even the rules of heathen honesty require? If so, have I the very *outside* of a Christian? The form of godliness? Do I abstain from evil, from whatsoever is forbidden in the written Word of God? Do I, whatever good my hand findeth to
10 do, do it with my might?[60] Do I seriously use all the ordinances of God at all opportunities? And is all this done with a sincere design and desire to please God in all things?'

8. Are not many of you conscious that you never came thus far? That you have not been even 'almost a Christian'? That you have
15 not come up to the standard of heathen honesty? At least, not to the form of Christian godliness? Much less hath God seen sincerity in you, a real design of pleasing him in all things. You never so much as intended to devote all your words and works, your business, studies, diversions to his glory. You never even
20 designed or desired that whatsoever you did should be done 'in the name of the Lord Jesus',[61] and as such should be a 'spiritual sacrifice, acceptable to God through Christ.'[62]

9. But supposing you had, do good designs and good desires make a Christian? By no means, unless they are brought to good
25 effect. 'Hell is paved', saith one, 'with good intentions.'[63] The great question of all, then, still remains. Is the love of God shed abroad in your heart? Can you cry out, 'My God and my all'? Do

times: twice in 1741, once in 1742 and 1747, twice in 1750, once in 1755, four times in 1760, three times in 1761, and once in 1787.

   Cf. Jeremy Taylor, *'Fides Formata; Or, Faith Working by Love'*, in *Works* (1844), II. 19-28. For Luther's denunciation of the distinction between 'formed' and 'unformed' faith, see his *Commentary on Galatians*, 3:11. See also W. P. Stephens, *The Holy Spirit in the Theology of Martin Bucer* (London, Cambridge University Press, 1970), pp. 51-68, for an analysis of the issues between *iustitia simplex, iustitia duplex*, etc.

   [59] Cf. Prov. 15:11.   [60] Eccles. 9:10.
   [61] Col. 3:17.   [62] Cf. 1 Pet. 2:5.

   [63] This proverb was, of course, a commonplace in Wesley's time; cf. Richard Whitlock, Ζωοτορία (1654); George Herbert, *Jacula Prudentum* (1651); and John Ray, *English Proverbs* (1670); it has a blurred history. St. Francis de Sales attributes it to St. Bernard of Clairvaux, in a letter to the Barrone de Chantal (Nov. 21, 1604) and in another letter to the Mother Superior of the Visitations in Lyons (Apr. 17, 1616); cf. Elisabeth Stopp, tr., *St. Francis de Sales; Selected Letters* (London, Faber and Faber, 1960), Letters 8, 92. The proverb itself has not yet been located in St. Bernard's published works. Cf. JWJ, July 10, 1736. See also No. 125, 'On a Single Eye', III.5, where Wesley cites St. Chrysostom as saying that 'Hell is paved with the skulls of Christian priests.'

you desire nothing but him? Are you happy in God? Is he your glory, your delight, your crown of rejoicing? And is this commandment written in your heart, 'that he who loveth God love his brother also'?[64] Do you then love your neighbour as yourself? Do you love every man, even your enemies, even the enemies of God, as your own soul? As Christ loved you? Yea, dost thou believe that Christ loved *thee*, and gave himself for thee? Hast thou faith in his blood? Believest thou the Lamb of God hath taken away *thy* sins,[65] and cast them as a stone into the depth of the sea? That he hath blotted out the handwriting that was against *thee*, taking it out of the way, nailing it to his cross? Hast *thou* indeed redemption through his blood, even the remission of *thy* sins?[66] And doth his Spirit bear witness with *thy* spirit, that thou art a child of God?[67]

10. The God and Father of our Lord Jesus Christ, who now standeth in the midst of us, knoweth that if any man die without this faith and this love, good it were for him that he had never been born.[68] Awake, then, thou that sleepest, and call upon thy God: call in the day when he may be found. Let him not rest till he 'make his goodness to pass before thee, till he proclaim unto thee the name of the Lord'[69]—'the Lord, the Lord God, merciful and gracious, long-suffering, and abundant in goodness and truth; keeping mercy for thousands, forgiving iniquity, and transgression, and sin.'[70] Let no man persuade thee by vain words to rest short of this prize of thy high calling.[71] But cry unto him day and night who 'while we were without strength died for the ungodly',[72] until thou knowest in whom thou hast believed, and canst say, 'My Lord and my God.'[73] Remember 'always to pray and not to faint',[74] till thou also canst lift up thy hand unto heaven and declare to him that liveth for ever and ever, 'Lord, thou knowest all things; thou knowest that I love thee.'[75]

11. May we all thus experience what it is to be not almost only, but altogether Christians! Being justified freely by his grace, through the redemption that is in Jesus, knowing we have peace with God through Jesus Christ, rejoicing in hope of the glory of God, and having the love of God shed abroad in our hearts by the Holy Ghost given unto us![76]

---

[64] 1 John 4:21. [65] See John 1:29. [66] See Eph. 1:7; Col. 1:14.
[67] See Rom. 8:16. [68] Cf. Mark 14:21. [69] Cf. Exod. 33:19.
[70] Exod. 34:6-7. [71] Phil. 3:14. [72] Rom. 5:6.
[73] John 20:28. [74] Luke 18:1. [75] John 21:17. [76] See Rom. 5:1, 2, 5.

A Sermon preached on Sunday, April 4, 1742,

before the University of Oxford.
By Charles Wesley, M.A.,
Student of Christ Church.[1]

Ephesians 5:14

Awake, thou that sleepest, and arise from the dead,
and Christ shall give thee light.

In discoursing on these words I shall, with the help of God,
First, describe the sleepers to whom they are spoken;
10 Secondly, enforce the exhortation, 'Awake thou that sleepest,
and arise from the dead;' and,
Thirdly, explain the promise made to such as do awake and
arise—'Christ shall give thee light.'

I.1. And first, as to the sleepers here spoken to. By sleep is
15 signified the natural state of man:[2] that deep sleep of the soul into
which the sin of Adam hath cast all who spring from his loins; that
supineness, indolence, and stupidity, that insensibility of his real
condition, wherein every man comes into the world, and
continues till the voice of God awakes him.
20 2. Now 'they that sleep, sleep in the night.'[3] The state of nature
is a state of utter darkness, a state wherein 'darkness covers the

---

[1] Half-title reproduced from *SOSO*, I (1746). The drop-title prefixed to the individual
editions of the sermon was simply 'Ephes. v. 14'; some variant of this continued in all
subsequent editions until 1795, when its present full title, *'Awake, Thou That Sleepest'*,
appeared for the first time. See 'Intro. Com.', pp. 111-12 above.
[2] An allegorical interpretation following a line established by St. Augustine, *Expositions
on the Psalms* (*NPNF*, I, VIII. 7, 159, 175, 259), and echoed in Poole, *Annotations, loc. cit.*
The source of the quotation is unknown; it may have come from a then familiar Christian
liturgical passage. In *Notes* Wesley shies away from allegory and comes nearer to Matthew
Henry's comment in *Exposition, loc. cit.:* 'God calls upon sinners . . . that they would break
off their sins by repentance and enter on a course of holy obedience, and he encourages
them to essay and do their utmost that way.'
[3] 1 Thess. 5:7.

earth, and gross darkness the people.'[4] The poor unawakened sinner, how much knowledge soever he may have as to other things, has no knowledge of himself. In this respect 'he knoweth nothing yet as he ought to know.'[5] He knows not that he is a fallen spirit, whose only business in the present world is to recover from 5 his fall, to regain that image of God[6] wherein he was created. He sees *no necessity* for 'the one thing needful',[7] even that inward universal change, that 'birth from above'[8] (figured out by baptism) which is the beginning of that total renovation, that sanctification of spirit, soul, and body, 'without which no man shall see the 10 Lord'.[9]

3. Full of all diseases as he is, he fancies himself in perfect health. Fast bound in misery and iron, he dreams that he is happy and at liberty. He says, 'Peace, peace,'[10] while the devil as 'a strong man armed'[11] is in full possession of his soul. He sleeps on still, 15 and takes his rest, though hell is moved from beneath to meet him;[12] though the pit, from whence there is no return,[13] hath opened its mouth to swallow him up.[14] A fire is kindled around him, yet he knoweth it not; yea, it burns him, yet he lays it not to heart. 20

4. By one who sleeps we are therefore to understand (and would to God we might all understand it!) a sinner satisfied in his sins, contented to remain in his fallen state, to live and die without the image of God; one who is ignorant both of his disease and of the only remedy for it; one who never was warned, or never 25 regarded the warning voice of God 'to flee from the wrath to come';[15] one that never yet saw he was in danger of hell-fire, or

---

[4] Cf. Isa. 60:2.

[5] 1 Cor. 8:2.

[6] Cf. No. 1, *Salvation by Faith*, §1 and n.

[7] Cf. Luke 10:42. This is the famous *unum necessarium*, the interpretation of which had exercised Anglicans and Puritans alike. See Jeremy Taylor's treatise with this title, *Works*, II. 419-646; also the *Christian Lib.*, XXXVIII. 57-58. It was a favourite text for Charles and John Wesley; John Wesley records that he preached from it at least fifty times during his ministry. Cf. his early sermon (May 1734) on this text, No. 146.

[8] Cf. John 3:3; ἄνωθεν here would seem to imply 'anew', i.e., a *new* birth ('from above', of course). There is an old puzzle as to the ambiguous meaning of ἄνωθεν continuing still as between Bultmann, Schnackenburg, Brown, and others. In Greek it has a double usage: 'from above' (as of place) and 'anew' (as in time). This ambiguity is absent from all its Aramaic and Hebrew equivalents. In John 19:23 it clearly means 'from the top'. Cf. Nos. 43, *The Scripture Way of Salvation*, I.4; and 45, 'The New Birth', II.3.

[9] Heb. 12:14.   [10] Jer. 6:14; 8:11.   [11] Luke 11:21.

[12] See Isa. 14:9.   [13] See Job 10:21; 16:22.

[14] See Num. 16:30.   [15] Matt. 3:7.

cried out in the earnestness of his soul, 'What must I do to be saved?'[16]

5. If this sleeper be not outwardly vicious, his sleep is usually the deepest of all: whether he be of the Laodicean spirit, 'neither cold nor hot',[17] but a quiet, rational, inoffensive, good-natured professor of the religion of his fathers; or whether he be zealous and orthodox, and 'after the most straitest sect of our religion lives a Pharisee';[18] that is, according to the scriptural account, one that *justifies himself,* one that labours 'to establish his own righteousness'[19] as the ground of his acceptance with God.

6. This is he who 'having a form of godliness, denies the power thereof';[20] yea, and probably reviles it, wheresoever it is found, as mere extravagance and delusion. Meanwhile the wretched self-deceiver thanks God that he 'is not as other men are, adulterers, unjust, extortioners'.[21] No, he doth no wrong to any man. He 'fasts twice in the week',[22] uses all the means of grace, is constant at church and sacrament; yea, and 'gives tithes of all that he has',[23] does all the good that he can. 'Touching the righteousness of the law', he is 'blameless':[24] he wants nothing of godliness but the power; nothing of religion but the spirit; nothing of Christianity but the truth and the life.

7. But know ye not that however highly esteemed among men such a Christian as this may be, he is an abomination in the sight of God,[25] and an heir of every woe which the Son of God yesterday, today, and for ever denounces against 'scribes and Pharisees, hypocrites'?[26] He hath 'made clean the outside of the cup and the platter',[27] but within is full of all filthiness. 'An evil disease cleaveth' still 'unto him,'[28] so that 'his inward parts are very wickedness'.[29] Our Lord fitly compares him to a 'painted sepulchre', which 'appears beautiful without', but nevertheless is 'full of dead men's bones and of all uncleanness'.[30] The bones

---

[16] Acts 16:30.   [17] Rev. 3:15.

[18] Cf. Acts 26:5.   [19] Cf. Rom. 10:3.

[20] Cf. 2 Tim. 3:5; see above, No. 2, *The Almost Christian,* I.4 and n.

[21] Cf. Luke 18:11.   [22] Cf. Luke 18:12.

[23] *Ibid.*   [24] Cf. Phil. 3:6.

[25] Cf. Luke 16:15, and note Charles Wesley's agreement with his brother in the early years of the Revival that even the best of the 'almost Christians' are 'abominations in the sight of God'. For later assuagements of this harsh judgment see III.6 and n. 179.

[26] Matt. 23:13.   [27] Cf. Matt. 23:25.

[28] Cf. Ps. 41:8.   [29] Cf. Ps. 5:9.

[30] Cf. Matt. 23:27; Wesley is here following Wycliffe, Tyndale, and the 'Great Bible' in translating κεκονιαμένοις (lit., 'whitewashed') as 'painted'. See III.11.

indeed are no longer dry; 'the sinews and flesh are come up upon them, and the skin covers them above: but there is no breath in them,'[31] no Spirit of the living God. And 'if any man have not the Spirit of Christ, he is none of his.'[32] 'Ye are Christ's',[33] 'if so be that the Spirit of God dwell in you.'[34] But if not, God knoweth that 5 ye abide in death, even until now.

8. This is another character of the sleeper here spoken to. He abides in death, though he knows it not. He is dead unto God, 'dead in trespasses and sins'.[35] 'For to be carnally minded is death.'[36] Even as it is written, 'By one man sin entered into the 10 world, and death by sin; and so death passed upon all men'[37]—not only temporal death, but likewise spiritual and eternal. 'In the day thou eatest (said God to Adam) thou shalt surely die.'[38] Not bodily (unless as he then became mortal) but spiritually: thou shalt lose the life of thy soul; thou shalt die to God, shalt be separated from 15 him, thy essential life and happiness.

9. Thus first was dissolved the vital union of our soul with God,[39] insomuch that 'in the midst of' natural 'life we are' now 'in' spiritual 'death'.[40] And herein we remain till the Second Adam becomes a quickening spirit to us, till he raises the dead, the dead 20 in sin, in pleasure, riches, or honours. But before any dead soul can live, he 'hears (hearkens to) the voice of the Son of God':[41] he is made sensible of his lost estate, and receives the sentence of death in himself. He knows himself to be 'dead while he liveth',[42] dead to God and all the things of God; having no more power to 25 perform the actions of a living Christian than a dead body to perform the functions of a living man.

10. And most certain it is that one dead in sin has not 'senses exercised to discern' spiritual 'good and evil'.[43] 'Having eyes, he sees not; he hath ears, and hears not.'[44] He doth not 'taste and see 30 that the Lord is gracious'.[45] He 'hath not seen God at any time',[46] nor 'heard his voice',[47] nor 'handled the Word of life'.[48] In vain is

---

[31] Cf. Ezek. 37:8.   [32] Rom. 8:9.   [33] 1 Cor. 3:23.
[34] Rom 8:9.   [35] Eph. 2:1.   [36] Rom. 8:6.
[37] Rom. 5:12.   [38] Cf. Gen. 2:17.
[39] Both Wesleys were body-soul dualists, and the notion of the Fall as a radical disruption of the aboriginal body-soul equilibrium goes back at least to Wesley's early MS sermon on Gen. 1:27; see Nos. 141, 'The Image of God'; and 41, *Wandering Thoughts*, III.5 and n.
[40] An echo from the committal service in the BCP, Burial.
[41] Cf. John 5:25.   [42] Cf. 1 Tim. 5:6.   [43] Cf. Heb. 5:14.
[44] Cf. Mark 8:18.   [45] Ps. 34:8 (BCP).   [46] John 1:18; 1 John 4:12.
[47] John 5:37.   [48] 1 John 1:1.

the name of Jesus 'like ointment poured forth',[49] and 'all his garments smell of myrrh, aloes, and cassia'.[50] The soul that sleepeth in death hath no perception of any objects of this kind. His heart is 'past feeling',[51] and understandeth none of these
5 things.

11. And hence, having no spiritual senses, no inlets of spiritual knowledge,[52] the natural man receiveth not the things of the Spirit of God; nay, he is so far from receiving them that whatsoever is spiritually discerned is mere foolishness unto him. He is not
10 content with being utterly ignorant of spiritual things, but he denies the very existence of them. And spiritual sensation itself is to him the foolishness of folly.[53] 'How', saith he, 'can these things be?'[54] How can any man *know* that he is alive to God? Even as you know that your body is now alive. Faith is the life of the soul: and if
15 ye have this life abiding in you, ye want no marks to evidence it *to yourself*, but that ἔλεγχος Πνεύματος,[55] that divine consciousness, that 'witness of God',[56] which is more and greater than ten thousand human witnesses.

12. If he doth not now bear witness with thy spirit that thou art
20 a child of God,[57] O that he might convince thee, thou poor unawakened sinner, by his demonstration and power, that thou art a child of the devil! O that as I prophesy there might now be 'a

[49] S. of S. 1:3.　　　　　　[50] Cf. Ps. 45:8.　　　　　[51] Eph. 4:19.

[52] An especial emphasis in the Wesleys' theory of religious knowledge derived from Descartes and Malebranche through John Norris. The human spirit is a 'spiritual sensorium', analogous to our physical senses, and thus the capacity for intuitions of spiritual reality is comparable to sight and sound. Cf. No. 10, 'The Witness of the Spirit, I', I.12 and n. Sin ('sleep', 'death') deadens all spiritual stimuli ('inlets of spiritual knowledge'). Thus, conversion or awakening is, by analogy, the discovery of a new world.

[53] See Prov. 14:24.

[54] John 3:9.

[55] Cf. Heb. 11:1. Where had Charles come across this reading? The *Textus Receptus* here reads πραγμάτων ἔλεγχος, and this agrees with all the critical editions. For the translation 'evidence and conviction', cf. John's note in *Notes*; for John's repeated use of 'divine consciousness', see Nos. 4, *Scriptural Christianity*, I.2; 5, 'Justification by Faith', IV.2; 12, 'The Witness of Our Own Spirit', §8; 17, 'The Circumcision of the Heart', I.7; 43, *The Scripture Way of Salvation*, II.1; 46, 'The Wilderness State', I.1; 70, 'The Case of Reason Impartially Considered', II.1; 106, 'On Faith, Heb. 11:6', §1; 108, 'On Riches', I.1; 119, 'Walking by Sight and Walking by Faith', §10; 132, 'On Faith, Heb. 11:1', §1. Cf. also *An Earnest Appeal*, §§6-7, and *A Farther Appeal*, Pt. I, I.4 (11: 46, 106-7 of this edn.). J. Clifford Hindley has studied the Wesleys' religious epistemology in his 'Philosophy of Enthusiasm . . .' in *The London Quarterly and Holborn Review*, Vol. 182, Nos. 2 and 3 (April and July 1957), pp. 99-109, 199-210; see also Umphrey Lee, *The Historical Backgrounds of Early Methodist Enthusiasm* (New York, Columbia University Press, 1931).

[56] 1 John 5:9.　　　　　　　　　　　　　　　　　[57] See Rom. 8:16.

noise and a shaking', and may 'the bones come together, bone to his bone'.[58] Then 'come from the four winds, O breath, and breathe on these slain that they may live!'[59] And do not ye harden your hearts and resist the Holy Ghost, who even now is come to 'convince you of sin',[60] 'because you believe not on the name of the only-begotten Son of God'.[61]

II.1. Wherefore, 'Awake, thou that sleepest, and arise from the dead.' God calleth thee now by my mouth; and bids thee know thyself,[62] thou fallen spirit, thy true state and only concern below: 'What meanest thou, O sleeper? Arise! Call upon thy God, if so be thy God will think upon thee, that thou perish not.'[63] A mighty tempest is stirred up round about thee, and thou art sinking into the depths of perdition, the gulf of God's judgments. If thou wouldst escape them, cast thyself into them. 'Judge thyself', and thou shalt 'not be judged of the Lord.'[64]

2. Awake, awake! Stand up this moment, lest thou 'drink at the Lord's hand the cup of his fury'.[65] Stir up thyself 'to lay hold on the Lord',[66] 'the Lord thy righteousness, mighty to save!'[67] 'Shake thyself from the dust.'[68] At least, let the earthquake of God's threatenings shake thee. Awake and cry out with the trembling gaoler, 'What must I do to be saved?'[69] And never rest till thou believest on the Lord Jesus, with a faith which is his gift, by the operation of his Spirit.

3. If I speak to any one of you more than to another it is to thee who thinkest thyself unconcerned in this exhortation. 'I have a message from God unto thee.'[70] In his name I 'warn *thee* to flee from the wrath to come'.[71] Thou unholy soul, see thy picture in condemned Peter, lying in the dark dungeon between the soldiers, bound with two chains, the keepers before the door keeping the prison.[72] The night is far spent, the morning is at hand[73] when thou art to be brought forth to execution. And in these dreadful circumstances thou art fast asleep; thou art fast asleep in the devil's arms, on the brink of the pit, in the jaws of everlasting destruction.[74]

[58] Cf. Ezek. 37:7.　　　　　　　　　　　　[59] Ezek. 37:9.
[60] Cf. John 8:46.　　　　　　　　　　　　[61] Cf. John 3:18.
[62] For this Wesleyan correlation of self-knowledge and repentance, see No. 7, 'The Way to the Kingdom', II.1 and n.
[63] Cf. Jonah 1:6.　　　　[64] Cf. 1 Cor. 11:31.　　　　[65] Cf. Isa. 51:17.
[6] Cf. 2 Chr. 7:22.　　　　[67] Cf. Jer. 23:6; Isa. 63:1.　　　　[68] Isa. 52:2.
[69] Acts 16:30.　　　　[70] Judg. 3:20.　　　　[71] Cf. Matt. 3:7.
[72] See Acts 12:6.　　　　[73] See Rom. 13:12.　　　　[74] 2 Thess. 1:9.

4. O may 'the angel of the Lord come upon thee, and the light shine into thy prison'![75] And mayst thou feel the stroke of an almighty hand raising thee with, 'Arise up quickly, gird thyself, and bind on thy sandals, cast thy garment about thee, and follow
5 me.'[76]

5. Awake, thou everlasting spirit, out of thy dream of worldly happiness. Did not God create thee for himself? Then thou canst not rest till thou restest in him.[77] Return, thou wanderer. Fly back to thy ark.[78] 'This is not thy home.'[79] Think not of building
10 tabernacles here. Thou art but 'a stranger, a sojourner upon earth';[80] a creature of a day,[81] but just launching out into an unchangeable state. Make haste; eternity is at hand. Eternity depends on this moment: an eternity of happiness, or an eternity of misery!

15 6. In what state is thy soul? Was God, while I am yet speaking, to require it of thee, art thou ready to meet death and judgment? Canst thou stand in his sight, 'who is of purer eyes than to behold

---

[75] Cf. Acts 12:7.   [76] Cf. Acts 12:7-8.

[77] See Augustine, *Confessions*, I.1: '*Fecisti nos ad te et inquietum est cor nostrum, donec requiescat in te*' ('Thou hast made us for thyself, and restless is our heart till it comes to rest in thee'). Cf. also Nos. 22, 'Sermon on the Mount, II', II.4; 33, 'Sermon on the Mount, XIII', II.2; 73, 'Of Hell', I.4; 77, 'Spiritual Worship', III.1; 78, 'Spiritual Idolatry', II.2; 84, *The Important Question*, III.3. For a quotation of the Latin, and the translation, cf. No. 120, 'The Unity of the Divine Being', §9. Cf. also Charles Wesley's hymn in *A Collection of Hymns*, No. 335, ll. 5-6:

My heart is pained, nor can it be
At rest, till it finds rest in thee.

[78] See Gen. 8:9.

[79] Charles Wesley uses a similar phrase at least three different times. Cf. 'After the Death of a Friend', ver. 7, l. 2: 'This earth, I know, is not my place.' The same line also occurs in 'Desiring to be Dissolved', ver. 5. Both poems were printed in John Wesley, *A Collection of Moral and Sacred Poems* (1744, *Bibliog*, No. 78), III. 266, 270. Cf. also Charles Wesley's Hymn No. 41, 'The Traveller', st. 2, l. 2, in *Hymns for Those That Seek and Those That Have Redemption* (1747), p. 51: 'This earth, we know, is not our place.' John Wesley closes his correspondence with 'John Smith', Mar. 22, 1748, by quoting the entire stanza:

Strangers and pilgrims here below,
   This earth, we know, is not our place:
And hasten through the vale of woe,
   And restless to behold thy face,
Swift to our heavenly country move,
Our everlasting home above.

Cf. also Nos. 15, *The Great Assize*, IV.4; and 108, 'On Riches', II.12.

[80] 1 Chr. 29:15.

[81] Note the echoes here of a familiar theme in Augustan literature, oft-repeated by both Wesleys; cf. Pindar, *Pythian Odes*, viii. 95-96 ('Creatures of a day . . . man is but a dream'); see also No. 124, 'Human Life a Dream', §2 and n.

iniquity'?[82] Art thou 'meet to be partaker of the inheritance of the saints in light'?[83] Hast thou 'fought a good fight and kept the faith'?[84] Hast thou secured 'the one thing needful'?[85] Hast thou recovered the image of God, even 'righteousness and true holiness'?[86] Hast thou 'put off the old man and put on the new'?[87]   5 Art thou 'clothed upon with Christ'?[88]

7. Hast thou oil in thy lamp?[89] Grace in thy heart? Dost thou 'love the Lord thy God with all thy heart, and with all thy mind, and with all thy soul, and with all thy strength'?[90] Is 'that mind in thee which was also in Christ Jesus'?[91] Art thou a Christian   10 indeed? That is, a new creature? Are 'old things passed away, and all things become new'?[92]

8. Art thou 'partaker of the divine nature'?[93] 'Knowest thou not that Christ is in thee, except thou be reprobate?'[94] Knowest thou that 'God dwelleth in thee, and thou in God, by his Spirit which   15 he hath given thee'?[95] Knowest thou not that 'thy body is a temple of the Holy Ghost, which thou hast of God'?[96] Hast thou 'the witness in thyself',[97] 'the earnest of thine inheritance'?[98] Art thou 'sealed by that Spirit of promise unto the day of redemption'?[99] 'Hast thou received the Holy Ghost?' Or dost thou start at the   20 question, not knowing whether there be any Holy Ghost?[100]

9. If it offends thee, be thou assured that thou neither art a Christian nor desirest to be one. Nay, thy 'very prayer is turned into sin';[101] and thou hast solemnly mocked God this very day by praying for 'the inspiration of his Holy Spirit',[102] when thou didst   25 not believe there was any such thing to be received.

10. Yet on the authority of God's Word and our own Church I must repeat the question, 'Hast thou received the Holy Ghost?' If thou hast not thou art not yet a Christian; for a Christian is a man that is 'anointed with the Holy Ghost and with power'.[103] Thou art   30 not yet made a partaker of pure religion and undefiled.[104] Dost

---

[82] Cf. Hab. 1:13.   [83] Col. 1:12.   [84] Cf. 2 Tim. 4:7.
[85] Cf. Luke 10:42.   [86] Eph. 4:24.   [87] Cf. Eph. 4:22, 24; Col. 3:9, 10.
[88] Cf. 2 Cor. 5:2.   [89] See Matt. 25:4.   [90] Cf. Mark 12:30.
[91] Cf. Phil. 2:5.   [92] Cf. 2 Cor. 5:17.   [93] Cf. 2 Pet. 1:4.
[94] Cf. 2 Cor. 13:5.   [95] Cf. 1 John 3:24; 4:12, 13.   [96] Cf. 1 Cor. 6:19.
[97] 1 John 5:10.   [98] Cf. Eph. 1:14.   [99] Cf. Eph. 1:13; 4:30.
[100] Acts 19:2.   [101] Cf. Ps. 109:6 (BCP).
[102] Cf. the first collect in The Order for Holy Communion, BCP: 'Almighty God, unto whom all hearts are open . . .'; note the assumption here that most in the audience had already shared in a eucharistic liturgy.
[103] Acts 10:38.   [104] Jas. 1:27.

thou know what religion is? That it is a participation of the divine nature, the life of God in the soul of man:[105] 'Christ formed in the heart',[106] 'Christ in thee, the hope of glory';[107] happiness and holiness; heaven begun upon earth;[108] 'a kingdom of God within
5 thee',[109] 'not meat and drink', no outward thing, 'but righteous-

[105] Cf. 2 Pet. 1:4: ἵνα διὰ τούτων γένησθε θείας κοινωνοὶ φύσεως, a phrase which sums up the catholic tradition of human participation in 'the divine nature'. Cf. St. Irenaeus, *Adversus Haereses*, III.xi.1, xix.6; IV.xxxiv. 3-4; and also J. T. Nielsen, *Adam and Christ in the Theology of Irenaeus of Lyons* (Assen, Van Gorcum, 1968); see also Origen's *De Principiis*, I.i.8-9; III.vi.1; IV.iv.9-10; and Hal Koch, *Pronoia und Paideusis* . . . (Berlin, Walter de Gruyter, 1932), ch.iii. See also, espec., Balas, *Metousia Theou:* (pp. 72-73 above). This theme had come to the Wesleys through such favourite sources in the Epworth rectory as Lorenzo Scupoli, *Pugna Spiritualis* . . . (1589), reckoned by both Susanna and John to have been the work of Juan de Castañiza; cf. Richard Lucas's English translation, *The Spiritual Combat* (1698), and many translations thereafter; see No. 107, 'On God's Vineyard', I.5 and n.; and Henry Scougal, *The Life of God in the Soul of Man* (cf. Wesley's abridgement in 1744; see also Winthrop S. Hudson's edn. [Philadelphia, The Westminster Press, 1948]). Other crucial sources in their Oxford days included Jeremy Taylor, Thomas à Kempis, William Law (cf. Wesley's references in *A Plain Account of Christian Perfection*, §4), and Richard Lucas (Wesley read his *Enquiry After Happiness* in Mar. 1730, and other works in 1733).

It is not incidental that John Wesley's carefully crafted account of his Aldersgate experience (JWJ, May 24, 1738) begins with the opening of his New Testament to 2 Pet. 1:4 (the longest Greek quotation in the *Journal*). He condenses both the original text and his translation of it so as to emphasize 'the exceeding great and precious promises, even that ye should be partakers of the divine nature' (cf. this with the AV and with the translation in the *Notes*). For further discussion, cf. Reginald Kissack, 'Wesley's Conversion', WHS, XXII.1-6.

For other references to the participation theme in the Wesley corpus, cf. Nos. 24, 'Sermon on the Mount, IV', III.1; 43, *The Scripture Way of Salvation*, I.4; 135, 'On Guardian Angels', II.2; 146, 'The One Thing Needful', III.1. Cf. also, in Wesley's *Notes*, his commentaries on Matt. 7:12; John 20:17; Rom. 3:23, 5:21; 1 John 2:5, 4:21. See also his letter to Richard Morgan, Jan.14, 1734; to 'John Smith', June 25, 1746; and to William Dodd, Mar. 12, 1756. Wesley emphasized this theme in his selections for the *Christian Lib.*, e.g., XIX. 193-97, 269-72; XXXIX. 44-61; L. 369-73. He even took care to preserve a MS sermon of John Gambold's among his own papers, from 1738 until his death, on 'The Holy Spirit' (see below, Vol. 4, Appendix B). Its dominant theme is participation.
[106] Cf. Gal. 4:19.
[107] Cf. Col. 1:27.
[108] A line which appears frequently in Charles Wesley's hymns. Cf., e.g., his hymn on Ps. 65, st. 4, ll. 7-8 (*Poet. Wks.*, VIII. 142):

Heaven begun on earth we feel,
The heaven of Jesu's love.

Cf. also the hymn on Ps. 31, Pt. II, st. 12, ll. 7-8 (*Poet. Wks.*, VIII. 64):

Enjoy a paradise of love
A heaven on earth begun.

Cf. also J. Wakelin, *Christ and Nicodemus*, ver. xxx, l. 1 (2nd edn., 1760, p. 19): 'A little heav'n begun on earth.'
[109] Cf. Luke 17:21.

ness, and peace, and joy in the Holy Ghost';[110] an everlasting kingdom brought into thy soul, a 'peace of God that passeth all understanding';[111] a 'joy unspeakable and full of glory'?[112]

11. Knowest thou that 'in Jesus Christ neither circumcision availeth anything, nor uncircumcision; but faith that worketh by love;'[113] but a new creation?[114] Seest thou the necessity of that inward change, that spiritual birth, that life from the dead, that holiness? And art thou thoroughly convinced that 'without it no man shall see the Lord'?[115] Art thou labouring after it? 'Giving all diligence to make thy calling and election sure'?[116] 'Working out thy salvation with fear and trembling'?[117] 'Agonizing to enter in at the strait gate'?[118] Art thou *in earnest* about thy soul? And canst thou tell the Searcher of hearts, 'Thou, O God, art the thing that I long for!'[119] 'Lord, thou knowest all things! Thou knowest that I *would* love thee!'[120]

12. Thou hopest to be saved. But what reason hast thou to give of the hope that is in thee?[121] Is it because thou hast done no harm? Or because thou hast done much good? Or because thou art not like other men,[122] but wise, or learned, or honest, and morally good? Esteemed of men, and of a fair reputation? Alas, all this will never bring thee to God. It is in his account lighter than vanity.[123] Dost thou 'know Jesus Christ whom he hath sent'?[124] Hath he taught thee that 'by grace we are saved through faith? And that not of ourselves: it is the gift of God; not of works, lest any man should boast'?[125] Hast thou received the faithful saying as the whole foundation of thy hope, that 'Jesus Christ came into the world to save sinners'?[126] Hast thou learned what that meaneth, 'I came not to call the righteous, but sinners to repentance'?[127] 'I am not sent but to the lost sheep'?[128] Art thou (he that heareth, let him understand!) lost, dead, *damned already*? Dost thou know thy deserts? Dost thou feel thy wants? Art thou 'poor in spirit'?[129] Mourning for God and refusing to be comforted?[130] Is the prodigal 'come to himself',[131] and well content to be therefore

---

[110] Rom. 14:17.   [111] Cf. Phil. 4:7.   [112] Cf. 1 Pet. 1:8.

[113] Gal. 5:6.   [114] Gal. 6:15.   [115] Cf. Heb. 12:14.

[116] Cf. 2 Pet. 1:10.   [117] Cf. Phil. 2:12.   [118] Cf. Luke 13:24.

[119] Cf. Job 6:8.   [120] Cf. John 21:17.   [121] See 1 Pet. 3:15.

[122] See Luke 18:11.   [123] Ps. 62:9.   [124] Cf. John 17:3.

[125] Cf. Eph. 2:8, 9.   [126] Cf. 1 Tim. 1:15.   [127] Mark 2:17.

[128] Matt. 15:24; note Charles Wesley's omission of the concluding phrase, 'of the house of Israel'.

[129] Matt. 5:3.   [130] See Matt. 5:4.   [131] Cf. Luke 15:17.

thought 'beside himself'[132] by those who are still feeding upon the husks which he hath left?[133] Art thou willing to 'live godly in Christ Jesus'? And dost thou therefore 'suffer persecution'?[134] Do 'men say all manner of evil against thee falsely, for the Son of man's sake'?[135]

13. O that in all these questions ye may hear the voice that wakes the dead, and feel that hammer of the Word which 'breaketh the rock in pieces'![136] 'If ye will hear his voice today, while it is called today, harden not your hearts.'[137] Now 'awake, thou that sleepest' in spiritual death, that thou sleep not in death eternal! Feel thy lost estate, and 'arise from the dead.' Leave thine old companions in sin and death. Follow thou Jesus, and 'let the dead bury their dead.'[138] 'Save thyself from this untoward generation.'[139] 'Come out from among them, and be thou separate, and touch not the unclean thing; and the Lord shall receive thee.'[140] 'Christ shall give thee light.'[141]

III.1. This promise I come, lastly, to explain. And how encouraging a consideration is this, that whosoever thou art who obeyest his call, thou canst not seek his face in vain. If thou even now 'awakest and arisest from the dead', he hath bound himself to 'give thee light'. 'The Lord shall give thee grace and glory;'[142] the light of his grace here, and the light of his glory when thou receivest the 'crown that fadeth not away.'[143] 'Thy light shall break forth as the morning,'[144] and thy darkness be as the noonday.[145] 'God, who commanded the light to shine out of darkness', shall 'shine in thy heart, to give the knowledge of the glory of God in the face of Jesus Christ.'[146] 'On them that fear the Lord shall the Sun of righteousness arise with healing in his wings.'[147] And 'in that day it shall be said unto thee',[148] 'Arise, shine; for thy light is come, and the glory of the Lord is risen upon thee.'[149] For Christ shall reveal himself in thee. And he is 'the true light'.[150]

2. God is light,[151] and will give himself to every awakened sinner that waiteth for him. And thou shalt then be a temple of the living God,[152] and Christ shall 'dwell in thy heart by faith'. And,

[132] Mark 3:21.   [133] Cf. Luke 15:16-17.   [134] 2 Tim. 3:12.
[135] Cf. Matt. 5:11.   [136] Jer. 23:29.   [137] Cf. Heb. 3:8, 15, etc.
[138] Matt. 8:22.   [139] Acts 2:40.   [140] Cf. 2 Cor. 6:17.
[141] Eph. 5:14.   [142] Cf. Ps. 84:11 (AV).   [143] Cf. 1 Pet. 5:4.
[144] Cf. Isa. 58:8.   [145] Isa. 58:10.   [146] Cf. 2 Cor. 4:6.
[147] Cf. Mal. 4:2.   [148] Cf. Zeph. 3:16.   [149] Isa. 60:1.
[150] John 1:9; 1 John 2:8.   [151] 1 John 1:5.   [152] 2 Cor. 6:16.

'being rooted and grounded in love', thou shalt 'be able to comprehend with all saints what is the breadth, and length, and depth, and height' of that 'love of Christ which passeth knowledge, that thou mayest be filled with all the fullness of God.'[153]   5

3. Ye see your calling, brethren. We are called to be 'an habitation of God through his Spirit';[154] and through his Spirit dwelling in us 'to be saints'[155] here, 'and partakers of the inheritance of the saints in light'.[156] So 'exceeding great are the promises which are given unto us',[157] actually given unto us who   10 believe. For by faith 'we receive, not the spirit of the world, but the Spirit which is of God'—the sum of all the promises—'that we may know the things that are freely given to us of God.'[158]

4. The Spirit of Christ is that great gift of God which at sundry times and in divers manners[159] he hath promised to man, and hath   15 fully bestowed since the time that Christ was glorified. Those promises before made to the fathers he hath thus fulfilled: 'I will put my Spirit within you, and cause you to walk in my statutes.'[a] 'I will pour water upon him that is thirsty, and floods upon the dry ground: I will pour my Spirit upon thy seed, and my blessing upon   20 thine offspring.'[b]

5. Ye may all be living witnesses of these things, of remission of sins, and the gift of the Holy Ghost.[160] 'If thou canst believe, all things are possible to him that believeth.'[161] 'Who among you is there that feareth the Lord', and yet 'walketh on in darkness, and   25 hath no light?'[162] I ask thee in the name of Jesus, believest thou that 'his arm is not shortened at all'?[163] That he is still 'mighty to save'?[164] That he is 'the same yesterday, today, and for ever'?[165] That 'he hath *now* power on earth to forgive sins'?[166] 'Son, be of good cheer; thy sins are forgiven.'[167] God, for Christ's sake, hath   30

[a] Ezek. 36:27.
[b] Isa. 44:3.

---

[153] Cf. Eph. 3:17-19.
[154] Cf. Eph. 2:22.
[155] Rom 1·7; 1 Cor. 1:2.
[156] Col. 1:12.
[157] Cf. 2 Pet. 1:4.
[158] Cf. 1 Cor. 2:12.
[159] Heb. 1:1.
[160] Cf. Acts 2:38; 10:43; note the implied rejection here of the patristic notion of 'the seal of the Spirit' in baptism (cf. 2 Cor. 1:22; Eph. 1:13; 4:30).
[161] Mark 9:23.
[162] Cf. Isa. 50:10.
[163] Cf. Isa. 50:2; 59:1.
[164] Isa. 63:1.
[165] Heb. 13:8.
[166] Cf. Matt. 9:6, etc.
[167] Cf. Matt. 9:2.

forgiven thee. Receive this, 'not as the word of man; but as it is, indeed, the word of God';[168] and thou art 'justified freely through faith'.[169] Thou shalt be sanctified also through faith which is in Jesus,[170] and shalt set to thy seal,[171] even thine, 'that God hath
5 given unto us eternal life, and this life is in his Son'.[172]

6. Men and brethren, let me freely speak unto you,[173] and 'suffer ye the word of exhortation',[174] even from one the least esteemed in the church. Your conscience beareth you witness in the Holy Ghost[175] that these things are so, 'if so be ye have tasted
10 that the Lord is gracious'.[176] 'This is eternal life, to know the only true God, and Jesus Christ whom he hath sent.'[177] This experimental knowledge,[178] and this alone, is true Christianity. He is a Christian who hath received the Spirit of Christ. He is not a Christian who hath not received him. Neither is it possible to
15 have received him and not know it. For 'at that day' (when he cometh, saith the Lord) 'ye shall know that I am in my Father, and you in me, and I in you.'[c] This is that 'Spirit of truth, whom the world cannot receive, because it seeth him not, neither knoweth him. But ye know him; for he dwelleth with you, and shall be in
20 you.'[179]

[c] John 14:20.

---

[168] Cf. 1 Thess. 2:13.   [169] Cf. Rom. 3:24.
[170] See Acts 26:18.   [171] See John 3:33.
[172] Cf. 1 John 5:11.   [173] Acts 2:29.
[174] Cf. Heb. 13:22.   [175] See Rom. 9:1.
[176] 1 Pet. 2:3.   [177] Cf. John 17:3.

[178] *Viz.*, 'personal', 'existential'. Cf. Bishop Joseph Hall, Epistle VII, 'To Mr. William Bedell', in *Select Works* (London, 1811), IV. 138; and Bishop Laurence Womock, *The Examination of Tilenus* (1661), p. 85. This distinction between 'speculative' and 'practical' religion is pervasive in the writings of both Wesley brothers. Note the implied either/or here; this, too, will soften as the Revival matures.

[179] John 14:17. Note the radical either/or here: either a clear and full assurance of justifying faith or none at all. Southey, I. 150-53, observes that it was this stark disjunction between full assurance and none at all that prompted many of the hysterical symptoms reported in the early years of the Revival. Bernard G. Holland confirms this thesis and extends it in 'The Conversions of John and Charles Wesley', WHS, XXXVIII. 53, 65-71, but also points to the fact that both brothers rather quickly modified this all-or-nothing emphasis by allowing for *degrees* of assurance. This softening may be seen in John Wesley's letter to Dr. Rutherford, Mar. 28, 1768; and in Nos. 89, 'The More Excellent Way', §§7, 8; and 106, 'On Faith, Heb. 11:6', I.11 (and for John's numerous references to the plerophory or 'full assurance of faith' cf. No. 117, 'On the Discoveries of Faith', §15 and n.).

Melville Horne, once an active Methodist itinerant, reports a 'final' word from John Wesley on this subject (either from a letter or a conversation that must be dated somewhere close to 1789): 'When fifty years ago my brother Charles and I, in the

7. The world cannot receive him, but utterly rejecteth the promise of the Father, contradicting and blaspheming. But every spirit which confesseth not this is not of God. Yea, 'this is that spirit of antichrist, whereof ye have heard that it should come into the world; and even now it is in the world.'[180] He is antichrist whosoever denies the inspiration of the Holy Ghost, or that the indwelling Spirit of God is the common privilege of all believers, the blessing of the gospel, the unspeakable gift, the universal promise, the criterion of a real Christian.[181]

8. It nothing helps them to say, 'We do not deny the *assistance* of God's Spirit, but only this *inspiration*,[182] this "receiving the Holy Ghost" and being *sensible* of it. It is only this *feeling* of the Spirit, this being *moved* by the Spirit, or *filled* with it, which we deny to have any place in sound religion.' But in 'only' denying this you deny the whole Scriptures, the whole truth and promise and testimony of God.

9. Our own excellent Church knows nothing of this devilish distinction; but speaks plainly of 'feeling the Spirit of Christ';[d] of

---

[d] Article 17 ['Of Predestination and Election': ' . . . and such as feel in themselves the working of the Spirit of Christ . . .'].

---

simplicity of our hearts, told the good people of England that unless they *knew* their sins were forgiven, they were under the wrath and curse of God, I marvel, Melville, they did not stone us!'; cf. Melville Horne, *An Investigation of the Definition of Justifying Faith* . . . (1809), p. 3; and Thomas Coke's reply to it in *A Series of Letters Addressed to the Methodist Connexion* . . . (1810). See also Southey, I. 216-17; and Semmel, *Methodist Revolution*, p. 100.

[180] Cf. 1 John 4:3.

[181] For a careful statement of the general teaching about the gifts of the Holy Spirit as extraordinary and exceptional, cf. Arthur Bedford, *The Doctrine of Assurance* . . . (1738). For another claim that such gifts are the common privilege of *all* believers, cf. Moore, I. 269, reporting a conversation between John Wesley and Joseph Butler in Bristol, Aug. 18, 1739, about faith and assurance. The bishop's complaint was candid: 'Sir, the pretending to extraordinary revelations and gifts of the Holy Ghost is a horrid thing, a very horrid thing.' Wesley's reply was meant to be disarming: 'My lord, . . . I pretend to no extraordinary revelations or gifts of the Holy Ghost—none but what *every* Christian may receive, and ought to expect and pray for . . . .' See p. 13, n. 47 above; see also No. 4, *Scriptural Christianity*, §4.

[182] Moore also prints (II. 277-322) a twelve-letter exchange between Wesley and a pseudonymous 'John Smith'. (See *Letters* II, Vol. 26 of this edn.) Though an acute theologian, 'Smith' almost certainly was not Thomas Secker as Tyerman (*JW*), I. 409-10); Sugden (I. 82); and Telford (*Letters*, II. 42) have suggested. Wesley's letter of Mar. 22, 1748, to 'Smith' indicates that he was a pastor of a parish ('If a single parish takes up your whole time and care, and you spend and are spent upon it, well'). 'Smith' was deeply disturbed by what he took to be a Wesleyan doctrine of assurance as 'perceptible inspiration' (cf. Letter III, Nov. 27, 1745, and Letter V, Feb. 26, 1746). Wesley's reply (Letter VI, June 25, 1746) rehearses once again the claim that the gifts of the Spirit are meant for all truly converted Christians. See also, below, Nos. 10 and 11, 'The Witness of the Spirit', Discourses I and II.

being 'moved by the Holy Ghost',^e and knowing and 'feeling there is no other name than that of Jesus whereby we can receive any salvation'.^f She teaches us also to pray for the 'inspiration of the Holy Spirit',^g yea, that we may be 'filled with the Holy Ghost'.^h
5 Nay, and every presbyter of hers professes to 'receive the Holy Ghost by the imposition of hands'.[183] Therefore to deny any of these is in effect to renounce the Church of England, as well as the whole Christian revelation.

10. But 'the wisdom of God' was always 'foolishness with
10 men'.[184] No marvel, then, that the great mystery of the gospel should be now also 'hid from the wise and prudent',[185] as well as in the days of old; that it should be almost universally denied, ridiculed, and exploded as mere frenzy, and all who dare avow it still branded with the names of madmen and enthusiasts.[186] This
15 is that 'falling away'[187] which was to come—that general apostasy of all orders and degrees of men which we even now find to have overspread the earth. 'Run to and fro in the streets of Jerusalem, and see if you can find a man,'[188] a man that loveth the Lord his God with all his heart, and serveth him with all his strength. How
20 does our own land mourn (that we look no farther) under the overflowings of ungodliness![189] What villainies of every kind are committed day by day; yea, too often with impunity by those who sin with a high hand, and glory in their shame![190] Who can reckon up the oaths, curses, profaneness, blasphemies; the lying,
25 slandering, evil speaking; the sabbath-breaking, gluttony, drunkenness, revenge; the whoredoms, adulteries, and various uncleanness; the frauds, injustice, oppression, extortion, which overspread our land as a flood?[191]

11. And even among those who have kept themselves pure
30 from those grosser abominations, how much anger and pride,

---

^e Office of consecrating Priests [BCP, The Ordering of Deacons].
^f Visitation of the Sick [*ibid.*, Of the Sick].
^g Collect before the Holy Communion [*ibid.*].
^h Order of Confirmation [*ibid.* However, the words do not occur there but in Collects, St. Stephen's Day].

---

[183] Cf. BCP, Ordering of Priests.
[184] Cf. 1 Cor. 1:21-25.   [185] Matt. 11:25.
[186] For samplings of eighteenth-century denunciations of enthusiasm, cf. Lee, *Early Methodist Enthusiasm*, chs. 2–3.
[187] 2 Thess. 2:3.   [188] Cf. Jer. 5:1.
[189] Ps. 18:4 (BCP).   [190] Phil. 3:19.
[191] See Ps. 69:2, and No. 4, *Scriptural Christianity*, IV.11. See also Rom. 1:18-32.

how much sloth and idleness, how much softness and effeminacy, how much luxury and self-indulgence, how much covetousness and ambition, how much thirst of praise,[192] how much love of the world, how much fear of man is to be found! Meanwhile, how little of true religion! For where is he that loveth either God or his 5 neighbour, as he hath given us commandment? On the one hand are those who have not so much as the form of godliness; on the other, those who have the form only:[193] there stands the open, there the painted sepulchre.[194] So that, in very deed, whosoever were earnestly to behold any public gathering together of the 10 people (I fear those in our churches are not to be excepted) might easily perceive 'that the one part were Sadducees, and the other Pharisees':[195] the one having almost as little concern about religion as if there were 'no resurrection, neither angel nor spirit';[196] and the other making it a mere lifeless form, a dull round 15 of external performances without either true faith, or the love of God, or joy in the Holy Ghost.[197]

12. Would to God I could except us of this place. 'Brethren, my heart's desire and prayer to God for you is that ye may be saved'[198] from this overflowing of ungodliness,[199] and that here 20 may its proud waves be stayed![200] But is it so indeed? God knoweth, yea, and our own conscience, it is not. We have not kept ourselves pure.[201] Corrupt are we also and abominable; and few are there that understand any more, few that worship God in spirit and in truth.[202] We too are 'a generation that set not our 25 hearts aright, and whose spirit cleaveth not steadfastly unto God'.[203] He hath appointed us indeed to be 'the salt of the earth. But if the salt have lost its savour, it is thenceforth good for nothing but to be cast out, and to be trodden under foot of men.'[204]

13. And 'shall I not visit for these things? saith the Lord. Shall 30 not my soul be avenged on such a nation as this?'[205] Yea, we know not how soon he may say to the sword, 'Sword, go through this land!'[206] He hath given us long space to repent. He lets us alone this year also. But he warns and awakens us by thunder. His

---

[192] For John Wesley's references to the common thirst for fame and glory (*gloria sitis*), see No. 14, *The Repentance of Believers*, I.7 and n.

[193] Cf. 2 Tim. 3:5, and No. 2, *The Almost Christian*, I.4 and n.

[194] Cf. Matt. 23:27, and I.7 and n., above.

[195] Acts 23:6. [196] Acts 23:8. [197] Rom. 14:17.

[198] Cf. Rom. 10:1. [199] Ps. 18:4 (BCP). [200] See Job 38:11.

[201] See 1 Tim. 5:22. [202] John 4:24. [203] Cf. Ps. 78:9 (BCP).

[204] Matt. 5:13. [205] Jer. 5:9, 29. [206] Cf. Ezek. 14:17.

judgments are abroad in the earth.[207] And we have all reason to expect that heaviest of all, even 'that he should come unto us quickly, and remove our candlestick out of its place, except we repent and do the first works';[208] unless we return to the principles
5 of the Reformation, the truth and simplicity of the gospel. Perhaps we are now resisting the last effort of divine grace to save us. Perhaps we have wellnigh 'filled up the measure of our iniquities'[209] by rejecting the counsel of God against ourselves, and casting out his messengers.

10   14. O God, 'in the midst of wrath remember mercy'![210] Be glorified in our reformation, not in our destruction. Let us 'hear the rod, and him that appointed it'.[211] Now that 'thy judgments are abroad in the earth',[212] let 'the inhabitants of the world learn righteousness'.[213]

15   15. My brethren, it is high time for us to awake out of sleep; before 'the great trumpet of the Lord be blown',[214] and our land become a field of blood.[215] O may we speedily see the things that make for our peace, before they are hid from our eyes![216] 'Turn thou us, O good Lord, and let thine anger cease from us.'[217] 'O
20 Lord, look down from heaven, behold and visit this vine';[218] and cause us to know the time of our visitation.[219] 'Help us, O God of our salvation, for the glory of thy name; O deliver us, and be merciful to our sins, for thy name's sake.'[220] 'And so will we not go back from thee: O let us live, and we shall call upon thy name.
25 Turn us again, O Lord God of hosts, show the light of thy countenance, and we shall be whole.'[221]

'Now unto him that is able to do exceeding abundantly above all that we can ask or think, according to the power that worketh in us, unto him be glory in the church by Christ Jesus throughout all
30 ages, world without end.   Amen.'[222]

---

[207] Cf. Ps. 105:7 (AV). III.13-15 are echoes of the compound crises in Europe in general and England in particular; Charles Wesley could expect most of his hearers to share his alarm, even if for different reasons. Sir Robert Walpole's cynical reign had ended only two months before, and a dangerous new future loomed ahead with the War of the Austrian Succession (1739-48) which had engulfed an ineptly led Britain; Charles Edward Stuart ('Bonnie Prince Charlie') was waiting in the wings. In 1745-46 England and, much more tragically, Scotland became 'a field of blood' (as at Culloden, Apr. 15, 1746). Cf. Robertson, *England Under the Hanoverians*, pp. 80-111; and Williams, *The Whig Supremacy*, pp. 220-51.

[208] Cf. Rev. 2:5.   [209] Cf. Matt. 23:32.   [210] Hab. 3:2.
[211] Cf. Mic. 6:9.   [212] Cf. 1 Chr. 16:14; Ps. 105:7.   [213] Isa. 26:9.
[214] Isa. 27:13.   [215] Matt. 27:8.   [216] See Luke 19:42.
[217] Cf. Ps. 85:4 (BCP).   [218] Cf. Ps. 80:14.   [219] See Jer. 8:12, etc.
[220] Ps. 79:9 (BCP).   [221] Ps. 80:18-19 (BCP).   [222] Eph. 3:20-21.

Scriptural Christianity

A Sermon preached at St. Mary's, Oxford,
before the University,
August 24, 1744[1]

To the Reader.

It was not my design when I wrote ever to print the latter part of the following sermon. But the false and scurrilous accounts[2] of it which have been published almost in every corner of the nation constrain me to publish the whole, just as it was preached, that men of reason may judge for themselves.   10

OCTOBER 20   JOHN WESLEY[3]
1744

Acts 4:31

And they were all filled with the Holy Ghost

1. The same expression occurs in the second chapter, where we 15
read, 'When the day of Pentecost was fully come, they were all'
(the apostles, with the women, and the mother of Jesus, and his
brethren) 'with one accord in one place. And suddenly there
came a sound from heaven, as of a rushing mighty wind. . . . And
there appeared unto them cloven tongues, like as of fire, and it sat 20
upon each of them. And they were all filled with the Holy Ghost.'[a]
One immediate effect whereof was, they 'began to speak with
other tongues';[b] insomuch that both the 'Parthians, Medes,

---

[a] Acts 2:1-4.
[b] Ver. 4.

---

[1] Half-title reproduced from *Sermons*, 1746. The drop-title prefixed to the individual editions of the sermon was simply 'Acts iv. 31'.

[2] See above, 'Intro. Com.', pp. 113-15.

[3] This foreword was omitted from the collected editions of *SOSO*.

Elamites', and the other strangers who 'came together' 'when this was noised abroad', 'heard them speak' in their several 'tongues, the wonderful works of God.'[c]

2. In this chapter we read that when the apostles and brethren had been praying and praising God, 'the place was shaken where they were assembled together, and they were all filled with the Holy Ghost.'[d] Not that we find any visible appearance here, such as had been in the former instance: nor are we informed that the *extraordinary* gifts of the Holy Ghost were then given to all or any of them, such as 'the gifts of healing, of working other miracles, of prophecy, of discerning spirits', the speaking with 'divers kinds of tongues', and 'the interpretation of tongues'.[e]

3. Whether these gifts of the Holy Ghost were designed to remain in the church throughout all ages, and whether or not they will be restored at the nearer approach of the 'restitution of all things',[1] are questions which it is not needful to decide. But it is needful to observe this, that even in the infancy of the church God divided them with a sparing hand. 'Were all' even then 'prophets?' Were 'all workers of miracles? Had all the gifts of healing? Did all speak with tongues?' No, in no wise. Perhaps not one in a thousand. Probably none but the teachers in the church, and only some of them.[f] It was therefore for a more excellent purpose than this that 'they were all filled with the Holy Ghost.'

4. It was to give them (what none can deny to be essential to all Christians in all ages)[2] 'the mind which was in Christ',[3] those holy 'fruits of the Spirit'[4] which whosoever hath not 'is none of his';[5] to fill them with 'love, joy, peace, long-suffering, gentleness, goodness'; to endue them with 'faith' (perhaps it might be rendered 'fidelity'), with 'meekness and temperance'; to enable them to 'crucify the flesh with its affections and lusts',[g] its passions and desires; and, in consequence of that *inward change*,

---

[c] Ver. 6 [9,11].
[d] Acts 4:31.
[e] 1 Cor. 12:9-10.
[f] 1 Cor. 12:28-30.
[g] Gal. 5:22-24.

---

[1] Acts 3:21.
[2] Another claim that the ordinary gifts of the Holy Spirit are designed for ordinary Christians; see above, p. 155, n. 181. What is important here is Wesley's view that the gifts of the Spirit are to be normed by the 'fruits'; cf. Nos. 10, 'The Witness of the Spirit, I', II.12; 37, 'The Nature of Enthusiasm', §§19-26; 89, 'The More Excellent Way', §2; and his letters to Dr. Middleton, Jan. 4, 1749; to Dr. Warburton, Nov. 26, 1762, and to George Fleury, May 18, 1771. See also, *Notes*, Acts 19:2.
[3] Cf. Phil. 2:5.
[4] Gal. 5:22.
[5] Rom. 8:9.

to fulfil all *outward* righteousness, 'to walk as Christ also walked',[6] in the 'work of faith, the patience of hope, the labour of love'.[h]

5. Without busying ourselves then in curious, needless inquiries touching those *extraordinary* gifts of the Spirit, let us take a nearer view of these his *ordinary* fruits, which we are 5 assured will remain throughout all ages: of that great work of God among the children of men which we are used to express by one word, 'Christianity'; not as it implies a set of opinions, a system of doctrines, but as it refers to men's hearts and lives. And this Christianity it may be useful to consider under three distinct 10 views:

I. As beginning to exist in individuals.

II. As spreading from one to another.

III. As covering the earth.

I design to close these considerations with a plain practical 15 application.

I. And first, let us consider Christianity in its rise, as beginning to exist in individuals.

[1.] Suppose then one of those who heard the Apostle Peter preaching 'repentance and remission of sins'[7] was 'pricked to the 20 heart',[8] was convinced of sin, repented, and then 'believed in Jesus'.[9] By this 'faith of the operation of God',[10] which was the very 'substance', or subsistence, 'of things hoped for', the demonstrative 'evidence of invisible things',[i] he instantly 'received the Spirit of adoption, whereby he (now) cried Abba, 25 Father.'[j] Now first it was that he could 'call Jesus Lord, by the Holy Ghost',[k] 'the Spirit itself bearing witness with his spirit that he was a child of God'.[l] Now it was that he could truly say, 'I live not, but Christ liveth in me; and the life which I now live in the flesh I live by faith in the Son of God, who loved me and gave 30 himself for me.'[m]

2. This then was the very essence of his faith, a divine ἔλεγχος[n] of the love of God the Father, through the Son of his love, to him

---

[h] 1 Thess. 1:3. [i] Heb. 11:1.
[j] Rom. 8:15. [k] 1 Cor. 12:3.
[l] Rom. 8:16. [m] [Cf.] Gal. 2:20.
[n] Evidence or conviction. [See Heb. 11:1; cf. No. 3, '*Awake, Thou That Sleepest*', I.11 and n.].

---

[6] Cf. 1 John 2:6. [7] Luke 24:47. [8] Cf. Acts 2:37.
[9] Gal. 2:16. [10] Col. 2:12.

a sinner, now 'accepted in the beloved'.[11] And 'being justified by faith, he had peace with God',[o] yea, 'the peace of God ruling in his heart';[12] a peace 'which, passing all understanding' ($\pi\acute{\alpha}\nu\tau\alpha$ $\nu o\hat{\upsilon}\nu$, all barely rational conception), 'kept his heart and mind'[13] from all
5 doubt and fear, through the 'knowledge of him in whom he had believed'.[14] He could not therefore 'be afraid of any evil tidings';[15] for his 'heart stood fast, believing in the Lord'.[16] He feared not what man could do unto him, knowing 'the very hairs of his head were all numbered'.[17] He feared not all the powers of darkness,
10 whom God was daily 'bruising under his feet'.[18] Least of all was he afraid to die; nay, he 'desired to depart and be with Christ';[p] who 'through death had destroyed him that had the power of death, even the devil, and delivered them who through fear of death were all their lifetime', till then, 'subject to bondage'.[q]
15 3. 'His soul' therefore 'magnified the Lord, and his spirit rejoiced in God his Saviour.'[19] He rejoiced in him 'with joy unspeakable',[20] who 'had reconciled him to God, even the Father';[21] 'in whom he had redemption through his blood, the forgiveness of sins.'[22] He rejoiced in that 'witness of God's Spirit
20 with his spirit that he was a child of God';[23] and more abundantly 'in hope of the glory of God';[24] in hope of the glorious image of God, the full 'renewal of his soul in righteousness and true holiness';[25] and in hope of that 'crown of glory',[26] that 'inheritance incorruptible, undefiled, and that fadeth not away'.[27]
25 4. 'The love of God' was also 'shed abroad in his heart by the Holy Ghost which was given unto him.'[r] 'Because he was a son,

---

[o] Rom. 5:1.　　　　　　　　　　　　　　　　　　[p] Phil. 1:23.
[q] Heb. 2:14-15.　　　　　　　　　　　　　　　　　　[r] Rom. 5:5.

---

[11] Eph. 1:6.　　　　　　　　　　　　　　　　　　　[12] Cf. Col. 3:15.
[13] Cf. Phil. 4:7. Wesley's translation of $\nu o\hat{\upsilon}\varsigma$ here as 'barely rational conception' is faithful to his own general distinction between mere reason and spiritual intuition, but it is misleading, even in this verse. Cf. Arndt and Gingrich, *A Greek-English Lexicon*, 1957 (entries on $\nu o\hat{\upsilon}\varsigma$ and its cognates); see also Liddell and Scott, *A Greek-English Lexicon* (9th edn., 1940). Cf. *The Epistle of Barnabas*, 6:10, where $\nu o\hat{\upsilon}\varsigma$ means an 'understanding' of *divine* 'secrets'. Thus, the 'peace' of Phil. 4:7 is a divine bestowal, surpassing the utmost outreach of 'rational conception'.
[14] Cf. 2 Tim. 1:12.　　　　　　　　　　　　　　　[15] Ps. 112:7 (BCP).
[16] Cf. Phil. 4:1; 1 Thess. 3:8.　　　　　　　　　[17] Cf. Matt. 10:30.
[18] Cf. Rom. 16:20.　　　　　　　　　　　　　　　[19] Cf. Luke 1:46-47.
[20] 1 Pet. 1:8.　　　　　　　　　[21] Cf. 2 Cor. 5:18; 1 Cor. 15:24, etc.
[22] Col. 1:14; cf. Eph. 1:7.　　　　[23] Cf. Rom. 8:16.　　　[24] Rom. 5:2.
[25] Cf. Eph. 4:23, 24.　　　　　　[26] 1 Pet. 5:4.　　　　　[27] 1 Pet. 1:4.

God had sent forth the Spirit of his Son into his heart, crying Abba, Father!'[s] And that filial love of God was continually increased by the 'witness he had in himself'[t] of God's pardoning love to him, by 'beholding what manner of love it was which the Father had bestowed upon him, that he should be called a child of God'.[u] So that God was the desire of his eyes, and the joy of his heart; his portion in time and in eternity.[28]

5. He that thus 'loved God' could not but 'love his brother also';[29] and 'not in word only, but in deed and in truth'.[30] 'If God', said he, 'so loved us, we ought also to love one another;'[v] yea, every soul of man, as the 'mercy' of God 'is over all his works'.[w] Agreeably hereto, the affection of this lover of God embraced all mankind for his sake; not excepting those whom he had never seen in the flesh, or those of whom he knew nothing more than that they were 'the offspring of God',[31] for whose souls his Son had died; not excepting the *evil* and *unthankful*, and least of all his enemies, those who 'hated, or persecuted, or despitefully used'[32] him for his Master's sake. These had a peculiar place both in his heart and his prayers. He loved them 'even as Christ loved us'.[33]

6. And 'love is not puffed up'.[x] It abases to the dust every soul wherein it dwells. Accordingly he was 'lowly of heart',[34] little and mean and vile in his own eyes. He neither sought nor received the 'praise of men',[35] 'but that which cometh of God only'.[36] He was meek and long-suffering, gentle to all, and easy to be entreated.[37] Faithfulness and truth never forsook him; they were 'bound about his neck, and wrote on the table of his heart'.[38] By the same Spirit he was enabled to be 'temperate in all things',[39] 'refraining his soul even as a weaned child'.[40] He was 'crucified to the world, and the world crucified to him'[41]—superior to 'the desire of the flesh, the

---

[s] Gal. 4:6.　　　　　　[t] 1 John 5:10.　　　　　　[u] 1 John 3:1.
[v] 1 John 4:11.　　　　　[w] Ps. 145:9.　　　　　　　[x] 1 Cor. 13:4.

---

[28] See Ps. 16:5; 73:25-26 (AV).　　　　　　　　　　　　[29] 1 John 4:21.
[30] Cf. 1 John 3:18.　　　　　　　　　　　　　　　　　　[31] Acts 17:29.
[32] Cf. Matt. 5:44.　　　　　　　　　　　　　　　　　　[33] Cf. Eph. 5:2.
[34] Matt. 11:29.　　　　　　　　　　　　　　　　　　　[35] John 12:43.
[36] Cf. John 5:44. Cf. also Nos. 17, 'The Circumcision of the Heart', I.1, II.1-2; 26, 'Sermon on the Mount, VI', I.3; 136, 'On Mourning for the Dead', ¶14; 3, '*Awake, Thou That Sleepest*', III.11 and n.; and 14, *The Repentance of Believers*, 1.7 and n.
[37] Jas. 3:17.　　　　　　　　[38] Cf. Prov. 3:3.　　　　　　[39] 1 Cor. 9:25.
[40] Cf. Ps. 131:3 (BCP), and Ps. 131:2 (AV); a rare instance of Wesley's combining the AV and BCP Psalters.
[41] Cf. Gal. 6:14.

desire of the eye, and the pride of life.'[42] By the same almighty love
was he saved both from passion and pride, from lust and vanity,
from ambition and covetousness, and from every temper which
was not in Christ.

5　　7. It may be easily believed, he who had this love in his heart
would 'work no evil to his neighbour'.[43] It was impossible for him
knowingly and designedly to do harm to any man. He was at the
greatest distance from cruelty and wrong, from any unjust or
unkind action. With the same care did he 'set a watch before his
10 mouth, and keep the door of his lips',[44] lest he should offend in
tongue either against justice, or against mercy or truth. He 'put
away all lying',[45] falsehood, and fraud; 'neither was guile found in
his mouth'.[46] He 'spake evil of no man';[47] nor did an unkind word
ever come out of his lips.

15　　8. And as he was deeply sensible of the truth of that word,
'without me ye can do nothing',[48] and consequently of the need he
had to be 'watered' of God 'every moment';[49] so he 'continued
daily'[50] in all the ordinances of God, the stated channels of his
grace to man: 'in the apostles' doctrine' or teaching, receiving that
20 food of the soul with all readiness of heart; 'in the breaking of
bread', which he found to be 'the communion of the body of
Christ';[51] and 'in the prayers'[52] and praises offered up by the great
congregation. And thus he daily 'grew in grace',[53] increasing in
strength, in the knowledge and love of God.

25　　9. But it did not satisfy him barely to abstain from doing evil.
His soul was athirst to do good. The language of his heart
continually was, 'My Father worketh hitherto, and I work.'[54] My
Lord 'went about doing good';[55] and shall not I 'tread in his
steps'?[56] 'As he had opportunity',[57] therefore, if he could do no
30 good of a higher kind, he fed the hungry, clothed the naked,
helped the fatherless or stranger, visited and assisted them that
were sick or in prison.[58] He 'gave all his goods to feed the poor'.[59]
He rejoiced to labour or to suffer for them; and whereinsoever he
might profit another, there especially to 'deny himself'.[60] He

[42] 1 John 2:16. Cf. No. 7, 'The Way to the Kingdom', II.2 and n.
[43] Cf. Ps. 15:3.　　　　[44] Cf. Ps. 141:3.　　　　[45] Cf. Eph. 4:25.
[46] 1 Pet. 2:22.　　　　[47] Titus 3:2.　　　　　[48] John 15:5.
[49] Isa. 27:3.　　　　[50] Acts 2:42, 46.　　　　[51] 1 Cor. 10:16.
[52] Acts 2:42.　　　　[53] Cf. 2 Pet. 3:18.　　　　[54] John 5:17.
[55] Acts 10:28; note the echoes here from the first two *General Rules*.
[56] Cf. 1 Pet. 2:21.　　　　[57] Cf. Gal. 6:10.　　　　[58] See Matt. 25:35-39.
[59] Cf. 1 Cor. 13:3.　　　　　　　　　　　　[60] Matt. 16:24, etc.

counted nothing too dear to part with for them, as well
remembering the word of his Lord, 'Inasmuch as ye have done it
unto one of the least of these my brethren, ye have done it unto
me.'[y]

10. Such was Christianity in its rise.[61] Such was a Christian in
ancient days. Such was every one of those who, 'when they heard'
the threatenings of 'the chief priests and elders', 'lifted up their
voice to God with one accord, . . . and were all filled with the
Holy Ghost. . . . The multitude of them that believed were of
one heart and of one soul' (so did the love of him in whom they
had believed constrain them to love one another). 'Neither said
any of them that ought of the things which he possessed was his
own; but they had all things common.'[62] So fully were they
crucified to the world and the world crucified to them.[63] 'And they
continued steadfastly . . .' 'with one accord . . .' 'in the apostles'
doctrine, and in the breaking of bread, and in prayers.'[64] 'And
great grace was upon them all; neither was there any among them
that lacked: for as many as were possessors of lands or houses sold
them, and brought the prices of the things that were sold, and laid
them down at the apostles' feet; and distribution was made unto
every man according as he had need.'[z]

II.1. Let us take a view, in the second place, of this Christianity
as spreading from one to another, and so gradually making its way
into the world. For such was the will of God concerning it, who
'did not light a candle to put it under a bushel, but that it might
give light to all that were in the house'. And this our Lord had
declared to his first disciples, 'Ye are the salt of the earth, . . . the
light of the world,' at the same time that he gave that general
command, 'Let your light so shine before men that they may see
your good works, and glorify your Father which is in heaven.'[aa]

2. And, indeed, supposing a few of these lovers of mankind to
see 'the whole world lying in wickedness',[65] can we believe they

---

[y] Matt. 25:40.   [z] Acts 4:31-5.   [aa] Matt. 5:13-16.

---

[61] Note the close correspondence between this description of apostolic Christianity and
Wesley's own conception of the *ordo salutis* in its successive stages from repentance to
experienced holiness.

[62] Acts 4:23-24, 31-32; for 'ought' see below, p. 171, n. 117.

[63] See Gal. 6:14.

[64] Acts 2:1, 42.

[65] Cf. 1 John 5:19.

would be unconcerned at the sight? At the misery of those for
whom their Lord died? Would not their bowels yearn over them,
and their hearts 'melt away for very trouble'?[66] Could they then
stand idle all the day long?[67] Even were there no command from
him whom they loved? Rather, would they not labour, by all
possible means, to 'pluck some of these brands out of the
burning'?[68] Undoubtedly they would: they would spare no pains to
bring back whomsoever they could of those poor 'sheep that had
gone astray' 'to the great Shepherd and Bishop of their souls.'[bb]

3. So the Christians of old did. They laboured, having
opportunity, to 'do good unto all men',[cc] warning them to 'flee
from the wrath to come';[69] now, now, to 'escape the damnation of
hell'.[70] They declared, 'The times of ignorance God winked at;
but now he calleth all men everywhere to repent.'[dd] They cried
aloud, 'Turn ye, turn ye from your evil ways;'[71] 'so iniquity shall
not be your ruin'.[ee] They 'reasoned' with them 'of temperance
and righteousness', or justice, of the virtues opposite to their
reigning sins, and 'of judgment to come',[ff] of the wrath of God
which would surely be executed on evil-doers in that day when he
should judge the world.

4. They endeavoured herein to speak to every man severally as
he had need. To the careless, to those who lay unconcerned in
darkness and in the shadow of death,[72] they thundered, 'Awake,
thou that sleepest; . . . arise from the dead, and Christ shall give
thee light.'[73] But to those who were already awakened out of sleep,
and groaning under a sense of the wrath of God, their language
was, 'We have an advocate with the Father; . . . he is the

[bb] 1 Pet. 2:25. [cc] Gal. 6:10.
[dd] Acts 17:30. ['Winked at' is the AV rendering; Wesley's text for his *Notes* has it
'overlooked'.]
[ee] Ezek. 18:30. [ff] Acts 24:25.

---

[66] Cf. Ps. 107:26; 6:7 (BCP). [67] See Matt. 20:6.
[68] Cf. Amos 4:11; Zech. 3:2. An autobiographical note here: Wesley and his mother had
regarded *him* as 'a brand plucked out of the burning' since the Epworth rectory fire of
1709. Cf. Wesley's personal account of Miss Sophy Hopkey, 1736-37 (MSS. III. 5, MA;
also quoted in Curnock, I. 328), and other frequent references in the *Journal* and *Letters*;
also Nos. 30, 'Sermon on the Mount, X', §17; 65, 'The Duty of Reproving our
Neighbour', III.12; 80, 'On Friendship with the World', §10; 107, 'On God's Vineyard',
II.1; 110, *Free Grace*, §18.
[69] Matt. 3:7; Luke 3:7. [70] Matt. 23:33.
[71] Ezek. 33:11. [72] Ps. 107:10; Luke 1:79.
[73] Eph. 5:14. An echo of Charles Wesley's sermon; cf. No. 3, *'Awake, Thou That
Sleepest'*.

propitiation for our sins.'[74] Meantime those who had believed they 'provoked to love and to good works';[75] to 'patient continuance in well-doing';[76] and to 'abound more and more'[77] in that 'holiness, without which no man can see the Lord'.[gg]

5. And their labour was not in vain in the Lord.[78] His 'word ran 5 and was glorified'.[79] It 'grew mightily and prevailed'.[80] But so much the more did offences prevail also. The world in general were offended, 'because they testified of it that the works thereof were evil'.[hh] The men of pleasure were offended, not only because these men were 'made', as it were, 'to reprove their thoughts' ('He 10 professeth', said they, 'to have the knowledge of God; he calleth himself the child of the Lord;' 'his life is not like other men's; his ways are of another fashion; he abstaineth from our ways, as from filthiness; he maketh his boast that God is his Father');[ii] but much more because so many of their companions were taken away and 15 would no more 'run with them to the same excess of riot'.[jj] The men of reputation were offended, because as the gospel spread they declined in the esteem of the people; and because many no longer dared to 'give them flattering titles',[81] or to pay man the homage due to God only. The men of trade called one another 20 together and said, 'Sirs, ye know that by this craft we have our wealth. But ye see and hear that these men have persuaded and turned away much people; . . . so that this our craft is in danger to be set at nought.'[kk] Above all the men of religion, so called—the men of *outside* religion, 'the saints of the world'[82]—were offended, 25

[gg] Heb. 12:14. [hh] John 7:7. [ii] Wisd. 2:13-16.
[jj] 1 Pet. 4:4. [kk] Acts 19:25-27.

---

[74] 1 John 2:1-2. Here, very early, is Wesley's distinction between preaching stern judgment to the unawakened or complacent and the gospel word of pardon and consolation to those under conviction of sin. Cf. his fuller exposition of this in his letter of Dec. 20, 1751, 'Of Preaching Christ', see *Letters* II, Vol. 26 of this edn.

[75] Cf. Heb. 10:24. [76] Rom. 2:7. [77] 1 Thess. 4:1.
[78] See 1 Cor. 15:58. [79] Cf. 2 Thess. 3:1. [80] Cf. Acts 19:20.
[81] Cf. Job 32:21, 22.

[82] In a letter to his father, Dec. 10, 1734, Wesley identifies the author of this phrase as Juan de Valdés: 'I never come from among these "saints of the world" (as J. Valdesso calls them) faint, dissipated, and shorn of all my strength, but I say, "God deliver us from an half-Christian"' (see above, No. 2, *The Almost Christian*, proem and n.) His diaries indicate that he first read Valdés in Oct. 1733, again in Nov. 1734 with the Holy Club, and to Sophy Hopkey, Nov. 1, 1736.

For the phrase in Valdés, cf. 'Consideraziones' LXXVI and LXXXI in *Reformistas Antiguos Españoles*, Tomo XVII: *Ziento I Diez Consideraziones* (1550), pp. 258, 261, 285; cf. also George Herbert's translation, *The Hundred and Ten Considerations of Signior J. Valdesso*

and ready at every opportunity to cry out, 'Men of Israel, help!'[ll]
'We have found these men pestilent fellows, movers of sedition
throughout the world.'[mm] 'These are the men that teach all men
everywhere against the people and against the law.'[nn]

5   6. Thus it was that the heavens grew black with clouds, and the
storm gathered amain. For the more Christianity spread, 'the
more hurt was done', in the account of those who received it not;
and the number increased of those who were more and more
enraged at these 'men who (thus) turned the world upside
10 down';[oo] insomuch that they more and more cried out, 'Away with
such fellows from the earth; it is not fit that they should live;'[83] yea,
and sincerely believed that 'whosoever' should 'kill them would
do God service'.[84]

       7. Meanwhile they did not fail to 'cast out their name as evil';[pp]
15 so that this 'sect was everywhere spoken against'.[qq] 'Men said all
manner of evil of them', even as had been done of 'the prophets
that were before them'.[rr] And whatever any would affirm, others
would believe; so that offences grew as the stars of heaven for
multitude.[85] And hence arose, at the time foreordained of the
20 Father, persecution in all its forms. Some, for a season, suffered
only shame and reproach; some, 'the spoiling of their goods';[ss]
some 'had trial of mocking and scourging'; some 'of bonds and
imprisonment';[tt] and others 'resisted unto blood'.[86]

       8. Now it was that the pillars of hell were shaken, and the
25 kingdom of God spread more and more. Sinners were
everywhere 'turned from darkness to light, and from the power of
Satan unto God'.[87] He gave his children 'such a mouth, and such
wisdom, as all their adversaries could not resist'.[88] And their lives
were of equal force with their words. But above all, their
30 sufferings spake to all the world. They 'approved themselves' the
servants of God 'in afflictions, in necessities, in distresses; in

[ll] Acts 21:28.   [mm] Acts 24:5.   [nn] Acts 21:28.
[oo] Acts 17:6.   [pp] Luke 6:22.   [qq] Acts 28:22.
[rr] Matt. 5:11,12.   [ss] Heb. 10:34.   [tt] Heb. 11:36.

(1638). For Wesley's other uses of this metaphor, cf. Nos. 18, 'The Marks of the New
Birth', IV.4; 31, 'Sermon on the Mount, XI', I.5; 61, 'The Mystery of Iniquity', §28; 94,
'On Family Religion', III.18; and see JWJ, Jan. 4, 1739; and *Notes* on Mark 2:16. For his
comments on 'the religion of the world', cf. No. 22, 'Sermon on the Mount, II', II.4 and n.
[83] Cf. Acts 22:22.   [84] Cf. John 16:2.
[85] Deut. 1:10.   [86] Heb. 12:4.
[87] Cf. Acts 26:18.   [88] Cf. Luke 21:15.

stripes, in imprisonments, in tumults, in labours';[uu] 'in perils in the sea, in perils in the wilderness; in weariness and painfulness, in hunger and thirst, in cold and nakedness'.[89] And when, having 'fought the good fight',[90] they were 'led as . . . sheep to the slaughter',[91] and 'offered upon the sacrifice and service of their 5 faith',[92] then the blood of each found a voice, and the heathen owned, 'He being dead, yet speaketh.'[93]

9. Thus did Christianity spread itself in the earth. But how soon did the tares appear with the wheat![94] And 'the mystery of iniquity'[95] work as well as 'the mystery of godliness'![96] How soon 10 did Satan find a seat, even 'in the temple of God'![97] Till 'the woman fled into the wilderness',[98] and 'the faithful were (again) minished from the children of men.'[99] Here we tread a beaten path: the still increasing corruptions of the succeeding generations have been largely described from time to time, by 15 those witnesses God raised up, to show that he had 'built his church upon a rock, and the gates of hell should not' wholly 'prevail against her.'[vv]

III.1. But shall we not see greater things than these?[100] Yea, greater than have been yet from the beginning of the world? Can 20 Satan cause the truth of God to fail? Or his promises to be of none effect? If not, the time will come when Christianity will prevail over all, and cover the earth. Let us stand a little, and survey (the third thing which was proposed) this strange sight, a *Christian world*. 'Of this the prophets of old inquired and searched 25 diligently:' of this 'the Spirit which was in them testified':[ww] 'It shall come to pass in the last days, that the mountain of the Lord's house shall be established in the top of the mountains, and shall be exalted above the hills, and all nations shall flow unto it. . . . And they shall beat their swords into ploughshares, and their 30 spears into pruning-hooks. Nation shall not lift up sword against nation; neither shall they learn war any more.'[xx] 'In that day there

[uu] 2 Cor. 6:4-5.   [vv] Matt. 16:18.
[ww] 1 Pet. 1:10,11, etc.   [xx] Isa. 2:2,4.

---

[89] 2 Cor. 11:26-27.   [90] Cf. 1 Tim. 6:12.   [91] Acts 8:32.
[92] Cf. Phil. 2:17.   [93] Heb. 11:4.   [94] Cf. Matt. 13:25-40.
[95] 2 Thess. 2:7.   [96] 1 Tim. 3:16.
[97] 2 Thess. 2:4.   [98] Rev. 12:6.
[99] Cf. Ps. 12:1 (BCP). Cf. *OED* for other eighteenth-century usages of 'minished'.
[100] For a fuller summary of Wesley's eschatology, cf. No. 15, *The Great Assize*.

shall be a root of Jesse, which shall stand for an ensign of the people. To it shall the Gentiles seek, and his rest shall be glorious. And it shall come to pass in that day, that the Lord shall set his hand again to recover the remnant of his people; . . . and he shall
5 set up an ensign for the nations, and shall assemble the outcasts of Israel, and gather together the dispersed of Judah, from the four corners of the earth.'ʸʸ 'The wolf shall (then) dwell with the lamb, and the leopard shall lie down with the kid; and the calf, and the young lion, and the fatling together; and a little child shall lead
10 them. . . . They shall not hurt nor destroy (saith the Lord) in all my holy mountain: for the earth shall be full of the knowledge of the Lord, as the waters cover the sea.'ᶻᶻ

2. To the same effect are the words of the great Apostle, which it is evident have never yet been fulfilled: 'Hath God cast away his
15 people? God forbid. . . . But through their fall, salvation is come to the Gentiles. And if the diminishing of them be the riches of the Gentiles, how much more their fullness? . . . For I would not, brethren, that ye should be ignorant of this mystery; . . . that blindness in part is happened to Israel, until the fullness of the
20 Gentiles be come in: and so all Israel shall be saved.'ᵃᵃᵃ

3. Suppose now the fullness of time to be come, and the prophecies to be accomplished—what a prospect is this! All is 'peace, quietness, and assurance forever'.[101] Here is no din of arms, no 'confused noise', no 'garments rolled in blood'.[102]
25 'Destructions are come to a perpetual end:'[103] wars are ceased from the earth. Neither is there any intestine jar [104] remaining: no brother rising up against brother; no country or city divided against itself, and tearing out its own bowels. Civil discord is at an end for evermore, and none is left either to destroy or hurt his
30 neighbour. Here is no oppression to 'make (even) the wise man mad';[105] no extortion to 'grind the face of the poor';[106] no robbery or wrong; no rapine or injustice; for all are 'content with such

---

ʸʸ Isa. 11:10-12.   ᶻᶻ Isa. 11:6,9.   ᵃᵃᵃ Rom. 11:1,11-12,25-6.

---

[101] Cf. Isa. 32:17.   [102] Cf. Isa. 9:5.   [103] Ps. 9:6.
[104] Cf. Matthew Prior, 'An Ode . . . on the late glorious success of Her Majesty's arms . . .' (1706): 'Their own intestine feuds and mutual jars . . .'. See also Shakespeare, *Comedy of Errors*, I.i.11-12:

the mortal and intestine jars
'Twixt thy seditious countrymen and us . . .

[105] Cf. Eccles. 7:7.   [106] Cf. Isa. 3:15.

things as they possess'.[107] Thus 'righteousness and peace have kissed each other';[bbb] they have 'taken root and filled the land';[108] righteousness flourishing out of the earth, and 'peace looking down from heaven'.[109]

4. And with righteousness or justice, mercy is also found. The earth is no longer 'full of cruel habitations'.[110] 'The Lord hath destroyed both the bloodthirsty'[111] and malicious, the envious and revengeful man. Were there any provocation, there is none that now knoweth to 'return evil for evil':[112] but indeed there is none doth evil, no not one;[113] for all are 'harmless as doves';[114] and being 'filled with peace and joy in believing',[115] and united in one body, by one Spirit, they all 'love as brethren';[116] they are all 'of one heart, and of one soul, neither saith any of them that ought of the things which he possesseth is his own'.[117] There is none among them that lacketh; for every man loveth his neighbour as himself. And all walk by one rule: 'Whatever ye would that men should do unto you, even so do unto them.'[118]

5. It follows that no unkind word can ever be heard among them—no 'strife of tongues',[119] no contention of any kind, no railing, or evil speaking—but everyone 'opens his mouth with wisdom, and in his tongue there is the law of kindness'.[120] Equally incapable are they of fraud or guile: their 'love is without dissimulation';[121] their words are always the just expression of their thoughts, opening a window into their breast,[122] that whosoever desires may look into their hearts and see that only love and God are there.

[hhh] Ps. 85:10.

---

[107] Cf. Heb. 13:5.   [108] Cf. Ps. 80:9 (BCP).   [109] Cf. Ps. 80:14.
[110] Cf. Ps. 74:21 (BCP).   [111] Cf. Ps. 5:6 (BCP).
[112] Cf. 1 Thess. 5:15, etc.   [113] See Rom. 3:10.
[114] Matt. 10:16.   [115] Cf. Rom. 15:13.   [116] 1 Pet. 3:8.
[117] Acts 4:32; in Shakespeare, Milton, and Pope 'ought' and 'aught' appear indiscriminately (in their original texts).
[118] Cf. Matt. 7:12.   [119] Ps. 31:20 (AV).
[120] Cf. Prov. 31:26.   [121] Cf. Rom. 12:9.
[122] A standard metaphor in illuminist mysticism; here it reflects Wesley's own intuitionism (cf. No. 10, 'The Witness of the Spirit, I', I.12 and n.). It occurs again in No. 100, 'On Pleasing All Men', II.7, where Christians are exhorted, in speaking '*the* truth', to 'open the window of their breasts'. Cf. also Edward Young (the elder), 'The Nature and Use of Self-Denial' (which Wesley published in the *Christian Lib.*, XLVI. 133-34): 'Were our breasts but for awhile that "sea of glass, clear as crystal" to one another (as St. John in his Revelation tells us, they always are unto God); were our breasts so laid open for awhile, that each could see the natural propensions of another's heart, in the same form that they

6. Thus, where 'the Lord God omnipotent taketh to himself his mighty power, and reigneth',[123] doth he 'subdue all things to himself',[124] cause every heart to overflow with love, and fill every mouth with praise. 'Happy are the people that are in such a case; 5 yea, blessed are the people who have the Lord for their God.'[ccc] 'Arise, shine (saith the Lord), for thy light is come, and the glory of the Lord is risen upon thee. . . . Thou hast known that I the Lord am thy Saviour and thy Redeemer, the mighty God of Jacob. . . . I have made thy officers peace, and thy exactors 10 righteousness. Violence shall no more be heard in thy land, wasting nor destruction within thy borders; but thou shalt call thy walls "Salvation", and thy gates "Praise". . . . Thy people are all righteous; they shall inherit the land for ever, the branch of my planting, the work of my hands, that I may be glorified.'[ddd] 'The 15 sun shall no more be thy light by day; neither for brightness shall the moon give light unto thee: but the Lord shall be unto thee an everlasting light, and thy God thy glory.'[eee]

IV. Having thus briefly considered Christianity as beginning, as going on, and as covering the earth, it remains only that I 20 should close the whole with a plain practical application.

1. And first I would ask, Where does this Christianity now exist? Where, I pray, do the Christians live?[125] Which is the

---

[ccc] Ps. 144:15 [BCP].　　　　　[ddd] Isa. 60:1,16-18 [,21].　　　　　[eee] Isa. 60:19.

now . . . stand; how should we be glad to run away from ourselves, and be ashamed to own our own appearances!'

In No. 90, 'An Israelite Indeed', II. 10, Wesley cites 'that arrogant King of Castile (Alphonso X [1221–84]) as having said that God ought to have made man with a window in his breast (so as to inhibit dissimulation; see Nos. 138A, 138B, 'On Dissimulation'). Originally, however, the jibe had come from Momus, the Greek god of wit and ridicule; cf. Joseph Addison in *The Guardian*, No. 106, July 13, 1713. The same point had been made by Bishop Robert Sanderson, 'Fifth Sermon *Ad Populum*', (1624), in *Sermons*, Vol. I, p. 277, with an involved reference to Lucian, *Hermotimus* (Loeb, 430: 297-99).

[123] Cf. Rev. 19:6.

[124] Cf. Phil. 3:21.

[125] Wesley's lifelong interest in primitive Christianity and its restoration is well analysed by Schmidt, *Wesley, passim*. Wesley had been deeply impressed by Johannes Arndt's *True Christianity* (Eng. tr., 1712, 1714) and its pietistic visions of renewal; there are echoes of the theme in Charles Wesley's hymn, 'Primitive Christianity', first published in *An Earnest Appeal*, 1743 (11:90-94 of this edn.). Wesley had read Antoinette Bourignon's *Light of the World* (Eng. tr. 1696); cf. her childhood queries and pleas: 'Where are the Christians? Let us go to the country where the Christians live' (Intro., xvi). Cf. Wesley's reply to the Duke of Weimar (?) to a query as to the purposes of his journey to Herrnhut: 'I answered, "To see the place where the Christians live"' (JWJ, July 22, 1738; cf. also Curnock's n., II. 15). One of Wesley's favourite church histories was Claude Fleury, *An Historical Account of the*

country, the inhabitants whereof are 'all (thus) filled with the Holy Ghost'?[126] Are all 'of one heart and of one soul'?[127] Cannot suffer one among them to 'lack anything', but continually give 'to every man as he hath need'?[128] Who one and all have the love of God filling their hearts, and constraining them to love their 5 neighbour as themselves? Who have all 'put on bowels of mercies, humbleness of mind, gentleness, long-suffering'?[129] Who offend not in any kind, either by word or deed, against justice, mercy, or truth, but in every point do unto all men as they would these should do unto them?[130] With what propriety can we term any a 10 Christian country which does not answer this description? Why then, let us confess we have never yet seen a Christian country upon earth.

    2. I beseech you, brethren, by the mercies of God, if ye do account *me* a madman or a fool,[131] yet 'as a fool bear with me.'[132] It 15

Manners and Behaviour of the Christians . . . (1698); indeed, he would presently edit and publish an abridged translation of it (*The Manners of the Ancient Christians*) in 1749; see *Bibliog*, No. 157.

    This primitivist orientation goes with Wesley's conviction that the Constantinian emancipation of Christianity was a sort of fall of the church; see No. 61, 'The Mystery of Iniquity', §27 and n.

  [126] Acts 2:4.

  [127] Acts 4:32. Cf. also Charles Wesley, 'Primitive Christianity', Pt. I, ll. 15-16:

> They all were of one heart and soul,
> And only love inspired the whole.

Cf. also No. 63, 'The General Spread of the Gospel', §20.

  [128] Cf. Acts 4:34-35.   [129] Cf. Col. 3:12.

  [130] See Matt. 7:12; Luke 6:31.

  [131] The Oxford Methodists had already been labelled with this commonplace eighteenth-century epithet in *Fog's Weekly Journal*, Nov. 5, 1732. John Hutchinson would apply it to England's most distinguished scientist, John Newton, in *Works* (3rd edn. 1748–49), V. 142. William Law had used it (though not of the Methodists) in *A Practical Treatise Upon Christian Perfection* (1726), *Works* (1762), III. 99: 'A good man who enjoys the use of his reason is offended at madmen and fools because they both act contrary to the reason of things. The madman fancies himself, and everything about him, to be different from what they are; the fool knows nothing of the value of things, is ridiculous in his choices and prefers a shell before the most useful things in life;' see also *ibid.*, III. 245. John Locke, *Essay Concerning Human Understanding* (1690), ch. xi, §§12-13, had distinguished between madmen (men who 'reason right from . . . wrong propositions') and fools (who 'reason scarce at all'). *The Tatler*, No. 127 (Jan. 28-31, 1709), quotes Terence, *Hic homines ex stultis facit insanos* ('This fellow has the art of converting fools into madmen').

    Wesley made his peace with this epithet as with the others; cf. *A Collection of Hymns* (1780), Hymn 388, l.25: 'Fools and madmen let us be'; see also Sermons 84, *The Important Question*, III.14; and 125, 'On a Single Eye', III.5. But in No. 11, *The Witness of the Spirit*, II, IV.2, Wesley himself speaks of the 'French prophets [i.e., the Camisards] and enthusiasts' as 'madmen'.

  [132] Cf. 2 Cor. 11:16.

is utterly needful that someone should use great plainness of speech toward you. It is more especially needful at *this* time; for who knoweth but it is the *last*? Who knoweth how soon the righteous judge may say, 'I will no more be entreated for this
5 people'?[133] 'Though Noah, Daniel, and Job, were in this land, they should but deliver their own souls.'[134] And who will use this plainness if I do not? Therefore I, even I, will speak. And I adjure you, by the living God, that ye steel not your breasts against receiving a blessing at *my* hands. Do not say in your heart, *Non*
10 *persuadebis, etiamsi persuaseris*;[135] or, in other words, Lord, thou shalt not 'send by whom thou wilt send'![136] Let me rather perish in my blood than be saved by this man!

3. 'Brethren, I am persuaded better things of you, though I thus speak.'[137] Let me ask you, then, in tender love, and in the spirit of
15 meekness, Is this city a *Christian* city? Is Christianity, *scriptural* Christianity, found here? Are we, considered as a community of men, so 'filled with the Holy Ghost'[138] as to enjoy in our hearts, and show forth in our lives, the genuine fruits of that Spirit? Are all the magistrates, all heads and governors of colleges and halls,
20 and their respective societies (not to speak of the inhabitants of the town), 'of one heart and of one soul'?[139] Is 'the love of God shed abroad in our hearts'?[140] Are our tempers the same that were

---

[133] Cf. Exod. 8:8, 9, 29-31; Jer. 7:16, etc.; and Ps. 77:7 (BCP).

[134] Cf. Ezek. 14:20.

[135] 'You cannot persuade me, even though you have been persuasive.' This aphorism appears, in Greek, in Aristophanes, *Plutus* (which Wesley had read), l. 600. By Wesley's time it had been turned into a sort of Latin proverb; cf. South, *Sermons* (1823), I. 170: 'Where the heart is bent upon . . . a vicious cause [even a miracle] would end in a *non persuadebit etiamsi persuaseris* . . . .' See also Sanderson, *Sermons*, II. 188. Joseph Addison (one of Wesley's favourite essayists) had used it in *The Freeholder*, No. 32 (Apr. 9, 1712): '"Make us believe that if you can", which is in Latin, if I may be allowed the pedantry, *Non persuadebis etiamsi persuaseris.*' For a later usage (1773), cf. Oliver Goldsmith, *She Stoops to Conquer*, III. i.

It reappears in Wesley in a letter to Francis Okeley, Oct. 4, 1758; in English it turns up in the Preface to the *Journal*, Pt. III. In Nos. 83, 'On Patience', §11; and 88, 'On Dress', §8, it appears as a somewhat incongruous paraphrase of Agrippa's comment to St. Paul in Acts 26:28 (the text of No. 2, *The Almost Christian*).

[136] Cf. Exod. 4:13; John 3:34; 5:38; 6:29; 7:28; 14:26; 17:3, all of which served as warrants for Wesley's self-understanding of his own 'extraordinary ministry' and that of his preachers. The theme reappears in Nos. 38, 'A Caution against Bigotry', I.14; 104, 'On Attending the Church Service', §21; 107, 'On God's Vineyard', V. 5; 121, 'Prophets and Priests', §3. See also Charles Wesley's *Hymns on the Four Gospels*, No. 1705 (on John 4:39), st. 1, l.6: 'The Almighty sends by whom he will' (cf. *Poet. Wks.*, XI. 361).

[137] Cf. Heb. 6:9.

[138] Acts 2:4; 4:31.

[139] Cf. Acts 4:32.

[140] Cf. Rom. 5:5.

in him? And are our lives agreeable thereto? Are we 'holy as he which hath called us is holy, in all manner of conversation'?[141]

4. I entreat you to observe that here are no *peculiar notions* now under consideration; that the question moved is not concerning *doubtful opinions* of one kind or another; but concerning the undoubted, fundamental branches (if there be any such) of our *common Christianity*. And for the decision thereof I appeal to your own conscience, guided by the Word of God. He therefore that is not condemned by his own heart, let him go free.

5. In the fear, then, and in the presence of the great God before whom both you and I shall shortly appear, I pray you that are in authority over us, whom I reverence for your office' sake, to consider (and not after the manner of dissemblers with God), are you 'filled with the Holy Ghost'?[142] Are ye lively portraitures of him whom ye are appointed to represent among men? 'I have said, Ye are gods,'[143] ye magistrates and rulers; ye are by office so nearly allied to the God of heaven! In your several stations and degrees ye are to show forth unto us 'the Lord our Governor'.[144] Are all the thoughts of your hearts, all your tempers and desires, suitable to your high calling? Are all your words like unto those which come out of the mouth of God? Is there in all your actions dignity and love? A greatness which words cannot express, which can flow only from an heart full of God—and yet consistent with the character of 'man that is a worm, and the son of man that is a worm'![145]

6. Ye venerable men who are more especially called to form the tender minds of youth, to dispel thence the shades of ignorance and error, and train them up to be wise unto salvation, are you 'filled with the Holy Ghost'? With all those 'fruits of the Spirit'[146] which your important office so indispensably requires? Is your heart whole with God? Full of love and zeal to set up his kingdom on earth? Do you continually remind those under your care that the one rational end of all our studies is to know, love, and serve 'the only true God, and Jesus Christ whom he hath sent'?[147] Do you inculcate upon them day by day that 'love alone never faileth'? Whereas, 'whether there be tongues, they shall fail', or

[141] Cf. 1 Pet. 1:15.
[142] Acts 2:4; 4:31.
[143] Ps. 82:6; cf. John 10:34.
[144] Cf. Ps. 8:1 (BCP).
[146] Cf. Gal. 5:22.
[145] Cf. Job 25:6.
[147] John 17:3.

philosophical 'knowledge, it shall vanish away';[148] and that
without love all learning is but splendid ignorance,[149] pompous
folly, vexation of spirit. Has all you teach an actual tendency to the
love of God, and of all mankind for his sake? Have you an eye to
5 this end in whatever you prescribe touching the kind, the manner,
and the measure of their studies; desiring and labouring that
wherever the lot of these young soldiers of Christ is cast they may
be so many 'burning and shining lights',[150] 'adorning the gospel of
Christ in all things'?[151] And permit me to ask, Do you put forth all
10 your strength in the vast work you have undertaken? Do you
labour herein with all your might? Exerting every faculty of your
soul? Using every talent which God hath lent you, and that to the
uttermost of your power?[152]

7. Let it not be said that I speak here as if all under your care
15 were intended to be clergymen. Not so; I only speak as if they
were all intended to be Christians. But what example is set them
by us who enjoy the beneficence of our forefathers; by fellows,
students, scholars; more especially those who are of some rank
and eminence? Do ye, brethren, abound in the fruits of the Spirit,
20 in lowliness of mind, in self-denial and mortification, in
seriousness and composure of spirit, in patience, meekness,
sobriety, temperance, and in unwearied, restless endeavours to
do good in every kind unto all men, to relieve their outward wants,
and to bring their souls to the true knowledge and love of God?[153]
25 Is this the general character of fellows of colleges? I fear it is not.
Rather, have not pride and haughtiness of spirit, impatience and
peevishness, sloth and indolence, gluttony and sensuality, and
even a proverbial uselessness, been objected to us, *perhaps* not
always by our enemies, nor *wholly* without ground? O that God
30 would roll away this reproach from us,[154] that the very memory of
it might perish for ever!

---

[148] 1 Cor. 13:8.
[149] In his earlier university sermon on Luke 10:42 (1734), No. 146, 'The One Thing
Needful', III.1, Wesley had described learning as 'that fairest earthly fruit'.
[150] Cf. John 5:35.
[151] Cf. Titus 2:10.
[152] Cf. these questions with those that had been put to Wesley himself on Feb. 8, 1736,
by the Moravian leader, A. G. Spangenberg (see JWJ for the reported conversation): 'Do
you know yourself? Have you the witness within yourself? Does the Spirit of God bear
witness with your spirit that you are a child of God?' Wesley records that he 'was surprised
and knew not what to answer'.
[153] A list clearly reminiscent of the goals of the earlier Holy Club.
[154] See Josh. 5:9.

8. Many of us are more immediately consecrated to God, called to 'minister in holy things'.[155] Are we then patterns to the rest, 'in word, in conversation, in charity; in spirit, in faith, in purity'?[fff] Is there written on our forehead and on our heart, 'Holiness to the Lord'?[156] From what motives did we enter upon this office? Was it 5 indeed with a single eye 'to serve God, trusting that we were inwardly moved by the Holy Ghost to take upon us this ministration, for the promoting of his glory, and the edifying of his people'?[157] And have we 'clearly determined, by God's grace, to give ourselves wholly to this office? Do we forsake and set aside, 10 as much as in us lies, all worldly cares and studies? Do we apply ourselves wholly to this one thing, and draw all our cares and studies this way'?[158] Are we 'apt to teach'?[159] Are we 'taught of God',[160] that we may be able to teach others also? Do we know God? Do we know Jesus Christ? Hath God 'revealed his Son in 15 us'?[161] And hath he 'made us able ministers of the new covenant'?[162] Where then are 'the seals of our apostleship'?[163] Who that 'were dead in trespasses and sins'[164] have been quickened by our word? Have we a burning zeal to save souls from death,[165] so that for their sake we often forget even to eat our 20 bread?[166] Do we speak plain, 'by manifestation of the truth commending ourselves to every man's conscience in the sight of God'?[ggg] Are we dead to the world and the things of the world, 'laying up all our treasure in heaven'?[167] 'Do we lord it over God's heritage'?[168] Or are we the least, the 'servants of all'?[169] When we 25 bear the reproach of Christ,[170] does it sit heavy upon us, or do we rejoice therein? When we are 'smitten on the one cheek', do we resent it? Are we impatient of affronts? Or do we 'turn the other also'; 'not resisting the evil',[171] but 'overcoming evil with good'?[172] Have we a bitter zeal, inciting us to strive sharply and passionately 30

[fff] 1 Tim. 4:12.   [ggg] 2 Cor. 4:2.

---

[155] Cf. 1 Cor. 9:13.   [156] Cf. Exod. 28:36.
[157] Cf. BCP, Ordering of Deacons, Bishop's examination, Q.1 (511).
[158] BCP, Ordering of Priests, Bishop's exhortation (532).
[159] 2 Tim. 2:24.   [160] John 6:45.
[161] Cf. Gal. 1:16.   [162] Cf. 2 Cor. 3:6.
[163] Cf. 1 Cor. 9:2.   [164] Eph. 2:1.
[165] Cf. Jas. 5:20.   [166] Cf. Ps. 102:4.
[167] Cf. Matt. 6:20.   [168] Cf. 1 Pet. 5:3.
[169] Cf. Mark 9:35.   [170] Heb. 11:26.
[171] Cf. Matt. 5:39.   [172] Cf. Rom. 12:21.

with them 'that are out of the way'?[173] Or is our zeal the flame of
love? So as to direct all our words with sweetness, lowliness, and
meekness of wisdom?

9. Once more: what shall we say concerning the youth of this
place? Have *you* either the form or the power of Christian
godliness? Are you humble, teachable, advisable; or stubborn,
self-willed, heady, and high-minded? Are you obedient to your
superiors as to parents; or do you despise those to whom you owe
the tenderest reverence? Are you diligent in your easy business,
pursuing your studies with all your strength? Do you 'redeem the
time',[174] crowding as much work into every day as it can contain?
Rather, are ye not conscious to yourselves that you waste away day
after day, either in reading what has no tendency to Christianity,
or in gaming, or in—you know not what?[175] Are you better
managers of your fortune than of your time? Do you, out of
principle, take care to 'owe no man anything'?[176] Do you
'remember the sabbath day to keep it holy';[177] to spend it in the
more immediate worship of God? When you are in his house do
you consider that God is there? Do you behave 'as seeing him that
is invisible'?[178] Do you know how to 'possess your bodies in
sanctification and honour'?[179] Are not drunkenness and uncleanness found among you? Yea, are there not of you who 'glory in
their shame'?[180] Do not many of you 'take the name of God in
vain',[181] perhaps habitually, without either remorse or fear? Yea,
are there not a multitude of you that are forsworn? I fear, a swiftly
increasing multitude. Be not surprised, brethren: before God and
this congregation I own myself to have been of that number;
solemnly swearing to 'observe all those customs' which I then

---

[173] Heb. 5:2.

[174] Cf. Eph. 5:16; Col. 4:5; see also No. 93, 'On Redeeming the Time'.

[175] The background here would have been the Statutes of the University, *Parecbolae sive Excerpta è Corpore Statutorum Universitatis Oxoniensis . . .* (1729). See also G. R. M. Ward, tr., *Oxford University Statutes*, Vol. I: *Containing the Caroline Code or Laudian Statutes, Promulgated, A.D. 1636. Titulus XV, De Moribus Conformandis* ('Concerning Appropriate Behaviour'), spells out prohibited behaviour in detail: e.g., §4, *De Domibus Oppidanorum non frequentandis* ('Concerning Types of Houses in the City Not to be Frequented'); §5, *De Oenopolis, sive Taberniis Vinariis, Popinis, et Diversionis non frequentandis* ('Concerning Wine-Shops or Taverns, Eating Houses and Diversions Not to be Frequented'); §6, *De Nocturna Vagatione reprimenda* ('Concerning the Restraint of Nocturnal Excursions'); §7, *De Ludis Prohibitis* ('Concerning Prohibited Amusements'); §8, *De famosis Libellis cohibendis* ('Concerning the Repression of Scandalous Books'), etc. See Nos. 150, 151, 'Hypocrisy in Oxford'.

[176] Rom. 13:8.

[177] Exod. 20:8.

[178] Heb. 11:27.

[179] Cf. 1 Thess. 4:4.

[180] Phil. 3:19.

[181] Exod. 20:7.

knew nothing of, 'and those statutes' which I did not so much as read over, either then, or for some years after.[182] What is perjury, if this is not? But if it be, O what a weight of sin, yea, sin of no common dye, lieth upon us! And doth not 'the Most High regard it'?[183]

10. May it not be one of the consequences of this that so many of you are a generation of *triflers*; triflers with God, with one another, and with your own souls? For how few of you spend, from one week to another, a single hour in private prayer? How few have any thought of God in the general tenor of your conversation? Who of you is in any degree acquainted with the work of his Spirit? His supernatural work in the souls of men? Can you bear, unless now and then in a church, any talk of the Holy Ghost? Would you not take it for granted if one began such a conversation that it was either 'hypocrisy' or 'enthusiasm'? In the name of the Lord God Almighty I ask, What religion are *you* of? Even the talk of Christianity ye cannot, will not, bear! O my brethren! What a Christian city is this? 'It is time for thee, Lord, to lay to thine hand!'[184]

11. For indeed what probability—what possibility rather (speaking after the manner of men)—is there that Christianity, scriptural Christianity, should be again the religion of this place? That all orders of men among us should speak and live as men 'filled with the Holy Ghost'? By whom should this Christianity be restored? By those of you that are in authority? Are you convinced then that this is scriptural Christianity? Are you desirous it should be restored? And do ye not count your fortune, liberty, life, dear unto yourselves, so ye may be instrumental in the restoring it? But suppose ye have this desire, who hath any power proportioned to the effect? Perhaps some of you have made a few faint attempts, but with how small success! Shall Christianity then be restored by young, unknown, inconsiderable men? I know not whether ye yourselves could suffer it. Would not some of you cry out, 'Young man, in so doing thou reproachest us!' But there is no danger of your being put to the proof, so hath 'iniquity overspread us like a flood'.[185] Whom then shall God send? The famine, the pestilence

---

[182] Not till Nov. 1726 (as the early diaries show), after his graduation as AB and his election as Fellow of Lincoln (Mar. 17, 1726).

[183] Cf. Ps. 73:11; 94:7.

[184] Ps. 119:126 (BCP). Wesley's own answer here had already been given (in No. 150, 'Hypocrisy in Oxford'): 'How has this city become an harlot!' (Isa. 1:21).

[185] Cf. Ps. 69:2; see also No. 3, *'Awake, Thou That Sleepest'*, III.10 and n.

(the last messengers of God to a guilty land), or the sword?[186] 'The armies of the' Romish 'aliens',[187] to reform us into our first love? Nay, rather 'let us fall into thy hand, O Lord, and let us not fall into the hand of man.'[188]

5   Lord, save, or we perish![189] Take us out of the mire, that we sink not! O help us against these enemies! For vain is the help of man. Unto thee all things are possible.[190] According to the greatness of thy power, preserve thou those that are appointed to die. And preserve us in the manner that seemest thee good; not as we will,
10 but as thou wilt![191]

---

[186] Cf. Jer 14:12, etc.; Ezek. 6:11, etc.

[187] Cf. Heb. 11:34; the 'Romish aliens' were, of course, the French. Britain was already deeply involved in the anti-Bourbon coalition led by Frederick II, and had already celebrated the victory of Dettingen the year before. But after the naval defeat at Toulon and the appearance of a French fleet off Dungeness (both in Feb. 1744), fears of a French invasion had aroused the country. War had been declared, officially, in March. A year later came 'the Rising of '45' under 'Bonnie Prince Charlie' (Stuart), aided by the French.

[188] Cf. 2 Sam. 24:14.

[189] See Matt. 8:25.

[190] See Mark 14:36.

[191] See Matt. 26:39.

JUSTIFICATION BY FAITH

AN INTRODUCTORY COMMENT

There was no mistaking the minatory tone and spirit of the 'prefixed'
university sermons; they measure Wesley's move from pious don to
itinerant evangelist. In 'Justification by Faith', however, we come to his
first fully positive exposition of his 'new' soteriology—'faith alone', 'the
article by which the Church stands or falls' (see No. 20, The Lord Our
Righteousness, *§4 and n.). Wesley's claim (in his letters to William*
Law, May 14 and 20, 1738; see Letters I *[Vol. 25 of this edn.], pp.*
540-50, for Wesley's letters and Law's replies) that he had never heard
of the doctrine of sola fide *is scarcely credible, since a wide-ranging*
controversy on this very point had been raging in the Church of England
between Puritans and Anglicans since the latter half of the sixteenth
century (cf. proem, §2). In 1739 Wesley had extracted and published
Robert Barnes's Treatise on Justification by Faith Only, According
to the Doctrine of the Eleventh Article of the Church of England,
from Barnes's Works, 1573 *(cf. above, p. 37); he had long known the*
Articles (specifically IX-XIV) and the Homilies (specifically the first five
of the Edwardian set, 1547). What is credible is that his preoccupations
with 'holy living' and 'the means of grace' before 1738 had obscured the
priority of justifying faith as antecedent to, and the ground of, 'the faith
that works by love'. In Holy Communion he had prayed, countless
times, for 'grace so to follow [the] good example . . . [of God's] servants
departed this life in [true] faith and fear . . . for Jesus Christ's sake, our
only Mediator and Advocate'; now he is prepared to explain how
Christ's mediation and advocacy effect the pardon of a repentant sinner.
The explanation is 'plain' enough for 'plain people', but III.3 and IV.6
give evidence that this essay was also addressed to the theological
community at large.

The first record in the Journal *of an oral sermon on justification from*
this text is for May 28, 1738 (at the chapel in Long Acre, London).
Later entries suggest that Wesley preached from Rom. 4:5 at least eight
more times before June 8, 1742, when he preached at Epworth
(probably from his father's tombstone): 'At eight I largely enforced at
Epworth the great truth (so little understood in what is called a

Christian country), "Unto him that worketh not, but believeth on him that justifieth the ungodly, his faith is counted to him for righteousness." ' This written sermon was first published in 1746, and it stands as the earliest full summary of Wesley's soteriology in the basic form in which it will continue. In this sense, it is a landmark sermon to which all subsequent ones may be compared. It was not reprinted separately during Wesley's lifetime, in common with many others first published in Wesley's SOSO, *for whose publishing history and variant readings see the Appendix, 'Wesley's Text', in Vol. 4 of this edn. It has been noted earlier that items which were printed separately before being collected into one of the volumes of* SOSO *are italicized in the notes and in Appendix C, and for these only are separate stemmata given in the Appendix, along with a few which were reprinted separately after originally appearing in* SOSO.

Justification by Faith

Romans 4:5

To him that worketh not, but believeth on him that justifieth the ungodly, his faith is counted to him for righteousness.

5

    1. How a sinner may be justified before God, the Lord and Judge of all, is a question of no common importance to every child of man. It contains the foundation of all our hope, inasmuch as while we are at enmity with God there can be no true peace, no
10 solid joy, either in time or in eternity. What peace can there be while our own heart condemns us? And much more he that 'is greater than our heart, and knoweth all things'?[1] What solid joy, either in this world or that to come, while 'the wrath of God abideth on us'?[2]
15   2. And yet how little hath this important question been understood! What confused notions have many had concerning it! Indeed not only confused, but often utterly false, contrary to the truth as light to darkness; notions absolutely inconsistent with

---

[1] 1 John 3:20.
[2] Cf. John 3:36.

the oracles of God,[3] and with the whole analogy of faith.[4] And hence, erring concerning the very foundation, they could not possibly build thereon; at least, not 'gold, silver, or precious stones', which would endure when 'tried as by fire', but only 'hay and stubble',[5] neither acceptable to God nor profitable to man. 5

3. In order to do justice, as far as in me lies, to the vast importance of the subject, to save those that seek the truth in sincerity from 'vain jangling'[6] and 'strife of words',[7] to clear the confusedness of thought into which so many have already been led thereby, and to give them true and just conceptions of this 10 great mystery of godliness,[8] I shall endeavour to show,

First, what is the general ground of this whole doctrine of justification;

[3] I.e., the Holy Scriptures taken as a whole; cf. Rom. 3:2, Heb. 5:12, 1 Pet. 4:11, and Acts 7:38. See also the agreement here between Matthew Poole and Matthew Henry, but notice that Poole (on Heb. 5:11) adds the 'ancient creeds' in which he sees 'God's oracles in the Scriptures' as being 'summed up'. This metaphor of the Scriptures as 'oracles' is a favourite with Wesley, a basic presupposition in his hermeneutics (it is also one of the premises of his early practice of bibliomancy); it appears in at least fifteen other sermons and more times than that in his other writings.

[4] The general and true sense of Scripture (both the truths revealed in Scripture and solid inferences drawn from them, as in the creeds and biblically-grounded theology); cf. John Gerhard, who had summed up their consensus in his *Loci Theologici* (1621), I. 55, and II. 424: 'All the interpretation of Scripture should be according to the analogy of faith . . .' (i.e., the general and essential truth of Scripture taken as a whole). See also Francis Turrentin, *Institutio Theologiae Elencticae* (1686), Eng. tr. J. Beardslee (1981), I. xii. 6-7; II. xix. 2-6; and add the summary analyses of Lutheran views in Schmid, *Doctrinal Theology of the Evangelical Lutheran Church* (Philadelphia, Lutheran Publication Society, 1889, 3rd edn. rev.; Minneapolis, Minn., Augsburg Publishing House, 1961), pp. 70, 76; and Heinrich Heppe, *Reformed Dogmatics* (London, George Allen and Unwin, 1950), pp. 30-31.

In his comment on Rom. 12:6 (in *Notes*) Wesley connects 'the analogy of faith' with 'the oracles of God' and cites 1 Pet. 4:11 as his authority. He then sums up its particulars: 'that grand scheme of doctrine which is delivered [in the Scriptures], touching original sin, justification by faith, and present inward salvation'. He then stipulates that 'any question should be determined by this rule; every doubtful Scripture interpreted according to the grand truths which run through the whole.'

For other usages of this phrase, see Nos. 21, 'Sermon on the Mount, I', §6 and n.; 62, 'The End of Christ's Coming', III.5 and n.; 64, 'The New Creation', §2; 115, 'Dives and Lazarus', III.7; 122, 'Causes of the Inefficacy of Christianity', §6; 135, 'On Guardian Angels', III.1. See also Susanna's letter to John, Aug. 18, 1725, where she concludes a long paragraph on the Calvinist doctrine of predestination: 'This is the sum of what I believe concerning predestination, which I think is agreeable to the analogy of faith' (see *Letters*, I, Vol. 25 of this edn., p. 180).

[5] Cf. 1 Cor. 3:12, 13.
[6] 1 Tim. 1:6.
[7] Cf. 1 Tim. 6:4.
[8] See 1 Tim. 3:16.

Secondly, what justification is;
Thirdly, who they are that are justified; and,
Fourthly, on what terms they are justified.

I. I am first to show what is the general ground of this whole
5 doctrine of justification.

1. In the image of God was man made;[9] holy as he that created
him is holy, merciful as the author of all is merciful, perfect as his
Father in heaven is perfect.[10] As God is love, so man dwelling in
love dwelt in God, and God in him.[11] God made him to be 'an
10 image of his own eternity',[12] an incorruptible picture of the God of
glory. He was accordingly pure, as God is pure, from every spot of
sin. He knew not evil in any kind or degree, but was inwardly and
outwardly sinless and undefiled. He 'loved the Lord his God with
all his heart, and with all his mind, and soul, and strength'.[13]

15 2. To man thus upright and perfect God gave a perfect law, to
which he required full and perfect obedience. He required full
obedience in every point, and this to be performed without any
intermission from the moment man became a living soul till the
time of his trial should be ended. No allowance was made for any
20 falling short. As, indeed, there was no need of any, man being
altogether equal to the task assigned, and thoroughly furnished
for every good word and work.[14]

3. To the entire law of love which was written in his heart
(against which, perhaps, he could not sin directly) it seemed good
25 to the sovereign wisdom of God to superadd one positive law:
'Thou shalt not eat of the fruit of the tree that groweth in the
midst of the garden;'[15] annexing that penalty thereto, 'In the day
thou eatest thereof, thou shalt surely die.'[16]

4. Such then was the state of man in paradise.[17] By the free,

---

[9] Gen. 1:27; 9:6. See Nos. 1, *Salvation by Faith*, §1 and n.; and 141, 'The Image of God',
on Gen. 1:27.

[10] See Matt. 5:48.   [11] See 1 John 4:16.

[12] Wisd. 2:23.

[13] Cf. Mark 12:30; Luke 10:27.

[14] See 2 Tim. 3:17; 2 Thess. 2:17.

[15] Cf. Gen. 3:3.   [16] Gen. 2:17.

[17] A similar (and even more detailed) account of human perfection in man's first
creation had already been expounded in No. 141, 'The Image of God' (Gen. 1:27). In both
sermons Wesley takes the perfection of the paradisaical state as normal and normative for
human existence. Its restoration is the goal of 'the order of salvation'; indeed, salvation is
defined as the restoration of the image of God; see No. 1, *Salvation by Faith*, §1 and n.; also
No. 44, *Original Sin*, III.5 and n.

unmerited love of God he was holy and happy;[18] he knew, loved, enjoyed God, which is (in substance) life everlasting. And in this life of love he was to continue for ever if he continued to obey God in all things. But if he disobeyed him in any he was to forfeit all. 'In that day (said God) thou shalt surely die.'

5. Man did disobey God; he 'ate of the tree of which God commanded him, saying, Thou shalt not eat of it.'[19] And in that day he was condemned by the righteous judgment of God. Then also the sentence whereof he was warned before began to take place upon him. For the moment he tasted that fruit he died. His soul died, was separated from God; separate from whom the soul has no more life than the body has when separate from the soul. His body likewise became corruptible and mortal, so that death then took hold on this also. And being already dead in spirit, dead to God, dead in sin, he hastened on to death everlasting, to the destruction both of body and soul in the fire never to be quenched.[20]

6. Thus 'by one man sin entered into the world, and death by sin. And so death passed upon all men,' as being contained in him who was the common father and representative of us all. Thus 'through the offence of one' all are dead, dead to God, dead in sin, dwelling in a corruptible, mortal body, shortly to be dissolved, and under the sentence of death eternal. For as 'by one man's disobedience all were made sinners', so by that offence of one 'judgment came upon all men to condemnation.'[a]

7. In this state we were, even all mankind, when 'God so loved the world that he gave his only begotten Son, to the end we might not perish but have everlasting life.'[21] In the fullness of time he

[a] Rom. 5:12, etc.

---

[18] Holiness and happiness had long been linked in the Anglican (catholic) tradition as reciprocals (as in John Norris, Richard Lucas, John Tillotson, and William Tilly). Here, in a staunchly Protestant exposition of 'faith alone', Wesley finds it easy and natural to presuppose the integrity of God's design for humanity (happiness) and his demand upon it (holiness). This linkage—'holy *and* happy'— is one of Wesley's most consistent themes, early, middle, and late, with nuances very much worth noting, for if holiness is active love toward God and neighbour, then happiness is one's enjoyment and security in such love. Cf. above, p. 35.

[19] Cf. Gen. 3:17.

[20] See Mark 9:43. For Wesley's interesting explanation as to how Adam's body *became* corruptible and mortal, see No. 141, 'The Image of God', II.1; it represents his concern to apply his understanding of current advances in medical knowledge to exegetical and soteriological problems.

[21] Cf. John 3:16.

was made man, another common head of mankind, a second general parent and representative of the whole human race.[22] And as such it was that 'he bore our griefs', the Lord 'laying upon him the iniquities of us all'. Then 'was he wounded for our
5   transgressions, and bruised for our iniquities.'[23] 'He made his soul an offering for sin.'[24] He poured out his blood for the transgressors. He 'bare our sins in his own body on the tree', that 'by his stripes we might be healed'.[25] And 'by that one oblation of himself once offered'[26] he 'hath redeemed me and all mankind';[27]
10 having thereby 'made a full, perfect, and sufficient sacrifice and satisfaction for the sins of the whole world'.[28]

8. In consideration of this, that the Son of God hath 'tasted death for every man',[29] God hath now 'reconciled the world to himself, not imputing to them their former trespasses'.[30] And
15 thus, 'as by the offence of one judgment came upon all men to condemnation, even so by the righteousness of one the free gift came upon all men unto justification.'[31] So that for the sake of his well-beloved Son, of what he hath done and suffered for us, God now vouchsafes on one only condition (which himself also
20 enables us to perform) both to remit the punishment due to our sins, to reinstate us in his favour, and to restore our dead souls to spiritual life, as the earnest of life eternal.[32]

---

[22] An echo here of the Christological views of Hugo Grotius of Christ as the 'Federal Head' of the whole body of humanity; cf. his *De Veritate Religionis Christianae* (1642; though Wesley probably knew it in Le Clerc's revision of 1709), Bks. II and III. In Charles Wesley's hymn (see No.125 in *A Collection of Hymns*, Vol. 7 in this edn.), it appears applied to the Pauline analogy between the First and Second Adams:

> Adam, descended from above,
> Federal head of all mankind.

The metaphor is developed at greater length in Wesley's *Doctrine of Original Sin* (1757), Sect. VI, pp. 366-68, against John Taylor's denial of the orthodox interpretations. In his conclusion Wesley quotes James Hervey approvingly: 'That as Adam was the first general representative of mankind, so Christ was the second and last . . . .'

[23] Cf. Isa. 53:4-6.
[24] Isa. 53:10.
[25] Cf. 1 Pet. 2:24; Isa. 53:5.
[26] BCP, Communion, Prayer of Consecration; note Wesley's 'that one oblation . . .' in place of 'his one oblation of himself '.
[27] *Ibid.*, Catechism.
[28] *Ibid.*, Communion, Prayer of Consecration; note Wesley's omission of the term 'oblation'.
[29] Cf. Heb. 2:9.
[30] Cf. 2 Cor. 5:19.   [31] Rom. 5:18.
[32] Cf. No. 20, *The Lord Our Righteousness*, II.8, for a cross-reference to this passage.

9. This therefore is the general ground of the whole doctrine of justification. By the sin of the first Adam, who was not only the father but likewise the representative of us all, we all 'fell short of the favour of God',[33] we all became 'children of wrath';[34] or, as the Apostle expresses it, 'Judgment came upon all men to condemnation.'[35] Even so by the sacrifice for sin made by the second Adam, as the representative of us all, God is so far reconciled to all the world that he hath given them a new covenant. The plain condition whereof being once fulfilled, 'there is no more condemnation for us',[36] but we are 'justified freely by his grace through the redemption that is in Jesus Christ'.[37]

II.1. But what is it to be 'justified'? What is 'justification'? This was the second thing which I proposed to show. And it is evident from what has been already observed that it is not the being made actually just and righteous. This is *sanctification;* which is indeed in some degree the immediate *fruit* of justification, but nevertheless is a distinct gift of God, and of a totally different nature.[38] The one implies what God *does for us* through his Son; the other what he *works in us* by his Spirit. So that although some rare instances may be found wherein the term 'justified' or 'justification' is used in so wide a sense as to include sanctification also, yet in general use they are sufficiently distinguished from each other both by St. Paul and the other inspired writers.

2. Neither is that far-fetched conceit that justification is the clearing us from accusation, particularly that of Satan, easily

---

[33] Cf. Rom. 3:23.
[34] Eph. 2:3.
[35] Rom. 5:18.
[36] Cf. Rom. 8:1.   [37] Cf. Rom. 3:24.
[38] The relation between justification and sanctification—and the problem of their order of precedence—was an old bone of contention between Puritans and Anglicans. Lutherans and Calvinists, as a rule, understood justification (in the forensic sense of pardon and acquittal) as antecedent to sanctification (in the sense of 'renovation'); cf. Schmid, *Doctrinal Theology*, Pt. III, ch. iii, §48 (pp. 486 ff.). Anglicans, like Jeremy Taylor, insisted that some evidence of sanctification (e.g., repentance and 'works meet for repentance') should precede justification. Wesley stressed the difference between the two (justification as 'what God does *for* us'; sanctifcation as 'what he works *in* us'; cf. No. 45, 'The New Birth', §1) and, after 1738, insists on the priority of justification in the order of salvation (cf. No. 19, 'The Great Privilege of those that are Born of God', I.1 and n.). But see the Minute of 1770 for an interesting recurrence of the holy living theme (*secundum merita operum*), and also the comment on the contrast between Lutherans, Catholics, and Methodists on this issue in No. 107, 'On God's Vineyard', I.5.

provable from any clear text of Holy Writ.[39] In the whole
scriptural account of this matter, as above laid down, neither that
accuser nor his accusation appears to be at all taken in. It cannot
indeed be denied that he is the 'accuser of men',[40] emphatically so
5 called. But it does in no wise appear that the great Apostle hath
any reference to this, more or less, in all that he hath written
touching justification either to the Romans or the Galatians.

3. It is also far easier to take for granted than to prove from any
clear Scripture testimony that justification is the clearing us from
10 the accusation brought against us by *the law*. At least, if this
forced, unnatural way of speaking mean either more or less than
this, that whereas we have transgressed the law of God and
thereby deserved the damnation of hell, God does not inflict on
those who are justified the punishment which they had
15 deserved.[41]

4. Least of all does justification imply that God is *deceived* in
those whom he justifies; that he thinks them to be what in fact
they are not, that he accounts them to be otherwise than they are.
It does by no means imply that God judges concerning us
20 contrary to the real nature of things, that he esteems us better
than we really are, or believes us righteous when we are
unrighteous.[42] Surely no. The judgment of the all-wise God is
always according to truth. Neither can it ever consist with his
unerring wisdom to think that I am innocent, to judge that I am
25 righteous or holy, because another is so. He can no more in this
manner confound me with Christ than with David or Abraham.
Let any man to whom God hath given understanding weigh this

[39] It has been supposed (e.g., by Sugden) that this is the Origenistic soteriology (and that of other Eastern Fathers; e.g., Athanasius, Gregory of Nyssa). It is, of course, a misreading of Origen; cf. Gustaf Aulén, *Christus Victor* (London, SPCK, 1945), pp. 54, 63-71.

[40] Cf. Rev. 12:10.

[41] This was typical Reformation teaching, as in John Gerhard, *op. cit.*, VII. 4-5: 'The *Law* accuses the sinner before the judgment-seat of God . . .'; cf. Martin Chemnitz, *Loci Theologici*, II. 250, where it is argued that 'the conscience of the sinner [is] accused by the divine Law before the tribunal of God . . . .' Note the mild tone of Wesley's rejection of this tradition.

[42] A mild distortion of the typical Puritan doctrine of forensic justification in which Christ's imputed righteousness allows the Father justly to pardon the elect and therefore regard them as if they were righteous. The ruling metaphor, in that view, is a forensic one: 'the heavenly tribunal'. Cf. Calvin, *Institutes*, III. 12; see also John Davenant, *A Treatise on Justification* (1631), I. 227-36, and George Downham [Downame], *A Treatise of Justification* (1639), pp. 15-45. For a larger survey of the Puritan thesis that imputation is the formal cause of justification (in Davenant, Downham, Joseph Hall, James Ussher, John Donne, Lancelot Andrewes, *et al.*), cf. Allison, *The Rise of Moralism*, *passim*.

without prejudice, and he cannot but perceive that such a notion of justification is neither reconcilable to reason nor Scripture.

5. The plain scriptural notion of justification is pardon,[43] the forgiveness of sins. It is that act of God the Father whereby, for the sake of the propitiation made by the blood of his Son, he 'showeth forth his righteousness (or mercy) by the remission of the sins that are past'.[44] This is the easy, natural account of it given by St. Paul throughout his whole Epistle. So he explains it himself, more particularly in this and in the following chapter. Thus in the next verses but one to the text, 'Blessed are they (saith he) whose iniquities are forgiven, and whose sins are covered. Blessed is the man to whom the Lord will not impute sin.'[45] To him that is justified or forgiven God 'will not impute sin' to his condemnation. He will not condemn him on that account either in this world or in that which is to come. His sins, all his past sins,

---

[43] The fulcrum of Wesley's evangelical soteriology. No such definition of justification appears anywhere in the early Wesley. The idea is normative after 1738—but see No. 86, *A Call to Backsliders*, II.2(3), where Wesley speaks of those who 'had been sanctified in the first degree . . .', i.e., before 'remission of sins'. For the early Wesley, see, e.g., his letter to his mother, Feb. 28, 1730, where he accepts Jeremy Taylor's correlation of 'pardon of sins in the gospel [with] sanctification'. Contrast this with Nos. 19, 'The Great Privilege of those that are Born of God' (1748), §2; and 43, *The Scripture Way of Salvation* (1765), I.3. It was in this sense that Wesley could maintain, in a letter to John Newton, May 14, 1765: 'I think on justification just as I have done any time these seven and twenty years—and just as Mr. Calvin does. In this respect I do not differ from him an hair's breadth.' Earlier (Apr. 24,1765), he wrote to Dr. Erskine, 'In . . . justification by faith I have not wavered a moment for these seven and twenty years.' Later (May 23, 1768), he would reassure the Revd. Mr. Plenderlieth: 'Since I believed justification by faith, which I have done upwards of thirty years, I have constantly maintained that we are pardoned and accepted wholly and solely for the sake of what Christ hath both *done and suffered* for us.' Cf. also *Notes* on Rom. 3:24; 5:18, and *Minutes*, 1746.

If the difference between Wesley and Calvin were only a hair's breadth, that hair's breadth was crucial—and the Calvinists always recognized it as such. In the *Institutes*, III. xx. 5, Calvin asserts expressly that 'in justification, faith is *merely passive* . . .'; whereas Wesley understood justifying faith as 'active' in some sense (prompted, as it is, by the Spirit's prevenient activity). In this, he was nearer to Richard Lucas (*Enquiry*, III. 33), John Goodwin (*Imputatio Fidei; Or a Treatise of Justification* [1642], p.77), or even to Thomas Cockman (*Salvation by Jesus Christ Alone . . . in two sermons preached before the University of Oxford, January 2 and 6, 1732)* than to Calvin, Davenant, or Bunyan. There is also his letter to Charles (July 31, 1747), which outlines *'a genesis problematica* on justifying faith', with its first formal question, 'Is justifying faith a sense of pardon?'—and the formal answer, *'Negatur'!* The ensuing explanation would seem to contradict the central thesis of 'Justification by Faith' and the claim to consensus with Calvin. A closer look, however, suggests a somewhat imprecise elision of justification as pardon with the *'sense of pardon'* here defined as 'a distinct, explicit assurance that my sins are forgiven'. Thus, for all of these variants, *justification as pardon* continues as Wesley's baseline definition.

[44] Cf. Rom. 3:25.

[45] Rom. 4:7, 8; cf. Ps. 32:1, 2.

in thought, word, and deed, 'are covered', are blotted out; shall not be remembered or mentioned against him, any more than if they had not been. God will not inflict on that sinner what he deserved to suffer, because the Son of his love hath suffered for
5 him. And from the time we are 'accepted through the Beloved', 'reconciled to God through his blood',[46] he loves and blesses and watches over us for good, even as if we had never sinned.

Indeed the Apostle in one place seems to extend the meaning of the word much farther, where he says: 'Not the hearers of the
10 law, but the doers of the law shall be justified.'[47] Here he appears to refer our justification to the sentence of the great day.[48] And so our Lord himself unquestionably doth when he says, 'By thy words thou shalt be justified;' proving thereby that 'for every idle word men shall speak they shall give an account in the day of
15 judgment.'[49] But perhaps we can hardly produce another instance of St. Paul's using the word in that distant sense. In the general tenor of his writings it is evident he doth not; and least of all in the text before us, which undeniably speaks, not of those who have already 'finished their course',[50] but of those who are now just
20 setting out, just beginning 'to run the race which is set before them'.[51]

III.1. But this is the third thing which was to be considered, namely, who are they that are justified? And the Apostle tells us expressly, the ungodly: he, that is, God, 'justifieth the ungodly';[52]
25 the ungodly of every kind and degree, and none but the ungodly. As 'they that are righteous need no repentance',[53] so they need no forgiveness. It is only sinners that have any occasion for pardon: it is sin alone which admits of being forgiven. Forgiveness therefore has an immediate reference to sin and (in this respect) to nothing
30 else. It is our 'unrighteousness' to which the pardoning God is 'merciful'; it is our 'iniquity' which he 'remembereth no more'.[54]

---

[46] Cf. Eph. 1:6, 7; Rom. 5:9, 10.
[47] Rom. 2:13.
[48] I.e., to our 'final justification' (*iustitia duplex*); this, then, is an echo of Wesley's doctrine of a 'double justification', already rejected by the Lutherans (cf. Schmid, *Doctrinal Theology*, Pt. III, ch. iii, §42, and, more specifically, pp. 430 ff.).
[49] Matt. 12:36, 37.
[50] 2 Tim. 4:7.
[51] Cf. Heb. 12:1. Another echo of the idea of 'double justification', which Wesley will argue for in the next sermon, 'The Righteousness of Faith' (see I.7 and n.).
[52] Rom. 4:5.
[53] Cf. Luke 5:32; 15:7; etc.
[54] Cf. Heb. 8:12.

2. This seems not to be at all considered by those who so vehemently contend that man must be sanctified, that is, holy, before he can be justified; especially by such of them as affirm that universal holiness or obedience must precede justification[55] (unless they mean that justification at the last day which is wholly out of the present question); so far from it, that the very supposition is not only flatly impossible (for where there is no love of God there is no holiness, and there is no love of God but from a sense of his loving us) but also grossly, intrinsically absurd, contradictory to itself. For it is not a *saint* but a *sinner* that is *forgiven,* and under the notion of a sinner. God *justifieth* not the godly, but the *ungodly;* not those that are holy already, but the unholy. Upon what condition he doth this will be considered quickly; but whatever it is, it cannot be holiness. To assert this is to say the Lamb of God takes away only those sins which were taken away before.[56]

3. Does then the good Shepherd seek and save only those that are found already? No. He seeks and saves that which is lost.[57] He pardons those who need his pardoning mercy. He saves from the guilt of sin (and at the same time from the power) sinners of every kind, of every degree: men who till then were altogether ungodly; in whom the love of the Father was not; and consequently in

---

[55] An unsympathetic reference to the typical assumption by those in the 'holy living' tradition that 'repentance and works meet for repentance' (Acts 26:20) were normal antecedents to justification—and certainly to anything like 'final justification' (since the doctrine of 'double justification' had come to them from Erasmus, Bucer, and others). Jeremy Taylor had spoken for many in espousing this view in a letter to Bishop John Warner of Rochester (Taylor, *Works,* II, 678–80; see also *Unum Necessarium,* ch. ix, 'The Effect of Repentance', *ibid.,* pp. 598 ff.); he had expounded it at greater length in *The Rule and Exercises of Holy Living* (1650), *Works,* I. 399–515. Bishop Thomas Barlow of Lincoln had accused George Bull of such a teaching in the *Harmonia Apostolica* (1669), despite Robert Nelson's denials of any such intention on Bull's part; cf. his *Life of Bull* (1713), pp. 90, 181, 211. Despite Nelson's protestations, Wesley had joined Barlow in denouncing both Bull and Tillotson as having taught such a doctrine of works-righteousness (cf. Nos. 150, 151, 'Hypocrisy in Oxford'). Thomas Tully thought he had found such a heresy in Richard Baxter's *Aphorisms on Justification,* and had roundly condemned it in *Justificatio Paulina* (1674). The point is that here Wesley has reversed his earlier stand and now is stressing the primacy of justification in the *ordo salutis* even as Baxter had sought to do in his *Aphorisms* and *Confession.* Even John Turner in his Boyle Lecture of 1708, 'The Wisdom of God in the Redemption of Man', *Sermons at the Boyle Lectures* (1739), II. 359, had asserted that universal or perfect obedience to the Law is impossible to fallen man. What everybody was trying to avoid was the Council of Trent's bald identification of justification as 'inherent and infused righteousness' (cf. Sessions VI, ch. vii). Thus, Wesley here is concerned to set down his new doctrine as clearly and firmly as possible.

[56] An echo of the *Agnus Dei* and 1 John 2:2.

[57] See Luke 19:10.

whom dwelt no good thing, no good or truly Christian temper, but all such as were evil and abominable—pride, anger, love of the world, the genuine fruits of that 'carnal mind which is enmity against God'.[58]

5   4. These 'who are sick', the 'burden of whose sins is intolerable',[59] are they that 'need a physician';[60] these who are guilty, who groan under the wrath of God, are they that need a pardon. These who are 'condemned already',[61] not only by God but also by their own conscience, as by a thousand witnesses, of all
10 their ungodliness, both in thought, and word, and work, cry aloud for him that 'justifieth the ungodly'[62] 'through the redemption that is in Jesus'[63]—'the ungodly and him that worketh not', that worketh not before he is justified anything that is good, that is truly virtuous or holy, but only evil continually. For his heart is
15 necessarily, essentially evil, till the love of God is shed abroad therein.[64] And while the tree is corrupt so are the fruits, 'for an evil tree cannot bring forth good fruit'.[65]

    5. If it be objected, 'Nay, but a man, before he is justified, may feed the hungry, or clothe the naked;[66] and these are good works,'
20 the answer is easy. He *may* do these, even before he is justified. And these are in one sense 'good works'; they are 'good and profitable to men'.[67] But it does not follow that they are, strictly speaking, good in themselves, or good in the sight of God. All truly 'good works' (to use the words of our Church) 'follow after
25 justification', and they are therefore 'good and acceptable to God in Christ', because they 'spring out of a true and living faith'.[68] By a parity of reason all 'works done before justification are not good', in the Christian sense, 'forasmuch as they spring not of faith in Jesus Christ' (though from some kind of faith in God they
30 may spring), 'yea, rather for that they are not done as God hath willed and commanded them to be done, we doubt not' (how

---

[58] Cf. Rom. 8:7.
[59] BCP, Communion, General Confession.
[60] Cf. Matt. 9:12.
[61] John 3:18.
[62] Rom. 4:5.
[63] Rom. 3:24.
[64] Rom. 5:5.
[65] Cf. Matt. 7:18; Luke 6:43.
[66] Cf. Matt. 25:37-38.   [67] Titus 3:8.
[68] *The Thirty-nine Articles*, Art. XII, 'Of Good Works'; also 'Of the True and Lively Faith', Pts. I-III, in *Homilies*, pp. 29-40, and 'Of Good Works Annexed Unto Faith', Pt. I, *ibid.*, pp. 41-44.

strange soever it may appear to some) 'but they have the nature of sin.'[69]

6. Perhaps those who doubt of this have not duly considered the weighty reason which is here assigned why no works done before justification can be truly and properly good. The argument 5 runs thus:

No works are good which are not done as God hath willed and commanded them to be done:

But no works done before justification are done as God hath willed and commanded them to be done: 10

Therefore no works done before justification are good.

The first proposition is self-evident. And the second, that no works done before justification are done as God hath willed and commanded them to be done, will appear equally plain and undeniable if we only consider God hath willed and commanded 15 that 'all our works should be done in charity' ($\dot{\epsilon}\nu$ $\dot{\alpha}\gamma\dot{\alpha}\pi\eta$),[70] in love, in that love to God which produces love to all mankind. But none of our works can be done in this love while the love of the Father (of God as our Father) is not in us. And this love cannot be in us till we receive the 'Spirit of adoption, crying in our hearts, 20 Abba, Father'.[71] If therefore God doth not 'justify the ungodly', and him that (in this sense) 'worketh not', then hath Christ died in vain; then, notwithstanding his death, can no flesh living be justified.

IV.1. But on what terms then is he justified who is altogether 25 'ungodly', and till that time 'worketh not'? On one alone, which is faith. He 'believeth in him that justifieth the ungodly', and 'he that believeth is not condemned';[72] yea, he 'is passed from death unto life'.[73] For 'the righteousness (or mercy) of God is by faith of Jesus Christ unto all and upon all them that believe; . . . whom 30 God hath set forth to be a propitiation through faith in his blood',

---

[69] Cf. *The Thirty-nine Articles*, Art. XIII, 'Of Works Before Justification', and see *The Doctrine of Salvation, Faith, and Good Works*, II. 6 (p. 4 above). In the homily, 'Of Good Works', *Homilies*, p. 43, Cranmer cites St. Chrysostom's *De Fide, Lege et Spiritu* . . .: 'they which glister and shine in good works without faith in God be like dead men which had goodly and precious tombs and yet it availeth them nothing.' Cf. Migne, *PG*, 48: 1081-83, where *De Lege* comes under the rubric 'Spuria'; even so, the passage faithfully reflects St. Chrysostom's views on the point. Also, see No. 99, *The Reward of Righteousness*, I.4 and n.

[70] Cf. 1 Cor. 16:14. For Wesley's preference for 'love' rather than 'charity' as a translation of $\dot{\alpha}\gamma\dot{\alpha}\pi\eta$, cf. No. 17, 'The Circumcision of the Heart', I.2 and n.

[71] Cf. Rom. 8:15.

[72] John 3:18.   [73] John 5:24; cf. 1 John 3:14.

that 'he might be just, and (consistently with his justice) the justifier of him which believeth in Jesus. . . . Therefore we conclude that a man is justified by faith without the deeds of the law'[74]—without previous obedience to the moral law, which
5 indeed he could not till now perform. That it is the moral law, and that alone, which is here intended, appears evidently from the words that follow: 'Do we then make void the law through faith? God forbid! Yea, we establish the law.'[75] What law do we establish by faith? Not the ritual law; not the ceremonial law of Moses. In
10 no wise; but the great, unchangeable law of love, the holy love of God and of our neighbour.

2. Faith in general is a divine, supernatural ἔλεγχος, 'evidence' or conviction 'of things not seen',[76] not discoverable by our bodily senses as being either past, future, or spiritual.[77]
15 Justifying faith implies, not only a divine evidence or conviction that 'God was in Christ, reconciling the world unto himself',[78] but a sure trust and confidence that Christ died for *my* sins, that he loved *me,* and gave himself for *me.*[79] And at what time soever a sinner thus believes, be it in early childhood, in the strength of his
20 years, or when he is old and hoary-haired, God justifieth that ungodly one; God for the sake of his Son pardoneth and absolveth him who had in him till then no good thing. Repentance indeed God had given him before. But that repentance was neither more nor less than a deep sense of the want of all good,
25 and the presence of all evil. And whatever good he hath or doth from that hour when he first believes in God through Christ, faith does not *find* but *bring.* This is the fruit of faith. First the tree is good, and then the fruit is good also.

---

[74] Rom. 3:22, 25-26, 28.

[75] Rom. 3:31; see Nos. 34, 'The Original, Nature, Properties, and Use of the Law', and 35, 36, 'The Law Established through Faith', Discourses I and II, for a full exposition of Wesley's views on 'Law and Gospel'.

[76] Heb. 11:1. Cf. No. 3, *'Awake, Thou That Sleepest',* I.11 and n.

[77] Is there an echo here of St. Augustine's famous distinction between three orders of time (*Confessions,* XI. xi-xxxi—*memoria, expectatio,* and *contuitus*)? Wesley's 'spiritual' is a rough equivalent to St. Augustine's 'contuitive'. See No. 29, 'Sermon on the Mount, IX', §28 and n.

[78] 2 Cor. 5:19.

[79] See 1 Cor. 15:3 and Gal. 2:20. This is Wesley's definition of the 'testimony' or 'witness of the Spirit'. See Nos. 10, 'The Witness of the Spirit, I', I.7; 11, *The Witness of the Spirit,* II, II.2; 17, 'The Circumcision of the Heart', II.5; 58, *On Predestination,* §12; 106, 'On Faith, Heb. 11:6', I.12. There is also here an echo of 'Aldersgate', JWJ, May 24, 1738. See also Wesley's *Notes* on 1 John 3:14.

3. I cannot describe the nature of this faith better than in the words of our own Church: 'The only instrument of salvation' (whereof justification is one branch) 'is faith: that is [. . .] a sure trust and confidence [. . .] that God both hath and will forgive our sins, that he hath accepted us again into his favour, [. . .] for the merits of Christ's death and Passion. . . . But here we must take heed that we do not halt with God through an inconstant, wavering faith. [. . .] Peter coming to Christ upon the water, because he fainted in faith, was in danger of drowning. So we, if we begin to waver or doubt, it is to be feared that we should sink as Peter did, not into the water but into the bottomless pit of hell-fire.'[b]

Therefore have 'a sure and constant faith, not only that the death of Christ is available for [. . .] all the world, [. . .] but [. . .] that he hath made [. . .] a full and sufficient sacrifice for *thee*, a perfect cleansing of *thy* sins, so that [. . .] thou mayst say with the Apostle, [. . .] he loved *thee*, and gave himself for *thee*.[80] For this is [. . .] to make Christ *thine own*, and to apply his merits unto *thyself.*[c]

4. By affirming that this faith is the term or *condition* of justification I mean, first, that there is no justification without it. 'He that believeth not is condemned already;'[81] and so long as he believeth not that condemnation cannot be removed, 'but the wrath of God abideth on him'.[82] As 'there is no other name given under heaven than that of Jesus of Nazareth,' no other merit whereby a condemned sinner can ever be saved from the guilt of sin;[83] so there is no other way of obtaining a share in his merit than 'by faith in his name'.[84] So that as long as we are without this faith we are 'strangers to the covenant of promise', we are 'aliens from the commonwealth of Israel', and 'without God in the world'.[85] Whatsoever virtues (so called) a man may have—I speak of those unto whom the gospel is preached; 'for what have I to do to judge them that are without?'[86]—whatsoever good works (so accounted) he may do, it profiteth not: he is still a 'child of wrath',[87] still under the curse, till he believes in Jesus.

---

[b] [Cf.] Second Sermon on the Passion [*Homilies*, pp. 382-83].
[c] [Cf.] Sermon on the Sacrament, First Part [*ibid.*, p. 399].

---

[80] Cf. Gal. 2:20. [81] John 3:18.
[82] John 3:36. [83] See Acts 4:10, 12. [84] Cf. Acts 3:16.
[85] Eph. 2:12. [86] 1 Cor. 5:12. [87] Cf. Eph. 2:3.

5. Faith therefore is the *necessary* condition of justification. Yea, and the *only necessary* condition thereof. This is the second point carefully to be observed: that the very moment God giveth faith (for 'it is the gift of God')[88] to the 'ungodly', 'that worketh
5　not', that 'faith is counted to him for righteousness'.[89] He hath no righteousness at all antecedent to this, not so much as negative righteousness[90] or innocence. But 'faith is imputed to him for righteousness' the very moment that he believeth. Not that God (as was observed before) thinketh him to be what he is not. But as
10　'he made Christ to be sin for us'[91] (that is, treated him as a sinner, punished him for our sins), so he counteth us righteous from the time we believe in him (that is, he doth not punish us for our sins, yea, treats us as though we were guiltless and righteous).

6. Surely the difficulty of assenting to this proposition, that
15　faith is the *only condition* of justification, must arise from not understanding it. We mean thereby thus much: that it is the only thing without which none is justified, the only thing that is immediately, indispensably, absolutely requisite in order to pardon. As on the one hand, though a man should have
20　everything else, without faith, yet he cannot be justified; so on the other, though he be supposed to want everything else, yet if he hath faith he cannot but be justified. For suppose a sinner of any kind or degree, in a full sense of his total ungodliness, of his utter inability to think, speak, or do good, and his absolute meetness for
25　hell-fire—suppose, I say, this sinner, helpless and hopeless, casts himself wholly on the mercy of God in Christ (which indeed he cannot do but by the grace of God)—who can doubt but he is forgiven in that moment? Who will affirm that any more is *indispensably required* before that sinner can be justified?
30　　Now if there ever was one such instance from the beginning of the world (and have there not been, and are there not ten

---

[88] Eph. 2:8; thus faith is not a meritorious 'work'.
[89] Cf. Rom. 4:5.
[90] I.e., Adam's state before temptation and its bearing on the problem of 'original righteousness'; cf. St. Irenaeus, *Against Heresies*, III. xxii.v., and St. Athanasius, *Contra Gentes*, 3. The Lutheran theologians had discussed *iustitia originalis* and had rejected any correlation of that with any *status purorum naturalium* (cf. Schmid, *Doctrinal Theology*, pp. 230-31, and see his citations of Gerhard, Calixtus, and Quenstedt). For the phrase, 'negative righteousness', cf. William Allen, *The Glass of Justification* (1658), p. 20.
[91] Cf. 2 Cor. 5:21.

thousand times ten thousand?)[92] it plainly follows that faith is, in the above sense, the sole condition of justification.[93]

7. It does not become poor, guilty, sinful worms, who receive whatsoever blessings they enjoy (from the least drop of water that cools our tongue[94] to the immense riches of glory in eternity) of grace, of mere favour, and not of debt, to ask of God the reasons of his conduct. It is not meet for us to call him in question 'who giveth account to none of his ways';[95] to demand, 'Why didst thou make faith the condition, the only condition of justification? Wherefore didst thou decree, "He that believeth", and he only, "shall be saved"?'[96] This is the very point on which St. Paul so strongly insists in the ninth chapter of this Epistle, *viz.*, that the terms of pardon and acceptance must depend, not on us, but 'on him that calleth us'; that there is no 'unrighteousness with God' in fixing his own terms, not according to ours, but his own good pleasure: who may justly say, 'I will have mercy on whom I will have mercy,' namely, on him who believeth in Jesus. 'So then it is not of him that willeth, nor of him that runneth', to choose the condition on which he shall find acceptance, 'but of God that showeth mercy,' that accepteth none at all but of his own free love, his unmerited goodness. 'Therefore hath he mercy on whom he will have mercy,' *viz.*, on those who believe on the Son of his love; 'and whom he will', that is, those who believe not, 'he hardeneth'—leaves at last to the hardness of their hearts.[97]

8. One reason, however, we may humbly conceive, of God's fixing this condition of justification—'If thou believest in the Lord Jesus Christ thou shalt be saved'[98]—was to 'hide pride from man'.[99] Pride had already destroyed the very angels of God, had

---

[92] Dan. 7:10.

[93] Wesley's starkest assertion, in any of his writings, of the *sola fide*, for here he excludes even *repentance*, which elsewhere he conjoins with faith as the human components of justification. See, e.g., No. 14, *The Repentance of Believers*, II.6; *Minutes*, 1745; *Principles of a Methodist Farther Explained*, VI.4; and his *Letter to a Gentleman at Bristol*, Jan. 6, 1758. See also Wesley's extracts of the lives of Henry and James Fraser in the *Christian Lib.*, L. 98-99, and XLIX. 299. For a doctrine of *sola fide* nuanced rather differently and yet still in the same tradition, cf. Joseph Mede, *Discourse XXVI*, *Works* (1677), pp. 113-15, and also Cockman, *Salvation by Jesus Christ Alone* . . . .

[94] See Luke 16:24.

[95] Cf. Job 33:13.

[96] Mark 16:16.

[97] Rom. 9:11, 14-16, 18.   [98] Cf. Acts 16:31.

[99] Job 33:17. This is one of Calvin's main points, in the *Institutes*, III, xii. 3-7, where (after quoting Augustine) he identifies pride as the chief obstacle to faith. See also *ibid.*, xiii. 2, 4.

cast down a 'third part of the stars of heaven'.[100] It was likewise in great measure owing to this, when the tempter said, 'Ye shall be as gods,'[101] that Adam fell from his own steadfastness and brought sin and death into the world. It was therefore an instance of wisdom worthy of God to appoint such a condition of reconciliation for him and all his posterity as might effectually humble, might abase them to the dust. And such is faith. It is peculiarly fitted for this end. For he that cometh unto God by this faith must fix his eye singly on his own wickedness, on his guilt and helplessness, without having the least regard to any supposed good in himself, to any virtue or righteousness whatsoever. He must come as a *mere sinner* inwardly and outwardly, self-destroyed and self-condemned, bringing nothing to God but ungodliness only, pleading nothing of his own but sin and misery. Thus it is, and thus alone, when his 'mouth is stopped', and he stands utterly 'guilty before God',[102] that he can 'look unto Jesus'[103] as the whole and sole 'propitiation for his sins'.[104] Thus only can he be 'found in him'[105] and receive the 'righteousness which is of God by faith'.[106]

9. Thou ungodly one who hearest or readest these words, thou vile, helpless, miserable sinner, I charge thee before God, the judge of all, go straight unto him with all thy ungodliness.[107] Take heed thou destroy not thy own soul by pleading thy righteousness, more or less. Go as altogether ungodly, guilty, lost, destroyed, deserving and dropping into hell, and thou shalt then find favour in his sight, and know that he justifieth the ungodly. As such thou

---

[100] Rev. 8:12; 12:4.

[101] Gen. 3:5; see also Nos. 141, 'The Image of God'; and 45, 'The New Birth', I.4 and n., for further interpretations of the Fall.

[102] Rom. 3:19.

[103] Cf. Heb. 12:2.   [104] Cf. 1 John 2:2; 4:10.

[105] Phil. 3:9.   [106] Cf. Rom. 3:22.

[107] Note the abrupt change here from exposition to direct and sustained exhortation. Cf. Wesley's letter to Joseph Taylor, Feb. 14, 1787: 'A sermon should be all application.' Also, No. 20, *The Lord Our Righteousness*, II.20. This, then, is the carryover into a written sermon of a dominant feature of Wesley's oral preaching.

This, of course, was not original with Wesley; English preaching was strong on 'application'. Cf., e.g., John Selden, *Table Talk* (1689), p. 92: 'Nothing is text but what was spoken in the Bible, and meant there for person, and place; the rest is *application*, which a discreet man may do well; but 'tis his Scripture, not the Holy Ghost.' See also Tillotson, *Works*, I. 560; Samuel Annesley's sermon 'On Conscience' in *The Morning Exercise at Cripplegate* (1661), p. 7; and Robert South's sermon on 1 Sam. 25:32, 33, preached at Christ Church, Oxford, Nov. 10, 1673, which Wesley extracted for the *Christian Lib.*, XLIII. 141-49.

shalt be brought unto the 'blood of sprinkling'[108] as an undone, helpless, damned sinner. Thus 'look unto Jesus'![109] There is 'the Lamb of God, who taketh away *thy* sins'![110] Plead thou no works, no righteousness of thine own; no humility, contrition, sincerity! In no wise. That were, in very deed, to deny the Lord that bought 5 thee. No. Plead thou singly the blood of the covenant,[111] the ransom paid for thy proud, stubborn, sinful soul. Who art thou that now seest and feelest both thine inward and outward ungodliness? Thou art the man![112] I want thee for my Lord. I challenge *thee* for a child of God by faith. The Lord hath need of 10 thee.[113] Thou who feelest thou art just fit for hell art just fit to advance his glory: the glory of his free grace, justifying the ungodly and him that worketh not. O come quickly. Believe in the Lord Jesus; and *thou*, even *thou*, art reconciled to God.

---

[108] Cf. Heb. 12:24.
[109] Cf. Heb. 12:2.
[110] Cf. John 1:29.
[111] Cf. Exod. 24:8; Heb. 10:29.
[112] 2 Sam. 12:7.
[113] Cf. Matt. 21:3, etc.

THE RIGHTEOUSNESS OF FAITH

AN INTRODUCTORY COMMENT

John Wesley was not as ebullient an orator as George Whitefield or even his brother Charles. And yet his preaching in the years just after 1738 seems to have been attended with more hysterical responses from his hearers. In the Journal, *June 12, 1742, he records preaching on 'the righteousness of faith' from his father's tombstone at Epworth. 'While I was speaking several dropped down as dead; and among the rest such a cry was heard of sinners groaning for the righteousness of faith as almost drowned my voice.' An even more tumultuous scene in Wapping is recounted in the* Journal, *June 15, 1739. Hysterical phenomena, as side effects of his preaching, receive an occasional mention in the* Journal *from 1739 through 1744. They seem to have tapered off thereafter.*

A credible hypothesis concerning these phenomena—and the contrast between the effects of John Wesley's preaching in this period and that of other evangelicals—has been offered by Bernard Holland, ' "A Species of Madness": The Effect of John Wesley's Early Preaching', WHS, XXXIX. 77-85, and this is confirmed in large part in this sermon on 'the righteousness of faith'. Holland's point is that whereas Whitefield and Charles Wesley sought consciously (and fervently) to drive their hearers to a 'conviction of sin', they spared them the extremes of despair by suggesting that once penitents began to 'groan' for faith, this was in itself a proleptic sign of their acceptance even before their conscious sense of assurance of forgiveness. Robert Philip, in his Life and Times of . . . Whitefield *(1837), pp. 580-83, stresses this distinction, and Melville Horne, John Fletcher's curate at Madeley, who had heard Whitefield and both the Wesleys, reached much the same conclusion: '[Charles Wesley, rather than] denouncing wrath on sincere penitents . . . comforted them by insinuating that they were in a salvable state. . . . To the best of my knowledge, Mr. John Wesley did not admit this distinction into his pulpit;' cf.* An Investigation . . . of Justifying Faith, *pp. 28 ff.*

Holland, op. cit., p. 81, suggests that it was on principle that John drove his penitent and half-penitent hearers out of any refuge of hope to real despair: 'In spite of their longing to be reconciled to God, they were nevertheless still damned until faith was given them. It was this that so intensified the feeling of helplessness and anxiety . . . that some fell down, or cried out or became delirious.' Cf. William Sargant, Battle for the Mind *(New York, Doubleday, 1957), p. 78, for a psychiatric comment on John Wesley's impact on guilt-ridden audiences in this period; but see also Ian Ramage,* Battle for the Free Mind *(London, Allen and Unwin, 1967), pp. 238-59, for a useful critique of Sargant. It is in this sense that we can understand Wesley's candid admission in* A Farther Appeal *that 'it is my endeavour to drive all I can into what* you *may term another species of "madness", . . . which I term "repentance" or "conviction" ' as preparatory to the gift of faith (see Pt. I, VII.12; also VII.11, 13-15, in Vol. 11, pp. 196-99 of this edn.). Later, the starkness of this demand for despair was softened, and with it came a proportional decrease in hysterical concomitants. In 1746 it is asked in Conference, 'But can it be conceived that God has any regard to* the sincerity *of an unbeliever?' The answer, now, is different from earlier ones: 'Yes; so much that if he persevere therein, God will infallibly give him faith;' cf. MS Minutes, 1746, §20.*

The following year the efficacy of sincerity *in repentance is actually emphasized;* ibid., *June 16, 1747. In 1767, in light of his experiences in the Revival and in reaction to the polemics of the Calvinists, Wesley came round to what amounts to an abandonment of his insistences of 1739-44: 'It is high time for us . . . to return to the plain word, "He that feareth God and worketh righteousness is* accepted *with him" ' (JWJ, Dec. 30, 1767). And in a very late sermon (1791) he actually deplores deliberate efforts to drive persons to despair as a means of bringing them to faith (see No. 106, 'On Faith, Heb. 11:6', I.11-12; see also No. 117, 'On the Discoveries of Faith', §§11-15).*

This present sermon, however, is focused on a radical contrast between 'the righteousness of the law' *and 'the righteousness of* faith', *between the two covenants of works and of grace. The righteousness of the law, with its corresponding covenant of works, demands absolute and perfected perfection; nothing short of this is worth anything at all. The unmistakable inference is that since Adam's sin this righteousness is utterly unattainable; hence, despair. The righteousness of faith, on the other hand, is God's mercy freely given. It is God's pardon warranted by Christ's atonement, and therefore both just and justifying. It is worth noticing how relentlessly Wesley builds up the demands of the law, reducing the moralist to despair, and how thoroughly he refutes all objections to a repentant sinner's eager acceptance of God's sheer, unmerited mercy (cf. Charlotte Elliott's later hymn [1834]: 'Just as I am, without one plea').* Here, then, sola fide *is once again unnuanced. Yet also, the residues of Wesley's holy living tradition reassert themselves and remind us of his constant search for an alternative to any of the traditional polarities.*

Wesley preached on the passage in Rom. 10:5-8 at least seven times between 1740 and 1789, twice before this present sermon which was, apparently, written expressly for SOSO. *For a list of variant readings in the editions published in Wesley's lifetime, see Appendix, Vol. 4, 'Wesley's Text'.*

The Righteousness of Faith

Romans 10:5-8

Moses describeth the righteousness which is of the law, that the man which doeth those things shall live by them.

5 *But the righteousness which is of faith speaketh on this wise: Say not in thine heart, Who shall ascend into heaven? (that is, to bring Christ down from above;)*

Or, Who shall descend into the deep? (that is, to bring Christ again from the dead.)

10 *But what saith it? The word is nigh thee, even in thy mouth and in thy heart; that is, the word of faith which we preach.*[1]

1. The Apostle does not here oppose the covenant given by Moses to the covenant given by Christ. If we ever imagined this it was for want of observing that the latter as well as the former part
15 of these words were spoken by Moses himself to the people of Israel, and that concerning the covenant which then was.[a] But it is

---

[a] Deut. 30:11, 12, 14.

---

[1] Matthew Henry had recognized the echoes here of Isa. 59:21, '. . . in thy mouth', and Jer. 31:33, '. . . in thy heart'; Poole and Wesley (in his *Notes*) ignore these texts. All ignore the remarkable parallel in the Septuagint translation of Deut. 30:11-14, which St. Paul would have known as a matter of course and would have taken as a reference to Torah: 'For this Torah which I give thee this day is not too great nor too far from thee. It is not in heaven saying, "Who shall go up for us to heaven and take it for us?" . . . Nor is it beyond the sea saying, "Who will cross beyond the sea for us and receive it for us?" . . . But the word [i.e., God's Torah] is near to thee, in thy mouth and in thy heart and in thy hands, to do it [i.e., obey it].' In Baruch 3:29 and 4 Esd. 4:7-9, it is denied that wisdom is so accessible to human grasp; see R. H. Charles, *Pseudepigrapha* (Oxford, Clarendon Press,

the covenant of *grace* which God through Christ hath established with men in all ages (as well before, and under the Jewish dispensation, as since God was manifest in the flesh), which St. Paul here opposes to the covenant of *works*, made with Adam while in paradise, but commonly supposed to be the only 5 covenant which God had made with man, particularly by those Jews of whom the Apostle writes.[2]

2. Of these it was that he so affectionately speaks in the beginning of this chapter. 'My heart's desire and prayer to God for Israel is, that they may be saved. For I bear them record that 10 they have a zeal for God, but not according to knowledge. For they, being ignorant of God's righteousness' (of the justification that flows from his mere grace and mercy, freely forgiving our sins through the Son of his love, through the redemption which is in Jesus),[3] 'and seeking to establish their own righteousness' 15 (their own holiness, antecedent to faith in 'him that justifieth the ungodly',[4] as the ground of their pardon and acceptance), 'have not submitted themselves unto the righteousness of God',[5] and consequently seek death in the error of their life.[6]

3. They were ignorant that 'Christ is the end of the law for 20 righteousness to everyone that believeth;'[7] that by the oblation of

---

1913), ll. 564-65. The parallel, cited by Sugden, I. 132, to Jubilees 24:32, is merely verbal. The point here for Wesley is that St. Paul had then set the 'righteousness of the law' and the 'righteousness of faith' in antithesis as the contrast between the Adamic 'covenant of works' and the 'covenant of grace which God through Christ hath established with men in all ages'. It is this contrast Wesley intends to stress here.

[2] This dialectic between the two covenants of works and grace had not been central in Latin or Lutheran theologies, but had been for Reformed dogmatics in general (see Heinrich Heppe, *Reformed Dogmatics*, ch. xvi, pp. 371-409); Wesley would have come by it through the Puritans (Ames and Perkins, and espec. the *Westminster Confession*, VII. 2 ff.). A classical statement of 'covenant soteriology' was in Cocceius, *Summa doctrinae* (1648); see above, p. 81. For Wesley's interest in this idea see in his selections in the *Christian Lib.*, especially John Preston, 'The New Covenant or the Saints' Portion' (1629), x. 81-84; Isaac Ambrose, 'Looking Unto Jesus' (1658), Bk. II, ch. ii, Sect. II, in XIV. 85-99; Jeremy Taylor, *Holy Dying* (ch. v, Sect. iv, XVI.200-3; William Beveridge, 'Thoughts on Religion', Arts. IX, X, XLVII. 61-78. Wesley's own variations on this theme may be seen in Nos. 12, 'The Witness of Our Own Spirit', §20; 35, 'The Law Established through Faith, I', II.3-4; 127, 'On the Wedding Garment', §19. Cf. also *Minutes*, May 13, 1746, and *Notes* on Heb. 8:8.

[3] See Rom. 3:24.   [4] Rom. 4:5.
[5] Cf. Rom. 10:1-3.
[6] See Wisd. 1:12. For Wesley's other uses of this text from an Apocryphal book, cf. Nos. 21, 'Sermon on the Mount, I', §3; 40, *Christian Perfection*, I.4; 65, 'The Duty of Reproving our Neighbour', II.3; 115, 'Dives and Lazarus', III.2; and 127, 'On the Wedding Garment', §11.
[7] Rom. 10:4.

himself once offered[8] he had put an end to the first law or covenant (which indeed was not given by God to Moses, but to Adam in his state of innocence), the strict tenor whereof, without any abatement, was, 'Do this and live;'[9] and at the same time
5 purchased for us that better covenant, 'Believe and live:' 'Believe and thou shalt be saved;'[10] now saved both from the guilt and power of sin, and of consequence from the wages of it.

4. And how many are equally ignorant now, even among those who are called by the name of Christ? How many who have now a
10 'zeal for God', yet have it not 'according to knowledge', but are still 'seeking to establish their own righteousness' as the ground of their pardon and acceptance, and therefore vehemently refuse to 'submit themselves unto the righteousness of God'?[11] Surely my heart's desire and prayer to God for you, brethren, is that ye
15 may be saved.[12] And in order to remove this grand stumbling-block out of your way I will endeavour to show, first, what 'the righteousness' is 'which is of the law', and what 'the righteousness which is of faith'; secondly, the folly of trusting in 'the righteousness . . . of the law', and the wisdom of 'submitting to
20 that which is of faith'.

I.1. And, first, 'The righteousness which is of the law saith, The man which doth these things shall live by them.' Constantly and perfectly observe all these things, to do them, and then thou shalt live for ever.[13] This law or covenant (usually called the
25 covenant of *works*) given by God to man in paradise, required an obedience perfect in all its parts, entire and wanting nothing, as the condition of his eternal continuance in the holiness and happiness wherein he was created.

2. It required that man should fulfil all righteousness, inward
30 and outward, negative and positive: that he should not only abstain from every idle word, and avoid every evil work, but

---

[8] BCP, Communion, Prayer of Consecration.

[9] Cf. Gen. 42:18; Luke 10:28. In the Colman Collection Vol. XX, there is a MS in Wesley's hand entitled, 'The Duty of Receiving the Lord's Supper', extracted (in part) from Robert Nelson, *The Great Duty of Frequenting the Christian Sacrifice* (1711), but with additions from Wesley himself and other authors. The 'covenant' idea does not appear in Nelson but does in Wesley's MS, fol. 18–23; see espec. fol. 18–19, where he has '*Try* to do this, and live.' See *Bibliog*, No. 412, and Vol. 8 of this edn.

[10] Cf. Acts 16:31.　　　　　　　　　　　　　　[11] Cf. Rom. 10:2-3.

[12] See Rom. 10:1.

[13] Cf. this text expounded literally in Wesley's sermon on Gen. 1:27, No. 141, 'The Image of God', II.1.

should keep every affection, every desire, every thought, in obedience to the will of God; that he should continue holy, as he which had created him was holy, both in heart and in all manner of conversation; that he should be pure in heart, even as God is pure, perfect as his Father in heaven was perfect;[14] that he should love the Lord his God with all his heart, with all his soul, with all his mind, and with all his strength;[15] that he should love every soul which God had made even as God had loved him; that by this universal benevolence he should 'dwell in God (who is love) and God in him';[16] that he should serve the Lord his God with all his strength, and in all things singly aim at his glory.

3. These were the things which the righteousness of the law required, that he who did them might live thereby. But it farther required that this entire obedience to God, this inward and outward holiness, this conformity both of heart and life to his will, should be perfect in *degree*. No abatement, no allowance could possibly be made for falling short in any degree as to any jot or tittle either of the outward or the inward law. If every commandment relating to outward things was obeyed, yet that was not sufficient unless every one was obeyed with all the strength, in the highest measure and most perfect manner. Nor did it answer the demand of this covenant to love God with every power and faculty, unless he were loved with the full capacity of each, with the whole possibility of the soul.

4. One thing more was indispensably required by the righteousness of the law, namely that this universal obedience, this perfect holiness both of heart and life, should be perfectly uninterrupted also, should continue without any intermission from the moment wherein God created man, and breathed into his nostrils the breath of life, until the days of his trial should be ended, and he should be confirmed in life everlasting.

5. The righteousness, then, which is of the law speaketh on this wise. 'Thou, O man of God, stand fast in love, in the image of God wherein thou art made. If thou wilt remain in life, keep the commandments which are now written in thy heart. Love the Lord thy God with all thy heart. Love as thyself every soul that he hath made. Desire nothing but God. Aim at God in every thought, in every word and work. Swerve not in one motion of

---

[14] See Matt. 5:48.
[15] See Matt. 22:37, etc.
[16] Cf. 1 John 4:16.

body or soul from him, thy mark, and the prize of thy high calling.[17] And let all that is in thee praise his holy name,[18] every power and faculty of thy soul, in every kind, in every degree, and at every moment of thine existence. "This do, and thou shalt
5 live;"[19] thy light shall shine, thy love shall flame more and more, till thou art received up into the house of God in the heavens, to reign with him for ever and ever.'[20]

6. 'But the righteousness which is of faith speaketh on this wise: Say not in thine heart, Who shall ascend into heaven? that is,
10 to bring down Christ from above' (as though it were some impossible task which God required thee previously to perform in order to thine acceptance); 'or, Who shall descend into the deep? that is, to bring up Christ from the dead' (as though that were still remaining to be done for the sake of which thou wert to be
15 accepted). 'But what saith it? The word' (according to the tenor of which thou mayest now be accepted as an heir of life eternal) 'is nigh thee, even in thy mouth and in thy heart; that is, the word of faith which we preach,' the new covenant which God hath now established with sinful man through Christ Jesus.[21]

20 7. By 'the righteousness which is of faith' is meant that condition of justification (and in consequence of present and final salvation, if we endure therein unto the end)[22] which was given by God to *fallen man* through the merits and mediation of his only begotten Son. This was in part revealed to Adam soon after his
25 fall, being contained in the original promise made to him and his seed concerning the seed of the woman, who should 'bruise the serpent's head'.[b] It was a little more clearly revealed to Abraham

---

[b] Gen. 3:15.

---

[17] See Phil. 3:14.　　　　　　　　　　　　　　　　[18] See Ps. 103:1.
[19] Luke 10:28. Cf. Ezek. 18:19, 22; 33:13.
[20] Wesley belabours this demand for absolute perfection to underscore the glaring contrast between human aspirations and the human actuality. But he also believed that since the ideal had been actual in Adam (see Nos. 141, 'The Image of God'; and 76, 'On Perfection', I.1 ff.), we may look forward to its restoration as the *'fullness* of salvation'. This notion of salvation as the recovery of the *imago Dei* is a basic Wesleyan theme; cf. No. 1, *Salvation by Faith*, §1 and n.
[21] Cf. Heb. 8:8, 13; 12:24. See also Jer. 31:31; 32:40.
[22] I.e., double justification. See above, No. 5, 'Justification by Faith', II.5 and n; see also Wesley's letters to Thomas Church, Feb. 2, 1745, and June 17, 1746, and his *Letter to a Gentleman at Bristol*, Jan. 6, 1758. Cf. his *Remarks on Mr. Hill's Review* and *Remarks on Mr. Hill's Farrago Double-Distilled (Bibliog,* Nos. 341, 345, both in Vol. 13 of this edn.)
For some of Wesley's sources here, cf. Richard Baxter, *Confession* (1655), pp. 297, 344 ff., 362-63; John Goodwin, *Imputatio Fidei,* ch. 3(1); *Common Places of Martin Bucer,*

by the angel of God from heaven, saying, 'By myself have I sworn, saith the Lord', that 'in thy seed shall all the nations of the earth be blessed.'[23] It was yet more fully made known to Moses, to David, and to the prophets that followed; and through them to many of the people of God in their respective generations. But still the bulk even of these were ignorant of it; and very few understood it clearly. Still 'life and immortality' were not so 'brought to light' to the Jews of old as they are now unto us 'by the gospel'.[24]

8. Now this covenant saith not to sinful man, 'Perform unsinning obedience and live.' If this were the term, he would have no more benefit by all which Christ hath done and suffered for him than if he was required, in order to life,[25] to 'ascend into heaven and bring down Christ from above'; or to 'descend into the deep', into the invisible world, and 'bring up Christ from the dead'. It doth not require any impossibility to be done (although to mere man what it requires would be impossible, but not to man assisted by the Spirit of God); this were only to mock human weakness. Indeed, strictly speaking, the covenant of *grace* doth not require us to *do* anything at all, as absolutely and indispensably necessary in order to our justification, but only to *believe* in him who for the sake of his Son and the propitiation which he hath made, 'justifieth the ungodly that worketh not', and 'imputes his faith to him for righteousness'.[26] Even so Abraham 'believed in the Lord; and he counted it to him for righteousness'.[c] 'And he received the sign of circumcision, a seal of the righteousness of faith . . .; that he might be the father of all them that believe . . .; that righteousness might be imputed unto them also.'[d] 'Now it was not written for his sake alone that it (i.e. faith) was imputed to him; but for us also, to whom it shall be imputed' (to whom faith shall be imputed for righteousness, shall stand in the stead of

[c] Gen. 15:6.
[d] Rom. 4:11.

---

tr. and ed. by D. F. Wright, in *The Courtenay Library of Reformation Classics* (Appleford, Abingdon, Berks., England, The Sutton Courtenay Press, 1972), IV. 162.

[23] Gen. 22:16, 18.

[24] 2 Tim. 1:10.

[25] 'Life' rather than an expected 'live' appears in all edns. Wesley is evidently here balancing the noun 'life', as a state of being against its antonym, 'the dead'.

[26] Cf. Rom. 4:5.

perfect obedience, in order to our acceptance with God) 'if we
believe on him who raised up Jesus our Lord from the dead; who
was delivered' to death 'for our offences, and was raised again for
our justification',ᵉ 'for the assurance of the remission of our sins,
5　and of a second life to come to them that believe.'²⁷

9. What saith then the covenant of forgiveness, of unmerited
love, of pardoning mercy? 'Believe in the Lord Jesus Christ, and
thou shalt be saved.'²⁸ In the day thou believest, thou shalt surely
live. Thou shalt be restored to the favour of God; and in his
10　pleasure is life. Thou shalt be saved from the curse and from the
wrath of God. Thou shalt be quickened from the death of sin into
the life of righteousness. And if thou endure to the end, believing
in Jesus, thou shalt never taste the second death, but having
suffered with the Lord shalt also live and reign with him for ever
15　and ever.

10. Now 'this word is nigh thee'. This condition of life is plain,
easy, always at hand. 'It is in thy mouth and in thy heart' through
the operation of the Spirit of God. The moment 'thou believest in
thine heart in him whom God hath raised from the dead, and
20　confessest with thy mouth the Lord Jesus as thy Lord and thy
God, thou shalt be saved'²⁹ from condemnation, from the guilt
and punishment of thy *former* sins, and shalt have power to serve
God in true holiness all the *remaining* days of thy life.

11. What is the difference then between the 'righteousness
25　which is of the law' and the 'righteousness which is of faith'?
Between the first covenant, or the covenant of works, and the
second, the covenant of grace? The essential, unchangeable
difference is this: the one supposes him to whom it is given to be
already holy and happy,³⁰ created in the image and enjoying the
30　favour of God; and prescribes the condition whereon he may
continue therein, in love and joy, life and immortality. The other
supposes him to whom it is given to be now unholy and unhappy;
fallen short of the glorious image of God, having the wrath of God
abiding on him,³¹ and hastening through sin, whereby his soul is

ᵉ Rom. 4:23-25.

---

²⁷ π; The same point, in nearly these words, is made by John Goodwin, *Imputatio Fidei*,
pp. 15-18.
²⁸ Acts 16:31.　　　　　　　　　　　　　　　²⁹ Cf. Rom. 10:8-9.
³⁰ Cf. No. 5, 'Justification by Faith', I.4 and n.
³¹ See John 3:36.

dead, to bodily death and death everlasting. And to man in this state it prescribes the condition whereon he may regain the pearl he has lost; may recover the favour, and the image of God, may retrieve the life of God in his soul, and be restored to the knowledge and the love of God, which is the beginning of life 5 eternal.

12. Again, the covenant of works, in order to man's *continuance* in the favour of God, in his knowledge and love, in holiness and happiness, required of perfect man a *perfect* and uninterrupted *obedience* to every point of the law of God; whereas the covenant of 10 grace, in order to man's *recovery* of the favour and life of God, requires only *faith*—living faith in him who through God justifies him that *obeyed not.*

13. Yet again: the covenant of works required of Adam and all his children to *pay the price themselves*, in consideration of which 15 they were to receive all the future blessings of God. But in the covenant of grace, seeing we have nothing to pay, God 'frankly forgives us all';[32] provided only that we believe in him who hath *paid the price for us*; who hath given himself a 'propitiation for our sins, for the sins of the whole world'.[33]   20

14. Thus the first covenant required what is now *afar off* from all the children of men, namely, unsinning obedience, which is far from those who are 'conceived and born in sin';[34] whereas the second requires what is nigh at hand, as though it should say, Thou art sin: God is love. Thou by sin art fallen short of the glory 25 of God; yet there is mercy with him. Bring then all thy sins to the pardoning God, and they shall vanish away as a cloud. If thou wert not ungodly there would be no room for him to justify thee as ungodly. But now draw near, in full assurance of faith. He speaketh, and it is done. Fear not, only believe; for even the just 30 God 'justifieth all that believe in Jesus'.[35]

II.1. These things considered, it will be easy to show, as I proposed to do in the second place, the folly of trusting in the 'righteousness which is of the law', and the wisdom of 'submitting to the righteousness which is of faith'.   35

---

[32] Cf. Luke 7:42.   [33] 1 John 2:2.
[34] Cf. Ps. 51:5. See also BCP, Baptism, Exhortation. This phrase, borrowed by Cranmer from Archbishop Herman von Wied, remains in the Church of England text. The idea in altered forms is retained in the Scottish and South African rites; the phrase was dropped from the American Episcopal Prayer Book in 1928.
[35] Cf. Rom. 4:5.

The folly of those who still trust in the 'righteousness which is of the law', the terms of which are, 'Do this and live,' may abundantly appear from hence.[36] They set out wrong. Their very first step is a fundamental mistake. For before they can ever think
5 of claiming any blessing on the terms of this covenant, they must suppose themselves to be in his state with whom this covenant was made. But how vain a supposition is this, since it was made with Adam in a state of innocence. How weak therefore must that whole building be which stands on such a foundation! And how
10 foolish are they who thus build on the sand![37] Who seem never to have considered that the covenant of works was not given to man when he was dead in trespasses and sins,[38] but when he was alive to God, when he knew no sin, but was holy as God is holy;[39] who forget that it was never designed for the *recovery* of the favour and
15 life of God once lost, but only for the *continuance* and increase thereof, till it should be complete in life everlasting.[40]

2. Neither do they consider, who are thus 'seeking to establish their own righteousness which is of the law', what manner of obedience or righteousness that is which the law indispensably
20 requires. It must be perfect and entire in every point, or it answers not the demand of the law. But which of you is able to perform such obedience? Or, consequently, to live thereby? Who among you fulfils every jot and tittle even of the outward commandments of God? Doing nothing, great or small, which God forbids?
25 Leaving nothing undone which he enjoins? Speaking no 'idle word'?[41] Having your conversation always 'meet to minister grace to the hearers'?[42] And 'whether you eat or drink, or whatever you do, doing all to the glory of God'?[43] And how much less are you able to fulfil all the inward commandments of God? Those which
30 require that every temper and motion of your soul should be holiness unto the Lord? Are you able to 'love God with all your

---

[36] Orig. (1746 and 1754), 'thence', altered in Wesley's hand in Vol. 1 of his *Works*, and in the printed errata to that volume; in this instance the revision had also been made in 1769 (followed by 1787), while the *Works* followed the text of 1754.

[37] See Matt. 7:26-27.   [38] Eph. 2:1.

[39] 2 Cor. 5:21; cf. 1 Pet. 1:16.

[40] Note how the covenant of works is reinstated here, by implication, for those who have been justified (who have thus recovered 'the favour and life of God once lost') and have thus been started on their way to sanctification. Cf. Nos. 27, 'Sermon on the Mount, VII', § 2; 35, 'The Law Established through Faith, I', II.6; and 45, 'The New Birth', III.1. Cf. also JWJ, Jan. 11, 1744, and *Notes* for Jas. 2:22.

[41] Matt. 12:36.

[42] Cf. Eph. 4:29.   [43] Cf. 1 Cor. 10:31.

heart'?[44] To love all mankind as your own soul? To 'pray without ceasing'? 'In everything to give thanks'?[45] To have God always before you? And to keep every affection, desire, and thought in obedience to his law?

3. You should farther consider that the righteousness of the law requires, not only the obeying every command of God, negative and positive, internal and external, but likewise in the perfect degree. In every instance whatever the voice of the law is, 'Thou shalt serve the Lord thy God with all thy strength.'[46] It allows no abatement of any kind. It excuses no defect. It condemns every coming short of the full measure of obedience, and immediately pronounces a curse on the offender. It regards only the invariable rules of justice, and saith, 'I know not to show mercy.'[47]

4. Who then can appear before such a Judge, who is 'extreme to mark what is done amiss'?[48] How weak are they who desire to be tried at the bar where 'no flesh living can be justified'![49]—none of the offspring of Adam. For suppose we did now keep every commandment with all our strength; yet one single breach which ever was utterly destroys our whole claim to life. If we have ever offended, in any one point, this righteousness is at an end. For the law condemns all who do not perform uninterrupted as well as perfect obedience. So that according to the sentence of this, for him who hath once sinned, in any degree, 'there remaineth only a fearful looking for of fiery indignation which shall devour the adversaries'[50] of God.

5. Is it not then the very foolishness of folly[51] for fallen man to seek life by this righteousness? For man, who was 'shapen in wickedness', and 'in sin did his mother conceive him';[52] man, who

---

[44] Cf. Deut. 6:5; Matt. 22:37, etc.

[45] 1 Thess. 5:17-18.   [46] Cf. Mark 12:30; Luke 10:27.

[47] This, of course, was the point at issue in Shakespeare, *The Merchant of Venice*, which Wesley not only knew but annotated; cf. IV. i. 179-82:

> . . . In the course of justice none of us
> Should see salvation: we do pray for mercy,
> And that same prayer doth teach us all to render
> The deeds of mercy.

See also Jas. 2:13.

[48] Ps. 130:3 (BCP).

[49] Cf. Ps. 143:2; Rom. 3:20; Gal. 2:16.

[50] Cf. Heb. 10:26-27.

[51] Cf. Prov. 14:24; 15:2, 14.

[52] Ps. 51:5 (BCP).

is by nature all 'earthly, sensual, devilish';[53] altogether 'corrupt and abominable';[54] in whom, till he find grace, 'dwelleth no good thing';[55] nay, who cannot of himself think one good thought? Who is indeed all sin, a mere lump of ungodliness, and who commits
5 sin in every breath he draws; whose actual transgressions, in word and deed, are more in number than the hairs of his head! What stupidity, what senselessness must it be for such an unclean, guilty, helpless worm as this to dream of seeking acceptance by 'his own righteousness', of living by 'the righteousness which is of
10 the law'!

6. Now whatsoever considerations prove the folly of trusting in the 'righteousness which is of the law' prove equally the wisdom of submitting to 'the righteousness which is of God by faith'.[56] This were easy to be shown with regard to each of the preceding
15 considerations. But to waive this, the wisdom of the first step hereto, the disclaiming our own righteousness, plainly appears from hence, that it is acting according to truth, to the real nature of things. For what is it more than to acknowledge with our heart as well as lips the true state wherein we are?[57] To acknowledge
20 that we bring with us into the world a corrupt, sinful nature; more corrupt indeed than we can easily conceive, or find words to express? That hereby we are prone to all that is evil, and averse from all that is good; that we are full of pride, self-will, unruly passions, foolish desires; vile and inordinate affections; lovers of
25 the world, lovers of pleasure more than lovers of God?[58] That our lives have been no better than our hearts, but many ways ungodly and unholy, insomuch that our actual sins, both in word and deed, have been as the stars of heaven for multitude?[59] That on all these accounts we are displeasing to him who is of purer eyes than to
30 behold iniquity,[60] and deserve nothing from him but indignation and wrath and death, the due wages of sin?[61] That we cannot by any of our righteousness (for indeed we have none at all) nor by any of our works (for they are as the tree from which they grow) appease the wrath of God, or avert the punishment we have justly
35 deserved? Yea, that if left to ourselves we shall only wax worse and

---

[53] Jas. 3:15.
[54] Cf. Ps. 53:1 (AV).
[55] Rom. 7:18.
[56] Phil. 3:9.
[57] I.e., repentance; cf. No. 7, 'The Way to the Kingdom', II.1 and n.
[58] See 2 Tim. 3:4.
[59] Deut. 1:10; 10:22; 28:62.
[60] See Hab. 1:13.
[61] See Rom. 6:23.

worse, sink deeper and deeper into sin, offend God more and more both with our evil works and with the evil tempers of our carnal mind, till we fill up the measure of our iniquities, and bring upon ourselves swift destruction?[62] And is not this the very state wherein by nature we are? To acknowledge this, then, both with 5 our heart and lips, that is, to disclaim our own righteousness, 'the righteousness which is of the law', is to act according to the real nature of things, and consequently is an instance of true wisdom.

7. The wisdom of submitting to 'the righteousness of faith' appears farther from this consideration, that it is 'the 10 righteousness of God'. I mean here, it is that method of reconciliation with God which hath been chosen and established by God himself, not only as he is the God of wisdom, but as he is the sovereign Lord of heaven and earth, and of every creature which he hath made. Now as it is not meet for man to say unto 15 God, 'What dost thou?'—as none who is not utterly void of understanding will contend with one that is mightier than he, with him whose kingdom ruleth over all—so it is true wisdom, it is a mark of a sound understanding, to acquiesce in whatever he hath chosen, to say in this as in all things, 'It is the Lord; let him do 20 what seemeth him good.'[63]

8. It may be farther considered that it was of mere grace, of free love, of undeserved mercy, that God hath vouchsafed to sinful man any way of reconciliation with himself; that we were not cut away from his hand, and utterly blotted out of his remembrance. 25 Therefore whatever method he is pleased to appoint, of his tender mercy, of his unmerited goodness, whereby his enemies, who have so deeply revolted from him, so long and obstinately rebelled against him, may still find favour in his sight, it is doubtless our wisdom to accept it with all thankfulness. 30

9. To mention but one consideration more. It is wisdom to aim at the best end by the best means.[64] Now the best end which any creature can pursue is happiness in God.[65] And the best end a

[62] Cf. 2 Pet. 2:1. [63] 1 Sam. 3:18.
[64] Cf. St. Thomas, *Summa Theologica*, II.ii, Q. 45.
[65] Here Wesley's eudaemonism is explicitly stated and linked to its premise 'in God' (μετουσία θεοῦ). This, too, is one of Wesley's favourite themes. Cf. Nos. 17, 'The Circumcision of the Heart', I.12; 77, 'Spiritual Worship', III.6, 7; 87, 'The Danger of Riches', I.12 (for a negative statement); and 149, 'On Love', III.4. See also Wesley's letters to Frances Godfrey, Aug. 2, 1789, and to Thomas Broadbent, Jan. 29, 1791.
Susanna Wesley held the same view. In a letter to her brother, Samuel Annesley, Jan. 20, 1722, she had written: 'Unspeakable are the blessings of privacy and leisure when the

fallen creature can pursue is the recovery of the favour and image of God.[66] But the best, indeed the only means under heaven given to man whereby he may regain the favour of God, which is better than life itself, or the image of God, which is the true life of the
5 soul, is the submitting to the 'righteousness which is of faith', the believing in the only-begotten Son of God.[67]

III.1. Whosoever therefore thou art who desirest to be forgiven and reconciled to the favour of God, do not say in thy heart, 'I must *first do this:* I must *first* conquer every sin, break off every evil
10 word and work, and do all good to all men; or I must *first* go to Church, receive the Lord's Supper, hear more sermons, and say more prayers.'[68] Alas, my brother, thou art clean gone out of the way. Thou art still 'ignorant of the righteousness of God', and art 'seeking to establish thy own righteousness'[69] as the ground of thy
15 reconciliation. Knowest thou not that thou canst do nothing but sin till thou art reconciled to God? Wherefore then dost thou say, I must do this and this *first,* and then I shall believe? Nay, but *first believe.* Believe in the Lord Jesus Christ, the propitiation for thy sins.[70] Let this good foundation *first* be laid, and then thou shalt do
20 all things well.[71]
2. Neither say in thy heart, 'I can't be accepted yet because I am not *good enough.*' Who is good enough, who ever was, to merit acceptance at God's hands? Was ever any child of Adam good enough for this? Or will any, till the consummation of all things?
25 And as for thee, thou art not good at all; there dwelleth in thee no

---

mind emerges from the corrupt animality to which she is united, and by a flight peculiar to her nature, soars beyond the bounds of time and place, in contemplation of the Invisible Supreme, whom she perceives to be her only happiness, her proper centre!' (Moore, I. 328). Cf. also John Norris, 'Contemplation and Love', in *A Collection of Miscellanies* (1723), pp. 238–39, and Bishop Francis Gastrell, *The Certainty of Necessity of Religion in General* (1697), 315, 317, 336. See also No. 5, 'Justification by Faith', I.4 and n.

[66] A distinctive emphasis here on justification as the recovery of the favour of God (the standard Protestant emphasis) but also the restoration of the lost image of God (the standard catholic emphasis); cf. above, No. 1, *Salvation by Faith*, §1 and n.

[67] See John 3:18.

[68] Cf. Wesley's controversy with Philip Molther in JWJ, Dec. 31, 1739, over 'the way to faith', where Wesley takes a different line: 'I believe [by contrast with Molther and the Moravians] it right for him who knows he has not faith . . . to go to church, to communicate, to fast', etc. Here, then, is an illustration of Wesley's way of shifting ground according to his opposition. Moravian antinomianism provoked him to defend 'the means of grace'; Anglican over-confidence in the means of grace calls for a rebuke against any false reliance on them as *necessary conditions* of justification.

[69] Cf. Rom. 10:3. [70] See 1 John 2:2; 4:10.
[71] See Mark 7:37.

good thing.[72] And thou never wilt be till thou believe in Jesus. Rather thou wilt find thyself worse and worse. But is there any need of being worse in order to be accepted?[73] Art thou not *bad enough* already? Indeed thou art, and that God knoweth. And thou thyself canst not deny it. Then delay not. All things are now ready. 5 'Arise, and wash away thy sins.'[74] The fountain is open. Now is the time to wash thee white in the blood of the Lamb. Now he shall 'purge thee as with hyssop, and thou shalt be clean; he shall wash thee, and thou shalt be whiter than snow'.[75]

3. Do not say, 'But I am not *contrite enough:* I am not sensible 10 enough of my sins.' I know it. I would to God thou wert more sensible of them, more contrite a thousandfold than thou art. But do not stay for this. It may be God will make thee so, not before thou believest, but by believing. It may be thou wilt not weep much till thou lovest much,[76] because thou hast had much 15 forgiven. In the meantime, look unto Jesus.[77] Behold how he loveth thee![78] What could he have done more for thee which he hath not done?

> O Lamb of God, was ever pain,
> Was ever love like thine![79]   20

Look steadily upon him till he looks on thee, and breaks thy hard heart. Then shall thy 'head be waters, and thy eyes fountains of tears'.[80]

4. Nor yet do thou say, 'I must *do* something more before I come to Christ.' I grant, supposing thy Lord should delay his 25 coming, it were meet and right to wait[81] for his appearing in doing,

---

[72] See Rom. 7:18.

[73] See Rom. 6:1, and Nos. 35, 36, 'The Law Established through Faith', Discourses I and II.

[74] Acts 22:16.   [75] Cf. Ps. 51:7.   [76] See Luke 7:47-48.

[77] See Heb. 12:2.   [78] See John 11:36.

[79] Samuel Wesley, Sen. (1662–1735) closes 'On the Crucifixion' with these two lines. The poem was a favourite of the Wesleys, first published in John Wesley's *Collection of Psalms and Hymns* (Charleston, 1737)—where his father's authorship is not credited—and frequently reprinted thereafter. Adam Clarke first identified the author and entitled the poem, 'A Hymn on the Passion'. Sugden says that the MS of it was found in the Epworth Rectory garden after the fire of 1709. Cf. Wesley's letter to Lady Maxwell, July 10, 1764.

[80] Cf. Jer. 9:1.

[81] Another characteristic usage. 'To wait', for Wesley, was not at all a passive stance; he speaks of 'waiting' as active obedience to God's commands and rejects 'quietism' on principle. Even so, good works done while 'waiting' are not 'meritorious'; thus he rejects moralism with equal consistency. Cf. MS Minutes for Aug. 2, 1745 (§ 50): 'Q.11. How shall we wait for the fulfilling of this promise [of sanctification]? A. In universal obedience;

so far as thou hast power, whatsoever he hath commanded thee. But there is no necessity for making such a supposition. How knowest thou that he will delay? Perhaps he will appear as the day-spring from on high,[82] before the morning light. O do not set

5 him a time. Expect him every hour. Now, he is nigh! Even at the door!

5. And to what end wouldst thou wait for *more sincerity*[83] before thy sins are blotted out? To make thee more worthy of the grace of God? Alas, thou art still 'establishing thy own righteousness'. He

10 will have mercy, not because thou art worthy of it, but because his compassions fail not;[84] not because thou art righteous, but because Jesus Christ hath atoned for thy sins.

Again, if there be anything good in *sincerity*, why dost thou expect it *before* thou hast faith?—seeing faith itself is the only root

15 of whatever is really good and holy.

Above all, how long wilt thou forget that whatsoever thou dost, or whatsoever thou hast, before thy sins are forgiven thee, it avails nothing with God toward the procuring of thy forgiveness? Yea, and that it must all be cast behind thy back, trampled under foot,

20 made no account of, or thou wilt never find favour in God's sight? Because until then thou canst not ask it as a mere sinner, guilty, lost, undone, having nothing to plead, nothing to offer to God but only the merits of his well-beloved Son, 'who loved *thee*, and gave himself for *thee*'.[85]

25 6. To conclude. Whosoever thou art, O man, who hast the sentence of death in thyself, who feelest thyself a condemned sinner, and hast the wrath of God abiding on thee:[86] unto thee said the Lord, not 'Do this; perfectly obey all my commands and live:' but, 'Believe in the Lord Jesus Christ, and thou shalt be saved.'[87]

30 'The word of faith is nigh unto thee.' Now, at this instant, in the present moment, and in thy present state, sinner as thou art, just as thou art, believe the gospel,[88] and 'I will be merciful unto thy unrighteousness, and thy iniquities will I remember no more.'[89]

---

in keeping all the commandments; in denying ourselves, and taking up our cross daily; [with] prayer, searching the Scripture, communicating, and fasting.' Cf. also No. 16, 'The Means of Grace', III.1.

[82] Luke 1:78.

[83] 'Sincerity' was a much discussed virtue, valued more highly by the pietists than the moralists. Cf. above, No. 2, *The Almost Christian*, I.9 and n.

[84] Lam. 3:22.   [85] Cf. Gal. 2:20.   [86] See John 3:36.

[87] Acts 16:31; cf. Rom. 10:9.   [88] Mark 1:15.   [89] Cf. Heb. 8:12.

THE WAY TO THE KINGDOM

AN INTRODUCTORY COMMENT

This sermon has a double text. The second one (Rom. 14:17) is invoked informally in I.1, and reminds us of Wesley's first 'tombstone sermon' at Epworth, June 6, 1742, which was never published but probably has its residues here (cf. JWJ):

After [the rector's] sermon [against 'enthusiasm'] John Taylor stood in the churchyard, and gave notice as the people were coming out, 'Mr. Wesley, not being permitted to preach in the church, designs to preach here at six o'clock.'

Accordingly at six I came, and found such a congregation as I believe Epworth never saw before. I stood near the east end of the church, upon my father's tombstone, and cried, 'The Kingdom of heaven is not meats and drinks, but righteousness, and peace, and joy in the Holy Ghost.'

Wesley records having preached from Rom. 14:17 seventeen times in the half-decade of 1739–43, and only twelve times thereafter (the last in 1791).

The formal text here is Mark 1:15, a favourite of Wesley's in his oral preaching (he records having used it one hundred and ninety times in the forty-eight-year span, 1742–90). The result, however, is a single sermon with an integrated, cumulative argument that progresses from a negative comment on what true religion is not (viz., correct praxis and doctrine) to a positive definition of it (viz., love of God and neighbour, both as empowered by grace). These lead into an exhortation to repentance and belief which includes another summary statement about repentance as true self-knowledge and authentic contrition (as in No. 6, 'The Righteousness of Faith', II.6). Belief is never 'bare assent' but rather an assenting trust whose first-fruits are reconciliation and peace. All this points to the conclusion: a celebration of Christian joy 'in the Holy Ghost'.

It is worth comparing this sermon with Wesley's later published sermon on the same text (No. 14, The Repentance of Believers). The latter makes the rather different point that becomes important once the sola fide *has been accepted (especially if also misconstrued), viz., that the Christian's progress in sanctification does not preclude repentance. Indeed, since repentance means self-knowledge, the farther Christians are along their way to sanctification, the more sensitive they are to their shortfalls in faith, hope, and love.*

The Way to the Kingdom

Mark 1:15

The kingdom of God is at hand: repent ye,
and believe the gospel.

5   These words naturally lead us to consider, first, the nature of true religion, here termed by our Lord 'the kingdom of God', which, saith he, 'is at hand'; and secondly, the way thereto, which he points out in those words, 'Repent ye, and believe the gospel.'

    I.1 We are, first, to consider the nature of true religion, here
10 termed by our Lord 'the kingdom of God'. The same expression the great Apostle uses in his Epistle to the Romans, where he likewise explains his Lord's words, saying, 'The kingdom of God is not meat and drink; but righteousness, and peace, and joy in the Holy Ghost.'[a]
15   2. 'The kingdom of God', or true religion, 'is not meat and drink.' It is well known that not only the unconverted Jews, but great numbers of those who had received the faith of Christ, were notwithstanding 'zealous of the law',[b] even the ceremonial law of Moses. Whatsoever therefore they found written therein, either
20 concerning meat and drink offerings, or the distinction between clean and unclean meats, they not only observed themselves, but vehemently pressed the same even on those 'among the Gentiles' (or heathens) 'who were turned to God'.[1] Yea, to such a degree that some of them taught, wheresoever they came among them,
25 'Except ye be circumcised, and keep the law' (the whole ritual law), 'ye cannot be saved.'[c]
    3. In opposition to these the Apostle declares, both here and in many other places, that true religion does not consist in *meat* and *drink*, or in any ritual observances; nor indeed in any outward
30 thing whatever, in anything exterior to the heart; the whole

---

[a] Rom. 14:17 [cf. 2 Tim. 2:22; Heb. 12:11].
[b] Acts 21:20.
[c] Acts 15:1, 24.

---

[1] Cf. Acts 15:19.

substance thereof lying in 'righteousness, peace, and joy in the Holy Ghost'.

4. Not in any *outward thing*, such as *forms* or *ceremonies*, even of the most excellent kind. Supposing these to be ever so decent and significant, ever so expressive of inward things; supposing them ever so helpful, not only to the vulgar, whose thought reaches little farther than their sight, but even to men of understanding, men of strong capacities, as doubtless they may sometimes be; yea, supposing them, as in the case of the Jews, to be appointed by God himself; yet even during the period of time wherein that appointment remains in force, true religion does not principally consist therein—nay, strictly speaking, not at all. How much more must this hold concerning such rites and forms as are only of human appointment! The religion of Christ rises infinitely higher and lies immensely deeper than all these. These are good in their place; just so far as they are in fact subservient to true religion.[2] And it were superstition to object against them while they are applied only as occasional helps to human weakness. But let no man carry them farther. Let no man dream that they have any intrinsic worth; or that religion cannot subsist without them. This were to make them an abomination to the Lord.[3]

5. The nature of religion is so far from consisting in these, in forms of worship, or rites and ceremonies, that it does not properly consist in any outward actions of what kind so ever.[4] It is true a man cannot have any religion who is guilty of vicious, immoral actions; or who does to others what he would not they should do to him if he were in the same circumstance. And it is also true that he can have no real religion who 'knows to do good, and doth it not'.[5] Yet may a man both abstain from outward evil, and do good, and still have no religion. Yea, two persons may do

[2] That Wesley himself did not dispense wih symbols and ceremonials would appear from his insistence on wearing his gown and cassock both for his field preaching and in his meetings with the societies; see JWJ, Sept. 9, 1743. His exhortations to 'use all the means of grace' were turned into the third of his *General Rules* for all Methodists. This is a reflection of his firm distinction between vestments and ceremonies being *used,* and their being *relied* on; cf. George Whitefield, *A Short Account of God's Dealings with the Reverend Mr. Whitefield* (London, Strahan, 1740), p. 44. It was also a sign of Wesley's quiet negation of the famous Puritan rejection of vestments, prelacy, and the BCP as 'popish remnants'. Thus, he could deny all *intrinsic* value to any external sign and still avoid any radical iconoclasm.
[3] Deut. 7:25, etc.
[4] A parallel rejection of moralism, on the one hand, and of antinomianism, on the other.
[5] Cf. Jas. 4:17.

the same outward work—suppose, feeding the hungry, or clothing the naked—and in the meantime one of these may be truly religious and the other have no religion at all; for the one may act from the love of God, and the other from the love of
5 praise. So manifest it is that although true religion naturally leads to every good word and work, yet the real nature thereof lies deeper still, even in 'the hidden man of the heart'.[6]

6. I say of the *heart*. For neither does religion consist in *orthodoxy* or *right opinions*;[7] which, although they are not properly
10 outward things, are not in the heart, but the understanding. A man may be orthodox in every point; he may not only espouse right opinions, but zealously defend them against all opposers; he may think justly concerning the incarnation of our Lord, concerning the ever blessed Trinity, and every other doctrine
15 contained in the oracles of God.[8] He may assent to all the three creeds—that called the Apostles', the Nicene, and the Athanasian—and yet 'tis possible he may have no religion at all, no more than a Jew, Turk, or pagan. He may be almost as orthodox as the devil (though indeed not altogether; for every man errs in

---

[6] 1 Pet. 3:4.

[7] Wesley's attitudes toward 'orthodoxy' and 'heresy' were complex. Here, his thesis is that orthodoxy—like ceremonialism and moralism—is not of the essence of true religion, and he belabours the point that the devil is more orthodox than the soundest Christian theologian. This is a favourite point with him, as in Nos. 33, 'Sermon on the Mount, XIII', III.1; 62, 'The End of Christ's Coming', III.5; 120, 'The Unity of the Divine Being', §15; 127, 'On the Wedding Garment', §15. Cf. also Wesley's *Plain Account of the People called Methodists*, I.2; and his letters to James Clark, July 3 and Sept. 18, 1756; Bishop Warburton, Nov. 26, 1762; and John Erskine, Apr. 24, 1765. Cf. also *Some Remarks on a Defence of . . . Aspasio Vindicated* (*Bibliog*, No. 296, Vol. 13 of this edn.) See also Glanvill, *Defence of Preaching*, p. 83; and Norris, *Miscellanies*, pp. 173-202.

To these may be added his slogan for theological pluralism ('to think and let think'): cf. Nos. 20, *The Lord Our Righteousness*, II.20; 37, 'The Nature of Enthusiasm', §36; 38, 'A Caution against Bigotry', II.3; 39, 'Catholic Spirit' (entire); 53, *On the Death of George Whitefield*, III.1; 55, *On the Trinity*, §2; 74, 'Of the Church', §19; 127, 'On the Wedding Garment', §14; 130, 'On Living without God', §15. See also JWJ, May 29, 1745; Dec. 3, 1776; Oct. 3, 1783; and Wesley's letters to Miss March, Mar. 29, 1760; Dr. Warburton, Nov. 26, 1762; Henry Venn, June 22, 1763; John Newton, Apr. 9, 1765; Philothea Briggs, June 20, 1772; Thomas Wride, Mar. 9, 1780; Joseph Benson, May 21, 1781; Mr. Howton, Oct. 3, 1783; Dr. Tomline, Mar. 1790. See also *The Character of a Methodist*, §1; and *Some Observations on Liberty*, §1 (*Bibliog*, No. 360, Vol. 15 of this edn.).

To conclude from all this, however, that Wesley was indifferent to the issues involved in sound doctrine is to misunderstand him. He had a clear view of heresy as deviation from the core of 'standing revelation'; and had no hesitation in denouncing views that threatened this core. See his *Doctrine of Original Sin* III.i, vii; IV. iv ('First Essay'). If Methodism may rightly be charged with theological indifferentism, this has no valid grounds in Wesley himself.

[8] Cf. No. 5, 'Justification by Faith', §2 and n.

something, whereas we can't well conceive him[9] to hold any erroneous opinion) and may all the while be as great a stranger as he to the religion of the heart.

7. This alone is religion, truly so called: this alone is in the sight of God of great price. The Apostle sums it all up in three particulars—'righteousness, and peace, and joy in the Holy Ghost'.[10] And first, *righteousness*.[11] We cannot be at a loss concerning this if we remember the words of our Lord describing the two grand branches thereof, on which 'hang all the law and the prophets':[12] 'Thou shalt love the Lord thy God with all thy heart, and with all thy mind, and with all thy soul, and with all thy strength. This is the first and great commandment,'[d] the first and great branch of Christian righteousness. Thou shalt delight thyself in the Lord thy God; thou shalt seek and find all happiness in him. He shall be 'thy shield, and thy exceeding great reward',[13] in time and in eternity. All thy bones shall say, 'Whom have I in heaven but thee? And there is none upon earth that I desire beside thee!'[14] Thou shalt hear and fulfil his word who saith, 'My son, give me thy heart.'[15] And having given him thy heart, thy inmost soul, to reign there without a rival, thou mayest well cry out in the fullness of thy heart, 'I will love thee, O Lord, my strength. The Lord is my strong rock and my defence: my Saviour, my God, and my might, in whom I will trust; my buckler, the horn also of my salvation, and my refuge.'[16]

8. And the second commandment is like unto this; the second great branch of Christian righteousness is closely and inseparably connected therewith, even 'Thou shalt love thy neighbour as thyself.'[17] 'Thou shalt love'—thou shalt embrace with the most tender goodwill, the most earnest and cordial affection, the most inflamed desires of preventing or removing all evil and of procuring for him every possible good—'thy neighbour'; that is, not only thy friend, thy kinsman, or thy acquaintance; not only the

---

[d] Mark 12:30 [actually Matt. 22:37-38].

---

[9] I.e., the devil.   [10] Cf. Rom. 14:17.
[11] Cf. No. 29, 'Sermon on the Mount, IX', §20.
[12] Matt. 22:40.   [13] Gen. 15:1.
[14] Ps. 73:25.
[15] Cf. Prov. 23:26.
[16] Cf. Ps. 18:1 (BCP), where the text reads 'stony rock', and Ps. 31:3 (BCP), 'And be thou my strong rock, and house of defence. . . .'
[17] Matt. 22:39, etc.

virtuous, the friendly, him that loves thee, that prevents[18] or returns thy kindness; but every child of man, every human creature,[19] every soul which God hath made: not excepting him whom thou never hast seen in the flesh, whom thou knowest not
5 either by face or name; not excepting him whom thou knowest to be evil and unthankful, him that still despitefully uses and persecutes thee.[20] Him thou shalt 'love as thyself'; with the same invariable thirst after his happiness in every kind,[21] the same unwearied care to screen him from whatever might grieve or hurt
10 either his soul or body.

9. Now is not this love 'the fulfilling of the law'?[22] The sum of all Christian righteousness? Of all inward righteousness; for it necessarily implies 'bowels of mercies, humbleness of mind'[23] (seeing 'love is not puffed up'),[24] 'gentleness, meekness,
15 long-suffering'[25] (for love 'is not provoked', but 'believeth, hopeth, endureth all things'):[26] and of all outward righteousness, for 'love worketh no evil to his neighbour',[27] either by word or deed. It cannot willingly either hurt or grieve anyone. And it is zealous of good works.[28] Every lover of mankind, as he hath
20 opportunity, 'doth good unto all men',[29] being ('without partiality and without hypocrisy') 'full of mercy and good fruits'.[30]

---

[18] Note in this one paragraph the use of 'preventing' in the sense of *hinder* and of 'prevent' in its more literal sense of *precede*.

[19] Wesley's standard definition of neighbour, as appears from Nos. 2, *The Almost Christian*, II.2; 18, 'The Marks of the New Birth', III.3; 52, *The Reformation of Manners*, III.8; 65, 'The Duty of Reproving our Neighbour', II.2; 84, *The Important Question*, III.2; 100, 'On Pleasing All Men', §1; 107, 'On God's Vineyard', I.9; 112, *On Laying the Foundation of the New Chapel*, II.1; 114, *On the Death of John Fletcher*, I.3. No such definition appears in the *OED*. But Wesley could have found it in Thomas Sprat, *Sermons Preached on Several Occasions* (1722), p. 101; in Poole's *Annotations* (on Ps. 15:3); in Law's *Serious Call* (*Works*, IV. 188, 216-25); and in Fleury, *The Manners . . . of the Christians*, p. 19.

[20] Matt. 5:44.

[21] Note here the 'socialization' of eudaemonism: the subjective 'thirst for happiness' is understood as interdependent with the Christian's readiness to seek and serve his neighbour's 'happiness in every kind' . . . 'procuring for him every possible good'. Cf. No. 5, 'Justification by Faith', I.4 and n. This premise of Wesley's social ethic was revolutionary in both its intention and partial effect; cf. Semmel, *Methodist Revolution*, chs. 1 and 3.

[22] Rom. 13:10.

[23] Col. 3:12.

[24] 1 Cor. 13:4; note Wesley's preference for 'love' instead of the AV's 'charity'; cf. No. 17, 'The Circumcision of the Heart', I.2 and n.

[25] Col. 3:12.

[26] 1 Cor. 13:5, 7.

[27] Rom. 13:10.

[28] Titus 2:14.

[29] Cf. Gal. 6:10.

[30] Jas. 3:17.

10. But true religion, or a heart right toward God and man, implies happiness as well as holiness.[31] For it is not only righteousness, but also 'peace and joy in the Holy Ghost'.[32] What peace? 'The peace of God', which God only can give, and the world cannot take away; the peace 'which passeth all under- 5 standing',[33] all (barely) rational conception; being a supernatural sensation, a divine taste of 'the powers of the world to come';[34] such as the natural man knoweth not, how wise soever in the things of this world; nor, indeed, can he know it in his present state, 'because it is spiritually discerned'.[35] It is a peace that 10 banishes all doubt, all painful uncertainty, the Spirit of God 'bearing witness with the spirit' of a Christian that he is 'a child of God'.[36] And it banishes fear, all such fear as hath torment;[37] the fear of the wrath of God, the fear of hell, the fear of the devil, and, in particular, the fear of death: he that hath the peace of God 15 'desiring' (if it were the will of God) 'to depart and to be with Christ'.[38]

11. With this peace of God, wherever it is fixed in the soul, there is also 'joy in the Holy Ghost';[39] joy wrought in the heart by the Holy Ghost, by the ever-blessed Spirit of God. He it is that 20 worketh in us that calm, humble rejoicing in God, through Christ Jesus, 'by whom we have now received the atonement',[40] καταλλαγήν, the reconciliation with God; and that enables us boldly to confirm the truth of the royal Psalmist's declaration, 'Blessed is the man' (or rather, *happy*, אשרי היש) 'whose 25 unrighteousness is forgiven, and whose sin is covered.'[41] He it is

---

[31] 'Holiness', here and everywhere in Wesley, denotes *active love*—to God ('inward holiness') and to neighbour ('outward holiness'). Such love yields happiness less as an end product than as a by-product; see below, I.11-12. Cf. Nos. 6, 'The Righteousness of Faith', II.9 and n.; 18, 'The Marks of the New Birth', III.3; 24, 'Sermon on the Mount, IV', III.1; 45, 'The New Birth', III.1; 83, 'On Patience', §§9, 10; 84, *The Important Question*, III.2; 85, 'On Working Out Our Own Salvation', I.2; 107, 'On God's Vineyard', I.9; and 112, *On Laying the Foundation of the New Chapel*, II.1.

[32] Rom. 14:17.   [33] Phil. 4:7.
[34] Heb. 6:5.   [35] Cf. 1 Cor. 2:14.
[36] Cf. Rom. 8:16.   [37] See 1 John 4:18.
[38] Cf. Phil. 1:23.   [39] Rom. 14:17.   [40] Rom. 5:11.
[41] Cf. Ps. 32:1 (BCP). Wesley would appear to be quoting here from memory or else 'back-translating', since the Hebrew text omits היש ('the one'), presumably as understood; cf. Rudolf Kittel, ed., *Biblia Hebraica* (New York, American Bible Society, 1937), and his *apparatus technicus*. In the pamphlet editions of this sermon, in *Works*, and in Benson, Jackson, and Sugden, the Hebrew phrase is omitted altogether. For further comments on Wesley's use of Hebrew, cf. *A Farther Appeal*, Pt. I, I.6, III.5 (11:108, 125 of this edn.).

that inspires the Christian soul with that even, solid joy which arises from the testimony of the Spirit that he is a child of God; and that gives him to 'rejoice with joy unspeakable',[42] 'in hope of the glory of God'[43] —hope both of the glorious image of God,
5 which is in part and shall be fully 'revealed in him',[44] and of that crown of glory which fadeth not away, reserved in heaven for him.[45]

12. This holiness and happiness, joined in one, are sometimes styled in the inspired writings, 'the kingdom of God' (as by our
10 Lord in the text), and sometimes, 'the kingdom of heaven'. It is termed 'the kingdom of God' because it is the immediate fruit of God's reigning in the soul. So soon as ever he takes unto himself his mighty power, and sets up his throne in our hearts, they are instantly filled with this 'righteousness, and peace, and joy in the
15 Holy Ghost'.[46] It is called 'the kingdom of heaven' because it is (in a degree) heaven opened in the soul.[47] For whosoever they are that experience this, they can aver before angels and men,

> Everlasting life is won:
> Glory is on earth begun;[48]

20 according to the constant tenor of Scripture, which everywhere bears record, 'God hath given unto us eternal life, and this life is in his Son. He that hath the Son' (reigning in his heart) 'hath life,' even life everlasting.[e] For 'this is life eternal, to know thee, the only true God, and Jesus Christ, whom thou hast sent. . . .'[f] And
25 they to whom this is given may confidently address God, though they were in the midst of a fiery furnace,[49]

> Thee . . . , Lord, safe-shielded by thy power,
> Thee, Son of God, Jehovah, we adore,
> In form of man descending to appear:
30 To thee be ceaseless hallelujahs given.
> Praise, as in heaven thy throne, we offer here;
> For where thy presence is displayed, is heaven.[50]

[e] 1 John 5:11-12.
[f] John 17:3.

---

[42] 1 Pet. 1:8. [43] Rom. 5:2. [44] Cf. Rom. 8:18.
[45] 1 Pet. 1:4; 5:4. [46] Rom. 14:17.
[47] Cf. above, No. 4, *Scriptural Christianity*, III.5 and n.
[48] Charles Wesley, 'Hymn After the Sacrament,' st. 6, ll. 3-4, in *Hymns and Sacred Poems*, 1739, p. 191 (*Poet. Wks.*, I. 170).
[49] See Dan. 3:8-30.
[50] Mark Le Pla (1650–1715), vicar of Finchingfield (Essex), *A Paraphrase on the Song of*

13. And this 'kingdom of God', or of heaven, 'is at hand'. As these words were originally spoken they implied that 'the time' was then 'fulfilled',[51] God being made 'manifest in the flesh',[52] when he would set up his kingdom among men, and reign in the hearts of his people. And is not the time now fulfilled? For 'Lo 5 (saith he), I am with you always', you who preach remission of sins in my name, 'even unto the end of the world.'[g] Wheresoever therefore the gospel of Christ is preached, this his 'kingdom is nigh at hand'.[53] It is not far from every one of you. Ye may this hour enter thereinto, if so be ye hearken to his voice, 'Repent ye, 10 and believe the gospel.'

II.1. This is the way: walk ye in it.[54] And first, repent, that is, know yourselves.[55] This is the first repentance, previous to faith, even conviction, or self-knowledge. Awake, then, thou that sleepest.[56] Know thyself to be a sinner, and what manner of sinner 15 thou art. Know that corruption of thy inmost nature, whereby thou art very far gone from original righteousness, whereby 'the flesh lusteth' always 'contrary to the Spirit',[57] through that 'carnal mind which is enmity against God', which 'is not subject to the law of God, neither indeed can be'.[58] Know that thou art 20 corrupted in every power, in every faculty of thy soul, that thou art totally corrupted in every one of these, all the foundations being out of course. The eyes of thine understanding are darkened, so that they cannot discern God or the things of God.[59] The clouds

[g] Matt. 28:20.

---

the *Three Children* (1724), concluding stanza. John Wesley included it in *A Collection of Moral and Sacred Poems*, II. 101-34. This quotation appears in 'O Ananias, Azarias, and Misael. . .', st. xliv, ll. 14-19, p. 134.

[51] Mark 1:15.   [52] 1 Tim. 3:16.
[53] Luke 21:31.   [54] Isa. 30:21.
[55] Wesley's distinctive view of repentance as that self-knowledge which leads to contrition and to casting oneself on God's pardoning mercy in Christ ('trust' rather than 'assent'). Variations on this basic theme may be seen in Nos. 3, *'Awake, Thou That Sleepest'*, II.1; 6, 'The Righteousness of Faith', II.6; 14, *The Repentance of Believers*, III.2; 17, 'The Circumcision of the Heart', I.2; 21, 'Sermon on the Mount, I', I.4; 30, 'Sermon on the Mount, X', §7; 33, 'Sermon on the Mount, XIII', III.6; 78, 'Spiritual Idolatry', II.4; see also, below, II.6-7; and Wesley's *Notes* on Matt. 5:3. In No. 79, 'On Dissipation', §19, Wesley comments on William Law's inversion of faith and repentance in the *ordo salutis* in Law's *Spirit of Prayer* (*Works*, VII.3-143). For Wesley's denunciation of Bishop Bull's doctrine of repentance, see Nos. 150 and 151, 'Hypocrisy in Oxford' (Eng. text, I.7; Lat. text, I.6).
[56] Eph. 5:14.   [57] Cf. Gal. 5:17.
[58] Cf. Rom. 8:7.   [59] See Eph. 1:18; 4:18.

of ignorance and error rest upon thee, and cover thee with the shadow of death. Thou knowest nothing yet as thou oughtest to know, neither God, nor the world, nor thyself. Thy will is no longer the will of God, but is utterly perverse and distorted,
5 averse from all good, from all which God loves, and prone to all evil, to every abomination which God hateth. Thy affections are alienated from God, and scattered abroad over all the earth. All thy passions, both thy desires and aversions, thy joys and sorrows, thy hopes and fears, are out of frame, are either undue in their
10 degree, or placed on undue objects. So that there is no soundness in thy soul, but 'from the crown of the head to the sole of the foot' (to use the strong expression of the prophet) there are only 'wounds, and bruises, and putrefying sores'.[60]

2. Such is the inbred corruption of thy heart, of thy very inmost
15 nature. And what manner of branches canst thou expect to grow from such an evil root? Hence springs unbelief, ever departing from the living God; saying, 'Who is the Lord that I should serve him?'[61] 'Tush! Thou, God, carest not for it.'[62] Hence independence, affecting to be like the Most High; hence pride, in all its
20 forms, teaching thee to say, 'I am rich, and increased in goods, and have need of nothing.'[63] From this evil fountain flow forth the bitter streams of vanity, thirst of praise, ambition, covetousness, the lust of the flesh, the lust of the eye, and the pride of life.[64]

---

[60] Cf. Isa. 1:6.   [61] Cf. Judg. 9:28, 38; Job 21:15.
[62] Ps. 10:14 (BCP).   [63] Rev. 3:17.
[64] 1 John 2:16. Wesley's favourite blanket reference to what St. Augustine had already identified as the *triplex concupiscentia* which, as he and Wesley agreed, 'includes all sin' (cf. St. Augustine, *Confessions*, X.xxx.41, *et seq.*, and *Expositions on the Psalms*, VIII. 13; see also the letter, CCXX, to Boniface [427], §§5-9; and *On Patience*, 14-16, 'the concupiscence of the bad'). Wesley repeats the text tirelessly, and its suggestion to him that sin is overreach of what in themselves are innocent appetites (as in the animals) reinforced his notion of our human responsibility in all sin. For this text related especially to the greed for money, cf. John Cardinal Bona, *Precepts and Practical Rules for a Truly Christian Life*, p. 38. See also Law, *Serious Call*, (Works, IV, 18, 178).
Cf. also Nos. 2, *The Almost Christian*, II. (i.) 1; 4, *Scriptural Christianity*, I.6; 9, 'The Spirit of Bondage and of Adoption', I.5, III.7; 14, *The Repentance of Believers*, I.5; 17, 'The Circumcision of the Heart', I.13, II.9; 28, 'Sermon on the Mount, VIII', §14; 41, *Wandering Thoughts*, III.4; 44, *Original Sin*, II.9, 10; 50, 'The Use of Money', II.1-2; 68, 'The Wisdom of God's Counsels', §16; 78, 'Spiritual Idolatry', I.5-15; 80, 'On Friendship with the World', §16; 81, 'In What Sense we are to Leave the World', §11; 83, 'On Patience', §9; 84, *The Important Question*, I.3, III.10; 86, *A Call to Backsliders*, §4; 87, 'The Danger of Riches', I.12-16; 90, 'An Israelite Indeed', I.1; 95, 'On the Education of Children', §§8, 19; 107, 'On God's Vineyard', V. 3; 108, 'On Riches', II.2-3; 109, *The Trouble and Rest of Good Men*, I.3; 119, 'Walking by Sight and Walking by Faith', §17; 120, 'The Unity of the Divine Being', §12; 122, 'Causes of the Inefficacy of Christianity', §8;

From this arise anger, hatred, malice, revenge, envy, jealousy, evil surmisings;[65] from this, all the foolish and hurtful lusts that now 'pierce thee through with many sorrows', and if not timely prevented will at length 'drown thy soul in everlasting perdition'.[66]

3. And what fruits can grow on such branches as these? Only such as are bitter and evil continually. Of pride cometh contention,[67] vain boasting, seeking and receiving praise of men, and so robbing God of that glory which he cannot give unto another. Of the lust of the flesh come gluttony or drunkenness, luxury or sensuality, fornication, uncleanness, variously defiling that body which was designed for a temple of the Holy Ghost:[68] of unbelief, every evil word and work. But the time would fail, shouldst thou reckon up all; all the idle words thou hast spoken, provoking the Most High, grieving the Holy One of Israel; all the evil works thou hast done, either wholly evil in themselves, or at least not done to the glory of God. For thy actual sins are more than thou art able to express, more than the hairs of thy head. Who can number the sands of the sea, or the drops of rain, or thy iniquities?

4. And knowest thou not that 'the wages of sin is death'?[69]—death not only temporal, but eternal. 'The soul that sinneth, it shall die;'[70] for the mouth of the Lord hath spoken it.[71] It shall die the second death.[72] This is the sentence, to 'be punished' with never-ending death, 'with everlasting destruction from the presence of the Lord, and from the glory of his power'.[73] Knowest thou not that every sinner ἔνοχος ἐστι τῇ γεέννῃ τοῦ πυρός, not properly is 'in danger of hell-fire'[74]—that expression

---

125, 'On a Single Eye', II.1; 128, 'The Deceitfulness of the Human Heart', I.4; 131, 'The Danger of Increasing Riches', I.9, 10, 12, 15; 143, 'Public Diversions Denounced', III.2.

See also Wesley's *Notes* on 1 John 2:16, and his letters to Mrs. Pendarves, Feb. 11, 1731; to Dr. Burton, Oct. 10, 1735; to his brother Samuel, Oct. 15, 1735; and to James Hutton, Apr. 30, 1739.

[65] 1 Tim. 6:4.   [66] Cf. 1 Tim. 6:9, 10.
[67] Prov. 13:10.   [68] 1 Cor. 6:19.
[69] Rom. 6:23.   [70] Ezek. 18:4, 20.
[71] Isa. 1:20, etc.   [72] See Rev. 2:11; 20:6, 14; 21:8.   [73] 2 Thess. 1:9.

[74] See Matt 5:22; another quotation from memory since Wesley's own Greek text (*TR*) read ἔνοχος ἔσται εἰς τὴν γέενναν τοῦ πυρός. It would seem that ἐστι for ἔσται and τῇ γεέννῃ for τὴν γέενναν are typographical errors left reverently uncorrected by subsequent printers and editors. But translating ἔνοχος as 'under the sentence of hell-fire'—'doomed already'—ignores the *future* tense of ἔσται. For Wesley's more typical translation or exegeses of ἔνοχος (i.e., 'obnoxious' or 'liable to', 'subject to'), see Nos. 9, 'The Spirit of Bondage and of Adoption', II.2; 22, 'Sermon on the Mount, II', I.7, 9, 10; 62, 'The End of Christ's Coming', I.10; 92, 'On Zeal', III.1-4. The same usage may

is far too weak—but rather, 'is under the sentence of hell-fire'; doomed already, just dragging to execution? Thou art guilty of everlasting death. It is the just reward of thy inward and outward wickedness. It is just that the sentence should now take place.

5 Dost thou see, dost thou feel this? Art thou throughly convinced that thou deservest God's wrath and everlasting damnation? Would God do thee any wrong if he now commanded the earth to open and swallow thee up? If thou wert now to go down quick into the pit,[75] into the fire that never shall be quenched?[76] If God hath

10 given thee truly to repent, thou hast a deep sense that these things are so; and that it is of his mere mercy thou art not consumed, swept away from the face of the earth.

5. And what wilt thou do to appease the wrath of God, to atone for all thy sins, and to escape the punishment thou hast so justly

15 deserved? Alas, thou canst do nothing; nothing that will in any wise make amends to God for one evil work or word or thought. If thou couldst now do all things well, if from this very hour, till thy soul should return to God, thou couldst perform perfect, uninterrupted obedience, even this would not atone for what is

20 past. The not increasing thy debt would not discharge it. It would still remain as great as ever. Yea, the present and future obedience of all the men upon earth, and all the angels in heaven, would never make satisfaction to the justice of God for one single sin. How vain then was the thought of atoning for thy own sins by

25 anything thou couldst do! It costeth far more to redeem one soul than all mankind is able to pay. So that were there no other help for a guilty sinner, without doubt he must have perished everlastingly.[77]

6. But suppose perfect obedience for the time to come could

30 atone for the sins that are past, this would profit thee nothing; for thou art not able to perform it; no, not in any one point. Begin now. Make the trial. Shake off that outward sin that so easily besetteth thee.[78] Thou canst not. How then wilt thou change thy life from all evil to all good? Indeed, it is impossible to be done,

---

be found in Robert Gell's *Remaines: Or Several Select Scriptures of the New Testament Opened and Explained* (1676), I. 44; and Offspring Blackall, *Works*, I. 221. See also St. Thomas, *Summa Theologica*, II. ii, Q. 158. A.5, obj. 3, 'Of Anger'; and Macarius, Homily XXVIII, in *Homilies* (1721), p. 362. Cf. *OED* for the diversity of meanings for 'obnoxious'.

[75] See Num. 16:30.　　　　　　　　　　　　　　　[76] Mark 9:43, 45.

[77] Echoes here from Anselm, *Cur Deus Homo?*, Bk. I, chs. xix-xxv; note there, and elsewhere in Anselm, a similar equation of holiness and happiness, as later in Wesley.

[78] See Heb. 12:1.

unless first thy heart be changed. For so long as the tree remains evil, it cannot bring forth good fruit.[79] But art thou able to change thy own heart from all sin to all holiness? To quicken a soul that is dead in sin?[80] Dead to God and alive only to the world? No more than thou art able to quicken a dead body, to raise to life him that lieth in the grave. Yea, thou art not able to quicken thy soul in any degree, no more than to give any degree of life to the dead body. Thou canst do nothing, more or less, in this matter; thou art utterly without strength. To be deeply sensible of this, how helpless thou art, as well as how guilty and how sinful, this is that 'repentance not to be repented of'[81] which is the forerunner of the kingdom of God.

7. If to this lively conviction of thy inward and outward sins, of thy utter guiltiness and helplessness, there be added suitable affections—sorrow of heart for having despised thy own mercies; remorse and self-condemnation, having the mouth stopped, shame to lift up thine eyes to heaven;[82] fear of the wrath of God abiding on thee, of his curse hanging over thy head, and of the fiery indignation ready to devour those who forget God and obey not our Lord Jesus Christ; earnest desire to escape from that indignation, to cease from evil and learn to do well[83]—then I say unto thee, in the name of the Lord, 'Thou art not far from the kingdom of God.'[84] One step more and thou shalt enter in. Thou dost 'repent'. Now, 'believe the gospel'.

8. 'The gospel' (that is, good tidings, good news for guilty, helpless sinners) in the largest sense of the word means the whole revelation made to men by Jesus Christ; and sometimes the whole account of what our Lord did and suffered while he tabernacled among men.[85] The substance of all is, 'Jesus Christ came into the world to save sinners;'[86] or, 'God so loved the world that he gave his only begotten Son, to the end we might not perish, but have everlasting life;'[87] or, 'He was bruised for our transgressions, he was wounded for our iniquities; the chastisement of our peace was upon him, and with his stripes we are healed.'[88]

---

[79] See Matt. 7:18; Luke 6:43.
[80] See Eph. 2:1, 5.
[81] 2 Cor. 7:10. Cf. above, II.1 and n.   [82] See Luke 18:13.
[83] See Isa. 1:16, 17.   [84] Mark 12:34.
[85] A literal rendering of the ἐσκήνωσεν of John 1:14 (from σκῆνος, 'tent' or 'tabernacle').
[86] Cf. 1 Tim. 1:15.   [87] Cf. John 3:16.
[88] Cf. Isa. 53:5.

9. Believe this, and the kingdom of God is thine. By faith thou attainest the promise: 'He pardoneth and absolveth all that truly repent and unfeignedly believe his holy gospel.'[89] As soon as ever God hath spoken to thy heart, 'Be of good cheer, thy sins are
5 forgiven thee,'[90] his kingdom comes; thou hast righteousness, and peace, and joy in the Holy Ghost.[91]

10. Only beware thou do not deceive thy own soul with regard to the nature of this faith. It is not (as some have fondly conceived) a bare assent to the truth of the Bible, of the articles of our creed,
10 or of all that is contained in the Old and New Testament.[92] The devils believe[93] this, as well as I or thou; and yet they are devils still. But it is, over and above this, a sure trust in the mercy of God through Christ Jesus.[94] It is a confidence in a pardoning God. It is a divine evidence or conviction that 'God was in Christ,
15 reconciling the world to himself, not imputing to them their former trespasses;'[95] and in particular that the Son of God hath loved me and given himself for me;[96] and that I, even I, am now reconciled to God by the blood of the cross.[97]

11. Dost thou thus believe? Then the peace of God is in thy
20 heart, and sorrow and sighing flee away.[98] Thou art no longer in doubt of the love of God; it is clear as the noonday sun. Thou criest out, 'My song shall be always of the loving-kindness of the Lord: with my mouth will I ever be telling of thy truth, from one generation to another.'[99] Thou art no longer afraid of hell, or
25 death, or him that had once the power of death, the devil: no, nor painfully afraid of God himself; only thou hast a tender, filial fear of offending him. Dost thou believe? Then thy 'soul doth magnify

---

[89] BCP, Morning Prayer, Absolution (4).
[90] Cf. Matt. 9:2.   [91] Rom. 14:17.
[92] Cf. here the doctrines of John Glas (1695–1773) and Robert Sandeman (1718–71), Scottish independents who had rejected both the Calvinist doctrine of 'final perseverance' and the Methodist doctrine of 'conversion'. Faith, they taught, was the clear-headed intellectual acceptance of 'the Gospel history' as recorded in the New Testament, and this in itself was saving. Wesley knew of them from Glas's *A Plea for Pure and Undefiled Religion* (1741) and *A Treatise on the Lord's Supper* (1743). Wesley's diary of Mar. 8, 1741, records that he had 'read Glas'. Later, Sandeman (under the pseudonym of 'Palaemon') would expound his soteriology in *Letters on Theron and Aspasio. Addressed to the Author* [James Hervey] (1757), which drew an extended reply from Wesley in a letter dated Nov. 1, 1757, in which the notion of faith as bare assent is sharply denounced as 'stark, staring nonsense' (see *Bibliog*, No. 221, Vol. 13 of this edn.).
[93] See Jas. 2:19.   [94] Cf. Homily, 'Of Faith', and I.6-7, above.
[95] Cf. 2 Cor. 5:19.   [96] See Gal. 2:20.
[97] A conflation of Rom. 5:10 and Col. 1:20.
[98] Isa. 35:10.   [99] Ps. 89:1 (BCP).

the Lord, and thy spirit rejoiceth in God thy Saviour'.[100] Thou rejoicest in that thou hast 'redemption through his blood, even the forgiveness of sins'.[101] Thou rejoicest in that 'Spirit of adoption which crieth in thy heart, Abba, Father!'[102] Thou rejoicest in a 'hope full of immortality';[103] in reaching forth unto the 'mark of the prize of thy high calling';[104] in an earnest expectation of all the good things which God hath prepared for them that love him.[105]

12. Dost thou now believe? Then 'the love of God is' now 'shed abroad in thy heart.'[106] Thou lovest him, because he first loved us.[107] And because thou lovest God, thou lovest thy brother also.[108] And being filled with 'love, peace, joy', thou art also filled with 'long-suffering, gentleness, fidelity, goodness, meekness, temperance',[109] and all the other fruits of the same Spirit—in a word, with whatever dispositions are holy, are heavenly or divine. For while thou 'beholdest with open (uncovered) face' (the veil now being taken away) 'the glory of the Lord', his glorious love, and the glorious image wherein thou wast created, thou art 'changed into the same image, from glory to glory, by the Spirit of the Lord'.[110]

13. This repentance, this faith, this peace, joy, love; this change from glory to glory, is what the wisdom of the world has voted to be madness, mere enthusiasm, utter distraction.[111] But thou, O man of God, regard them not: be thou moved by none of these things. Thou knowest in whom thou hast believed.[112] See that no man take thy crown.[113] Whereunto thou hast already attained, hold fast, and follow, till thou attain all the great and precious promises. And thou who hast not yet known him, let not vain men make thee ashamed of the gospel of Christ. Be thou in nothing terrified by those who speak evil of the things which they know not. God will soon turn thy heaviness into joy. O let not thy hands

---

100 Cf. Luke 1:46-47.
101 Col. 1:14.
102 Cf. Rom. 8:15.
103 Wisd. 3:4.
104 Cf. Phil. 3:14.
105 1 Cor. 2:9.
106 Cf. Rom. 5:5.
107 See 1 John 4:19.
108 See 1 John 4:21.   109 Gal. 5:22-23.   110 2 Cor. 3:18.

111 An echo of charges, chiefly against Whitefield, by various critics like *The Weekly Advertiser* (June 13, 1741), Joseph Trapp, *The Nature, Folly, Sin, and Danger of Being Righteous Overmuch* (1739), Richard Smalbroke (Bishop of Lichfield), and others. Cf. Green, *Anti-Methodist Publications*, for 1739–45. See also No. 10, 'The Witness of the Spirit, I', §1 and n.

112 See 2 Tim. 1:12.   113 Rev. 3:11.

hang down. Yet a little longer, and he will take away thy fears, and give thee the spirit of a sound mind. 'He is nigh that justifieth:'[114] 'Who is he that condemneth? It is Christ that died; yea, rather, that rose again; who is even now at the right hand of God, making 5 intercession for thee.'[115] Now cast thyself on the Lamb of God, with all thy sins, how many soever they be; and 'an entrance shall *now* be ministered unto *thee* into the kingdom of our Lord and Saviour Jesus Christ'![116]

[114] Cf. Isa. 50:8.
[115] Cf. Rom. 8:34.
[116] Cf. 2 Pet. 1:11.

THE FIRST-FRUITS OF THE SPIRIT

AN INTRODUCTORY COMMENT

Wesley's accent on salvation by faith as salvation from sin had already raised the question of 'sin in believers' and had involved him in the tortured debates about the residues of sin in the believer (fomes peccati) *after justification and reconciliation. The classical Protestant doctrine of invincible concupiscence had supported Luther's characterization of the Christian as* simul justus et peccator *(see No. 13,* On Sin in Believers). *But this collided with Wesley's holy living tradition, and it deferred entire sanctification until* in statu gloriae *('in the state of glory only'). It also fed the flames of scrupulosity, so that one of the marks of Puritan examinations of conscience had come to be self-accusation and self-reproach.*

In this sermon (one of only five recorded uses of Rom. 8:1; another in 1741, two in 1745, and one in 1760) Wesley is wrestling with the problem of Christian self-accusation. It is a problem for those who already profess faith in Christ but who retain their guilty memories and are still aware of continued shortfallings.

Here, then, is an early statement of Wesley's 'third alternative' to two extremes: of Christians, on the one hand, who might continue in sin and still plead Christ's atoning mercies, and Christians, on the other, who sag toward despair under the weight of their guilt-ridden consciences. The crucial distinction is between wilful *sins—lapses for which guilt and repentance are the sinner's only hope—and the* residue *of sin in believers for which 'there is therefore now no condemnation in Christ Jesus'. It is this sort of surcease from guilt and anxiety that Wesley here identifies as 'the first-fruits of the Spirit'. This, then, is a preparatory essay on the paradox of a Christian's sensitivity (in repentance) and serenity (in grace). Thus it belongs with* Christian Perfection *and its qualifiers* (Wandering Thoughts, On Sin in Believers, *and* The Repentance of Believers) *as part of Wesley's composite doctrine of salvation as pardon and of its fruits as a deliverance of the Christian conscience from anxiety and guilt.*

Yet another angle of the same, ancient controversy may be seen in Wesley's rejection of the Calvinist contention for 'the perseverance of the saints'. For Wesley, the way from the threshold to the plerophory of faith is a risky one, chiefly because the residues of sin are forever capable of thrusting themselves up to the level of direct temptation or even something like unconscious control. Christians walk in the certainties of grace with the assurance that sins repented are always forgivable, but they must always be alert lest the 'remains of sin' turn into wilful sins (which, unrepented, lead to backsliding). Here then, is an early sample of Wesley's lifelong endeavour to hold both 'faith alone' and 'holy living' in the same integrated vision of Christian existence.

The First-fruits of the Spirit

Romans 8:1

There is therefore now no condemnation to them
which are in Christ Jesus, who walk not
5 *after the flesh, but after the Spirit.*

1. By 'them which are in Christ Jesus' St. Paul evidently means those who truly believe in him; those who 'being justified by faith, have peace with God, through our Lord Jesus Christ'.[1] They who thus believe do no longer 'walk after the flesh', no longer follow
10 the motions of corrupt nature, but 'after the Spirit'. Both their thoughts, words, and works are under the direction of the blessed Spirit of God.

2. 'There is therefore now no condemnation to' these. There is no condemnation to them from God, for he hath 'justified them
15 freely by his grace, through the redemption that is in Jesus'.[2] He hath forgiven all their iniquities, and blotted out all their sins. And there is no condemnation to them from within, for they 'have received, not the spirit of the world, but the Spirit which is of God, that they might know the things which are freely given to
20 them of God':[a] 'which Spirit beareth witness with their spirits that they are the children of God'.[3] And to this is added 'the testimony

---

[a] 1 Cor. 2:12.

---

[1] Rom. 5:1. [2] Cf. Rom. 3:24. [3] Cf. Rom. 8:16.

of their conscience, that in simplicity and godly sincerity, not with fleshly wisdom, but by the grace of God, they have had their conversation in the world'.[b]

3. But because this Scripture has been so frequently misunderstood, and that in so dangerous a manner; because such multitudes of 'unlearned and unstable men' (οἱ ἀμαθεῖς καὶ ἀστήρικτοι,[4] men untaught of God, and consequently unestablished in 'the truth which is after godliness')[5] have 'wrested it to their own destruction';[6] I propose to show as clearly as I can, first, who those are 'which are in Christ Jesus, and walk not after the flesh, but after the Spirit'; and secondly, how 'there is no condemnation to' these.[7] I shall conclude with some practical inferences.

I.1. First, I am to show who those are that 'are in Christ Jesus'. And are they not those who believe in his name? Those who are 'found in him, not having their own righteousness, but the righteousness which is of God by faith'?[8] These, who 'have redemption through his blood',[9] are properly said to be 'in him', for *they* 'dwell in Christ and Christ in them'.[10] They are 'joined unto the Lord in one Spirit'.[11] They are engrafted into him as branches into the vine.[12] They are united, as members to their head, in a manner which words cannot express, nor could it before enter into their hearts to conceive.[13]

2. Now 'whosoever abideth in him sinneth not,'[14] 'walketh not after the flesh'. The flesh, in the usual language of St. Paul, signifies corrupt nature. In this sense he uses the word, writing to the Galatians, 'The works of the flesh are manifest;'[c] and a little before, 'Walk in the Spirit, and ye shall not fulfil the lust (or desire) of the flesh.'[d] To prove which, namely, that those who 'walk by the Spirit do not fulfil the lust of the flesh', he immediately adds, 'For the flesh lusteth against the spirit; but the spirit lusteth against the flesh (for these are contrary to each other), that ye may not do the things which ye would.' So the

---

[b] 2 Cor. 1:12.
[c] Gal. 5:19.
[d] Ver. 16.

---

[4] Cf. 2 Pet. 3:16. [5] Titus 1:1. [6] Cf. 2 Pet. 3:16.
[7] Cf. Rom. 8:1. [8] Cf. Phil. 3:9. [9] Eph. 1:7; Col. 1:14.
[10] Cf. 1 John 4:13. [11] 1 Cor. 6:17. [12] See John 15:4-5.
[13] See 1 Cor. 12:12-27; John 15:1-8. [14] 1 John 3:6.

words are literally translated (ἵνα μὴ ἅ ἂν ϑέλητε, ταῦτα ποιῆτε);[15] not, 'So that ye cannot do the things that ye would,' as if the flesh overcame the spirit—a translation which hath not only nothing to do with the original text of the Apostle, but likewise makes his whole argument nothing worth, yea, asserts just the reverse of what he is proving.

3. 'They who are of Christ',[16] who 'abide in him',[17] 'have crucified the flesh with its affections and lusts.'[18] They abstain from all those works of the flesh: from 'adultery and fornication'; from 'uncleanness and lasciviousness'; from 'idolatry, witchcraft, hatred, variance'; from 'emulations, wrath, strife, sedition, heresies, envyings, murders, drunkenness, revellings'[19]—from every design, and word, and work to which the corruption of nature leads. Although they feel the root of bitterness[20] in themselves, yet are they endued with power from on high to trample it continually under foot, so that it cannot 'spring up to trouble them':[21] insomuch that every fresh assault which they undergo only gives them fresh occasion of praise, of crying out, 'Thanks be unto God, who giveth us the victory, through Jesus Christ our Lord.'[22]

4. They now 'walk after the Spirit' both in their hearts and lives. They are taught of him to love God and their neighbour with a love which is as 'a well of water, springing up into everlasting life'.[23] And by him they are led into every holy desire, into every divine and heavenly temper, till every thought which arises in their heart is holiness unto the Lord.[24]

5. They who 'walk after the Spirit' are also led by him into all holiness of conversation. Their speech is 'always in grace, seasoned with salt',[25] with the love and fear of God. 'No corrupt communication comes out of their mouth, but (only) that which is good;' that which is 'to the use of edifying', which is 'meet to

---

[15] Cf. Gal. 5:17, as in *TR*: Wesley's printers introduced a medley of variant breathings and accents (e.g., Pine [1771] ἵνα μὴ ἅ ἂν ϑέλητε). Modern critical edns. read ἐὰν instead of the contraction, ἂν, and most modern translators take the whole phrase as a negative subjunctive, meaning 'so that what you will to do you cannot do' (NEB); cf. Goodspeed, Knox, etc. Wesley will not have it so: our moral disabilities are *not* part of God's *original* design for mankind; always, a remnant of freedom (and, therefore, of responsibility) remains. Cf. Nos. 13, *On Sin in Believers*, I.3, IV.7; and 43, *The Scripture Way of Salvation*, III.6.

[16] Cf. Gal. 5:24.   [17] 1 John 2:27, 28.   [18] Cf. Gal. 5:24.
[19] Gal. 5:19-21.   [20] Heb. 12:15.   [21] Cf. *ibid.*
[22] Cf. 1 Cor. 15:57.   [23] John 4:14.
[24] See Zech. 14:20-21; Jer. 2:3.   [25] Cf. Col. 4:6.

minister grace to the hearers'.[26] And herein likewise do they exercise themselves day and night to do only the things which please God; in all their outward behaviour to follow him who 'left us an example that we might tread in his steps';[27] in all their intercourse with their neighbour to walk in justice, mercy, and truth; and 'whatsoever they do', in every circumstance of life, to 'do all to the glory of God.'[28]

6. These are they who indeed 'walk after the Spirit'. Being filled with faith and with the Holy Ghost, they possess in their hearts, and show forth in their lives, in the whole course of their words and actions, the genuine fruits of the Spirit of God, namely, 'love, joy, peace, long-suffering, gentleness, goodness, fidelity, meekness, temperance',[29] and whatsoever else is lovely or praiseworthy.[30] They 'adorn in all things the gospel of God our Saviour';[31] and give full proof to all mankind that they are indeed actuated by the same Spirit 'which raised up Jesus from the dead'.[32]

II.1. I proposed to show, in the second place, how 'there is no condemnation to them which are' thus 'in Christ Jesus', and thus 'walk, not after the flesh, but after the Spirit.'

And, first, to believers in Christ walking thus 'there is no condemnation' on account of their past sins. God condemneth them not for any of these; they are as though they had never been; they are 'cast as a stone into the depth of the sea',[33] and he remembereth them no more. God having 'set forth his Son to be a propitiation for them, through faith in his blood, hath declared unto them his righteousness, for the remission of the sins that are past'.[34] He layeth therefore none of these to their charge;[35] their memorial is perished with them.[36]

2. And there is no condemnation in their own breast, no sense of guilt, or dread of the wrath of God. They 'have the witness in themselves';[37] they are conscious of their interest in the blood of sprinkling.[38] They 'have not received again the spirit of bondage unto fear', unto doubt and racking uncertainty; but they 'have

---

[26] Cf. Eph. 4:29. [27] Cf. 1 Pet. 2:21. [28] Cf. 1 Cor. 10:31.
[29] Gal. 5:22-23. [30] See Phil. 4:8.
[31] Cf. Titus 2:10. [32] Cf. Rom. 8:11.
[33] Cf. Mic. 7:19. [34] Cf. Rom. 3:25.
[35] See Acts 7:60; Rom. 8:33. [36] Ps. 9:6.
[37] Cf. 1 John 5:10. [38] See Heb. 12:24.

received the Spirit of adoption, crying in their hearts, Abba,
Father'.[39] Thus 'being justified by faith, they have the peace'[40] of
God ruling in their hearts, flowing from a continual sense of his
pardoning mercy, and 'the answer of a good conscience toward
5 God'.[41]

3. If it be said, 'But sometimes a believer in Christ may lose his
sight of the mercy of God; sometimes such darkness may fall
upon him that he no longer sees him that is invisible,[42] no longer
feels that witness in himself of his part in the atoning blood; and
10 then he is inwardly condemned, he hath again "the sentence of
death in himself".'[43] I answer, supposing it so to be, supposing
him not to see the mercy of God, then he is not a believer; for faith
implies light, the light of God shining upon the soul. So far
therefore as anyone loses this light, he for the time loses his faith.
15 And no doubt a true believer in Christ may lose the light of faith.
And so far as this is lost he may for a time fall again into
condemnation. But this is not the case of them who now 'are in
Christ Jesus', who now believe in his name. For so long as they
believe and walk after the Spirit neither God condemns them nor
20 their own heart.[44]

4. They are not condemned, secondly, for any present sins, for
now transgressing the commandments of God. For they do not
transgress them; they do not 'walk after the flesh, but after the
Spirit'. This is the continual proof of their 'love of God, that they
25 keep his commandments':[45] even as St. John bears witness,
'Whosoever is born of God doth not commit sin. For his seed
remaineth in him, and he cannot sin, because he is born of God;'[46]
he cannot so long as that seed of God, that loving, holy faith,
remaineth in him. So long as 'he keepeth himself' herein 'that
30 wicked one toucheth him not.'[47] Now it is evident he is not
condemned for the sins which he doth not commit at all. They

[39] Cf. Rom. 8:15. [40] Cf. Rom. 5:1. [41] 1 Pet. 3:21.
[42] See Heb. 11:27. [43] Cf. 2 Cor. 1:9.

[44] Note the 'third alternative' here to the polarities of over-anxious consciences, on the one hand, and to the 'perseverance of the saints', on the other. Assurance ('the light of faith') is a *gift;* it may be lost and yet also recovered. It is interesting to see how tenaciously Wesley argued against 'final perseverance', as in *Predestination Calmly Considered,* 72-86, and Nos. 13, *On Sin in Believers;* 41, *Wandering Thoughts;* 46, 'The Wilderness State'; and 47, 'Heaviness through Manifold Temptations'. See also how skilfully he edits his Puritan authors in *A Christian Library,* quietly omitting their arguments for it, as in Manton (1620–77), *Sermons on Several Subjects,* in Vol. 12.

[45] Cf. 1 John 5:3 and *Notes.*
[46] 1 John 3:9. [47] 1 John 5:18.

therefore who are thus 'led by the Spirit are not under the law':[e] not under the curse or condemnation of it, for it condemns none but those who break it. Thus that law of God, 'Thou shalt not steal,'[48] condemns none but those who do steal. Thus, 'Remember the sabbath day to keep it holy'[49] condemns those only who do not keep it holy. But 'against' the fruits of the Spirit 'there is no law.'[f] As the Apostle more largely declares in those memorable words of his former Epistle to Timothy, 'We know that the law is good if a man use it lawfully; knowing this' (if while he uses the law of God, in order either to convince or direct, he know and remember this), ὅτι δικαίῳ νόμος οὐ κεῖται (not 'that the law is not made for a righteous man', but) 'that the law does not lie against a righteous man' (it has no force against him, no power to condemn him), 'but against the lawless and disobedient, against the ungodly and sinners, against the unholy and profane; . . . according to the glorious gospel of the blessed God.'[g]

5. They are not condemned, thirdly, for inward sin, even though it does now remain. That the corruption of nature does still remain, even in those who are the children of God by faith; that they have in them the seeds of pride and vanity, of anger, lust and evil desire, yea, sin of every kind, is too plain to be denied, being matter of daily experience. And on this account it is that St. Paul, speaking to those whom he had just before witnessed to be 'in Christ Jesus',[h] to have been 'called of God into the fellowship (or participation) of his Son Jesus Christ',[i] yet declares, 'Brethren, I could not speak unto you as unto spiritual, but as unto carnal; even as unto babes in Christ.'[j] 'Babes in Christ'—so we see they were 'in Christ'; they were believers in a low degree. And yet how much of sin remained in them! Of that 'carnal mind' which 'is not subject to the law of God'![50]

---

[e] Gal. 5:18. [f] Ver. 23.

[g] 1 Tim. 1:8-9, 11. [κεῖται, from κεῖμαι, means 'to lie' or 'to lean', as Wesley has it here (*pace* Sugden, I. 169 and n.). Its figurative meaning is 'to be valid' or 'relevant'. The clause may thus be translated, 'The Law has no valid bearing on behaviour at this level . . .' (which is Wesley's point). Cf. Arndt and Gingrich, *Greek-English Lexicon*, p. 428; see also Wesley's *Notes* on this ver.]

[h] 1 Cor. 1:2.

[i] Ver. 9.

[j] 1 Cor. 3:1.

---

[48] Exod. 20:15.

[49] Exod. 20:8.

[50] Rom. 8:7.

6. And yet for all this they are not condemned. Although they feel the flesh, the evil nature in them; although they are more sensible day by day that their 'heart *is* deceitful, and desperately wicked';[51] yet so long as they do not yield thereto, so long as they give no place to the devil, so long as they maintain a continual war with all sin, with pride, anger, desire, so that the flesh hath not dominion over them, but they still 'walk after the Spirit': there is 'no condemnation to them which are in Christ Jesus'. God is well-pleased with their sincere though imperfect obedience;[52] and they 'have confidence toward God', knowing they are his 'by the Spirit which he hath given them'.[k]

7. Nay, fourthly, although they are continually convinced of sin cleaving to all they do; although they are conscious of not fulfilling the perfect law, either in their thoughts, or words, or works; although they know they do not love the Lord their God with all their heart, and mind, and soul, and strength; although they feel more or less of pride or self-will stealing in and mixing with their best duties; although even in their more immediate intercourse with God, when they assemble themselves with the great congregation, and when they pour out their souls in secret to him who seeth all the thoughts and intents of the heart, they are continually ashamed of their wandering thoughts,[53] or of the deadness and dullness of their affections—yet there is no condemnation to them still, either from God or from their own heart. The consideration of these manifold defects only gives them a deeper sense that they have always need of that blood of sprinkling[54] which speaks for them in the ears of God, and that advocate with the Father[55] who 'ever liveth to make intercession for them.'[56] So far are these from driving them away from him in whom they have believed, that they rather drive them the closer to him, whom they feel the want of every moment. And at the same time, the deeper sense they have of this want the more earnest

---

[k] 1 John 3:[21], 24.

---

[51] Jer. 17:9.

[52] A reference to Wesley's crucial distinction between wilful or deliberate sin (*viz.*, 'a voluntary transgression of a known law of God' as in Nos. 19, 'The Great Privilege of those that are Born of God', II.2-3; and 76, 'On Perfection', III.9) and a faithful Christian's 'sincere but imperfect obedience'. See below, No. 13, *On Sin in Believers*, intro., III.1-9 and n.

[53] Cf. No. 41, *Wandering Thoughts*.   [54] Heb. 12:24.

[55] 1 John 2:1.   [56] Heb. 7:25.

desire do they feel, and the more diligent they are, as they 'have received the Lord Jesus, so to walk in him'.[57]

8. They are not condemned, fifthly, for 'sins of infirmity', as they are usually called.[58] (Perhaps it were advisable rather to call them *infirmities*, that we may not seem to give any countenance to sin, or to extenuate it in any degree by thus coupling it with infirmity.) But if we must retain so ambiguous and dangerous an expression, by 'sins of infirmity' I would mean such involuntary failings as the saying a thing we believe true, though in fact it prove to be false; or the hurting our neighbour without knowing or designing it, perhaps when we designed to do him good. Though these are deviations from the holy and acceptable and perfect will of God,[59] yet they are not properly sins, nor do they bring any guilt on the conscience of 'them which are in Christ Jesus'. They separate not between God and them, neither intercept the light of his countenance, as being no ways inconsistent with their general character of 'walking not after the flesh, but after the Spirit'.

9. Lastly, 'there is no condemnation' to them for anything whatever which it is not in their power to help; whether it be of an inward or outward nature, and whether it be doing something or leaving something undone. For instance, the Lord's Supper is to be administered, but you do not partake thereof. Why do you not? You are confined by sickness; therefore you cannot help omitting it—and for the same reason you are not condemned. There is no guilt, because there is no choice. As there is 'a willing mind, it is accepted, according to that a man hath, not according to that he hath not'.[60]

---

[57] Cf. Col. 2:6.

[58] Cf. Thomas Westfield, 'Sermon at St. Bartholomew the Great, on 2 Sam. 5:3' (1628); Richard Kidder (Bishop of Bath and Wells), 'A Discourse Concerning Sins of Infirmity and Wilful Sins' (1704), pp. 3-33; and Lucas, *Enquiry After Happiness*, II. 178; III. 23, 296. Reformed theologians, generally, rejected the Catholic distinction between 'mortal' (wilful) sins and 'venial' (involuntary) sins. But see the list of sins in Johannes Heidegger, *Corpus Theologiae* (1700), V. 61-71 (§§26-27), where No. 8 pertains to 'sins of weakness' (i.e., 'ignorance', etc.). See also J. A. Quendstedt, *Theologia Didactico-Polemica* (1685), II. 70: 'Sins of infirmity, which overtake the regenerate without any certain purpose of sinning. Such are sinful emotions of the mind, which have suddenly arisen without their will, and whatever unlawful words or deeds are the result of inadvertence or precipitancy, and contrary to the purposes of one's will.'

[59] See Rom. 12:1, 2.

[60] 2 Cor. 8:12.

10. A believer indeed may sometimes be *grieved* because he cannot do what his soul longs for. He may cry out, when he is detained from worshipping God in the great congregation, 'Like as the hart panteth after the water brooks, so panteth my soul after 5 thee, O God. My soul is athirst for God, yea even for the living God. When shall I come to appear in the presence of God?'[61] He may earnestly desire (only still saying in his heart, 'Not as I will, but as thou wilt'[62]) to 'go again with the multitude, and bring them forth into the house of God'.[63] But still, if he cannot go, he feels no 10 condemnation, no guilt, no sense of God's displeasure; but can cheerfully yield up those desires with, 'O my soul, put thy trust in God: for I will yet give him thanks, who is the help of my countenance and my God.'[64]

11. It is more difficult to determine concerning those which are 15 usually styled 'sins of surprise':[65] as when one who commonly in patience possesses his soul on a sudden and violent temptation speaks or acts in a manner not consistent with the royal law, 'Thou shalt love thy neighbour as thyself.'[66] Perhaps it is not easy to fix a general rule concerning transgressions of this nature. We 20 cannot say either that men are, or that they are not, condemned for sins of surprise in general. But it seems whenever a believer is by surprise overtaken in a fault there is more or less condemnation as there is more or less concurrence of his will. In proportion as a sinful desire or word or action is more or less 25 voluntary, so we may conceive God is more or less displeased, and there is more or less guilt upon the soul.

12. But if so, then there may be some sins of surprise which bring much guilt and condemnation. For in some instances our being surprised is owing to some wilful and culpable neglect; or to 30 a sleepiness of soul which might have been prevented, or shaken off before the temptation came. A man may be previously warned, either of God or man, that trials and danger are at hand, and yet may say in his heart, 'A little more slumber, a little more

---

[61] Cf. Ps. 42:1-2 (BCP). [62] Matt. 26:39, etc.
[63] Ps. 42:4 (BCP). [64] Cf. Ps. 42:6-7 (BCP).
[65] Cf. Law, *Serious Call*, (p. 21), where Law is sure that God 'will be merciful to our unavoidable weaknesses and infirmities', including those surprising discoveries of residual sins of which we have not yet repented. His aim is 'to excite [Christians] to an earnest examination of their lives . . . , etc.'. Wesley stresses, more stringently than Law, the dangers of such 'sudden assaults' (see below, II.13) and, consequently, the importance of constant alertness to their disclosures. But here, again, the crucial issue is the vexed question of the borderline between involuntary shortfallings and wilful sins.
[66] Lev. 19:18, etc.

folding of the hands to rest.'[67] Now if such an one afterwards fall, though unawares, into the snare which he might have avoided, that he fell unawares is no excuse—he might have foreseen and have shunned the danger. The falling even by surprise, in such an instance as this, is in effect a wilful sin; and as such must expose 5 the sinner to condemnation both from God and his own conscience.

13. On the other hand, there may be sudden assaults either from the world, or the god of this world, and frequently from our own evil hearts, which we did not, and hardly could foresee. And 10 by these even a believer, while weak in faith, may possibly be borne down, suppose into a degree of anger, or thinking evil of another, with scarce any concurrence of his will. Now in such a case the jealous God would undoubtedly show him that he had done foolishly. He would be convinced of having swerved from 15 the perfect law, from the mind which was in Christ,[68] and consequently *grieved* with a godly sorrow, and lovingly *ashamed* before God. Yet need he not come into condemnation. God layeth not folly to his charge, but hath compassion upon him, even 'as a father pitieth his own children'.[69] And his heart condemneth 20 him not; in the midst of that sorrow and shame he can still say, 'I will trust and not be afraid. For the Lord Jehovah is my strength and my song; he is also become my salvation.'[70]

III.1. It remains only to draw some practical inferences from the preceding considerations. 25

And, first, if there be 'no condemnation to them which are in Christ Jesus', and 'walk not after the flesh, but after the Spirit', on account of their past sins; then 'Why art thou fearful, O thou of little faith?'[71] Though thy sins were once more in number than the sand,[72] what is that to thee now thou art in Christ Jesus? 'Who 30 shall lay anything to the charge of God's elect? It is God that justifieth: who is he that condemneth?'[73] All the sins thou hast committed from thy youth up until the hour when thou wast 'accepted in the Beloved'[74] are driven away as chaff,[75] are gone, are lost, swallowed up, remembered no more. Thou art now 'born 35

[67] Cf. Prov. 6:10; 24:33.
[69] Ps. 103:13 (BCP).
[71] Cf. Matt. 8:26.
[73] Rom. 8:33-34.
[75] See Hos. 13:3.

[68] See Phil. 2:5.
[70] Isa. 12:2.
[72] Ps. 139:18.
[74] Eph. 1:6.

of the Spirit';[76] wilt thou be troubled or afraid for what was done before thou wert born? Away with thy fears! Thou art not called to fear, but to the 'spirit of love and of a sound mind'.[77] Know thy calling. Rejoice in God thy Saviour, and give thanks to God thy Father through him.

2. Wilt thou say, 'But I have again committed sin, since I had redemption through his blood;[78] and therefore it is that "I abhor myself, and repent in dust and ashes" '?[79] It is meet thou shouldst abhor thyself; and it is God who hath wrought thee to this selfsame thing. But dost thou now believe? Hath he again enabled thee to say, 'I know that my Redeemer liveth;'[80] 'and the life which I now live, I live by faith in the Son of God'?[81] Then that faith again cancels all that is past, and there is no condemnation to thee. At whatsoever time thou truly believest in the name of the Son of God, all thy sins antecedent to that hour vanish away as the morning dew. Now, then, 'Stand thou fast in the liberty wherewith Christ hath made thee free.'[82] He hath once more made thee free from the power of sin, as well as from the guilt and punishment of it. O 'be not entangled again with the yoke of bondage'![83] Neither the vile, devilish bondage of sin, of evil desires, evil tempers, or words, or works, the most grievous yoke on this side hell; nor the bondage of slavish tormenting fear, of guilt and self-condemnation.

3. But, secondly, do all they which abide 'in Christ Jesus walk not after the flesh, but after the Spirit'? Then we cannot but infer that whosoever now committeth sin hath no part or lot in this matter. He is even now condemned by his own heart. But 'if our heart condemn us',[84] if our own conscience beareth witness that we are guilty, undoubtedly God doth; for he 'is greater than our heart, and knoweth all things';[85] so that we cannot deceive him, if we can ourselves. And think not to say, 'I was justified once; my sins were once forgiven me.' I know not that; neither will I dispute whether they were or no. Perhaps, at this distance of time, 'tis next to impossible to know with any tolerable degree of certainty whether that was a true, genuine work of God, or whether thou didst only deceive thy own soul. But this I know with the utmost

---

[76] John 3:6, 8.
[78] Eph. 1:7; Col. 1:14.
[80] Job 19:25.
[82] Cf. Gal. 5:1.
[84] 1 John 3:20.

[77] 2 Tim. 1:7.
[79] Job 42:6.
[81] Cf. Gal. 2:20.
[83] *Ibid.*
[85] *Ibid.*

degree of certainty, 'He that committeth sin is of the devil.'[86] Therefore thou art of thy father the devil. It cannot be denied; for the works of thy father thou dost. O flatter not thyself with vain hopes. Say not to thy soul, 'Peace, peace!' For there is no peace.[87] Cry aloud! Cry unto God out of the deep,[88] if haply he may hear thy voice. Come unto him as at first, as wretched and poor, as sinful, miserable, blind, and naked. And beware thou suffer thy soul to take no rest till his pardoning love be again revealed, till he 'heal thy backslidings',[89] and fill thee again with the 'faith that worketh by love'.[90]

4. Thirdly, is there no condemnation to them which 'walk after the Spirit' by reason of *inward sin* still remaining, so long as they do not give way thereto; nor by reason of *sin cleaving* to all they do? Then fret not thyself because of ungodliness, though it still remain in thy heart.[91] Repine not because thou still comest short of the glorious image of God; nor yet because pride, self-will, or unbelief, cleave to all thy words and works. And be not afraid to know all the evil of thy heart, to know thyself as also thou art known.[92] Yea, desire of God that thou mayst not think of thyself more highly than thou oughtest to think.[93] Let thy continual prayer be:

> Show me, as my soul can bear,
> The depth of inbred sin:
> All the unbelief declare,
> The pride that lurks within![94]

But when he heareth thy prayer, and unveils thy heart, when he shows thee throughly what spirit thou art of; then beware that thy faith fail thee not, that thou suffer not thy shield to be torn from thee. Be abased. Be humbled in the dust. See thyself

---

[86] 1 John 3:8. A sharp denial of the notion popularly associated with Calvinism: 'once in grace, always in grace.' Here, again, is Wesley's insistence that only *wilful sin* forfeits grace. But even wilful sins may be repented and forgiven.

[87] See Jer. 6:14; 8:11.

[88] See Ps. 130:1 (BCP).

[89] Cf. Jer. 3:22.

[90] Cf. Gal. 5:6; cf. also, No. 2, *The Almost Christian*, II.6 and n.

[91] Notice Wesley's version here of Luther's *simul justus et peccator* and his different nuancing of it. See above, II.6; and No. 13, *On Sin in Believers*, intro., III.1-9 and n.

[92] See 1 Cor. 13:12.

[93] See Rom. 12:3.

[94] Charles Wesley, 'Waiting for Christ the Prophet', st. 5, in *Hymns and Sacred Poems* (1742), p. 209 (*Poet. Wks.*, II.263).

nothing, less than nothing, and vanity.[95] But still, 'let not thy heart be troubled, neither let it be afraid.'[96] Still hold fast, 'I', even I, 'have an advocate with the Father, Jesus Christ the righteous.'[97] And 'as the heavens are higher than the earth, so is his love higher

5 than even my sins.'[98] Therefore God is merciful to thee a sinner![99] Such a sinner as thou art! God is love; and Christ hath died. Therefore the Father himself loveth thee. Thou art his child. Therefore he will withhold from thee no manner of thing that is good.[100] Is it good that the whole body of sin which is now

10 crucified in thee should be destroyed? It shall be done. Thou shalt be 'cleansed from all filthiness both of flesh and spirit'.[101] Is it good that nothing should remain in thy heart but the pure love of God alone? Be of good cheer! 'Thou shalt love the Lord thy God with all thy heart and mind and soul and strength.'[102] 'Faithful is

15 he that hath promised, who also will do it.'[103] It is thy part patiently to continue in the work of faith, and in the labour of love; and in cheerful peace, in humble confidence, with calm, and resigned, and yet earnest expectation to wait till 'the zeal of the Lord of Hosts shall perform this'.[104]

20 5. Fourthly, if they that 'are in Christ and walk after the Spirit' are not condemned for *sins of infirmity,* as neither for *involuntary failings,* nor for anything whatever which they are not able to help; then beware, O thou that hast faith in his blood, that Satan herein 'gain no advantage over thee'.[105] Thou art still foolish and weak,

25 blind and ignorant; more weak than any words can express, more foolish than it can yet enter into thy heart to conceive, knowing nothing yet as thou oughtest to know. Yet let not all thy weakness and folly, or any fruit thereof which thou art not yet able to avoid, shake thy faith, thy filial trust in God, or disturb thy peace or joy in

30 the Lord. The rule which some give as to wilful sins, and which in that case may perhaps be dangerous, is undoubtedly wise and safe if it be applied only to the case of weakness and infirmities.[106] Art

---

[95] Cf. Isa. 40:17.   [96] Cf. John 14:27.   [97] 1 John 2:1.
[98] Cf. Ps. 103:11.   [99] See Luke 18:13.   [100] Matt. 7:11.
[101] Cf. 2 Cor. 7:1.   [102] Mark 12:30; Luke 10:27.   [103] Cf. Heb. 10:23.

[104] Cf. Isa. 9:7; note this whole paragraph as a comment on the meaning of a believer's assurance, despite the remains of sin in believers (for which, see No. 13). It is equally an exhortation to the *constant* repentance of believers (for which, see No. 14).

[105] Cf. 2 Cor. 2:11.

[106] An echo of Law's stress on God's *mercifulness* toward all Christians who hold to their trust in Christ's sufficient merit and grace: 'Weak and imperfect men shall, notwithstanding their frailties and defects, be received as having pleased God, if they have

thou fallen, O man of God?[107] Yet do not lie there, fretting thyself
and bemoaning thy weakness; but meekly say, 'Lord, I shall fall
thus every moment unless thou uphold me with thy hand.' And
then, arise! Leap and walk. Go on thy way. 'Run with patience the
race set before thee.'[108]   5

6. Lastly, since a believer need not come into condemnation,
even though he be *surprised* into what his soul abhors (suppose his
being surprised is not owing to any carelessness or wilful neglect
of his own); if thou who believest art thus overtaken in a fault,
then grieve unto the Lord: it shall be a precious balm. Pour out   10
thy heart before him,[109] and show him of thy trouble. And pray
with all thy might to him who is 'touched with the feeling of thy
infirmities'[110] that he would stablish and strengthen and settle[111]
thy soul, and suffer thee to fall no more. But still he condemneth
thee not. Wherefore shouldst thou fear? Thou hast no need of any   15
'fear that hath torment'.[112] Thou shalt love him that loveth thee,
and it sufficeth: more love will bring more strength. And as soon
as thou lovest him with all thy heart thou shall be 'perfect and
entire, lacking nothing'.[113] Wait in peace for that hour when 'the
God of peace shall sanctify thee wholly, so that thy whole spirit   20
and soul and body may be preserved blameless unto the coming of
our Lord Jesus Christ'![114]

done their *utmost* to please him. . . . We cannot offer to God the service of angels [or of]
man in a state of perfection; but fallen men can do their *best*, and *this* is the perfection that
is required of us' (*Serious Call*, *Works*, IV.23-24).

[107] See Isa. 14:12.
[108] Cf. Heb. 12:1.
[109] See Ps. 62:8.
[110] Cf. Heb. 4:15.
[111] See 1 Pet. 5:10.
[112] Cf. 1 John 4:18.
[113] Cf. Jas. 1:4.
[114] 1 Thess. 5:23.

THE SPIRIT OF BONDAGE
AND OF ADOPTION

AN INTRODUCTORY COMMENT

In this sermon Wesley returns to the theme of 'faith alone', now in the context of a borrowed typology about the three states of man: 'natural', 'legal', *and 'evangelical' (a scheme that presupposes man's original state as that of innocence). His 'classical' source for such a scheme is in St. Augustine's* Enchiridion, xxxi *(117-19). His 'modern' source here would have been Thomas Boston's* Human Nature in Its Fourfold State *(Edinburgh, 1720) —henceforth 'Boston'. Wesley's interest in such typologies may be seen in an early letter to his mother, February 14, 1735, and an interesting entry in Benjamin Ingham's diary for March 17, 1734: '7:00 a.m. Breakfast with John Robson and John Wesley; religious talk of three different states of man: natural, Jewish (or fearful), and evangelical—the two last only, salvable.'*

At this point in the development of his soteriology after 1738, the term 'natural' was understood by John Wesley (as it had been by Charles in 'Awake, Thou That Sleepest'*) as a condition of moral anomie. This sermon, then, is John's positive version of Charles's earlier sermon. Later (as in No. 85, 'On Working Out Our Own Salvation', III.4), he will revise his view and assert that 'there is no man that is in a state of mere nature, no man, unless he has quenched the Spirit, that is wholly void of the grace of God. No man living is entirely destitute of what is vulgarly called "natural conscience". But this is not natural: it is more properly termed "preventing grace". Every man has a greater or less measure of this. . . .' But notice that in I.2, 4-5, he pursues the self-excusing 'natural man' into the depths of his unconscious motives as if there were a conscience at their core. Sin is not defined as deliberate violations of known laws of God (as in No. 13,* On Sin in Believers, *intro., III.1-9 and n.): 'it extends to every temper, desire, thought, and motion of the heart.' This differs also from his views in No. 40,* Christian Perfection.

Wesley's main concern, however, is with the contrast between the harrowed conscience and spiritual despair of those who in their 'legal state' have been 'awakened' (but continue as guilt-ridden and unhappy, despite their best efforts at good works and religious observances) and the peace, joy, and good conscience of those who have heard *the gospel and are assured of God's justifying grace. Here he is echoing Thomas Boston's moving description of 'Peace with God and Peace of Conscience' (op. cit., State III, Head II). Thus, this sermon is Wesley's interpretation of the contrast delineated in Romans 7 and 8, with Romans 7 taken as a description of despair in the 'legal state' and Romans 8 as St. Paul's celebration of 'evangelical' grace. Thus, the sermon concludes with an invitation to those living under the Law to accept God's proffered pardon and to 'rejoice and love like the angels of God'.*

It is worth noting that of the six sermons that follow after the bloc of 'university sermons,' five (Nos. 5, 6, 8, 9, and 10) have their texts from Romans. This is not accidental, for these are the sermons in which Wesley has distilled the essence of his gospel of justification. He had already preached from Romans 8:15 thirteen times: three times in 1739, once in 1740, three times in 1741, four times in 1742, and twice in 1743—all in the early years of the Revival. He seems to have neglected it thereafter.

The Spirit of Bondage and of Adoption

Romans 8:15

Ye have not received the spirit of bondage again unto fear; but ye have received the Spirit of adoption, whereby we cry, Abba, Father.

1. St. Paul here speaks to those who are the children of God by faith.[1] Ye, saith he, who are indeed his children, have drunk into his Spirit.[2] 'Ye have not received the spirit of bondage again unto fear;' but 'because ye are sons, God hath sent forth the Spirit of his Son into your hearts.'[3] 'Ye have received the Spirit of adoption, whereby we cry, Abba, Father.'

[1] Gal. 3:26.
[2] See 1 Cor. 10:4.
[3] Gal. 4:6.

2. The spirit of bondage and fear is widely distant from this loving Spirit of adoption. Those who are influenced only by slavish fear cannot be termed the sons of God. Yet some of them may be styled his servants,[4] and 'are not far from the kingdom of
5 heaven'.[5]

3. But it is to be feared the bulk of mankind, yea, of what is called 'the Christian world', have not attained even this; but are still afar off, 'neither is God in all their thoughts.'[6] A few names may be found of those who love God; a few more there are that
10 fear him. But the greater part have neither the fear of God before their eyes,[7] nor the love of God in their hearts.

4. Perhaps most of you, who by the mercy of God now partake of a better spirit, may remember the time when ye were as they, when ye were under the same condemnation. But at first ye knew
15 it not, though ye were wallowing daily in your sins and in your blood; till in due time ye 'received the spirit of fear'[8] (ye *received;* for this also is the gift of God);[9] and afterwards fear vanished away, and the spirit of love filled your hearts.

5. One who is in the first state of mind, without fear or love, is in
20 Scripture termed 'a natural man'.[10] One who is under the spirit of bondage and fear is sometimes said to be 'under the law'[11] (although that expression more frequently signifies one who is under the Jewish dispensation, who thinks himself obliged to observe all the rites and ceremonies of the Jewish law). But one
25 who has exchanged the spirit of fear for the spirit of love is properly said to be 'under grace'.[12]

Now because it highly imports us to know what spirit we are of, I shall endeavour to point out distinctly, first, the state of a 'natural man'; secondly, that of one who is 'under the law'; and
30 thirdly, of one who is 'under grace'.

---

[4] The earliest instance in the published sermons of the distinction between the faith of 'servants' and of 'sons'/'children'. It had already appeared in the *Minutes* (May 13, 1746). It will be further developed after this to become a Wesleyan commonplace (as in No. 106, 'On Faith, Heb. 11:6', espec. I:10 and n.).

[5] Cf. Mark 12:34. [6] Cf. Ps. 10:4 (BCP).
[7] See Rom. 3:18. [8] Cf. Rom. 8:15; 2 Tim. 1:7.
[9] Cf. Ps. 111:10, 'The fear of the Lord is the *beginning* of wisdom.'
[10] 1 Cor. 2:14. Cf. Boston, State II, Head II, 'The State of Nature'. For other references to 'natural man', see No. 1, *Salvation by Faith*, I.1 and n.; and espec. No. 2, *The Almost Christian*. See also Nos. 17, 'The Circumcision of the Heart', §2; 19, 'The Great Privilege of those that are Born of God', I.3-10; 44, *Original Sin*, II.1-2; 45, 'The New Birth', I.4; 63, 'The General Spread of the Gospel', §§9-10; 130, 'On Living without God', §6.
[11] Rom. 6:14, 15. [12] *Ibid.*

I.1. And, first, the state of a 'natural man'. This the Scripture represents as a state of sleep. The voice of God to him is, 'Awake, thou that sleepest.'[13] For his soul is in a deep sleep. His spiritual senses are not awake; they discern neither spiritual good nor evil. The eyes of his understanding are closed;[14] they are sealed   5
together, and see not. Clouds and darkness continually rest upon them;[15] for he lies in the valley of the shadow of death.[16] Hence, having no inlets for the knowledge of spiritual things,[17] all the avenues of his soul being shut up, he is in gross, stupid ignorance of whatever he is most concerned to know. He is utterly ignorant   10
of God, knowing nothing concerning him as he ought to know. He is totally a stranger to the law of God, as to its true, inward, spiritual meaning. He has no conception of that evangelical holiness without which no man shall see the Lord;[18] nor of the happiness which they only find whose 'life is hid with Christ in   15
God'.[19]

2. And for this very reason, because he is fast *asleep*, he is in some sense at *rest*. Because he is *blind*, he is also *secure:* he saith, 'Tush, . . . there shall no harm happen unto me.'[20] The darkness which covers him on every side keeps him in a kind of peace—so   20
far as peace can consist with the works of the devil, and with an earthly, devilish mind.[21] He *sees* not that he stands on the edge of the pit; therefore he *fears* it not. He cannot tremble at the danger he does not know. He has not understanding enough to fear. Why is it that he is in no dread of God? Because he is totally ignorant of   25
him: if not 'saying in his heart, There is no God',[22] or that he 'sitteth on the circle of the heavens',[23] 'and humbleth' not 'himself

---

[13] Eph. 5:14. See No. 3, '*Awake, Thou That Sleepest*', on this text.

[14] See Eph. 1:18.

[15] This echoes a line in Addison's famous drama, *Cato*, V.i:

> The wide, the unbounded prospect lies before me;
> But shadows, clouds, and darkness rest upon it.

Wesley quotes these lines in other sermons. See below, No. 117, 'On the Discoveries of Faith', §8 and n.

[16] Ps. 23:4.

[17] This same phrase—reflecting the same epistemology—as above in Charles's sermon, No. 3, '*Awake, Thou That Sleepest*', I.11. Cf. also No. 10, 'The Witness of the Spirit, I', I.12 and n.

[18] Heb. 12:14.

[19] Col. 3:3; once again, the correlation between 'holiness' and 'happiness'.

[20] Ps. 10:6 (BCP).

[21] See Jas. 3:15.

[22] Cf. Ps. 14:1; 53:1.

[23] Cf. Isa. 40:22.

to behold the things'[24] which are done on earth; yet satisfying himself as well, to all Epicurean intents and purposes,[25] by saying, 'God is merciful;'[26] confounding and swallowing up at once in that unwieldy idea of mercy all his holiness and essential hatred of
5 sin, all his justice, wisdom, and truth. He is in no dread of the vengeance denounced against those who obey not the blessed law of God, because he understands it not. He imagines the main point is to *do thus,* to be *outwardly* blameless—and sees not that it extends to every temper, desire, thought, motion of the heart. Or
10 he fancies that the obligation hereto is ceased, that Christ came to 'destroy the law and the prophets',[27] to save his people *in,* not *from* their sins, to bring them to heaven without holiness;[28] notwithstanding his own words, 'Not one jot or tittle of the law shall pass away till all things are fulfilled,'[29] and, 'Not everyone
15 that saith unto me, Lord, Lord, shall enter into the kingdom of heaven; but he that doth the will of my Father which is in heaven.'[30]

3. He is secure, because he is utterly ignorant of himself. Hence he talks of 'repenting by and by'; he does not indeed
20 exactly know when; but some time or other before he dies—taking it for granted that this is quite in his own power.[31]

---

[24] Ps. 113:6 (AV).

[25] The typical eighteenth-century estimate of 'Epicurism' is reflected in Samuel Johnson's definition: 'sensual enjoyment; gross pleasure'. Wesley had this in mind when he labelled Horace an 'Epicurean poet', in No. 2, *The Almost Christian,* I. (III.)9. But he also knew of Cicero's more positive views in *De Natura Deorum (On the Nature of the Gods),* i.19, and also the interesting passage on Epicureanism in Chambers's *Cyclopaedia* (1728), where a distinction is made between 'rigid Epicureans' and the 'loose or remiss' ones. The former 'thought it above the majesty of the deity to concern himself with human affairs'. The latter 'placed all their happiness in pleasures of the body. . . .' For some of Wesley's other references to 'elegant Epicurism', cf. Nos. 50, 'The Use of Money', II.2; 78, 'Spiritual Idolatry', I.5; and 87, 'The Danger of Riches', I.13.

[26] Ps. 116:5. In ascribing to either the 'natural' or 'legal' man any idea of God as being merciful, etc., Wesley seems to have confounded the Epicureans with the Gnostics whom Plotinus had denounced along with the Christians—the latter, though, for rather different reasons; cf. Plotinus, 'Against the Gnostics' in the Ninth Tractate of *Enneads* II; see A. H. Armstrong, ed., *The Cambridge History of Later Greek and Early Medieval Philosophy* (1967), pp. 205-6, 243-45.

[27] Matt. 5:17.

[28] An oblique criticism of Christian antinomians (e.g., Agricola, the Moravians, William Cudworth, James Relly); see No. 13, *On Sin in Believers,* intro.

[29] Cf. Matt. 5:18.

[30] Matt. 7:21.

[31] In his Oxford days, Wesley had borrowed, abridged, and preached a sermon of Benjamin Calamy's against 'death-bed repentance' to the prisoners in the Castle; see Vol. 4, Appendix C.

For what should hinder his doing it if he will? If he does but once set a resolution, no fear but he will make it good.[32]

4. But this ignorance never so strongly glares as in those who are termed 'men of learning'. If a natural man be one of these, he can talk at large of his rational faculties, of the freedom of his will 5 and the absolute necessity of such freedom in order to constitute man a moral agent.[33] He reads and argues, and proves to a demonstration that every man may do as he will, may dispose his own heart to evil or good as it seems best in his own eyes. Thus the god of this world spreads a double veil of blindness over his 10 heart, lest by any means 'the light of the glorious gospel of Christ should shine'[34] upon it.

5. From the same ignorance of himself and God there may sometimes arise in the natural man a kind of joy in congratulating himself upon his own wisdom and goodness. And what the world 15 calls joy he may often possess. He may have pleasure in various kinds, either in gratifying the desires of the flesh, or the desire of the eye, or the pride of life[35]—particularly if he has large possessions, if he enjoy an affluent fortune.[36] Then he may 'clothe himself in purple and fine linen, and fare sumptuously every 20 day'.[37] And *so long as* he thus *doth well unto himself,* 'men will' doubtless 'speak good of'[38] him. They will say he is a happy man; for indeed this is the sum of worldly happiness to dress, and visit, and talk, and eat, and drink, and rise up to play.[39]

6. It is not surprising if one in such circumstances as these, 25 dozed[40] with the opiates of flattery and sin, should imagine, among his other waking dreams, that he walks in great *liberty.* How easily may he persuade himself that he is at liberty from all 'vulgar errors' and from the 'prejudice' of education, judging

---

[32] Note the flat rejection here of any notion of moral freedom (and the power not to sin) in 'the *natural* man'. The *posse non peccare,* then, is a divine *gift* of justifying and regenerating grace. For other references to liberty and will, cf. No. 60, 'The General Deliverance', I.4 and n.

[33] Cf. No. 63, 'The General Spread of the Gospel', §11.

[34] 2 Cor. 4:4.

[35] See 1 John 2:16. See also below, III.7; and cf. No. 7, 'The Way to the Kingdom', II.2 and n.

[36] The first instance in the *OED* of this sense of 'affluent' is from 'Junius', and dated 1769. Samuel Johnson cites it from Pope and Prior. Thus, it was a 'modern' usage in Wesley's time and a sample of his interest in current speech.

[37] Cf. Luke 16:19.   [38] Cf. Luke 6:26.   [39] See Exod. 32:6.

[40] It seems almost certain here that Wesley is using the participial adjective of 'dosed', of which *OED* cites examples from 1659 to 1849.

exactly right, and keeping clear of all extremes. 'I am free (may he
say) from all the *enthusiasm*[41] of weak and narrow souls; from
superstition, the disease of fools and cowards, always righteous
overmuch; and from *bigotry*,[42] continually incident to those who
5 have not a free and generous way of thinking.' And too sure it is
that he is altogether free from the 'wisdom which cometh from
above',[43] from holiness, from the religion of the heart, from the
whole mind which was in Christ.[44]

7. For all this time he is the servant of sin. He commits sin,
10 more or less, day by day. Yet he is not troubled; he 'is in no
bondage' (as some speak), he feels no condemnation. He
contents himself (even though he should profess to believe that
the Christian revelation is of God) with: 'Man is frail. We are all
weak. Every man has his infirmity.' Perhaps he quotes Scripture:
15 'Why, does not Solomon say, "The righteous man falls into sin
seven times a day"?[45] And doubtless they are all hypocrites or
enthusiasts who pretend to be better than their neighbours.' If at
any time a serious thought fix upon him, he stifles it as soon as
possible with, 'Why should I fear, since God is merciful, and
20 Christ died for sinners?'[46] Thus he remains a willing servant of
sin, content with the bondage of corruption;[47] inwardly and
outwardly unholy, and satisfied therewith; not only not
conquering sin, but not striving to conquer, particularly that sin
which doth so easily beset him.[48]

25   8. Such is the state of every 'natural man'; whether he be a
gross, scandalous transgressor, or a more reputable and decent

---

[41] Cf. No. 37, 'The Nature of Enthusiasm'.

[42] Cf. No. 38, 'A Caution against Bigotry'.

[43] Cf. Jas. 3:17.

[44] See Phil. 2:5.

[45] An ironic metaphrase of Prov. 24:16, where the original refers to the righteous man's
falling (lit. 'stumbling') into adversity and being delivered. But seventeenth- and
eighteenth-century Puritan exegetes had come to understand נפל as connoting a fall into
sin. Thus Poole, *Annotations*, and Henry, *Exposition*, ('The just man falls, sometimes falls
seven times, perhaps into sin, . . . but he rises again, by repentance finds mercy with God,
and regains his peace'). In *A Plain Account of Christian Perfection*, §12, Wesley will dispute
the point again: 'Here [Prov. 24:16] is no mention of "falling into sin" at all. What is here
mentioned is "falling into temporal affliction".'); in *Predestination Calmly Considered*,
§§69-79, he will argue the question of 'perseverance' with Dr. John Gill (1697–1771), a
Baptist minister at Horsleydown and author of *The Doctrine of the Saints' Final Perseverance
Asserted and Vindicated* (1752). Cf. also No. 40, *Christian Perfection*, II.9; and see the homily
on 'An Information for Them That Take Offence at Certain Places in the Holy Scripture',
Pt. II, *Homilies*, p. 335.

[46] Cf. Rom. 5:8.   [47] Rom. 8:21.   [48] See Heb. 12:1.

sinner, having the form though not the power of godliness.[49] But how can such an one be 'convinced of sin'?[50] How is he brought to *repent*? To be 'under the law'? To receive the 'spirit of bondage unto fear'? This is the point which is next to be considered.

II.1. By some awful providence, or by his Word applied with the demonstration of his Spirit, God touches the heart of him that lay asleep in darkness and in the shadow of death.[51] He is terribly shaken out of his sleep, and awakes into a consciousness of his danger. Perhaps in a moment, perhaps by degrees, the eyes of his understanding are opened,[52] and now first (the veil being in part removed) discern the real state he is in. Horrid light breaks in upon his soul; such light as may be conceived to gleam from the bottomless pit, from the lowest deep, from a lake of fire burning with brimstone.[53] He at last sees the loving, the merciful God is also 'a consuming fire';[54] that he is a just God and a terrible, rendering to every man according to his works,[55] entering into judgment with the ungodly for every idle word, yea, and for the imaginations of the heart. He now clearly perceives that the great and holy God is 'of purer eyes than to behold iniquity';[56] that he is an avenger of everyone who rebelleth against him, and repayeth the wicked to his face;[57] and that 'it is a fearful thing to fall into the hands of the living God.'[58]

2. The inward, spiritual meaning of the law of God now begins to glare upon him. He perceives the 'commandment is exceeding broad',[59] and 'there is nothing hid from the light thereof.'[60] He is convinced that every part of it relates not barely to outward sin or obedience, but to what passes in the secret recesses of the soul, which no eye but God's can penetrate. If he now hears, 'Thou shalt not kill,'[61] God speaks in thunder, 'He that hateth his brother is a murderer;'[62] he that saith unto his brother, 'Thou fool, is obnoxious to hellfire.'[63] If the law say, 'Thou shalt not

---

[49] See 2 Tim. 3:5, from whence it would follow that 'the almost Christian', as Wesley had already described him, was 'a natural man', '*utterly* ignorant of God, . . . *totally* a stranger to the law of God' (above, I.1).

[50] Cf. John 8:46.   [51] Ps. 107:10; Luke 1:79.

[52] See Eph. 1:18.   [53] Rev. 19:20.   [54] Deut. 4:24; Heb. 12:29.

[55] Prov. 24:12; cf. Ps. 62:12.   [56] Cf. Hab. 1:13.   [57] See Deut. 7:10.

[58] Heb. 10:31; note here an abrupt shift in mood and rhetoric.

[59] Ps. 119:96.   [60] Cf. Ps. 19:6.   [61] Exod. 20:13, etc.

[62] Cf. 1 John 3:15.

[63] Cf. Matt. 5:22, and see No. 7, 'The Way to the Kingdom', II.4 and n.

commit adultery,'[64] the voice of the Lord sounds in his ears, 'He that looketh on a woman to lust after her hath committed adultery with her already in his heart.'[65] And thus in every point he feels the Word of God 'quick and powerful, sharper than a two-edged
5 sword'.[66] It pierces 'even to the dividing asunder of his soul and spirit, his joints and marrow'.[67] And so much the more because he is conscious *to himself* of having neglected so great salvation;[68] of having 'trodden under foot the Son of God' who would have saved him from his sins, and 'counted the blood of the covenant
10 an unholy', a common, unsanctifying 'thing'.[69]

3. And as he knows 'all things are naked and opened unto the eyes of him with whom we have to do,'[70] so he sees himself naked, stripped of all the fig-leaves which he had sewed together, of all his poor pretences to religion or virtue, and his wretched excuses
15 for sinning against God. He now sees himself like the ancient sacrifices, τετραχηλισμένον,[71] 'cleft in sunder', as it were, from the neck downward, so that all within him stands confessed. His heart is bare, and he sees it is all sin, 'deceitful above all things, desperately wicked';[72] that it is altogether corrupt and abomina-
20 ble, more than it is possible for tongue to express; that there dwelleth there no good thing,[73] but unrighteousness and ungodliness only; every motion thereof, every temper and thought, being only evil continually.[74]

4. And he not only sees, but feels in himself, by an emotion of
25 soul which he cannot describe, that for the sins of his heart, were his life without blame (which yet it is not, and cannot be; seeing 'an evil tree cannot bring forth good fruit'),[75] he deserves to be cast into 'the fire that never shall be quenched'.[76] He feels that 'the wages', the just reward, 'of sin', of his sin above all, 'is
30 death;'[77] even the second death,[78] the death which dieth not, the destruction of body and soul in hell.[79]

---

[64] Exod. 20:14, etc.   [65] Matt. 5:28.   [66] Cf. Heb. 4:12.
[67] *Ibid.*   [68] See Heb. 2:3.
[69] Heb. 10:29.   [70] Heb. 4:13.
[71] A lexical oddity. Sugden, *Standard Sermons*, I.187, has confused it with the τομώτερος in Heb. 4:12. Wesley's term does not appear in Liddell and Scott, *Greek-English Lexicon*, Arndt and Gingrich, *Greek-English Lexicon*, nor Lampe, *A Patristic Greek Lexicon*. Its meaning is clear enough—'drawn and quartered'—but not its source.
[72] Jer. 17:9.   [73] See Rom. 7:18.
[74] See Gen. 6:5.   [75] Cf. Matt. 7:18; Luke 6:43.
[76] Mark 9:43.   [77] Rom. 6:23.
[78] Rev. 21:8.   [79] See Matt. 10:28.

5. Here ends his pleasing dream, his delusive rest, his false peace, his vain security. His joy now vanishes as a cloud; pleasures once loved delight no more. They pall upon the taste; he loathes the nauseous sweet;[80] he is weary to bear them. The shadows of happiness flee away, and sink into oblivion; so that he is stripped of all, and wanders to and fro seeking rest, but finding none.[81]

6. The fumes of those opiates being now dispelled, he feels the anguish of a wounded spirit.[82] He finds that sin let loose upon the soul (whether it be pride, anger, or evil desire; whether self-will, malice, envy, revenge, or any other) is perfect misery. He feels sorrow of heart for the blessings he has lost, and the curse which is come upon him; remorse for having thus destroyed himself, and despised his own mercies; fear, from a lively sense of the wrath of God, and of the consequences of his wrath; of the punishment which he has justly deserved, and which he sees hanging over his head; fear of death, as being to him the gate of hell, the entrance of death eternal; fear of the devil, the executioner of the wrath and righteous vengeance of God; fear of men, who if they were able to kill his body, would thereby plunge both body and soul into hell;[83] fear, sometimes arising to such a height that the poor, sinful, guilty soul is terrified with everything, with nothing, with shades,[84] with a leaf shaken of the wind.[85] Yea, sometimes it may even border upon distraction, making a man 'drunken, though not with wine',[86] suspending the exercise of the memory, of the understanding, of all the natural faculties. Sometimes it may approach to the very brink of despair; so that he who trembles at the name of death may yet be ready to plunge into it every moment, to 'choose strangling rather than life'.[87] Well may such a man 'roar', like him of old, 'for the very disquietness of his heart'.[88] Well may he cry out, 'The spirit of a man may sustain his infirmities; but a wounded spirit who can bear?'[89]

---

[80] Cf. Samuel Johnson's quotation from Denham (under 'nauseous'):
   Those trifles wherein children take delight,
   Grow nauseous to the young man's appetite.
[81] See Matt. 12:43; Luke 11:24.
[82] Cf. below, III.4.
[83] See Matt. 10:28.
[84] I.e., ghosts; cf. Johnson, *Dictionary*, No. 10, and his citations from Dryden and Tickell.
[85] See Lev. 26:36.   [86] Cf. Isa. 29:9; 51:21.
[87] Cf. Job 7:15.   [88] Cf. Ps. 38:8 (BCP).   [89] Cf. Prov. 18:14.

7. Now he truly desires to break loose from sin, and begins to struggle with it. But though he strive with all his might he cannot conquer; sin is mightier than he. He would fain escape; but he is so fast in prison that he cannot get forth. He resolves against sin,
5 but yet sins on; he sees the snare, and abhors— and runs into it. So much does his boasted reason avail— only to enhance his guilt, and increase his misery! Such is the freedom of his will—free only to evil; free to 'drink in iniquity like water';[90] to wander farther and farther from the living God, and do more
10 'despite to the Spirit of grace'![91]

8. The more he strives, wishes, labours to be free, the more does he feel his chains, the grievous chains of sin, wherewith Satan binds and 'leads him captive at his will'.[92] His servant he is, though he repine ever so much; though he rebel, he cannot
15 prevail. He is still in bondage and fear by reason of sin: generally of some outward sin, to which he is peculiarly disposed either by nature, custom, or outward circumstances; but always of some inward sin, some evil temper or unholy affection. And the more he frets against it, the more it prevails; he may bite, but cannot
20 break his chain. Thus he toils without end, repenting and sinning, and repenting and sinning again, till at length the poor sinful, helpless wretch is even at his wit's end, and can barely groan, 'O wretched man that I am, who shall deliver me from the body of this death?'[93]

25 9. This whole struggle of one who is 'under the law',[94] under the 'spirit of fear and bondage',[95] is beautifully described by the Apostle in the foregoing chapter, speaking in the person of an awakened man. 'I (saith he) was alive without the law once.' I had much life, wisdom, strength, and virtue—so I thought. 'But when
30 the commandment came, sin revived, and I died.'[a] When the commandment, in its spiritual meaning, came to my heart with the power of God my inbred sin was stirred up, fretted, inflamed, and all my virtue died away. 'And the commandment, which was ordained to life, I found to be unto death. For sin, taking occasion
35 by the commandment, deceived me, and by it slew me.'[b] It came

---

[a] [Rom. 7,] ver. 9.　　　　　　　　　　　　　　[b] Ver. 10-11.

---

[90] Cf. Job 15:16.
[91] Heb. 10:29.
[92] Cf. 2 Tim. 2:26.　　　　　　　　　　　　　[93] Rom. 7:24.
[94] Rom. 6:14, 15.　　　　　　　　　　　　　　[95] Rom. 8:15.

upon me unawares, slew all my hopes, and plainly showed, in the midst of life I was in death.[96] 'Wherefore the law is holy, and the commandment holy, and just, and good:'[c] I no longer lay the blame on this, but on the corruption of my own heart. I acknowledge that 'the law is spiritual; but I am carnal, sold under sin.'[d] I now see both the spiritual nature of the law, and my own carnal devilish heart, 'sold under sin', totally enslaved (like slaves bought with money, who were absolutely at their master's disposal). 'For that which I do, I allow not; for what I would, I do not; but what I hate, that I do.'[e] Such is the bondage under which I groan; such the tyranny of my hard master. 'To will is present with me, but how to perform that which is good I find not. For the good that I would I do not; but the evil which I would not, that I do.'[f] 'I find a law', an inward constraining power, 'that when I would do good, evil is present with me. For I delight in' (or consent to) 'the law of God, after the inward man.'[g] (In my mind: so the Apostle explains himself in the words that immediately follow; and so ὁ ἔσω ἄνθρωπος, 'the inward man', is understood in all other Greek writers.[97]) 'But I see another law in my members', another constraining power, 'warring against the law of my mind', or inward man, 'and bringing me into captivity to the law', or power, 'of sin,'[h] dragging me as it were at my conqueror's chariot-wheels into the very thing which my soul abhors. 'O wretched man that I am, who shall deliver me from the body of this death!'[i] Who shall deliver me from this helpless, dying life; from this bondage of sin and misery! Till this is done, 'I myself' (or rather, 'that I', αὐτὸς ἐγώ, *that man* I am now personating[98]) 'with the mind', or inward man, 'serve the law of

---

[c] Ver. 12.

[d] Ver. 14. [Cf. Wesley's *Notes* here on 'the whole process of a man reasoning, groaning, striving, and escaping from the legal to the evangelical state'.]

[e] Ver. 15.   [f] Ver. 18-19.

[g] Ver. 21-22.   [h] Ver. 23.

[i] Ver. 24.

---

[96] See BCP, Burial (477).

[97] I.e., in ver. 23, where St. Paul speaks of τῷ νόμῳ τοῦ νοός μου. As for 'other Greek writers', Wesley would have known of this same usage, in Plato, *Republic* IX. 589*a*, and IV. 439*d*, as well as Plotinus, *Enneads* I.i.10.

[98] Wesley had inherited the still controverted question of whether St. Paul, in Rom. 7, is speaking of his continuing moral struggles as believer (eased and 'covered' by grace) or of his earlier state of ineffectual moral earnestness before his conversion. The Lutherans and

God'; my mind, my conscience, is on God's side: 'but with the flesh', with my body, 'the law of sin,'ʲ being hurried away by a force I cannot resist.

10. How lively a portraiture is this of one 'under the law'! One
5 who feels the burden he cannot shake off; who pants after liberty, power, and love, but is in fear and bondage still! Until the time that God answers the wretched man crying out, 'Who shall deliver me' from this bondage of sin, from this body of death?—'The grace of God, through Jesus Christ thy Lord.'⁹⁹

10 III.1. Then it is that this miserable bondage ends, and he is no more 'under the law, but under grace'.¹⁰⁰ This state we are thirdly to consider; the state of one who has found 'grace', or favour in the sight of God, even the Father, and who has the 'grace', or power of the Holy Ghost, reigning in his heart; who has received,
15 in the language of the Apostle, 'the Spirit of adoption, whereby he now cries, Abba, Father'.¹⁰¹

2. 'He cried unto the Lord in his trouble, and God delivers him out of his distress.'¹⁰² His eyes are opened in quite another manner than before, even to see a loving, gracious God. While he
20 is calling, 'I beseech thee show me thy glory,'¹⁰³ he hears a voice in his inmost soul, 'I will make all my goodness pass before thee, and I will proclaim the name of the Lord; I will be gracious to whom I will be gracious, and I will show mercy to whom I will show mercy.'¹⁰⁴ And it is not long before 'the Lord descends in the
25 cloud, and proclaims the name of the Lord.'¹⁰⁵ Then he sees (but not with eyes of flesh and blood) 'The Lord, the Lord God;

ʲ Ver. 25.

Calvinists by and large took it as confirmation of the *simul justus et peccator*. Wesley understands that St. Paul is here 'personating' a hypothetical man in 'the legal state'; he holds to this later in his *Notes* on Rom. 7:7-8. On the other side, cf. Karl Barth, *Epistle to the Romans* (Oxford, Oxford University Press, 1933), p. 270: 'What Paul is here asserting [that 7:21-25 is his own experience] was well understood by the Reformers; it is misunderstood by those modern theologians who read him through the spectacles of their own piety.' But see W. Sanday and A. C. Headlam, *The Epistle to the Romans*, in *The International Critical Commentary* (New York, Charles Scribner's Sons, 1895), XXXIII. 186; also John Knox in *The Interpreter's Bible*, IX. 498-500. Obviously, one's exegesis here follows from one's soteriology and not from any decisive evidence within the Greek text.

⁹⁹ Cf. 1 Cor. 1:4.
¹⁰⁰ Rom. 6:14. See also Boston, State III, 'The State of Grace', and note the similarities between that text and this.
¹⁰¹ Cf. Rom. 8:15.   ¹⁰² Cf. Ps. 107:6.   ¹⁰³ Exod. 33:18.
¹⁰⁴ Cf. Exod. 33:19.   ¹⁰⁵ Cf. Exod. 34:5.

merciful and gracious, long-suffering, and abundant in goodness and truth; keeping mercy for thousands, and forgiving iniquities and transgression and sin.'[106]

3. Heavenly, healing light now breaks in upon his soul. He 'looks on him whom he had pierced',[107] and 'God, who out of darkness commanded light to shine, shineth in his heart.' He sees 'the light of the glorious love of God, in the face of Jesus Christ'.[108] He hath a divine 'evidence of things not seen'[109] by sense, even of 'the deep things of God';[110] more particularly of the love of God, of his pardoning love to him that believes in Jesus. Overpowered with the sight, his whole soul cries out, 'My Lord, and my God!'[111] For he sees all his iniquities laid on him who 'bare them in his own body on the tree';[112] he beholds the Lamb of God taking away his sins. How clearly now does he discern 'that God was in Christ, reconciling the world unto himself; . . . making him sin for us, who knew no sin, that we might be made the righteousness of God through him!'[113] And that he himself is reconciled to God by that blood of the covenant!

4. Here end both the guilt and power of sin.[114] He can now say, 'I am crucified with Christ. Nevertheless I live; yet not I, but Christ liveth in me. And the life which I now live in the flesh', even in this mortal body, 'I live by faith in the Son of God, who loved me and gave himself for me.'[115] Here end remorse and sorrow of heart, and the anguish of a wounded spirit.[116] 'God turneth his heaviness into joy.'[117] He 'made sore', and now 'his hands bind up'.[118] Here ends also that bondage unto fear; for 'his heart standeth fast, believing in the Lord.'[119] He cannot fear any longer the wrath of God; for he knows it is now turned away from him, and looks upon him no more as an angry judge, but as a loving Father. He cannot fear the devil, knowing he has 'no

---

[106] Cf. Exod. 34:6-7. Note this rare instance of Wesley's 'spiritualizing' of what stands as a historical record in Exod. 33–34.

[107] Cf. Zech. 12:10. [108] Cf. 2 Cor. 4:6.
[109] Heb. 11:1. [110] 1 Cor. 2:10.
[111] John 20:28. [112] Cf. 1 Pet. 2:24.
[113] Cf. 2 Cor. 5:19, 21.

[114] A hyperbole here, since Wesley will continue to recognize (as in No. 8, 'The First-fruits of the Spirit', II.4-13) that even in regeneration (as here) 'sin *remains* but no longer *reigns*' (cf. No. 13, *On Sin in Believers*, I.6 and n.). What *is* taken away is guilt and 'condemnation'.

[115] Cf. Gal. 2:20. [116] Cf. above, II.6.
[117] Cf. Jas. 4:9. [118] Cf. Job 5:18.
[119] Cf. Ps. 112:7 (BCP).

power, except it be given him from above'.[120] He fears not hell, being an heir of the kingdom of heaven. Consequently, he has no fear of death, by reason whereof he was in time past for so many years 'subject to bondage'.[121] Rather, knowing that 'if the earthly
5 house of this tabernacle be dissolved, he hath a building of God, a house not made with hands, eternal in the heavens, he groaneth earnestly, desiring to be clothed upon with that house which is from heaven.'[122] He groans to shake off this house of earth, that 'mortality may be swallowed up of life'; knowing that 'God hath
10 wrought him for the selfsame thing; who hath also given him the earnest of his Spirit.'[123]

5. And 'where the Spirit of the Lord is, there is liberty;'[124] liberty not only from guilt and fear, but from sin, from that heaviest of all yokes, that basest of all bondage. His labour is not
15 now in vain.[125] The snare is broken, and he is delivered.[126] He not only strives, but likewise prevails; he not only fights, but conquers also. 'Henceforth he doth not serve sin. . . . He is dead unto sin and alive unto God. . . . Sin doth not now reign, even in his mortal body', nor doth he 'obey it in the desires thereof'. He does
20 not 'yield his members as instruments of unrighteousness unto sin, but as instruments of righteousness unto God'. For 'being now made free from sin, he is become the servant of righteousness.'[k]

6. Thus 'having peace with God, through our Lord Jesus
25 Christ', 'rejoicing in hope of the glory of God',[127] and having power over all sin, over every evil desire and temper, and word and work, he is a living witness of the 'glorious liberty of the sons of God':[128] all of whom, being partakers of 'like precious faith',[129] bear record with one voice, 'We have received the Spirit of
30 adoption, whereby we cry, Abba, Father!'[130]

7. It is this Spirit which continually 'worketh in them, both to will and to do of his good pleasure'.[131] It is he that sheds the love of God abroad in their hearts,[132] and the love of all mankind; thereby purifying their hearts from the love of the world, from the lust of

[k] [Rom.]6:6[,11-13, 18].

---

[120] Cf. John 19:11.
[121] Heb. 2:15.
[122] Cf. 2 Cor. 5:1-2.
[123] Cf. 2 Cor. 5:4-5.
[124] 2 Cor. 3:17.
[125] See 1 Cor. 15:58.
[126] See Ps. 124:7.
[127] Cf. Rom. 5:1-2.
[128] Cf. Rom. 8:21.
[129] 2 Pet. 1:1.
[130] Rom. 8:15.
[131] Cf. Phil. 2:13.
[132] See Rom. 5:5.

the flesh, the lust of the eye, and the pride of life.[133] It is by him they are delivered from anger and pride, from all vile and inordinate affections.[134] In consequence, they are delivered from evil words and works, from all unholiness of conversation; doing no evil to any child of man, and being zealous of all good works.[135]

8. To sum up all. The 'natural man' neither fears nor loves God; one 'under the law' fears, one 'under grace' loves him. The first has no light in the things of God, but walks in utter darkness. The second sees the painful light of hell; the third, the joyous light of heaven. He that sleeps in death has a false peace. He that is awakened has no peace at all. He that believes has true peace, the peace of God, filling and ruling his heart. The heathen, baptized or unbaptized,[136] hath a fancied liberty, which is indeed licentiousness; the Jew (or one under the Jewish dispensation) is in heavy, grievous bondage; the Christian enjoys the true glorious liberty of the sons of God.[137] An unawakened child of the devil[138] sins willingly; one that is awakened sins unwillingly; a child of God 'sinneth not, but keepeth himself, and the wicked one toucheth him not'.[139] To conclude: the natural man neither conquers nor fights; the man under the law fights with sin, but cannot conquer; the man under grace fights and conquers, yea is 'more than conqueror, through him that loveth him'.[140]

IV.1. From this plain account of the threefold state of man—the 'natural', the 'legal', and the 'evangelical'—it appears that it is not sufficient to divide mankind into sincere and insincere.[141] A man may be sincere in any of these states; not only when he has the 'Spirit of adoption', but while he has the 'spirit of bondage unto fear'. Yea, while he has neither this fear, nor love. For undoubtedly there may be sincere heathens as well as sincere

---

[133] 1 John 2:16.　　　[134] See Col. 3:5.　　　[135] See Titus 2:14.

[136] 'Baptized or unbaptized': a strange usage, since elsewhere Wesley uses the term 'heathen' in its generally accepted sense of those never having made any sort of Christian profession (or Jewish or Moslem, for that matter); cf. his argument with John Taylor over the cultural status of 'the heathens' in *Doctrine of Original Sin*, Pt. I, II.2–5; see also Nos. 63, 'The General Spread of the Gospel', §1; 21, 'Sermon on the Mount, I', I.9; and No. 2, *The Almost Christian*, I.1. But for the salvability of 'heathens', cf. Large *Minutes*, in *Minutes*, London, 1862, 1.669–73; and No. 91, 'On Charity', I.3 and n.

[137] See Rom. 8:21.

[138] Acts 13:10.

[139] Cf. 1 John 5:18.

[140] Cf. Rom. 8:37.

[141] Cf. No. 2, *The Almost Christian*, I.9 and n.

Jews or Christians. This circumstance, then, does by no means prove that a man is in a state of acceptance with God.

'Examine yourselves', therefore, not only whether ye are sincere, but 'whether ye be in the faith.'[142] Examine narrowly; for
5 it imports you much. What is the ruling principle in your soul? Is it the love of God? Is it the fear of God? Or is it neither one nor the other? Is it not rather the love of the world? The love of pleasure? Or gain? Of ease; or reputation? If so, you are not come so far as a Jew. You are but a *heathen* still. Have you heaven in your heart?
10 Have you the Spirit of adoption, ever crying, 'Abba, Father'? Or do you cry unto God as 'out of the belly of hell',[143] overwhelmed with sorrow and fear? Or are you a stranger to this whole affair, and cannot imagine what I mean? Heathen, pull off the mask. Thou hast never put on Christ.[144] Stand barefaced. Look up to
15 heaven; and own before him that liveth for ever and ever, thou hast no part either among the sons or servants of God.

Whosoever thou art, dost thou commit sin, or dost thou not? If thou dost, is it willingly, or unwillingly? In either case God hath told thee whose thou art—'He that committeth sin is of the
20 devil.'[145] If thou committest it willingly thou art his faithful servant. He will not fail to reward thy labour. If unwillingly, still thou art his servant.[146] God deliver thee out of his hands!

Art thou daily fighting against all sin; and daily more than conqueror? I acknowledge thee for a child of God. O stand fast in
25 thy glorious liberty. Art thou fighting, but not conquering; striving for the mastery, but not able to attain? Then thou art not yet a believer in Christ.[147] But follow on; and thou shalt know the Lord. Art thou not fighting at all, but leading an easy, indolent, fashionable life? O how hast thou dared to name the name of
30 Christ! Only to make it a reproach among the heathen? Awake, thou sleeper! Call upon thy God, before the deep swallow thee up.[148]

2. Perhaps one reason why so many think of themselves more highly than they ought to think,[149] why they do not discern what
35 state they are in, is because these several states of soul are often

---

[142] 2 Cor. 13:5.   [143] Jonah 2:2.
[144] Gal. 3:27.   [145] 1 John 3:8.
[146] An apparent exception to Wesley's normal distinction between wilful and unwilled sins; it fits the mood of this particular exhortation and need not signify a basic shift.
[147] Note Wesley's reversion, in this 'application', to his earlier emphasis on a complete deliverance from sin and the state of full assurance, or none at all.
[148] See Ps. 69:15 (AV).   [149] See Rom. 12:3.

mingled together, and in some measure meet in one and the same person. Thus experience shows that the legal state, or state of fear, is frequently mixed with the natural; for few men are so fast asleep in sin but they are sometimes more or less awakened. As the Spirit of God does not 'wait for the call of man',[150] so at some times he *will* be heard. He puts them in fear, so that for a season at least the heathen 'know themselves to be but men'.[151] They feel the burden of sin, and earnestly desire to flee from the wrath to come.[152] But not long. They seldom suffer the arrows of conviction to go deep into their souls;[153] but quickly stifle the grace of God, and return to their wallowing in the mire.[154]

In like manner the evangelical state, or state of love, is frequently mixed with the legal. For few of those who have the spirit of bondage and fear remain always without hope.[155] The wise and gracious God rarely suffers this; for he remembereth that we are but dust.[156] And he willeth not that 'the flesh should fail before him, or the spirit which he hath made'.[157] Therefore, at such times as he seeth good he gives a dawning of light unto them that sit in darkness.[158] He causes a part of his goodness to pass before them,[159] and shows he is a 'God that heareth the prayer'.[160] They see the promise which is by faith in Christ Jesus, though it be yet afar off; and hereby they are encouraged to 'run with patience the race which is set before them'.[161]

3. Another reason why many deceive themselves is because they do not consider how far a man may go and yet be in a natural, or at best a legal state.[162] A man may be of a compassionate and a benevolent temper; he may be affable, courteous, generous, friendly; he may have some degree of meekness, patience, temperance, and of many other moral virtues; he may feel many desires of shaking off all vice, and attaining higher degrees of virtue; he may abstain from much evil—perhaps from all that is

---

[150] Cf. Micah 5:7.   [151] Ps. 9:20.   [152] Matt. 3:7; Luke 3:7.
[153] Cf. Matthew Henry's exegesis *(Exposition)* of Ps. 38:2 ('the arrows of the Almighty [are] the terrors of the Lord [which cause] a very melancholy frightful apprehension of the wrath of God . . .') and also of Ps. 45:5 ('convictions are like the arrows of a bow. . .').
[154] 2 Pet. 2:22.
[155] Wesley is more positive than this in the *Minutes*, May 13, 1746:
    Q. But can it be conceived that God has any regard to the sincerity of an unbeliever?
    A. Yes, so much that if he persevere therein, God will infallibly give him faith.
[156] Ps. 103:14.   [157] Cf. Isa. 57:16.   [158] See Luke 1:79.
[159] See Exod. 33:19.   [160] Cf. Prov. 15:29.   [161] Heb. 12:1.
[162] This and the following two paragraphs are a sort of reprise of No. 2, *The Almost Christian*.

grossly contrary to justice, mercy, or truth; he may do much good, may feed the hungry, clothe the naked,[163] relieve the widow and fatherless;[164] he may attend public worship, use prayer in private, read many books of devotion—and yet for all this he may be a
5 mere natural man, knowing neither himself nor God; equally a stranger to the spirit of fear and to that of love; having neither repented nor believed the gospel.[165]

But suppose there were added to all this a deep conviction of sin, with much fear of the wrath of God; vehement desires to cast
10 off every sin, and to fulfil all righteousness;[166] frequent rejoicing in hope, and touches of love often glancing upon the soul: yet neither do these prove a man to be 'under grace',[167] to have true, living, Christian faith, unless the Spirit of adoption abide in his heart, unless he can continually cry, 'Abba, Father!'

15 4. Beware, then, thou who art called by the name of Christ, that thou come not short of the mark of thy high calling.[168] Beware thou rest not, either in a natural state, with too many that are accounted 'good Christians', or in a legal state, wherein those who are 'highly esteemed of men'[169] are generally content to live
20 and die. Nay, but God hath prepared better things for thee, if thou follow on till thou attain. Thou art not called to fear and tremble, like devils,[170] but to rejoice and love, like the angels of God. 'Thou shalt love the Lord thy God with all thy heart, and with all thy soul, and with all thy mind, and with all thy strength.'[171]
25 Thou shalt 'rejoice evermore.'[172] Thou shalt 'pray without ceasing.'[173] Thou shalt 'in everything give thanks.'[174] Thou shalt do the will of God 'on earth, as it is done in heaven'.[175] O 'prove' thou 'what is that good and acceptable and perfect will of God.'[176] Now 'present' thyself 'a living sacrifice, holy, acceptable to
30 God.'[177] 'Whereunto thou hast already attained',[178] 'hold fast',[179] by 'reaching forth unto those things which are before';[180] until 'the God of peace . . . make thee perfect in every good work, working in thee that which is well-pleasing in his sight, through Jesus Christ, to whom be glory for ever and ever! Amen!'[181]

---

[163] See Matt. 25:35-36.   [164] See Ps. 146:9.   [165] See Mark 1:15.
[166] Matt. 3:15.   [167] Rom. 6:14.   [168] See Phil. 3:14.
[169] Cf. Luke 16:15.   [170] See Jas. 2:19.   [171] Mark 12:30, etc.
[172] 1 Thess. 5:16.   [173] 1 Thess. 5:17.   [174] 1 Thess. 5:18.
[175] Cf. Matt. 6:10; Luke 11:2.   [176] Rom. 12:2.   [177] Rom. 12:1.
[178] Cf. Phil. 3:16; 1 Tim. 4:6.   [179] 1 Thess. 5:21; Heb. 4:14.   [180] Phil. 3:13.
[181] Cf. Heb. 13:20-21. For Wesley's use of ascriptions, cf. No. 1, *Salvation by Faith*, III.9 and n.

THE WITNESS OF THE SPIRIT,

DISCOURSES I & II

AN INTRODUCTORY COMMENT

The following two essays were written and published more than twenty years apart (1746, 1767), but that they belong together was recognized by Wesley in the collection of his Works, I, *where they appear as Sermons 10 and 11. While there is no record that either of them was ever preached, the evidence is abundant that their shared and central concern—the ground and character of Christian assurance—was paramount in Wesley's mind. It was also a bone of contention with his critics. Already, in* A Farther Appeal *(1745), Pt. I, III-V, Wesley had entered the lists against men like Edmund Gibson, Bishop of London, Thomas Herring, Archbishop of York, and Richard Smalbroke, Bishop of Lichfield and Coventry—all of whom had understood Wesley's doctrines of assurance and of religious intuition as 'enthusiasm' (11:117-76 of this edn.). Presently, he would be denounced by George Lavington, Bishop of Exeter, in* The Enthusiasm of Methodists and Papists Compared *(1749). It was, therefore, important in 1746 for him to summarize the issues and to clarify his own position as simply and directly as possible.*

It was clear enough that Wesley's theory of religious knowledge was frankly intuitionist, but this had been all too easily misconstrued as a one-sided subjectivism. Thus, he had to clarify his distinction between the ways in which assurance might be felt *('the witness of our own spirit') and the objective ground of any such experience (viz., the prior and direct 'witness of the Holy Spirit'). The question at issue between 'enthusiasts' and 'rationalists' was whether a believer's consciousness of justification and reconciliation was an inference from his religious and moral feelings or whether those feelings, if valid, were first prompted by a free and direct testimony of the Spirit to one's divine sonship, promptings to which faith had responded and in which hope and love could participate. Characteristically, Wesley opts for a both/and solution, stressing the believer's own consciousness of God's favour but even more strongly the priority of the Spirit's prevenient and direct witness as the necessary precondition of any* feelings *of assurance. That this is the crucial point for Wesley would appear from the fact that he repeats the same basic argument for it in Discourse II.*

The controversy was as old as second-century Montanism at least, and Wesley's balanced stress on an objective witness and a subjective one was not new. He had already found a survey of it in an essay on Romans 8 by Alexander Hamilton, A Cordial for Christians Travelling Heaven-Ward *(1696). Hamilton's conclusion foreshadows Wesley's: 'The witness of the Spirit is a twofold testimony for our sonship: by the Spirit himself and from our conscience' (p. 105). Moreover, according to Hamilton, the Spirit's testimony is conveyed conjointly, through Scripture by divine illumination, and also by the Spirit's gracious, sanctifying presence. Wesley seeks to safeguard this notion from subjectivity by insisting that the gifts of the Spirit, including the gift of assurance, are always to be judged by reference to the* fruit *of the Spirit (Gal. 5:22-23).*

But why two discourses of this sort, on the same text, with most of the same arguments? An answer to this must be circumstantial; it will illustrate Wesley's understanding of the sermon genre as a way of repeating himself with fresh and refined nuances. Discourse I is the basic statement; it seeks a middle course between 'enthusiasm' and 'rationalism' by recourse to the idea of testimonium internum Spiritus Sancti *(the inner witness of the Holy Spirit), in Lutheran and Reformed traditions, linked as they had been to the notion of the inspiration of the Scriptures. But what Wesley had intended as a moderating formulation had drawn a storm of criticism, repeating the charge of 'enthusiasm' and ignoring Wesley's stress on objectivity (cf. Green,* Anti-Methodist Publications, *where more than twenty attacks are listed on this point alone, including major essays by John Parkhurst, Theophilus Evans, and William Warburton; see also Umphrey Lee,* Early Methodist Enthusiasm, *and R. A. Knox,* Enthusiasm). *Moreover, as the Revival was moving on into its second generation, there were cases of real enthusiasm that lent credence to these other criticisms (e.g., William Cudworth and James Relly). By the mid-sixties, then, the time was ripe for a restatement of the doctrine of the 'twofold testimony' and also for a rehearsal and refutation of the main objections that had been raised against it over the controversy's course. Discourse II is, therefore, more than a mere sequel; it is a significant revision of Discourse I. Thus, the two essays are designed to be read together with one eye on the arguments themselves and the other on their theological context in the ongoing Revival.*

The edited text of Discourse II is based on that of the first edition of 1767. For a stemma illustrating the transmission of that text through its six extant editions issued during Wesley's lifetime, together with the substantive variant readings from those editions, see the Appendix, Vol. IV. For further details see Bibliog, *No. 303.*

SERMON 10

The Witness of the Spirit, I

Romans 8:16

The Spirit itself beareth witness with our spirit, that we are the children of God.

1. How many vain men, not understanding what they speak, 5 neither whereof they affirmed, have wrested this Scripture to the great loss if not the destruction of their souls! How many have mistaken the voice of their own imagination for this 'witness of the Spirit' of God, and thence idly presumed they were the children of God while they were doing the works of the devil![1] 10 These are truly and properly *enthusiasts;* and, indeed, in the worst sense of the word.[2] But with what difficulty are they convinced thereof, especially if they have drank deep into that spirit of error![3] All endeavours to bring them to the knowledge of themselves they will then account 'fighting against God'.[4] And 15 that vehemence and impetuosity of spirit which they call 'contending earnestly for the faith'[5] sets them so far above all the

---

[1] 1 John 3:8.

[2] Wesley would have had in mind here the long tradition of this idea in Chambers's *Cyclopaedia,* and its history from the Messalians (fourth century) through the Joachimites (thirteenth century), the German 'Schwärmer' (sixteenth century), the 'French prophets' (eighteenth century), *et al.;* cf. Umphrey Lee, *op. cit.* But since Wesley himself lay under the constant charge of 'enthusiast' himself, he was careful to formulate a positive alternative; cf. No. 37, 'The Nature of Enthusiasm'. Cf. also the claim in Bishop Smalbroke's *Charge . . . to . . . the Clergy* (1744) that 'the witness of the Spirit . . . cannot possibly be applied to the private testimony of the Spirit given to our consciences, as is pretended by modern enthusiasts' (i.e., Methodists), and Wesley's reply in *A Farther Appeal,* Pt. I, V.4-29 (11:141-73 of this edn.). Cf. also No. 7, 'The Way to the Kingdom', II.13 and n.

[3] 1 John 4:6.   [4] Acts 5:39.   [5] Cf. Jude 3.

usual methods of conviction that we may well say, 'With men it is impossible.'[6]

2. Who can then be surprised if many reasonable men, seeing the dreadful effects of this delusion, and labouring to keep at the utmost distance from it, should sometimes lean toward another extreme? If they are not forward to believe any who speak of having this witness concerning which others have so grievously erred; if they are almost ready to set all down for 'enthusiasts' who use the expressions which have been so terribly abused? Yea, if they should question whether the witness or testimony here spoken of be the privilege of *ordinary* Christians, and not rather one of those *extraordinary* gifts which they suppose belonged only to the apostolic age?

3. But is there any necessity laid upon us of running either into one extreme or the other? May we not steer a middle course? Keep a sufficient distance from that spirit of error and enthusiasm without denying the gift of God and giving up the great privilege of his children? Surely we may. In order thereto, let us consider, in the presence and fear of God,

First: What is this 'witness (or testimony) of our spirit'? What is the 'testimony of God's Spirit'? And how does he 'bear witness with our spirit that we are the children of God'?

Secondly: How is this joint testimony of God's Spirit and our own clearly and solidly distinguished from the presumption of a natural mind, and from the delusion of the devil?

I.1. Let us first consider, what is the 'witness' or 'testimony of our spirit'? But here I cannot but desire all those who are for swallowing up the testimony of the Spirit of God in the rational testimony of our own spirit to observe that in this text the Apostle is so far from speaking of the testimony of our own spirit *only*, that it may be questioned whether he speaks of it *at all*—whether he does not speak *only* of the testimony of God's Spirit. It does not appear but the original text may fairly be understood thus. The Apostle had just said, in the preceding verse, 'Ye have received the Spirit of adoption, whereby we cry, Abba, Father,'[7] and immediately subjoins, Αὐτὸ τὸ πνεῦμα (some copies read τὸ αὐτὸ πνεῦμα) συμμαρτυρεῖ τῷ πνεύματι ἡμῶν, ὅτι

---

[6] Mark 10:27; cf. Matt. 19:26.
[7] Rom. 8:15.

ἐσμὲν τέκνα θεοῦ;[8] which may be translated, 'The same Spirit beareth witness to our spirit that we are the children of God' (the preposition σύν only denoting that he witnesses this *at the same time* that he enables us to cry, 'Abba, Father!').[9] But I contend not; seeing so many other texts, with the experience of all real 5 Christians, sufficiently evince that there is in every believer both the testimony of God's Spirit, and the testimony of his own, that he is a child of God.

2. With regard to the latter, the foundation thereof is laid in those numerous texts of Scripture which describe the marks of 10 the children of God; and that so plain that he which runneth may read them.[10] These are also collected together, and placed in the strongest light, by many both ancient and modern writers.[11] If any need farther light he may receive it by attending on the ministry of God's Word, by meditating thereon before God in secret, and by 15 conversing with those who have the knowledge of his ways. And by the reason or understanding that God has given him—which religion was designed not to extinguish, but to perfect, according to that [word] of the Apostle, 'Brethren, be not children in understanding; in malice (or wickedness) be ye children; but in 20 understanding be ye men.'[a] Every man applying those scriptural marks to himself may know whether he is a child of God. Thus if he know, first, 'As many as are led by the Spirit of God' into all

---

[a] 1 Cor. 14:20.

---

[8] A more complicated point than first appears; there are no early Greek texts that read τὸ αὐτὸ πνεῦμα, and it does not appear in the *TR.* However, four sixteenth-century English translations read 'the same Spirit' instead of 'the Spirit himself': (Tyndale [1525, 1535], Coverdale [1535], the Great Bible [1539], the Geneva Bible [1560]). Moreover, Luther's *Römerbriefvorlesung* and his *Deutsche Bibel* read *'derselbige Geist'* ('the same Spirit'). Only the Douai-Rheims (1582), the Bishops' Bible (1568, 1602), and the King James (1611) read 'the Spirit himself'. In his *Notes,* Wesley reads 'the same spirit' just as John Heylyn did in his *Theological Lectures.* Bengel, however, had the *TR* before him and still read 'the Spirit himself'.

The key to these variations would seem to lie in Erasmus's Latin translation in his Greek-Latin edn. of 1518–19, where we find *idem spiritus* in place of the Vulgate's *ipse spiritus.* In his Greek edn. of 1589 Beza notices Erasmus's *idem spiritus* and back-translates τὸ αὐτὸ πνεῦμα; this is the only Greek text with such a reading that I have found. Could Wesley have seen this edn. or have heard this textual problem discussed in a lecture or conversation?

[9] Wesley's unwillingness to contend for this particular exegesis of σύν is warranted; it is more curious than correct.

[10] See IIab. 2:2.

[11] Cf. John Owen, *Of Communion With God* (1657), Pt. III. ii (espec. §4); see also Arthur Bedford's sermon on *The Doctrine of Assurance . . .* , Appendix, p. 35.

holy tempers and actions, 'they are the sons of God' (for which he
has the infallible assurance of Holy Writ[12]); secondly, I am thus
'led by the Spirit of God'— he will easily conclude, 'Therefore I
am a "son of God".'

5   3. Agreeable to this are all those plain declarations of St. John
in his First Epistle, 'Hereby we know that we do know him, if we
keep his commandments.'[b] 'Whoso keepeth his word, in him
verily is the love of God perfected; hereby know we that we are in
him'[c]—that we are indeed the children of God. 'If ye know that he
10 is righteous, ye know that everyone that doth righteousness is
born of him.'[d] 'We know that we have passed from death unto life,
because we love the brethren.'[e] 'Hereby we know that we are of
the truth, and shall assure our hearts before him;' namely,
because we 'love' one another not 'in word, neither in tongue; but
15 in deed and in truth'.[f] 'Hereby know we that we dwell in him, . . .
because he hath given us of his (loving) Spirit.'[g] And, 'Hereby we
know that he abideth in us, by the (obedient) spirit which he hath
given us.'[h]

      4. It is highly probable there never were any children of God,
20 from the beginning of the world unto this day, who were farther
advanced in the grace of God and the knowledge of our Lord
Jesus Christ than the Apostle John at the time when he wrote
these words, and the 'fathers in Christ'[13] to whom he wrote.
Notwithstanding which, it is evident both the Apostle himself and
25 all those pillars in God's temple[14] were very far from despising
these marks of their being the children of God; and that they
applied them to their own souls for the confirmation of their faith.
Yet all this is no other than rational evidence: the 'witness of our
spirit', our reason or understanding. It all resolves into this: those
30 who have these marks, they are the children of God. But we have
these marks: therefore we are children of God.

      5. But how does it appear that we have these marks?[15] This is a
question which still remains. How does it appear that we do love

---

[b] [1 John] 2:3.   [c] Ver. 5.   [d] Ver. 29.
[e] Chap. 3, ver. 14.   [f] Ver. 18.   [g] Chap. 4, ver. 13.
[h] Chap. 3, ver. 24.

---

[12] Cf. Rom. 8:14.   [13] Cf. 1 John 2:13, 14.
[14] See Rev. 3:12.
[15] For this usage of 'how does it appear' as equivalent to 'how is it made evident', cf.
OED, 'appear', 9.

God and our neighbour? And that we keep his commandments? Observe that the meaning of the question is, How does it appear to *ourselves*—not to *others*. I would ask him then that proposes this question, How does it appear to you that you are alive?[16] And that you are now in ease and not in pain? Are you not immediately conscious of it? By the same immediate consciousness you will know if your soul is alive to God; if you are saved from the pain of proud wrath, and have the ease of a meek and quiet spirit.[17] By the same means you cannot but perceive if you love, rejoice, and delight in God. By the same you must be directly assured if you love your neighbour as yourself;[18] if you are kindly affectioned to all mankind,[19] and full of gentleness and longsuffering. And with regard to the outward mark of the children of God, which is (according to St. John) the keeping his commandments, you undoubtedly know in your own breast if, by the grace of God, it belongs to you. Your conscience informs you from day to day if you do not take the name of God within your lips unless with seriousness and devotion, with reverence and godly fear; if you remember the sabbath day to keep it holy;[20] if you honour your father and mother;[21] if you do to all as you would they should do unto you;[22] if you possess your body in sanctification and honour;[23] and if, whether you eat or drink, you are temperate therein, and do all to the glory of God.[24]

6. Now this is properly the 'testimony of our own spirit', even the testimony of our conscience,[25] that God hath given us to be holy of heart, and holy in outward conversation. It is a

---

[16] Another instance of Wesley's direct intuitionism in spiritual knowledge; it presupposes self-awareness as self-evident. But subjective consciousness must always be correlated with outward marks—*viz.*, good works: love in action to God and to neighbour.

[17] 1 Pet 3:4.   [18] See Matt. 19:19, etc.   [19] See Rom. 12:10.
[20] Exod. 20:8.   [21] See Exod. 20:12.
[22] See Matt. 7:12; Luke 6:31.   [23] See 1 Thess. 4:4.
[24] See 1 Cor. 10:31.

[25] The Puritans had been much concerned with both 'the testimony of conscience' and the careful 'examination of conscience'. Cf. William Perkins, *A Case of Conscience, the greatest that ever was: How a man may know whether he be the child of God, or no . . .* (1595). See also his *Discourse of Conscience . . .* (1597), along with William Ames, *Conscience, with the power and cases thereof . . .* (1643), Richard Alleine, *Vindiciae Pietatis* (1676), and Samuel Annesley's sermon on 'How We May Be Universally and Exactly Conscientious', in *The Morning Exercise at Cripplegate* (1661). Richard Baxter had distinguished the *forum conscientiae* from the *forum Dei* in his *Confession* (1655), p. 189; Robert South had used the phrase, *forum conscientiae*, in 'The Remorse Occasioned by the Rejection of Christ' (*Works*, III. 403). See also Wesley's fourth letter to 'John Smith' (Mar. 25, 1747), espec. §§6-7, and his sermon No. 105, 'On Conscience'.

consciousness of our having received, in and by the Spirit of adoption, the tempers mentioned in the Word of God as belonging to his adopted children; even a loving heart toward God and toward all mankind, hanging with childlike confidence
5 on God our Father, desiring nothing but him, casting all our care upon him,[26] and embracing every child of man with earnest, tender affection, so as to be ready to lay down our life for our brother, as Christ laid down his life for us[27]—a consciousness that we are inwardly conformed by the Spirit of God to the image of
10 his Son, and that we walk before him in justice, mercy, and truth; doing the things which are pleasing in his sight.[28]

7. But what is that testimony of God's Spirit which is superadded to and conjoined with this? How does he 'bear witness with our spirit that we are the children of God'? It is hard
15 to find words in the language of men to explain 'the deep things of God'.[29] Indeed there are none that will adequately express what the children of God experience. But perhaps one might say (desiring any who are taught of God to correct, to soften or strengthen the expression), the testimony of the Spirit is an
20 inward impression on the soul, whereby the Spirit of God directly 'witnesses to my spirit that I am a child of God'; that Jesus Christ hath loved me, and given himself for me;[30] that all my sins are blotted out,[31] and I, even I, am reconciled to God.[32]

8. That this 'testimony of the Spirit of God' must needs, in the
25 very nature of things, be antecedent to the 'testimony of our own spirit' may appear from this single consideration: we must be holy of heart and holy in life before we can be conscious that we are so, before we can have 'the testimony of our spirit' that we are inwardly and outwardly holy. But we must love God before we
30 can be holy at all; this being the root of all holiness. Now we cannot love God till we know he loves us: 'We love him, because he first loved us.'[33] And we cannot know his pardoning love to us till his Spirit witnesses it to our spirit. Since therefore this 'testimony of his Spirit' must precede the love of God and all
35 holiness, of consequence it must precede our inward conscious-

---

[26] See 1 Pet. 5:7.
[28] See 1 John 3:22.
[30] See Gal. 2:20.
[32] 2 Cor. 5:20. Cf. No. 5, 'Justification by Faith', IV.2 and n.
[33] 1 John 4:19.

[27] See 1 John 3:16.
[29] 1 Cor. 2:10.
[31] See Acts 3:19.

ness[34] thereof, or the 'testimony of our spirit' concerning them.

9. Then, and not till then—when the Spirit of God beareth that witness to our spirit, 'God hath loved thee and given his own Son to be the propitiation for thy sins;'[35] 'the Son of God hath loved thee, and hath washed thee from thy sins in his blood'[36]—'we love God, because he first loved us,' and for his sake we 'love our brother also'.[37] And of this we cannot but be conscious to ourselves: we 'know the things that are freely given to us of God';[38] we know that we love God and keep his commandments; and hereby also 'we know that we are of God.'[39] This is that testimony of our own spirit which, so long as we continue to love God and keep his commandments, continues joined with the testimony of God's Spirit, 'that we are the children of God'.

10. Not that I would by any means be understood by anything which has been spoken concerning it to exclude the operation of the Spirit of God, even from the 'testimony of our own spirit'. In no wise. It is he that not only worketh in us every manner of thing that is good, but also shines upon his own work, and clearly shows what he has wrought. Accordingly this is spoken of by St. Paul as one great end of our receiving the Spirit, 'that we may know the things which are freely given to us of God';[40] that he may strengthen the testimony of our conscience touching our 'simplicity and godly sincerity',[41] and give us to discern in a fuller and stronger light that we now do the things which please him.

11. Should it still be inquired, 'How does the Spirit of God "bear witness with our spirit that we are the children of God" so as to exclude all doubt, and evince the reality of our sonship?'—the answer is clear from what has been observed above. And, first, as to the witness of our spirit: the soul as intimately and evidently perceives when it loves, delights, and rejoices in God, as when it loves and delights in anything on earth; and it can no more doubt whether it loves, delights, and rejoices,

---

[34] This reflects a shift (in 1738 and thereafter) from Wesley's earlier notion that holiness, in some degree and as intention, normally precedes justification in the *ordo salutis*. Here assurance (*viz.*, of pardon) 'must precede [our awareness] of the love of God and all holiness'. Note the stress on the *objective* aspects of the Spirit's prevenient action as the precondition of subjective experience. Cf. No. 2, *The Almost Christian*, II.6 and n.

[35] Cf. 1 John 4:10.
[36] Cf. Rev. 1:5.
[37] Cf. 1 John 4:19, 21.
[38] 1 Cor. 2:12.
[39] 1 John 5:19.
[40] 1 Cor. 2:12.
[41] 2 Cor. 1:12.

or no, than whether it exists, or no. If therefore this be just reasoning:

He that now loves God—that delights and rejoices in him with an humble joy, an holy delight, and an obedient love—is a child of
5 God;

But I thus love, delight, and rejoice in God;

Therefore I am a child of God;

then a Christian can in no wise doubt of his being a child of God. Of the former proposition he has as full an assurance as he has
10 that the Scriptures are of God. And of his thus loving God he has an inward proof, which is nothing short of self-evidence.[42] Thus the 'testimony of our own spirit' is with the most intimate conviction manifested to our hearts; in such a manner as beyond all reasonable doubt to evince the reality of our sonship.

15 12. The *manner* how the divine testimony is manifested to the heart I do not take upon me to explain. 'Such knowledge is too wonderful and excellent for me; I cannot attain unto it.'[43] 'The wind bloweth; and I hear the sound thereof'; but I cannot 'tell how it cometh, or whither it goeth'.[44] As no one knoweth the
20 things of a man save the spirit of a man that is in him, so the *manner* of the things of God knoweth no one save the Spirit of God.[45] But the fact we know: namely, that the Spirit of God does give a believer such a testimony of his adoption that while it is present to the soul he can no more doubt the reality of his sonship
25 than he can doubt of the shining of the sun while he stands in the full blaze of his beams.[46]

---

[42] Another instance of an either/or notion of assurance which Wesley will later soften to allow for *degrees* of assurance; see above, No. 3, *'Awake, Thou That Sleepest'*, III.6 and n.

[43] Ps. 139:5 (BCP).

[44] Cf. John 3:8.

[45] See 1 Cor. 2:11.

[46] What is here presupposed is Wesley's whole theory of religious knowledge with its notion of a 'spiritual sensorium' analogous to our physical senses and responsive to prior initiatives of the Holy Spirit. Typically, it is passive until acted upon by spiritual stimuli—e.g., divine light arouses our latent capacities for 'sight' and insight; revelation prompts us to insight and knowledge—always, however, as 're-actions' to initiatives beyond ourselves. Thus, no matter how intensely subjective our feelings may be in religious experiences, their source is prevenient, and in that sense, objective.

This, then, is Wesley's version of the intuitionist views of Christian Platonism as he had known that tradition from the Alexandrines, Bonaventura, the Cambridge Platonists, Malebranche, and, especially John Norris of Bemerton. It allowed him, without internal contradiction, to follow St. Thomas and John Locke in his theories of empirical knowledge (cf. No. 117, 'On the Discoveries of Faith', §1 and n.) and yet also to distinguish all such knowledge from our spiritual knowledge of God and 'of the deep

II.1. How this joint testimony of God's Spirit and our spirit may be clearly and solidly distinguished from the presumption of a natural mind, and from the delusion of the devil, is the next thing to be considered. And it highly imports all who desire the salvation of God to consider it with the deepest attention, as they 5 would not deceive their own souls. An error in this is generally observed to have the most fatal consequences; the rather, because he that errs seldom discovers his mistake till it is too late to remedy it.

2. And, first, How is this testimony to be distinguished from the 10 presumption of a natural mind? It is certain, one who was never convinced of sin is always ready to flatter himself, and to think of himself, especially in spiritual things, more highly than he ought to think.[47] And hence it is in no wise strange if one who is vainly puffed up by his fleshly mind, when he hears of this privilege of 15 true Christians, among whom he undoubtedly ranks himself, should soon work himself up into a persuasion that he is already possessed thereof. Such instances now abound in the world, and have abounded in all ages. How then may the real testimony of the Spirit with our spirit be distinguished from this damning 20 presumption?

3. I answer, the Holy Scriptures abound with marks whereby

---

things of God' (cf. 1 Cor. 2:10). This distinction, and its epistemological import, are pervasive throughout the Wesley corpus: cf. Nos. 3, *'Awake, Thou That Sleepest'*, I.11; 4, *Scriptural Christianity*, III.5; 9, 'The Spirit of Bondage and of Adoption', I.1; also, below, §II.9; 12, 'The Witness of Our Own Spirit', §§8, 18; 19, 'The Great Privilege of those that are Born of God', I. 4; 23, 'Sermon on the Mount, III', I. 6ff.; 34, 'The Original, Nature, Properties, and Use of the Law', I. 5; 36, 'The Law Established through Faith, II', II. 4; 43, *The Scripture Way of Salvation*, II. 1; 44, *Original Sin*, II. 2; 45, 'The New Birth', II.4; 62, 'The End of Christ's Coming', I.3, III.1; 69, 'The Imperfection of Human Knowledge', §§ 3-4; 71, 'Of Good Angels', I. 2; 96, 'On Obedience to Parents', § 1; 117, 'On the Discoveries of Faith', §§ 1-2; 118, 'On the Omnipresence of God', II.8; 119, 'Walking by Sight and Walking by Faith', §§ 1-2, 8, 11-12; 120, 'The Unity of the Divine Being', § 2; 125, 'On a Single Eye', I. 2; 130, 'On Living without God', § 9; 132, 'On Faith, Heb. 11: 1', § 18; 140, 'The Promise of Understanding', III. 2.

Cf. also his letter to Dr. Robertson, Sept. 24, 1753 (which seems contrary to his general theory); his letter to Richard Tompson, Mar. 16, 1756; and to Miss March, July 1, 1772; to Elizabeth Ritchie, Aug. 12, 1776; and to Joseph Benson, May 21, 1781. Cf. his *Earnest Appeal*, §§ 34-37 (11: 57-58 of this edn.); his *Farther Appeal*, Pt. I, I.4, V.28 (11: 106-7, 171-72). Also *Notes* on Matt. 13: 14; *A Short Address to the Inhabitants of Ireland*, § 6 (*Bibliog*, No. 167, Vol. 9 of this edn.; 'Of the Gradual Improvement of Natural Philosophy', § 24 (*Survey*, I. 21). Cf. also Jonathan Edwards, *A Treatise on Religious Affections*, Pt. II (see *Bibliog*, No. 334, Vol. 16 of this edn.); Lucas, *Enquiry After Happiness*, III. 79, 198; and Lee, *op. cit.*, pp. 140-41.

[47] See Rom. 12:3.

the one may be distinguished from the other. They describe in the plainest manner the circumstances which go before, which accompany, and which follow, the true, genuine testimony of the Spirit of God with the spirit of a believer. Whoever carefully

5 weighs and attends to these will not need to put darkness for light.[48] He will perceive so wide a difference with respect to all these, between the real and the pretended witness of the Spirit, that there will be no danger—I might say, no possibility—of confounding the one with the other.

10 4. By these, one who vainly presumes on the gift of God might surely know, if he really desired it, that he hath been hitherto 'given up to a strong delusion' and suffered to 'believe a lie'.[49] For the Scriptures lay down those clear, obvious marks as preceding, accompanying, and following that gift, which a little reflection

15 would convince him, beyond all doubt, were never found in his soul. For instance, the Scripture describes repentance, or conviction of sin, as constantly going before this witness of pardon. So, 'Repent; for the kingdom of heaven is at hand.'[i] 'Repent ye, and believe the Gospel.'[j] 'Repent, and be baptized

20 every one of you . . . for the remission of sins.'[k] 'Repent ye therefore, and be converted, that your sins may be blotted out.'[l] In conformity whereto our Church also continually places repentance before pardon or the witness of it: 'He pardoneth and absolveth all them that truly repent and unfeignedly believe his

25 holy gospel.'[50] 'Almighty God . . . hath promised forgiveness of sins to all them who with hearty repentance and true faith turn unto him.'[51] But he is a stranger even to this repentance. He hath never known 'a broken and a contrite heart'.[52] 'The remembrance of his sins' was never 'grievous unto' him, nor 'the burden of them

30 intolerable'.[53] In repeating those words he never meant what he

---

[i] Matt. 3:2.
[k] Acts 2:38.

[j] Mark 1:15.
[l] [Acts] 3:19.

---

[48] Isa. 5:20.
[49] Cf. 2 Thess. 2:11.
[50] BCP, Morning Prayer, Absolution (4).
[51] *Ibid.*, Communion, Absolution (349). Pardon precedes assurance, but repentance precedes pardon. Here, repentance (as self-knowledge of one's sinful state, plus a hope for pardon and amendment of life) is a fruit of the Spirit's prevenient stimulus; this gives the discussion of the antecedent conditions of justification by faith a distinctive Anglican nuance.
[52] Ps. 51:17.
[53] Cf. BCP, Communion, Confession (348).

said; he merely paid a compliment to God. And were it only from the want of this previous work of God he hath too great reason to believe that he hath grasped a mere shadow, and never yet known the real privilege of the sons of God.

5. Again, the Scriptures describe the being born of God, which must precede the witness that we are his children, as a vast and mighty change, a change 'from darkness to light', as well as 'from the power of Satan unto God';[54] as a 'passing from death unto life',[55] a resurrection from the dead. Thus the Apostle to the Ephesians: 'You hath he quickened, who were dead in trespasses and sins.'[m] And again, 'When we were dead in sins, he hath quickened us together with Christ; . . . and hath raised us up together, and made us sit together in heavenly places in Christ Jesus.'[n] But what knoweth he concerning whom we now speak of any such change as this? He is altogether unacquainted with this whole matter. This is a language which he does not understand. He tells you he always was a Christian. He knows no time when he had need of such a change. By this also, if he give himself leave to think, may he know that he is not born of the Spirit;[56] that he has never yet known God, but has mistaken the voice of nature for the voice of God.

6. But waiving the consideration of whatever he has or has not experienced in time past, by the present marks may we easily distinguish a child of God from a presumptuous self-deceiver. The Scriptures describe that joy in the Lord which accompanies the witness of his Spirit as an humble joy, a joy that abases to the dust; that makes a pardoned sinner cry out, 'I am vile![57] What am I or my father's house?—Now mine eye seeth thee I abhor myself in dust and ashes!'[58] And wherever lowliness is, there is meekness, patience, gentleness, long-suffering.[59] There is a soft, yielding spirit, a mildness and sweetness, a tenderness of soul which words cannot express.[60] But do these fruits attend that *supposed* testimony of the Spirit in a presumptuous man? Just the

---

[m] Eph. 2:1.   [n] Ver. 5, 6.

---

[54] Acts 26:18.   [55] Cf. John 5:24; 1 John 3:14.
[56] John 3:6, 8.   [57] Job 40:4.   [58] Cf. Job 42:5-6.
[59] See Gal. 5:22-23.
[60] Cf. Nos. 97, 'On Obedience to Pastors', III.3; 100, 'On Pleasing All Men', II.3; 108, 'On Riches', I.6-7; 120, 'The Unity of the Divine Being', §22. Cf. also *Notes*, especially for Phil. 4:5 and Jas. 3:17.

reverse. The more confident he is of the favour of God, the more is he lifted up. The more does he exalt himself, the more haughty and assuming is his whole behaviour. The stronger witness he imagines himself to have, the more overbearing is he to all around

5 him, the more incapable of receiving any reproof, the more impatient of contradiction. Instead of being more meek, and gentle, and teachable, more 'swift to hear, and slow to speak',[61] he is more slow to hear and swift to speak, more unready to learn of anyone, more fiery and vehement in his temper, and eager in his

10 conversation. Yea, perhaps, there will sometimes appear a kind of fierceness in his air, his manner of speaking, his whole deportment, as if he were just going to take the matter out of God's hands, and himself to 'devour the adversaries'.[62]

7. Once more: the Scriptures teach, 'This is the love of God'

15 (the sure mark thereof) 'that we keep his commandments.'[o] And our Lord himself saith, 'He that keepeth my commandments, he it is that loveth me.'[p] Love rejoices to obey, to do in every point whatever is acceptable to the Beloved.[63] A true lover of God hastens to do his will on earth as it is done in heaven.[64] But is this

20 the character of the presumptuous pretender to the love of God? Nay, but his love gives him a liberty to disobey, to break, not keep, the commandments of God. Perhaps when he was in fear of the wrath of God he did labour to do his will. But now, looking on himself as 'not under the law',[65] he thinks he is no longer obliged

25 to observe it. He is therefore less zealous of good works,[66] less careful to abstain from evil, less watchful over his own heart, less jealous over his tongue. He is less earnest to deny himself, and to take up his cross daily.[67] In a word, the whole form of his life is changed since he has fancied himself to be 'at liberty'. He is no

30 longer 'exercising himself unto godliness':[68] 'wrestling not only with flesh and blood, but with principalities and powers',[69] 'enduring hardships',[70] 'agonizing to enter in at the strait gate'.[71] No; he has found an easier way to heaven: a broad, smooth, flowery path, in which he can say to his soul, 'Soul, take thy ease;

---

[o] 1 John 5:3. [p] John 14:21.

[61] Jas. 1:19. [62] Heb. 10:27. [63] See Eph. 1:6.
[64] See Matt. 6:10; Luke 11:2. [65] Rom. 6:14, 15.
[66] Titus 2:14. [67] Cf. Luke 9:23.
[68] Cf. 1 Tim. 4:7. [69] Cf. Eph. 6:12.
[70] Cf. 2 Tim. 2:3. [71] Luke 13:24; cf. *Notes.*

eat, drink, and be merry.'[72] It follows with undeniable evidence that he has not the true testimony of his own spirit. He cannot be conscious of having those marks which he hath not, that lowliness, meekness, and obedience. Nor yet can the Spirit of the God of truth bear witness to a lie; or testify that he is a child of God when he is manifestly a child of the devil.[73]

8. Discover thyself, thou poor self-deceiver! Thou who art confident of being a child of God; thou who sayest, 'I have the witness in myself,' and therefore defiest all thy enemies. Thou art weighed in the balance and found wanting,[74] even in the balance of the sanctuary.[75] The Word of the Lord hath tried thy soul, and proved thee to be reprobate silver.[76] Thou art not lowly of heart; therefore thou hast not received the Spirit of Jesus unto this day. Thou art not gentle and meek; therefore thy joy is nothing worth: it is not joy in the Lord.[77] Thou dost not keep his commandments; therefore thou lovest him not, neither art thou partaker of the Holy Ghost.[78] It is consequently as certain and as evident as the oracles of God can make it, his Spirit doth not bear witness with thy spirit that thou art a child of God. O cry unto him, that the scales may fall off thine eyes;[79] that thou mayst know thyself as

---

[72] Cf. Luke 12:19.

[73] Acts 13:10.   [74] See Dan. 5:27.

[75] A familiar metaphor at that time signifying an earnest reflection upon a problem in the light of Holy Scripture and in the conscious presence of God *(coram Deo)*. Wesley would have known it from such sources as William Perkins, *A Golden Chaine*, where in his preface to the 2nd edn. of 1597 Perkins had written: 'This treatise being thus finished, I commit it to the weight of the ballance of the Sanctuarie. . .'. But see also Norris, *Miscellanies*, p. 184; Boston, State IV, Head VI; South, *Sermons* (1823), 7. 319. The phrase turns up in Wesley's 'Preface', §7, 'Extracts from the Works of the Puritans' (beginning with Bishop Joseph Hall's *Meditations and Vows*), in the *Christian Lib.*, VII; Nathaniel Culverwell, *ibid.*, XVII. 104; and Samuel Clarke, *ibid.*, XXVI. 171. The Quakers seem to have used it to denote the 'inner light', as in John Perrot, *An Epistle for the Most Pure Amity and Unity in the Spirit and Life of God to All Sincere-hearted Souls* (1662): 'Hear . . . the sound of the Spirit's voice . . . and let it enter into the balance of the sanctuary within you.' Littré, *Dictionnaire de la Langue Francaise*, III. 1683, refers the phrase to 'a conventional Jewish usage meaning the standard weights and scales kept in the Temple and supervised by the Temple priests', and cites Bourdaloue, Saci, and Fénelon as having borrowed it from thence; cf. William G. Braude, ed. and tr., 'Moses's Journey Through Heaven', Piska 20, in *Pesikta Rabbati: Discourses for Feasts, Fasts and Special Sabbaths* (New Haven, Yale University Press, 1968), p. 401.

It was a favourite figure of Wesley's and may first be found in his sermon 'Wiser than the Children of Light', §III (No. 147, below); see also JWJ, June 4, 1742; Nos. 32, 'Sermon on the Mount XII', III.9; 39, 'Catholic Spirit', III.2; see also *Predestination Calmly Considered*, §7; and his letter to Jasper Robinson, Nov. 17, 1790.

[76] I.e., worthless, inferior, or impure *(OED)*. Cf. Jer. 6:30.

[77] See Philem. 20.   [78] See Heb. 6:4.   [79] See Acts 9:18.

thou art known;[80] that thou mayst receive the sentence of death in thyself, till thou hear the voice that raises the dead, saying, 'Be of good cheer; thy sins are forgiven; thy faith hath made thee whole.'[81]

5 9. 'But how may one who has the real witness in himself distinguish it from presumption?' How, I pray, do you distinguish day from night? How do you distinguish light from darkness? Or the light of a star, or glimmering taper, from the light of the noonday sun? Is there not an inherent, obvious, essential

10 difference between the one and the other? And do you not immediately and directly perceive that difference, provided your senses are rightly disposed? In like manner, there is an inherent, essential difference between spiritual light and spiritual darkness; and between the light wherewith the sun of righteousness[82] shines

15 upon our heart, and that glimmering light which arises only from 'sparks of our own kindling'.[83] And this difference also is immediately and directly perceived, if our spiritual senses are rightly disposed.[84]

10. To require a more minute and philosophical account of the
20 *manner* whereby we distinguish these, and of the *criteria* or intrinsic marks whereby we know the voice of God, is to make a demand which can never be answered; no, not by one who has the deepest knowledge of God. Suppose, when Paul answered before Agrippa,[85] the wise Roman had said: 'Thou talkest of hearing the
25 voice of the Son of God. How dost thou know it was his voice? By what *criteria*, what intrinsic marks, dost thou know the voice of God? Explain to me the *manner* of distinguishing this from a human or angelic voice.' Can you believe the Apostle himself would have once attempted to answer so idle a demand? And yet
30 doubtless the moment he heard that voice he knew it was the voice of God. But *how* he knew this who is able to explain? Perhaps neither man nor angel.

11. To come yet closer: suppose God were now to speak to any soul, 'Thy sins are forgiven thee.'[86] He must be willing that soul
35 should know his voice; otherwise he would speak in vain. And he is able to effect this, for whenever he wills, to do is present with

---

[80] See 1 Cor. 13:12.
[81] Cf. Matt. 9:2, 22, etc.
[82] Mal. 4:2.   [83] Cf. Isa. 50:11.
[84] Cf. above, I.12 and n.; also No. 1, *Salvation by Faith*, §1 and n.
[85] Acts 26.   [86] Matt. 9:2, 5, etc.

him.[87] And he does effect it. That soul is absolutely assured, 'This voice is the voice of God.' But yet he who hath that witness in himself cannot explain it to one who hath not. Nor indeed is it to be expected that he should. Were there any natural medium to prove, or natural method to explain the things of God to unexperienced men, then the natural man might discern and know the things of the Spirit of God. But this is utterly contrary to the assertion of the Apostle that 'he cannot know them, because they are spiritually discerned;' even by spiritual senses which the natural man hath not.[88]

12. 'But how shall I know that my spiritual senses are rightly disposed?' This also is a question of vast importance; for if a man mistake in this he may run on in endless error and delusion. 'And how am I assured that this is not my case; and that I do not mistake the voice of the Spirit?' Even by the 'testimony of your own spirit';[89] by 'the answer of a good conscience toward God'.[90] By the fruits which he hath wrought in your spirit you shall know the 'testimony of the Spirit of God'.[91] Hereby you shall know that you are in no delusion; that you have not deceived your own soul. The immediate fruits of the Spirit ruling in the heart are 'love, joy, peace';[92] 'bowels of mercies, humbleness of mind, meekness, gentleness, long-suffering'.[93] And the outward fruits are the doing good to all men, the doing no evil to any, and the walking in the light—a zealous, uniform obedience to all the commandments of God.

13. By the same fruits shall you distinguish this voice of God from any delusion of the devil. That proud spirit cannot humble thee before God. He neither can nor would soften thy heart and melt it first into earnest mourning after God and then into filial love. It is not the adversary of God and man that enables thee to love thy neighbour; or to put on meekness, gentleness, patience, temperance, and the whole armour of God.[94] He is not divided

---

[87] An echo of Rom. 7:18-19; a conscious contrast between the human bondage depicted there and God's radical freedom.

[88] See 1 Cor. 2:14.   [89] Cf. Rom. 8:16.

[90] 1 Pet. 3:21.   [91] Cf. Rom. 8:16.

[92] Gal. 5:22. Wesley here ignores the fact that καρπόν, in the text, is singular (the 'fruit' of the Spirit). Elsewhere, as in the following sermon (Discourse II, §§II.1, 6-7) and in No. 76, 'On Perfection', I.6, III.3, he holds to the singular form. But cf. No. 4, *Scriptural Christianity*, §4 and n.

[93] Cf. Col. 3:12.

[94] Eph. 6:11, 13.

against himself,[95] or a destroyer of sin, his own work. No; it is none but the Son of God who cometh to 'destroy the works of the devil'.[96] As surely therefore as holiness is of God, and as sin is the work of the devil, so surely the witness thou hast in thyself is not of
5 Satan, but of God.

14. Well then mayst thou say, 'Thanks be unto God for his unspeakable gift!'[97] Thanks be unto God who giveth me to 'know in whom I have believed';[98] who 'hath sent forth the Spirit of his Son into my heart, crying Abba, Father',[99] and even now 'bearing
10 witness with my spirit that I am a child of God'![100] And see that not only thy lips, but thy life show forth his praise.[101] He hath sealed thee for his own; 'glorify him then in thy body and thy spirit which are'[102] his. Beloved, if thou 'hast this hope in thyself, purify thyself as he is pure'.[103] While thou 'beholdest what manner of love the
15 Father hath given thee, that thou shouldst be called a child of God',[104] 'cleanse thyself from all filthiness of flesh and Spirit, perfecting holiness in the fear of God;'[105] and let all thy thoughts, words, and works be a spiritual sacrifice, holy, acceptable to God through Christ Jesus![106]

---

[95] Matt. 12:26, etc.
[96] 1 John 3:8.
[97] 2 Cor. 9:15.
[98] Cf. 2 Tim. 1:12.
[99] Cf. Gal. 4:6.
[100] Cf. Rom. 8:16.
[101] See Ps. 51:15. See also BCP, Morning Prayer, General Thanksgiving.
[102] Cf. 1 Cor. 6:20.
[103] Cf. 1 John 3:3.
[104] Cf. 1 John 3:1.
[105] Cf. 2 Cor. 7:1.
[106] See Rom. 12:1; 1 Pet. 2:5.

The Witness of the Spirit, II

Romans 8:16

The Spirit itself beareth witness with our spirit,
that we are the children of God.

I.1. None who believes the Scriptures to be the Word of God 5
can doubt the *importance* of such a truth as this: a truth revealed
therein not once only, not obscurely, not incidentally, but
frequently, and that in express terms; but solemnly and of set
purpose, as denoting one of the peculiar privileges of the children
of God. 10

2. And it is the more necessary to explain and defend this truth,
because there is a danger on the right hand and on the left. If we
deny it, there is a danger lest our religion degenerate into mere
formality; lest, 'having a form of godliness', we neglect if not
'deny, the power of it'.[1] If we allow it, but do not understand what 15
we allow, we are liable to run into all the wildness of enthusiasm.[2]
It is therefore needful in the highest degree to guard those who
fear God from both these dangers by a scriptural and rational
illustration and confirmation of this momentous truth.

3. It may seem something of this kind is the more needful 20
because so little has been wrote on the subject with any clearness,
unless some discourses on the wrong side of the question, which
explain it quite away. And it cannot be doubted but these were
occasioned, at least in great measure, by the crude, unscriptural,
irrational explications of others, who 'knew not what they spake, 25
nor whereof they affirmed'.[3]

4. It more clearly concerns the Methodists, so called, clearly to
understand, explain, and defend this doctrine, because it is one
grand part of the testimony which God has given them to bear to
all mankind. It is by his peculiar blessing upon them in searching 30
the Scriptures, confirmed by the experience of his children, that

[1] 2 Tim. 3:5.
[2] Cf. No. 37, 'The Nature of Enthusiasm'.
[3] Cf. 1 Tim. 1:7.

this great evangelical truth has been recovered, which had been for many years wellnigh lost and forgotten.[4]

II.1. But what is 'the witness of the Spirit'? The original word, μαρτυρία, may be rendered either (as it is in several places) 'the
5 witness', or less ambiguously 'the testimony' or 'the record': so it is rendered in our translation, 'This is the record' (the testimony, the sum of what God testifies in all the inspired writings), 'that God hath given unto us eternal life, and this life is in his Son.'[a] The testimony now under consideration is given by the Spirit of
10 God to and with our spirit. He is the person testifying. What he testifies to us is 'that we are the children of God'. The immediate result of this testimony is 'the fruit of the Spirit'; namely, 'love, joy, peace; longsuffering, gentleness, goodness'.[5] And without these the testimony itself cannot continue. For it is inevitably
15 destroyed, not only by the commission of any outward sin, or the omission of known duty, but by giving way to any inward sin—in a word, by whatever grieves the Holy Spirit of God.
2. I observed many years ago:

[a] 1 John 5:11.

---

[4] For the Lutheran scholastics the *testimonium internum Spiritus Sancti* was chiefly related to the validation of the truth of Scripture: 'the supernatural act of the Holy Spirit through the Word of God . . . illuminating the heart of man and inciting it to obedience unto the faith; so that man, thus illuminated by internal spiritual influences, clearly perceives that the word proposed to him has indeed proceeded from God and thus gives it unyielding assent' (David Hollaz, *Examen Theologicum* [1707], p. 116). The notion of assurance was derived from this, but only by implication; cf. *ibid.*, pp. 117-18.

In the Reformed tradition, the inner witness was correlated more specifically with 'the perseverance and assurance of the saints'. Cf. Heppe, *Reformed Dogmatics*, pp. 581-87, and espec. Heidegger, *Corpus Theologiae*, XXIV. 72: '[The elect, assured by the Spirit's witness] trust that they are in a state of grace, not because of a deliberate intuition of their own dignity but of the divine conferring of it . . . not just for the present, but certain that they will also persevere in the same, though not without a struggle, . . . right to life's end—and so are infallibly salvable to the praise of the glory of God's grace and their own consolation amid the perpetual misery of life.'

In the Radical Reformation, the witness of the Spirit had been interiorized and turned toward what Wesley (and other Anglicans) had spoken of as 'all the wildness of enthusiasm'. Cf. Hugh Barbour and Arthur O. Roberts, eds., *Early Quaker Writings, 1650–1700* (Grand Rapids, Mich., William B. Eerdmans Publishing Co., 1973), pp. 261–62, and G. H. Williams *The Radical Reformation* (Philadelphia, The Westminster Press, 1962), chs. 18–19. In reaction, Anglicans tended to interpret assurance in terms of their *hope* of salvation rather than an inner certainty; e.g., cf. Wesley's reactions to Spangenberg's questions as to his sense of assurance in JWJ, Feb. 8, 1736; and his letter to Thomas Whitehead(?), Feb. 10, 1748; see also Isaac Barrow's 'Whitsunday Sermon', No. 77, in *Works*, III. 475–78.

[5] Cf. Gal. 5:22. Cf. No. 10, 'The Witness of the Spirit, I', II.12 and n.

It is hard to find words in the language of men to explain the deep things of God. Indeed there are none that will adequately express what the Spirit of God works in his children. But perhaps one might say (desiring any who are taught of God to correct, soften, or strengthen the expression), by 'the testimony of the Spirit' I mean an inward impression of the soul, whereby the Spirit of God immediately 5 and directly witnesses to my spirit that I am a child of God, that 'Jesus Christ hath loved me, and given himself for me;'[6] that all my sins are blotted out, and I, even I, am reconciled to God.[b]

3. After twenty years' farther consideration I see no cause to retract any part of this. Neither do I conceive how any of these 10 expressions may be altered so as to make them more intelligible. I can only add, that if any of the children of God will point out any other expressions which are more clear, and more agreeable to the Word of God, I will readily lay these aside.

4. Meantime let it be observed, I do not mean hereby that the 15 Spirit of God testifies this by any outward voice; no, nor always by an inward voice, although he may do this sometimes. Neither do I suppose that he always applies to the heart (though he often may) one or more texts of Scripture. But he so works upon the soul by his immediate influence, and by a strong though inexplicable 20 operation, that the stormy wind and troubled waves subside, and there is a sweet calm; the heart resting as in the arms of Jesus, and the sinner being clearly satisfied that God is reconciled, that all his 'iniquities are forgiven, and his sins covered'.[7]

5. Now what is the matter of dispute concerning this? Not 25 whether there be a witness or testimony of the Spirit? Not whether the Spirit does testify with our spirit that we are the children of God? None can deny this without flatly contradicting the Scripture, and charging a lie upon the God of truth. Therefore that there is a testimony of the Spirit is acknowledged 30 by all parties.

6. Neither is it questioned whether there is an *indirect* witness or testimony that we are the children of God. This is nearly, if not exactly, the same with 'the testimony of a good conscience toward God',[8] and is the result of reason or reflection on what we feel in 35 our own souls. Strictly speaking, it is a conclusion drawn partly

---

[b] *Sermons*, Vol.1 [No.10, 'The Witness of the Spirit, I', I.7. Note Wesley's revisions of his earlier text; another example of his habitual indifference to exact quotations].

---

[6] Cf. Gal. 2:20. See also No. 5, 'Justification by Faith', IV.2 and n.
[7] Rom. 4:7; cf. Ps. 32:1.   [8] Cf. 1 Pet. 3:21.

from the Word of God, and partly from our own experience. The Word of God says everyone who has the fruit of the Spirit[9] is a child of God. Experience, or inward consciousness, tells me that I have the fruit of the Spirit. And hence I rationally conclude:
5 therefore I am a child of God. This is likewise allowed on all hands, and so is no matter of controversy.

7. Nor do we assert that there can be any real testimony of the Spirit without the fruit of the Spirit.[10] We assert, on the contrary, that the fruit of the Spirit immediately springs from this
10 testimony. Not always, indeed, in the same degree, even when the testimony is first given, and much less afterwards. Neither joy nor peace are always at one stay; no, nor love; as neither is the testimony itself always equally strong and clear.

8. But the point in question is whether there be any *direct*
15 *testimony* of the Spirit at all; whether there be any other testimony of the Spirit than that which arises from a consciousness of the fruit.

III.1. I believe there is, because that is the plain, natural meaning of the text, 'The Spirit itself beareth witness with our
20 spirit, that we are the children of God.' It is manifest, here are two witnesses mentioned, who together testify the same thing—the Spirit of God, and our own spirit. The late Bishop of London, in his sermon on this text, seems astonished that anyone can doubt of this, which appears upon the very face of the words. Now 'the
25 testimony of our own spirit', says the bishop, is one which is 'the consciousness of our own sincerity';[11] or, to express the same thing a little more clearly, the consciousness of the fruit of the

---

[9] Cf. No. 10, 'The Witness of the Spirit, I', II. 12 and n.

[10] *Ibid.*

[11] This was Thomas Sherlock (cf. *DNB*) who was Bishop of London, 1748–61. Wesley's references here are to Sherlock's earlier sermon on Rom. 8:16, 'Discourse VIII', in *Several Discourses Preached at the Temple Church* (2nd edn., 1754), pp. 227-49. On p. 235, Sherlock concludes: 'So then the faithful Christian has two witnesses of his being the son of God: the Holy Spirit of God and his own mind and conscience.' On pp. 244-45, Sherlock insists that true Christians have 'the *utmost assurance* of being the children of God'. But his conclusion (pp. 246-47) differs significantly: 'So then you have two ways of judging yourselves which must both concur: you have the inward and outward signs of grace. The inward signs are a pure conscience, a sincere love of God. . . . The outward signs are acts of obedience conformable to the inward purity and love of your mind.' See also Sherlock, *Works* (1830), I. 157, 163. Cf. also *ibid.*, p. 155: '. . . there are therefore two witnesses; St. Paul, who witnessed his affection to his countrymen; and *his conscience, which witnessed for his sincerity.*'

Spirit. When our spirit is conscious of this—of love, joy, peace, long-suffering, gentleness, goodness—it easily infers from these premises that we are the children of God.

2. It is true, that great man supposes the other witness to be 'the consciousness of our own good works'. This, he affirms, is 'the testimony of God's Spirit'. But this is included in the testimony of our own spirit; yea, and in sincerity, even according to the common sense of the word. So the Apostle: 'Our rejoicing is this, the testimony of our conscience, that in simplicity and godly sincerity [. . .] we have had our conversation in the world:'[12] where, it is plain, sincerity refers to our words and actions at least as much as to our inward dispositions. So that this is not another witness, but the very same that he mentioned before, the consciousness of our good works being only one branch of the consciousness of our sincerity. Consequently here is only one witness still. If therefore the text speaks of two witnesses, one of these is not the consciousness of good works, neither of our sincerity, all this being manifestly contained in 'the testimony of our own spirit'.

3. What then is the other witness? This might easily be learned, if the text itself were not sufficiently clear, from the verse immediately preceding: 'Ye have received, not the spirit of bondage, but the Spirit of adoption, whereby we cry, Abba, Father.' It follows, 'The Spirit itself beareth witness with our spirit, that we are the children of God.'[13]

4. This is farther explained by the parallel text, 'Because ye are sons, God hath sent forth the Spirit of his Son into your hearts, crying Abba, Father.'[c] Is not this something *immediate* and *direct*, not the result of reflection or argumentation? Does not this Spirit cry 'Abba, Father', in our hearts the moment it is given—antecedently to any reflection upon our sincerity; yea, to any reasoning whatsoever? And is not this the plain, natural sense of the words, which strikes anyone as soon as he hears them? All these texts, then, in their most obvious meaning, describe a direct testimony of the Spirit.

5. That 'the testimony of the Spirit of God' must, in the very nature of things, be antecedent to 'the testimony of our own

[c] Gal. 4:6.

---

[12] 2 Cor. 1:12.　　　　　　　　　　　　　[13] Rom. 8:15-16.

spirit', may appear from this single consideration: we must be holy in heart and life before we can be conscious that we are so. But we must love God before we can be holy at all, this being the root of all holiness. Now we cannot love God till we know he loves us: 'We love him, because he first loved us.'[14] And we cannot know his love to us till his Spirit witnesses it to our spirit. Till then we cannot believe it; we cannot say, 'The life which I now live, I live by faith in the Son of God, who loved me, and gave himself for me.'[15]

> Then, only then we feel
> Our interest in his blood,
> And cry, with joy unspeakable,
> Thou art my Lord, my God.[16]

Since therefore the testimony of his Spirit must precede the love of God and all holiness, of consequence it must precede our consciousness thereof.[17]

6. And here properly comes in, to confirm this scriptural doctrine, the experience of the children of God—the experience not of two or three, not of a few, but of a great multitude which no man can number.[18] It has been confirmed, both in this and in all ages, by 'a cloud of' living and dying 'witnesses'.[19] It is confirmed by *your* experience and *mine*. The Spirit itself bore witness to my spirit that I was a child of God, gave me an *evidence* hereof, and I immediately cried, 'Abba, Father!' And this I did (and so did you) before I reflected on, or was conscious of, any fruit of the Spirit. It was from this testimony received that love, joy, peace, and the whole fruit of the Spirit flowed. First I heard,

> 'Thy sins are forgiven!   Accepted thou art!'
> I listened, and heaven   sprung up in my heart.[20]

---

[14] 1 John 4:19.

[15] Cf. Gal. 2:20.

[16] 'Spirit of Faith, Come Down', st. 2, ll. 5-8, in *Hymns of Petition and Thanksgiving for the Promise of the Father* (1746), 30 (*Poet. Wks.*, IV. 197).

[17] Cf. this para. with Discourse I, I.8, and note the slight shift in nuance in this later sermon.

[18] See Rev. 7:9.

[19] Heb. 12:1.

[20] Charles Wesley, 'After Preaching to the Newcastle Colliers', st. 9, ll. 3-4, beginning 'Ye neighbours and friends of Jesus, draw near', in *Hymns and Sacred Poems* (1749), I. 311 (*Poet. Wks.*, V. 116). Orig., 'They listen, and heaven springs up in their heart.'

7. But this is confirmed, not only by the experience of the children of God—thousands of whom can declare that they never did know themselves to be in the favour of God till it was directly witnessed to them by his Spirit—but by all those who are convinced of sin, who feel the wrath of God abiding on them.[21] These cannot be satisfied with anything less than a direct testimony from his Spirit that he is 'merciful to their unrighteousness, and remembers their sins and iniquities no more'.[22] Tell any of these, 'You are to know you are a child by reflecting on what he has wrought in you, on your love, joy, and peace;' and will he not immediately reply, 'By all this I know I am a child of the devil. I have no more love to God than the devil has; my carnal mind is enmity against God.[23] I have no joy in the Holy Ghost;[24] my soul is sorrowful even unto death.[25] I have no peace; my heart is a troubled sea; I am all storm and tempest.'[26] And which way can these souls possibly be comforted but by a divine testimony (not that they are good, or sincere, or conformable to the Scripture in heart and life, but) that God 'justifieth the ungodly'—[27] him that, till the moment he is justified, is all ungodly, void of all true holiness? 'Him that worketh not',[28] that worketh nothing that is truly good till he is conscious that he is accepted, 'not for any works of righteousness which he hath done',[29]

---

[21] See John 3:36.   [22] Cf. Heb. 8:12.   [23] Rom. 8:7.
[24] Rom. 14:17.   [25] Matt. 26:38.
[26] Is there an autobiographical reference here? Cf. JWJ, May 28, 1738, and Jan. 4, 1739. See also John's letter to his brother Charles, June 27, 1766 (where the double-bracketed words are in shorthand, meant for Charles's eyes only):

'[[I]] do not feel the wrath of God abiding on me. Nor can I believe it does. And yet (this is the mystery) [[I do not love God. I never did.]] Therefore [[I never]] *believed* in the Christian sense of the word. Therefore [[I am only an]] honest heathen, a proselyte of the Temple, one of the φοβούμενοι τὸν Θεόν ['God-fearers']. And yet, to be so employed of God! And so hedged in that I can neither get forward or backward! Surely there never was such an instance before, from the beginning of the world!

'If [[I ever had had]] *that faith*, it would not be so strange. But [[I never had any]] other ἔλεγχος of the eternal or the invisible world than [[I have]] now—and that is [[none at all]], unless such as faintly shines from reason's glimmering ray. [[I have no]] *direct* witness (I do not say, that [[I am a child of God]]), but of anything invisible or eternal.

'And yet I dare not preach otherwise than I do, either concerning faith, or love, or justification, or perfection. And yet I find rather an increase than a decrease of zeal, for the whole work of God, and every part of it. I am φερόμενος ['borne along'], I know not how, [so] that I can't stand still. I want all the world to come to ὃν οὐκ οἶδα ['what I do not know']. Neither am I impelled to this by fear of any kind. [[I have]] no more fear than love. Or if [[I have any fear, it is not that of falling]] into hell, but of falling into nothing!'
[27] Cf. Rom. 4:5.
[28] *Ibid.*
[29] Cf. Titus 3:5.

but by the mere free mercy of God? Wholly and solely for what the Son of God hath done and suffered for him? And can it be otherwise if 'a man is justified by faith, without the works of the law'?[30] If so, what inward or outward goodness can he be conscious of
5 antecedent to his justification? Nay, is not the 'having nothing to pay',[31] that is, the being conscious that 'there dwelleth in us no good thing,'[32] neither inward nor outward goodness, essentially, indispensably necessary before we can be 'justified freely through the redemption that is in Jesus Christ'?[33] Was ever any man
10 justified since his coming into the world, or can any man ever be justified till he is brought to that point,

> I give up every plea, beside
> 'Lord, I am damned—but thou hast died!'[34]

8. Everyone therefore who denies the existence of such a
15 testimony does, in effect, deny justification by faith.[35] It follows that either he never experienced this, either he never was justified, or that he has forgotten (as St. Peter speaks) τοῦ καθαρισμοῦ τῶν πάλαι [αὐτοῦ] ἁμαρτιῶν, 'the purification from his former sins',[36] the experience he then had himself, the
20 manner wherein God wrought in his own soul, when his former sins were blotted out.

9. And the experience even of the children of the world here confirms that of the children of God. Many of these have a desire to please God: some of them take much pains to please him. But
25 do they not, one and all, count it the highest absurdity for any to talk of *knowing* his sins are forgiven? Which of *them* even pretends to any such thing? And yet many of them are conscious of their own sincerity. Many of them undoubtedly have, in a degree, the testimony of their own spirit, a consciousness of their own
30 uprightness. But this brings them no consciousness that they are forgiven, no knowledge that they are the children of God. Yea,

---

[30] Rom. 3:28 (cf. *Notes*).   [31] Cf. Luke 7:42.
[32] Cf. Rom. 7:18.   [33] Cf. Rom 3:24.
[34] 'Galatians iii.22', st. 12, ll. 3-4, in *Hymns and Sacred Poems* (1739), p. 94 (*Poet. Wks.*, I. 85). A favourite hymn of Wesley's, quoted frequently. E.g., Nos.34, 'The Original, Nature, Properties, and Use of the Law', IV.2; and 122, 'Causes of the Inefficacy of Christianity', §19. See also the letter to Lady Maxwell, Sept. 22, 1764, and JWJ, Apr. 1, 1778.
[35] A clue to Wesley's purposes in this Discourse II: *viz.*, the reassertion of 'faith alone', but now as a proper precondition of 'holy living'.
[36] Cf. 2 Pet. 1:9. The omission of αὐτοῦ seems an inadvertence; the translation is Wesley's own (cf. *Notes*) and is more literal than the AV's 'purged from his old sins'.

the more sincere they are, the more uneasy they generally are for want of knowing it: plainly showing that this cannot be known in a satisfactory manner by the bare testimony of our own spirit, without God's directly testifying that we are his children.

IV. But abundance of objections have been made to this, the chief of which it may be well to consider.

1. It is objected, first, 'Experience is not sufficient to prove a doctrine which is not founded on Scripture.' This is undoubtedly true, and it is an important truth. But it does not affect the present question, for it has been shown that this doctrine is founded on Scripture. Therefore experience is properly alleged to confirm it.

2. 'But madmen, French prophets,[37] and enthusiasts of every kind have imagined they experienced this witness.' They have so, and perhaps not a few of them did, although they did not retain it long. But if they did not, this is no proof at all that others have not experienced it: as a madman's *imagining* himself a king does not prove that there are no *real* kings.

'Nay, many who pleaded strongly for this have utterly decried the Bible.' Perhaps so, but this was no necessary consequence: thousands plead for it who have the highest esteem for the Bible.

'Yea, but many have fatally deceived themselves hereby, and got above all conviction.'[38]

And yet a scriptural doctrine is no worse, though men abuse it to their own destruction.

---

[37] A popular English nickname for the Camisards who had suffered brutal persecution in southeastern France (the Cevennes and Dauphiné) in the first decade of the eighteenth century. The label 'Camisard' referred to their habit of wearing white shirts (*camisae*) as ritual symbols of their zeal for purity. But they were also visionaries and fanatics, strongly influenced by the apocalyptic emphasis of Pierre Jurieu (1637–1713), and laid claim to direct revelation and Spirit-possession; cf. André Ducasse, *La Guerre des Camisards* (Paris, 1946), and Charles Almeras, *La Révolte des Camisards* (Paris, 1960). Wesley shared the general feeling among Englishmen of his time that these 'French prophets' were 'enthusiasts' in the literal, pejorative sense of that term. His first meeting with them is recorded in JWJ, Jan. 28, 1739; see also June 6 and 22, 1739. Later (Apr. 3, 1786), he will compare them with 'the Jumpers in Wales' and some mountain folk near Chapel-en-le-Frith. See also his letter to Conyers Middleton, Jan. 4, 1749, and to *The London Magazine*, Dec. 12, 1750.

For accounts of their extravagances in England see Southey, ch. 8; and Knox, *Enthusiasm*, pp. 362, 376 ff.

[38] Cf. Wesley's own criticism of the enthusiastic opinions of Thomas Maxfield and George Bell in JWJ, Nov. 1, 1762 (and Nov. 24). Many of Wesley's erstwhile followers (John Cennick, Thomas Bissicks, *et al.*) had 'got above all conviction' without disconcerting his own more modest views of assurance and the Holy Spirit's witness in the human spirit. Cf. No. 37, 'The Nature of Enthusiasm'.

3. 'But I lay it down as an undoubted truth, the fruit of the Spirit is the witness of the Spirit.' Not undoubted; thousands doubt of, yea flatly deny it: but to let that pass, 'If this witness be sufficient there is no need of any other. But it is sufficient, unless in one of these cases: (1). The *total absence* of the fruit of the Spirit.' And this is the case when the direct witness is first given. '(2). The *not perceiving it*. But to contend for it in this case is to contend for being in the favour of God and not knowing it.' True, not knowing it at that time any otherwise than by the testimony which is given for that end. And this we do contend for: we contend that the direct witness may shine clear, even while the indirect one is under a cloud.

4. It is objected, secondly: 'the design of the witness contended for is to prove that the profession we make is genuine. But it does not prove this.' I answer, the proving this is not the design of it. It is antecedent to our making any profession at all, but that of being lost, undone, guilty, helpless sinners. It is designed to assure those to whom it is given that they are the children of God; that they are 'justified freely by his grace, through the redemption that is in Jesus Christ'.[39] And this does not suppose that their preceding thoughts, words, and actions are conformable to the rule of the Scripture. It supposes quite the reverse, namely, that they are sinners all over, sinners both in heart and life. Were it otherwise God would 'justify the godly', and their own works would be 'counted to them for righteousness'.[40] And I cannot but fear that a supposition of our being justified by works is at the root of all these objections. For whoever cordially believes that God *imputes*[41] to all that are justified 'righteousness without works',[42] will find no difficulty in allowing the witness of his Spirit preceding the fruit of it.

5. It is objected, thirdly: 'One evangelist says, "Your heavenly Father will give the Holy Spirit to them that ask him."'[43] The other evangelist calls the same thing "good gifts",[44] abundantly

---

[39] Cf. Rom. 3:24.   [40] Cf. Rom. 4:5.

[41] Note this appeal to the Puritan insistence on the imputation of Christ's righteousness as the crucial act in man's justification and Wesley's correlation of the witness of the Spirit with this imputation. It amounts to yet another linkage between the Protestant stress on 'faith alone' and a 'catholic' doctrine of prevenience (implied in the notion of *direct* witness).

[42] Rom. 4:6.
[43] Luke 11:13.
[44] Matt. 7:11.

demonstrating that the Spirit's way of bearing witness is by giving good gifts.' Nay, here is nothing at all about 'bearing witness', either in one text or the other. Therefore till this demonstration is more abundantly demonstrated, I let it stand as it is.

6. It is objected, fourthly: 'The Scripture says, "The tree is known by its fruit;"[45] "Prove all things;"[46] "Try the spirits;"[47] "Examine yourselves." '[48] Most true: therefore let every man who believes he 'hath the witness in himself' *try* whether it be of God. If the fruit follow, it is; otherwise, it is not. For certainly 'the tree is known by its fruit.' Hereby we *prove* if it be of God. 'But the direct witness is never referred to in the Book of God.' Not as standing alone, not as a single witness, but as connected with the other; as giving a *joint testimony*, testifying *with our spirit* that we are children of God. And who is able to prove that it is not *thus* referred to in this very Scripture: 'Examine yourselves whether ye be in the faith; prove your own selves. Know ye not your own selves that Jesus Christ is in you?'[49] It is by no means clear that they did not know this by a *direct* as well as a *remote* witness. How is it proved that they did not know it, first, by inward consciousness, and then by love, joy, and peace?

7. 'But the testimony arising from the internal and external change is constantly referred to in the Bible.' It is so. And we constantly refer thereto to confirm the testimony of the Spirit.

'Nay, all the marks *you* have given whereby to distinguish the operations of God's Spirit from delusion refer to the change wrought in us and upon us.' This likewise is undoubtedly true.

8. It is objected, fifthly, that 'the direct witness of the Spirit does not secure us from the greatest delusions. And is that a witness fit to be trusted whose testimony cannot be depended on, that is forced to fly to something else to prove what it asserts?' I answer: to secure us from all delusion, God gives us two witnesses that we are his children. And this they testify conjointly. Therefore 'what God hath joined together, let not man put asunder.'[50] And while they are joined we cannot be deluded: their testimony can be depended on. They are fit to be trusted in the highest degree, and need nothing else to prove what they assert.

'Nay, the direct witness only asserts, but does not prove anything.' By two witnesses shall every word be established.[51] And

---

[45] Matt. 12:33.　　[46] 1 Thess. 5:21.　　[47] 1 John 4:1.
[48] 2 Cor. 13:5.　　　　　　　　　　　　　　　　[49] *Ibid.*
[50] Matt. 19:6; Mark 10:9.　　　　　　　　　　[51] See Matt. 18:16.

when the Spirit 'witnesses with our spirit', as God designs it to do, then it fully proves that we are children of God.

9. It is objected, sixthly: 'You own the change wrought is a sufficient testimony, unless in the case of severe trials, such as that of our Saviour upon the cross. But none of us can be tried in that manner.' But you or I may be tried in such a manner, and so may any other child of God, that it will be impossible for us to keep our filial confidence in God without the direct witness of his Spirit.

10. It is objected, lastly, 'The greatest contenders for it are some of the proudest and most uncharitable of men.' Perhaps some of the *hottest* contenders for it are both proud and uncharitable. But many of the *firmest* contenders for it are eminently meek and lowly in heart,[52] and, indeed, in all other respects also,

True followers of their lamb-like Lord.[53]

The preceding objections are the most considerable that I have heard, and I believe contain the strength of the cause. Yet I apprehend whoever calmly and impartially considers those objections and the answers together, will easily see that they do not destroy, no, nor weaken the evidence of that great truth, that the Spirit of God does *directly* as well as *indirectly* testify that we are children of God.

V.1. The sum of all is this: the testimony of the Spirit is an inward impression on the souls of believers, whereby the Spirit of God directly testifies to their spirit that they are children of God. And it is not questioned whether there is a testimony of the Spirit, but whether there is any *direct testimony*, whether there is any other than that which arises from a consciousness of the fruit of the Spirit. We believe there is: because this is the plain, natural meaning of the text, illustrated both by the preceding words and by the parallel passage in the Epistle to the Galatians; because, in the nature of the thing, the testimony must precede the fruit which springs from it, and because this plain meaning of the

---

[52] Matt. 11:29.
[53] Hymn 146, st. 1, l. 4, in *Hymns on the Lord's Supper* (1745), p. 139, beginning, 'Happy the saints of former days'. For another quotation from this hymn see No. 61, 'The Mystery of Iniquity', §29.

Word of God is confirmed by the experience of innumerable children of God; yea, and by the experience of all who are convinced of sin, who can never rest till they have a direct witness; and even of the children of the world who, not having the witness in themselves, one and all declare none can *know* his sins forgiven. 5

2. And whereas it is objected that experience is not sufficient to prove a doctrine unsupported by Scripture; that madmen and enthusiasts of every kind have imagined such a witness; that the design of that witness is to prove our profession genuine, which design it does not answer; that the Scripture says, 'The tree is 10 known by its fruit,'[54] 'Examine yourselves: . . . prove your own selves,'[55] and meantime the direct witness is never referred to in all the Book of God; that it does not secure us from the greatest delusions; and, lastly, that the change wrought in us is a sufficient testimony, unless in such trials as Christ alone suffered—we 15 answer, (1). Experience is sufficient to *confirm* a doctrine which is grounded on Scripture. (2). Though many fancy they experience what they do not, this is no prejudice to real experience. (3). The design of that witness is to assure us we are children of God; and this design it does answer. (4). The true witness of the Spirit is 20 known by its fruit—love, peace, joy—not indeed preceding, but following it. (5). It cannot be proved that the direct as well as the indirect witness is not referred to in that very text, 'Know ye not your own selves . . . that Jesus Christ is in you?'[56] (6). The Spirit of God, 'witnessing with our spirit', does secure us from all 25 delusion. And, lastly, we are all liable to trials wherein the testimony of our own spirit is not sufficient, wherein nothing less than the direct testimony of God's Spirit can assure us we are his children.

3. Two inferences may be drawn from the whole. The first: let 30 none ever presume to rest in any supposed testimony of the Spirit which is separate from the fruit of it. If the Spirit of God does really testify that we are children of God, the immediate consequence will be the fruit of the Spirit, even 'love, joy, peace, long-suffering, gentleness, goodness, fidelity, meekness, tem- 35 perance'.[57] And however this fruit may be clouded for a while during the time of strong temptation, so that it does not appear to

---

[54] Matt. 12:33.
[55] 2 Cor. 13:5.
[56] *Ibid.*
[57] Gal. 5:22-23 (*Notes*).

the tempted person while 'Satan is sifting him as wheat,'[58] yet the substantial part of it remains, even under the thickest cloud. It is true, joy in the Holy Ghost[59] may be withdrawn during the hour of trial. Yea, the soul may be 'exceeding sorrowful'[60] while 'the hour
5 and power of darkness'[61] continues. But even this is generally restored with increase, and he rejoices 'with joy unspeakable and full of glory'.[62]

4. The second inference is: let none rest in any supposed fruit of the Spirit without the witness. There may be foretastes of joy,
10 of peace, of love—and those not delusive, but really from God —long before we have the witness in ourselves, before the Spirit of God witnesses with our spirits that we have 'redemption in the blood of Jesus, even the forgiveness of sins'.[63] Yea, there may be a degree of long-suffering, of gentleness, of fidelity, meekness,
15 temperance (not a shadow thereof, but a real degree, by the preventing grace of God)[64] before we are 'accepted in the Beloved',[65] and consequently before we have a testimony of our acceptance. But it is by no means advisable to rest here; it is at the peril of our souls if we do. If we are wise we shall be continually
20 crying to God, until his Spirit cry in our heart, 'Abba, Father!'[66] This is the privilege of all the children of God, and without this we can never be assured that we are his children. Without this we cannot retain a steady peace, nor avoid perplexing doubts and fears. But when we have once received this 'Spirit of adoption',[67]
25 that 'peace which passes all understanding', and which expels all painful doubt and fear, will 'keep our hearts and minds in Christ Jesus'.[68] And when this has brought forth its genuine fruit, all inward and outward holiness, it is undoubtedly the will of him that calleth us to give us always what he has once given. So that
30 there is no need that we should ever more be deprived of either the testimony of God's Spirit or the testimony of our own, the consciousness of our walking in all righteousness and true holiness.[69]

Newry, April 4, 1767

[58] Cf. Luke 22:31.   [59] Rom. 14:17.   [60] Matt. 26:22, 38.
[61] Cf. Luke 22:53.   [62] 1 Pet. 1:8.   [63] Cf. Eph. 1:7; Col. 1:14.
[64] Cf. Nos. 43, *The Scripture Way of Salvation*, I.2; and 85, 'On Working Out Our Own Salvation', II.1, III.3-4.
[65] Eph. 1:6.   [66] Cf. Gal. 4:6.   [67] Rom. 8:15.
[68] Cf. Phil. 4:7.   [69] Eph. 4:24.

THE WITNESS OF OUR OWN SPIRIT

AN INTRODUCTORY COMMENT

Here is a sequel to the two previous 'Discourses' and, like them, was apparently written expressly for publication rather than being a condensate of oral sermons already preached. For one thing, we have no records of Wesley's ever preaching an oral sermon on 2 Cor. 1:12. For another, this is one of Wesley's rare sermons with no 'heads'. Later, in 1788, he will write another sermon from the same text and with much the same argument; see No. 105, 'On Conscience'.

The main point to the discourses on 'The Witness of the Spirit' had been the objective ground of Christian assurance, viz., the direct 'witness of the Spirit' as revealing to and convincing the believer of God's pardoning, regenerating, adopting grace. Here, in the sequel, Wesley undertakes an analysis of the subjective side of this experience of grace. His distinctive emphasis, however, is his careful correlation of assurance with a good conscience. What we have, then, is a brief essay on conscience, its marks and norms—and the resultant joy of Christian living 'in simplicity and godly sincerity. . .'. Wesley recognizes the logical distinctions between adoption, justification, and regeneration but is even more concerned to show their psychological integration in the Christian experience of assurance and how the process of sanctification, begun with regeneration, is really aimed at 'the recovery of the image of God' (an equivalent phrase for holiness).

Note the clear anticipation here of Kant's notion of a universal, categorical moral imperative linked to a Puritan view of distinct guidelines for 'a good conscience': (1) Scripture, (2) self-understanding, and (3) an observed consonance between intentions and actual behaviour. There is an important identification of God's grace as his power: 'the Holy Ghost working in us both to will and to do of [the Father's] good pleasure' (§15). The essay concludes with a description of 'the nature of that joy whereby [a mature] Christian rejoiceth evermore' as a consequence of 'a conscience void of offence toward God and man'.

In 1771 Wesley added a postscript that suggests his awareness of the delicate balance between Christian conscience (as portrayed here) and Christian scrupulosity and unease: 'It may easily be observed that the preceding discourse describes the experience of those that are strong *in faith, but hereby those that are* weak *in faith may be discouraged; to prevent which the following discourse* [viz., On Sin in Believers] *may be of use.' This, then, is a 'bridge' sermon, and should be read with both what precedes and what follows it in mind.*

The Witness of Our Own Spirit

2 Corinthians 1:12

This is our rejoicing, the testimony of our conscience,
that in simplicity and godly sincerity, not with
fleshly wisdom, but by the grace of God, we
have had our conversation in the world.

1. Such is the voice of every true believer in Christ, so long as he abides in faith and love. 'He that followeth me', saith our Lord, 'walketh not in darkness.'[1] And while he hath the light he rejoiceth therein.[2] 'As he hath received the Lord Jesus Christ, so he walketh in him.'[3] And while he walketh in him, the exhortation of the Apostle takes place in his soul day by day: 'Rejoice in the Lord always; and again I say, rejoice.'[4]

2. But that we may not build our house upon the sand (lest when the rains descend, and the winds blow, and the floods arise and beat upon it, it fall, and great be the fall thereof)[5] I intend, in the following discourse, to show what is the nature and ground of a Christian's joy. We know, in general, it is that happy peace, that calm satisfaction of spirit, which arises from such a testimony of his conscience as is here described by the Apostle. But in order to understand this the more throughly,[6] it will be requisite to weigh all his words; whence will easily appear both what we are to

---

[1] Cf. John 8:12.　　　　　　　　　　　　　　[2] See John 5:35.
[3] Cf. Col. 2:6.　　　　　　　　　　　　　　　　[4] Phil. 4:4.
[5] See Matt. 7:26-27.

[6] Cf. Johnson's comment on the equivalence of 'throughly' and 'thoroughly' in his *Dictionary*. Although Wesley seems to have used both, he clearly preferred 'throughly'. In this edn., instead of standardizing one spelling, we use whichever form appears in the preferred printing.

understand by 'conscience', and what by the 'testimony' thereof; and also how he that hath this testimony rejoiceth evermore.

3. And, first, what are we to understand by 'conscience'? What is the meaning of this word that is in everyone's mouth? One would imagine it was an exceeding difficult thing to discover this, when we consider how large and numerous volumes have been from time to time wrote on this subject; and how all the treasures of ancient and modern learning have been ransacked in order to explain it. And yet it is to be feared it has not received much light from all those elaborate inquiries. Rather, have not most of those writers puzzled the cause, 'darkening counsel by words without knowledge',[7] perplexing a subject plain in itself, and easy to be understood? For set aside but hard words, and every man of an honest heart will soon understand the thing.[8]

4. God has made us thinking beings, capable of perceiving what is present, and of reflecting or looking back on what is past. In particular we are capable of perceiving whatsoever passes in our own hearts or lives; of knowing whatsoever we feel or do; and that either while it passes, or when it is past. This we mean when we say man is a 'conscious' being: he hath a 'consciousness' or inward perception both of things present and past relating to himself, of his own tempers and outward behaviour. But what we usually term 'conscience' implies somewhat more than this. It is not barely the knowledge of our present, or the remembrance of our preceding life. To remember, to bear witness either of past or

---

[7] Cf. Job 38:2.

[8] Wesley's habit of disparaging the existing literature on a given topic is more misleading here than usual. The fact is that 'conscience' had been a familiar theme for moralists since St. Thomas Aquinas at least. Joseph Butler had focused the second of his famous Rolls Chapel sermons on it in 1726. Wesley had read this, and Butler's definition of conscience is strikingly similar to his own (*viz.,* 'a superior principle of reflection in every man, which distinguishes between the internal principles of his heart as well as his external actions, which passes judgment upon himself and them, etc.'); cf. *Fifteen Sermons,* pp. 35-36. Wesley had also read Jean La Placette's *Divers traités sur des matières de conscience. . .* (1647) or, more likely, Basil Kennett's translation, *The Christian Casuist; or, a Treatise of Conscience* (1705). Besides these there were similar discussions of conscience in Henry Hammond, Robert South, and in Wesley's grandfather Samuel Annesley's sermon in *The Morning Exercise at Cripplegate* (1661). In his own later sermon (No. 105) 'On Conscience' (1788), Wesley will cite La Placette approvingly and will actually quote from Annesley's sermon extensively.

In Chambers's *Cyclopaedia*—one of Wesley's favourite reference books—a similar definition appears: 'a secret testimony or judgment of the soul where it gives its approbation to things it does that are good and reproaches itself for those that are evil'. Thus, early and late, the same basic notion appears, always with more obvious Anglican nuances than in any of the Lutheran or Reformed discussions of 'conscience'.

present things is only one, and the least, office of conscience. Its main business is to excuse or accuse, to approve or disapprove, to acquit or condemn.

5. Some late writers indeed have given a new name to this, and
5 have chose to style it a 'moral sense'.[9] But the old word seems preferable to the new, were it only on this account, that it is more common and familiar among men, and therefore easier to be understood. And to Christians it is undeniably preferable on another account also; namely, because it is scriptural; because it is
10 the word which the wisdom of God hath chose to use in the inspired writings.

And according to the meaning wherein it is generally used there, particularly in the epistles of St. Paul, we may understand by conscience a faculty or power, implanted by God in every soul
15 that comes into the world,[10] of perceiving what is right or wrong in his own heart or life, in his tempers, thoughts, words, and actions.

6. But what is the *rule* whereby men are to judge of right and wrong; whereby their conscience is to be directed? The rule of heathens (as the Apostle teaches elsewhere) is 'the law written in
20 their hearts'.[11] 'These (saith he) not having the (outward) law, are a law unto themselves: who show the work of the law', that which the outward law prescribes, 'written in their heart' by the finger of God; 'their conscience also bearing witness' whether they walk by this rule or not; 'and their thoughts the meanwhile accusing, or
25 even excusing', acquitting, defending them (ἢ καὶ ἀπολογου- μένων).[a] But the Christian rule of right and wrong is the Word of

---

[a] Rom. 2:14-15.

---

[9] The earliest of these was Anthony Ashley Cooper, the third Earl of Shaftesbury (cf. *DNB*). The phrase occurs in his *Inquiry Concerning Virtue or Merit* (1699), I.iii.1. Another 'late writer' was Francis Hutcheson (1694–1746), professor of philosophy at Glasgow, who had expanded and refined Shaftesbury's ideas. He used the phrase in *An Inquiry into the Original of our Ideas of Beauty and Virtue* (1725), Treatise II, Sect. I.v, viii (see also Sect. IV.), and incorporated it into the title of his *Essay on the Nature and Conduct of the Passions and Affections, with Illustrations Upon the Moral Sense* (1726). Especially in his later sermons, Wesley cites Hutcheson's as a horrible example of an autonomous ethical theory divorced from any theonomous ground. Cf. Nos. 49, 'The Cure of Evil-speaking', §4; 90, 'An Israelite Indeed', §§1-4; 92, 'On Zeal', §2; 105, 'On Conscience', I.8-10; 106, 'On Faith, Heb. 11:6', II.2; 120, 'The Unity of the Divine Being', §18; 128, 'The Deceitfulness of the Human Heart', I.2. See also Wesley's letters to Samuel Furly, Feb. 18, 1756, and Mar. 8, 1757.

[10] The notion of an innate conscience goes back to Plato, and even in Wesley's lifetime would become the linch-pin of Immanuel Kant's moral philosophy.

[11] Rom. 2:15.

God, the writings of the Old and New Testament: all which the prophets and 'holy men of old' wrote 'as they were moved by the Holy Ghost';[12] 'all' that 'Scripture' which was 'given by inspiration of God', and which is indeed 'profitable for doctrine', or teaching the whole will of God; 'for reproof' of what is contrary thereto; 'for correction' of error; and 'for instruction (or training us up) in righteousness'.[b]

This 'is a lantern unto a' Christian's 'feet, and a light in all his paths'.[13] This alone he receives as his rule of right or wrong, of whatever is really good or evil. He esteems nothing good but what is here enjoined, either directly or by plain consequence. He accounts nothing evil but what is here forbidden, either in terms or by undeniable inference. Whatever the Scripture neither forbids nor enjoins (either directly or by plain consequence) he believes to be of an indifferent nature, to be in itself neither good nor evil: this being the whole and sole outward rule whereby his conscience is to be directed in all things.[14]

7. And if it be directed thereby in fact, then hath he 'the answer of a good conscience toward God'.[15] A 'good conscience' is what is elsewhere termed by the Apostle a 'conscience void of offence'.[16] So what he at one time expresses thus, 'I have lived in all good conscience before God until this day,'[c] he denotes at another by that expression, 'Herein do I exercise myself, to have always a conscience void of offence toward God and toward man.'[d] Now in order to this there is absolutely required, first, a right understanding of the Word of God; of his 'holy and acceptable and perfect will'[17] concerning us, as it is revealed therein. For it is impossible we should walk by a rule if we do not

[b] 2 Tim. 3:16.
[c] Acts 23:1.
[d] Acts 24:16.

---

[12] Cf. 2 Pet. 1:21.
[13] Ps. 119:105 (cf. BCP).
[14] Here Wesley passes summary judgment on an ancient and vexed question of the dividing line between essentials and *adiaphora* (things indifferent); he favours the Melanchthonian tendency to allow a wide latitude in open questions not expressly settled by scriptural injunctions or prohibitions. Lutheran orthodoxy had tended to hold, with Flaccius Illyricus, that 'nothing is indifferent (ἀδιάφορον) in matters of confession and [potential] abuse *(in casu confessionalis et scandali)*'; cf. Seeberg, *History of Doctrines*, II.364. Reformed theologians took a more flexible position on this point (cf. Heppe, *Reformed Dogmatics*, p. 688); Wesley carried this view much further.
[15] 1 Pet. 3:21.   [16] Acts 24:16.   [17] Cf. Rom. 12:1, 2.

know what it means. There is, secondly, required (which how few have attained!) a true knowledge of ourselves; a knowledge both of our hearts and lives, of our inward tempers and outward conversation: seeing, if we know them not, it is not possible that
5 we should compare them with our rule. There is required, thirdly, an agreement of our hearts and lives, of our tempers and conversation, of our thoughts and words and works with that rule, with the written Word of God. For without this, if we have any conscience at all, it can be only an evil conscience. There is,
10 fourthly, required an inward perception of this agreement with our rule. And this habitual perception, this inward consciousness itself, is properly a 'good conscience'; or (in the other phrase of the Apostle) 'A conscience void of offence toward God and toward man'.
15 8. But whoever desires to have a conscience thus void of offence, let him see that he lay the right foundation. Let him remember, 'Other foundation' of this 'can no man lay than that which is laid, even Jesus Christ.'[18] And let him also be mindful that no man buildeth on him but by a living faith, that no man is a
20 partaker of Christ until he can clearly testify, 'The life which I now live . . . I live by faith in the Son of God,' in him who is now *revealed* in my heart, 'who loved me, and gave himself for me'.[19] Faith alone is that evidence, that conviction, that demonstration of things invisible, whereby the eyes of our understanding being
25 opened, and divine light poured in upon them,[20] we 'see the wondrous things of' God's 'law',[21] the excellency and purity of it; the height and depth and length and breadth thereof,[22] and of every commandment contained therein. It is by faith that beholding 'the light of . . . the glory of God in the face of Jesus
30 Christ'[23] we perceive, as in a glass, all that is in ourselves, yea, the inmost motions of our souls. And by this alone can that blessed love of God be 'shed abroad in our hearts',[24] which enables us so to love one another as Christ loved us. By this is that gracious promise fulfilled unto all the Israel of God, 'I will put my laws into

[18] Cf. 1 Cor. 3:11.
[19] Gal. 2:20; this is the *direct* witness of the Spirit so strongly stressed in the previous discourses.
[20] Cf. Nos. 3, '*Awake, Thou That Sleepest*', I.11 and n.; and 10, 'The Witness of the Spirit, I', I.12 and n.
[21] Ps. 119:18 (BCP).   [22] Cf. Eph. 3:18.
[23] 2 Cor. 4:6.   [24] Rom. 5:5.

their minds, and write (or engrave) them in their hearts;'ᵉ hereby producing in their souls an entire agreement with his holy and perfect law, and 'bringing into captivity every thought to the obedience of Christ'.²⁵

And as an evil tree cannot bring forth good fruit, so a good tree cannot bring forth evil fruit.²⁶ As the heart therefore of a believer, so likewise his life is throughly conformed to the rule of God's commandments. In a consciousness whereof he can give glory to God, and say with the Apostle, 'This is our rejoicing, the testimony of our conscience, that in simplicity and godly sincerity, not with fleshly wisdom, but by the grace of God, we have had our conversation in the world.'

9. 'We have had our conversation.' The Apostle in the original expresses this by one single word (ἀνεστράφημεν).²⁷ But the meaning thereof is exceeding broad, taking in our whole deportment, yea, every inward as well as outward circumstance, whether relating to our soul or body. It includes every motion of our heart, of our tongue, of our hands and bodily members. It extends to all our actions and words; to the employment of all our powers and faculties; to the manner of using every talent we have received, with respect either to God or man.

10. 'We have had our conversation in the world;' even in the world of the ungodly: not only among the children of God—that were, comparatively, a little thing—but among the children of the devil,²⁸ among those that 'lie in wickedness', ἐν τῷ πονηρῷ,²⁹ 'in the wicked one'.³⁰ What a world is this! How throughly impregnated with the spirit it continually breathes! As our God is good and doth good, so the god of this world and all his children are evil, and do evil (so far as they are suffered) to all the children of God. Like their father they are always lying in wait, or 'walking

ᵉ Heb. 8:10 [citing Jer. 31:33].

---

²⁵ 2 Cor. 10:5.   ²⁶ Matt. 7:18; cf. Luke 6:43.

²⁷ From ἀναστρέφειν, ἀναστρεφή, colloquial terms common in the papyri and signifying 'conduct' or 'lifestyle', usually with a qualifying adjective; cf. Arndt and Gingrich, *Greek-English Lexicon*. Cf. also Johnson's definition of 'conversation' (No. 4): 'Behaviour; manner of acting in common life.'

²⁸ 1 John 3:10.

²⁹ Cf. 1 John 5:19.

³⁰ 1 John 3:12 (ἐκ τοῦ πονηροῦ). Cf. also 'The Epistle of Barnabas', II.10, XXI.3, in *The Apostolic Fathers*, Loeb, 24:346, 408. See also Nos. 23, 'Sermon on the Mount, III', I.9; 26, 'Sermon on the Mount, VI', III.15; and 38, 'A Caution against Bigotry', I.1.

about, seeking whom they may devour';[31] using fraud or force, secret wiles or open violence, to destroy those who are not of the world; continually warring against our souls, and by old or new weapons and devices of every kind, labouring to bring them back
5 into the snare of the devil,[32] into the broad road that leadeth to destruction.[33]

11. 'We have had our whole conversation in such a world, in simplicity and godly sincerity.' First, 'in simplicity'.[34] This is what our Lord recommends under the name of a 'single eye'. 'The
10 light of the body (saith he) is the eye. If therefore thine eye be single, thy whole body shall be full of light.'[35] The meaning whereof is this: what the eye is to the body, that the intention is to all the words and actions.[36] If therefore this eye of thy soul be

[31] Cf. 1 Pet. 5:8.

[32] 1 Tim. 3:7; 2 Tim. 2:26. Wesley's view of 'the world' and its control is double-sided. When pointing to 'the mystery of iniquity', his view is satanocratic (under the dominion of Satan, or the devil—usually personified), as here and in Nos. 23, 'Sermon on the Mount, III', III.4; 72, 'Of Evil Angels', II.1; 129, 'Heavenly Treasure in Earthen Vessels', §2; 133, 'Death and Deliverance', §2; 138A, 'On Dissimulation', §II; see also No. 42, 'Satan's Devices'. But in his notions of creation, history, Providence, good angels, and eschatology, Wesley stresses the goodness of creation, the Lordship of Christ, the dominion of Providence. The result is an interesting dialectic between dualism and theomonism.

[33] See Matt. 7:13.

[34] The Erasmian text here reads ἁπλότητι ('simplicity'); Wesley could hardly have known that better manuscripts read ἁγιότητι ('holiness'), so that now ἁγιότητι is the preferred reading in D. Eberhard Nestle, ed., *Novum Testamentum Graece et Latine* (Stuttgart, 1932), and other modern texts. In any case, 'simplicity', 'sincerity', 'a single eye', are familiar terms in Wesley's lexicon; cf. Nos. 18, 'The Marks of the New Birth', II.2; 19, 'The Great Privilege of those that are Born of God', II.10; 30, 'Sermon on the Mount, X', §9; 79, 'On Dissipation', §17; 90, 'An Israelite Indeed', II.9; 95, 'On the Education of Children', §10; and 125, 'On a Single Eye', §1.

[35] Matt. 6:22; cf. Luke 11:34.

[36] Wesley's sources for this general notion would go back to Macarius, Homily IV, in *Spiritual Homilies* (1721), pp. 118-19, and would have included John Flavel, 'Touchstone of Sincerity: or, the Signs of Grace, and the Symptoms of Hypocrisy', ch. ii, §III (*Works*, II. 451), and Poole's *Annotations* on Luke 11:36: 'What the eye is to the body, that the soul, the mind, and affections are to the whole man. Now look, as the eye is the organ by which light is received to guide a man's steps, so that if that be perfect without any mixture of ill humours, etc., the body from it takes a full and right direction how to move and act. But if that be vitiated by ill humours, the man knows not how to direct his bodily steps. So if a man's soul (which answereth the bodily eye) more especially a man's understanding, or judgment be darkened, perverted, prejudiced, or his affections be debauched or depraved, he will not know how to move one step right in his duty; but if his understanding have a right notion of truths, he judgeth aright concerning the things and ways of God, and his affections be not depraved, then the whole man will be in a capacity to receive the light, the revelations of truth, as they shall be communicated to him, even as he who hath a perfect eye receiveth, and is able to make use of the bright shining of a candle.' This is strikingly similar to Wesley's general theory of illumination; cf. No. 10, 'The Witness of the Spirit, I', I.12 and n.

single, all thy actions and conversation shall be 'full of light', of the light of heaven, of love and peace and joy in the Holy Ghost.[37]

We are then simple of heart when the eye of our mind is singly fixed on God; when in all things we aim at God alone, as our God, our portion, our strength, our happiness, our exceeding great 5 reward,[38] our all in time and eternity. This is simplicity: when a steady view, a single intention of promoting his glory, of doing and suffering his blessed will, runs through our whole soul, fills all our heart, and is the constant spring of all our thoughts, desires, and purposes. 10

12. 'We have had our conversation in the world', secondly, 'in godly sincerity.'[39] The difference between simplicity and sincerity seems to be chiefly this: simplicity regards the intention itself, sincerity the execution of it. And this sincerity relates not barely to our words, but to our whole conversation, as described above. It is 15 not here to be understood in that narrow sense wherein St. Paul himself sometimes uses it, for speaking the truth, or abstaining from guile, from craft and dissimulation, but in a more extensive meaning, as actually hitting the mark which we aim at by simplicity. Accordingly it implies in this place that we do in fact 20 speak and do all to the glory of God;[40] that all our words are not only pointed at this, but actually conducive thereto; that all our actions flow on in an even stream, uniformly subservient to this great end; and that in our whole lives we are moving straight toward God, and that continually—walking steadily on in the 25 highway of holiness, in the paths of justice, mercy, and truth.[41]

13. This sincerity is termed by the Apostle 'godly sincerity', or the sincerity of God (εἰλικρινείᾳ Θεοῦ)[42] to prevent our mistaking or confounding it with the sincerity of the heathens (for they had also a kind of sincerity among them, for which they 30 professed no small veneration); likewise to denote the object and end of this, as of every Christian virtue; seeing whatever does not ultimately tend to God sinks among 'the beggarly elements of the world'.[43] By styling it 'the sincerity of God' he also points out the

---

[37] Rom. 14:17; cf. Gal. 5:22.
[38] Gen. 15:1.
[39] Cf. No. 2, *The Almost Christian*, I.9 and n.
[40] 1 Cor. 10:31.
[41] See Ps. 89:14 (AV).
[42] Thus the *TR*; modern texts read εἰλικρινείᾳ τοῦ Θεοῦ.
[43] Cf. Gal. 4:9.

author of it, the 'Father of lights, from whom every good and perfect gift descendeth';[44] which is still more clearly declared in the following words, 'not with fleshly wisdom, but by the grace of God'.[45]

5   14. 'Not with fleshly wisdom': as if he had said, 'We cannot thus converse in the world by any natural strength of understanding, neither by any naturally acquired knowledge or wisdom. We cannot gain this simplicity or practise this sincerity by the force either of good sense, good nature, or good breeding.

10 It overshoots all our native courage and resolution, as well as all our precepts of philosophy. The power of custom is not able to train us up to this, nor the most exquisite rules of human education. Neither could I, Paul, ever attain hereto, notwithstanding all the advantages I enjoyed, so long as I was "in the

15 flesh"[46] (in my natural state) and pursued it only by "fleshly", natural, "wisdom".'

And yet surely, if any man could, Paul himself might have attained thereto by that wisdom. For we can hardly conceive any who was more highly favoured with all the gifts both of nature and

20 education. Besides his natural abilities, probably not inferior to those of any person then upon the earth, he had all the benefits of learning, studying at the university of Tarsus,[47] afterwards 'brought up at the feet of Gamaliel',[48] the person of the greatest account both for knowledge and integrity that was then in the

25 whole Jewish nation. And he had all the possible advantages of religious education, being a Pharisee, the son of a Pharisee, trained up in the very straitest sect or profession, distinguished from all others by a more eminent strictness. And herein he had 'profited above many others who were his equals in years, being

30 more abundantly zealous'[49] of whatever he thought would please

---

[44] Cf. Jas. 1:17.   [45] 2 Cor. 1:12.   [46] Rom. 7:5, etc.

[47] An *urbs libera* ('free city') in the Syrian province of Cilicia. Jews living and educated there were in contact with a vigorous Hellenistic culture, but that there was a 'university of Tarsus' was, of course, Wesley's own 'modernization'. Cf. below, No. 25, 'Sermon on the Mount, V', IV.2.

[48] Cf. Acts 22:3. This was Gamaliel I, ha-Zaken ('the elder'), a grandson of Hillel and presiding officer of the Sanhedrin. He is credited, in the tradition of Hillel, with many *takkanot* (normative moral regulations) more tolerant than the rigorist rulings of Shammai. This would accord with his tolerant judgment upon the early Christian movement as reported in Acts 5:34-40. It conflicts with Paul's claim, emphasized here by Wesley, that he had been 'brought up at Gamaliel's feet', as if that amounted to his belonging 'to the very straitest sect' of the Pharisees. Cf. *Encyclopaedia Judaica* (Jerusalem, 1971), art. 'Gamaliel'.

[49] Cf. Gal. 1:14 (cf. *Notes*).

God, and 'as touching the righteousness of the law, blameless'.[50] But it could not be that he should hereby attain this simplicity and godly sincerity. It was all but lost labour; in a deep, piercing sense of which he was at length constrained to cry out: 'The things which were gain to me, those I counted loss for Christ. . . . Yea, doubtless, and I count all things but loss for the excellency of the knowledge of Christ Jesus my Lord.'[f]

15. It could not be that ever he should attain to this but by the 'excellent knowledge of Jesus Christ our Lord';[51] or 'by the grace of God'—another expression of nearly the same import. By 'the grace of God' is sometimes to be understood that free love, that unmerited mercy, by which I, a sinner, through the merits of Christ am now reconciled to God. But in this place it rather means that power of God the Holy Ghost which 'worketh in us both to will and to do of his good pleasure'.[52] As soon as ever the grace of God (in the former sense, his pardoning love) is manifested to our soul, the grace of God (in the latter sense, the power of his Spirit) takes place therein. And now we can perform, through God, what to man was impossible. Now we can order our conversation aright. We can do all things in the light and power of that love, through Christ which strengtheneth us.[53] We now have 'the testimony of our conscience', which we could never have by fleshly wisdom, 'that in simplicity and godly sincerity . . . we have our conversation in the world'.

16. This is properly the ground of a Christian's joy. We may now therefore readily conceive how he that hath this testimony in himself 'rejoiceth evermore'.[54] ' "My soul" (may he say) "doth magnify the Lord, and my spirit rejoiceth in God my Saviour."[55] I rejoice in him who, of his own unmerited love, of his own free and tender mercy, "hath called me into this state of salvation"[56] wherein through his power I now stand. I rejoice because his Spirit beareth witness to my spirit[57] that I am bought with the blood of the Lamb,[58] and that believing in him, "I am a member of

---

[f] Phil. 3:7-8.

---

[50] Cf. Phil. 3:6.
[51] Cf. main text and Phil. 3:8.
[52] Phil. 2:13. Cf. No. 85, 'On Working Out Our Own Salvation'.
[53] See Phil. 4:13.   [54] Cf. 1 Thess. 5:16.
[55] Cf. Luke 1:46-47.   [56] Cf. BCP, Catechism.
[57] See Rom. 8:16.   [58] Rev. 7:14; 12:11.

Christ, a child of God, and an inheritor of the kingdom of heaven."[59] I rejoice because the sense of God's love to me hath by the same Spirit wrought in me to love him, and to love for his sake every child of man, every soul that he hath made. I rejoice because
5 he gives me to feel in myself "the mind that was in Christ":[60] simplicity, a single eye to him in every motion of my heart; power always to fix the loving eye of my soul on him who "loved me, and gave himself for me",[61] to aim at him alone, at his glorious will, in all I think or speak or do; purity, desiring nothing more but God,
10 "crucifying the flesh with its affections and lusts",[62] "setting my affections on things above, not on things of the earth";[63] holiness, a recovery of the image of God,[64] a renewal of soul after his likeness; and godly sincerity, directing all my words and works so as to conduce to his glory. In this I likewise rejoice, yea and will
15 rejoice, because my conscience beareth me witness in the Holy Ghost, by the light he continually pours in upon it, that "I walk worthy of the vocation wherewith" I am "called";[65] that I "abstain from all appearance of evil",[66] "fleeing from sin as from the face of a serpent";[67] that as I have opportunity I do all possible good, in
20 every kind, to all men;[68] that I follow my Lord in all my steps, and do what is acceptable in his sight. I rejoice because I both see and feel, through the inspiration of God's Holy Spirit, that all my works are wrought in him, yea, and that it is he who worketh all my works in me. I rejoice in seeing, through the light of God which
25 shines in my heart, that I have power to walk in his ways, and that through his grace I turn not therefrom, to the right hand or to the left.'[69]

17. Such is the ground and the nature of that joy whereby a Christian rejoiceth evermore. And from all this we may easily
30 infer, first, that this is not a *natural* joy. It does not arise from any natural cause: not from any sudden flow of spirits. This may give a transient start of joy. But the Christian 'rejoiceth always'.[70] It cannot be owing to bodily health or ease, to strength and soundness of constitution. For it is equally strong in sickness and
35 pain; yea, perhaps far stronger than before. Many Christians have

---

[59] A composite paraphrase of 1 Cor. 6:15; Rom. 8:16, 17; and Jas. 2:5.
[60] Cf. Phil. 2:5.
[61] Gal. 2:20.   [62] Cf. Gal. 5:24.   [63] Cf. Col. 3:2.
[64] Gen. 1:27; 9:6. Cf. No. 44, *Original Sin*, III.5 and n.
[65] Cf. Eph. 4:1.   [66] 1 Thess. 5:22.   [67] Cf. Ecclus. 21:2.
[68] See *General Rules*, §5.   [69] Cf. Josh. 23:6.   [70] Cf. 2 Cor. 6:10.

never experienced any joy to be compared with that which then filled their soul, when the body was wellnigh worn out with pain, or consumed away with pining sickness. Least of all can it be ascribed to outward prosperity, to the favour of men, or plenty of worldly goods. For then chiefly when their faith has been tried as with fire, by all manner of outward afflictions, have the children of God rejoiced in him 'whom unseen they loved', even 'with joy unspeakable'.[71] And never surely did men rejoice like those who were used as 'the filth and offscouring of the world';[72] who wandered to and fro, being in want of all things, in hunger, in cold, in nakedness; who 'had trials', not only 'of cruel mockings', but 'moreover of bonds and imprisonments';[73] yea, who at last 'counted not their lives dear unto themselves, so they might finish their course with joy'.[74]

18. From the preceding considerations we may, secondly, infer that the joy of a Christian does not arise from any *blindness of conscience*, from his not being able to discern good from evil. So far from it that he was an utter stranger to this joy till the eyes of his understanding were opened,[75] that he knew it not until he had spiritual senses, fitted to discern spiritual good and evil.[76] And now the eye of his soul waxeth not dim. He was never so sharpsighted before. He has so quick a perception of the smallest things as is quite amazing to the natural man. As a mote is visible in the sunbeam, so to him who is walking in the light, in the beams of the uncreated sun, every mote of sin is visible.[77] Nor does he close the eyes of his conscience any more. That sleep is departed from him. His soul is always broad awake: no more slumber or folding of the hands in rest![78] He is always standing on the tower, and hearkening what his Lord will say concerning him;[79] and always rejoicing in this very thing, in 'seeing him that is invisible'.[80]

19. Neither does the joy of a Christian arise, thirdly, from any *dullness* or *callousness of conscience*. A kind of joy, it is true, may arise from this in those whose 'foolish hearts are darkened';[81] whose

[71] Cf. 1 Pet. 1:8.   [72] Cf. 1 Cor. 4:13.   [73] Cf. Heb. 11:36.
[74] Cf. Acts 20:24.   [75] See Eph. 1:18.
[76] See Heb. 5:14; cf. No. 10, 'The Witness of the Spirit, I', I.12 and n.
[77] Direct divine illumination; cf. §8 above.
[78] See Prov. 6:10; 24:33. See also No. 113, *The Late Work of God in North America*, II.12.
[79] See Isa. 21:8; 37:22. See also 2 Kgs. 19:21; 1 Chr. 17:23.
[80] Heb. 11:27.
[81] Cf. Rom. 1:21.

heart is callous, unfeeling, dull of sense, and consequently without spiritual understanding. Because of their senseless, unfeeling hearts, they may rejoice even in committing sin; and this they may probably call 'liberty'! Which is indeed mere
5 drunkenness of soul; a fatal numbness of spirit, the stupid insensibility of a seared conscience.[82] On the contrary, a Christian has the most exquisite sensibility, such as he would not have conceived before. He never had such a tenderness of conscience as he has had since the love of God has reigned in his heart. And
10 this also is his glory and joy, that God hath heard his daily prayer:

> O that my tender soul might fly
> The first abhorred approach of ill:
> Quick as the apple of an eye
> The slightest touch of sin to feel.[83]

15   20. To conclude. Christian joy is joy in obedience—joy in loving God and keeping his commandments. And yet not in keeping them as if we were thereby to fulfil the terms of the *covenant of works*;[84] as if by any works or righteousness of ours we were to *procure* pardon and acceptance with God. Not so: we are
20 already pardoned and accepted through the mercy of God in Christ Jesus—not as if we were by our own obedience to *procure* life, life from the death of sin. This also we have already through the grace of God. 'Us hath he quickened, who were dead in sin.'[85] And now we are 'alive to God, through Jesus Christ our Lord'.[86]
25 But we rejoice in walking according to the *covenant of grace*, in holy love and happy obedience. We rejoice in knowing that 'being justified through his grace',[87] we have 'not received that grace of God in vain';[88] that God having freely (not for the sake of our willing or running, but through the blood of the Lamb) reconciled
30 us to himself, we run in the strength which he hath given us the way of his commandments.[89] He hath 'girded us with strength

---

[82] See 1 Tim. 4:2; cf. Nos. 49, 'The Cure of Evil-speaking', I.6; 85, 'On Working Out Our Own Salvation', III.4; and 149, 'On Love', III.5.

[83] 'Watch in All Things', st. 10, in *Hymns and Sacred Poems* (1742), p. 218 (*Poet. Wks.*, II.273). Cf. also No. 105, 'On Conscience', I.15. For other quotations from this same hymn, cf. Nos. 95, 'On the Education of Children', §18; 106, 'On Faith, Heb. 11:6', II.4; and 126, 'On Worldly Folly', II.2.

[84] Cf. No. 6, 'The Righteousness of Faith', §1 and n.

[85] Cf. Eph. 2:1.   [86] Rom. 6:11.   [87] Cf. Rom. 3:24; Titus 3:7.

[88] Cf. 2 Cor. 6:1.   [89] See Ps. 119:32.

unto the war',[90] and we gladly 'fight the good fight of faith'.[91] We rejoice, through him who liveth in our hearts by faith, to 'lay hold of eternal life'.[92] This is our rejoicing; that as our 'Father worketh hitherto',[93] so (not by our own might or wisdom, but through the power of his Spirit freely given in Christ Jesus) we also work the works of God.[94] And may he work in us whatsoever is well-pleasing in his sight,[95] to whom be the praise for ever and ever![96]

[90] Cf. Ps. 18:39; 2 Sam. 22:40.
[91] 1 Tim. 6:12.
[92] *Ibid.*
[93] John 5:17.
[94] John 6:28.
[95] Heb. 13:21.
[96] See 1 Pet 4:11. For Wesley's use of ascriptions, cf. No. 1, *Salvation by Faith*, III.9 and n.

ON SIN IN BELIEVERS

THE REPENTANCE OF BELIEVERS

AN INTRODUCTORY COMMENT

In the first edition of SOSO, *I (1746), 'The Witness of the Spirit' (Discourse I), was followed by a sermon on 'The Means of Grace' to round out the volume.* Two years later, Wesley placed his third university sermon, 'The Circumcision of the Heart' (from 1733), as the first sermon in his second volume, following it with a new sermon on *'The Great Privilege of those that are Born of God'. The shared theme in this sequence (stressed in three of the sermons and implied in 'The Means of Grace') concerned the power bestowed on justified and regenerate believers* not to commit sin—*a crucial idea in the holy-living tradition, which then was given its climactic statement, up to that date, in* Christian Perfection *(1750); see No. 40.*

This idea of the Christian's grace-bestowed power not to commit sin was, however, bound to generate controversy and confusion among both critics and some disciples. With their doctrines of the ineradicable 'remains of sin' (fomes peccati), *the Lutherans had taught that the justified believer was* simul justus et peccator *but also that his repented sins were covered by the imputed righteousness of Christ and thus inculpable; cf.* The Apology of the Augsburg Confession *(1531), Article II, 'Original Sin', especially §§35-45. With similar premises with respect to the* fomes peccati *(the Christian is 'a sinner saved by grace'), the Calvinists stressed rigorous examination of consciences, repentance, the final perseverance of the elect, and the perfect and immutable freedom 'in the state of glory only'; cf.* The Westminster Confession *VI.v, IX.v; see also XIII-XVIII. On the other side, the Moravians and some of Wesley's own disciples (e.g., Thomas Maxfield, William Cudworth, James Relly) had taken the claim that 'those born of God do not commit sin' to its antinomian extreme of sinless—even guiltless—perfection, as if the power not to sin meant the extirpation of all 'remains of sin'. For an exposition of this view, see the Supplement to* The Christian Magazine for the Year 1762: *'for all who are united to Christ by the Holy Spirit's dwelling in them are delivered from the guilt, the power, or, in one word the being of* sin' *(p. 579; see also below, pp. 328-32). Moreover, they had appealed to Wesley's basic soteriology as the logical ground for their interpretation.*

Wesley, caught in the controversy generated by these two polarities, reacted typically and came up with what he regarded as a valid third alternative. Its root notion was a distinction between 'sin properly so called' (i.e., 'the [deliberate] violation of a known law of God'—mortal if unrepented) and all 'involuntary transgressions' (culpable only if unrepented and not discarded when discerned or entertained). This distinction already had a history in Catholic moral theory ('mortal' versus 'venial'); cf. Claude Fleury, Les Moeurs des Israélites *(1683; cf.* The Manners of the Ancient Israelites. . . , *ed. Adam Clarke [1852], p. 306). But it had also had a special development among Anglican moralists as well. Richard Lucas had analyzed it in his* Enquiry After Happiness *(1717), III. 299 301 (e.g., 'Mortal sin is a deliberate transgression of a known law of God tending to the dishonour of God and injury of our neighbour or the deprivation of our own nature'). John Kettlewell, in* The Measures of Christian Obedience *(1681), had spoken of 'voluntary' and 'involuntary' sins (see Bk. IV, chs. 3–4, pp. 330 ff., 335 ff.). Much more to the same effect had been found in Samuel Bradford's Boyle Lectures for 1699,* The Credibility of the Christian Revelation, from its intrinsic evidence; in eight sermons *(1700), Sermon II, p. 445; Hugh Binning,* Fellowship With God *(1671), pp. 216-18, and John Weemse [Weemes],* The Portraiture of God in Man . . . *(1627), p. 326 (cf. Weemes's formulation of the distinction as between 'sins forgiven' and 'sins passed by. . .').*

Thus, there was an unstable tension between the claims that a Christian may be delivered from sin's bondage, and that 'sin remains but no longer reigns' (see below, I.6 and n.); this continued to plague Wesley in many ways, as one can see from his frequent references to it; see below, II.3, III.1-9 and n.; and cf. Nos. 1, Salvation by Faith, *II.6; 8, 'The First-fruits of the Spirit', II.6, 9, III.4-5; 14,* The Repentance of Believers, *I.2-3; 18, 'The Marks of the New Birth', I.5-6; 19, 'The Great Privilege of those that are Born of God', II.8; 40,* Christian Perfection, *II.4-5; 41,* Wandering Thoughts, *III.6; 43,* The Scripture Way of Salvation, *III.6-8; 46, 'The Wilderness State', II.6, III.14; 58,* On Predestination, *§7; 62, 'The End of Christ's Coming', III.3; 65, 'The Duty of Reproving our Neighbour', III.14; 74, 'Of the Church', § 21; 76, 'On Perfection', II. 9; 82, 'On Temptation', I. 5; 104, 'On Attending the Church Service', § 18; 128,*

'*The Deceitfulness of the Human Heart*', *II. 5. Cf. also Wesley's letters to John Hosmer, June 7, 1761, to Mary Bishop, May 27, 1771, and to Mrs. Bennis, June 16, 1772.*

What matters most is that Wesley insisted on holding to both traditions—sola fide *and* holy living—*without forfeiting the good essence of either. Moreover, he saw no inconsistency in his shifting from one emphasis to the other as circumstances seemed to require. He was more concerned to face the dreadful realities of sin while never yielding to any defeatist notion that God's grace is intrinsically impotent to save souls 'to the utmost', in this life. That enough of his comments on this twin concern could have been misconstrued as a doctrine of 'sinless perfection' is apparent both in its exaggerations in Cudworth and others, and also in nineteenth-century developments—especially in American Methodism—in which 'entire sanctification' was interpreted as 'a second and separate work of grace' and normative for the Christian life; cf.* Peters, Christian Perfection and American Methodism.

In 1763, in a needed effort to counter the distortions and bring the controversy more nearly back to balance, Wesley wrote and published a sermon entitled A Discourse on Sin in Believers, '*in order to remove a mistake which some were labouring to propagate: that there is no sin in any that are justified' (see JWJ, Mar. 28, and* Bibliog, No. 257). *In 1767 he wrote out its sequel,* The Repentance of Believers, *and published it the following year (cf. JWJ, Apr. 17-24, and* Bibliog, No. 305).

Here, we find an interesting version of Wesley's doctrine of 'entire sanctification'; cf. Pt. II. Shortly after this, when he began to re-arrange the sequence of Vol. I of SOSO *for the edition of his* Works, *he quite deliberately inserted these two sermons as Nos. 13 and 14, between 'The Witness of Our Own Spirit' and 'The Means of Grace'. They are designed, as he says, for the encouragement of 'the weaker brethren' whose Christian assurance had been all too easily shaken by their awareness of sin's residues in their hearts, even in their uncertain pilgrimage of grace toward 'perfect love'.*

The present text of On Sin in Believers *is based on the first edition of 1763, and the text of* The Repentance of Believers *is from its first edition of 1767. For stemmata illustrating text transmissions through the editions published in Wesley's lifetime and the list of substantive variant readings found in these successive editions, see Appendix, 'Wesley's Text', in Vol. IV.*

On Sin in Believers

2 Corinthians 5:17

If any man be in Christ, he is a new creature.

I.1. Is there then sin in him that is in Christ? Does sin *remain* in one that 'believes in him'?[1] Is there any sin in them that are 'born of God',[2] or are they wholly delivered from it? Let no one imagine this to be a question of mere curiosity, or that it is of little importance whether it be determined one way or the other. Rather it is a point of the utmost moment to every serious Christian, the resolving of which very nearly concerns both his present and eternal happiness.

2. And yet I do not know that ever it was controverted in the primitive Church. Indeed there was no room for disputing concerning it, as all Christians were agreed. And so far as I have observed, the whole body of ancient Christians who have left us anything in writing declare with one voice that even believers in Christ, till they are 'strong in the Lord, and in the power of his might', have need to 'wrestle with flesh and blood', with an evil nature, as well as 'with principalities and powers'.[3]

3. And herein our own Church (as indeed in most points) exactly copies after the primitive;[4] declaring (in her Ninth

[1] Cf. John 9:36, 41.
[2] 1 John 3:9; 4:7, etc.
[3] Cf. Eph. 6:10, 12.
[4] A typical example of Wesley's unself-conscious Anglican triumphalism. Cf. also No. 33, 'Sermon on the Mount, XIII', III.1; 'Farther Thoughts on Separation from the Church', §1, dated Dec. 11, 1789 (*AM*, 1790); and his letter to Sir Harry Trelawney, Aug. 1780. He was 'anti-Establishment', to be sure, but never 'anti-Anglican' or even 'pro-Nonconformist'.

The Thirty-nine Articles were a set of doctrinal formulae first adopted by the Church of England in 1563. They gained full official approval in 1571, having evolved from a series of confessional statements in 1536 ('Ten Articles'), 1537, 1539 ('Six Articles'), 1543, and 1553 ('Forty-two Articles'). By design, they were more Reformed and anti-Roman than the Edwardian Homilies (1547) had been, and they had been added to the Elizabethan Prayer Book as an appendix, since they were never intended to be a 'confession' in the same sense as *The Augsburg Confession* (1530), etc. Even so, it was required that Anglican clergy, in Wesley's day, and even down till 1865, should subscribe to them. In the prayer

Article), 'Original sin [. . .] is the corruption of the nature of every man, [. . .] whereby man is [. . .] in his own nature inclined to evil, so that the flesh lusteth contrary to the Spirit.[5] [. . .] And this infection of nature doth remain, yea, in them that are
5 regenerated; whereby the lust of the flesh, called in Greek φρόνημα σαρκός,[6] [. . .] is not subject to the law of God.[7] And although there is no condemnation for them that believe [. . .], yet this lust hath of itself the nature of sin.'[8]

4. The same testimony is given by all other churches; not only
10 by the Greek and Romish Church, but by every Reformed Church in Europe, of whatever denomination. Indeed some of these seem to carry the thing too far; so describing the corruption of heart in a believer as scarce to allow that he has dominion over it, but rather is in bondage thereto.[9] And by this means they leave
15 hardly any distinction between a believer and an unbeliever.

5. To avoid this extreme many well-meaning men, particularly those under the direction of the late Count Zinzendorf,[10] ran into

book prepared by Wesley for the American Methodists in 1784 *(The Sunday Service)* he included a highly personal abridgement of them, reducing their number from thirty-nine to twenty-four; a twenty-fifth was added by the Americans. As in the BCP, Wesley's Articles were placed as an appendix; 'Of Original or Birth Sin' appears as Art. VII rather than IX.

[5] Cf. Gal. 5:17.

[6] Cf. No. 8, 'The First-fruits of the Spirit', I.2, and, below, IV.7; see also No. 43, *The Scripture Way of Salvation*, III.6.

[7] Rom. 8:7.

[8] Cf. The Thirty-nine Articles, Art. IX, 'Of Original or Birth Sin', and consider Wesley's omissions. For an even more drastic abridgement, cf. 'The Twenty-five Articles' of the Methodists, Art. VII, in Wesley's *Sunday Service*.

[9] Cf. No. 9, 'The Spirit of Bondage and of Adoption'. This is an obvious reference to the more one-sided versions of the *simul justus et peccator* as formulated by Matthias Flacius Illyricus and also as denounced by Trent, Session V.v. Cf. *The Formula of Concord* (Epitome), Art. I ('On Original Sin'), 'Affirmative', III: 'And we do indeed affirm that no one is able to dissever this [sinful] corruption of [human] nature from the nature itself except God alone—which will fully come to pass by means of death in the resurrection into blessedness,' in Philip Schaff, *The Creeds of Christendom* (New York, Harper and Brothers, 1881–82), III. 100–101.

Incidentally, this notion of sin's being destroyed by death is affirmed by the early Wesley in two sermons written before 1738 (cf. Nos. 109, *The Trouble and Rest of Good Men*, I, II.6; and 136, 'On Mourning for the Dead', ¶5, but the notion never reappears afterward. William Tilly had made the point in his sermon 'On Grieving the Holy Spirit' which Wesley extracted. This idea had appeared in Luther's *Treatise on the Holy Sacrament of Baptism* (1519), VII-VIII, XVII-XVIII, and had then been developed in classical Lutheran eschatology; cf. Schmid, *Doctrinal Theology*, pp. 625 ff. For references to Luther in the Wesley corpus, cf. No. 14, *The Repentance of Believers*, I.9 and n.

[10] Wesley's relations with Count Ludwig von Zinzendorf, the most prominent of the Moravians, were complex and unfortunate; cf. 'The Rift With the Moravians' in LPT,

another, affirming that 'all true believers are not only saved from the *dominion* of sin but from the *being* of inward as well as outward sin, so that it no longer *remains* in them.' And from them, about twenty years ago, many of our countrymen imbibed the same opinion, that even the corruption of nature *is no more* in those who 5 believe in Christ.

6. It is true that when the Germans[11] were pressed upon this head they soon allowed (many of them at least) that sin did still remain *in the flesh*, but not *in the heart* of a believer. And after a time, when the absurdity of this was shown, they fairly gave up the 10 point; allowing that sin did still *remain*, though not *reign*, in him that is born of God.[12]

7. But the English who had received it from them (some directly, some at second or third hand) were not so easily prevailed upon to part with a favourite opinion. And even when 15 the generality of them were convinced it was utterly indefensible, a few could not be persuaded to give it up, but maintain it to this day.[13]

II.1. For the sake of these who really fear God and desire to know 'the truth as it is in Jesus',[14] it may not be amiss to consider 20 the point with calmness and impartiality. In doing this I use indifferently the words 'regenerate', 'justified', or 'believers'; since, though they have not precisely the same meaning (the first

---

Wesley, pp. 347-76. The crucial difference between them, in Wesley's view, was that antinomianism was a natural consequence of the Moravian doctrines of 'perfect love', whereas his own doctrine of 'perfection' and 'holiness' was strongly moralized (*viz.*, 'love of God and neighbour'). Cf. below, III. 9-10 and V.1, as well as Nos. 48, 'Self-denial', III.2; 76, 'On Perfection', III.12; 107, 'On God's Vineyard', I.3. See also JWJ, July 12, 1739, and Sept. 3, 1741; Charles's letter to the Count, Nov. 26, 1737, and John's letter of Sept. 6, 1745. See also, *Dialogue between an Antinomian and his Friend*, *Bibliog*, No. 102, Vol. 13 of this edn.

[11] I.e., the Moravians.

[12] Cf. Nos. 1, *Salvation by Faith*, II.6; 14, *The Repentance of Believers*, I.2; 19, 'The Great Privilege of those that are Born of God', II.2; 43, *The Scripture Way of Salvation*, III.6-8; 74, 'Of the Church', §21; and 128, 'The Deceitfulness of the Human Heart', II.5. See also Wesley's account of Christian David's beliefs, in JWJ, Aug. 10, 1738, where the same phrase occurs: 'though it [sin] did not reign, it did remain in me.'

[13] E.g., John Gambold had been a lively member of the Holy Club and the author of a fine sermon, 'On the Holy Spirit' (1736), which Jackson published as Wesley's own (in his edn. of *Works*, VII. 508-20). Subsequently, Gambold became a pastor of the Moravians in England and, finally, their bishop. There is a poignant record of Wesley's last visit with him in JWJ, Nov. 5, 1763—very close to the date of the reference above.

[14] Eph. 4:21.

implying an inward, *actual* change; the second a *relative* one; and the third the means whereby both the one and the other are wrought) yet they come to one and the same thing, as everyone that 'believes' is both 'justified' and 'born of God'.[15]

5   2. By 'sin' I here understand inward sin:[16] any sinful temper, passion, or affection; such as pride, self-will, love of the world, in any kind or degree; such as lust, anger, peevishness; any disposition contrary to the mind which was in Christ.

3. The question is not concerning *outward sin*, whether a child
10   of God *commits sin* or no. We all agree and earnestly maintain, 'He that committeth sin is of the devil.'[17] We agree, 'Whosoever is born of God doth not commit sin.'[18] Neither do we now inquire whether inward sin will *always* remain in the children of God; whether sin will continue in the soul *as long as* it continues in the
15   body. Nor yet do we inquire whether a justified person may *relapse* either into inward or outward sin. But simply this: is a justified or regenerate man freed from *all sin* as soon as he is justified? Is there then no sin in his heart? Nor ever after, unless he fall from grace?

20   4. We allow that the state of a justified person is inexpressibly great and glorious. He is 'born again, not of blood, nor of the flesh, nor of the will of man, but of God'.[19] He is a child of God, a member of Christ, an heir of the kingdom of heaven. 'The peace of God which passeth all understanding keepeth his heart and
25   mind in Christ Jesus.'[20] His very 'body is a temple of the Holy Ghost',[21] and 'an habitation of God through the Spirit'.[22] He is 'created anew in Christ Jesus';[23] he is *washed;* he is *sanctified.* His 'heart is purified by faith';[24] he is cleansed from 'the corruption that is in the world'.[25] 'The love of God is shed abroad in his heart
30   by the Holy Ghost which is given unto him.'[26] And so long as he 'walketh in love'[27] (which he may always do) he 'worships God in

---

[15] But see below, No. 18, 'The Marks of the New Birth', where significant nuances of differentiation between these terms may be found.

[16] Wesley's inventory of 'inward' sins corresponds to what he speaks of elsewhere as 'involuntary' (as the Lutherans had in their *Formula of Concord*) and to what the Romans had grouped under the heading of 'venial' at Trent, Session V; see above, intro. and I.4 and n.

[17] 1 John 3:8.   [18] 1 John 3:9.
[19] Cf. John 1:13.   [20] Cf. Phil. 4:7.
[21] Cf. 1 Cor. 6:19.   [22] Eph. 2:22.
[23] Eph. 2:10.   [24] Cf. Acts 15:9.
[25] 2 Pet. 1:4.   [26] Cf. Rom. 5:5.
[27] Eph. 5:2.

spirit and in truth'.[28] He 'keepeth the commandments of God, and doth those things that are pleasing in his sight':[29] so 'exercising himself as to have a conscience void of offence toward God and toward man'.[30] And he has power both over outward and inward sin, even from the moment he is justified.

III.1. 'But was he not then "freed from all sin",[31] so that there is no sin in his heart?' I cannot say this: I cannot believe it, because St. Paul says the contrary. He is speaking to believers, and describing the state of believers in general, when he says, 'The flesh lusteth against the spirit, and the spirit against the flesh: these are contrary the one to the other.'[a] Nothing can be more express. The Apostle here directly affirms that 'the flesh', evil nature, opposes 'the spirit', even in believers; that even in the regenerate there are two principles 'contrary the one to the other'.

2. Again: when he writes to the believers at Corinth, to those who were 'sanctified in Christ Jesus',[b] he says: 'I, brethren, could not speak unto you as unto spiritual, but as unto carnal, as unto babes in Christ[32]. . . . Ye are yet carnal: for whereas there is among you envying and strife, [. . .] are ye not carnal?'[c] Now here the Apostle speaks unto those who were unquestionably believers, whom in the same breath he styles his 'brethren in Christ',[33] as being still in a measure *carnal*. He affirms there was 'envying' (an evil temper) occasioning 'strife' among them, and yet does not give the least intimation that they had lost their faith. Nay, he manifestly declares they had not; for then they would not

---

[a] Gal. 5:17.   [b] 1 Cor. 1:2.   [c] [1 Cor.] 3.1, 3.

[28] John 4: 23, 24.   [29] Cf. 1 John 3:22.
[30] Cf. Acts 24:16.   [31] Rom. 6:7.
[32] 'Babes' or 'children', 'young men', and 'fathers' in Christ is a frequent theme throughout Wesley's writings. E.g., cf. Nos. 24, 'Sermon on the Mount, IV', I.4; 40, *Christian Perfection*, II.1; 55, *On the Trinity*, §17; 83, 'On Patience', §10. See also JWJ, July 17, 1741, where Wesley records he preached a sermon from 1 Cor. 3: 'The school at Kingswood was throughly filled between eight and nine in the evening. I showed them from the example of the Corinthians what need we have to bear one with another, seeing we are not to expect "many fathers in Christ," no, nor young men among us, as yet. We then poured out our souls in prayer and praise, and our Lord did not hide his face from us.' Cf. also his letter to the Revd. Mr. Plenderlieth, May 23, 1768; to Joseph Benson, Mar. 16, 1771; to Elizabeth Briggs, May 31, 1771; and to John Fletcher, Mar. 22, 1775, and June 1, 1776. In his *Notes* on Heb. 5: 13-14, Wesley distinguishes the 'babes', 'who desire and can digest nothing but the doctrine of justification and imputed righteousness' from those 'of full age', who embrace the 'sublimer truths relating to "perfection"'.
[33] Col. 1:2.

have been 'babes in Christ'. And (what is most remarkable of all) he speaks of being 'carnal' and 'babes in Christ' as one and the same thing; plainly showing that every believer is (in a degree) 'carnal' while he is only a 'babe in Christ'.

5   3. Indeed this grand point, that there are two contrary principles in believers—nature and grace, the flesh and the spirit—runs through all the epistles of St. Paul, yea, through all the Holy Scriptures.[34] Almost all the directions and exhortations therein are founded on this supposition, pointing at wrong 10 tempers or practices in those who are, notwithstanding, acknowledged by the inspired writers to be believers. And they are continually exhorted to fight with and conquer these, by the power of the faith which was in them.

4. And who can doubt but there was faith in the angel of the 15 church of Ephesus[35] when our Lord said to him: 'I know thy works, and thy labour, and thy patience. . . . Thou hast patience, and for my name's sake hast laboured and hast not fainted.' But was there meantime no sin in his heart? Yea, or Christ would not have added, 'Nevertheless I have somewhat against thee, because 20 thou hast left thy first love.'[d] This was real sin[36] which God saw in his heart, of which accordingly he is exhorted to *repent*. And yet we have no authority to say that even then he had no faith.

5. Nay, the angel of the church at Pergamos also is exhorted to 'repent', which implies sin, though our Lord expressly says, 25 'Thou hast not denied my faith.'[e] And to the angel of the church in Sardis he says, 'Strengthen the things which remain that are ready to die.'[f] The good which remained was 'ready to die', but was not actually dead. So there was still a spark of faith even in him; which he is accordingly commanded to 'hold fast'.[g]

30   6. Once more: when the Apostle exhorts believers to 'cleanse' themselves 'from all filthiness of flesh and spirit',[h] he plainly

---

[d] Rev. 2:2-4.
[e] Ver. 13, 16.
[f] [Rev.] 3:2.
[g] Ver. 3.   [h] 2 Cor. 7:1.

---

[34] For a rather different view of the tension between nature and prevenient grace, see below, No. 85, 'On Working Out Our Own Salvation', III.3-4.

[35] I.e., the pastor and congregation considered as a single *persona;* cf. Wesley's *Notes* for Rev. 2:2-4.

[36] All the contemporary editions have 'a real sin', but the errata sheet in *Works* (1771) calls for the 'a' to be deleted, as does the MS correction in Wesley's personal copy.

teaches that those believers were not yet cleansed therefrom. Will you answer, 'He that "abstains from all appearance of evil"[37] does *ipso facto* cleanse himself from all filthiness'? Not in any wise. For instance, a man reviles me; I feel resentment, which is 'filthiness of spirit'; yet I say not a word. Here I 'abstain from all appearance of evil', but this does not cleanse me from that filthiness of spirit, as I experience to my sorrow.

7. And as this position, 'there is no sin in a believer, no carnal mind, no bent to backsliding,'[38] is thus contrary to the Word of God, so it is to the *experience* of his children. These continually feel an heart bent to backsliding, a natural tendency to evil, a proneness to depart from God, and cleave to the things of earth. They are daily sensible of sin remaining in their heart, pride, self-will, unbelief, and of sin cleaving to all they speak and do, even their best actions and holiest duties. Yet at the same time they 'know that they are of God';[39] they cannot doubt of it for a moment. They feel 'his Spirit clearly witnessing with their spirit that they are the children of God'.[40] They 'rejoice in God through Christ Jesus, by whom they have now received the atonement'.[41] So that they are equally assured that sin is in them and that 'Christ is in them, the hope of glory.'[42]

8. 'But can Christ be in the same heart where sin is?' Undoubtedly he can; otherwise it never could be saved therefrom. Where the sickness is, there is the physician,

> Carrying on his work within,
> Striving till he cast out sin.[43]

Christ indeed cannot *reign* where sin *reigns;* neither will he *dwell* where any sin is *allowed.* But he *is* and *dwells* in the heart of every believer who is fighting against all sin; although it be 'not' yet 'purified according to the purification of the sanctuary'.[44]

---

[37] Cf. 1 Thess. 5:22.

[38] The last phrase here is from Hos. 11:7; the entire quotation appears to be Wesley's own paraphrase of an antinomian view (as, e.g., from Cudworth and Relly).

[39] Cf. 1 John 5:19.   [40] Cf. Rom. 8:16.   [41] Cf. Rom. 5:11.

[42] Cf. Col. 1:27. The same point as Luther's *simul justus et peccator.*

[43] 'Hymn for Whitsunday', st. 4, ll. 3-4, *Hymns and Sacred Poems* (1739), p. 214 *(Poet. Wks.*, I. 188). The metaphors here of Christ the physician and of salvation as healing are significant; they distinguish Wesley's essentially interpersonal, therapeutic views of justification, regeneration, and sanctification from all their forensic alternatives; cf. No. 17, 'The Circumcision of the Heart', I.5.

[44] Cf. 2 Chr. 30:19.

9. It has been observed before, that the opposite doctrine, 'that there is no sin in believers', is quite *new* in the church of Christ; that it was never heard of for seventeen hundred years, never till it was discovered by Count Zinzendorf. I do not remember to have
5 seen the least intimation of it either in any ancient or modern writer, unless perhaps in some of the wild, ranting antinomians.[45] And these likewise say and unsay, acknowledging there is sin 'in their flesh', although no sin 'in their heart'.[46] But whatever doctrine is *new* must be *wrong;* for the *old* religion is the only *true*
10 one; and no doctrine can be right unless it is the very same 'which was from the beginning'.[47]

10. One argument more against this new, unscriptural doctrine may be drawn from the dreadful consequences of it. One says, 'I felt anger today.' Must I reply, 'Then you have no faith'? Another
15 says, 'I know what you advise is good; but my will is quite averse to it.' Must I tell him, 'Then you are an unbeliever, under the wrath and the curse of God'? What will be the natural consequence of this? Why, if he believe what I say, his soul will not only be grieved and wounded but perhaps utterly destroyed; inasmuch as he will
20 'cast away that confidence which hath great recompense of reward'.[48] And having cast away his shield, how shall he 'quench the fiery darts of the wicked one'?[49] How shall he overcome the world?[50] Seeing 'this is the victory that overcometh the world, even our faith.'[51] He stands disarmed in the midst of his enemies,

---

[45] Such as Johannes Agricola (1494–1566), Tobias Crisp (1600–43; cf. *DNB*, 'extremely unguarded in his expressions'), and John Saltmarsh (d. 1647; cf. *DNB*, 'champion of complete religious liberty').

[46] See I.5 above.

[47] 1 John 1:1. That Wesley took 'Christian antiquity' as a decisive guideline in theology and ethics may be seen, early and late, throughout the corpus. On Jan. 24, 1738 (see JWJ) he had invoked his own version of the 'canon' of Vincent of Lerins (first half of the fifth century) as 'a sure rule of interpreting Scripture, *viz.*: *Consensus veterum: quod ab omnibus, quod ubique, quod semper creditum . . .* ' ('the ancient consensus: what has been believed by all, everywhere and always . . .'); cf. *The Commonitory* of Vincent of Lerins (435), ch. II, §6. See also John Goodman, *The Old Religion* . . . (1684), 'To the Reader'. In No. 14, *The Repentance of Believers*, I.2, Wesley will list Scripture, reason, and Christian experience as his doctrinal norms. But in the Preface to his collected *Works*, I (1771), the list will read: 'Scripture, reason, and Christian antiquity'. See also his letter to Walter Churchey (June 20, 1789): 'In religion I am for as few innovations as possible;' for other references to doctrinal 'novelty', cf. No. 25, 'Sermon on the Mount, V' §1 and n.

[48] Cf. Heb. 10:35.

[49] Eph. 6:16 (cf. *Notes*).

[50] See John 16:33.

[51] 1 John 5:4.

open to all their assaults. What wonder then if he be utterly overthrown, if they take him captive at their will; yea, if he fall from one wickedness to another, and never see good any more? I cannot therefore by any means receive this assertion 'that there is no sin in a believer from the moment he is justified'. First, because it is contrary to the whole tenor of Scripture; secondly, because it is contrary to the experience of the children of God; thirdly, because it is absolutely new, never heard of in the world till yesterday; and lastly, because it is naturally attended with the most fatal consequences, not only grieving those whom God hath[52] not grieved, but perhaps dragging them into everlasting perdition.

IV.1. However, let us give a fair hearing to the chief arguments of those who endeavour to support it. And it is, first, from Scripture they attempt to prove that there is no sin in a believer. They argue thus: 'The Scripture says every believer is "born of God",[53] is "clean",[54] is "holy",[55] is "sanctified";[56] is "pure in heart",[57] has a new heart, is a temple of the Holy Ghost.[58] Now, as "that which is born of the flesh is flesh", is altogether evil, so "that which is born of the Spirit is spirit",[59] is altogether good. Again: a man cannot be clean, sanctified, holy, and at the same time unclean, unsanctified, unholy. He cannot be pure and impure, or have a new and an old heart together. Neither can his soul be unholy while it is a temple of the Holy Ghost.'[60]

I have put this objection as strong as possible, that its full weight may appear. Let us now examine it, part by part. And (1),

---

[52] Orig., 'had', altered to 'hath' in 1771 only.
[53] 1 John 3:9; 4:7.
[54] John 15:3, etc.
[55] Eph. 1:4, etc.
[56] Rom. 15:16, etc.
[57] Matt. 5:8.
[58] 1 Cor. 6:19.
[59] John 3:6.
[60] This pejorative summary of Moravian teachings should be compared with Zinzendorf's public teaching, as in *Nine Public Lectures on Important Subjects in Religion, Preached in Fetter Lane Chapel in London, 1746*, ed., G. W. Forell (Iowa City, Iowa, University of Iowa Press, 1973); see espec. Lecture IV, 'Concerning Saving Faith', and Lecture VII, 'On the Essential Character and Circumstances of the Life of a Christian'. Zinzendorf's words and Wesley's interpretation of them leave ground for pondering: was Wesley reading Zinzendorf in the light of the antinomian views of the *English* Moravians?

' "That which is born of the Spirit is spirit," is altogether good.' I allow the text, but not the comment; for the text affirms this, and no more, that every man who is 'born of the Spirit' is a *spiritual man*. He is so. But so he may be, and yet not be *altogether*
5 spiritual.[61] The Christians at *Corinth* were *spiritual* men; else they had been no Christians at all. And yet they were not *altogether* spiritual: they were still (in part) *carnal*. 'But they were fallen from grace.'[62] St. Paul says, 'No: they were even then "babes in Christ".'[63] (2). 'But a man cannot be clean, sanctified, holy, and at
10 the same time unclean, unsanctified, unholy.' Indeed he may. So the Corinthians were. 'Ye are washed,' says the Apostle, 'ye are sanctified;' namely cleansed from 'fornication, idolatry, drunkenness', and all other outward sin.[i] And yet at the same time, in another sense of the word, they were *unsanctified:* they were not
15 *washed*, not inwardly *cleansed* from envy, evil surmising, partiality. 'But sure they had not a new heart and an old heart together.' It is most sure they had; for at that very time their hearts were *truly*, yet not *entirely*, renewed. Their carnal mind was nailed to the cross; yet it was not wholly destroyed. 'But could they be *unholy* while
20 they were "temples of the Holy Ghost"?'[j] Yes, that they were 'temples of the Holy Ghost' is certain. And it is equally certain they were, in some degree, *carnal*, that is, *unholy*.

2. 'However, there is one Scripture more which will put the matter out of question: "If any man be (a believer) in Christ, he is
25 a new creature. Old things are passed away; behold all things are become new."[k] Now certainly a man cannot be a *new creature* and an *old creature* at once.' Yes, he may: he may be *partly renewed*, which was the very case with those at Corinth. They were doubtless 'renewed in the spirit of their mind',[64] or they could not
30 have been so much as 'babes in Christ'.[65] Yet they had not the whole mind which was in Christ,[66] for they *envied* one another. 'But it is said expressly, "Old things are passed away: all things

[i] 1 Cor 6:9, 10, 11.
[j] 1 Cor. 6:19.
[k] 2 Cor. 5:17.

---

[61] An interesting inversion of Wesley's earlier doctrine of the *radical* difference between 'almost' and 'altogether' Christians; cf. No. 2, *The Almost Christian*, proem.
[62] Cf. Gal. 5:4.   [63] 1 Cor. 3:1.
[64] Eph. 4:23.
[65] 1 Cor. 3:1.
[66] See Phil. 2:5.

are become new." ' But we must not so interpret the Apostle's words as to make him contradict himself. And if we will make him consistent with himself the plain meaning of the words is this: his *old judgment* (concerning justification, holiness, happiness, indeed concerning the things of God in general) is now 'passed away'; so are his *old desires, designs, affections, tempers,* and *conversation.* All these are undeniably 'become new', greatly changed from what they were. And yet, though they are *new,* they are not *wholly* new. Still he feels, to his sorrow and shame, remains of the 'old man',[67] too manifest taints of his former tempers and affections, a law in his members which frequently *fights* against that law of his mind,[68] though it cannot 'gain any advantage'[69] over him as long as he 'watches unto prayer'.[70]

3. This whole argument, 'If he is clean, he is clean,' 'if he is holy, he is holy' (and twenty more expressions of the same kind may easily be heaped together) is really no better than playing upon words: it is the fallacy of arguing from a *particular* to a *general,*[71] of inferring a general conclusion from particular premises. Propose the sentence entire, and it runs thus: 'If he is holy *at all,* he is holy *altogether.*' That does not follow: every babe in Christ is holy, and yet not altogether so. He is saved from sin; yet not entirely: it *remains,* though it does not *reign.* If you think it does not *remain* (in *babes* at least, whatever be the case with *young men,* or *fathers*) you certainly have not considered the height and depth and length and breadth of the law of God (even the law of love laid down by St. Paul in the thirteenth of Corinthians); and that 'every ἀνομία', disconformity to, or deviation from this law, 'is sin.'[77] Now, is there no disconformity to this in the heart or life of a believer? What may be in an adult Christian is another question. But what a stranger must he be to human nature who can possibly imagine that this is the case with every babe in Christ!

---

[67] Col. 3:9.
[68] See Rom. 7:23.
[69] 2 Cor. 2:11.
[70] 1 Pet. 4:7.
[71] Yet another reminder of Wesley's days as 'Moderator of the Classes' (i.e., logical disputations) at Lincoln College. He had mastered Dean Henry Aldrich's *Artis Logicae Compendiae* (1691) and, indeed, had translated it into English in 1750 for use in the Kingswood School; cf. *Bibliog,* No. 186 (Vol. 15 of this edn.).
[72] Cf. 1 John 3:4.

4. [1] 'But believers "walk after the Spirit",[m] and the Spirit of God *dwells* in them. Consequently they are delivered from the guilt, the power, *or, in one word,* the being of sin.'[73]

These are coupled together as if they were the same thing. But they are not the same thing. The *guilt* is one thing, the *power* another, and the *being* yet another. That believers are delivered from the *guilt* and *power* of sin we allow; that they are delivered from the *being* of it we deny. Nor does it in any wise follow from these texts. A man may have the Spirit of God *dwelling in* him, and may 'walk after the Spirit',[74] though he still feels 'the flesh lusting against the Spirit'.[75]

5. 'But the "church is the body of Christ".[n] This implies that its members are washed from all filthiness; otherwise it will follow that Christ and Belial are incorporated with each other.'[76]

Nay, it will not follow from hence—'Those who are the mystical body of Christ still feel the flesh lusting against the

---

[1] What follows for some pages is an answer to a paper published in the *Christian*'s [sic] *Magazine*, pp. 577-82. I am surprised Mr. Dodd should give such a paper a place in his magazine which is directly contrary to our Ninth Article.

[William Dodd is more famous for the spectacularly tragic ending of his career (his trial and execution as a forger) than for his earlier successes as a popular Anglican preacher whose 'eloquent and touching' sermons 'in the French style' were praised by Horace Walpole (*Letters*, III.282; cf. Leslie Stephens's biography of Dodd, *DNB*. Wesley had known him since 1756, and there had been a running controversy between them about Wesley's doctrine of Christian perfection and also about Wesley's separatist tendencies. Wesley's account of his pastoral visits with Dr. Dodd during his last days and at his execution was published in *AM*, 1783, pp. 358-60 (see Vol. 14 of this edn.).

[Dodd was editor of the *Christian Magazine*, 1760–67, and in its *Supplement . . . for the Year 1762* (pp. 577-82) published an article, 'Thoughts on Christianity', by one 'C.' (does this signify 'Christian' or, perhaps, William Cudworth?). Unsurprisingly, 'C.'s' arguments are more carefully nuanced than one could guess from Wesley's excerpts, even though their essential consequence is not misrepresented by much. And his stated aims (p. 582), to undercut hypocrisy, to abolish 'antinomianism', and to end 'the great contest about inherent and imputed righteousness', were not very different from Wesley's own, especially in his later years. What is most significant here is that when Wesley was confronted with a clear and forceful doctrine of sinless perfection, his repudiation of it was immediate and vigorous.]

[m] Rom. 8:1.   [n] Col. 1:24.

---

[73] 'C.'s' text (p. 579): '. . . all who are united to Christ by the holy spirits [sic] dwelling in them are delivered from the guilt, the power or, in one word, the being of sin.'
[74] Rom. 8:1.   [75] Cf. Gal. 5:17.
[76] 'C's' text: 'From the church being called "the body of Christ" (Col. 1:24), which undoubtedly implies that all the members of it are washed from all filthiness, or else that blasphemous consequence would follow, *viz.*, Christ and Belial are not only connected but in some sense incorporated with each other.'

Spirit'—that Christ has any fellowship with the devil, or with that sin which he enables them to resist and overcome.

6. 'But are not Christians "come to the heavenly Jerusalem", where "nothing defiled can enter"?'[77] Yes; 'and to an innumerable company of angels', 'and to the spirits of just men 5 made perfect':[o] that is,

> Earth and heaven all agree,
> All his one great family.[78]

And they are likewise holy and *undefiled* while they 'walk after the Spirit';[79] although sensible there is another principle in them, and 10 that 'these are contrary to each other'.[80]

7. 'But Christians are "reconciled to God".'[81] Now this could not be if any of the "carnal mind"[82] remained; for this "is enmity against God". Consequently no reconciliation can be effected but by its total destruction.' 15

We 'are reconciled to God through the blood of the cross'.[83] And in that moment, the $\varphi\rho\acute{o}\nu\eta\mu\alpha\ \sigma\alpha\rho\kappa\acute{o}\varsigma$,[84] the corruption of nature which is 'enmity with God',[85] is put under our feet. The flesh has 'no more dominion over us'.[86] But it still *exists;* and it is still in its nature enmity with God, lusting against his Spirit. 20

8. 'But "they that are Christ's have crucified the flesh, with its affections and lusts." '[p] They have so; yet it remains in them still, and often struggles to break from the cross. 'Nay, but they have

---

[o] Heb. 12:22-23.   [p] Gal. 5:24.

---

[77] Cf. Rev. 21:27. 'C.'s' text: 'It seems by the heavenly Jerusalem here we are to understand the Gospel church [i.e., on earth] . . . since it is said (Hebrews 12:22) that the kings of the earth shall bring their glory into this city, which cannot with propriety be said of the church triumphant, they having there no more glory than the meanest subject.'

[78] Cf. 'The Communion of Saints, Pt. VI', st. 1, last quatrain, in *Hymns and Sacred Poems* (1740), p. 198 *(Poet. Wks.*, I. 364). Orig.:

> Him let earth and heaven proclaim,
> Earth and heaven accord his name,
> Let us both in this agree,
> Both his one great family.

For quotations of other lines from this hymn, cf. Nos. 107, 'On God's Vineyard', II.6; and 132, 'On Faith, Heb. 11:1', §6.

[79] Rom. 8:1.   [80] Gal. 5:17.
[81] Rom. 5:10; 2 Cor. 5:20.   [82] Rom. 8:7.
[83] Cf. Col. 1:20.   [84] Rom. 8:7; cf. I.3 above and n.
[85] Jas. 4:4.   [86] Cf. Rom 6:9.

"put off the old man with his deeds." 'q They have; and in the
sense above-described, 'old things are passed away; all things are
become new.'87 An hundred texts may be cited to the same effect.
And they will all admit of the same answer. 'But, to say all in one
5 word, "Christ gave himself for the church, that . . . it might be
holy and without blemish." 'r And so it will be in the end: but it
never was yet, from the beginning to this day.

9. 'But let *experience* speak: all who are justified do at that time
find an absolute freedom from all sin.'88 That I doubt; but if they
10 do, do they find it ever after? Else you gain nothing. 'If they do
not, it is their own fault.' That remains to be proved.

10. 'But, in the very nature of things, can a man have pride in
him, and not be proud? Anger, and yet not be angry?'89

A man may have *pride* in him, may think of himself in *some*
15 *particulars* above what he ought to think (and so be *proud* in that
particular) and yet not be a proud man in his *general* character. He
may have *anger* in him, yea, and a strong propensity to furious
anger, without *giving way* to it. 'But can anger and pride be in that
heart where *only* meekness and humility are felt?' No; but *some*
20 pride and anger may be in that heart where there is *much* humility
and meekness.

'It avails not to say these tempers *are* there, but they do not
reign; for sin cannot in any kind or degree *exist* where it does not
reign; for *guilt* and *power* are essential properties of sin. Therefore
25 where one of them is, all must be.'90

Strange indeed! 'Sin cannot in any kind or degree *exist* where it

---

q Col. 3:9.
r Eph. 5:25, 27.

---

87 2 Cor. 5:17.
88 'C.'s' text (p. 581): 'nine out of ten, at least'.
89 'C.'s' text: 'Suppose anyone should assert that a man may have anger in him, yet not
be angry; pride in him, yet not be proud; the love of the world in him, yet not love the world;
what should we think of such an one's understanding?'
90 'C.'s' text (pp.581-82): 'It will not mend the matter at all to say, "these tempers *are*
there but they do not *reign*. . .". [This] implies a contradiction, for it is an infallible axiom
that sin cannot, in any kind or degree, *exist* where it does not *reign*, no more than fire can
live where it does not burn. Guilt and power being essential properties of sin, it follows that
where one of them is they all necessarily must be, and where anyone is wanting, none of
them can be there; for to separate these is to separate a thing from itself.' 'C.'s' contention
here is that conscious and unconscious sinful tempers cannot be dichotomized; on the
other hand, such a dichotomy is one of Wesley's crucial presuppositions.

does not *reign*'? Absolutely contrary this to all experience, all Scripture, all common sense. Resentment of an affront is sin. It is ἀνομία, disconformity to the law of love.[91] This has existed in me a thousand times. Yet it did not, and does not, *reign*. But '*guilt* and *power* are essential properties of sin; therefore where one is, all must be.' No; in the instance before us, if the resentment I feel is not yielded to, even for a moment, there is no *guilt* at all, no condemnation from God upon that account. And in this case it has no *power*: though it 'lusteth against the Spirit'[92] it cannot prevail. Here, therefore, as in ten thousand instances, there is *sin* without either *guilt* or *power*.

11. 'But the supposing sin in a believer is pregnant with everything frightful and discouraging. It implies the contending with a power that has the possession of our strength, maintains his usurpation of our hearts, and there prosecutes the war in defiance of our Redeemer.' Not so. The supposing sin is *in* us does not imply that it has the possession of our strength; no more than a man crucified has the possession of those that crucify him. As little does it imply that sin 'maintains its usurpation of our hearts'. The usurper is dethroned. He *remains* indeed where he once reigned; but remains *in chains*. So that he does in some sense 'prosecute the war', yet he grows weaker and weaker, while the believer goes on from strength to strength, conquering and to conquer.

12. 'I am not satisfied yet. He that has sin in him is a slave to sin. Therefore you suppose a man to be justified while he is a slave to sin. Now if you allow men may be justified while they have pride, anger, or unbelief in them—nay if you aver these are (at least for a time) in all that are justified—what wonder that we have so many proud, angry, unbelieving believers!'[93]

I do not suppose any man who is justified is a slave to sin. Yet I do suppose sin remains (at least for a time) in all that are justified. 'But if sin remains in a believer he is a sinful man: if pride, for instance, then he is proud; if self-will, then he is self-willed; if unbelief, then he is an unbeliever—consequently, no believer at

---

[91] See IV.3 above.　　　　　　　　　　　　　　　　[92] Gal. 5:17.

[93] 'C.'s' text: 'Is it to be wondered at if those who are prepossessed with such apprehensions should either decline the Christian warfare or faint in the day of battles; either not prepare to stand in the evil day or, having done so, not be able to stand?' Is Wesley's quotation here a very free paraphrase of his own, or is he quoting yet another source? The same question may be asked of the remaining quotations, since none of them appears verbatim in 'C.'s' text.

all. How then does he differ from unbelievers, from unregenerate men?'

This is still mere playing upon words. It means no more than, 'If there is sin, pride, self-will in him, then—there is sin, pride,
5 self-will.' And this nobody can deny. In *that sense*, then, he is proud or self-willed. But he is not proud or self-willed in the same sense that unbelievers are, that is, *governed* by pride or self-will. Herein he differs from unregenerate men. They *obey* sin; he does not. Flesh is in them both. But they 'walk after the
10 flesh'; he 'walks after the Spirit'.

'But how can *unbelief* be in a *believer?*' That word has two meanings. It means either *no faith*, or *little faith;* either the *absence* of faith, or the *weakness* of it. In the former sense, unbelief is not in a believer; in the latter, it is in all babes. Their faith is commonly
15 mixed with doubt or fear, that is (in the latter sense) with unbelief. 'Why are ye fearful,' says our Lord, 'O ye of little faith?'[94] Again, 'O thou of little faith, wherefore didst thou doubt?'[95] You see, here was *unbelief* in *believers:* little faith and much unbelief.[96]

13. 'But this doctrine—that sin remains in a believer, that a
20 man may be in the favour of God while he has sin in his heart—certainly tends to encourage men in sin.' Understand the proposition right, and no such consequence follows. A man may be in God's favour though he *feel* sin; but not if he *yields* to it. *Having sin* does not forfeit the favour of God; *giving way to sin*
25 does. Though the flesh in *you* 'lust against the Spirit', you may still be a child of God. But if you 'walk after the flesh', you are a child of the devil. Now, this doctrine does not encourage to *obey* sin, but to *resist* it with all our might.

V.1. The sum of all is this: there are in every person, even after
30 he is justified, two contrary principles, nature and grace, termed by St. Paul the 'flesh' and the 'spirit'. Hence although even babes in Christ are *sanctified*, yet it is only *in part*. In a degree, according to the measure of their faith, they are *spiritual;* yet in a degree they are *carnal*. Accordingly, believers are continually exhorted to

---

[94] Matt. 8:26.
[95] Matt. 14:31.
[96] Cf. this defence of gradations [degrees] of faith (and the validity of even a low degree of it) with No. 2, *The Almost Christian* and with Wesley's earlier either/or doctrine of assurance. Cf. also JWJ, May 29, June 6, 1738; the *Minutes*, Aug. 2, 1745 (answer to *Q.* 5) and June 16, 1747 (answer to *Q.* 2, 5); and his letters to Richard Tompson, July 25, 1755, and Feb. 5, 1756.

watch against the flesh, as well as the world and the devil.[97] And to this agrees the constant experience of the children of God. While they feel this witness in themselves they feel a will not wholly resigned to the will of God. They know they are in him, and yet find an heart ready to depart from him, a proneness to evil in 5 many instances, and a backwardness to that which is good. The contrary doctrine is wholly *new;* never heard of in the church of Christ from the time of his coming into the world till the time of Count Zinzendorf.[98] And it is attended with the most fatal consequences. It cuts off all watching against our evil nature, 10 against the Delilah which we are told is gone, though she is still lying in our bosom.[99] It tears away the shield of weak believers, deprives them of their faith,[100] and so leaves them exposed to all the assaults of the world, the flesh, and the devil.

2. Let us therefore hold fast the sound doctrine 'once delivered 15 to the saints',[101] and delivered down by them with the written word to all succeeding generations: that although we are renewed, cleansed, purified, sanctified, the moment we truly believe in Christ, yet we are not then renewed, cleansed, purified altogether; but the flesh, the evil nature, still remains (though 20 subdued) and wars against the Spirit.[102] So much the more let us use all diligence in 'fighting the good fight of faith'.[103] So much the

---

[97] BCP, Litany.

[98] See above, I.5 and n., and III.9 and n.

[99] Judg. 16. Cf. also Matthew Mead, *The Almost Christian Discovered*, p. 107: 'There is a natural man, let him go never so far, let him go never so much in matters of religion, but still he hath his Delilah, his bosom lust.' For Wesley's use of 'bosom sin', cf. No. 48, 'Self-denial', II.2 and n.

[100] Cf. Eph. 6:16.

[101] Jude 3.

[102] As explicit a version of the 'saved and yet also a sinner at one and the same time' as one might ask for. This should be compared to other passages where Wesley himself comes closer to claiming for Christians 'the power not to sin' or, indeed, close enough to a doctrine of sinless perfection as to allow for its development in some of his nineteenth-century followers, *in his name*. Cf. Nos. 14, *The Repentance of Believers*, I.20, III.2; 40, *Christian Perfection*, II. 1–30; 42, 'Satan's Devices', I.1; and see 109, *The Trouble and Rest of Good Men*, II.4 (which stands almost in contrast on this point to the sermon on *Christian Perfection*). Cf. also *A Plain Account of Christian Perfection; The Principles of a Methodist*, §§ 11–12; and *Some Remarks on a Defence of . . . Aspasio Vindicated*, §4. Wesley's prefaces to the earliest editions of the *Hymns and Sacred Poems* contain some of the strongest, least nuanced statements of perfection in the Wesley corpus; without the phrase itself, they come close to advocating 'sinless perfection' (see *Bibliog*, Nos. 13, 40, 54, and the text in Vol.12 of this edn.). Cf. also his letter to Revd. Mr. Plenderlieth, May 23, 1768, and to Thomas Olivers, Mar. 24, 1757.

[103] Cf. 1 Tim. 6:12.

more earnestly let us 'watch and pray'[104] against the enemy within. The more carefully let us 'take to' ourselves and 'put on the whole armour of God'; that although 'we wrestle' both with 'flesh and blood, and with principalities and powers, and wicked spirits in high places, we may be able to withstand in the evil day, and having done all, to stand'.[105]

[104] Matt. 26:41; Mark 13:33.
[105] Cf. Eph. 6:11-13.

The Repentance of Believers

Mark 1:15

Repent and believe the gospel.

1. It is generally supposed that repentance and faith are only the gate of religion;[1] that they are necessary only at the beginning of our Christian course, when we are setting out in the way of the kingdom. And this may seem to be confirmed by the great Apostle, where exhorting the Hebrew Christians to 'go on to perfection' he teaches them to 'leave' these first 'principles of the doctrine of Christ: not laying again the foundation of repentance from dead works and faith toward God';[2] which must at least mean that they should comparatively leave these, that at first took up all their thoughts, in order to 'press forward toward the prize of the high calling of God in Christ Jesus'.[3]

2. And this is undoubtedly true, that there is a repentance and a faith which are more especially necessary at the beginning: a repentance which is a conviction of our utter sinfulness and guiltiness[4] and helplessness, and which precedes our receiving that kingdom of God which our Lord observes 'is within us';[5] and

---

[1] Cf. Wesley's letter to Thomas Church, June 17, 1746; also William Tilly, Sermon XII, *Sermons*, p. 360: '. . . as one that was yet under the low dispensation, and detained in the *porch of repentance*'; and Edward Young (the elder), *A Sermon Preached Before His Majesty at White-Hall*, December 29, 1678, p. 24: 'Repentance was heretofore the porch of the Christian life but modern ages have made it the postern; it is the last thing men set themselves about.'
Wesley uses the metaphor of a porch in relating paradise to heaven ('paradise is the porch of heaven') in two sermons: 73, 'Of Hell', I.4; and 115, 'Dives and Lazarus', I.3. In No. 84, *The Important Question*, II.4, he calls paradise the 'antechamber' of heaven. Elsewhere, Fleury reports that the Mohammedan divines had called *fasting* 'the gate of religion'; cf. *The Manners of the Ancient Israelites*, pp. 176-77.

[2] Cf. Heb. 6:1.

[3] Cf. Phil. 3:14.

[4] This notion of repentance as realistic self-understanding is crucial in Wesley's evangelical soteriology. Cf. No. 7, 'The Way to the Kingdom', II.1 and n. What is most distinctive about it is Wesley's insistence that such repentance *precedes* justification as, in some sense, a precondition of it. Here again, we have a subtle qualification of the 'faith alone' theme; see below, II.6 and n.

[5] Cf. Luke 17:21.

a faith whereby we receive that kingdom, even 'righteousness, and peace, and joy in the Holy Ghost'.[6]

3. But notwithstanding this, there is also a repentance and a faith (taking the words in another sense, a sense not quite the same, nor yet entirely different) which are requisite after we have 'believed the gospel';[7] yea, and in every subsequent stage of our Christian course, or we cannot 'run the race which is set before us'.[8] And this repentance and faith are full as necessary, in order to our continuance and growth in grace, as the former faith and repentance were in order to our entering into the kingdom of God.[9]

But in what sense are we to repent and believe, after we are justified? This is an important question, and worthy of being considered with the utmost attention.

I. And first, in what sense are we to repent?

1. Repentance frequently means an inward change, a change of mind from sin to holiness. But we now speak of it in a quite different sense, as it is one kind of self-knowledge—the knowing ourselves sinners, yea, guilty, helpless sinners, even though we know we are children of God.

2. Indeed when we first know this, when we first find redemption in the blood of Jesus, when the love of God is first shed abroad in our hearts[10] and his kingdom set up therein, it is natural to suppose that we are no longer sinners, that all our sins are not only covered[11] but destroyed. As we do not then feel any evil in our hearts, we readily imagine none is there. Nay, some well-meaning men have imagined this, not only at that time, but ever after; having persuaded themselves that when they were justified they were entirely sanctified. Yea, they have laid it down as a general rule, in spite of Scripture, reason, and experience. These sincerely believe and earnestly maintain that all sin is destroyed when we are justified, and that there is no sin in the heart of a believer, but that it is altogether clean from that moment. But though we readily acknowledge, 'he that believeth is born of God,'[12] and 'he that is born of God doth not commit sin,'[13]

[6] Rom. 14:17.   [7] Cf. Mark 1:15.   [8] Cf. Heb. 12:1.

[9] An extension of the argument in the preceding sermon; cf. No. 13, *On Sin in Believers*, intro., III.1–9 and n.

[10] Rom. 5:5.   [11] See Pss. 32:1; 85:2; Rom. 4:7.

[12] Cf. 1 John 5:1.   [13] Cf. 1 John 3:9.

yet we cannot allow that he does not *feel* it within: it does not *reign*, but it does *remain*.[14] And a conviction of the sin which *remains* in our heart is one great branch of the repentance we are now speaking of.

3. For it is seldom long before he who imagined all sin was gone feels there is still *pride*[15] in his heart. He is convinced, both that in many respects he has thought of himself more highly than he ought to think, and that he has taken to himself the praise of something he had received, and gloried in it as though he had not received it. And yet he knows he is in the favour of God. He cannot and ought not to 'cast away his confidence'.[16] 'The Spirit still witnesses with his spirit, that he is a child of God.'[17]

4. Nor is it long before he feels *self-will* in his heart, even a will contrary to the will of God. A will every man must inevitably have, as long as he has an understanding. This is an essential part of human nature, indeed of the nature of every intelligent being.[18] Our blessed Lord himself had a will as a man; otherwise he had not been a man.[19] But his human will was invariably subject to the will of his Father. At all times, and on all occasions, even in the deepest affliction, he could say, 'Not as I will, but as thou wilt.'[20] But this is not the case at all times, even with a true believer in Christ. He frequently finds his will more or less exalting itself against the will of God. He wills something, because it is pleasing to nature, which is not pleasing to God. And he nills[21] (is averse

[14] Cf. No. 13, *On Sin in Believers*, I.6 and n.

[15] For Wesley, as for St. Augustine, pride is the primal sin—as also in Ecclus. 10:13 ('Pride is the beginning of all sin'). See also Nos. 15, *The Great Assize*, III.1; 21, 'Sermon on the Mount, I', I.4-5; 22, 'Sermon on the Mount, II', II.1, 62, 'The End of Christ's Coming', I.8, III.2; 88, 'On Dress', §§9-10; 92, 'On Zeal', III.2-4; 100, 'On Pleasing All Men', I.2, II.2; 111, *National Sins and Miseries*, §2; 113, *The Late Work of God in North America*, II.8; 128, 'The Deceitfulness of the Human Heart', I.1; 129, 'Heavenly Treasure in Earthen Vessels', II.5; cf also Wesley's letter to Mrs. Pendarves, Sept. 28, 1731, and to Mr.———, Sept. 3, 1756. For Wesley's references to 'bosom sin', cf. No. 48, 'Self-denial', II.2 and n.

[16] Cf. Heb. 10:35.

[17] Cf. Rom. 8:16.

[18] Cf. No. 60, 'The General Deliverance', I.4 and n.

[19] An echo of the Monothelite controversy and its resolution at the 'Sixth Ecumenical Council', in Constantinople, 680–81; cf. Henry R. Percival, *The Seven Ecumenical Councils, ... Canons and Dogmatic Decrees*, in *NPNF, II*, XIV. 325-54. See also Jaroslav Pelikan, *The Christian Tradition*, pp. 68-75.

[20] Matt. 26:39.

[21] Cf. Dr. Johnson's definition of 'to nill' ('to refuse; to reject') and his citation of its usage in Ben Jonson. That it was already an archaic negative in Wesley's time may be seen in the 1788 edn. of *SOSO*; the printer has it 'wills', without a care for its sense or meaning.

from) something because it is painful to nature, which is the will
of God concerning him. Indeed (suppose he continues in the
faith) he fights against it with all his might. But this very thing
implies that it really exists, and that he is conscious of it.

5   5. Now self-will, as well as pride, is a species of idolatry; and
both are directly contrary to the love of God. The same
observation may be made concerning *the love of the world*. But this
likewise even true believers are liable to feel in themselves; and
every one of them does feel it, more or less, sooner or later, in one
10 branch or another. It is true, when he first passes from death unto
life he desires nothing more but God. He can truly say, 'All my
desire is unto thee,'[22] 'and unto the remembrance of thy name.'[23]
'Whom have I in heaven but thee? And there is none upon earth
that I desire besides thee?'[24] But it is not so always. In process of
15 time he will feel again (though perhaps only for a few moments)
either 'the desire of the flesh, or the desire of the eye, or the pride
of life'.[25] Nay, if he does not continually watch and pray he may
find *lust* reviving, yea, and thrusting sore at him that he may fall,[26]
till he has scarce any strength left in him. He may feel the assaults
20 of *inordinate affection*,[27] yea, a strong propensity to 'love the
creature more than the Creator'[28]—whether it be a child, a
parent, an husband or wife, or 'the friend that is as his own soul'.[29]
He may feel in a thousand various ways a desire of earthly things
or pleasures. In the same proportion he will forget God, not
25 seeking his happiness in him, and consequently being a 'lover of
pleasure more than a lover of God'.[30]

     6. If he does not keep himself every moment he will again feel
'the desire of the eye', the desire of gratifying his imagination with
something great, or beautiful, or uncommon. In how many ways
30 does this desire assault the soul! Perhaps with regard to the
poorest trifles, such as dress, or furniture—things never designed
to satisfy the appetite of an immortal spirit. Yet how natural it is
for us, even after we 'have tasted of the powers of the world to
come',[31] to sink again into these foolish, low desires of things that
35 perish in the using! How hard is it, even for those who know in

---

[22] Cf. Ps. 38:9.   [23] Cf. Isa. 26:8.   [24] Ps. 73:25.
[25] Cf. 1 John 2:16 (*Notes*), and No. 7, 'The Way to the Kingdom', II.2 and n.
[26] Ps. 118:13.
[27] Col. 3:5. Cf. also Kempis, I.vi, II.iv.
[28] Cf. Rom. 1:25.   [29] Cf. Deut. 13:6.
[30] Cf. 2 Tim. 3:4.   [31] Cf. Heb. 6:5.

whom they have believed,[32] to conquer but one branch of the desire of the eye, curiosity; constantly to trample it under their feet, to desire nothing merely because it is new!

7. And how hard is it even for the children of God wholly to conquer 'the pride of life'! St. John seems to mean by this nearly the same with what the world terms 'the sense of honour'. This is no other than a desire of and delight in 'the honour that cometh of men'[33]—a desire and love of praise,[34] and (which is always joined with it) a proportionable *fear of dispraise*.[35] Nearly allied to this is *evil shame*, the being ashamed of that wherein we ought to glory. And this is seldom divided from 'the fear of man',[36] which brings a thousand snares upon the soul. Now where is he, even among those that seem strong in faith, who does not find in himself a degree of all these evil tempers? So that even these are but in part 'crucified to the world';[37] for the evil root remains in their heart.

8. And do we not feel other tempers, which are as contrary to the love of our neighbour as these are to the love of God? The love of our neighbour 'thinketh no evil'.[38] Do not we find anything of the kind? Do we never find any *jealousies*, any evil surmisings,[39] any groundless or unreasonable suspicions? He that is clear in these respects, let him cast the first stone at his neighbour.[40] Who does not sometimes feel other tempers or inward motions which he knows are contrary to brotherly love? If nothing of malice,

---

[32] See 2 Tim. 1:12.

[33] Cf. John 5.41, 44.

[34] Wesley makes frequent references to a 'desire', 'love', or 'thirst' of 'praise' or 'glory', Cf. Nos. 21, 'Sermon on the Mount, I', 1 4; 26, 'Sermon on the Mount, VI', I.2; 62, 'The End of Christ's Coming', §2; 84, *The Important Question*, I.4; 100, 'On Pleasing All Men', I.5.

[35] This was the main theme of A.H. Francke's then famous *Nicodemus: Or A Treatise Against the Fear of Man* (1706), which Wesley had read in Nov. 1733. Cf. Nos. 65, 'The Duty of Reproving our Neighbour', III.1; and 87, 'The Danger of Riches', §3. The idea is closely related to Wesley's emphasis on singularity as a mark of the Christian who is free from anxiety as to the world's approval or disapproval. For Wesley's frequent admonitions to be singular, cf. Nos. 31, 'Sermon on the Mount, XI', III.4 and n.; and 4, *Scriptural Christianity*, I.6 and n. For Wesley, the praise of men is equivalent to flattery, as in Nos. 65, 'The Duty of Reproving our Neighbour', III.6 ('that grand fashionable engine—flattery'); 100, 'On Pleasing All Men', I.5; and 107, 'On God's Vineyard', V.3. He knew that Cicero had spoken of flattery as 'the handmaid of vice' (*De Amicitia*, XXIV.89); see also Nos.35, 'The Law Established through Faith, I', II.6; 84, *The Important Question*, III. 9; 87, 'The Danger of Riches', §16.

[36] Prov. 29:25.   [37] Cf. Gal. 6:14.

[38] 1 Cor. 13:5.

[39] 1 Tim. 6:4.

[40] See John 8:7.

hatred, or bitterness, is there no touch of envy?[41] Particularly toward those who enjoy some (real or supposed) good which we desire but cannot attain? Do we never find any degree of *resentment* when we are injured or affronted? Especially by those
5 whom we peculiarly loved, and whom we had most laboured to help or oblige. Does injustice or ingratitude never excite in us any desire of *revenge*; any desire of returning evil for evil, instead of 'overcoming evil with good'?[42] This also shows how much is still in our heart which is contrary to the love of our neighbour.
10   9. *Covetousness* in every kind and degree is certainly as contrary to this as to the love of God. Whether φιλαργυρία, 'the love of money' which is too frequently 'the root of all evils',[43] or πλεονεξία,[44] literally, a desire of *having more*, or increasing in substance. And how few even of the real children of God are
15 entirely free from both! Indeed one great man, Martin Luther, used to say he 'never had any covetousness in him (not only in his converted state, but) ever since he was born'.[45] But if so, I would not scruple to say he was the only man born of a woman (except him that was God as well as man) who had not, who was born
20 without it. Nay, I believe, never was anyone born of God, that lived any considerable time after, who did not feel more or less of

---

[41] See Titus 3:3.

[42] Cf. Rom 12:21.

[43] Cf. 1 Tim. 6:10. Wesley will become very much more emphatic in his denunciations of the love of money and of the sin of surplus accumulation as the years wear on, and as many Methodists become more and more affluent. See below, No. 50,'The Use of Money', on Wesley's increasing alarm and despair over Methodist prosperity unaccompanied by equivalent philanthropy. Cf. also the intro. to No. 28, 'Sermon on the Mount, VIII'.

[44] I.e., covetousness; cf. Col. 3:5, etc., and Wesley's *Notes* thereon.

[45] Cf. Samuel Clarke, *Marrow of Ecclesiastical Historie*, pp. 98-99: 'Wellerus, also a disciple of Luther's, recordeth that he oft heard Luther say that he had been frequently assaulted and vexed with all kinds of temptations, except to the sin of covetousness. . . .' Cf. also John Gillies, *Historical Collections Relating to Remarkable Periods of the Success of the Gospel* (1754), Bk. II, ch. 1. A supporting witness here was Thomas Hayne, *Life and Death of Martin Luther* (1641), p. 115: 'Even the Papists agree that Luther was not covetous.' For other references to Luther, more often disparaging than not, cf. Nos. 1, *Salvation by Faith*, III. 9; 13, *On Sin in Believers*, I.4; 18, 'The Marks of the New Birth', IV.3; 38, 'A Caution against Bigotry', II.4; 63, 'The General Spread of the Gospel', §16; 68, 'The Wisdom of God's Counsels', §10; 94, 'On Family Religion', §3; 102, 'Of Former Times', §14; 104, 'On Attending the Church Service', §25; 107, 'On God's Vineyard', I.5; 122, 'Causes of the Inefficacy of Christianity', §17. See also Wesley's letters to Mrs. Hutton, Aug. 22, 1744; to Richard Tompson, Feb. 5, 1756; to John Fletcher, Aug. 18, 1775; to Elizabeth Ritchie, Feb. 12, 1779; JWJ, June 15-16, 1741; also his Preface to *Notes*, §12; *Farther Appeal*, Pt.III, IV. 6 (11: 318 of this edn.); and *Thoughts Upon a Late Phenomenon*, *AM* (1789), §4 (Vol. 9 of this edn.).

it many times, especially in the latter sense. We may therefore set it down as an undoubted truth that *covetousness*, together with pride, and self-will, and anger, *remain* in the hearts even of them that are justified.

10. It is their experiencing this which has inclined so many serious persons to understand the latter part of the seventh chapter to the Romans, not of them that 'are under the law'—that are convinced of sin, which is undoubtedly the meaning of the Apostle—but of them that 'are under grace',[46] that are 'justified freely, through the redemption that is in Jesus Christ'.[47] And it is most certain they are thus far right; there does still *remain*, even in them that are justified, a 'mind' which is in some measure 'carnal'[48] (so the Apostle tells even the believers at Corinth, 'Ye are carnal');[49] an heart 'bent to backsliding',[50] still ever ready to 'depart from the living God';[51] a propensity to pride, self-will, anger, revenge, love of the world, yea, and all evil: a root of bitterness[52] which, if the restraint were taken off for a moment, would instantly spring up; yea, such a depth of corruption as without clear light from God we cannot possibly conceive. And a conviction of all this sin *remaining* in their hearts is the repentance which belongs to them that are justified.

11. But we should likewise be convinced that as sin remains in our hearts, so it *cleaves* to our words and actions. Indeed it is to be feared that many of our words are more than mixed with sin, that they are sinful altogether. For such undoubtedly is all *uncharitable conversation*,[53] all which does not spring from brotherly love, all which does not agree with that golden rule, 'What ye would that others should do to you, even so do unto them.'[54] Of this kind is all backbiting, all talebearing, all whispering, all evil-speaking; that is, repeating the faults of absent persons—for none would have others repeat his faults when he is absent. Now how few are there, even among believers, who are in no degree guilty of this? Who steadily observe the good old rule, 'Of the dead and the absent—nothing but good.'[55] And suppose they do, do they

---

[46] Rom. 6:14, 15.   [47] Cf. Rom. 3:24.   [48] Rom. 8:7.   [49] 1 Cor. 3:3.
[50] Hos. 11:7.   [51] Cf. Heb. 3:12.   [52] Heb. 12:15.
[53] An echo of Wesley's *General Rules*, §4, in which 'uncharitable or unprofitable conversation' is interdicted.
[54] Cf. Matt. 7:12; Luke 6:31.
[55] This 'rule' was, in fact, an immemorial old aphorism. A version of it appears in Diogenes Laertius, 'Life of Chilon' in *Lives of Eminent Philosophers*, I.68-70 (Loeb, 184:69-73); another was attributed to Solon by Plutarch; a variant may be found in

likewise abstain from *unprofitable conversation?* Yet all this is unquestionably sinful, and 'grieves the Holy Spirit of God'.[56] Yea, and for 'every idle word that men shall speak they shall give an account in the day of judgment'.[57]

5   12. But let it be supposed that they continually 'watch and pray', and so do 'not enter into this temptation';[58] that they constantly set a watch before their mouth, and keep the door of their lips:[59] suppose they exercise themselves herein, that *all* their 'conversation may be in grace seasoned with salt',[60] and meet 'to
10 minister grace to the hearers';[61] yet do they not daily slide into useless discourse, notwithstanding all their caution? And even when they endeavour to speak for God, are their words pure, free from unholy mixtures? Do they find nothing wrong in their very *intention?* Do they speak merely to please God, and not partly to
15 please themselves? Is it wholly to do the will of God, and not their own will also? Or, if they begin with a single eye, do they go on 'looking unto Jesus',[62] and talking with him all the time they are with their neighbour? When they are reproving sin do they feel no anger or unkind temper to the sinner? When they are instructing
20 the ignorant do they not find any pride, any self-preference? When they are comforting the afflicted, or provoking one another to love and to good works,[63] do they never perceive any inward self-commendation—'Now you have spoken well'? Or any vanity, a desire that others should think so, and esteem them on the
25 account? In some or all of these respects how much sin *cleaves* to the best conversation even of believers! The conviction of which is another branch of the repentance which belongs to them that are justified.

       13. And how much sin, if their conscience is throughly awake,
30 may they find *cleaving to their actions* also? Nay, are there not many of these which, though they are such as the world would not condemn, yet cannot be commended, no, nor excused, if we judge by the Word of God? Are there not many of their actions which they themselves know are not 'to the glory of God'?[64] Many
35 wherein they did not even aim at this, which were not undertaken with an eye to God? And of those that were, are there not many

---

Propertius, *Elegies*, II. xix. 32: *absenti nemo non nocuisse velit* ('let no one be willing to speak evil of the absent'). Wesley recalls it with typical variations in Nos. 33, 'Sermon on the Mount, XIII', III.10; and 49, 'The Cure of Evil-speaking', §1.

[56] Cf. Eph. 4:30.   [57] Matt. 12:36.   [58] Cf. Matt. 26:41; Mark 14:38.
[59] See Ps. 141:3.   [60] Cf. Col. 4:6.   [61] Cf. Eph. 4:29.
[62] Heb. 12:2.   [63] See Heb. 10:24.   [64] 1 Cor. 10:31, etc.

wherein their eye is not singly fixed on God? Wherein they are
doing their own will at least as much as his, and seeking to please
themselves as much if not more than to please God? And while they
are endeavouring to do good to their neighbour, do they not feel
wrong tempers of various kinds? Hence their good actions, so 5
called, are far from being strictly such, being polluted with such a
mixture of evil! Such are their works of *mercy*! And is there not the
same mixture in their works of *piety*?[65] While they are hearing the
word which is able to save their souls, do they not frequently find
such thoughts as make them afraid lest it should turn to their 10
condemnation rather than their salvation? Is it not often the same
case while they are endeavouring to offer up their prayers to God,
whether in public, or private? Nay, while they are engaged in the
most solemn service. Even while they are at the table of the Lord,
what manner of thoughts arise in them? Are not their hearts 15
sometimes wandering to the ends of the earth, sometimes filled
with such imaginations as make them fear lest all their sacrifice
should be an abomination to the Lord?[66] So that they are more
ashamed of their best duties than they were once of their worst sins.

14. Again: how many *sins of omission* are they chargeable with? 20
We know the words of the Apostle, 'To him that knoweth to do
good, and doth it not, to him it is sin.'[67] But do they not know a
thousand instances wherein they might have done good, to
enemies, to strangers, to their brethren, either with regard to their
bodies or their souls, and they did it not? How many omissions 25
have they been guilty of in their duty toward God? How many
opportunities of communicating, of hearing his word, of public or
private prayer have they neglected? So great reason had even that
holy man Archbishop Ussher, after all his labours for God, to cry

---

[65] The distinction between 'works of piety' and of 'mercy' was an Anglican
commonplace, to be seen, e.g., in 'Of Good Works' in *Homilies*, p. 42, and in Joseph
Mede's Discourse XXVI (on Mark 1:15), in *Works*, pp. 81, 113, or in Law's *Serious Call*,
(pp. 18-19). 'Works of charity' is a phrase from Kempis, I. xv. 'Works of piety' is recorded
as a phrase attributed to 'Pulcheria' by Edward Gibbon in *The Decline and Fall of the
Roman Empire*, ch. 32; Gibbon cites Sozomen, ix. c. 1, 2, 3, and de Tillemont, *Mem. Eccles.*
xv. 171. For 'works of mercy', cf. St. Thomas, *Summa Theologica*, II-i, Q. 32, art. 2.
For Wesley's frequent usage of this pairing of Christian devotion and Christian social
action, cf. Nos. 22, 'Sermon on the Mount, II', I.10; 24, 'Sermon on the Mount, IV', II.7,
IV.4; 26, 'Sermon on the Mount, VI', I.1, II.1; 43, *The Scripture Way of Salvation*, III.10;
48, 'Self-denial', II.6; 87, 'The Danger of Riches', II.18; 91, 'On Charity', II.4; 92, 'On
Zeal', II.4, III.7, 12; 98, 'On Visiting the Sick', §§1, 2; 106, 'On Faith, Heb. 11:6', II.4;
126, 'On Worldly Folly', II.3. See also *A Plain Account of the People called Methodists*, I.2. It
is worth noting that he never set either over against the other.
[66] See Prov. 15:8.   [67] Jas. 4:17.

out, almost with his dying breath, 'Lord, forgive me my sins of omission.'[68]

15. But besides these outward omissions, may they not find in themselves *inward defects* without number? Defects of every kind:
5 they have not the love, the fear, the confidence they ought to have toward God. They have not the love which is due to their neighbour, to every child of man;[69] no, nor even that which is due to their brethren, to every child of God, whether those that are at a distance from them, or those with whom they are immediately
10 connected. They have no holy temper in the degree they ought; they are defective in everything: in a deep consciousness of which they are ready to cry out with Mr. de Renty, 'I am a ground all overrun with thorns;'[70] or with Job, 'I am vile;' 'I abhor myself, and repent as in dust and ashes.'[71]

15   16. A conviction of their *guiltiness* is another branch of that repentance which belongs to the children of God. But this is cautiously to be understood, and in a peculiar sense. For it is certain, 'there is no condemnation for them that are in Christ Jesus', that believe in him, and in the power of that faith 'walk not
20 after the flesh, but after the Spirit'.[72] Yet can they no more bear the *strict justice* of God now than before they believed. This pronounces them to be still *worthy of death* on all the preceding accounts. And it would absolutely condemn them thereto, were it not for the atoning blood. Therefore, they are throughly

---

[68] Cf. Richard Parr, *The Life of. . . James Usher, Late Lord Archbishop of Armagh* (1686), p. 77. Parr was Ussher's domestic chaplain and present at his deathbed. The saying had already appeared in Nicholas Bernard's *Life and Death of Archbishop Ussher, in a Sermon Preached at his Funeral at Westminster* (1656), which Wesley abridged and published in the *AM* (1779), II. 588 (Wesley preferred the simplified spelling of his name, 'Usher'). See also No. 98, 'On Visiting the Sick', III. 9; *A Plain Account of Christian Perfection*, §14 (6); and JWJ, Mar. 9, 1746. For Wesley's other references to 'sins of omission', cf. Nos. 19, 'The Great Privilege of those that are Born of God', III.1; 35, 'The Law Established through Faith, I', III. 8; and 46, 'The Wilderness State', II. 3.

[69] Cf. No. 7, 'The Way to the Kingdom', I. 8 and n.

[70] Cf. Jean-Baptiste de Saint-Jure, *The Holy Life of Monsr. de Renty, A Late Nobleman of France, and Sometimes Councellor to King Lewis the 13th* (Eng. tr. 1658, by E[dward] S[heldon,] Gent.), p. 274: 'In sum, I am a straggler from God, and a ground overrun with thorns.'

Wesley found de Renty's special combination of mysticism, asceticism, and civic involvement in philanthropy and practical affairs very congenial. Cf. the admiring references in Nos. 55, *On the Trinity*, § 17; 72, 'Of Evil Angels', II.15; 82, 'On Temptation', III. 5; 114, *On the Death of John Fletcher* (penultimate §); 117, 'On the Discoveries of Faith', § 17. See also the letter to Ann Granville, Oct. 3, 1741; to Lady Maxwell, Mar. 3, 1769; to Philothea Briggs, Aug. 31, 1772; to Ann Bolton, Jan. 14, 1780; to Hannah Ball, Feb. 17, 1780; to Adam Clarke, Jan. 3, 1791.

[71] Cf. Job 40:4; 42:6.   [72] Cf. Rom. 8:1.

convinced that they still *deserve* punishment, although it is hereby turned aside from them. But here there are extremes on one hand and on the other, and few steer clear of them. Most men strike on one or the other, either thinking themselves condemned when they are not, or thinking they *deserve* to be acquitted. Nay, the truth lies between: they still *deserve*, strictly speaking, only the damnation of hell. But what they deserve does not come upon them because they 'have an advocate with the Father'.[73] His life and death and intercession still interpose between them and condemnation.

17. A conviction of their *utter helplessness* is yet another branch of this repentance. I mean hereby two things: (1). That they are no more able now *of themselves* to think one good thought, to form one good desire, to speak one good word, or do one good work, than before they were justified; that they have still no kind or degree of strength *of their own*, no power either to do good or resist evil; no ability to conquer or even withstand the world, the devil, or their own evil nature. They 'can', it is certain, 'do all these things';[74] but it is not by *their own strength*. They have power to overcome all these enemies; 'for sin hath no dominion over'[75] them. But it is not from nature, either in whole or in part; 'it is the *mere* gift of God.'[76] Nor is it given all at once, as if they had a stock laid up for many years, but from moment to moment.

18. By this helplessness I mean, secondly, an absolute inability to deliver ourselves from that guiltiness or desert of punishment whereof we are still conscious; yea, and an inability to remove by all the grace we have (to say nothing of our natural powers) either the pride, self-will, love of the world, anger, and general proneness to *depart from God* which we experimentally know to *remain* in the heart, even of them that are regenerate; or the evil which, in spite of all our endeavours, *cleaves* to all our words and actions. Add to this an utter inability wholly to avoid *uncharitable* and, much more, *unprofitable conversation*. Add an inability to avoid *sins of omission*, or to supply the numberless *defects* we are convinced of, especially the want of love and other right tempers both to God and man.

---

[73] 1 John 2:1.   [74] Cf. Phil. 4:13.   [75] Cf. Rom. 6:14.
[76] Cf. Rom. 6:23. Cf. also No. 85, 'On Working Out Our Own Salvation', III.4: 'For, allowing that all the souls of men are dead in sin by "nature", this excuses none, seeing there is no man that is in a state of *mere* nature; there is no man, unless he has quenched the Spirit, that is wholly void of the grace of God.'

19. If any man is not satisfied of this, if any believes that whoever is justified is able to remove these sins out of his heart and life, let him make the experiment. Let him try whether, by the grace he has already received, he can expel pride, self-will, or
5 inbred sin in general. Let him try whether he can cleanse his words and actions from all mixture of evil; whether he can avoid all uncharitable and unprofitable conversation, with all sins of omission; and lastly, whether he can supply the numberless defects which he still finds in himself. Let him not be discouraged
10 by one or two experiments, but repeat the trial again and again. And the longer he tries the more deeply will he be convinced of his utter helplessness in all these respects.

20. Indeed this is so evident a truth that wellnigh all the children of God scattered abroad,[77] however they differ in other
15 points, yet generally agree in this, that although we may 'by the Spirit mortify the deeds of the body',[78] resist and conquer both outward and inward sin, although we may *weaken* our enemies day by day, yet we cannot *drive them out*. By all the grace which is given at justification we cannot extirpate them. Though we watch and
20 pray ever so much, we cannot wholly cleanse either our hearts or hands. Most sure we cannot, till it shall please our Lord to speak to our hearts again, to 'speak the second time, "Be clean"'.[79] And then only 'the leprosy is cleansed.'[80] Then only the evil root, the carnal mind, is destroyed, and inbred sin subsists no more.[81] But
25 if there be no such second change, if there be no instantaneous deliverance after justification, if there be none but a gradual work of God (that there is a gradual work none denies) then we must be content, as well as we can, to remain full of sin till death. And if so, we must remain *guilty* till death, continually *deserving* punishment.
30 For it is impossible the guilt or desert of punishment should be

---

[77] See John 11:52.   [78] Cf. Rom. 8:13.
[79] Charles Wesley, *Hymns and Sacred Poems* (1749), II.164; cf. *Collection of Hymns* (1780, Vol. 7 of this edn., No. 386:5).
[80] Cf. Matt. 8:3.
[81] Here, then is Wesley's resolution of the dilemma posed by his conflicting views on the *remains* of sin, even in the justified, and the Christian hope of their extirpation. '*We* cannot extirpate them,' but there is the possibility that God may do so as a special and instantaneous deliverance. Thus, Wesley clings to the *simul justus et peccator* as the general state of believers and yet also to the possibility of the extirpation of the root of sin in some by a special dispensation of grace. This may have been the ground for an implied doctrine of 'sinless perfection' which Wesley generally repudiates, and thus could be understood as the warrant for a post-Wesleyan doctrine of 'entire sanctification as a second and separate work of grace'.

removed from us as long as all this sin remains in our heart, and cleaves to our words and actions. Nay, in rigorous justice, all we think, and speak, and act, continually increases it.

II.1. In this sense we are to *repent* after we are justified. And till we do so we can go no farther. For till we are sensible of our 5 disease it admits of no cure. But supposing we do thus repent, then are we called to 'believe the gospel'.[82]

2. And this also is to be understood in a peculiar sense, different from that wherein we believed in order to justification. Believe the 'glad tidings of great salvation'[83] which God hath 10 prepared for all people. Believe that he who is 'the brightness of his Father's glory, the express image of his person',[84] 'is able to save unto the uttermost all that come unto God through him'.[85] He is able to save you from all the sin that still remains in your heart. He is able to save you from all the sin that cleaves to all your 15 words and actions. He is able to save you from sins of omission, and to supply whatever is wanting in you. It is true, 'This is impossible with man; but with [the] God-man all things are possible.'[86] For what can be too hard for him who hath 'all power in heaven and in earth'?[87] Indeed his bare power to do this is not a 20 sufficient foundation for our faith that he *will* do it, that he will thus exert his power, unless he hath promised it. But this he has done: he has promised it over and over, in the strongest terms. He has given us these 'exceeding great and precious promises',[88] both in the Old and the New Testament. So we read in the law, in the 25 most ancient part of the oracles of God, 'The Lord thy God will circumcise thy heart, and the heart of thy seed, to love the Lord thy God with all thy heart and all thy soul.'[a] So in the Psalms: 'He shall redeem Israel (the Israel of God) from all his sins.'[89] So in the Prophet: 'Then will I sprinkle clean water upon you, and ye 30 shall be clean; from all your filthiness, and from all your idols, will I cleanse you. . . . And I will put my Spirit within you, [. . .] and ye shall keep my judgments and do them. [. . .] I will also save you from all your uncleannesses.'[b] So likewise in the New Testament: 'Blessed be the Lord God of Israel; for he hath 35

---

[a] Deut. 30:6. [b] Ezek. 36:25, 27, 29.

---

[82] Mark 1:15.
[84] Cf. Heb. 1:3.
[87] Matt. 28:18.

[85] Cf. Heb. 7:25.
[88] 2 Pet. 1:4.

[83] Cf. Isa. 52:7; Rom. 10:15.
[86] Cf. Matt. 19:26.
[89] Ps. 130:8 (BCP).

visited and redeemed his people, and hath raised up an horn of salvation for us. . . . To perform [. . .] the oath which he swore to our father Abraham, that he would grant unto us that we, being delivered out of the hands of our enemies, should serve him 5 without fear, in holiness and righteousness before him, all the days of our life.'ᶜ

3. You have therefore good reason to believe he is not only able but *willing* to do this—to 'cleanse you from all your filthiness of flesh and spirit',⁹⁰ to 'save you from all your uncleannesses'.⁹¹ This 10 is the thing which you now long for: this is the faith which you now particularly need, namely, that the great physician, the lover of my soul, is willing to 'make me clean'.⁹² But is he willing to do this tomorrow or today? Let him answer for himself: 'Today, if ye will hear my voice, harden not your hearts.'⁹³ If you put it off till 15 tomorrow, you 'harden your hearts'; you refuse to 'hear his voice'. Believe therefore that he is willing to save you *today*. He is willing to save you *now*. 'Behold, now is the accepted time.'⁹⁴ He now saith, 'Be thou clean!'⁹⁵ Only believe; and you also will immediately find, 'All things are possible to him that believeth.'⁹⁶

20 4. Continue to believe in him 'that loved thee, and gave himself for thee',⁹⁷ that 'bore all thy sins in his own body on the tree';⁹⁸ and he saveth thee from all condemnation, by his blood continually applied. Thus it is that we continue in a justified state. And when we go 'from faith to faith',⁹⁹ when we have a faith to be cleansed 25 from indwelling sin, to be saved from all our uncleannesses,¹⁰⁰ we are likewise saved from all that *guilt*, that *desert* of punishment, which we felt before. So that then we may say, not only,

> Every moment, Lord, I *want*
> The merit of thy death:

30 but likewise, in the full assurance of faith,

> Every moment, Lord, I *have*
> The merit of thy death.¹⁰¹

ᶜ Luke 1:68-69, 72-75 [also BCP, Morning Prayer, Benedictus].

---

⁹⁰ Cf. 2 Cor. 7:1.   ⁹¹ Ezek. 36:29.   ⁹² Matt. 8:2, etc.
⁹³ Cf. Ps.95:7-8 (AV); Heb. 3:15; 4:7.   ⁹⁴ 2 Cor. 6:2.
⁹⁵ Matt. 8:3, etc.   ⁹⁶ Mark 9:23.   ⁹⁷ Cf. Gal. 2:20.
⁹⁸ Cf. 1 Pet. 2:24.   ⁹⁹ Rom. 1:17.   ¹⁰⁰ Ezek. 36:29.
¹⁰¹ Hymn on Isaiah 32:2, 'And a Man shall be as an Hiding-Place . . . ', st. 5, ll. 7-8, in *Hymns and Sacred Poems* (1742), p. 146 (*Poet. Wks.*, II. 207). The second version is John Wesley's deliberate revision. See also No. 76, 'On Perfection', I.3; and cf. Wesley's letters

For by that faith in his life, death, and intercession for us, renewed from moment to moment, we are every whit clean, and there is not only now no condemnation for us, but no such desert of punishment as was before, the Lord cleansing both our hearts and lives. 5

5. By the same faith we feel the power of Christ every moment resting upon us,[102] whereby alone we are what we are, whereby we are enabled to continue in spiritual life, and without which, notwithstanding all our present holiness, we should be devils the next moment. But as long as we retain our faith in him we 'draw 10 water out of the wells of salvation'.[103] Leaning on our Beloved, even Christ in us the hope of glory,[104] who dwelleth in our hearts by faith,[105] who likewise is ever interceding for us at the right hand of God,[106] we receive help from him to think and speak and act what is acceptable in his sight.[107] Thus does he 'prevent them that 15 believe in all their doings, and further them with his continual help', so that all their designs, conversations, and actions are 'begun, continued, and ended in him'.[108] Thus doth he 'cleanse the thoughts of their hearts, by the inspiration of his Holy Spirit, that they may perfectly love him, and worthily magnify his holy 20 name'.[109]

6. Thus it is that in the children of God repentance and faith exactly answer each other.[110] By repentance we feel the sin remaining in our hearts, and cleaving to our words and actions. By faith we receive the power of God in Christ, purifying our 25 hearts and cleansing our hands. By repentance we are still sensible that we deserve punishment for all our tempers and words and actions. By faith we are conscious that our advocate with the Father[111] is continually pleading for us, and thereby continually turning aside all condemnation and punishment from 30 us. By repentance we have an abiding conviction that there is no

---

to James Hervey, Oct. 15, 1756; to Samuel Furly, May 21, 1762; to Miss March, Apr. 7, 1763; and to Edward Lewly, Jan. 12, 1791.

[102] See 2 Cor. 12:9.   [103] Isa. 12:3.   [104] See Col. 1:27.
[105] See Eph. 3:17.   [106] See Rom. 8:34.   [107] See Ps. 19:14.
[108] BCP, Communion, Fourth Collect after Offertory (371).
[109] *Ibid.*, Collect for Purity (337).
[110] Wesley's most explicit and definitive summary of repentance as prerequisite to justifying faith, and as the groundtone of the continuing Christian life. Cf. above, Nos. 5, 'Justification by Faith', IV.6 and n.; and 7, 'The Way to the Kingdom', II.1 and n.; see also 43, *The Scripture Way of Salvation*, III.2; Wesley's letter to Thomas Church, June 17, 1746, and to Dr. Horne, Mar. 10, 1762, as well as his *Notes* on Luke 16:31.
[111] Cf. 1 John 2:1.

help in us. By faith we receive not only mercy, but 'grace to help in *every* time of need'.[112] Repentance disclaims the very possibility of any other help. Faith accepts all the help we stand in need of from him that hath all power in heaven and earth.[113] Repentance says,
5 'Without him I can do nothing:' faith says, 'I can do all things through Christ strengthening me.'[114] Through him I cannot only overcome, but expel all the enemies of my soul. Through him I can 'love the Lord my God with all my heart, mind, soul, and strength';[115] yea, and walk in holiness and righteousness before
10 him all the days of my life.[116]

III.1. From what has been said we may easily learn the mischievousness of that opinion that we are *wholly* sanctified when we are justified; that our hearts are then cleansed from all sin. It is true we are then delivered (as was observed before) from
15 the dominion of outward sin: and at the same time the power of inward sin is so broken that we need no longer follow or be led by it. But it is by no means true that inward sin is then totally destroyed, that the root of pride, self-will, anger, love of the world, is then taken out of the heart, or that the carnal mind[117] and
20 the heart bent to backsliding[118] are entirely extirpated. And to suppose the contrary is not, as some may think, an innocent, harmless mistake. No: it does immense harm; it entirely blocks up the way to any farther change. For it is manifest, 'They that are whole do not need a physician, but they that are sick.'[119] If
25 therefore we think we are quite made whole already, there is no room to seek any farther healing. On this supposition it is absurd to expect a farther deliverance from sin, whether gradual or instantaneous.

2. On the contrary, a deep conviction that we are not yet whole,
30 that our hearts are not fully purified, that there is yet in us 'a carnal mind' which is still in its nature 'enmity against God';[120] that a whole body of sin remains in our heart, weakened indeed, but not destroyed, shows beyond all possibility of doubt the absolute necessity of a farther change. We allow that at the very
35 moment of justification we are 'born again':[121] in that instant we

---

[112] Cf. Heb. 4:16.   [113] See Matt. 28:18.   [114] Phil. 4:13; cf. *Notes*.
[115] Cf. Mark 12:30; Luke 10:27.   [116] Cf. Luke 1:75.   [117] Rom. 8:7.
[118] Hosea 11:7.   [119] Cf. Luke 5:31.   [120] Rom. 8:7.
[121] John 3:3, 7; 1 Pet. 1:23. Cf. Nos. 1, *Salvation by Faith*, II.7; 19, 'The Great Privilege of those that are Born of God', §§1–2; 45, 'The New Birth' (entire sermon); 57, 'On the

experience that inward change from 'darkness into marvellous light';[122] from the image of the brute and the devil into the image of God,[123] from the earthly, sensual, devilish mind, to the mind which was in Christ Jesus.[124] But are we then *entirely* changed? Are we *wholly* transformed into the image of him that created us? Far 5 from it: we still retain a depth of sin; and it is the consciousness of this which constrains us to groan for a full deliverance to him that is mighty to save.[125] Hence it is that those believers who are not convinced of the deep corruption of their hearts, or but slightly and as it were notionally convinced, have little concern about 10 *entire sanctification.* They may possibly hold the opinion that such a thing is to be, either at death, or some time (they know not when) before it. But they have no great uneasiness for the want of it, and no great hunger or thirst after it. They cannot, until they know themselves better, until they repent in the sense above described, 15 until God unveils the inbred monster's face, and shows them the real state of their souls.[126] Then only, when they feel the burden, will they groan for deliverance from it. Then and not till then will they cry out, in the agony of their soul,

> Break off the yoke of inbred sin, 20
> And fully set my spirit free!
> I cannot rest till pure within,
> Till I am wholly lost in thee![127]

3. We may learn from hence, secondly, that a deep conviction of our *demerit* after we are accepted (which in one sense may be 25 termed *guilt*) is absolutely necessary in order to our seeing the true value of the atoning blood; in order to our feeling that we need this as much after we are justified as ever we did before. Without this conviction we cannot but account the blood of the covenant[128] *as a common thing*, something of which we have not 30 now any great need, seeing all our past sins are blotted out.[129] Yea, but if both our hearts and lives are thus unclean, there is a kind of guilt which we are contracting every moment, and which of

---

Fall of Man', II.9 10; 83, 'On Patience', §9. Cf. also Wesley's letter to the Editor of *Lloyd's Evening Post*, Feb. 26, 1771.
  [122] 1 Pet. 2:9.   [123] See No. 1, *Salvation by Faith*, §1 and n.   [124] See Phil. 2:5.
  [125] Isa. 63:1.   [126] Cf. No. 7, 'The Way to the Kingdom', II.1 and n.
  [127] 'Come unto me . . . Matt. xi. 28', st. 5, *Hymns and Sacred Poems* (1742), p. 91 (*Poet. Wks.*, II. 145; No. 377 in *Collection*). Here is an aspiration to sinless perfection that implies its possibility and, as we know from other passages, *in this life*. Cf. above, I.20, and No. 13, *On Sin in Believers*, V.2 and n.
  [128] Exod. 24:8; Heb. 10:29.   [129] See Acts 3:19.

consequence would every moment expose us to fresh condemnation, but that

> He ever lives above,
> For us to intercede,
> His all-atoning love,
> His precious blood to plead.[130]

It is this repentance, and the faith intimately connected with it, which are expressed in those strong lines:

> I sin in every breath I draw,
> Nor do thy will, nor keep thy law
> On earth as angels do above:
> But still the Fountain open stands,
> Washes my feet, my heart, my hands,
> Till I am perfected in love.[131]

4. We may observe, thirdly, a deep conviction of our utter *helplessness*—of our total inability to retain anything we have received, much more to deliver ourselves from the world of iniquity[132] remaining both in our hearts and lives—teaches us truly to live upon Christ by faith, not only as our Priest, but as our King. Hereby we are brought to 'magnify him', indeed, to 'give him all the glory of his grace',[133] to 'make him a whole Christ, an entire Saviour', and truly to 'set the crown upon his head'. These excellent words, as they have frequently been used,[134] have little or no meaning. But they are fulfilled in a strong and a deep sense when we thus, as it were, go out of ourselves, in order to be swallowed up in him; when we sink into nothing that he may be all in all.[135] Then, his almighty grace having abolished 'every high thing which exalted itself against' him, every temper, and thought, and word, and work is 'brought to the obedience of Christ'.[136]

Londonderry, April 24, 1767

---

[130] 'Behold the Man!' (beginning 'Arise my soul, arise'), ver. 2, ll. 1-4, in *Hymns and Sacred Poems* (1742), p. 264 (*Poet. Wks.*, II. 323; No. 194 in *Collection*). Orig., 'For me to intercede', and 'all-redeeming love'.

[131] 'A Thanksgiving', st. 16 in *Hymns and Sacred Poems* (1742), p. 171 (*Poet. Wks.*, II. 234, No. 355 in *Collection*). Orig., 'Washes my feet, and head, and hands'.

[132] Jas. 3:6.   [133] Eph. 1:6.

[134] Presumably, by the antinomians (e.g., Maxfield, Bell, Cudworth) and, quite possibly, by the English Moravians; but Sugden could not locate their literary sources and neither have I, thus far.

[135] See 1 Cor. 15:28.   [136] 2 Cor. 10:5.

The Great *Assize* :

A

SERMON

PREACHED

At the ASSIZES, in St. *Paul's*
Church, BEDFORD: on Friday,
March 10, 1758.

By *JOHN WESLEY*, M. A.
Late Fellow of *Lincoln College*, OXFORD.

LONDON,

Printed : and fold by T. TRYE, near Gray's-
Inn-Gate, Holbourn ; by G. KEITH, in
Gracechurch-ftreet ; by T. JAMES, under
the Royal-Exchange, and at the Foundery.

THE GREAT ASSIZE

AN INTRODUCTORY COMMENT

The Journal *entry for February 27, 1758, identifies the origins of this sermon: 'Having a sermon to write against the Assizes at Bedford, I retired for a few days to Lewisham'—i.e., to the home of his friend and benefactor, Ebenezer Blackwell. There he wrote his only published sermon* ad magistratum *(to a civil court) and also the only one in what may fairly be labelled an ornate style. The occasion had been arranged by the High Sheriff of Bedfordshire, William Cole, and the sermon itself was preached in Bedford's finest church, St. Paul's, on Friday, March 10, before the presiding Judge of Common Pleas, Sir Edward Clive (1704–71). Mr. Justice Clive, incidentally, appears in William Hogarth's scornful caricature, 'The Bench', 1758; cf. Ronald Paulson,* Hogarth's Graphic Works *(New Haven and London, Yale University Press, 1965), Vol. I, No. 205; Vol. II, Nos. 226-27; note that Paulson and Sugden have different identifications of Hogarth's characters (see Sugden, II. 399). Of the service itself, Wesley reports (JWJ): 'The congregation at St. Paul's was very large and attentive. The Judge, immediately after sermon, sent me an invitation to dine with him; but having no time [since he was already late for an appointment the next day in Epworth, some ninety miles away], I was obliged to send my excuse, and set out between one and two . . . .' The sermon was published, by request, in the summer of 1758 and then inserted into the 1771 edn. of* SOSO, *I. Twenty years later (JWJ, Sept. 1, 1778), Wesley remembered the sermon with some satisfaction, avowing that even then he could not 'write a better sermon on the Great Assize than I did [in 1758]'.*

The most striking feature of this sermon is the ease with which Wesley has accommodated his carefully cultivated 'plain style' to a new and special occasion; very little of the revival preacher appears here. There are no hymn-quotations, and, save for the controlling analogy between an earthly court in Bedford and God's Final Judgment, there is scant recourse to any evangelical emphasis. There are no polemics, no reference to Methodism, and only a passing hat-tipping to 'faith alone' (II.11). Virgil and Ovid are quoted once apiece, and the then widely popular Edward Young is quoted twice. The analogy between earthly assizes and 'the Great Assize' was at least as old in English preaching as The Pricke of Conscience, *line 5514, formerly attributed to Richard Rolle of Hampole (c.1300–1349). The rhetoric of the introduction and conclusion is frankly exalted, and an earthly commonplace becomes the analogue for the cosmic climax of human destiny and the occasion for Wesley's most explicit exposition of his eschatology.*

This, of course, is the central concern of the sermon: Wesley's vivid sense of the Christian life as lived under God's constant judgment and oriented toward his Final Judgment. The dominant metaphors are all forensic, and Wesley's depiction of the end-time is as stark and decisive as he could make it. The reader must judge as to the consonance of Wesley's views of 'The Last Day' with New Testament and traditional Christian eschatologies as they have evolved. But it would be well to recognize the influence of Joseph Mede and J. A. Bengel, his main sources for eschatology besides the Scriptures. 'The Great Assize' may better be appraised as an implicit statement about the Christian ordo salutis rather than a speculation reaching out beyond faith's basic surety that God's final purposes for his human creation are already validly revealed in Jesus Christ.

The edited text here is based on the first edition of 1758. For a stemma showing its textual history, together with a list of variant readings in the nine editions published in Wesley's lifetime, see Vol. IV, Appendix, 'Wesley's Text'. For bibliographical details, see Bibliog, No. 224.

The Great Assize

Romans 14:10

We shall all stand before the judgment seat of Christ.

1. How many circumstances concur to raise the awfulness of the present solemnity! The general concourse of people of every 5 age, sex, rank, and condition of life, willingly or unwillingly gathered together, not only from the neighbouring, but from distant parts: *criminals*, speedily to be brought forth, and having no way to escape; *officers*, waiting in their various posts to execute the orders which shall be given; and the *representative* of our 10

gracious Sovereign, whom we so highly reverence and honour.[1]
The *occasion* likewise of this assembly adds not a little to the
solemnity of it: to hear and determine causes of every kind, some
of which are of the most important nature; on which depends no
5 less than life or death—death, that uncovers the face of eternity!
It was doubtless in order to increase the serious sense of these
things, and not in the minds of the vulgar only, that the wisdom of
our forefathers did not disdain to appoint even several minute
circumstances of this solemnity. For these also, by means of the
10 eye or ear, may more deeply affect the heart. And when viewed in
this light, trumpets, staves, apparel, are no longer trifling or
insignificant, but subservient in their kind and degree to the most
valuable ends of society.

2. But as awful as this solemnity is, one far more awful is at
15 hand. For yet a little while and 'we shall all stand before the
judgment seat of Christ. For, As I live, saith the Lord, every knee
shall bow to me, and every tongue shall confess to God.' And in
that day 'every one of us shall give account of himself to God.'[2]

3. Had all men a deep sense of this, how effectually would it
20 secure the interests of society! For what more forcible motive can
be conceived to the practice of genuine morality? To a steady
pursuit of solid virtue, an uniform walking in justice, mercy, and
truth? What could strengthen our hands in all that is good, and
deter us from all evil, like a strong conviction of this—'The judge
25 standeth at the door,'[3] and we are shortly to *stand before* him?

4. It may not therefore be improper, or unsuitable to the design
of the present assembly, to consider,

---

[1] This is more than the nominal profession of a lifelong Tory. Wesley had special
reasons for gratitude to the aging George II, who would die two years later in 1760, aged
seventy-eight. Much earlier, in 1741, George II had ordered the Middlesex magistrates to
protect the Methodists from persecuting mobs and had declared, in Council, that there
would be no persecution in his dominions on account of religion while he sat on the throne
(cf. Moore, II. 2-3). During the agitations preceding the Stuart 'Rising of '45', the loyalties
of the Methodists were suspect and Wesley composed an 'Humble Address' to the King,
avowing his own loyalty and that of the Methodist people to both Crown and Church (JWJ,
Mar. 5, 1744); Charles persuaded him that such a letter might have the unintended effect
of setting the Methodists apart more separately from the Church of England than they
actually were and so the address was never sent. When George died, Wesley recorded a
pathetic valedictory (JWJ, Oct. 25, 1760): 'King George was gathered to his fathers. When
will England have a better Prince?' A strange question about the man whose private life
was less than exemplary and who had abetted Robert Walpole's venalities. Cf. Nos. 107,
'On God's Vineyard', IV. 2; and 127, 'On the Wedding Garment', §14.

[2] Rom. 14:10-12.

[3] Cf. Jas. 5:9.

I. The chief circumstances which will precede our standing before the judgment seat of Christ.

II. The judgment itself, and

III. A few of the circumstances which will follow it.

I. Let us, in the first place, consider the chief circumstances 5 which will precede our standing before the judgment seat of Christ.

And first, 1. 'God will show signs in the earth beneath:'[a] particularly, he will 'arise to shake terribly the earth'.[4] 'The earth shall reel to and fro like a drunkard, and shall be removed like a 10 cottage.'[5] 'There shall be earthquakes κατὰ τόπους (not in divers only, but) 'in all places'[b]—not in one only, or a few, but in every part of the habitable world—even 'such as were not since men were upon the earth, so mighty earthquakes and so great'.[6] In one of these 'every island shall flee away, and the mountains will not 15 be found.'[c] Meantime all the waters of the terraqueous globe[7] will feel the violence of those concussions: 'the sea and waves roaring',[d] with such an agitation as had never been known before since the hour that 'the fountains of the great deep were broken up,'[8] to destroy the earth which then 'stood out of the water and in 20 the water'.[9] The air will be all storm and tempest, full of dark

---

[a] Acts 2:19.

[b] Luke 21:11. [The suggestion here that κατὰ τόπους means 'in all places' is eccentric; in the *Notes* Wesley translates it literally, 'in divers places'.]

[c] Rev. 16:20.   [d] Luke 21:25.

---

[4] Isa. 2:19.   [5] Isa. 24:20.

[6] Cf. Rev. 16:18. The eighteenth century's interest in earthquakes was intense; there had been major quakes in Sicily and Jamaica in 1692; one in Lima, Peru, on Oct. 28, 1746; two in London in 1750 (Feb. 8 and Mar. 8); and another in Lisbon, Nov. 1, 1755. Cf. Burnet, *History of His Own Times*, II. 101; and John Ray, *Three Physico-Theological Discourses* (1693). In 1750 Charles Wesley had written a sermon on 'The Cause and Cure of Earthquakes' upon the occasion of the London shocks. That John shared Charles's interest and views in this matter may be seen in his *Serious Thoughts Occasioned by the Late Earthquake at Lisbon* (1755); cf. *Bibliog*, No. 213 and Vol. 15 of this edn. There are obvious parallels between the essay and the sermon. Another stimulus to this preoccupation with earthquakes came from the infant science of geology and theological reactions to it, as in Whiston's *A New Theory of the Earth* and Burnet's *Sacred Theory of the Earth* and the controversies engendered by them. (Burnet had been Master of Charterhouse during Wesley's time there).

[7] An eighteenth-century cliché and a favourite of Wesley's; see below, III.3; and Nos. 56, 'God's Approbation of His Works', I.8, 10; 69, 'The Imperfection of Human Knowledge', I.8; 103, 'What is Man? Ps. 8:3-4', I.2. Also, Wesley's *Survey*, III.3; IV. 55.

[8] Gen. 7:11.   [9] Cf. 2 Pet. 3:5.

'vapours and pillars of smoke';[e] resounding with thunder from pole to pole, and torn with ten thousand lightnings. But the commotion will not stop in the region of the air: 'The powers of heaven also shall be shaken.' 'There shall be signs in the sun and

5 in the moon and in the stars'[f]—those fixed as well as those that move round them. 'The sun shall be turned into darkness and the moon into blood, before the great and terrible day of the Lord come.'[g] 'The stars shall withdraw their shining,'[h] yea and 'fall from heaven',[10] being thrown out of their orbits. And then shall be

10 heard the universal 'shout' from all the companies of heaven, followed by 'the voice of the archangel' proclaiming the approach of the Son of God and man, 'and the trumpet of God'[i] sounding an alarm to all 'that sleep in the dust of the earth'.[11] In consequence of this all the graves shall open, and the bodies of

15 men arise.[12] 'The sea also shall give up the dead which are therein,'[j] and everyone shall rise *with his own body*—his own in substance, although so changed in its properties as we cannot now conceive. For 'this corruptible will then put on incorruption, and this mortal put on immortality.'[k] Yea, 'death and Hades', the

20 invisible world, shall 'deliver up the dead that are in them';[l] so that all who ever lived and died since God created man shall be raised incorruptible and immortal.

2. At the same time 'the Son of man shall send forth his angels' over all the earth, 'and they shall gather his elect from the four

25 winds, from one end of heaven to the other.'[m] And the Lord himself shall 'come with clouds,[13] in his own glory and the glory of his Father,[14] with ten thousand of his saints,[15] even myriads of angels',[16] and 'shall sit upon the throne of his glory. And before him shall be gathered all nations, and he shall separate them one

30 from another, and shall set the sheep' (the good) 'on his right hand, and the goats' (the wicked) 'upon the left.'[n] Concerning this general assembly it is that the beloved disciple speaks thus: 'I saw the dead' (all that had been dead) 'small and great, stand before

---

[e] Joel 2:30 [cf. Acts 2:19].
[f] Luke 21:25, 26.
[g] Joel 2:31.
[h] Joel 3:15.
[i] 1 Thess. 4:16.
[j] Rev. 20:13.
[k] 1 Cor. 15:53.
[l] Rev. 20:13.
[m] Matt. 24:31.
[n] Matt. 25:31-33.

---

[10] Matt. 24:29.
[11] Dan. 12:2.
[12] See Ezek. 37:12-13; Matt. 27:52-53.
[13] Cf. Matt. 24:30, etc.
[14] Cf. Luke 9:26.
[15] Jude 14.
[16] Cf. Heb. 12:22.

God. And the books were opened (a figurative expression, plainly referring to the manner of proceeding among men), and the dead were judged out of those things which were written in the books according to their works.'[o]

II. These are the chief circumstances which are recorded in the oracles of God as preceding the general judgment. We are, secondly, to consider the judgment itself, so far as it hath pleased God to reveal it.

1. The person by whom God 'will judge the world'[17] is his only-begotten Son, whose 'goings forth are from everlasting',[18] 'who is God over all, blessed for ever'.[19] Unto him, 'being the out-beaming of his Father's glory, the express image of his person',[p] the Father 'hath committed all judgment, [. . .] because he is the Son of man';[q] because, though he was 'in the form of God, and thought it not robbery to be equal with God, yet he emptied himself, taking upon him the form of a servant, being made in the likeness of men'.[r] Yea, because 'being found in fashion as a man, he humbled himself' yet farther, 'becoming obedient unto death, even the death of the cross. Wherefore God hath highly exalted him,'[20] even in his human nature, and 'ordained him'[21] as man to try the children of men, to be the 'judge both of the quick and dead';[22] both of those who shall be found alive at his coming, and of those who were before 'gathered to their fathers'.[23]

2. The time termed by the prophet 'the great and the terrible day'[24] is usually in Scripture styled 'the day of the Lord'.[25] The space from the creation of man upon the earth to the end of all things is *the day of the sons of men*. The time that is now passing over us is properly *our day*. When this is ended, the day of the Lord will begin. But who can say how long it will continue? 'With

---

[o] Rev. 20:12.
[p] Heb. 1:3 [This translation of ἀπαύγασμα as 'out-beaming' appealed to Wesley. Although he does not use it in his *Notes*, it appears in Nos. 24, 'Sermon on the Mount, IV', §1; and 34, 'The Original, Nature, Properties, and Use of the Law', II.3. Cf. Poole's *Annotations, loc. cit.*].
[q] John 5:22, 27.   [r] Phil. 2:6-7.

---

[17] Cf. Rom. 3:6; 1 Cor. 6:2.   [18] Cf. Mic. 5:2.
[19] Cf. Rom. 9:5.   [20] Cf. Phil. 2:8-9.   [21] Cf. Acts 17:31.
[22] Cf. 1 Pet. 4:5.   [23] Cf. Judg. 2:10.   [24] Joel 2:31.
[25] Joel 1:15, etc.

the Lord one day is as a thousand years, and a thousand years as one day.'⁵ And from this very expression some of the ancient Fathers drew that inference, that what is commonly called 'the day of judgment'²⁶ would be indeed a thousand years.²⁷ And it ⁵ seems they did not go beyond the truth; nay, probably they did not come up to it. For if we consider the number of persons who are to be judged, and of actions which are to be inquired into, it does not appear that a thousand years will suffice for the transactions of that day. So that it may not improbably comprise several ₁₀ thousand years. But God shall reveal this also in its season.²⁸

3. With regard to the place where mankind will be judged we have no explicit account in Scripture. An eminent writer²⁹ (but not he alone; many have been of the same opinion) supposes it will be on earth, where the works were done according to which they ₁₅ shall be judged, and that God will in order thereto employ the angels of his strength,

> To smooth and lengthen out the boundless space,
> And spread an area for all human race.³⁰

---

⁵ 2 Pet. 3:8.

---

²⁶ Matt. 10:15, etc.

²⁷ As in the 'Epistle of Barnabas' (xv), Justin Martyr (*Dialogue with Trypho*, lxx), Melito of Sardis (in Eusebius, *Ecclesiastical History*, xxiv. 5), Papias (in Irenaeus, *Against Heresies*, V.xxxiii, and Eusebius, *op. cit.*, III.xxxix), Irenaeus (*Against Heresies*, V.xxxii), Methodius of Olympus (*Symposium*, Disc. 9 and 10), Lactantius (*Epitome of the Divine Institutes*, LXXI-LXXII). Origen had criticized these chiliastic interpretations of Rev. 20:1-15, and St. Augustine, having championed such a view (as in *De Civ. Dei*, xx.7), abandoned it in Sermon CCLIX (Migne, *PL*, XXXVIII.1197). Apocalyptic visions continued throughout the Middle Ages, but chiliasm proper had few explicit champions. It was, however, renewed in the 'radical reformation' (Hoffman and the Munsterites in Cromwell's England and thereafter (Jane Leade), and in the writings of Joseph Mede and J. A. Bengel; for Bengel's influence on Wesley, cf. *Notes*, Preface, §7, and Rev. 20:1-15.

²⁸ Wesley's reticence here is as significant as his proposed revision of chiliastic thought, since he knew the history of millenarianism and had a sympathetic interest in Montanus; cf. Nos. 61, 'The Mystery of Iniquity', §24; and 68, 'The Wisdom of God's Counsels', §9; see also 'The Real Character of Montanus' (Vol. 12 of this edn.). His reaction to Jurieu and 'the French Prophets' was cautious. He also knew, but chose to ignore, William Whiston's prediction that the 'Last Day' was scheduled in the year 1720, as in his essay on the *Revelation of St. John* (1706). He had already used in his *Notes* (1755) Bengel's *Erklärte Offenbarung Johannis* . . . (1740; Eng. tr., 1757), with its predicted date for the millennium as 1836, and indeed reproduced Bengel's chronological appendix in his own work.

²⁹ Cf. Boston, State IV, Head IV; and Bengel, *Gnomon* (on Rev. 20), §§3-11; see also Joseph Mede, *Works*, III. 430-32, and espec. his chart, pp. 431-32 ('ΒΙΒΛΑΡΙΔΙΟΝ').

³⁰ Young, *Last Day*, ii.19-20; orig. 'th' unbounded space'; cf. Wesley, *Collection of Moral and Sacred Poems* (1744), II.76.

But perhaps it is more agreeable to our Lord's own account of his 'coming in the clouds'[31] to suppose it will be above the earth, if not 'twice a planetary height'.[32] And this supposition is not a little favoured by what St. Paul writes to the Thessalonians. 'The dead in Christ shall rise first. Then we who remain alive shall be caught 5 up together with them, in the clouds, to meet the Lord in the air.'[*] So that it seems most probable the 'great white throne'[33] will be high exalted above the earth.

4. The persons to be judged who can count, any more than the drops of rain or the sands of the sea? I beheld, saith St. John, 'a 10 great multitude which no man can number, clothed with white robes, and palms in their hands'.[34] How immense then must be the total multitude of all nations, and kindreds, and people, and tongues![35] Of all that have sprung from the loins of Adam since the world began, till time shall be no more! If we admit the 15 common supposition, which seems noways absurd, that the earth bears at any one time no less than four hundred millions of living souls—men, women, and children—what a congregation must all those generations make who have succeeded each other for seven thousand years![36] 20

---

[*] 1 Thess. 4:16-17.

---

[31] Matt. 24:30; Mark 13:26.
[32] Young, *Last Day*, ll. 274; cf. Wesley, *Collection of Moral and Sacred Poems*, II. 82.
[33] Rev. 20:11.
[34] Cf. Rev. 7:9.
[35] *Ibid.*
[36] Wesley had found this 'common supposition' in Brerewood's *Enquiries*, pp. 120-45. It would be repeated by Richard Price in a letter to Benjamin Franklin published in *Philosophical Transactions* (of the Royal Society) in 1768. Current estimates of the world's population in 1750 are based largely on the work of A. M. Carr-Saunders, *World Population* (Oxford, Oxford University Press, 1936), p. 42; W. S. Thompson, *Population and Progress in the Far East* (Chicago, University of Chicago Press, 1959), p.12; and W. F. Willcox, *Studies in American Demography* (Ithaca, N.Y., Cornell University Press, 1940), p. 45. The average of their estimates would put the round figure of world population in 1750 at seven hundred millions. Cf. W. D. Borrie, *The Growth and Control of World Population* (London, Weidenfeld and Nicolson, 1970), pp. 6-7; Gerhard and Jean Lenski, *Human Societies* (New York, McGraw Hill, 1974), p. 319; and Annabelle Desmond, 'How Many People Have Ever Lived on Earth?' in *Population Bulletin*, 18:1 (Feb. 1962), pp. 1-19. For some of Wesley's other references to population, cf. Nos. 63, 'The General Spread of the Gospel', §1; 69, 'The Imperfection of Human Knowledge', II.8; 103, 'What is Man? Ps. 8:3-4', I.2; 122, 'Causes of the Inefficacy of Christianity', §3. Cf. also, *The Doctrine of Original Sin*, II.1; *Some Observations on Liberty*, §11; his letter to the Bishop of Gloucester, Nov. 26, 1762; and JWJ, Sept. 9, 1776.

> Great Xerxes' world in arms, proud Cannae's host, . . .
> They all are here, and here they all are lost:
> Their numbers swell to be discerned in vain;
> Lost as a drop in the unbounded main.[37]

5 Every man, every woman, every infant of days that ever breathed the vital air will then hear the voice of the Son of God, and start into life, and appear before him. And this seems to be the natural import of that expression, 'the dead, small and great':[38] all universally, all without exception, all of every age, sex, or degree;
10 all that ever lived and died, or underwent such a change as will be equivalent with death. For long before that day the phantom of human greatness disappears and sinks into nothing. Even in the moment of death that vanishes away. Who is rich or great in the grave?[39]

15 5. And every man shall there 'give an account of his own works',[40] yea, a full and true account of all that he ever did while in the body, whether it was good or evil. O what a scene will then be disclosed in the sight of angels and men! While not the fabled Rhadamanthus, but the Lord God Almighty, who knoweth all
20 things in heaven and earth,

> *Castigatque, auditque dolos; subigitque fateri*
> *Quae quis apud superos, furto laetatus inani,*
> *Distulit in seram commissa piacula mortem.*[41]

Nor will all the actions alone of every child of man be then
25 brought to open view, but all their words, seeing 'every idle word

---

[37] Young, *Last Day*, ii.189, 194-96; orig., 'Their millions swell' and 'Lost as a billow in th' unbounded main'. Cf. Wesley, *Collection of Moral and Sacred Poems*, II.80. See also No. 103, 'What is Man? Ps. 8:3-4', I.1, where Wesley uses this last line again.

[38] Rev. 20:12.

[39] The grave as a great 'leveller' was a commonplace theme in poetry and preaching, as in Thomas Gray's contemporary *Elegy Written in a Country Churchyard* just seven years previously.

[40] Cf. Luke 16:2; Rom. 14:12; Rev. 20:12.

[41] Virgil, *Aeneid*, vi. 567-69; Wesley offers no translation, but in the 'Explanation of the Latin Sentences' added to Vol. 32 of his *Works* (1774) Wesley prefixed the preceding line, '*Haec Rhadamanthus habet durissima regna*', and furnished his own translation of the quatrain:

> O'er these drear realms stern Rhadamanthus reigns,
> Detects each artful villain, and constrains
> To own the crimes, long veiled from human sight:
> In vain! Now all stand forth in hated light.

See above, Intro., pp. 71-72, for evidence that Wesley continued to read Virgil 'for pleasure', even into his old age. Thus, he may have had a copy of the *Aeneid* at hand, which would explain this rare verbatim quotation.

which men shall speak, they shall give account thereof in the day of judgment.' So that, 'By thy words' (as well as works) 'thou shalt be justified; or by thy words thou shalt be condemned'.[u] Will not God then bring to light every circumstance also that accompanied every word or action, and if not altered the nature, yet lessened or increased the goodness or badness of them? And how casy is this to him who is 'about our bed and about our path, and spieth out all our ways'![42] We know 'the darkness is no darkness to him, but the night shineth as the day.'[43]

6. Yea, he 'will bring to light' not 'the hidden works of darkness'[44] only, but the very 'thoughts and intents of the heart'.[45] And what marvel? For he 'searcheth the reins',[46] and 'understandeth all our thoughts'.[47] 'All things are naked and open to the eyes of him with whom we have to do.'[48] 'Hell and destruction are before him' without a covering; 'how much more the hearts of the children of men!'[49]

7. And in that day shall be discovered every inward working of every human soul: every appetite, passion, inclination, affection, with the various combinations of them, with every temper and disposition that constitute the whole complex character of each individual. So shall it be clearly and infallibly scen who was righteous, and who unrighteous; and in what degree every action or person or character was either good or evil.

8. 'Then the king will say to them upon his right hand, Come, ye blessed of my Father. For I was hungry and ye gave me meat; thirsty and ye gave me drink; I was a stranger and ye took me in; naked and ye clothed me.'[50] In like manner, all the good they did upon earth will be recited before men and angels: whatsoever they had done either 'in word or deed, in the name', or for the sake 'of the Lord Jesus'.[51] All their good desires, intentions, thoughts, all their holy dispositions, will also be then remembered; and it will appear that though they were unknown or forgotten among men, yet God 'noted' them 'in his book'.[52] All

---

[u] Matt. 12:36-37.

---

[42] Ps. 139:2 (BCP).
[43] An interesting conflation of Ps. 139:11-12: ver. 11 is from the BCP; ver. 12 is AV.
[44] Cf. 1 Cor. 4:5.   [45] Heb. 4:12.   [46] Rev. 2:23.
[47] Cf. Ps. 139:2 (AV).   [48] Cf. Heb. 4:13.
[49] Cf. Prov. 15:11.   [50] Cf. Matt. 25:34-36.
[51] Col. 3:17.   [52] Cf. Isa. 30:8.

their sufferings likewise for the name of Jesus and for the
testimony of a good conscience will be displayed, unto their *praise*
from the righteous judge,[53] their *honour* before saints and angels,
and the increase of that 'far more exceeding and eternal weight of
5 glory'.[54]

9. But will their evil deeds too—since if we take in his whole life
'there is not a man on earth that liveth and sinneth not'[55]—will
these be remembered in that day, and mentioned in the great
congregation? Many believe they will not, and ask, 'Would not
10 this imply that their sufferings were not at an end, even when life
ended? Seeing they would still have sorrow, and shame, and
confusion of face to endure?' They ask farther, 'How can this be
reconciled with God's declaration by the Prophet, "If the wicked
will turn from all his sins that he hath committed, and keep all my
15 statutes, and do that which is lawful and right; . . . all his
transgressions that he hath committed, they shall not be once
mentioned unto him"?[v] How is it consistent with the promise
which God has made to all who accept of the gospel covenant, "I
will forgive their iniquities, and remember their sin no more"?[w]
20 Or as the Apostle expresses it, "I will be merciful to their
unrighteousness, and their sins and iniquities will I remember no
more"?'[x]

10. It may be answered, it is apparently and absolutely
necessary, for the full display of the glory of God, for the clear and
25 perfect manifestation of his wisdom, justice, power, and mercy
toward the heirs of salvation,[56] that all the circumstances of their
life should be placed in open view, together with all their tempers,
and all the desires, thoughts, and intents of their hearts.[57]
Otherwise how would it appear out of what a depth of sin and
30 misery the grace of God had delivered them? And, indeed, if the
whole lives of all the children of men were not manifestly
discovered, the whole amazing contexture of divine providence
could not be manifested; nor should we yet be able in a thousand

---

[v]   Ezek. 18:21-22.
[w] Jer. 31:34.
[x]   Heb. 8:12 [cf. Boston, State IV, Head V, 'The Kingdom of Heaven'].

---

[53] 2 Tim. 4:8.
[54] 2 Cor. 4:17.
[55] Cf. Eccles. 7:20.
[56] Heb. 1:14.   [57] Heb. 4:12.

instances to 'justify the ways of God to man'.[58] Unless our Lord's words were fulfilled in their utmost sense, without any restriction or limitation, 'there is nothing covered that shall not be revealed, or hid that shall not be known,'[y] abundance of God's dispensations under the sun would still appear without their 5 reasons. And then only when God hath brought to light all the hidden things of darkness,[59] whosoever were the actors therein, will it be seen that wise and good were all his ways; that he 'saw through the thick cloud',[60] and governed all things by the wise 'counsel of his own will';[61] that nothing was left to chance or the 10 caprice of men, but God disposed all 'strongly and sweetly',[62] and wrought all into one connected chain of justice, mercy, and truth.

11. And in the discovery of the divine perfections the righteous will rejoice with joy unspeakable; far from feeling any painful sorrow or shame for any of those past transgressions which were 15 long since blotted out as a cloud,[63] washed away by the blood of the Lamb.[64] It will be abundantly sufficient for them that 'all the transgressions which they had committed shall not be once mentioned unto them'[65] to their disadvantage; that 'their sins and transgressions and iniquities shall be remembered no more'[66] to 20 their condemnation. This is the plain meaning of the promise; and this all the children of God shall find true, to their everlasting comfort.

[y] Matt. 10:26.

---

[58] Cf. Milton, *Paradise Lost*, i. 26. Cf. also Nos. 56, 'God's Approbation of His Works', II.3; 57, 'On the Fall of Man', §2, and 140, 'The Promise of Understanding', I.1. See also Wesley's letter to Elizabeth Ritchie, Jan. 17, 1775.

[59] 1 Cor. 4:5.

[60] A paraphrase of Job 22:12-14, espec. ver. 13.

[61] Eph. 1:11.

[62] Cf. George Herbert, *The Temple*, 'Providence', ll. 1-2 and, espec., 29-32:

> We all acknowledge both thy power and love
> To be exact, transcendent, and divine;
> Who dost so strongly and so sweetly move,
> While all things have their will, yet none but thine.

Cf. also Kempis, IV.i.8: 'How sweetly and graciously dost thou dispose of all things with thine elect, ... This strongly draweth the hearts of the devout . . . .'. See Nos. 118, 'On the Omnipresence of God', II.2, where Wesley again pairs 'strongly and sweetly' in speaking of God's influencing his creatures without destroying their liberty; and 66, 'The Signs of the Times', II.9, where he speaks of the grace of God, 'strongly and sweetly working on every side'.

[63] See Isa. 44:22.   [64] Rev. 12:11.
[65] Cf. Ezek. 18:22.   [66] Cf. Heb. 8:12; 10:17.

12. After the righteous are judged, the king will turn to them upon his left hand, and they shall also be judged, every man 'according to his works'.[67] But not only their outward works will be brought into the account, but all the evil words which they have
5 ever spoken; yea, all the evil desires, affections, tempers, which have or have had a place in their souls, and all the evil thoughts or designs which were ever cherished in their hearts. The joyful sentence of acquittal will then be pronounced upon those on the right hand, the dreadful sentence of condemnation upon those on
10 the left—both of which must remain fixed and unmovable as the throne of God.

III.1. We may, in the third place, consider a few of the circumstances which will follow the general judgment. And the first is the execution of the sentence pronounced on the evil and
15 on the good. 'These shall go away into eternal punishment, and the righteous into life eternal.'[68] It should be observed, it is the very same word which is used both in the former and the latter clause: it follows that either the punishment lasts for ever, or the reward too will come to an end.[69] No, never, unless God could
20 come to an end, or his mercy and truth could fail. 'Then shall the righteous shine forth as the sun in the kingdom of their Father,'[70] and shall 'drink of those rivers of pleasure which are at God's right hand for evermore'.[71] But here all description falls short; all human language fails! Only one who is caught up into the third
25 heaven[72] can have a just conception of it. But even such an one cannot express what he hath seen—these things 'it is not possible for man to utter.'[73]

'The wicked', meantime, 'shall be turned into hell,' even 'all the people that forget God'.[74] They will be 'punished with
30 everlasting destruction from the presence of the Lord, and from the glory of his power'.[75] They will be 'cast into the lake of fire burning with brimstone',[76] originally 'prepared for the devil and

---

[67] Matt. 16:27.

[68] Cf. Matt. 25:46.

[69] Wesley's doctrine of 'a middle state' for souls after death but before the Final Judgment (as in No. 115, 'Dives and Lazarus', I.3 and n.) did not allow for further amelioration of the state of those who died in unrepented ('mortal') sins; human destinies are, therefore, predetermined at death and thus before 'The Great Assize'.

[70] Matt. 13:43.   [71] Cf. Pss. 16:11; 36:8.   [72] 2 Cor. 12:2.

[73] 2 Cor. 12:4 (cf. *Notes*).   [74] Cf. Ps. 9:17 (BCP).

[75] 2 Thess. 1:9.   [76] Cf. Rev. 19:20.

his angels';[77] where they will 'gnaw their tongues'[78] for anguish and pain; they will 'curse God, and look upward':[79] there the dogs of hell[80]—pride,[81] malice, revenge, rage, horror, despair—continually devour them. There 'they have no rest day or night, but the smoke of their torment ascendeth for ever and ever.'[82] 'For their worm dieth not, and the fire is not quenched.'[83]

2. Then the heavens will be shrivelled up 'as a parchment scroll',[84] and 'pass away with a great noise';[85] they will 'flee from the face of him that sitteth on the throne, and there will be found no place for them'.[z] The very manner of their passing away is disclosed to us by the Apostle Peter: 'In the day of God, the heavens, being on fire, shall be dissolved.'[aa] The whole beautiful fabric will be overthrown by that raging element, the connection of all its parts destroyed, and every atom torn asunder from the others. By the same 'the earth also and the works that are therein shall be burnt up.'[bb] The enormous works of nature, 'the everlasting hills',[86] mountains that have defied the rage of time, and stood unmoved so many thousand years, will sink down in fiery ruin. How much less will the works of art, though of the most durable kind, the utmost efforts of human industry—tombs, pillars, triumphal arches, castles, pyramids—be able to withstand the flaming conqueror. All, all will die, perish, vanish away, like a dream when one awaketh!

3. It has indeed been imagined by some great and good men that as it requires that same almighty power to annihilate things as to create, to speak into nothing or out of nothing; so no part of, no

---

[z] [Cf.] Rev. 20.11.   [aa] 2 Pet. 3:12.   [bb] 2 Pet. 3:10.

---

[77] Matt. 25:41.   [78] Rev. 16:10.   [79] Cf. Isa. 8:21.

[80] An odd metaphor, as if Wesley had confused the three *heads* of Cerberus (cf. Homer, *Iliad* viii. 367; Euripides, *Hercules Furens*, 611; and Virgil, *Aeneid*, vi. 417-22) with three dogs. In any case, there is no correlation between the roles of Cerberus and of the 'worms' (cf. Isa. 66:24; Judith 16:17; and Mark 9:44-49). In his *Notes* on Mark 9:44 Wesley had recently written of the 'worm' (of conscience) 'that gnaweth the soul (pride, self-will, desire, malice, envy, shame, sorrow, despair)'. For a classic text on the eternity of divine punishments, see St. Augustine, *De Civ. Dei*, xxi. chs. 9–14. Cf. Nos. 73, 'Of Hell', II.2; and 84, *The Important Question*, III.10; also *Advice to a Soldier*, §4, *Bibliog*, No. 72 (Vol. 14 of this edn.). See also Milton, *Paradise Lost*, x.616, and Henry Brooke, *Gustavus Vasa*, Act IV, sc. 2.

[81] Cf. No. 14, *The Repentance of Believers*, I.3 and n.

[82] Cf. Rev. 14:11.

[83] Cf. Mark 9:44; cf. also No. 73, 'Of Hell', III.3, where endless torment is also affirmed.

[84] Cf. Rev. 6:14.   [85] 2 Pet. 3:10.   [86] Gen. 49:26.

atom in the universe will be totally or finally destroyed.[87] Rather, they suppose that as the last operation of fire which we have yet been able to observe is to reduce into glass what by a smaller force it had reduced to ashes; so in the day God hath ordained the
5 whole earth, if not the material heavens also, will undergo this change, after which the fire can have no farther power over them. And they believe this is intimated by that expression in the Revelation made to St. John: 'Before the throne there was a sea of glass like unto crystal.'[cc] We cannot now either affirm or deny this;
10 but we shall know hereafter.

4. If it be inquired by the scoffers, the minute philosophers:[88] 'How can these things be? Whence should come such an immense quantity of fire[89] as would consume the heavens and the

---

[cc] [Rev.] 4:6. [But see also Rev. 15:2 and Wesley's *Notes* on these two verses. For a further reference to Jacob Behmen (Wesley's preferred spelling for Jakob Boehme) and his apocalyptic vision based on these verses, see No. 64, 'The New Creation', §13 and n. See also Wesley's letter to William Law, Jan. 6, 1756, in which he had criticized Law's dependence on Boehme and had denounced his 'superfluous, uncertain, dangerous, irrational, unscriptural philosophy'.]

---

[87] Seventeenth- and eighteenth-century scientists were agreed on the principle of 'the conservation of matter'; cf. Chambers's *Cyclopaedia* on 'Matter', and Singer, *Scientific Ideas*, pp. 332-33 (for citations of Francis Bacon, Robert Boyle, and Sir Isaac Newton); see also pp. 271-72. Wesley returns frequently to the point, as in Nos. 26, 'Sermon on the Mount, VI', III.7; 60, 'The General Deliverance', I.1; 68, 'The Wisdom of God's Counsels', §4; 70, 'The Case of Reason Impartially Considered', II.2; 77, 'Spiritual Worship', I.5; 118, 'On the Omnipresence of God', II.3. See also 'Some Thoughts on an Expression of St. Paul in the First Epistle to the Thessalonians . . .', *AM*, 1786, 543-44; *Notes* on Act 17:18 ('The stoics held that matter was eternal . . . '), and *Survey*, I. 178.

But cf. Laurence Echard, *A General Ecclesiastical History* (5th edn., 1719), III. iii. 345, for a reminder that when Hermogenes (*c.* A.D. 178) first proposed the idea as valid for a Christian doctrine of creation, he was denounced (by Tertullian and others) as an 'heresiarch'. Indeed, the obvious conflict between the doctrines of the eternity of matter, on the one side, and of the 'creation from nothing', on the other, has been a long-standing problem for Christian theologians.

[88] Cf. Cicero, *De Senectute (On Old Age)*, xxiii. 85: '*quidam minuti philosophi*' ('certain petty philosophers'). See also Berkeley's description and appraisal of these narrow-visioned thinkers in *Alciphron, or the Minute Philosopher* (1732; in the 3rd edn. [1752], Dial. I.ii, he says of them, 'They are, amongst the great thinkers, as the Dutch painters are amongst the men of the grand style'). Wesley mentions them again in No. 56, 'God's Approbation of His Works', II.1; *A Farther Appeal*, Pt. II, II.14 (11:226-27 of this edn.); and *Thoughts Upon Necessity, Bibliog*, No. 351 (Vol. 12 of this edn.).

[89] The primeval element of fire had, in Wesley's time, come to be often identified as 'ethereal fire'; cf. William Jones, *An Essay on the First Principles of Natural Philosophy* (1762), p. 210, where Zoroaster is cited as the source of the idea. See also Shakespeare, *Othello*, V.ii.280, 'steep-down gulfs of liquid fire'. Wesley was much interested in such popular scientific notions as 'ethereal fire' and the newly discovered phenomena of 'electric fire' and electricity; cf. Nos. 54, 'On Eternity', §7; 55, *On the Trinity*, §9; 56, 'God's Approbation of His Works', I.8; 57, 'On the Fall of Man', II.1; 64, 'The New

whole terraqueous globe?'[90] we would beg leave, first, to remind
them that this difficulty is not peculiar to the Christian system.
The same opinion almost universally obtained among the
unbigoted[91] heathens. So one of those celebrated 'free-thinkers'
speaks according to the generally received sentiment: 5

> *Esse quoque in fatis reminiscitur, afforc tempus,*
> *Quo mare, quo tellus, correptaque regia coeli*
> *Ardeat, et mundi moles operosa laboret.*[92]

But, secondly, it is easy to answer, even from our slight and
superficial acquaintance with natural things, that there are 10
abundant magazines of fire ready prepared, and treasured up
against the day of the Lord. How soon may a comet,
commissioned by him, travel down from the most distant parts of
the universe? And were it to fix upon the earth in its return from
the sun, when it is some thousand times hotter than a red-hot 15
cannon-ball,[93] who does not see what must be the immediate
consequence? But, not to ascend so high as the ethereal heavens,
might not the same lightnings which give 'shine to the world',[94] if
commanded by the Lord of nature give ruin and utter
destruction? Or, to go no farther than the globe itself, who knows 20
what huge reservoirs of liquid fire are from age to age contained
in the bowels of the earth? Aetna, Hecla, Vesuvius,[95] and all the

Creation', §10; 69, 'The Imperfection of Human Knowledge', I.7; 77, 'Spiritual
Worship', I.5; 116, 'What is Man? Ps. 8:4', §§2, 8; 124, 'Human Life a Dream', §7. See
also Wesley's *Survey*, III. 186, 246; 'Some Thoughts' on 1 Thess. (4M, 1786, 448);
'Thought on Nervous Disorders', *ibid*, 54; *Survey*, V. 235-55.

[90] Cf. above, I.1 and n.

[91] Wesley's spelling: 'unbigotted'; but cf. *OED* for spelling variations in the seventeenth
and eighteenth centuries.

[92] Ovid, *Metamorphoses*, i. 256-58: 'He remembered also that 'twas in the fates that a
time would come when sea and land, the unkindled palace of the sky, and the beleaguered
structure of the universe, should be destroyed by fire.'

[93] Cf. *Notes* on 2 Pet. 3:10, where Wesley uses almost the same words as here in this
paragraph. Cf. also No. 56, 'God's Approbation of His Works', I.10 and n.

[94] Ps. 97:4 (BCP).

[95] Wesley's 'favourite' volcanoes. The phrase, 'burning mountains', goes back to Pliny
the Elder, *Natural History*, II. 106-7, and to Macarius, *Spiritual Homilies*, XIV. 212. It
occurs in Goldsmith's *History of the Earth and Animated Nature* (1774), I. 291 (where
Buffon is cited). Cf. the long passage on 'burning mountains' in Wesley's *Survey*, III.
107-52, where the 'fire in caverns of the earth' (p. 131) is correlated with the phenomena
of volcanoes. Isaac Watts also used the term in his *Ruin and Recovery of Mankind* (p. 15),
which Wesley quoted in his *Doctrine of Original Sin*. Cf. also Nos. 56, 'God's Approbation
of His Works', I.3; 64, 'The New Creation', §15; and 69, 'The Imperfection of Human
Knowledge', I.8.

other volcanoes that belch out flames and coals of fire, what are they but so many proofs and mouths of those fiery furnaces? And at the same time so many evidences that God hath in readiness wherewith to fulfil his word. Yea, were we to observe no more
5 than the surface of the earth, and the things that surround us on every side, it is most certain (as a thousand experiments prove beyond all possibility of denial) that we ourselves, our whole bodies, are full of fire, as well as everything round about us. Is it not easy to make this ethereal fire visible even to the naked eye?
10 And to produce thereby the very same effects on combustible matter which are produced by culinary fire? Needs there then any more than for God to unloose that secret chain whereby this irresistible agent is now bound down, and lies quiescent in every particle of matter? And how soon would it tear the universal frame
15 in pieces, and involve all in one common ruin?

5. There is one circumstance more which will follow the judgment that deserves our serious consideration. 'We look', says the Apostle, 'according to his promise, for new heavens and a new earth, wherein dwelleth righteousness.'dd The promise stands in
20 the prophecy of Isaiah: 'Behold, I create new heavens and a new earth. And the former shall not be remembered;'ee so great shall the glory of the latter be. These St. John did behold in the visions of God. 'I saw', saith he, 'a new heaven and a new earth; for the first heaven and the first earth were passed away.'ff And only
25 'righteousness dwelt therein.'96 Accordingly he adds, 'And I heard a great voice from' the third 'heaven, saying, Behold, the tabernacle of God is with men, and he will dwell with them, and they shall be his people, and God himself shall be with them, and be their God.'gg Of necessity, therefore, they will all be happy:
30 'God shall wipe away all tears from their eyes, and there shall be no more death, neither sorrow, nor crying; neither shall there be any more pain.'hh 'There shall be no more curse; but [. . .] they shall see his face,'ii shall have the nearest access to, and thence the

dd [2 Pet.] 3:13.
ee [Isa.] 65:17.
ff Rev. 21:1.
gg Ver. 3.
hh Ver. 4.
ii [Rev.] 22:3,4.

---

96 Cf. 2 Pet. 3:13.

highest resemblance of him. This is the strongest expression in the language of Scripture to denote the most perfect happiness. 'And his name shall be on their foreheads.'[97] They shall be openly acknowledged as God's own property; and his glorious nature shall most visibly shine forth in them. 'And there shall be no night there; and they need no candle, neither light of the sun; for the Lord God giveth them light, and they shall reign for ever and ever.'[98]

IV. It remains only to apply the preceding considerations to all who are here before God. And are we not directly led so to do by the present solemnity, which so naturally points us to that day when the Lord 'will judge the world in righteousness'?[99] This, therefore, by reminding us of that more awful season, may furnish many lessons of instruction. A few of these I may be permitted just to touch on. May God write them on all our hearts!

1. And, first, 'how beautiful are the feet'[100] of those who are sent by the wise and gracious providence of God to execute justice on earth, to defend the injured, and punish the wrongdoer! Are they not 'the ministers of God to us for good',[101] the grand supporters of the public tranquillity, the patrons of innocence and virtue, the great security of all our temporal blessings? And does not every one of these represent not only an earthly prince, but the Judge of the earth;[102] him whose 'name is written upon his thigh, King of Kings, and Lord of Lords'![103] O that all these sons 'of the right hand of the Most High'[104] may be holy as he is holy![105] Wise with the 'wisdom that sitteth by his throne',[106] like him who is the eternal wisdom of the Father! No respecters of persons, as he is none; but 'rendering to every man according to his works':[107] like him inflexibly, inexorably just, though pitiful and of tender mercy![108] So shall they be terrible indeed to them that do evil, as 'not bearing the sword in vain'.[109] So shall the laws of our land have their full use and due honour, and the throne of our King be still 'established in righteousness'.[110]

---

97 Rev. 22:4.
99 Cf. Ps. 9:8.
101 Cf. Rom. 13:4.
103 Cf. Rev. 19:16.
105 See 1 Pet. 1:15-16.
107 Prov. 24:12; Matt. 16:27.
109 Cf. Rom. 13:4.

98 Rev. 22:5.
100 Isa. 52:7.
102 Ps. 94:2.
104 Ps. 77:10.
106 Wisd. 9:4.
108 Jas. 5:11.
110 Prov. 25:5.

2. Ye truly honourable men, whom God and the King have commissioned in a lower degree to administer justice, may not ye be compared to those ministering spirits who will attend the Judge coming in the clouds? May you, like them, burn with love to
5 God and man! May you love righteousness and hate iniquity![111] May ye all minister in your several spheres (such honour hath God given you also!) to them that shall be heirs of salvation,[112] and to the glory of your great Sovereign! May ye remain the establishers of peace, the blessing and ornaments of your country,
10 the protectors of a guilty land, the guardian angels of all that are round about you!

3. You whose office it is to execute what is given you in charge by him before whom you stand, how nearly are you concerned to resemble those that stand before the face of the Son of man!
15 Those 'servants of his that do his pleasure',[113] 'and hearken to the voice of his words'.[114] Does it not highly import *you* to be as uncorrupt as *them*? To approve yourselves the servants of God? To do justly and love mercy;[115] to do to all as ye would they should do to you?[116] So shall that great Judge, under whose eye you
20 continually stand, say to you also, 'Well done, good and faithful servants: enter ye into the joy of your Lord!'[117]

4. Suffer me to add a few words to all of you who are this day present before the Lord. Should not you bear it in your minds all the day long that a more awful day is coming? A large assembly
25 this! But what is it to that which every eye will then behold—the general assembly of all the children of men that ever lived on the face of the whole earth![118] A few will stand at the judgment seat this day, to be judged touching what shall be laid to their charge. And they are now reserved in prison, perhaps in chains, till they
30 are brought forth to be tried and sentenced. But we shall all, I that speak and you that hear, 'stand at the judgment seat of Christ'.[119] And we are now reserved on this earth, which is not our home,[120] in this prison of flesh and blood, perhaps many of us in chains of darkness too,[121] till we are ordered to be brought forth. Here a

---

[111] See Heb. 1:9.
[113] Ps. 103:21 (BCP).
[115] Mic. 6:8.
[117] Cf. Matt. 25:21, 23.
[118] Cf. Tertullian, *De spectaculis*, xxx.
[119] Cf. Rom. 14:10.
[120] Cf. No. 3, '*Awake, Thou That Sleepest*', II.5 and n.
[121] 2 Pet. 2:4.

[112] See Heb. 1:14.
[114] Ps. 103:20 (BCP).
[116] See Matt. 7:12; Luke 6:31.

man is questioned concerning one or two facts[122] which he is supposed to have committed. There we are to give an account of all our works, from the cradle to the grave:[123] of all our words; of all our desires and tempers, all the thoughts and intents of our hearts;[124] of all the use we have made of our various talents, 5 whether of mind, body, or fortune, till God said, 'Give an account of thy stewardship; for thou mayest be no longer steward.'[125] In this court it is possible some who are guilty may escape for want of evidence. But there is no want of evidence in that court. All men with whom you had the most secret intercourse, who were privy to 10 all your designs and actions, are ready before your face. So are all the spirits of darkness, who inspired evil designs, and assisted in the execution of them. So are all the angels of God—those 'eyes of the Lord that run to and fro over all the earth'[126]—who watched over your soul, and laboured for your good so far as you would 15 permit. So is your own conscience, a thousand witnesses in one,[127] now no more capable of being either blinded or silenced, but constrained to know and to speak the naked truth touching all your thoughts and words and actions. And is conscience as a thousand witnesses? Yea, but God is as a thousand consciences! 20 O who can stand before the face of 'the great God, even our Saviour, Jesus Christ'![128]

See, see! He cometh! He maketh the clouds his chariots. He rideth upon the wings of the wind! A devouring fire goeth before him, and after him a flame burneth! See, he sitteth upon his 25 throne, clothed with light as with a garment, arrayed with majesty and honour![129] Behold his eyes are as a flame of fire, his voice as the sound of many waters![130]

How will ye escape? Will ye call to the mountains to fall on you, the rocks to cover you?[131] Alas, the mountains themselves, the 30

---

[122] An already obsolescent synonym for 'acts' or 'deeds'; cf. *OED* and Johnson's *Dictionary*.

[123] Cf. John Dyer, 'Grongar Hill' (1726), line 89.

[124] See Heb. 4:12.

[125] Luke 16:2.

[126] Cf. Zech. 4:10.

[127] Cf. Quintillian, *Institut. Oratoriae*, V. xi. 41 (quoting a proverb): '*Conscientiam mille testes*' ('conscience is a thousand witnesses'). Cf. Robert Greene, *Philomela* (1592), and Thomas Fuller, *The Holy State of Recreations* (1642), 'He that sinnes against his conscience sinnes with a witness.' There was an old Latin tag, '*in foro conscientiae*' ('in conscience's court'); see also No. 105, 'On Conscience', espec. I.7 and n.

[128] Cf. Titus 2:13.

[129] See Ps. 104:1-3.

[130] See Rev. 1:14-15.

[131] See Rev. 6:16.

rocks, the earth, the heavens, are just ready to flee away! Can ye prevent the sentence? Wherewith? With all the substance of thy house,[132] with thousands of gold and silver? Blind wretch! Thou camest naked from thy mother's womb, and [shalt move][133] naked
5   into eternity.[134] Hear the Lord, the Judge! 'Come ye blessed of my Father! Inherit the kingdom prepared for you from the foundation of the world.'[135] Joyful sound! How widely different from that voice which echoes through the expanse of heaven, 'Depart, ye cursed, into everlasting fire, prepared for the devil
10 and his angels!'[136] And who is he that can prevent or retard the full execution of either sentence? Vain hope! Lo, 'hell is moved from beneath'[137] to receive those who are ripe for destruction! And the 'everlasting doors lift up their heads' that the heirs of glory may come in![138]

15 5. 'What manner of persons (then) ought we to be, in all holy conversation and godliness?'[139] We know it cannot be long before the Lord will descend 'with the voice of the archangel, and the trumpet of God';[140] when every one of us shall appear before him and 'give account of his own works'.[141] 'Wherefore, beloved,
20 seeing ye look for these things',[142] seeing ye know he will come and will not tarry,[143] 'be diligent that ye may be found of him in peace, without spot, and blameless.'[144] Why should ye not? Why should one of you be found on the left hand at his appearing? He 'willeth not that any should perish, but that all should come to
25 *repentance*';[145] by repentance to faith in a bleeding Lord; by faith to spotless love, to the full image of God renewed in the heart, and producing all holiness of conversation. Can you doubt of this

---

[132] See Prov. 6:31; S. of S. 8:7.

[133] Orig., 'and more naked' (as also the text of 1771), altered in the separate edns. of 1782 and thereafter to 'shalt go'. But it seems likely that the printer had omitted 'shalt' in error, that 'move' was then misprinted as 'more', and this then had gone unnoticed by Wesley.

[134] See Job 1:21.

[135] Matt. 25:34.

[136] Matt. 25:41.

[137] Cf. Isa. 14:9.

[138] See Ps. 24:7,9.

[139] Cf. 2 Pet. 3:11.

[140] Cf. 1 Thess. 4:16.

[141] Cf. Luke 16:2; Rev. 20:12.

[142] 2 Pet. 3:14.

[143] Heb. 10:37.

[144] Cf. 2 Pet. 3:14.

[145] Cf. 2 Pet. 3:9.

when you remember the Judge of all[146] is likewise 'the Saviour of all'?[147] Hath he not bought you with his own blood,[148] that ye might 'not perish, but have everlasting life'?[149] O make proof of his mercy rather than his justice! Of his love rather than the thunder of his power![150] 'He is not far from every one of us;'[151] and he is now come, 'not to condemn, but to save the world'.[152] He standeth in the midst! Sinner, doth he not now, even now, knock at the door of thy heart?[153] O that thou mayst know, at least *in this thy day*, the things that belong unto thy peace![154] O that ye may now give yourselves to him who 'gave himself for you',[155] in humble faith, in holy, active, patient love! So shall ye rejoice with exceeding joy[156] *in his day*, when he cometh in the clouds of heaven.[157]

[146] Heb. 12:23.
[147] 1 Tim. 4:10.
[148] See Acts 20:28.
[149] John 3:16.
[150] Job 26:14.
[151] Cf. Acts 17:27.
[152] Cf. John 3:17.
[153] See Rev. 3:20.
[154] See Luke 19:42.
[155] Cf. Gal. 2:20.
[156] See Matt. 2:10.
[157] See Matt. 24:30, etc.

THE MEANS OF GRACE

AN INTRODUCTORY COMMENT

This sermon carries us back to Wesley's earlier conflicts with the Moravians and other 'quietists' about the role and function of 'ordinances' in general and their relation to the spontaneous experience of 'assurance' in particular. There is no way of dating it exactly; Wesley has only a single mention of preaching on Malachi 3:7 (JWJ, June 22, 1741). What is clear, however, is that a sizeable group of Methodists in 1746 still continued to regard all 'outward observances' as superfluous, or even harmful, in their spiritual life. Considering themselves to be true evangelicals, they understood their conversions and 'baptisms of the Spirit' as having superseded their water baptisms, the Eucharist, and all other sacramental acts (or 'ordinances' as they preferred to call them). It is these Methodist *'quietists' who are the primary audience for this sermon. Wesley's purpose is to enforce upon them the validity, and even the necessity, of 'the means of grace' as taught and administered in the Church of England.*

He could remember, better than they, how disruptive this issue had been in the early days of the Revival, beginning with the new society in Fetter Lane. Actually, the Fourth Extract from his Journal *is a circumstantial account of his rift with the Moravians—and this question of ordinances is a crucial issue in that dispute. Wesley's view of the Moravian position is summarized in his entry for Sunday, November 4, 1739:*

In the evening I met the women of our society at Fetter Lane, where some of our brethren strongly intimated that none of them had any true faith, and then asserted, in plain terms, (1), that till they had true faith, they ought to be still, that is (as they explained themselves), 'to abstain from "the means of grace", as they are called—the Lord's Supper in particular'; (2), 'that the ordinances are not means of grace, there being no other means than Christ'.

His own, Anglican, conclusion is given in the entry for the following Wednesday (November 7):

What is to be inferred from this undeniable matter of fact—one that had not faith received it in the Lord's Supper? Why (1), that there are 'means of grace', i.e., outward ordinances, whereby the inward grace of God is ordinarily conveyed to man, *whereby the faith that brings salvation is conveyed to them who before had it not; (2), that* one of these means is the Lord's Supper; *and (3), that* he who has not this faith ought to wait for it in the use both of this and of the other means which God hath ordained.

The upshot of this controversy had been Wesley's abandonment of the Fetter Lane society, his forming of the new society in Upper Moorfields at the Foundery, and his constant advocacy thereafter of an equal emphasis upon 'conversion' and 'assurance', on the one hand, and a faithful, expectant usage of all 'the means of grace', on the other. The result is a sort of 'high-church' evangelicalism—a rare combination, then and since.

The controverted phrase, 'the means of grace', appears (apparently for the first time) in 'The General Thanksgiving' in the BCP of 1661–62 and was, quite probably, the contribution of Bishop Edward Reynolds of Norwich, a former Nonconformist and still something of a 'puritan' in his theology. Wesley also cites a phrase from the Catechism as composed for the Prayer Book of James I and re-incorporated in the 1662 version. The question, 'What meanest thou by this word Sacrament?' is answered thus: 'I mean an outward and visible sign of an inward and spiritual grace given unto us, ordained by Christ himself, as a means whereby we receive the same, and a pledge to assure us thereof' (emphasis added). Following the Ordinal (1550, and only slightly revised in 1661–62) used at Wesley's own ordination as priest, he had vowed 'always . . . to minister the doctrine and Sacraments, and the discipline, of Christ . . .' and to 'be diligent in prayers, and in the reading of the Holy Scriptures and in such studies as help to the knowledge of the same. . . .'. Finally, he knew how carefully intertwined faith, prayer, the Sacraments, and Scripture had been in the Edwardian Homilies. An eminent Anglican liturgiologist, Professor Massey Shepherd, has written, in response to a personal inquiry on this point: 'Wesley's threefold "means of grace" have a sound basis in the official Anglican formularies: Prayer Book, Ordinal, Homilies, Catechism.'

But how to appropriate this tradition for people whose sacramental sense had atrophied and whose spontaneous experiences of grace were so much more vivid than their usual experiences of its ordinances and means? How to make clear the difference between the proper use and possible abuse of such means or to suggest how strenuous a 'waiting upon the Lord' (II.7, III.1, IV.4-5) can, and should be, in the Christian life? These are the tasks attempted in this 'discourse' (II.1).

The Means of Grace

Malachi 3:7

Ye are gone away from mine ordinances,
and have not kept them.

5   [I].1. But are there any 'ordinances' now, since life and
immortality were brought to light by the gospel?[1] Are there, under
the Christian dispensation, any 'means' ordained of God as the
usual channels of his grace? This question could never have been
proposed in the apostolical church unless by one who openly
10   avowed himself to be a heathen, the whole body of Christians
being agreed that Christ had ordained certain outward means for
conveying his grace into the souls of men. Their constant practice
set this beyond all dispute; for so long as 'all that believed were
together, and had all things common,'[a] 'they continued
15   steadfastly in the teaching of the apostles, and in the breaking of
bread, and in prayers.'[b]
   2. But in process of time, when 'the love of many waxed cold,'[2]
some began to mistake the *means* for the *end*, and to place religion
rather in doing those outward works than in a heart renewed after
20   the image of God. They forgot that 'the end of' every
'commandment is love, out of a pure heart, with faith unfeigned:'[3]
the loving the Lord their God with all their heart, and their
neighbour as themselves;[4] and the being purified from pride,
anger, and evil desire, by a 'faith of the operation of God'.[5] Others
25   seemed to imagine that though religion did not principally consist
in these outward means, yet there was something in them
wherewith God was well-pleased, something that would still
make them acceptable in his sight, though they were not exact in
the weightier matters of the law, in justice, mercy, and the love of
30   God.[6]

[a] Acts 2:44.   [b] Ver. 42 [cf. *Notes*].

[1] See 2 Tim. 1:10.   [2] Cf. Matt. 24:12.
[3] Cf. 1 Tim. 1:5.
[4] See Matt. 22:37, 39, etc.
[5] Col. 2:12.
[6] See Matt. 23:23.

3. It is evident, in those who abused them thus, they did not conduce to the end for which they were ordained. Rather, the things which should have been for their health were to them an occasion of falling.[7] They were so far from receiving any blessing therein, that they only drew down a curse upon their head; so far from growing more heavenly in heart and life, that they were twofold more the children of hell than before.[8] Others clearly perceiving that these means did not convey the grace of God to those children of the devil, began from this particular case to draw a general conclusion, 'that they were not means of conveying the grace of God.'

4. Yet the number of those who *abused* the ordinances of God was far greater than of those who *despised* them, till certain men arose, not only of great understanding (sometimes joined with considerable learning), but who likewise appeared to be men of love, experimentally acquainted with true, inward religion. Some of these were burning and shining lights,[9] persons famous in their generations,[10] and such as had well deserved of the church of Christ for standing in the gap[11] against the overflowings of ungodliness.

It cannot be supposed that these holy and venerable men intended any more at first than to show that outward religion is nothing worth without the religion of the heart; that 'God is a Spirit, and they who worship him must worship him in spirit and truth;'[12] that, therefore, external worship is lost labour without a heart devoted to God; that the outward ordinances of God then profit much when they advance inward holiness, but when they advance it not are unprofitable and void, are lighter than vanity;[13] yea, that when they are used, as it were, *in the place* of this, they are an utter abomination to the Lord.[14]

5. Yet is it not strange if some of these, being strongly convinced of that horrid profanation of the ordinances of God which had spread itself over the whole church, and wellnigh driven true religion out of the world,[15] in their fervent zeal for the

---

[7] See Rom. 14:13.
[8] See Matt. 23:15.
[9] See John 5:35.   [10] See Eccles. 44:1-7.
[11] See Ezek. 22:30.   [12] Cf. John 4:24.
[13] Ps. 62:9.   [14] See Deut. 7:25, etc.
[15] An echo from the Preface, §6 (above, p. 106): 'formality, . . . mere outside religion, which has almost driven heart-religion out of the world'. See also No. 25, 'Sermon on the Mount, V', IV.13 and n.

glory of God and the recovery of souls from that fatal delusion, spake as if outward religion were *absolutely nothing*, as if it had *no* place in the religion of Christ. It is not surprising at all if they should not always have expressed themselves with sufficient
5 caution; so that unwary hearers might believe they condemned all outward means as altogether unprofitable, and as not designed of God to be the ordinary channels of conveying his grace into the souls of men.[16]

Nay, it is not impossible some of these holy men did at length
10 themselves fall into this opinion: in particular those who, not by choice, but by the providence of God, were cut off from all these ordinances—perhaps wandering up and down, having no certain abiding-place, or dwelling in dens and caves of the earth.[17] These, experiencing the grace of God in themselves, though they were
15 deprived of all outward means,[18] might infer that the same grace would be given to them who of set purpose abstained from them.

6. And experience shows how easily this notion spreads, and insinuates itself into the minds of men: especially of those who are throughly awakened out of the sleep of death,[19] and begin to feel
20 the weight of their sins a burden too heavy to be borne.[20] These are usually impatient of their present state, and trying every way to escape from it. They are always ready to catch at any new thing, any new proposal of ease or happiness. They have probably tried most outward means, and found no ease in them—it may be,
25 more and more of remorse and fear and sorrow and condemnation. It is easy, therefore, to persuade these that it is better for them to abstain from all those means. They are already weary of striving (as it seems) in vain, of labouring in the fire;[21] and are therefore glad of any pretence to cast aside that wherein their
30 soul had no pleasure; to give over the painful strife, and sink down into an indolent inactivity.

---

[16] As among the Quakers and at least some of the English Moravians. Cf. Francis Higginson's attack, *A Brief Relation of the Irreligion of the Northern Quakers* (1653), vii. 30-33. See also George Fox and James Nayler on 'ordinances' in Barbour and Roberts, *Early Quaker Writings*, pp. 256, 258, as well as Robert Barclay's *Apology*, ch. xi, 'Concerning Baptism, and Bread and Wine'. As for the Moravians, cf. JWJ, Dec. 3, 1739.
[17] Heb. 11:38.
[18] See below, No. 106, 'On Faith, Heb. 11:6', I.4, for the story of the Moslem, Ibn ben Yokdan, as an example of this same circumstance.
[19] Ps. 13:3.
[20] See Ps. 38:4.
[21] See Hab. 2:13.

II.1. In the following discourse I propose to examine at large whether there are any means of grace.

— By 'means of grace' I understand outward signs, words, or actions ordained of God, and appointed for this end—to be the *ordinary* channels whereby he might convey to men preventing, 5 justifying, or sanctifying grace.

— I use this expression, 'means of grace', because I know none better, and because it has been generally used in the Christian church for many ages: in particular by our own church, which directs us to bless God both for the 'means of grace and hope of 10 glory';[22] and teaches us that a sacrament is 'an outward sign of inward *grace*, and a *means* whereby we receive the same'.[23]

The chief of these means are prayer, whether in secret or with the great congregation; searching the Scriptures (which implies reading, hearing, and meditating thereon) and receiving the 15 Lord's Supper, eating bread and drinking wine in remembrance of him; and these we believe to be ordained of God as the ordinary channels of conveying his grace to the souls of men.[24]

2. But we allow that the whole value of the means depends on their actual subservience to the end of religion; that consequently 20 all these means, when separate from the end, are less than nothing, and vanity;[25] that if they do not actually conduce to the knowledge and love of God they are not acceptable in his sight; yea, rather, they are an abomination before him; a stink in his nostrils; he is weary to bear them—above all if they are used as a 25 kind of 'commutation'[26] for the religion they were designed to subserve. It is not easy to find words for the enormous folly and wickedness of thus turning God's arms against himself, of

---

[22] BCP, 'A General Thanksgiving' (57). Cf. Massey H. Shepherd, Jr., *American Prayer Book Commentary* (New York, Oxford University Press, 1950), pp. 17-19.

[23] BCP, Catechism, answer to Q., 'What meanest thou by this word "Sacrament"?' For sources of the idea of sacraments as signs, cf. St. Thomas, *Summa Theologica*, III, Q. 60, arts. 2 and 4; Hugh of St. Victor, *De sacramentis*; and St. Augustine, in his *First Catechetical Instruction* (*De catechezandis rudibus*), xxvi. 50: '. . . these symbols of divine things are, it is true, visible, but invisible realities are honoured thereby'. Cf. *De Civ.Dei*, X.v: 'An external offering is a visible sacrament of an invisible grace, i.e., a holy sign'.

[24] Note Wesley's omission of baptism from his listing of the 'chief means of grace'.

[25] Isa. 40:17.

[26] A forensic term, defined by Chambers's *Cyclopaedia* as 'a change of penalty or punishment, . . . as when death is commuted for, by banishment or perpetual imprisonment . . .'. The same sense is given the term by Dr. Johnson; see also *OED*. For another instance in Wesley, see below, No. 22, 'Sermon on the Mount, II', I.10.

keeping Christianity out of the heart by those very means which were ordained for the bringing it in.

3. We allow likewise that all outward means whatever, if separate from the Spirit of God, cannot profit at all, cannot conduce in any degree either to the knowledge or love of God. Without controversy, the help that is done upon earth, he doth it himself.[27] It is he alone who, by his own almighty power, worketh in us what is pleasing in his sight.[28] And all outward things, unless he work in them and by them, are mere weak and beggarly elements.[29] Whosoever therefore imagines there is any intrinsic *power* in any means whatsoever does greatly err, not knowing the Scriptures, neither the power of God.[30] We know that there is no inherent power in the words that are spoken in prayer, in the letter of Scripture read, the sound thereof heard, or the bread and wine received in the Lord's Supper; but that it is God alone who is the giver of every good gift,[31] the author of all grace; that the whole power is of him, whereby through any of these there is any blessing conveyed to our soul. We know likewise that he is able to give the same grace, though there were no means on the face of the earth. In this sense we may affirm that with regard to God there is no such thing as means, seeing he is equally able to work whatsoever pleaseth him by any or by none at all.[32]

4. We allow farther that the use of all means whatever will never atone for one sin; that it is the blood of Christ alone whereby any sinner can be reconciled to God;[33] there being no other propitiation for our sins,[34] no other fountain for sin and uncleanness. Every believer in Christ is deeply convinced that there is no *merit* but in him; that there is no *merit* in any of his own works; not in uttering the prayer, or searching the Scripture, or hearing the Word of God, or eating of that bread and drinking of that cup;[35] so that if no more be intended by the expression some have used, 'Christ is the only means of grace,'[36] than this—that he

---

[27] See Ps. 74:13, but only in the BCP; see also AV, ver. 12.
[28] 1 John 3:22.
[29] See Gal. 4:9.
[30] Matt. 22:29.
[31] Jas. 1:17.
[32] See Eccles. 8:3. See also St. Thomas, *Summa Theologica*, III, Q. 61, art. 1.
[33] See Rom. 5:10.
[34] 1 John 2:2; 4:10.				[35] See 1 Cor. 11:28.
[36] Cf. JWJ, Apr. 25, 1740, where Molther is reported as maintaining that there is 'no such thing as means of grace, but Christ only'. See also below, IV.3.

is the only *meritorious cause* of it[37]—it cannot be gainsaid by any who know the grace of God.

5. Yet once more. We allow (though it is a melancholy truth) that a large proportion of those who are called Christians do to this day abuse the means of grace to the destruction of their souls. This is doubtless the case with all those who rest content in the form of godliness without the power.[38] Either they fondly presume they are Christians already, because they do thus and thus, although Christ was never yet revealed in their hearts, nor the love of God shed abroad[39] therein: or else they suppose they shall infallibly be so, barely because they use these means; idly dreaming (though perhaps hardly conscious thereof) either that there is some kind of *power* therein whereby sooner or later (they know not when) they shall certainly be made holy; or that there is a sort of *merit* in using them, which will surely move God to give them holiness or accept them without it.

6. So little do they understand that great foundation of the whole Christian building, 'By grace ye are saved.'[40] Ye are saved from your sins, from the guilt and power thereof, ye are restored to the favour and image of God, not for any works, merits, or deservings of yours, but by the free *grace*, the mere mercy of God through the merits of his well-beloved Son.[41] Ye are thus saved, not by any power, wisdom, or strength which is in you or in any other creature, but merely through the grace or power of the Holy Ghost,[42] which worketh all in all.[43]

7. But the main question remains. We know this salvation is the gift and the work of God. But how (may one say, who is convinced he hath it not) may I attain thereto? If you say, 'Believe, and thou shalt be saved,'[44] he answers, 'True; but how shall I believe?' You reply, 'Wait upon God.' 'Well. But how am I to wait? In the means of grace, or out of them? Am I to wait for the grace of God which bringeth salvation[45] by using these means, or by laying them aside?'

[37] For Wesley's decisive stand for the doctrine of Christ as the 'meritorious cause' of grace (as over against its 'formal cause'), see above, Intro., pp. 80-81, and below, No. 20, *The Lord Our Righteousness*.
[38] See 2 Tim. 3:5.
[39] See Rom. 5:5.
[40] Eph. 2:5, 8; cf. above, No. 1, *Salvation by Faith*, text, and III. 7-8.
[41] See Mark 12:6.
[42] Rom. 15:13.
[43] 1 Cor. 12:6.
[44] Cf. Acts 16:31.
[45] Titus 2:11.

8. It cannot possibly be conceived that the Word of God should give no direction in so important a point; or that the Son of God who came down from heaven for us men and for our salvation[46] should have left us undetermined with regard to a question wherein our salvation is so nearly concerned.

And in fact he hath not left us undetermined; he hath shown us the way wherein we should go. We have only to consult the oracles of God, to inquire what is written there. And if we simply abide by their decision, there can no possible doubt remain.

III.1. According to this, according to the decision of Holy Writ, all who desire the grace of God are to wait for it in the means which he hath ordained; in using, not in laying them aside.[47]

And first, all who desire the grace of God are to wait for it in the way of *prayer*. This is the express direction of our Lord himself. In his Sermon upon the Mount, after explaining at large wherein religion consists, and describing the main branches of it, he adds: 'Ask, and it shall be given you; seek, and ye shall find; knock, and it shall be opened unto you. For everyone that asketh, receiveth; and he that seeketh, findeth; and to him that knocketh, it shall be opened.'[c] Here we are in the plainest manner directed to ask in order to, or as a *means* of, receiving; to seek in order to find the grace of God, the pearl of great price;[48] and to knock, to continue asking and seeking, if we would enter into his kingdom.

2. That no doubt might remain our Lord labours this point in a more peculiar manner. He appeals to every man's own heart: 'What man is there of you, who, if his son ask bread, will give him a stone? Or if he ask a fish, will he give him a serpent? If ye then, being evil, know how to give good gifts unto your children, how much more shall your Father which is in heaven'—the Father of angels and men, the Father of the spirits of all flesh—'give good things to them that ask him?'[d] Or, as he expresses himself on

---

[c] Matt. 7:7-8.   [d] Ver. 9-11.

---

[46] BCP, Communion, Nicene Creed.

[47] Wesley's idea of 'waiting upon the Lord' is characteristically dynamic; it never meant 'quietism' or 'stillness'. The Christian believer is to be zealous in *all* works of piety and mercy. None of these affects God's gratuities, but they can help prepare our own hearts to receive God's gifts as given; see below, IV.5. See also, above, No. 6, 'The Righteousness of Faith', III.4 and n. For a longer account of the controversy about 'waiting', prayer, searching the Scriptures and a Christian's need of the Sacraments, see JWJ, Dec. 31, 1739, and June 22-28, 1740.   [48] Matt. 13:46.

another occasion, including all good things in one, 'How much more shall your heavenly Father give the Holy Spirit to them that ask him?'[e] It should be particularly observed here that the persons directed to ask had not then received the Holy Spirit. Nevertheless our Lord directs them to use this means, and promises that it should be effectual; that upon asking they should receive the Holy Spirit from him whose mercy is over all his works.

3. The absolute necessity of using this means if we would receive any gift from God yet farther appears from that remarkable passage which immediately precedes these words: 'And he said unto them' (whom he had just been teaching how to pray) 'which of you shall have a friend, and shall go unto him at midnight, and shall say unto him, Friend, lend me three loaves; . . . and he from within shall answer, Trouble me not. . . . I cannot rise and give thee: I say unto you, though he will not rise and give him, because he is his friend, yet because of his importunity he will rise, and give him as many as he needeth. And I say unto you, ask and it shall be given you.'[f] 'Though he will not give him because he is his friend, yet because of his importunity he will rise and give him as many as he needeth.' How could our blessed Lord more plainly declare that we may receive of God by this means, by importunately asking, what otherwise we should not receive at all!

4. 'He spake also another parable to this end, that men ought always to pray, and not to faint,' till through this means they should receive of God whatsoever petition they asked of him: 'There was in a city a judge which feared not God, neither regarded man. And there was a widow in that city, and she came unto him, saying, Avenge me of my adversary. And he would not for a while; but afterward he said within himself, Though I fear not God, nor regard man, yet because this widow troubleth me I will avenge her, lest by her continual coming she weary me.'[g] The application of this our Lord himself hath made. 'Hear what the unjust judge saith!' Because she continues to ask, because she will take no denial, therefore I will avenge her. 'And shall not God avenge his own elect which cry day and night unto him? I tell you

---

[e] Luke 11:13.
[f] Luke 11: 5, 7-9.
[g] Luke 18:1-5.

he will avenge them speedily'⁴⁹—if they 'pray and faint not'.⁵⁰

5. A direction equally full and express to wait for the blessings of God in private prayer, together with a positive promise that by this means we shall obtain the request of our lips, he hath given us in those well-known words: 'Enter into thy closet; and when thou hast shut thy door, pray to thy Father which is in secret; and thy Father which seeth in secret shall reward thee openly.'ʰ

6. If it be possible for any direction to be more clear, it is that which God hath given us by the Apostle with regard to prayer of every kind, public and private, and the blessing annexed thereto. 'If any of you lack wisdom, let him ask of God, that giveth to all men liberally' (if they ask; otherwise 'ye have not, because ye ask not'ⁱ), 'and upbraideth not, and it shall be given him.'ʲ

If it be objected, 'But this is no direction to unbelievers, to them who know not the pardoning grace of God; for the Apostle adds, "But let him ask in faith;"otherwise, "let him not think that he shall receive anything of the Lord." '⁵¹ I answer, the meaning of the word 'faith' in this place is fixed by the Apostle himself (as if it were on purpose to obviate this objection) in the words immediately following: 'Let him ask in faith, nothing wavering,' nothing *doubting, μηδὲν διακρινόμενος*—not doubting God heareth his prayer, and will fulfil the desire of his heart.

The gross, blasphemous absurdity of supposing 'faith' in this place to be taken in the full Christian meaning appears hence: it is supposing the Holy Ghost to direct a man who knows he has not this faith (which is here termed 'wisdom') to ask it of God, with a positive promise that 'it shall be given him';⁵² and then immediately to subjoin that it shall not be given him unless he have it before he asks for it! But who can bear such a supposition? From this Scripture, therefore, as well as those cited above, we must infer that all who desire the grace of God are to wait for it in the way of prayer.

7. Secondly, all who desire the grace of God are to wait for it in 'searching the Scriptures'.

ʰ Matt. 6:6.   ⁱ Jas. 4:2.
ʲ [Jas.] 1:5.

---

⁴⁹ Luke 18:7-8.
⁵⁰ Luke 18:1.
⁵¹ Cf. Jas. 1:6-7.
⁵² Jas. 1:5.

Our Lord's direction with regard to the use of this means is likewise plain and clear. 'Search the Scriptures', saith he to the unbelieving Jews, 'for [. . .] they [. . .] testify of me.'ᵏ And for this very end did he direct them to search the Scriptures, that they might *believe in him.*

The objection that this is not a command, but only an assertion that they did 'search the Scriptures', is shamelessly false. I desire those who urge it to let us know how a command can be more clearly expressed than in those terms, Ἐρευνᾶτε τὰς γραφάς. It is as peremptory as so many words can make it.⁵³

And what a blessing from God attends the use of this means appears from what is recorded concerning the Bereans, who, after hearing St. Paul, 'searched the Scriptures daily, whether those things were so. Therefore many of them believed'—found the grace of God in the way which he had ordained.¹

It is probable, indeed, that in some of those who had 'received the word with all readiness of mind',⁵⁴ 'faith came (as the same Apostle speaks) by hearing,'⁵⁵ and was only confirmed by *reading* the Scriptures. But it was observed above that under the general term of 'searching the Scriptures' both hearing, reading, and meditating are contained.

8. And that this is a means whereby God not only gives, but also confirms and increases true wisdom, we learn from the words of St. Paul to Timothy: 'From a child thou hast known the Holy

---

ᵏ John 5:39.
¹ Acts 17:11-12.

---

⁵³ The second person plural *indicative* has the same form in Greek as the *imperative*. It is, therefore, a matter of interpretation as to whether ἐρευνᾶτε is a command or an indicative statement. In his third edition of the *Notes* (but not in the first two) Wesley had decided that it meant 'a plain command to all men'; here he was following the *tendency* of the early Fathers (e.g., Irenaeus, Tertullian, Origen, and the Latin Vulgate). Henry, *Exposition, loc. cit.*, stresses the fact that there is an open question here, though he inclined to the imperative; but Poole, *Annotations, loc. cit.*, had recognized that 'the words may be read imperatively (as our translation [AV] readeth them) *or* indicatively', and preferred the latter. Most modern commentators read ἐρευνᾶτε as indicative—thus emphasizing the point that the Scriptures may be *searched* without any prior guarantees of valid understanding in the search alone. Cf. J. H. Bernard, *Gospel According to St. John* (1928) in the *International Critical Commentary*.

For a further comment on Wesley's usage of imperatives and futures, cf. Nos. 21, 'Sermon on the Mount, I', §5 and n.; and 25, 'Sermon on the Mount, V', II.1.
⁵⁴ Acts 17:11.
⁵⁵ Cf. Rom. 10:17.

Scriptures, which are able to make thee wise unto salvation, through faith which is in Christ Jesus.'[m] The same truth (namely, that this is the great means God has ordained for conveying his manifold grace to man) is delivered, in the fullest manner that can
5 be conceived, in the words which immediately follow: 'All Scripture is given by inspiration of God' (consequently, all Scripture is infallibly true), 'and is profitable for doctrine, for reproof, for correction, for instruction in righteousness;' to the end 'that the man of God may be perfect, throughly furnished
10 unto all good works.'[n]

9. It should be observed that this is spoken primarily and directly of the Scriptures which Timothy had 'known from a child'; which must have been those of the Old Testament, for the New was not then wrote. How far then was St. Paul (though he
15 was 'not a whit behind the very chief of the apostles',[56] nor therefore, I presume, behind any man now upon earth) from making light of the Old Testament! Behold this, lest ye one day 'wonder and perish',[57] ye who make so small account of one half of the oracles of God![58] Yea, and that half of which the Holy Ghost
20 expressly declares that it is 'profitable', as a means ordained of God for this very thing, 'for doctrine, for reproof, for correction, for instruction in righteousness': to the end [that] 'the man of God may be perfect, throughly furnished unto all good works'.

10. Nor is this profitable only for the men of God, for those
25 who walk already in the light of his countenance,[59] but also for those who are yet in darkness, seeking him whom they know not. Thus St. Peter: 'We have also a more sure word of prophecy'[60]—literally, 'And we have the prophetic word more sure' ($\kappa\alpha\grave{\iota}$ $\check{\epsilon}\chi o\mu\epsilon\nu$ $\beta\epsilon\beta\alpha\iota\acute{o}\tau\epsilon\rho o\nu$ $\tau\grave{o}\nu$ $\pi\rho o\varphi\eta\tau\iota\kappa\grave{o}\nu$ $\lambda\acute{o}\gamma o\nu$),
30 confirmed by our being 'eye-witnesses of his majesty', and 'hearing the voice which came from the excellent glory'[61]—'unto which (prophetic word; so he styles the Holy Scriptures) ye do well that ye take heed, as unto a light that shineth in a dark place,

---

[m] 2 Tim. 3:15. [n] 2 Tim. 3:16-17.

---

[56] Cf. 2 Cor. 11:5. [57] Acts 13:41.
[58] There was a Marcionite tendency in many Protestant traditions 'to make light of the Old Testament' and to focus on the gospel as over against the law. Wesley's response here is typically Anglican in its substance, if not in its hermeneutic.
[59] See Ps. 89:16 (BCP). [60] Cf. 2 Pet. 1:19.
[61] Cf. 2 Pet. 1:16-17.

until the day dawn, and the day-star arise in your hearts.'[o] Let all, therefore, who desire that day to dawn upon their hearts, wait for it in 'searching the Scriptures'.

11. Thirdly, all who desire an increase of the grace of God are to wait for it in partaking of the Lord's Supper. For this also is a direction himself hath given: 'The same night in which he was betrayed, he took bread, and brake it, and said, Take, eat; this is my body' (that is, the sacred sign of my body). 'This do in remembrance of me. Likewise he took the cup, saying, This cup is the New Testament' (or covenant) 'in my blood' (the sacred sign of that covenant): 'this do ye . . . in remembrance of me. For as often as ye eat this bread and drink this cup, ye do show forth the Lord's death till he come'[p]—ye openly exhibit the same by these visible signs, before God, and angels, and men; ye manifest your solemn remembrance of his death, till he cometh in the clouds of heaven.

Only 'let a man (first) examine himself,' whether he understand the nature and design of this holy institution, and whether he really desire to be himself made conformable to the death of Christ; 'and so (nothing doubting) let him eat of that bread and drink of that cup.'[q]

Here then the direction first given by our Lord is expressly repeated by the Apostle: 'Let him eat,' 'let him drink' (ἐσθιέτω, πινέτω—both in the imperative mood); words not implying a bare permission only, but a clear explicit command; a command to all those either who already are filled with peace and joy in believing, or who can truly say, 'The remembrance of our sins is grievous unto us; the burden of them is intolerable.'[62]

12. And that this is also an ordinary stated means of receiving the grace of God is evident from those words of the Apostle which occur in the preceding chapter: 'The cup of blessing which we bless, is it not the communion (or communication) of the blood of Christ? The bread which we break, is it not the communion of the body of Christ?'[r] Is not the eating of that bread, and the drinking of that cup, the outward, visible means whereby God conveys into our souls all that spiritual grace, that righteousness, and peace,

[o] 2 Pet. 1:19.
[p] 1 Cor. 11:23-26.
[q] Ver. 28.
[r] 1 Cor. 10:16.

---

[62] BCP, Communion, General Confession.

and joy in the Holy Ghost,[63] which were purchased by the body of
Christ once broken and the blood of Christ once shed for us? Let
all, therefore, who truly desire the grace of God, eat of that bread
and drink of that cup.

5   IV.1. But as plainly as God hath pointed out the way wherein he
will be inquired after, innumerable are the objections which men
wise in their own eyes have from time to time raised against it. It
may be needful to consider a few of these; not because they are of
weight in themselves, but because they have so often been used,
10   especially of late years, to turn the lame out of the way;[64] yea, to
trouble and subvert those who did run well, till Satan appeared as
an angel of light.[65]

      The first and chief of these is, 'You cannot use these means (as
you call them) without *trusting* in them.' I pray, where is this
15   written? I expect you should show me plain Scripture for your
assertion; otherwise I dare not receive it, because I am not
convinced that you are wiser than God.

      If it really had been as you assert, it is certain Christ must have
known it. And if he had known it, he would surely have warned us;
20   he would have revealed it long ago. Therefore, because he has
not, because there is no tittle of this in the whole revelation of
Jesus Christ, I am as fully assured your assertion is false as that
this revelation is of God.

      'However, leave them off for a short time to see whether you
25   trusted in them or no.' So I am to disobey God in order to know
whether I trust in obeying him! And do you avow this advice? Do
you deliberately teach to 'do evil, that good may come'? O tremble
at the sentence of God against such teachers! Their 'damnation is
just'.[66]

30   'Nay, if you are troubled when you leave them off, it is plain you
trusted in them.' By no means. If I am troubled when I wilfully
disobey God, it is plain his Spirit is still striving with me. But if I
am not troubled at wilful sin, it is plain I am given up to a
reprobate mind.[67]

35   But what do you mean by '*trusting* in them'? Looking for the

63 Rom. 14:17.
64 See Heb. 12:13.
65 See 2 Cor. 11:14.
66 Rom. 3:8.
67 See Rom. 1:28.

blessing of God therein? Believing that if I wait in this way I shall attain what otherwise I should not? So I do. And so I will, God being my helper, even to my life's end. By the grace of God I will *thus* trust in them till the day of my death; that is, I will believe that whatever God hath promised he is faithful also to perform. And seeing he hath promised to bless me in this way, I *trust* it shall be according to his Word.

2. It has been, secondly, objected, 'This is seeking salvation by works.' Do you know the meaning of the expression you use? What is 'seeking salvation by works'? In the writings of St. Paul it means either seeking to be saved by observing the ritual works of the Mosaic law, or expecting salvation for the sake of our own works, by the merit of our own righteousness. But how is either of these implied in my waiting in the way God has ordained, and expecting that he will meet me there because he has promised so to do?

I do expect that he will fulfil his Word, that he will meet and bless me in this way. Yet not for the sake of any works which I have done, nor for the merit of my righteousness; but merely through the merits and sufferings and love of his Son, in whom he is always well-pleased.[68]

3. It has been vehemently objected, thirdly, that Christ is the only means of grace.[69] I answer, this is mere playing upon words. Explain your term, and the objection vanishes away. When we say, 'Prayer is a means of grace,' we understand a channel through which the grace of God is conveyed. When you say, 'Christ is the means of grace,' you understand the sole price and purchaser of it; or, that 'no man cometh unto the Father, but through him.'[70] And who denies it? But this is utterly wide of the question.

4. But does not the Scripture (it has been objected, fourthly) direct us to *wait* for salvation? Does not David say, 'My soul waiteth upon God; for of him cometh my salvation'?[71] And does not Isaiah teach us the same thing, saying, 'O Lord, [. . .] we have waited for thee'?[72] All this cannot be denied. Seeing it is the gift of God, we are undoubtedly to *wait* on him for salvation. But how

[68] See Matt. 3:17, etc.
[69] See above, II.4 and n.
[70] Cf. John 14:6.
[71] Cf. Ps. 62:1.
[72] Isa. 33:2.

shall we wait? If God himself has appointed a way, can you find a better way of waiting for him? But that he hath appointed a way hath been shown at large, and also what that way is. The very words of the Prophet which you cite put this out of the question.

5 For the whole sentence runs thus: 'In the way of thy judgments' (or ordinances), 'O Lord, have we waited for thee.'[s] And in the very same way did David wait, as his own words abundantly testify: 'I have waited for thy saving health, O Lord, and have kept thy law.'[73] 'Teach me, O Lord, the way of thy statutes, and I shall

10 keep it unto the end.'[74]

5. 'Yea', say some, 'but God has appointed another way—"Stand still and see the salvation of God." '[75]

Let us examine the Scriptures to which you refer. The first of them, with the context, runs thus: 'And when Pharaoh drew nigh,

15 the children of Israel lifted up their eyes . . . , and they were sore afraid.[. . .] And they said unto Moses, Because there were no graves in Egypt, hast thou taken us away to die in the wilderness? And Moses said unto the people, Fear ye not: stand still, and see the salvation of the Lord. [. . .] And the Lord said unto Moses,

20 [. . .] Speak unto the children of Israel that they go forward. But lift thou up thy rod, and stretch out thine hand over the sea, and divide it. And the children of Israel shall go on dry ground through the midst of the sea.'[t]

This was the 'salvation' of God which they 'stood still' to

25 see—by 'marching forward' with all their might!

The other passage wherein this expression occurs stands thus:

'There came some that told Jehoshaphat, saying, There cometh a great multitude against thee, from beyond the sea. [. . .] And Jehoshaphat feared, and set himself to seek the Lord, and proclaimed a fast throughout all Judah. And

30 Judah gathered themselves together to ask help of the Lord; even out of all the cities they came to seek the Lord. And Jehoshaphat stood in the congregation, in the house of the Lord. . . . Then upon Jahaziel [. . .] came the Spirit of the Lord. . . . And he said, . . . Be not dismayed by reason of this great multitude. . . . Tomorrow go ye down against them; [. . .] ye shall not need to fight in this

[s] Isa. 26:8.
[t] Exod. 14:10-11, 13, 15-16.

---

[73] Cf. Ps. 119:166, 174 (BCP).   [74] Ps. 119:33.
[75] Cf. Exod. 14:13; there is an echo here of Wesley's discussion of 'stillness' and 'waiting upon the Lord' with Benjamin Ingham (JWJ, Sept. 8, 1746). See also below, No. 24, 'Sermon on the Mount, IV', for another criticism of quietism, 'stillness'—and its connection with antinomianism.

battle. Set yourselves: stand ye still, and see the salvation of the Lord. . . . And they rose early in the morning and went forth. [. . .] And when they began to sing and to praise, the Lord set ambushments against the children of Moab, Ammon, and Mount Seir, . . . and everyone helped to destroy another.'[u]

Such was the salvation which the children of Judah saw. But how does all this prove that we ought not to wait for the grace of God in the means which he hath ordained?

6. I shall mention but one objection more, which indeed does not properly belong to this head. Nevertheless, because it has been so frequently urged, I may not wholly pass it by.

'Does not St. Paul say, "If ye be dead with Christ, why are ye subject to *ordinances*?"[v] Therefore a Christian, one that is "dead with Christ", need not use the ordinances any more.'

So you say, 'If I am a Christian I am not subject to the ordinances of Christ!' Surely, by the absurdity of this you must see at the first glance that the ordinances here mentioned cannot be the ordinances of Christ! That they must needs be the Jewish ordinances, to which it is certain a Christian is no longer subject.

And the same undeniably appears from the words immediately following, 'Touch not, taste not, handle not'[76]—all evidently referring to the ancient ordinances of the Jewish law.

So that this objection is the weakest of all. And in spite of all, that great truth must stand unshaken: that all who desire the grace of God are to wait for it in the means which he hath ordained.

V.1. But this being allowed—that all who desire the grace of God are to wait for it in the means he hath ordained—it may still be inquired how those means should be used, both as to the *order* and the *manner* of using them.

With regard to the former, we may observe there is a kind of order wherein God himself is generally pleased to use these means in bringing a sinner to salvation. A stupid, senseless wretch is going on in his own way, not having God in all his thoughts, when God comes upon him unawares,[77] perhaps by an awakening sermon or conversation, perhaps by some awful providence; or it may be an immediate stroke of his convincing Spirit, without any

---

[u] 2 Chron. 20:2-5, 14-17, 20, 22-23.
[v] Col. 2:20.

---

[76] Col. 2:21.   [77] I.e., preveniently.

outward means at all. Having now a desire to flee from the wrath to come,[78] he purposely goes to *hear* how it may be done. If he finds a preacher who speaks to the heart, he is amazed, and begins 'searching the Scriptures',[79] whether these things are so. The
5 more he *hears* and *reads*, the more convinced he is; and the more he *meditates* thereon day and night.[80] Perhaps he finds some other book which explains and enforces what he has heard and read in Scripture. And by all these means the arrows of conviction sink deeper into his soul. He begins also to *talk* of the things of God,
10 which are ever uppermost in his thoughts; yea, and to talk with God, to *pray* to him, although through fear and shame he scarce knows what to say. But whether he can speak or no, he cannot but pray, were it only in 'groans which cannot be uttered'.[81] Yet being in doubt whether 'the high and lofty One that inhabiteth
15 eternity'[82] will regard such a sinner as him, he wants to pray with those who know God, with the faithful 'in the great congrega- tion'.[83] But here he observes others go up to 'the table of the Lord'.[84] He considers, Christ has said, 'Do this.'[85] How is it that I do not? I am too great a sinner. I am not fit. I am not worthy. After
20 struggling with these scruples a while, he breaks through. And thus he continues in God's way—in hearing, reading, meditating, praying, and partaking of the Lord's Supper—till God, in the manner that pleases him, speaks to his heart, 'Thy faith hath saved thee; go in peace.'[86]
25   2. By observing this order of God we may learn what means to recommend to any particular soul. If any of these will reach a stupid, careless sinner, it is probably *hearing* or *conversation*. To such therefore we might recommend these, if he has ever any thought about salvation. To one who begins to feel the weight of
30 his sins, not only hearing the Word of God but *reading* it too, and perhaps other *serious books*, may be a means of deeper conviction. May you not advise him also to *meditate* on what he reads, that it may have its full force upon his heart? Yea, and to *speak* thereof, and not be ashamed, particularly among those who walk in the
35 same path. When trouble and heaviness take hold upon him, should you not then earnestly exhort him to pour out his soul

---

[78] Matt. 3:7; Luke 3:7.
[79] Cf. John 5:39.
[80] See Josh. 1:8.
[81] Cf. Rom. 8:26.
[82] Isa. 57:15.
[83] Ps. 22:25, etc.
[84] Mal. 1:7,12.
[85] Cf. 1 Cor. 11:24.
[86] Luke 7:50.

before God?[87] 'Always to pray and not to faint'?[88] And when he feels the worthlessness of his own prayers, are you not to work together with God and remind him of going up into 'the house of the Lord',[89] and praying with all them that fear him? But if he does this, the *dying word*[90] of his Lord will soon be brought to his remembrance: a plain intimation that this is the time when we should second the motions of the blessed Spirit. And thus may we lead him step by step through all the means which God has ordained; not according to our own will, but just as the providence and the Spirit of God go before and open the way.

3. Yet as we find no command in Holy Writ for any particular order to be observed herein, so neither do the providence and the Spirit of God adhere to any, without variation: but the means into which different men are led, and in which they find the blessing of God, are varied, transposed, and combined together a thousand different ways. Yet still our wisdom is to follow the leadings of his providence and his Spirit; to be guided herein (more especially as to the means wherein we ourselves seek the grace of God) partly by his outward providence, giving us the opportunity of using sometimes one means, sometimes another; partly by our experience, which it is whereby his free Spirit is pleased most to work in our heart. And in the meantime the sure and general rule for all who groan for the salvation of God is this—whenever opportunity serves, use all the means which God has ordained. For who knows in which God will meet thee with the grace that bringeth salvation?[91]

4. As to the *manner* of using them, whereon indeed it wholly depends whether they should convey any grace at all to the user, it behoves us, first, always to retain a lively sense that God is above all means. Have a care therefore of limiting the Almighty. He doth whatsoever and whensoever it pleaseth him. He can convey his grace, either in or out of any of the means which he hath appointed. Perhaps he will. 'Who hath known the mind of the Lord? Or who hath been his counsellor?'[92] Look then every moment for his appearing! Be it at the hour you are employed in

---

[87] See 1 Sam. 1:15.
[88] Luke 18:1.
[89] Ps. 122:1, etc.
[90] *Viz.*, 'Do this, in remembrance of me . . .' (Luke 22:19); cf. 1 Cor. 11:24-26.
[91] See Titus 2:11.
[92] Rom. 11:34.

his ordinances; or before, or after that hour; or when you are hindered therefrom—he is not hindered. He is always ready; always able, always willing to save. 'It is the Lord, let him do what seemeth him good!'[93]

5   Secondly, *before* you use any means let it be deeply impressed on your soul: There is no *power* in this. It is in itself a poor, dead, empty thing: separate from God, it is a dry leaf, a shadow. Neither is there any *merit* in my using this, nothing intrinsically pleasing to God, nothing whereby I deserve any favour at his hands, no, not a 10 drop of water to cool my tongue.[94] But because God bids, therefore I do; because he directs me to wait in this way, therefore here I wait for his free mercy, whereof cometh my salvation.[95]

Settle this in your heart, that the *opus operatum*,[96] the mere work done, profiteth nothing; that there is no *power* to save but in the 15 Spirit of God, no *merit* but in the blood of Christ; that consequently even what God ordains conveys no grace to the soul if you trust not in him alone. On the other hand, he that does truly trust in him cannot fall short of the grace of God, even though he were cut off from every outward ordinance, though he were shut 20 up in the centre of the earth.

Thirdly, in using all means, seek God alone. In and through every outward thing look singly to the *power* of his Spirit and the *merits* of his Son. Beware you do not stick in the *work* itself; if you do, it is all lost labour. Nothing short of God can satisfy your soul. 25 Therefore eye him in all, through all, and above all.[97]

Remember also to use all means *as means*; as ordained, not for their own sake, but in order to the renewal of your soul in

---

[93] 1 Sam. 3:18.

[94] See Luke 16:24.

[95] See Ps. 62:1.

[96] I.e., the ritual observance itself. The Reformers had charged that the Roman Catholics taught that the bare, ritual observance of the Mass conferred saving grace, *apart from faith*. It was this charge to which Canon VIII of Trent (Seventh Session) was responding: *Si quis dixerit per ipsa novae legis sacramenta ex opere operato non conferri gratiam* . . . ('against those who say that, under the New Law, grace is not conferred by the sacraments on the basis of the ritual observance itself . . .'). The Roman position was that *some* benefit is conveyed by the Eucharist even when not received in *conscious* faith, since the sacraments are, in some sense, converting ordinances and thus means of grace in yet another sense. Cf. Canon George D. Smith, ed., *The Teaching of the Catholic Church*, 2 vols. (London, Burns, Oates and Washbourne, 1948), II.755-58; but see also Richard P. McBrien, *Catholicism* (Minneapolis, Winston Press, 1980), II.735-43).

[97] See Eph. 4:6.

righteousness and true holiness.[98] If therefore they actually tend to this, well; but if not, they are dung and dross.

Lastly, after you have used any of these, take care how you value yourself thereon; how you congratulate yourself as having done some great thing. This is turning all into poison. Think, 'If God was not there, what does this avail? Have I not been adding sin to sin? How long, O Lord! Save, or I perish![99] O lay not this sin to my charge!'[100] If God was there, if his love flowed into your heart, you have forgot, as it were, the outward work. You see, you know, you feel, God is all in all.[101] Be abased. Sink down before him. Give him all the praise. Let God 'in all things be glorified through Christ Jesus'.[102] Let 'all your bones cry out',[103] 'My song shall be always of the loving-kindness of the Lord: With my mouth will I ever be telling of thy truth, from one generation to another!'[104]

---

[98] Eph. 4:24.
[99] See Matt. 8:25.
[100] Cf. Acts 7:60.
[101] See 1 Cor. 15:28.
[102] Cf. 1 Pet. 4:11.
[103] Cf. Ps. 35:10.
[104] Ps. 89:1 (BCP).

THE CIRCUMCISION OF THE HEART

AN INTRODUCTORY COMMENT

This is a landmark sermon in more ways than one. First, it is the earliest of Wesley's sermons in SOSO *and carefully placed at the beginning of his second volume (1748) as an updated version of a sermon written fifteen years earlier for delivery in St. Mary's, Oxford, on January 1, 1733. Second, it is one of Wesley's most careful and complete statements of his doctrine of holiness, and he continued to regard it as such thereafter. In a later summary statement of his theological development to John Newton (May 14, 1765) he would write: 'Jan. 1, 1733, I preached the sermon on "The Circumcision of the Heart", which contains all that I now teach concerning salvation from* all *sin,* and loving God with an undivided heart.' *Still later, (JWJ, September 1, 1778), he would recall: 'I know not that I can write a better [sermon] on "The Circumcision of the Heart" than I did five and forty years ago. Perhaps, indeed, I may have read five or six hundred books more than I had then, and may know a little more history or natural philosophy than I did. But I am not sensible that this has made any essential addition to my knowledge of divinity. Forty years ago [i.e., 1738] I knew and preached every Christian doctrine which I preach now.' Third, it supports the thesis that the basic elements of Wesley's soteriology (with the exception of the Moravian emphases on 'faith* alone' *and on* 'assurance') *were already in place long before his Aldersgate experience. Original sin is there (though more as a disease than an obliterated* imago Dei) *and so also is the* non posse non peccare *(I.3: 'without the Spirit of God we can do nothing but add sin to sin'). Christ's atonement is affirmed as the sole ground of our redemption, and in I.7, he can add (in 1748) a personal confession in the language of his Aldersgate experience without disturbing the rhetoric or sense in any noticeable way: 'I have an advocate with the Father . . . Jesus Christ the righteous is* my *Lord and the propitiation for* my *sins. I know . . . he hath reconciled* me, *even* me, *to God; and I have redemption through his blood, even the forgiveness of sins.' The theme of the Christian's participation in God is lovingly spelled out as the essence of Christian existence: 'the being joined to the Lord in one Spirit. One design . . . to pursue to the end of time: the enjoyment of God in time and*

398

eternity.' The means *to this single end are also delineated—not faith* alone, *but humility (i.e., repentance), faith, hope,* and *love. Fourth, it helped to establish Wesley as a man of mark in the university. How else could one explain those* six *university sermons in the next two-and-one-half years* (viz., *out of proportion to the regular rotations; see above, Intro. to Sermon I, pp. 109-11 above).*

Wesley's diary entries show that he began to plan this sermon in late November and began to write it on December 8. The project was then complicated by the appearance of a derogatory letter in Fog's Weekly Journal, *Saturday, December 9, about 'this Sect called Methodists', on the various grounds of their 'absurd and perpetual melancholy', their 'very near affinity to the Essenes among the Jews and the pietists among the Christians in Switzerland* [sic]', *their 'proposition that no action whatever is indifferent [which] is the chief hinge on which their whole scheme of religion turns', and their 'hypocrisy', since "tis certain that their Founder took formerly no small liberty in indulging his appetites . . .'. The obvious effect of any such defamation was the arousal of still more popular curiousity about the Methodists and their founder, and this assured him of a larger or more attentive audience than he might have expected otherwise. But it also made the occasion more crucial for Wesley's career as a theologian, and this helps to explain the uncommon carefulness of his preparations. He spent close to thirty hours during the following fortnight writing a first draft; he then added as much more time in consultations with others about its further refinement: his brother Charles, his friend Hudson Martin, Euseby Isham (Rector of Lincoln), Dr. Joseph Smith (of Queen's), Jonathan Colley (chaplain of Christ Church), and Emmanuel Langford (also of Christ Church).*

Finally, on Monday, January 1, he mounted St. Mary's pulpit to expound what would thenceforth become his most distinctive doctrine: Christian perfection understood as perfect love of God and neighbour, rooted in a radical faith in Christ's revelation of that love and its power. His text was suggested by the occasion, the Feast of the Circumcision of Christ, and its Collect: '. . . Grant us the true circumcision of the spirit that, our hearts and all our members being mortified from all worldly and carnal lusts, we may in all things obey thy blessed will . . . .' Afterwards, he records his post-sermon mood as 'chearfull' and notes that the sermon had 'found favour with the Rector [Isham] and the Vice-Chancellor' (William Holmes of St. John's). He seems not to have realized that Thomas Cockman, a prominent Latinist in the university, famed as the editor and translator of Cicero's De Officiis (On Moral Obligations), *1699, had already preached two sermons before the university, January 2 and 6, 1731, on* Salvation by Jesus Christ Alone . . . , *both thoroughly Christocentric and both remarkably like 'The Circumcision of the Heart' on many basic points. The diaries show that Wesley had been out of town on the 2nd and had failed to attend the university service on the 6th. But Cockman's sermons make clear that there was more evangelical teaching in Oxford than one would surmise from Wesley's later descriptions of the place. There were those, however, who were unimpressed. A contemporary, Thomas Wilson, Jun. (1703–84), son of the famed Bishop of Sodor and Man, spoke for many in his curt evaluation of this sermon as 'enthusiastic'; see* The Diaries of Thomas Wilson, D. D.; 1731–37 and 1750, *ed. C. L. S. Linnell (London, SPCK, 1964), p. 87.*

'The Circumcision of the Heart' *may profitably be paired with* 'Justification by Faith' *as two halves of the same 'gospel', and as twin foundation stones in Wesley's theology as a whole. Moreover, Wesley's deliberate placement of the two, out of chronological order but with a clear eye to his reader's interest in the right order of Christian experience and life, is very much worth pondering.*

The Circumcision of the Heart

A Sermon preached at St. Mary's, Oxford,
before the University,
on January 1, 1733.

Romans 2:29

*Circumcision is that of the heart, in the spirit
and not in the letter.*

1. 'Tis the melancholy remark of an excellent man that 'he who now preaches the most essential duties of Christianity runs the hazard of being esteemed by a great part of his hearers "a setter forth of new doctrines".'[1] Most men have so *lived away* the substance of that religion, the profession whereof they still retain, that no sooner are any of those truths proposed which difference the Spirit of Christ from the spirit of the world than they cry out, 'Thou bringest strange things to our ears; we would know what these things mean'[2]—though he is only preaching to them 'Jesus, and the resurrection',[3] with the necessary consequence of it. If Christ be risen, ye ought then to die unto the world, and to live wholly unto God.

2. A hard saying this to the 'natural man'[4] who is alive unto the world, and dead unto God, and one that he will not readily be persuaded to receive as the truth of God, unless it be so qualified

---

[1] Cf. Acts 17:18-19. The 'excellent man' is probably William Law, whose recent *Serious Call* would have been widely familiar in Oxford: 'And if in these days we want examples of these several degrees of perfection, if neither clergy nor laity are enough of this spirit; if we are so far departed from it that a man seems, like St. Paul at Athens, *a setter forth of strange doctrines* when he recommends self-denial, renunciation of the world, regular devotion, retirement, virginity, and voluntary poverty [the gist of Law's ethical agenda], it is because we are fallen into an age where the love, not of many but of most, is waxed cold' (*Works*, IV. 80).

For further comments of this sort by Wesley himself, see Nos. 25, 'Sermon on the Mount, V', §1; and 150, 'Hypocrisy in Oxford', I.1; JWJ, May 28, 1738; and 'A Short History of the People Called Methodists', §11.

[2] Cf. Acts 17:20.

[3] Acts 17:18.

[4] Cf. No. 9, 'The Spirit of Bondage and of Adoption', §5 and n.

in the interpretation as to have neither use nor significancy left. He 'receiveth not the' words 'of the Spirit of God', taken in their plain and obvious meaning. 'They are foolishness unto him; neither' indeed 'can he know them, because they are spiritually
5   discerned:'[5] they are perceivable only by that spiritual sense which in him was never yet awakened, for want of which he must reject as idle fancies of men what are both the 'wisdom' and the 'power of God'.[6]

3. That 'circumcision is that of the heart, in the spirit, and not
10 in the letter', that the distinguishing mark of a true follower of Christ, of one who is in a state of acceptance with God, is not either outward circumcision or baptism, or any other outward form, but a right state of soul—a mind and spirit renewed after the image of him that created it—is one of those important truths
15 that can only be 'spiritually discerned'. And this the Apostle himself intimates in the next words: 'Whose praise is not of men, but of God.'[7] As if he had said, 'Expect not, whoever thou art who thus followest thy great Master, that the world, the men who follow him not, will say, "Well done, good and faithful servant!"[8]
20 Know that the "circumcision of the heart", the seal of thy calling, is "foolishness with the world".[9] Be content to wait for thy applause till the day of thy Lord's appearing. In that day shalt thou "have praise of God"[10] in the great assembly of men and angels.'

I design, first, particularly to inquire wherein this circumcision
25 of the heart[11] consists; and secondly to mention some reflections that naturally arise from such an inquiry.

I.1. I am first to inquire wherein that circumcision of the heart consists which will receive the praise of God. In general we may observe it is that habitual disposition of soul which in the Sacred
30 Writings is termed 'holiness', and which directly implies the being cleansed from sin, 'from all filthiness both of flesh and

---

[5] 1 Cor. 2:14.
[6] 1 Cor. 1:24.
[7] Cf. Rom. 2:29; this is a subjective genitive: 'praise from God'. See also John 12:43 and 1 Cor. 4:5; the stress is on God's approval of Christian virtue in the 'renewed' creature. Cf. No. 4, *Scriptural Christianity*, I.6 and n.
[8] Matt. 25:23.
[9] Cf. 1 Cor. 1:20-21.
[10] 1 Cor. 4:5; cf. Rom. 2:29.
[11] All printed edns. up to *SOSO, II* (1787), read 'circumcision of heart' here and in I.1, below; Wesley's final reading quietly restores the definite article.

spirit',[12] and by consequence the being endued with those virtues which were also in Christ Jesus, the being so 'renewed in the image of our mind'[13] as to be 'perfect, as our Father in heaven is perfect'.[14]

2. To be more particular, circumcision of heart implies humility, faith, hope, and charity.[15] Humility, a right judgment of ourselves,[16] cleanses our minds from those high conceits of our own perfections, from the undue opinions of our own abilities and attainments which are the genuine fruit of a corrupted nature. This entirely cuts off that vain thought, 'I am rich, and wise, and have need of nothing;' and convinces us that we are by nature 'wretched, and poor, and miserable, and blind, and naked'.[17] It convinces us that in our best estate we are of ourselves all sin and vanity; that confusion, and ignorance, and error, reign over our understanding; that unreasonable, earthly, sensual, devilish passions usurp authority over our will: in a word, that there is no whole part in our soul, that all the foundations of our nature are out of course.[18]

3. At the same time we are convinced that we are not sufficient of ourselves to help ourselves; that without the Spirit of God we can do nothing but add sin to sin; that it is he alone 'who worketh

---

[12] Cf. 2 Cor. 7:1.

[13] Cf. Eph. 4:23.

[14] Cf. Matt. 5:48.

[15] Cf. 1 Cor. 13:13 (where 'humility' does not appear). Note that here Wesley uses the AV translation of ἀγάπη ('charity'), whereas in II.9, below, he shifts to his much preferred usage, 'love'. Cf. No. 91, 'On Charity' for his arguments for 'love'; but see above, No. 5, 'Justification by Faith', III.6, where he uses 'charity', and below, No. 22, 'Sermon on the Mount, II', III.3, where he speaks of '"charity" or love'; see also the MS sermon, No. 149, 'On Love', II.1-2, where he discusses 'the true meaning of the word "charity"'. Later, in JWJ, July 4, 1776, he will record: 'In the evening I showed, to a still more crowded audience, the nature and necessity of Christian love, ἀγάπη, vilely rendered "charity" to confound poor English readers.' For all that, 'charity' was standard usage among the generality of those same 'poor English readers'; four of their principal translations read 'charity'. Wesley, therefore, seems to have bowed to common usage where it seemed needful, but continued to advocate 'love' as a happier choice than 'charity' for ἀγάπη. Cf. his *Notes*, and Nos. 7, 'The Way to the Kingdom', I.9; 65, 'The Duty of Reproving our Neighbour', III.2; 76, 'On Perfection', I.4; 80, 'On Friendship with the World', §24; 83, 'On Patience', §10. Cf. also his letter to Ann Bolton, Dec. 5, 1772.

[16] An echo here, and in this whole para., of William Law, *Christian Perfection, Works*, III.103-4. See also Nos. 7, 'The Way to the Kingdom', II.1 and n.; and 21, 'Sermon on the Mount, I', I.7 and n. This stress on humility, and the equation of humility, self-knowledge, and repentance, is one of Law's main themes, but so also it had been in Jeremy Taylor and other Anglican divines.

[17] Cf. Rev. 3:17.

[18] Cf. Jonathan Swift, *Gulliver's Travels*, II. viii.

in us' by his almighty power, either 'to will or do'[19] that which is good—it being as impossible for us even to think a good thought without the supernatural assistance of his Spirit as to create ourselves, or to renew our whole souls in righteousness and true
5 holiness.

4. A sure effect of our having formed this right judgment of the sinfulness and helplessness of our nature is a disregard of that 'honour which cometh of man'[20] which is usually paid to some supposed excellency in us. He who knows himself neither desires
10 nor values the applause which he knows he deserves not. It is therefore 'a very small thing with him to be judged by man's judgment'.[21] He has all reason to think, by comparing what it has said either for or against him with what he feels in his own breast, that the world, as well as the god of this world, was 'a liar from the
15 beginning'.[22] And even as to those who are not of the world, though he would choose (if it were the will of God) that they should account of him as of one desirous to be found a faithful steward of his Lord's goods,[23] if haply this might be a means of enabling him to be of more use to his fellow-servants, yet as this is
20 the one end of his wishing for their approbation, so he does not at all rest upon it. For he is assured that whatever God wills he can never want instruments to perform; since he is able, even of these stones, to raise up servants[24] to do his pleasure.

5. This is that lowliness of mind which they have learned of
25 Christ who follow his example and tread in his steps. And this knowledge of their disease, whereby they are more and more cleansed from one part of it, pride and vanity, disposes them to embrace with a willing mind the second thing implied in 'circumcision of heart'—that faith which alone is able to make
30 them whole, which is the one medicine given under heaven to heal their sickness.[25]

6. The best guide of the blind, the surest light of them that are in darkness, the most perfect instructor of the foolish,[26] is faith. But it must be such a faith as is 'mighty through God, to the
35 pulling down of strongholds',[27] to the overturning all the

---

[19] Cf. Phil. 2:13. Cf. No. 85, 'On Working Out Our Own Salvation', I.1-4.
[20] Cf. John 5:41, 44.   [21] Cf. 1 Cor. 4:3.   [22] Cf. John 8:44.
[23] See Luke 12:42.   [24] See Matt. 3:9.
[25] Note the correlations here of faith, wholeness, and the theme of θεραπεία ψυχῆς. Cf. No. 13, *On Sin in Believers*, III.8 and n.
[26] See Rom. 2:19-20.   [27] 2 Cor. 10:4.

prejudices of corrupt reason, all the false maxims revered among men, all evil customs and habits, all that 'wisdom of the world' which 'is foolishness with God';[28] as 'casteth down imaginations' (reasonings) 'and every high thing that exalteth itself against the knowledge of God, and bringeth into captivity every thought to 5 the obedience of Christ'.[29]

7. 'All things are possible to him that' thus 'believeth:'[30] 'the eyes of his understanding being enlightened,' he *sees* what is his calling,[31] even to 'glorify God, who hath bought him with' so high 'a price, in his body and in his spirit, which now are God's'[32] by 10 redemption, as well as by creation. He feels what is 'the exceeding greatness of his power'[33] who, as he raised up Christ from the dead, so is able to quicken us—'dead in sin'[34]—'by his Spirit which dwelleth in us'.[35] 'This is the victory which overcometh the world, even our faith:'[36] that faith which is not only an unshaken 15 assent to all that God hath revealed in Scripture, and in particular to those important truths, 'Jesus Christ came into the world to save sinners;'[37] he 'bare our sins in his own body on the tree';[38] 'he is the propitiation for our sins; and not for ours only, but also for the sins of the whole world;'[a] but likewise the revelation of Christ 20 in our hearts: a divine evidence or conviction of his love, his free, unmerited love to me a sinner;[39] a sure confidence in his pardoning mercy, wrought in us by the Holy Ghost—a confidence whereby every true believer is enabled to bear witness, 'I know that my Redeemer liveth;'[40] that *I* 'have an 25 advocate with the Father', that 'Jesus Christ the righteous is' *my* Lord, and 'the propitiation for *my* sins.'[41] I know he 'hath loved *me*, and given himself for *me*'.[42] He 'hath reconciled *me*, even *me* to God';[43] and *I* 'have redemption through his blood, even the forgiveness of sins'.[44] 30

[a] N.B. The following part of this paragraph is now added to the sermon formerly preached. [The preceding quotation is from 1 John 2:2.]

---

[28] 1 Cor. 3:19. [29] 2 Cor. 10:5. [30] Mark 9:23.
[31] Eph. 1:18. [32] Cf. 1 Cor. 6:20. [33] Eph. 1:19.
[34] Cf. Eph. 2:1, 5. [35] Rom. 8:11. [36] 1 John 5:4.
[37] 1 Tim. 1:15. [38] 1 Pet. 2:24.
[39] See Heb. 11:1. This definition of faith is one that Wesley came to regard as normative; cf. No. 3, *'Awake, Thou That Sleepest'*, I.11 and n.
[40] Job 19:15. [41] 1 John 2:1-2.
[42] Cf. Eph. 5:2. [43] Cf. Rom. 5:10.
[44] Col. 1:14. In 1732 Wesley was still preoccupied with holy living. Here, in 1748, he has added his discovery of *justifying* faith as unmerited mercy and as the assurance of forgiveness through the merits of Christ's propitiatory death.

8. Such a faith as this cannot fail to show evidently the power of him that inspires it, by delivering his children from the yoke of sin, and 'purging their consciences from dead works';[45] by strengthening them so that they are no longer constrained to 'obey sin in
5 the desires thereof'; but instead of 'yielding their members unto' it, 'as instruments of unrighteousness', they now 'yield' themselves entirely 'unto God, as those that are alive from the dead'.[46]

9. Those who are thus by faith 'born of God'[47] have also 'strong consolation through hope'.[48] This is the next thing which the
10 'circumcision of the heart' implies—even the testimony of their own spirit with the Spirit which witnesses in their hearts, that they are the children of God.[49] Indeed it is the same Spirit who works in them that clear and cheerful confidence that their heart is upright toward God; that good assurance that they now do,
15 through his grace, the things which are acceptable in his sight; that they are now in the path which leadeth to life, and shall, by the mercy of God, endure therein to the end. It is he who giveth them a lively expectation of receiving all good things at God's hand—a joyous prospect of that 'crown of glory' which is
20 'reserved in heaven'[50] for them. By this anchor a Christian is kept steady in the midst of the waves of this troublesome world, and preserved from striking upon either of those fatal rocks, presumption or despair. He is neither discouraged by the misconceived severity of his Lord, nor does he 'despise the
25 richness of his goodness'.[51] He neither apprehends the difficulties of the race set before him[52] to be greater than he has strength to conquer, nor expects them to be so little as to yield him the conquest till he has put forth all his strength. The experience he already has in the Christian warfare, as it assures
30 him his 'labour is not in vain'[53] if 'whatever his hand findeth to do, he doth it with his might,'[54] so it forbids his entertaining so vain a thought as that he can otherwise gain any advantage, as that any virtue can be shown, any praise attained, by 'faint hearts and feeble hands'[55]—or indeed by any but those who pursue the same

---

[45] Cf. Heb. 9:14.   [46] Cf. Rom. 6:12-13.
[47] 1 John 3:9, etc.   [48] Cf. Heb. 6:18.
[49] Rom. 8:16; see above, Nos. 10 and 11, 'The Witness of the Spirit', Discourses I and II; and No. 12, 'The Witness of Our Own Spirit.'
[50] 1 Pet. 1:4; 5:4.   [51] Rom. 2:4.
[52] See Heb. 12:1.   [53] 1 Cor. 15:58.
[54] Cf. Eccles. 9:10.   [55] Ecclus. 2:12; cf. Ezek. 7:12.

course with the great Apostle of the Gentiles: 'I (says he) so run, not as uncertainly; so fight I, not as one that beateth the air. But I keep under my body, and bring it into subjection; lest by any means when I have preached to others, I myself should be a castaway.'[56]

10. By the same discipline is every good soldier of Christ to 'inure himself to endure hardships'.[57] Confirmed and strengthened by this, he will be able not only to renounce 'the works of darkness',[58] but every appetite, too, and every affection which is not subject to the law of God. For 'everyone', saith St. John, 'who hath this hope purifieth himself, even as he is pure.'[59] It is his daily care, by the grace of God in Christ, and through the blood of the covenant, to purge the inmost recesses of his soul from the lusts that before possessed and defiled it: from uncleanness, and envy, and malice, and wrath, from every passion and temper that is 'after the flesh',[60] that either springs from or cherishes his native corruption; as well knowing that he whose very 'body is the temple of God'[61] ought to admit into it nothing common or unclean; and that 'holiness becometh' that 'house for ever'[62] where the Spirit of holiness vouchsafes to dwell.[63]

11. Yet lackest thou one thing, whosoever thou art, that to a deep humility and a steadfast faith hast joined a lively hope, and thereby in a good measure cleansed thy heart from its inbred pollution. If thou wilt be perfect, add to all these charity: add love, and thou hast the 'circumcision of the heart'. 'Love is the fulfilling of the law,'[64] 'the end of the commandment'.[65] Very excellent things are spoken of love; it is the essence, the spirit, the life of all virtue. It is not only the first and great command,[66] but it is all the commandments in one. Whatsoever things are just, whatsoever things are pure, whatsoever things are amiable or honourable; if there be any virtue, if there be any praise,[67] they are all comprised in this one word—love. In this is perfection and glory and happiness. The royal law of heaven and earth is this, 'Thou shalt love the Lord thy God with all thy heart, and with all thy soul, and with all thy mind, and with all thy strength.'[68]

[56] 1 Cor. 9:26-27.   [57] Cf. 2 Tim. 2:3.   [58] Rom. 13:12.
[59] Cf. 1 John 3:3.   [60] John 8:15, etc.
[61] Cf.1 Cor. 6:19.   [62] Ps. 93:6 (BCP).
[63] An echo of the Puritan stress on self-examination and of Jeremy Taylor's doctrine of repentance; cf. his *Unum Necessarium* (*Works*, II. 419-646).
[64] Rom. 13:10.   [65] 1 Tim. 1:5.   [66] Matt. 22:38.
[67] Phil. 4:8.   [68] Mark 12:30.

12. Not that this forbids us to love anything besides God: it implies that we 'love our brother also'.[69] Not yet does it forbid us (as some have strangely imagined) to take pleasure in anything but God.[70] To suppose this is to suppose the fountain of holiness
5 is directly the author of sin, since he has inseparably annexed pleasure to the use of those creatures which are necessary to sustain the life he has given us. This therefore can never be the meaning of his command. What the real sense of it is both our blessed Lord and his apostles tell us too frequently and too plainly
10 to be misunderstood. They all with one mouth bear witness that the true meaning of those several declarations—'The Lord thy God is one Lord; thou shalt have no other gods but me,'[71] 'Thou shalt love the Lord thy God with all thy strength,'[72] 'Thou shalt cleave unto him;'[73] 'The desire of thy soul shall be to his
15 name'[74]—is no other than this. The one perfect good shall be your ultimate end. One thing shall ye desire for its own sake—the fruition of him that is all in all.[75] One happiness shall ye propose to your souls, even an union with him that made them, the having 'fellowship with the Father and the Son',[76] the being 'joined to the
20 Lord in one Spirit'.[77] One design ye are to pursue to the end of time—the enjoyment of God in time and in eternity.[78] Desire other things so far as they tend to this. Love the creature—as it leads to the Creator. But in every step you take be this the glorious point that terminates your view. Let every affection, and thought,
25 and word, and work, be subordinate to this. Whatever ye desire or fear, whatever ye seek or shun, whatever ye think, speak, or do, be it in order to your happiness in God,[79] the sole end as well as source of your being.

13. Have no end, no ultimate end, but God. Thus our Lord:
30 'One thing is needful.'[80] And if thine eye be singly fixed on this

---

[69] Cf. 1 John 4:21.

[70] An obvious rejoinder to the accusation in the letter to *Fog's Weekly Journal* that the Oxford Methodists 'avoid, as much as is possible, every object that may affect them with any pleasant and grateful sensation . . . , fancying . . . that religion was designed to contradict nature.'

[71] Cf. Deut. 6:4, 14; Mark 12:29, 32.

[72] Mark 12:30, etc.   [73] Deut. 13:4; Acts 11:23.

[74] Isa. 26:8.   [75] See 1 Cor. 15:20-28.

[76] Cf. 1 John 1:3.   [77] Cf. 1 Cor. 6:17.

[78] Note here the combination of the theme of participation *and* of 'the enjoyment of God'; cf. the Westminster Catechism, Q. and A. 1.

[79] Cf. No. 6, 'The Righteousness of Faith', II.9 and n.

[80] Luke 10:42.

one thing, 'thy whole body shall be full of light.'[81] Thus St. Paul: 'This one thing I do; [. . .] I press toward the mark, for the prize of the high calling in Christ Jesus.'[82] Thus St. James: 'Cleanse your hands, ye sinners, and purify your hearts, ye double-minded.'[83] Thus St. John: 'Love not the world, neither the things that are in the world. [. . .] For all that is in the world, the lust of the flesh, the lust of the eye, and the pride of life, is not of the Father, but is of the world.'[84] The seeking happiness in what gratifies either the desire of the flesh, by agreeably striking upon the outward senses; the desire of the eye, of the imagination, by its novelty, greatness, or beauty; or the pride of life,[85] whether by pomp, grandeur, power, or the usual consequence of them, applause and admiration: 'is not of the Father'—cometh not from, neither is approved by, the Father of spirits—'but of the world'—it is the distinguishing mark of those who will not have him reign over them.

II.1. Thus have I particularly inquired what that 'circumcision of the heart' is which will obtain the praise of God.[86] I am in the second place to mention some reflections that naturally arise from such an inquiry, as a plain rule whereby every man may judge himself whether he be of the world or of God.

And, first, it is clear from what has been said that no man has a title to the praise of God unless his heart is circumcised by humility, unless he is little, and base, and vile in his own eyes; unless he is deeply convinced of that inbred 'corruption of his nature, whereby he is very far gone from original righteousness',[87] being prone to all evil, averse to all good, corrupt and abominable; having a 'carnal mind', which 'is enmity against God, and is not subject to the Law of God, nor indeed can be';[88] unless he continually feels in his inmost soul that without the Spirit of God resting upon him he can neither think, nor desire, nor speak, nor act, anything good or well-pleasing in his sight.[89]

---

[81] Matt. 6:22.
[82] Phil. 3:13-14.
[83] Jas. 4:8.
[84] 1 John 2:15-16. See below, II.9; also No. 7, 'The Way to the Kingdom', II.2 and n.
[85] Cf. 1 John 2:16—Wesley's favourite text for an inclusive triad of sinful passions. Cf. No. 7, 'The Way to the Kingdom', II.2 and n.
[86] Cf. above, §3 and n.
[87] Cf. Art. IX, 'Of Original or Birth Sin' in the Thirty-nine Articles.
[88] Cf. Rom. 8:7.   [89] Heb. 13:21.

No man, I say, has a title to the praise of God till he feels his want of God: nor indeed till he seeketh that 'honour, which cometh of God only',[90] and neither desires nor pursues that which cometh of man, unless so far only as it tends to this.

5   2. Another truth which naturally follows from what has been said is that none shall obtain the honour that cometh of God unless his heart be circumcised by faith, even a 'faith of the operation of God';[91] unless, refusing to be any longer led by his senses, appetites, or passions, or even by that blind leader of the

10 blind,[92] so idolized by the world, natural reason, he lives and 'walks by faith',[93] directs every step as 'seeing him that is invisible',[94] 'looks not at the things that are seen, which are temporal, but at the things that are not seen, which are eternal';[95] and governs all his desires, designs, and thoughts, all his actions

15 and conversations, as one who is entered in within the veil,[96] where Jesus sits at the right hand of God.[97]

    3. It were to be wished that they were better acquainted with this faith who employ much of their time and pains in laying another foundation, in grounding religion on 'the eternal *fitness* of

20 things', on 'the intrinsic *excellence* of virtue', and the *beauty* of actions flowing from it—on the *reasons*, as they term them, of good and evil, and the *relations* of beings to each other.[98] Either these accounts of the grounds of Christian duty coincide with the scriptural or not. If they do, why are well-meaning men

25 perplexed, and drawn from the weightier matters of the law by a cloud of terms whereby the easiest truths are explained into obscurity? If they are not, then it behoves them to consider who is the author of this new doctrine, whether he is likely to be 'an angel

---

[90] John 5:44. Cf. above, §3 and n.
[91] Col. 2:12.
[92] Matt. 15:14.
[93] 2 Cor. 5:7.   [94] Heb. 11:27.
[95] 2 Cor. 4:18.   [96] Heb. 6:19.
[97] See Col. 3:1; Mark 16:19; Acts 7:55.
[98] The men complained of here range from the third Earl of Shaftesbury (cf. his *Inquiry Concerning Virtue or Merit*, and his *Characteristics of Men, Manners, Opinions, Times* [1st edn., 1711; 4th edn., 1727]), to Samuel Clarke (*Discourse Concerning the Unchangeable Obligations of Natural Religion and the Truth and Certainty of the Christian Revelation* [1706], espec. pp. 46 ff.; see also his *Demonstration of the Being and Attributes of God* [1705], Prop. XII, and espec. pp. 247-48), to Richard Fiddes (*A General Treatise of Morality* [1724]), to Francis Hutcheson's *Inquiry*, and *Essay*. They include both deists and rationalists; cf. John Leland, *A View of the Principal Deistical Writers . . .* , 1754-56, 3 vols. (3rd edn., 1757). See also *Notes and Queries* (6th series), VIII. 79, 138. For more complaints of the same sort, cf. No. 34, 'The Original, Nature, Properties, and Use of the Law', II.5.

from heaven' who 'preacheth another gospel'[99] than that of Christ Jesus—though if he were, God, not we, hath pronounced his sentence: 'Let him be accursed!'[100]

4. Our gospel, as it knows no other foundation of good works than faith, or of faith than Christ, so it clearly informs us we are not his disciples while we either deny him to be the author or his Spirit to be the inspirer and perfecter both of our faith and works. 'If any man have not the Spirit of Christ, he is none of his.'[101] He alone can quicken those who are dead unto God, can breathe into them the breath of Christian life, and so prevent, accompany, and follow them with his grace as to bring their good desires to good effect. And 'as many as are thus led by the Spirit of God, they are the sons of God.'[102] This is God's short and plain account of true religion and virtue; and 'other foundation can no man lay.'[103]

5. From what has been said we may, thirdly, learn that none is truly 'led by the Spirit' unless that 'Spirit bear witness with his spirit, that he is a child of God';[104] unless he see the prize and the crown before him, and 'rejoice in hope of the glory of God':[105] so greatly have they erred who have taught that in serving God we ought not to have a view to our own happiness. Nay, but we are often and expressly taught of God to have 'respect unto the recompense of reward',[106] to balance the toil with the 'joy set before us',[107] these 'light afflictions' with that 'exceeding weight of glory'.[108] Yea, we are 'aliens to the covenant of promise', we are 'without God in the world',[109] until God of 'his abundant mercy hath begotten us again unto a living hope' of the 'inheritance incorruptible, undefiled, and that fadeth not away'.[110]

6. But if these things are so, 'tis high time for those persons to deal faithfully with their own souls—who are so far from finding in themselves this joyful assurance, that they fulfil the terms and shall obtain the promises of that covenant, as to quarrel with the covenant itself, and blaspheme the terms of it, to complain they are too severe, and that no man ever did or shall live up to them!

[99] Cf. Gal. 1:8.
[100] *Ibid.*
[101] Rom. 8:9.
[102] Rom. 8:14.
[103] 1 Cor. 3:11.
[104] Rom. 8:16. Cf. No. 5, 'Justification by Faith', IV.2 and n.
[105] Rom. 5:2.
[106] Heb. 11:26.
[107] Cf. Heb. 12:2.
[108] 2 Cor. 4:17.
[109] Eph. 2:12.
[110] 1 Pet. 1:3-4.

What is this but to reproach God, as if he were an hard master requiring of his servants more than he enables them to perform; as if he had mocked the helpless works of his hands by binding them to impossibilities, by commanding them to overcome where neither their own strength nor his grace was sufficient for them?

7. These blasphemers might almost persuade those to imagine themselves guiltless who, in the contrary extreme, hope to fulfil the commands of God without taking any pains at all.[111] Vain hope! that a child of Adam should ever expect to see the kingdom of Christ and of God without striving, without '*agonizing*' first 'to enter in at the strait gate'![112] That one who was 'conceived and born in sin',[113] and whose 'inward parts are very wickedness',[114] should once entertain a thought of being 'purified as his Lord is pure'[115] unless he 'tread in his steps',[116] and 'take up his cross daily';[117] unless he 'cut off the right hand', and 'pluck out the right eye and cast it from him';[118] that he should ever dream of shaking off his old opinions, passions, tempers, of being 'sanctified throughout in spirit, soul, and body',[119] without a constant and continued course of general self-denial!

8. What less than this can we possibly infer from the above cited words of St. Paul, who, 'living in "infirmities, in reproaches, in necessities, in persecutions, in distresses" for Christ's sake, who being full of "signs, and wonders, and mighty deeds", who having been "caught up into the third heaven", yet reckoned' (as a late author strongly expresses it) that 'all his virtues' would be 'insecure, and' even 'his salvation in danger, without this constant self-denial.[. . .] "So run I", says he, "not as uncertainly; so fight I, not as one that beateth the air." By which he plainly teaches us that he who does not thus run, who does not thus' deny himself daily, does 'run uncertainly, and fighteth to as little purpose as he that "beateth the air".'[120]

---

[111] Note this early version of what will become Wesley's definition of enthusiasm; cf. No. 37, 'The Nature of Enthusiasm', §27.

[112] Luke 13:24. Note Wesley's preference here for 'agonizing' over 'striving' as a translation of ἀγωνίζεσθε; cf. *Notes*, and Nos. 25, 'Sermon on the Mount, V', III.6; 31, 'Sermon on the Mount, XI', III.1, 5, 6; 89, 'The More Excellent Way', §5.

[113] Cf. Ps. 51:5.   [114] Ps. 5:9.

[115] Cf. 1 John 3:3.   [116] Cf. 1 Pet. 2:21.

[117] Luke 9:23.   [118] Cf. Matt. 18:8-9.   [119] Cf. 1 Thess. 5:23.

[120] Cf. Law, *Christian Perfection* (*Works*, III. 117), who quotes in turn 2 Cor. 12: 10, 12; ver. 2, and 1 Cor. 9: 26. Note how close Law comes to turning St. Paul's triad ('faith, hope, and love') into a quartet by his addition of 'self-denial' as an equal theological virtue; Wesley follows him here in his stress on its equivalent, 'humility'. Cf. John Worthington,

9. To as little purpose does he talk of 'fighting the fight of faith',[121] as vainly hope to attain the crown of incorruption (as we may, lastly, infer from the preceding observations), whose heart is not circumcised by love. Cutting off both the lust of the flesh, the lust of the eye, and the pride of life,[122] engaging the whole man, body, soul, and spirit, in the ardent pursuit of that one object, is so essential to a child of God that 'without it whosoever liveth is counted dead before him.'[123] 'Though I speak with the tongues of men and angels, and have not love, I am as sounding brass, or a tinkling cymbal. Though I have the gift of prophecy, and understand all mysteries, and all knowledge, and though I have all faith so as to remove mountains, and have not love, I am nothing. Nay, though I give all my goods to feed the poor, and my body to be burned, and have not love, it profiteth me nothing.'[124]

10. Here then is the sum of the perfect law: this is the true 'circumcision of the heart'. Let the spirit return to God that gave it, with the whole train of its affections. 'Unto the place from whence all the rivers came, thither'[125] let them flow again. Other sacrifices from us he would not; but the living sacrifice of the heart he hath chosen. Let it be continually offered up to God through Christ, in flames of holy love. And let no creature be suffered to share with him: for he is a jealous God.[126] His throne will he not divide with another; he will reign without a rival. Be no design, no desire admitted there but what has him for its ultimate object. This is the way wherein those children of God once walked, who being dead still speak to us:[127] 'Desire not to live but to praise his name; let all your thoughts, words, and works tend to his glory. Set your heart firm on him, and on other things only as they are in and from him.'[128] 'Let your soul be filled with so entire a love of him that you may love nothing but for his sake.' 'Have a

whose *Great Duty of Self-Resignation to the Divine Will* (1675, 1689) was extracted by Wesley for his *Christian Lib.*, XXIII–XXIV.

[121] 1 Tim. 6:12.

[122] 1 John 2:16; see above, I.13 and n.

[123] Cf. BCP, Collects, Quinquagesima, which speaks of charity as 'that most excellent gift, . . . the very bond of peace and of all virtues.'

[124] Cf. 1 Cor. 13:1-3.

[125] Cf. Eccles. 1:7.

[126] Exod. 20:5, etc.

[127] See Heb. 11:4.

[128] Is this, and are the following three quotations, an imagined summary of what the saints have to tell us? More probably they are quotations from older devotional texts known to Wesley and to at least some of his audience, but not yet located in this context.

pure intention of heart, a steadfast regard to his glory in all your actions.' 'Fix your eye upon the blessed hope of your calling, and make all the things of the world minister unto it.' For then, and not till then, is that 'mind in us which was also in Christ Jesus',[129]
5 when in every motion of our heart, in every word of our tongue, in every work of our hands, we 'pursue nothing but in relation to him, and in subordination to his pleasure'; when we, too, neither think, or speak, nor act, to fulfil our 'own will, but the will of him that sent us';[130] when whether we 'eat, or drink, or whatever we do,
10 we do all to the glory of God'.[131]

---

[129] Cf. Phil. 2:5.
[130] Cf. John 5: 30; 6:38.
[131] Cf. 1 Cor. 10:31.

THE MARKS OF THE NEW BIRTH
THE GREAT PRIVILEGE OF THOSE
THAT ARE BORN OF GOD

AN INTRODUCTORY COMMENT

With SOSO, *I, Wesley could suppose that he had established the basis for his doctrine of justification by faith alone, understood as the threshold of true religion. Taking this then as given—with occasional short reaffirmations, as in I.3 below—he was free to devote the remainder of his collection to the problems of the ongoing Christian life, from its beginnings in saving faith to its fullness in perfect love. This is evident in the ordering of the sermons; they are out of their chronological sequence, but they have their own logic. Thus, after 'The Circumcision of the Heart' Wesley adds a pair of sermons about* regeneration, *understood as that act of grace concurrent with justification but not at all identical to it—a 'vast inward change' that opens up the lifelong quest for holiness.*

In the first of the pair (as also later in No. 45, 'The New Birth') Wesley wrestles with an unresolved dilemma in his beliefs and teachings. He had been brought up to take baptismal regeneration for granted, *as in the office for Baptism in the BCP, in Art. XXVII ('Of Baptism'), and in his father's 'Of Baptism' in* The Pious Communicant Rightly Prepared *(1700), which he would thereafter abridge and publish in his own name (1758). John seems always to have believed that something 'happens' in baptism (and in infant baptism at that) that validates its propriety and necessity as the sacrament of Christian initiation; he rejected the logic of 'believer's baptism' which always presupposes 'conversion' before baptism.*

Even so, his own experience and the dramatic conversions in the Revival had forced on him a recognition of yet another sort of regeneration, more decisive and subjective, more nearly correlated with justification and assurance than with water baptism. Thus, somewhat as he had explained 'the circumcision of the heart' as a personal transformation following baptism, so now, in 'The Marks of the New Birth' and 'The Great Privilege of those that are Born of God' (and again, later, in No. 45, 'The New Birth'), he was in search of a doctrine of regeneration that would take seriously the realities of evangelical conversions and yet not repudiate his own sacramental traditions. Whether he ever fully succeeded is an open question; it is undeniable that the doctrine of infant baptism as an objective divine action has never had more than a tenuous place in the Methodist tradition. (For a fuller probing of the theological problem of baptism and regeneration, cf. Robert E. Cushman, 'Baptism and the Family of God', in Dow Kirkpatrick, ed., The Doctrine of the Church *[New York, Abingdon, 1964], pp. 79-102.)*

All this, then, was part of the context of Wesley's direct concern in these two sermons, the special 'powers' (or 'privileges', as Wesley prefers to translate ἐξουσία in John 1:12) of justified and regenerated Christians. To this end, he borrows from the analogy of latency from physical birth to point to the latent powers in the human spirit when enlivened by its Creator Spirit (cf. the 'title' of the Holy Spirit in the Latin text of the Nicene Creed: Vivificator*). Just as the 'circumcision of the heart' had involved 'humility, faith, hope, and charity', so also 'the [distinctive] marks of the New Birth' are 'faith, hope, and love'.*

In expounding this Christian commonplace, however, Wesley comes, under the heading of 'faith', to his crucial assertion that the regenerate believer receives real power (or 'the privilege') not to commit sin, *and so to enjoy unanxious peace in heart and mind. Here Wesley comes as close as he ever will to an unnuanced notion of Christian existence as sinless; he even goes on to denounce those who try to qualify this with the more modest claim that the regenerate 'do not commit sin* habitually*' (I.5). He must have realized, however, that he had laid himself open to misinterpretation, and so he proceeded to add 'The Great Privilege of those that are Born of God', and with it a more careful distinction between 'sin properly so called' and other shortfallings, i.e., between voluntary and involuntary sins, where 'voluntary' sounds suspiciously like 'habitual'. After that he can develop his metaphor of a spiritual sensorium and his concept of human 're-actions' to divine 'actions'. This would suggest that the two sermons are better read as a pair than apart.*

Both seem to have been written versions of Wesley's oral preaching, reaching back to the beginnings of the Revival. It is recorded that he had preached from John 3:8 as early as June 10, 1739, and frequently thereafter (fourteen times in all until December 1757). His first recorded sermon from 1 John 3:9 comes on September 23, 1739; a second comes on January 17, 1740; its last usage as a sermon text seems to have been in November 1756. Even in 1748, however, with these twin sermons, Wesley had laid out one of the undergirding premises of his unfolding vision of Christian existence.

The Marks of the New Birth

John 3:8

So is everyone that is born of the Spirit.

1. How is everyone that is 'born of the Spirit'? That is, 'born again', 'born of God'?[1] What is meant by the being 'born again'? The being 'born of God'? Or, being 'born of the Spirit'? What is implied in the being a 'son' or a 'child of God'? Or, having the 'Spirit of adoption'?[2] That these privileges, by the free mercy of God, are ordinarily annexed to baptism (which is thence termed by our Lord in the preceding verse the being 'born of water and of the Spirit') we know; but we would know what these privileges are. What is 'the new birth'?

2. Perhaps it is not needful to give a definition of this, seeing the Scripture gives none. But as the question is of the deepest concern to every child of man (since 'except a man be born again', 'born of the Spirit', he 'cannot see the kingdom of God'), I propose to lay down the marks of it in the plainest manner, just as I find them laid down in Scripture.

I.1. The first of these (and the foundation of all the rest) is faith. So St. Paul, 'Ye are all the children of God by faith in Christ Jesus.'[a] So St. John, 'To them gave he power' (ἐξουσίαν, right, or privilege, it might rather be translated)[4] 'to become the sons of God, even to them that believe on his name: which were born', when they believed, ('not of blood, nor of the will of the flesh', not by natural generation, 'nor of the will of man', like those children adopted by men, in whom no inward change is thereby wrought,

---

[a] Gal. 3:26.

---

[1] John 3:3, 6.
[2] Rom. 8:14-16.   [3] John 3:3.
[4] Cf. *Notes, loc. cit.,* and also Poole, *Annotations, loc. cit.* The idea of ἐξουσία as 'a right' includes 'the right *to act* . . .' and also 'the ability *to act* . . .'; cf. Arndt and Gingrich, *Greek-English Lexicon.*

'but) of God.'^b And again in his General Epistle, 'Whosoever believeth that Jesus is the Christ is born of God.'^c

2. But it is not a barely notional[5] or speculative faith that is here spoken of by the apostles. It is not a bare assent to this
5 proposition, 'Jesus is the Christ;' nor indeed to all the propositions contained in our creed, or in the Old and New Testament. It is not merely 'an assent to any, or all these credible things, as credible'. To say this were to say (which who could hear?) that the devils were born of God. For they have their faith.[6]
10 They trembling believe both that Jesus is the Christ and that all Scripture, having been given by inspiration of God, is true as God is true.[7] It is not only 'an assent to divine truth, upon the testimony of God', or 'upon the evidence of miracles'.[8] For they also heard the words of his mouth, and knew him to be a faithful and true
15 witness. They could not but receive the testimony he gave, both of himself and of the Father which sent him. They saw likewise the mighty works which he did, and thence believed that he 'came forth from God'.[9] Yet notwithstanding this faith they are still 'reserved in chains of darkness unto the judgment of the great
20 day'.[10]

3. For all this is no more than a dead faith.[11] The true, living, Christian faith, which whosoever hath is 'born of God', is not only an assent, an act of the understanding, but a disposition which God hath wrought in his heart; 'a sure trust and confidence in
25 God that through the merits of Christ his sins are forgiven, and he

^b John 1:12-13.
^c 1 John 5:1.

---

[5] Cf. the citation of this actual passage in *OED* ('notional'); but note also that this distinction between 'notional' and 'real' was already established long before Wesley's time (by Hooker, Bacon, Theophilus Gale, *et al.*). See also Samuel Johnson's quotation from 'Bentley's *Sermons*': 'We must be wary, lest we ascribe any real substance or personality to this nature or chance; for it is merely a *notional* and imaginary thing; an abstract universal, which is properly nothing; a conception of our own making, occasioned by our reflecting upon the settled course of things; according to their essential properties, without any consciousness or intention of so doing.'

[6] See Jas. 2:19.
[7] See 2 Tim. 3:16; cf. also 'Of Faith', *Homilies*, p. 29.
[8] Cf. St. Thomas, *Summa Theologica*, II.ii, Q.1.
[9] Cf. John 16:30.
[10] Cf. Jude 6.
[11] See also 'Of Faith', Pt. I, *Homilies*, p. 29; and Wesley's *Notes* on Jas. 2:17. For 'living faith', cf. his letters to his mother, June 18 and Nov. 22, 1725; to William Law, May 14, 1738; and to Dr. Henry Stebbing, July 31, 1739, §6.

reconciled to the favour of God'.[12] This implies that a man first *renounce himself*; that, in order to be 'found in Christ',[13] to be accepted through him, he totally reject all 'confidence in the flesh';[14] that, 'having nothing to pay',[15] having no trust in his own works or righteousness of any kind, he come to God as a lost, 5 miserable, self-destroyed, self-condemned, undone, helpless sinner, as one whose 'mouth' is utterly 'stopped', and who is altogether 'guilty before God'.[16] Such a sense of sin (commonly called 'despair' by those who speak evil of the things they know not), together with a full conviction, such as no words can express, 10 that of Christ only cometh our salvation, and an earnest desire of that salvation must precede a living faith: a trust in him who 'for us paid our ransom by his death, and for us fulfilled the law of his life'.[17] This faith, then, whereby we are born of God, is 'not only a belief of all the articles of our faith, but also a true confidence of 15 the mercy of God, through our Lord Jesus Christ'.[18]

4. An immediate and constant fruit of this faith whereby we are born of God, a fruit which can in no wise be separated from it, no, not for an hour, is power over sin: power over outward sin of every kind; over every evil word and work; for wheresoever the blood of 20 Christ is thus applied it 'purgeth the conscience from dead works'.[19] And over inward sin; for it 'purifieth the heart'[20] from every unholy desire and temper. This fruit of faith St. Paul has largely described in the sixth chapter of his Epistle to the Romans: 'How shall we (saith he) who' by faith 'are dead to sin, 25 live any longer therein?'[21] 'Our old man is crucified with Christ, that the body of sin might be destroyed, that henceforth we should not serve sin.'[22] 'Likewise reckon ye yourselves to be dead unto sin, but alive unto God through Jesus Christ our Lord. . . . Let not sin therefore reign', even 'in your mortal body, [. . .] but 30 yield yourselves unto God, as those that are alive from the dead.[. . .] For sin shall not have dominion over you. . . . God be thanked that ye were the servants of sin . . . , but being made

---

[12] 'Of Salvation', Pt. III, *Homilies*, p. 26.
[13] Cf. Phil. 3:9.
[14] Phil. 3:3, 4.
[15] Cf. Luke 7:42.
[16] Rom. 3:19.
[17] 'Of Salvation', Pt. I, *Homilies*, p. 20, which reads 'for them . . .'.
[18] *Ibid.*, Pt. III, summarized.
[19] Cf. Heb. 9:14.
[20] Cf. Acts 15:9; Jas. 4:8.
[21] Rom. 6:2.
[22] Cf. Rom. 6:6.

free'—the plain meaning is, God be thanked that though ye were in the time past the servants of sin, yet now—'being free from sin, ye are become the servants of righteousness.'[23]

5. The same invaluable privilege of the sons of God is as strongly asserted by St. John; particularly with regard to the former branch of it, namely, power over outward sin. After he had been crying out as one astonished at the depth of the riches of the goodness of God, 'Behold what manner of love the Father hath bestowed upon us, that we should be called the sons of God! [. . .] Beloved, now are we the sons of God; and it doth not yet appear what we shall be; but we know that when he shall appear we shall be like him; for we shall see him as he is'—he soon adds, 'Whosoever is born of God doth not commit sin; for his seed remaineth in him, and he cannot sin because he is born of God.'[d] But some men will say, 'True; "whosoever is born of God doth not commit sin"[e] *habitually*.'[24] *Habitually*! Whence is that? I read it not.[25] It is not written in the Book. God plainly saith, he 'doth not commit sin'. And thou addest, 'habitually'! Who art thou that *mendest* the oracles of God? That 'addest to the words of this Book'?[26] Beware, I beseech thee, lest God 'add to thee all the plagues that are written therein'![27] Especially when the comment thou addest is such as quite swallows up the text: so that by this μεθοδεία πλάνης, this artful method of deceiving, the precious promise is utterly lost; by this κυβεία ἀνθρώπων,[28] this tricking

---

[d] 1 John 3:1-2, 9.   [e] Ver. 6[i.e.,9].

---

[23] Cf. Rom. 6:11-14, 17-18. See also No. 13, *On Sin in Believers*, intro., III.1-9 and n.

[24] For a later example of this usage, cf. James Hervey, *Eleven Letters . . . to . . . John Wesley* (1765), p. 128: 'True, he [the believer described in 1 John 5:18] sinneth not habitually. It is not his customary practice.' This evidently was an echo from a conventional usage. Cf. No. 40, *Christian Perfection*, II.6 and n.

[25] Cf. South, *Sermons* (1823), VI. 81, where he quotes 'that maxim: whatsoever is sinful is also voluntary,' and then comments on those who restrict sin (properly so called) to 'sinful habits'. See also Richard Hill, *Logica Wesleiensis . . .* p. 61, where he accuses Wesley of contradicting himself between his sermon on Eph. 2:8 (*Salvation by Faith*) and this sermon on John 3:8; see above, No. 1. In the former, says Hill, Wesley says, 'By any habitual sin', etc.; in the latter, Wesley denounces those who add 'habitually' to the text. But see below, No. 19, 'The Great Privilege of those that are Born of God', II.1, where Wesley himself restricts the definition of sin to that which is 'voluntary'. See also, No. 40, *Christian Perfection*, II.6.

[26] Cf. Rev. 22:18.   [27] *Ibid.*

[28] Eph. 4:14, 'the slight of men'. In his *Notes* Wesley translates this into the vernacular as 'cogging the dice'. For 'cogging' as a synonym for 'cheating', see *OED*. Cf. also No. 36, 'The Law Established through Faith, II', I.1 and n.

and shuffling of men, the Word of God is made of none effect. O beware thou that thus takest from the words of this Book, that taking away the whole meaning and spirit from them leavest only what may indeed be termed a dead letter, lest God take away thy part out of the book of life![29]   5

6. Suffer we the Apostle to interpret his own words by the whole tenor of his discourse. In the fifth verse of this chapter he had said, 'Ye know that he (Christ) was manifested to take away our sins; and in him is no sin.'[30] What is the inference he draws from this? 'Whosoever abideth in him sinneth not; whosoever 10 sinneth hath not seen him, neither known him.' To his enforcement of this important doctrine he premises an highly necessary caution: 'Little children, let no man deceive you' (for many will endeavour so to do; to persuade you that you may be unrighteous, that you may commit sin, and yet be children of 15 God). 'He that doth righteousness is righteous, even as he is righteous. He that committeth sin is of the devil; for the devil sinneth from the beginning.' Then follows, 'Whosoever is born of God doth not commit sin; for his seed remaineth in him: and he cannot sin, because he is born of God. In this (adds the Apostle) 20 the children of God are manifest, and the children of the devil.'[f] By this plain mark (the committing or not committing sin) are they distinguished from each other. To the same effect are those words in his fifth chapter. 'We know that whosoever is born of God sinneth not; but he that is begotten of God keepeth himself, 25 and that wicked one toucheth him not.'[g]

7. Another fruit of this living faith is peace. For 'being justified by faith', having all our sins blotted out, 'we have peace with God, through our Lord Jesus Christ.'[h] This indeed our Lord himself, the night before his death, solemnly bequeathed to all his 30 followers. 'Peace (saith he) I leave with you;' (you who 'believe in God', and 'believe also in me'[31]) 'my peace I give unto you. Not as the world giveth, give I unto you. Let not your heart be troubled, neither let it be afraid.'[i] And again, 'These things have I spoken unto you, that in me ye might have peace.'[j] This is that 'peace of 35

[f] Ver. 7[-10].
[g] Ver. 18.
[h] Rom. 5:1.
[i] John 14:27.   [j] [John] 16:33.

---

[29] See Rev. 22:19.   [30] 1 John 3:5.   [31] John 14:1.

God which passeth all understanding';[32] that serenity of soul which it hath not entered into the heart of a natural man to conceive,[33] and which it is not possible for even the spiritual man to utter. And it is a peace which all the powers of earth and hell are
5 unable to take from him. Waves and storms beat upon it, but they shake it not; for it is founded upon a rock.[34] It keepeth the hearts and minds[35] of the children of God at all times and in all places. Whether they are in ease or in pain, in sickness or health, in abundance or want, they are happy in God. In every state they
10 have learned to be content,[36] yea, to give thanks unto God through Christ Jesus; being well assured that 'whatsoever is, is best;'[37] because it is his will concerning them. So that in all the vicissitudes of life their 'heart standeth fast, believing in the Lord'.[38]

15 II.1. A second scriptural mark of those who are born of God is hope. Thus St. Peter, speaking to all the children of God who were then 'scattered abroad',[39] saith, 'Blessed be the God and Father of our Lord Jesus Christ, who according to his abundant mercy hath begotten us again unto a lively hope.'ᵏ Ἐλπίδα
20 ζῶσαν, a *lively* or *living* hope, saith the Apostle: because there is also a *dead* hope (as well as a dead faith), a hope which is not from God but from the enemy of God and man—as evidently appears by its fruits. For as it is the offspring of pride, so it is the parent of every evil word and work. Whereas every man that hath in him
25 this living hope is 'holy as he that calleth him is holy'.[40] Every man that can truly say to his brethren in Christ, 'Beloved, now are we the sons of God; [. . .] and we shall see him as he is'—'purifieth himself, even as he is pure'.[41]

ᵏ 1 Pet. 1:3.

---

[32] Phil. 4:7.
[33] See 1 Cor. 2:9, 14.
[34] See Matt. 7:25; Luke 6:48.
[35] See Phil. 4:7.
[36] See Phil. 4:11.
[37] Cf. Diogenes Laertius, 'Democritus', *Lives*, ix. 45, but see also, Pope, 'Whatever is, is right' (*Essay on Man*, i. 294). Charles Wesley had already borrowed this in his *Hymns and Sacred Poems* (1749); see also his *Funeral Hymns*, 1759 (*Poet. Wks.*, V. 428, VI.251). Cf. Wesley's letter to Ebenezer Blackwell, Jan. 5, 1754; also 'God's time is the best time,' in No. 42, 'Satan's Devices', II.2.
[38] Cf. Ps. 112:7 (BCP).
[39] Cf. 1 Pet. 1:1.
[40] Cf. 1 Pet. 1:15.
[41] 1 John 3: 2-3.

2. This hope (termed in the Epistle to the Hebrews πληροφορία πίστεως,[1] and elsewhere πληροφορία ἐλπίδος[m]—in our translation, the 'full assurance of faith', and the 'full assurance of hope'; expressions the best which our language could afford, although far weaker than those in the original), as described in Scripture,[42] implies, (1): the testimony of our own spirit or conscience that we walk 'in simplicity and godly sincerity';[43] but, secondly and chiefly, the testimony of the Spirit of God, 'bearing witness with', or to, 'our spirit, that we are the children of God; and if children, then heirs; heirs of God, and joint-heirs with Christ'.[44]

3. Let us well observe what is here taught us by God himself touching this glorious privilege of his children. Who is it that is here said to 'bear witness'? Not our spirit only, but another; even the Spirit of God. He it is who 'beareth witness with our spirit'. What is it he beareth witness of? 'That we are the children of God; and if children, then heirs; heirs of God, and joint-heirs with Christ'—'if so be that we suffer with him' (if we deny ourselves, if we take up our cross daily,[45] if we cheerfully endure persecution or reproach for his sake) 'that we may be also glorified together.'[46] And in whom doth the Spirit of God bear this witness? In all who are the children of God. By this very argument does the Apostle prove in the preceding verses that they are so: 'As many', saith he, 'as are led by the Spirit of God, they are the sons of God. For ye have not received the spirit of bondage again to fear; but ye have received the Spirit of adoption, whereby we cry, Abba, Father!' It follows, 'The Spirit itself beareth witness with our spirit, that we are the children of God.'[n]

4. The variation of the phrase in the fifteenth verse is worthy our observation. '*Ye* have received the Spirit of adoption, whereby *we* cry, Abba, Father!' *Ye*—as many [as] are the sons of God—have, in virtue of your sonship, received that selfsame

[1] Heb. 10:22.
[m] Heb. 6:11.
[n] Rom. 8:14-16.

---

[42] *Works* (1771), omits 'termed . . . Scripture'.
[43] 2 Cor. 1:12. Cf. No. 2, *The Almost Christian*, I.9 and n.
[44] Cf. Rom. 8:16-17. See Nos. 10 and 11, 'The Witness of the Spirit', Discourses I and II on this text; and also 12, 'The Witness of Our Own Spirit'.
[45] See Luke 9:23.
[46] Rom. 8:17.

Spirit of adoption whereby *we* cry, Abba, Father. *We*, the apostles, prophets, teachers (for so the word may not improperly be understood); we, through whom you have believed, the 'ministers of Christ, and stewards of the mysteries of God'.[47] As *we* and *you*

5 have one Lord, so we have one Spirit; as we have one faith, so have we one hope also.[48] We and you are sealed with one 'Spirit of promise', the earnest of *yours* and of *our* inheritance:[49] the same Spirit bearing witness with yours and with our spirit, 'that we are the children of God'.

10 5. And thus is the Scripture fulfilled: 'Blessed are they that mourn, for they shall be comforted.'[50] For 'tis easy to believe that though sorrow may precede this witness of God's Spirit with our spirit (indeed *must* in some degree while we groan under fear and a sense of the wrath of God abiding on us), yet as soon as any man

15 feeleth it in himself his 'sorrow is turned into joy'.[51] Whatsoever his pain may have been before, yet as soon as that 'hour is come, he remembereth the anguish no more, for joy'[52] that he is born of God. It may be many of *you* have now sorrow, because you are 'aliens from the commonwealth of Israel', because you are

20 conscious to yourselves that you have not this Spirit, that you are 'without hope and without God in the world'.[53] But when the Comforter is come, then 'your heart shall rejoice'; yea, 'your joy shall be full', 'and that joy no man taketh from you.'[o] 'We joy in God', will ye say, 'through our Lord Jesus Christ, by whom we

25 have now received the atonement:'[p] 'by whom we have access into this grace'; this state of grace, of favour, of reconciliation with God, 'wherein we stand, and rejoice in hope of the glory of God.'[54] Ye, saith St. Peter, whom God 'hath begotten again unto a lively hope', 'are kept by the power of God unto salvation. . . .

30 Wherein ye greatly rejoice, though now for a season, if need be, ye are in heaviness through manifold temptations; that the trial of your faith . . . may be found unto praise, and honour, and glory, at the appearing of Jesus Christ, . . . in whom, though now ye see him not, ye rejoice with joy unspeakable, and full of glory.'[q]

[o] John 16:22 [cf. 16:24].　　　　　　　　　　　　[p] Rom. 5:11.
[q] 1 Pet. 1:3-8.

---

[47] 1 Cor. 4:1.　　　　　　　　　　　　　　　[48] See Eph. 4:4, 5.
[49] See Eph. 1:13-14.　　　　　　　　　　　　　[50] Matt. 5:4.
[51] Cf. John 16:20.　　　　　　　　　　　　　　[52] Cf. John 16:21.
[53] Eph. 2:12.　　　　　　　　　　　　　　　　[54] Rom. 5:2.

Unspeakable indeed! It is not for the tongue of man to describe this joy in the Holy Ghost. It is 'the hidden manna, [. . .] which no man knoweth save he that receiveth it'.[55] But this we know, it not only remains, but overflows, in the depth of affliction. 'Are the consolations of God small'[56] with his children, when all earthly comforts fail? Not so. But when sufferings most abound, the consolation of his Spirit doth much more abound: insomuch that the sons of God 'laugh at destruction when it cometh';[57] at want, pain, hell and the grave; as knowing him who 'hath the keys of death and hell',[58] and will shortly 'cast them into the bottomless pit';[59] as hearing even now the 'great voice out of heaven' saying, 'Behold, the tabernacle of God is with men, and he will dwell with them, and they shall be his people, and God himself shall be with them, and be their God. And God shall wipe away all tears from their eyes, and there shall be no more death, neither sorrow, nor crying; neither shall there be any more pain; for the former things are passed away.'[r]

III.1. A third scriptural mark of those who are born of God, and the greatest of all, is love: even 'the love of God shed abroad in their hearts by the Holy Ghost which is given unto them'.[s] 'Because they are sons, God hath sent forth the Spirit of his Son into their hearts, crying, Abba Father!'[t] By this Spirit, continually looking up to God as their reconciled and loving Father, they cry to him for their daily bread, for all things needful whether for their souls or bodies. They continually pour out their hearts before him, knowing 'they have the petitions which they ask of him'.[u] Their delight is in him. He is the joy of their heart, 'their shield, and their exceeding great reward'.[60] The desire of their soul is toward him; it is their 'meat and drink to do his will';[61] and they are 'satisfied as with marrow and fatness, while their mouth praiseth him with joyful lips'.[v]

[r] Rev. 21:3-4.
[s] Rom. 5:5.
[t] Gal. 4:6.
[u] 1 John 5:15.
[v] Ps. 63:5.

---

[55] Cf. Rev. 2:17.
[56] Job 15:11.
[58] Cf. Rev. 1:18.
[60] Cf. Gen. 15:1.

[57] Cf. Job 5:22.
[59] Cf. Rev. 20:3.
[61] Cf. John 4:34.

2. And in this sense also 'everyone who loveth him that begat, loveth him that is begotten of him.'ʷ His spirit rejoiceth in God his Saviour.⁶² He 'loveth the Lord Jesus Christ in sincerity'.⁶³ He is so 'joined unto the Lord' as to be 'one spirit'.⁶⁴ His soul hangeth
5 upon him, and chooseth him as altogether lovely, 'the chiefest among ten thousand'.⁶⁵ He knoweth, he feeleth, what that means, 'My Beloved is mine, and I am his.'ˣ 'Thou art fairer than the children of men; full of grace are thy lips, because God hath anointed thee for ever!'ʸ

10 3. The necessary fruit of this love of God is the love of our neighbour, of every soul which God hath made;⁶⁶ not excepting our enemies, not excepting those who are now 'despitefully using and persecuting us';⁶⁷ a love whereby we love every man *as ourselves*—as we love our own souls. Nay, our Lord has expressed
15 it still more strongly, teaching us to 'love one another even as he hath loved us'.⁶⁸ Accordingly the commandment written in the hearts of all those that love God is no other than this, 'As I have loved you, so love ye one another.'⁶⁹ Now 'herein perceive we the love of God, in that he laid down his life for us. We ought', then,
20 as the Apostle justly infers, 'to lay down our lives for our brethren.'ᶻ If we feel ourselves ready to do this, then do we truly love our neighbour. Then 'we know that we have passed from death unto life, because we' thus 'love our brethren.'ᵃᵃ 'Hereby know we' that we are born of God, 'that we dwell in him, and he in
25 us, because he hath given us of his loving Spirit.'ᵇᵇ 'For love is of God, and everyone that' thus 'loveth is born of God, and knoweth God.'ᶜᶜ

ʷ 1 John 5:1.
ˣ Cant. 2:16.
ʸ Ps. 45:2[BCP].
ᶻ 1 John 3:16.
ᵃᵃ Ver. 14.
ᵇᵇ [1 John] 4:13.
ᶜᶜ 1 John 4:7.

---

⁶² See Luke 1:47.
⁶³ Cf. Eph. 6:24. ⁶⁴ 1 Cor. 6:17.
⁶⁵ S. of S. 5:10; cf. 5:16 (usage in this edn. for what Wesley cited as 'Canticles', note x. above).
⁶⁶ For Wesley's definition of neighbour, cf. No. 7, 'The Way to the Kingdom', I.8 and n. Just as the love of God is the substance of inward holiness, so also the love of neighbour is the substance of outward holiness; cf. *ibid.*, I.10 and n.
⁶⁷ Cf. Matt. 5:44. ⁶⁸ Cf. John 13:34. ⁶⁹ Cf. John 15:12.

4. But some may possibly ask, 'Does not the Apostle say, "This is the love of God, that we keep his commandments"?'[dd] Yea; and this is the love of our neighbour also, in the same sense as it is the love of God. But what would you infer from hence? That the keeping the outward commandments is all that is implied in loving God with all your heart, with all your mind, and soul, and strength, and in loving your neighbour as yourself?[70] That the love of God is not an affection of the soul, but merely an *outward service*? And that the love of our neighbour is not a disposition of the heart, but barely a course of *outward works*? To mention so wild an interpretation of the Apostle's words is sufficiently to confute it. The plain indisputable meaning of that text is: 'this is the' sign or proof of the 'love of God', of our keeping the first and great commandment—to keep the rest of his commandments. For true love, if it be once shed abroad in our heart, will constrain us so to do; since whosoever loves God with all his heart cannot but serve him with all his strength.

5. A second fruit then of the love of God (so far as it can be distinguished from it) is universal obedience to him we love, and conformity to his will; obedience to all the commands of God, internal and external; obedience of the heart and of the life, in every temper and in all manner of conversation.[71] And one of the tempers most obviously implied herein is the being 'zealous of good works';[72] the hungering and thirsting to do good, in every possible kind, unto all men; the rejoicing to 'spend and be spent for them',[73] for every child of man, not looking for any recompense in this world, but only in the resurrection of the just.[74]

IV.1. Thus have I plainly laid down those marks of the new birth which I find laid down in Scripture. Thus doth God himself answer that weighty question what it is to be born of God. Such, if the appeal be made to the oracles of God, is 'everyone that is born of the Spirit'.[75] This it is, in the judgment of the Spirit of God, to be a son or a child of God. It is so to believe in God through Christ

---

[dd] 1 John 5:3.

[70] Luke 10:27.
[71] 1 Pet. 1:15.
[72] Titus 2:14.
[74] Luke 14:14.
[73] Cf. 2 Cor. 12:15.
[75] John 3:8.

as 'not to commit sin',[76] and to enjoy, at all times and in all places, that 'peace of God which passeth all understanding'.[77] It is so to *hope* in God through the Son of his love as to have not only the 'testimony of a good conscience',[78] but also 'the Spirit of God
5 bearing witness with your spirits that ye are the children of God':[79] whence cannot but spring the 'rejoicing evermore in him through whom ye have received the atonement'.[80] It is so to *love* God, who hath thus loved you, as you never did love any creature: so that ye are constrained to love all men as yourselves; with a love not only
10 ever burning in your hearts, but flaming out in all your actions and conversations, and making your whole life one 'labour of love',[81] one continued obedience to those commands, 'Be ye merciful, as God is merciful;'[82] 'Be ye holy, as I the Lord am holy;'[83] 'Be ye perfect, as your Father which is in heaven is perfect.'[84]

15 2. Who then are ye that are *thus* born of God? Ye 'know the things which are given to you of God'.[85] Ye well know that ye are the children of God, and 'can assure your hearts before him'.[86] And every one of you who has observed these words cannot but feel and know of a truth whether at this hour (answer to God and
20 not to man!) you are thus a child of God or no! The question is not what you was made in baptism (do not evade!) but what you are now. Is the Spirit of adoption now in your heart? To your own heart let the appeal be made. I ask not whether you *was* born of water and the Spirit.[87] But *are* you *now* the temple of the Holy
25 Ghost which dwelleth in you?[88] I allow you was 'circumcised with the circumcision [. . .] of Christ' (as St. Paul emphatically terms baptism).[89] But does the Spirit of Christ and of glory *now* rest upon you? Else 'your circumcision is become uncircumcision'.[90]

3. Say not then in your heart, I *was once* baptized; therefore I *am*

---

[76] Cf. 1 John 3:9.
[77] Phil. 4:7.
[78] Cf. 2 Cor. 1:12; 1 Pet. 3:21.
[79] Cf. Rom. 8:16.
[80] Cf. 1 Thess. 5:16; Rom. 5:11.
[81] 1 Thess. 1:3; Heb. 6:10.
[82] Cf. Luke 6:36.
[83] Cf. 1 Pet. 1:16; Lev. 11:44, 45. [84] Matt. 5:48.
[85] Cf. 1 Cor. 2:12. [86] Cf. 1 John 3:19.
[87] John 3:5. Orig., in all edns. except *Works* (1771), 'and of spirit'.
[88] See 1 Cor. 6:19. [89] Col. 2:11.
[90] Rom. 2:25. An indirect allusion to the Calvinist doctrine of perseverance and an implied rejection of it. Cf. the longer analysis of that doctrine and Wesley's detailed refutation of it in *Predestination Calmly Considered*, §§63-83.

now a child of God.[91] Alas, that consequence will by no means hold. How many are the baptized gluttons and drunkards, the baptized liars and common swearers, the baptized railers and evil-speakers, the baptized whoremongers, thieves, extortioners! What think you? Are these now the children of God? Verily I say unto you, whosoever you are, unto whom any of the preceding characters belong, 'Ye are of your father the devil, and the works of your father ye do.'[92] Unto you I call in the name of him whom you crucify afresh, and in his words to your circumcised predecessors, 'Ye serpents, ye generation of vipers, how can you escape the damnation of hell?'[93]

4. How indeed, except ye be born again![94] For ye are now dead in trespasses and sins.[95] To say then that ye cannot be born again, that there is no new birth but in baptism, is to seal you all under damnation, to consign you to hell, without any help, without hope. And perhaps some may think this just and right. In their zeal for the Lord of Hosts they may say, 'Yea, cut off the sinners, the Amalekites![96] Let these Gibeonites be utterly destroyed!'[97] They deserve no less.' No; nor I, nor you—mine and your desert, as well as theirs, is hell.[98] And it is mere mercy, free undeserved mercy, that *we* are not now in unquenchable fire.[99] You will say, 'But we are washed, we were born again of water and of the Spirit.' So *were* they. This therefore hinders not at all, but that ye may *now* be even as they. Know ye not that 'what is highly esteemed of men is an abomination in the sight of God'?[100] Come forth, ye 'saints of the world',[101] ye that are honoured of men, and see who will cast the first stone at them, at these wretches not fit to live upon the earth, these common harlots, adulterers, murderers. Only learn ye first what that meaneth, 'He that hateth his brother is a murderer'[ee]— 'He that looketh on a woman to lust

---

[ee] 1 John 3:15.

---

[91] Cf. Luther, *Baptism*, XI, XV, but also, XX; see also Roland Bainton, *Here I Stand; A Life of Martin Luther* (New York and Nashville, Abingdon-Cokesbury Press, 1950), p. 367. See above, No. 14, *The Repentance of Believers*, I.9 and n.
[92] Cf. John 8:44.
[93] Cf. Matt. 23:33. See also No. 45, 'The New Birth', IV. 1, 2, 4.
[94] See John 3:3.   [95] Eph. 2:1.   [96] Cf. 1 Sam. 15:18.
[97] Cf. 1 Sam. 15:6-20; but see also 2 Sam. 21:1-9.
[98] Cf. No. 26, 'Sermon on the Mount, VI', III.12 and n.
[99] Matt. 3:12; cf. Luke 3:17.   [100] Cf. Luke 16:15.
[101] Juan de Valdés—as above, No. 4, *Scriptural Christianity*, II.5 and n.

after her hath committed adultery with her already in his heart'[ff]—'Ye adulterers and adulteresses, know ye not that the friendship of the world is enmity with God?'[gg]

5. 'Verily, verily, I say unto you, ye also must be born again.'[102] 'Except' ye also 'be born again, ye cannot see the kingdom of God.'[103] Lean no more on the staff of that broken reed,[104] that ye *were* born again in baptism. Who denies that ye were then made 'children of God, and heirs of the kingdom of heaven'?[105] But notwithstanding this, ye are now children of the devil; therefore ye must be born again. And let not Satan put it into your heart to cavil at a word, when the thing is clear. Ye have heard what are the marks of the children of God; all ye who have them not on your souls, baptized or unbaptized, must needs receive them, or without doubt ye will perish everlastingly. And if ye have been baptized, your only hope is this: that those who were made the children of God by baptism, but are now the children of the devil, may yet again receive 'power to become the sons of God';[106] that they may receive again what they have lost, even the 'Spirit of adoption, crying in their hearts, Abba, Father'![107]

6. Amen, Lord Jesus! May everyone who prepareth his heart yet again to seek thy face receive again that Spirit of adoption, and cry out, Abba, Father! Let him now again have power to believe in thy name as to become a child of God; as to know and feel he hath 'redemption in thy blood, even the forgiveness of sins',[108] and that he 'cannot commit sin, because he is born of God'.[109] Let him be now 'begotten again unto a living hope',[110] so as to 'purify himself, as thou art pure'![111] And 'because he is a son',[112] let the Spirit of love and of glory rest upon him, cleansing him 'from all filthiness of flesh and spirit', and teaching him to 'perfect holiness in the fear of God'![113]

[ff] Matt. 5:28.
[gg] Jas. 4:4.

---

[102] Cf. John 3:3.   [103] *Ibid.*
[104] Isa. 36:6.
[105] Cf. 'Of Salvation', Pt. I, ¶2, *Homilies*, p. 17: 'infants being baptized . . . are . . . brought to God's favour and made his children and inheritors of his kingdom of heaven.' See also Rom. 8:16-17.
[106] John 1:12.   [107] Cf. Rom. 8:15.
[108] Cf. Col. 1:14.   [109] Cf. 1 John 3:9.
[110] Cf. 1 Pet. 1:3.   [111] Cf. 1 John 3:3.
[112] Cf. Gal. 4:6.   [113] Cf. 2 Cor. 7:1.

The Great Privilege of those that are Born of God

1 John 3:9

Whosoever is born of God doth not commit sin.

1. It has been frequently supposed that the being born of God 5 was all one with the being justified; that the new birth and justification were only different expressions denoting the same thing:[1] it being certain on the one hand that whoever is justified is also born of God, and on the other that whoever is born of God is also justified; yea, that both these gifts of God are given to every 10 believer in one and the same moment. In one point of time his sins are blotted out and he is born of God.

2. But though it be allowed that justification and the new birth are in point of time inseparable from each other, yet are they easily distinguished as being not the same, but things of a widely 15 different nature. Justification implies only a relative, the new birth a real, change.[2] God in justifying us does something *for* us: in

---

[1] As in William Law, *The Grounds and Reasons of Christian Regeneration, or the New Birth* (1739), §§22-31 (*Works*, V. 155-66). But see also, even if in a differently nuanced statement, Arthur Bedford's sermon, *The Doctrine of Justification by Faith* (1741). The longer tradition to which Wesley here refers goes back to the Reformation, as in Quenstedt, *Theologia Didactico Polemica*, where, in III. 477, it is affirmed that regeneration may be 'taken *strictly* for the remission of sins or justification (Gal. 3:11), in which sense the Formula of Concord states it to be very frequently used in the *Apology of the Augsburg Confession*; or for renovation as it shows it to be frequently used by Luther.' In the Reformed tradition regeneration was more closely related to '*calling*' (the *applicatio salutis*) and thus rooted in the doctrine of election (*vocatio*). See Heppe, *Reformed Dogmatics*, ch. xx, pp. 510-30.

See also No. 1, *Salvation by Faith*, II.7: 'Justification . . . implies a deliverance from guilt and punishment,' and is *followed by* the new birth, which is its fullness, cf. the later sermon 'On Patience' (No. 83), §9. This correlation (and differentiation) between justification and regeneration was crucial for Wesley's distinction between God's action in pardoning the repentant and the human effect of this action ('regeneration', 'new birth', 'conversion'). Cf. No. 14, *The Repentance of Believers*, III.2 and n.

[2] Cf. No. 43, *The Scripture Way of Salvation*, I.4. In both places, and generally, Wesley sees justification as a change in the relationship between God and the believer, whereas regeneration is a '*real change*' of heart. Thus it is the threshold of the process of holy living, logically consequent upon justification and the beginning of sanctification. The two, then, are concurrent and yet decisively different.

begetting us again he does the work *in* us. The former changes
our outward relation to God, so that of enemies we become
children; by the latter our inmost souls are changed, so that of
sinners we become saints. The one restores us to the favour, the
5 other to the image of God. The one is the taking away the guilt,
the other the taking away the power, of sin. So that although they
are joined together in point of time, yet are they of wholly distinct
natures.

3. The not discerning this, the not observing the wide
10 difference there is between being justified and being born again,
has occasioned exceeding great confusion of thought in many
who have treated on this subject; particularly when they have
attempted to explain this great privilege of the children of God, to
show how 'whosoever is born of God doth not commit sin.'[3]
15 4. In order to apprehend this clearly it may be necessary, first,
to consider what is the proper meaning of that expression,
'whosoever is born of God'; and, secondly, to inquire in what
sense he 'doth not commit sin'.

I.1. First, we are to consider what is the proper meaning of that
20 expression, 'whosoever is born of God'.[4] And in general, from all
the passages of Holy Writ wherein this expression, the being
'born of God', occurs, we may learn that it implies not barely the
being baptized, or any outward change whatever; but a vast
inward change; a change wrought in the soul by the operation of
25 the Holy Ghost, a change in the whole manner of our existence;
for from the moment we are 'born of God' we live in quite another
manner than we did before; we are, as it were, in another world.[5]

2. The ground and reason of the expression is easy to be
understood. When we undergo this great change we may with
30 much propriety be said 'to be born again', because there is so near
a resemblance between the circumstances of the natural and of
the spiritual birth; so that to consider the circumstances of the
natural birth[6] is the most easy way to understand the spiritual.

3. The child which is not yet born subsists indeed by the air, as

---

[3] 1 John 3:9.

[4] An echo here from the Elizabethan Homilies, XVI, 'The Coming Down of the Holy
Ghost', *Homilies*, pp. 409-10. Cf. No. 45, 'The New Birth', II.1 ff.

[5] For this concept of the kinds of changes wrought in regeneration see Nos. 43, *The
Scripture Way of Salvation*, I.4; 45, 'The New Birth', II.5; 83, 'On Patience', §9; see also
No. 5, 'Justification by Faith', II.1.

[6] Cf. No. 9, 'The Spirit of Bondage and of Adoption', §5 and n.

does everything which has life; but *feels* it not, nor anything else, unless in a very dull and imperfect manner. It *hears* little, if at all, the organs of hearing being as yet closed up. It *sees* nothing, having its eyes fast shut, and being surrounded with utter darkness. There are, it may be, some faint beginnings of life when 5 the time of its birth draws nigh, and some motion consequent thereon, whereby it is distinguished from a mere mass of matter. But it has no *senses*; all these avenues of the soul are hitherto quite shut up. Of consequence it has scarce any intercourse with this visible world, nor any knowledge, conception, or idea of the 10 things that occur therein.

4. The reason why he that is not yet born is wholly a stranger to the visible world is not because it is afar off—it is very nigh; it surrounds him on every side—but partly because he has not those senses (they are not yet opened in his soul) whereby alone it is 15 possible to hold commerce with the material world; and partly because so thick a veil is cast between, through which he can discern nothing.[7]

5. But no sooner is the child born into the world than he exists in a quite different manner. He now *feels* the air with which he is 20 surrounded, and which pours into him from every side, as fast as he alternately breathes it back, to sustain the flame of life. And hence springs a continual increase of strength, of motion, and of sensation; all the bodily senses being now awakened and furnished with their proper objects. 25

His eyes are now opened to perceive the light, which silently flowing in upon them discovers not only itself but an infinite variety of things with which before he was wholly unacquainted. His ears are unclosed, and sounds rush in with endless diversity. Every sense is employed upon such objects as are peculiarly 30 suitable to it. And by these inlets the soul, having an open intercourse with the visible world, acquires more and more knowledge of sensible things, of all the things which are under the sun.

6. So it is with him that is born of God. Before that great change is wrought, although he subsists by him in whom all that have life 35

---

[7] This latency metaphor is one of Wesley's favourites; it stands as a premise of his religious epistemology (based as that was on ideas derived from Descartes through Malebranche, the Cambridge Platonists and John Norris); cf. No. 10, 'The Witness of the Spirit, I', I.12 and n. See also No. 130, 'On Living without God', §§2-12, for a striking illustration about an immured toad.

'live and move and have their being',[8] yet he is not *sensible* of God. He does not *feel*, he has no inward consciousness of his presence. He does not perceive that divine breath of life without which he cannot subsist a moment. Nor is he sensible of any of the things of God. They make no impression upon his soul. God is continually calling to him from on high, but he heareth not; his ears are shut; so that 'the voice of the charmer' is lost to him, 'charm he never so wisely'.[9] He seeth not the things of the Spirit of God, the eyes of his understanding being closed,[10] and utter darkness covering his whole soul, surrounding him on every side. It is true he may have some faint dawnings of life, some small beginnings of spiritual motion; but as yet he has no spiritual senses capable of discerning spiritual objects. Consequently, he 'discerneth not the things of the Spirit of God. He cannot know them; because they are spiritually discerned.'[11]

7. Hence he has scarce any knowledge of the invisible world, as he has scarce any intercourse with it. Not that it is afar off. No; he is in the midst of it: it encompasses him round about. The 'other world', as we usually term it, is not far from every one of us. It is above, and beneath, and on every side.[12] Only the natural man discerneth it not; partly because he has no spiritual senses, whereby alone we can discern the things of God; partly because so thick a veil is interposed as he knows not how to penetrate.

8. But when he is born of God, born of the Spirit, how is the manner of his existence changed! His whole soul is now sensible of God, and he can say by sure experience, 'Thou art about my bed, and about my path;' I feel thee in 'all my ways'.[13] 'Thou besettest me behind and before, and layest thy hand upon me.'[14] The Spirit or breath of God is immediately inspired, breathed into the new-born soul; and the same breath which comes from, returns to God. As it is continually received by faith, so it is continually rendered back by love, by prayer, and praise, and thanksgiving—love and praise and prayer being the breath of every soul which is truly born of God. And by this new kind of spiritual respiration, spiritual life is not only sustained but increased day by day, together with spiritual strength and motion

---

[8] Acts 17:28.
[9] Ps. 58:5 (BCP).
[10] See Eph. 1:18.
[11] Cf. 1 Cor. 2:14.
[13] Ps. 139:2 (BCP).

[12] See Acts 17:23-28.
[14] Ps. 139:5 (AV).

and sensation; all the senses of the soul being now awake, and capable of 'discerning' spiritual 'good and evil'.[15]

9. 'The eyes of his understanding'[16] are now open, and he 'seeth him that is invisible'.[17] He sees what is 'the exceeding greatness of his power'[18] and of his love toward them that believe. He sees that God is merciful to him a sinner;[19] that he is reconciled through the Son of his love. He clearly perceives both the pardoning love of God and all his 'exceeding great and precious promises'.[20] 'God, who commanded the light to shine out of the darkness, hath shined' and doth shine 'in his heart, to enlighten him with the knowledge of the glory of God in the face of Jesus Christ.'[21] All the darkness is now passed away, and he abides in the light of God's countenance.

10. His ears are now opened, and the voice of God no longer calls in vain. He hears and obeys the heavenly calling; he 'knows the voice of his shepherd'.[22] All his spiritual senses being now awakened, he has a clear intercourse with the invisible world. And hence he knows more and more of the things which before it 'could not enter into his heart to conceive'.[23] He now knows what the peace of God is; what is joy in the Holy Ghost; what the love of God which is shed abroad in the hearts[24] of them that believe through Christ Jesus. Thus the veil being removed which before interrupted the light and voice, the knowledge and love of God, he who is born of the Spirit, 'dwelling in love, dwelleth in God and God in him'.[25]

II.1. Having considered the meaning of that expression, 'whosoever is born of God', it remains in the second place to inquire in what sense he 'doth not commit sin'.

Now one who is so born of God as hath been above described, who continually receives into his soul the breath of life from God, the gracious influence of his Spirit, and continually renders it back; one who thus believes and loves, who by faith perceives the continual actings of God upon his spirit, and by a kind of spiritual

[15] Cf. Heb. 5:14.
[16] Cf. Eph. 1:18.
[17] Heb. 11:27.
[18] Eph. 1:19.
[19] See Luke 18:13.   [20] 2 Pet. 1:4.
[21] 2 Cor. 4:6; orig. 'both shined', altered to 'hath shined' in 1771, 1787.
[22] Cf. John 10:4.   [23] Cf. 1 Cor. 2:9.
[24] See Rom. 5:5.   [25] Cf. 1 John 4:16.

re-action[26] returns the grace he receives in unceasing love, and praise, and prayer; not only 'doth not commit sin'[27] while he thus 'keepeth himself',[28] but so long as this 'seed remaineth in him he cannot sin',[29] because he is born of God.

5   2. By 'sin' I here understand outward sin, according to the plain, common acceptation of the word: an actual, voluntary 'transgression of the law';[30] of the revealed, written law of God; of any commandment of God acknowledged to be such at the time that it is transgressed. But 'whosoever is born of God', while he
10 abideth in faith and love and in the spirit of prayer and thanksgiving, not only 'doth not', but 'cannot' thus 'commit sin'.[31] So long as he thus believeth in God through Christ and loves him, and is pouring out his heart before him, he cannot voluntarily transgress any command of God, either by speaking or acting
15 what he knows God hath forbidden—so long that 'seed' which 'remaineth in him'[32] (that loving, praying, thankful faith) compels him to refrain from whatsoever he knows to be an abomination in the sight of God.

3. But here a difficulty will immediately occur, and one that to
20 many has appeared insuperable, and induced them to deny the plain assertion of the Apostle, and give up the privilege of the children of God.

It is plain, in fact, that those whom we cannot deny to have been truly 'born of God' (the Spirit of God having given us in his Word
25 this infallible testimony concerning them) nevertheless not only could but did commit sin, even gross, outward sin. They did transgress the plain, known laws of God, speaking or acting what they knew he had forbidden.

4. Thus David was unquestionably born of God or ever he was
30 anointed king over Israel. He knew in whom he had believed;[33] he was strong in faith, giving glory to God.[34] 'The Lord', saith he, 'is

---

[26] Wesley's own hyphen here, for emphasis; cf. III.2, below, 'a continual action of God upon the soul and a re-action of the soul upon God' (and see the *OED's* misdated citation of this—as 1771 instead of 1748—as a pioneer usage). See also, below, III.3.

[27] 1 John 3:9.

[28] 1 John 5:18.

[29] 1 John 3:9.

[30] 1 John 3:4. Cf. No. 13, *On Sin in Believers*, intro., I.6 and n.

[31] Cf. 1 John 3:9. For another discussion of this same point cf. No. 40, *Christian Perfection*, II.14 ff.

[32] Cf. 1 John 3:9.

[33] See 2 Tim. 1:12.

[34] Rom. 4:20.

my shepherd; therefore can I lack nothing. He shall feed me in green pastures, and lead me forth beside the waters of comfort.[. . .] Yea, though I walk through the valley of the shadow of death, I will fear no evil; for thou art with me.'a He was filled with love, such as often constrained him to cry out, 'I will love 5 thee, O Lord, my God; the Lord is my stony rock, and my defence; the horn also of my salvation, and my refuge.'b He was a man of prayer, pouring out his soul before God in all circumstances of life; and abundant in praises and thanksgiving. 'Thy praise', saith he, 'shall be ever in my mouth.'c 'Thou art my 10 God, and I will thank thee; thou art my God, and I will praise thee.'d And yet such a child of God could and did commit sin; yea, the horrid sins of adultery and murder.

5. And even after the Holy Ghost was more largely given, after 'life and immortality were brought to light by the gospel',35 we 15 want not instances of the same melancholy kind, which were also doubtless written for our instruction.36 Thus he who (probably from his selling all that he had, and bringing the price for the relief of his poor brethren) was 'by the apostles' themselves 'surnamed Barnabas', that is, 'the son of consolation';e who was 20 so honoured at Antioch as to be selected with Saul out of all the disciples to carry their 'relief unto the brethren in Judea':f this Barnabas, who at his return from Judea was by the peculiar direction of the Holy Ghost solemnly 'separated' from the other 'prophets and teachers' 'for the work whereunto God had called 25 him',g even to accompany the great Apostle among the Gentiles, and to be his fellow-labourer in every place; nevertheless was afterward so 'sharp' in his 'contention' with St. Paul37 (because he 'thought it not good to take with them' John in his 'visiting the brethren' a second time, 'who had departed from them from 30

---

a Ps. 23:1, 2, 4 [BCP].
b Ps. 18:1, 2 [BCP].
c Ps. 34:1 [BCP].
d Ps. 118:28 [BCP].
e Acts 4:36-37.
f [Acts] 11:29.
g [Acts] 13:1-2.

---

35 Cf. 2 Tim. 1:10.   36 See 1 Cor. 9:10; 10:11; 2 Tim. 3:16-17.
37 Wesley returns repeatedly to this incident (Acts 15:36-41), always to the same point: that while Barnabas may have lost *his* temper in the contention, St. Paul never did; cf. No. 22, 'Sermon on the Mount, II', III.10 and n.

Pamphylia, and went not with them to the work') that he himself
also departed from the work; that he 'took John, and sailed unto
Cyprus',ʰ forsaking him to whom he had been in so immediate a
manner joined by the Holy Ghost.

5   6. An instance more astonishing than both these is given by St.
Paul in his Epistle to the Galatians. 'When Peter', the aged, the
zealous, the first of the apostles, one of the three most highly
favoured by his Lord, 'was come to Antioch, I withstood him to
the face, because he was to be blamed. For before that certain
10   came from James he did eat with the Gentiles'³⁸—the heathens
converted to the Christian faith—as having been peculiarly
taught of God that he 'should not call any man common or
unclean'.ⁱ But 'when they were come, [. . .] he separated himself,
fearing them which were of the circumcision. And the other Jews
15   dissembled likewise with him; insomuch that Barnabas also was
carried away with their dissimulation. But when I saw that they
walked not uprightly according to the truth of the gospel, I said
unto Peter before them all, If thou, being a Jew, livest after the
manner of the Gentiles', not regarding the ceremonial law of
20   Moses, 'why compellest thou the Gentiles to live as do the Jews?'ʲ
Here is also plain undeniable sin, committed by one who was
undoubtedly 'born of God'. But how can this be reconciled with
the assertion of St. John, if taken in the obvious literal meaning,
that 'whosoever is born of God doth not commit sin'?

25   7. I answer, what has been long observed is this: so long as 'he
that is born of God keepeth himself' (which he is able to do, by the
grace of God) 'the wicked one toucheth him not.'³⁹ But if he
keepeth not himself, if he abide not in the faith, he may commit
sin even as another man.⁴⁰

30   It is easy therefore to understand how any of these children of
God might be moved from his own steadfastness, and yet the
great truth of God, declared by the Apostle, remain steadfast and
unshaken. He did not keep himself by that grace of God which

ʰ [Acts] 15:35, 38, 39.
ⁱ Acts 10:28.
ʲ Gal. 2:12-14.

---

³⁸ Gal. 2:11-12.   ³⁹ 1 John 5:18 (*Notes*).
⁴⁰ This idea of backsliding is integral to Wesley's distinction between voluntary and
involuntary sins and to his rejection of 'perseverance' as well. See Nos. 14, *The Repentance
of Believers;* and 13, *On Sin in Believers.*

was sufficient for him.[41] He fell step by step, first into negative, inward sin—not 'stirring up the gift of God'[42] which was in him, not 'watching unto prayer',[43] not 'pressing on to the mark of the prize of his high calling';[44] then into positive, inward sin—inclining to wickedness with his heart, giving way to some evil desire or temper. Next he lost his faith, his sight of a pardoning God, and consequently his love of God. And being then weak and like another man he was capable of committing even outward sin.

8. To explain this by a particular instance. David was born of God, and saw God by faith. He loved God in sincerity. He could truly say, 'Whom have I in heaven but thee? And there is none upon earth' (neither person or thing) 'that I desire in comparison to thee!'[45] But still there remained in his heart that corruption of nature which is the seed of all evil.[46]

He was 'walking upon the roof of his house',[k] probably praising the God whom his soul loved, when he looked and saw Bathsheba. He felt a temptation, a thought which tended to evil. The Spirit of God did not fail to convince him of this. He doubtless heard and knew the warning voice. But he yielded in some measure to the thought, and the temptation began to prevail over him. Hereby his spirit was sullied. He saw God still; but it was more dimly than before. He loved God still; but not in the same degree, not with the same strength and ardour of affection. Yet God checked him again, though his spirit was grieved; and his voice, though fainter and fainter, still whispered, 'Sin lieth at the door;'[47] 'look unto me, and be thou saved.'[48] But he would not hear. He looked again, not unto God, but unto the forbidden object, till nature was superior to grace, and kindled lust in his soul.

The eye of his mind was now closed again, and God vanished out of his sight. Faith, the divine, supernatural intercourse with

---

[k] 2 Sam. 11:2.

---

[41] See 2 Cor. 12:9.　　　　[42] Cf. 2 Tim. 1:6.　　　　[43] Cf. 1 Pet. 4:7.
[44] Cf. Phil. 3:14.　　　　　　　　　　　　　　　　　[45] Ps. 73:25 (BCP).
[46] Cf. Luther, *Baptism*, VIII: 'Thus, St. Paul in Romans vii, and all the saints with him, lament that they are sinners and have sin in their nature, although they were baptized and were holy; and they lament thus because their natural sinful appetites are always active so long as we live.' Wesley was caught here between two extremes, rejecting not only all Lutheran and Calvinist versions of *invincible concupiscence* but also all counterclaims to 'sinless perfection'. See No. 8, 'The First-fruits of the Spirit', II.6 and n.
[47] Gen. 4:7.　　　　　　　　　　　　　　　　　　　　[48] Cf. Isa. 45:22.

God, and the love of God ceased together. He then rushed on as a horse into the battle,[49] and knowingly committed the outward sin.[50]

9. You see the unquestionable progress from grace to sin. Thus it goes on, from step to step. (1). The divine seed of loving, conquering faith remains in him that is 'born of God'. 'He keepeth himself ', by the grace of God, and 'cannot commit' sin; (2). A temptation arises, whether from the world, the flesh, or the devil, it matters not; (3). The Spirit of God gives him warning that sin is near, and bids him more abundantly watch unto prayer; (4). He gives way in some degree to the temptation, which now begins to grow pleasing to him; (5). The Holy Spirit is grieved; his faith is weakened, and his love of God grows cold; (6). The Spirit reproves him more sharply, and saith, 'This is the way; walk thou in it.'[51] (7). He turns away from the painful voice of God and listens to the pleasing voice of the tempter; (8). Evil desire begins and spreads in his soul, till faith and love vanish away; (9). He is then capable of committing outward sin, the power of the Lord being departed from him.

10. To explain this by another instance. The Apostle Peter was full of faith and of the Holy Ghost;[52] and hereby keeping himself he had a conscience void of offence toward God and toward man.[53]

Walking thus in simplicity and godly sincerity,[54] 'before that certain came from James he did eat with the Gentiles',[55] knowing that what God had cleansed was not common or unclean.

But 'when they were come' a temptation arose in his heart to 'fear those of the circumcision'[56] (the Jewish converts who were zealous for circumcision and the other rites of the Mosaic law) and regard the favour and praise of these men more than the praise of God.

He was warned by the Spirit that sin was near. Nevertheless, he yielded to it in some degree, even to sinful fear of man, and his faith and love were proportionably weakened.

God reproved him again for giving place to the devil. Yet he

---

[49] See Jer. 8:6.
[50] Cf. No. 13, *On Sin in Believers*, intro., III. 1-9 and n.
[51] Cf. Isa. 30:21.
[52] Acts 6:5 where the reference is to Stephen.
[53] Acts 24:16 where the reference is to Paul.
[54] 2 Cor. 1:12. Cf. No. 2, *The Almost Christian*, I.9 and n.
[55] Gal. 2:12; cf. Wesley's revision in *Notes*.
[56] *Ibid.*

would not hearken to the voice of his Shepherd, but gave himself up to that slavish fear, and thereby quenched the Spirit.[57]

Then God disappeared, and faith and love being extinct he committed the outward sin. 'Walking not uprightly, not according to the truth of the gospel', he 'separated himself' from his Christian brethren, and by his evil example, if not advice also, 'compelled' even 'the Gentiles to live after the manner of the Jews';[58] to entangle themselves again with that 'yoke of bondage' from which 'Christ had set them free'.[59]

Thus it is unquestionably true that he who is born of God, keeping himself, doth not, cannot commit sin; and yet if he keepeth not himself he may commit all manner of sin with greediness.

III.1. From the preceding considerations we may learn, first, to give a clear and incontestable answer to a question which has frequently perplexed many who were sincere of heart. Does sin precede or follow the loss of faith? Does a child of God first commit sin, and thereby lose his faith? Or does he lose his faith first, before he can commit sin?

I answer: some sin, of omission at least, must necessarily precede the loss of faith—some inward sin. But the loss of faith must precede the committing outward sin.[60]

The more any believer examines his own heart, the more will he be convinced of this: that 'faith working by love'[61] excludes both inward and outward sin from a soul 'watching unto prayer';[62] that nevertheless we are even then liable to temptation, particularly to the sin that did easily beset us;[63] that if the loving eye of the soul be steadily fixed on God the temptation soon vanishes away. But if not, if we are ἐξελκόμενοι (as the Apostle James speaks), 'drawn out' of God by our 'own desire', and δελεαζόμενοι, 'caught by the bait'[64] of present or promised

---

[57] See 1 Thess. 5:19.
[58] Gal. 2:12, 14.
[59] Gal. 5:1.
[60] This distinction between 'omission' and 'commission' is also essential to the doctrine of 'sin in believers' and the necessary 'repentance of believers'. But the line between involuntary and voluntary omissions is easy to slide across, in one direction or the other, and this never ceased to be a problem for Wesley. Cf. No. 14, *The Repentance of Believers*, I.14 and n.
[61] Gal. 5:6. Cf. No. 2, *The Almost Christian*, II.6 and n.
[62] Cf. 1 Pet. 4:7.   [63] Heb. 12:1.
[64] Jas. 1:14. Cf. *Notes*, and also No. 26, 'Sermon on the Mount, VI', III.15.

pleasure: then that 'desire conceived' in us 'brings forth sin';[65] and having by that inward sin destroyed our faith, it casts us headlong into the snare of the devil, so that we may commit any outward sin whatever.

5 2. From what has been said we may learn, secondly, what the life of God in the soul of a believer is, wherein it properly consists, and what is immediately and necessarily implied therein. It immediately and necessarily implies the continual inspiration of God's Holy Spirit: God's breathing into the soul, and the soul's
10 breathing back what it first receives from God; a continual action of God upon the soul, the re-action of the soul upon God; an unceasing presence of God, the loving, pardoning God, manifested to the heart, and perceived by faith; and an unceasing return of love, praise, and prayer, offering up all the thoughts of
15 our hearts, all the words of our tongues, all the works of our hands, all our body, soul, and spirit, to be an holy sacrifice, acceptable unto God[66] in Christ Jesus.

3. And hence we may, thirdly, infer the absolute necessity of this re-action of the soul (whatsoever it be called) in order to the
20 continuance of the divine life therein. For it plainly appears God does not continue to act upon the soul unless the soul re-acts upon God. He prevents us indeed with the blessings of his goodness. He first loves us, and manifests himself unto us. While we are yet afar off he calls us to himself, and shines upon our
25 hearts.[67] But if we do not then love him who first loved us;[68] if we will not hearken to his voice; if we turn our eye away from him, and will not attend to the light which he pours upon us: his Spirit will not always strive; he will gradually withdraw, and leave us to the darkness of our own hearts. He will not continue to breathe
30 into our soul unless our soul breathes toward him again; unless our love, and prayer, and thanksgiving return to him, a sacrifice wherewith he is well pleased.

4. Let us learn, lastly, to follow that direction of the great Apostle: 'Be not high-minded, but fear.'[69] Let us fear sin more
35 than death or hell. Let us have a jealous (though not painful) fear,

---

[65] Cf. Jas. 1:15.
[66] See Rom. 12:1.
[67] See Luke 15:20.
[68] See 1 John 4:19.
[69] Rom. 11:20.

lest we should lean to our own deceitful hearts.[70] 'Let him that standeth take heed lest he fall.'[71] Even he who now standeth fast in the grace of God, in the faith that 'overcometh the world',[72] may nevertheless fall into inward sin, and thereby 'make shipwreck of his faith'.[73] And how easily then will outward sin regain its dominion over him! Thou, therefore, O man of God, watch always, that thou mayest always hear the voice of God. Watch that thou mayest pray without ceasing,[74] at all times and in all places pouring out thy heart before him. So shalt thou always believe, and always love, and never commit sin.

---

[70] Cf. Charles Wesley's hymn, 'For a Tender Conscience', st. 2:

> I want a principle within
> Of jealous, godly fear,
> A sensibility of sin,
> A pain to feel it near.

(*Hymns and Sacred Poems* (1749), II. 230.)
[71] 1 Cor. 10:12.
[72] 1 John 5:4.
[73] Cf. 1 Tim. 1:19.
[74] 1 Thess. 5:17.

THE LORD OUR RIGHTEOUSNESS

AN INTRODUCTORY COMMENT

The preceding sermon had been written in 1747 or 1748 and for SOSO, *II (1748); there it had been followed directly by Wesley's thirteen-sermon series 'Upon our Lord's Sermon on the Mount'. At that time, it seemed natural enough to progress directly from the negative powers of faith ('not to sin') to an extended comment on faith's positive fruits. This present sermon, from a later period, was inserted in this particular place by Wesley in his collected* Works *(1771), II, and, at first glance, it might seem intrusive. A closer look, however, suggests that in 1771 Wesley could see the need for a clearer soteriological restatement between his sermon on faith's 'privileges' and his series on its 'duties'. There would be a good reason for this: in the interval between 1748 and 1771 the conflict with the Calvinists had worsened, and there was an obvious need at this particular juncture for a clearer statement of his counterposition on 'imputation' and 'impartation' in justification by faith.*

The conflict stretched back to the breach between the Wesleys and George Whitefield, with John's sermon on Free Grace *(1739) and Charles's thirty-six stanza poem, 'The Horrible Decree'. Characteristically, Wesley never understood why the Calvinists should have taken offence at his criticisms, and thus continued to repeat his sincere but unrealistic appeals to them for closer fellowship, as in his letter to Henry Venn, June 22, 1763: 'I desire to have a league offensive and defensive with every soldier of Christ.' It baffled him that, in response, he got more criticism than cooperation.*

The criticism came from such men as Jonathan Warne and John Cennick and was climaxed in 1755 by a three-volume 'dialogue' by a former pupil and fellow 'Oxford Methodist', James Hervey, since turned Calvinist, and rector of Weston Flavell. Hervey was already well known for his Meditations Among the Tombs. *Now, in his long, drawn-out* Theron and Aspasio, *he had laid out the differences between 'Theron' (his eponym for Arminians, generally) and 'Aspasio' (i.e., himself as a representative English Calvinist arguing plausibly for 'the imputed righteousness of Christ' as the prime reality in justification); needless to*

444

say, 'Theron' comes off rather badly in the 'dialogue'. Hervey had sent a pre-publication copy of his manuscript to Wesley who, like an old tutor attempting to improve the revision, had dashed off a set of critical annotations for Hervey's private eyes. The dialogues appeared unrevised and Wesley, somewhat peevishly, proceeded to publish his annotations on them, as 'A Letter to the Rev. Mr. ———', in his Preservative Against Unsettled Notions in Religion *(1758), pp. 211-36.*

This unexpected attack wounded the gentle-spirited Hervey and prompted him to reply in a series of long letters to Wesley that he wisely left unposted and unpublished at his death in 1758 (with explicit instructions that they should never be published). However, they fell into the hands of William Cudworth, who promptly put them in print in a form, as Hervey's brother William complained, 'so faulty and incorrect that little judgment can be formed from it of the propriety and force of my brother's answers to Mr. Westley'. Hence, an 'official' edition of Eleven Letters from the late Rev. Mr. Hervey to the Rev. Mr. John Wesley; containing an Answer to that Gentleman's Remarks on Theron and Aspasio *(1765).* The Lord Our Righteousness *was Wesley's prompt response.*

It was preached on Sunday, November 24, 1765, in the chapel in West Street, near Seven Dials (a chapel which belonged to the parish of St. Clement Dane's; earlier, it had been loaned to the Huguenots and then to the Methodists; its old pulpit is still preserved in the nearby church of St. Giles-in-the-Fields). This sermon represents Wesley in as irenic a mood as the circumstances allowed, viz., given the need for an unmistakable rejection of all one-sided emphases on 'imputation'.

There was, of course, much more at stake in this affair than an unhappy rift between two former friends. Its central issue was whether Christ's atoning death is to be understood as the 'formal' or the 'meritorious' cause of a sinner's justification. This had divided British theologians since the days of Davenant and Downame; cf. C. F. Allison, The Rise of Moralism *(chs. 1–3); but see also Alexander Hamilton's obscure* Cordial for Christians Travelling Heavenward *(1696), p. 69. The doctrine of 'formal cause' implied some sort of correlated view of predestination and irresistible grace. The idea of 'meritorious cause', while still 'evangelical', allowed for prevenience, free will, and 'universal redemption'. To the Calvinists, however, this was merely a subtler form of works-righteousness, indeed of 'popery' or something very like it. For his part, Hervey is generous enough to discount the insinuations he had heard, 'that Mr. Wesley is a Jesuit in disguise' (p. 122). Yet he felt it proper to suggest that Wesley's principles halt* '*between Protestantism and Popery*' (*p. 123*), that '*Wesley is pleased to associate with the Papists in ascribing our salvation partly to inherent, partly to imputed, righteousness*' (*p. 228*), that *Wesley's views are markedly similar to those of Bellarmine* (*p. 228, n.*). *Finally, Hervey stresses the contrast between Wesley's misleading notion that 'God's great end is to impart happiness to his creatures' and the Calvinist vision of man's chief end as the enhancement of God's glory* (*p. 291*).

Hervey and his friends had found abundant evidence of Wesley's synergism, particularly in 'The Marks of the New Birth' and 'The Great Privilege of those that are Born of God' (cf. Eleven Letters, p. 197, 'Sin remains in us till the Day of Judgment'). In 1771, therefore, when the breach with the Calvinists had become irreparable, it seemed urgent for Wesley to place The Lord Our Righteousness *between 'The Great Privilege . . .' and the discourses on the Sermon on the Mount, out of chronological order but in response to a pressing need for clarity on a particular point. He begins with an assertion of the premises of faith alone which is as clear and forceful as any he had ever made before. And yet his conclusions develop quite differently from anything in the Lutheran and Calvinist traditions based on those same premises. It is in this sense, then, that* The Lord Our Righteousness *may be reckoned as yet another 'landmark sermon'. It signals the end of Wesley's efforts to avoid an open rift with the Calvinists; it signals the beginning of that stage in his career that we have labelled 'the later Wesley'. Moreover, in its own right, it is a revealing sample of Wesley's earnest, even if largely unavailing, efforts to agree and disagree in matters of 'theological opinions' while still holding fast to the Christian unity made possible by shared beliefs in what he understood to be the* essentials *of Christian doctrine.*

The present text is based on that of the first edition of 1766. For a stemma illustrating the textual history of the nine extant editions issued during Wesley's lifetime and a list of substantive variant readings, see Appendix, 'Wesley's Text', Vol. IV. See also Bibliog, *No. 295.*

The LORD our RIGHTEOUSNESS

A

SERMON

PREACHED AT THE

Chappel in West-Street, Seven-Dials,

On SUNDAY, Nov. 24, 1765.

By JOHN WESLEY,

LONDON:

Printed for the Benefit of the Poor,

And sold by J. FLETCHER, at the Oxford
Theatre, St. Paul's Church-Yard; G. KEITH
at the Bible, Grace-Church-Street; E. CABE,
Ave-Mary-Lane, and M. ENGLEFIELD, at
the Bible, West-Street, Seven-Dials, 1766.

The Lord Our Righteousness

Jeremiah 23:6

This is his name whereby he shall be called,
The Lord our righteousness.

1. How dreadful and how innumerable are the contests which 5
have arisen about religion! And not only among the children of
this world,[1] among those who knew not what true religion was; but
even among the children of God, those who had experienced 'the
kingdom of God within them',[2] who had tasted of 'righteousness,
and peace, and joy in the Holy Ghost'.[3] How many of these in all 10
ages, instead of joining together against the common enemy, have
turned their weapons against each other, and so not only wasted
their precious time but hurt one another's spirits, weakened each
other's hands, and so hindered the great work of their common
Master! How many of the weak have hereby been offended! How 15
many of the 'lame turned out of the way'![4] How many sinners
confirmed in their disregard of all religion, and their contempt of
those that profess it! And how many of 'the excellent ones upon
earth'[5] have been constrained to 'weep in secret places'![6]

2. What would not every lover of God and his neighbour do, 20
what would he not suffer, to remedy this sore evil? To remove
contention from the children of God? To restore or preserve
peace among them? What but a good conscience would he think
too dear to part with in order to promote this valuable end? And
suppose we cannot 'make these wars to cease in all the world',[7] 25
suppose we cannot reconcile all the children of God to each
other; however, let each do what he can, let him contribute if it be
but two mites toward it.[8] Happy are they who are able in any

---

[1] Luke 16:8; 20:34. See also No. 4, *Scriptural Christianity,* II.5 and n., for an equivalent
phrase, 'saints of the world' (Juàn de Valdés's *'santos del mundo'*).
[2] Cf. Luke 17:21.   [3] Rom. 14:17.
[4] Heb. 12:13.   [5] Cf. Ps. 16:3.
[6] Jer. 13:17.   [7] Cf. Ps. 46:9 (BCP).
[8] See Mark 12:41-44.

degree to promote 'peace and goodwill among men'![9] Especially among good men; among those that are all listed under the banner of 'the Prince of Peace';[10] and are therefore peculiarly engaged, 'as much as lies in them, to live peaceably with all men'.[11]

5   3. It would be a considerable step toward this glorious end if we could bring good men to understand one another. Abundance of disputes arise purely from the want of this, from mere misapprehension. Frequently neither of the contending parties understands what his opponent means; whence it follows that
10 each violently attacks the other while there is no real difference between them.[12] And yet it is not always an easy matter to convince them of this. Particularly when their passions are moved: it is then attended with the utmost difficulty. However, it is not impossible; especially when we attempt it, not trusting in ourselves, but
15 having all our dependence upon him with whom all things are possible.[13] How soon is he able to disperse the cloud, to shine upon their hearts, and to enable them both to understand each other and 'the truth as it is in Jesus'![14]

4. One very considerable article of this truth is contained in the
20 words above recited, 'This is his name whereby he shall be called, The Lord our righteousness:' a truth this which enters deep into the nature of Christianity, and in a manner supports the whole frame of it. Of this undoubtedly may be affirmed what Luther affirms of a truth closely connected with it: it is *articulus stantis vel*
25 *cadentis ecclesiae*[15]—the Christian church stands or falls with it. It is

---

[9] Cf. Luke 2:14.   [10] Isa. 9:6.
[11] Cf. Rom. 12:18.

[12] An echo of John Locke's account of the motivations for his *Essay Concerning Human Understanding* (see his 'Epistle to the Reader', dated 1689, pp. xlvi-xlvii); *viz.*, that more confusion results from misunderstanding than from actual disagreement. A marginal note in James Tyrrell's copy of the *Essay* reports that the whole project was prompted by a discussion amongst Locke's 'group of friends' concerning the issues of 'morality and revealed religion'. It was Locke's hope to show that misunderstandings can usually be reduced if the disputants will agree on their terms and eschew their biases.

[13] See Matt. 19:26, etc.

[14] Cf. Eph. 4:21.

[15] 'The doctrine on which the church stands or falls'. Wesley's attribution of this famous aphorism to Luther is an interesting sidelight on the life history of such aphorisms. He is obviously repeating a commonplace which he may have read in John Flavel's Πλανηλογία, published in *Mr. John Flavel's Remains . . .* (1691), p. 318: 'The article of justification is deservedly styled by our divines *articulus stantis vel cadentis religionis*', or in Michael Harrison, *Christ's Righteousness Imputed . . .* (n.d. but *c.* 1690), p. 1, where it is attributed to Chemnitz. In WHS, V. 51, C. L. Ford has a note which cites 'Bp. Harold Browne, Article XI' as having found it in Luther, with a further note by one 'F. R.', 'I have not found it *earlier* than Luther.' Franz Hildebrandt, *From Luther to Wesley*, p. 16n., cites it

certainly the pillar and ground of that faith of which alone cometh salvation—of that *catholic* or universal faith which is found in all the children of God, and which 'unless a man keep whole and undefiled, without doubt he shall perish everlastingly'.[16]

5. Might not one therefore reasonably expect, that however they differed in others, all those who name the name of Christ[17] should agree in this point? But how far is this from being the case! There is scarce any wherein they are so little agreed, wherein those who all profess to follow Christ seem so widely and irreconcilably to differ. I say 'seem', because I am throughly convinced that many of them only seem to differ. The disagreement is more in words than in sentiments: they are much nearer in judgment than in language. And a wide difference in language there certainly is, not only between Protestants and Papists, but between Protestant and Protestant; yea, even between those who all believe justification by faith, who agree as well in this as every other fundamental doctrine of the gospel.

6. But if the difference be more in *opinion* than real *experience*, and more in *expression* than in *opinion*, how can it be that even the

as from 'Luther, *Art. Smalcaldi*, Pt. II, §1', without noting that its sense is affirmed in the *Smalkald Articles* (in II, XIII, etc.) but not the literal text.

Wesley will repeat the phrase, without an attribution, JWJ, Dec. 1, 1767; cf. his letter to William Law, Jan. 6, 1756; his *Remarks* on Hill's *Review* and *Farrago Double-Distilled*.

On the point of Luther's coining of the aphorism, Friedrich Loofs tried to puzzle it out in a notable essay, 'Der articulus stantis vel cadentis ecclesiae' in *Theologisches Studien und Kritiken* (1917), 90:323-420. Having found its sense in many places throughout the Luther corpus (e.g., his 'Argument of the Epistle to the Galatians' [*W.A.*, Vol. 40, Pt I, p. 49]), he concludes that its *verbatim* text is not there. Then, following a review of the Lutheran dogmaticians (ignoring Harrison's attribution, above), Loofs concludes (pp. 344-45) that the phrase as such first appears (and clearly he means in Lutheran circles) in one Valentin E. Löscher, *Timotheus Verinus* (1712), pp. 1027-28, and, again, in *Vollständiger Timotheus Verinus* (1718), pp. 342-43. Löscher was involved with Zinzendorf, the Moravians, and the Halle pietists, though not a pietist himself; cf. *The New Schaff-Herzog Encyclopedia of Religious Knowledge* (New York, Funk and Wagnalls Company, 1908–12), *loc. cit.* Would Wesley have heard the aphorism in Herrnhut, associated with Luther?

The 'Bp. Browne' noted above was Bishop Harold Browne, whose assertion (without citation) in his *Exposition of the Thirty-nine Articles* (1871) illustrates the persistence of the slogan: 'Luther strongly propounded his doctrine [of *sola fide*] in its strongest possible form, as the *articulus stantis aut cadentis ecclesiae*.' None of this would have troubled Wesley or many of his first readers, although Hervey was speaking for others besides himself in his comment that 'Mr. Wesley is so unfair in his quotations and so magisterial in his manner that I find it no small difficulty to preserve the decency of the gentleman and the meekness of the Christian in my intended answer' (cf. *Eleven Letters*, Pref., p. v.).

[16] Cf. the so-called Athanasian Creed or *Quicunque Vult* (BCP), and Schaff, *Creeds*, II.66.

[17] See 2 Tim. 2:19.

children of God should so vehemently contend with each other on the point? Several reasons may be assigned for this: the chief is their not understanding one another, joined with too keen an attachment to their *opinions* and particular modes of *expression*.

5   In order to remove this, at least in some measure, in order to our understanding one another on this head, I shall by the help of God endeavour to show,

     I. What is the righteousness of Christ;

     II. When, and in what sense, it is imputed to us;

10   And conclude with a short and plain application.

     And, I. What is the righteousness of Christ? It is twofold, either his divine or his human righteousness.

     1. His divine righteousness belongs to his divine nature, as he is ὁ ὤν, 'He that existeth, over all, God, blessed for ever:'[18] the
15 supreme, the eternal, 'equal with the Father as touching his godhead, though inferior to the Father as touching his manhood'.[19] Now this is his eternal, essential, immutable holiness; his infinite justice, mercy, and truth: in all which 'he and the Father are one.'[20]

20   But I do not apprehend that the divine righteousness of Christ is immediately concerned in the present question. I believe few, if any, do now contend for the *imputation* of *this* righteousness to us. Whoever believes the doctrine of imputation understands it chiefly, if not solely, of his human righteousness.

25   2. The *human righteousness* of Christ belongs to him in his human nature, as he is 'the mediator between God and man, the man Christ Jesus'.[21] This is either *internal* or *external*. His internal righteousness is the image of God[22] stamped on every power and faculty of his soul. It is a copy of his divine righteousness, as far as
30 it can be imparted to a human spirit. It is a transcript of the divine purity, the divine justice, mercy, and truth. It includes love, reverence, resignation to his Father; humility, meekness, gentleness; love to lost mankind, and every other holy and

---

[18] Cf. Rom. 9:5.

[19] Cf. the Athanasian Creed, §33 (Schaff, *Creeds*, II. 69); but see also the significantly different affirmation in the Definition of Chalcedon, *viz.*, that the Son is 'of the same οὐσία as the Father touching his godhead, and of the same οὐσία as we ourselves, touching his manhood' (Schaff, *ibid.*, II.62).

[20] Cf. John 10:30.

[21] Cf. 1 Tim. 2:5. See No. 85, 'On Working Out Our Own Salvation', §4 and n.

[22] Gen. 1:27; 9:6; 2 Cor. 4:4. See No. 1, *Salvation by Faith*, §1 and n.

heavenly temper: and all these in the highest degree, without any defect, or mixture of unholiness.

3. It was the least part of his *external righteousness* that he did nothing amiss; that he knew no outward sin of any kind, 'neither was guile found in his mouth';[23] that he never spoke one improper word, nor did one improper action. Thus far it is only a *negative* righteousness, though such an one as never did nor ever can belong to anyone that is born of a woman, save himself alone. But even his outward righteousness was *positive* too. 'He did all things well.'[24] In every word of his tongue, in every work of his hands, he did precisely the 'will of him that sent him'.[25] In the whole course of his life he did the will of God on earth as the angels do it in heaven.[26] All he acted and spoke was exactly right in every circumstance. The whole and every part of his obedience was complete. 'He fulfilled all righteousness.'[27]

4. But his obedience implied more than all this. It implied not only doing, but suffering: suffering the whole will of God from the time he came into the world till 'he bore our sins in his own body upon the tree;'[28] yea, till having made a full atonement for them 'he bowed his head and gave up the ghost.'[29] This is usually termed the *passive* righteousness of Christ, the former, his *active* righteousness. But as the active and passive righteousness of Christ were never in fact separated from each other, so we never need separate them at all, either in speaking or even in thinking. And it is with regard to both these conjointly that Jesus is called, 'the Lord our righteousness'.[30]

II. But when is it that any of us may truly say, 'the Lord our righteousness'? In other words, when is it that the righteousness of Christ is *imputed* to us, and in what sense is it imputed?

---

[23] 1 Pet. 2:22.   [24] Cf. Mark 7:37.   [25] Cf. John 4:34; 6:38.
[26] An echo of the Lord's Prayer, Matt. 6:10.
[27] Cf. Matt. 3:15.   [28] Cf. 1 Pet. 2:24.   [29] John 19:30.
[30] A popular restatement of a controversial issue between the Lutherans and Calvinists, on the one side, and the Anglicans on the other—*viz*, 'the active and passive obedience of Christ' and its import for soteriology. The former stressed Christ's passive obedience (his vicarious satisfaction of God's just judgment against sinful mankind) as the sole ground of our salvation (cf. Schmid, *Doctrinal Theology*, pp. 355-70, 449; see also Heppe, *Reformed Dogmatics*, ch. xviii). The Anglicans sought to avoid any separation between Christ's active obedience (Wesley: Christ's 'external righteousness') and his 'passive righteousness' (I.3-4); cf. More and Cross, *Anglicanism*, pp. 283-316. Puritans like William Perkins had maintained a strong Anselmian doctrine of 'substitutionary atonement'; Richard Baxter and John Goodwin, even more (cf. *Imputatio Fidei*), sound almost like Anglicans on this point (cf. Goodwin's 'Preface', pp. 22-23, and Pts. I. 36-37, and II. 230). The point here is

1. Look through all the world, and all the men therein are either believers or unbelievers. The first thing then which admits of no dispute among reasonable men is this: to all believers the righteousness of Christ is imputed; to unbelievers it is not.

5　'But when is it imputed?' When they believe. In that very hour the righteousness of Christ is theirs. It is imputed to every one that believes, as soon as he believes: faith and the righteousness of Christ are inseparable. For if he believes according to Scripture, he believes in the righteousness of Christ. There is no true faith,
10　that is, justifying faith, which hath not the righteousness of Christ for its object.

2. It is true believers may not all speak alike; they may not all use the same language. It is not to be expected that they should; we cannot reasonably require it of them. A thousand circum-
15　stances may cause them to vary from each other in the manner of expressing themselves. But a difference of expression does not necessarily imply a difference of sentiment. Different persons may use different expressions, and yet mean the same thing. Nothing is more common than this, although we seldom make
20　sufficient allowance for it. Nay, it is not easy for the same persons, when they speak of the same thing at a considerable distance of time, to use exactly the same expressions, even though they retain the same sentiments. How then can we be rigorous in requiring others to use just the same expressions with us?

25　3. We may go a step farther yet. Men may differ from us in their opinions as well as their expressions, and nevertheless be partakers with us of the same precious faith. 'Tis possible they may not have a *distinct apprehension* of the very blessing which they enjoy. Their *ideas* may not be so *clear*, and yet their experience
30　may be as sound as ours. There is a wide difference between the natural faculties of men, their understandings in particular. And that difference is exceedingly increased by the manner of their education. Indeed, this alone may occasion an inconceivable difference in their opinions of various kinds. And why not upon
35　this head as well as on any other? But still, though their opinions as well as expressions may be confused and inaccurate, their hearts may cleave to God through the Son of his love, and be truly interested in his righteousness.[31]

that Wesley is well aware that he is having to thread a careful way through a soteriological minefield.

[31] In part, this is a sample of Wesley's understanding of what 'catholic spirit' means in

4. Let us then make all that allowance to others which, were we in their place, we would desire for ourselves. Who is ignorant (to touch again on that circumstance only) of the amazing power of education? And who that knows it can expect, suppose, a member of the Church of Rome either to think or speak clearly on this subject? And yet if we had heard even dying Bellarmine cry out, when he was asked, 'Unto which of the saints wilt thou turn?'[32]—'*Fidere meritis Christi tutissimum:* It is safest to trust in the merits of Christ'—would we have affirmed that notwithstanding his wrong opinions he had no share in his righteousness?[33]

5. 'But in what sense is this righteousness imputed to believers?' In this: all believers are forgiven and accepted, not for the sake of anything in them, or of anything that ever was, that is, or ever can be done by them, but wholly and solely for the sake of what Christ hath done and suffered for them. I say again, not for the sake of anything in them or done by them, of their own righteousness or works. 'Not for works of righteousness which we have done, but of his own mercy he saved us.'[34] 'By grace ye are saved through faith. . . . Not of works, lest any man should boast;'[35] but wholly and solely for the sake of what Christ hath done and suffered for us. We are 'justified freely by his grace, through the redemption that is in Jesus Christ'.[36] And this is not only the means of our *obtaining* the favour of God, but of our

---

theological dialogue (see No. 39, 'Catholic Spirit'; cf. also No. 7, 'The Way to the Kingdom', I.6 and n.). But it also reflects his ideas about the radical ambiguity of religious language: no single form of words, in Wesley's view, could ever suffice to exhaust, or even accurately express, the full meaning of an authentic religious truth, to the exclusion of other equally valid statements.

[32] Cf. Job 5:1.

[33] None of Bellarmine's biographers records these as his 'dying words'; cf. Edward Coffin, S. J., *A True Relation of the Last Sickness and Death of Cardinal Bellarmine. Who dyed in Rome the seavententh day of September 1621. And of such things as happened in, or since, his Buriall* (1623). But the story had become folklore at least by the time of Christopher Nesse; cf. *A Protestant Antidote Against the Poyson of Popery* . . . (1679), ch. 3, pp. 80-81: '. . . such as those though they live papists, yet they dye protestants, to wit, to the principal foundation of our faith. This Bellarmine himself (their great champion) was driven to for succour when the terrors of death were upon him . . .'. Nesse's reference here is to Bellarmine, *De Justificatione*, lib. 5, cap. 7; but the only relevant passage in that chapter (or elsewhere in the essay) reads: '*Sit tertia propositio: "Propter incertitudinem propriae justitiae, et periculum inanis gloriae tutissimum est, fiduciam totam in sola Dei misericordia et benignitate reponere"* ' ('A third proposition: "Because of the uncertainty of our own true righteousness and the danger of our 'glory' turning out to be empty, our safest course by far is to rest our entire trust solely in the mercy of God and in his lovingkindness" '); see Bellarmine, *Works* (1873),6:359.

[34] Cf. Titus 3:5.   [35] Eph. 2:8-9.   [36] Cf. Rom. 3:24.

continuing therein. It is thus we come to God at first: it is by the same we come unto him ever after. We walk in one and the same 'new and living way'[37] till our spirit returns to God.

6. And this is the doctrine which I have constantly believed and taught for near eight and twenty years.[38] This I published to all the world in the year 1738, and ten or twelve times since, in those words, and many others to the same effect, extracted from the *Homilies* of our Church:

These things must necessarily go together in our justification: upon God's part his great mercy and grace, upon Christ's part the satisfaction of God's justice, and on our part faith in the merits of Christ. So that the grace of God doth not shut out the righteousness of God in our justification, but only shutteth out the righteousness of man, as to *deserving* our justification.[39]

That we are justified by faith alone is spoken to take away clearly all merit of our works, and wholly to ascribe the *merit* and *deserving* of our justification to Christ only. Our justification comes freely of the mere mercy of God. For whereas all the world was not able to pay any part toward our ransom, it pleased him, without any of our deserving, to prepare for us Christ's body and blood, whereby our ransom might be paid, and his justice satisfied. Christ therefore is now the righteousness of all them that truly believe in him.[40]

7. The hymns published a year or two after this, and since republished several times (a clear testimony that my judgment was still the same) speak full to the same purpose. To cite all the passages to this effect would be to transcribe a great part of the volumes. Take one for all, which was reprinted seven years ago, five years ago, two years ago, and some months since:

Jesu, thy blood and righteousness
My beauty are, my glorious dress:
Midst flaming worlds in these arrayed
With joy shall I lift up my head.[41]

The whole expresses the same sentiment from the beginning to the end.

[37] Heb. 10:20.
[38] Note Wesley's insistence on his unswerving fidelity to the doctrine of justification by faith since 1738, despite all Calvinist charges to the contrary. But note also his grounding of that doctrine, yet once again, in the Anglican standards of doctrine.
[39] Cf. *The Doctrine of Salvation, Faith, and Good Works*, I.5. See the original text in the homily 'Of the Salvation of All Mankind', Pt. I, in *Homilies*, pp. 19-20. At least fifteen edns. of Wesley's abridgement were extant when this sermon was preached.
[40] *Ibid.*, I.7.
[41] John Wesley, 'The Believer's Triumph', st. 1 (tr. from Zinzendorf's German), in *Hymns and Sacred Poems* (1740), p. 177 *(Poet. Wks.*, I.346).

8. In the sermon on justification published nineteen, and again seven or eight years ago, I express the same thing in these words:

In consideration of this, that the Son of God hath 'tasted death for every man',[42] God hath now 'reconciled the world unto himself, not imputing to them their former trespasses'.[43] [. . .] So that for the sake of his well-beloved Son, of what he hath done and suffered for us, God now vouchsafes on one only condition (which himself also enables us to perform) both to remit the punishment due to our sins, to reinstate us in his favour, and to restore our dead souls to spiritual life, as the earnest of life eternal.[a]

9. This is more largely and particularly expressed in the *Treatise on Justification* which I published last year:

If we take the phrase of 'imputing Christ's righteousness' for the bestowing (as it were) the righteousness of Christ, including his obedience, as well passive as active, in the return of it—that is, in the privileges, blessings, and benefits purchased by it—so a believer may be said to be justified by *the righteousness of Christ imputed*. The meaning is, God justifies the believer for the sake of Christ's righteousness, and not for any righteousness of his own. [. . .] So Calvin: 'Christ by his obedience procured and merited for us grace or favour with God the Father.'[b] Again, 'Christ by his obedience procured or purchased righteousness for us.'[44] And yet again: 'All such expressions as these—that we are justified by the grace of God, that Christ is our righteousness, that righteousness was procured for us by the death and resurrection of Christ—import the same thing:'[45] namely, that the righteousness of Christ, both his active and passive righteousness, is the meritorious cause[46] of our justification, and has procured for us at God's hand that upon our believing we should be accounted righteous by him.[c]

---

[a] p. 87 [*Sermons on Several Occasions* I (1746); cf. No. 5, 'Justification by Faith', I.8; 2nd edn., by W. Bowyer, 1754].

[b] *Institutes* [Vol. I], II.xvii. [3; cf. LCC, Vol. XX.530-31].

[c] p. 5. [Not Wesley's own work but an abridgement of John Goodwin's *Imputatio Fidei* (1642); cf. *Bibliog*, No. 266. Wesley's unusually long Preface registers his basic agreement with Goodwin against his detractors—and ignores Toplady's reference to 'that Arminian Ranter and Fifth Monarchy Man' (see Augustus M. Toplady, *Works*, II.342-43). Wesley's quotation here is further abridgement from his original extract; its locus in Goodwin is pp. 8-10.]

---

[42] Cf. Heb. 2:9.   [43] Cf. 2 Cor. 5:19.

[44] *Institutes*, III. xiv. 17 (LCC, Vol. XX.784). But note Calvin's full text: 'Surely the material cause [of justification] is Christ, with his [passive] obedience, through which he acquired righteousness for us. What shall we say is the *formal* or instrumental cause but faith?' It is this thesis that Wesley is here rejecting.

[45] Wesley's translation of Calvin's commentary on Gal. 3:6; cf. William Pringle's translation, *Commentaries on the Epistles of Paul to the Galatians and Ephesians* (1849), p. 85. See also Goodwin's translation of the same passage, p. 9.

[46] Wesley has here altered Goodwin to his own purpose. Goodwin reads: 'the

10. But perhaps some will object, 'Nay, but you affirm that "faith is imputed to us for righteousness." '[47] St. Paul affirms this over and over; therefore I affirm it too. Faith is imputed for righteousness to every believer; namely, faith in the righteousness
5 of Christ. But this is exactly the same thing which has been said before. For by that expression I mean neither more nor less than that we are justified by faith, not by works;[48] or that every believer is forgiven and accepted merely for the sake of what Christ has done and suffered.

10 11. 'But is not a believer invested or clothed with the righteousness of Christ?' Undoubtedly he is. And accordingly the words above-recited are the language of every believing heart:

> Jesu, thy blood and righteousness
> My beauty are, my glorious dress.[49]

15 That is, for the sake of thy active and passive righteousness I am forgiven and accepted of God.

'But must not we put off the filthy rags of our own righteousness[50] before we can put on the spotless righteousness of Christ?' Certainly we must; that is, in plain terms, we must
20 'repent' before we can 'believe the gospel'.[51] We must be cut off from dependence upon ourselves before we can truly depend upon Christ. We must cast away all confidence in our own righteousness, or we cannot have a true confidence in his. Till we are delivered from trusting in anything that we do, we cannot
25 throughly trust in what he has done and suffered. First 'we receive the sentence of death in ourselves;'[52] then we trust in him that lived and died for us.

12. 'But do not you believe *inherent* righteousness?' Yes, in its proper place; not as the *ground* of our acceptance with God, but as
30 the *fruit* of it; not in the place of *imputed* righteousness, but as consequent upon it. That is, I believe God *implants* righteousness in every one to whom he has *imputed* it. I believe 'Jesus Christ is

---

righteousness of Christ, meaning chiefly his *passive* obedience or righteousness, is the meritorious cause . . . .' But Wesley is concerned to include '*both* his active *and* passive righteousness as the meritorious cause . . .'. In this way he reasserts his Anglican 'both/and' and also rejects Calvin's thesis about 'formal or instrumental cause' which, in Wesley's view, carried predestination as a necessary implication.

[47] Cf. Rom. 4:22.　　　　　　　　　　　　　　　　[48] See Gal. 2:16.
[49] See above, II.7 and n.
[50] See Isa. 64:6. See also No. 127, 'On the Wedding Garment'.
[51] Mark 1:15.　　　　　　　　　　　　　　　　　　[52] Cf. 2 Cor. 1:9.

made of God unto us sanctification'[53] as well as righteousness; or that God sanctifies, as well as justifies, all them that believe in him. They to whom the righteousness of Christ is imputed are made righteous by the spirit of Christ, are renewed in the image of God 'after the likeness wherein they were created, in 5 righteousness and true holiness'.[54]

13. 'But do not you put faith in the room of Christ, or of his righteousness?' By no means. I take particular care to put each of these in its proper place. The righteousness of Christ is the whole and sole *foundation* of all our hope. It is by faith that the Holy 10 Ghost enables us to build upon this foundation. God gives this faith. In that moment we are accepted of God; and yet not for the sake of that faith, but of what Christ has done and suffered for us. You see, each of these has its proper place, and neither clashes with the other: we believe, we love; we endeavour to walk in all the 15 commandments of the Lord blameless.[55] Yet,

> While thus we bestow
> Our moments below,
> Ourselves we forsake,
> And refuge in Jesus's righteousness take. 20

> His passion alone,
> The foundation we own:
> And pardon we claim,
> And eternal redemption in Jesus's name.[56]

14. I therefore no more deny the righteousness of Christ than I 25 deny the godhead of Christ. And a man may full as justly charge me with denying the one as the other. Neither do I deny *imputed righteousness:* this is another unkind and unjust accusation. I always did, and do still continually affirm, that the righteousness of Christ is imputed to every believer. But who do deny it? Why, 30 all *infidels*, whether baptized or unbaptized; all who affirm the glorious gospel of our Lord Jesus Christ[57] to be a *cunningly devised fable;*[58] all Socinians and Arians;[59] all who deny the

---

[53] Cf. 1 Cor. 1:30.   [54] Cf. Eph. 4:24.   [55] See Luke 1:6.
[56] Charles Wesley, 'Hymns for Christian Friends', No. 14, st. 4, in *Hymns and Sacred Poems* (1749), II.281 (*Poet. Wks.*, V.424). Orig., 'Thus while we bestow', and *'The foundation'.*
[57] See 2 Cor. 4:4. Here again is Wesley's prime thesis: that 'imputation' is normally followed by 'implantation'. Thus the typical fruit of imputed righteousness (i.e., pardon) is a 'renewal [of the soul] in the image of God' (i.e., holy living).
[58] See 2 Pet. 1:16.
[59] The followers of Lelio (1525–67) and Faustus Socinus (1539-1604), who had

supreme godhead of the Lord that bought them. They of consequence deny his divine righteousness, as they suppose him to be a mere creature. And they deny his human righteousness as imputed to any man, seeing they believe everyone is accepted *for*
5 *his own righteousness.*

15. The human righteousness of Christ, at least the imputation of it as the whole and sole meritorious cause of the justification of a sinner before God, is likewise denied by the members of the Church of Rome—by all of them who are true to the principles of
10 their own church.[60] But undoubtedly there are many among them whose experience goes beyond their principles; who, though they are far from expressing themselves justly, yet feel what they know not how to express. Yea, although their conceptions of this great truth be as crude as their expressions, yet 'with their heart they
15 believe'; they rest on Christ alone, both 'unto' present and eternal 'salvation'.[61]

16. With these we may rank those even in the Reformed Churches who are usually termed *mystics*. One of the chief of these in the present century (at least in England) was Mr. Law.[62] It
20 is well known that he absolutely and zealously denied the imputation of the righteousness of Christ; as zealously as Robert Barclay, who scruples not to say, 'Imputed righteousness, imputed nonsense!'[63] The body of the people known by the name

rejected trinitarian orthodoxy and had expounded a unitarian Christology and a moralistic soteriology; they were dubbed 'Arians' by their orthodox critics, although they themselves rejected the label. Their views are best summarized in the *Racovian Catechism* (1605, 1608, 1609); cf. Earl Morse Wilbur, *A History of Unitarianism* (Cambridge, Mass., Harvard University Press, 1945), chs. xxix-xxxii. John Biddle (1615–62) is reckoned as 'the father of English Unitarianism'; in Wesley's time its most prominent spokesmen were John Taylor of Norwich and Joseph Priestley (see below, II. 16, and n. 65).

[60] How Wesley got this from the canons of Trent (Session Six, ch. vii) is not clear. That text reads: 'Justification is not merely the remission of sins but also the renewal of the inward man [Wesley's point about 'the renewed image']. . . . Its meritorious cause is God's most beloved, only-begotten Son, our Lord Jesus Christ, who, when we were enemies . . . merited justification for us by his most holy passion on the wood of the cross and made satisfaction for us unto God his Father. . . .' Is Wesley's complaint here more than that Trent had declined the absolute designation, 'whole and sole'?

[61] Cf. Rom. 10:10.

[62] William Law had just recently died (1761). As early as 1739, he had turned against 'faith alone' in *The Grounds and Reasons of Christian Regeneration*. Then, as he grew older, he had been drawn more and more into the orbit of Jacob Boehme. The books that Wesley has here in mind are *The Spirit of Prayer* and *The Spirit of Love* (1752, 1754), *Works*, VIII. 3-133, where Law stresses 'the indwelling Christ in the soul' to the exclusion of the doctrine of justification by faith.

[63] It is well known that Robert Barclay rejected 'imputed righteousness' out of hand (cf. his *Apology*, I. 141-44, 188-90; III. 360-74, 410-22); in his *Works* (1718), I. 142, there is a

of Quakers espouse the same sentiment. Nay, the generality of those who profess themselves members of the Church of England are either totally ignorant of the matter and know nothing about *imputed righteousness,* or deny this and justification by faith together as destructive of good works. To these we may add a 5 considerable number of the people vulgarly styled Anabaptists,[64] together with thousands of Presbyterians and Independents lately enlightened by the writings of Dr. Taylor.[65] On the last I am not called to pass any sentence: I leave them to him that made them. But will anyone dare to affirm that all mystics (such as was Mr. 10 Law in particular), all Quakers, all Presbyterians or Independents, and all members of the Church of England, who are not clear in their opinions or expressions, are void of all Christian experience? That consequently they are all in a state of damnation, 'without hope, without God in the world'?[66] However 15 confused their ideas may be, however improper their language, may there not be many of them whose heart is right toward God and who effectually know 'the Lord our righteousness'?

17. But, blessed be God, we are not among those who are so dark in their conceptions and expressions. We no more deny the 20 *phrase* than the *thing;* but we are unwilling to obtrude it on other men. Let them use either this or such other expressions as they judge to be more exactly scriptural, provided their *heart* rests only on what Christ hath done and suffered for pardon, grace, and glory. I cannot express this better than in Mr. Hervey's words, 25 worthy to be wrote in letters of gold: 'We are not solicitous as to

marginal rubric: 'Imputed righteousness a cloak for wickedness.' But Professors Hugh Barbour and Elton Trueblood, both Barclay specialists, agree that Wesley's quotation is not in Barclay's text nor even in Barclay's style.

[64] 'Anabaptists': a blanket term for radical Protestants of various sorts who rejected the official churches and coercive social institutions; cf. Williams, *The Radical Reformation,* ch. 33; and Claus-Peter Clasen, *Anabaptism: A Social History* (Ithaca, N.Y., Cornell University Press, 1972). They had flourished in England during the tumults of the Civil War and had survived into Wesley's time as Baptists, Congregationalists, Familists, etc. The 'Strict and Particular Baptists' taught a rigorous doctrine of election and imputation while the 'General Baptists' allowed for universal redemption as a possibility by Christ's atonement. Cf. A. C. Underwood, *History of the English Baptists* (London, Kingsgate Press, 1947).

[65] Dr. John Taylor of Norwich, a leader in the development of eighteenth-century Dissent from orthodoxy to the sort of unitarianism that one may see full blown in Joseph Priestley, Richard Price, *et al.;* cf. Gerald R. Cragg, *The Church and the Age of Reason (1648–1789),* (Baltimore, Md., Penguin Books, 1960). Taylor and Wesley had dueled over their contrary views of original sin; see above, II. 14, and n. 59.

[66] Cf. Eph. 2:12.

any *particular set of phrases*. Only let men be humbled as repenting criminals at Christ's feet, let them rely as devoted pensioners on his merits, and they are undoubtedly in the way to a blessed immortality.'[67]

5   18. Is there any need, is there any possibility of saying more? Let us only abide by this declaration, and all the contention about this or that 'particular phrase' is torn up by the roots. Keep to this: 'All who are humbled as repenting criminals at Christ's feet and rely as devoted pensioners on his merits are in the way to a blessed
10 immortality.' And what room for dispute? Who denies this? Do we not all meet on this ground? What then shall we wrangle about? A man of peace here proposes terms of accommodation to all the contending parties. We desire no better. We accept of the terms. We subscribe to them with heart and hand. Whoever
15 refuses so to do, set a mark upon that man! He is an enemy of peace, and a troubler of Israel,[68] a disturber of the church of God.[69]

19. In the meantime what we are afraid of is this: lest any should use the phrase, 'the righteousness of Christ', or, 'the
20 righteousness of Christ is "imputed to me",' as a cover for his unrighteousness. We have known this done a thousand times. A man has been reproved, suppose, for drunkenness. 'Oh, said he, I pretend to no righteousness of *my own:* Christ is *my righteousness.'* Another has been told that 'the extortioner, the unjust, shall not
25 inherit the kingdom of God.'[70] He replies with all assurance, 'I am unjust in myself, but I have a spotless righteousness in Christ.' And thus though a man be as far from the practice as from the tempers of a Christian, though he neither has the mind which was in Christ[71] nor in any respect walks as he walked, yet he has
30 armour of proof against all conviction in what he calls the 'righteousness of Christ'.[72]

20. It is the seeing so many deplorable instances of this kind which makes us sparing in the use of these expressions. And I cannot but call upon all of you who use them frequently, and

---

[67] Cf. James Hervey, *Theron and Aspasio*, Dial. II (4th edn., 1761, I. 55); this is clearly an olive branch to Hervey's memory, a reconciling gesture to his friends.

[68] 1 Chr. 2:7.

[69] An echo of Canon II of the Dedication Council of Antioch, A.D. 341 (*In Encaeniis*); cf. No. 27, 'Sermon on the Mount, VII', III.7 and n.

[70] Cf. 1 Cor. 6:9-10.

[71] See Phil. 2:5.

[72] Cf. 2 Pet. 1:1.

beseech you in the name of God our Saviour, whose you are and whom you serve,[73] earnestly to guard all that hear you against this accursed abuse of it. O warn them (it may be they will hear *your* voice) against 'continuing in sin that grace may abound'![74] Warn them against making 'Christ the minister of sin'![75] Against making void that solemn decree of God, 'without holiness no man shall see the Lord,'[76] by a vain imagination of being *holy in Christ*. O warn them that if they remain unrighteous, the righteousness of Christ will profit them nothing! Cry aloud (is there not a cause?) that for this very end the righteousness of Christ is imputed to us, that 'the righteousness of the law may be fulfilled in us,'[77] and that we may 'live soberly, religiously, and godly in this present world.'[78]

It remains only to make a short and plain application.[79] And first I would address myself to you who violently oppose these expressions, and are ready to condemn all that use them as antinomians. But is not this bending the bow too much the other way?[80] Why should you condemn all who do not speak just as you do? Why should you quarrel with *them* for using the phrases they like, any more than they with *you* for taking the same liberty? Or if they do quarrel with you upon that account, do not imitate the bigotry which you blame. At least allow *them* the liberty which they ought to allow *you*. And why should you be angry at an *expression*? 'Oh, it has been abused.' And what expression has not? However, the abuse may be removed, and at the same time the use remain.[81] Above all be sure to retain the important sense which is couched under that expression. All the blessings I enjoy,

---

[73] See Acts 27:23.   [74] Cf. Rom. 6:1.

[75] Gal. 2:17.   [76] Cf. Heb. 12:14.

[77] Rom. 8:4. Cf. Nos. 34, 'The Original, Nature, Properties, and Use of the Law'; and 35 and 36, 'The Law Established through Faith', Discourses I and II.

[78] Titus 2:12.

[79] Cf. No. 5, 'Justification by Faith', IV.9 and n.

[80] Cf. the memorandum of Jan. 25, 1738, noted in JWJ. See also Echard, *Eccles. Hist.*, III.vi.426: 'He bent the stick too much the contrary way.'

[81] This aphorism on 'use and abuse' is a favourite of Wesley's, cf., e.g., Nos. 24, 'Sermon on the Mount, IV', III.6; 33, 'Sermon on the Mount, XIII', II.2; 42, 'Satan's Devices', II.8; 78, 'Spiritual Idolatry', I.14; 108, 'On Riches', II.12. It appears often in seventeenth- and eighteenth-century literature. Cf. George Chapman's translation of Homer's *Odyssey* (Bk. xxiv), p. 526:

> It is the ground of age, when cares abuse it,
> To know life's end, and, as 'tis sweet so use it.

Cf. also Richard Graves, *Spiritual Quixote* (1772), Vol. II, ch. 2 (see 1820 edn., II.7): 'Our master does not deny us the use but only the abuse of his good creatures.'

all I hope for in time and in eternity, are given wholly and solely for the sake of what Christ has done and suffered for me.

I would, secondly, add a few words to you who are fond of these expressions. And permit me to ask, Do not I allow enough? What
5 can any reasonable man desire more? I allow the whole *sense* which you contend for: that we have every blessing 'through the righteousness of God our Saviour'.[82] I allow *you* to use whatever expressions you choose, and that a thousand times over; only guarding them against that dreadful abuse which you are as
10 deeply concerned to prevent as I am. I myself frequently use the expression in question, 'imputed righteousness'; and often put this and the like expressions into the mouth of a whole congregation. But allow me liberty of conscience herein: allow me the right of private judgment.[83] Allow me to use it just as often as I
15 judge it preferable to any other expression. And be not angry with me if I cannot judge it proper to use any one expression every two minutes. *You* may if you please; but do not condemn me because I do not. Do not for this represent me as a Papist, or 'an enemy to the righteousness of Christ'.[84] Bear with *me,* as I do with *you;* else
20 how shall we 'fulfil the law of Christ'?[85] Do not make tragical outcries, as though I was 'subverting the very foundations of Christianity'. Whoever does this does me much wrong: the Lord lay it not to his charge![86] I lay, and have done for many years, the very same foundation with you. And indeed 'other foundation can
25 no man lay than that which is laid, even Jesus Christ.'[87] I build inward and outward holiness thereon, as you do, even by faith. Do not therefore suffer any distaste, or unkindness, no, nor any shyness or coldness in your heart. If there were *a difference of opinion,* where is our religion if we cannot *think and let think?*[88]
30 What hinders but you may forgive *me* as easily as I may forgive *you?* How much more when there is only *a difference of expression?* Nay, hardly so much as that—all the dispute being only whether a particular mode of expression shall be used *more or less frequently!*

---

[82] Cf. 2 Pet. 1:1.

[83] Cf. JWJ, Mar. 25, 1743; see also *The Old Whig: Or, the Consistent Protestant* (1739), No. 4, in Vol. I, pp. 32-33.

[84] Cf. Wesley's letter to John Erskine, Apr. 24, 1765; see also his *Remarks on A Defence of . . . Aspasio Vindicated.*

[85] Gal. 6:2.

[86] See Acts 7:60.

[87] Cf. 1 Cor. 3:11.

[88] Cf. No. 7, 'The Way to the Kingdom', I.6 and n.

Surely we must earnestly desire to contend with one another before we can make this a bone of contention! O let us not any more for such very trifles as these give our common enemies room to blaspheme![89] Rather let us at length cut off occasion for them that seek occasion![90] Let us at length (O why was it not done 5 before?) join hearts and hands in the service of our great Master. As we have 'one Lord, one faith, one hope of our calling',[91] let us all strengthen each other's hands in God, and with one heart and one mouth declare to all mankind, 'the Lord our righteousness'.

---

[89] See 2 Sam. 12:14.
[90] See 2 Cor.11:12.
[91] Cf. Eph. 4:4-5.

UPON OUR LORD'S SERMON ON THE MOUNT

AN INTRODUCTORY COMMENT

The unifying theme of these next thirteen 'discourses' on the Sermon on the Mount, with all their variations and nuancings, is the Christian life understood as the fruit of justifying faith. But given such faith, what follows? Wesley's answer is given in this extended exposition of the Christian life based on the locus classicus *of evangelical ethics, 'The Sermon on the Mount' (i.e., Matthew 5–7). Since Tyndale, this 'sermon' had been understood as 'the epitome of God's laws and promises' for Christian believers; cf. Clebsch,* England's Earliest Protestants, *p. 184; see also William Burkitt,* Expository Notes . . . on the New Testament *(eleven editions between 1700 and 1739), Preface to chapter 5: 'Christ's famous Sermon on the Mount comprehends the sum and substance of both the Old and New Testaments.'*

Taken together, the following sermons are not a thirteen-part essay, tightly organized and argued. Instead, they are separate sermons, drawn from materials running back to 1725, arranged in a triadic pattern that seems to have been original with Wesley. Each is a discourse in its own right; yet the series is designed so that each appears as a part of a whole. This means that the sermons may be read singly or together, but with an eye on their shared aim: 'to assert and prove every branch of gospel obedience *as indispensably necessary to eternal salvation'; cf. Wesley's open letter (Nov. 17, 1759) to John Downes in reply to the latter's* abusive Methodism Examined and Exposed *(1759).*

Many of the great and near-great commentators of the seventeenth and eighteenth centuries had devoted their talents to the interpretation of Matthew 5–7 as the principal summary of Christian ethics, or, in Henry Hammond's phrase, as 'an abstract of Christian philosophy'; cf. his Practical Catechism *(1st edn., c. 1644), II. 1, in the* Library of Anglo-Catholic Theology *(1847), p. 83. Chief among these earlier works, in the order of their influences upon Wesley's thought, were Bishop Offspring Blackall, 'Eighty-Seven Practical Discourses Upon Our Saviour's Sermon on the Mount',* Works, I.1-561; II.609-939;

466

John Norris, Practical Discourses; *the American, James Blair*, Our
Saviour's Divine Sermon on the Mount in IV Volumes *(1722; 2nd
edn., 1740, with a preface by Daniel Waterland); John Cardinal Bona*,
Guide to Eternity . . . *(six editions in English between 1672 and
1712); and Henry Hammond*, op. cit. *Echoes of all these are scattered
along the way, together with lesser borrowings from Bengel, Poole, and
Henry. This makes it all the more remarkable that Wesley came up with
a model of his own, both in form and substance. This series thus reminds
us, yet again, of Wesley's ready appeal to tradition—even while he
maintains his own originality and independence.*

*Benjamin Ingham records in his Journal that 'during the voyage [to
Georgia] Wesley went over our Saviour's Sermon on the Mount' with
the ship's company aboard the* Simmonds. *There are also other records
of his preaching, very early on, from one or another text in Matthew
5–7. For example, his second sermon was preached at Binsey (near
Oxford), November 21, 1725, on Matt. 6:33. A first draft of the sermon
which appears here as 'Discourse VIII' seems to have been written out in
1736. Later, it was the example of the Sermon on the Mount that
encouraged Wesley to break out of his High Church prejudices in Bristol,
April 1, 1739: 'In the evening (Mr. Whitefield being gone) I begun
expounding our Lord's Sermon on the Mount (one pretty remarkable
precedent of* field preaching, *though I suppose* there were churches
at that time also) to a little society which was accustomed to meet once or
twice a week in Nicholas Street;' cf. *Journal entries for this whole story
of the unplanned outbreak of the Wesleyan Revival.*

*The records show that, between 1739 and 1746, Wesley preached
more than one hundred sermons from separate texts in the Sermon on
the Mount. There is, however, no recorded instance of his having treated
that Sermon as a whole anywhere else. Evidently, he was prepared to
allow this series, once published, to stand as his sufficient comment on
the subject.*

*In his introduction to 'Discourse X', §§1–3, Wesley repeats his
explanation (cf. 'Discourse I', Proem, §10) of how he had conceived the
design of Matthew 5–7, according to its three unfolding themes: (1) 'the
sum of true religion'; (2) 'rules touching that right intention which we
are to preserve in all our outward actions'; and (3) 'the main hindrances
of this religion'. He then adds a clarifying summary: 'In the fifth chapter
[of St. Matthew] our great Teacher . . . has laid before us those
dispositions of the soul* which constitute real Christianity. . . . *In the
sixth [chapter] he has shown how all our* actions . . . *may be made holy,
and good, and acceptable to God, by a pure and holy intention. . . . In*

the former part of [ch. 7] he points out the most common and fatal hindrances of this holiness; in the latter [part] he exhorts us, by various motives, to break through all [such hindrances] and secure that prize of our high calling [of God in Christ Jesus]' (cf. Phil. 3:14).

The thirteen discourses are divided almost equally over the three chapters of St. Matthew: five for chapter five, four each for six and seven. Of the first five, Discourse I is devoted to the first two Beatitudes; Discourse II to Beatitudes three through five (with a hymn to love based on 1 Cor. 13); Discourse III to the remainder of the Beatitudes; Discourse IV turns to Christianity as 'a social religion' in which inward holiness (our love of God) prompts outward holiness (love of neighbour); Discourse V is a balancing of law and gospel. Discourses VI–IX are based on chapter six: VI to the problems of purity and holiness of intention (to the 'works of piety and of mercy'); VII to fasting; VIII to a denunciation of greed and surplus accumulation; IX to the mutually exclusive services of God and Mammon. Discourses X–XIII turn to various hindrances to holy living and to their avoidance: X to 'judging' (contrary to love), 'intemperate zeal', 'neglect of prayer', 'neglect of charity'; XI to the noxious influences of ill-example and ill-advice with which the world deludes us; XII to false prophets and unedifying preachers (and yet also our duties to attend church nonetheless and to avail ourselves of all means of grace); XIII is an inevitable comment on the parable of the houses built on sand and rock. Discourse XII was also published separately in the same year that it appeared in SOSO, III (1750), under the title, 'A Caution Against False Prophets. A Sermon on Matt. vii. 15-20. Particularly recommended to the People Called Methodists'. This went through seven editions during Wesley's lifetime. For a stemma delineating the publishing history of that sermon ('collected' and 'separate') and a list of variant readings, see Appendix, 'Wesley's Text', Vol. IV; see also Bibliog, Nos. 130 and 130.i.

Obviously there is no interest, in any of these sermons, in critical textual problems or in the historical context. Everywhere it is assumed that in St. Matthew's text we are dealing with divine ipsissima verba—i.e., with a direct address from τὸ ὢν, 'the self-existent, the Supreme, the God who is over all, blessed for ever' (§ 9 below). The Sermon on the Mount, in Wesley's view, is the only Gospel passage where Christ designed 'to lay down at once the whole plan of his religion, to give us a full prospect of Christianity'. What matters most in our reading, therefore, is an awareness of Wesley's sense of the wholeness of the message he is interpreting, of his conviction of the honest integration of an evangel profoundly ethical with an ethic that is also vividly *evangelical. Maybe more than anywhere else in* SOSO *this particular bloc displays Wesley's distinctive concern for integration and balance—between the faith that justifies and the faith that works by love.*

SERMON 21

Upon our Lord's Sermon on the Mount

Discourse the First

Matthew 5:1-4

And seeing the multitudes, he went up into a mountain, and when he
was set, his disciples came unto him: 5
And he opened his mouth and taught them, saying,
Blessed are the poor in spirit; for theirs is the kingdom of heaven.
Blessed are they that mourn; for they shall be comforted.

1. Our Lord had now 'gone about all Galilee',[a] beginning at the time 'when John was cast into prison',[b] not only 'teaching in their 10 synagogues, and preaching the gospel of the kingdom', but likewise 'healing all manner of sickness, and all manner of disease among the people'.[1] It was a natural consequence of this that 'there followed him great multitudes from Galilee and from Decapolis, and from Jerusalem and from Judea, and from the 15 region beyond Jordan.'[c] 'And seeing the multitudes', whom no synagogue could contain, even had there been any at hand, 'he went up into a mountain',[d] where there was room for all that 'came unto him from every quarter'.[2] 'And when he was set', as the manner of the Jews was, 'his disciples came unto him. And he 20 opened his mouth' (an expression denoting the beginning of a solemn discourse) 'and taught them, saying. . . .'

----

  [a] Matt. 4:23.
  [b] Ver. 12.
  [c] Ver. 25.
  [d] Matt. 5:1, etc.

----

  [1] Matt. 4:23.
  [2] Mark 1:45.

2. Let us observe who it is that is here speaking, that we may 'take heed how we hear'.[3] It is the Lord of heaven and earth, the Creator of all, who, as such, has a right to dispose of all his creatures; the Lord our Governor, whose kingdom is from
5 everlasting, and ruleth over all; the great Lawgiver, who can well enforce all his laws, 'being able to save and to destroy';[4] yea, to punish with everlasting destruction from his presence and from the glory of his power.[5] It is the eternal Wisdom of the Father, who knoweth whereof we are made,[6] and understands our inmost
10 frame: who knows how we stand related to God, to one another, to every creature which God hath made; and consequently, how to adapt every law he prescribes to all the circumstances wherein he hath placed us. It is he who is 'loving unto every man, whose mercy is over all his works':[7] the God of love, who, having emptied
15 himself of his eternal glory, is come forth from his Father to declare his will to the children of men, and then goeth again to the Father; who is sent to God to 'open the eyes of the blind',[8] 'to give light to them that sit in darkness'.[9] It is the great Prophet of the Lord, concerning whom God had solemnly declared long ago,
20 'Whosoever will not hearken unto my words, which he shall speak in my name, I will require it of him;'[e] or, as the Apostle expresses it, 'Every soul which will not hear that prophet shall be destroyed from among the people.'[f]

3. And what is it which he is teaching? The Son of God, who
25 came from heaven, is here showing us the way to heaven,[10] to the place which he hath prepared for us,[11] the glory he had before the world began.[12] He is teaching us the true way to life everlasting, the royal way which leads to the kingdom. And the only true way; for there is none besides—all other paths lead to destruction.
30 From the character of the speaker we are well assured that he hath declared the full and perfect will of God.[13] He hath uttered

---

[e] Deut. 18:19.

[f] Acts 3:23. ['The Apostle' here is St. Peter. Note the direct correlation beween the human Jesus and the Second Person of the Trinity: no kenosis here, but more than a hint of Wesley's practical monophysitism; cf. §9, below.]

---

[3] Cf. Luke 8:18. [4] Cf. Jas. 4:12.
[5] See. 2 Thess. 1:9. [6] Ps. 103:14 (BCP).
[7] Ps. 145:9 (BCP). [8] John 10:21; cf. 11:37. [9] Luke 1:79.
[10] Cf. Wesley's Pref. to *SOSO*, §5: 'I want to know one thing—the way to heaven. . . . God himself has condescended to teach the way. . . .'
[11] See John 14:2, 3. [12] John 17:5. [13] Rom. 12:2.

not one tittle too much: nothing more than he had received of the Father. Nor too little: he hath not shunned to declare the whole counsel of God.[14] Much less hath he uttered anything wrong, anything contrary to the will of him that sent him.[15] All his words are true and right concerning all things, and shall stand fast for 5 ever and ever.

And we may easily remark that in explaining and confirming these faithful and true sayings he takes care to refute not only the mistakes of the scribes and Pharisees which then were, the false comments whereby the Jewish teachers of that age had perverted 10 the Word of God, but all the practical mistakes that are inconsistent with salvation which should ever arise in the Christian Church; all the comments whereby the Christian teachers (so called) of any age or nation should pervert the Word of God, and teach unwary souls to seek death in the error of their 15 life.[16]

4. And hence we are naturally led to observe whom it is that he is here teaching. Not the apostles alone; if so, he had no need to have gone 'up into the mountain'. A room in the house of Matthew, or any of his disciples, would have contained the 20 Twelve. Nor does it in any wise appear that the 'disciples who came unto him' were the Twelve only. Οἱ μαθηταὶ αὐτοῦ, without any force put upon the expression, may be understood of all who desired to 'learn of him'.[17] But to put this out of all question, to make it undeniably plain that where it is said, 'He 25 opened his mouth and taught them,' the word 'them' includes all the multitudes who went up with him into the mountain, we need only observe the concluding verses of the seventh chapter: 'And it came to pass, when Jesus had ended these sayings, the multitudes, οἱ ὄχλοι, were astonished at his doctrine (or 30 teaching). For he taught *them* (the multitudes) as one having authority, and not as the scribes.'[18]

---

[14] Acts 20:27.   [15] See John 4:34; 6:38, 40.

[16] See Wisd. 1:12. Cf. also No. 6, 'The Righteousness of Faith', §2 and n

[17] Cf. Matt. 11:29.

[18] Cf. Matt. 7:28-29 ('the multitudes were astonished'). This question of the intended auditory of the Sermon on the Mount had exercised most of the commentators. Henry, *Exposition, loc. cit.*, had insisted that the 'discourse was directed to the disciples [only], though in the hearing of the multitudes'; Blackall, *Works*, I. 2, had suggested that the 'sermon was designed only for his own disciples . . .'; later, John Heylyn makes the distinction even more sharply in *Theological Lectures*, I. 74. But Hammond, *Practical Catechism*, p. 84, had remarked that the term 'disciple' was 'of latitude enough to contain *all* Christians . . .; what is said in this sermon, all Christians are concerned in . . .'; and

Nor was it only those multitudes who were with him on the mount to whom he now taught the way of salvation,[19] but all the children of men, the whole race of mankind, the children that were yet unborn—all the generations to come even to the end of
5 the world who should ever hear the words of this life.

5. And this all men allow with regard to some parts of the ensuing discourse. No man, for instance, denies that what is said of 'poverty of spirit' relates to all mankind. But many have supposed that other parts concerned only the apostles, or the first
10 Christians, or the ministers of Christ; and were never designed for the generality of men,[20] who consequently have nothing at all to do with them.

But may we not justly inquire who told them this—that some parts of this discourse concerned only the apostles, or the
15 Christians of the apostolic age, or the ministers of Christ? Bare assertions are not a sufficient proof to establish a point of so great importance. Has then our Lord himself taught us that some parts of his discourse do not concern all mankind? Without doubt had it been so he would have told us; he could not have omitted so
20 necessary an information. But has he told us so? Where? In the discourse itself? No: here is not the least intimation of it. Has he said so elsewhere? In any other of his discourses? Not one word so much as glancing this way can we find in anything he ever spoke, either to the multitudes or to his disciples. Has any of the
25 apostles, or other inspired writers, left such an instruction upon record? No such thing. No assertion of this kind is to be found in all the oracles of God. Who then are the men who are so much wiser than God? Wise so far above that [which] is written?[21]

6. Perhaps they will say that the reason of the thing requires
30 such a restriction to be made. If it does, it must be on one of these

---

Poole, *Annotations, loc. cit.*, had lumped the disciples together, 'both those strictly so called and others also'. Later, in *Notes* on Matt. 5:1, Wesley will repeat his point here: 'His disciples: not only his twelve disciples, but *all* who desired to learn of him.'

[19] Acts 16:17.

[20] I.e., the monastic tradition of 'the counsels of perfection' based on Matt. 5:48, which, incidentally, Wesley translated as a future tense ('Therefore ye shall be perfect . . .') rather than its usual reading as an imperative. But he accepts Blackall's qualification that 'it would be very absurd for any *private* discourse to be given so prominent a place in a public Gospel. . . . This sermon was spoken by our Lord to all his disciples . . . , i.e., *to all Christians*; . . . every one of the flock as well as every *pastor* of the flock is obliged to lead his life according to those rules and prescriptions which are here given by our Saviour' (cf. *Works*, I. 3).

[21] 1 Cor. 4:6.

two accounts: because without such a restriction the discourse would either be apparently absurd, or would contradict some other Scripture. But this is not the case. It will plainly appear, when we come to examine the several particulars, that there is no absurdity at all in applying all which our Lord hath here delivered 5 to all mankind. Neither will it infer any contradiction to anything else he has delivered, nor to any other Scripture whatever. Nay, it will farther appear that either all the parts of this discourse are to be applied to men in general or no part; seeing they are all connected together, all joined as the stones in an arch, of which 10 you cannot take one away without destroying the whole fabric.[22]

7. We may, lastly, observe how our Lord teaches here. And surely, as at all times, so particularly at this, he speaks 'as never man spake'.[23] Not as the holy men of old; although they also spoke 'as they were moved by the Holy Ghost'.[24] Not as Peter, or James, 15 or John, or Paul. They were indeed wise masterbuilders in his church.[25] But still in this, in the degrees of heavenly wisdom, the servant is not as his Lord.[26] No, nor even as himself at any other time, or on any other occasion. It does not appear that it was ever his design, at any other time or place, to lay down at once the 20 whole plan of his religion, to give us a full prospect of Christianity, to describe at large the nature of that holiness without which no man shall see the Lord.[27] Particular branches of this he has indeed described on a thousand different occasions. But never besides here did he give, of set purpose, a general view of the whole. Nay, 25 we have nothing else of this kind in all the Bible; unless one should except that short sketch of holiness delivered by God in those ten words or commandments to Moses on Mount Sinai. But even here how wide a difference is there between one and the

---

[22] A crucial example of Wesley's twin principles of hermeneutics. The first is that Scripture is Scripture's own best interpreter; thus, 'the analogy of faith' (i.e., one's sense of the whole) should govern one's exegesis of each part; cf. No. 5, 'Justification by Faith', §2 and n.). The second is that one begins, always, with a literal translation and holds to it unless it should lead into a palpable absurdity; in which case, analogy and even allegory become allowable options. Cf. Nos. 74, 'Of the Church', §12; 84, *The Important Question*, I.1; 86, *A Call to Backsliders*, I.2(4); 87, 'The Danger of Riches', §2; 139, 'On the Sabbath', II.1; and 144, 'The Love of God', II.5. Cf. also Wesley's letter to Lady Cox, Mar. 7, 1738; to Samuel Furly, May 10, 1755; and to Dr. Lavington, Dec. 1751. For exceptions cf. Nos. 48, 'Self-denial', I.7; 99, *The Reward of Righteousness*, §4; and 110, *Free Grace*, §20.

[23] Cf. John 7:46.
[24] 2 Pet. 1:21.
[25] See 1 Cor. 3:10.
[26] See John 15:20.   [27] Heb. 12:14.

other! 'Even that which was made glorious had no glory in this respect, by reason of the glory that excelleth.'ᵍ

8. Above all, with what amazing love does the Son of God here reveal his Father's will to man! He does not bring us again 'to the mount that [. . .] burned with fire, nor unto blackness, and darkness, and tempest'.²⁸ He does not speak as when he 'thundered out of heaven, when the highest gave his thunder, hailstones, and coals of fire'.²⁹ He now addresses us with his still, small voice.³⁰ 'Blessed (or happy) are the poor in spirit.' Happy are the mourners, the meek; those that hunger after righteousness; the merciful, the pure in heart: happy in the end and in the way; happy in this life and in life everlasting! As if he had said, 'Who is he that lusteth to live, and would fain see good days? Behold, I show you the thing which your soul longeth for; see the way you have so long sought in vain! The way of pleasantness; the path to calm, joyous peace,³¹ to heaven below and heaven above!'

9. At the same time with what authority does he teach! Well might they say, 'not as the scribes'.³² Observe the manner (but it cannot be expressed in words), the air with which he speaks! Not as Moses, the servant of God; not as Abraham, his friend; not as any of the prophets; nor as any of the sons of men. It is something more than human; more than can agree to any created being. It speaks the Creator of all—a God, a God appears! Yea, ὁ ὤν, the being of beings, Jehovah, the self-existent, the supreme, the God who is over all, blessed for ever!³³

10. This divine discourse, delivered in the most excellent method, every subsequent part illustrating those that precede, is commonly, and not improperly, divided into three principal branches: the first contained in the fifth, the second in the sixth, and the third in the seventh chapter. In the first the sum of all true religion is laid down in eight particulars, which are explained and guarded against the false glosses of man in the following parts of the fifth chapter. In the second are rules for that right intention which we are to preserve in all our outward actions, unmixed with

---

ᵍ 2 Cor. 3:10.

²⁸ Heb. 12:18.
²⁹ Ps. 18:14 (BCP).
³⁰ 1 Kgs. 19:12.
³¹ See Prov. 3:17.
³² Matt. 7:29; Mark 1:22.   ³³ See Rom. 9:5.

worldly desires, or anxious cares for even the necessaries of life. In the third are cautions against the main hindrances of religion, closed with an application of the whole.[34]

I. 1. Our Lord, first, lays down the sum of all true religion in eight particulars, which he explains and guards against the false glosses of men, to the end of the fifth chapter.

Some have supposed that he designed in these to point out the several stages of the Christian course, the steps which a Christian successively takes in his journey to the promised land; others, that all the particulars here set down belong at all times to every Christian. And why may we not allow both the one and the other?[35] What inconsistency is there between them? It is undoubtedly true that both 'poverty of spirit'[36] and every other temper which is here mentioned are at all times found in a greater or less degree in every real Christian. And it is equally true that real Christianity always begins in poverty of spirit, and goes on in the order here set down till the 'man of God' is made 'perfect'.[37] We begin at the lowest of these gifts of God; yet so as not to relinquish this when we are called of God to come up higher:[38] but 'whereunto we have already attained'[39] we 'hold fast',[40] while we 'press on'[41] to what is yet before, to the highest blessings of God in Christ Jesus.

2. The foundation of all is 'poverty of spirit'.[42] Here therefore our Lord begins: 'Blessed (saith he) are the poor in spirit, for theirs is the kingdom of heaven.'

It may not improbably be supposed that our Lord, looking on those who were round about him, and observing that not many rich were there, but rather the poor of the world, took occasion from thence to make a transition from temporal to spiritual things. 'Blessed', saith he (or *happy:* so the word should be rendered both in this and the following verses) 'are the poor in spirit.' He does not say they that are poor as to *outward circumstances* (it being not impossible that some of these may be as far from happiness as a monarch upon his throne) but 'the poor in

---

[34] See below, Discourse X, §§1–3, for a recapitulation of this same outline.
[35] Cf. Wesley's *Dialogues between an Antinomian and his Friend*, 1745 (*Bibliog*, Nos. 102, 106, and 226; see Vol. 13 of this edn.).
[36] Cf. Matt. 5:3.   [37] 2 Tim. 3:17.
[38] Cf. Luke 14:10.   [39] Phil. 3:16.
[40] Heb. 3:6, etc.   [41] Cf. Phil. 3:14.
[42] A positive transvaluation of William Law; cf. *Serious Call, Works*, IV. 170–80.

spirit'; they who, whatever their outward circumstances are, have that disposition of heart which is the first step to all real, substantial happiness, either in this world or that which is to come.[43]

5   3. Some have judged that by the 'poor in spirit' here are meant those who love poverty; those who are free from covetousness, from the love of money; who fear rather than desire riches. Perhaps they have been induced so to judge by wholly confining their thought to the very term, or by considering that weighty
10 observation of St. Paul, that 'the love of money is the root of all evil.'[44] And hence many have wholly divested themselves, not only of riches, but of all worldly goods. Hence also the vows of voluntary poverty seem to have arisen in the Romish Church; it being supposed that so eminent a degree of this fundamental
15 grace must be a large step toward the kingdom of heaven.[45]

But these do not seem to have observed, first, that the expression of St. Paul must be understood with some restriction; otherwise it is not true. For the love of money is not 'the root'—the sole root—'of all evil'. There are a thousand other
20 roots of evil in the world, as sad experience daily shows. His meaning can only be, it is the root of very many evils; perhaps of more than any single vice besides. Secondly, that this sense of the expression 'poor in spirit' will by no means suit our Lord's present design, which is to lay a general foundation whereon the
25 whole fabric of Christianity may be built; a design which would be in no wise answered by guarding against one particular vice: so that even if this were supposed to be one part of his meaning, it could not possibly be the whole. Thirdly, that it cannot be supposed to be any part of his meaning unless we charge him with

[43] See No. 17, 'The Circumcision of the Heart', I.2.
[44] 1 Tim. 6:10.
[45] Cf. Blackall, *Works*, I.7: '. . . the Papists . . . who do so much magnify voluntary poverty. . . . And in this sense Maldonate, and divers others of the popish commentators, do expound this passage. . . . But this interpretation is perfectly groundless and also manifestly false.' The reference here is to Johannes Maldonatus (1534–83), Spanish exegete and theologian, whose chief work was *Commentarii in Quattuor Evangelistas* (2 vols., 1596–97, and many later edns., none in English until 1888). It is worth noting that Wesley has already begun to inveigh against surplus accumulation and 'the danger of riches'; cf. Discourse VIII, below, reflecting as it does the counsels of Richard Lucas and William Law against greed and self-indulgence—and about voluntary poverty as the Christian counterweight to the dangers of riches. This will become a lifelong theme of Wesley's, and his emphasis on it will increase with the passing years and growing affluence amongst the Methodists.

manifest tautology: seeing if 'poverty of spirit' were only freedom from covetousness, from the love of money, or the desire of riches, it would coincide with what he afterwards mentions; it would be only a branch of 'purity of heart'.[46]

4. Who then are the 'poor in spirit'? Without question, the humble;[47] they who know themselves, who are convinced of sin; those to whom God hath given that first repentance which is previous to faith in Christ.[48]

One of these can no longer say, 'I am rich, and increased in goods, and have need of nothing:' as now knowing that he is 'wretched, and poor, and miserable, and blind, and naked'.[49] He is convinced that he is spiritually poor indeed; having no spiritual good abiding in him. 'In me (saith he) dwelleth no good thing;'[50] but whatsoever is evil and abominable. He has a deep sense of the loathsome leprosy of sin, which he brought with him from his mother's womb, which overspreads his whole soul, and totally corrupts every power and faculty thereof. He sees more and more of the evil tempers which spring from that evil root: the pride and haughtiness of spirit,[51] the constant bias to think of himself more highly than he ought to think;[52] the vanity, the thirst after the esteem or honour that cometh from men;[53] the hatred or envy, the jealousy or revenge, the anger, malice, or bitterness; the inbred

---

[46] Cf. Matt. 5:8.

[47] This equivalence of 'the poor in spirit' and 'the humble' is also Blackall's line. Wesley compresses his exposition into six duodecimo pages; the bishop's runs to twenty-two folio pages. See also Hammond, *Practical Catechism*, p. 85.

[48] The notion of self-knowledge as that 'first repentance which is previous to faith in Christ' is crucial in Wesley's doctrine of justification. It is, regularly, a prevenient work of the Holy Spirit, but it involves human 're-action', viz., recognition of one's alienation from God and acknowledgement of the truth of one's sinful affections. Cf. John Norris, *Practical Discourses*, I. 4: 'Poverty of spirit . . . is not a state of *life* but a state of *mind*, and we may take it either in opposition to covetousness or . . . to pride and highmindedness.' On p. 16 the phrase is more clearly defined as 'humility', although for Norris 'poverty of spirit' is more nearly self-abasement than self-knowledge as in Wesley. Norris, p. 28: 'Humility is the proper foundation of grace and the theatre of all divine operations.' See Nos. 7, 'The Way to the Kingdom', II.1 and n.; and 17, 'The Circumcision of the Heart', I.2 and n.; see also Wesley's extract from Edward Young (the elder) in the *Christian Lib.*, XLVI.144-45. This notion of humility as a 'right judgment of ourselves' (i.e., authentic self-knowledge) is one of William Law's salient themes. Wesley goes a step further and correlates it with 'true repentance'.

[49] Rev. 3:17.

[50] Rom. 7:18.

[51] Cf. No. 14, *The Repentance of Believers*, I.3 and n.

[52] Rom. 12:3.

[53] Cf. No. 14, *The Repentance of Believers*, I.7 and n.

enmity both against God and man[54] which appears in ten thousand shapes; the love of the world, the self-will, the foolish and hurtful desires[55] which cleave to his inmost soul.[56] He is conscious how deeply he has offended by his tongue; if not by
5 profane, immodest, untrue, or unkind words, yet by discourse which was not 'good to the use of edifying', not 'meet to minister grace to the hearers';[57] which consequently was all *corrupt* in God's account, and grievous to his Holy Spirit. His evil works are now likewise ever in his sight; if he tell them 'they are more than
10 he is able to express'.[58] He may as well think to number the 'drops of rain, the sands of the sea, or the days of eternity'.[59]

5. His guilt is now also before his face: he knows the punishment he has deserved, were it only on account of his 'carnal mind',[60] the entire, universal corruption of his nature; how
15 much more on account of all his evil desires and thoughts, of all his sinful words and actions! He cannot doubt for a moment but the least of these deserves the damnation of hell, 'the worm that dieth not', and 'the fire that never shall be quenched'.[61] Above all, the guilt of 'not believing on the name of the only-begotten Son of
20 God'[62] lies heavy upon him. 'How (saith he) shall I escape, who neglect so great salvation!'[63] 'He that believeth not is condemned already', and 'the wrath of God abideth on him.'[64]

6. But what shall he give in exchange for his soul,[65] which is forfeit to the just vengeance of God? 'Wherewithal shall he come
25 before the Lord?'[66] How shall he pay him that he oweth? Were he from this moment to perform the most perfect obedience to every command of God, this would make no amends for a single sin, for any one act of past disobedience: seeing he owes God all the service he is able to perform from this moment to all eternity,
30 could he pay this it would make no manner of amends for what he ought to have done before. He sees himself therefore utterly helpless with regard to atoning for his past sins; utterly unable to make any amends to God, to pay any ransom for his own soul.

But if God would forgive him all that is past,[67] on this one
35 condition, that he should sin no more, that for the time to come he

---

[54] See Rom. 8:7.   [55] 1 Tim. 6:9.
[56] Note this impromptu catalogue of the classical 'deadly sins'.
[57] Cf. Eph. 4:29.   [58] Cf. Ps. 40:7 (BCP).   [59] Cf. Ecclus. 1:2.
[60] Rom. 8:7.   [61] Cf. Mark 9:43,45.   [62] Cf. John 3:18.
[63] Cf. Heb. 2:3.   [64] John 3:18, 36.   [65] See Matt. 16:26.
[66] Cf. Mic. 6:6.   [67] Cf. BCP, Communion, General Confession.

should entirely and constantly obey all his commands: he well knows that this would profit him nothing, being a condition he could never perform. He knows and feels that he is not able to obey even the outward commands of God; seeing these cannot be obeyed while his heart remains in its natural sinfulness and corruption—inasmuch as an evil tree cannot bring forth good fruit.[68] But he cannot cleanse a sinful heart: with men this is impossible.[69] So that he is utterly at a loss even how to begin walking in the path of God's commandments.[70] He knows not how to get one step forward in the way. Encompassed with sin and sorrow and fear, and finding no way to escape, he can only cry out, 'Lord, save, or I perish!'[71]

7. 'Poverty of spirit'[72], then, as it implies the first step we take in running the race which is set before us,[73] is a just sense of our inward and outward sins, and of our guilt and helplessness. This some have monstrously styled the 'virtue of humility';[74] thus teaching us to be proud of knowing we deserve damnation. But our Lord's expression is quite of another kind; conveying no idea to the hearer but that of mere want, of naked sin, of helpless guilt and misery.

8. The great Apostle, where he endeavours to bring sinners to God, speaks in a manner just answerable to this. 'The wrath of God (saith he) is revealed from heaven against all ungodliness and unrighteousness of men'[h]—a charge which he immediately fixes on the heathen world, and thereby proves they were under the wrath of God. He next shows that the Jews were no better than they, and were therefore under the same condemnation: and all this not in order to their attaining 'the noble virtue of humility',

---

[h] Rom. 1:18.

---

[68] See Matt. 7:18; Luke 6:43.
[69] Matt. 19:26.
[70] See Ps. 119:35.
[71] Cf. Matt. 8:25.
[72] Cf. above, I.4 and n.   [73] See Heb. 12:1.
[74] This phrase had been used almost casually by Law in *Christian Perfection* (*Works*, III. 67), and before him by John Selden, *Table Talk* (1689), p. 54: 'The master thinks the virtue of humility is good doctrine for his servant, the laity for the clergy and the clergy for the laity;' cf. Robert Burton in *The Anatomy of Melancholy* (1st edn., 1621; 8th edn., 1676), I. ii. 3-14. See also St. Francis de Sales, *An Introduction to the Devout Life* (1608), Pt. III, iv. For other references to humility in the sermons, cf. below, I.9; and Nos. 17, 'The Circumcision of the Heart', I.2; 65, 'The Duty of Reproving our Neighbour', III.3; 92, 'On Zeal', II.1; 108, 'On Riches', I.6; 120, 'The Unity of the Divine Being', §22.

'but that every mouth might be stopped, and all the world become guilty before God'.[75]

He proceeds to show that they were helpless as well as guilty; which is the plain purport of all those expressions—'Therefore by
5 the deeds of the law there shall no flesh be justified'[76]—'But now the righteousness of God, which is by faith of Jesus Christ, without the law is manifested'[77]—'We conclude that a man is justified by faith, without the deeds of the law'[78]—expressions all tending to the same point, even to 'hide pride from man';[79] to
10 humble him to the dust, without teaching him to reflect upon his humility as a virtue; to inspire him with that full piercing conviction of his utter sinfulness, guilt, and helplessness, which casts the sinner, stripped of all, lost, and undone, on his strong helper, 'Jesus Christ the righteous'.[80]

15 9. One cannot but observe here that Christianity begins just where heathen morality ends: 'poverty of spirit', 'conviction of sin',[81] the 'renouncing ourselves',[82] the 'not having our own righteousness',[83] the very first point in the religion of Jesus Christ, leaving all pagan religion behind. This was ever hid from the wise
20 men of this world;[84] insomuch that the whole Roman language, even with all the improvements of the Augustan age, does not afford so much as a name for *humility* (the word from whence we borrow this, as is well known, bearing in Latin a quite different meaning): no, nor was one found in all the copious language of
25 Greece till it was *made* by the great Apostle.[85]

10. O that we may feel what they were not able to express! Sinner, awake! Know thyself! Know and feel that thou 'wert shapen in wickedness, and that in sin did thy mother conceive thee',[86] and that thou thyself hast been heaping sin upon sin ever
30 since thou couldst discern good from evil. Sink under the mighty

[75] Cf. Rom. 3:19.   [76] Rom. 3:20.
[77] Rom. 3:21, 22.   [78] Rom. 3:28.
[79] Job 33:17. Cf. No. 129, 'Heavenly Treasure in Earthen Vessels', II.5.
[80] 1 John 2:1.
[81] Cf. John 8:46.   [82] Cf. 2 Cor. 4:2; See also Mark 8:34.
[83] Cf. Phil. 3:9.   [84] See Matt. 11:25.
[85] In classical Latin the meaning of *humilitas* ranges between 'lowness' (of stature or status) to 'insignificance' to 'baseness'. By the time of Lactantius (*c.* 240–*c.* 320) and Sulpicius Severus (*c.* 360–*c.* 420), it had acquired a specific Christian connotation. In the light of the lexical evolution of ταπεινοφροσύνη and *humilitas* in patristic Christian literature Wesley has an important point here for the history of Christian ethics. Cf. above, I.7.
[86] Cf. Ps. 51:5 (BCP).

hand of God, as guilty of death eternal; and cast off, renounce, abhor all imagination of ever being able to help thyself! Be it all thy hope to be washed in his blood and renewed by his almighty Spirit 'who himself bare all our sins in his own body on the tree'.[87] So shalt thou witness, 'Happy are the poor in spirit; for theirs is 5 the kingdom of heaven.'

11. This is that kingdom of heaven or of God which is 'within' us,[88] even 'righteousness, and peace, and joy in the Holy Ghost'.[89] And what is righteousness but the life of God in the soul, the mind which was in Christ Jesus,[90] the image of God stamped upon 10 the heart, now renewed after the likeness of him that created it? What is it but the love of God because he first loved us,[91] and the love of all mankind for his sake?

And what is this peace, the peace of God, but that calm serenity of soul, that sweet repose in the blood of Jesus, which leaves no 15 doubt of our acceptance in him? Which excludes all fear but the loving, filial fear of offending our Father which is in heaven?

This inward kingdom implies also 'joy in the Holy Ghost',[92] who seals upon our hearts 'the redemption which is in Jesus', the righteousness of Christ, imputed to us[93] for 'the remission of the 20 sins that are past':[94] who giveth us now 'the earnest of our inheritance'[95] of the crown which the Lord, the righteous Judge, will give at that day.[96] And well may this be termed 'the kingdom of heaven'; seeing it is heaven already opened in the soul, the first springing up of those rivers of pleasure[97] which flow at God's right 25 hand for evermore.

---

[87] 1 Pet. 2:24.
[88] Luke 17:21.
[89] Rom. 14:17.
[90] See Phil. 2:5.
[91] 1 John 4:19.   [92] Rom. 14:17.
[93] Here, and again in Discourse IX, §21, Wesley uses this commonplace Puritan phrase about the imputation of Christ's righteousness to the pardoned sinner in justification with studied indifference to its controversial overtones—with no indication that, later, he will reject it as misleading (see No. 20, *The Lord Our Righteousness*, II.19-20). Still later, when the Calvinists had made it one of their shibboleths, Wesley will renounce the phrase itself as 'ambiguous, unscriptural, . . . so liable to be misinterpreted'; cf. *Some Remarks on Mr. Hill's Review. . .* , 1772 (Vol. 13 of this edn.). In the following year Wesley repeated the point against Hill's *Farrago Double-Distilled (ibid.)*, §25: 'The doctrine which I believe has done immense hurt is that of the imputed righteousness of Christ in the antinomian [Hill's] sense. The doctrine which I have constantly held and preached is that faith is imputed [to us] for righteousness.'
[94] Rom. 3:24-25.   [95] Eph. 1:14.
[96] 2 Tim. 4:8.   [97] See Ps. 36:8.

12. 'Theirs is the kingdom of heaven.' Whosoever thou art to whom God hath given to be 'poor in spirit', to feel thyself lost, thou hast a right thereto, through the gracious promise of him who cannot lie.[98] It is purchased for thee by the blood of the 5 Lamb.[99] It is very nigh: thou art on the brink of heaven. Another step, and thou enterest into the kingdom of righteousness, and peace, and joy.[100] Art thou all sin? 'Behold the Lamb of God who taketh away the sin of the world.'[101] All unholy? See thy 'advocate with the Father, Jesus Christ the righteous'.[102] Art thou unable to 10 atone for the least of thy sins? 'He is the propitiation for' all thy 'sins.'[103] Now believe on the Lord Jesus Christ, and all thy sins are blotted out. Art thou totally unclean in soul and in body? Here is the 'fountain for sin and uncleanness'.[104] 'Arise, [. . .] and wash away thy sins:'[105] stagger no more at the promise through unbelief. 15 Give glory to God. Dare to believe! Now cry out, from the ground of thy heart:

> Yes, I yield, I yield at last,
> Listen to thy speaking blood;
> Me with all my sins I cast
> 20   On my atoning God![106]

13. Then thou learnest of him to be 'lowly of heart'.[107] And this is the true, genuine, Christian humility, which flows from a sense of the love of God, reconciled to us in Christ Jesus.[108] 'Poverty of spirit', in this meaning of the word, begins where a sense of guilt 25 and of the wrath of God ends; and is a continual sense of our total dependence on him for every good thought or word or work; of our utter inability to all good unless he 'water us every moment':[109] and an abhorrence of the praise of men, knowing that all praise is due unto God only. With this is joined a loving shame, a tender 30 humiliation before God, even for the sins which we know he hath forgiven us, and for the sin which still remaineth in our hearts, although we know it is not imputed to our condemnation. Nevertheless the conviction we feel of inbred sin[110] is deeper and deeper every day. The more we grow in grace the more do we see

---

[98] See Titus 1:2.   [99] Rev. 7:14; 12:11.
[100] Rom. 14:17.   [101] John 1:29.   [102] 1 John 2:1.
[103] Cf. 1 John 2:2.   [104] Zech. 13:1.   [105] Acts 22:16.
[106] 'Waiting for Christ the Prophet' (the second hymn with this title), st. 5, last 4 ll. in *Hymns and Sacred Poems* (1742), p. 211 (*Poet. Wks.*, II.265).
[107] Cf. Matt. 11:29.   [108] See 2 Cor. 5:18.
[109] Cf. Isa. 27:3.   [110] Cf. 2 Pet. 2:14; See also Rom. 7:14-23.

of the desperate wickedness of our heart. The more we advance in the knowledge and love of God, through our Lord Jesus Christ (as great a mystery as this may appear to those who know not the power of God unto salvation),[111] the more do we discern of our alienation from God, of the enmity that is in our carnal mind,[112] and the necessity of our being entirely renewed in righteousness and true holiness.[113]

II. 1. It is true, he has scarce any conception of this who now begins to know the inward kingdom of heaven. 'In his prosperity he saith, I shall never be moved; Thou, Lord, hast made my hill so strong.'[114] Sin is so utterly bruised beneath his feet that he can scarce believe it remaineth in him. Even temptation is silenced and speaks not again; it cannot approach, but stands afar off. He is borne aloft on the chariots of joy and love; he soars 'as upon the wings of an eagle'.[115] But our Lord well knew that this triumphant state does not often continue long. He therefore presently subjoins, 'Blessed are they that mourn; for they shall be comforted.'[116]

2. Not that we can imagine this promise belongs to those who mourn only on some worldly account; who are in sorrow and heaviness merely on account of some worldly trouble or disappointment, such as the loss of their reputation, or friends, or the impairing of their fortune. As little title to it have they who are afflicting themselves, through fear of some temporal evil; or who pine away with anxious care, or that desire of earthly things which 'maketh the heart sick'.[117] Let us not think these 'shall receive any thing from the Lord':[118] he is not in all their thoughts.[119] Therefore it is that they thus 'walk in a vain shadow, and disquiet themselves in vain'.[120] And 'This shall ye have of mine hand;' saith the Lord, 'ye shall lie down in sorrow.'[121]

3. The mourners of whom our Lord here speaks are those that mourn on quite another account: they that mourn after God, after him in whom they did 'rejoice with joy unspeakable'[122] when he gave them to 'taste the good', the pardoning 'word, and the

---

[111] Cf. the intro. to No. 44, *Original Sin*.   [112] See Rom. 8:7.

[113] Eph. 4:24. Cf. No. 45, 'The New Birth', I.1.

[114] Cf. Ps. 30:6 (BCP).

[115] Cf. Isa. 40:31.   [116] Matt. 5:4.

[117] Prov. 13:12.   [118] Jas. 1:7.

[119] See Ps. 10:4.   [120] Cf. Ps. 39:7 (BCP).

[121] Isa. 50:11.   [122] 1 Pet. 1:8.

powers of the world to come'.[123] But he now 'hides his face, and they are troubled';[124] they cannot see him through the dark cloud. But they see temptation and sin—which they fondly supposed were gone never to return—arising again, following after them
5 amain, and holding them in on every side. It is not strange if their soul is now disquieted within them,[125] if trouble and heaviness take hold upon them.[126] Nor will their great enemy fail to improve the occasion; to ask, 'Where is now thy God?[127] Where is now the blessedness whereof thou spakest?[128] The beginning of the
10 kingdom of heaven? Yea, hath God said, "Thy sins are forgiven thee"?[129] Surely God hath not said it. It was only a dream, a mere delusion, a creature of thy own imagination. If thy sins are forgiven, why art thou thus? Can a pardoned sinner be thus unholy?' And if then, instead of immediately crying to God, they
15 reason with him that is wiser than they, they will be in heaviness indeed, in sorrow of heart, in anguish not to be expressed. Nay, even when God shines again upon the soul, and takes away all doubt of his past mercy, still he that is 'weak in faith'[130] may be tempted and troubled on account of what is to come; especially
20 when inward sin revives, and thrusts sore at him that he may fall. Then may he again cry out:

> I have a sin of fear, that when I've spun
> My last thread, I shall perish on the shore![131]—

lest I should make shipwreck of the faith,[132] and my last state be
25 worse than the first[133]—

> Lest all my bread of life should fail,
> And I sink down unchanged to hell.[134]

[123] Heb. 6:5.   [124] Cf. Ps. 104:29.   [125] See Ps. 42:5,11; 43:5.
[126] See below, No. 47, 'Heaviness through Manifold Temptations', Proem and II.1-3.
[127] Ps. 42:10.   [128] See Gal. 4:15.
[129] Luke 5:20.   [130] Cf. 1 Cor. 8:7-12.
[131] John Donne, 'A Hymn to God the Father'; cf. JWJ, Jan. 24, 1738; see also, *AM*, 1779, 459-60, where Wesley again quotes this couplet in his extract from Donne's biography.
[132] See 1 Tim. 1:19.   [133] See Luke 11:26.
[134] 'Groaning for Redemption', Pt. II, ver. 3, last two ll., in *Hymns and Sacred Poems* (1742), p. 106 (*Poet. Wks.*, II.161). Could 'bread' here be an uncorrected misprint of 'breath'?
     This equivalence of 'mourning' and 'heaviness of spirit' is rather different from Blackall's exegesis of this passage (*Works*, I.24-31). The bishop takes it to refer both to those who are in 'trouble, sorrow, or affliction' and also to those 'full of sorrow and trouble in their own minds, on account of their sins which lie as a heavy load on them'. But

4. Sure it is that this affliction 'for the present is not joyous, but grievous. Nevertheless afterward it bringeth forth peaceable fruit unto them that are exercised thereby.'[135] 'Blessed' therefore 'are they that' thus 'mourn,' if they 'tarry the Lord's leisure',[136] and suffer not themselves to be turned out of the way[137] by the miserable comforters[138] of the world; if they resolutely reject all the comforts of sin, of folly, and vanity; all the idle diversions and amusements of the world, all the pleasures which 'perish in the using',[139] and which only tend to benumb and stupefy the soul, that it may neither be sensible of itself nor God. Blessed are they who 'follow on to know the Lord',[140] and steadily refuse all other comfort. They shall be comforted by the consolations of his Spirit, by a fresh manifestation of his love: by such a witness of his accepting them in the Beloved[141] as shall never more be taken away from them. This 'full assurance of faith'[142] swallows up all doubt, as well as all tormenting fear, God now giving them a sure hope of an enduring substance and 'strong consolation through grace'.[143] Without disputing whether it be possible for any of those to 'fall away'[144] 'who were once enlightened and [. . .] made partakers of the Holy Ghost',[145] it suffices them to say, by the power now resting upon them, 'Who shall separate us from the love of Christ? [. . .] I am persuaded, that neither death nor life, [. . .] nor things present, nor things to come; nor height nor depth . . . , shall be able to separate us from the love of God, which is in Christ Jesus our Lord!'[i]

5. This whole process, both of mourning for an absent God[146] and recovering the joy of his countenance, seems to be shadowed out in what our Lord spoke to his apostles the night before his

---

[i] Rom. 8:35, 38-39. [The comment here about 'falling away' (cf. 2 Thess. 2:3) is related to Wesley's rejection of the Calvinists' doctrine of final perseverance, and he returns to it again and again; cf. No. 1, *Salvation by Faith*, II.4 and n.]

Hammond, *Practical Catechism*, p. 86, had defined mourning as 'contrition' both for our 'spiritual wants' and also for our 'actual sins'. Later, John Heylyn, *Theological Lectures*, I.65 ff., will follow the same line.

[135] Cf. Heb. 12:11.
[136] Ps. 27:16 (BCP).   [137] Job 31:7; Heb. 12:13.
[138] Job 16:2.   [139] Col. 2:22 (cf. *Notes*).
[140] Hos. 6:3.   [141] See Eph. 1:6.
[142] Heb. 10:22. Cf. No. 117, 'On the Discoveries of Faith', §15 and n.
[143] Cf. 2 Thess. 2:16.   [144] Heb. 6:6.   [145] Heb. 6:4.
[146] Cf. Luther's notion of *Deus absconditus*, as well as the mystical idea about 'the dark night of the soul'.

Passion: 'Do ye inquire of that I said, a little while and ye shall not see me, and again a little while and ye shall see me? Verily, verily, I say unto you, that ye shall weep and lament,' namely, when ye do not see me; 'but the world shall rejoice,' shall triumph over you, as

5 though your hope were now come to an end. 'And ye shall be sorrowful,' through doubt, through fear, through temptation, through vehement desire; 'but your sorrow shall be turned into joy,' by the return of him whom your soul loveth. 'A woman when she is in travail hath sorrow because her hour is come. But as soon

10 as she is delivered of the child, she remembereth no more the anguish, for joy that a man is born into the world. And ye now have sorrow:' ye mourn and cannot be comforted. 'But I will see you again; and your heart shall rejoice' with calm, inward joy, 'and your joy no man taketh from you.'[j]

15 6. But although this mourning is at an end, is lost in holy joy, by the return of the Comforter, yet is there another, and a blessed mourning it is, which abides in the children of God. They still mourn for the sins and miseries of mankind: they 'weep with them that weep'.[147] They weep for them that weep not for themselves,

20 for the sinners against their own souls. They mourn for the weakness and unfaithfulness of those that are in some measure saved from their sins. 'Who is weak and they are not weak? Who is offended, and they burn not?'[148] They are grieved for the dishonour continually done to the Majesty of heaven and earth.

25 At all times they have an awful sense of this, which brings a deep seriousness upon their spirit; a seriousness which is not a little increased since the eyes of their understanding were opened[149] by their continually seeing the vast ocean of eternity,[150] without a bottom or a shore,[151] which has already swallowed up millions of

30 millions of men, and is gaping to devour them that yet remain. They see here the house of God eternal in the heavens; there, hell and destruction without a covering;[152] and thence feel the importance of every moment, which just appears, and is gone for ever.

35 7. But all this wisdom of God is foolishness with the world.[153] The whole affair of 'mourning' and 'poverty of spirit' is with them

---

[j] John 16:19-22.

---

[147] Rom. 12:15. [148] Cf. 2 Cor. 11:29. [149] See Eph. 1:18.
[150] Cf. No. 54, 'On Eternity', §4 and n. [151] *Ibid.*, §18 and n.
[152] See Job 26:6. [153] See 1 Cor. 3:19.

stupidity and dullness. Nay, 'tis well if they pass so favourable a judgment upon it, if they do not vote it to be mere moping and melancholy, if not downright lunacy and distraction. And it is no wonder at all that this judgment should be passed by those who know not God. Suppose as two persons were walking together one should suddenly stop, and with the strongest signs of fear and amazement cry out: 'On what a precipice do we stand! See, we are on the point of being dashed in pieces! Another step and we fall into that huge abyss. Stop! I will not go on for all the world.' When the other, who seemed to himself at least equally sharp-sighted, looked forward and saw nothing of all this, what would he think of his companion but that 'he was beside himself ',[154] that his head was out of order, that much religion (if he was not guilty of much learning) had certainly 'made him mad'?[155]

8. But let not the children of God, 'the mourners in Zion',[156] be moved by any of these things. Ye whose eyes are enlightened, be not troubled by those who walk on still in darkness. Ye do not walk on in a vain shadow:[157] God and eternity are real things. Heaven and hell are in very deed open before you: and ye are on the edge of the great gulf. It has already swallowed up more than words can express, nations and kindreds and peoples and tongues,[158] and still yawns to devour, whether they see it or no, the giddy, miserable children of men. O cry aloud! Spare not! Lift up your voice[159] to him who grasps both time and eternity, both for yourselves and your brethren, that ye may be counted worthy to escape the destruction that cometh as a whirlwind![160] That ye may be brought safe, through all the waves and storms, into the haven where you would be.[161] Weep for yourselves, till he wipes away the tears from your eyes.[162] And even then weep for the miseries that come upon the earth, till the Lord of all shall put a period to misery and sin, shall wipe away the tears from all faces, and 'the knowledge of the Lord shall cover the earth, as the waters cover the sea.'[163]

[154] Cf. Mark 3:21.
[155] Cf. Acts 26:24.
[156] Cf. Isa. 61:3.
[157] See Ps. 39:7 (BCP).
[158] See Rev. 14:6.
[159] See Isa. 58:1.
[160] See Prov. 1:27.
[161] See Ps. 107:30.
[162] See Rev. 7:17; 21:4.
[163] Cf. Isa. 11:9; Hab. 2:14. Cf. No. 47, 'Heaviness through Manifold Temptations', V. 2-4.

Upon our Lord's Sermon on the Mount
Discourse the Second

Matthew 5:5-7

Blessed are the meek; for they shall inherit the earth.
5   *Blessed are they which do hunger and thirst after righteousness; for they shall be filled.*
Blessed are the merciful; for they shall obtain mercy.

I. 1. When 'the winter is past', when 'the time of singing is come, and the voice of the turtle is heard in the land';[1] when he
10 that comforts the mourners is now returned, 'that he may abide with them for ever';[2] when at the brightness of his presence the clouds disperse, the dark clouds of doubt and uncertainty, the storms of fear flee away, the waves of sorrow subside, and their spirit again 'rejoiceth in God their Saviour':[3] then is it that this
15 word is eminently fulfilled; then those whom he hath comforted can bear witness, 'Blessed (or happy) are the meek; for they shall inherit the earth.'[4]

2. But who are the meek? Not those who grieve at nothing because they know nothing, who are not discomposed at the evils
20 that occur because they discern not evil from good. Not those who are sheltered from the shocks of life by a stupid insensibility; who have either by nature or art the virtue of stocks and stones, and resent nothing because they feel nothing. Brute philosophers[5] are

---

[1] S. of S. 2:11-12.
[2] Cf. John 14:16.
[3] Cf. Luke 1:47.
[4] Matt. 5:5.
[5] Cf. Nicholas Rowe's lines from the prologue to *The Ambitious Step-Mother* (inaccurately cited in the *OED*), quoted by Wesley in No. 84, *The Important Question*, III.3:

> Let not the Stoic boast his mind unmoved,
> The brute philosopher, who ne'er has proved
> The joy of loving, or of being loved.

See below, No. 136, 'On Mourning for the Dead', and Wesley's assertions that Christians

wholly unconcerned in this matter. Apathy[6] is as far from meekness as from humanity. So that one would not easily conceive how any Christians of the purer ages, especially any of the Fathers of the Church, could confound these, and mistake one of the foulest errors of heathenism for a branch of true 5 Christianity.

3. Nor does Christian meekness imply the being without zeal for God, any more than it does ignorance or insensibility. No; it keeps clear of every extreme, whether in excess or defect. It does not destroy but balance the affections, which the God of nature 10 never designed should be rooted out by grace, but only brought and kept under due regulations.[7] It poises the mind aright. It holds an even scale with regard to anger and sorrow and fear; preserving the mean in every circumstance of life, and not declining either to the right hand or the left.[8] 15

4. Meekness therefore seems properly to relate to ourselves. But it may be referred either to God or our neighbour. When this due composure of mind has reference to God it is usually termed resignation—a calm acquiescence in whatsoever is his will concerning us, even though it may not be pleasing to nature, 20 saying continually, 'It is the Lord; let him do what seemeth him good.'[9] When we consider it more strictly with regard to ourselves we style it patience or contentedness. When it is exerted toward

---

ought not feel deep grief. Is the disposition recommended there Christian meekness or stoicism?

[6] ἀπάθεια: a crowning virtue in Stoic ethics signifying the ideal state of freedom from passion (πάθεια) or any other disturbing emotions. Cf. primary sources (Dionysius, Arrian, Plutarch) in Liddell and Scott, *Greek-English Lexicon;* see also Lampe, *Patristic Greek Lexicon*, espec. the citations from Clement of Alexandria.

[7] The familiar Thomist principle that grace does not destroy nature but perfects it (*gratia non tollit naturam sed perfecit*).

[8] See 2 Chr. 34:2.

[9] 1 Sam. 3:18. Note this composite definition of a familiar theme of the mystics. Its nearest source was Law's *Serious Call*, (*Works*, IV. 242): 'Resignation to the divine will signifies a cheerful approbation and acceptance of everything that comes from God. . . .' But in the *Christian Lib.* (cf. the Index in the 2nd edn., 1837, Vol. XXX) Wesley cites the same idea in almost the same words from Molinos, De Renty, Antoinette Bourignon, and *The Country Parson's Advice* (cf. XLV. 169-291). E.g., in Miguel Molinos, *The Spiritual Guide Which Disentangles the Soul*, 1688 (*ibid.*, XXXVIII. 249-93), resignation is defined as 'a total and absolute consignment of thyself into the hands of God, with a perfect submission to his holy will. . . .' See also Nos. 69, 'The Imperfection of Human Knowledge', IV, ¶3; 82, 'On Temptation', III.10; and 83, 'On Patience', §10; see also the Diary for Sept. 2, 1736, for his report of reading 'Worthington on Resignation'; this would have been John Worthington, Cambridge Platonist and advocate of theological pluralism, *The Great Duty of Self-Resignation to the Divine Will* (1675).

other men then it is mildness to the good and gentleness to the evil.[10]

5. They who are truly meek can clearly discern what is evil; and they can also suffer it. They are *sensible* of everything of this kind; but still meekness holds the reins. They are exceeding 'zealous for the Lord of hosts';[11] but their zeal is always guided by knowledge, and tempered in every thought and word and work with the love of man as well as the love of God. They do not desire to extinguish any of the passions which God has for wise ends implanted in their nature. But they have the mastery of all; they hold them all in subjection, and employ them only in subservience to those ends. And thus even the harsher and more unpleasing passions are applicable to the noblest purposes. Even hate and anger and fear, when engaged against sin, and regulated by faith and love, are as walls and bulwarks to the soul, so that the wicked one cannot approach to hurt it.

6. 'Tis evident this divine temper is not only to abide but to increase in us day by day. Occasions of exercising, and thereby increasing it, will never be wanting while we remain upon earth. We 'have need of patience, that after we have done' and suffered 'the will of God, we may receive the promise'.[12] We have need of resignation, that we may in all circumstances say, 'Not as I will,

---

[10] Wesley is here digesting and adjudicating a very large literature on the theme of 'Christian meekness'. His sources here include Joseph Trapp, *Sermons on Moral and Practical Subjects* (1725), I. 145; Joseph Mede, 'Discourse XXXII', in *Works*, pp. 160-61; William Bates, 'Sermon on the Mount', in *Works*, II. 193-94; and, of course, Offspring Blackall and Henry Hammond. For Blackall meekness is chiefly 'the mastery of passion'; the Christian who 'can show *anger* when there is just cause for it' still keeps it under control (Discourse V, *Works*, I. 42 ff.; there follows an interesting analysis of anger amongst the 'Christian tempers'). Hammond defines meekness as 'a softness and mildness and quietness of spirit' in relation to God and our submission to his will and in relation to our fellows, 'whether superiors, equals or inferiors' (*Practical Catechism*, pp. 87-95). John Norris cites Aristotle's *Ethics* (IV) which defines meekness as *moderation* but then proceeds to identify it 'as an instance of charity, . . . since charity obliges us to promote both our own and our neighbour's happiness. It must, consequently, oblige us to moderate and govern [our] passion' (*Practical Discourses*, III. 59). Anger is especially difficult to control in a degree that is Plato's τὸ μέτριον ('the just right'): hence meekness is a *necessary* Christian virtue. See also Heylyn, *Theological Lectures*, pp. 60-61: 'The immediate office of meekness is to govern the passions.'
   For other comments on meekness in the Wesley corpus, cf. Nos. 23, 'Sermon on the Mount, III', III.12; 65, 'The Duty of Reproving our Neighbour', III.4; 83, 'On Patience', §4; 92, 'On Zeal', II.2; 110, *Free Grace*, §12; 120, 'The Unity of the Divine Being', §22; also his letter to the Bishop of Gloucester, Nov. 26, 1762.
[11] Cf. 2 Kgs. 19:31; Isa. 9:7; 37:32.
[12] Cf. Heb. 10:36.

but as thou wilt.'[13] And we have need of 'gentleness toward all men';[14] but especially toward the evil and the unthankful; otherwise we shall be overcome of evil, instead of overcoming evil with good.[15]

7. Nor does meekness restrain only the outward act, as the scribes and Pharisees taught of old, and the miserable teachers who are not taught of God will not fail to do in all ages. Our Lord guards us against this, and shows the true extent of it, in the following words: 'Ye have heard that it was said by them of old time, Thou shalt not kill; and whosoever shall kill shall be in danger of the judgment. But I say unto you, that whosoever shall be angry with his brother without a cause shall be in danger of the judgment; and whosoever shall say to his brother, Raca, shall be in danger of the council; but whosoever shall say, Thou fool, shall be in danger of hell-fire.'[a]

8. Our Lord here ranks under the head of murder even that anger which goes no farther than the heart; which does not show itself by an outward unkindness, no, not so much as a passionate word.

'Whosoever is angry with his brother'—with any man living, seeing we are all brethren; whosoever feels any unkindness in his heart, any temper contrary to love; whosoever is angry 'without a cause'—without a sufficient cause, or farther than that cause requires—'shall be in danger of the judgment', ἔνοχος ἔσται, 'shall' in that moment 'be obnoxious to'[16] the righteous judgment of God.

But would not one be inclined to prefer the reading of those copies which omit the word εἰκῇ, 'without a cause'?[17] Is it not entirely superfluous? For if *anger at persons* be a temper contrary to love, how can there be a cause, a sufficient cause for it? Any that will justify it in the sight of God?

Anger at sin we allow. In this sense we may 'be angry and' yet we 'sin not'.[18] In this sense our Lord himself is once recorded to have

---

[a] Matt. 5:21-22. [Cf. No. 7, 'The Way to the Kingdom', II.4 and n.]

---

[13] Matt. 26:39. [14] Cf. 2 Tim. 2:24. [15] See Rom. 12:21.

[16] Cf. Nos. 7, 'The Way to the Kingdom', II.4 and n.; and 9, 'The Spirit of Bondage and of Adoption', II.2 and n.

[17] εἰκῇ appears in many good manuscripts, including the *Codex Bezae* and the *TR;* Bengel and others rejected it as a gloss and Wesley followed them in the *Notes.* Modern critical texts and translations omit it.

[18] Eph. 4:26.

been angry: 'He looked round about upon them with anger, being grieved for the hardness of their hearts.'[19] He was grieved at the sinners, and angry at the sin.[20] And this is undoubtedly right before God.

5   9. 'And whosoever shall say to his brother, Raca.' Whosoever shall give way to anger, so as to utter any contemptuous word. It is observed by commentators that *Raca* is a Syriac word which properly signifies empty, vain, foolish: so that it is as inoffensive an expression as can well be used toward one at whom we are displeased.[21] And yet whosoever shall use this, as our Lord assures us, 'shall be in danger of the council'—rather, 'shall be obnoxious thereto'. He shall be liable to a severer sentence from the Judge of all the earth.

'But whosoever shall say, Thou fool'—whosoever shall so give place to the devil as to break out into reviling, into designedly reproachful and contumelious language, 'shall be obnoxious to hell-fire'—shall in that instant be liable to the highest condemnation. It should be observed that our Lord describes all these as obnoxious to capital punishment: the first to strangling, usually inflicted on those who were condemned in one of the inferior courts; the second to stoning, which was frequently inflicted on those who were condemned by the Great Council at

---

[19] Cf. Mark 3:5.

[20] Cf. Wesley's *Notes* for Matt. 5:22: 'We ought not for any cause to be angry at the *person* of the sinner, but at his *sin* only.' Law makes the same point in *Serious Call (Works,* IV. 224). In his section on loving all men (the good and the bad) equally, he says we must learn to distinguish between *actions* and *persons,* that we must always love persons, *all* persons—good and bad—for reasons that never change, in the same way that justice and truth never change, because they are grounded in God's love. Cf. also Seneca, *Moral Essays: 'De Ira' ('On Anger'),* ii. 28: '*Magna pars hominum est, quae non peccatis irascitur sed peccatibus*' ('The greater part of mankind are angry not with the sin but with the sinner'). Cf. Wesley's early sermon (133), 'Death and Deliverance', ¶11; and No. 33, 'Sermon on the Mount, XIII', III.8. See also Hymn 262, ll. 27-32, in *A Collection of Hymns* (1780):

> Thou hatest all iniquity,
> But nothing thou hast made.
> O may I learn the art,
> With meekness to reprove,
> *To hate the sin with all my heart,*
> *But still the sinner love.*

[21] 'Raca' (ῥάχα) is clearly more than this. If, as Poole had suggested *(Annotations, loc. cit.),* it is Syriac, then its verbal root signifies 'spitting' as a sign of contempt. Cf. Bengel, *Gnomon, loc. cit.,* and the papyri references in Arndt and Gingrich, *Greek-English Lexicon.* Also, cf. Nos. 7, 'The Way to the Kingdom', II.4 and n.; and 9, 'The Spirit of Bondage and of Adoption', II.2 and n.

Jerusalem; the third to burning alive, inflicted only on the highest offenders, in the 'valley of the sons of Hinnom', Γῆ Ἐννών, from which that word is evidently taken which we translate hell.[22]

10. And whereas men naturally imagine that God will excuse their defect in some duties for their exactness in others, our Lord next takes care to cut off that vain though common imagination. He shows that it is impossible for any sinner to *commute* with God, who will not accept one duty for another, nor take a part of obedience for the whole.[23] He warns us that the performing our duty to God will not excuse us from our duty to our neighbour; that works of piety, as they are called, will be so far from commending us to God if we are wanting in charity, that on the contrary that want of charity will make all those works an abomination to the Lord.[24]

'Therefore, if thou bring thy gift to the altar, and there rememberest that thy brother hath ought against thee'—on account of thy unkind behaviour toward him, of thy calling him 'Raca', or 'Thou fool'—think not that thy gift will atone for thy anger, or that it will find any acceptance with God so long as thy conscience is defiled with the guilt of unrepented sin. 'Leave there thy gift before the altar, and go thy way; first be reconciled to thy brother' (at least do all that in thee lies toward being reconciled) 'and then come and offer thy gift.'[b]

11. And let there be no delay in what so nearly concerneth thy soul. 'Agree with thine adversary quickly'—now; upon the spot—'while thou art in the way with him'—if it be possible, before he go out of thy sight—'lest at any time the adversary deliver thee to the judge'—lest he appeal to God, the Judge of all—'and the judge deliver thee to the officer'—to Satan, the executioner of the wrath of God—'and thou be cast into prison'[25]—into hell, there to be reserved to the judgment of the great day.[26] 'Verily I say unto thee, thou shalt by no means come out thence till thou hast paid the uttermost farthing.'[27] But this it is

---

[b]   Matt. 5:[22,] 23-24.

[22] See Josh. 15:8, גיא הנם; Wesley's Greek here is neither the Septuagint's nor St. Matthew's; cf. *Notes*, Matt. 5:22.

[23] Cf. No. 16, 'The Means of Grace', II.2 and n.

[24] Cf. No. 14, *The Repentance of Believers*, I.13 and n.

[25] Matt. 5:25.

[26] See Jude 6.   [27] Matt. 5:26.

impossible for thee ever to do; seeing thou hast nothing [with which] to pay.[28] Therefore if thou art once in that prison the smoke of thy torment must 'ascend up for ever and ever'.[29]

12. Meantime, 'the meek shall inherit the earth.'[30] Such is the foolishness of worldly wisdom! The wise of the world had warned them again and again that if they did not resent such treatment, if they would tamely suffer themselves to be thus abused, there would be no living for them upon earth; that they would never be able to procure the common necessaries of life, nor to keep even what they had; that they could expect no peace, no quiet possession, no enjoyment of anything. Most true—suppose there were no God in the world; or suppose he did not concern himself with the children of men. But 'when God ariseth to judgment, and to help all the meek upon earth',[31] how doth he laugh all this heathen wisdom to scorn, and turn the 'fierceness of man to his praise'![32] He takes a peculiar care to provide them with all things needful for life and godliness.[33] He secures to them the provision he hath made, in spite of the force, fraud, or malice of men. And what he secures he 'gives them richly to enjoy'.[34] It is sweet to them, be it little or much. As 'in patience they possess their souls',[35] so they truly possess whatever God hath given them. They are always content, always pleased with what they have. It pleases them because it pleases God; so that while their heart, their desire, their joy is in heaven, they may truly be said to 'inherit the earth'.

13. But there seems to be a yet farther meaning in these words, even that they shall have a more eminent part in the 'new earth, wherein dwelleth righteousness',[36] in that inheritance, a general description of which (and the particulars we shall know hereafter) St. John has given in the twentieth chapter of the Revelation. 'And I saw an angel come down from heaven. . . . And he laid hold on the dragon, that old serpent, . . . and bound him a thousand years. . . . And I saw the souls of them that were

---

[28] See Luke 7:42.
[29] Cf. Rev. 14:11.
[30] Ps. 37:11; cf. Matt. 5:5.
[31] Cf. Ps. 76:9 (BCP).
[32] Cf. Ps. 76:10 (BCP).
[33] See 2 Pet. 1:3.
[34] Cf. 1 Tim. 6:17.
[35] Cf. Luke 21:19. Cf. No. 83, 'On Patience', and espec. §5 and n.
[36] 2 Pet. 3:13.

beheaded for the witness of Jesus, and for the Word of God, and of them which had not worshipped the beast, neither his image, neither had received his mark upon their foreheads or in their hands; and they lived and reigned with Christ a thousand years. But the rest of the dead lived not again until the thousand years were expired. This is the first resurrection. Blessed and holy is he that hath part in the first resurrection: on such the second death hath no power; but they shall be priests of God and of Christ, and shall reign with him a thousand years.'[37]

II. 1. Our Lord has hitherto been more immediately employed in removing the hindrances of true religion: such is pride,[38] the first, grand hindrance of all religion, which is taken away by 'poverty of spirit';[39] levity and thoughtlessness, which prevent any religion from taking root in the soul till they are removed by holy *mourning*; such are anger, impatience, discontent, which are all healed by Christian *meekness*. And when once these hindrances are removed—these evil diseases of the soul which were continually raising false cravings therein, and filling it with sickly appetites—the native appetite of a heaven-born spirit returns; it hungers and thirsts after righteousness. And 'blessed are they which do hunger and thirst after righteousness; for they shall be filled.'[40]

2. Righteousness (as was observed before) is the image of God, the mind which was in Christ Jesus.[41] It is every holy and heavenly temper in one; springing from as well as terminating in the love of God as our Father and Redeemer, and the love of all men for his sake.[42]

3. 'Blessed are they which do hunger and thirst after' this; in order fully to understand which expression we should observe,

---

[37] Rev. 20:1-2, 4-6. For Wesley's 'last words' on 'the millennium', cf. his letter to Christopher Hopper, June 3, 1788, and to Walter Churchey, June 26, 1788.

[38] Cf. No. 14, *The Repentance of Believers*, I.3 and n.

[39] Cf. Matt. 5:3.

[40] Matt. 5:6.

[41] See Phil. 2:5.

[42] Cf. Blackall's definition of righteousness as 'twofold': both 'actual, personal, and inherent righteousness' (always imperfect) and 'imputed righteousness . . . , i.e., our justification and acquittal by God . . . for the sake of Christ' (*Works*, I.61). Here he follows Hammond, who had drawn the same distinction in his *Practical Catechism*, p. 96. Wesley pushes beyond their point and interprets righteousness as holiness: the perfect love of God and 'of all men for *his sake*'. Cf. Nos. 83, 'On Patience', §10; and 85, 'On Working Out Our Own Salvation', §§2, 3.

first, that hunger and thirst are the strongest of all our bodily appetites. In like manner this hunger in the soul, this thirst after the image of God, is the strongest of all our spiritual appetites when it is once awakened in the heart; yea, it swallows up all the
5 rest in that one great desire to be renewed after the likeness of him that created us. We should, secondly, observe that from the time we begin to hunger and thirst those appetites do not cease, but are more and more craving and importunate till we either eat and drink, or die. And even so, from the time that we begin to
10 hunger and thirst after the whole mind which was in Christ[43] these spiritual appetites do not cease, but cry after their food with more and more importunity. Nor can they possibly cease before they are satisfied, while there is any spiritual life remaining. We may, thirdly, observe that hunger and thirst are satisfied with nothing
15 but meat and drink. If you would give to him that is hungry all the world beside, all the elegance of apparel, all the trappings of state, all the treasure upon earth, yea thousands of gold and silver; if you would pay him ever so much honour, he regards it not; all these things are then of no account with him. He would still say, 'These
20 are not the things I want; give me food, or else I die.'[44] The very same is the case with every soul that truly hungers and thirsts after righteousness. He can find no comfort in anything but this: he can be satisfied with nothing else. Whatever you offer beside, it is lightly esteemed; whether it be riches, or honour, or pleasure, he
25 still says, 'This is not the thing which I want. Give me love or else I die!'

4. And it is as impossible to satisfy such a soul, a soul that is athirst for God, the living God, with what the world accounts religion, as with what they account happiness. The religion of the
30 world implies three things: first, the doing no harm, the abstaining from outward sin—at least from such as is scandalous, as robbery, theft, common swearing, drunkenness; secondly, the doing good—the relieving the poor, the being charitable, as it is called; thirdly, the using the means of grace—at least the going to
35 church and to the Lord's Supper.[45] He in whom these three

---

[43] See Phil. 2:5.   [44] Cf. Gen. 25:29-34; 30:1.
[45] An interesting summary of 'the [invalid] religion of the world' (an earlier account of which had been given in No. 2, *The Almost Christian;* cf. espec. I. 6). Note, however, that it is also a précis of Wesley's own *General Rules*, the seed of which can be found in his early sermon (Sept. 3, 1732), 'Public Diversions Denounced', II.2 (No. 143). Thus, the *Rules* by themselves, outside the context of faith, are no better than any other set of moralistic dicta.

marks are found is termed by the world a religious man. But will this satisfy him who hungers after God? No. It is not food for his soul. He wants a religion of a nobler kind, a religion higher and deeper than this. He can no more feed on this poor, shallow, formal thing, than he can 'fill his belly with the east wind'.[46] True, he is careful to abstain from the very appearance of evil.[47] He is zealous of good works.[48] He attends all the ordinances of God. But all this is not what he longs for. This is only the outside of that religion which he insatiably hungers after. The knowledge of God in Christ Jesus; 'the life that is hid with Christ in God';[49] the being 'joined unto the Lord in one Spirit';[50] the having 'fellowship with the Father and the Son';[51] the 'walking in the light as God is in the light';[52] the being 'purified even as he is pure'[53]—this is the religion, the righteousness he thirsts after. Nor can he rest till he thus rests in God.[54]

5. 'Blessed are they who' thus 'hunger and thirst after righteousness; for they shall be filled.' They shall be filled with the thing which they long for, even with righteousness and true holiness.[55] God shall satisfy them with the blessings of his goodness, with the felicity of his chosen. He shall feed them with the bread of heaven, with the manna of his love.[56] He shall give them to drink of his pleasures, as out of the river[57] which he that drinketh of shall never thirst[58]—only for more and more of the water of life.[59] This thirst shall endure for ever.

Cf. also Nos. 23, 'Sermon on the Mount, III', II.4; 25, 'Sermon on the Mount, V', IV.7, 11; 33, 'Sermon on the Mount, XIII', I.2, II. 2-4; 85, 'On Working Out Our Own Salvation', II. 4 (where Wesley has an approving reference); 89, 'The More Excellent Way', §5; 98, 'On Visiting the Sick', §1; 115, 'Dives and Lazarus', II. 7; 119, 'Walking by Sight and Walking by Faith', §§15 ff.; cf. also *A Blow at the Root*, §4 (*Bibliog*, No. 250, Vol. 13 of this edn.); and JWJ, Nov. 25, 1739. For Wesley's comments on 'the saints of the world' cf. No. 4, *Scriptural Christianity*, II. 5 and n.

[46] Job 15:2.
[47] See 1 Thess. 5:22.
[48] Titus 2:14.
[49] Cf. Col. 3:3.
[50] Cf. 1 Cor. 6:17.
[51] Cf. 1 John 1:3.
[52] Cf. 1 John 1:7.
[53] Cf. 1 John 3:3.
[54] Yet another usage of Wesley's favourite line from St. Augustine, *Confessions*, I.1; cf. No. 3, *'Awake, Thou That Sleepest'*, II.5 and n.
[55] Eph. 4:24.   [56] See John 6:58.
[57] See Ps. 36:8 (BCP).
[58] See John 4:14.
[59] Rev. 21:6; 22:1,17.

> The painful thirst, the fond desire,
> Thy joyous presence shall remove;
> But my full soul shall still require
> A whole eternity of love.[60]

5   6. Whosoever then thou art to whom God hath given to 'hunger and thirst after righteousness', cry unto him that thou mayst never lose that inestimable gift, that this divine appetite may never cease. If many rebuke thee, and bid thee hold thy peace, regard them not; yea, cry so much the more, ' "Jesus, Master, have
10 mercy on me!"[61] Let me not live but to be holy as thou art holy!' No more 'spend thy money for that which is not bread', nor thy 'labour for that which satisfieth not'.[62] Canst thou hope to dig happiness out of the earth? To find it in the things of the world? O trample under foot all its pleasures, despise its honours, count its
15 riches as dung and dross—yea, and all the things which are beneath the sun—'for the excellency of the knowledge of Christ Jesus';[63] for the entire renewal of thy soul in that image of God wherein it was originally created.[64] Beware of quenching that blessed hunger and thirst by what the world calls religion—a
20 religion of form, of outward show, which leaves the heart as earthly and sensual as ever.[65] Let nothing satisfy thee but the power of godliness, but a religion that is spirit and life; the dwelling in God and God in thee,[66] the being an inhabitant of eternity;[67] the entering in by the blood of sprinkling[68] 'within the
25 veil',[69] and 'sitting in heavenly places with Christ Jesus'.[70]

---

[60] Charles Wesley, 'Pleading the Promise of Sanctification', st. 22. This was first published as an appendix to No. 40, *Christian Perfection* (1741), and was reprinted in the brothers' *Hymns and Sacred Poems* (1742), p. 263 (*Poet. Wks.*, II. 322). Orig.,

> While my full soul doth still require
> The whole eternity of love.

[61] Luke 17:13.
[62] Cf. Isa. 55:2.
[63] Phil. 3:8.
[64] Cf. No. 1, *Salvation by Faith*, §1 and n.
[65] Cf. No. 23, 'Sermon on the Mount, III', IV.1. Wesley's usage of the term 'religion' varies. More often than not, he equates it with 'Christianity', as 'the true religion'. But he will also, as here, use 'religion' with a naturalistic connotation and, thus, as antithetical to Christianity.
[66] See 1 John 4:12-13.
[67] See Isa. 57:15.
[68] Heb. 12:24.
[69] Heb. 6:19.
[70] Cf. Eph. 2:6.

III. 1. And the more they are filled with the life of God, the more tenderly will they be concerned for those who are still without God in the world,[71] still dead in trespasses and sins.[72] Nor shall this concern for others lose its reward. 'Blessed are the merciful; for they shall obtain mercy.'[73]

The word used by our Lord more immediately implies the compassionate, the tender-hearted; those who, far from despising, earnestly grieve for those that do not hunger after God. This eminent part of brotherly love is here (by a common figure) put for the whole; so that 'the merciful', in the full sense of the term, are they who 'love their neighbours as themselves'.[74]

2. Because of the vast importance of this love—without which, 'though we spake with the tongues of men and angels, though we had the gift of prophecy and understood all mysteries and all knowledge, though we had all faith so as to remove mountains; yea, though we gave all our goods to feed the poor, and our very bodies to be burned, it would profit us nothing'[75]—the wisdom of God has given us by the Apostle Paul a full and particular account of it, by considering which we shall most clearly discern who are 'the merciful that shall obtain mercy'.

3. *Charity,* or love (as it were to be wished it had been rendered throughout, being a far plainer and less ambiguous word),[76] the love of our neighbour as Christ hath loved us, 'suffereth long',[77] is patient toward all men. It suffers all the weakness, ignorance, errors, infirmities, all the frowardness and littleness of faith in the children of God; all the malice and wickedness of the children of the world. And it suffers all this, not only for a time, for a short season, but to the end: still feeding our enemy when he hungers; if he thirst, still giving him drink; thus continually 'heaping coals of fire', of melting love, 'upon his head'.[78]

4. And in every step toward this desirable end, the 'overcoming evil with good',[79] 'love is kind' ($\chi\rho\eta\sigma\tau\varepsilon\acute{\nu}\varepsilon\tau\alpha\iota$, a word not easily

---

[71] Eph. 2:12.
[72] Eph. 2:1.
[73] Matt. 5:7.
[74] Cf. Matt. 19:19, etc. Cf. below, III.3 and n.
[75] Cf. 1 Cor. 13:1-3.
[76] Cf. No. 17, 'The Circumcision of the Heart', I.2 and n. Notice how οἱ ἐλεήμονες here reminds Wesley of ἀγάπη in 1 Cor. 13, and provides him with the occasion for this extended comment on the latter.
[77] 1 Cor. 13:4.
[78] Cf. Rom. 12:20.   [79] Cf. Rom. 12:21.

translated)[80]—it is soft, mild, benign. It stands at the utmost distance from moroseness, from all harshness or sourness of spirit; and inspires the sufferer at once with the most amiable sweetness and the most fervent and tender affection.

5. Consequently, 'Love envieth not.'[81] It is impossible it should; it is directly opposite to that baneful temper. It cannot be that he who has this tender affection to all, who earnestly wishes all temporal and spiritual blessings, all good things in this world and the world to come, to every soul that God hath made, should be pained at his bestowing any good gift on any child of man. If he has himself received the same he does not grieve but rejoice that another partakes of the common benefit. If he has not he blesses God that his brother at least has, and is herein happier than himself. And the greater his love, the more does he rejoice in the blessings of all mankind, the farther is he removed from every kind and degree of envy toward any creature.

6. Love οὐ περπερεύεται: not 'vaunteth not itself', which coincides with the very next words, but rather (as the word likewise properly imports) 'is not rash' or 'hasty' in judging.[82] It will not hastily condemn anyone. It does not pass a severe sentence on a slight or sudden view of things. It first weighs all the evidence, particularly that which is brought in favour of the accused. A true lover of his neighbour is not like the generality of men, who, even in cases of the nicest nature, 'see a little, presume a great deal, and so jump to the conclusion'.[83] No; he proceeds with wariness and circumspection, taking heed to every step; willingly subscribing to that rule of the ancient heathen (O where

---

[80] Cf. 1 Cor. 13:4. χρηστεύσμαι ('to be kind or merciful') and its cognates occur in *Christian* texts (e.g., 1 Clement 14:3; Eusebius, *Ecclesiastical History*, V., I. 46, etc.) and in the Psalms of Solomon 9:11; cf. Lampe, *Patristic Greek Lexicon*. Its original sense was 'pleasant', 'comfortable' (as of well-fitting clothes); hence its remarkable usage in Rom. 2:4.

[81] Cf. 1 Cor. 13:4.

[82] *Ibid.* In classical Greek πέρπερος means 'braggart, windbag'. Its cognate forms (even here) have more of a connotation of boasting than hasty judgment. Bengel, *Gnomon*, *loc. cit.*, had taken it thus. Even so, Wesley *(Notes)* translates it 'rashly', and adds: 'does not hastily condemn anyone.' Cf. III.10, below; also No. 149, 'On Love', II.7.

[83] Wesley had found this aphorism in an essay by Henry Grove (1648–1738) in *The Spectator*, No. 626 (Nov. 29, 1714), where it is attributed to John Locke. It can be found in 'Of the Conduct of the Understanding' (§16, on 'Haste'), written in 1697 but not included in any of Locke's published writings until 1762 (fourteen years after this sermon!). It may be found in modern edns. of Locke's *Works*—e.g., the 1963 Scientia Verlag Aalen reprint of the London, 1823 edn. (III. 238). Grove was a disciple of Locke and obviously had access to the unpublished MS of 'Conduct. . .'. He and *The Spectator* thus were Wesley's source for this bit of Lockean wisdom which Wesley quotes here *exactly*.

will the modern Christian appear!): 'I am so far from lightly believing what one man says against another that I will not easily believe what a man says against himself. I will always allow him second thoughts, and many times counsel too.'[84]

7. It follows, love 'is not puffed up'.[85] It does not incline or suffer any man 'to think more highly of himself than he ought to think', but rather 'to think soberly'.[86] Yea, it humbles the soul unto the dust. It destroys all high conceits engendering pride, and makes us rejoice to be as nothing, to be little and vile, the lowest of all, the servant of all.[87] They who are 'kindly affectioned one to another with brotherly love' cannot but 'in honour prefer one another'.[88] Those who, 'having the same love, are of one accord', do 'in lowliness of mind each esteem other better than themselves'.[89]

8. It 'doth not behave itself unseemly'.[90] It is not rude or willingly offensive to any. It 'renders to all their due: fear to whom fear, honour to whom honour';[91] courtesy, civility, humanity to all the world, in their several degrees 'honouring all men'.[92] A late writer defines good breeding, nay, the highest degree of it, politeness: 'A continual desire to please, appearing in all the behaviour.'[93] But if so, there is none so well-bred as a Christian, a lover of all mankind; for he cannot but desire to 'please all men',[94] 'for their good to edification'.[95] And this desire cannot be hid: it will necessarily appear in all his intercourse with men. For his 'love is without dissimulation';[96] it will appear in all his actions and

---

[94] In No. 30, 'Sermon on the Mount, X', §13, Wesley cites Seneca as the source for a slightly different version of this quotation. This is confirmed by Susanna Wesley's quotation of it as a 'rule of Seneca's' but with no more specific citation; cf. Adam Clarke, *Memoirs*, p. 317. But *where* in Seneca?

[85] 1 Cor. 13:4.   [86] Rom. 12:3.
[87] See Mark 9:35.   [88] Cf. Rom. 12:10.
[89] Cf. Phil. 2:2-3.   [90] 1 Cor. 13:5.
[91] Cf. Rom. 13:7.   [92] Cf. 1 Pet. 2:17.

[93] In No. 100, 'On Pleasing All Men', II.4, Wesley quotes 'Mr. Addison's well-known definition of politeness: "A constant desire of pleasing all men, appearing through the whole conversation" '—obviously a repetition of this definition here. The characterization of it as 'well-known' poses a problem, though, for I have yet to locate it in any of Addison's published works or in any of the indexes of *The Spectator*, *The Guardian*, or *The Tatler*. Nor is it cited in *OED*, Johnson's *Dictionary*, or Chambers's *Cyclopaedia*. Something very like it may be seen in *The Spectator*, No. 386 (May 23, 1712), but the author was Richard Steele; see also Steele in *The Spectator*, No. 33 (Apr. 11, 1711), for a similar phrasing; cf. Addison in *The Freeholder*, No. 38 (Apr. 30, 1712), for the same sentiment in different words.

[94] 1 Cor. 10:33.   [95] Rom. 15:2.   [96] Cf. Rom. 12:9.

conversation. Yea, and will constrain him, though without guile, to 'become all things to all men, if by any means he may save some'.[97]

9. And in becoming all things to all men 'love seeketh not her own.'[98] In striving to please all men the lover of mankind has no eye at all to his own temporal advantage. He covets no man's silver, or gold, or apparel: he desires nothing but the salvation of their souls. Yea, in some sense he may be said 'not to seek his own'[99] spiritual, any more than temporal advantage. For while he is on the full stretch to save their souls from death he as it were forgets himself. He does not think of himself so long as that zeal for the glory of God swallows him up. Nay, at some times he may almost seem, through an excess of love, to give up himself, both his soul and his body; while he cries out with Moses, 'Oh! this people have sinned a great sin[. . .]! Yet now, if thou wilt, forgive their sin. And if not, blot me out of the book which thou hast written.'[c] Or with St. Paul, 'I could wish that myself were accursed from Christ for my brethren, my kinsmen according to the flesh!'[d]

10. No marvel that 'such love is not provoked,'[100] οὐ παροξύνεται. Let it be observed, the word 'easily', strangely inserted in the translation, is not in the original. St. Paul's words are absolute: 'Love is not provoked'—it is not provoked to unkindness toward anyone.[101] Occasions indeed will frequently occur, outward provocations of various kinds. But love does not yield to provocation. It triumphs over all. In all trials it looketh unto Jesus, and is more than conqueror in his love.

'Tis not improbable that our translators inserted that word as it were to *excuse* the Apostle, who, as they supposed, might otherwise appear to be wanting in the very love which he so beautifully describes. They seem to have supposed this from a

---

[c] Exod. 32:31-32. [Both 1771 and 1787 edns. have an exclamation mark here.]
[d] Rom. 9:3.

---

[97] 1 Cor. 9:22.
[98] 1 Cor. 13:5.   [99] Cf. 1 Cor. 10:24.
[100] 1 Cor. 13:5. Cf. also Nos. 91, 'On Charity', I.5 and n. (see also, above, III.6); and 149, 'On Love', II.7.
[101] In classical Greek παροξύνεται means 'irritable' or 'quick-tempered' or, literally, 'in a paroxysm' (as in a fever). Most modern translations tilt away from Wesley's absolute, as in Arndt and Gingrich, *Greek-English Lexicon*, the RSV ('not irritable'), NEB ('not quick to take offence') or Phillips's colloquial ('not touchy').

phrase in the Acts of the Apostles, which is likewise very inaccurately translated. When Paul and Barnabas disagreed concerning John, the translation runs thus: 'And the contention was so sharp between them that they departed asunder.'[e] This naturally induces the reader to suppose that they were equally 5 sharp therein; that St. Paul, who was undoubtedly right with regard to the point in question (it being quite improper to take John with them again, who had deserted them before) was as much provoked as Barnabas, who gave such a proof of his anger as to leave 'the work' for which he had been 'set apart by the Holy 10 Ghost'.[102] But the original imports no such thing; nor does it affirm that St. Paul was provoked at all. It simply says, καὶ ἐγένετο παροξυσμός,[103] 'And there was a sharpness, a paroxysm' of anger; in consequence of which Barnabas left St. Paul, took John, and went his own way. 'Paul' then 'chose Silas 15 and departed, being recommended by the brethren to the grace of God' (which is not said concerning Barnabas), 'and he went through Syria and Cilicia', as he had proposed, 'confirming the churches'.[104] But to return.

11. Love prevents a thousand provocations which would 20 otherwise arise, because it 'thinketh no evil'.[105] Indeed the merciful man cannot avoid knowing many things that are evil, he cannot but see them with his own eyes and hear them with his own ears. For love does not put out his eyes, so that it is impossible for him not to see that such things are done. Neither does it take away 25 his understanding, any more than his senses, so that he cannot but know that they are evil. For instance: when he sees a man strike his neighbour, or hears him blaspheme God, he cannot either question the thing done or the words spoken, or doubt of their being evil. Yet οὐ λογίζεται τὸ κακόν. The word 30

---

[e] Acts 15:39.

---

[102] Cf. Acts 13:2.

[103] Acts 15:39; the original reads ἐγένετο δὲ παροξυσμός. It may be that St. Paul was not 'provoked at all', but the point that the disagreement was very sharp is quite clear. Wesley's interest here is to safeguard his doctrine of 'perfect love', even though he is not firmly supported on *lexical* grounds. But the point about St. Paul's equanimity is made repeatedly, e.g., Nos. 19, 'The Great Privilege of those that are Born of God', II.5; 61, 'The Mystery of Iniquity', §17; 91, 'On Charity', I.6. Cf. also the *Notes*, as well as *Remarks on A Defence of . . . Aspasio Vindicated*, §4; see, finally, the extract from Bolton's *Discourse . . . of True Happiness* (1631), in the *Christian Lib.*, VII. 273-74.

[104] Acts 15:40-41.   [105] 1 Cor. 13:5.

λογίζεται ('thinketh') does not refer either to our seeing and hearing, or to the first and involuntary acts of our understanding; but to our willingly thinking what we need not; our *inferring* evil where it does not appear: to our *reasoning* concerning things
5 which we do not see, our *supposing* what we have neither seen nor heard.[106] This is what true love absolutely destroys. It tears up, root and branch, all *imagining* what we have not known. It casts out all jealousies, all evil surmisings, all readiness to believe evil. It is frank, open, unsuspicious; and as it cannot design, so neither
10 does it fear, evil.

　　12. It 'rejoiceth not in iniquity',[107] common as this is, even among those who bear the name of Christ; who scruple not to rejoice over their enemy when he falleth either into affliction, or error, or sin. Indeed, how hardly can they avoid this who are
15 zealously attached to any party! How difficult is it for them not to be pleased with any fault which they discover in those of the opposite party! With any real or supposed blemish, either in their principles or practice! What warm defender of any cause is clear of these? Yea, who is so calm as to be altogether free? Who does
20 not rejoice when his adversary makes a false step which he thinks will advantage his own cause? Only a man of love. He alone weeps over either the sin or folly of his enemy, takes no pleasure in hearing or in repeating it, but rather desires that it may be forgotten for ever.

25 　　13. But he 'rejoiceth in the truth',[108] wheresoever it is found, in the 'truth which is after godliness',[109] bringing forth its proper fruit, holiness of heart and holiness of conversation. He rejoices to find that even those who oppose him, whether with regard to opinions or some points of practice, are nevertheless lovers of
30 God, and in other respects unreprovable. He is glad to hear good of them, and to speak all he can, consistently with truth and justice. Indeed, good in general is his glory and joy, wherever diffused throughout the race of mankind. As a citizen of the world[110] he claims a share in the happiness of all the inhabitants of

---

[106] An eccentric interpretation of λογίζομαι; normally, it means 'to reckon, calculate, consider, or ponder'; cf. Arndt and Gingrich, *Greek-English Lexicon;* and Liddell and Scott, *Greek-English Lexicon.*
[107] 1 Cor. 13:6.
[108] *Ibid.*　　　　　　　　　　　　　　　　　　　　　　　[109] Titus 1:1.
[110] Cf. Francis Bacon, 'Goodness and Goodness of Nature', No. 13, in *Essays:* 'If a man be gracious and courteous to strangers, it shows he is a citizen of the world.' The phrase goes back to Plutarch's anecdote about Socrates's claim to being a 'cosmian' (κόσμιος)

it. Because he is a man he is not unconcerned in the welfare of any man; but enjoys whatsoever brings glory to God and promotes peace and goodwill among men.[111]

14. This love 'covereth all things'.[112] (So without all doubt πάντα στέγει should be translated; for otherwise it would be the very same with πάντα ὑπομένει, 'endureth all things'.)[113] Because the merciful man 'rejoiceth not in iniquity', neither does he willingly make mention of it. Whatever evil he sees, hears, or knows, he nevertheless conceals so far as he can without making himself 'partaker of other men's sins'.[114] Wheresoever or with whomsoever he is, if he sees anything which he approves not it goes not out of his lips unless to the person concerned, if haply he may gain his brother. So far is he from making the faults or failures of others the matter of his conversation, that of the absent he never does speak at all unless he can speak well. A talebearer, a backbiter, a whisperer, an evil-speaker, is to him all one as a murderer. He would just as soon cut his neighbour's throat as thus murder his reputation. Just as soon would he think of diverting himself by setting fire to his neighbour's house as of thus 'scattering abroad arrows, firebrands, and death, and saying, Am I not in sport?'[115]

He makes one only exception. Sometimes he is convinced that it is for the glory of God or (which comes to the same) the good of his neighbour that an evil should not be covered. In this case, for the benefit of the innocent he is constrained to declare the guilty. But even here: (1). He will not speak at all till love, superior love, constrains him; (2). He cannot do it from a general confused view of doing good or of promoting the glory of God, but from a clear sight of some particular end, some determinate good which he pursues; (3). Still he cannot speak unless he be fully convinced

---

rather than a citizen of Athens only; cf. Plutarch, 'On Exile', ll. 600-601, in *Moralia* (Loeb, 405:28-29). A similar story is told of Diogenes; cf. Diogenes Laertius, 'Diogenes' in *Lives*, VI. 63 (Loeb, 185:64-65). In Cicero, *De Legibus (Laws)*, I. xxiii. 61, he speaks of a liberated mind realizing itself 'not bound by walls, like people in a single town, but *civem urbis mundi quasi unius urbis*' ('a citizen of the whole world as if it were one great city').

[111] See Luke 2:14.
[112] 1 Cor. 13:7.
[113] Did Wesley suppose that none of his readers would know that στέγω had so wide a range of meanings (including 'to cover', but more usually 'to endure') that no single usage is 'without all doubt', even here? Cf. Liddell and Scott, *Greek-English Lexicon*, and Arndt & Gingrich, *Greek-English Lexicon, loc. cit.*
[114] 1 Tim. 5:22.
[115] Cf. Prov. 26:18-19.

that this very means is necessary to that end—that the end cannot be answered, at least not so effectually, by any other way; (4). He then doth it with the utmost sorrow and reluctance, using it as the last and worst medicine, a desperate remedy in a desperate case, a kind of poison never to be used but to expel poison; consequently, (5). He uses it as sparingly as possible. And this he does with fear and trembling, lest he should transgress the law of love by speaking too much, more than he would have done by not speaking at all.

15. Love 'believeth all things'.[116] It is always willing to think the best, to put the most favourable construction on everything. It is ever ready to believe whatever may tend to the advantage of anyone's character. It is easily convinced of (what it earnestly desires) the innocence or integrity of any man; or, at least, of the sincerity of his repentance, if he had once erred from the way. It is glad to excuse whatever is amiss, to condemn the offender as little as possible, and to make all the allowance for human weakness which can be done without betraying the truth of God.

16. And when it can no longer believe, then love 'hopeth all things'.[117] Is any evil related of any man? Love hopes that the relation is not true, that the thing related was never done. Is it certain it was?—'But perhaps it was not done with such circumstances as are related; so that, allowing the fact, there is room to hope it was not so ill as it is represented.' Was the action apparently, undeniably evil? Love hopes the intention was not so. Is it clear the design was evil too?—'Yet might it not spring, [not][118] from the settled temper of the heart, but from a start of passion, or from some vehement temptation, which hurried the man beyond himself?' And even when it cannot be doubted but all the actions, designs, and tempers are equally evil; still love hopes that God will at last make bare his arm, and get himself the victory; and that there shall be 'joy in heaven over this one sinner that repenteth, more than over ninety and nine just persons that need no repentance.'[119]

17. Lastly, it 'endureth all things'.[120] This completes the

---

[116] 1 Cor. 13:7.   [117] *Ibid.*

[118] All published edns. (including Sugden's) read, '. . . might it not spring from the settled temper of the heart, but . . .'—which clearly is not what Wesley meant.

[119] Cf. Luke 15:7.

[120] 1 Cor. 13:7. ὑπομένει here is not merely a synonym for στέγει. Its nuance is 'to stand one's ground' rather than to flee; thus 'to remain steadfast' in difficulties.

character of him that is truly merciful. He endureth not some, not many things only, not most, but absolutely 'all things'. Whatever the injustice, the malice, the cruelty of men can inflict, he is able to suffer. He calls nothing intolerable; he never says of anything, 'This is not to be borne.' No; he can not only do but suffer all 5 things through Christ which strengtheneth him.[121] And all he suffers does not destroy his love, nor impair it in the least. It is proof against all. It is a flame that burns even in the midst of the great deep. 'Many waters cannot quench his love, neither can the floods drown it.'[122] It triumphs over all. It 'never faileth', either in 10 time or in eternity.

> In obedience to what heaven decrees,
> Knowledge shall fail and prophecy shall cease.
> But lasting charity's more ample sway,
> Nor bound by time, nor subject to decay,   15
> In happy triumph shall for ever live,
> And endless good diffuse, and endless praise receive.[123]

So shall 'the merciful obtain mercy';[124] not only by the blessing of God upon all their ways, by his now repaying the love they bear to their brethren a thousandfold into their own bosom, but 20 likewise by an 'exceeding and eternal weight of glory'[125] in the 'kingdom prepared for them from the beginning of the world'.[126]

18. For a little while you may say, 'Woe is me, that I am constrained to dwell with Mesech, and to have my habitation among the tents of Kedar!'[127] You may pour out your soul, and 25 bemoan the loss of true genuine love in the earth. Lost indeed! You may well say (but not in the ancient sense), 'See how *these* Christians love one another!'[128] These Christian kingdoms that

---

[121] See Phil. 4:13.   [122] S. of S. 8:7.

[123] Matthew Prior, 'Charity,' 31-36. Cf. Wesley, *Collection of Moral and Sacred Poems*, I. 87-89. See also No. 36, 'The Law Established through Faith, II', II.1, where Wesley again quotes the last two lines as well as two later ones.

[124] Cf. Matt. 5:7.   [125] 2 Cor. 4:17.

[126] Cf. Matt. 25:34.   [127] Ps. 120:4 (BCP).

[128] 'The ancient sense' here refers to the famous claim in Tertullian's *Apology*, ch. 39, §7: 'see how the Christians love one another!'; this was echoed by Julian, *Epistle* 49, as reported in Sozomen, *Ecclesiastical History*, V. xvi: 'Ought we not to consider that the progress of Atheism [i.e., Christianity] has been principally owing to the humanity evinced by Christians *towards strangers* . . . ? It is, therefore, requisite that each of us be diligent in the discharge of *our* duty.'

Wesley was fond of this claim about Christian benevolence and repeats it, as in Nos. 41, *Wandering Thoughts*, I.4; 49, 'The Cure of Evil-speaking', II.5; 53, *On the Death of George Whitefield*, III.9; 110, *Free Grace* ('To the Reader'). Cf. also Wesley's letter to his mother, July 6, 1738.

are tearing out each other's bowels, desolating one another with fire and sword! These Christian armies that are sending each other by thousands, by ten thousands, quick into hell![129] These Christian nations that are all on fire with intestine broils, party

5 against party, faction against faction! These Christian cities where deceit and fraud, oppression and wrong, yea, robbery and murder, go not out of their streets! These Christian families, torn asunder with envy, jealousy, anger, domestic jars—without number, without end! Yea, what is most dreadful, most to be

10 lamented of all, these Christian churches!—churches ('Tell it not in Gath;'[130] but alas, how can we hide it, either from Jews, Turks, or pagans?) that bear the name of Christ, 'the Prince of Peace',[131] and wage continual war with each other! That convert sinners by burning them alive: that are 'drunk with the blood of the saints'![132]

15 Does this praise belong only to 'Babylon the great, the mother of harlots and abominations of the earth'?[133] Nay, verily; but Reformed churches (so called) have fairly learned to tread in her steps. Protestant churches, too, know to persecute, when they have power in their hands, even unto blood. And meanwhile, how

20 do they also anathematize each other! Devote each other to the nethermost hell! What wrath, what contention, what malice, what bitterness is everywhere found among them! Even when they agree in essentials, and only differ in opinions, or in the circumstantials of religion.[134] Who 'follows after' only 'the things

25 that make for peace, and things wherewith one may edify another'?[135] O God! How long? Shall thy promise fail? Fear it not, ye little flock.[136] Against hope believe in hope.[137] It is your Father's

---

[129] Ps. 55:15 (AV).

[130] 2 Sam. 1:20.

[131] Isa. 9:6.

[132] Cf. Rev. 17:6.

[133] Rev. 17:5.

[134] Wesley is painfully sensitive to Christianity's bloody record, and the horrors of war are frequently recounted in the sermons. E.g., cf. Nos. 102, 'Of Former Times', §13, where he speaks of 'that savage barbarity'; 111, *National Sins and Miseries*, I.4, 'that fell monster, war'; 128, 'The Deceitfulness of the Human Heart', II.4, the 'foul monster, war'. Cf. also Nos. 92, 'On Zeal', §1, where he cites 'an eminent German writer' who has written about the persecutions; and 102, 'Of Former Times', §14, where he is identified only as 'an eminent writer'. Chambers's *Cyclopaedia* says the persecutions were usually reckoned as ten in number. See also Bishop Joseph Hall, *Soliloquies*, X, in *Select Works*, III.346. And cf. No. 39, 'Catholic Spirit', as a counterweight to this spirit of persecution.

[135] Cf. Rom. 14:19.

[136] See Luke 12:32.

[137] See Rom. 4:18.

good pleasure[138] yet to renew the face of the earth.[139] Surely all
these things shall come to an end,[140] and the inhabitants of the
earth shall learn righteousness.[141] 'Nation shall not lift up sword
against nation, neither shall they know war any more.'[142] 'The
mountain of the Lord's house shall be established in the top of the   5
mountains;'[143] and all the kingdoms of the world shall become the
kingdoms of our God.[144] 'They shall not' then 'hurt or destroy in
all his holy mountain;'[145] but 'they shall call their walls salvation
and their gates praise.'[146] They shall all be without spot or
blemish,[147] loving one another, even as Christ hath loved us.[148] Be   10
thou part of the first-fruits, if the harvest is not yet. Do thou love
thy neighbour as thyself.[149] The Lord God fill thy heart with such
a love to every soul that thou mayst be ready to lay down thy life for
his sake! May thy soul continually overflow with love, swallowing
up every unkind and unholy temper, till he calleth thee up into the   15
region of love, there to reign with him for ever and ever!

[138] Luke 12:32.
[139] Ps. 104:30 (BCP).
[140] See Ps. 7:9.
[141] See Isa. 26:9.
[142] Cf. Isa. 2:4.
[143] Isa. 2:2.
[144] Rev. 11:15.
[145] Cf. Isa. 11:9.
[146] Cf. Isa. 60:18.
[147] See 1 Pet. 1:19.
[148] See John 15:12.
[149] Lev. 19:18; Matt. 19:19, etc.

Upon our Lord's Sermon on the Mount
Discourse the Third

Matthew 5:8-12

Blessed are the pure in heart: for they shall see God.
5   *Blessed are the peacemakers: for they shall be called the children of God.*

Blessed are they which are persecuted for righteousness' sake: for theirs is the kingdom of heaven.

Blessed are ye when men shall revile you, and persecute you, and shall
10 *say all manner of evil against you falsely for my sake.*

Rejoice, and be exceeding glad; for great is your reward in heaven: for so persecuted they the prophets which were before you.

I. 1. How excellent things are spoken of the love of our neighbour! It is 'the fulfilling of the law',[1] 'the end of the
15 commandment'.[2] Without this all we have, all we do, all we suffer, is of no value in the sight of God. But it is that love of our neighbour which springs from the love of God; otherwise itself is nothing worth. It behoves us therefore to examine well upon what foundation our love of our neighbour stands: whether it is really
20 built upon the love of God; whether 'we' do 'love him because he first loved us;'[3] whether we are 'pure in heart'.[4] For this is the foundation which shall never be moved: 'Blessed are the pure in heart: for they shall see God.'

2. 'The pure in heart' are they whose hearts God hath 'purified
25 even as he is pure';[5] who are purified through faith in the blood of Jesus from every unholy affection; who, being 'cleansed from all filthiness of flesh and spirit, perfect holiness in the' loving 'fear of God'.[6] They are, through the power of his grace, purified from pride by the deepest poverty of spirit; from anger, from every

---

[1] Rom. 13:10.   [2] 1 Tim. 1:5.
[3] 1 John 4:19.   [4] Matt. 5:8.
[5] Cf. 1 John 3:3.   [6] Cf. 2 Cor. 7:1.

unkind or turbulent passion, by meekness and gentleness; from every desire but to please and enjoy God, to know and love him more and more, by that hunger and thirst after righteousness which now engrosses their whole soul:[7] so that now they love the Lord their God with all their heart, and with all their soul, and mind, and strength.[8]

3. But how little has this 'purity of heart' been regarded by the false teachers of all ages! They have taught men barely to abstain from such outward impurities as God hath forbidden by name. But they did not strike at the heart; and by not guarding against, they in effect countenanced inward corruptions.

A remarkable instance of this our Lord has given us in the following words: 'Ye have heard that it was said by them of old time, Thou shalt not commit adultery.'[a] And in explaining this those blind leaders of the blind[9] only insist on men's abstaining from the outward act. 'But I say unto you, whosoever looketh on a woman to lust after her hath committed adultery with her already in his heart.'[b] For God requireth truth in the inward parts.[10] He searcheth the heart and trieth the reins.[11] And 'if thou incline unto iniquity with thy heart, the Lord will not hear thee.'[12]

4. And God admits no excuse for retaining anything which is an occasion of impurity. Therefore 'if thy right eye offend thee, pluck it out and cast it from thee, for it is profitable for thee that one of thy members should perish, and not that thy whole body should be cast into hell.'[c] If persons as dear to thee as thy right eye be an occasion of thy thus offending God, a means of exciting unholy desire in thy soul, delay not—forcibly separate from them. 'And if thy right hand offend thee, cut it off, and cast it from thee; for it is profitable for thee that one of thy members should perish, and not that thy whole body should be cast into hell.'[d] If any who

---

[a]   [Matt. 5,] ver. 27.   [b]   Ver. 28.
[c]   Ver. 29.   [d]   Ver. 30.

[7] Cf. Blackall, Discourse IX, *Works*, I.79: 'By heart it is most obvious to understand the soul with all its faculties, the understanding, the will and the affections. . . . The "pure in heart" are they who . . . as strictly forbear all *inward* acts of sin . . . as they would be to forbear and avoid the open practice of wickedness. . . .' See also, Hammond, *Practical Catechism*, pp. 99-100, for a similar view and another Anglican source for Wesley's ideas about holy living.

[8] See Mark 12:30; Luke 10:27.   [9] Matt. 15:14.
[10] See Ps. 51:6 (BCP).   [11] See Ps. 7:10; see Jer. 11:20.
[12] Cf. Ps. 66:16 (BCP).

seem as necessary to thee as thy right hand be an occasion of sin, of impure desire, even though it were never to go beyond the heart, never to break out in word or action, constrain thyself to an entire and final parting: cut them off at a stroke; give them up to
5 God. Any loss, whether of pleasure, or substance, or friends, is preferable to the loss of thy soul.

Two steps only it may not be improper to take before such an absolute and final separation. First, try whether the unclean spirit may not be driven out by fasting and prayer,[13] and by carefully
10 abstaining from every action and word and look which thou hast found to be an occasion of evil. Secondly, if thou art not by this means delivered, ask counsel of him that watcheth over thy soul,[14] or at least of some who have experience in the ways of God, touching the time and manner of that separation. But confer not
15 with flesh and blood,[15] lest thou be 'given up to a strong delusion to believe a lie'.[16]

5. Nor may marriage itself, holy and honourable as it is, be used as a pretence for giving a loose to our desires.[17] Indeed 'It hath been said, Whosoever will put away his wife, let him give her a
20 writing of divorcement.' And then all was well, though he alleged no cause but that he did not like her, or liked another better. 'But I say unto you, That whosoever shall put away his wife, saving for the case of fornication' (that is adultery, the word πορνεία signifying unchastity in general, either in the married or
25 unmarried state) 'causeth her to commit adultery' if she marry again; 'and whosoever shall marry her that is put away committeth adultery.'[e]

All polygamy is clearly forbidden in these words, wherein our Lord expressly declares that for any woman who has a husband
30 alive, to marry again is adultery. By parity of reason it is adultery for any man to marry again so long as he has a wife alive. Yea, although they were divorced—unless that divorce had been for the cause of adultery. In that only case there is no Scripture which forbids to marry again.[18]

---

e Ver. 31-32.

---

[13] Matt. 17:21; Mark 9:29.
[14] Note the assumption here that every Christian should have his or her own 'spiritual director'.
[15] Gal. 1:16.   [16] Cf. 2 Thess. 2:11.
[17] Cf. No. 138A, 'On Dissimulation', II and n.
[18] A point long debated by Anglican casuists; cf. More and Cross, *Anglicanism*, pp.

6. Such is the purity of heart which God requires, and works in those who believe on the Son of his love. And 'blessed' are they who are thus 'pure in heart; for they shall see God'. He will 'manifest himself unto them', not only 'as he doth not unto the world',[19] but as he doth not always to his own children. He will bless them with the clearest communications of his Spirit, the most intimate 'fellowship with the Father and with the Son'.[20] He will cause his presence to go continually before them, and the light of his countenance to shine upon them.[21] It is the ceaseless prayer of their heart, 'I beseech thee, show me thy glory:'[22] and they have the petition they ask of him. They now see him by faith (the veil of the flesh being made, as it were, transparent[23]) even in these his lowest works, in all that surrounds them, in all that God has created and made. They see him in the height above, and in the depth beneath; they see him filling all in all.[24]

The pure in heart see all things full of God.[25] They see him in the firmament of heaven, in the moon walking in brightness,[26] in the sun when he rejoiceth as a giant to run his course.[27] They see him 'making the clouds his chariots, and walking upon the wings of the wind'.[28] They see him 'preparing rain for the earth',[29] 'and blessing the increase of it';[30] 'giving grass for the cattle, and green herb for the use of man'.[31] They see the Creator of all wisely

---

661 66. The governing canon was No. 107 of 1604 (*Constitutions and Canons Ecclesiastical*, E. Cardwell, *Synodalia*, I. 307-8); it would seem to prevent remarriage of divorced persons in any case. Lancelot Andrewes had declared against remarriage, 'notwithstanding [one party] hath profaned marriage with another'; cf. *A Discourse . . . Against Second Marriage, After Sentence of Divorce . . .* (1601), in *Minor Works* (in LACT), pp. 106-7. Hammond, in his *Practical Catechism*, II. vii, had made no allowance for remarriage after divorce, even 'in the case of fornication'. But Bishops John Cosin and Joseph Hall had allowed for the remarriage of the innocent party in the case of a divorce on the grounds of adultery; cf. Cosin's *Works* (in LACT), IV. 489-93, and Hall, *Works* (ed. Peter Hall, 1837), VII. 474.

[19] Cf. John 14:22.   [20] Cf. 1 John 1:3.
[21] See Ps. 4:6, etc.   [22] Exod. 33:18.
[23] Cf. No. 10, 'The Witness of the Spirit, I', I.12 and n.
[24] See Eph. 1:23.
[25] Aristotle, *De Anima*, I.5, 411a, ll. 9-10, attributes this idea to the philosopher Thales; cf. *The Basic Works of Aristotle*, tr. by Richard McKeon (New York, Random House, 1941), p. 553. Cicero, *De Legibus*, II. xi. 26, also says that it was Thales's opinion, '*Homines existimare oportere deos omnia cernere, deorum omnia esse plena*' ('Men ought to believe that everything they see is full of gods'). Cf. also Virgil, *Eclogues*, iii.60: '*Jovis omnia plena*', which Wesley quotes exactly in No. 118, 'On the Omnipresence of God', II.3. Cf. also, I.11, below; and No. 69, 'The Imperfection of Human Knowledge', I.2. See also Q. Aurelius Symmachus, *Epistularum ad Diversos*, Lib. X (Pareus edn., 1617, p. 441): *Omnia quidem Deo plena sunt . . .* [Seeck edn., 1888, pp. 281-82].

[26] Job 31:26.   [27] See Ps. 19:5 (BCP).   [28] Cf. Ps. 104:3.
[29] Cf. Ps. 147:8.   [30] Cf. Ps. 65:11 (BCP).   [31] Cf. Ps. 104:14.

governing all, and 'upholding all things by the word of his power'.[32] 'O Lord, our Governor, how excellent is thy name in all the world!'[33]

7. In all his providences relating to themselves, to their souls or bodies, the pure in heart do more particularly see God. They see his hand ever over them for good; giving them all things in weight, and measure, numbering the hairs of their head,[34] making a hedge round about them and all that they have,[35] and disposing all the circumstances of their life according to the depth both of his wisdom and mercy.

8. But in a more especial manner they see God in his ordinances.[36] Whether they appear in the great congregation to 'pay him the honour due unto his name, and worship him in the beauty of holiness';[37] or 'enter into their closets' and there pour out their souls before their 'Father which is in secret';[38] whether they search the oracles of God, or hear the ambassadors of Christ proclaiming glad tidings of salvation; or by eating of that bread and drinking of that cup[39] 'show forth his death till he come'[40] in the clouds of heaven.[41] In all these his appointed ways they find such a near approach as cannot be expressed. They see him, as it were, face to face, and 'talk with him as a man talking with his friend'[42]—a fit preparation for those mansions above wherein they shall 'see him as he is'.[43]

9. But how far were they from seeing God, who having 'heard that it had been said by them of old time, Thou shalt not forswear thyself, but shalt perform unto the Lord thine oaths',[f] interpreted it thus: thou shalt not forswear thyself when thou swearest by the Lord Jehovah; thou 'shalt perform unto the Lord *these* thine oaths'—but as to other oaths, he regardeth them not.

So the Pharisees taught. They not only allowed all manner of swearing in common conversation; but accounted even forswearing a little thing, so they had not sworn by the peculiar name of God.

[f] Ver. 33.

---

[32] Heb. 1:3.
[33] Ps. 8:1, 9 (BCP).
[34] See Matt. 10:30.
[35] See Job 1:10.
[36] Cf. No. 16, 'The Means of Grace'.
[37] Cf. Ps. 96:8, 9 (BCP).
[38] Matt. 6:6.
[39] See 1 Cor. 11:28.
[40] 1 Cor. 11:26.
[41] Matt. 26:64; Mark 14:62.
[42] Cf. Exod. 33:11.
[43] 1 John 3:2.

But our Lord here absolutely forbids all common swearing as well as all false swearing; and shows the heinousness of both by the same awful consideration, that every creature is God's, and he is everywhere present, in all, and over all.

'I say unto you, Swear not at all; neither by heaven, for it is God's throne'ᵍ—and therefore this is the same as to swear by him who sitteth upon the circle of the heavens[44]—'nor by the earth, for it is his footstool,' and he is as intimately present in earth as heaven; 'neither by Jerusalem, for it is the city of the great King',ʰ and 'God is well known in her palaces.'[45] 'Neither shalt thou swear by thy head, because thou canst not make one hair white or black;'ⁱ because even this, it is plain, is not thine but God's, the sole disposer of all in heaven and earth. 'But let your communication'—your conversation, your discourse with each other—'be, Yea, yea; Nay, nay' a bare serious affirming or denying—'for whatsoever is more than these cometh of evil'ʲ—ἐκ τοῦ πονηροῦ ἐστιν, ('is the evil one',[46] proceedeth from the devil and is a mark of his children).

10. That our Lord does not here forbid the 'swearing in judgment and truth'[47] when we are required so to do by a magistrate may appear: (1). From the occasion of this part of his discourse, the abuse he was here reproving, which was false swearing and common swearing, the swearing before a magistrate being quite out of the question. (2) From the very words wherein he forms the general conclusion, 'Let your communication', or discourse, 'be, Yea, yea; Nay, nay.' (3). From his own example;

ᵍ Ver. 34.
ʰ Ver. 35.
ⁱ Ver. 36.
ʲ Ver. 37.

---

[44] See Isa. 40:22.
[45] Ps. 48:2 (BCP).
[46] Cf. No. 12, 'The Witness of Our Own Spirit', §10 and n.
[47] Cf. Thirty-nine Articles, Art. XXXIX, 'Of a Christian Man's Oath', to which Wesley subscribed so wholeheartedly that he reproduced it, intact, in his later abridgement of the Articles. The issue here had been posed by the Anabaptist's stubborn refusal to take such oaths, chiefly on the grounds of this New Testament prohibition. See Williams, *The Radical Reformation*, pp. 125, 185, 194 ff., 594, 785; for the later controversy in England over this article itself, cf. Barbour and Roberts, *Early Quaker Writings*, p. 354, and the 'testimonies against the oath' by George Fox (p. 406) and William Penn (pp. 448-50). But see also the section on 'Oaths' in More and Cross, *Anglicanism*, pp. 672-76, where Tillotson, Taylor, and Beveridge are quoted in support of the position here taken by Wesley.

for he answered himself upon oath when required by a magistrate. When 'the High Priest said unto him, I adjure thee by the living God that thou tell us whether thou be the Christ, the Son of God,' Jesus immediately answered in the affirmative,
5 'Thou hast said' (i.e., the truth). 'Nevertheless' (or rather, 'Moreover'[48]) 'I say unto you, Hereafter shall ye see the Son of man sitting on the right hand of power, and coming in the clouds of heaven.'[k] (4). From the example of God, even the Father, who 'willing the more abundantly to show unto the heirs of promise
10 the immutability of his counsel, confirmed it by an oath.'[l] (5). From the example of St. Paul, who we 'think had the Spirit of God',[49] and well understood the mind of his Master. 'God is my witness', saith he to the Romans, 'that without ceasing I make mention of you always in my prayers;'[m] to the Corinthians, 'I call
15 God to record upon my soul, that to spare you I came not as yet unto Corinth;'[n] and to the Philippians, 'God is my record, how greatly I long after you in the bowels of Jesus Christ.'[o] (Hence it undeniably appears that if the Apostle knew the meaning of his Lord's words, they do not forbid swearing on weighty occasions,
20 even to one another—how much less before a magistrate!) And lastly, from that assertion of the great Apostle concerning solemn swearing in general (which it is impossible he could have mentioned without any touch of blame if his Lord had totally forbidden it): 'Men verily swear by the greater' (by one greater
25 than themselves), 'and an oath for confirmation is to them the end of all strife.'[p]

11. But the great lesson which our blessed Lord inculcates here, and which he illustrates by this example, is that God is in all things,[50] and that we are to see the Creator in the glass of every
30 creature;[51] that we should use and look upon nothing as separate

---

[k] Matt. 26:63-64.
[l] Heb. 6:17.
[m] Rom. 1:9.
[n] 2 Cor. 1:23.
[o] Phil. 1:8.   [p] Heb. 6:16.

---

[48] Wesley's translation in *Notes* on Matt. 26:63-64; but cf. Poole, *Annotations,* for Jesus's reply to Caiaphas, 'Thou hast said the Truth . . . ,' and Henry's comment, 'It is as thou hast said' *(Exposition).*
[49] Cf. 1 Cor. 7:40.   [50] Cf. I.6, above, and n.
[51] This will be the central theme of Wesley's *Survey of the Wisdom of God . . .* in its three successive edns. (1763, 1770, 1777).

from God, which indeed is a kind of practical atheism;[52] but with a true magnificence of thought survey heaven and earth and all that is therein as contained by God in the hollow of his hand, who by his intimate presence holds them all in being, who pervades and actuates the whole created frame, and is in a true sense the soul of 5 the universe.[53]

II. 1. Thus far our Lord has been more directly employed in teaching the religion of the heart. He has shown what Christians are to be. He proceeds to show what they are to do also: how inward holiness is to exert itself in our outward conversation. 10 'Blessed', saith he, 'are the peacemakers; for they shall be called the children of God.'[54]

2. 'The peacemakers'—the word in the original is οἱ εἰρηνοποιοί. It is well known that εἰρήνη in the sacred writings implies all manner of good—every blessing that relates either to 15 the soul or the body, to time or eternity. Accordingly, when St. Paul in the titles of his epistles wishes 'grace and peace' to the Romans or the Corinthians it is as if he had said, 'As a fruit of the free, undeserved love and favour of God, may you enjoy all blessings, spiritual and temporal, all the good things "which God 20 hath prepared for them that love him." '[55]

3. Hence we may easily learn in how wide a sense the term 'peacemakers' is to be understood. In its literal meaning it implies those lovers of God and man who utterly detest and abhor all strife and debate, all variance and contention; and accordingly 25

---

[52] A phrase from John Norris, 'Concerning Practical Atheism', in *Practical Discourses*, IV. 100-24. Wesley habitually used 'practical atheism', 'idolatry', and 'dissipation' as working synonyms. Cf. below, III.4, as well as Nos. 41, *Wandering Thoughts*, III.1; 44, *Original Sin*, II.7; 69, 'The Imperfection of Human Knowledge', III.2; 108, 'On Riches', II.1; 119, 'Walking by Sight and Walking by Faith', §20; 120, 'The Unity of the Divine Being', §§19, 20; 127, 'On the Wedding Garment', §12; 128, 'The Deceitfulness of the Human Heart', I.3, 4; and 130, 'On Living without God', §§1, 6, 7. Cf. also Nos. 79, 'On Dissipation', §1; and 78, 'Spiritual Idolatry'. See also Charles Hickman, *Sermon Before the Queen at Whitehall, Sunday, October 2, 1692*, p. 7: 'When men have conquered their conscience . . . they may for a while enjoy their sins in peace and live as if there were no God in the world.'

[53] *Viz.*, the *'anima mundi'*, one of the oldest notions of both Platonists and Stoics; it will presently be re-echoed by Wordsworth in *The Prelude*, I. 401-4:

> Wisdom and Spirit of the Universe!
> Thou Soul that art the Eternity of thought!
> And giv'st to forms and images a breath
> And everlasting motion!

[54] Matt. 5:9.   [55] 1 Cor. 2:9.

labour with all their might either to prevent this fire of hell from being kindled, or when it is kindled from breaking out, or when it is broke out from spreading any farther.[56] They endeavour to calm the stormy spirits of men, to quiet their turbulent passions, to
5 soften the minds of contending parties, and if possible reconcile them to each other. They use all innocent arts, and employ all their strength, all the talents which God has given them, as well to preserve peace where it is as to restore it where it is not. It is the joy of their heart to promote, to confirm, to increase mutual
10 goodwill among men, but more especially among the children of God, however distinguished by things of smaller importance; that as they have all 'one Lord, one faith', as they are all 'called in one hope of their calling', so they may all 'walk worthy of the vocation wherewith they are called': 'with all lowliness and meekness, with
15 long-suffering, forbearing one another in love; endeavouring to keep the unity of the Spirit in the bond of peace.'[57]

4. But in the full extent of the word a 'peacemaker' is one that as he hath opportunity 'doth good unto all men';[58] one that being filled with the love of God and of all mankind cannot confine the
20 expressions of it to his own family, or friends, or acquaintance, or party; or to those of his own opinions; no, nor those who are partakers of like precious faith;[59] but steps over all these narrow bounds that he may do good to every man; that he may some way or other manifest his love to neighbours and strangers, friends
25 and enemies. He doth good to them all as he hath opportunity, that is, on every possible occasion; 'redeeming the time'[60] in order thereto, 'buying up every opportunity',[61] improving every hour, losing no moment wherein he may profit another. He does good, not of one particular kind, but good in general: in every possible
30 way, employing herein all his talents of every kind, all his powers and faculties of body and soul, all his fortune, his interest, his

---

[56] In this entire section (II.2-7) Wesley continues the hermeneutical tradition reflected in Blackall, Discourse XII, *Works*, I.105-14, and in Hammond, *Practical Catechism*, pp. 101-3.

[57] Eph. 4:1-5.

[58] Cf. Gal. 6:10.Cf. John Norris, *Practical Discourses*, I.126: 'The "peacemakers" are persons of "peaceable dispositions". And this requires: "First, that the [peacemaker] be free from all inordinate self-love; it being impossible that he who prefers his own little private concerns before the public interest should be at peace with the public when that tender part comes once to be touched. No, such an one will balance self against the world, will not care what becomes of the public when it stands in competition; but will embroil all the world in war and mischief, if he can, for the least self-advantage. . .".'

[59] See 2 Pet. 1:1.   [60] Eph. 5:16; Col. 4:5.   [61] Cf. Gal. 6:10.

reputation; desiring only that when his Lord cometh he may say, 'Well done, good and faithful servant!'[62]

5. He doth good, to the uttermost of his power, even to the bodies of all men. He rejoices to 'deal his bread to the hungry', and to 'cover the naked with a garment'.[63] Is any a stranger? He takes him in, and relieves him according to his necessities. Are any sick or in prison? He visits them, and administers such help as they stand most in need of. And all this he does, not as unto man, but remembering him that hath said, 'Inasmuch as ye have done it unto one of the least of these my brethren, ye have done it unto me.'[64]

6. How much more does he rejoice if he can do any good to the soul of any man! This power indeed belongeth unto God. It is he only that changes the heart, without which every other change is lighter than vanity.[65] Nevertheless it pleases him who worketh all in all[66] to help man chiefly by man, to convey his own power and blessing and love through one man to another. Therefore, although it be certain that 'the help which is done upon earth, God doth it himself,'[67] yet has no man need on this account to stand idle in his vineyard. The peacemaker cannot: he is ever labouring therein, and as an instrument in God's hand preparing the ground for his Master's use, or sowing the seed of the kingdom, or watering what is already sown, if haply God may give the increase.[68] According to the measure of grace which he has received he uses all diligence either to reprove the gross sinner, to reclaim those who run on headlong in the broad way of destruction[69], or 'to give light to them that sit in darkness'[70] and are ready to 'perish for lack of knowledge';[71] or to 'support the weak',[72] to 'lift up the hands that hang down, and the feeble knees';[73] or to bring back and heal that which was 'lame and turned out of the way'.[74] Nor is he less zealous to confirm those who are already striving to enter in at the strait gate;[75] to strengthen those that stand, that they may 'run with patience the race which is set before them';[76] to 'build up in their most holy

---

[62] Matt. 25:23.
[63] Cf. Isa. 58:7; Ezek. 18:7, 16.
[64] Matt. 25:40.
[65] Ps. 62:9.
[66] 1 Cor. 12:6.
[67] Cf. Ps. 74:13 (BCP).
[68] See 1 Cor. 3:6-7.
[69] See Matt. 7:13.
[70] Luke 1:79.
[71] Cf. Hos. 4:6.
[72] Acts 20:35; 1 Thess. 5:14.
[73] Heb. 12:12.
[74] Heb. 12:13.
[75] See Luke 13:24.
[76] Cf. Heb. 12:1.

faith'[77] those that know in whom they have believed;[78] to exhort them to stir up the gift of God which is in them,[79] that daily 'growing in grace',[80] 'an entrance may be ministered unto them abundantly into the everlasting kingdom of our Lord and Saviour
5 Jesus Christ'.[81]

7. Blessed are they who are thus continually employed in the work of faith and the labour of love; 'for they shall be called'—that is 'shall be' (a common Hebraism[82])—'the children of God.'[83] God shall continue unto them the Spirit of adoption,[84] yea, shall
10 pour it more abundantly into their hearts. He shall bless them with all the blessings of his children. He shall acknowledge them as sons before angels and men; 'and if sons, then heirs; heirs of God, and joint heirs with Christ.'[85]

III. 1. One would imagine such a person as has been above
15 described, so full of genuine humility, so unaffectedly serious, so mild and gentle, so free from all selfish design, so devoted to God, and such an active lover of men, should be the darling of mankind.[86] But our Lord was better acquainted with human nature in its present state. He therefore closes the character of
20 this man of God with showing him the treatment he is to expect in the world. 'Blessed', saith he, 'are they which are persecuted for righteousness' sake; for theirs is the kingdom of heaven.'[87]

2. In order to understand this throughly, let us first inquire who are they that are persecuted.[88] And this we may easily learn from
25 St. Paul: 'As of old he that was born after the flesh persecuted him

---

[77] Cf. Jude 20.
[78] See 2 Tim. 1:12.
[79] See 2 Tim. 1:6.
[80] Cf. 2 Pet. 3:18.
[81] Cf. 2 Pet. 1:11.
[82] Generally true but with important exceptions, as in Gen. 2:23; Isa. 35:8; 47:1; 54:5; 58:12; 62:2, 4, 12; Jer. 7:32; 19:6; 23:6; 33:16. But cf. Heylyn, *Theological Lectures*, I.71: ' "to be called" is a frequent Hebraism signifying only an assertion that such a thing really *is*, or *becomes*, what is said to be "called".'
[83] Matt. 5:9.
[84] Rom. 8:15.
[85] Cf. Rom. 8:17.
[86] Cf. Suetonius, *Lives of the Caesars* ('The Deified Titus', I): 'Titus, with the same surname as his father, was the delight and darling of mankind' *('deliciae humani generis')*.
[87] Matt. 5:10.
[88] Here Wesley departs from both Blackall and Hammond, who stress that 'the persecuted' are those who offend the world by their 'strict and close adherence to the profession and practice of the Christian Church'; Cf. Blackall, Discourse XV, *Works*, I. 134-41.

that was born after the Spirit, even so it is now.'q 'Yea', saith the
Apostle, 'and all that will live godly in Christ Jesus shall suffer
persecution.'r The same we are taught by St. John: 'Marvel not,
my brethren, if the world hate you. We know that we have passed
from death unto life, because we love the brethren.'s As if he had   5
said, The brethren, the Christians, cannot be loved but by them
who have passed from death unto life. And most expressly by our
Lord: 'If the world hate you, ye know that it hated me before it
hated you. If ye were of the world, the world would love its own;
but because ye are not of the world, . . . therefore the world 10
hateth you. Remember the word that I said unto you, The servant
is not greater than the Lord. If they have persecuted me, they will
also persecute you.'t

By all these Scriptures it manifestly appears who they are that
are persecuted, namely the righteous: 'he that is born after the 15
Spirit';89 'all that will live godly in Christ Jesus';90 they that are
'passed from death unto life';91 those who 'are not of the world';92
all those who are meek and lowly in heart, that mourn for God,
that hunger after his likeness; all that love God and their
neighbour, and therefore as they have opportunity do good unto 20
all men.93

3. If it be, secondly, inquired why they are persecuted, the
answer is equally plain and obvious. It is 'for righteousness'
sake':94 because they are righteous; because they are 'born after
the Spirit';95 because they 'will live godly in Christ Jesus';96 25
because they 'are not of the world'.97 Whatever may be pretended,
this is the real cause; be their infirmities more or less, still if it
were not for this they would be borne with, and the world would
love its own. They are persecuted because they are 'poor in
spirit':98 that is, say the world, 'poor-spirited, mean, dastardly 30
souls, good for nothing, not fit to live in the world'; because they

q Gal. 4:29.
r 2 Tim. 3:12.
s 1 John 3:13-14.
t John 15:18-20.

89 Cf. Gal. 4:29.
90 2 Tim. 3:12.
91 1 John 3:14.
93 Gal. 6:10.
95 Gal. 4:29.
97 John 15:19.

92 John 15:19.
94 Matt. 5:10.
96 2 Tim. 3:12.
98 Matt. 5:3.

'mourn': 'They are such dull, heavy, lumpish creatures,[99] enough
to sink anyone's spirits that sees them! They are mere
death's-heads; they kill innocent mirth, and spoil company
wherever they come;' because they are *meek:* 'Tame, passive
5 fools, just fit to be trampled upon;' because they 'hunger and
thirst after righteousness':[100] 'A parcel of hot-brained enthusiasts,
gaping after they know not what, not content with rational
religion, but running mad after raptures and inward feelings;'
because they are 'merciful', lovers of all, lovers of the evil and
10 unthankful: 'Encouraging all manner of wickedness; nay,
tempting people to do mischief by impunity; and men who, it is to
be feared, have their own religion still to seek; very loose in their
principles;' because they are 'pure in heart':[101] 'Uncharitable
creatures that damn all the world but those that are of their own
15 sort! Blasphemous wretches that pretend to make God a liar, to
live without sin!' Above all because they are 'peacemakers',
because they take all opportunities of doing good to all men. This
is the grand reason why they have been persecuted in all ages, and
will be till the restitution of all things.[102]
20   'If they would but keep their religion to themselves it would be
tolerable. But it is this spreading their errors, this infecting so
many others, which is not to be endured. They do so much
mischief in the world that they ought to be tolerated no longer. It
is true the men do some things well enough; they relieve some of
25 the poor. But this, too, is only done to gain the more to their party;
and so in effect to do the more mischief.' Thus the men of the
world sincerely think and speak. And the more the kingdom of
God prevails, the more the peacemakers are enabled to propagate
lowliness, meekness, and all other divine tempers, the more
30 mischief is done—in their account. Consequently the more are
they enraged against the authors of this, and the more vehemently
will they persecute them.
    4. Let us, thirdly, inquire who are they that persecute them. St.
Paul answers, 'He that is born after the flesh'; everyone who is not
35 'born of the Spirit',[103] or at least desirous so to be; all that do not at

---

[99] Cf. *Address to the Clergy*, II.1 (*Bibliog*, No. 216, Vol. 14 of this edn.), where Wesley
speaks of 'dull, heavy, blockish ministers'.
[100] Matt. 5:6.
[101] Matt. 5:8.
[102] See Acts 3:21.
[103] Cf. Gal. 4:29.

least labour to 'live godly in Christ Jesus';[104] all that are not 'passed from death unto life', and consequently cannot 'love the brethren';[105] 'the world', that is, according to our Saviour's account, 'they who know not him that sent me';[106] they who know not God, even the loving, pardoning God, by the teaching of his own Spirit.

The reason is plain. The spirit which is in the world is directly opposite to the Spirit which is of God. It must therefore needs be that those who are of the world will be opposite to those who are of God. There is the utmost contrariety between them in all their opinions, their desires, designs, and tempers. And hitherto 'the leopard and the kid' cannot 'lie down in peace together.'[107] The proud, because he is proud, cannot but persecute the lowly; the light and airy, those that mourn: and so in every other kind, the unlikeness of disposition (were there no other) being a perpetual ground of enmity. Therefore (were it only on this account) all the servants of the devil will persecute the children of God.

5. Should it be inquired, fourthly, how they will persecute them, it may be answered in general, just in that manner and measure which the wise Disposer of all sees will be most for his glory, will tend most to his children's growth in grace and the enlargement of his own kingdom. There is no one branch of God's government of the world which is more to be admired than this. His ear is never heavy to the threatenings of the persecutor or the cry of the persecuted. His eye is ever open and his hand stretched out to direct every the minutest circumstance. When the storm shall begin, how high it shall rise, which way it shall point its course, when and how it shall end, are all determined by his unerring wisdom.[108] The ungodly are only a sword of his; an instrument which he uses as it pleaseth him, and which itself,

---

[104] 2 Tim. 3:12.

[105] 1 John 3:14.

[106] Cf. John 15:21. Ὁ κόσμος as the community of those at enmity with God is a special New Testament usage (cf. 7 in Arndt and Gingrich, *Greek-English Lexicon*), but it was one of Wesley's favourites; the notable exception, of course, is in his *Notes* on John 3:16, 17. Generally, however, he followed the mystical tradition of *contemptus mundi* (Kempis, De Renty, Law); cf. Nos. 4, *Scriptural Christianity*, II.5 and n., for Wesley's comments on 'saints of the world'; and 22, 'Sermon on the Mount, II', II.4 and n., for 'religion of the world'; see also No. 80, 'On Friendship with the World', §5. For Wesley's satanocratic views about the world, cf. No. 12, 'The Witness of Our Own Spirit', §10 and n.

[107] Cf. Isa. 11:6.

[108] Cf. No. 67, 'On Divine Providence', §23 and n.

Sermon 23

when the gracious ends of his providence are answered, is cast into the fire.

 At some rare times, as when Christianity was planted first, and while it was taking root in the earth, as also when the pure
5 doctrine of Christ began to be planted again in our nation, God permitted the storm to rise high, and his children were called to resist unto blood.[109] There was a peculiar reason why he suffered this with regard to the apostles—that their evidence might be the more unexceptionable. But from the annals of the church we
10 learn another and a far different reason why he suffered the heavy persecutions which rose in the second and third centuries: namely, because the mystery of iniquity did so strongly work, because of the monstrous corruptions which even then reigned in the church; these God chastised, and at the same time strove to
15 heal, by those severe but necessary visitations.

 Perhaps the same observation may be made with regard to the grand persecution in our own land.[110] God had dealt very graciously with our nation; he had poured out various blessings upon us. He had given us peace abroad and at home; and a king
20 wise and good beyond his years.[111] And above all he had caused

---

[109] See Heb. 12:4. Cf. Tertullian, *Apology*, 50, §13: '. . . *semen est sanguis Christianorum*' ('nothing whatever is accomplished by your cruelties. . . . They are the bait that wins men for our sect. We multiply whenever we are mown down by you; *the blood of Christians is seed*'). This evolved into the familiar aphorism: 'The blood of the martyrs is the seed of the Church.'

[110] Any Englishman of the time would have recognized this as a reference to 'Bloody Mary' Tudor (1553–58), since John Foxe's *Book of Martyrs* (first Eng. edn. in 1563) had indelibly fixed the image of Roman Catholic zeal and cruelty in English minds; John Knox's contemptuous epithet ('that wicked Jezebel of England') had focused their feelings on Mary. Her cruelties, however, were scarcely more ruthless than those of her acclaimed half-sister, 'Good Queen Bess'. But in JWJ for Mar. 13, 1747, Wesley records having read Daniel Neal's *History of the Puritans* (1732–38) and being 'amaze[d]': 'First, at the execrable spirit of persecution which drove [the Puritans] out of the Church, and with which Queen Elizabeth's clergy were as deeply tinctured as ever Queen Mary's were.' On Apr. 26, 1786, he recounts his 'discovery' of Queen Elizabeth's cruel treatment of Mary Stuart: 'But what then was Queen Elizabeth? As just and merciful as Nero and as good a Christian as Mahomet.' In his old age, however, he wrote to Henry Fisher (Nov. 7, 1781): 'I do not remember that Queen Elizabeth or King James (bad as they were) burnt any heretics.' Here he conveniently ignored the 'forty English martyrs' (later to be canonized in Rome in 1968). The Roman martyrology reckons 183 persons martyred for their faith during Elizabeth's reign. Cf. No. 92, 'On Zeal', §1. The last Englishman burnt for heresy (by James I) was Edward Wightman (in Lichfield, Apr. 1612), a month after Bartholomew Legate had been burnt in Smithfield; the Roman Catholics martyred by Charles II were formally charged with sedition.

[111] The boy-king, Edward VI (1547–53), who succeeded his father, Henry VIII, at the age of ten. Under guidance by the Lords Protector (first the Earl of Somerset and then the Earl of Northumberland), Edward aided the Protestant reform, chiefly by his

the pure light of his gospel to arise and shine amongst us. But what return did he find? 'He looked for righteousness; but behold a cry!'[112] A cry of oppression and wrong, of ambition and injustice, of malice and fraud and covetousness. Yea, the cry of those who even then expired in the flames entered into the ears of the Lord of sabaoth.[113] It was then God arose to maintain his own cause against those that held the truth in unrighteousness.[114] Then he sold them into the hands of their persecutors, by a judgment mixed with mercy, an affliction to punish and yet a medicine to heal the grievous backslidings of his people.

6. But it is seldom God suffers the storm to rise so high as torture or death or bonds or imprisonment. Whereas his children are frequently called to endure those lighter kinds of persecution: they frequently suffer the estrangement of kinsfolk, the loss of the friends that were as their own soul.[115] They find the truth of their Lord's word (concerning the event, though not the design of his coming): 'Suppose ye that I am come to give peace on earth? I tell you, Nay, but rather division.'[u] And hence will naturally follow loss of business or employment, and consequently of substance. But all these circumstances likewise are under the wise direction of God, who allots to everyone what is most expedient for him.

7. But the persecution which attends all the children of God is that our Lord describes in the following words: 'Blessed are ye, when men shall revile you, and persecute you (shall persecute by reviling you), and say all manner of evil against you falsely, for my sake.'[116] This cannot fail: it is the very badge of our discipleship; it is one of the seals of our calling. It is a sure portion entailed on all the children of God; if we have it not we are bastards and not

---

[u] Luke 12:51.

---

encouragement of reformers like Thomas Cranmer, John Hooper, Nicholas Ridley. The results included the *Homilies* (1547), clerical marriage, and communion in both kinds (1548), a 'reformed' BCP (1549), followed by an even more 'reformed' version (1552), a Protestant Catechism and Christian Primer (1553). Wesley rightly infers that the young king had taken a personal interest in these reform measures. With his early death and the counter-reform measures of Queen Mary, the Protestant cause had been imperilled but also had become heroic. For a rather different perspective, see Carolly Erickson, *Bloody Mary*, pp. 226-84, 450 ff.

[112] Isa. 5:7.
[113] Jas. 5:4.
[114] See Rom. 1:18.
[115] See Deut. 13:6.
[116] Matt. 5:11.

sons. Straight through 'evil report' as well as 'good report'[117] lies
the only way to the kingdom. The meek, serious, humble, zealous
lovers of God and man are of good report among their brethren;
but of evil report with the world, who count and treat them 'as the
5 filth[. . .]and offscouring of all things'.[118]

8. Indeed some have supposed that before the fullness of the
Gentiles shall come in[119] the scandal of the cross will cease; that
God will cause Christians to be esteemed and loved, even by
those who are as yet in their sins.[120] Yea, and sure it is that even
10 now he at some times suspends the contempt as well as the
fierceness of men. 'He makes a man's enemies to be at peace with
him'[121] for a season, and gives him favour with his bitterest
persecutors. But setting aside this exempt case, 'the scandal of the
cross is' not yet 'ceased':[122] but a man may say still, 'If I please
15 men, I am not the servant of Christ.'[123] Let no man therefore
regard that pleasing suggestion (pleasing doubtless to flesh and
blood), that 'Bad men only *pretend* to hate and despise them that
are good, but do indeed love and esteem them in their hearts.'
Not so: they may employ them sometimes, but it is for their own
20 profit. They may put confidence in them, for they know their ways
are not like other men's. But still they love them not, unless so far
as the Spirit of God may be striving with them. Our Saviour's
words are express: 'If ye were of the world, the world would love
its own: but because ye are not of the world,[. . .]therefore the
25 world hateth you.'[124] Yea (setting aside what exceptions may be
made by the preventing grace[125] or the peculiar providence of
God) it hateth them as cordially and sincerely as ever it did their
Master.

9. It remains only to inquire, 'How are the children of God to
30 behave with regard to persecution?' And first, they ought not
knowingly or designedly to bring it upon themselves. This is

---

[117] 2 Cor. 6:8.
[118] 1 Cor. 4:13.
[119] See Rom. 11:25.
[120] Cf. Joseph Mede, *Commentationum Apocalypticarum*, in *Works*, III. 530-32; and 'Remains', XI, XII, *ibid.*, 602-5.
[121] Cf. Prov. 16:7.
[122] Cf. Gal. 5:11.
[123] Cf. Gal. 1:10.
[124] John 15:19.
[125] An illuminating correlation of 'preventing' (prevenient) grace and providence. But note that here, 'preventing' has its more nearly common meaning of 'hindering' as well as 'anticipating'.

contrary both to the example and advice of our Lord and all his apostles, who teach us not only not to seek, but to avoid it as far as we can without injuring our conscience, without giving up any part of that righteousness which we are to prefer before life itself. So our Lord expressly saith, 'When they persecute you in this 5 city, flee ye into another'[126]—which is indeed, when it can be taken, the most unexceptionable way of avoiding persecution.

10. Yet think not that you can always avoid it, either by this or any other means. If ever that idle imagination steals into your heart, put it to flight by that earnest caution: 'Remember the word 10 that I said unto you, The servant is not greater than his Lord. If they have persecuted me, they will also persecute you.'[127] 'Be ye wise as serpents, and harmless as doves.'[128] But will this screen you from persecution? Not unless you have more wisdom than your Master, or more innocence than the Lamb of God. 15

Neither desire to avoid it, to escape it wholly; for if you do, you are none of his. If you escape the persecution you escape the blessing, the blessing of those who are persecuted for righteousness' sake.[129] If you are not persecuted for righteousness' sake you cannot enter into the kingdom of heaven. 'If we 20 suffer with him we shall also reign with him. But if we deny him he will also deny us.'[130]

11. Nay, rather, 'rejoice and be exceeding glad'[131] when men persecute you for his sake, when 'they persecute you by reviling' you, and by 'saying all manner of evil against you falsely' (which 25 they will not fail to mix with every kind of persecution; they must blacken you to excuse themselves): 'for so persecuted they the prophets which were before you,'[132] those who were most eminently holy in heart and life; yea, and all the righteous which ever have been from the beginning of the world. Rejoice, because 30 by his mark also ye know unto whom ye belong. And because 'great is your reward in heaven,'[133] the reward purchased by the blood of the covenant, and freely bestowed in proportion to your sufferings, as well as to your holiness of heart and life. 'Be exceeding glad,'[134] knowing that 'these light afflictions, which are 35 but for a moment, work out for you a far more exceeding and eternal weight of glory.'[135]

---

[126] Matt. 10:23.   [127] John 15:20.
[128] Matt. 10:16.   [129] Matt. 5:10.
[130] Cf. 2 Tim. 2:12.   [131] Matt. 5:12.   [132] *Ibid.*
[133] *Ibid.*   [134] *Ibid.*   [135] Cf. 2 Cor. 4:17.

12. Meantime, let no persecution turn you out of the way of lowliness and meekness, of love and beneficence. 'Ye have heard' indeed 'that it hath been said, An eye for an eye and a tooth for a tooth.'ᵛ And your miserable teachers have hence allowed you to
5 avenge yourselves, to return evil for evil.

'But I say unto you, that ye resist not evil'—not thus: not by returning it in kind. 'But' (rather than do this) 'whosoever smiteth thee on thy right cheek, turn to him the other also. And if any man will sue thee at the law, and take away thy coat, let him have thy
10 cloak also. And whosoever shall compel thee to go a mile, go with him twain.'¹³⁶

So invincible let thy meekness be.¹³⁷ And be thy love suitable thereto. 'Give to him that asketh thee, and from him that would borrow of thee turn not thou away.'¹³⁸ Only give not away that
15 which is another man's, that which is not thine own. Therefore, (1). Take care to owe no man anything.¹³⁹ For what thou owest is not thy own, but another man's. (2). Provide for those of thine own household.¹⁴⁰ This also God hath required of thee: and what is necessary to sustain them in life and godliness is also not thine
20 own. Then, (3), give or lend all that remains from day to day, or from year to year: only first, seeing thou canst not give or lend to all, remember the household of faith.¹⁴¹

13. The meekness and love we are to feel, the kindness we are to show to them which persecute us for righteousness' sake, our
25 blessed Lord describes farther in the following verses. O that they were graven upon our hearts!

'Ye have heard that it hath been said, Thou shalt love thy neighbour, and hate thy enemy.'ʷ (God indeed had said only the former part, 'Thou shalt love thy neighbour;'¹⁴² the children of the
30 devil¹⁴³ had added the latter, 'and hate thy enemy.') 'But I say unto you:' (1). 'Love your enemies.'¹⁴⁴ See that you bear a tender

---

ᵛ [Matt. 5,] ver. 38, etc.
ʷ Ver. 43, etc.

---

¹³⁶ Matt. 5:39-41.
¹³⁷ Cf. No. 22, 'Sermon on the Mount, II', I.4 and n.
¹³⁸ Matt. 5:42.   ¹³⁹ Rom. 13:8.
¹⁴⁰ See 1 Tim. 5:8.
¹⁴¹ Gal. 6:10. This paragraph is an anticipation of 'give all you can . . .'; cf. No. 50, 'The Use of Money'.
¹⁴² Lev. 19:18, etc.
¹⁴³ 1 John 3:10.   ¹⁴⁴ Matt. 5:43-44.

goodwill to those who are most bitter of spirit against you, who wish you all manner of evil. (2). 'Bless them that curse you.'[145] Are there any whose bitterness of spirit breaks forth in bitter words? Who are continually cursing and reproaching you when you are present, and 'saying all evil against you'[146] when absent? So much the rather do you bless. In conversing with them use all mildness and softness of language. Reprove them by repeating a better lesson before them, by showing them how they ought to have spoken. And in speaking of them say all the good you can without violating the rules of truth and justice. (3). 'Do good to them that hate you.'[147] Let your actions show that you are as real in love as they in hatred. Return good for evil. 'Be not overcome of evil, but overcome evil with good.'[148] (4). If you can do nothing more, at least 'pray for them that despitefully use you and persecute you.'[149] You can never be disabled from doing this; nor can all their malice or violence hinder you. Pour out your souls to God, not only for those who did this once but now repent. This is a little thing. 'If thy brother seven times a day turn and say unto thee, I repent'—that is, if after ever so many relapses he give thee reason to believe that he is really and throughly changed—then 'thou shalt forgive him,'[x] so as to trust him, to put him in thy bosom, as if he had never sinned against thee at all. But pray for, wrestle with God for those that do not repent, that now despitefully use thee and persecute thee. Thus far forgive them, 'not until seven times only, but until seventy times seven'.[y] Whether they repent or no, yea, though they appear farther and farther from it, yet show them this instance of kindness: 'that ye may be the children', that ye may approve yourselves the genuine children, 'of your Father which is in heaven', who shows his goodness by giving such blessings as they are capable of even to his stubbornest enemies; who 'maketh his sun to rise on the evil and on the good, and sendeth rain on the just and on the unjust.'[150] 'For if ye love them which love you, what reward have ye? Do not even the publicans the same?'[z]—who pretend to no religion, whom ye yourselves

---

[x]   Luke 17:3-4.
[y]   Matt. 18:22.
[z]   [Matt. 5,] ver. 46.

---

[145]   Matt. 5:44.   [146]   Cf. Matt. 5:11.   [147]   Matt. 5:44.
[148]   Rom. 12:21.   [149]   Matt. 5:44.   [150]   Matt. 5:45.

acknowledge to be without God in the world. 'And if ye salute', show kindness in word or deed to 'your brethren', your friends or kinsfolk, 'only, what do ye more than others?' Than those who have no religion at all? 'Do not even the publicans so?'[aa] Nay, but
5 follow ye a better pattern than them. In patience, in longsuffering, in mercy, in beneficence of every kind, to all, even to your bitterest persecutors: 'Be ye' Christians 'perfect' (in kind though not in degree) even 'as your Father which is in heaven is perfect.'[bb]

IV. Behold Christianity in its native form, as delivered by its
10 great Author! This is the genuine religion of Jesus Christ. Such he presents it to him whose eyes are opened. See a picture of God, so far as he is imitable by man! A picture drawn by God's own hand! 'Behold, ye despisers, and wonder and perish!'[151] Or rather, wonder and adore! Rather cry out, 'Is this the religion of
15 Jesus of Nazareth? The religion which I persecuted! Let me no more be found even to fight against God. Lord, what wouldst thou have me to do?'[152] What beauty appears in the whole! How just a symmetry! What exact proportion in every part! How desirable is the happiness here described! How venerable, how
20 lovely the holiness! This is the *spirit* of religion; the quintessence of it. These are indeed the *fundamentals* of Christianity. O that we may not be hearers of it only![153] 'Like a man beholding his own face in a glass, who goeth his way, and straightway forgetteth what manner of man he was.'[154] Nay, but let us steadily 'look into this
25 perfect law of liberty, and continue therein'.[155] Let us not rest until every line thereof is transcribed into our own hearts. Let us watch and pray and believe and love, and 'strive for the mastery',[156] till every part of it shall appear in our soul, graven there by the finger of God; till we are 'holy as he which hath called us is holy',[157]
30 'perfect as our Father which is in heaven is perfect'![158]

[aa] Ver. 47.
[bb] Ver. 48.

---

[151] Acts 13:41.
[152] A composite of echoes from Acts 22:4; 5:39; 23:9; 9:6.
[153] Cf. Jas. 1:22.
[154] Cf. Jas. 1:23-24.
[155] Cf. Jas. 1:25.
[156] Cf. 1 Cor. 9:25.   [157] Cf. 1 Pet. 1:15.
[158] Cf. Matt. 5:48. Notice the positive reference to 'religion' here by contrast with No. 22, 'Sermon on the Mount, II', II.4.

Upon our Lord's Sermon on the Mount
Discourse the Fourth

Matthew 5:13-16

Ye are the salt of the earth. But if the salt hath lost its savour,
wherewith shall it be salted? It is thenceforth good for nothing but to be 5
cast out, and trodden under foot of men.

Ye are the light of the world. A city that is set on an hill cannot be hid.

Neither do men light a candle and put it under a bushel, but on a
candlestick; and it giveth light to all that are in the house.

Let your light so shine before men that they may see your good works, 10
and glorify your Father which is in heaven.

1. The beauty of holiness, of that inward man of the heart
which is renewed after the image of God,[1] cannot but strike every
eye which God hath opened, every enlightened understanding.
The ornament of a meek, humble, loving spirit will at least excite 15
the approbation of all those who are capable in any degree of
discerning spiritual good and evil. From the hour men begin to
emerge out of the darkness which covers the giddy, unthinking
world, they cannot but perceive how desirable a thing it is to be
thus transformed into the likeness of him that created us. This 20
inward religion bears the shape of God so visibly impressed upon
it that a soul must be wholly immersed in flesh and blood when he
can doubt of its divine original. We may say of this, in a secondary
sense, even as of the Son of God himself, that it is 'the brightness
of his glory, the express image of his person': ἀπαύγασμα τῆς 25
δόξης [. . .] αὐτοῦ, 'the beaming forth of his' eternal 'glory'; and
yet so tempered and softened that even the children of men may
herein see God and live: χαρακτὴρ τῆς ὑποστάσεως
αὐτοῦ, 'the character, the stamp, the living impression, of his

---

[1] See 2 Cor. 4:16.

person' who is the fountain of beauty and love, the original source of all excellency and perfection.[2]

2. If religion therefore were carried no farther than this they could have no doubt concerning it—they should have no objection against pursuing it with the whole ardour of their souls. But why, say they, is it clogged with other things? What need of loading it with *doing* and *suffering?* These are what damps the vigour of the soul and sinks it down to earth again. Is it not enough to 'follow after charity'?[3] To soar upon the wings of love? Will it not suffice to worship God, who is a Spirit,[4] with the spirit of our minds, without encumbering ourselves with outward things, or even thinking of them at all? Is it not better that the whole extent of our thought should be taken up with high and heavenly contemplation? And that instead of busying ourselves at all about externals, we should only commune with God in our hearts?

3. Many eminent men have spoken thus: have advised us 'to cease from all outward actions'; wholly to withdraw from the world; to leave the body behind us; to abstract ourselves from all sensible things—to have no concern at all about outward religion, but to 'work all virtues in the will', as the far more excellent way, more perfective of the soul, as well as more acceptable to God.[5]

4. It needed not that any should tell our Lord of this masterpiece of the wisdom from beneath, this fairest of all the devices wherewith Satan hath ever perverted the right ways of the Lord![6] And Oh! what instruments hath he found from time to time to employ in this his service! To wield this grand engine of hell against some of the most important truths of God! Men that 'would deceive, if it were possible, the very elect',[7] the men of faith

---

[2] Heb. 1:3. Cf. Nos. 15, *The Great Assize,* II.1; and 34, 'The Original, Nature, Properties, and Use of the Law', II.3.

[3] 1 Cor. 14:1.

[4] John 4:24.

[5] A composite reference to the tradition of 'will-mysticism' and its spokesmen with whom Wesley was familiar (Zinzendorf, Law, De Renty, Gregory Lopez, Lorenzo Scupoli, and others). The admonition 'to cease from all outward action' may be Wesley's summary of Philip Molther's quietistic beliefs, presumed to represent Zinzendorf's, as outlined in JWJ, Dec. 31, 1739. The idea behind the aphorism, 'to work all virtues in the will' had been stated in Scupoli's *Spiritual Combat,* ch. 13; cf. William Lester and Robert Mohan, trs. (Westminster, Md., The Newman Press, 1950), p. 40: 'Evangelical perfection is attained by repeated acts of the will conforming itself to the will of God, who moved it to practice different virtues at different times.' The implication that pure intentions may suffice for the Christian 'withdrawn from the world' was already familiar in Kempis and William Law.

[6] Cf. No. 42, 'Satan's Devices'.

[7] Cf. Matt. 24:24.

and love. Yea, that have for a season deceived and led away no inconsiderable number of them who have fallen in all ages into the gilded snare,[8] and hardly escaped with the skin of their teeth.[9]

5. But has our Lord been wanting on his part? Has he not sufficiently guarded us against this pleasing delusion? Has he not armed us here with armour of proof against Satan 'transformed into an angel of light'?[10] Yea, verily. He here defends, in the clearest and strongest manner, the active, patient religion he had just described. What can be fuller and plainer than the words he immediately subjoins to what he had said of doing and suffering? 'Ye are the salt of the earth. But if the salt have lost its savour, wherewith shall it be salted? It is thenceforth good for nothing but to be cast out and trodden under foot of men. Ye are the light of the world. A city that is set on an hill cannot be hid. Neither do men light a candle and put it under a bushel, but on a candlestick; and it giveth light to all that are in the house. Let your light so shine before men that they may see your good works, and glorify your Father which is in heaven.'[11]

In order fully to explain and enforce these important words I shall endeavour to show, first, that Christianity is essentially a social religion, and that to turn it into a solitary one is to destroy it;[12] secondly, that to conceal this religion is impossible, as well as utterly contrary to the design of its author. I shall, thirdly, answer some objections; and conclude the whole with a practical application.

I. 1. First, I shall endeavour to show that Christianity is essentially a social religion, and that to turn it into a solitary religion is indeed to destroy it.

By Christianity I mean that method of worshipping God which is here revealed to man by Jesus Christ. When I say this is essentially a social religion, I mean not only that it cannot subsist so well, but that it cannot subsist at all without society, without

---

[8] Cf. No. 87, 'The Danger of Riches', I.10 and n.

[9] Cf. Job 19:20.

[10] 2 Cor. 11:14.   [11] Matt. 5:13-16.

[12] Cf. I.3-4, below; and see Wesley's later letter to Lady Maxwell, Aug. 17, 1764. Bishop Blackall had brought out the same point in Discourse XVII, *Works*, I. 153 ff., where 'the solitary religious life' is condemned. 'For there is no virtue practised by those that live reclusely but what may also be practised by such as live and converse in the world.' But Wesley, here and elsewhere, is more activist in his interpretation of social religion than Blackall, or any of the other commentators on the Sermon on the Mount that he had read.

living and conversing with other men. And in showing this I shall confine myself to those considerations which will arise from the very discourse before us. But if this be shown, then doubtless to turn this religion into a solitary one is to destroy it.

5 Not that we can in any wise condemn the intermixing solitude or retirement with society. This is not only allowable but expedient; nay, it is necessary, as daily experience shows, for everyone that either already is or desires to be a real Christian. It can hardly be that we should spend one entire day in a continued 10 intercourse with men without suffering loss in our soul, and in some measure grieving the Holy Spirit of God. We have need daily to retire from the world, at least morning and evening, to converse with God, to commune more freely with our Father which is in secret.[13] Nor indeed can a man of experience condemn 15 even longer seasons of religious retirement, so they do not imply any neglect of the worldly employ wherein the providence of God has placed us.

2. Yet such retirement must not swallow up all our time; this would be to destroy, not advance, true religion. For that the 20 religion described by our Lord in the foregoing words cannot subsist without society, without our living and conversing with other men, is manifest from hence, that several of the most essential branches thereof can have no place if we have no intercourse with the world.

25 3. There is no disposition, for instance, which is more essential to Christianity than meekness. Now although this, as it implies resignation to God, or patience in pain and sickness, may subsist in a desert, in a hermit's cell, in total solitude; yet as it implies (which it no less necessarily does) mildness, gentleness, and 30 long-suffering, it cannot possibly have a being, it has no place under heaven, without an intercourse with other men. So that to attempt turning this into a solitary virtue is to destroy it from the face of the earth.

4. Another necessary branch of true Christianity is peacemak-
35 ing, or doing of good. That this is equally essential with any of the other parts of the religion of Jesus Christ there can be no stronger argument to evince (and therefore it would be absurd to allege any other) than that it is here inserted in the original plan he has laid down of the fundamentals of his religion. Therefore to set aside

[13] Matt. 6:6, 18.

this is the same daring insult on the authority of our great Master as to set aside mercifulness, purity of heart, or any other branch of his institution. But this is apparently set aside by all who call us to the wilderness, who recommend entire solitude either to the babes, or the young men, or the fathers in Christ.[14] For will any man affirm that a solitary Christian (so called, though it is little less than a contradiction in terms)[15] can be a merciful man—that is, one that takes every opportunity of doing all good to all men? What can be more plain than that this fundamental branch of the religion of Jesus Christ cannot possibly subsist without society, without our living and conversing with other men?

5. But is it not expedient, however (one might naturally ask), to converse only with good men? Only with those whom we know to be meek and merciful, holy of heart and holy of life? Is it not expedient to refrain from any conversation or intercourse with men of the opposite character? Men who do not obey, perhaps do not believe, the gospel of our Lord Jesus Christ? The advice of St. Paul to the Christians at Corinth may seem to favour this: 'I wrote unto you in an epistle not to company with fornicators.'[a] And it is certainly not advisable so to company with them, or with any of the workers of iniquity, as to have any particular familiarity, or any strictness of friendship with them. To contract or continue an intimacy with any such is no way expedient for a Christian. It must necessarily expose him to abundance of dangers and snares, out of which he can have no reasonable hope of deliverance.[16]

But the Apostle does not forbid us to have any intercourse at all, even with the men that know not God. For then, says he, 'ye

---

[a] 1 Cor. 5:9. [Cf. Wesley's tr. in *Notes:* '. . . not to converse with lewd persons'].

---

[14] See above, No. 13, *On Sin in Believers*, III.2 and n. Is there an echo here of William Law's withdrawal into near solitude, first at Stepney and then even more completely at King's Cliffe? Cf. Walker, *William Law*, ch. 16, *et passim*.

[15] See above, §5.

[16] Cf. JWJ, May 24, 1738: 'Removing soon after [ordination as deacon] to another college [Lincoln], I executed a resolution which I was before convinced was of the utmost importance, shaking off at once all my trifling acquaintance. . . .' Cf. also No. 81, 'In What Sense we are to Leave the World' (1784), §23: 'Entering now, as it were, into a new world [i.e., Lincoln College], I resolved to have no acquaintance by chance, but by choice; and to choose such only as I had reason to believe would help me on in my way to heaven. . . . I narrowly observed the temper and behaviour of all that visited me. I saw no reason to think that the greater part of these truly loved or feared God. Such acquaintance, therefore, I did not choose. . . . I bless God, this has been my invariable rule for about threescore years.'

must needs go out of the world,'[17] which he could never advise them to do. But, he subjoins, 'If any man that is called a brother', that professes himself a Christian, 'be a fornicator, or covetous, or an idolator, or a railer, or a drunkard, or an extortioner', 'now I
5 have written unto you not to keep company' with him; 'with such an one, no, not to eat.'[b] This must necessarily imply that we break off all familiarity, all intimacy of acquaintance with him. 'Yet count him not', saith the Apostle elsewhere, 'as an enemy, but admonish him as a brother:'[c] plainly showing that even in such a
10 case as this we are not to renounce all fellowship with him; so that here is no advice to separate wholly, even from wicked men. Yea, these very words teach us quite the contrary.

6. Much more the words of our Lord, who is so far from directing us to break off all commerce with the world that without
15 it, according to his account of Christianity, we cannot be Christians at all. It would be easy to show that some intercourse even with ungodly and unholy men is absolutely needful in order to the full exertion of every temper which he has described as the way of the kingdom;[18] that it is indispensably necessary in order to
20 the complete exercise of poverty of spirit, of mourning, and of every other disposition which has a place here in the genuine religion of Jesus Christ. Yea, it is necessary to the very being of several of them; of that meekness, for example, which instead of demanding 'an eye for an eye, or a tooth for a tooth', doth 'not
25 resist evil', but causes us rather, when smitten 'on the right cheek, to turn the other also';[19] of that mercifulness whereby 'we love our enemies, bless them that curse us, do good to them that hate us, and pray for them which despitefully use us and persecute us;'[20] and of that complication of love and all holy tempers which is
30 exercised in suffering for righteousness' sake.[21] Now all these, it is clear, could have no being were we to have no commerce with any but real Christians.

7. Indeed, were we wholly to separate ourselves from sinners, how could we possibly answer that character which our Lord
35 gives us in these very words: 'Ye' (Christians, ye that are lowly,

---

[b] Ver. 11.   [c] 2 Thess. 3:15.

---

[17] Cf. 1 Cor. 5:10.
[18] In *Works*, II.170, this becomes 'the way to the kingdom'; cf. No. 7, 'The Way to the Kingdom'.
[19] Cf. Matt. 5:38-39.   [20] Cf. Matt. 5:44.   [21] See Matt. 5:10.

serious and meek; ye that hunger after righteousness, that love God and man, that do good to all, and therefore suffer evil: Ye) 'are the salt of the earth.'[22] It is your very nature to season whatever is round about you. It is the nature of the divine savour which is in you to spread to whatsoever you touch; to diffuse itself on every side, to all those among whom you are. This is the great reason why the providence of God has so mingled you together with other men, that whatever grace you have received of God may through you be communicated to others; that every holy temper, and word, and work of yours, may have an influence on them also. By this means a check will in some measure be given to the corruption which is in the world; and a small part, at least, saved from the general infection, and rendered holy and pure before God.

8. That we may the more diligently labour to season all we can with every holy and heavenly temper, our Lord proceeds to show the desperate state of those who do not impart the religion they have received; which indeed they cannot possibly fail to do, so long as it remains in their own hearts. 'If the salt have lost its savour, wherewith shall it be salted? It is thenceforth good for nothing but to be cast out, and trodden under foot of men.'[23] If ye who were holy and heavenly-minded, and consequently zealous of good works, have no longer that savour in yourselves, and do therefore no longer season others; if you are grown flat, insipid, dead, both careless of your own soul and useless to the souls of other men, 'wherewith shall' ye 'be salted?' How shall ye be recovered? What help? What hope? Can tasteless salt be restored to its savour? No; 'it is thenceforth good for nothing but to be cast out', even as the mire in the streets, 'and to be trodden under foot of men,' to be overwhelmed with everlasting contempt. If ye had never known the Lord there might have been hope—if ye had never been 'found in him'.[24] But what can you now say to that his solemn declaration, just parallel to what he hath here spoken? 'Every branch in me that beareth not fruit, he (the Father) taketh away. . . . He that abideth in me, and I in him, bringeth forth much fruit. . . . If a man abide not in me' (or, do not bring forth fruit) 'he is cast out as a branch, and withered; and men gather them' (not to plant them again, but) 'to cast them into the fire.'[d]

---

[d] John 15:2, 5-6.

[22] Matt. 5:13.   [23] *Ibid.*   [24] Phil. 3:9.

9. Toward those who have never tasted of the good word[25] God is indeed pitiful and of tender mercy.[26] But justice takes place with regard to those who have tasted that the Lord is gracious, and have afterwards 'turned back from the holy commandment then
5 delivered to them'.[27] 'For it is impossible for those who were once enlightened', in whose hearts God had once shined, to enlighten them with the knowledge of the glory of God in the face of Jesus Christ; who 'have tasted of the heavenly gift' of redemption in his blood, the forgiveness of sins; 'and were made partakers of the
10 Holy Ghost'—of lowliness, of meekness, and of the love of God and man shed abroad in their hearts by the Holy Ghost which was given unto them—'and have fallen away', καὶ παραπεσόντας (here is not a supposition, but a flat declaration of matter of fact),[28] 'to renew them again unto repentance; seeing they crucify to
15 themselves the Son of God afresh, and put him to an open shame.'[e]

But that none may misunderstand these awful words it should be carefully observed, (1), who they are that are here spoken of; namely they, and they only, who 'were once' thus 'enlightened';
20 they only 'who did taste of that heavenly gift, and were' thus 'made partakers of the Holy Ghost'. So that all who have not experienced these things are wholly unconcerned in this Scripture. (2). What that falling away is which is here spoken of. It is an absolute, total apostasy. A believer may fall, and not fall
25 away. He may fall and rise again. And if he should fall, even into sin, yet this case, dreadful as it is, is not desperate. For 'we have an advocate with the Father, Jesus Christ the righteous; and he is the propitiation for our sins.'[29] But let him above all things beware lest his 'heart be hardened by the deceitfulness of sin';[30] lest he should
30 sink lower and lower till he wholly fall away, till he become as 'salt that hath lost its savour': 'For if we thus sin wilfully, after we have received the' experimental 'knowledge of the truth, there remaineth no more sacrifice for sins; but a certain, fearful looking for of fiery indignation, which shall devour the adversaries.'[31]

[e] Heb. 6:4, etc.

---

[25] See Heb. 6:5. [26] Jas. 5:11. [27] Cf. 2 Pet. 2:21.
[28] See 2 Thess. 2:3; for an extended analysis of this question of 'falling away', see *Predestination Calmly Considered*, §§ 69-79. See also No. 1, *Salvation by Faith*, II.4 and n.
[29] 1 John 2:1-2. [30] Cf. Heb. 3:13.
[31] Heb. 10:26-27.

II. 1. 'But although we may not wholly separate ourselves from mankind; although it be granted we ought to season them with the religion which God has wrought in our hearts; yet may not this be done insensibly? May we not convey this into others in a secret and almost imperceptible manner? So that scarce anyone shall be 5 able to observe how or when it is done? Even as salt conveys its own savour into that which is seasoned thereby, without any noise, and without being liable to any outward observation. And if so, although we do not go out of the world, yet we may lie hid in it. We may thus far keep our religion to ourselves, and not offend 10 those whom we cannot help.'[32]

2. Of this plausible reasoning of flesh and blood our Lord was well aware also. And he has given a full answer to it in those words which come now to be considered: in explaining which I shall endeavour to show, as I proposed to do in the second place, that 15 so long as true religion abides in our hearts it is impossible to conceal it, as well as absolutely contrary to the design of its great author.

And, first, it is impossible for any that have it to conceal the religion of Jesus Christ. This our Lord makes plain beyond all 20 contradiction by a twofold comparison: 'Ye are the light of the world. A city set upon an hill cannot be hid.'

'Ye' Christians 'are the light of the world,'[33] with regard both to your tempers and actions. Your holiness makes you as conspicuous as the sun in the midst of heaven. As ye cannot go 25 out of the world, so neither can ye stay in it without appearing to all mankind. Ye may not flee from men, and while ye are among them it is impossible to hide your lowliness and meekness and those other dispositions whereby ye aspire to be perfect, as your Father which is in heaven is perfect.[34] Love cannot be hid any 30 more than light;[35] and least of all when it shines forth in action, when ye exercise yourselves in the labour of love, in beneficence of every kind. As well may men think to hide a city as to hide a

---

[32] Apparently a composite paraphrase of the general quietist view that the manifestation of 'a Christian presence' is the most effective means of Christian witness; cf. Wesley's account of his controversy with the Moravians on this point in JWJ, Pt. IV, from Nov. 1, 1739, to Sept. 3, 1741.

[33] Matt. 5:14.

[34] Matt. 5:48.

[35] Cf. James Kelly, *A Complete Collection of Scottish Proverbs* (1721), 242, 103: 'Love and light cannot be hid.'

Christian: yea, as well may they conceal a city set upon a hill[36] as a holy, zealous, active lover of God and man.

3. It is true, men who love darkness rather than light, because their deeds are evil,[37] will take all possible pains to prove that the
5 light which is in you is darkness. They will say evil, all manner of evil, falsely,[38] of the good which is in you: they will lay to your charge that which is farthest from your thoughts, which is the very reverse of all you are and all you do. And your patient continuance in well-doing, your meek suffering all things for the Lord's sake,
10 your calm, humble joy in the midst of persecution, your unwearied labour to overcome evil with good,[39] will make you still more visible and conspicuous than ye were before.

4. So impossible it is to keep our religion from being seen, unless we cast it away; so vain is the thought of hiding the light,
15 unless by putting it out. Sure it is that a secret, unobserved religion cannot be the religion of Jesus Christ. Whatever religion can be concealed is not Christianity. If a Christian could be hid, he could not be compared to a city set upon an hill; to the light of the world, the sun shining from heaven and seen by all the world
20 below. Never therefore let it enter into the heart of him whom God hath renewed in the spirit of his mind to hide that light, to keep his religion to himself; especially considering it is not only impossible to conceal true Christianity, but likewise absolutely contrary to the design of the great Author of it.
25 5. This plainly appears from the following words: 'Neither do men light a candle, to put it under a bushel.'[40] As if he had said, 'As men do not light a candle only to cover or conceal it, so neither does God enlighten any soul with his glorious knowledge and love to have it covered or concealed, either by prudence, falsely so
30 called, or shame, or voluntary humility; to have it hid either in a desert, or in the world; either by avoiding men, or in conversing with them. "But they put it on a candlestick, and it giveth light to all that are in the house." ' In like manner it is the design of God that every Christian should be in an open point of view; that he
35 may give light to all around; that he may visibly express the religion of Jesus Christ.

36 See Matt. 5:14.
37 See John 3:19.
38 See Matt. 5:11.
39 Rom. 12:21.
40 Cf. Matt. 5:15.

6. Thus hath God in all ages spoken to the world, not only by precept but by example also. He hath 'not left himself without witness'[41] in any nation where the sound of the gospel hath gone forth, without a few who testified his truth by their lives as well as their words. These have been 'as lights shining in a dark place'.[42]   5
And from time to time they have been the means of enlightening some, of preserving a remnant, a little seed, which was 'counted unto the Lord for a generation'.[43] They have led a few poor sheep out of the darkness of the world, and guided their feet into the way of peace.[44]   10

7. One might imagine that where both Scripture and the reason of things speak so clearly and expressly there could not be much advanced on the other side, at least not with any appearance of truth. But they who imagine thus know little of the depths of Satan. After all that Scripture and reason have said, so exceeding   15
plausible are the pretences for solitary religion, for a Christian's going out of the world, or at least hiding himself in it, that we need all the wisdom of God to see through the snare, and all the power of God to escape it—so many and strong are the objections which have been brought against being social, open, active Christians.   20

III. 1. To answer these was the third thing which I proposed. And, first, it has been often objected that religion does not lie in outward things but in the heart, the inmost soul; that it is the union of the soul with God, the life of God in the soul of man;[45] that outside religion is nothing worth; seeing God 'delighteth not   25
in burnt offerings', in outward services, but a pure and holy heart is 'the sacrifice he will not despise'.[46]

I answer, it is most true that the root of religion lies in the heart, in the inmost soul; that this is the union of the soul with God, the life of God in the soul of man. But if this root be really in the heart   30
it cannot but put forth branches. And these are the several

---

[41] Cf. Acts 14:17.
[42] Cf. 2 Pet. 1:19.
[43] Ps. 22:31 (BCP).
[44] See Luke 1:79.
[45] Cf. No. 3, *'Awake, Thou That Sleepest'*, II.10 and n.
[46] Cf. Ps. 51:16-17 (BCP). A typical example of Wesley's habit of rejecting 'either/or' disjunctions and opting for 'both/and'. Cf. JWJ, Jan. 3, 1740, and his letter to Richard Bailey, Aug. 15, 1751. Also Nos. 27, 'Sermon on the Mount, VII', §1; 77, 'Spiritual Worship', III.4; and 85, 'On Working Out Our Own Salvation', I.2-3. For the 'love of God' as the substance of inward holiness and the 'love of neighbour' as the substance of outward holiness, cf. No. 7, 'The Way to the Kingdom', I.10 and n.

instances of outward obedience, which partake of the same nature with the root, and consequently are not only marks or signs, but substantial parts of religion.

It is also true that bare, outside religion, which has no root in the heart, is nothing worth; that God delighteth not in *such* outward services, no more than in Jewish burnt offerings, and that a pure and holy heart is a sacrifice with which he is always well pleased. But he is also well pleased with all that outward service which arises from the heart; with the sacrifice of our prayers (whether public or private), of our praises and thanksgivings; with the sacrifice of our goods, humbly devoted to him, and employed wholly to his glory; and with that of our bodies, which he peculiarly claims; which the Apostle 'beseeches us, by the mercies of God, to present unto him, a living sacrifice, holy, acceptable to God'.[47]

2. A second objection, nearly related to this, is that love is all in all: that it is 'the fulfilling of the law',[48] 'the end of the commandment',[49] of every commandment of God; that all we do and all we suffer, if we have not charity or love, profiteth us nothing;[50] and therefore the Apostle directs us to 'follow after charity',[51] and terms this, the 'more excellent way'.[52]

I answer, it is granted that the love of God and man arising from 'faith unfeigned'[53] is all in all 'the fulfilling of the law',[54] the end of every commandment of God. It is true that without this whatever we do, whatever we suffer, profits us nothing. But it does not follow that love is all [in all] in such a sense as to supersede either faith or good works. It is 'the fulfilling of the law', not by releasing us from but by constraining us to obey it. It is 'the end of the commandment' as every commandment leads to and centres in it. It is allowed that whatever we do or suffer, without love, profits us nothing. But withal whatever we do or suffer in love, though it were only the suffering reproach for Christ, or the giving a cup of cold water in his name,[55] it shall in no wise lose its reward.

3. 'But does not the Apostle direct us to "follow after charity"?

---

[47] Cf. Rom. 12:1.
[49] 1 Tim. 1:5.
[51] 1 Cor. 14:1.
[53] 1 Tim. 1:5.
[54] Rom. 13:10.
[55] See Mark 9:41.

[48] Rom. 13:10.
[50] See 1 Cor. 13:2, 3.
[52] Cf. 1 Cor. 12:31.

And does he not term it "a more excellent way"? He does direct us to 'follow after charity;' but not after that alone. His words are, 'Follow after charity; and desire spiritual gifts.'[f] Yea, 'follow after charity,' and desire to spend and to be spent for your brethren. 'Follow after charity;' and as you have opportunity do good to all men.[56]

In the same verse also wherein he terms this, the way of love, 'a more excellent way', he directs the Corinthians to desire other gifts besides it; yea, to desire them earnestly. 'Covet earnestly', saith he, 'the best gifts: and yet I show unto you a more excellent way.'[g] More excellent than what? Than the gifts of 'healing', of 'speaking with tongues', and of 'interpreting', mentioned in the preceding verse. But not more excellent than the way of obedience. Of this the Apostle is not speaking; neither is he speaking of outward religion at all. So that this text is quite wide of the present question.

But suppose the Apostle had been speaking of outward as well as inward religion, and comparing them together; suppose in the comparison he had given the preference ever so much to the latter; suppose he had preferred (as he justly might) a loving heart before all outward works whatever. Yet it would not follow that we were to reject either one or the other. No; God hath joined them together from the beginning of the world. And let not man put them asunder.[57]

4. 'But "God is a Spirit, and they that worship him must worship him in spirit and in truth".[58] And is not this enough? Nay, ought we not to employ the whole strength of our mind herein? Does not attending to outward things clog the soul,[59] that it cannot soar aloft in holy contemplation? Does it not damp the vigour of our thought? Has it not a natural tendency to encumber and distract the mind? Whereas St. Paul would have us "to be without

[f] 1 Cor. 14:1.
[g] 1 Cor. 12:31.

---

[56] See Gal. 6:10.
[57] See Matt. 19:6; Mark 10:9; cf. BCP, Matrimony (440).
[58] John 4:24.
[59] A key metaphor for Wesley. See below, III.5; and Nos. 71, 'Of Good Angels', I.1; 81, 'In What Sense we are to Leave the World', §24; 140, 'The Promise of Understanding', proem. Cf. also Law, *Christian Perfection* (*Works*, III.118). Johnson's *Dictionary* cites Sir Kenelm Digby, *On the Soul* (Dedication), 'Let a man wean himself from these worldly impediments that here clog his soul's flight.'

carefulness", and to "wait upon the Lord without distraction".[60]

I answer, 'God is a Spirit, and they that worship him must worship him in spirit and in truth.' Yea, and this is enough: we ought to employ the whole strength of our mind therein. But then
5 I would ask, 'What is it to worship God, a Spirit, in spirit and in truth?' Why, it is to worship him with our spirit; to worship him in that manner which none but spirits are capable of. It is to believe in him as a wise, just, holy being, of purer eyes than to behold iniquity;[61] and yet merciful, gracious, and longsuffering; forgiving
10 iniquity and transgression and sin; casting all our sins behind his back, and accepting us in the beloved.[62] It is to love him, to delight in him, to desire him, with all our heart and mind and soul and strength;[63] to imitate him we love by purifying ourselves, even as he is pure;[64] and to obey him whom we love, and in whom we
15 believe, both in thought and word and work. Consequently one branch of the worshipping God in spirit and in truth is the keeping his outward commandments. To glorify him therefore with our bodies as well as with our spirits, to go through outward work with hearts lifted up to him, to make our daily employment a
20 sacrifice to God, to buy and sell, to eat and drink to his glory:[65] this is worshipping God in spirit and in truth as much as the praying to him in a wilderness.

5. But if so, then contemplation is only one way of worshipping God in spirit and in truth. Therefore to give ourselves up entirely
25 to this would be to destroy many branches of spiritual worship, all equally acceptable to God, and equally profitable, not hurtful, to the soul. For it is a great mistake to suppose that an attention to those outward things whereto the providence of God hath called us is any clog to a Christian,[66] or any hindrance at all to his always
30 seeing him that is invisible. It does not at all damp the ardour of his thought; it does not encumber or distract his mind; it gives him no uneasy or hurtful care who does it all as unto the Lord: who hath learned whatsoever he doth, in word or deed, to do all in the name of the Lord Jesus;[67] having only one eye of the soul
35 which moves round on outward things, and one immovably fixed on God.[68] Learn what this meaneth, ye poor recluses, that you

---

[60] Cf. 1 Cor. 7:32, 35.
[61] See Hab. 1:13.
[62] See Eph. 1:6.
[63] See Mark 12:30; Luke 10:27.
[64] See 1 John 3:3.
[65] See 1 Cor. 10:31.
[66] See above, III.4 and n.
[67] See Col. 3:17.
[68] A strained ocular metaphor; is it Wesley's own coinage or borrowed?

may clearly discern your own littleness of faith. Yea, that you may no longer judge others by yourselves, go and learn what that meaneth:

> Thou, O Lord, in tender love
> Dost all my burdens bear; 5
> Lift my heart to things above,
> And fix it ever there.
> Calm on tumult's wheel I sit,
> Midst busy multitudes alone,
> Sweetly waiting at thy feet, 10
> Till all thy will be done.[69]

6. But the grand objection is still behind. 'We appeal', say they, 'to experience. Our light did shine: we used outward things many years; and yet they profited nothing. We attended on all the ordinances; but we were no better for it—nor indeed anyone else. 15 Nay, we were the worse. For we fancied ourselves Christians for so doing, when we knew not what Christianity meant.'[70]

I allow the fact. I allow that you and ten thousand more have thus abused the ordinances of God, mistaking the means for the end, supposing that the doing these or some other outward works 20 either was the religion of Jesus Christ or would be accepted in the place of it. But let the abuse be taken away and the use remain.[71] Now use all outward things; but use them with a constant eye to the renewal of your soul in righteousness and true holiness.[72]

7. But this is not all. They affirm: 'Experience likewise shows 25 that the trying to do good is but lost labour. What does it avail to feed or clothe men's bodies if they are just dropping into everlasting fire? And what good can any man do to their souls? If these are changed, God doth it himself. Besides, all men are either good, at least desirous so to be, or obstinately evil. Now the 30 former have no need of us. Let them ask help of God, and it shall be given them. And the latter will receive no help from us. Nay, and our Lord forbids to "cast our pearls before swine".'[73]

---

[69] 'For a Believer, in Worldly Business', ver. 3, in *Hymns for those that seek, and those that have Redemption* (1747), p. 8 (*Poet. Wks.*, IV. 215).

[70] See above, No. 16, 'The Means of Grace'. See also JWJ, Nov. 1, 1739–Sept. 3, 1741 (the account of Wesley's struggle with the Moravians). Most of the quotations in Wesley's text here are paraphrases of statements he recalled from the Moravians in Fetter Lane and elsewhere.

[71] Cf. No. 20, *The Lord Our Righteousness*, II.20 and n.

[72] Eph. 4:24.

[73] Cf. Matt. 7:6.

I answer, (1), whether they will finally be lost or saved, you are expressly commanded to feed the hungry and clothe the naked. If you can and do not, whatever becomes of them, you shall go away into everlasting fire. (2). Though it is God only changes hearts,
5 yet he generally doth it by man. It is our part to do all that in us lies as diligently as if we could change them ourselves, and then to leave the event to him. (3). God, in answer to their prayers, builds up his children by each other in every good gift, nourishing and strengthening the whole 'body by that which every joint
10 supplieth'.[74] So that 'the eye cannot say to the hand, I have no need of thee;' no, nor even 'the head to the feet, I have no need of you'.[75] Lastly, how are you assured that the persons before you are dogs or swine? Judge them not until you have tried. 'How knowest thou, O man, but thou mayst gain thy brother,'[76] but thou mayst,
15 under God, save his soul from death? When he spurns thy love and blasphemes the good word, then it is time to give him up to God.

8. 'We have tried. We have laboured to reform sinners. And what did it avail? On many we could make no impression at all.
20 And if some were changed for a while, yet their goodness was but as the morning dew, and they were soon as bad, nay worse than ever. So that we only hurt them—and ourselves too; for our minds were hurried and discomposed; perhaps filled with anger instead of love. Therefore we had better have kept our religion to
25 ourselves.'

It is very possible this fact also may be true, that you have tried to do good and have not succeeded; yea, that those who seemed reformed relapsed into sin, and their last state was worse than the first.[77] And what marvel? Is the servant above his master?[78] But
30 how often did he strive to save sinners! And they would not hear; or when they had followed him awhile they turned back as a dog to his vomit.[79] But he did not therefore desist from striving to do good. No more should you, whatever your success be. It is your part to do as you are commanded: the event is in the hand of God.
35 You are not accountable for this: leave it to him who orders all things well.[80] 'In the morning sow thy seed, and in the evening

---

[74] Eph. 4:16.
[76] Cf. 1 Cor. 7:16; Matt. 18:15.
[78] See Matt. 10:24; John 13:16; 15:20.
[79] See Prov. 26:11; 2 Pet. 2:22.
[80] See Mark 7:37.

[75] 1 Cor. 12:21.
[77] See Matt. 12:45.

withhold not thy hand; for thou knowest not whether shall prosper.'[h]

'But the trial hurries and frets your own soul.' Perhaps it did so for this very reason, because you thought you was accountable for the event—which no man is, nor indeed can be. Or perhaps because you was off your guard; you was not watchful over your own spirit. But this is no reason for disobeying God. Try again; but try more warily than before. Do good (as you forgive) 'not seven times only; but until seventy times seven.'[81] Only be wiser by experience: attempt it every time more cautiously than before. Be more humbled before God, more deeply convinced that of yourself you can do nothing.[82] Be more jealous over your own spirit, more gentle and watchful unto prayer. Thus 'cast your bread upon the waters, and you shall find it again after many days.'[83]

IV. 1. Notwithstanding all these plausible pretences for hiding it, 'Let your light so shine before men that they may see your good works, and glorify your Father which is in heaven.'[84] This is the practical application which our Lord himself makes of the foregoing considerations.

'Let your light so shine'—your lowliness of heart, your gentleness and meekness of wisdom;[85] your serious, weighty concern for the things of eternity, and sorrow for the sins and miseries of men; your earnest desire of universal holiness and full happiness in God; your tender goodwill to all mankind, and fervent love to your supreme benefactor. Endeavour not to conceal this light wherewith God hath enlightened your soul, but let it 'shine before men', before all with whom you are, in the whole tenor of your conversation. Let it shine still more eminently in your actions, in your doing all possible good to all men;[86] and in

---

[h] Eccles. 11:6 ['. . . whether shall prosper, either this or that'].

---

[81] Cf. Matt. 18:22.
[82] See John 15:5.
[83] Cf. Eccles. 11:1.
[84] Matt. 5:16.
[85] See 2 Cor. 10:1.
[86] See Gal. 6:10; note how often these *General Rules* of the Methodists are deprecated as 'almost Christian' when they are not grounded in living, loving faith. They are, however, positively recommended in Wesley's early sermon (No. 143), 'Public Diversions Denounced' (a source of the *General Rules* of 1743), and thereafter in Nos. 80, 'On Friendship with the World', §6; 85, 'On Working Out Our Own Salvation', II.4; 99, *The Reward of Righteousness*, I.5; 107, 'On God's Vineyard', III.1.

your suffering for righteousness' sake, while you 'rejoice and are exceeding glad, knowing that great is your reward in heaven'.[87]

2. 'Let your light so shine before men that they may see your good works:' so far let a Christian be from ever designing or desiring to conceal his religion. On the contrary let it be your desire not to conceal it, not to put the 'light under a bushel'. Let it be your care to place it 'on a candlestick, that it may give light to all that are in the house'. Only take heed not to seek your own praise herein, not to desire any honour to yourselves. But let it be your sole aim that all who see your good works may 'glorify your Father which is in heaven'.

3. Be this your one ultimate end in all things. With this view be plain, open, undisguised. Let your love be without dissimulation.[88] Why should you hide fair, disinterested love? Let there be no guile found in your mouth:[89] let your words be the genuine picture of your heart. Let there be no darkness or reservedness in your conversation, no disguise in your behaviour. Leave this to those who have other designs in view—designs which will not bear the light. Be ye artless and simple to all mankind, that all may see the grace of God which is in you. And although some will harden their hearts, yet others will take knowledge that ye have been with Jesus,[90] and by returning themselves 'to the great Bishop of their souls',[91] 'glorify your Father which is in heaven'.

4. With this one design, that men may 'glorify God in you', go on in his name and in the power of his might.[92] Be not ashamed even to stand alone, so it be in the ways of God. Let the light which is in your heart shine in all good works, both works of piety and works of mercy.[93] And in order to enlarge your ability of doing good, renounce all superfluities.[94] Cut off all unnecessary expense, in food, in furniture, in apparel. Be a good steward of

---

[87] Cf. Matt. 5:12.

[88] See Rom. 12:9. 'Dissimulation' is a theme that runs throughout the Wesley sermons from early to late. Cf. his early sermon 'On Dissimulation' and a fragment on the same subject (Nos. 138A, 138B) as well as Nos. 52, *The Reformation of Manners*, IV. 4-5; 90, 'An Israelite Indeed', II.5-7; 100, 'On Pleasing All Men', §§3, 4, 5, II.4; 128, 'The Deceitfulness of the Human Heart', II.7. Cf. also his letter to Sophy Hopkey, July 5, 1737, and to the Moravian Church, Sept. 1738.

[89] See 1 Pet. 2:22; Rev. 14:5.

[90] See Acts 4:13.

[91] Cf. 1 Pet. 2:25.

[92] Eph. 6:10.

[93] Cf. Sermon 14, *The Repentance of Believers*, I.13 and n.

[94] An early instance of Wesley's consistent denunciation of the essential sinfulness of

every gift of God,[95] even of these his lowest gifts. Cut off all unnecessary expense of time, all needless or useless employments. And 'whatsoever thy hand findeth to do, do it with thy might.'[96] In a word, be thou full of faith and love; do good; suffer evil. And herein be thou 'steadfast, unmovable'; yea, 'always 5 abounding in the work of the Lord; forasmuch as thou knowest that thy labour is not in vain in the Lord.'[97]

all surplus accumulation. It will be repeated, ever more emphatically, by the late Wesley, as more and more Methodists became more and more affluent. Cf. Nos. 28, 'Sermon on the Mount, VIII', §§9-27; and 50, 'The Use of Money', intro.

[95] See 1 Pet. 4:10.
[96] Eccles. 9:10.
[97] Cf. 1 Cor. 15:58.

Upon our Lord's Sermon on the Mount
Discourse the Fifth
Matthew 5:17-20

Think not that I am come to destroy the law or the prophets: I am not
5 *come to destroy, but to fulfil.*

For verily I say unto you, Till heaven and earth pass, one jot or one tittle shall in no wise pass from the law, till all be fulfilled.

Whosoever therefore shall break one of these least commandments, and shall teach men so, he shall be called the least in the kingdom of
10 *heaven; but whosoever shall do and teach them, the same shall be called great in the kingdom of heaven.*

For verily I say unto you, That except your righteousness shall exceed the righteousness of the scribes and Pharisees, ye shall in no case enter into the kingdom of heaven.

15   1. Among the multitude of reproaches which fell upon him who was 'despised and rejected of men',[1] it could not fail to be one that he was a teacher of novelties, an introducer of a *new religion.*[2] This might be affirmed with the more colour because many of the expressions he had used were not common among the Jews:
20 either they did not use them at all, or not in the same sense, not in so full and strong a meaning. Add to this that the worshipping

---

[1] Isa. 53:3.

[2] Such a charge, if true, would have been devastating in Wesley's eyes, since he regarded novelty in doctrine as prima facie evidence of error; cf. No. 13, *On Sin in Believers*, III.9 ('Whatever doctrine is *new* must be *wrong*'); and his letter to Mary Stokes, Aug. 10, 1772: a thing that is 'wholly new is therefore wholly wrong'. In No. 17, 'The Circumcision of the Heart', §1, he had emphatically denied that *he* was 'a setter forth of new doctrine' and would warn against doctrinal innovations in later sermons; cf. Nos. 78, 'Spiritual Idolatry', I.7 ff.; and 84, *The Important Question*, III.8; and see also a very late letter to Walter Churchey, June 20, 1789: 'In religion I am for as few innovations as possible.' In all this he was reflecting the basic Anglican attitude toward *tradition* ('Christian antiquity'); the same perspective had been echoed by Stillingfleet, Addison, South, and others—harking back to the Vincentian Canon, '*Consensus veterum: quod ab omnibus, quod ubique, quod semper creditum* ('the ancient consensus: what has been believed by all, everywhere and always'). Cf. *The Commonitory of Vincent of Lerins* (A.D. 435), §6 [ch. II].

God 'in spirit and in truth'[3] must always appear a new religion to those who have hitherto known nothing but outside worship, nothing but the 'form of godliness'.[4]

2. And 'tis not improbable some might hope it was so, that he was abolishing the old religion and bringing in another, one which they might flatter themselves would be an easier way to heaven. But our Lord refutes in these words both the vain hopes of the one and the groundless calumnies of the other.

I shall consider them in the same order as they lie, taking each verse for a distinct head of discourse.

I. 1. And, first, 'think not that I am come to destroy the law or the prophets. I am not come to destroy, but to fulfil.'

The ritual or ceremonial law delivered by Moses to the children of Israel, containing all the injunctions and ordinances which related to the old sacrifices and service of the temple, our Lord indeed did come to destroy, to dissolve and utterly abolish. To this bear all the apostles witness: not only Barnabas and Paul, who vehemently withstood those who taught that Christians ought 'to keep the law of Moses';[a] not only St. Peter, who termed the insisting on this, on the observance of the ritual law, a[s] 'tempting God, and putting a yoke upon the neck of the disciples which neither our fathers (saith he) nor we were able to bear';[b] but 'all the apostles, elders, and brethren,[. . .]being assembled with one accord', declared that to command them to keep this law was to 'subvert their souls'; and that 'it seemed good to the Holy Ghost and to them to lay no such burden upon them.'[c] This 'handwriting of ordinances our Lord did blot out, take away, and nail to his cross.'[5]

2. But the moral law, contained in the Ten Commandments, and enforced by the prophets, he did not take away. It was not the design of his coming to revoke any part of this. This is a law which never can be broken, which 'stands fast as the faithful witness in heaven'.[6] The moral stands on an entirely different foundation from the ceremonial or ritual law, which was only designed for a temporary restraint upon a disobedient and stiff-necked people;

[a] Acts 15:5.
[b] Acts 15:10.
[c] Ver. 24, etc. [Acts 15:22-28.]

[3] John 4:23, 24.
[5] Cf. Col. 2:14.
[4] 2 Tim. 3:5.
[6] Ps. 89:36 (BCP).

whereas this was from the beginning of the world, being 'written not on tables of stone'[7] but on the hearts of all the children of men when they came out of the hands of the Creator. And however the letters once wrote by the finger of God[8] are now in a great

5　measure defaced by sin, yet can they not wholly be blotted out while we have any consciousness of good and evil. Every part of this law must remain in force, upon all mankind, and in all ages; as not depending either on time or place, or any other circumstances liable to change, but on the nature of God and the nature of man,

10　and their unchangeable relation to each other.

3. 'I am not come to destroy, but to fulfil.' Some have conceived our Lord to mean, I am come to fulfil this by my entire and perfect obedience to it. And it cannot be doubted but he did in this sense fulfil every part of it.[9] But this does not appear to be what he

15　intends here, being foreign to the scope of his present discourse. Without question his meaning in this place is (consistently with all that goes before and follows after): I am come to establish it in its fullness, in spite of all the glosses of men; I am come to place in a full and clear view whatsoever was dark or obscure therein; I am

20　come to declare the true and full import of every part of it; to show the length and breadth, the entire extent of every commandment contained therein, and the height and depth, the inconceivable purity and spirituality of it in all its branches.[10]

4. And this our Lord has abundantly performed in the

25　preceding and subsequent parts of the discourse before us, in which he has not introduced a new religion into the world, but the same which was from the beginning: a religion the substance of which is, without question, 'as old as the creation';[11] being coeval

---

[7] Cf. 2 Cor. 3:3.　　　　　　　　　　　　　　[8] See Exod. 31:18; Deut. 9:10.

[9] A special point of Blackall's in Discourse XIX, *Works*, I. 174-77.

[10] A move beyond the prevailing interpretations, as in Tillotson, Henry, and Poole; cf. Poole, *Annotations*, where Jesus's word is paraphrased thus, 'I am come to fulfil [the Moral Law] by yielding myself a personal obedience to it, by giving a fuller and stricter interpretation of it.' Henry's comment here is to the same effect. For Wesley's view of the exalted status of 'the Moral Law', see below, Nos. 34-36, but especially the passage on 'the nature of the Law' in No. 34, 'The Original, Nature, Properties, and Use of the Law', II.1-6.

[11] Cf. Eusebius, *Ecclesiastical History*, I.4(4-10): 'Our [Christian] manner of life and mode of conduct, together with our religious principles, have not been just now invented by us, but from the first creation of man were established by the innate ideas of those men of old whom God loved. . . .' Matthew Tindal had given this old idea a deistic twist in his *Christianity as Old as Creation* (1730); Wesley harks back to the original—the moral law *is* 'coeval with man' but is, and has always been, *supernatural* in its origins and sanctions.

with man, and having proceeded from God at the very time when
'man became a living soul'.[12] (The substance, I say, for some
circumstances of it now relate to man as a fallen creature); a
religion witnessed to both by the law and by the prophets in all
succeeding generations. Yet was it never so fully explained nor so 5
throughly understood till the great Author of it himself
condescended to give mankind this authentic comment on all the
essential branches of it; at the same time declaring it should never
be changed, but remain in force to the end of the world.

II. 1. 'For verily I say unto you' (a solemn preface, which 10
denotes both the importance and certainty of what is spoken),
'Till heaven and earth pass, one jot or one tittle shall in no wise
pass from the law till all be fulfilled.'[13]

'One jot'—it is literally, *not one iota*, not the most inconsiderable vowel; 'or one tittle', μία κεραία, one corner, or point of a 15
consonant. It is a proverbial expression which signifies that no
one commandment contained in the moral law, nor the least part
of one, however inconsiderable it might seem, should ever be
disannulled.[14]

'Shall in no wise pass from the law;' οὐ μὴ παρέλθῃ ἀπὸ τοῦ 20
νόμου. The double negative here used strengthens the sense so
as to admit of no contradiction. And the word παρέλθῃ, it may
be observed, is not barely *future*, declaring what *will* be; but has
likewise the force of an *imperative*, ordering what *shall* be. It is a
word of authority, expressing the sovereign will and power of him 25
that spake, of him whose word is the law of heaven and earth, and
stands fast for ever and ever.[15]

'One jot or one tittle shall in no wise pass till heaven and earth
pass;' or as it is expressed immediately after, ἕως ἂν πάντα
γένηται, 'till all' (or rather, *all things*) 'be fulfilled', till the 30
consummation of all things. Here is therefore no room for that
poor evasion (with which some have delighted themselves greatly)
that 'no part of the law was to pass away till *all the law* was fulfilled;
but it has been fulfilled by Christ, and therefore now must pass,

---

[12] Gen. 2:7.
[13] Matt. 5:18.
[14] I.e., 'cancelled'; cf. III.8, below, for a similar usage. See also *OED*.
[15] Cf. Isa. 40:8. For Wesley's overconfident way with future indicative and imperative
forms in Greek, cf. No. 16, 'The Means of Grace', III.7 and n.

for the gospel to be established.'[16] Not so; the word 'all' does not mean all the law, but all things in the universe; as neither has the term 'fulfilled' any reference to the law, but to all things in heaven and earth.

5　2. From all this we may learn that there is no contrariety at all between the law and the gospel; that there is no need for the law to pass away in order to the establishing of the gospel. Indeed neither of them supersedes the other, but they agree perfectly well together. Yea, the very same words, considered in different respects, are parts both of the law and of the gospel. If they are considered as commandments, they are parts of the law: if as promises, of the gospel. Thus, 'Thou shalt love the Lord thy God with all thy heart,'[17] when considered as a commandment, is a branch of the law; when regarded as a promise, is an essential part of the gospel—the gospel being no other than the commands of the law proposed by way of promises.[18] Accordingly poverty of spirit, purity of heart, and whatever else is enjoined in the holy law of God, are no other, when viewed in a gospel light, than so many great and precious promises.[19]

20　3. There is therefore the closest connection that can be conceived between the law and the gospel.[20] On the one hand the law continually makes way for and points us to the gospel; on the other the gospel continually leads us to a more exact fulfilling of the law. The law, for instance, requires us to love God, to love our neighbour, to be meek, humble, or holy. We feel that we are not sufficient for these things, yea, that 'with man this is impossible.'[21] But we see a promise of God to give us that love, and to make us humble, meek, and holy. We lay hold of this gospel, of these glad tidings: it is done unto us according to our faith, and 'the righteousness of the law is fulfilled in us'[22] through faith which is in Christ Jesus.

We may yet farther observe that every command in Holy Writ is

---

[16] Wesley's paraphrase of the substance of the antinomian argument cast in the form of a syllogism.

[17] Deut. 6:5; Matt. 22:37, etc.

[18] A prime rule for Wesley's hermeneutics: no command apart from a promise of grace; no promise without an implied moral responsibility. Its probable source: Thomas Drayton, *The Proviso or Condition of the Promises* (1657), pp. 1-2. Cf. also Nos. 27, 'Sermon on the Mount, VII', II.12; 76, 'On Perfection', II.1-2, 11; and 101, 'The Duty of Constant Communion', II.3. See also Wesley's letter to Ebenezer Blackwell (?), Dec. 20, 1751.

[19] See 2 Pet. 1:4.

[20] For a fuller development of this thesis, see below, Nos. 34-36.

[21] Cf. Matt. 19:26.　　　　　　　　　　　　　　　　　[22] Cf. Rom. 8:4.

only a covered promise. For by that solemn declaration, 'This is
the covenant I will make after those days, saith the Lord; I will put
my laws in your minds, and write them in your hearts,'[23] God hath
engaged to give whatsoever he commands. Does he command us
then to 'pray without ceasing'?[24] To 'rejoice evermore'?[25] To be 5
'holy as he is holy'?[26] It is enough. He will work in us this very
thing. It shall be unto us according to his word.[27]

4. But if these things are so, we cannot be at a loss what to think
of those who in all ages of the church have undertaken to change
or supersede some commands of God, as they professed, by the 10
peculiar direction of his Spirit. Christ has here given us an
infallible rule whereby to judge of all such pretentions.
Christianity, as it includes the whole moral law of God, both by
way of injunction and of promise, if we will hear him, is designed
of God to be the last of all his dispensations. There is no other to 15
come after this. This is to endure till the consummation of all
things. Of consequence all such new revelations are of Satan, and
not of God; and all pretences to another more perfect
dispensation fall to the ground of course. 'Heaven and earth shall
pass away; but this word shall not pass away.'[28] 20

III. 1. 'Whosoever therefore shall break one of these least
commandments, and shall teach men so, he shall be called the
least in the kingdom of heaven; but whosoever shall do and teach
them, the same shall be called great in the kingdom of heaven.'[29]

Who, what are they that make 'the preaching of the law' a 25
character of reproach? Do they not see on whom their reproach
must fall? On whose head it must light at last? Whosoever on this
ground despiseth us, despiseth him that sent us.[30] For did ever
any man preach the law like him? Even when he 'came not to
condemn but to save the world';[31] when he came purposely to 30
bring 'life and immortality to light through the gospel'.[32] Can any
'preach the law' more expressly, more rigorously, than Christ
does in these words? And who is he that shall amend them? Who
is he that shall instruct the Son of God how to preach? Who will
teach him a better way of delivering the message which he hath 35
received of the Father?

---

23 Cf. Heb. 10:16.   24 1 Thess. 5:17.   25 1 Thess. 5:16.
26 Cf. 1 Pet. 1:16.   27 See Luke 1:38.   28 Cf. Luke 21:33.
29 Matt. 5:19.   30 See Luke 10:16.
31 Cf. John 3:17; 12:47.   32 2 Tim. 1:10.

2. 'Whosoever shall break one of these least commandments', or one of the least of these commandments. 'These commandments', we may observe, is a term used by our Lord as equivalent with 'the law', or the 'law and the prophets', which is the same
5 thing, seeing the prophets added nothing to the law, but only declared, explained, or enforced it, as they were moved by the Holy Ghost.[33]

'Whosoever shall break one of these least commandments', especially if it be done wilfully or presumptuously. *One*—for 'he
10 that keepeth the whole law and' thus 'offends in one point, is guilty of all:'[34] the wrath of God abideth on him[35] as surely as if he had broken every one. So that no allowance is made for one darling lust;[36] no reserve for one idol; no excuse for refraining from all besides, and only giving way to one bosom sin. What God
15 demands is an entire obedience; we are to have an eye to all his commandments; otherwise we lose all the labour we take in keeping some, and our poor souls for ever and ever.

'One of these least', or one of the least of these 'commandments'. Here is another excuse cut off, whereby many, who
20 cannot deceive God, miserably deceive their own souls. 'This sin, saith the sinner, is it not a little one? Will not the Lord spare me in this thing? Surely he will not be extreme to mark this, since I do not offend in the greater matters of the law.' Vain hope! Speaking after the manner of men we may term these great, and those little
25 commandments. But in reality they are not so. If we use propriety of speech there is no such thing as a little sin, every sin being a transgression of the holy and perfect law, and an affront of the great majesty of heaven.

3. 'And shall teach men so'—In some sense it may be said that
30 whosoever openly breaks any commandment teaches others to do

---

[33] 2 Pet. 1:21.
[34] Cf. Jas. 2:10.
[35] John 3:36.
[36] A seventeenth- and eighteenth-century cliché repeated by John Bunyan, John Dryden, Francis Atterbury, Samuel Annesley, Robert Bolton, Thomas Fuller, Richard Lucas, Robert South, and others, with such variations as 'darling sins', 'bosom sins', etc. Cf. Matthew Mead, *The Almost Christian Discovered*, p. 107: 'There is a natural man, let him go never so far, let him go never so much in matters of religion; but still he hath his Dalilah, his bosom-lust;' on p. 130 he repeats the point: '. . . every lust, every darling, every beloved sin. . .'). For other usages in Wesley, cf. Nos. 48, 'Self-denial', II.2-3; 62, 'The End of Christ's Coming', §1; and 142, 'The Wisdom of Winning Souls', II.7. In No. 135, 'On Guardian Angels', proem, ¶2, Wesley speaks of 'darling bodies'; in No. 31, 'Sermon on the Mount, XI', I.3, he speaks of 'parent sins'.

the same; for example speaks, and many times louder than precept. In this sense it is apparent every open drunkard is a teacher of drunkenness; every sabbath-breaker is constantly teaching his neighbour to profane the day of the Lord. But this is not all; an habitual breaker of the law is seldom content to stop here. He generally teaches other men to do so too, by word as well as example; especially when he hardens his neck, and hateth to be reproved. Such a sinner soon commences[37] an advocate for sin: he defends what he is resolved not to forsake. He excuses the sin which he will not leave, and thus directly teaches every sin which he commits.

'He shall be called least in the kingdom of heaven'—that is, shall have no part therein.[38] He is a stranger to the kingdom of heaven which is on earth; he hath no portion in that inheritance; no share of that righteousness and peace and joy in the Holy Ghost.[39] Nor by consequence can he have any part in the glory which shall be revealed.[40]

4. But if those who even thus break and teach others to break one of the least of these commandments shall be called least in the kingdom of heaven, shall have no part in the kingdom of Christ and of God; if even these 'shall be cast into outer darkness', where is 'wailing and gnashing of teeth',[41] then where will they appear whom our Lord chiefly and primarily intends in these words? They who, bearing the character of teachers sent from God, do nevertheless themselves break his commandments, yea and openly teach others so to do, being corrupt both in life and doctrine?

5. These are of several sorts. Of the first sort are they who live in some wilful, habitual sin. Now if an ordinary sinner teaches by his example, how much more a sinful minister, even if he does not attempt to defend, excuse, or extenuate his sin! If he does he is a murderer indeed, yea, the murderer-general of his congregation![42] He peoples the regions of death. He is the choicest

---

[37] This is the academic usage of 'commence'; i.e., 'graduates to the status of . . .'. Cf. No. 41, *Wandering Thoughts*, III.4, where Wesley again uses 'commence' in this sense.

[38] Heylyn's point: *'minimus in regno caelorum'* has here the force of *minimé* and imports an exclusion from the gospel dispensation (*Theological Lectures*, I. 76). Wesley repeats his own phrase here in his *Notes*.

[39] Rom. 14:17.   [40] Rom. 8:18.   [41] Matt. 8:12.

[42] This stark metaphor occurs in a letter written at the same time with this sermon (to 'John Smith', Mar. 25, 1747): 'a lifeless, unconverting minister is the murderer-general of his congregation.' Cf. the much later No. 104, 'On Attending the Church

instrument of the prince of darkness. When he goes hence 'hell from beneath is moved to meet him at his coming.'[43] Nor can he sink into the bottomless pit[44] without dragging a multitude after him.

5　　6. Next to these are the good-natured, good sort of men: who live an easy, harmless life, neither troubling themselves with outward sin, nor with inward holiness; men who are remarkable neither one way nor the other, neither for religion nor irreligion; who are very regular both in public and private, but don't pretend to be any stricter than their neighbours. A minister of this kind breaks not one, or a few only, of the least commandments of God, but all the great and weighty branches of his law which relate to the power of godliness, and all that require us to 'pass the time of our sojourning in fear';[45] to 'work out our salvation with fear and trembling';[46] to have our 'loins always girt and our lights burning';[47] to 'strive or "agonize" to enter in at the strait gate'.[48] And he 'teaches men so',[49] by the whole form of his life and the general tenor of his preaching, which uniformly tends to soothe those in their pleasing dream who imagine themselves Christians and are not; to persuade all who attend upon his ministry to sleep on and take their rest.[50] No marvel, therefore, if both he and they that follow him wake together in everlasting burnings.[51]

7. But above all these, in the highest rank of the enemies of the gospel of Christ are they who openly and explicitly 'judge the law' itself, and 'speak evil of the law';[52] who teach men to break ($\lambda\tilde{v}\sigma\alpha\iota$, to dissolve, to loose, to untie the obligation of) not one only—whether of the least or of the greatest—but all the

Service',§§19 ff., where unworthy ministers are viewed less harshly. See also Art. XXVI, 'Of the unworthiness of the ministers, which hinders not the effect of the sacraments'.

[43] Cf. Isa. 14:9.

[44] See Rev. 9:11; 20:1. Cf. also No. 32, 'Sermon on the Mount, XII', I.7 and n.

[45] Cf. 1 Pet. 1:17.

[46] Phil. 2:12.

[47] Cf. Luke 12:35.

[48] Luke 13:24. The Greek imperative is $\dot{\alpha}\gamma\omega\nu\dot{\iota}\zeta\varepsilon\sigma\vartheta\varepsilon$, and Wesley is fond of stressing the metaphor of 'agonizing' as a characteristic of Christian moral discipline, since it had the double meaning of 'struggle' (as in athletics) and also of 'suffering' (as in martyrdom). Cf. No. 17, 'The Circumcision of the Heart', II.7 and n.

[49] Cf. Matt. 5:19.

[50] An ironic echo of Matt. 26:45 and Mark 14:41.

[51] Isa. 33:14. Another favourite metaphor; cf. below, IV.13 and n.; and No. 33, 'Sermon on the Mount, XIII', III.12, where Wesley links it with 'everlasting glory'; see also Downey, *Eighteenth Century Pulpit*, p. 162.

[52] Cf. Jas. 4:11.

commandments at a stroke; who teach, without any cover, in so many words: 'What did our Lord do with the law? He abolished it.' 'There is but one duty, which is that of believing.' 'All commands are unfit for our times.' 'From any demand of the law no man is obliged now to go one step, to give away one farthing, to eat or omit one morsel.'[53] This is indeed carrying matters with a high hand.[54] This is withstanding our Lord to the face, and telling him that he understood not how to deliver the message on which he was sent. 'O Lord, lay not this sin to their charge!'[55] 'Father, forgive them; for they know not what they do!'[56]

8. The most surprising of all the circumstances that attend this strong delusion is that they who are given up to it really believe that they honour Christ by overthrowing his law, and that they are magnifying his office while they are destroying his doctrine! Yea, they honour him just as Judas did when he 'said, Hail, Master, and kissed him'.[57] And he may as justly say to every one of them, 'Betrayest thou the Son of man with a kiss?'[58] It is no other than betraying him with a kiss to talk of his blood and take away his crown; to set light by any part of his law under pretence of advancing his gospel. Nor indeed can anyone escape this charge who preaches faith in any such manner as either directly or indirectly tends to set aside any branch of obedience; who preaches Christ so as to disannul or weaken in any wise the least of the commandments of God.

9. It is impossible indeed to have too high an esteem for 'the faith of God's elect'.[59] And we must all declare, 'By grace ye are saved through faith: . . . not of works, lest any man should boast.'[60] We must cry aloud to every penitent sinner, 'Believe in the Lord Jesus Christ, and thou shalt be saved.'[61] But at the same time we must take care to let all men know we esteem no faith but

---

[53] Again, a catena of quotations or paraphrases from the favourite dicta of the antinomians running back to Tobias Crisp and James Saltmarsh (targets of Richard Baxter's), to the Moravians and even to schismatic Methodists like James Wheatley, William Cudworth, *et al.* In the *Minutes* of 1744, the question is asked: '*Q.* 19. What is antinomianism? *A.* The doctrine which makes void the law through faith.' This is followed by '*Q.* 20. What are the main pillars thereof?' The answer lists six of them (No. 1, 'That Christ abolished the moral law'); one might compare that list with the quotations Wesley has collected here. Cf. also below, Nos. 34-36.

[54] See Num. 33:3 (especially in the Wycliffe translation); see also *OED* ('high', 17*b*).

[55] Cf. Acts 7:60.

[56] Luke 23:34.

[57] Matt. 26:49.

[58] Luke 22:48.

[59] Titus 1:1.

[60] Eph. 2:8-9.

[61] Acts 16:31.

that 'which worketh by love';[62] and that we are not 'saved by faith' unless so far as we are delivered from the power as well as the guilt of sin.[63] And when we say, 'Believe, and thou shalt be saved,' we do not mean, 'Believe, and thou shalt step from sin to heaven, 5 without any holiness coming between, faith supplying the place of holiness;' but, believe and thou shalt be holy; believe in the Lord Jesus, and thou shalt have peace and power together. Thou shalt have power from him in whom thou believest to trample sin under thy feet; power to love the Lord thy God with all thy heart,[64] and to 10 serve him with all thy strength. Thou shalt have power 'by patient continuance in well-doing' to 'seek for glory and honour and immortality'.[65] Thou shalt both 'do and teach'[66] all the commandments of God, from the least even to the greatest. Thou shalt teach them by thy life as well as thy words, and so 'be called 15 great in the kingdom of heaven'.[67]

IV. 1. Whatever other way we teach to the kingdom of heaven, to glory, honour, and immortality,[68] be it called 'the way of faith' or by any other name, it is in truth the way to destruction.[69] It will not bring a man peace at the last.[70] For thus saith the Lord, 'Verily I 20 say unto you, except your righteousness shall exceed the righteousness of the scribes and Pharisees, ye shall in no case enter into the kingdom of heaven.'[71]

The *scribes*, mentioned so often in the New Testament as some of the most constant and vehement opposers of our Lord, were 25 not secretaries, or men employed in writing only, as that term might incline us to believe. Neither were they *lawyers*, in our common sense of the word (although the word νομικοί is so rendered in our translation).[72] Their employment had no affinity

---

[62] Gal. 5:6. Cf. No. 2, *The Almost Christian*, II.6 and n.

[63] A bald claim of salvation from the *power* of sin. Cf. No. 13, *On Sin in Believers*, I.6: 'sin *remains* but no longer *reigns*', and n.

[64] See Mark 12:30; Luke 10:27.   [65] Rom. 2:7.   [66] Matt. 5:19.

[67] *Ibid.*   [68] Rom. 2:7.   [69] See Matt. 7:13.

[70] Was this phrase Wesley's own coinage? If not, what was its common source with J. H. Newman, who would use it for the close of his best known prayer in 'Wisdom and Innocence', 1843: 'Then in thy mercy, grant us a safe lodging and a holy rest, and peace at the last'? See Newman, *Sermons Bearing on Subjects of the Day* (London and New York, Longmans, Green, and Co., 1918), p. 307.

[71] Matt. 5:20.

[72] Wesley here takes the English law and English lawyers, as he knew them, as the popular paradigm for νομικός. Actually, amongst Greek-speaking Jews, the term would have denoted a man who was learned both in the written Torah and the unwritten legal interpretations of *Halakah*; cf. *The Jewish Encyclopedia*.

at all to that of a lawyer among us. They were conversant with the laws of God, and not with the laws of man. These were their study: it was their proper and peculiar business to read and expound the law and the prophets, particularly in the synagogues. They were the ordinary, stated preachers among the Jews; so that if the sense of the original word was attended to we might render it, the divines.[73] For these were the men who made divinity their profession; and they were generally (as their name literally imports) men of letters; men of the greatest account for learning that were then in the Jewish nation.

2. The Pharisees were a very ancient sect or body of men among the Jews: originally so called from the Hebrew word פרש, which signifies to 'separate' or 'divide'.[74] Not that they made any formal separation from or division in the national church. They were only distinguished from others by greater strictness of life, by more exactness of conversation. For they were zealous of the law in the minutest points, paying tithes of mint, anise, and cummin.[75] And hence they were had in honour of all the people and generally esteemed the holiest of men.

Many of the scribes were of the sect of the Pharisees. Thus St. Paul himself, who was educated for a scribe, first at the university of Tarsus,[76] and after that in Jerusalem at the feet of Gamaliel[77] (one of the most learned scribes or doctors of the law that were then in the nation), declares of himself before the council, 'I am a Pharisee, the son of a Pharisee;'[d] and before King Agrippa, 'after the straitest sect of our religion I lived a Pharisee.'[e] And the whole body of the scribes generally esteemed and acted in concert with the Pharisees. Hence we find our Saviour so frequently coupling them together, as coming in many respects under the same consideration. In this place they seem to be mentioned together

---

[d] Acts 23:6.   [e] [Acts] 26:5.

---

[73] Cf. No. 104, 'On Attending the Church Service', §12, where Wesley again equates 'scribe' with 'divine' (i.e., theologian) and then defines 'divine' as meaning a public teacher (and, by inference, the term 'divinity' as the church's public teaching); cf. *OED*.

[74] The literal meaning of the Hebrew verb, *perush*, is to 'disperse' or 'scatter'; in a figurative sense it meant to separate. The Pharisees *(perushim, perishaya)* were those who had separated themselves from those who did not strictly observe both Torah and *Halakah*.

[75] See Matt. 23:23.

[76] Cf. No. 12, 'The Witness of Our Own Spirit', §14 and n.

[77] Acts 22:3.

as the most eminent professors of religion: the former of whom were accounted the wisest, the latter the holiest of men.

3. What 'the righteousness of the scribes and Pharisees' really was it is not difficult to determine. Our Lord has preserved an authentic account which one of them gave of himself. And he is clear and full in describing his own righteousness, and cannot be supposed to have omitted any part of it. He 'went up' indeed 'into the temple to pray', but was so intent upon his own virtues that he forgot the design upon which he came.[78] For 'tis remarkable he does not properly pray at all. He only tells God how wise and good he was. 'God, I thank thee that I am not as other men are, extortioners, unjust, adulterers; or even as this publican. I fast twice in the week: I give tithes of all that I possess.'[79] His righteousness therefore consisted of three parts: first, saith he, 'I am not as other men are.' I am not an 'extortioner', not 'unjust', not an 'adulterer'; not 'even as this publican'. Secondly, 'I fast twice in the week;' and thirdly, 'give tithes of all that I possess.'

'I am not as other men are.' This is not a small point. It is not every man that can say this. It is as if he had said, I do not suffer myself to be carried away by that great torrent, custom.[80] I live not by custom but by reason; not by the examples of men but the word

---

[78] Cf. Luke 18:10; this parable was one of Wesley's favourites in the Revival's early days. He used it thirteen times between 1739-47, but only five times thereafter for a total of eighteen times in all. For a sample of conventional wisdom about the Pharisees in Wesley's time, see Chambers's *Cyclopaedia:* 'a celebrated sect among the ancient Jews . . . separated from the rest by the austerity of their life, by their professing a greater degree of holiness. . .'.

[79] Luke 18:11-12.

[80] A favourite phrase; cf. IV.7 and IV.12, below. Cf. also Nos. 52, *The Reformation of Manners*, I.6; 88, 'On Dress', §21; and 94, 'On Family Religion', III.18. In No. 97, 'On Obedience to Pastors', III.11, Wesley defines its synonym, 'fashion' as 'that tyrant of fools'; in No. 108, 'On Riches', II.3, he calls it 'the mistress of fools'. See also his letter to Miss March, June 29, 1767: 'Fashion and custom are nothing to you: you have a more excellent rule.' Also his letter to John Fletcher, Mar. 20, 1786; to Mary Bishop, Nov. 22, 1769. The idea is also found in Law's *Serious Call* (*Works*, IV.170): 'the vogue and fashion of the world by which we have been carried away as in a torrent'. Cf. also, Edward Stillingfleet, Sermon II, in *Sermons on Several Occasions* (1696), I.66-67: 'custom of the world . . . a torrent of wickedness'; James Garden, *Comparative Theology* (1700), p. 70: 'that vulgar maxim: Custom is a second nature'—which Bartlett, *Familiar Quotations*, attributes to Caesar Augustus, *Rules for the Preservation of Health*, 18. Cf. also Guillaume de Salluste, Seigneur du Bartas (1544–90), *Divine Weekes and Workes, Second Week, Third Day, Part 2:* 'Only that he may conform/To tyrant custom.' So also Shakespeare, *Othello*, I. iii. 231: 'The tyrant custom. . .'. Addison made 'custom' the topic of an essay for the *Spectator;* cf. No. 447, Aug. 2, 1712 (see No. 81, 'In What Sense we are to Leave the World', §17 and n.). See also No. 31, 'Sermon on the Mount, XI', II.5, where Wesley uses the phrase, 'the torrent of example'.

of God. 'I am not an extortioner, not unjust, not an adulterer;' however common these sins are, even among those who are called the people of God (extortion, in particular, a kind of legal injustice, not punishable by any human law, the making gain of another's ignorance or necessity, having filled every corner of the land); 'nor even as this publican', not guilty of any open or presumptuous sin, not an outward sinner, but a fair, honest man, of blameless life and conversation.

4. 'I fast twice in the week.' There is more implied in this than we may at first be sensible of. All the stricter Pharisees observed the weekly fasts, namely, every Monday and Thursday. On the former day they fasted in memory of Moses receiving on that day (as their tradition taught) the two tables of stone written by the finger of God;[81] on the latter in memory of his casting them out of his hand when he saw the people dancing round the golden calf.[82] On these days they took no sustenance at all till three in the afternoon, the hour at which they began to offer up the evening sacrifice in the temple. Till that hour it was their custom to remain in the temple—in some of the corners, apartments, or courts thereof—that they might be ready to assist at all the sacrifices and to join in all the public prayers. The time between they were accustomed to employ partly in private addresses to God, partly in searching the Scriptures, in reading the law and the prophets, and in meditating thereon. Thus much is implied in, 'I fast twice in the week', the second branch of the righteousness of a Pharisee.[83]

5. 'I give tithes of all that I possess.' This the Pharisees did with the utmost exactness. They would not except the most inconsiderable thing, no, not mint, anise, or cummin.[84] They would not keep back the least part of what they believed properly to belong to God, but gave a full tenth of their whole substance yearly, and of all their increase, whatsoever it was.

Yea, the stricter Pharisees (as has been often observed by those who are versed in the ancient Jewish writings), not content with giving one tenth of their substance to God in his priests and Levites, gave another tenth to God in the poor, and that continually. They gave the same proportion of all they had in alms

---

[81] See Exod. 31:18; Deut. 9:10.
[82] Exod. 32:19; Deut. 9:17.
[83] Cf. Chambers's *Cyclopaedia*, 'Pharisees'.
[84] See Matt. 23:23.

as they were accustomed to give in tithes. And this likewise they adjusted with the utmost exactness, that they might not keep back any part, but might fully render unto God the things which were God's,[85] as they accounted this to be. So that upon the whole they
5 gave away from year to year an entire fifth of all that they possessed.

6. This was 'the righteousness of the scribes and Pharisees': a righteousness which in many respects went far beyond the conception which many have been accustomed to entertain
10 concerning it. But perhaps it will be said it was all false and feigned; for they were all a company of hypocrites. Some of them doubtless were; men who had really no religion at all, no fear of God, or desire to please him; who had no concern for the honour that cometh of God,[86] but only for the praise of men. And these
15 are they whom our Lord so severely condemns, so sharply reproves, on many occasions. But we must not suppose, because many Pharisees were hypocrites, therefore all were so. Nor indeed is hypocrisy by any means essential to the character of a Pharisee. This is not the distinguishing mark of their sect. It is
20 rather this (according to our Lord's account)—they 'trusted in themselves that they were righteous, and despised others'.[87] This is their genuine badge. But the Pharisee of this kind cannot be a hypocrite. He must be, in the common sense, sincere; otherwise he could not 'trust in himself that he is righteous'. The man who
25 was here commending himself to God unquestionably thought himself righteous. Consequently, he was no hypocrite—he was not conscious to himself of any insincerity. He now spoke to God just what he thought, namely, that he was abundantly better than other men.
30 But the example of St. Paul, were there no other, is sufficient to put this out of all question. He could not only say, when he was a Christian, 'Herein do I exercise myself, to have always a conscience void of offence toward God and toward men;'[f] but even concerning the time when he was a Pharisee, 'Men and
35 brethren, I have lived in all good conscience before God until this day.'[g] He was therefore sincere when he was a Pharisee, as well as

---

[f] Acts 24:16.
[g] [Acts] 23:1.

---

[85] See Matt. 22:21; Mark 12:17.   [86] See John 5:44.   [87] Luke 18:9.

when he was a Christian. He was no more an hypocrite when he persecuted the church than when he preached the faith which once he persecuted. Let this then be added to 'the righteousness of the scribes and Pharisees'—a sincere belief that they are righteous, and in all things 'doing God service'.[88]

7. And yet, 'Except your righteousness', saith our Lord, 'shall exceed the righteousness of the scribes and Pharisees, ye shall in no case enter into the kingdom of heaven.' A solemn and weighty declaration! And which it behoves all who are called by the name of Christ seriously and deeply to consider. But before we inquire how our righteousness may exceed theirs, let us examine whether at present we come up to it.[89]

First, a Pharisee was 'not as other men are'.[90] In externals he was singularly good. Are we so? Do we dare to be singular at all?[91] Do we not rather swim with the stream? Do we not many times dispense with religion and reason together because we would not 'look particular'? Are we not often more afraid of being out of the fashion[92] than of being out of the way of salvation? Have we courage to stem the tide? To run counter to the world? 'To obey God rather than man'?[93] Otherwise the Pharisee leaves us behind at the very first step. 'Tis well if we overtake him any more.

But to come closer. Can we use his first plea with God, which is in substance, 'I do no harm.[94] I live in no outward sin. I do nothing for which my own heart condemns me.' Do you not? Are you sure of that? Do you live in no practice for which your own heart condemns you? If you are not an adulterer, if you are not unchaste either in word or deed, are you not unjust? The grand measure of justice, as well as of mercy, is, Do unto others as thou wouldst they should do unto thee.[95] Do you walk by this rule? Do you

---

[88] Cf. John 16:2.

[89] Blackall had devoted two entire discourses to this question (XXII-XXIII, *Works*, I.212-18), and his answer is summed up (p. 216): 'This was [the Pharisees'] righteousness. Some things they did which, as to the matter of them, were good, but then they spoiled them by a wrong intention. . . ; they sought their own glory thereby, not the glory of God. . . . [They had] no design . . . to recommend themselves to his grace and favour. . . . That our righteousness may exceed theirs, it is necessary not only that we do the thing that is good, but that we do it with a right intention; i.e., that we design it to the glory of God, and that we do it out of a principle of obedience to the will of God. . . .'

[90] Luke 18:11.

[91] Cf. No. 31, 'Sermon on the Mount, XI', III.4 and n.

[92] Cf. above, IV.3 and n.   [93] Cf. Acts 5:29.

[94] Cf. IV.11, below; and No. 22, 'Sermon on the Mount, II'. II.4 and n.

[95] See Matt. 7:12; Luke 6:31.

never do unto any what you would not they should do unto you? Nay, are you not grossly unjust? Are you not an extortioner? Do you not make a gain of anyone's ignorance or necessity? Neither in buying nor selling? Suppose you are engaged in trade, do you
5　demand, do you receive, no more than the real value of what you sell? Do you demand, do you receive, no more of the ignorant than of the knowing; of a little child than of an experienced trader? If you do, why does not your heart condemn you? You are a barefaced extortioner. Do you demand no more than the usual
10　price of the goods of any who is in pressing want? Who must have, and that without delay, the things which you only can furnish him with? If you do, this also is flat extortion. Indeed you do not come up to the righteousness of a Pharisee.

8. A Pharisee, secondly (to express his sense in our common
15　way), used all the means of grace. As he fasted *often* and *much*, 'twice in every week',[96] so he attended all the sacrifices. He was constant in public and private prayer, and in reading and hearing the Scriptures. Do you go as far as this? Do you fast *much* and *often?* Twice in the week? I fear not! Once, at least: 'On all Fridays
20　in the year.' (So our church clearly and peremptorily enjoins all her members to do, to observe all these as well as the vigils and the forty days of Lent as 'days of fasting, or abstinence'.)[97] Do you fast twice in the year? I am afraid some among us cannot plead even this! Do you neglect no opportunity of attending and partaking of
25　the Christian sacrifice? How many are they who call themselves Christians and yet are utterly regardless of it; yet do not eat of that bread or drink of that cup for months, perhaps years together? Do you every day either hear the Scriptures or read them and meditate thereon? Do you join in prayer with the great
30　congregation?[98] Daily, if you have opportunity? If not, whenever you can, particularly on that day which you 'remember to keep it holy'?[99] Do you strive to *make* opportunities? Are you 'glad when they say unto you, we will go into the house of the Lord'?[100] Are you zealous of, and diligent in, private prayer? Do you suffer no
35　day to pass without it? Rather are not some of you so far from spending therein (with the Pharisee) several hours in one day that

---

[96]　Luke 18:12; cf. Matt. 9:14.
[97]　BCP, 'Tables and Rules': 'All the Fridays in the year except Christmas Day and The Epiphany, or any Friday which may intervene between these feasts.'
[98]　See Ps. 35:18; also 22:25.
[99]　Exod. 20:8.　　　　　　　　　　　　　　　　　　　[100]　Cf. Ps. 122:1.

you think one hour full enough, if not too much? Do you spend an hour in a day, or in a week, in praying to your Father which is in secret?[101] Yea, an hour in a month? Have you spent one hour together in private prayer ever since you was born? Ah, poor Christian! Shall not the Pharisee rise up in the judgment against thee and condemn thee?[102] His righteousness is as far above thine as the heaven is above the earth.

9. The Pharisee, thirdly, 'paid tithes' and gave alms 'of all that he possessed'. And in how ample a manner! So that he was (as we phrase it) 'a man that did much good'. Do we come up to him here? Which of us is so abundant as he was in good works? Which of us gives a fifth of all his substance to God? Both of the principal and of the increase? Who of us out of (suppose) an hundred pounds a year, gives twenty to God and the poor; out of fifty, ten: and so in a larger or a smaller proportion? When shall our righteousness, in using all the means of grace, in attending all the ordinances of God, in avoiding evil and doing good, equal at least the righteousness of the scribes and Pharisees?

10. Although if it only equalled theirs what would that profit? 'For verily I say unto you, except your righteousness shall exceed the righteousness of the scribes and Pharisees, ye shall in no case enter into the kingdom of heaven.' But how can it exceed theirs? Wherein does the righteousness of a Christian exceed that of a scribe or Pharisee?

Christian righteousness exceeds theirs, first, in the extent of it. Most of the Pharisees, though they were rigorously exact in many things, yet were emboldened by the traditions of the elders to dispense with others of equal importance. Thus they were extremely punctual in keeping the fourth commandment—they would not even 'rub an ear of corn'[103] on the sabbath day—but not at all in keeping the third, making little account of light, or even false swearing. So that their righteousness was partial—whereas the righteousness of a real Christian is universal. He does not observe one, or some parts, of the law of God, and neglect the rest; but keeps all his commandments, loves them all, values them above gold or precious stones.[104]

11. It may be indeed that some of the scribes and Pharisees

101   See Matt. 6:6, 18.
102   See Matt. 12:41, 42; Luke 11:31, 32.
103   Cf. Luke 6:1.
104   See Rev. 17:4; 18:16.

endeavoured to keep all the commandments, and consequently
were, as touching the righteousness of the law, that is, according
to the letter of it, blameless.[105] But still the righteousness of a
Christian exceeds all this righteousness of a scribe or Pharisee by
5 fulfilling the spirit as well as the letter of the law, by inward as
well as outward obedience. In this, in the spirituality of it, it
admits of no comparison. This is the point which our Lord has so
largely proved in the whole tenor of this discourse. Their
righteousness was external only; Christian righteouness is in the
10 inner man. The Pharisee 'cleansed the outside of the cup and the
platter';[106] the Christian is clean within. The Pharisee laboured to
present God with a good life; the Christian with a holy heart. The
one shook off the leaves, perhaps the fruits of sin; the other 'lays
the axe to the root',[107] as not being content with the outward form
15 of godliness,[108] how exact soever it be, unless the life, the spirit,
the power of God unto salvation,[109] be felt in the inmost soul.

Thus to do no harm, to do good, to attend the ordinances of
God (the righteousness of a Pharisee)[110] are all external; whereas,
on the contrary, poverty of spirit, mourning, meekness, hunger
20 and thirst after righteousness, the love of our neighbour, and
purity of heart[111] (the righteousness of a Christian) are all internal.
And even peacemaking (or doing good) and suffering for
righteousness' sake,[112] stand entitled to the blessings annexed to
them only as they imply these inward dispositions, as they spring
25 from, exercise, and confirm them. So that whereas the
righteousness of the scribes and Pharisees was external only, it
may be said in some sense that the righteousness of a Christian is
internal only—all his actions and sufferings being as nothing in
themselves, being estimated before God only by the tempers from
30 which they spring.

12. Whosoever therefore thou art who bearest the holy and

---

[105] See Phil. 3:6.
[106] Cf. Matt. 23:25; Luke 11:39.
[107] Cf. Luke 3:9.
[108] See 2 Tim. 3:5.
[109] Rom. 1:16.
[110] But also the righteousness of the *General Rules* of the Methodist Societies (as also above, IV.7; and No. 22, 'Sermon on the Mount, II', II.4 and n.). What were the Methodists supposed to make of these denigrations of their disciplinary rules? This much at least: Wesley himself was clear of any charge of 'mere moralism' and wanted none of it for his people.
[111] See Matt. 5:3-8.
[112] See Matt. 5:9-10.

venerable name of a Christian, see, first, that thy righteousness fall not short of the righteousness of the scribes and Pharisees. Be not thou 'as other men are'.[113] Dare to stand alone, to be

> Against example, singularly good![114]

If thou 'follow a multitude' at all it must be 'to do evil'.[115] Let not 5 custom or fashion[116] be thy guide, but reason and religion. The practice of others is nothing to thee: 'Every man must give an account of himself to God.'[117] Indeed if thou canst save the soul of another, do; but at least save one, thy own. Walk not in the path of death because it is broad, and many walk therein.[118] Nay, by this 10 very token thou mayst know it. Is the way wherein thou now walkest a broad, well-frequented, fashionable way? Then it infallibly leads to destruction. O be not thou 'damned for company'[119]—'cease from evil';[120] fly from sin as from the face of a serpent.[121] At least, do no harm. 'He that committeth sin is of the 15 devil.'[122] Be not thou found in that number. Touching outward sins, surely the grace of God is even now sufficient for thee. 'Herein' at least 'exercise thyself to have a conscience void of offence toward God and toward men.'[123]

Secondly, let not thy righteousness fall short of theirs with 20 regard to the ordinances of God. If thy labour or bodily strength will not allow of thy fasting 'twice in the week', however, deal faithfully with thy own soul, and fast as often as thy strength will

---

[113] Luke 18:11.

[114] Apparently a conflation of two lines of verse from Samuel Wesley, Jun.: the first from 'The Battle of the Sexes', st. xxxv, l. 3 ('Against example resolutely good'), in *Poems on Several Occasions* (1736; hereafter cited as *Poems*), p. 38; the second from 'To the Memory of the Rt. Rev. Francis Gastrell', l. 226 ('Adverse against a world, and singly good'), *ibid.*, p. 135. But see also, Milton, *Paradise Regained*, iii.57 ('His lot who dares be singularly good'). Cf. No. 88, 'On Dress', §23.

[115] Exod. 23:2.

[116] Cf. above, IV.3 and n.

[117] Cf. Rom. 14:12.

[118] See Matt. 7:13.

[119] Mark Le Pla, *A Paraphrase on the Song of the Three Children, op. cit.*, st. 12:

> You who from vice, as from infection fly,
> And care not to be damned for company.

See also Wesley, *Collection of Moral and Sacred Poems*, II.132.

[120] Cf. Isa. 1:16.   [121] See Rev. 12:14.

[122] 1 John 3:8.

[123] Cf. Acts 24:16.

permit. Omit no public, no private opportunity of pouring out thy soul in prayer. Neglect no occasion of eating that bread and drinking that cup which is the communion of the body and blood of Christ.[124] Be diligent in searching the Scriptures: read as thou

5 mayst, and meditate therein day and night. Rejoice to embrace every opportunity of hearing 'the word of reconciliation'[125] declared by the 'ambassadors of Christ, the stewards of the mysteries of God'.[126] In using all the means of grace, in a constant and careful attendance on every ordinance of God, live up to (at

10 least, till thou canst go beyond) 'the righteousness of the scribes and Pharisees'.

Thirdly, fall not short of a Pharisee in doing good. Give alms of all thou dost possess. Is any hungry? Feed him. Is he athirst? Give him drink. Naked? Cover him with a garment.[127] If thou hast this

15 world's goods, do not limit thy beneficence to a scanty proportion. Be merciful to the uttermost of thy power. Why not, even as this Pharisee? 'Now make thyself friends', while the time is, 'of the mammon of unrighteousness,[128] that when thou failest', when this earthly tabernacle is dissolved, 'they may receive thee into

20 everlasting habitations.'[129]

13. But rest not here. Let thy 'righteousness exceed the righteousness of the scribes and Pharisees'. Be not thou content to 'keep the whole law, and offend in one point'.[130] 'Hold thou fast all his commandments, and all false ways do thou utterly abhor.'[131]

25 Do all the things whatsoever he hath commanded, and that with all thy might. Thou canst do all things through Christ strengthening thee,[132] though without him thou canst do nothing.[133]

Above all, let thy righteousness exceed theirs in the purity and

30 spirituality of it. What is the exactest form of religion to thee? The most perfect outside righteousness? Go thou higher and deeper

---

[124] See 1 Cor. 11:28; 10:16.

[125] 2 Cor. 5:19.

[126] Cf. 1 Cor. 4:1.

[127] See Matt. 25:35-38.

[128] An anticipation of the third of Wesley's three rules for 'the use of money'; cf. below, Nos. 28, 'Sermon on the Mount, VIII', §§23-28, and 50, 'The Use of Money', III.1-7 and n.

[129] Cf. Luke 16:9.

[130] Jas. 2:10.

[131] Cf. Ps. 119:128 (BCP).

[132] See Phil. 4:13.

[133] See John 15:5.

than all this. Let thy religion be the religion of the heart.[134] Be thou poor in spirit; little and base and mean and vile in thy own eyes; amazed and humbled to the dust at the love of God which is in Christ Jesus thy Lord.[135] Be serious: let the whole stream of thy thoughts, words, and works, be such as flows from the deepest 5 conviction that thou standest on the edge of the great gulf, thou and all the children of men, just ready to drop in, either into everlasting glory, or everlasting burnings.[136] Be meek: let thy soul be filled with mildness, gentleness, patience, long-suffering toward all men; at the same time that all which is in thee is athirst 10 for God, the living God,[137] longing to awake up after his likeness, and to be satisfied with it. Be thou a lover of God and of all mankind. In this spirit do and suffer all things. Thus 'exceed the righteousness of the scribes and Pharisees', and thou shalt be 'called great in the kingdom of heaven'.   15

[134] Cf. JWJ, Aug. 12, 1771: 'The very thing which Mr. Stinstra calls fanaticism is no other than heart religion—in other words, "righteousness and peace and joy in the Holy Ghost" '; cf. John Stinstra, *A Pastoral Letter Against Fanaticism* . . . (1753). See also Wesley's letter to James Knox, May 30, 1765: 'You saw what heart-religion meant, and the gate of it, justification. . . . True religion is not a negative or an external thing, but the life of God in the soul of man [Scougal], the image of God stamped upon the heart.'

Cf. above, Wesley's Preface, §6, (p. 106); and Nos. 7, 'The Way to the Kingdom', I.6; 16, 'The Means of Grace', I.5; 33, 'Sermon on the Mount, XIII', III.12; 36, 'The Law Established through Faith, II', I.5; 37, 'The Nature of Enthusiasm', §§1, 10; 102, 'Of Former Times', §11. Cf. also *Remarks on a Defence of . . . Aspasio Vindicated:* 'the grand points—the religion of the heart and salvation by faith.' See also Harald Höffding, *A History of Modern Philosophy,* I.252.

[135] See Rom. 8:39.

[136] See Isa. 33:14; cf. Jonathan Edwards, 'Sinners in the Hands of an Angry God' (ten years earlier), *Works* (1843), IV.318-19. For the phrase, 'everlasting glory', cf. BCP, Burial (481), as well as the Collect for St. Peter's Day (312). It occurs frequently in Kempis, *Imitation,* e.g., IV. iii. 2. Cf. above, III.6 and n.; and Nos. 26, 'Sermon on the Mount, VI', III.8; and 33, 'Sermon on the Mount, XIII', III.12.

[137] See Ps. 42:2.

Upon our Lord's Sermon on the Mount

Discourse the Sixth

Matthew 6:1-15

Take heed that ye do not your alms before men, to be seen of them;
5 *otherwise ye have no reward of your Father which is in heaven.*

Therefore when thou dost thine alms, do not sound a trumpet before thee, as the hypocrites do in the synagogues and in the streets, that they may have praise of men. Verily, I say unto you, they have their reward.

But when thou dost alms, let not thy left hand know what thy right
10 *hand doth: that thine alms may be in secret; and thy Father which seeth in secret, himself shall reward thee openly.*

And when thou prayest, thou shalt not be as the hypocrites are; for they love to pray standing in the synagogues and in the corners of the streets, that they may be seen of men. Verily I say unto you, They have
15 *their reward.*

But thou, when thou prayest, enter into thy closet, and when thou hast shut the door, pray to thy Father which is in secret; and thy Father which seeth in secret, he shall reward thee openly.

But when ye pray, use not vain repetitions, as the heathen do; for they
20 *think that they shall be heard for their much speaking.*

Be not ye therefore like unto them; for your Father knoweth what things ye have need of before you ask him.

After this manner therefore pray ye: Our Father, which art in heaven, hallowed be thy name. Thy kingdom come. Thy will be done on
25 *earth as it is in heaven. Give us this day our daily bread. And forgive us our trespasses, as we forgive them that trespass against us. And lead us not into temptation, but deliver us from evil. For thine is the kingdom and the power and the glory, for ever and ever. Amen.*

For if ye forgive men their trespasses, your heavenly Father will also
30 *forgive you.*

But if ye forgive not men their trespasses, neither will your Father forgive your trespasses.

1. In the preceding chapter our Lord has described inward religion in its various branches. He has laid before us those

dispositions of soul which constitute real Christianity: the inward tempers contained in that holiness 'without which no man shall see the Lord'[1]—the affections which, when flowing from their proper fountain, from a living faith in God through Christ Jesus, are intrinsically and essentially good, and acceptable to God. He proceeds to show in this chapter how all our actions likewise, even those that are indifferent in their own nature, may be made holy and good and acceptable to God, by a pure and holy intention. Whatever is done without this, he largely declares, is of no value before God. Whereas whatever outward works are thus consecrated to God, they are, in his sight, of great price.

2. The necessity of this purity of intention[2] he shows, first, with regard to those which are usually accounted religious actions, and indeed are such when performed with a right intention. Some of these are commonly termed works of piety; the rest, works of charity or mercy.[3] Of the latter sort he particularly names almsgiving; of the former, prayer and fasting. But the directions given for these are equally to be applied to every work, whether of charity or mercy.

I. 1. And, first, with regard to works of mercy.[4] 'Take heed', saith he, 'that ye do not your alms before men, to be seen of them. Otherwise ye have no reward of your Father which is in heaven.' 'That ye do not your alms'—although this only is named, yet is every work of charity included, everything which we give, or speak, or do, whereby our neighbour may be profited, whereby another man may receive any advantage, either in his body or soul. The feeding the hungry, the clothing the naked, the entertaining or assisting the stranger, the visiting those that are sick or in prison,[5] the comforting the afflicted, the instructing the ignorant, the reproving the wicked, the exhorting and encouraging the well-doer; and if there be any other work of mercy, it is equally included in this direction.

---

[1] Heb. 12:14.
[2] The central theme in the holy living tradition; cf. Kempis, II. vi. 3: 'Man considereth the *deeds*, but God weigheth the *intention*.' Cf. also Nos. 12, 'The Witness of Our Own Spirit', §11 and n.; 30, 'Sermon on the Mount, X', §§1-2; 104, 'On Attending the Church Service', §30; 105, 'On Conscience', I.3; 146, 'The One Thing Needful', III.3; 148, 'A Single Intention', I.4. See also *An Address to the Clergy*, I.3(1); and Wesley's *Notes* on Matt. 6:1, 22.
[3] See above, No. 14, *The Repentance of Believers*, I.13 and n.; see also, below, II.1.
[4] *Ibid.*   [5] See Matt. 25:35-38.

2. 'Take heed that ye do not your alms before men, to be seen of them.' The thing which is here forbidden is not barely the doing good in the sight of men. This circumstance alone, that others see what we do, makes the action neither worse nor better, but the doing it before men, 'to be seen of them'—with this view, from this intention only. I say, 'from this intention only', for this may in some cases be a part of our intention; we may design that some of our actions should be seen, and yet they may be acceptable to God. We may intend that our 'light' should 'shine before men', when our conscience bears us witness in the Holy Ghost that our ultimate end in designing they should 'see our good works' is 'that they may glorify our Father which is in heaven'.[6] But take heed that ye do not the least thing with a view to your own glory. Take heed that a regard to the praise of men[7] have no place at all in your works of mercy. If ye seek your own glory, if you have any design to gain the honour that cometh of men, whatever is done with this view is nothing worth; it is not done unto the Lord; he accepteth it not; 'ye have no reward' for this 'of our Father which is in heaven'.

3. 'Therefore when thou dost thine alms, do not sound a trumpet before thee, as the hypocrites do in the synagogues and in the streets, that they may have praise of men.' The word 'synagogue' does not here mean a place of worship, but any place of public resort, such as the market-place or exchange.[8] It was a common thing among the Jews who were men of large fortunes, particularly among the Pharisees, to cause a trumpet to be sounded before them in the most public parts of the city when they were about to give any considerable alms. The pretended reason for this was to call the poor together to receive it, but the

---

[6] Cf. Matt. 5:16.

[7] A reflection of Wesley's fear of vanity and 'thirst for fame'; cf. No. 14, *The Repentance of Believers*, I.7 and n.

[8] An unconventional opinion echoing an obscure controversy marked by the studies of Carolus Signorius (1524–84) and Campegius Vitringa (1659–1722). For the view here offered by Wesley, and the views of Hugo Grotius and the majority of the Christian and Jewish commentators of the period on the other side; *viz.*, that synagogues were 'pre-eminently places of worship', see *Encyclopedia Judaica*, XV. 587, 594. Wesley's view would be urged again a century later by the eminent Hungarian rabbi, Leopold Löw, who believed that the synagogue (lit. 'the place of meeting') was designed as a public centre for many functions in the community: the study of Torah, liturgical worship, and social intercourse. For a contemporary discussion of this problem, cf. I. Sonne, 'Synagogue', in *The Abingdon Dictionary of the Bible*.

real design that they might have praise of men. But be not thou like unto them. Do not thou cause a trumpet to be sounded before thee. Use no ostentation in doing good. Aim at the honour which cometh of God only. 'They' who seek the praise of men 'have their reward.' They shall have no praise of God.[9]

4. 'But when thou dost alms, let not thy left hand know what thy right hand doth.' This is a proverbial expression, the meaning of which is, do it in as secret a manner as is possible: as secret as is consistent with the doing it at all (for it must not be left undone: omit no opportunity of doing good, whether secretly or openly) and with the doing it in the most effectual manner. For here is also an exception to be made. When you are fully persuaded in your own mind that by your not concealing the good which is done either you will yourself be enabled, or others excited, to do the more good, then you may not conceal it: then let your light appear, and 'shine to all that are in the house'.[10] But unless where the glory of God and the good of mankind oblige you to the contrary, act in as private and unobserved a manner as the nature of the thing will admit: 'That thy alms may be in secret; and thy Father which seeth in secret, he shall reward thee openly.' Perhaps in the present world—many instances of this stand recorded in all ages— but infallibly in the world to come, before the general assembly of men and angels.

II. 1. From works of charity or mercy our Lord proceeds to those which are termed works of piety.[11] 'And when thou prayest', saith he, 'thou shalt not be as the hypocrites are; for they love to pray standing in the synagogues, and in the corners of the streets, that they may be seen of men.' 'Thou shalt not be as the hypocrites are.' Hypocrisy then, or insincerity, is the first thing we are to guard against in prayer. Beware not to speak what thou dost not mean. Prayer is the lifting up of the heart to God: all words of prayer without this are mere hypocrisy. Whenever therefore thou attemptest to pray, see that it be thy one design to commune with God, to lift up thy heart to him, to pour out thy soul before him. Not 'as the hypocrites', who 'love', or are wont, 'to pray standing in the synagogues', the exchange or market-places, 'and in the corners of the streets', wherever the most people are, 'that they

---

[9] Cf. No. 4, *Scriptural Christianity*, I.6 and n.

[10] Cf. Matt. 5:15.

[11] Cf. I.1, above, and No. 14, *The Repentance of Believers*, I.13 and n.

may be seen of men': this was the sole design, the motive and end, of the prayers which they there repeated. 'Verily I say unto you, They have their reward.' They are to expect none from your Father which is in heaven.

5 2. But it is not only the having an eye to the praise of men which cuts us off from any reward in heaven, which leaves us no room to expect the blessing of God upon our works, whether of piety or mercy; purity of intention is equally destroyed by a view to any temporal reward whatever. If we repeat our prayers, if we attend
10 the public worship of God, if we relieve the poor, with a view to gain or interest, it is not a whit more acceptable to God than if it were done with a view to praise.[12] Any temporal view, any motive whatever on this side eternity, any design but that of promoting the glory of God, and the happiness of men for God's sake, makes
15 every action, however fair it may appear to men, an abomination unto the Lord.

3. 'But when thou prayest, enter into thy closet; and when thou hast shut the door, pray to thy Father which is in secret.' There is a time when thou art openly to glorify God, to pray and praise him
20 in the great congregation.[13] But when thou desirest more largely and more particularly to make thy requests known unto God,[14] whether it be in the evening or in the morning or at noonday,[15] 'enter into thy closet and shut the door.' Use all the privacy thou canst. (Only leave it not undone, whether thou hast any closet, any
25 privacy, or no. Pray to God if it be possible when none seeth but he; but if otherwise, pray to God.) Thus 'pray to thy Father which is in secret;' pour out thy heart before him; 'and thy Father which seeth in secret, he shall reward thee openly.'

4. 'But when ye pray', even in secret, 'use not vain repetitions,
30 as the heathen do.' Μὴ βατταλογήσητε.[16] Do not use abundance of words without any meaning. Say not the same thing over and over again; think not the fruit of your prayers depends on the length of them, like the heathens; 'for they think they shall be heard for their much speaking.'

---

[12] See 1 Cor. 13:2-3.
[13] See Ps. 40:9, etc.
[14] See Phil. 4:6.
[15] See Ps. 55:17 (BCP).
[16] Cf. Blackall, Discourse XLVII, *Works*, I.479-82, on 'Vain Repetitions' or 'Battology'; note the extent to which Blackall has already made the very same distinctions that Wesley repeats here. In III.1, below, he will recommend the *Lord's* Prayer, however, as worthy of constant repetition.

The thing here reproved is not simply the length, no more than the shortness of our prayers. But, first, length without meaning: the speaking much, and meaning little or nothing; the using (not all repetitions; for our Lord himself prayed thrice, repeating the same words; but) vain repetitions, as the heathens did, reciting the names of their gods over and over; as they do among Christians (vulgarly so called) and not among the Papists only, who say over and over the same string of prayers without ever feeling what they speak. Secondly, the thinking to be heard for our much speaking: the fancying God measures prayers by their length, and is best pleased with those which contain the most words, which sound the longest in his ears. These are such instances of superstition and folly as all who are named by the name of Christ should leave to the heathens, to them on whom the glorious light of the gospel hath never shined.[17]

5. 'Be not ye therefore like unto them.' Ye who have tasted of the grace of God in Christ Jesus are throughly convinced 'your Father knoweth what things ye have need of before ye ask him.' So that the end of your praying is not to inform God, as though he knew not your wants already; but rather to inform yourselves, to fix the sense of those wants more deeply in your hearts, and the sense of your continual dependence on him who only is able to supply all your wants. It is not so much to move God—who is always more ready to give than you to ask—as to move yourselves, that you may be willing and ready to receive the good things he has prepared for you.[18]

III. 1. After having taught the true nature and ends of prayer our Lord subjoins an example of it: even that divine form of prayer which seems in this place to be proposed by way of pattern chiefly, as the model and standard of all our prayers—'After this manner therefore pray ye.' Whereas elsewhere he enjoins the use of these very words: 'He said unto them, When ye pray, say. . . .'[a]

2. We may observe in general concerning this divine prayer, first, that it contains all we can reasonably or innocently pray for. There is nothing which we have need to ask of God, nothing which we can ask without offending him, which is not included

[a] Luke 11:2.

---

[17] See 2 Cor. 4:4.
[18] See 1 Cor. 2:9.

either directly or indirectly in this comprehensive form. Secondly, that it contains all we can reasonably or innocently desire; whatever is for the glory of God, whatever is needful or profitable, not only for ourselves, but for every creature in heaven
5 and earth. And indeed our prayers are the proper test of our desires, nothing being fit to have a place in our desires which is not fit to have a place in our prayers; what we may not pray for, neither should we desire. Thirdly, that it contains all our duty to God and man; whatsoever things are pure and holy,[19] whatsoever
10 God requires of the children of men, whatsoever is acceptable in his sight,[20] whatsoever it is whereby we may profit our neighbour, being expressed or implied therein.

3. It consists of three parts: the preface, the petitions, and the doxology or conclusion.[21] The preface, 'Our Father which art in
15 heaven', lays a general foundation for prayer; comprising what we must first know of God before we can pray in confidence of being heard. It likewise points out to us all those tempers with which we are to approach to God, which are most essentially requisite if we desire either our prayers or our lives should find acceptance with
20 him.

4. 'Our *Father.*' If he is a Father, then he is good, then he is loving to his children. And here is the first and great reason for prayer. God is willing to bless; let us ask for a blessing. 'Our *Father*'—our Creator, the Author of our being; he who raised us
25 from the dust of the earth, who breathed into us the breath of life, and we became living souls.[22] But if he made us, let us ask, and he will not withhold any good thing from the work of his own hands. 'Our *Father*'—our Preserver, who day by day sustains the life he has given; of whose continuing love we now and every moment
30 receive life and breath and all things. So much the more boldly let us come to him, and 'we shall find mercy and grace to help in time of need.'[23] Above all, the Father of our Lord Jesus Christ, and of all that believe in him; who justifies us 'freely by his grace, through the redemption that is in Jesus';[24] who hath 'blotted out

[19] See Phil. 4:8.
[20] See Ps. 19:14.
[21] Cf. Blackall, *Works*, I.502: 'In [the Lord's Prayer] there are three principal parts: the Preface, the Body of the Prayer and the Conclusion. . . . The conclusion contains a Doxology, or a solemn recognition of the power and majesty of God.'
[22] See Gen. 2:7.
[23] Cf. Heb. 4:16.
[24] Rom. 3:24.

all our sins',[25] 'and healed all our infirmities';[26] who hath received us for 'his own children, by adoption and grace',[27] 'and because we are sons, hath sent forth the Spirit of his Son into our hearts, crying Abba, Father;'[28] 'who hath begotten us again of incorruptible seed',[29] and 'created us anew in Christ Jesus'.[30] Therefore we know that he heareth us always; therefore we 'pray' to him 'without ceasing'.[31] We pray, because we love. And 'we love him, because he first loved us.'[32]

5. '*Our* Father'—not *mine* only who now cry unto him; but *ours*, in the most extensive sense. The 'God and Father of the spirits of all flesh';[33] the Father of angels and men (so the very heathens acknowledged him to be, Πατὴρ ἀνδρῶν τε θεῶν τε),[34] the Father of the universe, of all the families both in heaven and earth. Therefore with him there is no respect of persons.[35] He loveth all that he hath made. He 'is loving unto every man, and his mercy is over all his works'.[36] And 'the Lord's delight is in them that fear him, and put their trust in his mercy;'[37] in them that trust in him through the Son of his love, knowing they are 'accepted in the Beloved'.[38] But 'if God so loved us, we ought also to love one another.'[39] Yea, all mankind; seeing 'God so loved the world, that he gave his only-begotten Son', even to die the death, that they 'might not perish, but have everlasting life'.[40]

6. 'Which art in heaven'—high and lifted up; God over all, blessed for ever.[41] Who, sitting on the circle of the heavens,[42] beholdeth all things both in heaven and earth. Whose eye pervades the whole sphere of created being; yea, and of uncreated

---

[25] Cf. Ps. 51:9.   [26] Cf. Ps. 103:3 (BCP).

[27] BCP, Collects, Sunday after Christmas.

[28] Cf. Gal. 4:6.

[29] Cf. 1 Pet. 1:3, 23.

[30] Cf. Eph. 2:10.

[31] 1 Thess. 5:17.

[32] 1 John 4:19.

[33] Cf. 2 Cor. 1:2, etc.; see also Num. 16:22; 27:16.

[34] Cf. Homer, *Iliad*, i. 544 ('father of men and gods'); see also Hesiod, *Works and Days*, l. 59.

[35] See Acts 10:34 and 1 Pet. 1:17.

[36] Ps. 145:9 (BCP).

[37] Ps. 147:11 (BCP).

[38] Eph. 1:6.

[39] 1 John 4:11.

[40] John 3:16.

[41] See Rom. 9:5.

[42] See Wisd. 13:2.

night;[43] unto whom 'known are all his works',[44] and all the works of every creature, not only 'from the beginning of the world'[45] (a poor, low, weak translation) but ἀπ' αἰῶνος, from all eternity, from everlasting to everlasting. Who constrains the host of
5 heaven, as well as the children of men, to cry out with wonder and amazement, O the depth!—'the depth of the riches both of the wisdom and of the knowledge of God!'[46] 'Which art in heaven'—the Lord and ruler of all, superintending and disposing all things; who art the King of kings and Lord of lords,[47] the
10 blessed and only potentate;[48] who art strong and girded about with power,[49] doing whatsoever pleaseth thee! The Almighty, for whensoever thou willest, to do is present with thee.[50] 'In heaven'—eminently there. Heaven is thy throne, the place where thine honour particularly dwelleth. But not there alone; for thou
15 fillest heaven and earth, the whole expanse of space. Heaven and earth are full of thy glory. Glory be to thee, O Lord, most high![51]

Therefore should we 'serve the Lord with fear, and rejoice unto him with reverence'.[52] Therefore should we think, speak, and act, as continually under the eye, in the immediate presence
20 of the Lord, the King.

7. 'Hallowed be thy name.' This is the first of the six petitions whereof the prayer itself is composed.[53] The name of God is God himself—the nature of God so far as it can be discovered to man. It means, therefore, together with his existence, all his attributes
25 or perfections—his eternity, particularly signified by his great and incommunicable name Jehovah, as the Apostle John translates it, τὸ Ἀ καὶ τὸ Ω, ἀρχὴ καὶ τέλος, ὁ ὢν καὶ ὁ ἦν καὶ ὁ ἐρχόμενος,[54] 'the Alpha and Omega, the Beginning and the End; he which is, and which was, and which is to come.' His
30 'fullness of being',[55] denoted by his other great name, 'I am that I

---

[43] Wesley uses this phrase at least four times in the sermons, three times without quotation marks. See the versification of Ps. 46 [by Henry Pitt?] in John's letter to his brother Samuel, Apr. 4, 1726, later printed in *A Collection of Psalms and Hymns* (1737), p. 4, and *Hymns and Sacred Poems* (1739), p. 135: '. . . the pathless realms . . . of uncreated night'. Cf. also *AM*, 1779, 157; and Milton, *Paradise Lost*, ii. 149-50. Cf. Nos. 118, 'On the Omnipresence of God', I.1; 120, 'The Unity of the Divine Being', §6; and 132, 'On Faith, Heb.11:1', §7.

[44] Cf. Acts 15:18 and *Notes, loc. cit.*

[45] *Ibid.*   [46] Rom. 11:33.   [47] Rev. 19:16.

[48] 1 Tim. 6:15.   [49] Ps. 65:6.   [50] Cf. Phil. 2:13.

[51] BCP, Communion, Sanctus.   [52] Ps.2:11 (BCP).

[53] Bengel, *Gnomon*, reckons seven petitions in the Prayer; Poole, *Annotations*, Henry, *Exposition*, and Blackall, list only six.

[54] Cf. Rev. 21:6.   [55] Cf. Eph. 3:19; Col. 2:9.

am;'[56] his omnipresence;—his omnipotence;—who is indeed the only agent in the material world, all matter being essentially dull and inactive,[57] and moving only as it is moved by the finger of God.[58] And he is the spring of action in every creaturè, visible and invisible, which could neither act nor exist without the continued influx and agency of his almighty power;—his wisdom, clearly deduced from the things that are seen, from the goodly order of the universe;—his Trinity in Unity and Unity in Trinity, discovered to us in the very first line of his Written Word, אלהים ברא[59]—literally 'the Gods created', a plural noun joined with a verb of the singular number; as well as in every part of his subsequent revelations, given by the mouth of all his holy prophets and apostles;—his essential purity and holiness;—and above all his love, which is the very brightness of his glory.[60]

In praying that God, or his 'name', may 'be hallowed' or glorified, we pray that he may be known, such as he is, by all that are capable thereof, by all intelligent beings, and with affections suitable to that knowledge: that he may be duly honoured and feared and loved by all in heaven above and in the earth beneath;[61] by all angels and men, whom for that end he has made capable of knowing and loving him to eternity.

8. 'Thy kingdom come.' This has a close connection with the preceding petition. In order that the name of God may be hallowed, we pray that his kingdom, the kingdom of Christ, may come. This kingdom then comes to a particular person when he 'repents and believes the gospel';[62] when he is taught of God not only to know himself but to know Jesus Christ and him crucified.[63] As 'this is life eternal, to know the only true God, and Jesus Christ whom he hath sent',[64] so it is the kingdom of God begun below, set up in the believer's heart. The Lord God omnipotent then reigneth,[65] when he is known through Christ Jesus. He taketh unto himself his mighty power; that he may subdue all things unto himself.[66] He goeth on in the soul conquering and to conquer,[67]

[56] Exod. 3.14
[57] Cf. No. 15, *The Great Assize*, III.3.
[58] See Exod. 8:19; Luke 11:20.
[59] Gen. 1:1; note that all of Wesley's Hebrew quotations are unpointed.
[60] Heb. 1:3.
[61] Josh. 2:11. Cf. Blackall, *Works*, I.514-17, clearly a fruitful source for what Wesley has compressed here.
[62] Cf. Mark 1:15. [63] See 1 Cor. 2:2. [64] Cf. John 17:3.
[65] See Rev. 19:6. [66] Phil. 3:21. [67] See Rev. 6:2.

till he hath put all things under his feet, till 'every thought' is 'brought into captivity to the obedience of Christ'.[68]

When therefore God shall 'give his Son the heathen for his inheritance, and the utmost parts of the earth for his possession';[69]
5 when 'all kingdoms shall bow before him, and all nations shall do him service';[70] when 'the mountain of the Lord's house', the church of Christ, 'shall be established in the top of the mountains';[71] when 'the fullness of the Gentiles shall come in, and all Israel shall be saved'[72]—then shall it be seen that 'the Lord
10 is King, and hath put on glorious apparel',[73] appearing to every soul of man as King of kings, and Lord of lords.[74] And it is meet for all those who 'love his appearing'[75] to pray that he would hasten the time; that this his kingdom, the kingdom of grace, may come quickly, and swallow up all the kingdoms of the earth; that
15 all mankind receiving him for their king, truly believing in his name, may be filled with righteousness and peace and joy,[76] with holiness and happiness, till they are removed hence into his heavenly kingdom, there to reign with him for ever and ever.

For this also we pray in those words, 'Thy kingdom come.' We
20 pray for the coming of his everlasting kingdom, the kingdom of glory in heaven, which is the continuation and perfection of the kingdom of grace on earth. Consequently this, as well as the preceding petition, is offered up for the whole intelligent creation, who are all interested in this grand event, the final
25 renovation of all things by God's putting an end to misery and sin, to infirmity and death, taking all things into his own hands, and setting up the kingdom which endureth throughout all ages.

Exactly answerable to this are those awful words in the prayer at the burial of the dead: 'Beseeching thee, that it may please thee,
30 of thy gracious goodness, shortly to accomplish the number of thine elect, and to hasten thy kingdom; that we, with all those that are departed in the true faith of thy holy name, may have our perfect consummation and bliss, both in body and soul, in thy everlasting glory.'[77]

---

[68] Cf. 2 Cor. 10:5.
[69] Ps. 2:8 (BCP).
[70] Ps. 72:11 (BCP).
[71] Isa. 2:2.
[72] Cf. Rom. 11:25-26.
[73] Ps. 93:1 (BCP).
[74] Rev. 19:16, etc.
[75] 2 Tim. 4:8.
[76] Rom. 14:17.
[77] BCP, Burial (481); note how later Prayer Books have altered this; see also No. 25, 'Sermon on the Mount, V', IV.13 and n.

9. 'Thy will be done on earth,[78] as it is in heaven.' This is the necessary and immediate consequence wherever the kingdom of God is come; wherever God dwells in the soul by faith, and Christ reigns in the heart by love.

It is probable many, perhaps the generality of men, at the first 5 view of these words are apt to imagine they are only an expression of, or petition for, resignation; for a readiness to suffer the will of God, whatsoever it be concerning us. And this is unquestionably a divine and excellent temper, a most precious gift of God. But this is not what we pray for in this petition, at least not in the chief 10 and primary sense of it. We pray, not so much for a passive as for an active conformity to the will of God in saying, 'Thy will be done on earth as it is done in heaven.'

How is it done by the angels of God in heaven? Those who now circle his throne rejoicing? They do it *willingly;* they love his 15 commandments, and gladly hearken to his words. It is their meat and drink to do his will;[79] it is their highest glory and joy. They do it *continually;* there is no interruption in their willing service. They rest not day nor night,[80] but employ every hour (speaking after the manner of men—otherwise our measures of duration, days and 20 nights and hours, have no place in eternity)[81] in fulfilling his commands, in executing his designs, in performing the counsel of his will. And they do it *perfectly.* No sin, no defect belongs to angelic minds. It is true, 'the stars are not pure in his sight,'[82] even the morning stars that sing together before him.[83] 'In his sight', 25 that is, in comparison of him, the very angels are not pure. But this does not imply that they are not pure *in themselves.* Doubtless they are; they are without spot and blameless. They are altogether devoted to his will, and perfectly obedient in all things.

If we view this in another light, we may observe the angels of 30 God in heaven do *all* the will of God. And they do nothing else,

---

[78] Note Wesley's punctuation of this phrase, thus accenting the petition that God's will should 'be done *on earth*' as it is, of course, in heaven. For this, he has the authority of the AV and the 1662 BCP. Law's *Serious Call, (Works,* IV.47), follows the AV and the BCP. Blackall, *Works,* I.532, follows the punctuation of the Bishops' Bible: 'thy will be done, [as well] in earth, as it is in heaven.' But see John Norris, *Practical Discourses,* the last of which is entitled, 'Concerning Doing God's Will on Earth . . .'. Wesley may have had Norris's description of 'angelic obedience' here in mind.

[79] See John 4:34.

[80] Rev. 4:8.

[81] Cf. No. 54, 'On Eternity', §§5-8.

[82] Job 25:5.

[83] See Job 38:7.

nothing but what they are absolutely assured is his will. Again, they do all the will of God *as* he willeth, in the manner which pleases him, and no other. Yea, and they do this only *because* it is his will; for this and no other reason.

5   10. When therefore we pray that the 'will of God' may 'be done on earth as it is in heaven', the meaning is that all the inhabitants of the earth, even the whole race of mankind, may do the will of their Father which is in heaven as *willingly* as the holy angels; that these may do it *continually*, even as they, without any interruption

10 of their willing service. Yea, and that they may do it *perfectly;* that 'the God of peace, through the blood of the everlasting covenant, may make them perfect in every good work to do his will, and work in them all which is well-pleasing in his sight'.[84]

In other words, we pray that we, and all mankind, may do the

15 whole will of God in all things; and nothing else, not the least thing but what is the holy and acceptable will of God.[85] We pray that we may do the whole will of God *as* he willeth, in the manner that pleases him; and lastly, that we may do it *because* it is his will; that this may be the sole reason and ground, the whole and only

20 motive, of whatsoever we think, or whatsoever we speak, or do.

11. 'Give us this day our daily bread.' In the three former petitions we have been praying for all mankind. We come now more particularly to desire a supply for our own wants. Not that we are directed, even here, to confine our prayer altogether to

25 ourselves; but this and each of the following petitions may be used for the whole church of Christ upon earth.

By 'bread' we may understand all things needful, whether for our souls or bodies: $\tau\grave{\alpha}\ \pi\rho\grave{o}s\ \zeta\omega\grave{\eta}\nu\ \kappa\alpha\grave{\iota}\ \epsilon\grave{v}\sigma\acute{\epsilon}\beta\epsilon\iota\alpha\nu$,[86] 'the things pertaining to life and godliness'. We understand not barely the

30 outward bread, what our Lord terms 'the meat which perisheth'; but much more the spiritual bread, the grace of God, the food 'which endureth unto everlasting life'.[87] It was the judgment of many of the ancient Fathers that we are here to understand the sacramental bread also;[88] daily received in the beginning by the

35 whole church of Christ, and highly esteemed, till the love of many

[84] Cf. Heb. 13:20-21.   [85] See Rom. 12:1, 2.
[86] 2 Pet. 1:3.   [87] John 6:27.
[88] Wesley was well aware, with Blackall (*Works*, I.542), that 'concerning the strict and proper meaning of this word, $\grave{\epsilon}\pi\iota o\acute{v}\sigma\iota os$, there is a great dispute among the critics.' Origen, *On Prayer*, ch. 27, defines it as 'supersubstantial'; Tertullian, *On Prayer*, §6, and Cyprian, *On the Lord's Prayer*, §18, speak of *panem quotidianum* ('daily bread'). Ambrose, *On the Sacraments*, 5.4.24 (Migne, *PL*, XVI. 452A) is more emphatic than any of the other

waxed cold,[89] as the grand channel whereby the grace of his Spirit was conveyed to the souls of all the children of God.

'Our daily bread.' The word we render 'daily' has been differently explained by different commentators. But the most plain and natural sense of it seems to be this, which is retained in almost all translations, as well ancient as modern: what is sufficient for this day, and so for each day as it succeeds.

12. 'Give us;' for we claim nothing of right, but only of free mercy. We deserve not the air we breathe, the earth that bears, or the sun that shines upon us. All our desert, we own, is hell.[90] But God loves us freely. Therefore we ask him to *give* what we can no more *procure* for ourselves than we can *merit* it at his hands.

Not that either the goodness or the power of God is a reason for us to stand idle. It is his will that we should use all diligence in all things, that we should employ our utmost endeavours, as much as if our success were the natural effect of our own wisdom and strength. And then, as though we had done nothing, we are to depend on him, the giver of every good and perfect gift.[91]

'This day;' for we are to take no thought for the morrow.[92] For this very end has our wise Creator divided life into these little portions of time, so clearly separated from each other; that we might look on every day as a fresh gift of God, another life which we may devote to his glory; and that every evening may be as the close of life, beyond which we are to see nothing but eternity.

13. 'And forgive us our trespasses, as we forgive them that trespass against us.' As nothing but sin can hinder the bounty of God from flowing forth upon every creature, so this petition naturally follows the former; that all hindrances being removed, we may the more clearly trust in the God of love for every manner of thing which is good.

Latin Fathers that ἐπιουσία means 'supernatural' *(supersubstantialis)*. Jerome reports that the now lost 'Gospel according to the Hebrews' had ἡ ἐπιουσία ἤμερα ('sufficient for tomorrow'); cf. Gerhard Kittel, ed., *Theological Dictionary of the New Testament* (Grand Rapids, Mich., Wm. B. Eerdmans Publishing Company, 1964), II. 591. Cyril of Jerusalem, *Catechetical Lectures*, XXIII. 15, comes close to Wesley's point, but Chrysostom interprets it more mundanely as 'bread enough for one day' (*Homilies . . . on the Gospel of St. Matthew*, XIX. 8). In this he is supported by a fifth century papyrus in which ἐπιούσιος occurs with the sense of 'daily ration'; cf. W. M. Flinders Petrie, *Hawara, Biahmu, Arsinoë* (London, Field and Tuer, 1889), pp. 33-35.

[89] See Matt. 24:12.

[90] Cf. 'Hymns for a Protestant' (1745, at end of *A Word to a Protestant, Bibliog,* No. 113, Vol. 14 of this edn.), *Poet. Wks.,* VI.2, Hymn I, l. 40: 'My whole desert is hell.'

[91] Jas. 1:17.   [92] See Matt. 6:34.

'Our trespasses.' The word properly signifies 'our debts'.[93] Thus our sins are frequently represented in Scripture; every sin laying us under a fresh debt to God, to whom we already owe, as it were, ten thousand talents. What then can we answer when he
5 shall say, 'Pay me that thou owest'?[94] We are utterly insolvent; we have nothing to pay; we have wasted all our substance.[95] Therefore if he deal with us according to the rigour of his law, if he exact what he justly may, he must command us to be 'bound hand and foot',[96] 'and delivered over to the tormentors'.[97]
10 Indeed we are already bound hand and foot by the chains of our own sins. These, considered with regard to ourselves, are chains of iron and fetters of brass. They are wounds wherewith the world, the flesh, and the devil, have gashed and mangled us all over. They are diseases that drink up our blood and spirits, that
15 bring us down to the chambers of the grave.[98] But considered, as they are here, with regard to God, they are debts, immense and numberless. Well, therefore, seeing we have nothing to pay, may we cry unto him that he would 'frankly forgive'[99] us all.

The word translated 'forgive' implies either to forgive a debt,
20 or to unloose a chain. And if we attain the former, the latter follows of course: if our debts are forgiven, the chains fall off our hands. As soon as ever, through the free grace of God in Christ, we 'receive forgiveness of sins', we receive likewise 'a lot among those which are sanctified, by faith which is in him'.[100] Sin has lost
25 its power; it has no dominion over those who 'are under grace',[101] that is, in favour with God. As 'there is now no condemnation for them that are in Christ Jesus',[102] so they are freed from sin as well as from guilt. 'The righteousness of the law is fulfilled in them', and they 'walk not after the flesh, but after the Spirit'.[103]

---

[93] The only two instances of ὀφείλημα in the New Testament are here and in Rom. 4:4 (where, clearly, the single meaning is 'debt'). Bengel, *Gnomon*, translated 'our debts' without further comment; Blackall had translated and interpreted it as 'trespasses'; Poole *(Annotations)* and Henry *(Exposition)* had understood the phrase as 'our debts', but meaning 'our sins'; cf. Wesley's *Notes*. He could have joined Blackall's concluding prayer on this point: 'We humbly beseech thee to give us thy grace, that we may never forfeit our title to thy pardon upon our repentance, by denying pardon, by bearing hatred or malice, or a spirit of revenge to any who trespass against us' (cf. *Works*, I.556).

[94] Matt. 18:24, 28.　　　　　　　　　　　　[95] See Luke 15:13.
[96] John 11:44.　　　　　　　　　　　　　　[97] Cf. Matt. 18:34.
[98] Cf. Prov. 7:27.　　　　　　　　　　　　　[99] Cf. Luke 7:42.
[100] Cf. Acts 26:18.　　　　　　　　　　　　[101] Rom. 6:14, 15.
[102] Cf. Rom. 8:1.
[103] Cf. Rom. 8:4.

14. 'As we forgive them that trespass against us.' In these words our Lord clearly declares both on what condition and in what degree or manner we may look to be forgiven of God. All our trespasses and sins are forgiven us *if* we forgive, and *as* we forgive, others. First, God forgives us *if* we forgive others. This is a point 5 of the utmost importance. And our blessed Lord is so jealous lest at any time we should let it slip out of our thoughts that he not only inserts it in the body of his prayer, but presently after repeats it twice over: 'If', saith he, 'ye forgive men their trespasses, your heavenly Father will also forgive you. But if ye forgive not men 10 their trespasses, neither will your Father forgive your trespasses.'[b] Secondly, God forgives us *as* we forgive others. So that if any malice or bitterness, if any taint of unkindness or anger remains, if we do not clearly, fully, and from the heart, forgive all men their trespasses, we far cut short the forgiveness of our own. God 15 cannot clearly and fully forgive us. He may show us some degree of mercy. But we will not suffer him to blot out all our sins, and forgive all our iniquities.[104]

In the meantime, while we do not from our hearts forgive our neighbour his trespasses, what manner of prayer are we offering 20 to God whenever we utter these words? We are indeed setting God at open defiance: we are daring him to do his worst. 'Forgive us our trespasses, as we forgive them that trespass against us!' That is, in plain terms, 'Do not thou forgive us at all; we desire no favour at thy hands. We pray that thou wilt keep our sins in 25 remembrance, and that thy wrath may abide upon us.' But can you seriously offer such a prayer to God? And hath he not yet cast you quick into hell?[105] O tempt him no longer! Now, even now, by his grace, forgive as you would be forgiven! Now have compassion on thy fellow-servant, as God hath had and will have pity on thee! 30

15. 'And lead us not into temptation, but deliver us from evil.' 'Lead us not into temptation.' The word translated 'temptation' means trial of any kind.[106] And so the English word 'temptation' was formerly taken in an indifferent sense, although now it is usually understood of solicitation to sin.[107] St. James uses the 35

---

[b] [Matt. 6:] 14-15.

---

[104] See Jer. 18:23.   [105] Ps. 55:15 (AV).
[106] Cf. Blackall, *Works*, II.609: 'The word "temptation" signifies nothing else but only a trial or experiment made of any person to see what temper and disposition he is.'
[107] An echo of Johnson's definition: 'a solicitation to ill'.

word in both these senses: first in its general, then its restrained acceptation. He takes it in the former sense when he saith, 'Blessed is the man that endureth temptation; for when he is tried', or approved of God, 'he shall receive the crown of life.'ᶜ He
5 immediately adds, taking the word in the latter sense: 'Let no man say when he is tempted, I am tempted of God; for God cannot be tempted with evil, neither tempteth he any man. But every man is tempted, when he is drawn away of his own lust,' or desire, ἐξελκόμενος, drawn out of God, in whom alone he is safe, 'and
10 enticed', caught as a fish with a bait.¹⁰⁸ Then it is, when he is thus 'drawn away and enticed', that he properly 'enters into temptation'. The temptation covers him as a cloud; it overspreads his whole soul. Then how hardly shall he escape out of the snare! Therefore we beseech God 'not to lead us into temptation', that is
15 (seeing 'God tempteth no man'¹⁰⁹) not to suffer us to be led into it. 'But deliver us from evil'; rather 'from the evil one'; ἀπὸ τοῦ πονηροῦ.¹¹⁰ Ὁ πονηρός is unquestionably 'the wicked one',¹¹¹ emphatically so called, the prince and god of this world,¹¹² who works with mighty power in the children of disobedience.¹¹³ But
20 all those who are the children of God by faith are delivered out of his hands. He may fight against them; and so he will. But he cannot conquer, unless they betray their own souls. He may torment for a time, but he cannot destroy; for God is on their side, who will not fail in the end to 'avenge his own elect, that cry unto
25 him day and night':¹¹⁴ 'Lord, when we are tempted, suffer us not to enter into temptation. Do thou make a way for us to escape, that the wicked one touch us not.'¹¹⁵

16. The conclusion of this divine prayer,¹¹⁶ commonly called

ᶜ [Jas.] 1:12.

---

¹⁰⁸ Cf. Jas. 1:13-14. See also No. 19, 'The Great Privilege of those that are Born of God', III.1.
¹⁰⁹ Cf. Jas. 1:13.   ¹¹⁰ Matt. 6:13.
¹¹¹ 1 John 2:13, 14; 3:12; 5:18. Cf. No. 12, 'The Witness of Our Own Spirit', §10 and n.
¹¹² See John 12:31; 14:30; 16:11.   ¹¹³ Eph. 2:2.
¹¹⁴ Cf. Luke 18:7.   ¹¹⁵ Cf. 1 John 5:18.
¹¹⁶ Note that Wesley adds the doxology here, as in the AV and in Tyndale, Cranmer, and Geneva, but not in the *TR*, nor in Wycliffe or Douai. Blackall, *Works*, II.616-26, takes the doxology for granted, as had the BCP and Anglicans generally. It is, of course, lacking from the earliest MSS of St. Matthew; Origen (*On Prayer*, ch. 30, §3) seems unaware of any such addition. In the Latin Mass, the Paternoster ends with *Libera nos a malo*, with the succeeding collect picking up the phrase and repeating it. One may, therefore, wonder if Wesley knew the actual text of the Roman Mass.

the doxology, is a solemn thanksgiving, a compendious acknowledgement of the attributes and works of God. 'For thine is the kingdom'— the sovereign right of all things that are or ever were created; yea, thy kingdom is an everlasting kingdom, and thy dominion endureth throughout all ages.[117] 'The power'— the executive power whereby thou governest all things in thy everlasting kingdom, whereby thou dost whatsoever pleaseth thee, in all places of thy dominion. 'And the glory'— the praise due from every creature for thy power, and the mightiness of thy kingdom, and for all thy wondrous works which thou workest from everlasting, and shalt do, world without end, 'for ever and ever! Amen.'[118] So be it!

I believe it will not be unacceptable to the serious reader, to subjoin

A
Paraphrase
on the
Lord's Prayer

I

Father of all, whose powerful voice
    Called forth this universal frame,
Whose mercies over all rejoice,
    Through endless ages still the same:
Thou by thy word upholdest all;
    Thy bounteous LOVE to all is showed,
Thou hear'st thy every creature call,
    And fillest every mouth with good.

II

In heaven thou reign'st, enthroned in light,
    Nature's expanse beneath thee spread;
Earth, air, and sea before thy sight,
    And hell's deep gloom are open laid.
Wisdom, and might, and love are thine,
    Prostrate before thy face we fall,
Confess thine attributes divine,
    And hail the sovereign Lord of all.

---

[117] See Dan. 4:3.
[118] Matt. 6:13. See No. 145, 'In Earth as in Heaven' (a fragment) on Matt. 6:10 (1734).

III

Thee, sovereign Lord, let all confess
    That moves in earth, or air, or sky,
Revere thy power, thy goodness bless,
    Tremble before thy piercing eye.
All ye who owe to him your birth
    In praise your every hour employ;
Jehovah reigns! Be glad, O earth,
    And shout, ye morning stars, for joy.

IV

Son of thy sire's eternal love,
    Take to thyself thy mighty power;
Let all earth's sons thy mercy prove,
    Let all thy bleeding grace adore.
The triumphs of thy love display;
    In every heart reign thou alone,
Till all thy foes confess thy sway,
    And glory ends what grace begun.

V

Spirit of grace, and health, and power,
    Fountain of light and love below,
Abroad thine healing influence shower,
    O'er all the nations let it flow.
Inflame our hearts with perfect love,
    In us the work of faith fulfil;
So not heaven's hosts shall swifter move
    Than we on earth to do thy will.

VI

Father, 'tis thine each day to yield
    Thy children's wants a fresh supply;
Thou cloth'st the lilies of the field,
    And hearest the young ravens cry.
On thee we cast our care; we live
    Through thee, who know'st our every need;
O feed us with thy grace, and give
    Our souls this day the living bread.

VII

Eternal, spotless Lamb of God,
  Before the world's foundation slain,
Sprinkle us ever with thy blood,
  O cleanse and keep us ever clean.
To every soul (all praise to thee!)   5
  Our bowels of compassion more:
And all mankind by this may see
  God is in us; for God is love.

VIII

Giver and Lord of life, whose power
  And guardian care for all are free;   10
To thee in fierce temptation's hour
  From sin and Satan let us flee.
Thine, Lord, we are, and ours thou art;
  In us be all thy goodness showed;
Renew, enlarge, and fill our heart   15
  With peace, and joy, and heaven, and God.

IX

Blessing and honour, praise and love,
  Co-equal, co-eternal Three,
In earth below, in heaven above,
  By all thy works be paid to Thee.   20
Thrice holy, thine the kingdom is,
  The power omnipotent is thine;
And when created nature dies,
  Thy never-ceasing glories shine.[119]

---

[119] *Hymns and Sacred Poems* (1742), pp. 275-77, there entitled, 'The Lord's Prayer Paraphrased'.

Upon our Lord's Sermon on the Mount

Discourse the Seventh

Matthew 6:16-18

Moreover, when ye fast, be not as the hypocrites, of a sad countenance;
5 *for they disfigure their faces, that they may appear unto men to fast.*
Verily I say unto you, They have their reward.
But thou, when thou fastest, anoint thy head, and wash thy face;
That thou appear not unto men to fast, but unto thy Father which is
in secret; and thy Father, which seeth in secret, shall reward thee
10 *openly.*

1. It has been the endeavour of Satan from the beginning of the world to put asunder what God had joined together;[1] to separate inward from outward religion; to set one of these at variance with the other. And herein he has met with no small success among 15 those who were 'ignorant of his devices'.[2]

Many in all ages, having a zeal for God, but not according to knowledge,[3] have been strictly attached to the 'righteousness of the law',[4] the performance of outward duties, but in the meantime wholly regardless of inward righteousness, 'the righteousness 20 which is of God by faith'.[5] And many have run into the opposite extreme, disregarding all outward duties, perhaps even 'speaking evil of the law, and judging the law',[6] so far as it enjoins the performance of them.

2. It is by this very device of Satan that faith and works have 25 been so often set at variance with each other. And many who had a real zeal for God have for a time fallen into the snare on either hand. Some have magnified faith to the utter exclusion of good

---

[1] See Matt. 19:6; Mark 10:9.
[2] 2 Cor. 2:11. Cf. No. 42, 'Satan's Devices'.
[3] Rom. 10:2.
[4] Rom. 2:26; 8:4.
[5] Phil. 3:9. Cf. No. 24, 'Sermon on the Mount, IV', III.1 and n.
[6] Cf. Jas. 4:11.

works, not only from being the cause of our justification (for we know that man is 'justified freely by the redemption which is in Jesus')[7] but from being the necessary fruit of it—yea, from having any place in the religion of Jesus Christ. Others, eager to avoid this dangerous mistake, have run as much too far the contrary way; and either maintained that good works were the cause, at least the previous condition, of justification, or spoken of them as if they were all in all, the whole religion of Jesus Christ.

3. In the same manner have the end and the means of religion been set at variance with each other. Some well-meaning men have seemed to place all religion in attending the prayers of the church, in receiving the Lord's Supper, in hearing sermons, and reading books of piety; neglecting meantime the end of all these, the love of God and their neighbour. And this very thing has confirmed others in the neglect, if not contempt, of the ordinances of God, so wretchedly abused to undermine and overthrow the very end they were designed to establish.

4. But of all the means of grace there is scarce any concerning which men have run into greater extremes than that of which our Lord speaks in the above-mentioned words; I mean religious fasting. How have some exalted this beyond all Scripture and reason![8] And others utterly disregarded it, as it were revenging themselves by undervaluing as much as the former had overvalued it. Those have spoken of it as if it were all in all; if not the end itself, yet infallibly connected with it: these as if it were just nothing, as if it were a fruitless labour which had no relation at all thereto. Whereas it is certain the truth lies between them both.[9] It is not all; nor yet is it nothing. It is not the end; but it is a

---

[7] Rom. 3:24.

[8] Wesley's own asceticism, on this and other points, was moderate by comparison with the rigorous fasts of the Carthusians, Cistercians, and Carmelites, or such ascetics as Gregory Lopez, Peter of Alcántara, not to mention the innumerable 'Fast Days' proclaimed by the Puritan Parliaments (1642–59). He would also have known the curious justification for abstinence from *meat* on fast days provided by the Elizabethan Homily 'On Fasting', Pt. II (*Homilies*, p. 257): *viz.*, to encourage *the fishing industry* and for 'the sooner reducing of victuals to a more moderate price, to the better sustenance of the poor'.

[9] There is nothing more characteristically Anglican in Wesley than his avoidance, as here, of all stark disjunctions. Before him, Peter Heylyn had complained of 'how much truth was lost on both extremes and yet how easy to be found by those who went a middle way in search thereof. . .'; cf. *Historia Quinquarticularis* (1659), p. 508. Thomas Fuller had prayed that 'we may hit the golden mean and endeavour to avoid all extremes: the fanatic Anabaptists on the one side and the fiery zeal of the Jesuits on the other, so that we may be true Protestants or, which is far better, real Christians indeed' (*Good Thoughts in Bad Times; Mixt Contemplations in Better Times* [1645]; cf. *Thoughts and Contemplations*, ed.

precious means thereto, a means which God himself has ordained; and in which therefore, when it is duly used, he will surely give us his blessing.

In order to set this in the clearest light I shall endeavour to show, first, what is the nature of fasting, and what the several sorts and degrees thereof; secondly, what are the reasons, grounds, and ends of it; thirdly, how we may answer the most plausible objections against it; and fourthly, in what manner it should be performed.[10]

I. 1. I shall endeavour to show, first, what is the nature of fasting, and what the several sorts and degrees thereof. As to the nature of it, all the inspired writers, both in the Old Testament and the New, take the word to 'fast' in one single sense, for not to eat, to abstain from food. This is so clear that it would be labour lost to quote the words of David, Nehemiah, Isaiah, and the prophets which followed, or of our Lord and his apostles; all agreeing in this: that to fast is not to eat for a time prescribed.

2. To this other circumstances were usually joined by them of old, which had no necessary connection with it. Such were the neglect of their apparel, the laying aside those ornaments which they were accustomed to wear; the putting on mourning, the strewing ashes upon their head, or wearing sackcloth next their skin. But we find little mention made in the New Testament of any of these indifferent circumstances; nor does it appear that any stress was laid upon them by the Christians of the purer ages, however some penitents might voluntarily use them as outward signs of inward humiliation. Much less did the apostles or the Christians cotemporary with them beat or tear their own flesh. Such 'discipline' as this was not unbecoming the priests or worshippers of Baal. The gods of the heathens were but devils; and it was doubtless acceptable to their devil-god when his priests

James O. Wood [London, SPCK, 1964], p. 124). Wesley had himself borrowed William Tilly's dictum that 'the truth lies in the middle way between both these [antithetical] opinions;' cf. Tilly's Sermon VIII, in *Sermons*, p. 228.

In Wesley this principle of a third alternative may be seen further in Nos. 32, 'Sermon on the Mount, XII', II.5; 70, 'The Case of Reason Impartially Considered', §§1-5, II.10; 83, 'On Patience', §3; 97, 'On Obedience to Pastors', §2; 120, 'The Unity of the Divine Being', §25. Cf. also *Notes* on John 2:24; his letter to John Bennet, June 1744; to Miss March, Mar. 29, 1760; to Alexander Knox, Aug. 29, 1777. See also his Preface to *A Concise History of England* (*Bibliog*, No. 357, Vol. 15 of this edn.).

[10] Cf. the heads of Blackall's very similar Discourse LVII, 'Of the Nature and Duty of Fasting', in *Works*, II. 627-28, *et. seq.*

'cried aloud, and cut themselves after their manner, till the blood gushed out upon them'.[a] But it cannot be pleasing to him, nor become his followers, who 'came not to destroy men's lives, but to save them'.[11]

3. As to the degrees or measures of fasting, we have instances of some who have fasted several days together. So Moses, Elijah, and our blessed Lord, being endued with supernatural strength for that purpose, are recorded to have fasted without intermission 'forty days and forty nights'.[12] But the time of fasting more frequently mentioned in Scripture is one day, from morning till evening. And this was the fast commonly observed among the ancient Christians. But beside these they had also their half-fasts (*semi-jejunia*, as Tertullian styles them[13]) on the fourth and sixth days of the week (Wednesday and Friday) throughout the year; on which they took no sustenance till three in the afternoon, the time when they returned from the public service.[14]

4. Nearly related to this is what our Church seems peculiarly to mean by the term 'abstinence'; which may be used when we cannot fast entirely, by reason of sickness or bodily weakness. This is the eating little; the abstaining in part; the taking a smaller quantity of food than usual.[15] I do not remember any scriptural instance of this. But neither can I condemn it, for the Scripture does not. It may have its use, and receive a blessing from God.

5. The lowest kind of fasting, if it can be called by that name, is the abstaining from pleasant food. Of this we have several instances in Scripture, besides that of Daniel and his brethren: who from a peculiar consideration, namely, that they might 'not defile themselves with the portion of the king's meat, nor with the wine which he drank' (a 'daily provision' of which 'the king had

---

[a] 1 Kgs. 18:28.

---

[11] Cf. Luke 9:56.

[12] For Moses, see Exod. 34:38 and Deut. 9:9, 18; for Elijah, see 1 Kgs. 19:8; for Jesus, see Matt. 4:1-2. Cf. Poole, *Annotations* (Matt. 4:2): '. . . The like did Moses before the Law, Elijah *under* the law. Christ does the same in the beginning of the Gospel . . .'; see also Henry, *Exposition*. 'Christ . . . "fasted forty days and forty nights" in compliance with the type and example of Moses, the great Lawgiver, and of Elias, the great Reformer, of the Old Testament.'

[13] Cf. Tertullian, *On Fasting*, ch. ix, 'Partial Fasts and Xerophagies'.

[14] *Ibid.* ch. x, 'The Stations, and Hours of Prayer.' Wesley and the Holy Club had stressed stationary fasts (as distinguished from movable ones); he wrote a short piece on them—see Vol. 12 of this edn.

[15] Here, Chambers's *Cyclopaedia* and Wesley agree; Johnson's *Dictionary* ignores any such distinction (*viz.*, that 'abstaining' is less rigorous than 'fasting').

appointed for them'), 'requested' and obtained of 'the prince of the eunuchs' 'pulse to eat, and water to drink'.[b] Perhaps from a mistaken imitation of this might spring the very ancient custom of abstaining from flesh and wine during such times as were set
5 apart for fasting and abstinence; if it did not rather arise from a supposition that these were the most pleasant food, and a belief that it was proper to use what was least pleasing at those times of solemn approach to God.

6. In the Jewish church there were some *stated* fasts. Such was
10 the fast of the seventh month, appointed by God himself to be observed by all Israel under the severest penalty. 'The Lord spake unto Moses, saying, [. . .] on the tenth day of the seventh month there shall be a day of atonement; [. . .] and ye shall afflict your souls . . . to make an atonement for you before the Lord your
15 God. For whatsoever soul it be that shall not be afflicted in that same day, he shall be cut off from among his people.'[c] In after ages several other stated fasts were added to these. So mention is made by the prophet Zechariah of the fast, not only 'of the seventh', but also of 'the fourth, of the fifth, and of the tenth
20 month'.[d]

In the ancient Christian church there were likewise stated fasts, and those both annual and weekly. Of the former sort was that before Easter, observed by some for eight and forty hours; by others, for an entire week; by many for two weeks; taking no
25 sustenance till the evening of each day. Of the latter, those of the fourth and sixth days of the week, observed (as Epiphanius writes, remarking it as an undeniable fact) ἐν ὅλῃ τῇ οἰκουμένῃ—'in the whole habitable earth',[16] at least in every place where any

[b] Dan. 1:5, etc. [8, 12].
[c] Lev. 23:26-29.
[d] Zech. 8:19.

---

[16] This phrase appears, with slight variations, in Matt. 24:14; Acts 11:28; Rev. 3:10; and 16:14, but not, I think, in Epiphanius; cf. the latter's comments on the universality of catholic praxis in fasting in his *Against Seventy Heresies*, III. ii. 1104-6 ('*Expositio Fidei*', in Migne, *PG*, XLII. 826-28); but see also Migne, XLII. 353. In the Elizabethan Homily, 'Of Fasting', Pt. II (*Homilies*, p. 259), the phrase is credited to 'Eusebius, lib. 5, cap. 24' (actually it is V. 21: 1: '. . . peace embraced the churches throughout the whole world'); see also Eusebius, *Ecclesiastical History*, IV. 15: 15 ('the whole Catholic Church throughout the world . . .'); *The Didache*, 8; Tertullian, *Of Fasting*, ch. 2; Clement of Alexandria, *Stromateis*, VII. 12 (75.2).
Wesley also knew Claude Fleury, *An Historical Account of the Manners and Behaviour of the Christians* . . . ; cf. his extract of three of Fleury's chs. (viii-x, pp. 58-74) into ch. v, pp. 14-16 of his own *Manners* . . . (*Bibliog*, No. 157): 'The fasts of the ancients were either

Christians made their abode. The annual fasts in our Church are 'The forty days of Lent, the Ember days at the four seasons', the Rogation days, and the vigils or eves of several solemn festivals: the weekly, 'all Fridays in the year, except Christmas Day'.[17]

But beside those which were fixed, in every nation fearing God 5 there have always been occasional fasts appointed from time to time as the particular circumstances and occasions of each required. So when 'the children of Moab and the children of Ammon [. . .] came against Jehoshaphat to battle, [. . .] Jehoshaphat set himself to seek the Lord, and proclaimed a fast 10 throughout all Judah.'[e] And so 'in the fifth year of Jehoiakim the son of Josiah, in the ninth month', when they were afraid of the King of Babylon, the princes of Judah 'proclaimed a fast before the Lord to all the people of Jerusalem.'[f]

And in like manner particular persons who take heed unto their 15 ways, and desire to walk humbly and closely with God, will find frequent occasion for private seasons of thus afflicting their souls before their Father which is in secret. And it is to this kind of fasting that the directions here given do chiefly and primarily refer.

II. 1. I proceed to show, in the second place, what are the 20 grounds, the reasons, and ends of fasting.[18]

And first, men who are under strong emotions of mind, who are affected with any vehement passion such as sorrow or fear, are often swallowed up therein, and even 'forget to eat their bread'.[19]

---

[e] 2 Chr. 20:1, 3.
[f] Jer. 36:9.

---

yearly, as that of Lent, which they observed daily till six in the evening; or weekly, as those of Wednesday and Friday, which they observed till three in the afternoon. The yearly they kept in memory of their Lord, and in obedience to that command, "When the Bridegroom shall be taken away, then shall they fast in those days." And the weekly too were observed throughout the whole church in remembrance of his Passion: Because on Wednesday the Council against him was held, and on Friday he was put to death. During the whole Lent [they ate] only bread and water; some added thereto nuts and almonds. And others were obliged to use different food, according to their different infirmities. But all abstained from wine and delicate meats during whatever time was set apart for fasting, and spent as large a proportion of it as they could in retirement, reading, and prayer' (p. 14). Cf. also No. 122, 'Causes of the Inefficacy of Christianity', §14.

[17] Cf. BCP, 'Tables and Rules'. But see also Robert Nelson, *A Companion for the Festivals and Fasts of the Church of England* (1715; 19 edns. by 1748), p. xx.

[18] Blackall (*Works*, II. 628-29), speaks of 'the obligations [to fast], the good purposes fasting ministers to, and what good ends it serves for . . .'. The development of these points is similar, though not identical.

[19] Cf. Ps. 102:4.

At such seasons they have little regard for food, not even what is needful to sustain nature; much less for any delicacy or variety, being taken up with quite different thoughts. Thus when Saul said, 'I am sore distressed; for the Philistines make war against
5 me, and God is departed from me;' it is recorded, 'He had eaten no bread all the day, nor all the night.'ᵍ Thus those who were in the ship with St. Paul, 'when no small tempest lay upon them', and all 'hope that they should be saved was taken away', 'continued fasting, having taken nothing',ʰ no regular meal, for
10 fourteen days together. And thus 'David, [. . .] and all the men that were with him', when they heard that 'the people were fled from the battle, and that many of the people were fallen and dead, and Saul and Jonathan his son were dead also', 'mourned, and wept, and fasted until even, for Saul, and Jonathan, and for the
15 house of Israel.'ⁱ

Nay, many times they whose minds are deeply engaged are impatient of any interruption, and even loathe their needful food, as diverting their thoughts from what they desire should engross their whole attention. Even as Saul, when on the occasion
20 mentioned before he had 'fallen all along upon the earth, and there was no strength in him', yet 'said, I will not eat', till 'his servants, together with the woman, compelled him.'²⁰

2. Here then is the natural ground of fasting. One who is under deep affliction, overwhelmed with sorrow for sin, and a strong
25 apprehension of the wrath of God, would without any rule, without knowing or considering whether it were a command of God or not, 'forget to eat his bread', abstain not only from pleasant, but even from needful food. Like St. Paul, who after he was 'led into Damascus, was three days without sight, and neither
30 did eat nor drink'.ʲ

Yea, when the storm rose high, when 'an horrible dread overwhelmed'²¹ one who had long been without God in the world, his soul would 'loathe all manner of meat';²² it would be unpleasing and irksome to him. He would be impatient of
35 anything that should interrupt his ceaseless cry, 'Lord, save! or I perish.'²³

ᵍ 1 Sam. 28:15, 20.   ʰ Acts 27:[20,] 33.
ⁱ 2 Sam. 1:[11, 4,] 12.   ʲ Acts 9:[8,] 9.

---

²⁰ 1 Sam. 28:20, 23.   ²¹ Ps. 55:5 (BCP).
²² Cf. Ps. 107:18.   ²³ Cf. Matt. 8:25.

How strongly is this expressed by our Church in the first part of the homily on fasting!

> When men feel in themselves the heavy burden of sin, see damnation to be the reward of it, and behold with the eye of their mind the horror of hell, they tremble, they quake, and are inwardly touched with sorrowfulness of heart, and cannot but accuse themselves, and open their grief unto Almighty God, and call unto him for mercy. This being done seriously, their mind is so occupied (taken up), partly with sorrow and heaviness, partly with an earnest desire to be delivered from this danger of hell and damnation, that all desire of meat and drink is laid apart, and loathsomeness (or loathing) of all worldly things and pleasure cometh in place; so that nothing then liketh them more than to weep, to lament, to mourn, and both with words and behaviour of body to show themselves weary of life.[24]

3. Another reason or ground of fasting is this. Many of those who now fear God are deeply sensible how often they have sinned against him by the abuse of these lawful things. They know how much they have sinned by excess of food; how long they have transgressed the holy law of God with regard to temperance, if not sobriety too; how they have indulged their sensual appetites, perhaps to the impairing even their bodily health, certainly to the no small hurt of their soul. For hereby they continually fed and increased that sprightly folly, that airiness of mind, that levity of temper, that gay inattention to things of the deepest concern, that giddiness and carelessness of spirit, which were no other than drunkenness of soul, which stupefied all their noblest faculties, no less than excess of wine or strong drink. To remove therefore the effect they remove the cause; they keep at a distance from all excess. They abstain, as far as is possible, from what had wellnigh plunged them in everlasting perdition. They often wholly refrain; always take care to be sparing and temperate in all things.

4. They likewise well remember how fullness of bread[25] increased not only carelessness and levity of spirit but also foolish and unholy desires, yea, unclean and vile affections. And this experience puts beyond all doubt. Even a genteel, regular sensuality is continually sensualizing the soul, and sinking it into a level with the beasts that perish.[26] It cannot be expressed what an effect variety and delicacy of food have on the mind as well as the body; making it just ripe for every pleasure of sense, as soon as

---

[24] Cf. the Elizabethan Homily 'On Fasting', Pt. 1 (*Homilies*, p. 249); except for his two parenthetical asides, Wesley's only changes are slight omissions.

[25] Ezek. 16:49. [26] Ps. 49:12, 20.

opportunity shall invite. Therefore on this ground also every wise man will refrain his soul, and keep it low; will wean it more and more from all those indulgences of the inferior appetites which naturally tend to chain it down to earth, and to pollute as well as
5 debase it. Here is another perpetual reason for fasting: to remove the food of lust and sensuality, to withdraw the incentives of foolish and hurtful desires, of vile and vain affections.

5. Perhaps we need not altogether omit (although I know not if we should do well to lay any great stress upon it) another reason
10 for fasting which some good men have largely insisted on: namely, the punishing themselves for having abused the good gifts of God, by sometimes wholly refraining from them; thus exercising a kind of holy revenge upon themselves for their past folly and ingratitude, in turning the things which should have
15 been for their health into an occasion of falling. They suppose David to have had an eye to this when he said, 'I wept and chastened' or punished 'my soul with fasting;'[27] and St. Paul, when he mentions 'what revenge'[28] godly sorrow occasioned in the Corinthians.

20 6. A fifth and more weighty reason for fasting is that it is an help to prayer; particularly when we set apart larger portions of time for private prayer. Then especially it is that God is often pleased to lift up the souls of his servants above all the things of earth, and sometimes to rap them up, as it were, into the third heaven.[29] And
25 it is chiefly as it is an help to prayer that it has so frequently been found a means in the hand of God of confirming and increasing not one virtue, not chastity only (as some have idly imagined, without any ground either from Scripture, reason, or experience), but also seriousness of spirit, earnestness, sensibility, and
30 tenderness of conscience; deadness to the world, and consequently the love of God and every holy and heavenly affection.

7. Not that there is any natural or necessary connection between fasting and the blessings God conveys thereby. But he will have mercy as he will have mercy:[30] he will convey whatsoever
35 seemeth him good, by whatsoever means he is pleased to appoint.

---

[27] Ps. 69:10. [28] 2 Cor. 7:11.
[29] See 2 Cor. 12:2. *OED* (which cites this usage here) regards this as 'a back-formation from "rapt" ' and dates its first example from 1599. By Wesley's time, this spelling was rare; it so confused his printers that both Pine and Paramore spelled it 'wrap'; they also printed 'heavens' for 'heaven'.
[30] See Rom. 9:18.

And he hath in all ages appointed this to be a means of averting his wrath, and obtaining whatever blessings we from time to time stand in need of.

How powerful a means this is to avert the wrath of God we may learn from the remarkable instance of Ahab. 'There was none like him, who did sell himself'—wholly give himself up, like a slave bought with money—'to work wickedness.' Yet when he 'rent his clothes, and put sackcloth upon his flesh, and fasted, [. . .] and went softly, the word of the Lord came to Elijah, saying, Seest thou how Ahab humbleth himself before me? Because he humbleth himself before me, I will not bring the evil in his days.'[31]

It was for this end, to avert the wrath of God, that Daniel sought God 'with fasting and sackcloth and ashes'. This appears from the whole tenor of his prayer, particularly from the solemn conclusion of it: 'O Lord, according to all thy righteousnesses (or mercies), [. . .] let thy anger be turned away from thy holy mountain. . . . Hear the prayer of thy servant, and cause thy face to shine upon thy sanctuary that is desolate. . . . O Lord, hear! O Lord, forgive! O Lord, hearken and do, [. . .] for thine own sake.'[k]

8. But it is not only from the people of God that we learn when his anger is moved to seek him by fasting and prayer; but even from the heathens. When Jonah had declared, 'Yet forty days, and Nineveh shall be destroyed, the people of Nineveh proclaimed a fast, and put on sackcloth, from the greatest of them unto the least. For the King of Nineveh arose from his throne, and laid his robe from him, and covered him with sackcloth, and sat in ashes. And he caused it to be proclaimed and published through Nineveh, Let neither man nor beast, herd nor flock, taste anything. Let them not feed, nor drink water.' (Not that the beasts had sinned, or could repent; but that by their example man might be admonished, considering that for his sin the anger of God was hanging over all creatures.) 'Who can tell if God will turn and repent, and turn away from his fierce anger, that we perish not?' And their labour was not in vain. The fierce anger of God was turned away from them. 'God saw their works' (the fruits of that repentance and faith which he had wrought in them by his prophet), 'and God repented of the evil that he had said he would do unto them; and he did it not.'[l]

---

[k] Dan. 9:3, 16-19.   [l] Jonah 3:4-7, 9, 10.

---

[31] Cf. 1 Kgs. 21:25, 27-29.

9. And it is a means not only of turning away the wrath of God, but also of obtaining whatever blessings we stand in need of. So when the other tribes were smitten before the Benjamites, 'all the children of Israel went up unto the house of the Lord, and wept,
5 and fasted that day until even.' And then the Lord said, 'Go up again; for tomorrow I will deliver them into thine hand.'ᵐ So Samuel 'gathered all Israel together' when they were in bondage to the Philistines, 'and they fasted on that day before the Lord'. And when 'the Philistines drew near to battle against Israel, the
10 Lord thundered upon them with a great thunder, and discomfited them, and they were smitten before Israel.'ⁿ So Ezra: 'I proclaimed a fast at the river Ahava, that we might afflict ourselves before our God, to seek of him a right way for us, and for our little ones; . . . and he was entreated of us.'º So Nehemiah:
15 'I [. . .] fasted and prayed before the God of heaven, and said, [. . .] Prosper, I pray thee, thy servant this day, and grant him mercy in the sight of this man.'ᵖ And God granted him mercy in the sight of the king.

10. In like manner the apostles always³² joined fasting with
20 prayer when they desired the blessing of God on any important undertaking. Thus we read (Acts thirteen): 'There were in the church that was at Antioch certain prophets and teachers. . . . As they ministered to the Lord and fasted' (doubtless for direction in this very affair) 'the Holy Ghost said, Separate me Barnabas and
25 Saul for the work whereunto I have called them. And when they had' (a second time) 'fasted and prayed, and laid their hands on them, they sent them away.'�q

Thus also Paul and Barnabas themselves, as we read in the following chapter, when they 'returned again to Lystra, Iconium,
30 and Antioch, confirming the souls of the disciples; [. . .] and when they had ordained them elders in every church, and had prayed with fasting, commended them to the Lord.'ʳ

Yea, that blessings are to be obtained in the use of his means

---

ᵐ Judg. 20:26, 28.
ⁿ 1 Sam. 7:5, 6, 10.
º Ezra 8:21, 23.
ᵖ [Neh.] 1:4, 11.
q [Acts 13:] ver. 1-3.　　　　　　　　　　ʳ [Acts 14:] ver. [21-]23.

---

³² An inference from Matt. 17:21 (a verse missing from the best texts), Mark 9:29; Luke 2:37; Acts 14:23; 1 Cor. 7:5. Cf. *Notes* on Matt. 17:21.

which are no otherwise attainable our Lord expressly declares in his answer to his disciples, asking, 'Why could not we cast him out? Jesus said unto them, Because of your unbelief; for verily I say unto you, if ye have faith as a grain of mustard seed, ye shall say unto this mountain, Remove hence to yonder place, and it 5 shall remove; and nothing shall be impossible unto you. Howbeit, this kind' (of devils) 'goeth not out but by prayer and fasting'ˢ—these being the appointed means of attaining that faith whereby the very devils are subject unto you.

11. These were the *appointed* means; for it was not merely by 10 the light of reason, or of natural conscience (as it is called), that the people of God have been in all ages directed to use fasting as a means to these ends. But they have been from time to time taught it of God himself, by clear and open revelations of his will. Such is that remarkable one by the prophet Joel: 'Therefore thus saith the 15 Lord, Turn you unto me with all your heart, and with fasting, and with weeping, and with mourning. . . . Who knoweth if the Lord will return and repent, and leave a blessing behind him? [. . .] Blow the trumpet in Zion, sanctify a fast, call a solemn assembly. . . . Then will the Lord be jealous over his land, and 20 will spare his people. Yea, [. . .] I will send you corn and wine and oil. . . . I will no more make you a reproach among the heathen.'ᵗ

Nor are they only temporal blessings which God directs his people to expect in the use of these means. For at the same time that he promised to those who should seek him with fasting, and 25 weeping, and mourning, 'I will render you the [y]ears which the grasshopper hath eaten, the canker-worm, and the caterpillar, and the palmer-worm, my great army,' he subjoins: 'So shall ye eat and be satisfied, and praise the name of the Lord your God. . . . Ye shall also know that I am in the midst of Israel, and 30 that I am the Lord your God.'³³ And then immediately follows the great gospel promise: 'I will pour out my Spirit upon all flesh, and your sons and your daughters shall prophesy, your old men shall dream dreams, and your young men shall see visions. And also

---

ˢ Matt. 17:19-21.
ᵗ [Joel] 2:12, 14, 15, 18-19.

---

³³ Joel 2:25 (Geneva Bible). Wesley's MS must have read 'years', since he would have had no warrant, in the Hebrew text or any English translation, for 'ears'. But his first printer set it down as 'ears', and this was followed in every subsequent edition until 1811, when Joseph Benson corrected it silently.

upon the servants and upon the handmaids in those days will I pour out my Spirit.'[34]

12. Now whatsoever reasons there were to quicken those of old in the zealous and constant discharge of this duty, they are of equal force still to quicken us. But above all these we have a peculiar reason for being 'in fastings often',[35] namely the command of him by whose name we are called. He does not indeed in this place *expressly* enjoin either fasting, giving of alms, or prayer. But his directions how to fast, to give alms, and to pray, are of the same force with such injunctions. For the commanding us to do anything *thus* is an unquestionable command to do that thing; seeing it is impossible to perform it *thus* if it be not performed *at all*. Consequently the saying, Give alms, pray, fast in *such a manner*, is a clear command to perform all those duties; as well as to perform them in that *manner* which shall in no wise lose its reward.

And this is a still farther motive and encouragement to the performance of this duty; even the promise which our Lord has graciously annexed to the due discharge of it: 'Thy Father, which seeth in secret, shall reward thee openly.'[36] Such are the plain grounds, reasons, and ends of fasting; such our encouragement to persevere therein, notwithstanding abundance of objections which men, wiser than their Lord, have been continually raising against it.

III. 1. The most plausible of these I come now to consider. And, first, it has been frequently said, 'Let a Christian fast from sin, and not from food: this is what God requires at his hands.'[37] So he does; but he requires the other also. Therefore this ought to be done, and that not left undone.[38]

View your argument in its full dimensions, and you will easily judge of the strength of it:

> If a Christian ought to abstain from sin, then he ought not to abstain from food;

---

[34] Joel 2:25-29.

[35] 2 Cor. 11:27.

[36] Matt. 6:18. For other comments by Wesley on this point of 'commands', and 'covered promises', see above, No. 25, 'Sermon on the Mount, V', II.2 and n.

[37] Probably an echo of the Moravian rejection of fasting; cf. JWJ, Dec. 31, 1739. For more on the Anglican tradition on this point, cf. Robert Nelson, *Festivals and Fasts*, pp. 362-67.

[38] See Matt. 23:23, and III.2, below.

> But a Christian ought to abstain from sin;
> Therefore he ought not to abstain from food.

That a Christian ought to abstain from sin is most true. But how does it follow from hence that he ought not to abstain from food? Yea, let him do both the one and the other. Let him, by the 5 grace of God, always abstain from sin; and let him often abstain from food, for such reasons and ends as experience and Scripture plainly show to be answered thereby.

2. 'But is it not better' (as it has, secondly, been objected) 'to abstain from pride and vanity, from foolish and hurtful desires,[39] 10 from peevishness, and anger, and discontent, than from food?' Without question it is. But here again we have need to remind you of our Lord's words, 'These things ought ye to have done, and not to leave the other undone.'[40] And indeed the latter is only in order to the former; it is a means to that great end. We abstain from food 15 with this view, that by the grace of God, conveyed into our souls through this outward means, in conjunction with all the other channels of his grace which he hath appointed, we may be enabled to abstain from every passion and temper which is not pleasing in his sight. We refrain from the one that, being endued 20 with power from on high,[41] we may be able to refrain from the other. So that your argument proves just the contrary to what you designed. It proves that we ought to fast. For if we ought to abstain from evil tempers and desires, then we ought thus to abstain from food; since these little instances of self-denial are 25 the ways God hath[42] chose wherein to bestow that great salvation.

3. 'But we do not find it so in fact.' (This is a third objection.) 'We have fasted much and often. But what did it avail? We were not a whit better: we found no blessing therein. Nay, we have found it an hindrance rather than an help. Instead of preventing 30 anger, for instance, or fretfulness, it has been a means of increasing them to such a height that we could neither bear others nor ourselves.' This may very possibly be the case. 'Tis possible either to fast or pray in such a manner as to make you much worse than before; more unhappy, and more unholy. Yet the fault does 35 not lie in the means itself, but in the *manner* of using it. Use it still, but use it in a different manner. Do what God commands *as* he

---

[39] 1 Tim. 6:9.
[40] Matt. 23:23; Luke 11:42.
[41] See Luke 24:49. [42] Orig., 1748, 'has'.

commands it, and then doubtless his promise shall not fail; his blessing shall be withheld no longer; but 'when thou fastest in secret, he that seeth in secret shall reward thee openly.'

4. 'But is it not mere superstition' (so it has been, fourthly,
5 objected) 'to imagine that God regards such little things as these?' If you say it is, you condemn all the generation of God's children. But will you say, These were all weak superstitious men? Can you be so hardy as to affirm this both of Moses and Joshua, of Samuel and David, of Jehoshaphat, Ezra, Nehemiah, and all the
10 prophets? Yea, of a greater than all—the Son of God himself? It is certain both our Master and all these his servants did imagine that fasting is not a little thing, and that he who is higher than the highest doth regard it.[43] Of the same judgment, it is plain, were all his apostles, after they were 'filled with the Holy Ghost and with
15 wisdom'.[44] When they had 'the unction of the Holy One',[45] 'teaching' them 'all things',[46] they still 'approved themselves the ministers of God, by fastings', as well as 'by the armour of righteousness on the right hand and on the left'.[47] After 'the bridegroom was taken from them, then did they fast in those
20 days'.[48] Nor would they attempt anything (as we have seen above) wherein the glory of God was nearly concerned, such as the sending forth labourers into the harvest, without solemn fasting as well as prayer.

5. 'But if fasting be indeed of so great importance, and
25 attended with such a blessing, is it not best', say some, fifthly, 'to fast always? Not to do it now and then, but to keep a continual fast? To use as much abstinence at all times as our bodily strength will bear?' Let none be discouraged from doing this. By all means use as little and plain food, exercise as much self-denial herein at
30 all times, as your bodily strength will bear. And this may conduce, by the blessing of God, to several of the great ends above-mentioned. It may be a considerable help not only to chastity, but also to heavenly-mindedness; to the weaning your affections from things below, and setting them on things above.[49]
35 But this is not fasting, scriptural fasting; it is never termed so in all the Bible. It in some measure answers some of the ends thereof, but still it is another thing. Practise it by all means; but not so as

---

[43] See Eccles. 5:8.
[44] Cf. Acts 6:3.
[45] Cf. 1 John 2:20.
[46] Cf. John 14:26.
[47] Cf. 2 Cor. 6:4-5, 7.
[48] Cf. Mark 2:20.
[49] See Col. 3:2.

thereby to set aside a command of God, and an instituted means of averting his judgments, and obtaining the blessings of his children.

6. Use continually then as much abstinence as you please; which taken thus is no other than Christian temperance. But this need not at all interfere with your observing solemn times of fasting and prayer. For instance: your habitual abstinence or temperance would not prevent your fasting in secret if you was suddenly overwhelmed with huge sorrow and remorse, and with horrible fear and dismay. Such a situation of mind would almost constrain you to fast; you would loathe your dainty food; you would scarce endure even to take such supplies as were needful for the body, till God lifted you up 'out of the horrible pit, and set your feet upon a rock, and ordered your goings'.[50] The same would be the case if you was in agony of desire, vehemently wrestling with God for his blessing.[51] You would need none to instruct you not to eat bread till you had obtained the request of your lips.

7. Again, had you been at Nineveh when it was proclaimed throughout the city, 'Let neither man nor beast, herd nor flock, taste anything. Let them not feed, nor drink water; but let them cry mightily unto God:'[52] would your continual fast have been any reason for not bearing part in that general humiliation? Doubtless it would not. You would have been as much concerned as any other not to taste food on that day.

No more would abstinence, or the observing a continual fast, have excused any of the children of Israel from fasting on the tenth day of the seventh month, the great annual day of atonement. There was no exception for these in that solemn decree, 'Whatsoever soul it shall be that shall not be afflicted' (shall not fast) 'in that day, he shall be cut off from among his people.'[53]

Lastly, had you been with the brethren in Antioch at the time when they fasted and prayed before the sending forth of Barnabas and Saul, can you possibly imagine that your temperance or abstinence would have been a sufficient cause for not joining

---

[50] Cf. Ps. 40:2 (BCP).
[51] See Gen. 32:24-32.
[52] Jonah 3:7-8.
[53] Cf. Lev. 23:29.

therein? Without doubt, if you had not, you would soon have been cut off from the Christian community. You would have deservedly been cast out from among them 'as bringing confusion into the church of God'.[54]

5 IV. 1. I am, in the last place, to show in what manner we are to fast, that it may be an acceptable service unto the Lord. And, first, let it be done *unto the Lord*, with our eye singly fixed on him. Let our intention herein be this, and this alone, to glorify our Father which is in heaven; to express our sorrow and shame for our 10 manifold transgressions of his holy law; to wait for an increase of purifying grace, drawing our affections to things above; to add seriousness and earnestness to our prayers; to avert the wrath of God, and to obtain all the great and precious promises which he hath made to us in Christ Jesus.

15 Let us beware of mocking God, of turning our fast as well as our prayer into an abomination unto the Lord, by the mixture of any temporal view, particularly by seeking the praise of men. Against this our blessed Lord more peculiarly guards us in the words of the text: 'Moreover, when ye fast, be ye not as the 20 hypocrites' (such were too many who were called the people of God), 'of a sad countenance'; sour, affectedly sad, putting their looks into a peculiar form; 'for they disfigure their faces', not only by unnatural distortions, but also by covering them with dust and ashes, 'that they may appear unto men to fast'. This is their chief, 25 if not only design. 'Verily, I say unto you, they have their reward'—even the admiration and praise of men. 'But thou, when thou fastest, anoint thy head, and wash thy face'—do as thou art accustomed to do at other times—'that thou appear not unto men to fast' (let this be no part of thy intention: if they know it without 30 any desire of thine it matters not; thou art neither the better nor the worse), 'but unto thy Father which is in secret; and thy Father which seeth in secret shall reward thee openly.'[55]

2. But if we desire this reward, let us beware, secondly, of fancying we *merit* anything of God by our fasting. We cannot be 35 too often warned of this; inasmuch as a desire to 'establish our own righteousness',[56] to procure salvation of *debt*, and not of *grace*,

---

[54] Cf. Canon II of the Dedication Council of Antioch *('in Encaeniis')*, A.D. 341 Cf. No. 101, 'The Duty of Constant Communion', I.4 and n.
[55] Matt. 6:16-18.
[56] Cf. Rom. 10:3.

is so deeply rooted in all our hearts. Fasting is only a way which God hath ordained wherein we wait for his *unmerited* mercy; and wherein, without any desert of ours, he hath promised *freely* to give us his blessing.

3. Not that we are to imagine the performing the bare outward act will receive any blessing from God. 'Is it such a fast that I have chosen?' saith the Lord. 'A day for a man to afflict his soul? Is it to bow down his head as a bulrush, and to spread sackcloth and ashes under him?' Are these outward acts, however strictly performed, all that is meant by a man's 'afflicting his soul'? 'Wilt thou call this a fast, and an acceptable day to the Lord?'[57] No, surely. If it be a mere external service, it is all but lost labour. Such a performance may possibly afflict the body. But as to the soul, it profiteth nothing.

4. Yea, the body may sometimes be afflicted too much, so as to be unfit for the works of our calling. This also we are diligently to guard against; for we ought to preserve our health, as a good gift of God. Therefore care is to be taken, whenever we fast, to proportion the fast to our strength. For we may not offer God murder for sacrifice, or destroy our bodies to help our souls.

But at these solemn seasons we may, even in great weakness of body, avoid that other extreme for which God condemns those who of old expostulated with him for not accepting their fast. 'Wherefore have we fasted, say they, and thou seest not?' 'Behold, in the day of your fast you find pleasure,' saith the Lord.[58] If we cannot wholly abstain, we may at least abstain from pleasant food; and then we shall not seek his face in vain.

5. But let us take care to afflict our souls as well as our bodies.[59] Let every season, either of public or private fasting, be a season of exercising all those holy affections which are implied in a broken and contrite heart.[60] Let it be a season of devout mourning, of godly sorrow for sin: such a sorrow as that of the Corinthians, concerning which the Apostle saith, 'I rejoice, not that ye were made sorry, but that ye sorrowed to repentance. For ye were made sorry after a godly manner, that ye might receive damage by us in nothing.'[61] 'For godly sorrow' (ἡ [γὰρ] κατὰ θεὸν λύπη),

[57] Isa. 58:5.
[58] Isa. 58:3.
[59] See Lev. 23:27-32; Isa. 58:5.
[60] See Ps. 51:17.
[61] 2 Cor. 7:9.

the sorrow which is according to God, which is a precious gift of his Spirit, lifting the soul to God from whom it flows, 'worketh repentance to salvation, not to be repented of'.[62] Yea, and let our sorrowing after a godly sort work in us the same inward and
5 outward repentance; the same entire change of heart, renewed after the image of God,[63] in righteousness and true holiness;[64] and the same change of life, till we are holy as he is holy in all manner of conversation.[65] Let it work in us the same *carefulness* to be found in him without spot and blameless;[66] the same 'clearing of
10 ourselves'[67] by our lives rather than words, by our abstaining from all appearance of evil;[68] the same *indignation*, vehement abhorrence of every sin; the same *fear* of our own deceitful hearts; the same *desire* to be in all things conformed to the holy and acceptable will of God;[69] the same *zeal* for whatever may be a
15 means of his glory, and of our growth in the knowledge of our Lord Jesus Christ; and the same *revenge* against Satan and all his works, against all filthiness both of flesh and spirit.[u]

6. And with fasting let us always join fervent prayer, pouring out our whole souls before God, confessing our sins with all their
20 aggravations, humbling ourselves under his mighty hand,[70] laying open before him all our wants, all our guiltiness and helplessness. This is a season for enlarging our prayers, both in behalf of ourselves and of our brethren. Let us now bewail the sins of our people, and cry aloud for the city of our God: that the Lord may
25 build up Zion, and cause his face to shine on her desolations.[71] Thus we may observe the men of God in ancient times always joined prayer and fasting together; thus the apostles in all the instances cited above; and thus our Lord joins them in the discourse before us.

30 7. It remains only, in order to our observing such a fast as is acceptable to the Lord, that we add alms thereto: works of mercy, after our power, both to the bodies and souls of men. 'With such sacrifices' also 'God is well pleased.'[72] Thus the angel declares to

---

[u] 2 Cor. 7:9-11.

[62] 2 Cor. 7:10.
[63] See Col. 3:10.
[64] Eph. 4:24.
[65] See 1 Pet. 1:15.
[66] See 2 Pet. 3:14.
[67] Cf. 2 Cor. 7:11.
[68] See 1 Thess. 5:22.
[69] See Rom. 12:1.
[70] See 1 Pet. 5:6.
[71] See Dan. 9:16-18.
[72] Heb. 13:16.

Cornelius, fasting and praying in his house, 'Thy prayers and thine alms are come up for a memorial before God.'ᵛ And this God himself expressly and largely declares: 'Is not this the fast that I have chosen: . . . to undo the heavy burdens, to let the oppressed go free, and that ye break every yoke? Is it not to deal 5 thy bread to the hungry, and that thou bring the poor that are cast out to thy house? When thou seest the naked, that thou cover him, and that thou hide not thyself from thy own flesh? Then shall thy light break forth as the morning, and thine health shall spring forth speedily; and thy righteousness shall go before thee; the 10 glory of the Lord shall be thy rereward.⁷³ Then shalt thou call, and the Lord shall answer; thou shalt cry, and he shall say, Here I am. . . . If (when thou fastest) thou draw out thy soul to the hungry, and satisfy the afflicted soul; then shall thy light rise in obscurity, and thy darkness be as the noonday. And the Lord shall 15 guide thee continually, and satisfy thy soul in drought, and make thy bones fat: and thou shalt be like a watered garden, and like a spring . . . whose waters fail not.'ʷ

ᵛ Acts. 10:4.
ʷ Isa. 58:6-11.

---

⁷³ Orig., 'rearward', i.e., 'rearguard'; the errata sheet in Wesley's *Works*, (1771), as in his own annotated copy, II. 276 (correcting the mis-spelling 'rare-ward') calls for 'rereward', which is also the spelling in 1787, and in AV; see also *OED*, where 'rereward' is listed as a variant of 'rearward'.

Upon our Lord's Sermon on the Mount

Discourse the Eighth

Matthew 6:19-23

Lay not up for yourselves treasures upon earth, where moth and rust
5 *doth corrupt, and where thieves break through and steal:*

But lay up for yourselves treasures in heaven, where neither moth nor rust doth corrupt, and where thieves do not break through nor steal;

For where your treasure is, there will your heart be also.

The light of the body is the eye: if therefore thine eye be single, thy
10 *whole body shall be full of light.*

But if thine eye be evil, thy whole body shall be full of darkness. If therefore the light that is in thee be darkness, how great is that darkness!

1. From those which are commonly termed 'religious
15 actions', and which are real branches of true religion where they spring from a pure and holy intention and are performed in a manner suitable thereto, our Lord proceeds to the actions of 'common life', and shows that the same purity of intention is as indispensably required in our ordinary business as in giving alms,
20 or fasting, or prayer.

And without question the same purity of intention 'which makes our alms and devotions acceptable must also make our labour or employment a proper offering to God. If a man [. . .] pursues his business that he may raise himself to a state of honour
25 and riches in the world, he is no longer serving God in his employment, [. . .] and has no more title to a reward from God than he who gives alms that he may be *seen*, or prays that he may be *heard* of men. For vain and earthly designs are no more allowable in our employments than in our alms and devo-
30 tions.[. . .] They are not only evil when they mix with our good works', with our religious actions, 'but they have the same evil nature [. . .] when they enter into the common business of our employments. If it were allowable to pursue them in our worldly

employments, it would be allowable to pursue them in our devotions. But as our alms and devotions are not an acceptable service but when they proceed from a pure intention, so our common employment cannot be reckoned a service to him but when it is performed with the same piety of heart.'[1]

2. This our blessed Lord declares in the liveliest manner in those strong and comprehensive words which he explains, enforces, and enlarges upon throughout this whole chapter. 'The light of the body is the eye. If therefore thine eye be single, thy whole body shall be full of light: but if thine eye be evil, thy whole body shall be full of darkness.' The eye is the intention: what the eye is to the body, the intention is to the soul.[2] As the one guides all the motions of the body, so does the other those of the soul. This eye of the soul is then said to be 'single' when it looks at one thing only; when we have no other design but to 'know God, and Jesus Christ whom he hath sent';[3] to know him with suitable affections, loving him as he hath loved us; to please God in all things; to serve God (as we love him) with all our heart and mind and soul and strength;[4] and to enjoy God in all and above all things, in time and in eternity.

3. 'If thine eye be' thus 'single', thus fixed on God, 'thy whole body shall be full of light.' 'Thy whole body'—all that is guided by the intention, as the body is by the eye. All thou art, all thou dost: thy desires, tempers, affections; thy thoughts and words and actions. The whole of these 'shall be full of light'; full of true, divine knowledge. This is the first thing we may here understand by light. 'In his light thou shalt see light.'[5] 'He which' of old 'commanded light to shine out of darkness, shall shine in thy heart.'[6] He shall enlighten the eyes of thy understanding[7] with the knowledge of the glory of God. His Spirit shall reveal unto thee the deep things of God.[8] The inspiration of the Holy One shall

---

[1] A quotation from Law's *Serious Call*, (*Works*, IV. 33); but note Wesley's alterations (e.g., 'earthly designs' in place of 'earthly desires'). Wesley had already published an abridged edn. of *Serious Call* in 1744 (cf. *Bibliog*, No. 86); here he abridges that abridgement still further.

[2] Cf. No. 12, 'The Witness of Our Own Spirit', §11 and n.

[3] John 17:3.

[4] See Mark 12:30.

[5] Cf. Ps. 36:9.

[6] Cf. 2 Cor. 4:6.

[7] See Eph. 1:18.

[8] See 1 Cor. 2:10.

give thee understanding, and cause thee to know wisdom secretly. Yea, the anointing which thou receivest of him 'shall abide in thee and teach thee of all things'.[9]

How does experience confirm this? Even after God hath
5 opened the eyes of our understanding, if we seek or desire anything else than God, how soon is our foolish heart darkened! Then clouds again rest upon our souls. Doubts and fears again overwhelm us. We are tossed to and fro, and know not what to do, or which is the path wherein we should go. But when we desire
10 and seek nothing but God, clouds and doubts vanish away. We 'who were sometime darkness are now light in the Lord'.[10] The night now shineth as the day;[11] and we find 'the path of the upright is light.'[12] God showeth us the path wherein we should go, and 'maketh plain the way before our face'.[13]

15   4. The second thing which we may here understand by 'light' is holiness. While thou seekest God in all things thou shalt find him in all, the fountain of all holiness, continually filling thee with his own likeness, with justice, mercy, and truth. While thou lookest unto Jesus and him alone thou shalt be filled with the mind that
20 was in him.[14] Thy soul shall be renewed day by day after the image of him that created it. If the eye of thy mind be not removed from him, if thou endurest 'as seeing him that is invisible',[15] and seeking nothing else in heaven or earth, then as thou beholdest the glory of the Lord thou shalt be 'transformed into the same
25 image, from glory to glory, by the Spirit of the Lord'.[16]

And it is also matter of daily experience that 'by grace we are thus saved through faith.'[17] It is by faith that the eye of the mind is opened to see the light of the glorious love of God. And as long as it is steadily fixed thereon, on God in Christ, reconciling the
30 world unto himself,[18] we are more and more filled with the love of God and man, with meekness, gentleness, long-suffering; with all the fruits of holiness, which are, through Christ Jesus, to the glory of God the Father.

[9] Cf. 1 John 2:27.   [10] Cf. Eph. 5:8.
[11] See Ps. 139:12.
[12] Cf. Prov. 4:18.
[13] Cf. Ps. 5:8 (BCP).
[14] See Phil. 2:5.
[15] Cf. Heb. 11:27.
[16] 2 Cor. 3:18.
[17] Cf. Eph. 2:8.
[18] See 2 Cor. 5:19.

5. This light which fills him who has a single eye implies, thirdly, happiness as well as holiness. Surely 'light is sweet, and a pleasant thing it is to see the sun.'[19] But how much more to see the sun of righteousness continually shining upon the soul! And if there be any consolation in Christ, if any comfort of love,[20] if any peace that passeth all understanding,[21] if any rejoicing in hope of the glory of God,[22] they all belong to him whose eye is single. Thus is his 'whole body full of light'.[23] He walketh in the light as God is in the light,[24] rejoicing evermore, praying without ceasing, and in everything giving thanks, *enjoying* whatever is the will of God concerning him in Christ Jesus.[25]

6. 'But if thine eye be evil, thy whole body shall be full of darkness.'[26] 'If thine eye be evil': we see there is no medium between a single and an evil eye. If the eye be not single, then it is evil. If the intention in whatever we do be not singly to God, if we seek anything else, then our 'mind and conscience are defiled'.[27]

Our eye therefore is evil if in anything we do we aim at any other end than God; if we have any view but to know and to love God, to please and serve him in all things; if we have any other design than to enjoy God, to be happy in him both now and for ever.[28]

7. If thine eye be not singly fixed on God, 'thy whole body shall be full of darkness.' The veil shall still remain on thy heart. Thy mind shall be more and more blinded by 'the God of this world, lest the light of the glorious gospel of Christ should shine upon thee'.[29] Thou wilt be full of ignorance and error touching the things of God, not being able to receive or discern them. And even when thou hast some desire to serve God, thou wilt be full of uncertainty as to the manner of serving him; finding doubts and difficulties on every side, and not seeing any way to escape.

---

[19] Cf. Eccles. 11:7. Cf. No. 91, 'On Charity', III.10, where Wesley relates an anecdote of a victim of the Inquisition brought out of prison to execution. Having not seen the sun in many years, looking up, he cried out in surprise, 'O how can anyone who sees that glorious luminary worship any but the God that made it!'

[20] Phil. 2:1.

[21] See Phil. 4:7.

[22] See Rom. 5:2.

[23] Matt. 6:22.

[24] See 1 John 1:7.

[25] See 1 Thess. 5:16-18.

[26] Matt. 6:23.

[27] Cf. Titus 1:15. Cf. No. 125, 'On a Single Eye'.

[28] Note the echo here of the answer to *Q*.1 in the Westminster *Shorter Catechism* of 1647.

[29] Cf. 2 Cor. 4:4.

Yea, if thine eye be not single, if thou seek any of the things of earth, thou shalt be full of ungodliness and unrighteousness, thy desires, tempers, affections, being all out of course, being all dark, and vile, and vain. And thy conversation will be evil as well as thy heart, not 'seasoned with salt',[30] or 'meet to minister grace unto the hearers',[31] but idle, unprofitable, corrupt, grievous to the Holy Spirit of God.

8. Both 'destruction and unhappiness are in thy ways;' for 'the way of peace hast thou not known.'[32] There is no peace, no settled, solid peace, for them that know not God. There is no true nor lasting content for any who do not seek him with their whole heart. While thou aimest at any of the things that perish, 'all that cometh is vanity.'[33] Yea, not only vanity, but 'vexation of spirit',[34] and that both in the pursuit and the enjoyment also. Thou walkest indeed in a vain shadow, and disquietest thyself in vain.[35] Thou walkest in darkness that may be felt.[36] 'Sleep on;' but thou canst not 'take thy rest.'[37] The dreams of life can give pain, and that thou knowest; but ease they cannot give. There is no rest in this world or the world to come, but only in God, the centre of spirits.

'If the light which is in thee be darkness, how great is that darkness!' If the intention which ought to enlighten the whole soul, to fill it with knowledge, and love, and peace, and which in fact does so as long as it is single, as long as it aims at God alone—if this be darkness; if it aim at anything beside God, and consequently cover the soul with darkness instead of light, with ignorance and error, with sin and misery—O how great is that darkness! It is the very smoke which ascends out of the bottomless pit![38] It is the essential night which reigns in the lowest deep, in the land of the shadow of death.[39]

9. Therefore 'lay not up for yourselves treasures upon earth, where moth and rust doth corrupt, and where thieves break through and steal.'[40] If you do, it is plain your eye is evil; it is not singly fixed on God.

With regard to most of the commandments of God, whether

---

[30] Col. 4:6.
[31] Cf. Eph. 4:29.
[32] Cf. Rom. 3:16-17.
[33] Eccles. 11:8.
[34] Eccles. 1:14, etc.
[35] See Ps. 39:6.
[36] See Exod. 10:21.
[37] Cf. Matt. 26:45.
[38] See Rev. 11:7; 17:8.
[39] See Isa. 9:1-2; Matt. 4:16.
[40] Matt. 6:19.

relating to the heart or life, the heathens of Africa[41] or America stand much on a level with those that are called Christians. The Christians observe them (a few only being excepted) very near as much as the heathens. For instance: the generality of the natives of England, commonly called Christians, are as sober and as temperate as the generality of the heathens near the Cape of Good Hope. And so the Dutch or French Christians are as humble and as chaste as the Choctaw or Cherokee Indians. It is not easy to say, when we compare the bulk of the nations in Europe with those in America, whether the superiority lies on the one side or the other. At least the American has not much the advantage. But we cannot affirm this with regard to the command now before us. Here the heathen has far the pre-eminence.[42] He desires and seeks nothing more than plain food to eat and plain raiment to put on. And he seeks this only from day to day. He reserves, he lays up nothing; unless it be as much corn at one season of the year as he will need before that season returns. This command, therefore, the heathens, though they know it not, do constantly and punctually observe. They 'lay up for themselves no treasures upon earth'; no stores of purple or fine linen, of gold or silver, which either 'moth or rust may corrupt', or 'thieves break through and steal'. But how do the Christians observe what they profess to receive as a command of the most high God? Not at all; not in any degree; no more than if no such command had ever been given to man. Even the *good* Christians, as they are accounted by others as well as themselves, pay no manner of

---

[41] Most of what Wesley knew of Africa came from the published accounts of travellers and was confined largely to the 'dark continent's' southern tip. Cf. Peter Kolben, *The Present State of the Cape of Good Hope* (1731) and Thomas Salmon, *Modern History*. The general label at that time for the natives of the Cape Colony and its hinterlands was 'Hottentots', and they are described in quite various lights (as 'noble savages' by some and as uncivilized by others). Wesley's concern here, however, is to use 'the heathens of Africa or America' as foils in his scornful comparisons between nominal Christians and so-called heathens. Cf. JWJ, Dec. 2, 1737 (§§21-28); and Nos. 69, 'The Imperfection of Human Knowledge', II.5; 105, 'On Conscience', §5. See also *The Doctrine of Original Sin*, Pt. II, II.1-10; *Thoughts upon Slavery*, II.1-2 (*Bibliog*, No. 350, Vol. 15); *Survey*, IV. 109; and *AM*, 1789, 377-83. Wesley seems never to have used the name 'Africa', but always, as here, 'Africk' (1748) or 'Afric' (1771, 1787).

[42] Wesley's lifelong rejection of surplus accumulation as an economic moral principle would intensify in the last decade of his life; see below, No. 87, 'The Danger of Riches' (1781). Here, before Adam Smith's *Wealth of Nations* (1776) and in sharp contrast, he is suggesting that, in terms of freedom from the greed that expresses itself in 'laying up treasures . . .', the heathens are morally superior to European Christians who, long since, had lost their 'natural' scruples against hoarding and amassing wealth without stint. Cf. No. 50, 'The Use of Money', espec. I.8-9, III.1.

regard thereto. It might as well be still hid in its original Greek for any notice they take of it. In what Christian city do you find one man of five hundred who makes the least scruple of laying up just as much treasure as he can? Of increasing his goods just as far as he is able? There are indeed those who would not do this unjustly; there are many who will neither rob nor steal; and some who will not defraud their neighbour; nay, who will not gain either by his ignorance or necessity. But this is quite another point. Even these do not scruple the thing, but the manner of it. They do not scruple the 'laying up treasures upon earth', but the laying them up by dishonesty.

They do not start at disobeying Christ, but at a breach of heathen morality. So that even these honest men do no more obey this command than a highwayman or a housebreaker. Nay, they never designed to obey it. From their youth up it never entered into their thoughts. They were bred up by their Christian parents, masters, and friends, without any instruction at all concerning it; unless it were this, to break it as soon and as much as they could, and to continue breaking it to their life's end.

10. There is no one instance of spiritual infatuation in the world which is more amazing than this. Most of these very men read or hear the Bible read, many of them every Lord's day. They have read or heard these words an hundred times, and yet never suspect that they are themselves condemned thereby, any more than by those which forbid parents to offer up their sons or daughters unto Moloch.

O that God would speak to these miserable self-deceivers with his own voice, his mighty voice! That they may at last awake out of the snare of the devil,[43] and the scales may fall from their eyes![44]

11. Do you ask what it is to 'lay up treasures on earth'? It will be needful to examine this thoroughly. And let us, first, observe what is not forbidden in this command, that we may then clearly discern what is.

We are not forbidden in this command, first, to 'provide things honest in the sight of all men,'[45] to provide wherewith we may 'render unto all their due,'[46] whatsoever they can justly demand of us. So far from it that we are taught of God to 'owe no man anything'.[47] We ought therefore to use all diligence in our calling,

---

[43] See 2 Tim. 2:26.
[45] Cf. 2 Cor. 8:21.   [46] Cf. Rom. 13:7.   [44] See Acts 9:18.
[47] Rom. 13:8.

in order to owe no man anything: this being no other than a plain law of common justice which our Lord came 'not to destroy but to fulfil'.[48]

Neither, secondly, does he here forbid the providing for ourselves such things as are needful for the body; a sufficiency of plain, wholesome food to eat, and clean raiment to put on. Yea, it is our duty, so far as God puts it into our power, to provide these things also; to the end we may 'eat our own bread',[49] and be 'burdensome to no man'.[50]

Nor yet are we forbidden, thirdly, to provide for our children and for those of our own household. This also it is our duty to do, even upon principles of heathen morality. Every man ought to provide the plain necessaries[51] of life both for his own wife and children, and to put them into a capacity of providing these for themselves when he is gone hence and is no more seen. I say, of providing *these*, the plain necessaries of life—not delicacies, not superfluities—and that by their *diligent labour*; for it is no man's duty to furnish them any more than himself with the means either of luxury or idleness. But if any man provides not thus far for his own children (as well as for 'the widows of his own house',[52] of whom primarily St. Paul is speaking in those well-known words to Timothy), 'he hath' practically 'denied the faith, and is worse than an infidel,'[53] or heathen.

Lastly, we are not forbidden in these words to lay up from time to time what is needful for the carrying on our worldly business in such a measure and degree as is sufficient to answer the foregoing purposes: in such a measure as, first, to 'owe no man anything';[54] secondly, to procure for ourselves the necessaries of life; and, thirdly, to furnish those of our own house with them while we live, and with the means of procuring them when we are gone to God.

12. We may now clearly discern (unless we are unwilling to discern it) what that is which is forbidden here. It is the designedly procuring more of this world's goods than will answer the foregoing purposes; the labouring after a larger measure of worldly substance, a larger increase of gold and silver; the laying up any more than these ends require is what is here expressly and absolutely forbidden. If the words have any meaning at all, it must

---

[48] Matt. 5:17.   [49] Cf. 2 Thess. 3:12.   [50] Cf. 2 Cor. 11:9.
[51] Cf. No. 30, 'Sermon on the Mount, X', §26 and n.
[52] Cf. 1 Tim. 5:3, 8.   [53] 1 Tim. 5:8.
[54] Rom. 13:8.

be this, for they are capable of no other. Consequently whoever he is that, owing no man anything, and having food and raiment for himself and his household, together with a sufficiency to carry on his worldly business so far as answers these reasonable purposes—whosoever, I say, being already in these circumstances, seeks a still larger portion on earth—he lives in an open habitual denial of the Lord that bought him. He hath practically 'denied the faith, and is worse than an' African or American 'infidel'.

13. Hear ye this, all ye that dwell in the world, and love the world wherein ye dwell. Ye may be 'highly esteemed of men'; but ye are an 'abomination in the sight of God'.[55] How long shall your souls cleave to the dust?[56] How long will ye load yourselves with thick clay?[57] When will ye awake and see that the open, speculative heathens are nearer the kingdom of heaven than you?[58] When will ye be persuaded to choose the better part; that which cannot be taken away from you?[59] When will ye seek only to 'lay up treasures in heaven',[60] renouncing, dreading, abhorring all other? If you aim at 'laying up treasures on earth'[61] you are not *barely* losing your time and spending your strength for that which is not bread:[62] for what is the fruit if you succeed? You have murdered your own soul. You have extinguished the last spark of spiritual life therein. Now indeed, in the midst of life you are in death.[63] You are a living man, but a dead Christian. 'For where your treasure is, there will your heart be also.'[64] Your heart is sunk into the dust; your soul cleaveth to the ground.[65] Your affections are set, not on things above, but on things of the earth;[66] on poor husks that may poison, but cannot satisfy an everlasting spirit made for God. Your love, your joy, your desire are all placed on the things which perish in the using. You have thrown away the treasure in heaven: God and Christ are lost. You have gained riches, and hell-fire.

14. O 'how hardly shall they that have riches enter into the kingdom of God!'[67] When our Lord's disciples were astonished at

---

[55] Cf. Luke 16:15.   [56] See Ps. 119:25.   [57] See Hab. 2:6.

[58] Aristotle, *Nicomachean Ethics*, had been Wesley's undergraduate textbook in ethics, along with the ethical writings of Seneca and Cicero; with one voice they had condemned greed and covetousness.

[59] See Luke 10:42.

[60] Matt. 6:20.

[62] See Isa. 55:2.

[64] Matt. 6:21.

[66] See Col. 3:2.

[61] Cf. Matt. 6:19.

[63] BCP, Burial (477).

[65] See Ps. 119:25.

[67] Mark 10:23.

his speaking thus he was so far from retracting it that he repeated the same important truth in stronger terms than before. 'It is easier for a camel to go through the eye of a needle, than for a rich man to enter into the kingdom of God.'[68] How hard is it for them whose very word is applauded not to be wise in their own eyes! 5 How hard for them not to think themselves better than the poor, base, uneducated herd of men! How hard not to seek happiness in their riches, or in things dependent upon them; in gratifying the desire of the flesh, the desire of the eye, or the pride of life![69] O ye rich, how can ye escape the damnation of hell?[70] Only, with 10 God all things are possible.[71]

15. And even if you do not succeed, what is the fruit of your *endeavouring* to lay up treasures on earth? 'They that will be rich' (οἱ βουλόμενοι πλουτεῖν, they that desire, that endeavour after it, whether they succeed or no) 'fall into a temptation and a snare', 15 a gin, a trap of the devil, 'and into many foolish and hurtful lusts'—ἐπιθυμίας [πολλὰς] ἀνοήτους, desires with which reason hath nothing to do, such as properly belong, not to rational and immortal beings, but only to the brute beasts which have no understanding; 'which drown men in destruction and perdi- 20 tion',[72] in present and eternal misery. Let us but open our eyes, and we may daily see the melancholy proofs of this: men who desiring, resolving to be rich, 'coveting after money, the root of all evil, have already pierced themselves through with many sorrows',[73] and anticipated the hell to which they are going. 25

The cautiousness with which the Apostle here speaks is highly observable. He does not affirm this absolutely of *the rich;* for a man may possibly be rich without any fault of his, by an overruling providence, preventing his own choice. But he affirms it of οἱ βουλόμενοι πλουτεῖν, 'those who desire' or seek 'to be rich'. 30 Riches, dangerous as they are, do not always 'drown men in destruction and perdition'. But the *desire of riches* does: those who calmly desire and deliberately seek to attain them, whether they do, in fact, gain the world or no, do infallibly lose their own souls. These are they that sell him who bought them with his blood, for a 35 few pieces of gold or silver.[74] These enter into a covenant with

---

68 Mark 10:25.
69 See 1 John 2:16. Cf. No. 7, 'The Way to the Kingdom', II.2 and n.
70 Matt. 23:33.
71 Matt. 19:26.
72 Cf. 1 Tim. 6:9.
73 Cf. 1 Tim. 6:10.
74 See Matt. 26:14-15.

death and hell: and their covenant shall stand. For they are daily
making themselves meet to partake of their inheritance with the
devil and his angels.[75]

16. O who shall warn this generation of vipers to flee from the
wrath to come![76] Not those who lie at their gate, or cringe at their
feet, desiring to be fed with the crumbs that fall from their
tables.[77] Not those who court their favour or fear their frown:
none of those who mind earthly things. But if there be a Christian
upon earth, if there be a man who hath overcome the world, who
desires nothing but God, and fears none but him that is able to
destroy both body and soul in hell[78]—thou, O man of God, speak
and spare not; lift up thy voice like a trumpet.[79] Cry aloud, and
show these honourable sinners the desperate condition wherein
they stand. It may be one in a thousand may have ears to hear, may
arise and shake himself from the dust; may break loose from these
chains that bind him to the earth, and at length lay up treasures in
heaven.

17. And if it should be that one of these, by the mighty power of
God, awoke and asked, What must I do to be saved?[80] the answer,
according to the oracles of God, is clear, full, and express. God
doth not say to thee, 'Sell all that thou hast.'[81] Indeed he who seeth
the hearts of men saw it needful to enjoin this in one peculiar
case, that of the *young, rich ruler.* But he never laid it down for a
general rule to all rich men, in all succeeding generations. His
general direction is, first, 'Be not highminded.'[82] 'God seeth not
as man seeth.'[83] He esteems thee not for thy riches, for thy
grandeur or equipage, for any qualification or accomplishment
which is directly or indirectly owing to thy wealth, which can be
bought or procured thereby. All these are with him as dung and
dross: let them be so with thee also. Beware thou think not thyself
to be one jot wiser or better for all these things. Weigh thyself in
another balance:[84] estimate thyself only by the measure of faith
and love which God hath given thee. If thou hast more of the

---

[75] Matt. 25:41.
[76] See Matt. 3:7.
[77] See Luke 16:20-21.
[78] See Matt. 10:28.
[79] Isa. 58:1.
[80] Acts 16:30.   [81] Luke 18:22.
[82] Rom. 11:20.   [83] Cf. 1 Sam. 16:7.
[84] I.e., 'in the balance of the sanctuary'; cf. No. 10, 'The Witness of the Spirit, I', II.8
and n.

knowledge and love of God than he, thou art on this account, and no other, wiser and better, more valuable and honourable than him who is with the dogs of thy flock.[85] But if thou hast not this treasure those art more foolish, more vile, more truly contemptible—I will not say, than the lowest servant under thy roof but—than the beggar laid at thy gate, full of sores.[86]

18. Secondly, 'Trust not in uncertain riches.'[87] Trust not in them for help; and trust not in them for happiness.

First, trust not in them for help. Thou art miserably mistaken if thou lookest for this in gold or silver. These are no more able to set thee *above the world* than to set thee above the devil. Know that both the world and the prince of this world[88] laugh at all such preparations against them. These will little avail in the day of trouble—even if they remain in the trying hour. But it is not certain that they will; for how oft do they 'make themselves wings and fly away'?[89] But if not, what support will they afford, even in the ordinary troubles of life? The desire of thy eyes,[90] the wife of thy youth,[91] thy son, thine only son, or the friend which was as thy own soul,[92] is taken away at a stroke.[93] Will thy riches reanimate the breathless clay, or call back its late inhabitant? Will they secure thee from sickness, diseases, pain? Do these visit the poor only? Nay; he that feeds thy flocks or tills thy ground has less sickness and pain than thou. He is more rarely visited by these unwelcome guests: and if they come there at all they are more easily driven away from the little cot than from 'the cloud-topped palaces'.[94] And during the time that thy body is chastened with pain, or consumes away with pining sickness, how do thy treasures help thee? Let the poor heathen answer:

Ut lippum pictae tabulae, fomenta podagrum,
Auriculas citharae collecta sorde dolentes.[95]

[85] Job 30:1.   [86] See Luke 16:20.   [87] Cf. 1 Tim. 6:17.
[88] John 14:30; 16:11.   [89] Cf. Prov. 23:5.
[90] See Ezek. 24:16, 21.   [91] Prov. 5:18; Mal. 2:14.
[92] Cf. Deut. 13:6; see also 1 Sam. 18:3.   [93] See Ezek. 24:16.
[94] Cf. Shakespeare, *The Tempest*, IV.i. 152—a conflation from memory of 'The cloud-capp'd towers, the gorgeous palaces'.
[95] Wesley seems to have held Horace in an especial contempt; cf., e.g., No. 2, *The Almost Christian*, III.9, where Wesley refers to him with two unflattering epithets ('a heathen Epicurean poet' and 'this poor wretch'). The quotation here is from the *Epistles*, I. ii. 52-53, and speaks of 'such pleasures as pictures can afford to weak eyes or bounty-laden tables to a man with gout'. Despite this disdain, however, Wesley quotes Horace at least twenty-nine times in the *Sermons*.

19. But there is at hand a greater trouble than all these. *Thou* art to die. *Thou* art to sink into dust; to return to the ground from which thou wast taken, to mix with common clay. *Thy* body is to go to the earth as it was, while thy spirit returns to God that gave it.[96]

5 And the time draws on: the years slide away with a swift though silent pace. Perhaps your day is far spent: the noon of life is past, and the evening shadows begin to rest upon you. You feel in yourself sure approaching decay. The springs of life wear away apace.[97] Now what help is there in your riches? Do they sweeten

10 death? Do they endear that solemn hour? Quite the reverse. 'O death, how bitter art thou to a man that liveth at rest in his possessions!'[98] How unacceptable to him is that awful sentence. 'This night shall thy soul be required of thee!'[99] Or will they prevent the unwelcome stroke, or protract the dreadful hour?

15 Can they deliver your soul that it should not see death?[100] Can they restore the years that are past? Can they add to your appointed time a month, a day, an hour, a moment? Or will the good things you have chosen for your portion here follow you over the great gulf? Not so: naked came you into this world; naked must you

20 return.[101]

> *Linquenda tellus, et domus et placens*
> *Uxor: nec harum quas seris arborum*
> *Te, praeter invisam cupressum,*
> *Ulla brevem dominum sequetur.*[102]

25 Surely, were not these truths too plain to be *observed*, because they are too plain to be *denied*, no man that is to die could possibly 'trust' for help 'in uncertain riches'.[103]

20. And trust not in them for happiness. For here also they will be found 'deceitful upon the weights'.[104] Indeed this every

---

[96] See Eccles. 12:7.

[97] Cf. John's later comment on his brother Charles's death (*Minutes* of Conference, 1788): 'He had no disease, but after a gradual decay of some months, "The weary wheels of life stood still at last";' the line of poetry is from John Dryden and Nathaniel Lee, *Oedipus*, Act IV, sc. 1.

[98] Cf. Ecclus. 41:1. [99] Cf. Luke 12:20.

[100] See Ps. 33:19 (AV). [101] See Job 1:21.

[102] Horace, again; this time from the *Odes*, II. xiv. 21-24. The orig. reads *colis* ('culture') instead of Wesley's *seris* ('planting') and, in l. 23, it reads *invisas cupressos* (i.e., the plural): 'You must take leave of lands, home, winsome wife; and no tree whose culture had pleased shall survive your brief reign except those mournful cypresses.' Cf. also, JWJ, July 4, 1756, and Oct. 13, 1779.

[103] 1 Tim. 6:17.

[104] Ps. 62:9 (BCP).

reasonable man may infer from what has been observed already. For if neither thousands of gold and silver, nor any of the advantages or pleasures purchased thereby, can prevent our being miserable, it evidently follows they cannot make us happy. What happiness can they afford to him who in the midst of all is ₅ constrained to cry out,

> To my new courts sad thought does still repair,
> And round my gilded roofs hangs hovering care.[105]

Indeed experience is here so full, strong, and undeniable, that it makes all other arguments needless. Appeal we therefore to fact. ₁₀ Are the rich and great the only happy men? And is each of them more or less happy in proportion to his measure of riches? Are they happy at all? I had wellnigh said, they are of all men most miserable![106] Rich man, for once, speak the truth from thy heart. Speak, both for thyself, and for thy brethren: ₁₅

> Amidst our plenty something still . . .
> To me, to thee, to him is wanting!
> That cruel something unpossessed
> Corrodes and leavens all the rest.[107]

Yea, and so it will, till thy wearisome days of vanity are shut up in ₂₀ the night of death.

Surely then, to trust in riches for happiness is the greatest folly of all that are under the sun! Are you not convinced of this? Is it possible you should still expect to find happiness in money or all it can procure? What! Can silver and gold, and eating and drinking, ₂₅ and horses and servants, and glittering apparel, and diversions and pleasures (as they are called) make thee happy? They can as soon make thee immortal.

21. These are all dead show. Regard them not. 'Trust' thou 'in the living God;'[108] so shalt thou be safe under the shadow of the ₃₀ Almighty;[109] his faithfulness and truth shall be thy shield and

---

[105] Matthew Prior, *Solomon*, ii. 53-54 (the orig. uses the past tense). Cf. Wesley, *Collection of Moral and Sacred Poems*, II. 129. Cf. Wesley's 'Thoughts on the Character and Writings of Mr. Prior', where he asserts that Prior's best passages 'do not yield to anything that has been wrote by Pope, or Dryden, or any English poet, except Milton' (*AM* 1782, 665).

[106] 1 Cor. 15:19.

[107] Matthew Prior, 'The Ladle', ll. 162, 164-66, with l. 163 omitted. See also No. 77, 'Spiritual Worship', III.1.

[108] 1 Tim. 4:10.   [109] See Ps. 91:1.

buckler.[110] He is a very present help in time of trouble;[111] such an help as can never fail. Then shalt thou say, if all thy other friends die, 'The Lord liveth, and blessed be my strong helper!'[112] He shall remember thee when thou liest sick upon thy bed;[113] when
5 vain is the help of man;[114] when all the things of earth can give no support, he will 'make all thy bed in thy sickness'.[115] He will sweeten thy pain; the consolations of God shall cause thee to clap thy hands in the flames. And even when this house of earth[116] is wellnigh shaken down, when it is just ready to drop into the dust,
10 he will teach thee to say, 'O death, where is thy sting? O grave, where is thy victory? [. . .] Thanks be unto God, who giveth me the victory, through my Lord Jesus Christ.'[117]

O trust in him for happiness as well as for help. All the springs of happiness are in him. Trust in him 'who giveth us all things
15 richly to enjoy', παρέχοντι [ἡμῖν] πλουσίως πάντα εἰς ἀπόλαυσιν;[118] who of his own rich and free mercy holds them out to us as in his own hand, that receiving them as his gift, and as pledges of his love, we may 'enjoy all' that we possess. It is his love gives a relish to all we taste, puts life and sweetness into all, while
20 every creature leads us up to the great Creator, and all earth is a scale to heaven.[119] He transfuses the joys that are at his own right hand into all he bestows on his thankful children; who, having fellowship with the Father and his Son Jesus Christ,[120] enjoy him in all and above all.

25 22. Thirdly, seek not to *increase in goods*. 'Lay not up for thyself treasures upon earth.'[121] This is a flat, positive command, full as clear as 'Thou shalt not commit adultery.'[122] How then is it

---

[110] Ps. 91:4 (BCP).   [111] See Ps. 46:1.   [112] Ps. 18:47 (BCP).
[113] See Ps. 41:3 (BCP).   [114] Ps. 60:11; 108:12.   [115] Cf. Ps. 41:3.
[116] See below, §26. Wesley's thoroughgoing dualism is reflected in his oft-repeated metaphors about the earthly body as temporary lodgement for the soul. His biblical sources would include Job 4:19 ('houses of clay') and 2 Cor. 5:1 ('the earthly house of this tabernacle'); and he uses one or another variant of the idea in other sermons (thirteen of them) and at least three letters, not to mention his early imitation of Horace (*Odes* I. xxiv), ver. 6, l. 4: '[The body's] ancient tenement of clay'. The metaphor had come to be a cliché in English poetry, from Thomas Carew ('On the Lady Mary Villiers': 'The purest soul that e'er was sent/Into a clayey tenement') to John Dryden ('Absalom and Achitophel', I. 144: 'And o'er informed the tenement of clay') to James Thomson ('Upon Happiness', l. 125: 'cage of clay'), and many others.
[117] 1 Cor. 15:55-57.
[118] A paraphrase of the meaning of 1 Tim. 6:17 in the *TR*; cf. the AV: 'who giveth us richly all things to enjoy'.
[119] Cf. No. 56, 'God's Approbation of His Works', I.14 and n.
[120] Cf. 1 John 1:3.   [121] Matt. 6:19.   [122] Exod. 20:14.

possible for a rich man to grow richer without denying the Lord that bought him? Yea, how can any man who has already the necessaries of life gain or aim at more, and be guiltless? 'Lay not up', saith our Lord, 'treasures upon earth.' If in spite of this you do and will lay up money or goods, what 'moth or rust' may 5 'corrupt, or thieves break through and steal';[123] if you will add house to house, or field to field,[124] why do you call yourself a Christian? You do not obey Jesus Christ. You do not design it. Why do you name yourself by his name? 'Why call ye me, Lord, Lord', saith he himself, 'and do not the things which I say?'[125] 10

23. If you ask, 'But what must we do with our goods, seeing we have more than we have occasion to use, if we must not lay them up? Must we throw them away?' I answer: if you threw them into the sea, if you were to cast them into the fire and consume them, they would be better bestowed than they are now.[126] You cannot 15 find so mischievous a manner of throwing them away as either the laying them up for your posterity or the laying them out upon yourselves in folly and superfluity. Of all possible methods of 'throwing them away' these two are the very worst—the most opposite to the gospel of Christ, and the most pernicious to your 20 own soul.

How pernicious to your own soul the latter of these is has been excellently shown by a late writer:

> If we waste our money we are not only guilty of wasting a talent which God has given us, [. . .] but we do ourselves this farther harm: we turn this useful talent 25 into a powerful means of corrupting ourselves; because so far as it is spent wrong, so far it is spent in the support of some wrong temper, in gratifying some vain and unreasonable desires, which as Christians we are obliged to renounce.
>
> As wit and fine parts cannot be only trifled away, but will expose those that have them to greater follies, so money cannot be only trifled away, but if it is not 30 used according to reason and religion, will make people live a more silly and extravagant life than they would have done without it. If therefore you don't spend your money in doing good to others, you must spend it to the hurt of yourself. You act like one that refuses the cordial to his sick friend which he cannot drink himself without inflaming his blood. For this is the case of 35 superfluous money; if you give it to those who want it it is a cordial; if you spend it upon yourself in something that you do not want it only inflames and disorders your mind.[. . .]

---

[123] Cf. Matt. 6:19.
[124] See Isa. 5:8.
[125] Luke 6:46.
[126] But see No. 50, 'The Use of Money', §§2-3, where certain positive uses of money are acknowledged.

In using riches where they have no real use, nor we any real want, we only use them to our great hurt, in creating unreasonable desires, in nourishing ill tempers, in indulging in foolish passions, and supporting a vain turn of mind. For high eating and drinking, fine clothes and fine houses, state and equipage,
5 gay pleasures and diversions, do all of them naturally hurt and disorder our heart. They are the food and nourishment of all the folly and weakness of our nature.[. . .] They are all of them the support of something that ought not to be supported. They are contrary to that sobriety and piety of heart which relishes divine things. They are so many weights upon our mind, that makes us less able
10 and less inclined to raise our thoughts and affections to things above.

So that money thus spent is not merely wasted or lost, but it is spent to bad purposes and miserable effects; to the corruption and disorder of our hearts; to the making us unable to follow the sublime doctrines of the gospel. It is but like keeping money from the poor to buy poison for ourselves.[127]

15   24. Equally inexcusable are those who *lay up* what they do not need for any reasonable purposes:

If a man had hands and eyes and feet that he could give to those that wanted them; if he should lock them up in a chest [. . .] instead of giving them to his brethren that were blind and lame, should we not justly reckon him an inhuman
20 wretch? If he should rather choose to amuse himself with hoarding them up than entitle himself to an eternal reward by giving them to those that wanted eyes and hands, might we not justly reckon him mad?

Now money has very much the nature of eyes and feet. If therefore we lock it up in chests [. . .] while the poor and distressed want it for their necessary uses
25 [. . .] we are not far from the cruelty of him that chooses rather to hoard up the hands and eyes than to give them to those that want them. If we choose to lay it up rather than to entitle ourselves to an eternal reward by disposing of our money well, we are guilty of his madness that rather chooses to lock up eyes and hands than to make himself for ever blessed by giving them to those that want
30 them.[128]

25. May not this be another reason why rich men shall so hardly enter into the kingdom of heaven?[129] A vast majority of them are under a curse, under the peculiar curse of God; inasmuch as in the general tenor of their lives they are not only
35 robbing God continually, embezzling and wasting their Lord's goods, and by that very means corrupting their own souls; but also robbing the poor, the hungry, the naked, wronging the widow and the fatherless, and making themselves accountable for all the

---

[127] Law, *Serious Call* (*Works*, IV.50-51); cf. above, §1 and n. See also No. 108, 'On Riches', II.3.

[128] More from Law; but note that Wesley reverses Law's ordering of the 'heads' of his argument; cf. *ibid.*, ch. vi; cf. §1, above, and n.

[129] See Matt. 19:23.

want, affliction, and distress which they may but do not remove. Yea, doth not the blood of all those who perish for want of what they either lay up or lay out needlessly, cry against them from the earth?[130] O what account will they give to him who is ready to judge both the quick and the dead![131]   5

26. The true way of employing what you do not want yourselves you may, fourthly, learn from those words of our Lord which are the counterpart of what went before: 'Lay up for yourselves treasures in heaven, where neither moth nor rust doth corrupt, and where thieves do not break through and steal.'[132] Put out 10 whatever thou canst spare upon better security than this world can afford. Lay up thy treasures in the bank of heaven; and God shall restore them in that day. 'He that hath pity upon the poor lendeth unto the Lord,' and look, 'what he layeth out, it shall be paid him again.'[133] Place that, saith he, unto my account. Howbeit, 15 'thou owest me thine own self also!'[134]

Give to the poor with a single eye, with an upright heart, and write, 'So much given to God.' For 'Inasmuch as ye did it unto one of the least of these my brethren, ye have done it unto me.'[135]

This is the part of a 'faithful and wise steward':[136] not to sell 20 either his houses or lands, or principal stock, be it more or less, unless some peculiar circumstance should require it; and not to desire or endeavour to increase it, any more than to squander it away in vanity; but to employ it wholly to those wise and reasonable purposes for which his Lord has lodged it in his 25 hands. The wise steward, after having provided his own houschold with what is needful for life and godliness,[137] 'makes' himself 'friends with' all that remains from time to time of the 'mammon of unrighteousness; that when he fails they may receive him into everlasting habitations;'[138] that whensoever his earthly 30 tabernacle[139] is dissolved, they who were before carried into Abraham's bosom,[140] after having eaten his bread, and worn the fleece of his flock, and praised God for the consolation, may welcome him into paradise, and to 'the house of God, eternal in the heavens'.[141]   35

---

[130] See Gen. 4:10.
[132] Matt. 6:20.
[134] Cf. Philem. 19.
[136] Luke 12:42.
[138] Cf. Luke 16:9.
[140] See Luke 16:22.

[131] See 1 Pet. 4:5.
[133] Cf. Prov. 19:17.
[135] Cf. Matt. 25:40.
[137] See 2 Pet. 1:3.
[139] See above, §21 and n.
[141] Cf. 2 Cor. 5:1.

27. We 'charge you', therefore, 'who are rich in this world',[142] as having authority from our great Lord and Master, ἀγαδοερ-γεῖν[143]—'to be habitually doing good', to live in a course of good works. 'Be ye merciful as your Father which is in heaven is
5 merciful,'[144] who doth good and ceaseth not. 'Be ye merciful'— 'How far?' *After your power,*[145] with all the ability which God giveth. Make this your only measure of doing good, not any beggarly maxims or customs of the world. We charge you to 'be rich in good works';[146] as you have much, to *give plenteously.* Freely ye
10 have received; freely give;[147] so as to lay up no treasure but in heaven. Be ye 'ready to distribute'[148] to everyone according to his necessity. Disperse abroad, give to the poor: deal your bread to the hungry.[149] Cover the naked with a garment,[150] entertain the stranger,[151] carry or send relief to them that are in prison. Heal the
15 sick; not by miracle, but through the blessing of God upon your seasonable support. Let the blessing of him that was ready to perish through pining want come upon thee.[152] Defend the oppressed, plead the cause of the fatherless, and make the widow's heart sing for joy.[153]

20 28. We exhort *you* in the name of the Lord Jesus Christ to be 'willing to communicate', κοινωνικούς εἶναι;[154] to be of the same spirit (though not in the same outward state) with those believers of ancient times, who 'remained steadfast' ἐν τῇ κοινωνίᾳ,[155] in that blessed and holy 'fellowship' wherein 'none
25 said that anything was his own, but they had all things common.'[156] Be a steward, a faithful and wise steward,[157] of God and of the poor; differing from them in these two circumstances only, that your wants are first supplied out of the portion of your Lord's goods which remains in your hands, and that you have the
30 blessedness of giving. Thus 'lay up for yourselves a good foundation', not in the world which now is, but rather 'for the time to come, that ye may lay hold on eternal life.'[158] The great

---

[142] Cf. 1 Tim. 6:17.   [143] 1 Tim. 6:18.   [144] Cf. Luke 6:36.
[145] Cf. the *General Rules,* §5: 'doing good, by being in every kind merciful *after their power'.*
[146] Cf. 1 Tim. 6:17-18.
[147] Matt. 10:8.   [148] 1 Tim. 6:18.
[149] See Isa. 58:7.   [150] See Ezek. 18:7.
[151] See Heb. 13:2.   [152] See Job 29:13.   [153] *Ibid.*
[154] Cf. 1 Tim. 6:18, . . . εὐμεταδότους εἶναι, κοινωνικούς, ...
[155] Acts 2:42. Note Wesley's ἐν for καὶ.
[156] Cf. Acts 4:32.   [157] Luke 12:42.   [158] Cf. 1 Tim. 6:19.

foundation indeed of all the blessings of God, whether temporal or eternal, is the Lord Jesus Christ, his righteousness and blood, what he hath done, and what he hath suffered for us. And 'other foundation', in this sense, 'can no man lay;'[159] no, not an apostle, no, not an angel from heaven.[160] But through his merits, whatever 5 we do in his name is a foundation for a good reward in the day when 'every man shall receive his own reward, according to his own labour.'[161] Therefore 'labour' thou, 'not for the meat that perisheth, but for that which endureth unto everlasting life.'[162] Therefore 'whatsoever thy hand' now 'findeth to do, do it with thy 10 might'.[163] Therefore let

> No fair occasion pass unheeded by;
> Snatching the golden moments as they fly,
> Thou by few fleeting years ensure eternity![164]

'By patient continuance in well-doing, seek' thou 'for glory and 15 honour and immortality.'[165] In a constant, zealous performance of all good works[166] wait thou for that happy hour when 'the King shall say, [. . .] I was an hungered, and ye gave me meat; I was thirsty, and ye gave me drink. I was a stranger, and ye took me in, naked, and ye clothed me. I was sick, and ye visited me; I was in 20 prison, and ye came unto me.'[167] 'Come, ye blessed of my Father, receive the kingdom prepared for you from the foundation of the world!'[168]

---

[159] 1 Cor. 3:11.
[160] See Gal. 1:8.
[161] 1 Cor. 3:8.
[162] John 6:27.
[163] Eccles. 9:10.
[164] An adaptation from Samuel Wesley, Jun., 'On the Death of Mr. Morgan . . .'; ll. 19-21, in *Poems* (1736), p. 108. Later, John will quote the first line here (with his own variations) in a letter to Ann Bolton, Nov. 28, 1772.
[165] Rom. 2:7.
[166] See Titus 2:14.
[167] Matt. 25:34-36.
[168] Cf. Matt. 25:34. Cf. No. 51, *The Good Steward*, III and IV.

Upon our Lord's Sermon on the Mount[1]

Discourse the Ninth

Matthew 6:24-34

No man can serve two masters; for either he will hate the one and love
5 *the other, or else he will hold to the one and despise the other. Ye cannot*
serve God and mammon.

Therefore I say unto you, Take no thought for your life, what ye shall
eat, or what ye shall drink; nor yet for your body, what ye shall put on. Is
not the life more than meat, and the body than raiment?

10 *Behold the fowls of the air: for they sow not, neither do they reap, nor*
gather into barns; yet your heavenly Father feedeth them. Are ye not
much better than they?

Which of you by taking thought can add one cubit unto his stature?

And why take ye thought for raiment? Consider the lilies of the field,
15 *how they grow; they toil not, neither do they spin:*

And yet I say unto you, that even Solomon in all his glory was not
arrayed like one of these.

Wherefore, if God so clothe the grass of the field, which today is, and
tomorrow is cast into the oven, shall he not much more clothe you, O ye of
20 *little faith?*

Therefore take no thought, saying, What shall we eat? or, What shall
we drink? or, Wherewithal shall we be clothed?

(For after all these things do the Gentiles seek); for your heavenly
Father knoweth that ye have need of all these things.

25 *But first seek ye the kingdom of God and his righteousness; and all*
these things shall be added unto you.

Take therefore no thought for the morrow; for the morrow shall take
thought for the things of itself: sufficient unto the day is the evil
thereof.

---

[1] Sugden, I. 495, says that 'the manuscript of this sermon has been preserved and is in
the Colman Collection; a facsimile was issued by the Wesleyan Methodist Book Room in
1903.' He also repeats the tradition that it was 'the first sermon preached by Wesley after
his ordination'. There *is* a MS sermon on Matt. 6:33 in the Colman Collection, and it is
published in Vol. 4 below (No. 133); readers will see that it is an altogether different
sermon. Moreover, it was not Wesley's 'first sermon', but rather his second; cf.
Heitzenrater, 'John Wesley's Early Sermons', (WHS, XXXVII.115).

1. It is recorded of the nations whom the King of Assyria, after he had carried Israel away into captivity, placed in the cities of Samaria: 'They feared the Lord, and served their own gods.' 'These nations', saith the inspired writer, 'feared the Lord,' performed an outward service to him (a plain proof that they had a fear of God, though not according to knowledge)[2] 'and served their graven images, both their children, and their children's children; as did their fathers, so did they unto this day.'[a]

How nearly does the practice of most modern Christians resemble this of the ancient heathens! 'They fear the Lord': they also perform an outward service to him, and hereby show they have some fear of God; but they likewise 'serve their own gods'. There are those who 'teach them' (as there were who taught the Assyrians) 'the manner of the God of the land';[3] the God whose name the country bears to this day, and who was once worshipped there with an holy worship. 'Howbeit', they do not serve him alone; they do not fear him enough for this; but 'every nation maketh gods of their own, every nation in the cities wherein they dwell.'[4] 'These nations fear the Lord', they have not laid aside the outward form of worshipping him. But 'they serve their graven images,' silver and gold, the work of men's hands. Money, pleasure, and praise, the gods of this world, more than divide their service with the God of Israel. This is the manner both of 'their children and their children's children; as did their fathers, so do they unto this day.'

2. But although, speaking in a loose way, after the common manner of men, those poor heathens were said to 'fear the Lord', yet we may observe the Holy Ghost immediately adds, speaking according to the truth and real nature of things: 'They fear not the Lord, neither do after the law and commandment which the Lord commanded the children of Jacob. With whom the Lord made a covenant, and charged them, saying, Ye shall not fear other gods nor serve them. . . . But the Lord your God ye shall fear, and he shall deliver you out of the hand of all your enemies.'[5]

The same judgment is passed by the unerring Spirit of God, and indeed by all, the eyes of whose understanding he hath opened[6] to discern the things of God, upon these poor Christians,

[a] 2 Kgs. 17:33, 41.

---

[2] See Rom. 10:2.   [3] 2 Kgs. 17:27.   [4] Cf. 2 Kgs. 17:29.
[5] 2 Kgs. 17:34, 35, 39.   [6] See Eph. 1:18.

commonly so called. If we speak according to the truth and real
nature of things, 'they fear not the Lord, neither do they serve
him.' For they do not 'after the covenant the Lord hath made with
them, neither after the law and commandment which he hath
5 commanded them', saying, Thou shalt worship the Lord thy
God, and him only shalt thou serve.[7] 'They serve other gods'[8]
unto this day. And 'no man can serve two masters.'[9]

3. How vain is it for any man to aim at this—to attempt the
serving of two masters! Is it not easy to foresee what must be the
10 unavoidable consequence of such an attempt? 'Either he will hate
the one, and love the other; or else he will hold to the one, and
despise the other.'[10] The two parts of this sentence, although
separately proposed, are to be understood in connection with
each other; for the latter part is a consequence of the former. He
15 will naturally 'hold to' him whom he loves. He will so cleave to
him as to perform to him a willing, faithful, and diligent service.
And in the meantime he will so far at least 'despise' the master he
hates as to have little regard to his commands, and to obey them, if
at all, in a slight and careless manner. Therefore, whatsoever the
20 wise men of the world may suppose, 'Ye cannot serve God and
mammon.'

4. Mammon was the name of one of the heathen gods, who was
supposed to preside over riches.[11] It is here understood of riches
themselves, gold and silver, or in general, money; and by a
25 common figure of speech, of all that may be purchased thereby,
such as ease, honour, and sensual pleasure.

But what are we here to understand by 'serving God'; and what
by 'serving mammon'?

We cannot 'serve God' unless we believe in him. This is the
30 only true foundation of serving him. Therefore believing in God

---

[7] Luke 4:8.   [8] Deut. 7:4.
[9] Matt. 6:24.   [10] *Ibid.*

[11] It was Milton who fixed the tradition that Mammon (Mamon) was the name of a
Syrian god; cf. *Paradise Lost*, i. 678-751, ii. 228-83; and see also *The Jewish Encyclopedia*.
Blackall, *Works*, II. 660-61, repeats this bit of lore: 'And 'tis agreed, I think, by all that the
word Mammon is a Syriac word signifying riches or treasure,' but in this place, 'signifies
not a thing but a person; Mammon is here plainly spoken of as a God, i.e., as an idol or false
god' and 'was accounted by the ancient heathens the god of *money*.'

The Greek μαμωνᾶ is more probably a transcription of the Aramaic māmônā, meaning
'gain' or 'riches'; cf. Sirach 31:8 and Enoch 63:10; see also *Pirke Aboth* 2:12. St.
Augustine, *On the Sermon on the Mount* (II.xiv.47), comments that its Punic equivalent is
'lucre'. Cf. Nos. 28, 'Sermon on the Mount, VIII', §26; 50, 'The Use of Money', §1; and
122, 'Causes of the Inefficacy of Christianity', §8.

as 'reconciling the world to himself'[12] through Christ Jesus, the believing in him as a loving, pardoning God, is the first great branch of his service.

And thus to believe in God implies to *trust* in him as our strength, without whom we can do nothing,[13] who every moment endues us with power from on high, without which it is impossible to please him; as our help, our only help in time of trouble, who compasseth us about with songs of deliverance;[14] as our shield, our defender, and the lifter up of our head above all our enemies that are round about us.[15]

It implies to trust in God as our happiness; as the centre of spirits, the only rest of our souls; the only good who is adequate to all our capacities, and sufficient to satisfy all the desires he hath given us.

It implies (what is nearly allied to the other) to trust in God as our end; to have an eye to him in all things; to use all things only as means of enjoying him; wheresoever we are, or whatsoever we do, to see him that is invisible looking on us well-pleased, and to refer all things to him in Christ Jesus.

5. Thus to believe is the first thing we are to understand by 'serving God'. The second is, to love him.

Now, to love God in the manner the Scripture describes, in the manner God himself requires of us, and by requiring engages to work in us, is to love him as the one God; that is, 'with all our heart, and with all our soul, and with all our mind, and with all our strength'.[16] It is to desire God alone for his own sake, and nothing else but with reference to him; to rejoice in God; to delight in the Lord; not only to seek, but find happiness in him; to enjoy God as the chiefest among ten thousand;[17] to rest in him as our God and our all—in a word, to have such a possession of God as makes us always happy.

6. A third thing we are to understand by 'serving God' is to resemble or imitate him.

So the ancient Father: *Optimus Dei cultus, imitari quem colis*[18]—'It is the best worship or service of God, to imitate him you worship.'

---

[12] 2 Cor. 5:19.   [13] See John 15:5.   [14] See Ps. 32:7 (AV).
[15] See Ps. 27:6.   [16] Cf. Mark 12:30.   [17] S. of S. 5:10.
[18] Is this Wesley's memory of St. Augustine, *De civ. Dei*, viii.17, *'religionis summa sit imitari quem colis'*? If not, 'the ancient father' remains unidentified. In his abridged edn. of Arndt's *True Christianity*, Wesley includes the aphorism: 'The whole of religion . . . is to

We here speak of imitating or resembling him in the spirit of our minds.[19] For here the true Christian imitation of God begins. God is a Spirit; and they that imitate or resemble him must do it in spirit and in truth.[20]

5 Now God is love;[21] therefore they who resemble him in the spirit of their minds are transformed into the same image. They are merciful even as he is merciful.[22] Their soul is all love. They are kind, benevolent, compassionate, tender-hearted; and that not only to the good and gentle, but also to the froward. Yea, they 10 are, like him, loving unto every man,[23] and their mercy extends to all his works.

7. One thing more we are to understand by 'serving God', and that is, the obeying him; the glorifying him with our bodies as well as with our spirits;[24] the keeping his outward commandments; the 15 zealously doing whatever he hath enjoined; the carefully avoiding whatever he hath forbidden; the performing all the ordinary actions of life with a single eye and a pure heart—offering them all in holy, fervent love, as sacrifices to God through Jesus Christ.

8. Let us consider now what we are to understand, on the other 20 hand, by 'serving mammon'. And first, it implies the *trusting* in riches, in money, or the things purchasable thereby, as our strength, the means whereby we shall perform whatever cause we have in hand; the trusting in them as our help, by which we look to be comforted in or delivered out of trouble.

25 It implies the trusting in the world for happiness; the supposing that 'a man's life consisteth' (the comfort of his life) 'in the abundance of the things which he possesseth;'[25] the looking for rest in the things that are seen; for content, in outward plenty; the expecting that satisfaction in the things of the world which can 30 never be found out of God.

And if we do this we cannot but make the world our end; the ultimate end, if not of all, at least of many of our undertakings,

---

imitate whom thou dost worship. . . . This was well understood by Plato, in whose school was the maxim, "The perfection of man consisteth in the imitation of God." ' (*Christian Lib.*, I.228-29). Wesley may also have remembered Tillotson's comment that '*Deus optimus maximus* was the constant title of God, both among the Greeks and Romans', and his added quotation from Seneca, *primus deorum cultus est deos credere*, etc. (*Works*, I.678). The idea is found in St. Cyprian (Migne, *PL*, IV.215) but not Wesley's actual phrase. See also Wesley's *Earnest Appeal*, §28 (11:55 of this edn.).

[19] See Eph. 4:23.   [20] See John 4:24.
[21] 1 John 4:8, 16.   [22] See Luke 6:36.
[23] Ps. 145:9 (BCP).   [24] See 1 Cor. 6:20.   [25] Cf. Luke 12:15.

many of our actions and designs—in which we shall aim only at an increase of wealth; at the obtaining pleasure or praise; at the gaining a larger measure of temporal things, without any reference to things eternal.

9. The 'serving mammon' implies, secondly, loving the world; 5 desiring it for its own sake; the placing our joy in the things thereof, and setting our hearts upon them; the seeking (what indeed it is impossible we should find) our happiness therein; the resting with the whole weight of our souls upon the staff of this broken reed, although daily experience shows it cannot support, 10 but will only 'enter into our hand and pierce it'.[26]

10. To resemble, to be conformed to the world, is the third thing we are to understand by 'serving mammon'; to have not only designs, but desires, tempers, affections suitable to those of the world; to be of an earthly, sensual mind, chained down to the 15 things of earth; to be self-willed, inordinate lovers of ourselves; to think highly of our own attainments; to desire and delight in the praise of men; to fear, shun, and abhor reproach; to be impatient of reproof, easy to be provoked, and swift to return evil for evil.

11. To 'serve mammon' is, lastly, to obey the world, by 20 outwardly conforming to its maxims and customs; to walk as other men walk, in the common road, in the broad, smooth, beaten path; to be in the fashion; to follow a multitude; to do like the rest of our neighbours; that is, to do the will of the flesh and the mind, to gratify our appetites and inclinations—to sacrifice to ourselves, 25 to aim at our own ease and pleasure in the general course both of our words and actions.

Now what can be more undeniably clear than that we 'cannot' thus 'serve God and mammon'?

12. Does not every man see that he cannot *comfortably* serve 30 both? That to trim between God and the world[27] is the sure way to be disappointed in both, and to have no rest either in one or the other? How uncomfortable a condition must he be in, who, having the fear but not the love of God, who, serving him, but not with all his heart, has only the toils and not the joys of religion! He 35 has religion enough to make him miserable, but not enough to

---

[26] Isa. 36:6.

[27] Johnson's definition of 'trim' is 'to balance; to fluctuate between two parties', and he gives a sample usage from South's *Sermons:* 'For men to pretend that their will obeys the law, while all besides their will serves the faction; what is this but a gross, fulsome juggling with their duty, and a kind of *trimming* it between God and the devil.'

make him happy: his religion will not let him enjoy the world, and the world will not let him enjoy God. So that by halting between both he loses both, and has no peace either in God or the world.

13. Does not every man see that he cannot serve both consistently with himself? What more glaring inconsistency can be conceived than must continually appear in his whole behaviour who is endeavouring to obey both these masters, striving to 'serve God and mammon'! He is indeed a 'sinner that goeth two ways'[28]—one step forward and another backward. He is continually building up with one hand and pulling down with the other. He loves sin, and he hates it: he is always seeking, and yet always fleeing from God. He would, and he would not. He is not the same man for one day, no, not for an hour together. He is a motley mixture of all sorts of contrarieties; a heap of contradictions jumbled in one. Oh, be consistent with thyself, one way or the other. Turn to the right hand or to the left.[29] If 'mammon' be God, serve thou him; if the Lord, then serve him.[30] But never think of serving either at all unless it be with thy whole heart.

14. Does not every reasonable, every thinking man see that he cannot *possibly* 'serve God and mammon'? Because there is the most absolute contrariety, the most irreconcilable enmity, between them. The contrariety between the most opposite things on earth, between fire and water, darkness and light, vanishes into nothing when compared to the contrariety between God and mammon. So that in whatsoever respect you serve the one, you necessarily renounce the other. Do you believe in God through Christ? Do you *trust* in him as your strength, your help, your shield, and your exceeding great reward?[31] As your happiness? Your end in all, above all things? Then you cannot *trust* in riches. It is absolutely impossible you should, so long as you have this faith in God. Do you thus 'trust in riches'?[32] Then you have denied the faith.[33] You do not trust in the living God.[34] Do you *love* God? Do you seek and find happiness in him? Then you cannot love the world, neither the things of the world. You are crucified to the world and the world crucified to you.[35] Do you 'love the

---

[28] Ecclus. 2:12.
[29] Gen. 24:49, etc.
[30] See 1 Kgs. 18:21.
[31] See Gen. 15:1.
[32] Mark 10:24.
[33] 1 Tim. 5:8.
[34] 1 Tim. 4:10; 6:17.
[35] See Gal. 6:14.

world'?[36] Are your affections set on things beneath?[37] Do you seek happiness in earthly things? Then it is impossible you should love God. Then the love of the Father is not in you. Do you *resemble* God? Are you merciful, as your Father is merciful?[38] Are you transformed by the renewal of your mind[39] into the image of him that created you? Then you cannot be conformed to the present world.[40] You have renounced all its affections and lusts. Are you conformed to the world? Does your soul still bear the image of the earthly?[41] Then you are not renewed in the spirit of your mind.[42] You do not bear the image of the heavenly.[43] Do you *obey God?* Are you zealous to do his will on earth as the angels do in heaven? Then it is impossible you should *obey mammon.* Then you set the world at open defiance. You trample its customs and maxims under foot, and will neither follow nor be led by them. Do you follow the world? Do you live like other men? Do you please men? Do you please yourself? Then you cannot be a servant of God. You are of your master and father, the devil.[44]

15. Therefore thou shalt worship the Lord thy God, and him only shalt thou serve.[45] Thou shalt lay aside all thoughts of obeying two masters, of serving God and mammon. Thou shalt propose to thyself no end, no help, no happiness, but God. Thou shalt seek nothing in earth or heaven but him; thou shalt aim at nothing but to know, to love, and enjoy him. And because this is all your business below, the only view you can reasonably have, the one design you are to pursue in all things, 'Therefore I say unto you' (as our Lord continues his discourse) 'Take no thought for your life, what ye shall eat, or what ye shall drink; nor yet for your body, what ye shall put on.'[46] A deep and weighty direction, which it imports us well to consider and throughly to understand.

16. Our Lord does not here require that we should be utterly without thought, even touching the concerns of this life. A giddy, careless temper is at the farthest remove from the whole religion of Jesus Christ. Neither does he require us to be 'slothful in business',[47] to be slack and dilatory therein. This likewise is contrary to the whole spirit and genius of his religion. A Christian abhors sloth as much as drunkenness, and flees from idleness as he does from adultery. He well knows that there is one kind of

[36] 1 John 2:15.
[37] See Col. 3:2.
[38] See Luke 6:36.
[39] See Rom. 12:2.
[40] *Ibid.*
[41] See 1 Cor. 15:49.
[42] Eph. 4:23.
[43] See 1 Cor. 15:49.
[44] See John 8:44.
[45] Luke 4:8.
[46] Matt. 6:25.
[47] Rom. 12:11.

thought and care with which God is well-pleased; which is absolutely needful for the due performance of those outward works unto which the providence of God has called him.

5 It is the will of God that every man should labour to 'eat his own bread';[48] yea, and that every man should provide for his own, for them of his own household. It is likewise his will that we should 'owe no man anything',[49] but 'provide things honest in the sight of all men'.[50] But this cannot be done without taking some thought, without having some care upon our minds; yea, often not without 10 long and serious thought, not without much and earnest care. Consequently this care to provide for ourselves and our household, this thought how to render to all their dues, our blessed Lord does not condemn. Yea, it is good and acceptable in the sight of God our Saviour.[51]

15 It is good and acceptable to God that we should so take thought concerning whatever we have in hand as to have a clear comprehension of what we are about to do, and to plan our business before we enter upon it. And it is right that we should carefully consider from time to time what steps we are to take 20 therein; as well as that we should prepare all things beforehand for the carrying it on in the most effectual manner. This care, termed by some, 'the care of the head', [π] it was by no means our Lord's design to condemn.

17. What he here condemns is 'the care of the heart': the 25 anxious, uneasy care; the care that hath torment; all such care as does hurt, either to the soul or body. What he forbids is that care which sad experience shows wastes the blood and drinks up the spirits;[52] which anticipates all the misery it fears, and comes to torment us before the time. He forbids only that care which 30 poisons the blessings of today by fear of what may be tomorrow; which cannot enjoy the present plenty through apprehensions of future want. This care is not only a sore disease, a grievous sickness of soul, but also an heinous offence against God, a sin of the deepest dye. It is an high affront to the gracious Governor and 35 wise Disposer of all things; necessarily implying that the great

---

[48] 2 Thess. 3:12.
[49] Rom. 13:8.
[50] Rom. 12:17.   [51] 1 Tim. 2:3.
[52] Cf. Chambers's *Cyclopaedia*, on 'Humours'; see also the poetic tradition on 'care', as in Spenser's *Mother Hubbard's Tale*, ll. 903-4, and Shakespeare's *Julius Caesar*, II.i.231-32 ('fantasies which busy care draws in the brains of men').

Judge does not do right,[53] that he does not order all things well.[54] It plainly implies that he is wanting either in wisdom, if he does not know what things we stand in need of, or in goodness, if he does not provide those things for all who put their trust in him. Beware, therefore, that you take not thought in this sense: be ye anxiously 5 careful for nothing.[55] Take no uneasy thought. This is a plain, sure rule—*uneasy* care is *unlawful* care. With a single eye to God, do all that in you lies to provide things honest in the sight of all men.[56] And then give up all into better hands: leave the whole event to God. 10

18. 'Take no thought' of this kind, no uneasy thought, even 'for your life, what ye shall eat, or what ye shall drink, nor yet for your body, what ye shall put on. Is not the life more than meat, and the body than raiment?' If then God gave you life, the greater gift, will he not give you food to sustain it? If he hath given you the body, 15 how can ye doubt but he will give you raiment to cover it? More especially if you give yourselves up to him, and serve him with your whole heart. 'Behold', see before your eyes, 'the fowls of the air: for they sow not, neither do they reap, nor gather into barns;' and yet they lack nothing, 'yet your heavenly Father feedeth them. 20 Are ye not much better than they?' Ye that are creatures capable of God? Are ye not of more account in the eyes of God? Of a higher rank in the scale of beings?[57] 'And which of you by taking thought can add one cubit to his stature?'[58] What profit have you then from this anxious thought? It is every way fruitless and 25 unavailing.

'And why take ye thought for raiment?' Have ye not a daily reproof wherever you turn your eyes? 'Consider the lilies of the field, how they grow; they toil not, neither do they spin. And yet I say unto you, that even Solomon in all his glory was not arrayed 30 like one of these. Wherefore if God so clothe the grass of the field, which today is, and tomorrow is cast into the oven', is cut down, burnt up, and seen no more, 'shall he not much more clothe you, O ye of little faith?' You, whom he made to endure for

---

[53] See Gen. 18:25.
[54] See Mark 7:37.   [55] See Phil. 4:6.
[56] Rom. 12:17. For Wesley's use of the *in se est* theme, see above, pp. 72-73.
[57] Cf. No. 56, 'God's Approbation of His Works', I.14 and n.
[58] Matt. 6:27. In both Johnson's *Dictionary* and *OED* 'cubit' is defined as a measure of *space*, the sense in which Wesley uses it here. Cf., however, his *Notes*, where he uses it as a measure of *time*: *'And which of you'*, if you are ever so careful, can even add a moment to your own life thereby? This seems by far the most easy and natural sense of the words.'

ever and ever, to be pictures of his own eternity![59] Ye are indeed of
little faith. Otherwise ye could not doubt of his love and care; no,
not for a moment.

19. 'Therefore take no thought, saying, What shall we eat,' if
we lay up no treasure upon earth? 'What shall we drink,' if we
serve God with all our strength, if our eye be singly fixed on him?
'Wherewithal shall we be clothed,' if we are not conformed to the
world, if we disoblige those by whom we might be profited? 'For
after all these things do the Gentiles seek,' the heathens who
know not God. But ye are sensible, 'your heavenly Father
knoweth that ye have need of all these things.' And he hath
pointed out to you an infallible way of being constantly supplied
therewith. 'Seek ye first the kingdom of God, and his
righteousness, and all these things shall be added unto you.'[60]

20. 'Seek ye first the kingdom of God.' Before ye give place to
any other thought or care let it be your concern that the God and
Father of our Lord Jesus Christ, who 'gave his only-begotten
Son, to the end that believing in him ye might not perish, but have
everlasting life',[61] may reign in your heart, may manifest himself in
your soul, and dwell and rule there: 'that he may cast down every
high thing which exalteth itself against the knowledge of God,
and bring into captivity every thought to the obedience of
Christ.'[62] Let God have the sole dominion over you. Let him reign
without a rival. Let him possess all your heart, and rule alone. Let
him be your one desire, your joy, your love; so that all that is
within you may continually cry out, 'The Lord God omnipotent
reigneth.'[63]

'Seek the kingdom of God and his righteousness.' Righteousness is the fruit of God's reigning in the heart. And what is
righteousness but love?[64] The love of God and of all mankind,
flowing from faith in Jesus Christ, and producing humbleness of
mind, meekness, gentleness, long-suffering, patience, deadness
to the world;[65] and every right disposition of heart toward God
and toward man. And by these it produces all holy actions,
whatsoever are lovely or of good report;[66] whatsoever works of

[59] Wisd. 2:23.   [60] Matt. 6:31-33.
[61] Cf. John 3:16.   [62] Cf. 2 Cor. 10:5.
[63] Rev. 19:6.
[64] Cf. No. 7, 'The Way to the Kingdom', I.7 and n.
[65] See Col. 3:12; see also Gal. 5:22-23.
[66] See Phil. 4:8.

faith and labour of love[67] are acceptable to God and profitable to man.

'His righteousness.' This is all *his* righteousness still: it is his own free *gift* to us, for the sake of Jesus Christ the righteous,[68] through whom alone it is purchased for us. And it is his *work:* it is he alone that worketh it in us by the inspiration of his Holy Spirit.

21. Perhaps the well observing this may give light to some other Scriptures which we have not always so clearly understood. St. Paul, speaking in his Epistle to the Romans concerning the unbelieving Jews, saith, 'They, being ignorant of God's righteousness, and going about to establish their own righteousness, have not submitted themselves unto the righteousness of God.'[69] I believe this may be one sense of the words:[70] they were 'ignorant of God's righteousness', not only of the righteousness of Christ, imputed to every believer,[71] whereby all his sins are blotted out, and he is reconciled to the favour of God; but (which seems here to be more immediately understood) they were ignorant of that inward righteousness, of that holiness of heart, which is with the utmost propriety termed 'God's righteousness', as being both his own free gift through Christ, and his own work, by his almighty Spirit.[72] And because they were ignorant of this they 'went about to establish their own righteousness'. They laboured to establish that outside righteousness which might very properly be termed 'their own'; for neither was it wrought by the Spirit of God nor was it owned or accepted of him. They might work this themselves, by their own natural strength; and when they had done, it was a stink in his nostrils. And yet, trusting in

---

[67] See 1 Thess. 1:3.
[68] 1 John 2:1.   [69] Rom. 10:3.
[70] This sentence is inserted only in the *Works*, 1771.
[71] Note Wesley's nearly casual use of this phrase, destined to become a bone of contention between him and the Calvinists; cf. Nos. 20, *The Lord Our Righteousness* (intro., pp. 444-46); and 21, 'Sermon on the Mount, I', I.11. See also Wesley's *Remarks on Mr. Hill's Review*, espec. 12:III, where Wesley weighs and balances the pros and cons of what he calls 'that ambiguous, unscriptural phrase, so liable to be misinterpreted' ('the imputed righteousness of Christ'). His conclusion (§44): 'With regard to [the doctrine] that we are justified merely for the sake of what Christ has *done* and *suffered*, I have constantly and earnestly maintained [that] above four and thirty years. And I have frequently used the *phrase* [*viz.*, 'the imputed righteousness of Christ'], hoping thereby to please others. . . . But it has had a contrary effect. . . . Therefore I will use it no more, unless it occur in an hymn, or steal upon me unawares. . . .'
[72] In this implied rejection of self-righteousness Wesley manages an indirect assertion of the *sola fide* and yet yoked, as always, with holiness of heart; cf. No. 21, 'Sermon on the Mount, I', I.11.

this, they would 'not submit themselves unto the righteousness of God'. Yea, they hardened themselves against that faith whereby alone it was possible to attain it. 'For Christ is the end of the law for righteousness to everyone that believeth.'[73] Christ, when he
5 said, 'It is finished,'[74] put an end to that law—to the law of external rites and ceremonies—that he might 'bring in a better righteousness'[75] through his blood, by that one oblation of himself once offered,[76] even the image of God, into the inmost soul of 'everyone that believeth'.

10 22. Nearly related to these are those words of the Apostle in his Epistle to the Philippians: 'I count all things but dung that I may win Christ,' an entrance into his everlasting kingdom, 'and be found in him', believing in him, 'not having mine own righteousness, which is of the law, but that which is through the
15 faith of Christ, the righteousness which is of God by faith'[77]—'not having my own righteousness, which is of the law', a barely external righteousness, the outside religion I formerly had when I hoped to be accepted of God because I was, 'touching the righteousness which is in the law, blameless'[78]—'but that which is
20 through the faith of Christ, the righteousness which is of God by faith:' that holiness of heart, that renewal of the soul in all its desires, tempers, and affections, 'which is of God'. It is the work of God and not of man, 'by faith'; through the faith of Christ, through the revelation of Jesus Christ[79] in us, and by faith in his
25 blood;[80] whereby alone we obtain the remission of our sins, and an inheritance among those that are sanctified.[81]

23. 'Seek ye first' this 'kingdom of God' in your hearts, this 'righteousness', which is the gift and work of God, the image of God renewed in your souls—'and all these things' shall be added
30 unto you: all things needful for the body; such a measure of all as God sees most for the advancement of his kingdom. These 'shall be added', they shall be thrown in, over and above. In seeking the peace and the love of God you shall not only find what you more immediately seek, even the kingdom that cannot be moved; but
35 also what you seek not, not at all for its own sake, but only in reference to the other. You shall find in your way to the kingdom all outward things, so far as they are expedient for you. This care

---

[73] Rom. 10:4. [74] John 19:30. [75] Cf. Heb. 7:19.
[76] BCP, Communion, Prayer of Consecration.
[77] Phil. 3:8-9. [78] Phil. 3:6.
[79] Gal. 1:12. [80] Rom. 3:25. [81] See Acts 20:32.

God hath taken upon himself: cast you all your care upon him.[82]
He knoweth your wants; and whatsoever is lacking he will not fail
to supply.

24. 'Therefore take no thought for the morrow.'[83] Not only,
take ye no thought how to lay up treasures on earth, how to 5
increase in worldly substance; take no thought how to procure
more food than you can eat, or more raiment than you can put on;
or more money than is required from day to day for the plain,
reasonable purposes of life: but take no *uneasy* thought even
concerning those things which are absolutely needful for the 10
body. Do not trouble yourself now with thinking what you shall do
at a season which is yet afar off. Perhaps that season will never
come; or it will be no concern of yours—before then you will have
passed through all the waves, and be landed in eternity. All those
distant views do not belong to *you*, who are but a creature of a 15
day.[84] Nay, what have you to do with 'the morrow', more strictly
speaking? Why should you perplex yourself without need? God
provides for you today what is needful to sustain the life which he
hath given you. It is enough. Give yourself up into his hands. If
you live another day he will provide for that also. 20

25. Above all, do not make the care of future things a pretence
for neglecting present duty. This is the most fatal way of 'taking
thought for the morrow'. And how common is it among men!
Many, if we exhort them to keep a conscience void of offence,[85] to
abstain from what they are convinced is evil, do not scruple to 25
reply: 'How then must we live? Must we not take care of ourselves
and of our families?' And this they imagine to be a sufficient
reason for continuing in known, wilful sin. They say, and perhaps
think, they would serve God now were it not that they should by
and by lose their bread. They would prepare for eternity; but they 30
are afraid of wanting the necessaries of life. So they serve the devil
for a morsel of bread; they rush into hell for fear of want; they
throw away their poor souls lest they should some time or other
fall short of what is needful for their bodies.

It is not strange that they who thus take the matter out of God's 35
hand should be so often disappointed of the very things they seek;
that while they throw away heaven to secure the things of earth

---

82 See 1 Pet. 5:7.
83 Cf. Matt. 6:34.
84 Pindar, *Pythian Odes*, viii. 95. Cf. Wesley's Pref., §5 and n.
85 Acts 24:16.

they lose the one, but do not gain the other. The jealous God, in the wise course of his providence, frequently suffers this. So that they who will not cast their care on God, who, taking thought for temporal things, have little concern for things eternal, lose the
5 very portion which they have chosen. There is a visible blast on all their undertakings: whatsoever they do it doth not prosper. Insomuch that after they have forsaken God for the world they lose what they sought, as well as what they sought not. They fall short of the kingdom of God and his righteousness; nor yet are
10 other things added unto them.

26. There is another way of 'taking thought for the morrow', which is equally forbidden in these words. It is possible to take thought in a wrong manner, even with regard to spiritual things; to be so careful about what may be by and by as to neglect what is
15 now required at our hands. How insensibly do we slide into this if we are not continually watching unto prayer![86] How easily are we carried away in a kind of waking dream,[87] projecting distant schemes, and drawing fine scenes in our own imagination! We think what good we will do when we are in such a place, or when
20 such a time is come! How useful we will be, how plenteous in good works, when we are easier in our circumstances! How earnestly we will serve God when once such an hindrance is out of the way!

Or, perhaps, you are now in heaviness of soul:[88] God as it were
25 hides his face from you. You see little of the light of his countenance; you cannot taste his redeeming love. In such a temper of mind how natural is it to say, 'O how I will praise God when the light of his countenance shall be again lifted up upon my soul![89] How will I exhort others to praise him when his love is
30 again shed abroad in my heart![90] Then I will do thus and thus: I will speak for God in all places; I will not be ashamed of the gospel of Christ.[91] Then I will redeem the time,[92] I will use to the uttermost every talent I have received.' Do not believe thyself. Thou wilt not do it then unless thou dost it now. 'He that is

---

[86] See 1 Pet. 4:7.

[87] Cf. Diogenes Laertius, *Lives*, V. 18 (Loeb, 184:460-61), where Aristotle is said to have spoken of hope as 'a kind of waking dream'.

[88] Johnson's *Dictionary* and the *OED* both define 'heaviness' as a 'dejection or dejectedness of mind'. Johnson adds 'depression of spirit'. Cf. Nos. 46 and 47: 'The Wilderness State' and 'Heaviness through Manifold Temptations'.

[89] See Num. 6:26.

[90] See Rom. 5:5.

[91] See Rom. 1:16.

[92] See Eph. 5:16.

faithful in that which is little', of whatsoever kind it be, whether it be worldly substance or the fear or love of God, 'will be faithful in that which is much.'[93] But if thou now hidest one talent in the earth, thou wilt then hide five.[94] That is, if ever they are given; but there is small reason to expect they ever will. Indeed 'unto him that hath', that is, uses what he hath, 'shall be given, and he shall have more abundantly. But from him that hath not', that is, uses not the grace which he hath already received, whether in a larger or smaller degree, 'shall be taken away even that which he hath.'[95]

27. And 'take no thought' for the temptations of tomorrow. This also is a dangerous snare. Think not, 'When such a temptation comes, what shall I do, how shall I stand? I feel I have not power to resist: I am not able to conquer that enemy.' Most true: you have not *now* the power which you do not *now* stand in need of. You are not able at *this time* to conquer that enemy; and at *this time* he does not assault you. With the grace you have now you could not withstand the temptations which you have not. But when the temptation comes the grace will come. In greater trials you will have greater strength. When sufferings abound, the consolations of God will in the same proportion abound also. So that in every situation the grace of God will be sufficient for you.[96] He doth not suffer you 'to be tempted' today 'above that ye are able to bear. And in every temptation he will make a way to escape.'[97] 'As thy day, so thy strength shall be.'[98]

28. 'Let the morrow' therefore 'take thought for the things of itself.' That is, when the morrow comes, then think of it. Live thou today. Be it thy earnest care to improve the present hour. This is your own, and it is your all. The past is as nothing, as though it had never been. The future is nothing to you. It is not yours; perhaps it never will be. There is no depending on what is yet to come; for you 'know not what a day may bring forth'.[99]

---

[93] Cf. Luke 16:10.

[94] See Matt. 25:18.

[95] Cf. Matt. 13:12. Both Poole *(Annotations)* and Henry *(Exposition)* explain this paradox in terms of election; cf. Poole's distinction between those who have 'the seed of God' or 'the root of grace' in them and those who do not. Henry reminds us 'that God is debtor to no man. His grace is his own; he gives or withholds it at pleasure. The difference must be resolved into God's sovereignty.' For Wesley's very different interpretation, cf. No. 85, 'On Working Out Our Own Salvation', III.4-6: 'No man sins because he has not grace, but because he does not use the grace which he hath. . . . Stir up the spark of grace which is now in you and he will give you more grace.'

[96] See 2 Cor. 12:9.

[97] Cf. 1 Cor. 10:13.

[98] Cf. Deut. 33:25.

[99] Cf. Prov. 27:1.

Therefore live today: lose not an hour; use this moment; for it is
your portion. 'Who knoweth the things which have been before
him,'[100] 'or which shall be after him under the sun?'[101] The
generations that were from the beginning of the world, where are
they now? Fled away, forgotten. They *were:* they lived their day;
they were shook off of the earth, as leaves off of their trees.[102]
They mouldered away into common dust. Another and another
race succeeded; then they 'followed the generation of their
fathers, and shall never' more 'see the light.'[103] Now is thy turn
upon the earth. 'Rejoice, O young man, in the days of thy
youth.'[104] Enjoy the very, very now;[105] by enjoying him 'whose
years fail not'.[106] Now let thine eye be singly fixed on him, in
'whom is no variableness, neither shadow of turning'.[107] Now give
him thy heart; now stay thyself on him; now be thou holy as he is
holy.[108] Now lay hold of the blessed opportunity of doing his
acceptable and perfect will.[109] Now 'rejoice to suffer the loss of all
things, so thou mayst win Christ.'[110]

29. Gladly suffer today, for his name's sake, whatsoever he
permits this day to come upon thee. But look not at the sufferings
of tomorrow. 'Sufficient unto the day is the evil thereof.'[111] Evil it
is, speaking after the manner of men; whether it be reproach or
want, pain or sickness. But in the language of God, all is blessing:
'It is a precious balm,'[112] prepared by the wisdom of God, and

[100] Cf. Ecclus. 23:20; Sus. 42.
[101] Cf. Eccles. 6:12.
[102] Cf. Homer, *Iliad*, vi. 146. See No. 70, 'The Case of Reason Impartially
Considered', II.2 and n.
[103] Cf. Ps. 49:19 (BCP).
[104] Eccles. 11:9.
[105] Cf. St. Augustine's analysis of time (past, future, and present) in *Confessions*, XI.
xi-xxxi, where times past and future signify determinate actions registered in either
memoria or *expectatio*, but where *time present* is grasped by 'contuition' in that 'moment'
which eludes clock-time and is the 'truly, truly *now*', the time of human freedom. Cf. John
Byrom, 'Time Past, Future, and Present', in *The Poems of John Byrom*, ed. A. W. Ward
(Manchester, printed for the Chetham Society, 1894), Vol. I, Pt. II, p. 567:
> Time present only is within thy pow'r:
> Now, now improve, then whilst thou can'st, the hour!
Cf. Nos. 5, 'Justification by Faith', IV.2 and n.; and 33, 'Sermon on the Mount, XIII', III.7.
[106] Cf. Heb. 1:12.
[107] Jas. 1:17.
[108] See 1 Pet. 1:15, 16.
[109] See Rom. 12:2.
[110] Cf. Phil. 3:8.
[111] Matt. 6:34.
[112] Cf. Ps. 141:6 (BCP).

variously dispensed among his children according to the various sicknesses of their souls. And he gives in one day sufficient for that day, proportioned to the want and strength of the patient. If therefore thou snatchest today what belongs to the morrow, if thou addest this to what is given thee already, it will be more than 5 thou canst bear: this is the way, not to heal, but to destroy thy own soul. Take therefore just as much as he gives thee today: today do and suffer his will. Today give up thyself, thy body, soul, and spirit, to God, through Christ Jesus; desiring nothing but that God may be glorified in all thou art, all thou dost, all thou 10 sufferest; seeking nothing but to know God, and his Son Jesus Christ, through the Eternal Spirit; pursuing nothing but to love him, to serve him, and to enjoy him, at this hour, and to all eternity!

Now unto God the Father, who hath made me and all the 15 world; unto God the Son, who hath redeemed me and all mankind; unto God the Holy Ghost, who sanctifieth me and all the elect people of God: be honour, and praise, majesty, and dominion, for ever and ever! Amen.[113]

---

[113] A rare instance of a formal ascription (cf. No. 1, *Salvation by Faith*, III.9 and n.); it is a conflation of fragments from 'A Catechism' in the BCP.

Upon our Lord's Sermon on the Mount

Discourse the Tenth

Matthew 7:1-12

Judge not, that ye be not judged.

5   *For with what judgment ye judge, ye shall be judged; and with what measure ye mete, it shall be measured to you again.*

   And why beholdest thou the mote that is in thy brother's eye, but considerest not the beam that is in thine own eye?

   Or how wilt thou say to thy brother, Let me pull out the mote out of
10 *thine eye; and, behold, a beam is in thine own eye?*

   Thou hypocrite, first cast out the beam out of thine own eye; and then thou shalt see clearly to cast out the mote out of thy brother's eye.

   Give not that which is holy unto dogs, neither cast your pearls before swine; lest they trample them under their feet, and turn again and rend
15 *you.*

   Ask, and it shall be given you; seek, and ye shall find; knock, and it shall be opened unto you.

   For everyone that asketh, receiveth; and he that seeketh, findeth; and to him that knocketh, it shall be opened.

20   *Or what man is there of you, who, if his son ask bread, will give him a stone? Or if he ask a fish, will give him a serpent?*

   If ye, then, being evil, know how to give good gifts unto your children, how much more shall your Father which is in heaven give good things to them that ask him!

25   *Therefore all things whatsoever ye would that men should do to you, do ye even so to them; for this is the law and the prophets.*

1. Our blessed Lord, having now finished his main design, having, first, delivered the sum of true religion, carefully guarded against those glosses of men whereby they would make the Word
30 of God of none effect; and having, next, laid down rules touching that right intention which we are to preserve in all our outward actions, now proceeds to point out the main hindrances of this religion, and concludes all with a suitable application.

2. In the fifth chapter our great Teacher has fully described inward religion in its various branches. He has there laid before us those dispositions of soul which constitute real Christianity; the tempers contained in that holiness 'without which no man shall see the Lord';[1] the affections which, when flowing from their proper fountain, from a living faith in God through Christ Jesus, are intrinsically and essentially good, and acceptable to God. In the sixth he has shown how all our actions likewise, even those that are indifferent in their own nature, may be made holy, and good, and acceptable to God, by a pure and holy intention.[2] Whatever is done without this he declares is of no value with God; whereas whatever outward works are thus consecrated to God are in his sight of great price.

3. In the former part of this chapter he points out the most common and most fatal hindrances of this holiness. In the latter he exhorts us by various motives to break through all and secure that prize of our high calling.[3]

4. The first hindrance he cautions us against is judging: 'Judge not, that ye be not judged.' Judge not others, that ye be not judged of the Lord, that ye bring not vengeance on your own heads. 'For with what judgment ye judge, ye shall be judged; and with what measure ye mete, it shall be measured to you again'—a plain and equitable rule, whereby God permits you to determine for yourselves in what manner he shall deal with you in the judgment of the great day.

5. There is no station of life, nor any period of time, from the hour of our first repenting and believing the gospel till we are made perfect in love, wherein this caution is not needful for every child of God. For occasions of judging can never be wanting. And the temptations to it are innumerable; many whereof are so artfully disguised that we fall into the sin before we suspect any danger. And unspeakable are the mischiefs produced hereby: always to him that judges another, thus wounding his own soul, and exposing himself to the righteous judgment of God; and frequently to those who are judged, whose hands hang down, who are weakened and hindered in their course, if not wholly turned out of the way,[4] and caused to draw back even to perdition. Yea,

---

[1] Heb. 12:14.
[2] Cf. No. 26, 'Sermon on the Mount, VI', §1 and n., for other comments on holy living understood as purity of intention.
[3] See Phil. 3:14. [4] See Heb. 12:13.

how often when this 'root of bitterness springs up', are 'many defiled thereby';[5] by reason whereof the way of truth itself is evil spoken of,[6] and that worthy name blasphemed whereby we are called.

5 6. Yet it does not appear that our Lord designed this caution only or chiefly for the children of God; but rather for the children of the world, for the men who know not God. These cannot but hear of those who are not of the world; who follow after the religion above described; who endeavour to be humble, serious, 10 gentle, merciful, and pure in heart; who earnestly desire such measures of these holy tempers as they have not yet attained, and wait for them in doing all good to all men, and patiently suffering evil. Whoever go but thus far cannot be hid, no more than 'a city set upon a hill'.[7] And why do not those who 'see' their 'good works 15 glorify their Father which is in heaven'?[8] What excuse have they for not treading in their steps? For not imitating their example, and being followers of them, as they are also of Christ?[9] Why, in order to provide an excuse for themselves, they condemn those whom they ought to imitate. They spend their time in finding out 20 their neighbour's faults,[10] instead of amending their own. They are so busied about others going out of the way, that themselves never come into it at all; at least, never get forward, never go beyond a poor dead form of godliness without the power.[11]

7. It is to these more especially that our Lord says, 'Why 25 beholdest thou the mote that is in thy brother's eye', the infirmities, the mistakes, the imprudence, the weakness of the children of God, 'but considerest not the beam that is in thine own eye?' Thou considerest not the damnable impenitence, the satanic pride, the accursed self-will, the idolatrous love of the 30 world, which are in thyself, and which make thy whole life an abomination to the Lord. Above all, with what supine carelessness and indifference art thou dancing over the mouth of hell! And 'how', then, with what grace, with what decency or

---

[5] Cf. Heb. 12:15.
[6] See 2 Pet.2:2.
[7] Cf. Matt. 5:14.
[8] Cf. Matt. 5:16.
[9] See 1 Cor. 11:1.
[10] Cf. this condemnation of fault-finding with No. 65, 'The Duty of Reproving our Neighbour'.
[11] See 2 Tim. 3:5.

modesty, 'wilt thou say to thy brother, Let me pull out the mote out of thine eye'—the excess of zeal for God, the extreme of self-denial, the too great disengagement from worldly cares and employments, the desire to be day and night in prayer, or hearing the words of eternal life—'And behold a beam is in thine own 5 eye!' Not a mote, like one of these. 'Thou hypocrite!' who pretendest to care for others, and hast no care for thy own soul; who makest a show of zeal for the cause of God, when in truth thou neither lovest nor fearest him! 'First cast out the beam out of thine own eye.' Cast out the beam of impenitence. Know thyself.[12] 10 See and feel thyself a sinner. Feel that thy inward parts are very wickedness,[13] that thou are altogether corrupt and abominable,[14] and that the wrath of God abideth on thee.[15] Cast out the beam of pride. Abhor thyself. Sink down as in dust and ashes. Be more and more little, and mean, and base, and vile in thine own eyes. 15 Cast out the beam of self-will. Learn what that meaneth, 'If any man will come after me, let him renounce himself.' Deny thyself and take up thy cross daily.[16] Let thy whole soul cry out, 'I came down from heaven' (for so thou didst, thou never-dying spirit, whether thou knowest it or no) 'not to do my own will, but the will 20 of him that sent me.'[17] Cast out the beam of love of the world. Love not the world, neither the things of the world.[18] Be thou crucified unto the world, and the world crucified unto thee.[19] Only *use* the world, but *enjoy* God.[20] Seek all thy happiness in him.

---

[12] Cf. No. 7, 'The Way to the Kingdom', II.1 and n.

[13] Ps. 5:9 (BCP).

[14] See Ps. 53.1 (BCP).

[15] See John 3:36.

[16] See Luke 9:23.

[17] John 6:38. Note this identification of the Christian with Christ; still another accent on 'participation'.

[18] See 1 John 2:15.   [19] See Gal. 6:14.

[20] Cf. Pascal, *Pensées*, ed. H. F. Stewart (London, Routledge and Kegan Paul, 1950), pp. 304-5 (French text with Eng. tr.). In the Modern Library and Everyman's Library edns., cf. Pensée 570. The translation Wesley knew, of course, was that of Basil Kennet, *Thoughts on Religion;* cf. 2nd edn., 1727, p. 79: 'For there are two principles which divide the wills of men, covetousness and charity. It is not indeed impossible that covetousness should subsist with faith, or charity with temporal possession. But here's the difference: the former imploys itself in using God and enjoying the world; the latter in using the world and enjoying God'. Cf. also, St. Augustine, *De doctrina christiana*, 1.3.3-35.39; *De diversis quaestionibus*, LXXXIII.30; *De civ. Dei*, 15:7; and *De Octoginta-tribus Quaestionibus*, XXX. See also St. Francis de Sales, *Devout Life*, III. xxxix. See also Nos. 108, 'On Riches', II.12; and 142, 'The Wisdom of Winning Souls', II.7, and Wesley's letter to Mrs. Pendarves, Feb. 11, 1731, where he attributes the aphorism to Pascal.

Above all cast out the grand beam, that supine carelessness and indifference. Deeply consider that 'one thing is needful',[21] the one thing which thou hast scarce ever thought of. Know and feel that thou art a poor, vile, guilty worm, quivering over the great gulf! What art thou? A sinner born to die; a leaf driven before the wind; a vapour ready to vanish away, just appearing, and then scattered into air, to be no more seen![22] See this. 'And then shalt thou see clearly to cast out the mote out of thy brother's eye.' Then, if thou hast leisure from the concerns of thy own soul, thou shalt know how to correct thy brother also.

8. But what is properly the meaning of this word, 'judge not'? What is the *judging* which is here forbidden? It is not the same as evil-speaking, although it is frequently joined therewith. Evil-speaking is the relating anything that is evil concerning an absent person; whereas judging may indifferently refer either to the absent or the present. Neither does it necessarily imply the speaking at all, but only the *thinking evil* of another. Not that all kind of thinking evil of others is that judging which our Lord condemns. If I see one commit robbery or murder, or hear him blaspheme the name of God, I cannot refrain from thinking ill of the robber or murderer. Yet this is not evil judging: there is no sin in this, nor anything contrary to tender affection.

9. The thinking of another in a manner that is contrary to love is that judging which is here condemned; and this may be of various kinds. For, first, we may think another to blame when he is not. We may lay to his charge (at least in our own mind) the things of which he is not guilty—the words which he has never spoke, or the actions which he has never done. Or we may think his *manner* of acting was wrong, although in reality it was not. And even where nothing can justly be blamed, either in the thing itself or in the manner of doing it, we may suppose his *intention* was not good, and so condemn him on that ground, at the same time that he who searches the heart sees his simplicity and godly sincerity.[23]

10. But we may not only fall into the sin of judging by condemning the innocent, but also, secondly, by condemning the guilty in a higher degree than he deserves. This species of judging

[21] Luke 10:42.

[22] See Luke 16:26, and Wesley's Pref., §5: 'I am a spirit come from God and returning to God; just hovering over the great gulf, till a few moments hence, I am no more seen.' See also Wisd. 5:9-14.

[23] 2 Cor. 1:12. Cf. Nos. 2, *The Almost Christian*, I.9 and n.; and 12, 'The Witness of Our Own Spirit', §11 and n.

is likewise an offence against justice as well as mercy; and yet such
an offence as nothing can secure us from but the strongest and
tenderest affection. Without this we readily suppose one who is
acknowledged to be in fault to be more in fault than he really is.
We undervalue whatever good is found in him. Nay, we are not　5
easily induced to believe that anything good can remain in him in
whom we have found anything that is evil.

11. All this shows a manifest want of that love which οὐ
λογίζεται κακόν, 'thinketh no evil';[24] which never draws an
unjust or unkind conclusion from any premises whatsoever. Love　10
will not infer from a person's falling once into an act of open sin
that he is accustomed so to do, that he is habitually guilty of it.
And if he was habitually guilty once, love does not conclude he is
so still; much less that if he is now guilty of this, therefore he is
guilty of other sins also. These evil reasonings all pertain to that　15
sinful judging which our Lord here guards us against; and which
we are in the highest degree concerned to avoid if we love either
God or our own souls.[25]

12. But supposing we do not condemn the innocent, neither
the guilty any farther than they deserve; still we may not be　20
altogether clear of the snare; for there is a third sort of sinful
judging, which is the condemning any person at all where there is
not sufficient evidence. And be the facts we suppose ever so true;
yet that does not acquit us. For they ought not to have been
supposed, but proved; and till they were we ought to have formed　25
no judgment. I say, till they were; for neither are we excused;
although the facts admit of ever so strong proof, unless that proof
be produced before we pass sentence, and compared with the
evidence on the other side. Nor can we be excused if ever we pass
a full sentence before the accused has spoken for himself. Even a　30
Jew might teach us this, as a mere lesson of justice abstracted
from mercy and brotherly love. 'Doth our law', says Nicodemus,
'judge any man before it hear him, and know what he doth?'[a] Yea,
a heathen could reply, when the chief of the Jewish nation desired
to have judgment against his prisoner, 'It is not the manner of the　35

---

[a] John 7:51.

---

[24] 1 Cor. 13:5; see above, No. 22, 'Sermon on the Mount, II', III.11 and n.
[25] Cf. this generous spirit of reserved judgment with Wesley's harsh judgments heaped
upon Oxford in Nos. 2, *The Almost Christian*, and 150, 'Hypocrisy in Oxford'; see also
Charles Wesley's critique of Oxford in No. 3, *'Awake, Thou That Sleepest.'*

Romans' to judge 'any man before he that is accused have the accusers face to face, and have licence to answer for himself concerning the crime laid against him.'[26]

13. Indeed we could not easily fall into sinful judging were we only to observe that rule which another of those heathen Romans affirms to have been the measure of his own practice. 'I am so far', says he, 'from lightly believing every man's or any man's evidence against another, that I do not easily or immediately believe a man's evidence against himself. I always allow him second thoughts, and many times counsel too.'[b] Go, thou who art called a Christian, and do likewise, lest the heathen rise and condemn thee in that day.[27]

14. But how rarely should we condemn or judge one another, at least how soon would that evil be remedied, were we to walk by that clear and express rule which our Lord himself has taught us! 'If thy brother shall trespass against thee' (or if thou hear, or believe that he hath) 'go and tell him of his fault, between him and thee alone.' This is the first step thou art to take. 'But if he will not hear, take with thee one or two more, that in the mouth of two or three witnesses every word may be established.' This is the second step. 'If he neglect to hear them, tell it unto the church;'[28] either to the overseers thereof, or to the whole congregation. Thou hast then done thy part. Then think of it no more, but commend the whole to God.

15. But supposing thou hast, by the grace of God, 'cast the beam out of thine own eye', and dost now 'clearly see the mote or the beam which is in thy brother's eye'; yet beware thou dost not receive hurt thyself by endeavouring to help him. Still 'give not that which is holy unto dogs.' Do not lightly account any to be of this number. But if it evidently appear that they deserve the title, then cast ye not 'your pearls before swine'. Beware of that zeal which is not according to knowledge;[29] for this is another great hindrance in their way who would be 'perfect as their heavenly Father is perfect'.[30] They who desire this cannot but desire that all

---

[b] Seneca [so identified by Wesley in *Works*, II.344; cf. No. 22, 'Sermon on the Mount, II', III.6 and n.].

[26] Acts 25:16. Cf. Wesley's *Notes:* 'How excellent a rule, to condemn no one unheard! A rule which, as it is common to all nations (courts of inquisition only excepted), so it ought to direct our proceedings in all affairs, not only in public but private life.'
[27] See Matt. 12:41-42.
[28] Matt. 18:15-17.
[29] See Rom. 10:2.
[30] Cf. Matt. 5:48.

mankind should partake of the common blessing. And when we ourselves first partake of the heavenly gift, the divine 'evidence of things not seen',[31] we wonder that all mankind do not see the things which we see so plainly; and make no doubt at all but we shall open the eyes of all we have any intercourse with. Hence we are for attacking all we meet without delay, and constraining them to see, whether they will or no. And by the ill success of this intemperate zeal, we often suffer in our own souls. To prevent this spending our strength in vain our Lord adds this needful caution (needful to all, but more especially to those who are now warm in their first love), 'Give not that which is holy unto the dogs, neither cast ye your pearls before swine; lest they trample them under foot, and turn again and rend you.'

16. 'Give not that which is holy unto the dogs.' Beware of thinking that any deserve this appellation till there is full and incontestable proof, such as you can no longer resist. But when it is clearly and indisputably proved that they are unholy and wicked men, not only strangers to, but enemies to God, to all righteousness and true holiness;[32] 'give not that which is holy', τὸ ἄγιον, the holy thing, emphatically so called, unto these. The holy, the peculiar doctrines of the gospel, such as were 'hid from the ages and generations'[33] of old, and are now made known to us only by the revelation of Jesus Christ and the inspiration of his Holy Spirit, are not to be prostituted unto these men who know not if there be any Holy Ghost.[34] Not indeed that the ambassadors of Christ can refrain from declaring them in the great congregation, wherein some of these may probably be. We must speak, whether men will hear or whether they will forbear.[35] But this is not the case with private Christians. They do not bear that awful character; nor are they under any manner of obligation to force these great and glorious truths on them who contradict and blaspheme, who have a rooted enmity against them. Nay, they ought not so to do, but rather to lead them as they are able to bear. Do not begin a discourse with these upon remission of sins and the gift of the Holy Ghost; but talk with them in their own manner, and upon their own principles. With the rational, honourable, unjust Epicure, 'reason of righteousness, temper-

---

[31] Heb. 11:1.
[32] Eph. 4:24.
[33] Cf. Col. 1:26.
[34] Acts 19:2.
[35] Ezek. 2.5, 7, 3.11. Note the distinction here between doctrinal preaching to large and mixed audiences and doctrinal teaching for individuals and small groups.

ance, and judgment to come'.[36] This is the most probable way to make 'Felix tremble'.[37] Reserve higher subjects for men of higher attainments.

17. 'Neither cast ye your pearls before swine.' Be very unwilling to pass this judgment on any man. But if the fact be plain and undeniable, if it is clear beyond all dispute, if the swine do not endeavour to disguise themselves, but rather glory in their shame, making no pretence to purity either of heart or life, but working all uncleanness with greediness;[38] then 'cast' not 'ye your pearls before' them. Talk not to them of the mysteries of the kingdom; of the things which 'eye hath not seen, nor ear heard';[39] which of consequence, as they have no other inlets of knowledge, no spiritual senses, it cannot enter into their hearts to conceive. Tell not them of the 'exceeding great and precious promises'[40] which God hath given us in the Son of his love. What conception can they have of being made 'partakers of the divine nature' who do not even desire to 'escape the corruption that is in the world through lust'?[41] Just as much knowledge as swine have of pearls, and as much relish as they have for them, so much relish have they for the deep things of God,[42] so much knowledge of the mysteries of the gospel, who are immersed in the mire of this world, in worldly pleasures, desires, and cares. 'O cast not' those 'pearls before' these, 'lest they trample them under their feet', lest they utterly despise what they cannot understand, and speak evil of the things which they know not. Nay, 'tis probable this would not be the only inconvenience[43] which would follow. It would not be strange if they were, according to their nature, to 'turn again, and rend you'; if they were to return you evil for good, cursing for blessing, and hatred for your goodwill. Such is the enmity of the carnal mind against God[44] and all the things of God. Such the treatment you are to expect from these, if you offer them the unpardonable affront of endeavouring to save their souls from death,[45] to pluck them as brands out of the burning![46]

---

[36] Cf. Acts 24:25. Cf. Wesley's own attempt at a similar sardonic discourse in *An Earnest Appeal*, 11:45-94, of this edn.

[37] Cf. Acts 24:25.   [38] See Eph. 4:19.   [39] 1 Cor. 2:9.

[40] 2 Pet. 1:4.   [41] *Ibid.*   [42] 1 Cor. 2:10.

[43] For 'inconvenience' as *serious* trouble, cf. *OED*, 3*b*. In Johnson's *Dictionary* it had come to be a synonym for 'disadvantageous'. Note Wesley's usage here in the older tradition.

[44] See Rom. 8:7.   [45] See Jas. 5:20.

[46] See Amos 4:11; Zech. 3:2. Cf. No. 4, *Scriptural Christianity*, II.2 and n.

18. And yet you need not utterly despair even of these, who for the present 'turn again and rend you'. For if all your arguments and persuasives fail, there is yet another remedy left; and one that is frequently found effectual when no other method avails. This is prayer. Therefore whatever you desire or want, either for others or for your own soul, 'Ask, and it shall be given you; seek, and ye shall find; knock, and it shall be opened unto you.'[47] The neglect of this is a third grand hindrance of holiness. Still we 'have not, because we ask not'.[48] O how meek and gentle, how lowly in heart, how full of love both to God and man, might ye have been at this day, if you had only asked! If you had 'continued instant in prayer'![49] Therefore now, at least, 'Ask, and it shall be given unto you.' 'Ask', that ye may throughly experience and perfectly practise the whole of that religion which our Lord has here so beautifully described. 'It shall' then 'be given you' to be holy as he is holy, both in heart and in all manner of conversation.[50] 'Seek', in the way he hath ordained, in searching the Scriptures, in hearing his Word, in meditating thereon, in fasting, in partaking of the Supper of the Lord, and surely 'ye shall find.' Ye shall find that pearl of great price,[51] that faith which overcometh the world,[52] that peace which the world cannot give,[53] that love which is the earnest of your inheritance.[54] 'Knock': continue in prayer, and in every other way of the Lord. Be not weary or faint in your mind. Press on to the mark.[55] Take no denial. Let him not go until he bless you.[56] And the door of mercy, of holiness, of heaven 'shall be opened unto you'.

19. It is in compassion to the hardness of our hearts, so unready to believe the goodness of God, that our Lord is pleased to enlarge upon this head, and to repeat and confirm what he hath spoken. 'For everyone', saith he, 'that asketh, receiveth;' so that none need come short of the blessing; 'and he that seeketh', even everyone that seeketh, 'findeth' the love and the image of God; 'and to him that knocketh', to everyone that knocketh, the gate of righteousness shall be opened.[57] So that here is no room for any to be discouraged, as though they might ask or seek or knock in vain. Only remember 'always to pray', to seek, to knock, 'and not to

[47] Matt. 7:7.
[48] Cf. Jas. 4:2.
[49] Cf. Rom. 12:12.
[50] See 1 Pet. 1:15.
[51] Matt. 13:46.
[52] See 1 John 5:4.
[53] See John 14:27.
[54] Eph. 1:14.
[55] Phil. 3:14.
[56] See Gen. 32:26.
[57] See Ps. 118:19.

faint'.[58] And then the promise standeth sure. It is firm as the pillars of heaven. Yea, more firm; for heaven and earth shall pass away; but his word shall not pass away.[59]

20. To cut off every pretence for unbelief, our blessed Lord in the following verses illustrates yet farther what he had said, by an appeal to what passes in our own breasts. 'What man', saith he, 'is there of you, who, if his son ask bread, will give him a stone?' Will even natural affection permit you to refuse the reasonable request of one you love? 'Or if he ask a fish, will he give him a serpent?'[60] Will he give him hurtful instead of profitable things? So that even from what you feel and do yourselves you may receive the fullest assurance, as on the one hand that no ill effect can possibly attend your asking, so on the other that it will be attended with that good effect, a full supply of all your wants. For 'if ye, being evil, know how to give good gifts unto your children, how much more shall your Father which is in heaven', who is pure, unmixed, essential goodness, 'give good things to them that ask him!' Or (as he expresses it on another occasion) 'give the Holy Ghost to them that ask him!'[61] In him are included all good things; all wisdom, peace, joy, love; the whole treasures of holiness and happiness; all that God hath prepared for them that love him.[62]

21. But that your prayer may have its full weight with God, see that ye be in charity with all men; for otherwise it is more likely to bring a curse than a blessing on your own head; nor can you expect to receive any blessing from God while you have not charity towards your neighbour. Therefore let this hindrance be removed without delay. Confirm your love towards one another and towards all men. And love them, not in word only, but in deed and in truth.[63] 'Therefore all things whatsoever ye would that men should do to you, do ye even so unto them; for this is the law and the prophets.'[64]

22. This is that royal law, that golden rule of mercy as well as justice, which even the heathen emperor[65] caused to be written

---

[58] Cf. Luke 18:1. Orig., 'and not to be faint', altered only by Wesley in his personal copy of the *Works*, II. 350.

[59] See Matt. 24:35.   [60] Matt. 7:10.   [61] Luke 11:13.

[62] 1 Cor. 2:9.   [63] 1 John 3:18.   [64] Matt. 7:12.

[65] Cf. Echard, *Eccles. Hist.*, III.iv. ('222 A.D.'), p. 389: 'Though Alexander [Severus—222-35] did not believe in Jesus Christ as a Saviour, yet he reverenced him as a Law-giver, whose institutions excelled all those of the Gentile Philosophers. That command, on which all the Law and the Prophets depend. DO NOT THAT TO ANOTHER, WHICH YOU WOULD NOT HAVE ANOTHER DO TO YOU, he was so fond of, that when he punished any man for

over the gate of his palace: a rule which many believe to be naturally engraved on the mind of everyone that comes into the world.[66] And thus much is certain, that it commends itself, as soon as heard, to every man's conscience and understanding; insomuch that no man can knowingly offend against it without carrying his condemnation in his own breast.

23. 'This is the law and the prophets.' Whatsoever is written in that law which God of old revealed to mankind, and whatsoever precepts God has given by 'his holy prophets which have been since the world began',[67] they are all summed up in these few words, they are all contained in this short direction. And this, rightly understood, comprises the whole of that religion which our Lord came to establish upon earth.

24. It may be understood either in a positive or negative sense. If understood in a negative sense the meaning is, 'Whatever ye would not that men should do to you, do not ye unto them.' Here is a plain rule, always ready at hand, always easy to be applied. In all cases relating to your neighbour, make his case your own. Suppose the circumstances to be changed, and yourself to be just as he is now. And then beware that you indulge no temper or thought, that no word pass out of your lips, that you take no step which you should have condemned in him, upon such a change of circumstances. If understood in a direct and positive sense, the plain meaning of it is, 'Whatsoever you could reasonably desire of him, supposing yourself to be in his circumstance, that do, to the uttermost of your power, to every child of man.'

25. To apply this in one or two obvious instances. It is clear to every man's own conscience, we would not that others should *judge* us, should causelessly or lightly think evil of us; much less would we that any should speak evil of us, should publish our real faults or infirmities. Apply this to yourself. Do not unto another what you would not he should do unto you; and you will never more judge your neighbour, never causelessly or lightly think evil of anyone; much less will you speak evil. You will never mention even the real fault of an absent person, unless so far as you are convinced it is absolutely needful for the good of other souls.

acts of injustice, the Crier was commanded publicly to announce it in the Court; and that it might be more regarded, he ordered it to be inscribed upon his palace, his courts of judicature, and his public works and buildings.' See also, below, §24; and Nos. 2, *The Almost Christian*, I.5 and n.; and 150, 'Hypocrisy in Oxford', I.10.

[66] Cf. John 1:9.　　　　　　　　　　　　　　　　　　　　　　　[67] Luke 1:70.

26. Again: we would that all men should love and esteem us, and behave towards us according to justice, mercy, and truth. And we may reasonably desire that they should do us all the good they can do without injuring themselves; yea, that in outward things (according to the known rule) their superfluities should give way to our conveniencies, their conveniencies to our necessities, and their necessities to our extremities.[68] Now then, let us walk by the same rule: let us do unto all as we would they should do to us. Let us love and honour all men. Let justice, mercy, and truth govern all our minds and actions. Let our superfluities give way to our neighbour's conveniencies (and who then will have any superfluities left?); our conveniencies to our neighbour's necessities; our necessities to his extremities.[69]

27. This is pure and genuine morality. This do, and thou shalt live.[70] 'As many as walk by this rule, peace be to them, and mercy;' for they are 'the Israel of God'.[71] But then be it observed, none can walk by this rule (nor ever did from the beginning of the world), none can love his neighbour as himself, unless he first love God. And none can love God unless he believe in Christ, unless he have redemption through his blood,[72] and the Spirit of God bearing witness with his spirit that he is a child of God.[73] Faith therefore is still the root of all, of present as well as future salvation. Still we must say to every sinner, Believe in the Lord

---

[68] Cf. South, *Sermons* (1823), I. 282-83: 'God does not accept the willingness of the mind instead of the liberality of the purse [when it is affluent]. No, assuredly, for the measures that God marks out to thy charity are these: thy superfluities must give place to thy neighbour's great convenience; thy convenience must vail to thy neighbour's necessity; and lastly, thy very necessities must yield to thy neighbour's extremity. . . . This is the gradual process that must be thy rule . . .'. Johnson's *Dictionary* quotes this as an example under the word 'vail' understood in the sense, 'to yield'. Cf. also No. 98, 'On Visiting the Sick', III.4, where Wesley again quotes 'this excellent rule'. This pairing of 'conveniences and necessaries of life' shows up in Nos. 28, 'Sermon on the Mount, VIII', §11; 68, 'The Wisdom of God's Counsels', §16; 87, 'The Danger of Riches', I.3, II.3; 108, 'On Riches', §4; 111, *National Sins and Miseries*, I,1; 113, *The Late Work of God in North America*, II.7; 133, 'Death and Deliverance' ¶9 (for the 'necessaries of life'); 134, 'Seek First the Kingdom', ¶¶5, 12, 15. Cf. also *Address to the Clergy*, II.3(1), *Bibliog*, No. 215 (Vol. 14 of this edn.); and *An Earnest Appeal*, §93 (11:86 of this edn.). It is a commonplace phrase in *The Guardian* and *The Spectator;* see also Francis Atterbury, *Fourteen Sermons* (1708), p. 303; and John Locke, *Essay Concerning Human Understanding*, Bk. 2, ch. 23, §12.

[69] For Wesley's views on surplus accumulation, cf. Nos. 28, 'Sermon on the Mount, VIII', §9 and n.; and 50, 'The Use of Money', intro., espec. I. 8-9 and III. 1.

[70] Luke 10:28.

[71] Cf. Gal. 6:16.

[72] Eph. 1:7; Col. 1:14.

[73] See Rom. 8:16.

Jesus Christ, and thou shalt be saved.[74] Thou shalt be saved now, that thou mayst be saved for ever; saved on earth, that thou mayst be saved in heaven. Believe in him, and thy faith will work by love.[75] Thou wilt love the Lord thy God because he hath loved thee; thou wilt love thy neighbour as thyself. And then it will be thy glory and joy to exert and increase this love, not barely by abstaining from what is contrary thereto—from every unkind thought, word, and action—but by showing all that kindness to every man which thou wouldst he should show unto thee.

[74] Acts 16:31.
[75] See Gal. 5:6.

Upon Our Lord's Sermon on the Mount

Discourse the Eleventh

Matthew 7:13-14

Enter ye in at the strait gate: for wide is the gate, and broad is the way,
5 *which leadeth to destruction, and many there be which go in thereat:*
Because strait is the gate, and narrow is the way, which leadeth unto
life, and few there be that find it.

1. Our Lord, having warned us of the dangers which easily
beset us at our first entrance upon real religion, the hindrances
10 which naturally arise from within, from the wickedness of our
own hearts, now proceeds to apprise us of the hindrances from
without, particularly ill example and ill advice. By one or the other
of these, thousands who once ran well have drawn back unto
perdition; yea, many of those who were not novices in religion,
15 who had made some progress in righteousness. His caution
therefore against these he presses upon us with all possible
earnestness, and repeats again and again, in variety of
expressions, lest by any means we should let it slip. Thus,
effectually to guard us against the former, 'Enter ye in', saith he,
20 'at the strait gate; for wide is the gate, and broad is the way, that
leadeth to destruction, and many there be which go in thereat:
because strait is the gate, and narrow is the way, which leadeth
unto life, and few there be that find it.' To secure us from the
latter, 'Beware', saith he, 'of false prophets.'[1] We shall at present
25 consider the former only.
2. 'Enter ye in', saith our blessed Lord, 'at the strait gate; for
wide is the gate, and broad is the way, that leadeth to destruction,
and many there be which go in thereat: because strait is the gate,
and narrow is the way, which leadeth unto life, and few there be
30 that find it.'
3. In these words we may observe, first, the inseparable

[1] Matt. 7:15.

properties of the way to hell: 'Wide is the gate, broad the way, that leadeth to destruction, and many there be that go in thereat;' secondly, the inseparable properties of the way to heaven: 'Strait is that gate, and narrow is the way, which leadeth unto life, and few there be that find it;' thirdly, a serious exhortation grounded thereon: 'Enter ye in at the strait gate.'

I. 1. We may observe, first, the inseparable properties of the way to hell: 'Wide is the gate, and broad is the way, that leadeth to destruction, and many there be that go in thereat.'

2. Wide indeed is the gate, and broad the way, that leadeth to destruction. For sin is the gate of hell, and wickedness the way to destruction. And how wide a gate is that of sin! How broad is the way of wickedness! The 'commandment' of God 'is exceeding broad',[2] as extending not only to all our actions, but to every word which goeth out of our lips, yea, every thought that rises in our heart. And sin is equally broad with the commandment, seeing any breach of the commandment is sin. Yea, rather, it is a thousand times broader, since there is only one way of keeping the commandment; for we do not properly keep it unless both the thing done, the manner of doing it, and all the other circumstances, are right. But there are a thousand ways of breaking every commandment; so that this gate is wide indeed.

3. To consider this a little more particularly. How wide do those parent sins[3] extend, from which all the rest derive their being: 'that carnal mind which is enmity against God',[4] pride of heart, self-will, and love of the world! Can we fix any bounds to them? Do they not diffuse themselves through all our thoughts, and mingle with all our tempers? Are they not the leaven which leavens, more or less, the whole mass of our affections? May we not, on a close and faithful examination of ourselves, perceive these roots of bitterness continually springing up,[5] infecting all our words, and tainting all our actions? And how innumerable an offspring do they bring forth, in every age and nation! Even enough to cover the whole earth with 'darkness and cruel habitations'.[6]

---

[2] Ps. 119:96.
[3] Cf. No. 25, 'Sermon on the Mount, V', III.2 and n.
[4] Cf. Rom. 8:7.
[5] See Heb. 12:15.
[6] Ps. 74:21 (BCP).

4. O who is able to reckon up their accursed fruits! To count all the sins, whether against God or our neighbour, not which imagination might paint, but which may be matter of daily, melancholy experience! Nor need we range over all the earth to 5 find them. Survey any one kingdom, any single country, or city, or town, and how plenteous is this harvest! And let it not be one of those which are still overspread with Mahometan or pagan darkness, but of those which name the name of Christ, which profess to see the light of his glorious gospel.⁷ Go no farther than 10 the kingdom to which we belong, the city wherein we are now.⁸ We call ourselves Christians; yea, and that of the purest sort; we are Protestants, reformed Christians! But alas! who shall carry on the reformation of our opinions into our hearts and lives? Is there not a cause? For how innumerable are our sins! And those of the 15 deepest dye! Do not the grossest abominations of every kind abound among us from day to day? Do not sins of every sort cover the land, as the waters cover the sea?⁹ Who can count them? Rather go and count the drops of rain, or the sands on the sea-shore. So 'wide is the gate', so 'broad is the way that leadeth 20 to destruction'.

5. 'And many there be who go in at' that gate, many who walk in that way—almost as many as go in at the gate of death, as sink into the chambers of the grave.¹⁰ For it cannot be denied (though neither can we acknowledge it but with shame and sorrow of 25 heart) that even in this which is called a Christian country the generality of every age and sex, of every profession and employment, of every rank and degree, high and low, rich and poor, are walking in the way of destruction. The far greater part of the inhabitants of this city to this day live in sin;¹¹ in some

---

⁷ See 2 Cor. 4:4. For Wesley's scorn of nominal Christianity in so-called Christian countries or Christian churches, cf. Nos. 49, 'The Cure of Evil-speaking', III.4; 61, 'The Mystery of Iniquity', §25; 63, 'The General Spread of the Gospel', §§1-2; 64, 'The New Creation', §§1-2; 69, 'The Imperfection of Human Knowledge', II.8-9; 122, 'Causes of the Inefficacy of Christianity', §6. Cf. also *A Plain Account of Christian Perfection*, III.8, and *A Farther Appeal*, Pt. II, II.28 (11:239-40 of this edn.).
⁸ The 'kingdom', of course, is England; 'the city', London.
⁹ Isa. 11:9; Hab. 2:14.   ¹⁰ See Prov. 7:27.
¹¹ Cf. Rudé, in *Hanoverian London*, ch. 5 ('The "Other" London') and ch. 10 ('Social Protest "From Below" '). Wesley makes no mention of having seen William Hogarth's famous engravings on 'modern moral subjects' (from 'A Harlot's Progress' [1732], to 'Gin Lane' [1751]); but they were famous, and Wesley was interested in such things. More importantly, he himself had seen what Hogarth saw and reacts to it here with words instead of pictures.

palpable, habitual, known transgression of the law they profess to observe;[12] yea, in some outward transgression, some gross, visible kind of ungodliness or unrighteousness; some open violation of their duty, either to God or man. These then, none can deny, are all in the way that leadeth to destruction. Add to these those who 'have a name, indeed, that they live',[13] but were never yet alive to God;[14] those that outwardly appear fair to men, but are inwardly full of all uncleanness;[15] full of pride or vanity, of anger or revenge, of ambition or covetousness; lovers of themselves, lovers of the world, lovers of pleasure more than lovers of God.[16] These indeed may be highly esteemed of men, but they are an abomination to the Lord. And how greatly will these saints of the world[17] swell the number of the children of hell! Yea, add all—whatever they be in other respects, whether they have more or less of the form of godliness[18]—who, 'being ignorant of God's righteousness, and seeking to establish their own righteousness' as the ground of their reconciliation to God and acceptance with him, of consequence have 'not submitted themselves unto the righteousness which is of God by faith.'[19] Now all these things joined together in one, how terribly true is our Lord's assertion, 'Wide is the gate and broad is the way that leadeth to destruction, and many there be who go in thereat.'

6. Nor does this only concern the vulgar herd, the poor, base, stupid part of mankind.[20] Nay; men of eminence in the world, men who have many fields and yoke of oxen, do not desire to be excused from this. On the contrary, 'many wise men after the

---

[12] Cf. No. 13, *On Sin in Believers*, intro., III.1-9, and n.
[13] Cf. Rev. 3:1.
[14] See Rom. 6:11.
[15] See Matt. 23:27.
[16] See 2 Tim. 3:2-4.
[17] Cf. No. 4, *Scriptural Christianity*, II.5 and n.
[18] See 2 Tim. 3:5.
[19] Cf. Rom. 10:3.
[20] Cf. Horace, *Odes*, III.1 *(odi profanum vulgus)*, and Abraham Cowley's 'imitation' in *Works* (11th edn., 1710), II.751. These epithets were commonplace in eighteenth-century English middle- and upper-class language; cf. *The Tatler*, No. 81 (Oct. 13-15, 1709), and *The Spectator*, No. 114 (July 11, 1711), and No. 472 (Sept. 1, 1712), three samples from hundreds. It is interesting that Wesley slips into them from time to time, despite his self-conscious identification with 'Christ's poor' (cf. No. 47, 'Heaviness through Manifold Temptations', III.3; JWJ, Sept. 28, 1765, and Apr. 5, 1782; his letter to Dorothy Furly, Sept. 25, 1757, to Brian Bury Collins, June 14, 1780, and to Freeborn Garrettson, Sept. 30, 1786).

Cf. II.6, 10; III.5, below; also Nos. 85, 'On Working Out Our Own salvation', §3; 108, 'On Riches', II.1; and 125, 'On a Single Eye', II.5. Cf. also his Pref. to the *Christian Lib.*, §5. For Wesley's use of 'beasts of the people' see No. 52, *The Reformation of Manners*, I.5 and n.

flesh', according to the human methods of judging, 'many mighty' in power, in courage, in riches, many 'noble are called';[21] called into the broad way, by the world, the flesh, and the devil;[22] and they are not disobedient to that calling. Yea, the higher they are
5 raised in fortune and power, the deeper do they sink into wickedness. The more blessings they have received from God, the more sins do they commit; using their honour or riches, their learning or wisdom, not as means of working out their salvation, but rather of excelling in vice, and so ensuring their own
10 destruction.[23]

II. 1. And the very reason why many of these go on so securely in the 'broad way' is because it is broad; not considering that this is the inseparable property of the way to destruction. 'Many there be', saith our Lord, 'who go in thereat'—for the very reason why
15 they should flee from it, even 'because strait is the gate and narrow the way that leadeth unto life, and few there be that find it.'

2. This is an inseparable property of the way to heaven. So narrow is the way that leadeth unto life, unto life everlasting, so
20 strait the gate, that nothing unclean, nothing unholy, can enter. No sinner can pass through that gate until he is saved from all his sins. Not only from his outward sins, from his evil 'conversation, received by tradition from his fathers'.[24] It will not suffice that he hath 'ceased to do evil' and 'learned to do well'.[25] He must not
25 only be saved from all sinful actions and from all evil and useless discourse; but inwardly changed, throughly renewed in the spirit of his mind.[26] Otherwise he cannot pass through the gate of life, he cannot enter into glory.

3. For 'narrow is the way that leadeth unto life'—the way of
30 universal holiness. Narrow indeed is the way of poverty of spirit, the way of holy mourning, the way of meekness, and that of hungering and thirsting after righteousness.[27] Narrow is the way of mercifulness, of love unfeigned; the way of purity of heart; of

---

[21] 1 Cor. 1:26.   [22] BCP, Litany.
[23] For later and more distanced views of England in the 1740s, see Williams, *The Whig Supremacy*, chs. ii, v, and Robertson, *England Under the Hanoverians*, chs. ii, iv. For vivid contemporary accounts to the same effect, cf. Henry Fielding, *The History of Tom Jones, A Foundling* (1749); Daniel Defoe, *The Fortune and Misfortune of the Famous Moll Flanders* (1722); and Samuel Richardson, *Clarissa, or, The History of a Young Lady* (1747–48).
[24] Cf. 1 Pet. 1:18.   [25] Cf. Isa. 1:16, 17.
[26] See Eph. 4:23.   [27] See Matt. 5:3-6.

doing good unto all men, and of gladly suffering evil, all manner of evil, for righteousness' sake.[28]

4. 'And few there be that find it.' Alas, how few find even the way of heathen honesty![29] How few are there that do nothing to another which they would not another should do unto them![30] How few that are clear before God from acts either of injustice or unkindness! How few that do not 'offend with their tongue';[31] that speak nothing unkind, nothing untrue! What a small proportion of mankind are innocent even of outward transgressions! And how much smaller a proportion have their hearts right before God, clean and holy in his sight! Where are they whom his all-searching eye discerns to be truly humble? To abhor themselves in dust and ashes[32] in the presence of God their Saviour? To be deeply and steadily serious, feeling their wants, and 'passing the time of their sojourning with fear'?[33] Truly meek and gentle, never 'overcome of evil, but overcoming evil with good'?[34] Throughly athirst for God, and continually panting[35] after a renewal in his likeness? How thinly are they scattered over the earth, whose souls are enlarged in love to all mankind; and who love God with all their strength; who have given him their hearts, and desire nothing else in earth or heaven![36] How few are those lovers of God and man that spend their whole strength in doing good unto all men;[37] and are ready to suffer all things, yea, death itself, to save one soul from eternal death!

5. But while so few are found in the way of life, and so many in the way of destruction, there is great danger lest the torrent of example[38] should bear us away with them. Even a single example, if it be always in our sight, is apt to make much impression upon us; especially when it has nature on its side, when it falls in with

---

[28] See Matt. 5:7-8, 10.

[29] For other uses of this phrase as synonymous with natural morality, cf. Nos. 1, *Salvation by Faith*, I.1, 2, 4; 2, *The Almost Christian*, I. (ii.) 4; 50, 'The Use of Money', II.2; 55, *On the Trinity*, §11. Cf. also the letter to a clergyman, June 18, 1787; and JWJ, Feb. 8, 1753. See also Lucas, *Enquiry After Happiness*, I. 101.

[30] See Matt. 7:12. [31] Cf. Ecclus. 19:16.
[32] See Job 42:6. [33] Cf. 1 Pet. 1:17.
[34] Cf. Rom. 12:21. [35] See Ps. 42:1-2 (AV).
[36] See Ps. 73:25. [37] See Gal. 6:10.

[38] An echo, here and elsewhere, of Francis Bacon's insight that human thought is more often warped by ingrained prejudices than it is guided by reason or good example; e.g., Bacon's famous 'four idols' of the 'tribe', the 'cave', the 'market-place', and the 'theatre', as in *Novum Organum* (1620), I, Aphorisms 38-69. For other instances of the phrase, 'torrents of custom', cf. No. 25, 'Sermon on the Mount, V', IV.3 and n.

our own inclinations. How great then must be the force of so numerous examples, continually before our eyes; and all conspiring together with our own hearts to carry us down the stream of nature! How difficult must it be to stem the tide, and to
5 keep ourselves 'unspotted in the world'![39]

6. What heightens the difficulty still more is that they are not the rude and senseless part of mankind,[40] at least not these alone, who set us the example, who throng the downward way; but the polite, the well-bred, the genteel, the wise, the men who
10 understand the world; the men of knowledge, of deep and various learning, the rational, the eloquent! These are all, or nearly all, against us. And how shall we stand against these? Do not their tongues drop manna?[41] And have they not learned all the arts of soft persuasion? And of reasoning too; for these are versed in all
15 controversies and strife of words. It is therefore a small thing with them to prove that the way is *right* because it is *broad;* that he who follows a multitude cannot do evil,[42] but only he who will not follow them; that your way must be *wrong* because it is *narrow* and because there are so few that find it. These will make it clear to a
20 demonstration that evil is good, and good is evil; that the way of holiness is the way of destruction, and the way of the world the only way to heaven.

7. O how can unlearned and ignorant men maintain their cause against such opponents! And yet these are not all with whom they
25 must contend, however unequal to the task; for there are many mighty and noble and powerful men, as well as wise, in the road that leadeth to destruction. And these have a shorter way of confuting than that of reason and argument. They usually apply, not to the understanding, but to the fears of any that oppose
30 them—a method that seldom fails of success, even where argument profits nothing, as lying level to the capacities of all men: for all can fear, whether they can reason or no. And all who have not a firm trust in God, a sure reliance both on his power and love, cannot but fear to give any disgust[43] to those who have the
35 power of the world in their hands. What wonder, therefore, if the example of these is a law to all who know not God!

[39] Cf. Jas. 1:27.   [40] Cf. above, I.6 and n.
[41] Milton, *Paradise Lost*, ii.112-13: 'His tongue dropt manna, and could make the worse appear the better reason.'
[42] See Exod. 23:2.
[43] I.e., an offence; a then contemporary usage which may be seen in both Johnson's *Dictionary* and the *OED*.

8. Many rich are likewise in the broad way. And these apply to the hopes of men, and to all their foolish desires, as strongly and effectually as the mighty and noble to their fears. So that hardly can you hold on in the way of the kingdom unless you are dead to all below, unless you are crucified to the world and the world 5 crucified to you,[44] unless you desire nothing more but God.

9. For how dark, how uncomfortable, how forbidding is the prospect on the opposite side! A strait gate! A narrow way! And few finding that gate! Few walking in the way. Besides, even those few are not wise men, not men of learning or eloquence. They are 10 not able to reason either strongly or clearly; they cannot propose an argument to any advantage. They know not how to prove what they profess to believe; or to explain even what they say they experience. Surely such advocates as these will never recommend, but rather discredit the cause they have espoused. 15

10. Add to this that they are not noble, not honourable men: if they were, you might bear with their folly. They are men of no interest, no authority, of no account in the world. They are mean and base, low in life;[45] and such as have no power, if they had the will, to hurt you. Therefore there is nothing at all to be feared 20 from them; and there is nothing at all to hope: for the greater part of them may say, 'Silver and gold have I none'[46]—at least a very moderate share. Nay, some of them have scarce food to eat or raiment to put on. For this reason, as well as because their ways are not like those of other men, they are everywhere spoken 25 against, are despised, have their names cast out as evil, are variously persecuted, and treated as the filth and offscouring of the world.[47] So that both your fears, your hopes, and all your desires (except those which you have immediately from God), yea, all your natural passions, continually incline you to return 30 into the broad way.

III. 1. Therefore it is that our Lord so earnestly exhorts, 'Enter ye in at the strait gate.' Or (as the same exhortation is elsewhere expressed) 'Strive to enter in': ἀγωνίζεσθε εἰσελθεῖν, strive as in an agony. 'For many', saith our Lord, 'shall seek to enter 35 in'—indolently strive—'and shall not be able.'[48]

---

[44] See Gal. 6:14.
[45] Cf. above, I.6 and n.
[46] Acts 3:6.   [47] See 1 Cor. 4:13.
[48] Luke 13:24. Cf. *Notes*, III.5, and No. 17, 'The Circumcision of the Heart', II.7 and n.

2. 'Tis true he intimates what may seem another reason for this, for their 'not being able to enter in', in the words which immediately follow these. For after he had said, 'Many, I say unto you, will seek to enter in, and shall not be able,' he subjoins: 'When once the master of the house is risen up and hath shut to the door, and ye begin to stand without' (ἄρξησθε ἔξω ἐστάναι: rather, 'ye stand without', for ἄρξησθε seems to be only an elegant expletive) 'and to knock at the door, saying, Lord, Lord, open unto us; he shall answer and say unto you, I know you not. Depart from me, all ye workers of iniquity.'[a]

3. It may appear, upon a transient view of these words, that their delaying to seek at all, rather than their manner of seeking, was the reason why they were not able to enter in. But it comes in effect to the same thing. They were therefore commanded to depart, because they had been 'workers of iniquity', because they had walked in the broad road; in other words, because they had not agonized to enter in at the strait gate. Probably they did *seek*, before the door was shut; but that did not suffice. And they did *strive*, after the door was shut; but then it was too late.

4. Therefore 'strive' ye now, in this your day, 'to enter in at the strait gate'. And in order hereto, settle it in your heart, and let it be ever uppermost in your thoughts, that if you are in a broad way, you are in the way that leadeth to destruction. If many go with you, as sure as God is true, both they and you are going to hell. If you are walking as the generality of men walk, you are walking to the bottomless pit. Are many wise, many rich, many mighty or noble[49] travelling with you in the same way? By this token, without going any farther, you know it does not lead to life. Here is a short, a plain, an infallible rule, before you enter into particulars. In whatever profession you are engaged, you must be singular or be damned.[50] The way to hell has nothing singular in it; but the way

---

[a] Luke 13:24-27.

---

[49] See 1 Cor. 1:26.

[50] One of Wesley's aims was to raise up men and women in his societies who could stand in their own dignity against the 'torrents of example' and 'custom' (cf. No. 25, 'Sermon on the Mount, V', IV.3 and n.); hence his 'infallible rule' of singularity. Cf. Nos. 14, *The Repentance of Believers*, I.7; 32, 'Sermon on the Mount, XII', I.3; 52, *The Reformation of Manners*, V.7; 66, 'The Signs of the Times', II.5; 125, 'On a Single Eye' (on Matt. 6:22-23); and 148, 'A Single Intention' (on the same text). Cf. also his letters to his father, June 13, 1733, and Dec. 10, 1734; to 'John Smith', 1745; and to Miss March, Sept. 16, 1774. Cf. also William Tilly, Sermon XVI, *Sermons*, p. 463; and John Norris,

to heaven is singularity all over. If you move but one step towards God you are not as other men are.[51] But regard not this. 'Tis far better to stand alone than to fall into the pit.[52] Run then with patience the race which is set before thee,[53] though thy companions therein are but few. They will not always be so. Yet a little while and thou wilt 'come to an innumerable company of angels, to the general assembly and church of the first-born, and to the spirits of just men made perfect'.[54]

5. Now, then, 'strive to enter in at the strait gate,' being penetrated with the deepest sense of the inexpressible danger your soul is in so long as you are in a broad way, so long as you are void of poverty of spirit and all that inward religion which the many, the rich, the wise, account madness. 'Strive to enter in,' being pierced with sorrow and shame for having so long run on with the unthinking crowd,[55] utterly neglecting if not despising that 'holiness, without which no man can see the Lord'.[56] *Strive* as in an agony of holy fear, lest 'a promise being made you of entering into his rest',[57] even that 'rest which remaineth for the people of God',[58] you should nevertheless 'come short of it'.[59] Strive in all the fervour of desire, with 'groanings which cannot be uttered'.[60] Strive by prayer without ceasing,[61] at all times, in all places lifting up your heart to God, and giving him no rest till you 'awake up after his likeness' and are 'satisfied with it'.[62]

6. To conclude: 'Strive to enter in at the strait gate,' not only by this agony of soul, of conviction, of sorrow, of shame, of desire, of

Discourse III, 'Concerning Singularity', *Practical Discourses*, II.45-70, and Discourse V, 'Of Walking by Faith', IV.125-71.

Johnson's *Dictionary* cites Robert South for an illustration of 'singularly'. 'Solitude and singularity can neither daunt nor disgrace him, unless we could suppose it a disgrace to be singularly good.' For an opposite viewpoint, cf. Ben Franklin, *Poor Richard's Almanac* (1757): 'Singularity . . . hath ruined many; happy those who are convinced of the general opinion.'

[51] Luke 18:11.
[52] Cf. No. 32, 'Sermon on the Mount, XII', I.7 and n.
[53] See Heb. 12:1.
[54] Heb. 12:22-23.
[55] Cf. above, I.6 and n.
[56] Heb. 12:14.
[57] Cf. Heb. 4:1. Cf. No. 17, 'The Circumcision of the Heart', II.7 and n. See also III.1, above, and III.6, below.
[58] Cf. Heb. 4:9.
[59] Heb. 4:1.
[60] Rom. 8:26.
[61] See 1 Thess. 5:17.
[62] Cf. Ps. 17:16 (BCP).

fear, of unceasing prayer, but likewise by 'ordering thy conversation aright',[63] by walking with all thy strength in all the ways of God, the way of innocence, of piety, and of mercy. Abstain from all appearance of evil;[64] do all possible good to all men;[65] deny thyself, thy own will, in all things, and take up thy cross daily.[66] Be ready to cut off thy right hand, to pluck out thy right eye and cast it from thee;[67] to suffer the loss of goods, friends, health, all things on earth, so thou mayst enter into the kingdom of heaven.

[63] Cf. Ps. 50:23.
[64] 1 Thess. 5:22.
[65] See Gal. 6:10.
[66] See Luke 9:23.
[67] See Matt. 5:29; 18:9.

Upon our Lord's Sermon on the Mount

Discourse the Twelfth

Matthew 7:15-20

Beware of false prophets, which come to you in sheep's clothing, but inwardly they are ravening wolves.

Ye shall know them by their fruits. Do men gather grapes of thorns, or figs of thistles?

Even so every good tree bringeth forth good fruit; but a corrupt tree bringeth forth evil fruit.

A good tree cannot bring forth evil fruit; neither can a corrupt tree bring forth good fruit.

Every tree that bringeth not forth good fruit is hewn down and cast into the fire.

Wherefore by their fruits ye shall know them.

1. It is scarce possible to express or conceive what multitudes of souls run on to destruction because they would not be persuaded to walk in a *narrow* way, even though it were the way to everlasting salvation. And the same thing we may still observe daily. Such is the folly and madness of mankind that thousands of men still rush on in the way to hell only because it is a broad way. They walk in it themselves because others do: because so many perish they will add to the number. Such is the amazing influence of example over the weak, miserable children of men! It continually peoples the regions of death, and drowns numberless souls in everlasting perdition.

2. To warn mankind of this, to guard as many as possible against this spreading contagion, God has commanded his watchmen to cry aloud, and show the people the danger they are in.[1] For this end he has sent his servants, the prophets, in their succeeding generations, to point out the narrow path, and exhort all men not to be conformed to this world.[2] But what if the

[1] See Isa. 58:1.
[2] See Rom. 12:2.

watchmen themselves fall into the snare against which they should warn others? What if 'the prophets prophesy deceits'?[3] If they 'cause the people to err from the way'?[4] What shall be done if they point out, as the way to eternal life, what is in truth the way to
5 eternal death? And exhort others to walk, as they do themselves, in the broad, not the narrow way?

3. Is this an unheard of, is it an uncommon thing? Nay, God knoweth it is not. The instances of it are almost innumerable. We may find them in every age and nation. But how terrible is this!
10 When the ambassadors of God turn agents for the devil! When they who are commissioned to teach men the way to heaven do in fact teach them the way to hell! These are like the locusts of Egypt 'which eat up the residue that had escaped', that had 'remained after the hail'.[5] They devour even the residue of men that had
15 escaped, that were not destroyed by ill example. It is not therefore without cause that our wise and gracious master so solemnly cautions us against them: 'Beware', saith he, 'of false prophets, which come to you in sheep's clothing, but inwardly they are ravening wolves.'
20 4. A caution this of the utmost importance. That it may the more effectually sink into our hearts, let us inquire, first, who these false prophets are; secondly, what appearance they put on; and, thirdly, how we may know what they really are, notwithstanding their fair appearance.

25 I. 1. We are, first, to inquire who these false prophets are. And this it is needful to do the more diligently because these very men have so laboured to 'wrest this Scripture to their own (though not only their own) destruction'.[6] In order therefore to cut off all dispute I shall raise no dust[7] (as the manner of some is) neither
30 use any loose, rhetorical exclamations to deceive the hearts of the simple, but speak rough, plain truths, such as none can deny who has either understanding or modesty left, and such truths as have the closest connection with the whole tenor of the preceding

---

[3] Cf. Isa. 30:10.
[4] Cf. Jer. 23:13, 32.
[5] Cf. Exod. 10:5.
[6] Cf. 2 Pet. 3:16.
[7] A rare instance of slang in Wesley; this usage is not noted in the *OED*. But cf. E. Partridge, *A Dictionary of Slang and Unconventional English* (1937), and E. C. Brewer's *Dictionary of Phrase and Fable* (1870, *et seq.*).

discourse; whereas too many have interpreted these words without any regard to all that went before, as if they bore no manner of relation to the sermon in the close of which they stand.

2. By 'prophets' here (as in many other passages of Scripture, particularly in the New Testament) are meant, not those who foretell things to come, but those who speak in the name of God; those men who profess to be sent of God to teach others the way to heaven.[8]

Those are 'false prophets' who teach a false way to heaven, a way which does not lead thither; or (which comes in the end to the same point) who do not teach the true.

3. Every broad way is infallibly a false one. Therefore this is one plain, sure rule, 'They who teach men to walk in a broad way, a way that many walk in, are false prophets.'

Again, the true way to heaven is a narrow way. Therefore this is another plain, sure rule, 'They who do not teach men to walk in a narrow way, to be singular, are false prophets.'[9]

4. To be more particular: the only true way to heaven is that pointed out in the preceding sermon. Therefore they are false prophets who do not teach men to walk in *this way*.

Now the way to heaven pointed out in the preceding sermon is the way of lowliness, mourning, meekness, and holy desire, love of God and of our neighbour, doing good, and suffering evil for Christ's sake. They are therefore false prophets who teach as the way to heaven any other way than *this*.

5. It matters not what they call that other way. They may call it 'faith', or 'good works'; or 'faith and works'; or 'repentance'; or 'repentance, faith, and new obedience'. All these are good words. But if under these, or any other terms whatever, they teach men any way distinct from *this*, they are properly false prophets.

6. How much more do they fall under that condemnation who speak evil of this good way! But above all they who teach the directly opposite way—the way of pride, of levity, of passion, of worldly desires, of loving pleasure more than God, of unkindness to our neighbour, of unconcern for good works, and suffering no evil, no persecution for righteousness' sake!

---

[8] The Puritans had identified prophecy as preaching-teaching ('forthtelling' rather than 'foretelling') and Wesley reflects that tradition here. Cf. William Perkins, *The Art of Prophesying*. See No. 121, 'Prophets and Priests', §6, which corresponds to Perkins's conception of prophecy and prophesying; cf. Wesley's *Notes* on 1 Thess. 5:20.

[9] Cf. No. 31, 'Sermon on the Mount, XI', III.4 and n.

7. If it be asked, 'Why, who ever did teach this?' Or, 'Who does teach it as the way to heaven?' I answer, Ten thousand wise and honourable men; even all those, of whatever denomination,[10] who encourage the proud, the trifler, the passionate, the lover of the 5 world, the man of pleasure, the unjust or unkind, the easy, careless, harmless, useless creature, the man who suffers no reproach for righteousness' sake, to imagine he is in the way to heaven. These are false prophets in the highest sense of the word. These are traitors both to God and man. These are no other than 10 the first-born of Satan, the eldest sons of Apollyon, the destroyer.[11] These are far above the rank of ordinary cut-throats; for they murder the souls of men. They are continually peopling the realms of night; and whenever they follow the poor souls whom they have destroyed, 'hell' shall be 'moved from beneath to 15 meet them at their coming'.[12]

II. 1. But do they come now in their own shape? By no means. If it were so they could not destroy. You would take the alarm and flee for your life. Therefore they put on a quite contrary appearance, which was the second thing to be considered: 'they 20 come to you in sheep's clothing,' although 'inwardly they are ravening wolves.'

[10] This usage, connoting an *ecclesial* entity, was rather new; the first instance of it in the *OED*, in this sense, is dated 1716. Even in 1755, Dr. Johnson would use it of 'sects' of philosophers without any ecclesial connotation at all. For other instances of Wesley's use of the term, see Nos. 104, 'On Attending the Church Service', §4, and 107, 'On God's Vineyard', II.8.

[11] See Rev. 9:11: 'the angel of the bottomless pit, whose name in the Hebrew tongue is Abaddon, but in the Greek tongue hath his name Apollyon'. In Enoch 20:2 the angel presiding over 'Tarturus' was named Uriel. Cf. John Bunyan, *Pilgrim's Progress* (1st edn., 1678; Philadelphia, Porter and Coates, n.d.), pp. 61-65. This metaphor of 'the bottomless pit' was one of Wesley's favourites; cf. e.g., III.4, below, and Nos. 25, 'Sermon on the Mount, V', III.5; 66, 'The Signs of the Times', II.7; 90, 'An Israelite Indeed', II.4; 96, 'On Obedience to Parents', II.4; 100, 'On Pleasing All Men', II.2; 102, 'Of Former Times', §16; 115, 'Dives and Lazarus', I.7; and 119, 'Walking by Sight and Walking by Faith', §18. For 'the first-born of Satan', cf. 'The Epistle of Polycarp to the Philippians', VII.1, in *The Apostolic Fathers*, Loeb, I:293 (quoting 1 John 4:2, 3, and 2 John 7): ' "For everyone who does not confess that Jesus Christ has come in the flesh is an antichrist;" and whosoever does not confess the testimony of the cross is of the devil; and whosoever perverts the oracles of the Lord for his own lusts, and says that there is neither resurrection nor judgment—this man is the first-born of Satan.' A footnote here says that, according to St. Irenaeus, *Against Heresies*, iii.3, 4, this phrase, 'first-born of Satan', was later applied by Polycarp specifically to Marcion. Cf. also Nos. 128, 'The Deceitfulness of the Human Heart', I.1; and 150, 'Hypocrisy in Oxford', I.3, where Wesley uses the Greek phrase, πρωτότοκοι τοῦ Σατανᾶ.

[12] Cf. Isa. 14:9.

2. 'They come to you in sheep's clothing;' that is, with an appearance of harmlessness.[13] They come in the most mild, inoffensive manner, without any mark or token of enmity. Who can imagine that these quiet creatures would do any hurt to anyone? Perhaps they may not be so zealous and active in doing 5 good as one would wish they were. However, you see no reason to suspect that they have even the desire to do any harm. But this is not all.

3. They come, secondly, with an appearance of usefulness. Indeed to this, to do good, they are particularly called. They are 10 set apart for this very thing. They are particularly commissioned to watch over your soul, and to train you up to eternal life. 'Tis their whole business to 'go about doing good, and healing those that are oppressed of the devil'.[14] And you have been always accustomed to look upon them in this light, as messengers of God 15 sent to bring you a blessing.

4. They come, thirdly, with an appearance of religion. All they do is for conscience' sake! They assure you it is out of mere zeal for God that they are making God a liar. It is out of pure concern for religion that they would destroy it root and branch. All they 20 speak is only from a love of truth, and a fear lest it should suffer. And, it may be, from a regard for the church, and a desire to defend her from all her enemies.

5. Above all, they come with an appearance of love. They take all these pains only for *your* good. They should not trouble 25 themselves about you, but that they have a kindness for you. They will make large professions of their goodwill, of their concern for the danger you are in, and of their earnest desire to preserve you from error, from being entangled in new and mischievous doctrines. They should be very sorry to see one who *means* so well 30 hurried into any extreme, perplexed with strange and unintelligible notions, or deluded into enthusiasm. Therefore it is that they advise you to keep still in the plain middle way;[15] and to beware of 'being righteous overmuch', lest you should 'destroy yourself'.[16]

35

---

[13] Wesley speaks frequently of 'harmlessness', often sarcastically, as here. Cf. Nos. 33, 'Sermon on the Mount, XIII', III.2; 52, *The Reformation of Manners*, III.3; 81, 'In What Sense we are to Leave the World', §23; 119, 'Walking by Sight and Walking by Faith', §18; and 127, 'On the Wedding Garment', §16.

[14] Cf. Acts 10:38.

[15] Cf. No. 27, 'Sermon on the Mount, VII', §4 and n.

[16] Eccles. 7:16. Cf. below, III.11. An oblique reference to Joseph Trapp, whose four

III. 1. But how may we know what they really are, notwithstanding their fair appearance? This was the third thing into which it was proposed to inquire.

Our blessed Lord saw how needful it was for all men to know
5 false prophets, however disguised. He saw likewise how unable most men were to deduce a truth through a long train of consequences. He therefore gives us a short and plain rule, easy to be understood by men of the meanest capacities, and easy to be applied upon all occasions: 'Ye shall know them by their fruits.'
10 2. Upon all occasions you may easily apply this rule. In order to know whether any who speak in the name of God are false or true prophets it is easy to observe, first, What are the fruits of their doctrine as to themselves? What effect has it had upon their lives? Are they holy and unblameable in all things? What effect has it
15 had upon their hearts? Does it appear by the general tenor of their conversation that their tempers are holy, heavenly, divine? That the mind is in them which was in Christ Jesus?[17] That they are meek, lowly, patient lovers of God and man, and zealous of good works?[18]
20 3. You may easily observe, secondly, what are the fruits of their doctrine as to those that hear them—in many, at least, though not in all; for the apostles themselves did not convert all that heard them. Have these the mind that was in Christ? And do they walk as he also walked? And was it by hearing these men that they
25 began so to do? Were they inwardly and outwardly wicked till they heard them? If so, it is a manifest proof that those are true prophets, teachers sent of God. But if it is not so, if they do not effectually teach either themselves or others to love and serve God, it is a manifest proof that they are false prophets; that God
30 hath not sent them.

4. An hard saying this! How few can bear it![19] This our Lord was sensible of, and therefore condescends to prove it at large by several clear and convincing arguments. 'Do men', says he, 'gather grapes of thorns, or figs of thistles?'[a] Do you expect that

[a] Ver. 16[of text].

---

sermons on *The Nature, Folly, Sin, and Danger of Being Righteous Overmuch* (1739) had ridiculed the Methodists and had, in turn, become an easy target for their scornful retorts. Wesley's description here of the ideal ministerial character is perfectionistic enough so as to encourage his people to expect more of their Church of England priests than they could realistically expect from their own Methodist preachers or class-leaders.

[17] Phil. 2:5.   [18] Titus 2:14.   [19] See John 6:60.

these evil men should bring forth good fruit? As well might you expect that thorns should bring forth grapes, or that figs should grow upon thistles! 'Every good tree bringeth forth good fruit; but a corrupt tree bringeth forth evil fruit.'[b] Every true prophet, every teacher whom I have sent, bringeth forth the good fruit of holiness. But a false prophet, a teacher whom I have not sent, brings forth only sin and wickedness. 'A good tree cannot bring forth evil fruit; neither can a corrupt tree bring forth good fruit.' A true prophet, a teacher sent from God, does not bring forth good fruit sometimes only, but always; not accidentally, but by a kind of necessity. In like manner, a false prophet, one whom God hath not sent, does not bring forth evil fruit accidentally or sometimes only, but always, and of necessity. 'Every tree that bringeth not forth good fruit is hewn down and cast into the fire.'[c] Such infallibly will be the lot of those prophets who bring not forth good fruit, who do not save souls from sin, who do not bring sinners to repentance. 'Wherefore' let this stand as an eternal rule: 'By their fruits ye shall know them.'[d] They who in fact bring the proud, passionate, unmerciful lovers of the world to be lowly, gentle lovers of God and man—they are true prophets, they are sent from God, who therefore confirms their word. On the other hand they whose hearers, if unrighteous before, remain unrighteous still, or at least void of any righteousness which 'exceeds the righteousness of the scribes and Pharisees'[20]—they are false prophets; they are not sent of God; therefore their word falls to the ground. And without a miracle of grace they and their hearers together will fall into the bottomless pit.

5. O 'beware of' these 'false prophets'! For though they 'come in sheep's clothing, yet inwardly they are ravening wolves'. They only destroy and devour the flock: they tear them in pieces if there is none to help them. They will not, cannot lead you in the way to heaven. How should they, when they know it not themselves? O beware they do not turn you out of the way, and cause you to 'lose what you have wrought'.[21]

6. But perhaps you will ask, 'If there is such danger in hearing

---

[b] Ver. 17.
[c] Ver. 19.
[d] Ver. 20.

---

[20] Cf. Matt. 5:20.
[21] Cf. 2 John 8.

them, ought I to hear them at all?' It is a weighty question, such as deserves the deepest consideration, and ought not to be answered but upon the calmest thought, the most deliberate reflection. For many years I have been almost afraid to speak at all concerning it;
5 being unable to determine one way or the other, or to give any judgment upon it. Many reasons there are which readily occur, and incline me to say, 'Hear them not.' And yet what our Lord speaks concerning the false prophets of his own times seems to imply the contrary. 'Then spake Jesus unto the multitude, and to
10 his disciples, saying, The scribes and the Pharisees sit in Moses' seat,' are the ordinary, stated teachers in your church: 'All therefore whatsoever they bid you observe, that observe and do. But do not ye after their works; for they say and do not.'²² Now that these were false prophets in the highest sense our Lord had
15 shown during the whole course of his ministry, as indeed he does in those very words, 'they say and do not.' Therefore by their fruits his disciples could not but know them, seeing they were open to the view of all men. Accordingly he warns them again and again to 'beware of' these 'false prophets'. And yet he does not
20 forbid them to hear even these. Nay, he in effect commands them so to do in those words: 'All therefore whatsoever they bid you observe, that observe and do.' For unless they heard them they could not know, much less 'observe, whatsoever they bade them do'. Here then our Lord himself gives a plain direction, both to
25 his apostles and the whole multitude, in some circumstances to hear even false prophets, known and acknowledged so to be.

7. But perhaps it will be said, he only directed to hear them when they read the Scripture to the congregation. I answer, at the same time that they thus read the Scripture they generally
30 expounded it too. And here is no kind of intimation that they were to hear the one and not the other also. Nay, the very terms, 'All things whatsoever they bid you observe', exclude any such limitation.

8. Again, unto them, unto false prophets, undeniably such, is
35 frequently committed (O grief to speak! for surely these things ought not so to be) the administration of the sacraments also. To direct men, therefore, not to hear them would be in effect to cut them off from the ordinance of God. But this we dare not do, considering the validity of the ordinance doth not depend on the

²² Matt. 23:1-3.

goodness of him that administers, but on the faithfulness of him that ordained it; who will and doth meet us in his appointed ways.[23] Therefore on this account likewise I scruple to say, 'Hear not even the false prophets.' Even by these who are under a curse themselves God can and doth give us his blessing. For the bread which they break we have experimentally known to be 'the communion of the body of Christ'; and the cup which God blessed, even by their unhallowed lips, was to us the communion of the blood of Christ.[24]

9. All, therefore, which I can say is this: in any particular case wait upon God by humble and earnest prayer, and then act according to the best light you have. Act according to what you are persuaded upon the whole will be most for your spiritual advantage. Take great care that you do not judge rashly; that you do not lightly think any to be false prophets. And when you have full proof, see that no anger or contempt have any place in your heart. After this, in the presence and in the fear of God, determine for yourself. I can only say, if by experience you find that the hearing them hurts your soul, then hear them not; then quietly refrain, and hear those that profit you. If on the other hand you find it does not hurt your soul, you then may hear them still. Only 'take heed how you hear.'[25] Beware of them and of their doctrine. Hear with fear and trembling, lest *you* should be deceived, and given up like them to a strong delusion. As they continually mingle truth and lies, how easily may you take in both together! Hear with fervent and continual prayer to him who alone teacheth man wisdom. And see that you bring whatever you hear 'to the law and to the testimony'.[26] Receive nothing untried, nothing till it is weighed in 'the balance of the sanctuary'.[27] Believe

[23] Cf. Art. XXVI, 'Of the unworthiness of the ministers, which hinders not the effect of the sacraments.' The background here is the bitter controversy that still centred in the Nonconformists' contention that it was *against conscience* (and, therefore, *sinful*) to accept the ministrations of unworthy priests or to participate in rituals that still smacked of popery. Wesley's toleration on this point was rooted in his ecclesiology. Cf. the longer explanation of his 'Reasons Against a Separation from the Church of England' in *A Preservative Against Unsettled Notions in Religion*. See also Nos. 97, 'On Obedience to Pastors', where Wesley argues a distinction between 'pastors' *(ex officio)* and 'spiritual guides'; and 104, 'On Attending the Church Service', §27. His concerns to keep his people within the sacramental environment of the Church of England and also to warn them against 'false prophets' were carefully balanced.

[24] 1 Cor. 10:16.

[25] Luke 8:18.

[26] Isa. 8:20.

[27] Cf. No. 10, 'The Witness of the Spirit, I', II.8 and n.

nothing they say unless it is clearly confirmed by plain passages of Holy Writ. Wholly reject whatsoever differs therefrom, whatever is not confirmed thereby. And in particular reject with the utmost abhorrence whatsoever is described as the way of salvation that is
5 either different from, or short of, the way our Lord has marked out in the foregoing discourse.

10. I cannot conclude without addressing a few plain words to those of whom we have now been speaking.[28] O ye false prophets, O ye dry bones, hear ye for once the word of the Lord.[29] How long
10 will ye lie in the name of God, saying God hath spoken, and God hath not spoken by you?[30] How long will ye pervert the right ways of the Lord,[31] putting darkness for light, and light for darkness?[32] How long will ye teach the way of death, and call it the way of life? How long will ye deliver to Satan the souls whom you profess to
15 bring unto God?

11. 'Woe unto you, ye blind leaders of the blind!'[33] 'For ye shut the kingdom of heaven against men: ye neither go in yourselves, neither suffer ye them that are entering to go in.'[34] Them that would strive to enter in at the strait gate ye call back into the broad
20 way. Them that have scarce gone one step in the ways of God you devilishly caution against 'going too far'. Them that just begin to hunger and thirst after righteousness you warn not to be 'righteous overmuch'.[35] Thus you cause them to stumble at the very threshold; yea, to fall and rise no more.[36] O wherefore do ye
25 this? What profit is there in their blood when they go down to the pit?[37] Miserable profit to *you*. They 'shall perish in their iniquity; but their blood will God require at *your* hands'![38]

12. Where are your eyes? Where is your understanding? Have ye deceived others till you have deceived yourselves also? Who
30 hath required this at your hands, to *teach* a way which ye never *knew?* Are you 'given up to' so 'strong a delusion' that ye not only teach but 'believe a lie'?[39] And can you possibly believe that God

---

[28] For still more 'plain words' to the Anglican clergy, cf. Wesley's *Address to the Clergy*, I.3–II.1, 3.
[29] Ezek. 37:4.
[30] See Ezek. 13:6-7.
[31] Acts 13:10.
[32] See Isa. 5:20.
[33] Cf. Matt. 15:14; 23:16.
[34] Matt. 23:13.
[35] Cf. above, II.5 and n.
[36] Jer. 25:27.
[37] Ps. 30:9.
[38] Cf. Ezek. 3:18; 33:8.
[39] Cf. Ps. 81:12; 2 Thess. 2:11.

hath sent you? That ye are *his* messengers? Nay, if the Lord had sent you, the 'work of the Lord', would 'prosper in your hands'.[40] As the Lord liveth, if ye were messengers of God he would 'confirm the word of his messengers'.[41] But the work of the Lord doth not prosper in your hand: you bring no sinners to 5 repentance. The Lord doth not confirm your word, for you save no souls from death.

13. How can you possibly evade the force of our Lord's words—so full, so strong, so express? How can ye evade 'knowing yourselves by your fruits'? Evil fruits of evil trees! And how should 10 it be otherwise? 'Do men gather grapes of thorns, or figs of thistles?' Take this to yourselves, ye to whom it belongs. O ye barren trees, why cumber ye the ground?[42] 'Every good tree bringeth forth good fruit.' See ye not that here is no exception? Take knowledge, then, ye are not good trees; for ye do not bring 15 forth good fruit. 'But a corrupt tree bringeth forth evil fruit.' And so have ye done from the beginning. Your speaking as from God has only confirmed them that heard you in the tempers, if not works, of the devil. O take warning of him in whose name ye speak, before the sentence he hath pronounced take place. 'Every 20 tree which bringeth not forth good fruit is hewn down, and cast into the fire.'

14. My dear brethren, harden not your hearts.[43] You have too long shut your eyes against the light. Open them now, before it is too late; before you are cast into outer darkness.[44] Let not any 25 temporal consideration weigh with you; for eternity is at stake. Ye have run before ye were sent. O go no farther. Do not persist to damn yourselves and them that hear you! You have no fruit of your labours. And why is this? Even because the Lord is not with you. But can you go this warfare at your own cost?[45] It cannot be. 30 Then humble yourselves before him. Cry unto him out of the dust, that he may first quicken *thy* soul, give *thee* the faith that worketh by love; that is lowly and meek, pure and merciful, zealous of good works;[46] rejoicing in tribulation, in reproach, in distress, in persecution for righteousness' sake. So shall 'the 35 Spirit of glory and of Christ rest upon thee',[47] and it shall appear

---

[40] Cf. Isa. 53:10.
[41] Cf. Ezek. 13:6.
[42] See Luke 13:7.
[43] Ps. 95:8; Heb. 3:8.
[44] See Matt. 8:12; 22:13.
[45] See 1 Cor. 9:7.
[46] Titus 2:14.
[47] Cf. 1 Pet. 4:14.

that God hath sent thee. So shalt thou indeed 'do the work of an evangelist, and make full proof of thy ministry.'[48] So shall the word of God in thy mouth be 'an hammer that breaketh the rocks in pieces'.[49] It shall then be known by thy fruits that thou art a
5 prophet of the Lord, even by the children whom God hath given thee.[50] And having 'turned many to righteousness, thou shalt shine as the stars for ever and ever'![51]

[48] Cf. 2 Tim. 4:5.
[49] Jer. 23:29.
[50] See Isa. 8:18.
[51] Cf. Dan. 12:3.

Upon our Lord's Sermon on the Mount

Discourse the Thirteenth

Matthew 7:21-27

Not everyone that saith unto me, Lord, Lord, shall enter into the kingdom of heaven; but he that doeth the will of my Father which is in heaven.

Many will say to me in that day, Lord, Lord, have we not prophesied in thy name? And in thy name have cast out devils? And in thy name done many wonderful works?

And then will I profess unto them, I never knew you: depart from me, ye that work iniquity.

Therefore whosoever heareth these sayings of mine, and doeth them, I will liken him unto a wise man, which built his house upon a rock;

And the rain descended, and the floods came, and the winds blew, and beat upon that house; and it fell not; for it was founded upon a rock.

And everyone that heareth these sayings of mine, and doeth them not, shall be likened unto a foolish man, which built his house upon the sand;

And the rain descended, and the floods came, and the winds blew, and beat upon that house; and it fell: and great was the fall of it.

1. Our divine Teacher, having declared the whole counsel of God with regard to the way of salvation, and observed the chief hindrance of those who desire to walk therein, now closes the whole with these weighty words; thereby, as it were, setting his seal to his prophecy, and impressing his whole authority on what he had delivered, that it might stand firm to all generations.

2. For thus saith the Lord, that none may ever conceive there is any other way than this: 'Not everyone that saith unto me, Lord, Lord, shall enter into the kingdom of heaven, but he that doeth the will of my Father which is in heaven. Many will say to me in that day, Lord, Lord, have we not prophesied in thy name? And in thy name have cast out devils? And in thy name done many wonderful works? And then will I profess unto them, I never knew you: depart from me, ye that work iniquity . [. . .] Therefore

everyone that heareth these sayings of mine and doeth them not, shall be likened unto a foolish man which built his house upon the sand. And the rain descended, and the floods came, and the winds blew, and beat upon that house; and it fell: and great was the fall of it.'

3. I design in the following discourse, first, to consider the case of him who thus builds his house upon the sand; secondly, to show the wisdom of him who builds upon a rock; and thirdly, to conclude with a practical application.

I. 1.And, first, I am to consider the case of him who builds his house upon the sand. It is concerning him our Lord saith, 'Not everyone that saith unto me, Lord, Lord! shall enter into the kingdom of heaven.' And this is a decree which cannot pass; which standeth fast for ever and ever.[1] It therefore imports us in the highest degree throughly to understand the force of these words. Now what are we to understand by that expression, 'that saith unto me, Lord, Lord'? It undoubtedly means, 'that thinks of going to heaven by any other way than that which I have now described'. It therefore implies (to begin at the lowest point) all good words, all verbal religion. It includes whatever creeds we may rehearse; whatever professions of faith we make; whatever number of prayers we may repeat, whatever thanksgivings we read or say to God. We may speak good of his name;[2] and declare his loving-kindness to the children of men.[3] We may be talking of all his mighty acts, and telling of his salvation from day to day. By comparing spiritual things with spiritual,[4] we may show the meaning of the oracles of God. We may explain the mysteries of his kingdom, which have been hid from the beginning of the world.[5] We may speak with the tongue of angels rather than men concerning the deep things of God.[6] We may proclaim to sinners, 'Behold the Lamb of God, who taketh away the sin of the world.'[7] Yea, we may do this with such a measure of the power of God, and such demonstration of his Spirit, as to save many souls from death,[8] and hide a multitude of sins.[9] And yet 'tis very possible all

---

[1] See Ps. 148:6.
[2] I.e., lead (or join in) the responses of the daily offices, beginning with the *'Jubilate Deo'*, Ps. 100:4, etc., in BCP, Morning Prayer.
[3] See another favourite Psalm in 'Morning Prayer': 107:8, 15, 21, 31 (BCP).
[4] See 1 Cor. 2:13.   [5] See Col. 1:26.
[6] See 1 Cor. 13:1.   [7] John 1:29.
[8] See Jas. 5:20.   [9] See 1 Pet.4:8.

this may be no more than 'saying, Lord, Lord!' After I have thus successfully preached to others, still I myself may be a castaway.[10] I may in the hand of God snatch many souls from hell, and yet drop into it when I have done. I may bring many others to the kingdom of heaven, and yet myself never enter there. Reader, if God hath ever blessed my word to *thy* soul, pray that he may be merciful to *me* a sinner.[11]

2. The 'saying, Lord, Lord!' may, secondly, imply the doing no harm.[12] We may abstain from every presumptuous sin, from every kind of outward wickedness. We may refrain from all those ways of acting or speaking which are forbidden in Holy Writ. We may be able to say to all those among whom we live, Which of you convinceth me of sin?[13] We may have a conscience void of any external offence towards God and towards man.[14] We may be clear of all uncleanness, ungodliness, and unrighteousness as to the outward act, or (as the Apostle testifies concerning himself) 'touching the righteousness of the law', i.e. outward righteousness, 'blameless';[15] but yet we are not hereby justified. Still this is no more than 'saying, Lord, Lord!' And if we go no farther than this we shall never 'enter into the kingdom of heaven'.

3. The 'saying, Lord, Lord!' may imply, thirdly, many of what are usually styled good works. A man may attend the Supper of the Lord, may hear abundance of excellent sermons, and omit no opportunity of partaking all the other ordinances of God. I may do good to my neighbour, deal my bread to the hungry, and cover the naked with a garment. I may be so zealous of good works as even to 'give all my goods to feed the poor'.[16] Yea, and I may do all this with a desire to please God and a real belief that I do please him thereby (which is undeniably the case of those our Lord introduces, 'saying unto him, Lord, Lord!'); and still I may have no part in the glory which shall be revealed.[17]

---

[10] A compounded echo here from 1 Cor. 9:27 and the shipboard memoranda back in January and February 1738; cf. JWJ, Jan. 8, Jan. 24, and Feb. 1; see also Moore, I.342-44. Note also the premonition here of John Wesley's later outburst to Charles, June 27, 1766: 'Neither am I impelled to [my evangelical mission] by fear of any kind. I have no more fear than love. Or if I have any fear, it is not that of falling into hell but of falling into nothing.' Cf. No. 2, *The Almost Christian*, I.13 and n.

[11] Luke 18:13; as we have seen, Wesley's 'assurance' of 1738 had been confirmed to him in 1739 when *others* received 'assurance' as a fruit of his preaching of it.

[12] Cf. below, III.2-4, and No. 22, 'Sermon on the Mount, II', II.4 and n.

[13] John 8:46. [14] See Acts 24:16.

[15] Cf. Phil. 3:6. [16] Cf. 1 Cor. 13:3.

[17] Rom. 8:18; another description of 'the almost Christian'.

4. If any man marvels at this, let him acknowledge he is a stranger to the whole religion of Jesus Christ; and in particular to that perfect portraiture thereof which he has set before us in this discourse. For how far short is all this of that righteousness and
5 true holiness[18] which he has described therein! How widely distant from that inward kingdom of heaven which is now opened in the believing soul! Which is first sown in the heart as a grain of mustard seed, but afterwards putteth forth great branches,[19] on which grow all the fruits of righteousness,[20] every good temper
10 and word and work.

5. Yet as clearly as he had declared this, as frequently as he had repeated that none who have not this kingdom of God within them shall enter into the kingdom of heaven, our Lord well knew that many would not receive this saying, and therefore confirms it
15 yet again. 'Many' (saith he; not one; not a few only; it is not a rare or an uncommon case) 'shall say unto me in that day'. Not only, we have said many prayers; we have spoken thy praise; we have refrained from evil; we have exercised ourselves in doing good; but what is abundantly more than this—'We have prophesied in
20 thy name. In thy name have we cast out devils; in thy name done many wonderful works.' 'We have prophesied': we have declared thy will to mankind; we have showed sinners the way to peace and glory. And we have done this 'in thy name', according to the truth of thy gospel. Yea, and by thy authority, who didst confirm the
25 Word with the Holy Ghost sent down from heaven. For 'in' (or *by*) 'thy name', by the power of thy Word and of thy Spirit, 'have we cast out devils;' out of the souls which they had long claimed as their own, and whereof they had full and quiet possession. 'And in thy name', by thy power, not our own, 'have we done many
30 wonderful works;' insomuch that even 'the dead heard the voice of the Son of God'[21] speaking by us, and lived. 'And then will I profess' even 'unto them, I never knew you:' no, not then, when you were 'casting out devils in my name'. Even then I did not know you as my own; for your heart was not right toward God. Ye
35 were not yourselves meek and lowly; ye were not lovers of God and of all mankind; ye were not renewed in the image of God.[22] Ye were not holy as I am holy.[23] 'Depart from me, ye' who,

---

[18] Eph. 4:24.
[19] See Matt. 13:31-32.
[20] Phil. 1:11.
[21] Cf. John 5:25.
[22] See Col. 3:10.
[23] See 1 Pet. 1:16.

notwithstanding all this, are 'workers of iniquity' (ἀνομία). Ye
are transgressors of my law—my law of holy and perfect love.

6. It is to put this beyond all possibility of contradiction that our
Lord confirms it by that opposite comparison. 'Everyone', saith
he, 'who heareth these sayings of mine and doeth them not, shall
be likened unto a foolish man which built his house upon the
sand. And the rain descended, and the floods came, and the
winds blew, and beat upon that house:' as they will surely do,
sooner or later, upon every soul of man; even the floods of
outward affliction, or inward temptation; the storms of pride,
anger, fear, or desire. 'And it fell: and great was the fall of it;' so
that it perished for ever and ever. Such must be the portion of all
who rest in anything short of that religion which is above
described. And the *greater* will their fall be because they 'heard
those sayings, and yet did them not'.

II. 1. I am, secondly, to show the wisdom of him that doth them,
that 'buildeth his house upon a rock'. He indeed is wise who
'doeth the will of my Father which is in heaven'. He is truly wise
whose 'righteousness exceeds the righteousness of the scribes
and Pharisees'.[24] He is poor in spirit;[25] knowing himself even as
also he is known.[26] He sees and feels all his sin, and all his guilt, till
it is washed away by the atoning blood. He is conscious of his lost
estate, of the wrath of God abiding on him,[27] and of his utter
inability to help himself till he is filled with peace and joy in the
Holy Ghost.[28] He is meek and gentle, patient toward all men,
never 'returning evil for evil, or railing for railing, but
contrariwise blessing',[29] till he overcomes evil with good.[30] His
soul is athirst for nothing on earth, but only for God, the living
God.[31] He has bowels of love for all mankind, and is ready to lay
down his life for his enemies. He loves the Lord his God with all
his heart, and with all his mind and soul and strength.[32] He alone
shall enter into the kingdom of heaven who in this spirit doth good
unto all men;[33] and who, being for this cause despised and

[24] Matt. 5:20.
[25] Matt. 5:3.
[26] See 1 Cor. 13:12.
[27] See John 3:36.
[28] Rom. 14:17.
[29] Cf. 1 Pet. 3:9.
[30] See Rom. 12:21.
[31] See Ps. 42:2.
[32] See Mark 12:30.
[33] See Gal. 6:10.

rejected of men,[34] being hated, reproached, and persecuted, 'rejoices and is exceeding glad',[35] knowing in whom he hath believed;[36] and being assured these light, momentary afflictions will 'work out for him an eternal weight of glory'.[37]

5 　2. How truly wise is this man! He knows himself: an everlasting spirit which came forth from God, and was sent down into an house of clay,[38] not to do his own will, but the will of him that sent him.[39] He knows the world: the place in which he is to pass a few days or years, not as an inhabitant, but as a stranger and sojourner 10 in his way to the everlasting habitations;[40] and accordingly he uses the world, as not abusing it, and as knowing the fashion of it passes away.[41] He knows God: his Father and his friend, the parent of all good, the centre of the spirits of all flesh, the sole happiness of all intelligent beings. He sees, clearer than the light 15 of the noonday sun, that this is the end of man: to glorify him who made him for himself, and to love and enjoy him for ever.[42] And with equal clearness he sees the means to that end, to the enjoyment of God in glory; even now to know, to love, to imitate God, and to believe in Jesus Christ whom he hath sent.[43]

20 　3. He is a wise man, even in God's account; for 'he buildeth his house upon a rock;' upon the Rock of Ages, the everlasting Rock, the Lord Jesus Christ. Fitly is he so called; for he changeth not.[44] He is 'the same yesterday, today, and for ever'.[45] To him both the man of God of old, and the Apostle citing his words, bear witness: 25 'Thou, Lord, in the beginning hast laid the foundation of the earth, and the heavens are the works of thine hands. They shall perish, but thou remainest; they all shall wax old as doth a garment: and as a vesture shalt thou fold them up, and they shall be changed: but thou art the same, and thy years shall not fail.'[a]

---

[a] Heb. 1:10-12 [quoting Ps. 102:25-27 (BCP)].

---

[34] Isa. 53:3.
[35] Cf. Matt. 5:12.
[36] See 2 Tim. 1:12.
[37] Cf. 2 Cor. 4:17.
[38] See Job 4:19. Cf. No. 28, 'Sermon on the Mount, VIII', §28 and n.
[39] See John 6:38.
[40] Luke 16:9.
[41] See 1 Cor. 7:31. See also No. 20, *The Lord Our Righteousness*, II.20 and n.
[42] An interesting conflation of two famous aphorisms: Q.1 and A. in the Westminster *Shorter Catechism* and St. Augustine's *Confessions*, I.i.; cf. No. 3, '*Awake, Thou That Sleepest*', II.5 and n.
[43] See John 6:29; 17:3.　　　　　[44] See Mal. 3:6.　　　　　[45] Heb. 13:8.

Wise therefore is the man who buildeth on him; who layeth him for his only foundation; who builds only upon his blood and righteousness, upon what he hath done and suffered for us. On this corner-stone he fixes his faith, and rests the whole weight of his soul upon it. He is taught of God to say, Lord I have sinned; I deserve the nethermost hell. But I am 'justified freely by thy grace, through the redemption that is in Jesus Christ'.[46] 'And the life I now live I live by faith in him who loved me and gave himself for me.'[47] 'The life I now live': namely, a divine, heavenly life, a life which is 'hid with Christ in God'.[48] I now live, even in the flesh, a life of love, of pure love both to God and man; a life of holiness and happiness, praising God and doing all things to his glory.

4. Yet let not such an one think that he shall not see war any more,[49] that he is now out of the reach of temptation. It still remains for God to prove the grace he hath given: he shall be tried as gold in the fire.[50] He shall be tempted not less than they who know not God; perhaps abundantly more. For Satan will not fail to try to the uttermost those whom he is not able to destroy. Accordingly 'the rain' will impetuously 'descend'; only at such times and in such a manner as seems good, not to the prince of the power of the air, but to him whose 'kingdom ruleth over all'.[51] 'The floods', or torrents, 'will come;' they will lift up their waves and rage horribly. But to them also the Lord that sitteth above the water-floods, that remaineth a King for ever,[52] will say, 'Hitherto shall ye come and no farther: here shall your proud waves be stayed.'[53] 'The winds will blow, and beat upon that house,' as though they would tear it up from the foundation. But they cannot prevail: it falleth not; for it is founded upon a rock. He buildeth on Christ by faith and love; therefore he shall not be cast down. 'He shall not fear, though the earth be moved, and though the hills be carried into the midst of the sea. Though the waters thereof rage and swell, and the mountains shake at the tempest of the same;'[54] still he 'dwelleth under the defence of the Most High, and is safe under the shadow of the Almighty'.[55]

[46] Cf. Rom. 3:24.
[47] Cf. Gal. 2:20.
[48] Col. 3:3.
[49] See Mic. 4:3.
[50] See Rev. 3:18.
[51] Ps. 103:19.
[52] See Ps. 29:9 (BCP).
[53] Cf. Job 38:11.
[54] Ps. 46:2-3 (BCP).
[55] Ps. 91:1 (BCP).

III. 1. How nearly then does it concern every child of man practically to apply these things to himself! Diligently to examine on what foundation he builds, whether on a rock or on the sand! How deeply are *you* concerned to inquire, What is the foundation
5 of *my* hope? Whereon do I build my expectation of entering into the kingdom of heaven? Is it not built on the sand? Upon my *orthodoxy* or right opinions (which by a gross abuse of words I have called *faith*);[56] upon my having a set of notions—suppose more rational or scriptural than many others have? Alas! What madness
10 is this? Surely this is building on the sand; or rather, on the froth of the sea! Say I am convinced of this. Am I not again building my hope on what is equally unable to support it? Perhaps on my belonging to 'so excellent a church; reformed after the true Scripture model; blessed with the purest doctrine, the most
15 primitive liturgy, the most apostolical form of goverment'.[57] These are doubtless so many reasons for praising God, as they may be so many helps to holiness. But they are not holiness itself. And if they are separate from it they will profit me nothing. Nay, they will leave me the more without excuse, and exposed to the
20 greater damnation. Therefore, if I build my hope upon this foundation I am still building upon the sand.

2. You cannot, you dare not, rest here. Upon what next will you build your hope of salvation? Upon your innocence? Upon your doing no harm?[58] Your not wronging or hurting anyone? Well;
25 allow this plea to be true. You are just in all your dealings; you are a downright honest man; you pay every man his own; you neither cheat nor extort; you act fairly with all mankind. And you have a conscience towards God; you do not live in any known sin. Thus far is well. But still it is not the thing. You may go thus far and yet
30 never come to heaven. When all this harmlessness[59] flows from a right principle it is the *least part* of the religion of Christ. But in you it does not flow from a right principle, and therefore is no part at all of religion. So that in grounding your hope of salvation on this you are still building upon the sand.

35 3. Do you go farther yet? Do you add to the doing no harm the attending all the ordinances of God? Do you at all opportunities

---

[56] Cf. No. 7, 'The Way to the Kingdom', I.6 and n.
[57] A sardonic reference here; but cf. No. 13, *On Sin in Believers*, I.3 and n., for samples of Wesley's own triumphalist sentiments on this very point.
[58] Cf. above, I.2; and No. 22, 'Sermon on the Mount, II', II.4 and n.
[59] Cf. No. 32, 'Sermon on the Mount, XII', II.2 and n.

partake of the Lord's Supper? Use public and private prayer? Fast often? Hear and search the Scriptures, and meditate thereon? These things likewise ought you to have done, from the time you first set your face towards heaven. Yet these things also are nothing, being alone. They are nothing without the weightier matters of the law.[60] And those you have forgotten. At least you experience them not: faith, mercy, and love of God; holiness of heart; heaven opened in the soul. Still therefore you build upon the sand.

4. Over and above all this, are you zealous of good works?[61] Do you, as you have time, do good to all men?[62] Do you feed the hungry and clothe the naked, and visit the fatherless and widow in their affliction?[63] Do you visit those that are sick? Relieve them that are in prison? Is any a stranger and you take him in? Friend, come up higher.[64] Do you 'prophesy in the name' of Christ?[65] Do you preach the truth as it is in Jesus?[66] And does the influence of his Spirit attend your word, and make it the power of God unto salvation?[67] Does he enable you to bring sinners from darkness to light, from the power of Satan unto God?[68] Then go and learn what thou hast so often taught, 'By grace ye are saved, through faith.'[69] 'Not by works of righteousness which we have done, but of his own mercy he saveth us.'[70] Learn to hang naked upon the cross of Christ, counting all thou hast done but dung and dross.[71] Apply to him just in the spirit of the dying thief,[72] of the harlot with her seven devils;[73] else thou art still on the sand, and after saving others thou wilt lose thy own soul.

5. Lord! Increase my faith, if I now believe! Else, give me faith, though but as a grain of mustard seed![74] But 'what doth it profit if a man say he hath faith, and have not works? Can' *that* 'faith save him?'[75] O no! That faith which hath not works, which doth not produce both inward and outward holiness, which does not stamp the whole image of God on the heart, and purify us as he is pure;[76]

---

[60] See Matt. 23:23.
[61] Titus 2:14.
[62] See Gal. 6:10.
[63] Jas. 1:27.
[64] See Luke 14:10.
[65] Cf. Matt. 7:22.
[66] See Eph. 4:21.
[67] Rom. 1:16.
[68] Acts 26:18.
[69] Cf. Eph. 2:8.
[70] Cf. Titus 3:5.
[71] See Phil. 3:8.
[72] See Luke 23:42.
[73] See Mark 16:9.
[74] See Matt. 17:20.
[75] Cf. Jas. 2:14.
[76] See 1 John 3:3.

that faith which does not produce the whole of the religion described in the foregoing chapters, is not the faith of the gospel, not the Christian faith, not the faith which leads to glory. O beware of this, above all other snares of the devil, of resting on
5 unholy, unsaving faith! If thou layest stress on this thou art lost for ever: thou still buildest thy house upon the sand. When 'the rain descends and the floods come it' will surely 'fall; and great' will be 'the fall of it.'

6. Now, therefore, build thou upon a rock. By the grace of God,
10 know thyself.[77] Know and feel that thou wast shapen in wickedness, and in sin did thy mother conceive thee;[78] and that thou thyself hast been heaping sin upon sin ever since thou couldst discern good from evil.[79] Own thyself guilty of eternal death; and renounce all hope of ever being able to save thyself. Be
15 it all thy hope to be washed in his blood and purified by his Spirit 'who himself bore all thy sins in his own body upon the tree'.[80] And if thou knowest he hath taken away thy sins, so much the more abase thyself before him in a continued sense of thy total dependence on him for every good thought and word and work,
20 and of thy utter inability to all good unless he 'water thee every moment'.[81]

7. Now weep for your sins, and mourn after God till he turns your heaviness into joy.[82] And even then weep with them that weep;[83] and for them that weep not for themselves. Mourn for the
25 sins and miseries of mankind. And see, but just before your eyes, the immense ocean of eternity,[84] without a bottom or a shore;[85] which has already swallowed up millions of millions of men, and is gaping to devour them that yet remain. See here the house of God, eternal in the heavens;[86] there, hell and destruction without
30 a covering.[87] And thence learn the importance of every moment, which just appears, and is gone for ever![88]

8. Now add to your seriousness, meekness of wisdom. Hold an even scale as to all your passions, but in particular as to anger, sorrow, and fear. Calmly acquiesce in whatsoever is the will of
35 God. Learn in every state wherein you are, therewith to be

---

[77] The prior human 're-action' in all true repentance; see No. 7, 'The Way to the Kingdom', II.1 and n.
[78] See Ps. 51:5 (BCP).   [79] See Heb. 5:14.   [80] 1 Pet. 2:24.
[81] Cf. Isa. 27:3.   [82] See Jas. 4:9.   [83] Rom. 12:15.
[84] Cf. No. 54, 'On Eternity', §4 and n.
[85] Cf. *ibid.*, §18 and n.   [86] See 2 Cor. 5:1.   [87] See Job 26:6.
[88] Cf. No. 29, 'Sermon on the Mount, IX', §28 and n.

content.[89] Be mild to the good; be gentle toward all men,[90] but especially toward the evil and the unthankful. Beware not only of outward expressions of anger, such as calling thy brother 'Raca', or 'Thou fool'[91] but of every inward emotion contrary to love, though it go no farther than the heart. Be angry at sin, as an affront offered to the majesty of heaven; but love the sinner still,[92] like our Lord who 'looked round about upon' the Pharisees 'with anger, being grieved for the hardness of their hearts'.[93] He was grieved at the sinners, angry at the sin. Thus 'be thou angry and sin not.'[94]

9. Now do thou hunger and thirst, not for 'the meat that perisheth, but for that which endureth unto everlasting life'.[95] Trample under foot the world and the things of the world—all these riches, honours, pleasures. What is the world to thee? Let the dead bury their dead: but follow thou after the image of God.[96] And beware of quenching that blessed thirst, if it is already excited in thy soul, by what is vulgarly called religion—a poor, dull farce, a religion of form, of outside show[97]—which leaves the heart still cleaving to the dust, as earthly and sensual as ever.[98] Let nothing satisfy thee but the power of godliness, but a religion that is spirit and life; the dwelling in God and God in thee; the being an inhabitant of eternity; the entering in by the blood of sprinkling[99] 'within the veil',[100] and 'sitting in heavenly places with Christ Jesus'.[101]

10. Now, seeing thou canst do all things through Christ strengthening thee,[102] be merciful as thy Father in heaven is merciful.[103] Love thy neighbour as thyself.[104] Love friends and enemies as thy own soul. And let thy love be *long-suffering*, and patient towards all men.[105] Let it be *kind*, soft, benign: inspiring thee with the most amiable sweetness, and the most fervent and tender affection. Let it 'rejoice in the truth',[106] wheresoever it is found, the truth that is after godliness.[107] Enjoy whatsoever brings

---

[89] See Phil. 4:11.   [90] 2 Tim. 2:24.   [91] Matt. 5:22.

[92] Cf. No. 22, 'Sermon on the Mount, II', I.8 and n.

[93] Cf. Mark 3:5.   [94] Eph. 4:26.   [95] John 6:27.

[96] Cf. Matt. 8:22; an interesting Christological note identifying Jesus Christ as the representative 'image of God'.

[97] Cf. Matthew Prior, 'An English Padlock', l. 60: ''Tis a dull farce, an empty show;' see No. 77, 'Spiritual Worship', III.5 and n.

[98] See Jas. 3:15.   [99] Heb. 12:24.   [100] Heb. 6:19.

[101] Cf. Eph. 2:6.   [102] See Phil. 4:13.   [103] See Luke 6:36.

[104] Lev. 19:18, etc.   [105] 1 Thess. 5:14.

[106] Cf. 1 Cor. 13:6.   [107] See 1 Tim. 6:3.

glory to God, and promotes peace and goodwill among men. In love 'cover all things', of the dead and the absent speaking nothing but good;[108] 'believe all things' which may any way tend to clear your neighbour's character; 'hope all things' in his favour;
5 and 'endure all things', triumphing over all opposition. For true 'love never faileth',[109] in time or in eternity.

11. Now be thou 'pure in heart'; purified through faith from every unholy affection, 'cleansing thyself from all filthiness of flesh and spirit, and perfecting holiness in the fear of God'.[110]
10 Being through the power of his grace purified from pride by deep poverty of spirit; from anger, from every unkind or turbulent passion by meekness and mercifulness; from every desire but to please and enjoy God by hunger and thirst after righteousness;[111] now love the Lord thy God with all thy heart and with all thy
15 strength.[112]

12. In a word: let thy religion be the religion of the heart.[113] Let it lie deep in thy inmost soul. Be thou little and base, and mean and vile (beyond what words can express) in thy own eyes; amazed and humbled to the dust by the love of God which is in Christ
20 Jesus.[114] Be serious. Let the whole stream of thy thoughts, words, and actions flow from the deepest conviction that thou standest on the edge of the great gulf, thou and all the children of men, just ready to drop in, either into everlasting glory or everlasting burnings.[115] Let thy soul be filled with mildness, gentleness,
25 patience, long-suffering towards all men, at the same time that all which is in thee is athirst for God, the living God;[116] longing to awake up after his likeness, and to be satisfied with it. Be thou a lover of God and of all mankind. In this spirit do and suffer all things. Thus show thy faith by thy works: thus 'do the will of thy
30 Father which is in heaven.'[117] And as sure as thou now walkest with God on earth, thou shalt also reign with him in glory.

---

[108] Cf. No. 14, *The Repentance of Believers*, I.11 and n.
[109] Cf. 1 Cor. 13:7-8.
[110] Cf. 2 Cor. 7:1.
[111] Matt. 5:6.
[112] See Mark 12:30.
[113] Cf. No. 25, 'Sermon on the Mount, V', IV.13 and n.
[114] Rom. 8:39.
[115] Isa. 33:14. Cf. No. 25, 'Sermon on the Mount, V', III.6, IV.13 and n.
[116] See Ps. 42:2.
[117] Cf. Matt. 7:21; 12:50.

APPENDIX A

The Sermons as Ordered in this Edition

(Included is the location of the text as it is to be found in Jackson's edition of Wesley's *Works* (1829-31), Vols. V-VII, which has been popularly reproduced during this generation from the 1872 edition.)

[This edition, Vol. 1]

Sermons on Several Occasions (1771), I-IV

[This edition, Vol. 2]

Sermons on Several Occasions (1788), V-VIII

Manuscript Sermons

*Sermons not by John Wesley, but included
in Jackson's edition (see Appendices B and C, Vol. 4)*

Appendix A
(Wesley's text: editions, transmission, presentation, and variant readings)

Appendix B
(Sermons ascribed to Wesley on inconclusive grounds)

Appendix C
(Manuscript sermons abridged from other authors)

Appendix D
(Samples of Wesley's sermon registers)

Bibliography

Indexes

APPENDIX B

The Sermons
in Chronological Sequence

APPENDIX C

The Sermons
in Alphabetical Order

(N.B. Where a title is italicized, the sermon was published as a separate item before being issued in a collection. Some of the titles thus italicized here, however, abridge the titles under which Wesley originally published them; others (Nos. 3, 55, 58, 99, 109, 111) are quite different. For detailed descriptions of all Wesley's contemporary editions of each sermon see the Bibliography in this edition, here noted as '*B*.50', etc. Titles supplied by the editor, whether to sermons separately published or to those first appearing in collected editions, or from manuscript sources, are given in this listing only within parentheses. These parentheses, however, are dropped from other listings, as from running titles and footnotes. Frequently the titles come from a lengthy tradition, which is noted, along with all the original titles used, in the introductory comment to the appropriate sermon. In alphabetizing the words 'a', 'an', 'of', 'on', 'the' are ignored. F.B.)

The Distribution of the Sermons in this Edition

Vol. 1, Nos. 1–33
Vol. 2, Nos. 34–76
Vol. 3, Nos. 77–114
Vol. 4, Nos. 115–51

Number	Title	Date
2.	*The Almost Christian* (*B*. 50)............................ Acts 26:28	1741, July 25
[App.	The Apostolic Ministry (Ben. Calamy)........... Mark 6:12	1732, Apr. 1-2]
104.	On Attending the Church Service.................. 1 Sam. 2:17	1787, Oct. 7
3.	(*'Awake, Thou That Sleepest'*) (CW) (*B*.59,...... *A Sermon preached on Sunday, April 4, 1742, before the University of Oxford*) Eph. 5:14	1742, Apr. 4
86.	*A Call to Backsliders* (*B*. 388)............................ Ps. 77:7-8	1778, May 20
70.	The Case of Reason Impartially Considered. 1 Cor. 14:20	1781, July 6
39.	Catholic Spirit... 2 Kgs. 10:15	(1750)
122.	(Causes of the Inefficacy of Christianity)....... Jer. 8:22	1789, July 2

Number	Title	Date

38. A Caution against Bigotry............................... (1750)
     Mark 9:38-39

91. On Charity... 1784, Oct. 15
    1 Cor. 13:1-3

[App. *(Christ Crucified) (B.624, A Sermon, preached...* 1774, Apr. 28]
     at the Opening of the New Meeting-House, at
     Wakefield. . .)
     1 Cor. 1:23

40. *Christian Perfection (B. 53)*............................ 1741
    Phil. 3:12

74. Of the Church...................................... 1785, Sept. 28
    Eph. 4:1-6

17. The Circumcision of the Heart...................... 1733, Jan. 1
    Rom. 2:29

105. On Conscience..................................... 1788, Apr. 8
     2 Cor. 1:12

137. (On Corrupting the Word of God)................. 1727, Oct. 6
     2 Cor. 2:17

49. The Cure of Evil-speaking........................... 1760
    Matt. 18:15-17

131. (The Danger of Increasing Riches)............... 1790, Sept. 21
     Ps. 62:10

87. The Danger of Riches................................. 1781, Jan.—Feb.
    1 Tim. 6:9

133. (Death and Deliverance)............................. 1725, Oct. 1
     Job 3:17

53. *On the Death of George Whitefield (B. 324,......* 1770, Nov. 18
    A Sermon on the Death of the Rev.
    Mr. George Whitefield . . .)
    Num. 23:10

114. *On the Death of John Fletcher (B. 442,............* 1785, Oct. 24
     A Sermon preached on occasion of the Death of
     the Rev. Mr. John Fletcher, Vicar of Madeley,
     Shropshire)
     Ps. 37:37

[App. The Death of the Righteous (Ben. Calamy).. 1732, Mar.
      Num. 23:10   11-12]

128. (The Deceitfulness of the Human Heart)...... 1790, Apr. 21
     Jer. 17:9
     [*A Discourse on Sin in Believers*—see *Sin in*
     . . .]
     [*Discourses* on the Sermon on the Mount—see
     'Upon Our Lord's Sermon on the Mount]

117. (On the Discoveries of Faith)........................ 1788, June 11
     Heb. 11:1

138A. (On Dissimulation)................................. 1728, Jan. 17
      John 1:47

138B-C. (Dissimulation, two fragments on)................. ?